Lectures and Office Hours Leave Off

Students choose MyEconLab:

In a recent study, 87 percent of students who used MyEconLab regularly felt it improved their grade.

"It was very useful because it had EVERYTHING, from practice exams to exercises to reading. Very helpful."

—**student, Northern Illinois University**

"I like how every chapter is outlined by vocabulary and flash cards. It helped me memorize equations and definitions. It was like having a study partner."

—**student, Temple University**

Chart 2. Helpfulness of Study Plan Practice Questions and Feedback
From a recent nationwide survey of students using MyEconLab (conducted by Contemporary Solutions)

90% of students surveyed who used the Study Plan practice questions and feedback felt it helped them to prepare for tests.

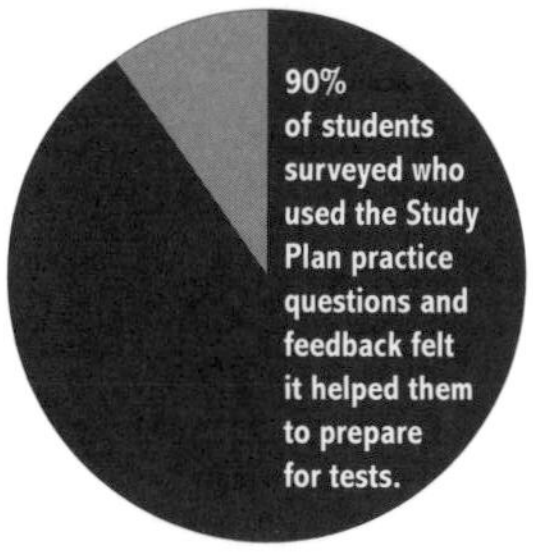

n = 227

"It made me look through the book to find answers so I did more reading."

—**student, Northern Illinois University**

"It was very helpful to get instant feedback. Sometimes I would get lost reading the book, and these individual problems would help me focus and see if I understood the concepts."

—**student, Temple University**

Chart 3. Recommendation to a Friend
From a recent survey of Texas A&M students using MyEconLab (conducted by Contemporary Solutions)

83.9% of students surveyed would recommend MyEconLab to a friend.

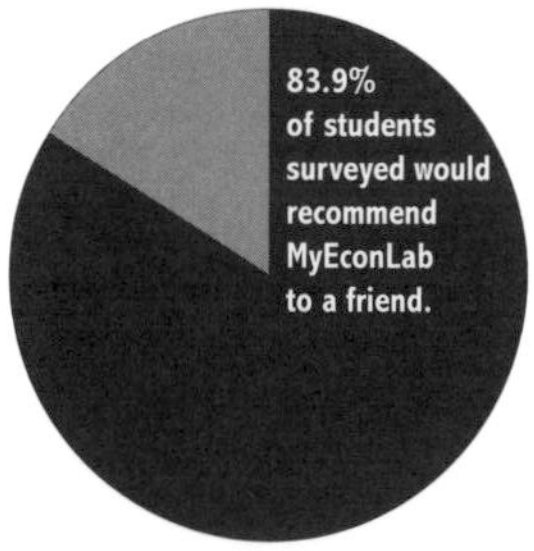

n = 33

"I really like the way MyEconLab took me through the graphs step-by-step. The Fast Track tutorials were the most helpful for the graph questions. I used the 1-2-3 buttons all the time."

—**student, Stephen F. Austin State University**

"I would recommend MyEconLab to a friend. It was really easy to use and helped in studying the material for class."

—**student, Northern Illinois University**

"I would recommend taking the quizzes on MyEconLab because it gives you a true account of whether or not you understand the material."

—**student, Montana Tech**

economics

Second Edition, Updated

economics

Second Edition, Updated

R. Glenn Hubbard
Columbia University

Anthony Patrick O'Brien
Lehigh University

Prentice Hall

Upper Saddle River, New Jersey 07458

Library of Congress Cataloging-in-Publication Data

Hubbard, R. Glenn.

    Economics/R. Glenn Hubbard, Anthony Patrick O'Brien. — 2nd ed. update.

      p. cm.

    Includes bibliographical references and index.

    ISBN-13: 978-0-13-609205-6

    ISBN-10: 0-13-609205-5

    1. Economics--Textbooks. I. O'Brien, Anthony Patrick. II. Title.

    HB171.5.H79 2009

    330--dc22

                              2008034185

VP/Publisher: Natalie E. Anderson
AVP/Executive Editor, Print: David Alexander
Senior Development Editor: Lena Buonanno
Production Project Manager: Carol O'Rourke
AVP/Executive Marketing Manager: Lori DeShazo
VP/Director of Development: Steve Deitmer
Editorial Assistant: Terenia McHenry
Production Media Project Manager: Lorena Cerisano
Marketing Assistant: Justin Jacob
Senior Managing Editor: Cynthia Zonneveld
Manager of Rights & Permissions: Charles Morris
Senior Operations Specialist: Nick Sklitsis
Operations Specialist: Natacha Moore
Senior Art Director: Jonathan Boylan
Interior Design: Blair Brown
Cover Design: Jonathan Boylan

Cover Illustration/Photo: iStockphoto/Oliver Hoffmann
Illustration (Interior): Fernando Quijano
Director, Image Resource Center: Melinda Patelli
Manager, Rights and Permissions: Zina Arabia
Manager, Visual Research: Beth Brenzel
Manager, Cover Visual Research & Permissions: Karen Sanatar
Image Permission Coordinator: Kathy Gavilanes
Composition: GGS Higher Education Resources, A Divison of Premedia Global, Inc.
Full-Service Project Management: GGS Higher Education Resources, A Divison of Premedia Global, Inc.
Printer/Binder: Courier Kendallville
Typeface: 10.5/12 Minion

Credits and acknowledgments borrowed from other sources and reproduced, with permission, in this textbook appear on page C-1.

Pearson Education LTD., London
Pearson Education Singapore, Pte. Ltd
Pearson Education, Canada, Inc.
Pearson Education–Japan
Pearson Education Australia PTY, Limited

Pearson Education North Asia Ltd., Hong Kong
Pearson Educación de Mexico, S.A. de C.V.
Pearson Education Malaysia, Pte. Ltd.
Pearson Education, Upper Saddle River, New Jersey

Prentice Hall
is an imprint of

www.pearsonhighered.com

10 9 8 7 6 5 4 3 2 1
ISBN-13: 978-0-13-609205-6
ISBN-10:   0-13-609205-5

For Constance, Raph, and Will
—R. Glenn Hubbard

For Cindy, Matthew, Andrew, and Daniel
—Anthony Patrick O'Brien

Authorship

Glenn Hubbard, policymaker, professor, and researcher.

R. Glenn Hubbard is the dean and Russell L. Carson Professor of Finance and Economics in the Graduate School of Business at Columbia University and professor of economics in Columbia's Faculty of Arts and Sciences. He is also a research associate of the National Bureau of Economic Research and a director of Automatic Data Processing, Black Rock Closed-End Funds, Duke Realty, Information Services Group, KKR Financial Corporation, MetLife, and Ripplewood Holdings. He received his Ph.D. in economics from Harvard University in 1983. From 2001 to 2003, he served as chairman of the White House Council of Economic Advisers and chairman of the OECD Economy Policy Committee, and from 1991 to 1993, he was deputy assistant secretary of the U.S. Treasury Department. He currently serves as co-chair of the nonpartisan committee on Capital Markets Regulation. Hubbard's fields of specialization are public economics, financial markets and institutions, corporate finance, macroeconomics, industrial organization, and public policy. He is the author of more than 100 articles in leading journals, including *American Economic Review, Brookings Papers on Economic Activity, Journal of Finance, Journal of Financial Economics, Journal of Money, Credit, and Banking, Journal of Political Economy, Journal of Public Economics, Quarterly Journal of Economics, RAND Journal of Economics*, and *Review of Economics and Statistics*. His research has been supported by grants from the National Science Foundation, the National Bureau of Economic Research, and numerous private foundations.

Tony O'Brien, award-winning professor and researcher.

Anthony Patrick O'Brien is a professor of economics at Lehigh University. He received his Ph.D. from the University of California, Berkeley, in 1987. He has taught principles of economics for more than 15 years, in both large sections and small honors classes. He received the Lehigh University Award for Distinguished Teaching. He was formerly the director of the Diamond Center for Economic Education and was named a Dana Foundation Faculty Fellow and Lehigh Class of 1961 Professor of Economics. He has been a visiting professor at the University of California, Santa Barbara, and the Graduate School of Industrial Administration at Carnegie Mellon University. O'Brien's research has dealt with such issues as the evolution of the U.S. automobile industry, the sources of U.S. economic competitiveness, the development of U.S. trade policy, the causes of the Great Depression, and the causes of black–white income differences. His research has been published in leading journals, including *American Economic Review, Quarterly Journal of Economics, Journal of Money, Credit, and Banking, Industrial Relations, Journal of Economic History*, and *Explorations in Economic History*. His research has been supported by grants from government agencies and private foundations. In addition to teaching and writing, O'Brien also serves on the editorial board of the *Journal of Socio-Economics*.

Brief Contents

Contents

CHAPTER 10 Appendix: Using Isoquants and Isocosts to Understand Production and Cost   364

PART 6: The Markets for Factors of Production

CHAPTER 16: The Markets for Labor and Other Factors of Production 534

PART 7: Information, Taxes, and the Distribution of Income

CHAPTER 17: The Economics of Information   574

CHAPTER 18: Public Choice, Taxes, and the Distribution of Income   598

PART 8: Macroeconomic Foundations and Long-Run Growth

CHAPTER 19: GDP: Measuring Total Production and Income   632

CHAPTER 20: Unemployment and Inflation   658

CHAPTER 21: Economic Growth, the Financial System, and Business Cycles   694

FLEXIBILITY CHART

The following chart helps you organize your syllabus based on your teaching preferences and objectives:

Core	Policy	Optional
CHAPTER 1: Economics: Foundations and Models *Uses the debate of outsourcing to discuss the role of models in economic analysis.* **CHAPTER 2:** Trade-offs, Comparative Advantage, and the Market System *Includes coverage of the role of the entrepreneur, property rights, and the legal system in a market system.* **CHAPTER 3:** Where Prices Come From: The Interaction of Demand and Supply **CHAPTER 6:** Elasticity: The Responsiveness of Demand and Supply **CHAPTER 8:** Comparative Advantage and the Gains from International Trade *This chapter may be delayed until after Chapter 28.* **CHAPTER 10:** Technology, Production, and Costs **CHAPTER 11:** Firms in Perfectly Competitive Markets **CHAPTER 12:** Monopolistic Competition: The Competitive Model in a More Realistic Setting **CHAPTER 13:** Oligopoly: Firms in Less Competitive Markets *Includes full coverage of game theory and unique coverage of Porter's Five Forces model of competition.* **CHAPTER 14:** Monopoly and Antitrust Policy *This chapter may be covered after Chapter 11.* **CHAPTER 16:** The Markets for Labor and Other Factors of Production *Covers all factors of production in one chapter and includes coverage of discrimination, unions, compensating differentials, and personnel economics.* **CHAPTER 17:** The Economics of Information *Covers asymmetric information and moral hazard.*	**CHAPTER 4:** Economic Efficiency, Government Price Setting, and Taxes **CHAPTER 5:** Externalities, Environmental Policy, and Public Goods *This chapter may be delayed until after Chapter 14.* **CHAPTER 18:** Public Choice, Taxes, and the Distribution of Income **CHAPTER 26:** Monetary Policy *Uses the aggregate demand and aggregate supply model to show the effects of monetary policy on real GDP and the price level. Chapter 26 is a self-contained discussion, so instructors may safely omit the material in Chapter 28.* **CHAPTER 27:** Fiscal Policy *Uses the aggregate demand and aggregate supply model to show how taxes and government spending affect the economy. Includes significant coverage of the supply-side effects of fiscal policy.*	**CHAPTER 1 Appendix:** Using Graphs and Formulas **CHAPTER 4 Appendix:** Quantitative Demand and Supply Analysis *Provides a quantitative analysis of rent control.* **CHAPTER 7:** Firms, the Stock Market, and Corporate Governance *Unique chapter that includes coverage of the Sarbanes-Oxley Act.* **CHAPTER 7 Appendix:** Tools to Analyze Firms' Financial Information *Covers present value and financial statements.* **CHAPTER 8 Appendix:** Multinational Firms *Covers the benefits and challenges of operating overseas businesses.* **CHAPTER 9:** Consumer Choice and Behavioral Economics *Covers utility theory and unique coverage of social influences on behavior and network externalities.* **CHAPTER 9 Appendix:** Using Indifference Curves and Budget Lines to Understand Consumer Behavior *Complete and intuitive coverage for instructors who prefer to cover indifference curves rather than utility theory.* **CHAPTER 10 Appendix:** Using Isoquants and Isocosts to Understand Production and Costs *Provides a formal analysis of how firms choose the combination of inputs to produce a given level of output.* **CHAPTER 15:** Pricing Strategy *A unique chapter that covers price discrimination, cost-plus pricing, and two-part tariffs.*

Core	Policy	Optional

Core

CHAPTER 19: GDP: Measuring Total Production and Income
Covers how total production is measured and the difference between real and nominal variables.

CHAPTER 20: Unemployment and Inflation
Covers the three types of unemployment, how inflation is measured, and the difference between real and nominal interest rates.

CHAPTER 21: Economic Growth, the Financial System, and Business Cycles
Provides an overview of key macroeconomic issues by discussing the business cycle in the context of long-run growth. Discusses the roles of entrepreneurship, financial institutions, and policy in economic growth.

CHAPTER 22: Long-Run Economic Growth: Sources and Policies
Highlights the importance of institutions, policies, and technological change for economic growth.

CHAPTER 24: Aggregate Demand and Aggregate Supply Analysis
Carefully develops the AD-AS model and then makes the model dynamic to better account for actual movements in real GDP and the price level.

CHAPTER 25: Money, Banks, and the Federal Reserve System
Explores the role of money in the economy, the money supply process, and the structure of the Federal Reserve.

Optional

CHAPTER 23: Output and Expenditure in the Short Run
Uses the Keynesian 45°-line aggregate expenditure model to introduce students to the short-run relationship between spending and production. The discussion of monetary and fiscal policy in later chapters uses only the aggregate demand and aggregate supply model, which allows instructors to omit Chapter 23.

CHAPTER 23 Appendix: The Algebra of Macroeconomic Equilibrium
Uses equations to represent the aggregate expenditure model described in the chapter.

CHAPTER 24 Appendix: Macroeconomic Schools of Thought
Covers the monetarist model, the new classical model, and the real business cycle model.

CHAPTER 28: Inflation, Unemployment, and Federal Reserve Policy
Discusses the short-run and long-run Phillips curves. Also covers the roles of expectations formation and central bank credibility in monetary policy.

CHAPTER 29: Macroeconomics in an Open Economy
Explains the linkages among countries at the macroeconomic level and how policymakers in all countries take these linkages into account when conducting monetary and fiscal policy.

CHAPTER 30: The International Financial System
Covers the international financial system and explores the role central banks play in the system.

Preface

When George Lucas was asked why he made *Star Wars*, he replied, "It's the kind of movie I like to see, but no one seemed to be making them. So, I decided to make one." We realized that no one seemed to be writing the kind of textbook we wanted to use in our classes. So, after years of supplementing texts with fresh, lively, real-world examples from newspapers, magazines, and professional journals, we decided to write an economics text that delivers complete economics coverage with many real-world business examples. Our goal was to keep our classes "widget free."

NEW TO THE SECOND EDITION, UPDATED

Much has happened in the economy since the Second Edition of this text went to press in late 2007. The intensity of the housing crisis increased, gasoline prices marched relentlessly upward—reaching well above $4.00 per gallon in many parts of the country—and the financial system continued to stagger under the impact of problems in the market for mortgage-backed securities. In response to these problems, Congress, the president, and the Federal Reserve enacted dramatic new policies. Our approach in the first two editions of this text has been to put applications at the forefront of the discussion. We believe that students find the study of economics more interesting and easier to master when they see economic analysis applied to the real-world issues that concern them. Given how much has happened recently in the economy, we believe we needed to update our Second Edition to provide students with a better understanding of recent economic events and the policy responses to them. The additional material included in this update has taken us into areas—such as investment banking and mortgage-backed securities—not often dealt with in principles texts. We believe, though, some background in these issues is necessary for students to understand the economic problems of recent months and the responses of policymakers.

Although we have taken the opportunity of this update edition to make many changes throughout the text, we have concentrated on three key areas:

- *The economic slowdown that began in 2007.* Although as of this writing it is still not certain that the economy will have officially experienced a recession, declining real GDP during the fourth quarter of 2007, and slow growth and rising unemployment during 2008 give a strong indication that the economic expansion that began in late 2001 has ended. In this updated edition, we discuss the reasons for this slowdown, in addition to showing how the slowdown is reflected in the most recent macroeconomic data.

- *New initiatives by the Federal Reserve.* During 2008, the Fed dramatically broke with precedent in making investment banks eligible for discount loans and in facilitating the purchase of Bear Stearns by JP Morgan Chase. In this updated edition, we provide students with a background on investment banks, the mortgage-backed securities market, including the roles of Fannie Mae and Freddie Mac, and the debate among economists concerning the Fed's new policies.

- *Fiscal policy, including the 2008 tax rebate.* The rapid enactment of a stimulus package in early 2008 led to tax rebate checks arriving in taxpayers' mailboxes a few months later. In discussing this policy, we look at the different effects on consumption spending that result from temporary and permanent tax changes. To gauge the likely effect of the tax cut, we look at evidence about the impact of the similar 2001 tax rebate.

Here are the key changes to Economics, Second Edition, Updated:

- Chapter 24, "Aggregate Demand and Aggregate Supply Analysis" includes a new section entitled "The Economy in 2008: A Growth Slowdown, Recession, or Stagflation?"
- Chapter 25, "Money, Banks, and the Federal Reserve System" covers how the Fed changed its discount policy in 2008 because of problems in the market for "subprime" mortgages.
- Chapter 26, "Monetary Policy," includes a new section entitled "The Fed Responds to the Crisis in the Housing Market" and all-new end-of-chapter problems for this section. This chapter also covers Fed policies during 2007 and 2008 to deal with instability in the financial system.
- Chapter 27, "Fiscal Policy," includes a new section entitled "Fiscal Policy in Action: The Tax Rebate of 2008."
- Four new *Making the Connections* on the following topics:

    Chapter 8, "Comparative Advantage and the Gains from International Trade," covers the president-elect's trade policies.

    Chapter 21, "Economic Growth, the Financial System, and Business Cycles," covers the effect of the 2008 economy on the presidential election.

    Chapter 27, "Fiscal Policy," covers fiscal policy and the new administration.

    Chapter 29, "Macroeconmics in an Open Economy," covers the reasons for the falling value of the U.S. dollar.
- About 70 figures and tables have been updated using the latest data available.
- Many chapter openers are updated with new information and data about the real-world business featured.

The Foundation:
Contextual Learning and Modern Organization

We believe a course is a success if students can apply what they have learned in both personal and business settings and if they have developed the analytical skills to understand what they read in the media. That's why we explain economic concepts by using many real-world business examples and applications in the chapter openers, graphs, *Making the Connection* feature, *An Inside Look* feature, and end-of-chapter problems. This approach helps both business majors and liberal arts majors become educated consumers, voters, and citizens. In addition to our widget-free approach, we also have a modern organization and place interesting policy topics early in the book to pique student interest.

Here are several chapters that illustrate our approach in both microeconomics and macroeconomics.

Microeconomics

We are convinced that students learn to apply economic principles best if they are taught in a familiar context. Whether they open an art studio, do social work, trade on Wall Street, work for the government, or tend bar, students would benefit from understanding the economic forces behind their work. And though business students will have many opportunities to see economic principles in action in various courses, liberal arts students may not. We therefore use many diverse real-world business and policy examples to illustrate economic concepts and to develop educated consumers, voters, and citizens.

Here are several chapters that illustrate our approach:

- **A STRONG SET OF INTRODUCTORY CHAPTERS.** The introductory chapters provide students with a solid foundation in the basics. We emphasize the key ideas of marginal analysis and economic efficiency. In Chapter 4, "Economic Efficiency, Government Price Setting, and Taxes," we use the concepts of consumer surplus and producer surplus to measure the economic effects of price ceilings and price floors as they relate to the familiar examples of rental properties and the minimum wage. (We revisit consumer surplus and producer surplus in Chapter 8, "Comparative Advantage and the Gains from International Trade," where we discuss outsourcing and analyze government policies that affect trade; in Chapter 14, "Monopoly and Antitrust Policy," where we examine the effect of market power on economic efficiency; and in Chapter 15, "Pricing Strategy," where we examine the effect of firm pricing policy on economic efficiency.) In Chapter 7, "Firms, the Stock Market, and Corporate Governance," we provide students with a basic understanding of how firms are organized, how they raise funds, and how they provide information to investors. We also illustrate how in a market system entrepreneurs meet consumer wants and efficiently organize production. To explore how government policy affects business, we cover the outcome of the 2002 Sarbanes-Oxley Act and how companies have responded to the act.

- **EARLY COVERAGE OF POLICY ISSUES.** To expose students to policy issues early in the course, we discuss outsourcing in Chapter 1, "Economics: Foundations and Models," rent control and the minimum wage in Chapter 4, "Economic Efficiency, Government Price Setting, and Taxes," air pollution, global warming, and whether the government should run the health care system in Chapter 5, "Externalities, Environmental Policy, and Public Goods," and government policy toward illegal drugs in Chapter 6, "Elasticity: The Responsiveness of Demand and Supply."

- **COMPLETE COVERAGE OF MONOPOLISTIC COMPETITION.** We devote a full chapter to monopolistic competition (Chapter 12, "Monopolistic Competition: The

Competitive Model in a More Realistic Setting") prior to covering oligopoly and monopoly in Chapter 13, "Oligopoly: Firms in Less Competitive Markets," and Chapter 14, "Monopoly and Antitrust Policy." Although many instructors cover monopolistic competition very briefly or dispense with it entirely, we think it is an overlooked tool for reinforcing the basic message of how markets work in a context that is much more familiar to students than are the agricultural examples that dominate other discussions of perfect competition. We use the monopolistic competition model to introduce the downward-sloping demand curve material usually introduced in the monopoly chapter. This helps students grasp the important point that nearly all firms—not just monopolies—face downward-sloping demand curves. Covering monopolistic competition directly after perfect competition also allows for the early discussion of topics such as brand management and the sources of competitive success. Nevertheless, we wrote the chapter so that instructors who prefer to cover monopoly (Chapter 14, "Monopoly and Antitrust Policy") directly after perfect competition (Chapter 11, "Firms in Perfectly Competitive Markets") can do so without loss of continuity.

- **EXTENSIVE, REALISTIC GAME THEORY COVERAGE.** In Chapter 13, "Oligopoly: Firms in Less Competitive Markets," we use game theory to analyze competition among oligopolists. Game theory helps students understand how companies with market power make strategic decisions in many competitive situations. We use familiar companies such as Wal-Mart, Target, Coca-Cola, PepsiCo, and Dell in our game theory applications.

- **UNIQUE COVERAGE OF PRICING STRATEGY.** In Chapter 15, "Pricing Strategy," we explore how firms use pricing strategies to increase profits. Students encounter pricing strategies everywhere—when they buy a movie ticket, book a flight for spring break, or research book prices online. We use these relevant, familiar examples to illustrate how companies use strategies such as price discrimination, cost-plus pricing, and two-part tariffs.

- **A CHAPTER DEVOTED TO THE ECONOMICS OF INFORMATION.** In Chapter 17, "The Economics of Information," we explore the important fact that consumers, firms, and governments must make decisions on the basis of incomplete information. Students face uncertainty and make decisions with incomplete information when they buy used cars or health insurance, or when they search for a job. We help students analyze these familiar situations and explore the perspective of the consumer and firm. We also apply the concepts of adverse selection and moral hazard to financial markets.

Macroeconomics

Students come to study macroeconomics with a strong interest in understanding events and developments in the economy. We try to capture that interest and develop students' economic intuition and understanding in this text. We present macroeconomics in a way that is modern and based in the real world of business and economic policy. And we believe we achieve this presentation without making the analysis more difficult. We avoid the recent trend of using simplified versions of intermediate models, which are often more detailed and more complex than what students need to understand the basic macroeconomic issues. Instead, we use a more realistic version of the familiar aggregate demand and aggregate supply model to analyze short-run fluctuations and monetary and fiscal policy. We also avoid the "dueling schools of thought" approach often used to teach macroeconomics at the principles level. We emphasize the many areas of macroeconomics where most economists agree. And we present throughout real business and policy situations to develop students' intuition.

Here are a few highlights of our approach to macroeconomics:

- **A BROAD DISCUSSION OF MACRO STATISTICS.** Many students pay at least some attention to the financial news and know that the release of statistics by federal agencies can cause movements in stock and bond prices. A background in macroeconomic statistics helps clarify some of the policy issues encountered in later chapters. In Chapter 19, "GDP: Measuring Total Production and Income," and Chapter 20, "Unemployment and Inflation," we provide students with an understanding of the uses and potential shortcomings of the key macroeconomic statistics, without getting bogged down in the minutiae of how the statistics are constructed. So, for instance, we discuss the important differences between the payroll survey and the household survey for understanding conditions in the labor market. We explain why the financial markets react more strongly to news from the payroll survey. Chapter 26, "Monetary Policy," discusses why the Federal Reserve prefers to measure inflation using the personal consumption expenditures price index rather than the consumer price index.

- **EARLY COVERAGE OF LONG-RUN TOPICS.** We place key macroeconomic issues in their long-run context in Chapter 21, "Economic Growth, the Financial System, and Business Cycles," and Chapter 22, "Long-Run Economic Growth: Sources and Policies." Chapter 21 puts the business cycle in the context of underlying long-run growth and discusses what actually happens during the phases of the business cycle. We believe this material is important if students are to have the understanding of business cycles they will need to interpret economic events, yet this material is often discussed only briefly or omitted entirely in other books. We know that many instructors prefer to have a short-run orientation to their macro courses, with a strong emphasis on policy. Accordingly, we have structured Chapter 21 so that its discussion of long-run growth would be sufficient for instructors who want to move quickly to short-run analysis. Chapter 22 uses a simple neoclassical growth model to explain important growth issues. We apply the model to topics such as the decline of the Soviet economy, the surprisingly strong growth performance of Botswana, and the failure of many developing countries to sustain high growth rates. And we challenge students with the discussion "Why Isn't the Whole World Rich?"

- **A DYNAMIC MODEL OF AGGREGATE DEMAND AND AGGREGATE SUPPLY.** We take a fresh approach to the standard aggregate demand and aggregate supply model. We realize there is no good, simple alternative to using the *AD-AS* model when explaining movements in the price level and in real GDP. But we know that more instructors are dissatisfied with the *AD-AS* model than with any other aspect of the macro principles course. The key problem, of course, is that *AD-AS* is a static model that attempts to account for dynamic changes in real GDP and the price level. Our approach retains the basics of the *AD-AS* model but makes it more accurate and useful by making it more dynamic. We emphasize two points: First, changes in the position of the short-run (upward-sloping) aggregate supply curve depend mainly on the state of expectations of the inflation rate. Second, the existence of growth in the economy means that the long-run (vertical) aggregate supply curve shifts to the right every year. This "dynamic" *AD-AS* model provides students with a more accurate understanding of the causes and consequences of fluctuations in real GDP and the price level.

Chapter 24 includes a three-layer, full-color acetate for the key introductory dynamic *AD-AS* graph (Figure 24-8, "A Dynamic Aggregate Demand and Aggregate Supply Model," on page 828). We created this acetate (which is reproduced at the top of the next page) to help students see how the graph builds step by step and to help make the graph easier for instructors to present. The acetate will help instructors who want to use dynamic *AD-AS* in class but believe the model needs to be developed carefully.

We introduce this model in Chapter 24, "Aggregate Demand and Aggregate Supply Analysis," and use it to discuss monetary policy in Chapter 26, "Monetary Policy," and fiscal policy in Chapter 27, "Fiscal Policy." Instructors may safely omit the sections on the dynamic *AD-AS* model without any loss in continuity to the discussion of macroeconomic theory and policy. Chapter 26,"Monetary Policy," includes a graph, Figure 26-7, "Monetary Policy," on page 900 that shows expansionary and contractionary policy using only the basic *AD-AS* model, which makes it possible to skip the dynamic *AD-AS* discussion of monetary policy. Chapter 27, "Fiscal Policy," also includes a graph, Figure 27-5, "Fiscal Policy," on page 935 that shows expansionary and contractionary policy using only the basic *AD-AS* model, which makes it possible to skip the dynamic *AD-AS*

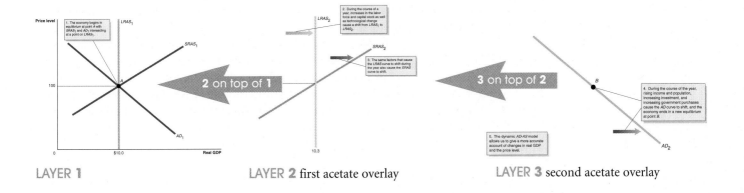

LAYER **1**   LAYER **2** first acetate overlay   LAYER **3** second acetate overlay

discussion of fiscal policy. Chapter 28, "Inflation, Unemployment, and Federal Reserve Policy," uses only the basic *AD-AS* model in discussing the Phillips curve.

- **EXTENSIVE COVERAGE OF MONETARY POLICY.** Because of the central role monetary policy plays in the economy and in students' curiosity about business and financial news, we devote two chapters—Chapters 26, "Monetary Policy," and 28, "Inflation, Unemployment, and Federal Reserve Policy"—to the topic. We emphasize the issues involved in the Fed's choice of monetary policy targets, and we include coverage of the Taylor rule. This updated edition includes coverage of the Fed's new policies aimed at dealing with the housing crisis and its effects on financial markets.

- **COVERAGE OF BOTH THE DEMAND-SIDE AND SUPPLY-SIDE EFFECTS OF FISCAL POLICY.** Our discussion of fiscal policy in Chapter 27, "Fiscal Policy," carefully distinguishes between automatic stabilizers and discretionary fiscal policy. We also provide significant coverage of the supply-side effects of fiscal policy.

- **A SELF-CONTAINED BUT THOROUGH DISCUSSION OF THE KEYNESIAN INCOME-EXPENDITURE APPROACH.** The Keynesian income-expenditure approach (the "45°-line diagram," or "Keynesian cross") is useful for introducing students to the short-run relationship between spending and production. Many instructors, however, prefer to omit this material. Therefore, we use the 45°-line diagram only in Chapter 23, "Output and Expenditure in the Short Run." The discussion of monetary and fiscal policy in later chapters uses only the *AD-AS* model, making it possible to omit Chapter 23.

- **EXTENSIVE INTERNATIONAL COVERAGE.** We include three chapters devoted to international topics: Chapter 8, "Comparative Advantage and the Gains from International Trade," Chapter 29, "Macroeconomics in an Open Economy," and Chapter 30, "The International Financial System." Having a good understanding of the international trading and financial systems is essential to understanding the macroeconomy and to satisfying students' curiosity about the economic world around them. In addition to the material in our three international chapters, we weave international comparisons into the narratives of several chapters, including our discussion of labor market policies in Chapter 28, "Inflation, Unemployment, and Federal Reserve Policy," and central banking in Chapter 25, "Money, Banks, and the Federal Reserve System."

- **FLEXIBLE CHAPTER ORGANIZATION.** Because we realize that there are a variety of approaches to teaching principles of macroeconomics, we have structured our chapters for maximum flexibility. For example, our discussion of long-run economic growth in Chapter 21, "Economic Growth, the Financial System, and Business Cycles," makes it possible for instructors to omit the more thorough discussion of these issues in Chapter 22, "Long-Run Economic Growth: Sources and Policies." Our discussion of the Keynesian 45°-line diagram is confined to Chapter 23 so that instructors who do not use this approach can proceed directly to aggregate demand and aggregate supply analysis in Chapter 24, "Aggregate Demand and Aggregate Supply Analysis." While we devote two chapters to monetary policy, the first of these—Chapter 26, "Monetary Policy"—is a self-contained discussion, so instructors may safely omit the material in Chapter 28, "Inflation, Unemployment, and Federal Reserve Policy," if they choose to. Finally, instructors may choose to omit all three of the international chapters (Chapter 8, "Comparative Advantage and the Gains from International Trade," Chapter 29, "Macroeconomics in an Open Economy," and Chapter 30, "The International Financial System"), cover just Chapter 8 on international trade; cover just Chapter 29; or cover Chapter 29 and Chapter 30, while omitting Chapter 8. Please refer to the flexibility chart on **pages xxvi and xxvii** to help select the chapters and order best suited to your classroom needs.

Special Features:
A Real-World, Hands-on Approach to Learning Economics

Business Cases and *Inside Look* News Articles

Each chapter-opening case provides a real-world context for learning, sparks students' interest in economics, and helps to unify the chapter. The case describes an actual company facing a real situation. The company is integrated in the narrative, graphs, and pedagogical features of the chapter. Many of the chapter openers focus on the role of the entrepreneur in developing new products and bringing them to the market. For example, Chapter 3 covers Steve Jobs of Apple, Chapter 12 covers Howard Schultz of Starbucks, and Chapter 22 covers Tom Anderson and Chris DeWolfe of MySpace.com. Here are a few examples of companies we explore in this Update Edition:

- Can Apple's iPod continue to dominate the market? (**Chapter 3**, "Where Prices Come From: The Interaction of Demand and Supply")

- How does a tariff on Brazilian ethanol producers affect U.S. corn farmers? (**Chapter 8**, "Comparative Advantage and the Gains from International Trade")

- What does activity at American Airlines tell us about the economy? (**Chapter 19**, "GDP: Measuring Total Production and Income")

- Will MySpace succeed in China? (**Chapter 22**, "Long-Run Economic Growth: Sources and Policies")

- How does the business cycle affect FedEx? (**Chapter 24**, "Aggregate Demand and Aggregate Supply Analysis")

An Inside Look is a two-page feature that shows students how to apply the concepts from the chapter to the analysis of a news article. Select articles deal with policy issues and are titled *An Inside Look at Policy*. Articles are from sources such as the *Wall Street Journal*, the *Economist*, and *BusinessWeek*. The feature presents an excerpt from an article, analysis of the article, graph(s), and critical thinking questions.

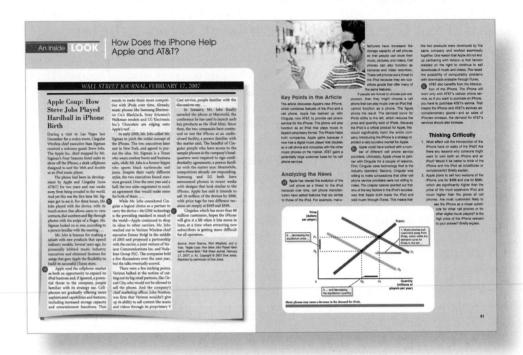

Here are some examples of the articles featured in *An Inside Look*:

- "Apple Coup: How Steve Jobs Played Hardball in iPhone Birth," *Wall Street Journal*, (**Chapter 3**, "Where Prices Come From: The Interaction of Demand and Supply")

- "The United States and South Korea Reach a Trade Deal," *New York Times*, (**Chapter 8**, "Comparative Advantage and the Gains from International Trade")

- "Entrepreneurship and Sustained Economic Growth in Europe," *Economist*, (**Chapter 22**, "Long-Run Economic Growth: Sources and Policies")

- "Freight Carrier Weakness Shows Retailer Uncertainty," *Wall Street Journal*, (**Chapter 24**, "Aggregate Demand and Aggregate Supply Analysis")

Economics in Your Life

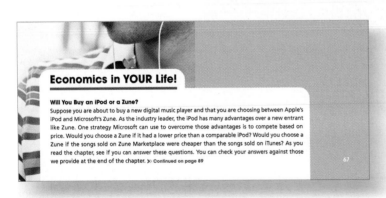

After the chapter-opening real-world business case, we have added a personal dimension to the chapter opener with a new feature titled *Economics in Your Life*, which asks students to consider how economics affects their own lives. The feature piques the interest of students and emphasizes the connection between the material they are learning and their own experiences.

At the end of the chapter, we use the chapter concepts to answer the questions asked at the beginning of the chapter.

Here are examples of the topics we cover in the new "Economics in Your Life" feature:

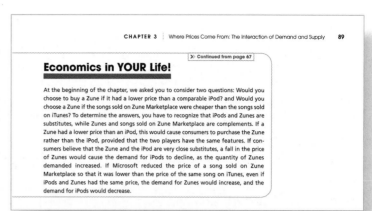

- Will you buy an iPod or a Zune? (**Chapter 3**, "Where Prices Come From: The Interaction of Demand and Supply")

- Does rent control make it easier to find an affordable apartment? (**Chapter 4**, "Economic Efficiency, Government Price Setting, and Taxes")

- What's the best country to work in? (**Chapter 19**, "GDP: Measuring Total Production and Income")

- Would you be better off without China? (**Chapter 22**, "Long-Run Economic Growth: Sources and Policies")

- Is an employer likely to cut your pay during a recession? (**Chapter 24**, "Aggregate Demand and Aggregate Supply Analysis")

Solved Problems

As we all know, many students have great difficulty handling applied economics problems. We help students overcome this hurdle by including two or three worked-out problems tied to select chapter-opening learning objectives. Our goals are to keep students focused on the main ideas of each chapter and to give students a model of how to solve an economic problem by breaking it down step by step. There are additional exercises in the end-of-chapter *Problems and Applications* section tied to every *Solved Problem*.

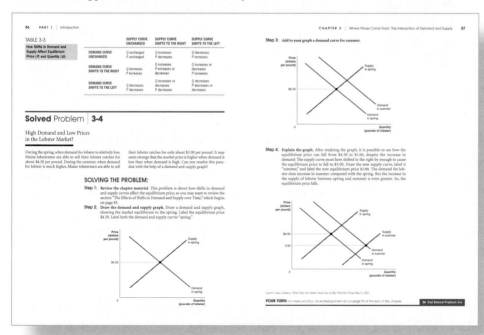

Additional *Solved Problems* appear in the following areas:

- The *Instructor's Manual*
- PowerPoint® slides
- The print *Study Guide*
- The *Test Item Files* includes problems tied to the *Solved Problems* in the main book.

Don't Let This Happen to You!

We know from many years of teaching which concepts students find most difficult. Each chapter contains a box feature called *Don't Let This Happen to You!* that alerts students to the most common pitfalls in that chapter's material. We follow up with a related question in the end-of-chapter *Problems and Applications* section.

Making the Connection

Each chapter includes two to four *Making the Connection* features that present real-world reinforcement of key concepts and help students learn how to interpret what they read on the Web or in newspapers. Most *Making the Connection* features use relevant, stimulating, and provocative news stories focused on businesses and policy issues. One-third of the *Making the Connection* features are new to this edition, and most others have been updated. Several *Making the Connection* features discuss health care, which remains a pressing policy issue. Each *Making the Connection* has at least one supporting end-of-chapter problem to allow students to test their understanding of the topic discussed. Here are some of the new *Making the Connection* features:

- The Market System in Action: How Do You Make an iPod? (**Chapter 2**, "Trade-offs, Comparative Advantage, and the Market System")

- Apple Computer Inc. Forecasts the Demand for Consumer Electronics (**Chapter 3**, "Where Prices Come From: The Interaction of Demand and Supply")

- Should the Government Run the Health Care System? (**Chapter 5**, "Externalities, Environmental Policy, and Public Goods")

- The President Elect's Trade Policies and How Expanding International Trade Has Helped Boeing (**Chapter 8**, "Comparative Advantage and the Gains from International Trade")

- Why Do Some Firms Like the Hilton Hotels Hide Their Prices? (**Chapter 9**, "Consumer Choice and Behavioral Economics")

- Is Being the First Firm in the Market a Key to Success? (**Chapter 12**, "Monopolistic Competition: The Competitive Model in a More Realistic Setting")

- Should the Government Prevent Banks from Becoming Too Big? (**Chapter 14**, "Monopoly and Antitrust Policy")

- Price Discrimination with a Twist at Netflix (**Chapter 15**, "Pricing Strategy")

- Does Adverse Selection Explain Why Some People Do Not Have Health Insurance? (**Chapter 17**, "The Economics of Information")

- Can FedEx and the U.S. Economy Withstand High Oil Prices? (**Chapter 24**, "Aggregate Demand and Aggregate Supply Analysis")

- In a Global Economy, How Can You Tell the Imports from the Domestic Goods? (**Chapter 24**)

- Do We Still Need the Penny? (**Chapter 25**, "Money, Banks, and the Federal Reserve System")

- The Inflation and Deflation of the Housing Market "Bubble" (**Chapter 26**, "Monetary Policy")

Will Apple's iPhone match the success of its iPod?

- Is Losing Your Job Good for Your Health? (**Chapter 27**, "Fiscal Policy")
- The Incredible Falling Dollar (**Chapter 29**, "Macroeconomics in an Open Economy")

Graphs and Summary Tables

Graphs are an indispensable part of the principles of economics course but are a major stumbling block for many students. Every chapter except Chapter 1 includes end-of-chapter problems that require students to draw, read, and interpret graphs. Interactive graphing exercises appear on the book's supporting Web site. We use four devices to help students read and interpret graphs:

1. Detailed captions
2. Boxed notes
3. Color-coded curves
4. Summary tables with graphs

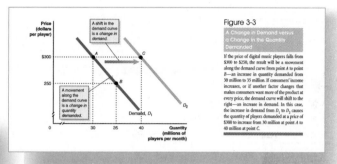

Figure 3-3

A Change in Demand versus a Change in the Quantity Demanded

If the price of digital music players falls from $300 to $250, the result will be a movement along the demand curve from point A to point B—an increase in quantity demanded from 30 million to 35 million. If consumers' income increases, or if another factor changes that makes consumers want more of the product at every price, the demand curve will shift to the right—an increase in demand. In this case, the increase in demand from D_1 to D_2 causes the quantity of players demanded at a price of $300 to increase from 30 million at point A to 40 million at point C.

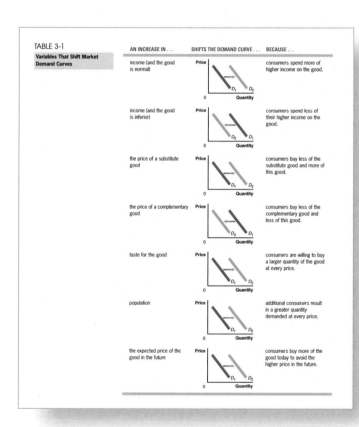

TABLE 3-1

Variables That Shift Market Demand Curves

AN INCREASE IN . . .	SHIFTS THE DEMAND CURVE . . .	BECAUSE . . .
income (and the good is normal)		consumers spend more of higher income on the good.
income (and the good is inferior)		consumers spend less of their higher income on the good.
the price of a substitute good		consumers buy less of the substitute good and more of this good.
the price of a complementary good		consumers buy less of the complementary good and less of this good.
taste for the good		consumers are willing to buy a larger quantity of the good at every price.
population		additional consumers result in a greater quantity demanded at every price.
the expected price of the good in the future		consumers buy more of the good today to avoid the higher price in the future.

New Review Questions and Problems and Applications—Grouped by Learning Objective to Improve Assessment

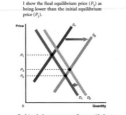

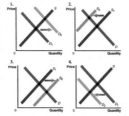

All the end-of-chapter material—*Summary, Review Questions,* and *Problems and Applications*—is grouped under learning objectives. The goals of this new organization are to make it easier for instructors to assign problems based on learning objectives, both in the book and in MyEconLab, and to help students efficiently review material that they find difficult. If students have difficulty with a particular learning objective, an instructor can easily identify which end-of-chapter questions and problems support that objective and assign them as homework or discuss them in class. Every exercise in a chapter's *Problems and Applications* section is available in MyEconLab. Using MyEconLab, students can complete these and many other exercises online, get tutorial help, and receive instant feedback and assistance on those exercises they answer incorrectly. Also, student learning will be enhanced by having the summary material and problems grouped together by learning objective, which will allow students to focus on the parts of the chapter they found most challenging. Each major section of the chapter, paired with a learning objective, has at least two review questions and three problems.

As in the first and second editions, we include one or more end-of-chapter problems that test the students' understanding of the content presented in the *Solved Problem, Making the Connection,* and *Don't Let This Happen to You!* special features in the chapter. Instructors can cover the feature in class and assign the corresponding problem for homework. The Test Item Files also include test questions that pertain to these special features.

Integrated Supplements

The authors and Prentice Hall have worked together to integrate the text, print, and media resources to make teaching and learning easier. The process of revising the supplements began with the Test Item File Review Board, which consisted of 30 instructors who reviewed each question in the first edition's Test Item Files. Many of these instructors became part of the supplement editor team. We are grateful to both the members of the Test Item Review Board and our creative and generous supplement authors. They participated in a two-day meeting with us to discuss ideas on how to improve the supplements and how to ensure that they are consistent with the main book. Ben Paris, Prentice Hall's Executive Producer of Assessment Programs, evaluated Test Item File questions and provided the Test Item File authors guidance on how to write effective questions.

Special thanks to Edward Scahill of the University of Scranton for accuracy checking and coordinating the revisions of the supplements for the Second Edition, Update.

The supplement author team from left to right: Iordanis Petsas, Cathleen Leue, Fernando Quijano, Yvonn Quijano, Ed Scahill, main book authors Glenn Hubbard and Tony OBrien, Kelly Blanchard, and Ratha Ramoo. Not pictured here are Robert Gillette, Wendine Thompson-Dawson, Nick Noble, Robert Holland, Rebecca Stein, and Jim Lee.

Resources for the Instructor

Instructor's Manuals

Edward Scahill of the University of Scranton prepared the *Instructor's Manual* for microeconomics, and Iordanis Petsas of the University of Scranton prepared the *Instructor's Manual* for macroeconomics. The *Instructor's Manuals* include chapter-by-chapter summaries, learning objectives, extended examples and class exercises, teaching outlines incorporating key terms and definitions, teaching tips, topics for class discussion, new *Solved Problems*, new *Making the Connections*, new *Economics in Your Life* scenarios, and solutions to all review questions and problems in the book. The *Instructor's Manuals* are available in print and for download from the Instructor's Resource Center. Rebecca Stein of University of Pennsylvania, Jim Lee of Texas A&M University, and the authors prepared the solutions to the end-of-chapter review questions and problems.

Four Test Item Files

Ratha Ramoo of Diablo Valley College and Edward Scahill of the University of Scranton prepared two Test Item File to accompany microeconomics. Cathleen Leue of the University of Oregon, Robert Gillette of the University of Kentucky, Kelly Blanchard of Purdue University, and Robert Holland of Purdue University prepared two Test Item Files to accompany macroeconomics. Each Test Item File includes 2,000 multiple-choice questions, true/false, short-answer, and graphing questions. There are questions to support each key feature in the book. Test questions are annotated with the following information:

- **Difficulty:** 1 for straight recall, 2 for some analysis, 3 for complex analysis
- **Type:** multiple-choice, true/false, short-answer, essay

- **Topic:** the term or concept the question supports
- **Skill:** fact, definition, analytical, conceptual
- **Learning objective**
- **AACSB** (see description that follows)
- **Page number**
- **Special feature in the main book:** chapter-opening business example, *Economics in Your Life, Solved Problem, Making the Connection, Don't Let this Happen to You!* and *An Inside Look.*

The Test Item Files were checked for accuracy by Thomas C. Kinnaman of Bucknell University; Randy Methenitis of Richland College; Norman C. Miller of Miami University; Brian Rosario of the University of California, Davis; Rachel Small of the University of Colorado, Boulder.

The Association to Advance Collegiate Schools of Business (AACSB)

The Test Item File authors have connected select questions to the general knowledge and skill guidelines found in the AACSB Assurance of Learning Standards.

What is the AACSB?

AACSB is a not-for-profit corporation of educational institutions, corporations, and other organizations devoted to the promotion and improvement of higher education in business administration and accounting. A collegiate institution offering degrees in business administration or accounting may volunteer for AACSB accreditation review. The AACSB makes initial accreditation decisions and conducts periodic reviews to promote continuous quality improvement in management education. Pearson Education is a proud member of the AACSB and is pleased to provide advice to help you apply AACSB Assurance of Learning Standards.

What are AACSB Assurance of Learning Standards?

One of the criteria for AACSB accreditation is the quality of the curricula. Although no specific courses are required, the AACSB expects a curriculum to include learning experiences in such areas as:

- Communication
- Ethical Reasoning
- Analytic Skills
- Use of Information Technology
- Multicultural and Diversity
- Reflective Thinking

These six categories are AACSB Assurance of Learning Standards. Questions that test skills relevant to these standards are tagged with the appropriate standard. For example, a question testing the moral questions associated with externalities would receive the Ethical Reasoning tag.

How Can Instructors Use the AACSB Tags?

Tagged questions help you measure whether students are grasping the course content that aligns with the AACSB guidelines noted above. This in turn may suggest enrichment activities or other educational experiences to help students achieve these skills.

TestGen

The computerized TestGen package allows instructors to customize, save, and generate classroom tests. The test program permits instructors to edit, add, or delete questions from the Test Item Files; edit existing graphics and create new graphics; analyze test results; and organize a database of tests and student results. This software allows for extensive flexibility and ease of use. It provides many options for organizing and displaying tests, along with search and sort features. The software and the Test Item Files can be downloaded from the Instructor's Resource Center (www.prenhall.com/hubbard).

PowerPoint® Lecture Presentation

There are three sets of PowerPoint® slides, prepared by Fernando and Yvonn Quijano, for instructors to use:

1. A comprehensive set of PowerPoint® slides that can be used by instructors for class presentations or by students for lecture preview or review. The presentation includes all the graphs, tables, and equations in the textbook. Two versions are available—the first is in step-by-step mode so that you can build graphs as you would on a blackboard, and in an automated mode, using a single click per slide.

2. A comprehensive set of PowerPoint® slides with Classroom Response Systems (CRS) questions built in so that instructors can incorporate CRS "clickers" into their classroom lectures. For more information on Prentice Hall's partnership with CRS, see the description below. Instructors may download these PowerPoint presentations from the Instructor's Resource Center (www.prenhall.com/hubbard).

3. A student version of the PowerPoints® slides is available as .pdf files from the book's companion website at www.prenhall.com. This version allows students to print the slides and bring them to class for note taking.

   Instructors may download these PowerPoint® presentations from the Instructor's Resource Center (www.prenhall.com/hubbard).

Instructor's Resource CD-ROM

The Instructor's Resource CD-ROM contains all the faculty and student resources that support this text. Instructors have the ability to access and edit the *Instructor's Manuals*, Test Item Files, and PowerPoint® presentations. By simply clicking on a chapter or searching for a keyword, faculty can access an interactive library of resources. Faculty can pick and choose from the various supplements and export them to their hard drives.

Classroom Response Systems

Classroom Response Systems (CRS) is an exciting new wireless polling technology that makes large and small classrooms even more interactive because it enables instructors to pose questions to their students, record results, and display the results instantly. Students can answer questions easily, using compact remote-control transmitters. Prentice Hall has partnerships with leading classroom response systems providers and can show you everything you need to know about setting up and using a CRS system. We'll provide the classroom hardware, text-specific PowerPoint slides, software, and support, and we'll also show you how your students can benefit! Learn more at www.prenhall.com/crs.

Blackboard and WebCT Course Content

Prentice Hall offers fully customizable course content for the Blackboard and WebCT Course Management Systems.

Resources for the Student

Study Guides

Wendine Thompson-Dawson of Monmouth College prepared the study guide to accompany microeconomics, and Nicholas Noble of Miami University prepared the study guide to accompany macroeconomics. The study guides reinforce the textbooks and provide students with the following:

- Chapter summary
- Discussion of each learning objective

- Section-by-section review of the concepts presented
- Helpful study hints
- Additional *Solved Problems* to supplement those in the text
- Key terms with definitions
- A self-test, including 40 multiple-choice questions, plus a number of short-answer and true/false questions, with accompanying answers and explanations

Companion Web site

The free companion Web site, www.prenhall.com/hubbard, gives students access to an interactive study guide that provides instant feedback, economics updates, student PowerPoint slides, and many other resources to promote success in the principles of economics course.

PowerPoint® Slides

For student use as a study aide or note-taking guide, PowerPoint® slides, prepared by Fernando and Yvonn Quijano, may be downloaded from the companion Web site, at www.prenhall.com/hubbard. The slides include:

- All graphs, tables, and equations in the text
- Figures in step-by-step, automated mode, using a single click per graph curve
- End-of-chapter key terms with hyperlinks to relevant slides

CourseSmart is an exciting new *choice* for students looking to save money. As an alternative to purchasing the print textbook, students can purchase an electronic version of the same content and save up to 50 percent off the suggested list price of the print text. With a CourseSmart etextbook, students can search the text, make notes online, print out reading assignments that incorporate lecture notes, and bookmark important passages for later review. For more information, or to purchase access to the CourseSmart eTextbook, visit www.coursesmart.com.

Vango Notes

Study on the go with VangoNotes (www.VangoNotes.com), detailed chapter reviews in downloadable MP3 format. Now, wherever you are and whatever you're doing, you can study on the go by listening to the following for each chapter of your textbook:

- **Big Ideas:** Your "need to know" for each chapter
- **Key Terms:** Audio "flashcards"—help you review key concepts and terms
- **Rapid Review:** Quick-drill sessions—use it right before your test

VangoNotes are **flexible**: Download all the material (or only the chapters you need) directly to your player. And *VangoNotes* are **efficient**: Use them in your car, at the gym, walking to class, wherever you go. So get yours today, and get studying.

Get Ahead of the Curve

For the Instructor

MyEconLab is an online course management, testing, and tutorial resource. Instructors can choose how much, or how little, time to spend setting up and using MyEconLab.

Each chapter contains two Sample Tests, Study Plan Exercises, and Tutorial Resources. Student use of these materials requires no initial set-up by their instructor. The online Gradebook records each student's performance and time spent on the Tests and Study Plan and generates reports by student or by chapter.

Instructors can assign Tests, Quizzes, and Homework in MyEconLab using four resources:

- pre-loaded Sample Test questions
- Problems similar to the end-of-chapter problems
- Test Item File questions
- Self-authored questions using Econ Exercise Builder

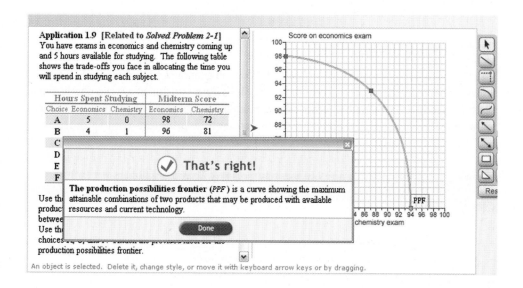

Exercises use multiple-choice, graph drawing, and free-response items, many of which are generated algorithmically so that each time a student works them, a different variation is presented.

MyEconLab grades every problem, even those with graphs. When working homework exercises, students receive immediate feedback with links to additional learning tools.

Customization and Communication

MyEconLab in CourseCompass provides additional optional customization and communication tools. Instructors who teach distance-learning courses or very large lecture sections find the CourseCompass format useful because they can upload course documents and assignments, customize the order of chapters, and use communication features such as Digital Dropbox and Discussion Board.

For the Student

MyEconLab puts students in control of their learning through a collection of testing, practice, and study tools tied to the online, interactive version of the textbook and other medial resources.

Within MyEconLab's structured environment, students practice what they learn, test their understanding, and pursue a personalized Study Plan generated from their performance on Sample Tests and tests created by their instructors. At the core of MyEconLab are the following features:

- Sample Tests, two per chapter
- Personal Study Plan
- Tutorial Instruction
- Graphing Tool

Sample Tests

Two Sample Tests for each chapter are pre-loaded in MyEconLab, enabling students to practice what they have learned, test their understanding, and identify areas in which they need to do further work. Students can study on their own, or they can complete assignments created by their instructor.

Personal Study Plan

Based on a student's performance on tests, MyEconLab generates a personal Study Plan that shows where he or she needs further study. The Study Plan consists of a series of additional practice exercises with detailed feedback and guided solutions and keyed to other tutorial resources.

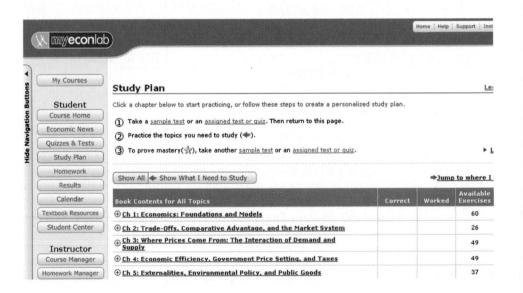

Tutorial Instruction

Launched from many of the exercises in the Study Plan, MyEconLab provides tutorial instruction in the form of step-by-step solutions and other media-based explanations.

Graphing Tool

A graphing tool is integrated into the Tests and Study Plan exercises to enable students to make and manipulate graphs. This feature helps students understand how concepts, numbers, and graphs connect.

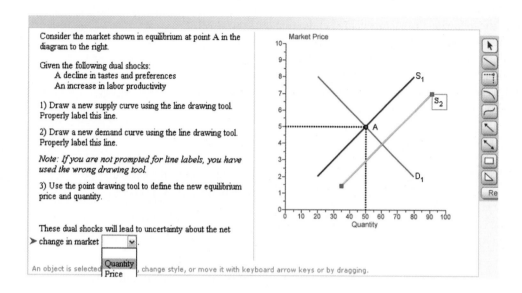

Additional MyEconLab Tools

MyEconLab also includes the following additional features:

1. **Economics in the News**—weekly news article updates during the school year of news items with links to sources for further reading and discussion questions

2. **eText**—While working in the Study Plan or completing homework assignments, part of the tutorial resources available is a link directly to the relevant page of the text so the student can review the appropriate material to help them complete the exercise

3. **Glossary**—a searchable version of the textbook glossary with additional examples and links to related terms

4. **Glossary Flashcards**—every key term is available as a flashcard, allowing students to quiz themselves on vocabulary from one or more chapters at a time

5. **Ask the Author**—e-mail economic related questions to the author

6. **Research Navigator (CourseCompass version only)**—extensive help on the research process and four exclusive databases of credible and reliable source material, including *The New York Times*, the *Financial Times*, and peer-reviewed journals

MyEconLab content has been created through the efforts of: Chris Annala, State University of New York–Geneseo; Charles Baum, Middle Tennessee State University; Sarah Ghosh, University of Scranton; Chris Kauffman, University of Tennessee–Knoxville; Russell Kellogg, University of Colorado–Denver; Noel Lotz, Middle Tennessee State University; Woo Jung, University of Colorado; Katherine McCann, University of Delaware; Christine Polek, University of Massachusetts–Boston; Leonie L. Stone, State University of New York–Geneseo; Bert G. Wheeler, Cedarville University; and Douglas A. Ruby, Pearson Education.

Consultant Board, Accuracy Review Board, and Reviewers

The guidance and recommendations of the following instructors helped us develop the revision plans for the second edition and the supplements package. While we could not incorporate every suggestion from every consultant board member, reviewer, or accuracy checker, we do thank each and every one of you, and acknowledge that your feedback was indispensable in developing this text. We greatly appreciate your assistance in making this the best text it could be—you have helped teach a whole new generation of students about the exciting world of economics.

Consultant Board

Kate Antonovics, University of California–San Diego

Robert Beekman, University of Tampa

Valerie Bencivenga, University of Texas–Austin

Kelly Blanchard, Purdue University

Robert Gillette, University of Kentucky

Robert Godby, University of Wyoming

William Goffe, State University of New York–Oswego

Jane S. Himarios, University of Texas–Arlington

Michael Potepan, San Francisco State University

Robert Whaples, Wake Forest University

Jonathan B. Wight, University of Richmond

Accuracy Review Board

Our accuracy checkers did a particularly painstaking and thorough job of helping us proof the graphs, equations, and features of the text and the supplements. We are grateful for their time and commitment:

Fatma Abdel-Raouf, Goldey-Beacom College

Mohammad S. Bajwa, Northampton Community College

Hamid Bastin, Shippensburg University

Kelly Blanchard, Purdue University

Don Bumpass, Sam Houston State University

Mark S. Chester, Reading Area Community College

Kenny Christianson, Binghamton University

Ishita Edwards, Oxnard College

Harry Ellis, University of North Texas

Can Erbil, Brandeis University

Marc Fusaro, East Carolina University

Sarah Ghosh, University of Scranton

Maria Giuili, Diablo Valley College

Carol Hogan, University of Michigan–Dearborn

Aaron Jackson, Bentley College

Nancy Jianakoplos, Colorado State University

Thomas C. Kinnaman, Bucknell University

Mary K. Knudson, University of Iowa

Stephan Kroll, California State University–Sacramento

Randy Methenitis, Richland College

Norman C. Miller, Miami University

Michael Potepan, San Francisco State University

Mary L. Pranzo, California State University–Fresno

Brian Rosario, the University of California–Davis

Joseph M. Santos, South Dakota State University

Mark V. Siegler, California State University–Sacramento

Rachel Small, University of Colorado–Boulder

Stephen Smith, Bakersfield College

Rajeev Sooreea, Pennsylvania State University–Altoona

Rebecca Stein, University of Pennsylvania

Wendine Thompson-Dawson, Monmouth College

Robert Whaples, Wake Forest University

Reviewers

The guidance and thoughtful recommendations of many instructors helped us develop and implement a revision plan that expanded the book's content, improved the figures, and strengthened assessment features. We extend special thanks to Joseph Santos of South Dakota State University, Matthew Rafferty of Quinnipiac University, and David Eaton of Murray State University for helping us revise the chapter openers and *Inside Look* features. We are grateful for the comments and many helpful suggestions received from the following reviewers:

ALABAMA

Doris Bennett, Jacksonville State University

Harold W. Elder, University of Alabama–Tuscaloosa

Wanda Hudson, Alabama Southern Community College

ARIZONA

Price Fishback, University of Arizona

ARKANSAS

Jerry Crawford, Arkansas State University

CALIFORNIA

Maneeza Aminy, Golden Gate University

Becca Arnold, Mesa College

Anoshua Chaudhuri, San Francisco State University

Jose Esteban, Palomar College

Craig Gallet, California State University–Sacramento

Maria Giuili, Diablo Valley College

Lisa Grobar, California State University–Long Beach

Dewey Heinsma, Mt. San Jacinto Community College

Jessica Howell, California State University–Sacramento

Greg Hunter, California State University–Pomona

Jonathan Kaplan, California State University–Sacramento

Philip King, San Francisco State University

Lori Kletzer, University of California, Santa Cruz

Stephan Kroll, California State University–Sacramento

David Lang, California State University–Sacramento

Carsten Lange, California State Polytechnic University–Pomona

Rose LeMont, Modesto Junior College

Kristen Monaco, California State University–Long Beach

Mary L. Pranzo, California State University–Fresno

Scott J. Sambucci, California State University–East Bay

Stephen Smith, Bakersfield College

Lea Templer, College of the Canyons

Kristin Vangaasbeck, California State University–Sacramento

Michael Visser, Sonoma State University

Kevin Young, Diablo Valley College

COLORADO

Dale DeBoer, University of Colorado–Colorado Springs

William G. Mertens, University of Colorado–Boulder

Rachael Small, University of Colorado–Boulder

CONNECTICUT

Matthew Rafferty, Quinnipiac University

DELAWARE

Fatma Abdel-Raouf, Goldey-Beacom College

Ali Ataiifar, Delaware County Community College

FLORIDA

Herman Baine, Broward Community College

Robert L. Beekman, University of Tampa

Eric P. Chiang, Florida Atlantic University

Brad Kamp, University of South Florida

Brian Kench, University of Tampa

Barbara A. Moore, University of Central Florida

Deborah Paige, Santa Fe Community College

Bob Potter, University of Central Florida

Zhiguang Wang, Florida International University

Joan Wiggenhorn, Barry University

GEORGIA

Constantin Ogloblin, Georgia Southern University

Dr. Greg Okoro, Georgia Perimeter College–Clarkston

ILLINOIS

Ali Akarca, University of Illinois at Chicago

Zsolt Becsi, Southern Illinois University–Carbondale

David Gordon, Illinois Valley Community College

Rosa Lea Danielson, College of DuPage

Scott Gilbert, Southern Illinois University

Rajeev K. Goel, Illinois State University

Alan Grant, Eastern Illinois University

Alice Melkumian, Western Illinois University

Jeff Reynolds, Northern Illinois University

Thomas R. Sadler, Western Illinois University

Kevin Sylwester, Southern Illinois University–Carbondale

Wendine Thompson-Dawson, Monmouth College

INDIANA

Robert B. Harris, Indiana University–Purdue University–Indianapolis

James K. Self, Indiana University–Bloomington

Arun K. Srinivasan, Indiana University–Southeast Campus

IOWA

John Solow, University of Iowa

Jonathan Warner, Dordt College

KANSAS

Guatam Bhattacharya, University of Kansas

Dipak Ghosh, Emporia State University

Alan Grant, Baker University

Wayne Oberle, St. Ambrose University

Martin Perline, Wichita State University

Joel Potter, Kansas State University

Joshua Rosenbloom, University of Kansas

Shane Sanders, Kansas State University

Bhavneet Walia, Kansas State University

KENTUCKY

David Eaton, Murray State University

Ann Eike, University of Kentucky

Barry Haworth, University of Louisville

Donna Ingram, Eastern Kentucky University

Waithaka Iraki, Kentucky State University

Martin Milkman, Murray State University

David Shideler, Murray State University

LOUISIANA

Sung Chul No, Southern University and A&M College

MARYLAND

Jill Caviglia-Harris, Salisbury University

Dustin Chambers, Salisbury University

Karl Einolf, Mount Saint Mary's University

Bruce Madariaga, Montgomery College

Gretchen Mester, Anne Arundel Community College

MASSACHUSETTS

Michael Enz, Western New England College

Can Erbil, Brandeis University

Lou Foglia, Suffolk University

Aaron Jackson, Bentley College
Ahmad Saranjam, Bridgewater State College
Howard Shore, Bentley College
Janet Thomas, Bentley College

MICHIGAN

Eric Beckman, Delta College
Jared Boyd, Henry Ford Community College
Victor Claar, Hope College
Dr. Sonia Dalmia, Grand Valley State University
Daniel Giedeman, Grand Valley State University
Gregg Heidebrink, Washtenaw Community College
Carol Hogan, University of Michigan–Dearborn
Marek Kolar, Delta College
Susan J. Linz, Michigan State University
James Luke, Lansing Community College
Ilir Miteza, University of Michigan–Dearborn
Norman P. Obst, Michigan State University
Laudo M. Ogura, Grand Valley State University
Michael J. Ryan, Western Michigan University
Charles A. Stull, Kalamazoo College
Michael J. Twomey, University of Michigan–Dearborn
Mark Wheeler, Western Michigan University
Wendy Wysocki, Monroe County Community College

MINNESOTA

Mary Edwards, Saint Cloud State University
Phillip J. Grossman, Saint Cloud State University
David J. O'Hara, Metropolitan State University–Minneapolis
Ken Rebeck, Saint Cloud State University
Kwang Woo (Ken) Park, Minnesota State University–Mankato

MISSISSIPPI

Becky Campbell, Mississippi State University

MISSOURI

Chris Azevedo, University of Central Missouri
Ariel Belasen, Saint Louis University
Catherine Chambers, University of Central Missouri
Paul Chambers, University of Central Missouri
Ben Collier, Northwest Missouri State University
John R. Crooker, University of Central Missouri
Mark Karscig, Central Missouri State University
Nicholas D. Peppes, Saint Louis Community College–Forest Park

MONTANA

Jeff Bookwalter, University of Montana–Missoula
Agnieszka Bielinska-Kwapisz, Montana State University–Bozeman

NEBRASKA

Allan Jenkins, University of Nebraska–Kearney
Kim Sosin, University of Nebraska–Omaha

NEVADA

Bernard Malamud, University of Nevada–Las Vegas

NEW JERSEY

Giuliana Campanelli-Andreopoulos, William Paterson University
Donna Thompson, Brookdale Community College

NEW MEXICO

Kate Krause, University of New Mexico
Curt Shepherd, University of New Mexico

NEW YORK

Seemi Ahmad, Dutchess Community College
Chris Annala, State University of New York–Geneseo
John Bockino, Suffolk County Community College–Ammerman
Sean Corcoran, New York University
Debra Dwyer, Stony Brook University
Glenn Gerstner, Saint John's University–Queens
Susan Glanz, Saint John's University–Queens
Leonie Stone, State University of New York–Geneseo

NORTH CAROLINA

Marc Fusaro, East Carolina University
Melissa Hendrickson, North Carolina State University
Jeff Sarbaum, University of North Carolina–Greensboro
Catherine Skura, Sandhills Community College

OHIO

Bolong Cao, Ohio University–Athens
Harley Gill, Ohio State University
Leroy Gill, Ohio State University
Steven Heubeck, Ohio State University
Ida A. Mirzaie, Ohio State University
Dennis C. O'Neill, University of Cincinnati
Joseph Palardy, Youngstown State University
Bert Wheeler, Cedarville University
Kathryn Wilson, Kent State University

OKLAHOMA

Ed Price, Oklahoma State University
Abdulhamid Sukar, Cameron University

PENNSYLVANIA

Bradley Andrew, Juniata College
Mohammad Bajwa, Northampton Community College
Howard Bodenhorn, Lafayette College
Milica Bookman, St Joseph's University
Eric Brucker, Widener University
Scott J. Dressler, Villanova University
Satyajit Ghosh, University of Scranton
Anthony Gyapong, Pennsylvania State University–Abington
Andrew Hill, Federal Reserve Bank of Philadelphia
James Jozefowicz, Indiana University of Pennsylvania
Stephanie Jozefowicz, Indiana University of Pennsylvania
Nicholas Karatjas, Indiana University of Pennsylvania
Mary Kelly, Villanova University
Thomas C. Kinnaman, Bucknell University
Christopher Magee, Bucknell University
Judy McDonald, Lehigh University

Ranganath Murthy, Bucknell University

Hong V. Nguyen, University of Scranton

Cristian Pardo, Saint Joseph's University

Rajeev Sooreea, Pennsylvania State University–Altoona

Rebecca Stein, University of Pennsylvania

Sandra Trejos, Clarion University

Ann Zech, Saint Joseph's University

Lei Zhu, West Chester University of Pennsylvania

RHODE ISLAND

Leonard Lardaro, University of Rhode Island

Nazma Latif-Zaman, Providence College

SOUTH CAROLINA

Calvin Blackwell, College of Charleston

Ward Hooker, Orangeburg-Calhoun Technical College

Woodrow W. Hughes, Jr., Converse College

John McArthur, Wofford College

SOUTH DAKOTA

Joseph M. Santos, South Dakota State University

Jason Zimmerman, South Dakota State University

TENNESSEE

Charles Baum, Middle Tennessee State University

Michael J. Gootzeit, University of Memphis

TEXAS

Carlos Aguilar, El Paso Community College

William Beaty, Tarleton State University

Klaus Becker Texas Tech University

Jack A. Bucco, Austin Community College–Northridge and Saint Edward's University

Don Bumpass, Sam Houston State University

Marilyn M. Butler, Sam Houston State University

Cesar Corredor, Texas A&M University

Patrick Crowley, Texas A&M University–Corpus Christi

Mark Frank, Sam Houston State University

Tina J. Harvell, Blinn College–Bryan Campus

Jane S. Himarios, University of Texas–Arlington

James Holcomb, University of Texas–El Paso

Jamal Husein, Angelo State University

Karen Johnson, Baylor University

Kathy Kelly, University of Texas–Arlington

Jim Lee, Texas A&M University–Corpus Christi

Ronnie W. Liggett, University of Texas–Arlington

Kimberly Mencken, Baylor University

Randy Methenitis, Richland College

Charles Newton, Houston Community College–Southwest College

Sara Saderion, Houston Community College–Southwest College

George E. Samuels, Sam Houston State University

Roger Wehr, University of Texas–Arlington

Jim Wollscheid, Texas A&M University–Kingsville

Dr. J. Christopher Wreh, I, North Central Texas College

David W. Yoskowitz, Texas A&M University–Corpus Christi

Inske Zandvliet, Brookhaven College

VERMONT

Nancy Brooks, University of Vermont

VIRGINIA

Philip Heap, James Madison University

George E. Hoffer, Virginia Commonwealth University

Oleg Korenok, Virginia Commonwealth University

Frances Lea, Germanna Community College

John Min, Northern Virginia Community College

Susanne Toney, Hampton University

George Zestos, Christopher Newport University

WASHINGTON

Stacey Jones, Seattle University

Dean Peterson, Seattle University

WISCONSIN

Marina Karabelas, Milwaukee Area Technical College

Elizabeth Sawyer Kelly, University of Wisconsin–Madison

John R. Stoll, University of Wisconsin–Green Bay

DISTRICT OF COLUMBIA

Michael Bradley, George Washington University

Colleen M. Callahan, American University

INTERNATIONAL

Minh Quang Dao, Carleton University–Ottawa, Canada

Previous Edition Class Testers, Accuracy Reviewers, and Consultants

Class Testers

We are grateful to both the instructors who class tested manuscript of the first edition and their students for providing clear-cut recommendations on how to make chapters interesting, relevant, and comprehensive:

Charles A. Bennett, Gannon University

Anne E. Bresnock, University of California, Los Angeles and California State Polytechnic University–Pomona

Linda Childs-Leatherbury, Lincoln University, Pennsylvania

John Eastwood, Northern Arizona University

David Eaton, Murray State University

Paul Elgatian, St. Ambrose University

Patricia A. Freeman, Jackson State University

Robert Godby, University of Wyoming

Frank Gunter, Lehigh University

Ahmed Ispahani, University of LaVerne

Brendan Kennelly, Lehigh University and National University of Ireland–Galway

Ernest Massie, Franklin University

Carol McDonough, University of Massachusetts–Lowell

Shah Mehrabi, Montgomery College

Sharon Ryan, University of Missouri–Columbia

Bruce G. Webb, Gordon College

Madelyn Young, Converse College

Susan Zumas, Lehigh University

Accuracy Review Board

We are grateful to the following first edition accuracy checkers for their hard work on the book and supplements:

Kelly Hunt Blanchard, Purdue University

Harold Elder, University of Alabama

Marc Fusaro, East Carolina University

Robert Gillette, University of Kentucky

William L. Goffe, State University of New York–Oswego

Travis Hayes, University of Tennessee–Chattanooga

Anisul M. Islam, University of Houston–Downtown

Faik A. Koray, Louisiana State University

Tony Lima, California State University–Hayward

James A. Moreno, Blinn College

Matthew Rafferty, Quinnipiac University

Jeff Reynolds, Northern Illinois University

Brian Rosario, University of California, Davis

Joseph M. Santos, South Dakota State University

Edward Scahill, University of Scranton

Robert Whaples, Wake Forest University

Consultant Board

We received guidance during the first edition development at several critical junctures from a dedicated consultant board. We relied on the board for input on content, figure treatment, and design:

Susan Dadres, Southern Methodist University

Harry Ellis, Jr., University of North Texas

Robert Godby, University of Wyoming

William L. Goffe, State University of New York–Oswego

Donn M. Johnson, Quinnipiac University

Mark Karscig, Central Missouri State University

Jenny Minier, University of Kentucky

Nicholas Noble, Miami University

Matthew Rafferty, Quinnipiac University

Helen Roberts, University of Illinois–Chicago

Robert Rosenman, Washington State University

Joseph M. Santos, South Dakota State University

Martin C. Spechler, Indiana University–Purdue University–Indianapolis

Robert Whaples–Wake Forest University

Reviewers

The guidance and recommendations of the following instructors helped us shape the first edition over the course of three years. We extend special thanks to Joseph Santos of South Dakota State University for helping prepare some of the *Inside Look* features and Robert Gillette of the University of Kentucky, Robert Whaples of Wake Forest University, Nicholas Noble of Miami University, and Lee Craig of North Carolina State University for preparing some of the review questions and problems and applications that appear at the ends of chapters.

ALABAMA

Doris Bennett, Jacksonville State University

Harold W. Elder, University of Alabama–Tuscaloosa

James L. Swofford, University of Southern Alabama

ARIZONA

    Doug Conway, Mesa Community College

    John Eastwood, Northern Arizona University

    Price Fishback, University of Arizona

CALIFORNIA

    Renatte Adler, San Diego State University

    Robert Bise, Orange Coast Community College

    Victor Brajer, California State University–Fullerton

    Anne E. Bresnock, University of California, Los Angeles and California State Polytechnic University–Pomona

    David Brownstone, University of California, Irvine

    Maureen Burton, California State Polytechnic University–Pomona

    James G. Devine, Loyola Marymount University

    Roger Frantz, San Diego State University

    Andrew Gill, California State University–Fullerton

    Lisa Grobar, California State University–Long Beach

    Steve Hamilton, California State University–Fullerton

    Ahmed Ispahani, University of LaVerne

    George A. Jouganatos, California State University–Sacramento

    Philip King, San Francisco State University–Chico

    Don Leet, California State University–Fresno

    Rose LeMont, Modesto Junior College

    Solina Lindahl, California Polytechnic State University–San Luis Obispo

    Kristen Monaco, California State University–Long Beach

    W. Douglas Morgan, University of California, Santa Barbara

    Joseph M. Pogodzinksi, San Jose State University

    Michael J. Potepan, San Francisco State University

    Ratha Ramoo, Diablo Valley College

    Ariane Schauer, Marymount College

    Frederica Shockley, California State University–Chico

    Mark Siegler, California State University–Sacramento

    Lisa Simon, California Polytechnic State University–San Louis Obispo

    Rodney B. Swanson, University of California, Los Angeles

    Kristin A. Van Gaasbeck, California State University–Sacramento

    Anthony Zambelli, Cuyamaca College

COLORADO

    Rhonda Corman, University of Northern Colorado

    Dale DeBoer, University of Colorado–Colorado Springs

    Murat Iyigun, University of Colorado at Boulder

    Nancy Jianakoplos, Colorado State University

    Jay Kaplan, University of Colorado–Boulder

    Stephen Weiler, Colorado State University

CONNECTICUT

    Christopher P. Ball, Quinnipiac University

    Donn M. Johnson, Quinnipiac University

    Judith Mills, Southern Connecticut State University

    Matthew Rafferty, Quinnipiac University

DELAWARE

    Fatma Abdel-Raouf, Goldey-Beacom College

    Andrew T. Hill, University of Delaware

FLORIDA

    Herm Baine, Broward Community College–Central

    Martine Duchatelet, Barry University

    Hadley Hartman, Santa Fe Community College

    Richard Hawkins, University of West Florida

    Barbara Moore, University of Central Florida

    Augustine Nelson, University of Miami

    Jamie Ortiz, Florida Atlantic University

    Robert Pennington, University of Central Florida

    Jerry Schwartz, Broward Community College–North

    William Stronge, Florida Atlantic University

    Nora Underwood, University of Central Florida

IDAHO

    Don Holley, Boise State University

ILLINOIS

    Teshome Abebe, Eastern Illinois University

    Ali Akarca, University of Illinois–Chicago

    James Bruehler, Eastern Illinois University

    Louis Cain, Loyola University Chicago and Northwestern University

    Rik Hafer, Southern Illinois University–Edwardsville

    Alla A. Melkumian, Western Illinois University

    Christopher Mushrush, Illinois State University

    Jeff Reynolds, Northern Illinois University

    Helen Roberts, University of Illinois–Chicago

    Eric Schulz, Northwestern University

    Charles Sicotte, Rock Valley Community College

    Neil T. Skaggs, Illinois State University

    Mark Witte, Northwestern University

    Laurie Wolff, Southern Illinois University–Carbondale

    Paula Worthington, Northwestern University

INDIANA

    Kelly Blanchard, Purdue University

    Cecil Bohanon, Ball State University

    Thomas Gresik, University of Notre Dame

    Fred Herschede, Indiana University–South Bend

    James K. Self, Indiana University–Bloomington

    Esther-Mirjam Sent, University of Notre Dame

    Virginia Shingleton, Valparaiso University

    Martin C. Spechler, Indiana University–Purdue University–Indianapolis

    Geetha Suresh, Purdue University–West Lafayette

IOWA

    Terry Alexander, Iowa State University

    Paul Elgatian, St. Ambrose University

KANSAS

Jodi Messer Pelkowski, Wichita State University

Josh Rosenbloom, University of Kansas

KENTUCKY

Tom Cate, Northern Kentucky University

Nan-Ting Chou, University of Louisville

David Eaton, Murray State University

Robert Gillette, University of Kentucky

Hak Youn Kim, Western Kentucky University

Jenny Minier, University of Kentucky

John Vahaly, University of Louisville

LOUISIANA

Faik Koray, Louisiana State University

Paul Nelson, University of Louisiana–Monroe

Tammy Parker, University of Louisiana–Monroe

Wesley A. Payne, Delgado Community College

MASSACHUSETTS

William L. Casey, Jr., Babson College

Arthur Schiller Casimir, Western New England College

Michael Enz, Western New England College

Todd Idson, Boston University

Russell A. Janis, University of Massachusetts–Amherst

Anthony Laramie, Merrimack College

Carol McDonough, University of Massachusetts–Lowell

William O'Brien, Worcester State College

Gregory H. Wassall, Northeastern University

Bruce G. Webb, Gordon College

Gilbert Wolpe, Newbury College

MARYLAND

Carey Borkoski, Anne Arundel Community College

Kathleen A. Carroll, University of Maryland–Baltimore County

Dustin Chambers, Salisbury University

Shah Mehrabi, Montgomery College

David Mitch, University of Maryland–Baltimore County

John Neri, University of Maryland

Henry Terrell, University of Maryland

MICHIGAN

John Nader, Grand Valley State University

Robert J. Rossana, Wayne State University

Mark Wheeler, Western Michigan University

MISSOURI

Jo Durr, Southwest Missouri State University

Julie H. Gallaway, Southwest Missouri State University

Terrel Galloway, Southwest Missouri State University

Mark Karscig, Central Missouri State University

Steven T. Petty, College of the Ozarks

Sharon Ryan, University of Missouri–Columbia

Ben Young, University of Missouri–Kansas City

MINNESOTA

Monica Hartman, University of St. Thomas

MISSISSIPPI

Randall Campbell, Mississippi State University

Patricia A. Freeman, Jackson State University

NEBRASKA

James Knudsen, Creighton University

Craig MacPhee, University of Nebraska–Lincoln

Mark E. Wohar, University of Nebraska–Omaha

NEW HAMPSHIRE

Evelyn Gick, Dartmouth College

Neil Niman, University of New Hampshire

NEW JERSEY

Len Anyanwu, Union County College

Maharuk Bhiladwalla, Rutgers University–New Brunswick

Gary Gigliotti, Rutgers University–New Brunswick

John Graham, Rutgers University–Newark

Berch Haroian, William Paterson University

Paul Harris, Camden County College

NEW MEXICO

Donald Coes, University of New Mexico

NEW YORK

Erol Balkan, Hamilton College

Ranjit S. Dighe, City University of New York–Bronx Community College

William L. Goffe, State University of New York–Oswego

Wayne A. Grove, LeMoyne College

Christopher Inya, Monroe Community College

Clifford Kern, State University of New York–Binghampton

Mary Lesser, Iona College

Howard Ross, Baruch College

Leonie Stone, State University of New York–Geneseo

Ganti Subrahmanyam, University of Buffalo

Jogindar S. Uppal, State University of New York–Albany

Susan Wolcott, Binghamton University

NORTH CAROLINA

Otilia Boldea, North Carolina State University

Robert Burrus, University of North Carolina–Wilmington

Lee A. Craig, North Carolina State University

Kathleen Dorsainvil, Winston-Salem State University

Marc Fusaro, East Carolina University

Salih Hakeem, North Carolina Central University

Haiyong Liu, East Carolina University

Kosmas Marinakis, North Carolina State University

Todd McFall, Wake Forest University

Shahriar Mostashari, Campbell University

Peter Schuhmann, University of North Carolina–Wilmington

Carol Stivender, University of North Carolina–Charlotte

Vera Tabakova, East Carolina University

Robert Whaples, Wake Forest University

Gary W. Zinn, East Carolina University

OHIO

John P. Blair, Wright State University
Kyongwook Choi, Ohio University
Darlene DeVera, Miami University
Tim Fuerst, Bowling Green University
Ernest Massie, Franklin University
Mike Nelson, University of Akron
Nicholas Noble, Miami University
Rochelle Ruffer, Youngstown State University
Kate Sheppard, University of Akron
Steve Szeghi, Wilmington College
Melissa Thomasson, Miami University
Yaqin Wang, Youngstown State University
Sourushe Zandvakili, University of Cincinnati

OKLAHOMA

David Hudgins, University of Oklahoma

OREGON

Bill Burrows, Lane Community College
Tom Carroll, Central Oregon Community College
Larry Singell, University of Oregon
Ayca Tekin-Koru, Oregon State University

PENNSYLVANIA

Gustavo Barboza, Mercyhurst College
Charles A. Bennett, Gannon University
Howard Bodenhorn, Lafayette College
Milica Bookman, St. Joseph's University
Robert Brooker, Gannon University
Linda Childs-Leatherbury, Lincoln University
Satyajit Ghosh, University of Scranton
Mehdi Haririan, Bloomsburg University
Nicholas Karatjas, Indiana University of Pennsylvania
Brendan Kennelly, Lehigh University
Iordanis Petsas, University of Scranton
Adam Renhoff, Drexel University
Edward Scahill, University of Scranton
Rajeev Sooreea, Pennsylvania State University–Altoona
Sandra Trejos, Clarion University
Peter Zaleski, Villanova University
Susan Zumas, Lehigh University

SOUTH CAROLINA

Calvin Blackwell, College of Charleston
Chad Turner, Clemson University
Madelyn Young, Converse College

SOUTH DAKOTA

Joseph M. Santos, South Dakota State University
Jason Zimmerman, South Dakota State University

TENNESSEE

Bichaka Fayissa, Middle Tennessee State University
Travis Hayes, University of Tennessee–Chattanooga
Christopher C. Klein, Middle Tennessee State University
Milicent Sites, Carson-Newman College

TEXAS

Rashid Al-Hmoud, Texas Tech University
Mike Cohick, Collin County Community College
Cesar Corredor, Texas A&M University
Susan Dadres, Southern Methodist University
Harry Ellis, Jr., University of North Texas
Paul Emberton, Texas State University
Diego Escobari, Texas A&M University
Nicholas Feltovich, University of Houston–Main
Charles Harold Fifield, Baylor University
Richard Gosselin, Houston Community College–Central
James W. Henderson, Baylor University
Ansul Islam, University of Houston–Downtown
Sheila Amin Gutierrez de Pineres, University of Texas–Dallas
James W. Henderson, Baylor University
Ansul Islam, University of Houston–Downtown
Kathy Kelly, University of Texas–Arlington
Thomas Kemp, Tarrant County College–Northwest
Akbar Marvasti, University of Houston–Downtown
James Mbata, Houston Community College
Carl Montano, Lamar University
James Moreno, Blinn College
John Pisciotta, Baylor University
Sara Saderion, Houston Community College–Southwest
Ivan Tasic, Texas A&M University

UTAH

Lowell Glenn, Utah Valley State College
Aric Krause, Westminster College
Arden Pope, Brigham Young University

VIRGINIA

Lee Badgett, Virginia Military Institute
Lee A. Coppock, University of Virginia
Carrie Meyer, George Mason University
James Roberts, Tidewater Community College–Virginia Beach
Araine A. Schauer, Mary Mount College
Sarah Stafford, The College of William & Mary
Michelle Vachris, Christopher Newport University
James Wetzel, Virginia Commonwealth University

WASHINGTON

Robert Rosenman, Washington State University

WASHINGTON, DC

Leon Battista, American Enterprise Institute

WISCONSIN

Pascal Ngoboka, University of Wisconsin–River Falls
Kevin Quinn, St. Norbert College
John R. Stoll, University of Wisconsin–Green Bay

WYOMING

Robert Godby, University of Wyoming

A Word of Thanks

Once again, we benefited greatly from the dedication and professionalism of the Prentice Hall team. Executive Editor David Alexander's energy and support were indispensable. David helped mold the presentation and provided words of encouragement whenever our energy flagged. Developmental Editor Lena Buonanno worked tirelessly to ensure that this text was as good as it could be. We remain literally astonished at the amount of time, energy, and unfailing good humor she brings to this project. As we worked on the first edition, Director of Key Markets David Theisen provided invaluable insight into how best to structure a principles text. His advice helped shape nearly every chapter. Executive Marketing Manager Lori DeShazo developed a unique and innovative marketing plan. Steve Deitmer, Director of Development, brought sound judgment to the many decisions required to create this book. Terenia McHenry managed the extensive supplement package that accompanies the book. Melissa Feimer, Blair Brown, and Jonathan Boylan turned our manuscript pages into a beautiful published book. Ben Paris, executive producer of assessment programs, evaluated Test Item File questions and provided the authors guidance on how to write effective questions. Photo researcher Rachel Lucas located photographs that captured the essence of key concepts. We received excellent research assistance from Ed Timmons, David Van Der Goes, and Jason Hockenberry.

A good part of the burden of a project of this magnitude is borne by our families. We appreciate the patience, support, and encouragement of our wives and children. We extend special thanks to Constance Hubbard for her diligent reading of page proofs.

economics

Second Edition, Updated

Economics:
Foundations and Models

What Happens When U.S. High-Technology Firms Move to China?

You have probably seen the words "Made in China" on a variety of the products you own, including running shoes, clothing, towels, and sheets. It may not be surprising that relatively simple products are manufactured in China, where workers receive much lower wages than in the United States. Until recently, though, most people would not have expected sophisticated, high-technology products to be designed and manufactured in China. That is why the movement of high-technology manufacturing and even high-technology research and development (R&D) to China has surprised many people. In recent years, U.S. firms such as Oracle, IBM, and Motorola have all opened R&D facilities in China. Harry Shum, who runs Microsoft's research center in Beijing, said, "For us, it's always been about finding the best people. China has 1.3 billion brains. The question is how you make them truly creative, truly innovative. This is the key to China becoming a real superpower in science."

3Com is a leading U.S. high-technology firm. The firm introduced a new network switch for corporate computer systems that not only was manufactured in China but had been designed by Chinese engineers. 3Com was able to charge a much lower price for the switch than competitors that designed and manufactured similar products in the United States. Because the salaries of engineers are so much lower in China, 3Com was able to use four times as many engineers to design its switch than did competing firms employing engineers in the United States. The cost to manufacture the switch was also much lower in China, where the average factory worker earns the equivalent of about $2.10 per hour, including benefits, compared with about $24.00 per hour earned by the average factory worker in the United States.

Many U.S., Japanese, and European firms have been moving the production of goods and services outside their home country, a process called *outsourcing* (sometimes also referred to as *off-shoring*). Articles on outsourcing appear frequently in business magazines and the financial pages of newspapers, and the issue has also been the subject of heated debate among political commentators, policymakers, and presidential candidates. The focus of the debate has been the question "Has outsourcing been good or bad for the U.S. economy?" This question is one of many that cannot be answered without using economics. In this chapter and the remainder of this book, we will see how economics helps in answering important questions about outsourcing, as well as many other issues. Economics provides us with tools for understanding why outsourcing has increased, why some firms are more likely to move production to other countries, and what the effects of outsourcing will be on the wages of U.S. workers, the profits of U.S. firms, and the overall ability of the U.S. economy to produce more and better goods and services. **AN INSIDE LOOK** on **page 18** discusses how developments in China and India are affecting the high-technology sector in the United States.

Sources: Charles Leadbeater and James Wilson, "Do Not Fear the Rise of World-Class Science Asia," *Financial Times*, October 12, 2005, p. 19; Pete Engardio and Dexter Roberts, "The China Price," *BusinessWeek*, December 6, 2004; and Judith Banister, "Manufacturing Earnings and Compensation in China," *Monthly Labor Review*, August 2006, pp. 22–40.

Economics in YOUR Life!

Are You Likely to Lose Your Job to Outsourcing?

An estimated 3.3 million jobs in the United States will have been outsourced between 2000 and 2015, according to a report by John McCarthy of Forrester Research, a private research firm. Other estimates of the number of U.S. jobs likely to be outsourced have been in the same range. More than 3 million jobs seems like a large number. Suppose you plan on working as an accountant, a software engineer, a lawyer, a business consultant, a financial analyst, or in another industry where some jobs have already been outsourced. Is it likely that during your career, your job will be outsourced to China, India, or some other foreign country? As you read the chapter, see if you can answer this question. You can check your answer against the one we provide at the end of the chapter.

>> **Continued on page 17**

In this book, we use economics to answer questions such as the following:

- How are the prices of goods and services determined?

- How does pollution affect the economy, and how should government policy deal with these effects?

- Why do firms engage in international trade, and how do government policies affect international trade?

- Why does government control the prices of some goods and services, and what are the effects of those controls?

Economists do not always agree on the answers to every question. In fact, as we will see, economists engage in lively debate on some issues. In addition, new problems and issues are constantly arising. So, economists are always at work developing new methods to analyze and answer these questions.

All the questions we discuss in this book illustrate a basic fact of life: People must make choices as they try to attain their goals. We must make choices because we live in a world of **scarcity**, which means that although our wants are unlimited, the resources available to fulfill those wants are limited. You might like to have a 60-inch plasma television in every room of your home, but unless you are a close relative of Bill Gates, you probably lack the money to purchase them. Every day, you must make choices about how to spend your limited income on the many goods and services available. The finite amount of time available to you also limits your ability to attain your goals. If you spend an hour studying for your economics midterm, you have one less hour available to study for your history midterm. Firms and the government are in the same situation as you: They have limited resources available as they attempt to attain their goals. **Economics** is the study of the choices consumers, business managers, and government officials make to attain their goals, given their scarce resources.

We begin this chapter by discussing three important economic ideas that we will return to many times in the book: *People are rational. People respond to incentives. Optimal decisions are made at the margin.* Then we consider the three fundamental questions that any economy must answer: *What* goods and services will be produced? *How* will the goods and services be produced? *Who* will receive the goods and services? Next we consider the role of *economic models* in helping analyze the many issues presented throughout this book. **Economic models** are simplified versions of reality used to analyze real-world economic situations. Later in this chapter, we explore why economists use models and how they construct them. Finally, we discuss the difference between microeconomics and macroeconomics, and we preview some important economic terms.

Scarcity The situation in which unlimited wants exceed the limited resources available to fulfill those wants.

Economics The study of the choices people make to attain their goals, given their scarce resources.

Economic model A simplified version of reality used to analyze real-world economic situations.

1.1 LEARNING OBJECTIVE

1.1 | Explain these three key economic ideas: People are rational. People respond to incentives. Optimal decisions are made at the margin.

Three Key Economic Ideas

As you try to achieve your goals, whether they are buying a new computer or finding a part-time job, you will interact with other people in *markets*. A **market** is a group of buyers and sellers of a good or service and the institution or arrangement by which they come together to trade. Most of economics involves analyzing what happens in markets.

Market A group of buyers and sellers of a good or service and the institution or arrangement by which they come together to trade.

Throughout this book, as we study how people make choices and interact in markets, we will return to three important ideas:

1 People are rational.

2 People respond to economic incentives.

3 Optimal decisions are made at the margin.

People Are Rational

Economists generally assume that people are rational. This assumption does *not* mean that economists believe everyone knows everything or always makes the "best" decision. It means that economists assume that consumers and firms use all available information as they act to achieve their goals. Rational individuals weigh the benefits and costs of each action, and they choose an action only if the benefits outweigh the costs. For example, if Microsoft charges a price of $239 for a copy of Windows, economists assume that the managers at Microsoft have estimated that a price of $239 will earn Microsoft the most profit. The managers may be wrong; perhaps a price of $265 would be more profitable, but economists assume that the managers at Microsoft have acted rationally on the basis of the information available to them in choosing the price. Of course, not everyone behaves rationally all the time. Still, the assumption of rational behavior is very useful in explaining most of the choices that people make.

People Respond to Economic Incentives

Human beings act from a variety of motives, including religious belief, envy, and compassion. Economists emphasize that consumers and firms consistently respond to *economic* incentives. This fact may seem obvious, but it is often overlooked. For example, according to an article in the *Wall Street Journal*, the FBI couldn't understand why banks were not taking steps to improve security in the face of an increase in robberies: "FBI officials suggest that banks place uniformed, armed guards outside their doors and install bullet-resistant plastic, known as a 'bandit barrier,' in front of teller windows." FBI officials were surprised that few banks took their advice. But the article also reported that installing bullet-resistant plastic costs $10,000 to $20,000, and a well-trained security guard receives $50,000 per year in salary and benefits. The average loss in a bank robbery is only about $1,200. The economic incentive to banks is clear: It is less costly to put up with bank robberies than to take additional security measures. That banks respond as they do to the threat of robberies may be surprising to the FBI—but not to economists.

In each chapter, the *Making the Connection* feature discusses a news story or another application related to the chapter material. Read the following *Making the Connection* for a discussion of whether people respond to economic incentives even when making the decision to have children.

Making
the
Connection | **Will Women Have More Babies if the Government Pays Them To?**

The populations of the United States, Japan, and most European countries are aging as birthrates decline and the average person lives longer. The governments of these countries have programs to pay money to retired workers, such as the Social Security system in the United States. Most of the money for these programs comes from taxes paid by people currently working. As the population ages, there are fewer workers paying taxes relative to the number of retired people receiving government payments. The result is a funding crisis that countries can solve only by either reducing government payments to retired workers or by raising the taxes paid by current workers.

In some European countries, birthrates have fallen so low that the total population will soon begin to decline, which will make the funding crisis for government retirement programs even worse. For the population of a country to be stable, the average woman must have 2.1 children, which is enough to replace both parents and account for children who die before reaching adulthood. In recent years, the birthrates in a number of countries, including France, Germany, and Italy, have fallen below this replacement level. The concern about falling birthrates has been particularly strong in the small European country of Estonia. In 2001, the United Nations issued a report in which it forecast that, given its current birthrate, by 2050, the population of Estonia would decline from 1.4 million to only about 700,000. The Estonian government responded by using economic incentives in an attempt to increase the birthrate. Beginning in 2007, the government began paying working women who take time off after having a baby their entire salary for up to 15 months. Women who do not work receive $200 per month, which is a substantial amount, given that the average income in Estonia is only $650 per month.

Will women actually have more babies as a result of this economic incentive? As the graph below shows, the birthrate in Estonia has increased from 1.3 children per woman in the late 1990s to 1.6 children per woman in 2007. This is still below the replacement level birthrate of 2.1 children, and it is too early to tell whether the increased birthrate is due to the economic incentives. But the Estonian government is encouraged by the results and is looking for ways to provide additional economic incentives to raise the birthrate further. And Estonia is not alone; more than 45 other countries in Europe and Asia have taken steps to try to raise their birthrates. People may respond to economic incentives even when making the very personal decision of how many children to have.

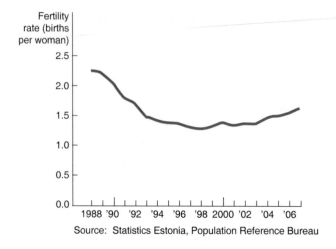

Source: Statistics Estonia, Population Reference Bureau

Source: Marcus Walker, "In Estonia, Paying Women to Have Babies Is Paying Off," *Wall Street Journal*, October 20, 2006, p. A1. Copyright © 2006 Dow Jones. Reprinted by permission of Dow Jones via Copyright Clearance Center; and Sharon Lerner, "The Motherhood Experiment," *New York Times*, March 4, 2007.

YOUR TURN: Test your understanding by doing related problem 1.7 on page 21 at the end of this chapter.

Optimal Decisions Are Made at the Margin

Some decisions are "all or nothing": An entrepreneur decides whether to open a new restaurant. He or she either starts the new restaurant or doesn't. You decide whether to enter graduate school or to take a job instead. You either enter graduate school or you don't. But most decisions in life are not all or nothing. Instead, most decisions involve doing a little more or a little less. If you are trying to decrease your spending and increase your saving, the decision is not really a choice between saving every dollar you earn or spending it all. Rather, many small choices are involved, such as whether to buy a caffè mocha at Starbucks every day or to cut back to three times per week.

Economists use the word *marginal* to mean an extra or additional benefit or cost of a decision. Should you watch another hour of TV or spend that hour studying? The *marginal benefit* (or, in symbols, *MB*) of watching more TV is the additional enjoyment you receive. The *marginal cost* (or *MC*) is the lower grade you receive from having studied a little less. Should Apple Computer produce an additional 300,000 iPods? Firms receive *revenue* from selling goods. Apple's marginal benefit is the additional revenue it receives from selling 300,000 more iPods. Apple's marginal cost is the additional cost—for wages, parts, and so forth—of producing 300,000 more iPods. *Economists reason that the optimal decision is to continue any activity up to the point where the marginal benefit equals the marginal cost—in symbols, where* MB = MC. Often we apply this rule without consciously thinking about it. Usually you will know whether the additional enjoyment from watching a television program is worth the additional cost involved in not spending that hour studying, without giving it a lot of thought. In business situations, however, firms often have to make careful calculations to determine, for example, whether the additional revenue received from increasing production is greater or less than the additional cost of the production. Economists refer to analysis that involves comparing marginal benefits and marginal costs as **marginal analysis**.

Marginal analysis Analysis that involves comparing marginal benefits and marginal costs.

In each chapter of this book, you will see the special feature *Solved Problem.* This feature will increase your understanding of the material by leading you through the steps of solving an applied economic problem. After reading the problem, you can test your understanding by working the related problems that appear at the end of the chapter and in the study guide that accompanies this book.

Solved Problem | 1-1

Apple Computer Makes a Decision at the Margin

Suppose Apple is currently selling 3,000,000 iPods per year. Managers at Apple are considering whether to raise production to 3,300,000 iPods per year. One manager argues, "Increasing production from 3,000,000 to 3,300,000 is a good idea because we will make a total profit of $100 million if we produce 3,300,000." Do you agree with her reasoning? What, if any, additional information do you need to decide whether Apple should produce the additional 300,000 iPods?

SOLVING THE PROBLEM:

Step 1: **Review the chapter material.** The problem is about making decisions, so you may want to review the section "Optimal Decisions Are Made at the Margin," which begins on page 6. Remember to think "marginal" whenever you see the word "additional" in economics.

Step 2: **Explain whether you agree with the manager's reasoning.** We have seen that any activity should be continued to the point where the marginal benefit is equal to the marginal cost. In this case, that involves continuing to produce iPods up to the point where the additional revenue Apple receives from selling more iPods is equal to the marginal cost of producing them. The Apple manager has not done a marginal analysis, so you should not agree with her reasoning. Her statement about the *total* profit of producing 3,300,000 iPods is not relevant to the decision of whether to produce the last 300,000 iPods.

Step 3: **Explain what additional information you need.** You will need additional information to make a correct decision. You will need to know the additional revenue Apple would earn from selling 300,000 more iPods and the additional cost of producing them.

YOUR TURN: For more practice, do related problems 1.4, 1.5, and 1.6 on pages 20–21 at the end of this chapter.

>> End Solved Problem 1-1

1.2 | Discuss how an economy answers these questions: *What* goods and services will be produced? *How* will the goods and services be produced? *Who* will receive the goods and services?

The Economic Problem That Every Society Must Solve

Trade-off The idea that because of scarcity, producing more of one good or service means producing less of another good or service.

Opportunity cost The highest-valued alternative that must be given up to engage in an activity.

We have already noted the important fact that we live in a world of scarcity. As a result, any society faces the economic problem that it has only a limited amount of economic resources—such as workers, machines, and raw materials—and so can produce only a limited amount of goods and services. Therefore, society faces **trade-offs**: Producing more of one good or service means producing less of another good or service. In fact, the best way to measure the cost of producing a good or service is the value of what has to be given up to produce it. The **opportunity cost** of any activity—such as producing a good or service—is the highest-valued alternative that must be given up to engage in that activity. The concept of opportunity cost is very important in economics and applies to individuals as much as it does to firms or to society as a whole. Consider the example of someone who could receive a salary of $80,000 per year working as a manager at a firm but opens her own firm instead. In that case, the opportunity cost of her managerial services to her own firm is $80,000, even if she does not explicitly pay herself a salary.

Trade-offs force society to make choices, particularly when answering the following three fundamental questions:

1 *What* goods and services will be produced?

2 *How* will the goods and services be produced?

3 *Who* will receive the goods and services produced?

Throughout this book, we will return to these questions many times. For now, we briefly introduce each question.

What Goods and Services Will Be Produced?

How will society decide whether to produce more economics textbooks or more Blu-ray players? More daycare facilities or more football stadiums? Of course, "society" does not make decisions; only individuals make decisions. The answer to the question of what will be produced is determined by the choices made by consumers, firms, and the government. Every day, you help decide which goods and services will be produced when you choose to buy an iPod rather than a Blu-ray player or a caffè mocha rather than a chai tea. Similarly, Apple must choose whether to devote its scarce resources to making more iPods or more MacBook laptop computers. The federal government must choose whether to spend more of its limited budget on breast cancer research or on homeland security. In each case, consumers, firms, and the government face the problem of scarcity by trading off one good or service for another. And each choice made comes with an opportunity cost measured by the value of the best alternative given up.

How Will the Goods and Services Be Produced?

Firms choose how to produce the goods and services they sell. In many cases, firms face a trade-off between using more workers or using more machines. For example, a local service station has to choose whether to provide car repair services using more diagnostic computers and fewer auto mechanics or more auto mechanics and fewer diagnostic computers. Similarly, movie studios have to choose whether to produce animated films using highly skilled animators to draw them by hand or fewer animators and more computers. In deciding whether to move production offshore to China, firms may be choosing between a production method in the United States that uses fewer workers and more machines and a production method in China that uses more workers and fewer machines.

Who Will Receive the Goods and Services Produced?

In the United States, who receives the goods and services produced depends largely on how income is distributed. Individuals with the highest income have the ability to buy the most goods and services. Often, people are willing to give up some of their income—and, therefore, some of their ability to purchase goods and services—by donating to charities to increase the incomes of poorer people. Each year, Americans donate more than $250 billion to charity, or an average donation of $2,100 for each household in the country. An important policy question, however, is whether the government should intervene to make the distribution of income more equal. Such intervention already occurs in the United States, because people with higher incomes pay a larger fraction of their incomes in taxes and because the government makes payments to people with low incomes. There is disagreement over whether the current attempts to redistribute income are sufficient or whether there should be more or less redistribution.

Centrally Planned Economies versus Market Economies

Societies organize their economies in two main ways to answer the three questions of what, how, and who. A society can have a **centrally planned economy** in which the government decides how economic resources will be allocated. Or a society can have a **market economy** in which the decisions of households and firms interacting in markets allocate economic resources.

From 1917 to 1991, the most important centrally planned economy in the world was that of the Soviet Union, which was established when Vladimir Lenin and his Communist Party staged a revolution and took over the Russian Empire. In the Soviet Union, the government decided what goods to produce, how to produce them, and who would receive them. Government employees managed factories and stores. The objective of these managers was to follow the government's orders rather than to satisfy the wants of consumers. Centrally planned economies like the Soviet Union have not been successful in producing low-cost, high-quality goods and services. As a result, the standard of living of the average person in a centrally planned economy tends to be quite low. All centrally planned economies have also been political dictatorships. Dissatisfaction with low living standards and political repression finally led to the collapse of the Soviet Union in 1991. Today, only a few small countries, such as Cuba and North Korea, still have completely centrally planned economies.

All the high-income democracies, such as the United States, Canada, Japan, and the countries of western Europe, are market economies. Market economies rely primarily on privately owned firms to produce goods and services and to decide how to produce them. Markets, rather than the government, determine who receives the goods and services produced. In a market economy, firms must produce goods and services that meet the wants of consumers, or the firms will go out of business. In that sense, it is ultimately consumers who decide what goods and services will be produced. Because firms in a market economy compete to offer the highest-quality products at the lowest price, they are under pressure to use the lowest-cost methods of production. For example, in the past 10 years, some U.S. firms, particularly in the electronics and furniture industries, have been under pressure to reduce their costs to meet competition from Chinese firms.

In a market economy, the income of an individual is determined by the payments he receives for what he has to sell. If he is a civil engineer and firms are willing to pay a salary of $85,000 per year for engineers with his training and skills, that is the amount of income he will have to purchase goods and services. If the engineer also owns a house that he rents out, his income will be even higher. One of the attractive features of markets is that they reward hard work. Generally, the more extensive the training a person

Centrally planned economy An economy in which the government decides how economic resources will be allocated.

Market economy An economy in which the decisions of households and firms interacting in markets allocate economic resources.

has received and the longer the hours the person works, the higher the person's income will be. Of course, luck—both good and bad—also plays a role here, as elsewhere in life. We can conclude that market economies answer the question "Who receives the goods and services produced?" with the answer "Those who are most willing and able to buy them."

The Modern "Mixed" Economy

In the nineteenth and early twentieth centuries, the U.S. government engaged in relatively little regulation of markets for goods and services. Beginning in the middle of the twentieth century, government intervention in the economy dramatically increased in the United States and other market economies. This increase was primarily caused by the high rates of unemployment and business bankruptcies during the Great Depression of the 1930s. Some government intervention was also intended to raise the incomes of the elderly, the sick, and people with limited skills. For example, in the 1930s, the United States established the Social Security system, which provides government payments to retired and disabled workers, and minimum wage legislation, which sets a floor on the wages employers can pay in many occupations. In more recent years, government intervention in the economy has also expanded to meet such goals as protection of the environment and the promotion of civil rights.

Mixed economy An economy in which most economic decisions result from the interaction of buyers and sellers in markets but in which the government plays a significant role in the allocation of resources.

Some economists argue that the extent of government intervention makes it no longer accurate to refer to the U.S., Canadian, Japanese, and western European economies as pure market economies. Instead, they should be referred to as *mixed economies*. A **mixed economy** is still primarily a market economy with most economic decisions resulting from the interaction of buyers and sellers in markets, but in a mixed economy the government plays a significant role in the allocation of resources. As we will see in later chapters, economists continue to debate the role government should play in a market economy.

One of the most important developments in the international economy in recent years has been the movement of China from being a centrally planned economy to being a more mixed economy. The Chinese economy had suffered decades of economic stagnation following the takeover of the government by Mao Zedong and the Communist Party in 1949. Although China remains a political dictatorship, production of most goods and services is now determined in the market rather than by the government. The result has been rapid economic growth that in the near future may lead to total production of goods and services in China surpassing total production in the United States.

Efficiency and Equity

Productive efficiency The situation in which a good or service is produced at the lowest possible cost.

Allocative efficiency A state of the economy in which production is in accordance with consumer preferences; in particular, every good or service is produced up to the point where the last unit provides a marginal benefit to society equal to the marginal cost of producing it.

Voluntary exchange The situation that occurs in markets when both the buyer and seller of a product are made better off by the transaction.

Market economies tend to be more efficient than centrally planned economies. There are two types of efficiency: *productive efficiency* and *allocative efficiency*. **Productive efficiency** occurs when a good or service is produced at the lowest possible cost. **Allocative efficiency** occurs when production is in accordance with consumer preferences. Markets tend to be efficient because they promote competition and facilitate voluntary exchange. **Voluntary exchange** refers to the situation in which both the buyer and seller of a product are made better off by the transaction. We know that the buyer and seller are both made better off because, otherwise, the buyer would not have agreed to buy the product or the seller would not have agreed to sell it. Productive efficiency is achieved when competition among firms in markets forces the firms to produce goods and services at the lowest cost. Allocative efficiency is achieved when the combination of competition among firms and voluntary exchange between firms and consumers results in firms producing the mix of goods and services that consumers prefer most. Competition will force firms to continue producing and selling goods and services as long as the additional benefit to consumers is greater than the additional cost of production. In this way, the mix of goods and services produced will be in accordance with consumer preferences.

Although markets promote efficiency, they don't guarantee it. Inefficiency can arise from various sources. To begin with, it may take some time to achieve an efficient outcome. When DVD players were introduced, for example, firms did not instantly achieve productive efficiency. It took several years for firms to discover the lowest-cost method of producing this good. As we will discuss in Chapter 4, governments sometimes reduce efficiency by interfering with voluntary exchange in markets. For example, many governments limit the imports of some goods from foreign countries. This limitation reduces efficiency by keeping goods from being produced at the lowest cost. The production of some goods damages the environment. In this case, government intervention can increase efficiency because without such intervention, firms may ignore the costs of environmental damage and thereby fail to produce the goods at the lowest possible cost.

Just because an economic outcome is efficient does not necessarily mean that society finds it desirable. Many people prefer economic outcomes that they consider fair or equitable, even if those outcomes are less efficient. **Equity** is harder to define than efficiency, but it usually involves a fair distribution of economic benefits. For some people, equity involves a more equal distribution of economic benefits than would result from an emphasis on efficiency alone. For example, some people support taxing people with higher incomes to provide the funds for programs that aid the poor. Although governments may increase equity by reducing the incomes of high-income people and increasing the incomes of the poor, efficiency may be reduced. People have less incentive to open new businesses, to supply labor, and to save if the government takes a significant amount of the income they earn from working or saving. The result is that fewer goods and services are produced, and less saving takes place. As this example illustrates, *there is often a trade-off between efficiency and equity.* In this case, the total amount of goods and services produced falls, although the distribution of the income to buy those goods and services is made more equal. Government policymakers often confront this trade-off.

Equity The fair distribution of economic benefits.

1.3 LEARNING OBJECTIVE

1.3 | Understand the role of models in economic analysis.

Economic Models

Economists rely on economic theories, or *models* (the words *theory* and *model* are used interchangeably), to analyze real-world issues, such as the economic effects of outsourcing. As mentioned earlier, economic models are simplified versions of reality. Economists are certainly not alone in relying on models: An engineer may use a computer model of a bridge to help test whether it will withstand high winds, or a biologist may make a physical model of a nucleic acid to better understand its properties. One purpose of economic models is to make economic ideas sufficiently explicit and concrete so that individuals, firms, or the government can use them to make decisions. For example, we will see in Chapter 3 that the model of demand and supply is a simplified version of how the prices of products are determined by the interactions among buyers and sellers in markets.

Economists use economic models to answer questions. For example, consider the question from the chapter opener: Has outsourcing been good or bad for the U.S. economy? For a complicated issue such as the effects of outsourcing, economists often use several models to examine different aspects of the issue. For example, they may use a model of how wages are determined to analyze how outsourcing affects wages in particular industries. They may use a model of international trade to analyze how outsourcing affects income growth in the countries involved. Sometimes economists use an existing model to analyze an issue, but in other cases, they must develop a new model. To develop a model, economists generally follow these steps:

1 Decide on the assumptions to be used in developing the model.

2 Formulate a testable hypothesis.

3 Use economic data to test the hypothesis.

4 Revise the model if it fails to explain well the economic data.

5 Retain the revised model to help answer similar economic questions in the future.

The Role of Assumptions in Economic Models

Any model is based on making assumptions because models have to be simplified to be useful. We cannot analyze an economic issue unless we reduce its complexity. For example, economic models make *behavioral assumptions* about the motives of consumers and firms. Economists assume that consumers will buy the goods and services that will maximize their well-being or their satisfaction. Similarly, economists assume that firms act to maximize their profits. These assumptions are simplifications because they do not describe the motives of every consumer and every firm. How can we know if the assumptions in a model are too simplified or too limiting? We discover this when we form hypotheses based on these assumptions and test these hypotheses using real-world information.

Forming and Testing Hypotheses in Economic Models

Economic variable Something measurable that can have different values, such as the wages of software programmers.

A *hypothesis* in an economic model is a statement that may be either correct or incorrect about an *economic variable*. An **economic variable** is something measurable that can have different values, such as the wages paid to software programmers. An example of a hypothesis in an economic model is the statement that outsourcing by U.S. firms reduces wages paid to software programmers in the United States. An economic hypothesis is usually about a *causal relationship*; in this case, the hypothesis states that outsourcing causes, or leads to, lower wages for software programmers.

Before accepting a hypothesis, we must test it. To test a hypothesis, we must analyze statistics on the relevant economic variables. In our example, we must gather statistics on the wages paid to software programmers, and perhaps on other variables as well. Testing a hypothesis can be tricky. For example, showing that the wages paid to software programmers fell at a time when outsourcing was increasing would not be enough to demonstrate that outsourcing *caused* the wage fall. Just because two things are *correlated*—that is, they happen at the same time—does not mean that one caused the other. For example, suppose that the number of workers trained as software engineers greatly increased at the same time that outsourcing was increasing. In that case, the fall in wages paid to software engineers might have been caused by the increased competition among workers for these jobs rather than by the effects of relocating programming jobs from the United States to India or China. Over a period of time, many economic variables change, which complicates testing hypotheses. In fact, when economists disagree about a hypothesis, such as the effect of outsourcing on wages, it is often because of disagreements over interpreting the statistical analysis used to test the hypothesis.

Note that hypotheses must be statements that could, in principle, turn out to be incorrect. Statements such as "Outsourcing is good" or "Outsourcing is bad" are value judgments rather than hypotheses because it is not possible to disprove them.

Economists accept and use an economic model if it leads to hypotheses that are confirmed by statistical analysis. In many cases, the acceptance is tentative, however, pending the gathering of new data or further statistical analysis. In fact, economists often refer to a hypothesis having been "not rejected," rather than having been "accepted," by statistical analysis. But what if statistical analysis clearly rejects a hypothesis? For example, what if a model leads to a hypothesis that outsourcing by U.S. firms lowers wages of U.S. software programmers, but this hypothesis is rejected by the data? In that case, the model must be reconsidered. It may be that an assumption used in the model was too simplified or too limiting. For example, perhaps the model used to determine the effect of outsourcing on wages paid to software programmers assumed that software programmers in China and India had the same training and experience as software programmers in the United States. If, in fact, U.S. software programmers have more training and experience than Chinese and Indian programmers, this difference may explain why our hypothesis was rejected by the economic statistics.

The process of developing models, testing hypotheses, and revising models occurs not just in economics but also in disciplines such as physics, chemistry, and biology. This process is often referred to as the *scientific method*. Economics is a *social science* because it applies the scientific method to the study of the interactions among individuals.

Making the Connection | When Economists Disagree: A Debate over Outsourcing

Does outsourcing by U.S. firms raise or lower incomes in the United States?

There is an old saying in the newspaper business that it's not news when a dog bites a man, but it is news when a man bites a dog. In 2004, many newspapers ran a "man bites dog" story concerning economics.

Most economists believe that international trade—including the trade that results when firms move production offshore—increases economic efficiency and raises incomes. It was news, then, when Paul Samuelson, an MIT economist and a winner of the Nobel Prize in Economics, wrote an article in the *Journal of Economic Perspectives* questioning whether incomes in the United States will be higher as a result of the outsourcing of jobs to India and China. Samuelson presented a model of the effects of outsourcing that can be illustrated with the following hypothetical case: Suppose a bank in New York has been using a company in South Dakota to handle its telephone customer service. The bank then switches to using a company in Bangalore, India, that pays its workers much lower wages. Samuelson argued that even when the workers fired by the South Dakota firm eventually find new jobs, the jobs may pay lower wages. If outsourcing becomes widespread enough, Samuelson argued, it may result in a significant decline in U.S. incomes.

Many economists objected to Samuelson's argument. One economist who wrote a rebuttal to Samuelson was Jagdish Bhagwati, a former student of Samuelson's and a professor of economics at Columbia University. Bhagwati argued that in Samuelson's example, the wages of South Dakota call center workers were reduced by outsourcing, but the costs to the bank were also reduced, which would allow the bank to reduce the prices it charged its customers. In Bhagwati's model, these gains to consumers from lower prices more than offset the loss to workers from lower wages, so the United States experiences a net gain from outsourcing. Samuelson argued, though, that if the United States exports the product—in this case banking services—to other countries, the lower price hurts the exporting firms. In that case, the United States might still be hurt by outsourcing.

This brief summary does not do full justice to the models of Samuelson and Bhagwati, which are too complicated for us to cover in this chapter. We can, however, discuss the sources of the disagreement between these two economists. We have seen that economists sometimes differ about the assumptions that should be used in building a model. That is not the case here: Samuelson and Bhagwati basically agree on the model and the assumptions to be used. Instead, they disagree over how to interpret the relevant economic statistics. Bhagwati argues that the number of U.S. jobs moving to other countries has been relatively small, amounting to about 1 percent of the jobs created in the U.S. economy each year. He also argues that the jobs lost to outsourcing tend to be low-wage jobs, such as telephone customer service or data entry, and are likely to be replaced by higher-wage jobs. Samuelson argues that the impact of outsourcing is greater than Bhagwati believes, and he is less optimistic that newly created jobs in the United States will pay higher wages than the jobs lost to outsourcing.

The debate between Samuelson and Bhagwati demonstrates that economics is an evolving discipline. New models are continually being introduced, and new hypotheses are being formulated and tested. We can expect the debate over the economic impact of outsourcing to continue to be lively.

Sources: Paul A. Samuelson, "Where Ricardo and Mill Rebut and Confirm Arguments of Mainstream Economists Supporting Globalization," *Journal of Economic Perspectives*, Vol. 18, No. 3, Summer 2004, pp. 135–146; Jagdish Bhagwati, Arvind Panagariya, and T. N. Srinivasan, "The Muddles Over Outsourcing," *Journal of Economic Perspectives*, Vol. 18, No. 4, Fall 2004, pp. 93–114; and Steve Lohr, "An Elder Challenges Outsourcing's Orthodoxy," *New York Times*, September 9, 2004, p. C1.

YOUR TURN: Test your understanding by doing related problem 3.7 on page 22 at the end of this chapter.

Normative and Positive Analysis

Positive analysis Analysis concerned with what is.

Normative analysis Analysis concerned with what ought to be.

Throughout this book, as we build economic models and use them to answer questions, we need to bear in mind the distinction between *positive analysis* and *normative analysis*. **Positive analysis** is concerned with *what is*, and **normative analysis** is concerned with *what ought to be*. Economics is about positive analysis, which measures the costs and benefits of different courses of action.

We can use the federal government's minimum wage law to compare positive and normative analysis. In 2008, under this law, it was illegal for an employer to hire a worker at a wage less than $6.55 per hour (the minimum wage is scheduled to increase to $7.25 per hour in 2009). Without the minimum wage law, some firms and some workers would voluntarily agree to a lower wage. Because of the minimum wage law, some workers have difficulty finding jobs, and some firms end up paying more for labor than they otherwise would have. A positive analysis of the federal minimum wage law uses an economic model to estimate how many workers have lost their jobs because of the law, its impact on the costs and profits of businesses, and the gains to workers receiving the minimum wage. After economists complete this positive analysis, the decision as to whether the minimum wage law is a good idea or a bad idea is a normative one and depends on how people evaluate the trade-off involved. Supporters of the law believe that the losses to employers and to workers who are unemployed as a result of the law are more than offset by the gains to workers who receive higher wages than they would without the law. Opponents of the law believe the losses are greater than the gains. The assessment by any individual would depend, in part, on that person's values and political views. The positive analysis provided by an economist would play a role in the decision but can't by itself decide the issue one way or the other.

In each chapter, you will see a *Don't Let This Happen to You!* box like the one below. These boxes alert you to common pitfalls in thinking about economic ideas. After reading the box, test your understanding by working the related problem that appears at the end of the chapter.

Economics as a Social Science

Because economics is based on studying the actions of individuals, it is a social science. Economics is therefore similar to other social science disciplines, such as psychology, political science, and sociology. As a social science, economics considers human behavior—particularly decision-making behavior—in every context, not just in the context of business. Economists have studied such issues as how families decide the number of children

---

Don't Let This Happen to **YOU!**

Don't Confuse Positive Analysis with Normative Analysis

"Economic analysis has shown that the minimum wage law is a bad idea because it causes unemployment." Is this statement accurate? As of 2008, the federal minimum wage law prevents employers from hiring workers at a wage of less than $6.55 per hour. This wage is higher than some employers are willing to pay some workers. If there were no minimum wage law, some workers who currently cannot find any firm willing to hire them at $6.55 per hour would be able to find employment at a lower wage. Therefore, positive economic analysis indicates that the minimum wage law causes unemployment (although economists disagree about how much unemployment is caused by the minimum wage). *But,*

those workers who still have jobs benefit from the minimum wage because they are paid a higher wage than they otherwise would be. In other words, the minimum wage law creates both losers (the workers who become unemployed and the firms that have to pay higher wages) and winners (the workers who receive higher wages).

Should we value the gains to the winners more than we value the losses to the losers? The answer to that question involves normative analysis. Positive economic analysis can only show the consequences of a particular policy; it cannot tell us whether the policy is "good" or "bad." So, the statement at the beginning of this box is inaccurate.

YOUR TURN: Test your understanding by doing related problem 3.9 on page 23 at the end of this chapter.

to have, why people have difficulty losing weight or attaining other desirable goals, and why people often ignore relevant information when making decisions. Economics also has much to contribute to questions of government policy. As we will see throughout this book, economists have played an important role in formulating government policies in areas such as the environment, health care, and poverty.

1.4 | Distinguish between microeconomics and macroeconomics.

Microeconomics and Macroeconomics

Economic models can be used to analyze decision making in many areas. We group some of these areas together as *microeconomics* and others as *macroeconomics*. **Microeconomics** is the study of how households and firms make choices, how they interact in markets, and how the government attempts to influence their choices. Microeconomic issues include explaining how consumers react to changes in product prices and how firms decide what prices to charge. Microeconomics also involves policy issues, such as analyzing the most efficient way to reduce teenage smoking, analyzing the costs and benefits of approving the sale of a new prescription drug, and analyzing the most efficient way to reduce air pollution.

Macroeconomics is the study of the economy as a whole, including topics such as inflation, unemployment, and economic growth. Macroeconomic issues include explaining why economies experience periods of recession and increasing unemployment and why over the long run, some economies have grown much faster than others. Macroeconomics also involves policy issues, such as whether government intervention can reduce the severity of recessions.

The division between microeconomics and macroeconomics is not hard and fast. Many economic situations have *both* a microeconomic and a macroeconomic aspect. For example, the level of total investment by firms in new machinery and equipment helps to determine how rapidly the economy grows—which is a macroeconomic issue. But to understand how much new machinery and equipment firms decide to purchase, we have to analyze the incentives individual firms face—which is a microeconomic issue.

Microeconomics The study of how households and firms make choices, how they interact in markets, and how the government attempts to influence their choices.

Macroeconomics The study of the economy as a whole, including topics such as inflation, unemployment, and economic growth.

1.5 | Become familiar with important economic terms.

A Preview of Important Economic Terms

In the following chapters, you will encounter certain important terms again and again. Becoming familiar with these terms is a necessary step in learning economics. Here we provide a brief introduction to some of these terms. We will discuss them all in greater depth in later chapters:

- *Entrepreneur.* An entrepreneur is someone who operates a business. In a market system, entrepreneurs decide what goods and services to produce and how to produce them. An entrepreneur starting a new business puts his or her own funds at risk. If an entrepreneur is wrong about what consumers want or about the best way to produce goods and services, the entrepreneur's funds can be lost. This is not an unusual occurrence: In the United States, about half of new businesses close within four years. Without entrepreneurs willing to assume the risk of starting and operating businesses, economic progress would be impossible in a market system.

- *Innovation.* There is a distinction between an *invention* and *innovation*. An invention is the development of a new good or a new process for making a good. An innovation is the practical application of an invention. (*Innovation* may also be used more broadly to refer to any significant improvement in a good or in the means of producing a good.) Much time often passes between the appearance of a new idea and its development for widespread use. For example, the Wright brothers first achieved self-propelled flight at Kitty Hawk, North Carolina, in 1903, but the Wright brothers' plane was very crude, and it wasn't until the introduction of the DC-3 by Douglas Aircraft in 1936 that regularly scheduled intercity airline flights became common in the United States. Similarly, the first digital electronic computer—the ENIAC—was developed in 1945, but the first IBM personal computer was not introduced until 1981, and widespread use of computers did not have a significant effect on the productivity of American business until the 1990s.

- *Technology.* A firm's technology is the processes it uses to produce goods and services. In the economic sense, a firm's technology depends on many factors, such as the skill of its managers, the training of its workers, and the speed and efficiency of its machinery and equipment.

- *Firm, company, or business.* A firm is an organization that produces a good or service. Most firms produce goods or services to earn profits, but there are also non-profit firms, such as universities and some hospitals. Economists use the terms *firm, company,* and *business* interchangeably.

- *Goods.* Goods are tangible merchandise, such as books, computers, or DVD players.

- *Services.* Services are activities done for others, such as providing haircuts or investment advice.

- *Revenue.* A firm's revenue is the total amount received for selling a good or service. It is calculated by multiplying the price per unit by the number of units sold.

- *Profit.* A firm's profit is the difference between its revenue and its costs. Economists distinguish between *accounting profit* and *economic profit.* In calculating accounting profit, we exclude the cost of some economic resources that the firm does not pay for explicitly. In calculating economic profit, we include the opportunity cost of all resources used by the firm. When we refer to *profit* in this book, we mean economic profit. It is important not to confuse *profit* with *revenue.*

- *Household.* A household consists of all persons occupying a home. Households are suppliers of factors of production—particularly labor—used by firms to make goods and services. Households also demand goods and services produced by firms and governments.

- *Factors of production or economic resources.* Firms use factors of production to produce goods and services. The main factors of production are labor, capital, human capital, natural resources—including land—and entrepreneurial ability. Households earn income by supplying the factors of production to firms.

- *Capital.* The word *capital* can refer to *financial capital* or to *physical capital.* Financial capital includes stocks and bonds issued by firms, bank accounts, and holdings of money. In economics, though, *capital* refers to physical capital, which includes manufactured goods that are used to produce other goods and services. Examples of physical capital are computers, factory buildings, machine tools, warehouses, and trucks. The total amount of physical capital available in a country is referred to as the country's *capital stock.*

- *Human capital.* Human capital refers to the accumulated training and skills that workers possess. For example, college-educated workers generally have more skills and are more productive than workers who have only high school degrees.

>> Continued from page 3

Economics in YOUR Life!

At the beginning of the chapter, we posed the question: "Is it likely that during your career, your job will be outsourced to China, India, or some other foreign country?" Some information helpful in answering this question appears in the *Making the Connection* on page 13. Economist Jagdish Bhagwati notes that the number of jobs moving to other countries each year is relatively small—probably less than 1 percent of the total jobs created in the U.S. economy each year. In fact, the U.S. economy is constantly creating and eliminating jobs as new firms open their doors and as existing firms get larger or smaller or go out of business. For example, from June 2006 to June 2007, the U.S. economy created 30.4 million jobs and eliminated 29.2 million jobs. The Forrester Research report cited at the beginning of the chapter indicated that as many as 3.3 million jobs might be lost to outsourcing between 2000 and 2015. But that number is very small compared with the more than 450 million jobs the economy is likely to create over that period, or in comparison with the more than 430 million jobs that will be lost due to all causes. So, you may lose your job one or more times during your career, but probably not because of outsourcing.

Conclusion

The best way to think of economics is as a group of useful ideas about how individuals make choices. Economists have put these ideas into practice by developing economic models. Consumers, business managers, and government officials use these models every day to help make choices. In this book, we explore many key economic models and give examples of how to apply them in the real world.

Most students taking an introductory economics course do not major in economics or become professional economists. Whatever your major may be, the economic principles you will learn in this book will improve your ability to make choices in many aspects of your life. These principles will also improve your understanding of how decisions are made in business and government.

Reading the newspaper and other periodicals is an important part of understanding the current business climate and learning how to apply economic concepts to a variety of real-world events. At the end of each chapter, you will see a two-page feature entitled *An Inside Look*. This feature consists of an excerpt of an article that relates to the company introduced at the start of the chapter and also to the concepts discussed throughout the chapter. A summary and analysis and supporting graphs highlight the economic key points of the article. Read *An Inside Look* on the next page to learn why some economists argue that fears about outsourcing to China are unjustified. Test your understanding by answering the *Thinking Critically* questions.

An Inside **LOOK**

Should the United States Worry about High-Tech Competition from India and China?

ECONOMIST, OCTOBER 7, 2006

Nightmare Scenarios

India's high-tech enclaves exude euphoria. Proud techies take their parents on tours of company campuses. Proud parents boast that their children earn more than the rest of the family combined. Mr Nilekani of Infosys says that his company's greatest achievement is not its $2 billion turnover but the fact that it has taught Indians to redefine the possible.

The mood in America, the country that is driving the outsourcing boom, could hardly be more different. People view the global war for talent with foreboding. Their fears take two forms. The first is that well-paying jobs in services will follow manufacturing jobs to the developing world. Norman Augustine, a former boss of Lockheed Martin, says that "virtually no one's job seems safe." Craig Barrett, the chairman of Intel, admits that "I worry for my grandchildren." The second fear is that America may no longer be able to attract more than its fair share of the world's brains. . . .

(a) Are Americans right to worry? One misconception is that the number of jobs is fixed, so if some of them go abroad there must be fewer left at home. If a farmer in Palo Alto in 1900 had been told that in a hundred years' time agricultural workers would account for only 2% of the American workforce, he would have expected the Valley to become a desert rather than a global technological hub. But even if the number of good jobs were fixed, the fears of a great job migration are exaggerated.

(b) The McKinsey Global Institute has conducted a large-scale study of the offshoring market and concluded that constraints on both the demand and the supply side will keep the number of service jobs moving offshore much lower than is widely believed. It will probably rise from 1.5m in 2003 to 4.1m in 2008, or 1.2% of the demand for labour in the developed world. That figure is dwarfed by the normal job churn in America, where 4.6m Americans start with a new employer every month.

There is clearly plenty of eager talent in the developing world. But McKinsey argues that only about 13% of that talent is capable of working for a Western multinational in a high-grade job at the moment (although the stock of suitable professionals is expanding a lot faster in developing than in rich countries). There are problems with cultural and language skills, particularly in China. The quality of education is often inadequate. China may have twice as many engineering graduates as America, but only 10% of them are equipped to work for a Western multinational. Geography also imposes limits. In large countries such as India and China many graduates live far away from international airports. In China only about half the talent pool is accessible to multinationals, according to McKinsey. . . .

India's difficulties have more to do with another intractable problem: poor government. The country's infrastructure is crumbling and the education system is hugely uneven. The Indian Institutes of Technology are very good at producing a highly educated elite, but run-of-the-mill colleges are often of poor quality. The result is graduate unemployment of 17% at a time when the high-tech economy is booming.

Americans are right to worry about losing out in the international competition for talented people, particularly as highly qualified Indians and Chinese based in America go home. America's immigration system is hopelessly antiquated, geared more towards reuniting families than attracting high-quality workers. The 2005 allocation for H1B visas for skilled workers ran out on the first day of the fiscal year. . . .

(c) But again these worries are exaggerated. America remains the world's number one destination for foreign students, soaking up almost 30% of the global supply. There is every reason to think that the absolute number of people from India and China who want to study in America will rise as those countries get richer. It is true that some foreigners who might have stayed in America a few years ago are going home. But David Zweig, of the Hong Kong University of Science and Technology, argues that the best Chinese students remain abroad. The pattern of geographical mobility is likely to get more complicated in the future as people divide their careers between the developed and the developing world, but America is unlikely to be denuded of talent. . . .

Key Points in the Article

This article discusses fears in the United States that as the Chinese and Indian economies grow, well-paying jobs will move overseas, and it will also become more difficult to attract high-skilled foreign workers to the United States. A decline in the number of high-skilled jobs in the United States could undermine economic growth and reduce increases in living standards. The article argues that these fears are exaggerated and that the United States has many advantages that should allow it to retain many high-skilled, high-wage jobs.

Analyzing the News

ⓐ We have seen in this chapter that economists use models to analyze economic issues such as the effects of outsourcing. One advantage of economic models is that they make explicit the assumptions being made. Models also generate hypotheses that can be tested against the real world. According to the article,

people who fear competition from China believe that it will result in a loss of jobs in the United States. People who make this argument are also using a model, but it is a model that is not explicitly stated. This model assumes "that the number of jobs is fixed, so if some of them go abroad there must be fewer left at home." We know this model is not useful because for many years the United States has been trading goods and services with other countries, and U.S. firms have had operations in other countries, and the total number of jobs available in the United States has continued to increase.

ⓑ The *Making the Connection* on page 13 presents the debate between economists Paul Samuelson and Jagdish Bhagwati over whether outsourcing has helped or hurt the U.S. economy. One key aspect of the debate concerns whether workers who lose their jobs because of outsourcing are eventually likely to find comparable or better jobs. The article cites a study from the McKinsey Global Institute that points out that the number of jobs lost to outsourcing is small relative to the total number of new jobs created in the United States each month.

ⓒ The figure below shows the trend in foreign-born doctoral scientists and engineers employed in the United States

from 1993 to 2004. Although the relative number of permanent resident scientists and engineers has declined somewhat, the relative number of scientists and engineers who were born in other countries but who have become naturalized citizens of the United States has increased over time. In fact, the share of foreign-born scientists and engineers in the United States increased from 17.9 percent in 1993 to 24.8 percent in 2004. The United States has retained the ability to attract scientists and engineers from other countries.

Thinking Critically

1. The article points out that a total of 4.1 million well-paying service-sector jobs will have moved from the developed world to China and India by 2008. However, the article argues that there are limits to the number of jobs that can move from developed countries to China and India. What determines those limits?

2. According to the article, some Americans worry that the United States is having more difficulty attracting highly skilled workers from China and India and that this will undermine the U.S. high-tech sector. What evidence from the article suggests that the lead of the United States in the high-tech sector is relatively secure?

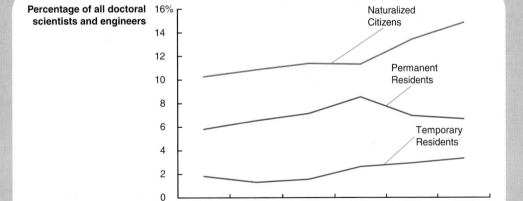

The United States has continued to attract foreign-born scientists and engineers.
Source: National Science Foundation, Division of Science Resources Statistics, *Characteristics of Doctoral Scientists and Engineers in the United States: 2003*, NSF 06-320, Project Officer, John Tsapogas (Arlington, VA, 2006).

Key Terms

1.1 LEARNING OBJECTIVE   1.1 | Explain these three key economic ideas: *People are rational. People respond to incentives. Optimal decisions are made at the margin,* **pages 4–7.**

Three Key Economic Ideas

Summary

Economics is the study of the choices consumers, business managers, and government officials make to attain their goals, given their scarce resources. We must make choices because of **scarcity**, which means that although our wants are unlimited, the resources available to fulfill those wants are limited. Economists assume that people are rational in the sense that consumers and firms use all available information as they take actions intended to achieve their goals. Rational individuals weigh the benefits and costs of each action and choose an action only if the benefits outweigh the costs. Although people act from a variety of motives, ample evidence indicates that they respond to economic incentives. Economists use the word **marginal** to mean extra or additional. The optimal decision is to continue any activity up to the point where the marginal benefit equals the marginal cost.

 Visit www.myeconlab.com to complete these exercises online and get instant feedback.

Review Questions

1.1 Briefly discuss each of the following economic ideas: People are rational. People respond to incentives. Optimal decisions are made at the margin.

1.2 What is scarcity? Why is scarcity central to the study of economics?

Problems and Applications

1.3 In the first six months of 2003, branches of Commerce Bank in New York City were robbed 14 times. The New York City Police Department recommended steps the bank could take to deter robberies, including the installation of plastic barriers called "bandit barriers." The police were surprised that the

bank did not take their advice. According to a deputy commissioner of police, "Commerce does very little of what we recommend. They've told our detectives they have no interest in ever putting in the barriers." Wouldn't Commerce Bank have a strong incentive to install bandit barriers to deter robberies? Why, then, wouldn't it do so?

Source: Dan Barry, "Friendly Bank Makes It Easy for Robbers," *New York Times,* July 5, 2003.

1.4 (Related to *Solved Problem 1-1* on page 7) Suppose Dell is currently selling 250,000 Penryn laptops per month. A manager at Dell argues, "The last 10,000 laptops we produced increased our revenue by $8.5 million and our costs by $8.9 million. However, because we are making a substantial total profit of $25 million from producing 250,000 laptops, I think we are producing the optimal number of laptops." Briefly explain whether you agree with the manager's reasoning.

1.5 (Related to *Solved Problem 1-1* on page 7) Two students are discussing Solved Problem 1-1:

> **Joe:** "I think the key additional information you need to know in deciding whether to produce 300,000 more iPods is the amount of profit you currently are making while producing 3,000,000. Then you can compare the profit earned from selling 3,300,000 iPods with the profit earned from selling 3,000,000. This information is more important than the additional revenue and additional cost of the last 300,000 iPods produced."
>
> **Jill:** "Actually, Joe, knowing how much profits change when you sell 300,000 more iPods is exactly the same as knowing the additional revenue and the additional cost."

Briefly evaluate their arguments.

1.6 (Related to *Solved Problem 1-1* on page 7) Late in the semester, a friend tells you, "I was going to drop my psychology course so I could concentrate on my other courses, but I had already put so much time into the course that I decided not to drop it." What do you think of your friend's reasoning? Would it make a difference to your answer if your friend has to pass the psychology course at some point to graduate? Briefly explain.

1.7 **(Related to the *Making the Connection* on page 5)** Estonia has attempted to increase the country's birthrate by making payments to women who have babies. According to an article in the *Wall Street Journal*, "Some demographers argue that paying people to have a baby simply makes them have one earlier; it doesn't necessarily make them have more." Reread the description of Estonia's programs. Could the program be changed in ways that might make it more likely that Estonian women will have more children, rather than simply changing the timing of when they have children? What

information would we need to have to resolve the question of whether Estonian women are responding to the government's incentives by having more children or simply by having them earlier?

Source: Marcus Walker, "In Estonia, Paying Women to Have Babies Is Paying Off," *Wall Street Journal*, October 20, 2006, p. A1.

1.8 In a column in the *Wall Street Journal*, Robert McTeer, Jr., former president of the Federal Reserve Bank of Dallas, wrote, "My take on training in economics is that it becomes increasingly valuable as you move up the career ladder. I can't think of a better major for corporate CEOs [chief executive officers], congressmen or American presidents." Why might studying economics be particularly good preparation for being the top manager of a corporation or a leader in government?

Source: Robert D. McTeer, Jr., "The Dismal Science? Hardly!" *Wall Street Journal*, June 4, 2003.

>> **End Learning Objective 1.1**

1.2 LEARNING OBJECTIVE 1.2 | Discuss how an economy answers these questions: *What* goods and services will be produced? *How* will the goods and services be produced? *Who* will receive the goods and services? **pages 8–11.**

The Economic Problem That Every Society Must Solve

Summary

Society faces **trade-offs**: Producing more of one good or service means producing less of another good or service. The **opportunity cost** of any activity—such as producing a good or service—is the highest-valued alternative that must be given up to engage in that activity. The choices of consumers, firms, and governments determine what goods and services will be produced. Firms choose how to produce the goods and services they sell. In the United States, who receives the goods and services produced depends largely on how income is distributed in the marketplace. In a **centrally planned economy**, most economic decisions are made by the government. In a **market economy**, most economic decisions are made by consumers and firms. Most economies, including that of the United States, are **mixed economies** in which most economic decisions are made by consumers and firms but in which the government also plays a significant role. There are two types of efficiency: productive efficiency and allocative efficiency. **Productive efficiency** occurs when a good or service is produced at the lowest possible cost. **Allocative efficiency** occurs when production is in accordance with consumer preferences. **Voluntary exchange** is the situation that occurs in markets when both the buyer and seller of a product are made better off by the transaction. **Equity** is more difficult to define than efficiency, but it usually involves a fair distribution of economic benefits. Government policymakers often face a trade-off between equity and efficiency.

 Visit www.myeconlab.com to complete these exercises online and get instant feedback.

Review Questions

2.1 What are the three economic questions that every society must answer? Briefly discuss the differences in how centrally planned, market, and mixed economies answer these questions.

2.2 What is the difference between productive efficiency and allocative efficiency?

2.3 What is the difference between efficiency and equity? Why do government policymakers often face a trade-off between efficiency and equity?

Problems and Applications

2.4 Does Bill Gates, the richest person in the world, face scarcity? Does everyone? Are there any exceptions?

2.5 Would you expect new and better machinery and equipment to be adopted more rapidly in a market economy or in a centrally planned economy? Briefly explain.

2.6 Centrally planned economies have been less efficient than market economies.
   a. Has this happened by chance, or is there some underlying reason?
   b. If market economies are more economically efficient than centrally planned economies, would there ever be a reason to prefer having a centrally planned economy rather than a market economy?

2.7 Thomas Sowell, an economist at the Hoover Institution at Stanford University, has written, "All economic systems not only provide people with goods and services, but also restrict or prevent them from getting as much of these goods and services as they wish." Why is it necessary for all economic systems to do this? How does a market system prevent people from getting as many goods and services as they wish?

Source: Thomas Sowell, *Applied Economics: Thinking Beyond Stage One*, New York: Basic Books, 2004, p. 16.

2.8 Suppose that your local police department recovers 100 tickets to a big NASCAR race in a drug raid. It decides to distribute these to residents and announces that tickets will be given away at 10 A.M. Monday at City Hall.
   a. What groups of people will be most likely to try to get the tickets? Think of specific examples and then generalize.
   b. What is the opportunity cost of distributing the tickets this way?
   c. Productive efficiency occurs when a good or service (such as the distribution of tickets) is produced at the lowest possible cost. Is this an efficient way to distribute the tickets? If possible, think of a more efficient method of distributing the tickets.
   d. Is this an equitable way to distribute the tickets? Explain.

>> **End Learning Objective 1.2**

1.3 LEARNING OBJECTIVE   1.3 | Understand the role of models in economic analysis, **pages 11–15.**

Economic Models

Summary

Economists rely on economic models when they apply economic ideas to real-world problems. **Economic models** are simplified versions of reality used to analyze real-world economic situations. Economists accept and use an economic model if it leads to hypotheses that are confirmed by statistical analysis. In many cases, the acceptance is tentative, however, pending the gathering of new data or further statistical analysis. Economics is a **social science** because it applies the scientific method to the study of the interactions among individuals. Economics is concerned with positive analysis rather than normative analysis. **Positive analysis** is concerned with what is. **Normative analysis** is concerned with what ought to be. Because economics is based on studying the actions of individuals, it is a social science. As a social science, economics considers human behavior in every context of decision making, not just in business.

myeconlab Visit www.myeconlab.com to complete these exercises
Get Ahead of the Curve online and get instant feedback.

Review Questions

3.1 Why do economists use models? How are economic data used to test models?

3.2 Describe the five steps by which economists arrive at a useful economic model.

3.3 What is the difference between normative analysis and positive analysis? Is economics concerned mainly with normative analysis or mainly with positive analysis? Briefly explain.

Problems and Applications

3.4 Do you agree or disagree with the following assertion: "The problem with economics is that it assumes consumers and firms always make the correct decision. But we know everyone's human, and we all make mistakes."

3.5 Suppose an economist develops an economic model and finds that "it works great in theory, but it fails in practice." What should the economist do next?

3.6 Dr. Strangelove's theory is that the price of mushrooms is determined by the activity of subatomic particles that exist in another universe parallel to ours. When the subatomic particles are emitted in profusion, the price of mushrooms is high. When subatomic particle emissions are low, the price of mushrooms also is low. How would you go about testing Dr. Strangelove's theory? Discuss whether this theory is useful.

3.7 (Related to the *Making the Connection* on page 13) The *Making the Connection* that discusses the debate between Paul Samuelson and Jagdish Bhagwati over outsourcing mentions that the two economists disagree over how to interpret the relevant economic statistics. What economic statistics would be most useful in evaluating the positions these economists hold? Assuming these statistics are available or could be gathered, are they likely to finally resolve the debate?

3.8 (Related to the *Chapter Opener* on page 2) Many large firms have begun outsourcing work to China.
  a. Why have large firms done this?
  b. Is outsourcing work to low-wage Chinese workers a risk-free proposition for large firms?

3.9 (Related to the *Don't Let This Happen to You!* on page 14) Explain which of the following statements represent positive analysis and which represent normative analysis.
  a. A 50-cent-per-pack tax on cigarettes will reduce smoking by teenagers by 12 percent.
  b. The federal government should spend more on AIDS research.
  c. Rising paper prices will increase textbook prices.
  d. The price of coffee at Starbucks is too high.

3.10 The American Bar Association has proposed a law that would prohibit anyone except lawyers from giving legal advice. Under the proposal, income tax preparers, real estate agents, hospitals, labor unions, and anyone else who offered legal advice would be penalized. One critic of the proposal argued that the proposal would protect attorneys more than it would protect consumers.
  a. How might the proposal protect consumers?
  b. Why did the critic of the proposal argue that it would protect attorneys more than it would protect consumers?
  c. Briefly discuss whether you consider the proposed law to be a good idea.

Source: Adam Liptak, "U.S. Opposes Proposal to Limit Who May Give Legal Advice," *New York Times*, February 3, 2003.

>> End Learning Objective 1.3

1.4 LEARNING OBJECTIVE 1.4 | Distinguish between microeconomics and macroeconomics, **page 15.**

Microeconomics and Macroeconomics

Summary

Microeconomics is the study of how households and firms make choices, how they interact in markets, and how the government attempts to influence their choices. **Macroeconomics** is the study of the economy as a whole, including topics such as inflation, unemployment, and economic growth.

myeconlab Visit www.myeconlab.com to complete these exercises online and get instant feedback.

Review Question

4.1 Briefly discuss the difference between microeconomics and macroeconomics.

Problems and Applications

4.2 Briefly explain whether each of the following is primarily a microeconomic issue or a macroeconomic issue.

  a. The effect of higher cigarette taxes on the quantity of cigarettes sold.
  b. The effect of higher income taxes on the total amount of consumer spending.
  c. The reasons for the economies of East Asian countries growing faster than the economies of sub-Saharan African countries.
  d. The reasons for low rates of profit in the airline industry.

4.3 Briefly explain whether you agree with the following assertion: "Microeconomics is concerned with things that happen in one particular place, such as the unemployment rate in one city. In contrast, macroeconomics is concerned with things that affect the country as a whole, such as how the rate of teenage smoking in the United States would be affected by an increase in the tax on cigarettes."

>> End Learning Objective 1.4

1.5 LEARNING OBJECTIVE 1.5 | Become familiar with important economic terms, **pages 15–16.**

A Preview of Important Economic Terms

Summary

Becoming familiar with important terms is a necessary step in learning economics. These important economic terms include *capital, entrepreneur, factors of production, firm, goods, household, human capital, innovation, profit, revenue,* and *technology.*

Appendix

Using Graphs and Formulas

LEARNING OBJECTIVE

Review the use of **graphs** and **formulas**.

Graphs are used to illustrate key economics ideas. Graphs appear not just in economics textbooks but also on Web sites and in newspaper and magazine articles that discuss events in business and economics. Why the heavy use of graphs? Because they serve two useful purposes: (1) They simplify economic ideas, and (2) they make the ideas more concrete so they can be applied to real-world problems. Economic and business issues can be complicated, but a graph can help cut through complications and highlight the key relationships needed to understand the issue. In that sense, a graph can be like a street map.

For example, suppose you take a bus to New York City to see the Empire State Building. After arriving at the Port Authority Bus Terminal, you will probably use a map similar to the one shown below to find your way to the Empire State Building.

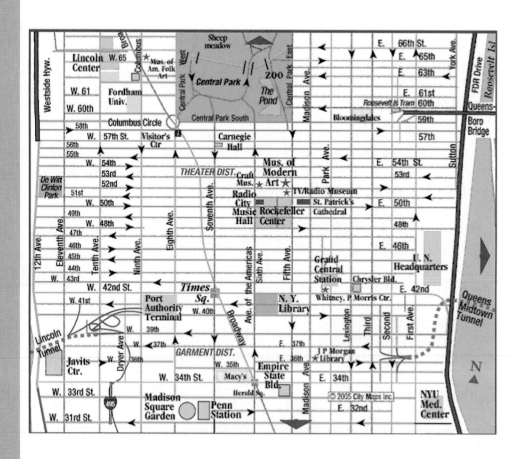

Maps are very familiar to just about everyone, so we don't usually think of them as being simplified versions of reality, but they are. This map does not show much more than the streets in this part of New York City and some of the most important buildings. The names, addresses, and telephone numbers of the people who live and work in the area aren't given. Almost none of the stores and buildings those people work and live in are shown either. The map doesn't tell which streets allow curbside parking and which don't. In fact, the map tells almost nothing about the messy reality of life in this section of New York City, except how the streets are laid out, which is the essential information you need to get from the Port Authority to the Empire State Building.

Think about someone who says, "I know how to get around in the city, but I just can't figure out how to read a map." It certainly is possible to find your destination in a city without a map, but it's a lot easier with one. The same is true of using graphs in economics. It is possible to arrive at a solution to a real-world problem in economics and business without using graphs, but it is usually a lot easier if you do use them.

Often, the difficulty students have with graphs and formulas is a lack of familiarity. With practice, all the graphs and formulas in this text will become familiar to you. Once you are familiar with them, you will be able to use them to analyze problems that would otherwise seem very difficult. What follows is a brief review of how graphs and formulas are used.

Graphs of One Variable

Figure 1A-1 displays values for *market shares* in the U.S. automobile market, using two common types of graphs. Market shares show the percentage of industry sales accounted for by different firms. In this case, the information is for groups of firms: the "Big Three"—Ford, General Motors, and DaimlerChrysler—as well as Japanese firms, European firms, and Korean firms. Panel (a) displays the information on market shares as a *bar graph*, where the market share of each group of firms is represented by the

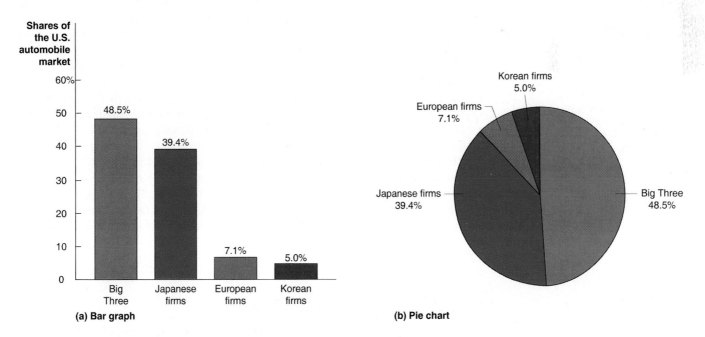

Figure 1A-1 | Bar Graphs and Pie Charts

Values for an economic variable are often displayed as a bar graph or as a pie chart. In this case, panel (a) shows market share data for the U.S. automobile industry as a bar graph, where the market share of each group of firms is represented by the height of its bar. Panel (b) displays the same information as a pie chart, with the market share of each group of firms represented by the size of its slice of the pie.
Source: "Auto Sales," *Wall Street Journal*, April 1, 2008.

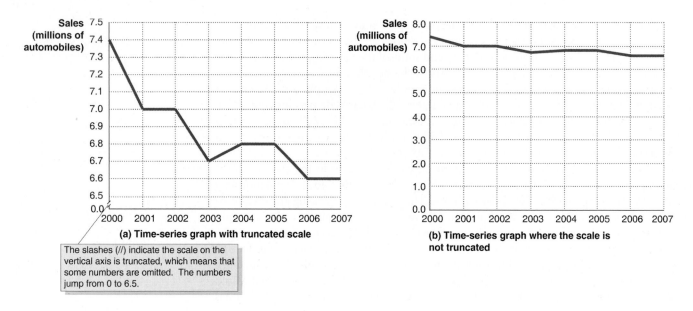

Figure 1A-2 | Time-Series Graphs

Both panels present time-series graphs of Ford Motor Company's worldwide sales during each year from 2000–2007. Panel (a) has a truncated scale on the vertical axis, and panel (b) does not. As a result, the fluctuations in Ford's sales appear smaller in panel (b) than in panel (a).
Source: Ford Motor Company, *Annual Report*, various years.

height of its bar. Panel (b) displays the same information as a *pie chart*, with the market share of each group of firms represented by the size of its slice of the pie.

Information on economic variables is also often displayed in *time-series graphs*. Time-series graphs are displayed on a coordinate grid. In a coordinate grid, we can measure the value of one variable along the vertical axis (or *y*-axis), and the value of another variable along the horizontal axis (or *x*-axis). The point where the vertical axis intersects the horizontal axis is called the *origin*. At the origin, the value of both variables is zero. The points on a coordinate grid represent values of the two variables. In Figure 1A-2, we measure the number of automobiles and trucks sold worldwide by the Ford Motor Company on the vertical axis, and we measure time on the horizontal axis. In time-series graphs, the height of the line at each date shows the value of the variable measured on the vertical axis. Both panels of Figure 1A-2 show Ford's worldwide sales during each year from 2000 to 2007. The difference between panel (a) and panel (b) illustrates the importance of the scale used in a time-series graph. In panel (a), the scale on the vertical axis is truncated, which means that it does not start with zero. The slashes (//) near the bottom of the axis indicate that the scale is truncated. In panel (b), the scale is not truncated. In panel (b), the decline in Ford's sales since 2000 appears smaller than in panel (a). (Technically, the horizontal axis is also truncated because we start with the year 2000, not the year 0.)

Graphs of Two Variables

We often use graphs to show the relationship between two variables. For example, suppose you are interested in the relationship between the price of a pepperoni pizza and the quantity of pizzas sold per week in the small town of Bryan, Texas. A graph showing the relationship between the price of a good and the quantity of the good demanded at each price is called a *demand curve*. (As we will discuss later, in drawing a demand curve for a good, we have to hold constant any variables other than price that might affect the

Price (dollars per pizza)	Quantity (pizzas per week)	Points
$15	50	A
14	55	B
13	60	C
12	65	D
11	70	E

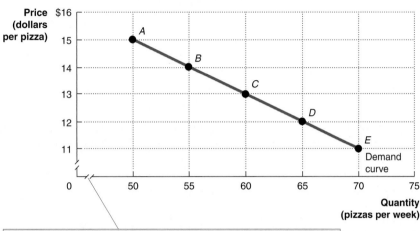

Figure 1A-3

Plotting Price and Quantity Points in a Graph

The figure shows a two-dimensional grid on which we measure the price of pizza along the vertical axis (or *y*-axis) and the quantity of pizza sold per week along the horizontal axis (or *x*-axis). Each point on the grid represents one of the price and quantity combinations listed in the table. By connecting the points with a line, we can better illustrate the relationship between the two variables.

As you learned in Figure 1A-2, the slashes (//) indicate the scales on the axes are truncated, which means that numbers are omitted: On the horizontal axis numbers jump from 0 to 50, and on the vertical axis numbers jump from 0 to 11.

willingness of consumers to buy the good.) Figure 1A-3 shows the data you have collected on price and quantity. The figure shows a two-dimensional grid on which we measure the price of pizza along the *y*-axis and the quantity of pizza sold per week along the *x*-axis. Each point on the grid represents one of the price and quantity combinations listed in the table. We can connect the points to form the demand curve for pizza in Bryan, Texas. Notice that the scales on both axes in the graph are truncated. In this case, truncating the axes allows the graph to illustrate more clearly the relationship between price and quantity by excluding low prices and quantities.

Slopes of Lines

Once you have plotted the data in Figure 1A-3, you may be interested in how much the quantity of pizza sold increases as the price decreases. The *slope* of a line tells us how much the variable we are measuring on the *y*-axis changes as the variable we are measuring on the *x*-axis changes. We can use the Greek letter delta (Δ) to stand for the change in a variable. The slope is sometimes referred to as the rise over the run. So, we have several ways of expressing slope:

$$\text{Slope} = \frac{\text{Change in value on the vertical axis}}{\text{Change in value on the horizontal axis}} = \frac{\Delta y}{\Delta x} = \frac{\text{Rise}}{\text{Run}}.$$

Figure 1A-4 reproduces the graph from Figure 1A-3. Because the slope of a straight line is the same at any point, we can use any two points in the figure to calculate the slope of the line. For example, when the price of pizza decreases from $14 to $12, the quantity of pizza sold increases from 55 per week to 65 per week. Therefore, the slope is:

$$\text{Slope} = \frac{\Delta \text{Price of pizza}}{\Delta \text{Quantity of pizza}} = \frac{(\$12 - \$14)}{(65 - 55)} = \frac{-2}{10} = -0.2.$$

Figure 1A-4

We can calculate the slope of a line as the change in the value of the variable on the *y*-axis divided by the change in the value of the variable on the *x*-axis. Because the slope of a straight line is constant, we can use any two points in the figure to calculate the slope of the line. For example, when the price of pizza decreases from $14 to $12, the quantity of pizza demanded increases from 55 per week to 65 per week. So, the slope of this line equals −2 divided by 10, or −0.2.

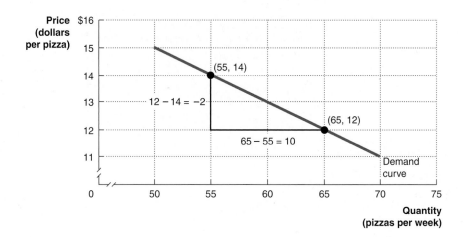

The slope of this line gives us some insight into how responsive consumers in Bryan, Texas, are to changes in the price of pizza. The larger the value of the slope (ignoring the negative sign), the steeper the line will be, which indicates that not many additional pizzas are sold when the price falls. The smaller the value of the slope, the flatter the line will be, which indicates a greater increase in pizzas sold when the price falls.

Taking into Account More Than Two Variables on a Graph

The demand curve graph in Figure 1A-4 shows the relationship between the price of pizza and the quantity of pizza sold, but we know that the quantity of any good sold depends on more than just the price of the good. For example, the quantity of pizza sold in a given week in Bryan, Texas, can be affected by such other variables as the price of hamburgers, whether an advertising campaign by local pizza parlors has begun that week, and so on. Allowing the values of any other variables to change will cause the position of the demand curve in the graph to change.

Suppose, for example, that the demand curve in Figure 1A-4 was drawn holding the price of hamburgers constant at $1.50. If the price of hamburgers rises to $2.00, then some consumers will switch from buying hamburgers to buying pizza, and more pizzas will be sold at every price. The result on the graph will be to shift the line representing the demand curve to the right. Similarly, if the price of hamburgers falls from $1.50 to $1.00, some consumers will switch from buying pizza to buying hamburgers, and fewer pizzas will be sold at every price. The result on the graph will be to shift the line representing the demand curve to the left.

The table in Figure 1A-5 shows the effect of a change in the price of hamburgers on the quantity of pizza demanded. For example, suppose at first we are on the line labeled *Demand curve₁*. If the price of pizza is $14 (point *A*), an increase in the price of hamburgers from $1.50 to $2.00 increases the quantity of pizzas demanded from 55 to 60 per week (point *B*) and shifts us to *Demand curve₂*. Or, if we start on *Demand curve₁* and the price of pizza is $12 (point *C*), a decrease in the price of hamburgers from $1.50 to $1.00 decreases the quantity of pizzas demanded from 65 to 60 per week (point *D*) and shifts us to *Demand curve₃*. By shifting the demand curve, we have taken into account the effect of changes in the value of a third variable—the price of hamburgers. We will use this technique of shifting curves to allow for the effects of additional variables many times in this book.

Positive and Negative Relationships

We can use graphs to show the relationships between any two variables. Sometimes the relationship between the variables is *negative*, meaning that as one variable increases in value, the other variable decreases in value. This was the case with the

Price (dollars per pizza)	Quantity (pizzas per week)		
	When the Price of Hamburgers = $1.00	When the Price of Hamburgers = $1.50	When the Price of Hamburgers = $2.00
$15	45	50	55
14	50	55	60
13	55	60	65
12	60	65	70
11	65	70	75

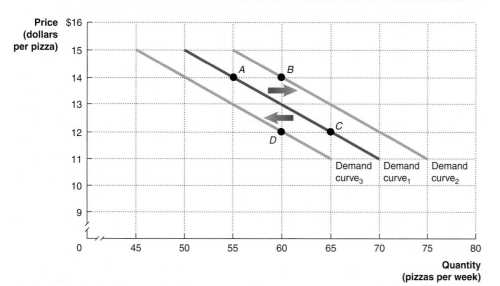

Figure 1A-5

Showing Three Variables on a Graph

The demand curve for pizza shows the relationship between the price of pizzas and the quantity of pizzas demanded, *holding constant other factors that might affect the willingness of consumers to buy pizza*. If the price of pizza is $14 (point *A*), an increase in the price of hamburgers from $1.50 to $2.00 increases the quantity of pizzas demanded from 55 to 60 per week (point *B*) and shifts us to Demand curve₂. Or, if we start on *Demand curve₁* and the price of pizza is $12 (point *C*), a decrease in the price of hamburgers from $1.50 to $1.00 decreases the quantity of pizza demanded from 65 to 60 per week (point *D*) and shifts us to *Demand curve₃*.

price of pizza and the quantity of pizzas demanded. The relationship between two variables can also be *positive*, meaning that the values of both variables increase or decrease together. For example, when the level of total income—or *disposable personal income*—received by households in the United States increases, the level of total *consumption spending*, which is spending by households on goods and services, also increases. The table in Figure 1A-6 shows the values for income and consumption spending for the years 2004–2007 (the values are in billions of dollars). The graph

Year	Disposable personal income (billions of dollars)	Consumption spending (billions of dollars)
2004	$8,681	$8,196
2005	9,092	8,708
2006	9,629	9,225
2007	10,177	9,734

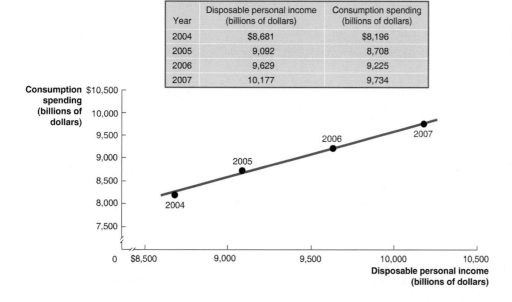

Figure 1A-6

Graphing the Positive Relationship between Income and Consumption

In a positive relationship between two economic variables, as one variable increases, the other variable also increases. This figure shows the positive relationship between disposable personal income and consumption spending. As disposable personal income in the United States has increased, so has consumption spending.
Source: U.S. Department of Commerce, Bureau of Economic Analysis.

plots the data from the table, with national income measured along the horizontal axis and consumption spending measured along the vertical axis. Notice that the four points do not all fall exactly on the line. This is often the case with real-world data. To examine the relationship between two variables, economists often use the straight line that best fits the data.

Determining Cause and Effect

When we graph the relationship between two variables, we often want to draw conclusions about whether changes in one variable are causing changes in the other variable. Doing so, however, can lead to incorrect conclusions. For example, suppose you graph the number of homes in a neighborhood that have a fire burning in the fireplace and the number of leaves on trees in the neighborhood. You would get a relationship like that shown in panel (a) of Figure 1A-7: The more fires burning in the neighborhood, the fewer leaves the trees have. Can we draw the conclusion from this graph that using a fireplace causes trees to lose their leaves? We know, of course, that such a conclusion would be incorrect. In spring and summer, there are relatively few fireplaces being used, and the trees are full of leaves. In the fall, as trees begin to lose their leaves, fireplaces are used more frequently. And in winter, many fireplaces are being used and many trees have lost all their leaves. The reason that the graph in Figure 1A-7 is misleading about cause and effect is that there is obviously an *omitted variable* in the analysis—the season of the year. An omitted variable is one that affects other variables, and its omission can lead to false conclusions about cause and effect.

Although in our example the omitted variable is obvious, there are many debates about cause and effect where the existence of an omitted variable has not been clear. For instance, it has been known for many years that people who smoke cigarettes suffer from higher rates of lung cancer than do nonsmokers. For some time, tobacco companies and some scientists argued that there was an omitted variable—perhaps psychological temperament—that made some people more likely to smoke and more likely to develop lung cancer. If this omitted variable existed, then the finding that smokers were

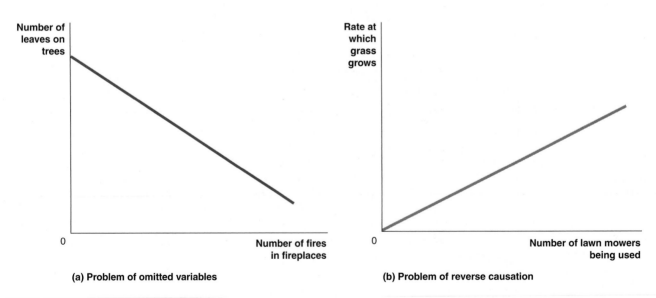

(a) Problem of omitted variables

(b) Problem of reverse causation

Figure 1A-7 | Determining Cause and Effect

Using graphs to draw conclusions about cause and effect can be hazardous. In panel (a), we see that there are fewer leaves on the trees in a neighborhood when many homes have fires burning in their fireplaces. We cannot draw the conclusion that the fires cause the leaves to fall because we have an *omitted variable*—the season of the year. In panel (b), we see that more lawn mowers are used in a neighborhood during times when the grass grows rapidly and fewer lawn mowers are used when the grass grows slowly. Concluding that using lawn mowers *causes* the grass to grow faster would be making the error of *reverse causality*.

more likely to develop lung cancer would not have been evidence that smoking *caused* lung cancer. In this case, however, nearly all scientists eventually concluded that the omitted variable did not exist and that, in fact, smoking does cause lung cancer.

A related problem in determining cause and effect is known as *reverse causality*. The error of reverse causality occurs when we conclude that changes in variable X cause changes in variable Y when, in fact, it is actually changes in variable Y that cause changes in variable X. For example, panel (b) of Figure 1A-7 plots the number of lawn mowers being used in a neighborhood against the rate at which grass on lawns in the neighborhood is growing. We could conclude from this graph that using lawn mowers *causes* the grass to grow faster. We know, however, that in reality, the causality is in the other direction: Rapidly growing grass during the spring and summer causes the increased use of lawn mowers. Slowly growing grass in the fall or winter or during periods of low rainfall causes decreased use of lawn mowers.

Once again, in our example, the potential error of reverse causality is obvious. In many economic debates, however, cause and effect can be more difficult to determine. For example, changes in the money supply, or the total amount of money in the economy, tend to occur at the same time as changes in the total amount of income people in the economy earn. A famous debate in economics was about whether the changes in the money supply caused the changes in total income or whether the changes in total income caused the changes in the money supply. Each side in the debate accused the other side of committing the error of reverse causality.

Are Graphs of Economic Relationships Always Straight Lines?

The graphs of relationships between two economic variables that we have drawn so far have been straight lines. The relationship between two variables is *linear* when it can be represented by a straight line. Few economic relationships are actually linear. For example, if we carefully plot data on the price of a product and the quantity demanded at each price, holding constant other variables that affect the quantity demanded, we will usually find a curved—or *nonlinear*—relationship rather than a linear relationship. In practice, however, it is often useful to approximate a nonlinear relationship with a linear relationship. If the relationship is reasonably close to being linear, the analysis is not significantly affected. In addition, it is easier to calculate the slope of a straight line, and it also is easier to calculate the area under a straight line. So, in this textbook, we often assume that the relationship between two economic variables is linear even when we know that this assumption is not precisely correct.

Slopes of Nonlinear Curves

In some situations, we need to take into account the nonlinear nature of an economic relationship. For example, panel (a) of Figure 1A-8 shows the hypothetical relationship between Apple's total cost of producing iPods and the quantity of iPods produced. The relationship is curved, rather than linear. In this case, the cost of production is increasing at an increasing rate, which often happens in manufacturing. Put a different way, as we move up the curve, its slope becomes larger. (Remember that with a straight line, the slope is always constant.) To see this effect, first remember that we calculate the slope of a curve by dividing the change in the variable on the *y*-axis by the change in the variable on the *x*-axis. As we move from point *A* to point *B*, the quantity produced increases by 1 million iPods, while the total cost of production increases by $50 million. Farther up the curve, as we move from point *C* to point *D*, the change in quantity is the same—1 million iPods—but the change in the total cost of production is now much larger: $250 million. Because the change in the *y* variable has increased, while the change in the *x* variable has remained the same, we know that the slope has increased.

To measure the slope of a nonlinear curve at a particular point, we must measure the slope of the *tangent line* to the curve at that point. A tangent line will only touch the curve at that point. We can measure the slope of the tangent line just as we would

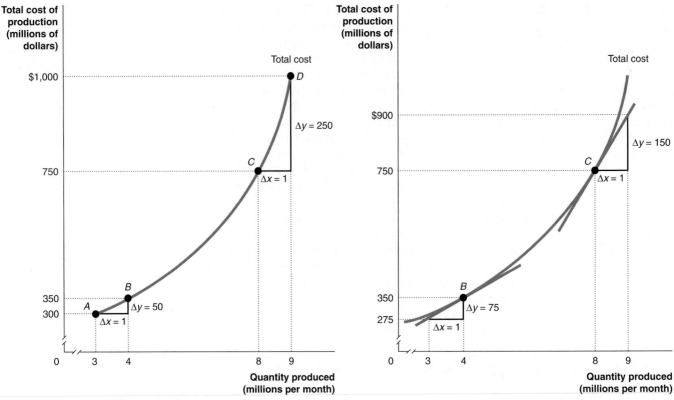

Figure 1A-8   The Slope of a Nonlinear Curve

The relationship between the quantity of iPods produced and the total cost of production is curved, rather than liner. In panel (a), in moving from point *A* to point *B*, the quantity produced increases by 1 million iPods, while the total cost of production increases by $50 million. Farther up the curve, as we move from point *C* to point *D*, the change in quantity is the same—1 million iPods—but the change in the total cost of production is now much larger: $250 million.

Because the change in the *y* variable has increased, while the change in the *x* variable has remained the same, we know that the slope has increased. In panel (b), we measure the slope of the curve at a particular point by the slope of the tangent line. The slope of the tangent line at point *B* is 75, and the slope of the tangent line at point *C* is 150.

the slope of any straight line. In panel (b), the tangent line at point *B* has a slope equal to:

$$\frac{\Delta\text{Cost}}{\Delta\text{Quantity}} = \frac{75}{1} = 75.$$

The tangent line at point *C* has a slope equal to:

$$\frac{\Delta\text{Cost}}{\Delta\text{Quantity}} = \frac{150}{1} = 150.$$

Once again, we see that the slope of the curve is larger at point *C* than at point *B*.

Formulas

We have just seen that graphs are an important economic tool. In this section, we will review several useful formulas and show how to use them to summarize data and to calculate important relationships.

Formula for a Percentage Change

One important formula is the percentage change. The *percentage change* is the change in some economic variable, usually from one period to the next, expressed as a percentage. An important macroeconomic measure is the real gross domestic product (GDP). *GDP* is the value of all the final goods and services produced in a country during a year. "Real" GDP is corrected for the effects of inflation. When economists say that the U.S. economy grew 2.2 percent during 2007, they mean that real GDP was 2.2 percent higher in 2007 than it was in 2006. The formula for making this calculation is:

$$\left(\frac{\text{GDP}_{2007} - \text{GDP}_{2006}}{\text{GDP}_{2006}} \right) \times 100$$

or, more generally, for any two periods:

$$\text{Percentage change} = \frac{\text{Value in the second period} - \text{Value in the first period}}{\text{Value in the first period}} \times 100.$$

In this case, real GDP was $11,319 billion in 2006 and $11,567 billion in 2007. So, the growth rate of the U.S. economy during 2007 was:

$$\left(\frac{\$11,567 - \$11,319}{\$11,319} \right) \times 100 = 2.2\%.$$

Notice that it didn't matter that in using the formula, we ignored the fact that GDP is measured in billions of dollars. In fact, when calculating percentage changes, *the units don't matter*. The percentage increase from $11,319 billion to $11,567 billion is exactly the same as the percentage increase from $11,319 to $11,567.

Formulas for the Areas of a Rectangle and a Triangle

Areas that form rectangles and triangles on graphs can have important economic meaning. For example, Figure 1A-9 shows the demand curve for Pepsi. Suppose that the price is currently $2.00 and that 125,000 bottles of Pepsi are sold at that price. A firm's *total revenue* is equal to the amount it receives from selling its product, or the quantity sold multiplied by the price. In this case, total revenue will equal 125,000 bottles times $2.00 per bottle, or $250,000.

The formula for the area of a rectangle is:

Area of a rectangle = Base × Height

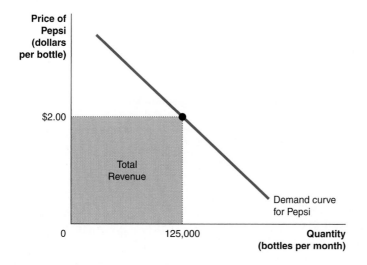

Figure 1A-9

Showing a Firm's Total Revenue on a Graph

The area of a rectangle is equal to its base multiplied by its height. Total revenue is equal to quantity multiplied by price. Here, total revenue is equal to the quantity of 125,000 bottles times the price of $2.00 per bottle, or $250,000. The area of the green-shaded rectangle shows the firm's total revenue.

Figure 1A-10

The Area of a Triangle

The area of a triangle is equal to ½ multiplied by its base multiplied by its height. The area of the blue-shaded triangle has a base equal to 150,000 − 125,000, or 25,000, and a height equal to $2.00 − $1.50, or $0.50. Therefore, its area equals ½ × 25,000 × $0.50, or $6,250.

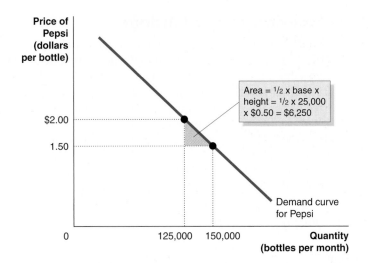

In Figure 1A-9, the green-shaded rectangle also represents the firm's total revenue because its area is given by the base of 125,000 bottles multiplied by the price of $2.00 per bottle.

We will see in later chapters that areas that are triangles can also have economic significance. The formula for the area of a triangle is:

$$\text{Area of a triangle} = \frac{1}{2} \times \text{Base} \times \text{Height}.$$

The blue-shaded area in Figure 1A-10 is a triangle. The base equals 150,000 − 125,000, or 25,000. Its height equals $2.00 − $1.50, or $0.50. Therefore, its area equals ½ × 25,000 × $0.50, or $6,250. Notice that the blue area is a triangle only if the demand curve is a straight line, or linear. Not all demand curves are linear. However, the formula for the area of a triangle will usually still give a good approximation, even if the demand curve is not linear.

Summary of Using Formulas

You will encounter several other formulas in this book. Whenever you must use a formula, you should follow these steps:

1 Make sure you understand the economic concept that the formula represents.

2 Make sure you are using the correct formula for the problem you are solving.

3 Make sure that the number you calculate using the formula is economically reasonable. For example, if you are using a formula to calculate a firm's revenue and your answer is a negative number, you know you made a mistake somewhere.

LEARNING OBJECTIVE   Review the use of graphs and formulas, **pages 24–34.**

myeconlab Visit www.myeconlab.com to complete these exercises
Get Ahead of the Curve online and get instant feedback.

Problems and Applications

1A.1 The following table gives the relationship between the price of custard pies and the number of pies Jacob buys per week.

PRICE	QUANTITY OF PIES	WEEK
$3.00	6	July 2
2.00	7	July 9
5.00	4	July 16
6.00	3	July 23
1.00	8	July 30
4.00	5	August 6

a. Is the relationship between the price of pies and the number of pies Jacob buys a positive relationship or a negative relationship?

b. Plot the data from the table on a graph similar to Figure 1A-3. Draw a straight line that best fits the points.

c. Calculate the slope of the line.

1A.2 The following table gives information on the quantity of glasses of lemonade demanded on sunny and overcast days. Plot the data from the table on a graph similar to Figure 1A-5. Draw two straight lines representing the two demand curves—one for sunny days and one for overcast days.

PRICE (DOLLARS PER GLASS)	QUANTITY (GLASSES OF LEMONADE PER DAY)	WEATHER
$0.80	30	Sunny
0.80	10	Overcast
0.70	40	Sunny
0.70	20	Overcast
0.60	50	Sunny
0.60	30	Overcast
0.50	60	Sunny
0.50	40	Overcast

1A.3 Using the information in Figure 1A-2, calculate the percentage change in auto sales from one year to the next. Between which years did sales fall at the fastest rate?

1A.4 Real GDP in 1981 was $5,292 billion. Real GDP in 1982 was $5,189 billion. What was the percentage change in real GDP from 1981 to 1982? What do economists call the percentage change in real GDP from one year to the next?

1A.5 Assume that the demand curve for Pepsi passes through the following two points:

PRICE PER BOTTLE OF PEPSI	NUMBER OF BOTTLES OF PEPSI SOLD
$2.50	100,000
1.25	200,000

a. Draw a graph with a linear demand curve that passes through these two points.

b. Show on the graph the areas representing total revenue at each price. Give the value for total revenue at each price.

1A.6 What is the area of the blue triangle shown in the following figure?

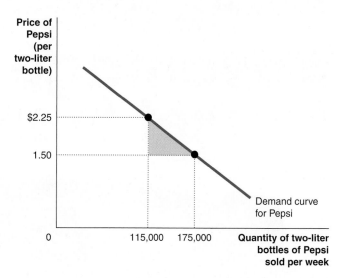

1A.7 Calculate the slope of the total cost curve at point *A* and at point *B* in the following figure.

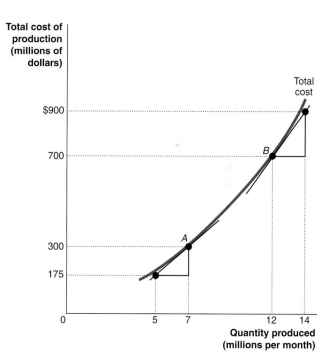

Chapter 2

Trade-offs, Comparative Advantage, and the Market System

Managers Making Choices at BMW

When you think of cars that combine fine engineering, high performance, and cutting-edge styling, you are likely to think of BMW. The Bayerische Motoren Werke, or Bavarian Motor Works, was founded in Germany in 1916. Today, BMW employs more than 100,000 workers in 23 factories in 15 countries to produce eight car models. In 2007, it had worldwide sales of nearly 1.5 million cars.

To compete in the automobile market, the managers of BMW must make many strategic decisions, such as whether to introduce a new car model. In 2006, for example, BMW announced that it would introduce a hydrogen-powered version of the 7-Series sedan and was also working on fuel-cell powered cars. Another strategic decision BMW's managers face is where to focus their advertising. In the late 1990s, for example, some of BMW's managers opposed advertising in China because they were skeptical about the country's sales potential.

Other managers, however, argued that rising incomes were rapidly increasing the size of the Chinese market. BMW decided to advertise in China, and it has become the company's eighth-largest market, with sales increasing by more than 35 percent in 2007 alone.

Over the years, BMW's managers have also faced the strategic decision of whether to concentrate production in factories in Germany or to build new factories in its overseas markets. Keeping production in Germany makes it easier for BMW's managers to supervise production and to employ German workers, who generally have high levels of technical training. Building factories in other countries, however, has two benefits. First, the lower wages paid to workers in other countries reduce the cost of manufacturing vehicles. Second, BMW can reduce political friction by producing vehicles in the same country in which it sells them. In 2003, BMW opened a plant at Shenyang, in northeast China, to build its 3-Series and 5-Series cars. Previously, in 1994, BMW opened a U.S. factory in Spartanburg, South Carolina, which currently produces the Z4 roadster and X5 sports utility vehicle (SUV) for sale both in the United States and worldwide.

Managers also face smaller-scale—or tactical—business decisions. For instance, for many years, BMW used two workers to attach the gearbox to the engine in each car. Then BMW engineers developed a new method of attaching the gearbox using a robot rather than workers. In choosing which method to use, managers at BMW faced a trade-off because the robot method had a higher cost, but installed the gearbox in exactly the correct position, which reduces engine noise when the car is driven. Ultimately, the managers decided to adopt the robot method. A similar tactical business decision must be made in scheduling production at BMW's Spartanburg, South Carolina, plant. The plant produces both the Z4 and the X5 models, and each month managers must decide the quantity of each model that should be produced. **AN INSIDE LOOK** on **page 58** discusses how BMW managers in the Spartanburg plant prepared to manufacture a new sports-activity coupe.

LEARNING Objectives

After studying this chapter, you should be able to:

2.1 Use a **production possibilities frontier** to analyze opportunity costs and trade-offs, page 38.

2.2 Understand **comparative advantage** and explain how it is the basis for **trade**, page 44.

2.3 Explain the basic idea of how a **market system** works, page 50.

Economics in YOUR Life!

The Trade-offs When You Buy a Car

When you buy a car, you probably consider factors such as safety and gas mileage. To increase gas mileage, automobile manufacturers make cars small and light. Large cars absorb more of the impact of an accident than do small cars. As a result, people are usually safer driving large cars than small cars. What can we conclude from these facts about the relationship between safety and gas mileage? Under what circumstances would it be possible for car manufacturers to make cars safer and more fuel efficient? As you read the chapter, see if you can answer these questions. You can check your answer against those provided at the end of the chapter. >> **Continued on page 56**

Scarcity The situation in which unlimited wants exceed the limited resources available to fulfill those wants.

I n a market system, managers at most firms must make decisions like those made by BMW's managers. The decisions managers face reflect a key fact of economic life: *Scarcity requires trade-offs.* **Scarcity** exists because we have unlimited wants but only limited resources available to fulfill those wants. Goods and services are scarce. So, too, are the economic resources, or *factors of production*—workers, capital, natural resources, and entrepreneurial ability—used to make goods and services. Your time is scarce, which means you face trade-offs: If you spend an hour studying for an economics exam, you have one less hour to spend studying for a psychology exam or going to the movies. If your university decides to use some of its scarce budget funds to buy new computers for the computer labs, those funds will not be available to buy new books for the library or to resurface the student parking lot. If BMW decides to devote some of the scarce workers and machinery in its Spartanburg assembly plant to producing more Z4 roadsters, those resources will not be available to produce more X5 SUVs.

Many of the decisions of households and firms are made in markets. One key activity that takes place in markets is trade. Trade involves the decisions of millions of households and firms spread around the world. By engaging in trade, people can raise their standard of living. In this chapter, we provide an overview of how the market system coordinates the independent decisions of these millions of households and firms. We begin our analysis of the economic consequences of scarcity and the working of the market system by introducing an important economic model: the *production possibilities frontier.*

2.1 LEARNING OBJECTIVE

2.1 | Use a production possibilities frontier to analyze opportunity costs and trade-offs.

Production Possibilities Frontiers and Opportunity Costs

As we saw in the opening to this chapter, BMW operates an automobile factory in Spartanburg, South Carolina, where it assembles Z4 roadsters and X5 SUVs. Because the firm's resources—workers, machinery, materials, and entrepreneurial skills—are limited, BMW faces a trade-off: Resources devoted to producing Z4s are not available for producing X5s and vice versa. Chapter 1 explained that economic models can be useful in analyzing many questions. We can use a simple model called the *production possibilities frontier* to analyze the trade-offs BMW faces in its Spartanburg plant. A **production possibilities frontier** (*PPF*) is a curve showing the maximum attainable combinations of two products that may be produced with available resources and current technology. In BMW's case, the two products are Z4 roadsters and X5 SUVs, and the resources are BMW's workers, materials, robots, and other machinery.

Production possibilities frontier (*PPF*) A curve showing the maximum attainable combinations of two products that may be produced with available resources and current technology.

Graphing the Production Possibilities Frontier

Figure 2-1 uses a production possibilities frontier to illustrate the trade-offs that BMW faces. The numbers from the table are plotted in the graph. The line in the graph is BMW's production possibilities frontier. If BMW uses all its resources to produce roadsters, it can produce 800 per day—point *A* at one end of the production possibilities frontier. If BMW uses all its resources to produce SUVs, it can produce 800 per day—point *E* at the other end of the production possibilities frontier. If BMW devotes resources to producing both vehicles, it could be at a point like *B*, where it produces 600 roadsters and 200 SUVs.

All the combinations either on the frontier—like *A*, *B*, *C*, *D*, and *E*—or inside the frontier—like point *F*—are *attainable* with the resources available. Combinations on

BMW's Production Choices at Its Spartanburg Plant		
Choice	Quantity of Roadsters Produced	Quantity of SUVs Produced
A	800	0
B	600	200
C	400	400
D	200	600
E	0	800

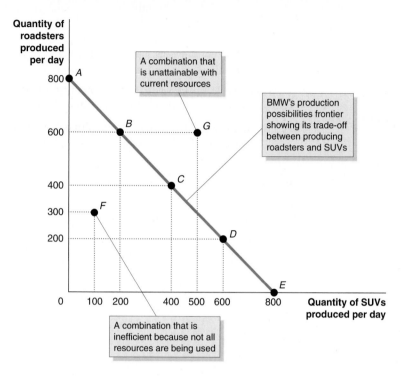

Figure 2-1

BMW's Production Possibilities Frontier

BMW faces a trade-off: To build one more roadster, it must build one less SUV. The production possibilities frontier illustrates the trade-off BMW faces. Combinations on the production possibilities frontier—like points *A, B, C, D,* and *E*—are *technically efficient* because the maximum output is being obtained from the available resources. Combinations inside the frontier—like point *F*—are *inefficient* because some resources are not being used. Combinations outside the frontier—like point *G*—are *unattainable* with current resources.

the frontier are *efficient* because all available resources are being fully utilized, and the fewest possible resources are being used to produce a given amount of output. Combinations inside the frontier—like point *F*—are *inefficient* because maximum output is not being obtained from the available resources—perhaps because the assembly line is not operating at capacity. BMW might like to be beyond the frontier—at a point like *G*, where it would be producing 600 roadsters and 500 SUVs—but points beyond the production possibilities frontier are *unattainable*, given the firm's current resources. To produce the combination at *G*, BMW would need more machines or more workers.

Notice that if BMW is producing efficiently and is on the production possibilities frontier, the only way to produce more of one vehicle is to produce less of the other vehicle. Recall from Chapter 1 that the **opportunity cost** of any activity is the highest valued alternative that must be given up to engage in that activity. For BMW, the opportunity cost of producing one more SUV is the number of roadsters the company will not be able to produce because it has shifted those resources to producing SUVs. For example, in moving from point *B* to point *C*, the opportunity cost of producing 200 more SUVs per day is the 200 fewer roadsters that can be produced.

What point on the production possibilities frontier is best? We can't tell without further information. If consumer demand for SUVs is greater than demand for roadsters, the company is likely to choose a point closer to *E*. If demand for roadsters is greater than demand for SUVs, the company is likely to choose a point closer to *A*.

Opportunity cost The highest-valued alternative that must be given up to engage in an activity.

Solved Problem | 2-1

Drawing a Production Possibilities Frontier for Rosie's Boston Bakery

Rosie's Boston Bakery specializes in cakes and pies. Rosie has 5 hours per day to devote to baking. In 1 hour, Rosie can prepare 2 pies or 1 cake.

a. Use the information given to complete the following table:

CHOICE	HOURS SPENT MAKING		QUANTITY MADE	
	CAKES	PIES	CAKES	PIES
A	5	0		
B	4	1		
C	3	2		
D	2	3		
E	1	4		
F	0	5		

b. Use the data in the table to draw a production possibilities frontier graph illustrating Rosie's trade-offs between making cakes and making pies. Label the vertical axis "Quantity of cakes made." Label the horizontal axis "Quantity of pies made." Make sure to label the values where Rosie's production possibilities frontier intersects the vertical and horizontal axes.

c. Label the points representing choice *D* and choice *E*. If Rosie is at choice *D*, what is her opportunity cost of making more pies?

SOLVING THE PROBLEM:

Step 1: **Review the chapter material.** This problem is about using production possibilities frontiers to analyze trade-offs, so you may want to review the section "Graphing the Production Possibilities Frontier," which begins on page 38.

Step 2: **Answer question (a) by filling in the table.** If Rosie can produce 1 cake in 1 hour, then with choice *A*, she will make 5 cakes and 0 pies. Because she can produce 2 pies in 1 hour, with choice *B*, she will make 4 cakes and 2 pies. Using similar reasoning, you can fill in the remaining cells in the table as follows:

CHOICE	HOURS SPENT MAKING		QUANTITY MADE	
	CAKES	PIES	CAKES	PIES
A	5	0	5	0
B	4	1	4	2
C	3	2	3	4
D	2	3	2	6
E	1	4	1	8
F	0	5	0	10

Step 3: **Answer question (b) by drawing the production possibilities frontier graph.** Using the data in the table in Step 2, you should draw a graph that looks like this:

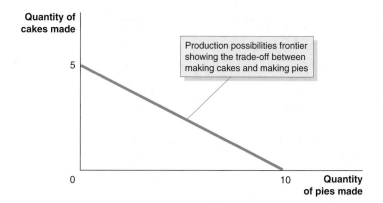

If Rosie devotes all 5 hours to making cakes, she will make 5 cakes. Therefore, her production possibilities frontier will intersect the vertical axis at 5 cakes made. If Rosie devotes all 5 hours to making pies, she will make 10 pies. Therefore, her production possibilities frontier will intersect the horizontal axis at 10 pies made.

Step 4: **Answer question (c) by showing choices _D_ and _E_ on your graph.** The points for choices _D_ and _E_ can be plotted using the information from the table:

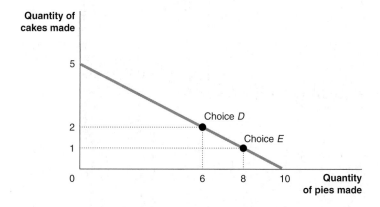

Moving from choice _D_ to choice _E_ increases Rosie's production of pies by 2 but lowers her production of cakes by 1. Therefore, her opportunity cost of making 2 more pies is making 1 less cake.

YOUR TURN: For more practice, do related problem 1.9 on page 61 at the end of this chapter.

>> End Solved Problem 2-1

Making the Connection

Trade-offs: Hurricane Katrina, Tsunami Relief, and Charitable Giving

When Hurricane Katrina hit the Gulf Coast region in August 2005, it resulted in massive flooding that destroyed large sections of New Orleans and other towns in Louisiana, Mississippi, Alabama, and Texas. More than 1,800 people lost their lives. In response, there was a massive outpouring of charitable donations to aid the victims. More than two-thirds of Americans donated money to hurricane relief. Although these funds helped to reduce the suffering of many hurricane victims, donations to some other causes actually declined. For instance, the head of the United Way in Alleghany County, Pennsylvania, indicated that it had suffered a decline in donations during 2005: "We're seeing declines this year, not all entirely due to the economy but also due to the effect of so much fund raising in August and September for hurricanes Katrina and Rita." The director of the Women's Center and Shelter of Great Pittsburgh

More funds for Katrina relief meant less funds for other charities.

had a similar experience: "What they've told us is there are so many important causes that they are aware of that they want to support. The choices are greater than what they've been faced with before."

Unfortunately, the trade-off of an increase in charitable giving to one cause resulting in a decrease in charitable giving to other causes is common following a disaster. In December 2004, an earthquake caused a tidal wave—or tsunami—to flood coastal areas of Indonesia, Thailand, Sri Lanka, and other countries bordering the Indian Ocean. More than 280,000 people died, and billions of dollars worth of property was destroyed. Governments and individuals around the world moved quickly to donate to relief efforts. The U.S. government donated $950 million, and individual U.S. citizens donated an additional $500 million. Both governments and individuals face limited budgets, however, and funds used for one purpose are unavailable to be used for another purpose. Although governments and individuals did increase their total charitable giving following the tsunami disaster, much of the funds spent on tsunami relief appear to have been diverted from other uses. A difficult trade-off resulted: Giving funds to victims of the tsunami meant fewer funds were available to aid other good causes.

For example, some of the funds provided by the U.S. government for reconstruction in the tsunami-devastated areas came from existing aid programs. As a result, spending on other aid projects in the region declined. Similarly, nonprofit organizations in New York City reported sharp declines in donations to the homeless and the poor, as donors gave funds for tsunami relief instead. According to a report in the newspaper *Crain's New York Business*, "Some groups such as Bailey House, which helps homeless people who have AIDS, have even started receiving letters from longtime donors warning that this year's gifts are being redirected to the tsunami relief effort." As one commentator observed, "The milk of human kindness is probably flowing at the usual rate in the United States. It's just getting channeled in different directions."

Sources: Steve Levin, "Disaster Aid Is Extra Giving," *Pittsburgh Post Gazette*, April 22, 2006; Jacqueline L. Salmon, "Katrina Compassion Drives Disaster Donations to a Record," *Washington Post*, June 19, 2006, p. A05; and Daniel Gross, "Zero-Sum Charity," *Slate*, January 20, 2005.

YOUR TURN: Test your understanding by doing related problem 1.10 on page 61 at the end of this chapter.

Increasing Marginal Opportunity Costs

We can use the production possibilities frontier to explore issues related to the economy as a whole. For example, suppose we divide all the goods and services produced in the economy into just two types: military goods and civilian goods. In Figure 2-2, we let tanks represent military goods and automobiles represent civilian goods. If all the country's

Figure 2-2

Increasing Marginal Opportunity Cost

As the economy moves down the production possibilities frontier, it experiences *increasing marginal opportunity costs* because increasing automobile production by a given quantity requires larger and larger decreases in tank production. For example, to increase automobile production from 0 to 200—moving from point *A* to point *B*—the economy has to give up only 50 tanks. But to increase automobile production by another 200 vehicles—moving from point *B* to point *C*—the economy has to give up 150 tanks.

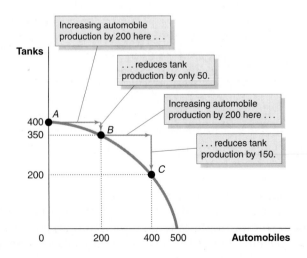

resources are devoted to producing military goods, 400 tanks can be produced in one year. If all resources are devoted to producing civilian goods, 500 automobiles can be produced in one year. Devoting resources to producing both goods results in the economy being at other points along the production possibilities frontier.

Notice that this production possibilities frontier is bowed outward rather than being a straight line. Because the curve is bowed out, the opportunity cost of automobiles in terms of tanks depends on where the economy currently is on the production possibilities frontier. For example, to increase automobile production from 0 to 200—moving from point *A* to point *B*—the economy has to give up only 50 tanks. But to increase automobile production by another 200 vehicles—moving from point *B* to point *C*—the economy has to give up 150 tanks.

As the economy moves down the production possibilities frontier, it experiences *increasing marginal opportunity costs* because increasing automobile production by a given quantity requires larger and larger decreases in tank production. Increasing marginal opportunity costs occurs because some workers, machines, and other resources are better suited to one use than to another. At point *A*, some resources that are well suited to producing automobiles are forced to produce tanks. Shifting these resources into producing automobiles by moving from point *A* to point *B* allows a substantial increase in automobile production, without much loss of tank production. But as the economy moves down the production possibilities frontier, more and more resources that are better suited to tank production are switched into automobile production. As a result, the increases in automobile production become increasingly smaller, while the decreases in tank production become increasingly larger. We would expect in most situations that production possibilities frontiers will be bowed outward rather than linear, as in the BMW example discussed earlier.

The idea of increasing marginal opportunity costs illustrates an important economic concept: *The more resources already devoted to any activity, the smaller the payoff to devoting additional resources to that activity.* For example, the more hours you have already spent studying economics, the smaller the increase in your test grade from each additional hour you spend—and the greater the opportunity cost of using the hour in that way. The more funds a firm has devoted to research and development during a given year, the smaller the amount of useful knowledge it receives from each additional dollar—and the greater the opportunity cost of using the funds in that way. The more funds the federal government spends cleaning up the environment during a given year, the smaller the reduction in pollution from each additional dollar—and, once again, the greater the opportunity cost of using the funds in that way.

Economic Growth

At any given time, the total resources available to any economy are fixed. Therefore, if the United States produces more automobiles, it must produce less of something else—tanks in our example. Over time, though, the resources available to an economy may increase. For example, both the labor force and the capital stock—the amount of physical capital available in the country—may increase. The increase in the available labor force and the capital stock shifts the production possibilities frontier outward for the U.S. economy and makes it possible to produce both more automobiles and more tanks. Panel (a) of Figure 2-3 shows that the economy can move from point *A* to point *B*, producing more tanks and more automobiles.

Similarly, technological advance makes it possible to produce more goods with the same amount of workers and machinery, which also shifts the production possibilities frontier outward. Technological advance need not affect all sectors equally. Panel (b) of Figure 2-3 shows the results of technological advance in the automobile industry that increases the quantity of automobile workers can produce per year while leaving unchanged the quantity of tanks that can be produced.

Shifts in the production possibilities frontier represent **economic growth** because they allow the economy to increase the production of goods and services, which ultimately raises the standard of living. In the United States and other high-income countries, the

Economic growth The ability of the economy to produce increasing quantities of goods and services.

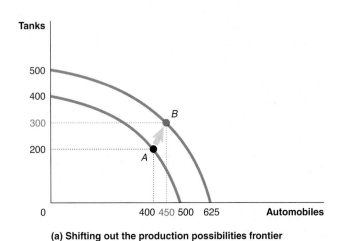

(a) Shifting out the production possibilities frontier

(b) Technological change in the automobile industry

Figure 2-3 | Economic Growth

Panel (a) shows that as more economic resources become available and technological change occurs, the economy can move from point A to point B, producing more tanks and more automobiles. Panel (b) shows the results of technological advance in the automobile industry that increases the quantity of vehicles workers can produce per year while leaving the maximum quantity of tanks that can be produced unchanged. Shifts in the production possibilities frontier represent *economic growth*.

market system has aided the process of economic growth, which over the past 200 years has greatly increased the well-being of the average person.

2.2 | Understand comparative advantage and explain how it is the basis for trade.

Comparative Advantage and Trade

Trade The act of buying or selling.

We can use the ideas of production possibilities frontiers and opportunity costs to understand the basic economic activity of *trade*. Markets are fundamentally about **trade**, which is the act of buying and selling. Sometimes we trade directly, as when children trade one baseball card for another baseball card. But often we trade indirectly: We sell our labor services as, say, an accountant, a salesperson, or a nurse for money, and then we use the money to buy goods and services. Although in these cases, trade takes place indirectly, ultimately the accountant, salesperson, or nurse is trading his or her services for food, clothing, and other goods and services. One of the great benefits to trade is that it makes it possible for people to become better off by increasing both their production and their consumption.

Specialization and Gains from Trade

Consider the following situation: You and your neighbor both have fruit trees on your property. Initially, suppose you have only apple trees and your neighbor has only cherry trees. In this situation, if you both like apples and cherries, there is an obvious opportunity for both of you to gain from trade: You trade some of your apples for some of your neighbor's cherries, making you both better off. But what if there are apple and cherry trees growing on both of your properties? In that case, there can still be gains from trade. For example, your neighbor might be very good at picking apples, and you might be very good at picking cherries. It would make sense for your neighbor to concentrate on picking apples and for you to concentrate on picking cherries. You can then trade some of the cherries you pick for some of the apples your neighbor picks. But what if your neighbor is actually better at picking both apples and cherries than you are?

We can use production possibilities frontiers (*PPFs*) to show how your neighbor can benefit from trading with you even though she is better than you are at picking both apples and cherries. (For simplicity, and because it will not have any effect on the conclusions we draw, we will assume that the *PPFs* in this example are straight lines.) The table in Figure 2-4 shows how many apples and how many cherries you and your neighbor can pick in one week. The graph in the figure uses the data from the table to construct *PPFs*. Panel (a) shows your *PPF*. If you devote all your time to picking apples, you can pick 20 pounds of apples per week. If you devote all your time to picking cherries, you can pick 20 pounds per week. Panel (b) shows that if your neighbor devotes all her time to picking apples, she can pick 30 pounds. If she devotes all her time to picking cherries, she can pick 60 pounds.

The production possibilities frontiers in Figure 2-4 show how many apples and cherries you and your neighbor can consume, *without trade*. Suppose that when you don't trade with your neighbor, you pick and consume 8 pounds of apples and 12 pounds of cherries per week. This combination of apples and cherries is represented by point *A* in panel (a) of Figure 2-5, on page 46. When your neighbor doesn't trade with you, she picks and consumes 9 pounds of apples and 42 pounds of cherries per week. This combination of apples and cherries is represented by point *B* in panel (b) of Figure 2-5.

After years of picking and consuming your own apples and cherries, suppose your neighbor comes to you one day with the following proposal: She offers to trade you 15 pounds of her cherries for 10 pounds of your apples next week. Should you accept this offer? You should accept because you will end up with more apples and more cherries to consume. To take advantage of her proposal, you should specialize in picking only apples rather than splitting your time between picking apples and picking cherries. We know this will allow you to pick 20 pounds of apples. You can trade 10 pounds of apples to your neighbor for 15 pounds of her cherries. The result is that you will be able to consume 10 pounds of apples and 15 pounds of cherries (point *A'* in panel (a) of Figure 2-5). You are clearly better off as a result of trading with your neighbor: You now can consume 2 more pounds of apples and 3 more pounds of cherries than you were consuming without trading. You have moved beyond your *PPF*!

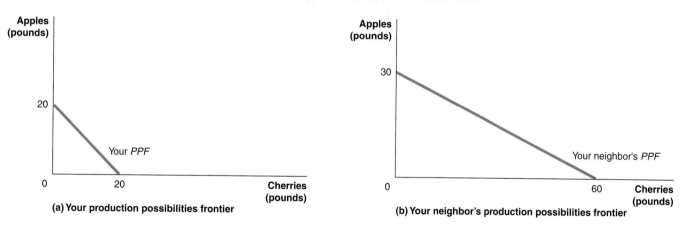

	You		**Your Neighbor**	
	Apples	Cherries	Apples	Cherries
Devote all time to picking apples	20 pounds	0 pounds	30 pounds	0 pounds
Devote all time to picking cherries	0 pounds	20 pounds	0 pounds	60 pounds

(a) Your production possibilities frontier

(b) Your neighbor's production possibilities frontier

Figure 2-4 | Production Possibilities for You and Your Neighbor, without Trade

The table in this figure shows how many pounds of apples and how many pounds of cherries you and your neighbor can each pick in one week. The graphs in the figure use the data from the table to construct production possibilities frontiers (*PPFs*) for you and your neighbor. Panel (a) shows your *PPF*. If you devote all your time to picking apples and none of your time to picking cherries, you can pick 20 pounds. If you devote all your time to picking cherries, you can pick 20 pounds. Panel (b) shows that if your neighbor devotes all her time to picking apples, she can pick 30 pounds. If she devotes all her time to picking cherries, she can pick 60 pounds.

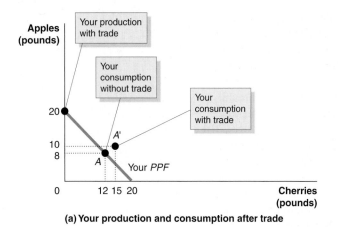

(a) Your production and consumption after trade

(b) Your neighbor's production and consumption with trade

Figure 2-5 | Gains from Trade

When you don't trade with your neighbor, you pick and consume 8 pounds of apples and 12 pounds of cherries per week—point *A* in panel (a). When your neighbor doesn't trade with you, she picks and consumes 9 pounds of apples and 42 pounds of cherries per week—point *B* in panel (b). If you specialize in picking apples, you can pick 20 pounds. If your neighbor specializes in picking cherries, she can pick

60 pounds. If you trade 10 pounds of your apples for 15 pounds of your neighbor's cherries, you will be able to consume 10 pounds of apples and 15 pounds of cherries—point *A'* in panel (a). Your neighbor can now consume 10 pounds of apples and 45 pounds of cherries—point *B'* in panel (b). You and your neighbor are both better off as a result of trade.

Your neighbor has also benefited from the trade. By specializing in picking only cherries, she can pick 60 pounds. She trades 15 pounds of cherries to you for 10 pounds of apples. The result is that she can consume 10 pounds of apples and 45 pounds of cherries (point *B'* in panel (b) of Figure 2-5). This is 1 more pound of apples and 3 more pounds of cherries than she was consuming before trading with you. She also has moved beyond her *PPF*. Table 2-1 summarizes the changes in production and consumption that result from your trade with your neighbor. (In this example, we chose one specific rate of trading cherries for apples—15 pounds of cherries for 10 pounds of apples. There are, however, many other rates of trading cherries for apples that would also make you and your neighbor better off.)

Absolute Advantage versus Comparative Advantage

Perhaps the most remarkable aspect of the preceding example is that your neighbor benefits from trading with you even though she is better than you at picking both apples and cherries. **Absolute advantage** is the ability of an individual, a firm, or a country to

Absolute advantage The ability of an individual, a firm, or a country to produce more of a good or service than competitors, using the same amount of resources.

TABLE 2-1

A Summary of the Gains from Trade

	YOU		YOUR NEIGHBOR	
	APPLES (IN POUNDS)	**CHERRIES (IN POUNDS)**	**APPLES (IN POUNDS)**	**CHERRIES (IN POUNDS)**
Production *and* consumption *without* trade	8	12	9	42
Production *with* trade	20	0	0	60
Consumption *with* trade	10	15	10	45
Gains from trade (increased consumption)	2	3	1	3

produce more of a good or service than competitors, using the same amount of resources. Your neighbor has an absolute advantage over you in producing both apples and cherries because she can pick more of each fruit than you can in the same amount of time. Although it seems that your neighbor should pick her own apples *and* her own cherries, we have just seen that she is better off specializing in cherry picking and leaving the apple picking to you.

We can consider further why both you and your neighbor benefit from specializing in picking only one fruit. First, think about the opportunity cost to each of you of picking the two fruits. We saw from the *PPF* in Figure 2-4 that if you devoted all your time to picking apples, you would be able to pick 20 pounds of apples per week. As you move down your *PPF* and shift time away from picking apples to picking cherries, you have to give up 1 pound of apples for each pound of cherries you pick (the slope of your *PPF* is −1). (For a review of calculating slopes, see the appendix to Chapter 1.) Therefore, your opportunity cost of picking 1 pound of cherries is 1 pound of apples. By the same reasoning, your opportunity cost of picking 1 pound of apples is 1 pound of cherries. Your neighbor's *PPF* has a different slope, so she faces a different trade-off: As she shifts time from picking apples to picking cherries, she has to give up 0.5 pound of apples for every 1 pound of cherries she picks (the slope of your neighbor's *PPF* is −0.5). As she shifts time from picking cherries to picking apples, she gives up 2 pounds of cherries for every 1 pound of apples she picks. Therefore, her opportunity cost of picking 1 pound of apples is 2 pounds of cherries, and her opportunity cost of picking 1 pound of cherries is 0.5 pound of apples.

Table 2-2 summarizes the opportunity costs for you and your neighbor of picking apples and cherries. Note that even though your neighbor can pick more apples in a week than you can, the *opportunity cost* of picking apples is higher for her than for you because when she picks apples, she gives up more cherries than you do. So, even though she has an absolute advantage over you in picking apples, it is more costly for her to pick apples than it is for you. The table also shows that her opportunity cost of picking cherries is lower than your opportunity cost of picking cherries. **Comparative advantage** is the ability of an individual, a firm, or a country to produce a good or service at a lower opportunity cost than competitors. In apple picking, your neighbor has an *absolute advantage* over you, but you have a *comparative advantage* over her. Your neighbor has both an absolute and a comparative advantage over you in picking cherries. As we have seen, you are better off specializing in picking apples, and your neighbor is better off specializing in picking cherries.

Comparative advantage The ability of an individual, a firm, or a country to produce a good or service at a lower opportunity cost than competitors.

Comparative Advantage and the Gains from Trade

We have just derived an important economic principle: *The basis for trade is comparative advantage, not absolute advantage.* The fastest apple pickers do not necessarily do much apple picking. If the fastest apple pickers have a comparative advantage in some other activity—picking cherries, playing major league baseball, or being industrial engineers—they are better off specializing in that other activity. Individuals, firms, and countries are better off if they specialize in producing goods and services for which they have a comparative advantage and obtain the other goods and services they need by trading. We will return to the important concept of comparative advantage in Chapter 18, which is devoted to the subject of international trade.

	OPPORTUNITY COST OF PICKING 1 POUND OF APPLES	OPPORTUNITY COST OF PICKING 1 POUND OF CHERRIES	TABLE 2-2
YOU	1 pound of cherries	1 pound of apples	**Opportunity Costs of Picking Apples and Cherries**
YOUR NEIGHBOR	2 pounds of cherries	0.5 pound of apples	

Don't Let This Happen to **YOU!**

Don't Confuse Absolute Advantage and Comparative Advantage

First, make sure you know the definitions:

- **Absolute advantage.** The ability of an individual, a firm, or a country to produce more of a good or service than competitors, using the same amount of resources. In our example, your neighbor has an absolute advantage over you in both picking apples and picking cherries.

- **Comparative advantage.** The ability of an individual, a firm, or a country to produce a good or service at a lower opportunity cost than competitors. In our example, your neighbor has a comparative advantage

in picking cherries, but you have a comparative advantage in picking apples.

Keep these two key points in mind:

1. It is possible to have an absolute advantage in producing a good or service without having a comparative advantage. This is the case with your neighbor picking apples.

2. It is possible to have a comparative advantage in producing a good or service without having an absolute advantage. This is the case with you picking apples.

YOUR TURN: Test your understanding by doing related problem 2.7 on page 63 at the end of this chapter.

Solved Problem | **2-2**

Comparative Advantage and the Gains from Trade

Suppose that Canada and the United States both produce maple syrup and honey. These are the combinations of the two goods that each country can produce in one day:

CANADA		UNITED STATES	
HONEY (IN TONS)	MAPLE SYRUP (IN TONS)	HONEY (IN TONS)	MAPLE SYRUP (IN TONS)
0	60	0	50
10	45	10	40
20	30	20	30
30	15	30	20
40	0	40	10
		50	0

a. Who has a comparative advantage in producing maple syrup? Who has a comparative advantage in producing honey?

b. Suppose that Canada is currently producing 30 tons of honey and 15 tons of maple syrup and the United States is currently producing 10 tons of honey and 40 tons of maple syrup. Demonstrate that Canada and the United States can both be better off if they specialize in producing only one good and engage in trade.

c. Illustrate your answer to question (b) by drawing a *PPF* for the United States and a *PPF* for Canada. Show on your *PPF*s the combinations of honey and maple syrup produced and consumed in each country before and after trade.

SOLVING THE PROBLEM:

Step 1: **Review the chapter material.** This problem concerns comparative advantage, so you may want to review the section "Absolute Advantage versus Comparative Advantage," which begins on page 46.

Step 2: **Answer question (a) by calculating who has a comparative advantage in each activity.** Remember that a country has a comparative advantage in producing a good if it can produce the good at the lowest opportunity cost. When

Canada produces 1 more ton of honey, it produces 1.5 fewer tons of maple syrup. On the one hand, when the United States produces 1 more ton of honey, it produces 1 less ton of maple syrup. Therefore, the United States's opportunity cost of producing honey—1 ton of maple syrup—is lower than Canada's—1.5 tons of maple syrup. On the other hand, when Canada produces 1 more ton of maple syrup, it produces 0.67 ton less of honey. When the United States produces 1 more ton of maple syrup, it produces 1 less ton of honey. Therefore, Canada's opportunity cost of producing maple syrup—0.67 ton of honey—is lower than that of the United States—1 ton of honey. We can conclude that the United States has a comparative advantage in the production of honey and Canada has a comparative advantage in the production of maple syrup.

Step 3: **Answer question (b) by showing that specialization makes Canada and the United States better off.** We know that Canada should specialize where it has a comparative advantage and the United States should specialize where it has a comparative advantage. If both countries specialize, Canada will produce 60 tons of maple syrup and 0 tons of honey, and the United States will produce 0 tons of maple syrup and 50 tons of honey. After both countries specialize, the United States could then trade 30 tons of honey to Canada in exchange for 40 tons of maple syrup. (Other mutually beneficial trades are possible as well.) We can summarize the results in a table:

	BEFORE TRADE		**AFTER TRADE**	
	HONEY (IN TONS)	**MAPLE SYRUP (IN TONS)**	**HONEY (IN TONS)**	**MAPLE SYRUP (IN TONS)**
CANADA	30	15	30	20
UNITED STATES	10	40	20	40

The United States is better off after trade because it can consume the same amount of maple syrup and 10 more tons of honey. Canada is better off after trade because it can consume the same amount of honey and 5 more tons of maple syrup.

Step 4: **Answer question (c) by drawing the *PPF*s.**

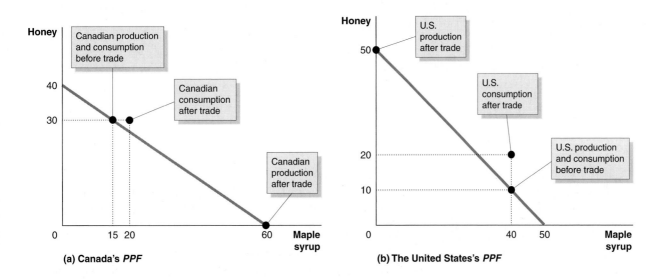

(a) Canada's *PPF*

(b) The United States's *PPF*

YOUR TURN: For more practice, do related problems 2.5 and 2.6 on pages 62 and 63 at the end of this chapter.

>> End Solved Problem 2-2

2.3 | Explain the basic idea of how a market system works.

The Market System

We have seen that households, firms, and the government face trade-offs and incur opportunity costs because of the scarcity of resources. We have also seen that trade allows people to specialize according to their comparative advantage. By engaging in trade, people can raise their standard of living. Of course, trade in the modern world is much more complex than the examples we have considered so far. Trade today involves the decisions of millions of people spread around the world. But how does an economy make trade possible, and how are the decisions of these millions of people coordinated? In the United States and most other countries, trade is carried out in markets. Markets also determine the answers to the three fundamental questions discussed in Chapter 1: *What* goods and services will be produced? *How* will the goods and services be produced? and *Who* will receive the goods and services?

Market A group of buyers and sellers of a good or service and the institution or arrangement by which they come together to trade.

Recall that the definition of **market** is a group of buyers and sellers of a good or service and the institution or arrangement by which they come together to trade. Markets take many forms: They can be physical places, like a local pizza parlor or the New York Stock Exchange, or virtual places, like eBay. In a market, the buyers are demanders of goods or services, and the sellers are suppliers of goods or services. Households and firms interact in two types of markets: *product markets* and *factor markets*. **Product markets** are markets for goods—such as computers—and services—such as medical treatment. In product markets, households are demanders, and firms are suppliers. **Factor markets** are markets for the *factors of production*. **Factors of production** are the inputs used to make goods and services. Factors of production are divided into four broad categories:

Product markets Markets for goods—such as computers—and services—such as medical treatment.

Factor markets Markets for the factors of production, such as labor, capital, natural resources, and entrepreneurial ability.

Factors of production The inputs used to make goods and services.

- *Labor* includes all types of work, from the part-time labor of teenagers working at McDonald's to the work of top managers in large corporations.

- *Capital* refers to physical capital, such as computers and machine tools, that is used to produce other goods.

- *Natural resources* include land, water, oil, iron ore, and other raw materials (or "gifts of nature") that are used in producing goods.

- An *entrepreneur* is someone who operates a business. *Entrepreneurial ability* is the ability to bring together the other factors of production to successfully produce and sell goods and services.

The Circular Flow of Income

Two key groups participate in markets:

- A *household* consists of all the individuals in a home. Households are suppliers of factors of production—particularly labor—used by firms to make goods and services. Households use the income they receive from selling the factors of production to purchase the goods and services supplied by firms. We are used to thinking of households as suppliers of labor because most people earn most of their income by going to work, which means they are selling their labor services to firms in the labor market. But households own the other factors of production as well, either directly or indirectly, by owning the firms that have these resources. All firms are owned by households. Small firms, like a neighborhood restaurant, might be owned by one person. Large firms, like Microsoft or BMW, are owned by millions of households who own shares of stock in them. (We discuss the stock market in Chapter 5.) When firms pay profits to the people who own them, the firms are paying for using the capital and natural resources that are supplied to them by those owners. So, we can generalize by saying that in factor markets, households are suppliers, and firms are demanders.

- *Firms* are suppliers of goods and services. Firms use the funds they receive from selling goods and services to buy the factors of production needed to make the goods and services.

We can use a simple economic model called the **circular-flow diagram** to see how participants in markets are linked. Figure 2-6 shows that in factor markets, households supply labor and other factors of production in exchange for wages and other payments from firms. In product markets, households use the payments they earn in factor markets to purchase the goods and services supplied by firms. Firms produce these goods and services using the factors of production supplied by households. In the figure, the blue arrows show the flow of factors of production from households through factor markets to firms. The red arrows show the flow of goods and services from firms through product markets to households. The green arrows show the flow of funds from firms through factor markets to households and the flow of spending from households through product markets to firms.

Like all economic models, the circular-flow diagram is a simplified version of reality. For example, Figure 2-6 leaves out the important role of government in buying goods from firms and in making payments, such as Social Security or unemployment insurance payments, to households. The figure also leaves out the roles played by banks, the stock and bond markets, and other parts of the *financial system* in aiding the flow of funds from lenders to borrowers. Finally, the figure does not show that some goods and services purchased by domestic households are produced in foreign countries and some goods and services produced by domestic firms are sold to foreign households. The government, the financial system, and the international sector are explored further in later chapters. Despite these simplifications, the circular-flow diagram in Figure 2-6 is useful for seeing how product markets, factor markets, and their participants are linked

Circular-flow diagram A model that illustrates how participants in markets are linked.

Figure 2-6

The Circular-Flow Diagram

Households and firms are linked together in a circular flow of production, income, and spending. The blue arrows show the flow of the factors of production. In factor markets, households supply labor, entrepreneurial ability, and other factors of production to firms. Firms use these factors of production to make goods and services that they supply to households in product markets. The red arrows show the flow of goods and services from firms to households. The green arrows show the flow of funds. In factor markets, households receive wages and other payments from firms in exchange for supplying the factors of production. Households use these wages and other payments to purchase goods and services from firms in product markets. Firms sell goods and services to households in product markets, and they use the funds to purchase the factors of production from households in factor markets.

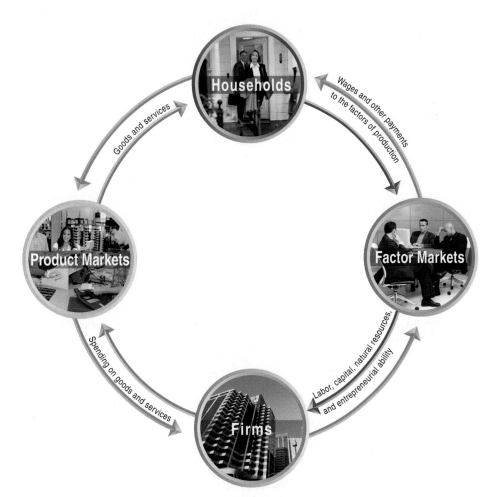

together. One of the great mysteries of the market system is that it manages to successfully coordinate the independent activities of so many households and firms.

The Gains from Free Markets

Free market A market with few government restrictions on how a good or service can be produced or sold or on how a factor of production can be employed.

A **free market** exists when the government places few restrictions on how a good or a service can be produced or sold or on how a factor of production can be employed. Governments in all modern economies intervene more than is consistent with a fully free market. In that sense, we can think of the free market as being a benchmark against which we can judge actual economies. There are relatively few government restrictions on economic activity in the United States, Canada, the countries of Western Europe, Hong Kong, Singapore, and Estonia. So these countries come close to the free market benchmark. In countries such as Cuba and North Korea, the free market system has been rejected in favor of centrally planned economies with extensive government control over product and factor markets. Countries that come closest to the free-market benchmark have been more successful than countries with centrally planned economies in providing their people with rising living standards.

The Scottish philosopher Adam Smith is considered the father of modern economics because his book *An Inquiry into the Nature and Causes of the Wealth of Nations*, published in 1776, was an early and very influential argument for the free market system. Smith was writing at a time when extensive government restrictions on markets were still very common. In many parts of Europe, the *guild system* still prevailed. Under this system, governments would give guilds, or organizations of producers, the authority to control the production of a good. For example, the shoemakers' guild controlled who was allowed to produce shoes, how many shoes they could produce, and what price they could charge. In France, the cloth makers' guild even dictated the number of threads in the weave of the cloth.

Smith argued that such restrictions reduced the income, or wealth, of a country and its people by restricting the quantity of goods produced. Some people at the time supported the restrictions of the guild system because it was in their financial interest to do so. If you were a member of a guild, the restrictions served to reduce the competition you faced. But other people sincerely believed that the alternative to the guild system was economic chaos. Smith argued that these people were wrong and that a country could enjoy a smoothly functioning economic system if firms were freed from guild restrictions.

The Market Mechanism

In Smith's day, defenders of the guild system worried that if, for instance, the shoemakers' guild did not control shoe production, either too many or too few shoes would be produced. Smith argued that prices would do a better job of coordinating the activities of buyers and sellers than the guilds could. A key to understanding Smith's argument is the assumption that *individuals usually act in a rational, self-interested way*. In particular, individuals take those actions most likely to make themselves better off financially. This assumption of rational, self-interested behavior underlies nearly all economic analysis. In fact, economics can be distinguished from other fields that study human behavior—such as sociology and psychology—by its emphasis on the assumption of self-interested behavior. Adam Smith understood—as economists today understand—that people's motives can be complex. But in analyzing people in the act of buying and selling, the motivation of financial reward usually provides the best explanation for the actions people take.

For example, suppose that a significant number of consumers switch from buying regular gasoline-powered cars to buying gasoline/electric-powered hybrid cars, such as the Toyota Prius, as in fact happened in the United States during the 2000s. Firms will find that they can charge relatively higher prices for hybrid cars than they can for regular cars. The self-interest of these firms will lead them to respond to consumers' wishes by producing more hybrids and fewer regular cars. Or suppose that consumers decide that they want to eat less bread, pasta, and other foods high in carbohydrates, as many did following the increase in popularity of the Atkins and South Beach diets. Then the prices firms can charge for bread and pasta will fall. The self-interest of firms will lead them to produce less bread and pasta, which in fact is what happened.

In the case where consumers want more of a product, and in the case where they want less of a product, the market system responds without a guild or the government giving orders about how much to produce or what price to charge. In a famous phrase, Smith said that firms would be led by the "invisible hand" of the market to provide consumers with what they wanted. Firms would respond to changes in prices by making decisions that ended up satisfying the wants of consumers.

Making the Connection	## A Story of the Market System in Action: How Do You Make an iPod?

The iPod is a product of Apple, which has its headquarters in Cupertino, California. It seems reasonable to assume that iPods are also manufactured in California. In fact, Apple produces none of the components of the iPod, nor does it assemble the components into a finished product. Far from being produced entirely by one company in one place, the iPod requires the coordinated activities of thousands of workers and dozens of firms, spread around the world.

The market coordinates the activities of the many people spread around the world who contribute to the making of an iPod.

Several Asian firms, including Asustek, Inventec Appliances, and Foxconn, assemble the iPod, which is then shipped to Apple for sale in the United States. But the firms doing final assembly don't make any of the components. For example, the iPod's hard drive is manufactured by the Japanese firm, Toshiba, although Toshiba actually assembles the hard drive in factories in China and the Philippines. Apple purchases the controller chip that manages the iPod's functions from PortalPlayer, which is based in Santa Clara, California. But PortalPlayer actually has the chip manufactured for it by Taiwan Semiconductor Manufacturing Corporation, and the chip's processor core was designed by ARM, a British company. Taiwan Semiconductor Manufacturing Corporation's factories are for the most part not in Taiwan, but in mainland China and Eastern Europe.

All told, the iPod contains 451 parts, designed and manufactured by firms around the world. Many of these firms are not even aware of which other firms are also producing components for the iPod. Few of the managers of these firms have met managers of the other firms or shared knowledge of how their particular components are produced. In fact, no one person from Steve Jobs, the head of Apple, on down possesses the knowledge of how to produce all of the components that are assembled into an iPod. Instead, the invisible hand of the market has led these firms to contribute their knowledge to the process that ultimately results in an iPod available for sale in a store in the United States. Apple has so efficiently organized the process of producing the iPod that you can order a custom iPod with a personal engraving and have it delivered from an assembly plant in China to your doorstep in the United States in as little as three days.

Hal Varian, an economist at the University of California, Berkeley, has summarized the iPod story: "Those clever folks at Apple figured out how to combine 451 mostly generic parts into a valuable product. They may not make the iPod, but they created it."

Sources: Hal Varian, "An iPod Has Global Value. Ask the (Many) Countries That Make It," *New York Times*, June 28, 2007; and Greg Linden, Kenneth L. Kraemer, Jaon Dedrick, "Who Captures Value in a Global Innovation System? The Case of Apple's iPod," Personal Computing Industry Center, June 2007.

YOUR TURN: Test your understanding by doing related problem 3.8 on page 64 at the end of this chapter.

The Role of the Entrepreneur

Entrepreneurs are central to the working of the market system. An **entrepreneur** is someone who operates a business. Entrepreneurs must first determine what goods and services they believe consumers want, and then they must decide how to produce those goods and services most profitably. Entrepreneurs bring together the factors of production—labor, capital, and natural resources—to produce goods and services. They put their own funds

Entrepreneur Someone who operates a business, bringing together the factors of production—labor, capital, and natural resources—to produce goods and services.

at risk when they start businesses. If they are wrong about what consumers want or about the best way to produce goods and services, they can lose those funds. In fact, it is not unusual for entrepreneurs who eventually achieve great success to fail at first. For instance, early in their careers, both Henry Ford and Sakichi Toyoda, who eventually founded the Toyota Motor Corporation, started companies that quickly failed.

The Legal Basis of a Successful Market System

In a free market, government does not restrict how firms produce and sell goods and services or how they employ factors of production, but the absence of government intervention is not enough for a market system to work well. Government has to provide secure rights to private property for a market system to work at all. In addition, government can aid the working of the market by enforcing contracts between private individuals through an independent court system. Many economists would also say the government has a role in facilitating the development of an efficient financial system as well as systems of education, transportation, and communication. The protection of private property and the existence of an independent court system to impartially enforce the law provide a *legal environment* that will allow a market system to succeed.

Protection of Private Property For a market system to work well, individuals must be willing to take risks. Someone with $250,000 can be cautious and keep it safely in a bank— or even in cash, if the person doesn't trust the banking system. But the market system won't work unless a significant number of people are willing to risk their funds by investing them in businesses. Investing in businesses is risky in any country. Many businesses fail every year in the United States and other high-income countries. But in the high-income countries, someone who starts a new business or invests in an existing business doesn't have to worry that the government, the military, or criminal gangs might decide to seize the business or demand payments for not destroying the business. Unfortunately, in many poor countries, owners of businesses are not well protected from having their businesses seized by the government or from having their profits taken by criminals. Where these problems exist, opening a business can be extremely risky. Cash can be concealed easily, but a business is difficult to conceal and difficult to move.

Property rights The rights individuals or firms have to the exclusive use of their property, including the right to buy or sell it.

Property rights are the rights individuals or firms have to the exclusive use of their property, including the right to buy or sell it. Property can be tangible, physical property, such as a store or factory. Property can also be intangible, such as the right to an idea.

Two amendments to the U.S. Constitution guarantee property rights: The 5th Amendment states that the federal government shall not deprive any person "of life, liberty, or property, without due process of law." The 14th Amendment extends this guarantee to the actions of state governments: "No state . . . shall deprive any person of life, liberty, or property, without due process of law." Similar guarantees exist in every high-income country. Unfortunately, in many developing countries, such guarantees do not exist or are poorly enforced.

In any modern economy, *intellectual property rights* are very important. Intellectual property includes books, films, software, and ideas for new products or new ways of producing products. To protect intellectual property, the federal government grants a *patent* that gives an inventor—which is often a firm—the exclusive right to produce and sell a new product for a period of 20 years from the date the product was invented. For instance, because Microsoft has a patent on the Windows operating system, other firms cannot sell their own versions of Windows. The government grants patents to encourage firms to spend money on the research and development necessary to create new products. If other companies could freely copy Windows, Microsoft would not have spent the funds necessary to develop it. Just as a new product or a new method of making a product receives patent protection, books, films, and software receive *copyright* protection. Under U.S. law, the creator of a book, film, or piece of music has the exclusive right to use the creation during the creator's lifetime. The creator's heirs retain this exclusive right for 50 years after the death of the creator.

Making the Connection

Property Rights in Cyberspace: YouTube and MySpace

The development of the Internet has led to new problems in protecting intellectual property rights. People can copy and e-mail songs, newspaper and magazine articles, and even entire motion pictures and television programs or post them on Web sites. Controlling unauthorized copying is more difficult today than it was when "copying" meant making a physical copy of a book, CD, or DVD. The popularity of YouTube and MySpace highlights the problem of unauthorized copying of videos and music. YouTube, founded in 2005, quickly became an enormous success because it provided an easy way to upload videos, which could then be viewed by anyone with an Internet connection. By 2008, thousands of new videos were being uploaded each day, and the site was receiving more than 20 million visitors per month. YouTube earned substantial profits from selling online advertising. Unfortunately, many of the videos on the site contained copyrighted material.

At first, YouTube's policy was to remove any video containing unauthorized material if the holder of the copyright complained. Then YouTube began to negotiate with the copyright holders to pay a fee in return for allowing the copyrighted material to remain on the site. For music videos, YouTube was usually able to obtain the needed permission directly from the

Some recording artists worry that the copyrights for their songs are not being protected on the Internet.

recording company. Things were more complicated when videos on YouTube used copyrighted songs as background music. In those cases, YouTube needed to obtain permissions from the songwriters as well as the record company, which could be a time-consuming process. Obtaining permission to use videos that contained material from television shows or movies was even more complicated because sometimes dozens of people—including the actors, directors, and composers of music—held rights to the television show or movie. YouTube's vice president for business development was quoted as saying, "It's almost like technology has pushed far beyond the business practices and the law, and now everything needs to kind of catch up." In November 2006, YouTube agreed to be purchased by Google for $1.65 billion, which made the young entrepreneurs who started the company very wealthy. The willingness of YouTube's owners to sell their company to Google was motivated at least partly by the expectation that Google had the resources to help them resolve their copyright problems.

MySpace had similar problems because many Web pages on the site contained copyrighted music or videos. Universal Music sued MySpace after music from rapper Jay-Z's latest album started appearing on the site even before the album was released. In its lawsuit, Universal claimed that the illegal use of its copyrighted music had "created hundreds of millions of dollars of value for the owners of MySpace."

Music, television, and movie companies believe that the failure to give the full protection of property rights to the online use of their material reduces their ability to sell CDs and DVDs.

Sources: Kevin J. Delaney, Ethan Smith, and Brooks Barnes, "YouTube Finds Signing Rights Deals Complex, Frustrating," *Wall Street Journal*, November 3, 2006, p. B1; and Ethan Smith and Julia Angwin, "Universal Music Sues MySpace Claiming Copyright Infringement," *Wall Street Journal*, November 18, 2006, p. A3.

YOUR TURN: Test your understanding by doing related problem 3.14 on page 64 at the end of this chapter.

Enforcement of Contracts and Property Rights Much business activity involves someone agreeing to carry out some action in the future. For example, you may borrow $20,000 to buy a car and promise the bank—by signing a loan contract—that you will pay back the money over the next five years. Or Microsoft may sign a licensing agreement with a small technology company, agreeing to use that company's technology for a period of several years in return for a fee. Usually these agreements take the form of legal contracts. For a market system to work, businesses and individuals have to rely on these contracts being carried out. If one party to a legal contract does not fulfill its obligations—perhaps the small company had promised Microsoft exclusive use of its technology but then began licensing it to other companies—the other party could go to court to have the agreement enforced. Similarly, if property owners in the United States believe that the federal or state government has violated their rights under the 5th or 14th Amendments, they can go to court to have their rights enforced.

But going to court to enforce a contract or private property rights will be successful only if the court system is independent and judges are able to make impartial decisions on the basis of the law. In the United States and other high-income countries, the court systems have enough independence from other parts of the government and enough protection from intimidation by outside forces—such as criminal gangs—that they are able to make their decisions based on the law. In many developing countries, the court systems lack this independence and will not provide a remedy if the government violates private property rights or if a person with powerful political connections decides to violate a business contract.

If property rights are not well enforced, fewer goods and services will be produced. This reduces economic efficiency, leaving the economy inside its production possibilities frontier.

Economics in YOUR Life!

>> Continued from page 37

At the beginning of the chapter, we asked you to think about two questions: When buying a new car, what is the relationship between safety and gas mileage? and Under what circumstances would it be possible for car manufacturers to make cars safer and more fuel efficient? To answer the first question, you have to recognize that there is a trade-off between safety and gas mileage. With the technology available at any particular time, an automobile manufacturer can increase gas mileage by making a car smaller and lighter. But driving a lighter car increases your chances of being injured if you have an accident. The trade-off between safety and gas mileage would look much like the relationship in Figure 2-1 on page 39. To get more of both safety and gas mileage, automobile makers would have to discover new technologies that allow them to make the car lighter and safer at the same time. Such new technologies would make points like *G* in Figure 2-1 attainable.

Conclusion

We have seen that by trading in markets, people are able to specialize and pursue their comparative advantage. Trading on the basis of comparative advantage makes all participants in trade better off. The key role of markets is to facilitate trade. In fact, the market system is a very effective means of coordinating the decisions of millions of consumers, workers, and firms. At the center of the market system is the consumer. To be successful, firms must respond to the desires of consumers. These desires are communicated to firms through prices. To explore how markets work, we must study the behavior of consumers and firms. We continue this exploration of markets in Chapter 3, when we develop the model of demand and supply.

Before moving on to Chapter 3, read *An Inside Look* on the next page to learn how BMW managers reallocate scarce resources in the firm's South Carolina plant to prepare to manufacture a new sports-activity coupe.

BMW Managers Change Production Strategy

KNIGHT RIDDER TRIBUNE BUSINESS NEWS, JANUARY 25, 2007

Redesigned X5 to lead increase; new coupe to debut in 2008

(a) BMW expects production to rise 58 percent this year, nearly reaching its record production of 2002 and ending the string of production declines since then. The plant's 4,500 workers [based in Spartanburg, South Carolina] are expected to make 165,000 vehicles this year, up from 104,632 in 2006, spokesman Bob Nitto said Wednesday. The redesigned X5 sport utility vehicle is expected to drive the increase, with its production nearly doubling to about 130,000 vehicles. Production of the Z4 and related coupes is expected to decline slightly to 35,000 cars, down from 38,756 last year.

And in 2008, the plant is expected to add a new coupe to the production line, one that BMW now refers to as a sports-activity coupe. The term is a variation of the moniker BMW adopted in 1999 for the X5—a sports-activity vehicle. The automotive press is referring to the new car as the BMW X6, the crossover vehicle company officials have said previously would be built at Greer.

But even with a third vehicle, plant employment is not likely to increase substantially, plant spokeswoman Bunny Richardson said. Production workers at the plant earn about $25 to $26 per hour.

(b) Richardson and Nitto spoke with about a dozen area journalists allowed to see the plant for the first time since November 2005. That winter, the facility was shut down for two months as its separate assembly lines for the X5 and Z4 were merged into a single line.

One reason for the change was the increasing imbalance in production. The Z4s are smaller cars with fewer parts than the large, complex X5s. Also, Z4 sales have flattened, while X5 sales have risen. As a result, X5s are expected to account for 80 percent of the cars made at the plant this year.

The plant continues to become more dense. When it opened in 1994, aisles were wide and heavy equipment thin. Now many parts move overhead, and robots have become more numerous.

(c) The appearance has changed as the plant's production has climbed:

- At the end of 1995, the first full year of production, the plant had 1,556 workers and made 13,943 cars, or about nine cars per worker.

- At the end of 2000—the first full year of production of the original X5—the plant had 4,058 workers and made 83,672 vehicles, about 21 vehicles per worker.

- Production peaked in 2003, when the plant's work force swelled to 4,700, making 166,090 vehicles, or about 35 per worker.

- This year, the plant is expected to exceed 2003 in productivity, with production of 37 cars per worker.

This will be all the more challenging because of the size and complexity of the new X5, which first reached U.S. dealers in November, and is being rolled out to the European market this year. The X5 is filled with gizmos designed to allow it to shift from trips to the grocery store to fording creeks. Even the tires are complex: Run-flat tires now are standard equipment. Those supplied by Michelin are made at its Lexington plant, Richardson said.

Journalists were allowed to test the cars driving on a test track and off-road trail near the plant. Some versions carried an option that BMW calls Active Steering, a form of power steering that varies response depending on speed.

In a parking lot, only a slight motion is needed to steer into a space, while at higher speeds, sharp turns require more turning.

"You don't want to sneeze and change lanes," said Larry Parmele, a 55-year-old former race car driver and instructor at BMW's Performance Center test tracks in Greer.

Source: Jim Duplessis, "BMW Expects Turnaround," *Knight Ridder Tribune Business News,* January 25, 2007, p.1. Reprinted by permission of the Permissions Group.

Key Points in the Article

The article discusses the trade-offs that BMW managers face when making production decisions, given the size of the manufacturing plant and the technology used at the plant. The article also points out that these production decisions depend on the characteristics of the cars being produced, the number of workers at the plant, the technology of production, and the sales of the different car models.

Analyzing the News

(a) BMW plans to produce about 60,000 more automobiles at the Spartanburg, South Carolina, plant during 2007. Even though the total number of automobiles produced is going to increase, BMW is going to cut back on the production of the Z4 and other coupes. Figure 1 shows the increase in total production as a movement toward the production possibilities frontier. Notice that even though BMW is producing more automobiles, it is choosing to produce fewer coupes, so total production of coupes is declining as the production at the plant is moving toward the frontier.

(b) Production at plants frequently responds to changes in the marketplace. If sales of one model decline, then automobile companies often reduce production of that model and expand production of the models that are selling. At this plant, production of the Z4 model is declining, while production of the X5 model is expanding. These changes in production decisions are a direct response to changes in the sales of these models. In addition, managers sometimes have to stop production so that they can retool the plant. In this case, managers closed the plant for two months during 2005, so that they could introduce a new assembly line that produced both the X5 and Z4 models. This allowed the managers to expand production at the plant and make it easier to introduce a new "sports-activity coupe" model that will begin production in 2008. The managers may have to close the plant again to prepare for production of the new sports-activity couple. In effect, the managers would be giving up production of existing models in 2007 while the plant is closed so that they can increase production of the new model in the future. Sometimes the trade-offs that managers face are trade-offs between the present and the future.

(c) As the demand for BMW models has increased, the automobile factory has changed. Managers introduced more machinery and workers and changed the layout of the factory. Moving the X5 and Z4 to the same assembly line so the plant can produce the new sports-activity coupe model is just the latest in a long line of changes that the managers have made. These changes provide the plant with more resources for producing BMW cars. We show this by shifting out the production possibilities frontier in Figure 2. You should also notice that as output at the plant expanded, BMW increased employment and the number of robots. As output at a firm or a plant expands, BMW tends to use more of all types of inputs, including labor.

Thinking Critically

1. Launching the new sports-activity coupe may require that the BMW managers shut down the Spartanburg plant for some period. Besides the direct costs of installing a new assembly line and new machinery, what would be the costs to BMW of shutting down the plant for a period of months? If shutting down the plant is costly, why would BMW do it?

2. Some BMWs are made in Germany, some in South Carolina, and some in other places. Should the United States government encourage the domestic production of BMWs by banning imports of BMWs?

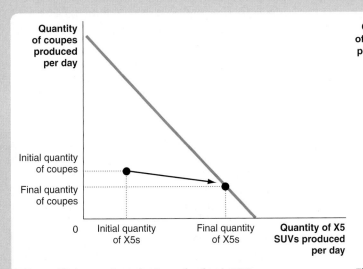

Figure 1. The increase in production at the plant in 2008.

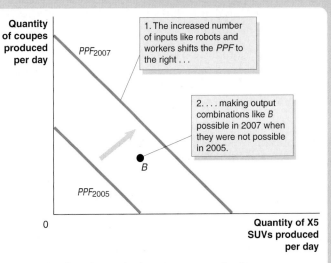

Figure 2. The effect of increasing inputs on output at the plant.

Key Terms

Absolute advantage, p. 46

Circular-flow diagram, p. 51

Comparative advantage, p. 47

Economic growth, p. 43

Entrepreneur, p. 53

Factor markets, p. 50

Factors of production, p. 50

Free market, p. 52

Market, p. 50

Opportunity cost, p. 39

Product markets, p. 50

Production possibilities frontier (*PPF*), p. 38

Property rights, p. 54

Scarcity, p. 38

Trade, p. 44

2.1 LEARNING OBJECTIVE   2.1 | Use a production possibilities frontier to analyze opportunity costs and trade-offs, pages 38–44.

Production Possibilities Frontiers and Opportunity Costs

Summary

The **production possibilities frontier (*PPF*)** is a curve that shows the maximum attainable combinations of two products that may be produced with available resources. The *PPF* is used to illustrate the trade-offs that arise from **scarcity**. Points on the frontier are technically efficient. Points inside the frontier are inefficient, and points outside the frontier are unattainable. The **opportunity cost** of any activity is the highest valued alternative that must be given up to engage in that activity. Because of increasing marginal opportunity costs, production possibilities frontiers are usually bowed out rather than straight lines. This illustrates the important economic concept that the more resources that are already devoted to any activity, the smaller the payoff to devoting additional resources to that activity is likely to be. **Economic growth** is illustrated by shifting a production possibilities frontier outward.

myeconlab Visit www.myeconlab.com to complete these exercises
Get Ahead of the Curve online and get instant feedback.

Review Questions

1.1 What do economists mean by scarcity? Can you think of anything that is not scarce according to the economic definition?

1.2 What is a production possibilities frontier? How can we show economic efficiency on a production possibilities frontier? How can we show inefficiency? What causes a production possibilities frontier to shift outward?

1.3 What does increasing marginal opportunity costs mean? What are the implications of this idea for the shape of the production possibilities frontier?

Problems and Applications

1.4 Draw a production possibilities frontier that shows the trade-off between the production of cotton and the production of soybeans.
   a. Show the effect that a prolonged drought would have on the initial production possibilities frontier.

   b. Suppose genetic modification makes soybeans resistant to insects, allowing yields to double. Show the effect of this technological change on the initial production possibilities frontier.

1.5 (Related to the *Chapter Opener* on page 36) One of the trade-offs BMW faces is between safety and gas mileage. For example, adding steel to a car makes it safer but also heavier, which results in lower gas mileage. Draw a hypothetical production possibilities frontier that BMW engineers face that shows this trade-off.

1.6 Suppose you win free tickets to a movie plus all you can eat at the snack bar for free. Would there be a cost to you to attend this movie? Explain.

1.7 Suppose we can divide all the goods produced by an economy into two types: consumption goods and capital goods. Capital goods, such as machinery, equipment, and computers, are goods used to produce other goods.
   a. Use a production possibilities frontier graph to illustrate the trade-off to an economy between producing consumption goods and producing capital goods. Is it likely that the production possibilities frontier in this situation would be a straight line (as in Figure 2-1 on page 39) or bowed out (as in Figure 2-2 on page 42)? Briefly explain.
   b. Suppose a technological advance occurs that affects the production of capital goods but not consumption goods. Show the effect on the production possibilities frontier.
   c. Suppose that country A and country B currently have identical production possibilities frontiers but that country A devotes only 5 percent of its resources to producing capital goods over each of the next 10 years, whereas country B devotes 30 percent. Which country is likely to experience more rapid economic growth in the future? Illustrate using a production possibilities frontier graph. Your graph should include production possibilities frontiers for country A today and in 10 years and production possibilities frontiers for country B today and in 10 years.

1.8 Use the production possibilities frontier for a country to answer the following questions.

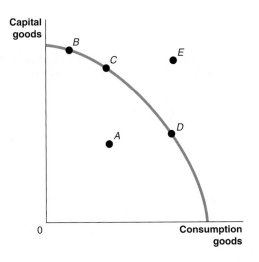

a. Which point(s) are unattainable? Briefly explain why.

b. Which point(s) are efficient? Briefly explain why.

c. Which point(s) are inefficient? Briefly explain why.

d. At which point is the country's future growth rate likely to be the highest? Briefly explain why.

1.9 (Related to *Solved Problem 2-1* on page 40) You have exams in economics and chemistry coming up and five hours available for studying. The following table shows the trade-offs you face in allocating the time you will spend in studying each subject.

| | HOURS SPENT STUDYING | | MIDTERM SCORE | |
CHOICE	ECONOMICS	CHEMISTRY	ECONOMICS	CHEMISTRY
A	5	0	95	70
B	4	1	93	78
C	3	2	90	84
D	2	3	86	88
E	1	4	81	90
F	0	5	75	91

a. Use the data in the table to draw a production possibilities frontier graph. Label the vertical axis "Score on economics exam" and label the horizontal axis "Score on chemistry exam." Make sure to label the values where your production possibilities frontier intersects the vertical and horizontal axes.

b. Label the points representing choice *C* and choice *D*. If you are at choice *C*, what is your opportunity cost of increasing your chemistry score?

c. Under what circumstances would *A* be a sensible choice?

1.10 (Related to the *Making the Connection* on page 41) Suppose the president is attempting to decide whether the federal government should spend more on research to find a cure for heart disease. He asks you, one of his economic advisors, to prepare a report discussing the relevant factors he should consider. Discuss the main issues you would deal with in your report.

1.11 Lawrence Summers served as secretary of the treasury in the Clinton administration and later as the president of Harvard University. He has been quoted as giving the following moral defense of the economic approach:

> There is nothing morally unattractive about saying: We need to analyze which way of spending money on health care will produce more benefit and which less, and using our money as efficiently as we can. I don't think there is anything immoral about seeking to achieve environmental benefits at the lowest possible costs.

Would it be more moral to reduce pollution without worrying about the cost or by taking the cost into account? Briefly explain.

Source: David Wessel, "Precepts from Professor Summers," *Wall Street Journal*, October 17, 2002.

1.12 In *The Wonderful Wizard of Oz* and his other books about the Land of Oz, L. Frank Baum observed that if people's wants were modest enough, most goods would not be scarce. According to Baum, this was the case in Oz:

> There were no poor people in the Land of Oz, because there was no such thing as money. . . . Each person was given freely by his neighbors whatever he required for his use, which is as much as anyone may reasonably desire. Some tilled the lands and raised great crops of grain, which was divided equally among the whole population, so that all had enough. There were many tailors and dressmakers and shoemakers and the like, who made things that any who desired them might wear. Likewise there were jewelers who made ornaments for the person, which pleased and beautified the people, and these ornaments also were free to those who asked for them. Each man and woman, no matter what he or she produced for the good of the community, was supplied by the neighbors with food and clothing and a house and furniture and ornaments and games. If by chance the supply ever ran short, more was taken from the great storehouses of the Ruler, which were afterward filled up again when there was more of any article than people needed. . . .

You will know, by what I have told you here, that the Land of Oz was a remarkable country. I do not suppose such an arrangement would be practical with us.

Do you agree with Baum that the economic system in Oz wouldn't work in the contemporary United States? Briefly explain why or why not.

Source: L. Frank Baum, *The Emerald City of Oz*, pp. 30–31. First edition published in 1910.

>> **End Learning Objective 2.1**

2.2 LEARNING OBJECTIVE   2.2 | Understand comparative advantage and explain how it is the basis for trade. pages 44–49.

Comparative Advantage and Trade

Summary

Fundamentally, markets are about **trade**, which is the act of buying or selling. People trade on the basis of comparative advantage. An individual, a firm, or a country has a **comparative advantage** in producing a good or service if it can produce the good or service at the lowest opportunity cost. People are usually better off specializing in the activity for which they have a comparative advantage and trading for the other goods and services they need. It is important not to confuse comparative advantage with absolute advantage. An individual, a firm, or a country has an **absolute advantage** in producing a good or service if it can produce more of that good or service from the same amount of resources. It is possible to have an absolute advantage in producing a good or service without having a comparative advantage.

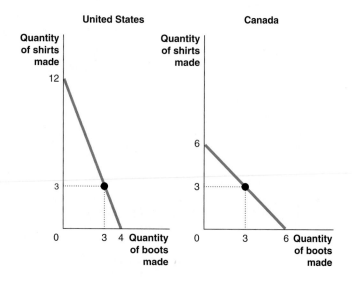

myeconlab Visit www.myeconlab.com to complete these exercises
Get Ahead of the Curve online and get instant feedback.

Review Questions

2.1 What is absolute advantage? What is comparative advantage? Is it possible for a country to have a comparative advantage in producing a good without also having an absolute advantage? Briefly explain.

2.2 What is the basis for trade? What advantages are there to specialization?

Problems and Applications

2.3 Look again at the information in Figure 2-4 on page 45. Choose a rate of trading cherries for apples different than the rate used in the text (15 pounds of cherries for 10 pounds of apples) that will allow you and your neighbor to benefit from trading apples and cherries. Prepare a table like Table 2-1 on page 46 to illustrate your answer.

2.4 Using the same amount of resources, the United States and Canada can both produce lumberjack shirts and lumberjack boots, as shown in the following production possibilities frontiers.

a. Who has a comparative advantage in producing lumberjack boots? Who has a comparative advantage in producing lumberjack shirts? Explain your reasoning.

b. Does either country have an absolute advantage in producing both goods? Explain.

c. Suppose that both countries are currently producing three pairs of boots and three shirts. Show that both can be better off if they specialize in producing one good and then engage in trade.

2.5 (Related to *Solved Problem 2-2* on page 48) Suppose Iran and Iraq both produce oil and olive oil. The following table shows combinations of both goods that each country can produce in a day, measured in thousands of barrels.

IRAQ		IRAN	
OIL	OLIVE OIL	OIL	OLIVE OIL
0	8	0	4
2	6	1	3
4	4	2	2
6	2	3	1
8	0	4	0

a. Who has the comparative advantage in producing oil? Explain.

b. Can these two countries gain from trading oil and olive oil? Explain.

2.6 (Related to *Solved Problem 2-2* on page 48) Suppose that France and Germany both produce schnitzel and wine. The following table shows combinations of the goods that each country can produce in a day.

FRANCE		GERMANY	
WINE (BOTTLES)	SCHNITZEL (POUNDS)	WINE (BOTTLES)	SCHNITZEL (POUNDS)
0	8	0	15
1	6	1	12
2	4	2	9
3	2	3	6
4	0	4	3
		5	0

a. Who has a comparative advantage in producing wine? Who has a comparative advantage in producing schnitzel?

b. Suppose that France is currently producing 1 bottle of wine and 6 pounds of schnitzel, and Germany is currently producing 3 bottles of wine and 6 pounds of schnitzel. Demonstrate that France and Germany can both be better off if they specialize in producing only one good and then engage in trade.

2.7 (Related to *Don't Let This Happen to You!* on page 48) In the 1950s, the economist Bela Balassa compared 28 manufacturing industries in the United States and Britain. In every one of the 28 industries, Balassa found that the United States had an absolute advantage. In these circumstances, would there have been any gain to the United States from importing any of these products from Britain? Explain.

2.8 In colonial America, the population was spread thinly over a large area, and transportation costs were very high because it was difficult to ship products by road for more than short distances. As a result, most of the free population lived on small farms where they not only grew their own food but also usually made their own clothes and very rarely bought or sold anything for money. Explain why the incomes of these farmers were likely to rise as transportation costs fell. Use the concept of comparative advantage in your answer.

2.9 During the 1928 presidential election campaign, Herbert Hoover, the Republican candidate, argued that the United States should only import those products that could not be produced here. Do you believe that this would be a good policy? Explain.

>> **End Learning Objective 2.2**

2.3 LEARNING OBJECTIVE 2.3 | Explain the basic idea of how a market system works, **pages 50–56.**

The Market System

Summary

A **market** is a group of buyers and sellers of a good or service and the institution or arrangement by which they come together to trade. **Product markets** are markets for goods and services, such as computers and medical treatment. **Factor markets** are markets for the **factors of production**, such as labor, capital, natural resources, and entrepreneurial ability. A **circular-flow diagram** shows how participants in product markets and factor markets are linked. Adam Smith argued in his 1776 book *The Wealth of Nations* that in a **free market** where the government does not control the production of goods and services, changes in prices lead firms to produce the goods and services most desired by consumers. If consumers demand more of a good, its price will rise. Firms respond to rising prices by increasing production. If consumers demand less of a good, its price will fall. Firms respond to falling prices by producing less of a good. An **entrepreneur** is someone who operates a business. In a market system, entrepreneurs are responsible for organizing the production of goods and services. A market system will work well only if there is protection for **property rights**, which are the rights of individuals and firms to use their property.

 Visit www.myeconlab.com to complete these exercises online and get instant feedback.

Review Questions

3.1 What is the circular-flow diagram, and what does it demonstrate?

3.2 What are the two main categories of participants in markets? Which participants are of greatest importance in determining what goods and services are produced?

3.3 What is a free market? In what ways does a free market economy differ from a centrally planned economy?

3.4 What is an entrepreneur? Why do entrepreneurs play a key role in a market system?

3.5 Under what circumstances are firms likely to produce more of a good or service? Under what circumstances are firms likely to produce less of a good or service?

3.6 What are private property rights? What role do they play in the working of a market system? Why are independent courts important for a well-functioning economy?

Problems and Applications

3.7 Identify whether each of the following transactions will take place in the factor market or in the product market and whether households or firms are supplying the good or service or demanding the good or service:
  a. George buys a BMW X5 SUV.
  b. BMW increases employment at its Spartanburg plant.
  c. George works 20 hours per week at McDonald's.
  d. George sells land he owns to McDonald's so it can build a new restaurant.

3.8 (Related to the *Making the Connection* on page 53) In *The Wealth of Nations*, Adam Smith wrote the following (Book I, Chapter II): "It is not from the benevolence of the butcher, the brewer, or the baker, that we expect our dinner, but from their regard to their own interest." Briefly discuss what he meant by this.

3.9 In a commencement address to economics graduates at the University of Texas, Robert McTeer, Jr., who was then the president of the Federal Reserve Bank of Dallas, argued, "For my money, Adam Smith's invisible hand is the most important thing you've learned by studying economics." What's so important about the idea of the invisible hand?

Source: Robert D. McTeer, Jr., "The Dismal Science? Hardly!" *Wall Street Journal*, June 4, 2003.

3.10 Evaluate the following argument: "Adam Smith's analysis is based on a fundamental flaw: He assumes that people are motivated by self-interest. But this isn't true. I'm not selfish, and most people I know aren't selfish."

3.11 Writing in the *New York Times*, Michael Lewis argued that "a market economy is premised on a system of incentives designed to encourage an ignoble human trait: self-interest." Do you agree that self-interest is an "ignoble human trait"? What incentives does a market system provide to encourage self-interest?

Source: Michael Lewis, "In Defense of the Boom," *New York Times*, October 27, 2002.

3.12 An editorial in *BusinessWeek* magazine offered this opinion: "Economies should be judged on a simple measure: their ability to generate a rising standard of living for all members of society, including people at the bottom." Briefly discuss whether you agree.

Source: "Poverty: The Bigger Picture," *BusinessWeek*, October 7, 2002.

3.13 An estimated 400 million to 600 million people worldwide are squatters who live on land to which they have no legal title, usually on the outskirts of cities in developing countries. Economist Hernando de Soto persuaded Peru's government to undertake a program to make it cheap and easy for such squatters to obtain a title to the land they had been occupying. How would this creation of property rights be likely to affect the economic opportunities available to these squatters?

Source: Alan B. Krueger, "A Study Looks at Squatters and Land Title in Peru," *New York Times*, January 9, 2003.

3.14 (Related to the *Making the Connection* on page 55) A columnist for the *Wall Street Journal* argued that most copyright holders are not damaged by having their material shown on YouTube:

> It's [laughable] to suggest that content owners are hurt by videos of teenagers lip-synching to hip-hop songs, that the market for sports DVDs is destroyed by fans being allowed to relive a team's great moment, or that artists reusing footage of famous televised events destroys interest in documentaries.

Do you agree with the argument that the copyright owners of the material mentioned should not be paid a fee if their material is on YouTube? Are there other types of material not mentioned by this columnist with which the copyright holders might suffer significant financial damages by having their material available on YouTube?

Source: Jason Fry, "The Revolution May Be Briefly Televised," *Wall Street Journal*, November 13, 2006.

>> End Learning Objective 2.3

Where Prices Come From: The Interaction of Demand and Supply

Apple and the Demand for iPods

During the first three months of 2008, Apple sold $1.82 billion worth of iPods. iPods seemed to be everywhere, but during 2008 it became clear that the market for digital music players was becoming much more competitive.

Steve Jobs and Steve Wozniak started Apple in 1976. Working out of Jobs's parents' garage, the two friends created the Apple I computer. By 1980, although Jobs was still only in his mid-twenties, Apple had become the first firm in history to join the Fortune 500 list of largest U.S. firms in less than five years. Apple's success in the computer business has been up and down, but when the company introduced the iPod digital music player in 2001, it had a runaway success on its hands. The most obvious reasons for the iPod's success are its ease of use and sleek design. But also important has been iTunes, Apple's online music store. Apple decided to offer individual songs, as well as whole albums, for download at a price of just $0.99 per song. After paying a royalty to the record company, Apple makes very little profit from the songs it sells on iTunes. Apple was willing to accept a small profit on the sale of each song to make the purchase of the iPod more attractive to consumers.

At a price of several hundred dollars, the iPod might be relatively expensive, but purchasing the music is very inexpensive. In addition, the songs on iTunes are playable only on iPods, and iPods can only play songs downloaded from iTunes (although with enough technical skill, it's possible to get around both restrictions). So, owners of other digital music players do not have easy access to iTunes, and iPod owners have little incentive to download music from other online sites. In addition, because Apple makes the iPod and owns iTunes, the two systems work smoothly together, which is not the case for many of Apple's competitors. Microsoft's Vice President Bryan Lee says, "That's something that Apple has played up very well. One brand, one device, one service."

By early 2008, more than 150 million iPods had been sold and more than 4 billion songs had been downloaded from iTunes. Clearly, the strategy of selling an expensive digital music player and selling the music cheaply has been very successful for Apple. But how long will the iPod's dominance last? By 2008, competitors were flooding into the market. New digital music players, such as Microsoft's Zune, Toshiba's Gigabeat, and iRiver's H10, among many others, were rapidly gaining customers. In addition, firms were introducing new "music phones" that combined the features of a cell phone with the features of a digital music player. Although this wave of competition might be bad news for Apple, it could be good news for consumers by increasing the choices available and lowering prices. **AN INSIDE LOOK** on **page 90** discusses how Apple responded to competition by teaming with AT&T to create its own music phone, the iPhone.

Sources: Nick Wingfield and Robert Guth, "iPod, TheyPod: Rivals Imitate Apple's Success," *Wall Street Journal*, September 18, 2006, p. B1; and Nick Wingfield, "iPod Demand Lifts Apple's Results," *Wall Street Journal*, January 18, 2007, p. A2.

LEARNING Objectives

After studying this chapter, you should be able to:

3.1 Discuss the variables that influence **demand**, page 68.

3.2 Discuss the variables that influence **supply**, page 75.

3.3 Use a graph to illustrate **market equilibrium**, page 79.

3.4 Use **demand and supply graphs** to predict changes in prices and quantities, page 83.

Economics in YOUR Life!

Will You Buy an iPod or a Zune?

Suppose you are about to buy a new digital music player and that you are choosing between Apple's iPod and Microsoft's Zune. As the industry leader, the iPod has many advantages over a new entrant like Zune. One strategy Microsoft can use to overcome those advantages is to compete based on price. Would you choose a Zune if it had a lower price than a comparable iPod? Would you choose a Zune if the songs sold on Zune Marketplace were cheaper than the songs sold on iTunes? As you read the chapter, see if you can answer these questions. You can check your answers against those we provide at the end of the chapter. **>> Continued on page 89**

I n Chapter 1, we explored how economists use models to predict human behavior. In Chapter 2, we used the model of production possibilities frontiers to analyze scarcity and trade-offs. In this chapter and the next, we explore the model of demand and supply, which is the most powerful tool in economics, and use it to explain how prices are determined.

Recall from Chapter 1 that economic models rely on assumptions and that these assumptions are simplifications of reality. In some cases, the assumptions of the model may not seem to describe exactly the economic situation being analyzed. For example, the model of demand and supply assumes that we are analyzing a *perfectly competitive market*. In a **perfectly competitive market**, there are many buyers and sellers, all the products sold are identical, and there are no barriers to new firms entering the market. These assumptions are very restrictive and apply exactly to only a few markets, such as the markets for wheat and other agricultural products. Experience has shown, however, that the model of demand and supply can be very useful in analyzing markets where competition among sellers is intense, even if there are relatively few sellers and the products being sold are not identical. In fact, in recent studies the model of demand and supply has been successful in analyzing markets with as few as four buyers and four sellers. In the end, the usefulness of a model depends on how well it can predict outcomes in a market. As we will see in this chapter, the model of demand and supply is often very useful in predicting changes in quantities and prices in many markets.

We begin considering the model of demand and supply by discussing consumers and the demand side of the market, then we turn to firms and the supply side. As you will see, we will apply this model throughout this book to understand business, the economy, and economic policy.

Perfectly competitive market
A market that meets the conditions of (1) many buyers and sellers, (2) all firms selling identical products, and (3) no barriers to new firms entering the market.

3.1 | Discuss the variables that influence demand.

The Demand Side of the Market

Chapter 2 explained that in a market system, consumers ultimately determine which goods and services will be produced. The most successful businesses are the ones that respond best to consumer demand. But what determines consumer demand for a product? Certainly, many factors influence the willingness of consumers to buy a particular product. For example, consumers who are considering buying a digital music player, such as Apple's iPod or Microsoft's Zune, will make their decisions based on, among other factors, the income they have available to spend and the effectiveness of the advertising campaigns of the companies that sell digital music players. The main factor in consumer decisions, though, will be the price of the digital music player. So, it makes sense to begin with price when analyzing the decisions of consumers to buy a product. It is important to note that when we discuss demand, we are considering not what a consumer *wants* to buy but what the consumer is both willing and *able* to buy.

Demand Schedules and Demand Curves

Tables that show the relationship between the price of a product and the quantity of the product demanded are called **demand schedules**. The table in Figure 3-1 shows the number of players consumers would be willing to buy over the course of a month at five different prices. The amount of a good or a service that a consumer is willing and able to purchase at a given price is referred to as the **quantity demanded**. The graph in Figure 3-1 plots the numbers from the table as a **demand curve**, a curve that shows the relationship between the price of a product and the quantity of the product demanded. (Note that for convenience, we made the demand curve in Figure 3-1 a straight line, or linear. There is no reason that all demand curves need to be straight lines.) The demand curve in Figure 3-1 shows the **market demand**, or the demand by all the consumers of a

Demand schedule A table showing the relationship between the price of a product and the quantity of the product demanded.

Quantity demanded The amount of a good or service that a consumer is willing and able to purchase at a given price.

Demand curve A curve that shows the relationship between the price of a product and the quantity of the product demanded.

Market demand The demand by all the consumers of a given good or service.

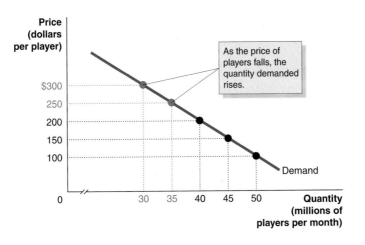

Demand Schedule	
Price (dollars per player)	Quantity (millions of players per month)
$300	30
250	35
200	40
150	45
100	50

Figure 3-1

A Demand Schedule and Demand Curve

As the price changes, consumers change the quantity of digital music players they are willing to buy. We can show this as a *demand schedule* in a table or as a *demand curve* on a graph. The table and graph both show that as the price of players falls, the quantity demanded rises. When the price of a player is $300, consumers buy 30 million. When the price drops to $250, consumers buy 35 million. Therefore, the demand curve for digital music players is downward sloping.

given good or service. The market for a product, such as restaurant meals, that is purchased locally would include all the consumers in a city or a relatively small area. The market for a product that is sold internationally, such as digital music players, would include all the consumers in the world.

The demand curve in Figure 3-1 slopes downward because consumers will buy more players as the price falls. When the price of players is $300, consumers buy 30 million players per month. If the price of players falls to $250, consumers buy 35 million players. Buyers demand a larger quantity of a product as the price falls because the product becomes less expensive relative to other products and because they can afford to buy more at a lower price.

The Law of Demand

The inverse relationship between the price of a product and the quantity of the product demanded is known as the **law of demand**: Holding everything else constant, when the price of a product falls, the quantity demanded of the product will increase, and when the price of a product rises, the quantity demanded of the product will decrease. The law of demand holds for any market demand curve. Economists have never found an exception to it. In fact, Nobel Prize–winning economist George Stigler once remarked that the surest way for an economist to become famous would be to discover a market demand curve that sloped upward rather than downward.

What Explains the Law of Demand?

It makes sense that consumers will buy more of a good when the price falls and less of a good when the price rises, but let's look more closely at why this is true. When the price of digital music players falls, consumers buy a larger quantity because of the *substitution effect* and the *income effect*.

Substitution Effect The **substitution effect** refers to the change in the quantity demanded of a good that results from a change in price, making the good more or less expensive *relative* to other goods that are *substitutes*. When the price of digital music players falls, consumers will substitute buying music players for buying other goods, such as radios or compact stereos.

The Income Effect The **income effect** of a price change refers to the change in the quantity demanded of a good that results from the effect of a change in the good's price on consumers' purchasing power. Purchasing power is the quantity of goods a consumer can buy with a fixed amount of income. When the price of a good falls, the increased purchasing power of consumers' incomes will usually lead them to purchase a larger quantity of the good. When the price of a good rises, the decreased purchasing power of consumers' incomes will usually lead them to purchase a smaller quantity of the good.

Note that although we can analyze them separately, the substitution effect and the income effect happen simultaneously whenever a price changes. Thus, a fall in the price

Law of demand The rule that, holding everything else constant, when the price of a product falls, the quantity demanded of the product will increase, and when the price of a product rises, the quantity demanded of the product will decrease.

Substitution effect The change in the quantity demanded of a good that results from a change in price, making the good more or less expensive relative to other goods that are substitutes.

Income effect The change in the quantity demanded of a good that results from the effect of a change in the good's price on consumers' purchasing power.

of digital music players leads consumers to buy more players, both because the players are now cheaper relative to substitute products and because the purchasing power of the consumers' incomes has increased.

Holding Everything Else Constant: The *Ceteris Paribus* Condition

Notice that the definition of the law of demand contains the phrase *holding everything else constant*. In constructing the market demand curve for digital music players, we focused only on the effect that changes in the price of players would have on the quantity of players consumers would be willing and able to buy. We were holding constant other variables that might affect the willingness of consumers to buy players. Economists refer to the necessity of holding all variables other than price constant in constructing a demand curve as the **ceteris paribus** condition; *ceteris paribus* is Latin for "all else equal."

What would happen if we allowed a change in a variable—other than price—that might affect the willingness of consumers to buy music players? Consumers would then change the quantity they demand at each price. We can illustrate this effect by shifting the market demand curve. A shift of a demand curve is *an increase or a decrease in demand*. A movement along a demand curve is *an increase or a decrease in the quantity demanded*. As Figure 3-2 shows, we shift the demand curve to the right if consumers decide to buy more of the good at each price, and we shift the demand curve to the left if consumers decide to buy less at each price.

Ceteris paribus ("all else equal")
The requirement that when analyzing the relationship between two variables—such as price and quantity demanded—other variables must be held constant.

Variables That Shift Market Demand

Many variables other than price can influence market demand. These five are the most important:

- Income

- Prices of related goods

- Tastes

- Population and demographics

- Expected future prices

We next discuss how changes in each of these variables affect the market demand curve for digital music players.

Figure 3-2

Shifting the Demand Curve

When consumers increase the quantity of a product they wish to buy at a given price, the market demand curve shifts to the right, from D_1 to D_2. When consumers decrease the quantity of a product they wish to buy at any given price, the demand curve shifts to the left, from D_1 to D_3.

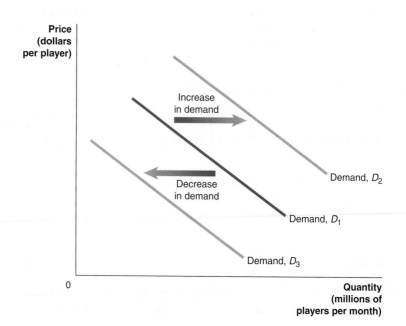

Income The income that consumers have available to spend affects their willingness and ability to buy a good. Suppose that the market demand curve in Figure 3-1 represents the willingness of consumers to buy digital music players when average household income is $43,000. If household income rises to $45,000, the demand for players will increase, which we show by shifting the demand curve to the right. A good is a **normal good** when demand increases following a rise in income and decreases following a fall in income. Most goods are normal goods, but the demand for some goods falls when income rises and rises when income falls. For instance, as your income rises, you might buy less canned tuna fish or fewer hot dogs and buy more shrimp or prime rib. A good is an **inferior good** when demand decreases following a rise in income and increases following a fall in income. So, for you hot dogs and tuna fish would be examples of inferior goods—not because they are of low quality but because you buy less of them as your income increases.

> **Normal good** A good for which the demand increases as income rises and decreases as income falls.

> **Inferior good** A good for which the demand increases as income falls and decreases as income rises.

Prices of Related Goods The prices of other goods can also affect consumers' demand for a product. Suppose that the market demand curve in Figure 3-1 represents the willingness and ability of consumers to buy digital music players during a year when the average price of compact stereos, such as the Bose Wave music system, is $500. If the average price of these stereo systems falls to $400, how will the market demand for digital music players change? Fewer players will be demanded at every price. We show this by shifting the demand curve for players to the left.

Goods and services that can be used for the same purpose—such as digital music players and compact stereos—are **substitutes**. When two goods are substitutes, the more you buy of one, the less you will buy of the other. A decrease in the price of a substitute causes the demand curve for a good to shift to the left. An increase in the price of a substitute causes the demand curve for a good to shift to the right.

> **Substitutes** Goods and services that can be used for the same purpose.

Many consumers play songs downloaded from a Web site, such as iTunes or Zune Marketplace, on their digital music players. Suppose the market demand curve in Figure 3-1 represents the willingness of consumers to buy players at a time when the average price to download a song is $0.99. If the price to download a song falls to $0.49, consumers will buy more song downloads *and* more digital music players: The demand curve for music players will shift to the right.

Products that are used together—such as digital music players and song downloads—are **complements**. When two goods are complements, the more consumers buy of one, the more they will buy of the other. A decrease in the price of a complement causes the demand curve for a good to shift to the right. An increase in the price of a complement causes the demand curve for a good to shift to the left.

> **Complements** Goods and services that are used together.

Making the Connection | Why Supermarkets Need to Understand Substitutes and Complements

Supermarkets sell what sometimes seems like a bewildering variety of goods. The first row of the following table shows the varieties of eight products stocked by five Chicago supermarkets.

	COFFEE	FROZEN PIZZA	HOT DOGS	ICE CREAM	POTATO CHIPS	REGULAR CEREAL	SPAGHETTI SAUCE	YOGURT
Varieties in five Chicago supermarkets	391	337	128	421	285	242	194	288
Varieties introduced in a 2-year period	113	109	47	129	93	114	70	107
Varieties removed in a 2-year period	135	86	32	118	77	75	36	51

Source: Juin-Kuan Chong, Teck-Hua Ho, and Christopher S. Tang, "A Modeling Framework for Category Assortment Planning," *Manufacturing & Service Operations Management*, 2001, Vol. 3, No. 3, pp. 191–210.

Supermarkets are also constantly adding new varieties of goods to their shelves and removing old varieties. The second row of the table shows that these five Chicago supermarkets added 113 new varieties of coffee over a two-year period, while the third row shows that they eliminated 135 existing varieties. How do supermarkets decide which varieties to add and which to remove?

Christopher Tang is a professor at the Anderson Graduate School of Management at the University of California, Los Angeles (UCLA). In an interview with the *Baltimore Sun*, Tang argues that supermarkets should not necessarily remove the slowest-selling goods from their shelves but should consider the relationships among the goods. In particular, they should consider whether the goods being removed are substitutes or complements with the remaining goods. A lobster bisque soup, for example, could be a relatively slow seller but might be a complement to other soups because it can be used with them to make a sauce. In that case, removing the lobster bisque would hurt sales of some of the remaining soups. Tang suggests the supermarket would be better off removing a slow-selling soup that is a substitute for another soup. For example, the supermarket might want to remove one of two brands of cream of chicken soup.

Source: Lobster bisque example from Lorraine Mirabella, "Shelf Science in Supermarkets," *Baltimore Sun*, March 17, 2002, p. 16.

YOUR TURN: For more practice, do problem 1.5 on page 92 at the end of this chapter.

Tastes Consumers can be influenced by an advertising campaign for a product. If Apple, Microsoft, Toshiba, and other makers of digital music players begin to heavily advertise on television and online, consumers are more likely to buy players at every price, and the demand curve will shift to the right. An economist would say that the advertising campaign has affected consumers' *taste* for digital music players. Taste is a catchall category that refers to the many subjective elements that can enter into a consumer's decision to buy a product. A consumer's taste for a product can change for many reasons. Sometimes trends play a substantial role. For example, the popularity of low-carbohydrate diets caused a decline in demand for some goods, such as bread and donuts, and an increase in demand for beef. In general, when consumers' taste for a product increases, the demand curve will shift to the right, and when consumers' taste for a product decreases, the demand curve for the product will shift to the left.

Demographics The characteristics of a population with respect to age, race, and gender.

Population and Demographics Population and demographic factors can affect the demand for a product. As the population of the United States increases, so will the number of consumers, and the demand for most products will increase. The **demographics** of a population refers to its characteristics, with respect to age, race, and gender. As the demographics of a country or region change, the demand for particular goods will increase or decrease because different categories of people tend to have different preferences for those goods. For instance, in 2006, a record 17 percent of the U.S. population was 60 years of age or older increasing the demand for health care and other products heavily used by older people.

Making *the* Connection │ **Companies Respond to a Growing Hispanic Population**

The spending power of Hispanic Americans is rapidly increasing. So, it is no surprise that firms have begun to respond: When Apple announced in early 2007 that it would sell a 90-minute video of highlights of the 2007 Super Bowl on its iTunes store, the download was made available in Spanish as well as in English. In early 2008, "Coffee Break Spanish," a weekly Spanish language podcast, was one of the most frequently downloaded podcasts on iTunes. Today, more than one third of all DVDs are sold to consumers whose first language is Spanish, and Blockbuster has responded by increasing its offerings of Spanish-language films. Kmart sells a clothing line named after Thalia, a Mexican singer. The Ford Motor Company hired Mexican actress Salma Hayek to appear in commercials. A used car dealer in Pennsylvania displayed a sign stating "Salga Manejando Hoy Mismo" (or "Drive Out Today" in English).

Blockbuster responds to a growing Hispanic population by featuring DVDs dubbed in Spanish.

The increase in spending by Hispanic households was due partly to increased population growth and partly to rising incomes. By 2020, the Hispanic share of the U.S. consumer market is expected to grow to more than 13 percent—almost twice what it was in 2000. The Selig Center for Economic Growth at the University of Georgia has forecast that spending by Hispanic households will increase about 70 percent more between 2006 and 2011 than spending by non-Hispanic households.

As the demand for goods purchased by Hispanic households increases, a larger quantity can be sold at every price. Firms have responded by devoting more resources to serving this demographic group.

Sources: "Apple Completes Pass for Super Bowl Highlights," *St. Petersburg* (Florida) *Times*, February 1, 2007; Catherine E. Shoichet and John Martin, "Downloading," *Houston Chronicle*, January 7, 2007; Jeffrey M. Humphreys, "The Multicultural Economy 2006," *Georgia Business and Economic Conditions*, Third Quarter 2006, Vol. 66, No. 3; and Eduardo Porter, "Buying Power of Hispanics Is Set to Soar," *Wall Street Journal*, April 18, 2003, p. B1.

YOUR TURN: For more practice, do problem 1.8 on page 93 at the end of this chapter.

Expected Future Prices Consumers choose not only which products to buy but also when to buy them. If enough consumers become convinced that digital music players will be selling for lower prices three months from now, the demand for players will decrease now, as some consumers postpone their purchases to wait for the expected price decrease. Alternatively, if enough consumers become convinced that the price of players will be higher three months from now, the demand for players will increase now, as some consumers try to beat the expected price increase.

Table 3-1 on page 74 summarizes the most important variables that cause market demand curves to shift. You should note that the table shows the shift in the demand curve that results from an *increase* in each of the variables. A *decrease* in these variables would cause the demand curve to shift in the opposite direction.

A Change in Demand versus a Change in Quantity Demanded

It is important to understand the difference between a *change in demand* and a *change in quantity demanded*. A change in demand refers to a shift of the demand curve. A shift occurs if there is a change in one of the variables, *other than the price of the product*, that affects the willingness of consumers to buy the product. A change in quantity demanded refers to a movement along the demand curve as a result of a change in the product's price. Figure 3-3 illustrates this important distinction. If the price of digital music players falls from $300 to $250, the result will be a movement along the demand curve from

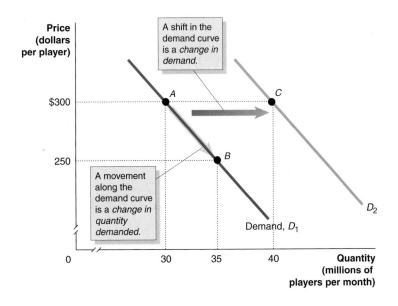

Price (dollars per player)

A shift in the demand curve is a *change in demand*.

A movement along the demand curve is a *change in quantity demanded*.

Demand, D_1

D_2

Quantity (millions of players per month)

Figure 3-3

A Change in Demand versus a Change in the Quantity Demanded

If the price of digital music players falls from $300 to $250, the result will be a movement along the demand curve from point *A* to point *B*—an increase in quantity demanded from 30 million to 35 million. If consumers' income increases, or if another factor changes that makes consumers want more of the product at every price, the demand curve will shift to the right—an increase in demand. In this case, the increase in demand from D_1 to D_2 causes the quantity of players demanded at a price of $300 to increase from 30 million at point *A* to 40 million at point *C*.

TABLE 3-1

Variables That Shift Market Demand Curves

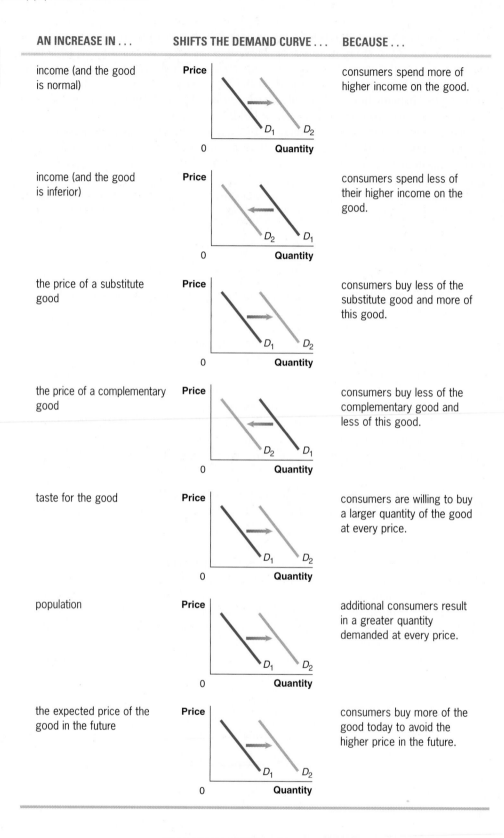

AN INCREASE IN . . .	SHIFTS THE DEMAND CURVE . . .	BECAUSE . . .
income (and the good is normal)		consumers spend more of higher income on the good.
income (and the good is inferior)		consumers spend less of their higher income on the good.
the price of a substitute good		consumers buy less of the substitute good and more of this good.
the price of a complementary good		consumers buy less of the complementary good and less of this good.
taste for the good		consumers are willing to buy a larger quantity of the good at every price.
population		additional consumers result in a greater quantity demanded at every price.
the expected price of the good in the future		consumers buy more of the good today to avoid the higher price in the future.

point A to point B—an increase in quantity demanded from 30 million to 35 million. If consumers' incomes increase, or if another factor changes that makes consumers want more of the product at every price, the demand curve will shift to the right—an increase in demand. In this case, the increase in demand from D_1 to D_2 causes the quantity of digital music players demanded at a price of $300 to increase from 30 million at point A to 40 million at point C.

Making the Connection

Apple Forecasts the Demand for iPhones and other Consumer Electronics

One of the most important decisions that the managers of any large firm have to make is which new products to develop. A firm must devote people, time, and money to designing the product, negotiating with suppliers, formulating a marketing campaign, and many other tasks. But any firm has only limited resources and so faces a trade-off: Resources used to develop one product will not be available to develop another product. Ultimately, the products a firm chooses to develop will be those which it believes will be the most profitable. So, to decide which products to develop, firms need to forecast the demand for those products.

David Sobotta, who worked at Apple for 20 years, eventually becoming its national sales manager, has described the strategy Apple has used to decide which consumer electronics products will have the greatest demand. Sobotta describes discussions at Apple during 2002 about whether to develop a tablet personal computer. A tablet PC is a laptop with a special screen that allows the computer to be controlled with a stylus or pen and that has the capability of converting handwritten input into text. The previous year, Bill Gates, chairman of Microsoft, had predicted that "within five years . . . [tablet PCs] will be the most popular form of PC sold in America." Representatives of the federal government's National Institutes of Health also urged Apple to develop a tablet PC, arguing that it would be particularly useful to doctors, nurses, and hospitals. Apple's managers decided not to develop a tablet PC, however, because they believed the technology was too complex for the average computer user and did not believe that the demand from doctors and nurses would be very large. This forecast turned out to be correct. Despite Bill Gates's prediction, in 2006, tablets made up only 1 percent of the computer market, and they were forecast to increase to only 5 percent by 2009.

According to Sobotta, "Apple executives had a theory that the route to success will not be through selling thousands of relatively expensive things, but millions of very inexpensive things like iPods." In fact, although many business analysts were skeptical that the iPod would succeed, demand grew faster than even Apple's most optimistic forecasts. By the beginning of 2007, 100 million iPods had been sold. So, it was not very surprising when in early 2007, Apple Chief Executive Officer Steve Jobs announced that the company would be combining the iPod with a cell phone to create the iPhone. With more than 900 million cell phones sold each year, Apple expects the demand for the iPhone to be very large. As Sobotta noted, "And there's an 'Apple gap': mobile phone users often find their interfaces confusing. . . . Apple's unique ability to simplify while innovating looks like a good fit there."

Apple forecasted that it would sell 10 million iPhones during the product's first year on the market, with much larger sales expected in future years. In July 2008, iPhone sales received a further boost when Apple released a new version that uses a faster cellular network.

Sources: David Sobotta, "Technology: What Jobs Told Me on the iPhone," *The Guardian* (London), January 4, 2007, p. 1; and Connie Guglielmo, "Apple First-Quarter Profit Rises on IPod, Mac Sales," Bloomberg.com, January 17, 2007.

YOUR TURN: For more practice, do problem 1.10 on page 93 at the end of this chapter.

Will Apple's iPhone match the success of its iPod?

3.2 | Discuss the variables that influence supply.

The Supply Side of the Market

Just as many variables influence the willingness and ability of consumers to buy a particular good or service, many variables also influence the willingness and ability of firms to sell a good or service. The most important of these variables is price. The amount of a good or service that a firm is willing and able to supply at a given price is the **quantity supplied**. Holding other variables constant, when the price of a good rises, producing

Quantity supplied The amount of a good or service that a firm is willing and able to supply at a given price.

the good is more profitable, and the quantity supplied will increase. When the price of a good falls, the good is less profitable, and the quantity supplied will decrease. In addition, as we saw in Chapter 2, devoting more and more resources to the production of a good results in increasing marginal costs. So, if, for example, Apple, Microsoft, and Toshiba increase production of digital music players during a given time period, they are likely to find that the cost of producing the additional players increases as they run existing factories for longer hours and pay higher prices for components and higher wages for workers. With higher marginal costs, firms will supply a larger quantity only if the price is higher.

Supply Schedules and Supply Curves

Supply schedule A table that shows the relationship between the price of a product and the quantity of the product supplied.

Supply curve A curve that shows the relationship between the price of a product and the quantity of the product supplied.

A **supply schedule** is a table that shows the relationship between the price of a product and the quantity of the product supplied. The table in Figure 3-4 is a supply schedule showing the quantity of digital music players that firms would be willing to supply per month at different prices. The graph in Figure 3-4 plots the numbers from the supply schedule as a *supply curve*. A **supply curve** shows the relationship between the price of a product and the quantity of the product supplied. The supply schedule and supply curve both show that as the price of players rises, firms will increase the quantity they supply. At a price of $250 per player, firms will supply 45 million players per year. At the higher price of $300, they will supply 50 million. (Once again, we are assuming for convenience that the supply curve is a straight line, even though not all supply curves are actually straight lines.)

The Law of Supply

Law of supply The rule that, holding everything else constant, increases in price cause increases in the quantity supplied, and decreases in price cause decreases in the quantity supplied.

The *market supply curve* in Figure 3-4 is upward sloping. We expect most supply curves to be upward sloping according to the **law of supply**, which states that, holding everything else constant, increases in price cause increases in the quantity supplied, and decreases in price cause decreases in the quantity supplied. Notice that the definition of the law of supply—like the definition of the law of demand—contains the phrase *holding everything else constant*. If only the price of the product changes, there is a movement along the supply curve, which is *an increase or a decrease in the quantity supplied*. As Figure 3-5 shows, if any other variable that affects the willingness of firms to supply a good changes, the supply curve will shift, which is *an increase or decrease in supply*. When firms increase the quantity of a product they wish to sell at a given price, the supply curve shifts to the right. The shift from S_1 to S_3 represents *an increase in supply*. When firms decrease the quantity of a product they wish to sell at a given price, the supply curve shifts to the left. The shift from S_1 to S_2 represents *a decrease in supply*.

Figure 3-4

A Supply Schedule and Supply Curve

As the price changes, Apple, Microsoft, Toshiba, and the other firms producing digital music players change the quantity they are willing to supply. We can show this as a *supply schedule* in a table or as a *supply curve* on a graph. The supply schedule and supply curve both show that as the price of players rises, firms will increase the quantity they supply. At a price of $250, firms will supply 45 million players. At a price of $300 per player, firms will supply 50 million players.

Supply Schedule	
Price (dollars per player)	Quantity (millions of players per month)
$300	50
250	45
200	40
150	35
100	30

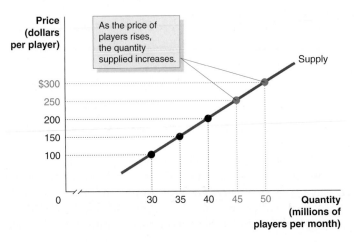

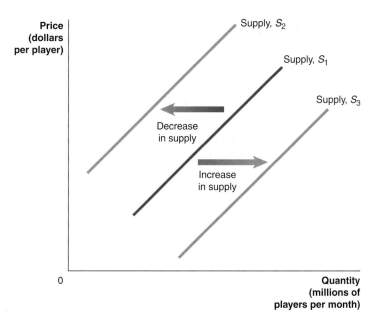

Figure 3-5

Shifting the Supply Curve

When firms increase the quantity of a product they wish to sell at a given price, the supply curve shifts to the right. The shift from S_1 to S_3 represents an *increase in supply*. When firms decrease the quantity of a product they wish to sell at a given price, the supply curve shifts to the left. The shift from S_1 to S_2 represents a *decrease in supply*.

Variables That Shift Supply

The following are the most important variables that shift supply:

- Prices of inputs
- Technological change
- Prices of substitutes in production
- Number of firms in the market
- Expected future prices

We next discuss how each of these variables affects the supply of digital music players.

Prices of Inputs The factor most likely to cause the supply curve for a product to shift is a change in the price of an *input*. An input is anything used in the production of a good or service. For instance, if the price of a component of digital music players, such as the microprocessor, rises, the cost of producing music players will increase, and players will be less profitable at every price. The supply of players will decline, and the market supply curve for players will shift to the left. Similarly, if the price of an input declines, the supply of players will increase, and the supply curve will shift to the right.

Technological Change A second factor that causes a change in supply is *technological change*. **Technological change** is a positive or negative change in the ability of a firm to produce a given level of output with a given quantity of inputs. Positive technological change occurs whenever a firm is able to produce more output using the same amount of inputs. This shift will happen when the *productivity* of workers or machines increases. If a firm can produce more output with the same amount of inputs, its costs will be lower, and the good will be more profitable to produce at any given price. As a result, when positive technological change occurs, the firm will increase the quantity supplied at every price, and its supply curve will shift to the right. Normally, we expect technological change to have a positive impact on a firm's willingness to supply a product. Negative technological change is relatively rare, although it could result from a natural disaster or a war that reduces the ability of a firm to supply as much output with a given amount of inputs. Negative technological change will raise a firm's costs, and the good will be less profitable to produce. Therefore, negative technological change causes a firm's supply curve to shift to the left.

Technological change A positive or negative change in the ability of a firm to produce a given level of output with a given quantity of inputs.

Prices of Substitutes in Production Firms often choose which good or service they will produce. Alternative products that a firm could produce are called *substitutes in production*. To this point, we have considered the market for all types of digital music players. But suppose we now consider separate markets for music players with screens capable of showing videos and for smaller players, without screens, that play only music. If the price of video music players increases, video music players will become more profitable, and Apple, Microsoft, and the other companies making music players will shift some of their productive capacity away from smaller players and toward video players. The companies will offer fewer smaller players for sale at every price, so the supply curve for smaller players will shift to the left.

Number of Firms in the Market A change in the number of firms in the market will change supply. When new firms *enter* a market, the supply curve shifts to the right, and when existing firms leave, or *exit*, a market, the supply curve for digital music players shifts to the left. For instance, when Microsoft introduced the Zune, the market supply curve for digital music players shifted to the right.

Expected Future Prices If a firm expects that the price of its product will be higher in the future than it is today, it has an incentive to decrease supply now and increase it in the future. For instance, if Apple believes that prices for digital music players are temporarily

TABLE 3-2

Variables That Shift Market Supply Curves

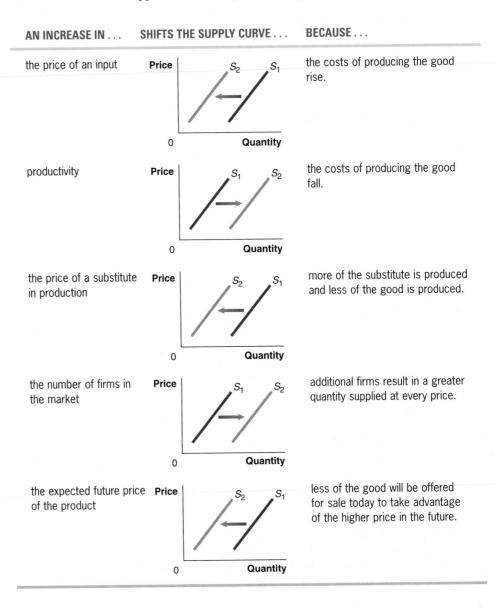

AN INCREASE IN ...	SHIFTS THE SUPPLY CURVE ...	BECAUSE ...
the price of an input		the costs of producing the good rise.
productivity		the costs of producing the good fall.
the price of a substitute in production		more of the substitute is produced and less of the good is produced.
the number of firms in the market		additional firms result in a greater quantity supplied at every price.
the expected future price of the product		less of the good will be offered for sale today to take advantage of the higher price in the future.

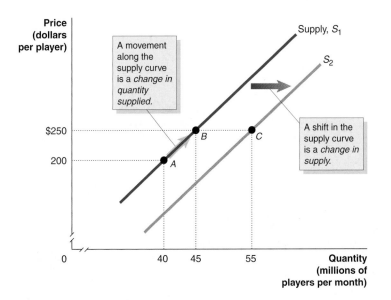

Figure 3-6

A Change in Supply versus a Change in the Quantity Supplied

If the price of digital music players rises from $200 to $250, the result will be a movement up the supply curve from point A to point B—an increase in quantity supplied by Apple, Microsoft, and Toshiba and the other firms from 40 million to 45 million. If the price of an input decreases or another factor changes that makes sellers supply more of the product at every price, the supply curve will shift to the right—an increase in supply. In this case, the increase in supply from S_1 to S_2 causes the quantity of digital music players supplied at a price of $250 to increase from 45 million at point B to 55 million at point C.

low—perhaps because of a price war among firms making players—it may store some of its production today to sell tomorrow, when it expects prices will be higher.

Table 3-2 on page 78 summarizes the most important variables that cause market supply curves to shift. You should note that the table shows the shift in the supply curve that results from an *increase* in each of the variables. A *decrease* in these variables would cause the supply curve to shift in the opposite direction.

A Change in Supply versus a Change in Quantity Supplied

We noted earlier the important difference between a change in demand and a change in quantity demanded. There is a similar difference between a *change in supply* and a *change in quantity supplied*. A change in supply refers to a shift of the supply curve. The supply curve will shift when there is a change in one of the variables, *other than the price of the product*, that affects the willingness of suppliers to sell the product. A change in quantity supplied refers to a movement along the supply curve as a result of a change in the product's price. Figure 3-6 illustrates this important distinction. If the price of music players rises from $200 to $250, the result will be a movement up the supply curve from point A to point B—an increase in quantity supplied from 40 million to 45 million. If the price of an input decreases or another factor makes sellers supply more of the product at every price change, the supply curve will shift to the right—an increase in supply. In this case, the increase in supply from S_1 to S_2 causes the quantity of digital music players supplied at a price of $250 to increase from 45 million at point B to 55 million at point C.

3.3 | Use a graph to illustrate market equilibrium.

3.3 LEARNING OBJECTIVE

Market Equilibrium: Putting Demand and Supply Together

The purpose of markets is to bring buyers and sellers together. As we saw in Chapter 2, instead of being chaotic and disorderly, the interaction of buyers and sellers in markets ultimately results in firms being led to produce those goods and services consumers desire most. To understand how this process happens, we first need to see how markets work to reconcile the plans of buyers and sellers.

In Figure 3-7, we bring together the market demand curve for digital music players and the market supply curve. Notice that the demand curve crosses the supply curve at

Figure 3-7

Market Equilibrium

Where the demand curve crosses the supply curve determines market equilibrium. In this case, the demand curve for digital music players crosses the supply curve at a price of $200 and a quantity of 40 million. Only at this point is the quantity of players consumers are willing to buy equal to the quantity of players Apple, Microsoft, Toshiba, and the other firms are willing to sell: The quantity demanded is equal to the quantity supplied.

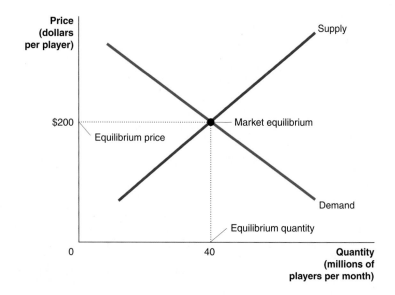

Market equilibrium A situation in which quantity demanded equals quantity supplied.

Competitive market equilibrium A market equilibrium with many buyers and many sellers.

only one point. This point represents a price of $200 and a quantity of 40 million players. Only at this point is the quantity of players consumers are willing to buy equal to the quantity of players firms are willing to sell. This is the point of **market equilibrium**. Only at market equilibrium will the quantity demanded equal the quantity supplied. In this case, the *equilibrium price* is $200, and the *equilibrium quantity* is 40 million. As we noted at the beginning of the chapter, markets that have many buyers and many sellers are competitive markets, and equilibrium in these markets is a **competitive market equilibrium**. In the market for digital music players, there are many buyers but fewer than 20 firms. Whether 20 firms is enough for our model of demand and supply to apply to this market is a matter of judgment. In this chapter, we are assuming that the market for digital music players has enough sellers to be competitive.

How Markets Eliminate Surpluses and Shortages

A market that is not in equilibrium moves toward equilibrium. Once a market is in equilibrium, it remains in equilibrium. To see why, consider what happens if a market is not in equilibrium. For instance, suppose that the price in the market for digital music players was $250, rather than the equilibrium price of $200. As Figure 3-8 shows, at a price of $250, the quantity of players supplied would be 45 million, and the quantity of players demanded would be 35 million. When the quantity supplied is greater than the quantity demanded, there is a **surplus** in the market. In this case, the surplus is equal to 10 million players (45 million − 35 million = 10 million). When there is a surplus, firms have unsold goods piling up, which gives them an incentive to increase their sales by cutting the price. Cutting the price will simultaneously increase the quantity demanded and decrease the quantity supplied. This adjustment will reduce the surplus, but as long as the price is above $200, there will be a surplus, and downward pressure on the price will continue. Only when the price has fallen to $200 will the market be in equilibrium.

Surplus A situation in which the quantity supplied is greater than the quantity demanded.

If, however, the price were $100, the quantity supplied would be 30 million, and the quantity demanded would be 50 million, as shown in Figure 3-8. When the quantity demanded is greater than the quantity supplied, there is a **shortage** in the market. In this case, the shortage is equal to 20 million digital music players (50 million − 30 million = 20 million). When a shortage occurs, some consumers will be unable to buy a digital music player at the current price. In this situation, firms will realize that they can raise the price without losing sales. A higher price will simultaneously increase the quantity supplied and decrease the quantity demanded. This adjustment will reduce the shortage, but as long as the price is below $200, there will be a shortage, and upward pressure on the price will continue. Only when the price has risen to $200 will the market be in equilibrium.

Shortage A situation in which the quantity demanded is greater than the quantity supplied.

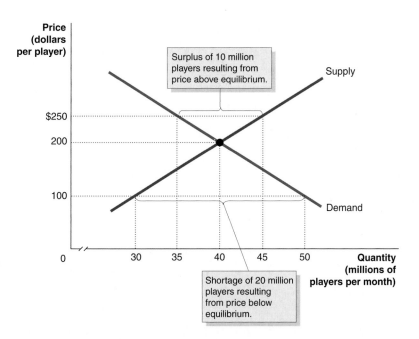

Price
(dollars
per player)

Surplus of 10 million
players resulting from
price above equilibrium.

Supply

$250

200

100

Demand

0   30   35   40   45   50

Quantity
(millions of
players per month)

Shortage of 20 million
players resulting
from price below
equilibrium.

Figure 3-8

The Effect of Surpluses and Shortages on the Market Price

When the market price is above equilibrium, there will be a *surplus*. In the figure, a price of $250 for digital music players results in 45 million being supplied but only 35 million being demanded, or a surplus of 10 million. As Apple, Microsoft, Toshiba, and the other firms cut the price to dispose of the surplus, the price will fall to the equilibrium of $200. When the market price is below equilibrium, there will be a *shortage*. A price of $100 results in 50 million players being demanded but only 30 million being supplied, or a shortage of 20 million. As consumers who are unable to buy a player offer to pay higher prices, the price will rise to the equilibrium of $200.

At a competitive market equilibrium, all consumers willing to pay the market price will be able to buy as much of the product as they want, and all firms willing to accept the market price will be able to sell as much of the product as they want. As a result, there will be no reason for the price to change unless either the demand curve or the supply curve shifts.

Demand and Supply Both Count

Always keep in mind that it is the interaction of demand and supply that determines the equilibrium price. Neither consumers nor firms can dictate what the equilibrium price will be. No firm can sell anything at any price unless it can find a willing buyer, and no consumer can buy anything at any price without finding a willing seller.

Solved Problem | **3-3**

Demand and Supply Both Count: A Tale of Two Letters

Which letter is likely to be worth more: one written by Abraham Lincoln or one written by his assassin, John Wilkes Booth? Lincoln is one of the greatest presidents, and many people collect anything written by him. The demand for letters written by Lincoln surely would seem to be much greater than the demand for letters written by Booth. Yet when R. M. Smythe and Co. auctioned off on the same day a letter written by Lincoln and a letter written by Booth, the Booth letter sold for $31,050, and the Lincoln letter sold for only $21,850. Use a demand and supply graph to explain how the Booth letter has a higher market price than the Lincoln letter, even though the demand for letters written by Lincoln is greater than the demand for letters written by Booth.

SOLVING THE PROBLEM:

Step 1: **Review the chapter material.** This problem is about prices being determined at market equilibrium, so you may want to review the section "Market Equilibrium: Putting Demand and Supply Together," which begins on page 79.

Step 2: **Draw demand curves that illustrate the greater demand for Lincoln's letters.** Begin by drawing two demand curves. Label one "Demand for Lincoln's letters" and the other "Demand for Booth's letters." Make sure that the Lincoln demand curve is much farther to the right than the Booth demand curve.

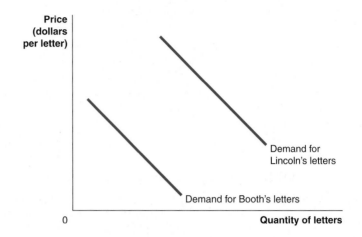

Step 3: **Draw supply curves that illustrate the equilibrium price of Booth's letters being higher than the equilibrium price of Lincoln's letters.** Based on the demand curves you have just drawn, think about how it might be possible for the market price of Lincoln's letters to be lower than the market price of Booth's letters. The only way this can be true is if the supply of Lincoln's letters is much greater than the supply of Booth's letters. Draw on your graph a supply curve for Lincoln's letters and a supply curve for Booth's letters that will result in an equilibrium price of Booth's letters of $31,050 and an equilibrium price of Lincoln's letters of $21,850. You have now solved the problem.

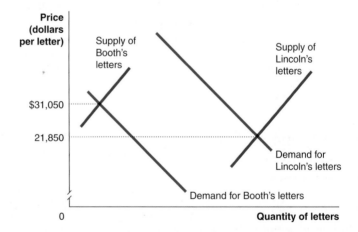

EXTRA CREDIT: The explanation for this puzzle is that both demand and supply count when determining market price. The demand for Lincoln's letters is much greater than the demand for Booth's letters, but the supply of Booth's letters is very small. Historians believe that only eight letters written by Booth exist today. (Note that the supply curves for letters written by Booth and by Lincoln slope up even though only a fixed number of each of these types of letters is available and, obviously, no more can be produced. The upward slope of the supply curves occurs because the higher the price, the larger the quantity of letters that will be offered for sale by people who currently own them.)

YOUR TURN: For more practice, do related problem 3.4 on page 94 at the end of this chapter.

The Effect of Demand and Supply Shifts on Equilibrium

We have seen that the interaction of demand and supply in markets determines the quantity of a good that is produced and the price at which it sells. We have also seen that several variables cause demand curves to shift, and other variables cause supply curves to shift. As a result, demand and supply curves in most markets are constantly shifting, and the prices and quantities that represent equilibrium are constantly changing. In this section, we see how shifts in demand and supply curves affect equilibrium price and quantity.

The Effect of Shifts in Supply on Equilibrium

When Microsoft decided to start selling the Zune music player, the market supply curve for music players shifted to the right. Figure 3-9 shows the supply curve shifting from S_1 to S_2. When the supply curve shifts to the right, there will be a surplus at the original equilibrium price, P_1. The surplus is eliminated as the equilibrium price falls to P_2, and the equilibrium quantity rises from Q_1 to Q_2. If existing firms exit the market, the supply curve will shift to the left, causing the equilibrium price to rise and the equilibrium quantity to fall.

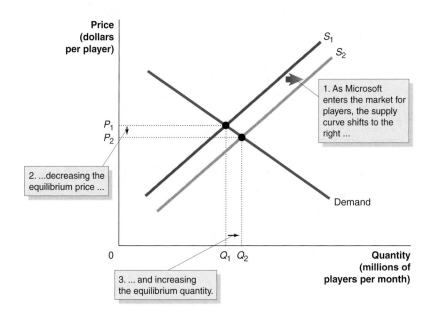

1. As Microsoft enters the market for players, the supply curve shifts to the right ...

2. ...decreasing the equilibrium price ...

3. ... and increasing the equilibrium quantity.

Figure 3-9

The Effect of an Increase in Supply on Equilibrium

If a firm enters a market, as Microsoft entered the market for digital music players when it launched the Zune, the equilibrium price will fall, and the equilibrium quantity will rise.

1. As Microsoft enters the market for digital music players, a larger quantity of players will be supplied at every price, so the market supply curve shifts to the right, from S_1 to S_2, which causes a surplus of players at the original price, P_1.
2. The equilibrium price falls from P_1 to P_2.
3. The equilibrium quantity rises from Q_1 to Q_2.

Making the Connection | The Falling Price of LCD Televisions

Research on flat-screen televisions using liquid crystal displays (LCDs) began in the 1960s. However, it was surprisingly difficult to use this research to produce a television priced low enough for many consumers to purchase. One researcher noted, "In the 1960s, we used to say 'In ten years, we're going to have the TV on the wall.' We said the same thing in the seventies and then in the eighties." A key technical problem in manufacturing LCD televisions was making glass sheets large enough, thin enough, and clean enough to be used as LCD screens. Finally, in 1999, Corning, Inc., developed a process to manufacture glass that was less than 1 millimeter thick and very clean because it was produced without being touched by machinery.

Corning's breakthrough led to what the *Wall Street Journal* described as a "race to build new, better factories." The firms producing the flat screens are all located in Taiwan, South Korea, and Japan. The leading firms are Korea's Samsung Electronics and LG Phillips LCD, Taiwan's AU Optronics, and Japan's Sharp Corporation. In 2004, AU Optronics opened a new factory with 2.4 million square feet of clean room in which the LCD screens are manufactured. This factory is nearly five times as large as the largest factory in which Intel makes computer chips. In all, 10 new factories manufacturing LCD screens came into operation between late 2004 and late 2005. The figure shows that this increase in supply drove the price of a typical large LCD television from $4,000 in the fall of 2004 to $1,600 at the end of 2006, increasing the quantity demanded worldwide from 8 million to 46 million.

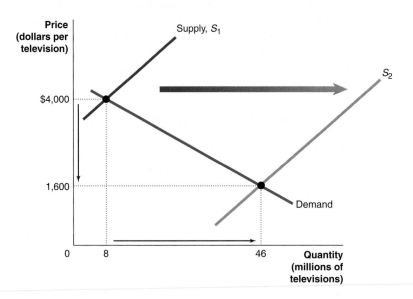

Sources: David Richards, "Sony and Panasonic Flat Screen Kings," Smarthouse.com, February 13, 2007; Evan Ramstad, "Big Display: Once a Footnote, Flat Screens Grow into Huge Industry," *Wall Street Journal*, August 30, 2004, p. A1; and Michael Schuman, "Flat Chance: Prices on Cool TVs Are Dropping as New Factories Come on Line," *Time*, October 18, 2004, pp. 64–66.

YOUR TURN: For more practice, do problem 4.7 on page 95 at the end of this chapter.

The Effect of Shifts in Demand on Equilibrium

When population growth and income growth occur, the market demand for music players shifts to the right. Figure 3-10 shows the effect of a demand curve shifting to the right, from D_1 to D_2. This shift causes a shortage at the original equilibrium price, P_1. To eliminate the shortage, the equilibrium price rises to P_2, and the equilibrium quantity

Figure 3-10

The Effect of an Increase in Demand on Equilibrium

Increases in income and population will cause the equilibrium price and quantity to rise:
1. As population and income grow, the quantity demanded increases at every price, and the market demand curve shifts to the right, from D_1 to D_2, which causes a shortage of digital music players at the original price, P_1.
2. The equilibrium price rises from P_1 to P_2.
3. The equilibrium quantity rises from Q_1 to Q_2.

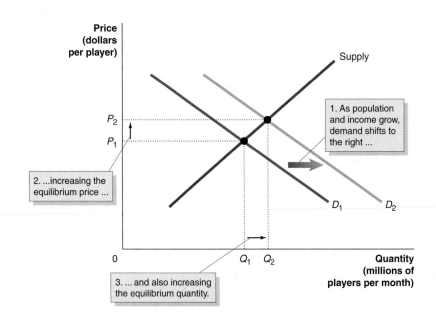

rises from Q_1 to Q_2. By contrast, if the price of a complementary good, such as downloads from music Web sites, were to rise, the demand for music players would decrease. This change would cause the demand curve for players to shift to the left, and the equilibrium price and quantity would both decrease.

The Effect of Shifts in Demand and Supply over Time

Whenever only demand or only supply shifts, we can easily predict the effect on equilibrium price and quantity. But what happens if *both* curves shift? For instance, in many markets, the demand curve shifts to the right over time, as population and income grow. The supply curve also often shifts to the right as new firms enter the market and positive technological change occurs. Whether the equilibrium price in a market rises or falls over time depends on whether demand shifts to the right more than does supply. Panel (a) of Figure 3-11 shows that when demand shifts to the right more than supply, the equilibrium price rises. But, as panel (b) shows, when supply shifts to the right more than demand, the equilibrium price falls.

Table 3-3 on page 86 summarizes all possible combinations of shifts in demand and supply over time and the effects of the shifts on equilibrium price (P) and quantity (Q). For example, the entry in red in the table shows that if the demand curve shifts to the right and the supply curve also shifts to the right, then the equilibrium quantity will increase, while the equilibrium price may increase, decrease, or remain unchanged. To make sure you understand each entry in the table, draw demand and supply graphs to check whether you can reproduce the predicted changes in equilibrium price and quantity. If the entry in the table says the predicted change in equilibrium price or quantity can be either an increase or a decrease, draw two graphs similar to panels (a) and (b) of Figure 3-11, one showing the equilibrium price or quantity increasing and the other showing it decreasing. Note also that in the ambiguous cases where either price or quantity might increase or decrease, it is also possible that price or quantity might remain unchanged. Be sure you understand why this is true.

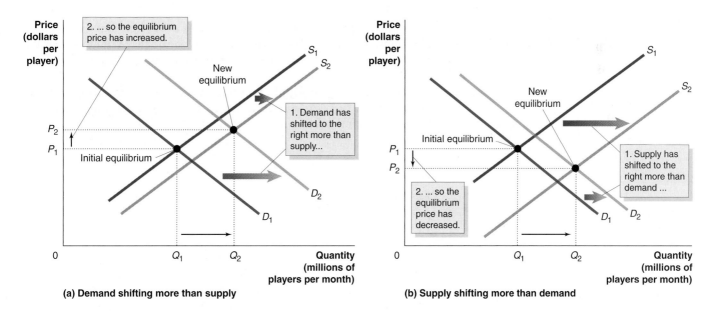

(a) Demand shifting more than supply

(b) Supply shifting more than demand

Figure 3-11 | Shifts in Demand and Supply over Time

Whether the price of a product rises or falls over time depends on whether demand shifts to the right more than supply.

In panel (a), demand shifts to the right more than supply, and the equilibrium price rises.
1. Demand shifts to the right more than supply.
2. Equilibrium price rises from P_1 to P_2.

In panel (b), supply shifts to the right more than demand, and the equilibrium price falls.
1. Supply shifts to the right more than demand.
2. Equilibrium price falls from P_1 to P_2.

TABLE 3-3

How Shifts in Demand and Supply Affect Equilibrium Price (*P*) and Quantity (*Q*)

	SUPPLY CURVE UNCHANGED	SUPPLY CURVE SHIFTS TO THE RIGHT	SUPPLY CURVE SHIFTS TO THE LEFT
DEMAND CURVE UNCHANGED	*Q* unchanged *P* unchanged	*Q* increases *P* decreases	*Q* decreases *P* increases
DEMAND CURVE SHIFTS TO THE RIGHT	*Q* increases *P* increases	*Q* increases *P* increases or decreases	*Q* increases or decreases *P* increases
DEMAND CURVE SHIFTS TO THE LEFT	*Q* decreases *P* decreases	*Q* increases or decreases *P* decreases	*Q* decreases *P* increases or decreases

Solved Problem | 3-4

High Demand and Low Prices in the Lobster Market?

During the spring, when demand for lobster is relatively low, Maine lobstermen are able to sell their lobster catches for about $4.50 per pound. During the summer, when demand for lobster is much higher, Maine lobstermen are able to sell their lobster catches for only about $3.00 per pound. It may seem strange that the market price is higher when demand is low than when demand is high. Can you resolve this paradox with the help of a demand and supply graph?

SOLVING THE PROBLEM:

Step 1: **Review the chapter material.** This problem is about how shifts in demand and supply curves affect the equilibrium price, so you may want to review the section "The Effect of Shifts in Demand and Supply over Time," which begins on page 85.

Step 2: **Draw the demand and supply graph.** Draw a demand and supply graph, showing the market equilibrium in the spring. Label the equilibrium price $4.50. Label both the demand and supply curves "spring."

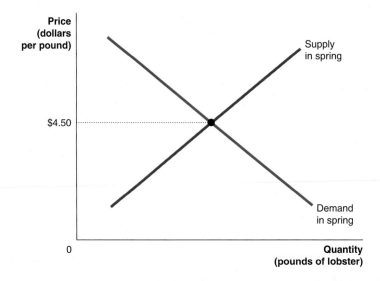

Step 3: **Add to your graph a demand curve for summer.**

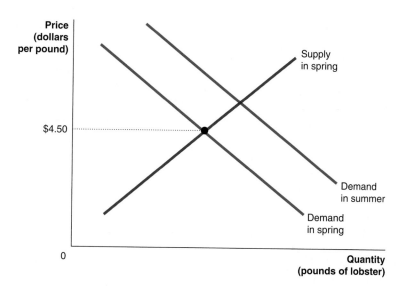

Step 4: **Explain the graph.** After studying the graph, it is possible to see how the equilibrium price can fall from $4.50 to $3.00, despite the increase in demand: The supply curve must have shifted to the right by enough to cause the equilibrium price to fall to $3.00. Draw the new supply curve, label it "summer," and label the new equilibrium price $3.00. The demand for lobster does increase in summer compared with the spring. But the increase in the supply of lobster between spring and summer is even greater. So, the equilibrium price falls.

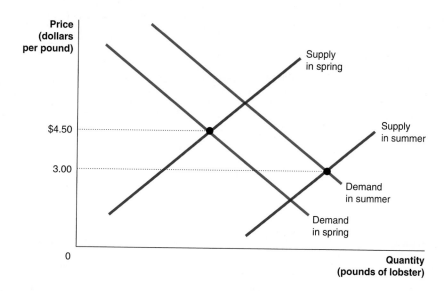

Source: Carey Goldberg, "Down East, the Lobster Hauls Are Up Big," *New York Times*, May 31, 2001.

YOUR TURN: For more practice, do related problem 4.5 on page 95 at the end of this chapter.

>> **End Solved Problem 3-4**

Shifts in a Curve versus Movements along a Curve

When analyzing markets using demand and supply curves, it is important to remember that *when a shift in a demand or supply curve causes a change in equilibrium price, the change in price does not cause a further shift in demand or supply*. For instance, suppose an increase in supply causes the price of a good to fall, while everything else that affects the willingness of consumers to buy the good is constant. The result will be an increase in the quantity demanded but not an increase in demand. For demand to increase, the whole curve must shift. The point is the same for supply: If the price of the good falls but everything else that affects the willingness of sellers to supply the good is constant, the quantity supplied decreases, but the supply does not. For supply to decrease, the whole curve must shift.

Don't Let This Happen to **YOU!**

Remember: A Change in a Good's Price Does *Not* Cause the Demand or Supply Curve to Shift

Suppose a student is asked to draw a demand and supply graph to illustrate how an increase in the price of oranges would affect the market for apples, other variables being constant. He draws the graph on the left below and explains it as follows: "Because apples and oranges are substitutes, an increase in the price of oranges will cause an initial shift to the right in the demand curve for apples, from D_1 to D_2. However, because this initial shift in the demand curve for apples results in a higher price for apples, P_2, consumers will find apples less desirable, and the demand curve will shift to the left, from D_2 to D_3, resulting in a final equilibrium price of P_3." Do you agree or disagree with the student's analysis?

You should disagree. The student has correctly understood that an increase in the price of oranges will cause the demand curve for apples to shift to the right. But the second

demand curve shift the student describes, from D_2 to D_3, will not take place. Changes in the price of a product do not result in shifts in the product's demand curve. Changes in the price of a product result only in movements along a demand curve.

The graph on the right below shows the correct analysis. The increase in the price of oranges causes the demand curve for apples to increase from D_1 to D_2. At the original price, P_1, the increase in demand initially results in a shortage of apples equal to $Q_3 - Q_1$. But, as we have seen, a shortage causes the price to increase until the shortage is eliminated. In this case, the price will rise to P_2, where the quantity demanded and the quantity supplied are both equal to Q_2. Notice that the increase in price causes a decrease in the *quantity demanded* from Q_3 to Q_2, but does *not* cause a decrease in demand.

YOUR TURN: Test your understanding by doing related problems 4.13 and 4.14 on page 96 at the end of this chapter.

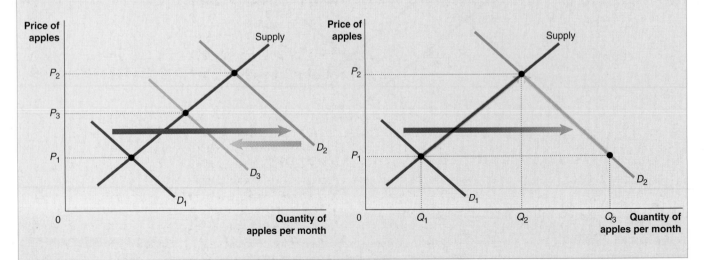

>> Continued from page 67

Economics in YOUR Life!

At the beginning of the chapter, we asked you to consider two questions: Would you choose to buy a Zune if it had a lower price than a comparable iPod? and Would you choose a Zune if the songs sold on Zune Marketplace were cheaper than the songs sold on iTunes? To determine the answers, you have to recognize that iPods and Zunes are substitutes, while Zunes and songs sold on Zune Marketplace are complements. If a Zune had a lower price than an iPod, this would cause consumers to purchase the Zune rather than the iPod, provided that the two players have the same features. If consumers believe that the Zune and the iPod are very close substitutes, a fall in the price of Zunes would cause the demand for iPods to decline, as the quantity of Zunes demanded increased. If Microsoft reduced the price of a song sold on Zune Marketplace so that it was lower than the price of the same song on iTunes, even if iPods and Zunes had the same price, the demand for Zunes would increase, and the demand for iPods would decrease.

Conclusion

The interaction of demand and supply determines market equilibrium. The model of demand and supply provides us with a powerful tool for predicting how changes in the actions of consumers and firms will cause changes in equilibrium prices and quantities. As we have seen in this chapter, the model can often be used to analyze markets that do not meet all the requirements for being perfectly competitive. As long as there is intense competition among sellers, the model of demand and supply can often successfully predict changes in prices and quantities. We will use the model in the next chapter to analyze economic efficiency and the results of government-imposed price floors and price ceilings. Before moving on, read *An Inside Look* on the next page to learn how Apple and AT&T benefit from collaborating on the iPhone.

WALL STREET JOURNAL, FEBRUARY 17, 2007

Apple Coup: How Steve Jobs Played Hardball in iPhone Birth

During a visit to Las Vegas last December for a rodeo event, Cingular Wireless chief executive Stan Sigman received a welcome guest: Steve Jobs. The Apple Inc. chief stopped by Mr. Sigman's Four Seasons hotel suite to show off the iPhone, a sleek cellphone designed to surf the Web and double as an iPod music player.

The phone had been in development by Apple and Cingular [now AT&T] for two years and was weeks away from being revealed to the world. And yet this was the first time Mr. Sigman got to see it. For three hours, Mr. Jobs played with the device, with its touch-screen that allows users to view contacts, dial numbers and flip through photos with the swipe of a finger. Mr. Sigman looked on in awe, according to a person familiar with the meeting . . .

Mr. Jobs is famous for making a splash with new products that upend industry models. Several years ago, he personally lobbied music industry executives and obtained licenses for songs that gave Apple the flexibility to build its successful iTunes store.

Apple eyed the cellphone market as both an opportunity to expand its iPod business and, if ignored, a potential threat to the company, people familiar with its strategy say. Cellphones are gradually offering more sophisticated capabilities and features, including increased storage capacity and entertainment functions. That stands to make them more competitive with iPods over time. Already, music phones like Samsung Electronics Co.'s BlackJack, Sony Ericsson's Walkman models and LG Electronic Inc.'s Chocolate are edging onto Apple's turf . . .

In early 2005, Mr. Jobs called Mr. Sigman to pitch the initial concept of the iPhone. The two executives later met in New York, and agreed to pursue the idea. Mr. Sigman is a Texan who wears cowboy boots and business suits, while Mr. Jobs is a former hippie who sports black turtlenecks and jeans. Despite their vastly different styles, the two executives found common ground. Over the next year and a half, the two sides negotiated to reach an agreement that would make sense for both of them . . .

While Mr. Jobs considered Cingular a logical choice as a partner to carry the device—its GSM technology is the prevailing standard in much of the world—Apple continued to shop its ideas to other carriers. Mr. Jobs reached out to Verizon Wireless chief executive Denny Strigl in the middle of 2005 and proposed a partnership with the carrier, a joint venture of Verizon Communications Inc. and Vodafone Group PLC. The companies held a few discussions over the next year, but the talks eventually soured.

There were a few sticking points. Verizon balked at the notion of cutting out its big retail partners, like Circuit City, who would not be allowed to sell the phone. And the company's chief marketing officer, John Stratton, was firm that Verizon wouldn't give up its ability to sell content like music and videos through its proprietary V Cast service, people familiar with the discussions say. . . .

In January, Mr. Jobs finally unveiled the phone at Macworld, the conference he has used to launch such key products as the iPod Mini. Since then, the two companies have continued to test the iPhone at an undisclosed facility, a person familiar with the matter said. The handful of Cingular people who have access to the sample phones at the company's headquarters were required to sign confidentiality agreements, a person familiar with the matter says. Meanwhile, competitors already are responding. Samsung and LG both have announced phones in recent weeks with designs that look similar to the iPhone. Apple has said it intends to sell 10 million of the devices by 2008, with price tags for two different versions set steeply at $499 and $599.

Cingular, which has more than 60 million customers, hopes the iPhone will give it a lift when it hits stores in June, at a time when attracting new subscribers is getting more difficult for all operators.

Key Points in the Article

The article discusses Apple's new iPhone, which combines features of the iPod and a cell phone. Apple has teamed up with Cingular, now AT&T, to provide cell phone service for the iPhone. The phone will also function as an iPod that plays music in Apple's proprietary format. The iPhone helps both companies. Apple gains because it now has a digital music player that doubles as a cell phone and competes with the other music phones on the market. AT&T gains a potentially large customer base for its cell phone services.

Analyzing the News

a Apple has viewed the evolution of the cell phone as a threat to the iPod because over time, cell phone manufacturers have added features that are similar to those of the iPod. For example, manu-

facturers have increased the storage capacity of cell phones so that people can store their music, pictures, and videos. Cell phones can also function as cameras and video recorders. These cell phones are a threat to the iPod because they are substitute goods that offer many of the same features.

If people are forced to choose just one product, then they might choose a cell phone that can play music over an iPod that cannot function as a phone. The figure shows the result. The demand curve for iPods shifts to the left, which reduces the price and quantity sold of iPods. Because the iPod is a critical product for Apple, this would significantly harm the entire company. Introducing the iPhone is a strategy to protect a very lucrative market for Apple.

b Apple could have worked with a number of different cell phone service providers. Ultimately, Apple chose to partner with Cingular for a couple of reasons. First, Cingular uses technology that is the industry standard. Second, Cingular was willing to make concessions that other cell phone service providers were not willing to make. The chapter opener pointed out that one of the key factors in the iPod's success was that Apple both made the iPod and sold music through iTunes. This means that

the two products were developed by the same company and worked seamlessly together. One reason that Apple did not end up partnering with Verizon is that Verizon insisted on the right to continue to sell downloads of music and videos. This raised the possibility of compatibility problems with downloads available through iTunes.

c AT&T also benefits from the introduction of the iPhone. The iPhone will work only with AT&T's cellular phone service, so if you want to purchase an iPhone, you have to purchase AT&T's service. That means the iPhone and AT&T's services are complementary goods—and as sales of iPhones increase, the demand for AT&T's services should also increase.

Thinking Critically

1. What effect will the introduction of the iPhone have on sales of the iPod? Are there any reasons why someone might want to own both an iPhone and an iPod? Would it be better to think of the iPhone and the iPod as substitutes or complements? Briefly explain.

2. Apple plans to sell two versions of the iPhone: one for $499 and one for $599, which are significantly higher than the price of the most expensive iPod and much higher than the prices of cell phones. Are most customers likely to see the iPhone as a closer substitute for other cell phones or for other digital music players? Is the high price of the iPhone relevant to your answer? Briefly explain.

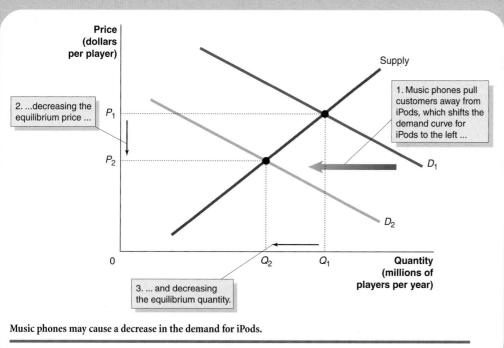

Music phones may cause a decrease in the demand for iPods.

Key Terms

Ceteris paribus ("all else equal"), p. 70

Competitive market equilibrium, p. 80

Complements, p. 71

Demand curve, p. 68

Demand schedule, p. 68

Demographics, p. 72

Income effect, p. 69

Inferior good, p. 71

Law of demand, p. 69

Law of supply, p. 76

Market demand, p. 68

Market equilibrium, p. 80

Normal good, p. 71

Perfectly competitive market, p. 68

Quantity demanded, p. 68

Quantity supplied, p. 75

Shortage, p. 80

Substitutes, p. 71

Substitution effect, p. 69

Supply curve, p. 76

Supply schedule, p. 76

Surplus, p. 80

Technological change, p. 77

3.1 LEARNING OBJECTIVE   3.1 | Discuss the variables that influence demand, **pages 68–75.**

The Demand Side of the Market

Summary

The model of demand and supply is the most powerful in economics. The model applies exactly only to **perfectly competitive markets**, where there are many buyers and sellers, all the products sold are identical, and there are no barriers to new sellers entering the market. But the model can also be useful in analyzing markets that don't meet all of these requirements. The **quantity demanded** is the amount of a good or service that a consumer is willing and able to purchase at a given price. A **demand schedule** is a table that shows the relationship between the price of a product and the quantity of the product demanded. A **demand curve** is a graph that shows the relationship between the price of a good and the quantity of the good consumers are willing and able to buy over a period of time. **Market demand** is the demand by all consumers of a given good or service. The **law of demand** states that *ceteris paribus*—holding everything else constant—the quantity of a product demanded increases when the price falls and decreases when the price rises. Demand curves slope downward because of the **substitution effect**, which is the change in quantity demanded that results from a price change making one good more or less expensive relative to another good, and the **income effect**, which is the change in quantity demanded of a good that results from the effect of a change in the good's price on consumer purchasing power. Changes in income, the prices of related goods, tastes, population and demographics, and expected future prices all cause the demand curve to shift. **Substitutes** are goods that can be used for the same purpose. **Complements** are goods that are used together. A **normal good** is a good for which demand increases as income increases. An **inferior good** is a good for which demand decreases as income increases. **Demographics** are the characteristics of a population with respect to age, race, and gender. A change in demand refers to a shift of the demand curve. A change in quantity demanded refers to a movement along the demand curve as a result of a change in the product's price.

 Visit www.myeconlab.com to complete these exercises online and get instant feedback.

Review Questions

1.1 What is a demand schedule? What is a demand curve?

1.2 What do economists mean when they use the Latin expression *ceteris paribus*?

1.3 What is the difference between a change in demand and a change in quantity demanded?

1.4 What is the law of demand? What are the main variables that will cause the demand curve to shift? Give an example of each.

Problems and Applications

1.5 (Related to the *Making the Connection* on page 71) For each of the following pairs of products, state which are complements, which are substitutes, and which are unrelated.
 a. Pepsi and Coke
 b. Oscar Mayer hot dogs and Wonder hot dog buns
 c. Jif peanut butter and Smucker's strawberry jam
 d. iPods and Texas Instruments financial calculators

1.6 (Related to the *Chapter Opener* on page 66) Suppose Apple discovers that it is selling relatively few downloads of television programs on iTunes. Are downloads of television programs substitutes or complements for downloads of music? For downloads of movies? How might the answers to these questions affect Apple's decision about whether to continue offering downloads of television programs on iTunes?

1.7 State whether each of the following events will result in a movement along the demand curve for McDonald's Big Mac hamburgers or whether it will cause the curve to shift. If the demand curve shifts, indicate whether it will shift to the left or to the right and draw a graph to illustrate the shift.
 a. The price of Burger King's Whopper hamburger declines.

b. McDonald's distributes coupons for $1.00 off on a purchase of a Big Mac.

c. Because of a shortage of potatoes, the price of French fries increases.

d. Kentucky Fried Chicken raises the price of a bucket of fried chicken.

1.8 **(Related to the** *Making the Connection* **on page 72)** Name three products whose demand is likely to increase rapidly if the following demographic groups increase at a faster rate than the population as a whole:

a. Teenagers

b. Children under five

c. People over age 65

1.9 Suppose the data in the following table present the price of a base model Ford Explorer sport-utility vehicle (SUV) and the quantity of Explorers sold. Do these data indicate that the demand curve for Explorers is upward sloping? Explain.

YEAR	PRICE	QUANTITY
2006	$27,865	325,265
2007	28,325	330,648
2008	28,765	352,666

1.10 **(Related to the** *Making the Connection* **on page 75)** In early 2007, Apple forecast that it would sell 10 million iPhones during the product's first year on the market. What factors could affect the accuracy of this forecast? Is the forecast likely to be more or less accurate than Apple's forecast of how many iPods they would sell during the same time period? Briefly explain.

>> **End Learning Objective 3.1**

3.2 LEARNING OBJECTIVE   3.2 | Discuss the variables that influence supply, **pages 75–79.**

The Supply Side of the Market

Summary

The **quantity supplied** is the amount of a good that a firm is willing and able to supply at a given price. A **supply schedule** is a table that shows the relationship between the price of a product and the quantity of the product supplied. A **supply curve** shows on a graph the relationship between the price of a product and the quantity of the product supplied. When the price of a product rises, producing the product is more profitable, and a greater amount will be supplied. The **law of supply** states that, holding everything else constant, the quantity of a product supplied increases when the price rises and decreases when the price falls. Changes in the prices of inputs, technology, the prices of substitutes in production, expected future prices, and the number of firms in a market all cause the supply curve to shift. **Technological change** is a positive or negative change in the ability of a firm to produce a given level of output with a given quantity of inputs. A change in supply refers to a shift of the supply curve. A change in quantity supplied refers to a movement along the supply curve as a result of a change in the product's price.

myeconlab Visit www.myeconlab.com to complete these exercises
Get Ahead of the Curve online and get instant feedback.

Review Questions

2.1 What is a supply schedule? What is a supply curve?

2.2 What is the law of supply? What are the main variables that will cause a supply curve to shift? Give an example of each.

Problems and Applications

2.3 Briefly explain whether each of the following statements describes a change in supply or a change in the quantity supplied.

a. To take advantage of high prices for snow shovels during a very snowy winter, Alexander Shovels, Inc., decides to increase output.

b. The success of Apple's iPod leads more firms to begin producing digital music players.

c. In the six months following Hurricane Katrina, production of oil in the Gulf of Mexico declined by 25 percent.

2.4 Will each firm in a given industry always supply the same quantity as every other firm at each price? What factors might cause the quantity of digital music players supplied by each firm at each price to be different?

2.5 If the price of a good increases, is the increase in the quantity of the good supplied likely to be smaller or larger, the longer the time period being considered? Briefly explain.

>> **End Learning Objective 3.2**

Market Equilibrium: Putting Demand and Supply Together

Summary

Market equilibrium occurs where the demand curve intersects the supply curve. A **competitive market equilibrium** has a market equilibrium with many buyers and many sellers. Only at this point is the quantity demanded equal to the quantity supplied. Prices above equilibrium result in **surpluses**, with the quantity supplied being greater than the quantity demanded. Surpluses cause the market price to fall. Prices below equilibrium result in **shortages**, with the quantity demanded being greater than the quantity supplied. Shortages cause the market price to rise.

myeconlab Visit www.myeconlab.com to complete these exercises
Get Ahead of the Curve online and get instant feedback.

Review Questions

3.1 What do economists mean by market equilibrium?

3.2 What happens in a market if the current price is above the equilibrium price? What happens if the current price is below the equilibrium price?

Problems and Applications

3.3 Briefly explain whether you agree with the following statement: "When there is a shortage of a good,

consumers eventually give up trying to buy it, so the demand for the good declines, and the price falls until the market is finally in equilibrium."

3.4 (Related to *Solved Problem 3-3* on page 81) In *The Wealth of Nations*, Adam Smith discussed what has come to be known as the "diamond and water paradox":

> Nothing is more useful than water: but it will purchase scarce anything; scarce anything can be had in exchange for it. A diamond, on the contrary, has scarce any value in use; but a very great quantity of other goods may frequently be had in exchange for it.

Graph the market for diamonds and the market for water. Show how it is possible for the price of water to be much lower than the price of diamonds, even though the demand for water is much greater than the demand for diamonds.

3.5 Briefly explain under what conditions zero would be the equilibrium quantity.

3.6 If a market is in equilibrium, is it necessarily true that all buyers and all sellers are satisfied with the market price? Briefly explain.

>> End Learning Objective 3.3

The Effect of Demand and Supply Shifts on Equilibrium

Summary

In most markets, demand and supply curves shift frequently, causing changes in equilibrium prices and quantities. Over time, if demand increases more than supply, equilibrium price will rise. If supply increases more than demand, equilibrium price will fall.

myeconlab Visit www.myeconlab.com to complete these exercises
Get Ahead of the Curve online and get instant feedback.

Review Questions

4.1 Draw a demand and supply curve to show the effect on the equilibrium price in a market in the following two situations:
   a. The demand curve shifts to the right.
   b. The supply curve shifts to the left.

4.2 If, over time, the demand curve for a product shifts to the right more than the supply curve does, what will happen to the equilibrium price? What will happen to the equilibrium price if the supply curve shifts to the right more than the demand curve? For each case, draw a demand and supply graph to illustrate your answer.

Problems and Applications

4.3 As oil prices rose during 2006, the demand for alternative fuels increased. Ethanol, one alternative fuel, is made from corn. According to an article in the *Wall Street Journal*, the price of tortillas, which are made from corn, also rose during 2006: "The price spike [in tortillas] is part of a ripple effect from the ethanol boom."

a. Draw a demand and supply graph for the corn market and use it to show the effect on this market of an increase in the demand for ethanol. Be sure to indicate the equilibrium price and quantity before and after the increase in the demand for ethanol.

b. Draw a demand and supply graph for the tortilla market and use it to show the effect on this market of an increase in the price of corn. Once again, be sure to indicate the equilibrium price and quantity before and after the increase in the demand for ethanol.

Source: Mark Gongloff, "Tortilla Soup," *Wall Street Journal*, January 25, 2007.

4.4 A recent study indicated that "stricter college alcohol policies, such as raising the price of alcohol, or banning alcohol on campus, decrease the number of students who use marijuana."

a. On the basis of this information, are alcohol and marijuana substitutes or complements?

b. Suppose that campus authorities reduce the supply of alcohol on campus. Use demand and supply graphs to illustrate the impact on the campus alcohol and marijuana markets.

Source: Jenny Williams, Rosalie Pacula, Frank Chaloupka, and Henry Wechsler, "Alcohol and Marijuana Use Among College Students: Economic Complements or Substitutes?" *Health Economics*, Volume 13, Issue 9, September 2005, pp. 825–843.

4.5 (Related to *Solved Problem 3-4* on page 86) The demand for watermelons is highest during summer and lowest during winter. Yet watermelon prices are normally lower in summer than in winter. Use a demand and supply graph to demonstrate how this is possible. Be sure to carefully label the curves in your graph and to clearly indicate the equilibrium summer price and the equilibrium winter price.

4.6 According to an article in the *Wall Street Journal*:

As occupancy rates at luxury hotels have grown 13% over the last five years, prices have risen by 19%, according to Smith Travel Research. (That comes despite an 18.5% increase in the number of rooms over the same period.)

Use a demand and supply graph to explain how these three things could be true: an increase in the equilibrium quantity of hotel rooms occupied, an increase in the equilibrium price of hotel rooms, and an increase in the number of hotel rooms available.

Source: Nancy Keates, "Cracking Down on Chair Hogs," *Wall Street Journal*, February 23, 2007, p. W1.

4.7 (Related to the *Making the Connection* on page 83) The average price of a high-definition plasma or LCD television fell between 2001 and 2006, from more than $8,000 to about $1,500. During that period, Sharp, Matsushita Electric Industrial, and Samsung all began producing plasma or LCD televisions. Use a demand and supply graph to explain what happened to the quantity of plasma and LCD televisions sold during this period.

4.8 According to an article in the *Wall Street Journal*, during 2006, the demand for full-size pickup trucks declined as a result of rising gas prices and a decline in housing construction (construction firms are an important part of the market for full-size pickup trucks). At the same time, Toyota began production of trucks at a new truck factory in Texas.

a. Draw a demand and supply graph illustrating these developments in the market for full-size pickup trucks. Be sure to indicate changes in the equilibrium price and equilibrium quantity.

b. Briefly discuss whether this problem provides enough information to determine whether the equilibrium quantity of trucks increased or decreased.

Source: Neal E. Boudette and Jeffrey C. McCracken, "Detroit's Cash Cow Stumbles," *Wall Street Journal*, August 1, 2006, p. B1.

4.9 Beginning in the late 1990s, many consumers were having their vision problems corrected with laser surgery. An article in the *Wall Street Journal* noted two developments in the market for laser eye surgery. The first involved increasing concerns related to side effects from the surgery, including blurred vision and, occasionally, blindness. The second development was that the companies renting eye-surgery machinery to doctors had reduced their charges. One large company had cut its charge from $250 per patient to $100. Use a demand and supply graph to illustrate the effects of these two developments on the market for laser eye surgery.

Source: Laura Johannes and James Bandler, "Slowing Economy, Safety Concerns Zap Growth in Laser Eye Surgery," *Wall Street Journal*, January 8, 2001, p. B1.

4.10 The market for autographs, including letters or other documents signed by famous people, is subject to frequent large price changes, as are markets for most collectibles. The following table is adapted from one that originally appeared in an article in the *Wall Street Journal*. It gives the 1997 price for an autograph, the 2001 price, and a brief comment by the *Wall Street Journal* reporter. Use the information contained in the Comment column of the table to draw a demand and supply graph for each of the three autographs listed that can account for the change in its market price from 1997 to 2001.

AUTOGRAPH	1997 PRICE	2001 PRICE	COMMENT
The Beatles	$2,500	$7,475	"As boomers get rich, so do prices for pieces . . . signed by the Fab Four."
Princess Diana	14,000	2,000	"Demand rose after her death in 1997, but now the market's full of items like her signed Christmas cards."
Robert E. Lee	200,000	100,000	"The Civil War's out."

Source: Brooks Barnes, "Signature Market: Hard to Read," *Wall Street Journal*, July 13, 2001.

4.11 Historically, the production of many perishable foods, such as dairy products, was highly seasonal. Thus, as the supply of those products fluctuated, prices tended to fluctuate tremendously—typically by 25 to 50 percent or more—over the course of the year. One impact of mechanical refrigeration, which was commercialized on a large scale in the last decade of the nineteenth century, was that suppliers could store perishables from one season to the next. Economists have estimated that as a result of refrigerated storage, wholesale prices rose by roughly 10 percent during peak supply periods, while they fell by almost the same amount during the off season. Use a demand and supply graph for each season to illustrate how refrigeration affected the market for perishable food.

Source: Lee A. Craig, Barry Goodwin, and Thomas Grennes, "The Effect of Mechanical Refrigeration on Nutrition in the U.S.," *Social Science History*, Vol. 28, No. 2 (Summer 2004), pp. 327–328.

4.12 Briefly explain whether each of the following statements is true or false.

a. If the demand and supply for a product both increase, the equilibrium quantity of the product must also increase.

b. If the demand and supply for a product both increase, the equilibrium price of the product must also increase.

c. If the demand for a product decreases and the supply of the product increases, the equilibrium price of the product may increase or decrease, depending on whether supply or demand has shifted more.

4.13 **(Related to the** *Don't Let This Happen to You!* **on page 88)** A student writes the following: "Increased production leads to a lower price, which in turn increases demand." Do you agree with his reasoning? Briefly explain.

4.14 **(Related to the** *Don't Let This Happen To You!* **on page 88)** A student was asked to draw a demand and supply graph to illustrate the effect on the laptop computer market of a fall in the price of computer hard drives, *ceteris paribus*. She drew the graph at the top of the next column and explained it as follows:

> Hard drives are an input to laptop computers, so a fall in the price of hard drives will cause the supply curve for personal computers to shift to the right (from S_1 to S_2). Because this shift in the supply curve results in a lower price (P_2), consumers will want to buy more laptops, and the demand curve will shift to the right (from D_1 to D_2). We know that more laptops will be sold, but we can't be sure whether the price of laptops will rise or fall. That depends on whether the supply curve or the demand curve has shifted farther to the right. I assume that the effect on supply is greater than the effect on demand, so

I show the final equilibrium price (P_3) as being lower than the initial equilibrium price (P_1).

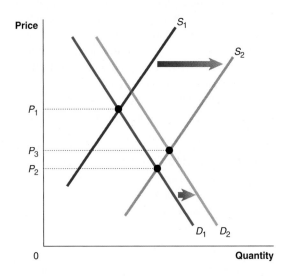

Explain whether you agree or disagree with the student's analysis. Be careful to explain exactly what—if anything—you find wrong with her analysis.

4.15 Following are four graphs and four market scenarios, each of which would cause either a movement along the supply curve for Pepsi or a shift of the supply curve. Match each scenario with the appropriate graph.

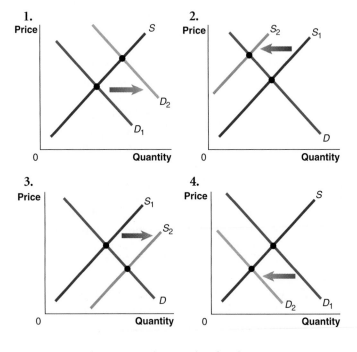

a. A decrease in the supply of Coke

b. A drop in the average household income in the United States from $42,000 to $41,000

c. An improvement in soft-drink bottling technology

d. An increase in the price of sugar

4.16 David Surdam, an economist at Loyola University of Chicago, makes the following observation of the world cotton market at the beginning of the Civil War:

> As the supply of American-grown raw cotton decreased and the price of raw cotton increased, there would be a *movement along* the supply curve of non-American raw cotton suppliers, and the quantity supplied by these producers would increase.

Illustrate this observation with one demand and supply graph for the market for American-grown cotton and another demand and supply graph for the market for non-American cotton. Make sure your graphs clearly show (1) the initial equilibrium before the decrease in the supply of American-grown cotton and (2) the final equilibrium. Also clearly show any shifts in the demand and supply curves for each market.

Source: David G. Surdam, "King Cotton: Monarch or Pretender? The State of the Market for Raw Cotton on the Eve of the American Civil War," *The Economic History Review*, Vol. 51, No. 1 (February 1998), p. 116.

4.17 Proposals have been made to increase government regulation of firms providing childcare services by, for instance, setting education requirements for childcare workers. Suppose that these regulations increase the quality of childcare and cause the demand for childcare services to increase. At the same time, assume that complying with the new government regulations increases the costs of firms providing childcare services. Draw a demand and supply graph to illustrate the effects of these changes in the market for childcare services. Briefly explain whether the total quantity of childcare services purchased will increase or decrease as a result of regulation.

4.18 Below are the supply and demand functions for two markets. One of the markets is for BMW automobiles, and the other is for a cancer-fighting drug, without which lung cancer patients will die. Briefly explain which diagram most likely represents which market.

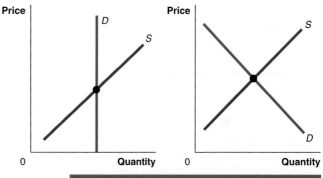

>> End Learning Objective 3.4

Chapter 4

Economic Efficiency, Government Price Setting, and **Taxes**

Should the Government Control Apartment Rents?

Robert F. Moss owns an apartment building in New York City. Unlike most other business owners, he is not free to charge the prices he would like for the service he offers. In New York, San Francisco, Los Angeles, and nearly 200 smaller cities, apartments are subject to rent control by the local government. Rent control puts a legal limit on the rent that landlords can charge for an apartment.

New York City has two million apartments, about one million of which are subject to rent control. The other one million apartments have their rents determined in the market by the demand and supply for apartments. Mr. Moss's building includes apartments that are rent controlled and apartments that are not. The market-determined rents are usually far above the controlled rents. The government regulations that determine what Mr. Moss can charge for a rent-controlled apartment are very complex. The following is Mr. Moss's description:

> When [an apartment] is vacated, state rent laws entitle landlords to raise rents in three primary ways: a vacancy increase of 20 percent for a new tenant's two-year lease (a bit less for a one-year lease); one-fortieth per month of the cost of any improvements, and a "longevity bonus" for longtime residents (calculated at six-tenths of 1 percent times the tenant's last legal rent multiplied by the number of years of residency beyond eight). . . . Apartments renting for $2,000 a month are automatically deregulated if they are vacant. Occupied apartments whose rent reaches that figure can be deregulated if the income of the tenants has been $175,000 or more for two years.

As this description shows, someone earning a living by renting out apartments in New York City has to deal with much more complex government regulation of prices than someone who owns, for instance, a McDonald's restaurant.

Larger companies also struggle with the complexity of rent-control regulations. This was the case for several companies that built multiple apartment buildings in New York during the 1970s. In exchange for renting apartments to moderate- and low-income tenants at controlled rents, the companies were allowed to charge market rents after 20 years. Unfortunately for the companies, when the 20 years were over, attempts to start charging market rents were often met with lawsuits from unhappy tenants. New York Mayor Michael Bloomberg proposed that the law be changed to keep many of these apartment buildings under rent control.

Tenants in rent-controlled apartments in New York are very reluctant to see rent control end because rents for rent-controlled apartments are much lower than rents for apartments that aren't rent controlled. As we will see in this chapter, however rent control can also cause significant problems for renters. **AN INSIDE LOOK AT POLICY** on **page 122** explores the debate over rent control laws in Los Angeles.

Source: Robert F. Moss, "A Landlord's Lot Is Sometimes Not an Easy One," *New York Times*, August 3, 2003, Section 11, p. 1.

LEARNING Objectives

After studying this chapter, you should be able to:

4.1 Distinguish between the concepts of **consumer surplus** and **producer surplus**, page 100.

4.2 Understand the concept of **economic efficiency**, page 105.

4.3 Explain the economic effect of government-imposed **price ceilings** and **price floors**, page 107.

4.4 Analyze the economic impact of **taxes**, page 115.

APPENDIX Use **quantitative** demand and supply **analysis**, page 131.

Economics in YOUR Life!

Does Rent Control Make It Easier to Find an Affordable Apartment?

Suppose you have job offers in two cities. One factor in deciding which job to accept is whether you can find an affordable apartment. If one city has rent control, are you more likely to find an affordable apartment in that city, or would you be better off looking for an apartment in a city without rent control? As you read the chapter, see if you can answer this question. You can check your answer against the one we provide at the end of the chapter. **>> Continued on page 120**

W e saw in Chapter 3 that, in a competitive market, the price adjusts to ensure that the quantity demanded equals the quantity supplied. Stated another way, in equilibrium, every consumer willing to pay the market price is able to buy as much of the product as the consumer wants, and every firm willing to accept the market price can sell as much as it wants. Even so, consumers would naturally prefer to pay a lower price, and sellers would prefer to receive a higher price. Normally, consumers and firms have no choice but to accept the equilibrium price if they wish to participate in the market. Occasionally, however, consumers succeed in having the government impose a **price ceiling**, which is a legally determined maximum price that sellers may charge. Rent control is an example of a price ceiling. Firms also sometimes succeed in having the government impose a **price floor**, which is a legally determined minimum price that sellers may receive. In markets for farm products such as milk, the government has been setting price floors that are above the equilibrium market price since the 1930s.

Another way in which the government intervenes in markets is by imposing taxes. The government relies on the revenue raised from taxes to finance its operations. As we will see, though, imposing taxes alters the equilibrium in a market.

Unfortunately, whenever the government imposes a price ceiling, a price floor, or a tax, there are predictable negative economic consequences. It is important for government policymakers and voters to understand these negative consequences when evaluating the effects of these policies. Economists have developed the concepts of *consumer surplus, producer surplus*, and *economic surplus*, which we discuss in the next section. In the sections that follow, we use these concepts to analyze the economic effects of price ceilings, price floors, and taxes. (As we will see in later chapters, these concepts are also useful in many other contexts.)

Price ceiling A legally determined maximum price that sellers may charge.

Price floor A legally determined minimum price that sellers may receive.

4.1 LEARNING OBJECTIVE

4.1 | Distinguish between the concepts of consumer surplus and producer surplus.

Consumer Surplus and Producer Surplus

Consumer surplus measures the dollar benefit consumers receive from buying goods or services in a particular market. Producer surplus measures the dollar benefit firms receive from selling goods or services in a particular market. Economic surplus in a market is the sum of consumer surplus plus producer surplus. As we will see, *when the government imposes a price ceiling or a price floor, the amount of economic surplus in a market is reduced*—in other words, price ceilings and price floors reduce the total benefit to consumers and firms from buying and selling in a market. To understand why this is true, we need to understand how consumer surplus and producer surplus are determined.

Consumer Surplus

Consumer surplus measures the difference between the highest price a consumer is willing to pay and the price the consumer actually pays. For example, suppose you are in Wal-Mart and you see a DVD of *Iron Man* on the rack. No price is indicated on the package, so you bring it over to the register to check the price. As you walk to the register, you think to yourself that $20 is the highest price you would be willing to pay. At the register, you find out that the price is actually $12, so you buy the DVD. Your consumer surplus in this example is $8: the difference between the $20 you were willing to pay and the $8 you actually paid.

We can use the demand curve to measure the total consumer surplus in a market. Demand curves show the willingness of consumers to purchase a product at different prices. Consumers are willing to purchase a product up to the point where the marginal benefit of consuming a product is equal to its price. The **marginal benefit** is the additional

Consumer surplus The difference between the highest price a consumer is willing to pay and the price the consumer actually pays.

Marginal benefit The additional benefit to a consumer from consuming one more unit of a good or service.

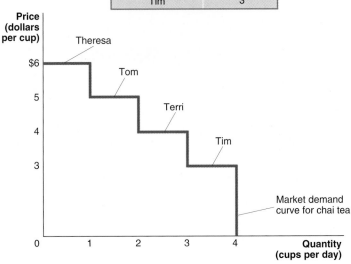

Consumer	Highest Price Willing to Pay
Theresa	$6
Tom	5
Terri	4
Tim	3

Figure 4-1

Deriving the Demand Curve for Chai Tea

With four consumers in the market for chai tea, the demand curve is determined by the highest price each consumer is willing to pay. For prices above $6, no tea is sold because $6 is the highest price any consumer is willing to pay. For prices of $3 and below, all four consumers are willing to buy a cup of tea.

benefit to a consumer from consuming one more unit of a good or service. As a simple example, suppose there are only four consumers in the market for chai tea: Theresa, Tom, Terri, and Tim. Because these four consumers have different tastes for tea and different incomes, the marginal benefit each of them receives from consuming a cup of tea will be different. Therefore, the highest price each is willing to pay for a cup of tea is also different. In Figure 4-1, the information from the table is used to construct a demand curve for chai tea. For prices above $6 per cup, no tea is sold because $6 is the highest price any of the consumers is willing to pay. At a price of $5, both Theresa and Tom are willing to buy, so two cups are sold. At prices of $3 and below, all four consumers are willing to buy, and four cups are sold.

Suppose the market price of tea is $3.50 per cup. As Figure 4-2 on page 102 shows, the demand curve allows us to calculate the total consumer surplus in this market. In panel (a), we can see that the highest price Theresa is willing to pay is $6, but because she pays only $3.50, her consumer surplus is $2.50 (shown by the area of rectangle *A*). Similarly, Tom's consumer surplus is $1.50 (rectangle *B*), and Terri's consumer surplus is $0.50 (rectangle *C*). Tim is unwilling to buy a cup of tea at a price of $3.50, so he doesn't participate in this market and receives no consumer surplus. In this simple example, the total consumer surplus is equal to $2.50 + $1.50 + $0.50 = $4.50 (or the sum of the areas of rectangles *A*, *B*, and *C*). Panel (b) shows that a lower price will increase consumer surplus. If the price of tea drops from $3.50 per cup to $3.00, Theresa, Tom, and Terri each receive $0.50 more in consumer surplus (shown by the shaded areas), so total consumer surplus in the market rises to $6.00. Tim now buys a cup of tea but doesn't receive any consumer surplus because the price is equal to the highest price he is willing to pay. In fact, Tim is indifferent between buying the cup or not—his well-being is the same either way.

The market demand curves shown in Figures 4-1 and 4-2 do not look like the smooth curves we saw in Chapter 3. This is because this example uses a small number of consumers, each consuming a single cup of tea. With many consumers, the market demand curve for chai tea will have the normal smooth shape shown in Figure 4-3. In this figure, the quantity demanded at a price of $2.00 is 15,000 cups per day. We can calculate total consumer surplus in Figure 4-3 the same way we did in Figures 4-1 and

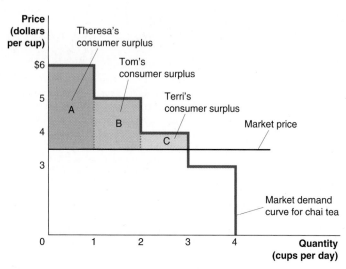

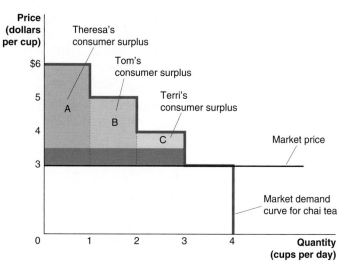

(a) Consumer surplus with a market price of $3.50

(b) Consumer surplus with a market price of $3.00

Figure 4-2 | Measuring Consumer Surplus

Panel (a) shows the consumer surplus for Theresa, Tom, and Terri when the price of tea is $3.50 per cup. Theresa's consumer surplus is equal to the area of rectangle *A* and is the difference between the highest price she would pay—$6—and the market price of $3.50. Tom's consumer surplus is equal to the area of rectangle *B*, and Terri's

consumer surplus is equal to the area of rectangle *C*. Total consumer surplus in this market is equal to the sum of the areas of rectangles *A*, *B*, and *C*, or the total area below the demand curve and above the market price. In panel (b), consumer surplus increases by the shaded area as the market price declines from $3.50 to $3.00.

4-2: by adding up the consumer surplus received on each unit purchased. Once again, we can draw an important conclusion: *The total amount of consumer surplus in a market is equal to the area below the demand curve and above the market price.* Consumer surplus is shown as the blue area in Figure 4-3 and represents the benefit to consumers in excess of the price they paid to purchase the product—in this case, chai tea.

Figure 4-3

Total Consumer Surplus in the Market for Chai Tea

The demand curve tells us that most buyers of chai tea would have been willing to pay more than the market price of $2.00. For each buyer, consumer surplus is equal to the difference between the highest price he or she is willing to pay and the market price actually paid. Therefore, the total amount of consumer surplus in the market for chai tea is equal to the area below the demand curve and above the market price. Consumer surplus represents the benefit to consumers in excess of the price they paid to purchase the product.

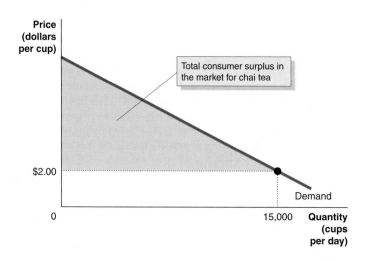

Making the Connection

The Consumer Surplus from Satellite Television

Consumer surplus allows us to measure the benefit consumers receive in excess of the price they paid to purchase a product. Recently, Austan Goolsbee and Amil Petrin, economists at the Graduate

School of Business at the University of Chicago, estimated the consumer surplus that households receive from subscribing to satellite television. To do this, they estimated the demand curve for satellite television and then computed the shaded area shown in the graph.

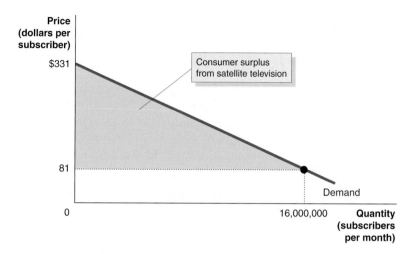

In 2001, the year for which the study was conducted, 16 million consumers paid an average price of $81 per month to subscribe to DIRECTV or DISH Network, the two main providers of satellite television. The demand curve shows that many consumers would have been willing to pay more than $81 rather than do without satellite television. Goolsbee and Petrin calculated that the consumer surplus for households subscribing to satellite television averaged $127 per month, which is the difference between the price they would have paid and the $81 they did pay. The shaded area on the graph represents the total consumer surplus in the market for satellite television. Goolsbee and Petrin estimate that the value of this area is $2 billion. This is one year's benefit to the consumers who subscribe to satellite television.

Source: Austan Goolsbee and Amil Petrin, "The Consumer Gains from Direct Broadcast Satellites and the Competition with Cable TV," *Econometrica*, Vol. 72, No. 2, March 2004, pp. 351–381.

YOUR TURN: Test your understanding by doing related problem 1.8 on page 124 at the end of this chapter.

Producer Surplus

Just as demand curves show the willingness of consumers to buy a product at different prices, supply curves show the willingness of firms to supply a product at different prices. The willingness to supply a product depends on the cost of producing it. Firms will supply an additional unit of a product only if they receive a price equal to the additional cost of producing that unit. **Marginal cost** is the additional cost to a firm of producing one more unit of a good or service. Consider the marginal cost to the firm Heavenly Tea of producing one more cup: In this case, the marginal cost includes the ingredients to make the tea and the wages paid to the worker preparing the tea. Often, the marginal cost of producing a good increases as more of the good is produced during a given period of time. This is the key reason—as we saw in Chapter 3—that supply curves are upward sloping.

Panel (a) of Figure 4-4 shows Heavenly Tea's producer surplus. For simplicity, we show Heavenly producing only a small quantity of tea. The figure shows that Heavenly's marginal cost of producing the first cup of tea is $1.00. Its marginal cost of producing

Marginal cost The additional cost to a firm of producing one more unit of a good or service.

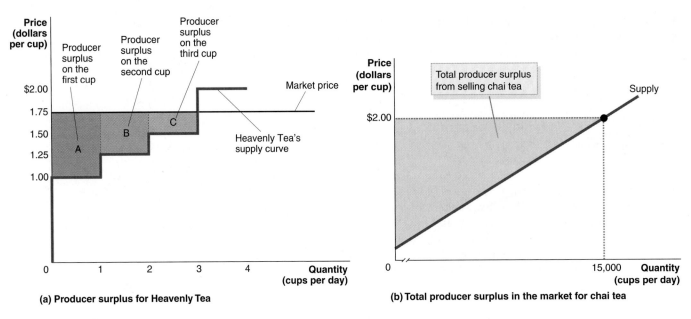

Figure 4-4 | Calculating Producer Surplus

Panel (a) shows Heavenly Tea's producer surplus. Producer surplus is the difference between the lowest price a firm would be willing to accept and the price it actually receives. The lowest price Heavenly Tea is willing to accept to supply a cup of tea is equal to its marginal cost of producing that cup. When the market price of tea is $1.75, Heavenly receives producer surplus of $0.75 on the first cup (the area of

rectangle A), $0.50 on the second cup (rectangle B), and $0.25 on the third cup (rectangle C). In panel (b), the total amount of producer surplus tea sellers receive from selling chai tea can be calculated by adding up for the entire market the producer surplus received on each cup sold. In the figure, total producer surplus is equal to the area above the supply curve and below the market price, shown in red.

Producer surplus The difference between the lowest price a firm would be willing to accept and the price it actually receives.

the second cup is $1.25, and so on. The marginal cost of each cup of tea is the lowest price Heavenly is willing to accept to supply that cup. The supply curve, then, is also a marginal cost curve. Suppose the market price of tea is $1.75 per cup. On the first cup of tea, the price is $0.75 higher than the lowest price Heavenly is willing to accept. **Producer surplus** is the difference between the lowest price a firm would be willing to accept and the price it actually receives. Therefore, Heavenly's producer surplus on the first cup is $0.75 (shown by the area of rectangle A). Its producer surplus on the second cup is $0.50 (rectangle B). Its producer surplus on the third cup is $0.25 (rectangle C). Heavenly will not be willing to supply the fourth cup because the marginal cost of producing it is greater than the market price. Heavenly Tea's total producer surplus is equal to $0.75 + $0.50 + $0.25 = $1.50 (or the sum of rectangles A, B, and C). A higher price will increase producer surplus. For example, if the market price of chai tea rises from $1.75 to $2.00, Heavenly Tea's producer surplus will increase from $1.50 to $2.25. (Make sure you understand how the new level of producer surplus was calculated.)

The supply curve shown in panel (a) of Figure 4-4 does not look like the smooth curves we saw in Chapter 3 because this example uses a single firm producing only a small quantity of tea. With many firms, the market supply curve for chai tea will have the normal smooth shape shown in panel (b) of Figure 4-4. In panel (b), the quantity supplied at a price of $2.00 is 15,000 cups per day. We can calculate total producer surplus in panel (b) the same way we did in panel (a): by adding up the producer surplus received on each cup sold. Therefore, *the total amount of producer surplus in a market is equal to the area above the market supply curve and below the market price*. The total producer surplus tea sellers receive from selling chai tea is shown as the red area in panel (b) of Figure 4-4.

What Consumer Surplus and Producer Surplus Measure

We have seen that consumer surplus measures the benefit to consumers from participating in a market, and producer surplus measures the benefit to producers from participating in a market. It is important, however, to be clear what we mean by this. In a sense, consumer surplus measures the *net* benefit to consumers from participating in a market rather than the *total* benefit. That is, if the price of a product were zero, the consumer surplus in a market would be all of the area under the demand curve. When the price is not zero, consumer surplus is the area below the demand curve and above the market price. So, consumer surplus in a market is equal to the total benefit received by consumers minus the total amount they must pay to buy the good.

Similarly, producer surplus measures the *net* benefit received by producers from participating in a market. If producers could supply a good at zero cost, the producer surplus in a market would be all of the area below the market price. When cost is not zero, producer surplus is the area below the market price and above the supply curve. So, producer surplus in a market is equal to the total amount firms receive from consumers minus the cost of producing the good.

4.2 | Understand the concept of economic efficiency.

The Efficiency of Competitive Markets

In Chapter 3, we defined a *competitive market* as a market with many buyers and many sellers. An important advantage of the market system is that it results in efficient economic outcomes. But what do we mean by *economic efficiency*? The concepts we have developed so far in this chapter give us two ways to think about the economic efficiency of competitive markets. We can think in terms of marginal benefit and marginal cost. We can also think in terms of consumer surplus and producer surplus. As we will see, these two approaches lead to the same outcome, but using both can increase our understanding of economic efficiency.

Marginal Benefit Equals Marginal Cost in Competitive Equilibrium

Figure 4-5 again shows the market for chai tea. Recall from our discussion that the demand curve shows the marginal benefit received by consumers, and the supply curve shows the marginal cost of production. To achieve economic efficiency in this market, the marginal

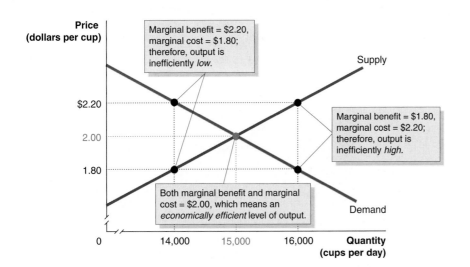

Figure 4-5

Marginal Benefit Equals Marginal Cost Only at Competitive Equilibrium

In a competitive market, equilibrium occurs at a quantity of 15,000 cups and price of $2.00 per cup, where marginal benefit equals marginal cost. This is the economically efficient level of output because every cup has been produced where the marginal benefit to buyers is greater than or equal to the marginal cost to producers.

benefit from the last unit sold should equal the marginal cost of production. The figure shows that this equality occurs at competitive equilibrium where 15,000 cups per day are produced, and marginal benefit and marginal cost are both equal to $2.00. Why is this outcome economically efficient? Because every cup of chai tea has been produced where the marginal benefit to buyers is greater than or equal to the marginal cost to producers.

Another way to see why the level of output at competitive equilibrium is efficient is to consider what would be true if output were at a different level. For instance, suppose that output of chai tea were 14,000 cups per day. Figure 4-5 shows that at this level of output, the marginal benefit from the last cup sold is $2.20, whereas the marginal cost is only $1.80. This level of output is not efficient because 1,000 more cups could be produced for which the additional benefit to consumers would be greater than the additional cost of production. Consumers would willingly purchase those cups, and tea sellers would willingly supply them, making both consumers and sellers better off. Similarly, if the output of chai tea were 16,000 cups per day, the marginal cost of the 16,000th cup is $2.20, whereas the marginal benefit is only $1.80. Tea sellers would only be willing to supply this cup at a price of $2.20, which is $0.40 higher than consumers would be willing to pay. In fact, consumers would not be willing to pay the price tea sellers would need to receive for any cup beyond the 15,000th.

To summarize, we can say this: *Equilibrium in a competitive market results in the economically efficient level of output, where marginal benefit equals marginal cost.*

Economic Surplus

Economic surplus The sum of consumer surplus and producer surplus.

Economic surplus in a market is the sum of consumer surplus and producer surplus. In a competitive market, with many buyers and sellers and no government restrictions, economic surplus is at a maximum when the market is in equilibrium. To see this, let's look one more time at the market for chai tea shown in Figure 4-6. The consumer surplus in this market is the blue area below the demand curve and above the line indicating the equilibrium price of $2.00. The producer surplus is the red area above the supply curve and below the price line.

Deadweight Loss

To show that economic surplus is maximized at equilibrium, consider the situation in which the price of chai tea is *above* the equilibrium price, as shown in Figure 4-7. At a price of $2.20 per cup, the number of cups consumers are willing to buy per day drops from 15,000 to 14,000. At competitive equilibrium, consumer surplus is equal to the sum of areas A, B, and C. At a price of $2.20, fewer cups are sold at a higher price, so consumer surplus declines to just the area of A. At competitive equilibrium, producer surplus is equal to the sum of areas D and E. At the higher price of $2.20, producer surplus changes to be equal to the sum of areas B and D. The sum of consumer and producer surplus—economic surplus—has been reduced to the sum of areas A, B, and D. Notice that this is less than the original economic surplus by an amount equal to areas C and E.

Figure 4-6

Economic Surplus Equals the Sum of Consumer Surplus and Producer Surplus

The economic surplus in a market is the sum of the blue area representing consumer surplus and the red area representing producer surplus.

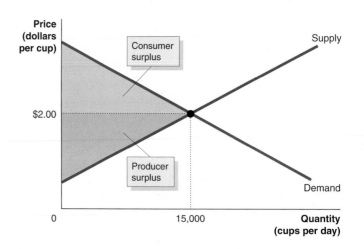

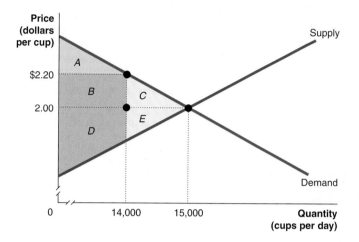

	At Competitive Equilibrium	At a Price of $2.20
Consumer Surplus	A + B + C	A
Producer Surplus	D + E	B + D
Deadweight Loss	None	C + E

Figure 4-7

Economic surplus is maximized when a market is in competitive equilibrium. When a market is not in equilibrium, there is a deadweight loss. When the price of chai tea is $2.20, instead of $2.00, consumer surplus declines from an amount equal to the sum of areas *A, B,* and *C* to just area *A.* Producer surplus increases from the sum of areas *D* and *E* to the sum of areas *B* and *D.* At competitive equilibrium, there is no deadweight loss. At a price of $2.20, there is a deadweight loss equal to the sum of areas *C* and *E.*

Economic surplus has declined because at a price of $2.20, all the cups between the 14,000th and the 15,000th, which would have been produced in competitive equilibrium, are not being produced. These "missing" cups are not providing any consumer or producer surplus, so economic surplus has declined. The reduction in economic surplus resulting from a market not being in competitive equilibrium is called the **deadweight loss.** In the figure, it is equal to the sum of areas *C* and *E.*

Deadweight loss The reduction in economic surplus resulting from a market not being in competitive equilibrium.

Economic Surplus and Economic Efficiency

Consumer surplus measures the benefit to consumers from buying a particular product, such as chai tea. Producer surplus measures the benefit to firms from selling a particular product. Therefore, economic surplus—which is the sum of the benefit to firms plus the benefit to consumers—is the best measure we have of the benefit to society from the production of a particular good or service. This gives us a second way of characterizing the economic efficiency of a competitive market: *Equilibrium in a competitive market results in the greatest amount of economic surplus, or total net benefit to society, from the production of a good or service.* Anything that causes the market for a good or service not to be in competitive equilibrium reduces the total benefit to society from the production of that good or service.

Now we can give a more general definition of *economic efficiency* in terms of our two approaches: **Economic efficiency** is a market outcome in which the marginal benefit to consumers of the last unit produced is equal to its marginal cost of production and in which the sum of consumer surplus and producer surplus is at a maximum.

Economic efficiency A market outcome in which the marginal benefit to consumers of the last unit produced is equal to its marginal cost of production and in which the sum of consumer surplus and producer surplus is at a maximum.

4.3 | Explain the economic effect of government-imposed price ceilings and price floors.

4.3 LEARNING OBJECTIVE

Government Intervention in the Market: Price Floors and Price Ceilings

Notice that we have *not* concluded that every *individual* is better off if a market is at competitive equilibrium. We have only concluded that economic surplus, or the *total* net benefit to society, is greatest at competitive equilibrium. Any individual producer would rather charge a higher price, and any individual consumer would rather pay a lower price, but usually producers can sell and consumers can buy only at the competitive equilibrium price.

Producers or consumers who are dissatisfied with the competitive equilibrium price can lobby the government to legally require that a different price be charged. The U.S. government only occasionally overrides the market outcome by setting prices. When the government does intervene, it can either attempt to aid sellers by requiring that a price be above equilibrium—a price floor—or aid buyers by requiring that a price be below equilibrium—a price ceiling. To affect the market outcome, a price floor must be set above the equilibrium price and a price ceiling must be set below the equilibrium price. Otherwise, the price ceiling or price floor will not be *binding* on buyers and sellers. The preceding section demonstrates that moving away from competitive equilibrium will reduce economic efficiency. We can use the concepts of consumer surplus, producer surplus, and deadweight loss to see more clearly the economic inefficiency of binding price floors and price ceilings.

Price Floors: Government Policy in Agricultural Markets

The Great Depression of the 1930s was the greatest economic disaster in U.S. history, affecting every sector of the U.S. economy. Many farmers were unable to sell their products or could sell them only at very low prices. Farmers were able to convince the federal government to intervene to raise prices by setting price floors for many agricultural products. Government intervention in agriculture—often referred to as the "farm program"—has continued ever since. To see how a price floor in an agricultural market works, suppose that the equilibrium price in the wheat market is $3.00 per bushel but the government decides to set a price floor of $3.50 per bushel. As Figure 4-8 shows, the price of wheat rises from $3.00 to $3.50, and the quantity of wheat sold falls from 2.0 billion bushels per year to 1.8 billion. Initially, suppose that production of wheat also falls to 1.8 billion bushels.

Just as we saw in the earlier example of the market for chai tea (refer to Figure 4-7), the producer surplus received by wheat farmers increases by an amount equal to the area of the red rectangle *A* and falls by an amount equal to the area of the yellow triangle *C*. The area of the red rectangle *A* represents a transfer from consumer surplus to producer surplus. The total fall in consumer surplus is equal to the area of the red rectangle *A* plus the area of the yellow triangle *B*. Wheat farmers benefit from this program, but consumers lose. There is also a deadweight loss equal to the areas of the yellow triangles *B* and *C*, which represents the decline in economic efficiency due to the price floor. There

Figure 4-8

The Economic Effect of a Price Floor in the Wheat Market

If wheat farmers convince the government to impose a price floor of $3.50 per bushel, the amount of wheat sold will fall from 2.0 billion bushels per year to 1.8 billion. If we assume that farmers produce 1.8 billion bushels, producer surplus then increases by the red rectangle *A*—which is transferred from consumer surplus—and falls by the yellow triangle *C*. Consumer surplus declines by the red rectangle *A* plus the yellow triangle *B*. There is a deadweight loss equal to the yellow triangles *B* and *C*, representing the decline in economic efficiency due to the price floor. In reality, a price floor of $3.50 per bushel will cause farmers to expand their production from 2.0 billion to 2.2 billion bushels, resulting in a surplus of wheat.

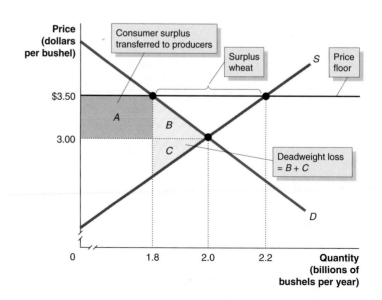

is a deadweight loss because the price floor has reduced the amount of economic surplus in the market for wheat. Or, looked at another way, the price floor has caused the marginal benefit of the last bushel of wheat to be greater than the marginal cost of producing it. We can conclude that a price floor reduces economic efficiency.

The actual federal government farm programs have been more complicated than just legally requiring farmers not to sell their output below a minimum price. We assumed initially that farmers reduce their production of wheat to the amount consumers are willing to buy. In fact, as Figure 4-8 shows, a price floor will cause the quantity of wheat that farmers want to supply to increase from 2.0 billion to 2.2 billion bushels. Because the higher price also reduces the amount of wheat consumers wish to buy, the result is a surplus of 0.4 billion bushels of wheat (the 2.2 billion bushels supplied minus the 1.8 billion demanded).

The federal government's farm programs have often resulted in large surpluses of wheat and other agricultural products. The government has usually either bought the surplus food or paid farmers to restrict supply by taking some land out of cultivation. Because both of these options are expensive, Congress passed the Freedom to Farm Act of 1996. The intent of the act was to phase out price floors and government purchases of surpluses and return to a free market in agriculture. To allow farmers time to adjust, the federal government began paying farmers *subsidies*, or cash payments based on the number of acres planted. Although the subsidies were originally scheduled to be phased out, Congress has continued to pay them.

<table>
<tr><td align="right">Making
the
Connection</td><td>### Price Floors in Labor Markets:
The Debate over Minimum
Wage Policy</td></tr>
</table>

The minimum wage may be the most controversial "price floor." Supporters see the minimum wage as a way of raising the incomes of low-skilled workers. Opponents argue that it results in fewer jobs and imposes large costs on small businesses.

In summer 2008, the national minimum wage as set by Congress is $6.55 per hour for most occupations. (The minimum wage is scheduled to increase to $7.25 per hour in 2009.) It is illegal for an employer to pay less than this wage in those occupations. For most workers, the minimum wage is irrelevant because it is well below the wage employers are voluntarily willing to pay them. But for low-skilled workers—such as workers in fast-food restaurants—the minimum wage is above the wage they would otherwise receive. The following figure shows the effect of the minimum wage on employment in the market for low-skilled labor.

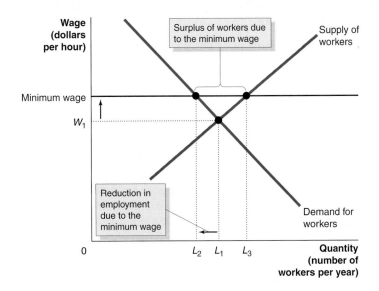

Without a minimum wage, the equilibrium wage would be W_1, and the number of workers hired would be L_1. With a minimum wage set above the equilibrium wage, the quantity of workers demanded by employers declines from L_1 to L_2, and the quantity of labor supplied increases to L_3, leading to a surplus of workers unable to find jobs equal to $L_3 - L_2$. The quantity of labor supplied increases because the higher wage attracts more people to work. For instance, some teenagers may decide that working after school is worthwhile at the minimum wage of $6.55 per hour but would not be worthwhile at a lower wage.

This analysis is very similar to our analysis of the wheat market in Figure 4-8. Just as a price floor in the wheat market leads to less wheat consumed, a price floor in the labor market should lead to fewer workers hired. Views differ sharply among economists, however, concerning how large a reduction in employment the minimum wage causes. For instance, David Card of the University of California, Berkeley, and Alan Krueger of Princeton University conducted a study of fast-food restaurants in New Jersey and Pennsylvania that indicates that the effect of minimum wage increases on employment is very small. Card and Krueger's study has been very controversial, however. Other economists have examined similar data and have come to the different conclusion that the minimum wage leads to a significant decrease in employment.

Whatever the extent of employment losses from the minimum wage, because it is a price floor, it will cause a deadweight loss, just as a price floor in the wheat market does. Therefore, many economists favor alternative policies for attaining the goal of raising the incomes of low-skilled workers. One policy many economists support is the *earned income tax credit*. The earned income tax credit reduces the amount of tax that low-income wage earners would otherwise pay to the federal government. Workers with very low incomes who do not owe any tax receive a payment from the government. Compared with the minimum wage, the earned income tax credit can increase the incomes of low-skilled workers without reducing employment. The earned income tax credit also places a lesser burden on the small businesses that employ many low-skilled workers, and it might cause a smaller loss of economic efficiency.

Sources: David Card and Alan B. Krueger, *Myth and Measurement: The New Economics of the Minimum Wage*, Princeton, NJ: Princeton University Press, 1995; David Neumark and William Wascher, "Minimum Wages and Employment: A Case Study of the Fast-Food Industry in New Jersey and Pennsylvania: Comment," *American Economic Review*, Vol. 90, No. 5, December 2000, pp. 1362–1396; and David Card and Alan B. Krueger, "Minimum Wages and Employment: A Case Study of the Fast-Food Industry in New Jersey and Pennsylvania: Reply," *American Economic Review*, Vol. 90, No. 5, December 2000, pp. 1397–1420.

YOUR TURN: Test your understanding by doing related problem 3.12 on page 127 at the end of this chapter.

Price Ceilings: Government Rent Control Policy in Housing Markets

Support for governments setting price floors typically comes from sellers, and support for governments setting price ceilings typically comes from consumers. For example, when there is a sharp increase in gasoline prices, there are often proposals for the government to impose a price ceiling on the market for gasoline. As we saw in the opener to this chapter, New York is one of the cities that imposes rent controls, which put a ceiling on the maximum rent that landlords can charge for an apartment. Figure 4-9 shows the market for apartments in a city that has rent controls.

Without rent control, the equilibrium rent would be $1,500 per month, and 2,000,000 apartments would be rented. With a maximum legal rent of $1,000 per month, landlords reduce the quantity of apartments supplied to 1,900,000. The fall in the quantity of apartments supplied is the result of some apartments being converted to offices or sold off as condominiums, some small apartment buildings being converted to single-family homes, and, over time, some apartment buildings being abandoned. In New York City, rent control has resulted in whole city blocks being abandoned by landlords who

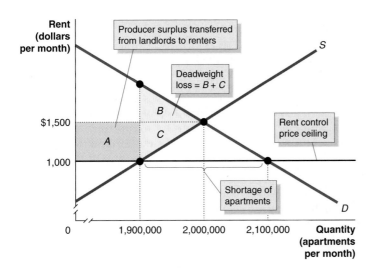

Figure 4-9

The Economic Effect of a Rent Ceiling

Without rent control, the equilibrium rent is $1,500 per month. At that price, 2,000,000 apartments would be rented. If the government imposes a rent ceiling of $1,000, the quantity of apartments supplied falls to 1,900,000, and the quantity of apartments demanded increases to 2,100,000, resulting in a shortage of 200,000 apartments. Producer surplus equal to the area of the blue rectangle *A* is transferred from landlords to renters, and there is a deadweight loss equal to the areas of yellow triangles *B* and *C*.

were unable to cover their costs with the rents they were allowed to charge. In London, when rent controls were applied to rooms and apartments located in a landlord's own home, the quantity of these apartments supplied dropped by 75 percent.

In Figure 4-9, with the rent ceiling of $1,000, the quantity of apartments demanded rises to 2,100,000. There is a shortage of 200,000 apartments. Consumer surplus increases by rectangle *A* and falls by triangle *B*. Rectangle *A* would have been part of producer surplus if rent control were not in place. With rent control, it is part of consumer surplus. Rent control causes the producer surplus received by landlords to fall by rectangle *A* plus triangle *C*. Triangles *B* and *C* represent the deadweight loss. There is a deadweight loss because rent control has reduced the amount of economic surplus in the market for apartments. Rent control has caused the marginal benefit of the last apartment rented to be greater than the marginal cost of supplying it. We can conclude that a price ceiling, such as rent control, reduces economic efficiency. The appendix to this chapter shows how we can make quantitative estimates of the deadweight loss, and it shows the changes in consumer surplus and producer surplus that result from rent control.

Renters as a group benefit from rent controls—total consumer surplus is larger—but landlords lose. Because of the deadweight loss, the total loss to landlords is greater than the gain to renters. Notice also that although renters as a group benefit, the number of renters is reduced, so some renters are made worse off by rent controls because they are unable to find an apartment at the legal rent.

Don't Let This Happen to **YOU!**

Don't Confuse "Scarcity" with a "Shortage"

At first glance, the following statement seems correct: "There is a shortage of every good that is scarce." In everyday conversation, we describe a good as "scarce" if we have trouble finding it. For instance, if you are looking for a present for a child, you might call the latest hot toy "scarce" if you are willing to buy it at its listed price but can't find it online or in any store. But recall from Chapter 2 that

economists have a broad definition of *scarce*. In the economic sense, almost everything—except undesirable things like garbage—is scarce. A shortage of a good occurs only if the quantity demanded is greater than the quantity supplied at the current price. Therefore, the preceding statement—"There is a shortage of every good that is scarce"—is incorrect. In fact, there is no shortage of most scarce goods.

YOUR TURN: Test your understanding by doing related problem 3.16 on page 128 at the end of this chapter.

Black Markets

To this point, our analysis of rent controls is incomplete. In practice, renters may be worse off and landlords may be better off than Figure 4-9 makes it seem. We have assumed that renters and landlords actually abide by the price ceiling, but sometimes they don't. Because rent control leads to a shortage of apartments, renters who would otherwise not be able to find apartments have an incentive to offer landlords rents above the legal maximum. When governments try to control prices by setting price ceilings or price floors, buyers and sellers often find a way around the controls. The result is a **black market** where buying and selling take place at prices that violate government price regulations.

Black market A market in which buying and selling take place at prices that violate government price regulations.

In a housing market with rent controls, the total amount of consumer surplus received by renters may be reduced and the total amount of producer surplus received by landlords may be increased if apartments are being rented at prices above the legal price ceiling.

Solved Problem | 4-3

What's the Economic Effect of a "Black Market" for Apartments?

In many cities with rent controls, the actual rents paid can be much higher than the legal maximum. Because rent controls cause a shortage of apartments, desperate tenants are often willing to pay landlords rents that are higher than the law allows, perhaps by writing a check for the legally allowed rent and paying an additional amount in cash. Look again at Figure 4-9 on page 111. Suppose that competition among tenants results in the black market rent rising to $2,000 per month. At this rent, tenants demand 1,900,000 apartments. Use a graph showing the market for apartments to compare this situation with the one shown in Figure 4-9. Be sure to note any differences in consumer surplus, producer surplus, and deadweight loss.

SOLVING THE PROBLEM:

Step 1: **Review the chapter material.** This problem is about price controls in the market for apartments, so you may want to review the section "Price Ceilings: Government Rent Control Policy in Housing Markets," which begins on page 110.

Step 2: **Draw a graph similar to Figure 4-9, with the addition of the black market price.**

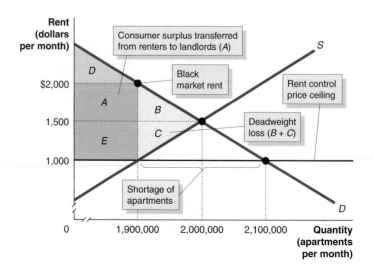

Step 3: **Analyze the changes from Figure 4-9.** Because the black market rent is now $2,000—even higher than the original competitive equilibrium rent of $1,500—compared with Figure 4-9, consumer surplus declines by an amount equal to the red rectangle *A* plus the red rectangle *E*. The remaining consumer surplus is the blue triangle *D*. Note that the rectangle *A*, which would have been part of consumer surplus without rent control, represents a transfer from renters to landlords. Compared with the situation shown in Figure 4-9, producer surplus has increased by an amount equal to rectangles *A* and *E*, and consumer surplus has declined by the same amount. Deadweight loss is equal to triangles *B* and *C*, the same as in Figure 4-9.

EXTRA CREDIT: This analysis leads to a surprising result: With an active black market in apartments, rent control may leave renters as a group worse off—with less consumer surplus—than if there were no rent control. There is one more possibility to consider, however. If enough landlords become convinced that they can get away with charging rents above the legal ceiling, the quantity of apartments supplied will increase. Eventually, the market could even end up at the competitive equilibrium, with an equilibrium rent of $1,500 and equilibrium quantity of 2,000,000 apartments. In that case the rent control price ceiling becomes nonbinding, not because it was set below the equilibrium price but because it was not legally enforced.

YOUR TURN: For more practice, do related problems 3.14 on page 127 and 3.23 on page 129 at the end of this chapter.

>> **End Solved Problem 4-3**

Rent controls can also lead to an increase in racial and other types of discrimination. With rent controls, more renters are looking for apartments than there are apartments to rent. Landlords can afford to indulge their prejudices by refusing to rent to people they don't like. In cities without rent controls, landlords face more competition, which makes it more difficult to turn down tenants on the basis of irrelevant characteristics, such as race.

Making
the
Connection

Does Holiday Gift Giving Have a Deadweight Loss?

The deadweight loss that results from rent control occurs, in part, because consumers rent fewer apartments than they would in a competitive equilibrium. Their choices are *constrained* by government. When you receive a gift, you are also constrained because the person who gave the gift has already chosen the product. In many cases, you would have chosen a different gift for yourself. Economist Joel Waldfogel of the University of Pennsylvania points out that gift giving results in a deadweight loss. The amount of the deadweight loss is equal to the difference between the gift's price and the dollar value the recipient places on the gift. Waldfogel surveyed his students, asking them to list every gift they had received for Christmas, to estimate the retail price of each gift, and to state how much they would have been willing to pay for each gift. Waldfogel's students estimated that their families and friends had paid $438 on average for the students' gifts. The students themselves, however, would have been willing to pay only $313 to buy the presents. If the deadweight losses experienced by Waldfogel's students were extrapolated to the whole population, the deadweight loss of Christmas gift giving could be as much as $13 billion.

Gift giving may lead to deadweight loss.

If the gifts had been cash, the people receiving the gifts would not have been constrained by the gift givers' choices, and there would have been no deadweight loss. If your sister had given you cash instead of that sweater you didn't like, you could have bought whatever you wanted. Why then do people continue giving presents rather than cash? One answer is that most people receive more satisfaction from giving or receiving a present than from giving or receiving cash. If we take this satisfaction into account, the deadweight loss from gift giving will be lower than in Waldfogel's calculations. In fact, a later study by economists John List of the University of Maryland and Jason Shogren of the University of Wyoming showed that as much as half the value of a gift to a recipient was its sentimental value. As Professor Shogren concluded, "People get a whole heck of a lot of value out of doing something for others and other people doing something for them. Aunt Helga gave you that ugly scarf, but hey, it's Aunt Helga."

Sources: Mark Whitehouse, "How Christmas Brings Out the Grinch in Economists," *Wall Street Journal*, December 23, 2006, p. A1; Joel Waldfogel, "The Deadweight Loss of Christmas," *American Economic Review*, Vol. 83, No. 4, December 1993, pp. 328–336; and John A. List and Jason F. Shogren, "The Deadweight Loss of Christmas: Comment," *American Economic Review*, Vol. 88, No, 5, 1998, pp. 1350–1355.

YOUR TURN: Test your understanding by doing related problem 3.15 on page 128 at the end of this chapter.

The Results of Government Price Controls: Winners, Losers, and Inefficiency

When the government imposes price floors or price ceilings, three important results occur:

- Some people win.

- Some people lose.

- There is a loss of economic efficiency.

The winners with rent control are the people who are paying less for rent because they live in rent-controlled apartments. Landlords may also gain if they break the law by charging rents above the legal maximum for their rent-controlled apartments, provided that those illegal rents are higher than the competitive equilibrium rents would be. The losers from rent control are the landlords of rent-controlled apartments who abide by the law and renters who are unable to find apartments to rent at the controlled price. Rent control reduces economic efficiency because fewer apartments are rented than would be rented in a competitive market (refer again to Figure 4-9). The resulting deadweight loss measures the decrease in economic efficiency.

Positive and Normative Analysis of Price Ceilings and Price Floors

Are rent controls, government farm programs, and other price ceilings and price floors bad? As we saw in Chapter 1, questions of this type have no right or wrong answers. Economists are generally skeptical of government attempts to interfere with competitive market equilibrium. Economists know the role competitive markets have played in raising the average person's standard of living. They also know that too much government intervention has the potential to reduce the ability of the market system to produce similar increases in living standards in the future.

But recall from Chapter 1 the difference between positive and normative analysis. Positive analysis is concerned with *what is*, and normative analysis is concerned with *what should be*. Our analysis of rent control and of the federal farm programs in this chapter is positive analysis. We discussed the economic results of these programs. Whether these programs are desirable or undesirable is a normative question. Whether the gains to the winners more than make up for the losses to the losers and for the decline in economic efficiency is a matter of judgment and not strictly an economic question. Price ceilings and price floors continue to exist partly because people who understand their downside still believe they are good policies and therefore support them. The policies also persist because many people who support them do not understand the economic analysis in this chapter and so do not understand the drawbacks to these policies.

4.4 | Analyze the economic impact of taxes.

The Economic Impact of Taxes

Supreme Court Justice Oliver Wendell Holmes once remarked, "Taxes are what we pay for a civilized society." When the government taxes a good, however, it affects the market equilibrium for that good. Just as with a price ceiling or price floor, one result of a tax is a decline in economic efficiency. Analyzing taxes is an important part of the field of economics known as *public finance*. In this section, we will use the model of demand and supply and the concepts of consumer surplus, producer surplus, and deadweight loss to analyze the economic impact of taxes.

The Effect of Taxes on Economic Efficiency

Whenever a government taxes a good or service, less of that good or service will be produced and consumed. For example, a tax on cigarettes will raise the cost of smoking and reduce the amount of smoking that takes place. We can use a demand and supply graph to illustrate this point. Figure 4-10 shows the market for cigarettes.

Without the tax, the equilibrium price of cigarettes would be $4.00 per pack, and 4 billion packs of cigarettes would be sold per year (point *A*). If the federal government requires sellers of cigarettes to pay a $1.00-per-pack tax, then their cost of selling cigarettes will increase by $1.00 per pack. This causes the supply curve for cigarettes to

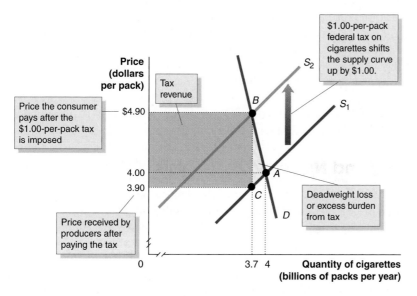

Figure 4-10 | The Effect of a Tax on the Market for Cigarettes

Without the tax, market equilibrium occurs at point *A*. The equilibrium price of cigarettes is $4.00 per pack, and 4 billion packs of cigarettes are sold per year. A $1.00-per-pack tax on cigarettes will cause the supply curve for cigarettes to shift up by $1.00, from S_1 to S_2. The new equilibrium occurs at point *B*. The price of cigarettes will increase by $0.90, to $4.90 per pack, and the quantity sold will fall to 3.7 billion packs. The tax on cigarettes has increased the price paid by consumers from $4.00 to $4.90 per pack. Producers receive a price of $4.90 per pack (point *B*), but after paying the $1.00 tax, they are left with $3.90 (point *C*). The government will receive tax revenue equal to the green shaded box. Some consumer surplus and some producer surplus will become tax revenue for the government and some will become deadweight loss, shown by the yellow-shaded area.

shift up by $1.00 because sellers will now require a price that is $1.00 greater to supply the same quantity of cigarettes. In Figure 4-10, for example, without the tax, sellers would be willing to supply a quantity of 3.7 billion packs of cigarettes at a price of $3.90 per pack (point *C*). With the tax, they will supply only 3.7 billion packs of cigarettes if the price is $4.90 per pack (point *B*). The shift in the supply curve will result in a new equilibrium price of $4.90 and a new equilibrium quantity of 3.7 billion packs (point *B*).

The federal government will collect tax revenue equal to the tax per pack multiplied by the number of packs sold, or $3.7 billion. The area shaded in green in Figure 4-10 represents the government's tax revenue. Consumers will pay a higher price of $4.90 per pack. Although sellers appear to be receiving a higher price per pack, after they have paid the tax, the price they receive falls from $4.00 per pack to $3.90 per pack. There is a loss of consumer surplus because consumers are paying a higher price. The price producers receive falls, so there is also a loss of producer surplus. Therefore, the tax on cigarettes has reduced *both* consumer surplus and producer surplus. Some of the reduction in consumer and producer surplus becomes tax revenue for the government. The rest of the reduction in consumer and producer surplus is equal to the deadweight loss from the tax, shown by the yellow-shaded triangle in the figure.

We can conclude that the true burden of a tax is not just the amount paid to government by consumers and producers but also includes the deadweight loss. The deadweight loss from a tax is referred to as the *excess burden* of the tax. *A tax is efficient if it imposes a small excess burden relative to the tax revenue it raises.* One contribution economists make to government tax policy is to provide advice to policymakers on which taxes are most efficient.

Tax Incidence: Who Actually Pays a Tax?

The answer to the question "Who pays a tax?" seems obvious: Whoever is legally required to send a tax payment to the government pays the tax. But there can be an important difference between who is legally required to pay the tax and who actually *bears the burden* of the tax. The actual division of the burden of a tax is referred to as **tax incidence**. The federal government currently levies an excise tax of 18.4 cents per gallon of gasoline sold. Gas station owners collect this tax and forward it to the federal government, but who actually bears the burden of the tax?

Tax incidence The actual division of the burden of a tax between buyers and sellers in a market.

Determining Tax Incidence on a Demand and Supply Graph Suppose that the retail price of gasoline—including the federal excise tax—is $4.08 per gallon, 140 billion gallons of gasoline are sold in the United States per year, and the federal excise tax is 10 cents per gallon. Figure 4-11 allows us to analyze the incidence of the tax.

Consider the market for gasoline if there were no federal excise tax on gasoline. This equilibrium occurs at the intersection of the demand curve and supply curve, S_1. The equilibrium price is $4.00 per gallon, and the equilibrium quantity is 144 billion gallons. If the federal government imposes a 10-cents-per-gallon tax, the supply curve for gasoline will shift up by 10 cents per gallon. At the new equilibrium, where the demand curve intersects the supply curve, S_2, the price has risen by 8 cents per gallon, from $4.00 to $4.08. Notice that only in the extremely unlikely case that demand is a vertical line will the market price rise by the full amount of the tax. Consumers are paying 8 cents more per gallon. Sellers of gasoline receive a new higher price of $4.08 per gallon, but after paying the 10-cents-per-gallon tax, they are left with $3.98 per gallon, or 2 cents less than they had been receiving in the old equilibrium.

Although the sellers of gasoline are responsible for collecting the tax and sending the tax receipts to the government, they do not bear most of the burden of the tax. In this case, consumers pay 8 cents of the tax because the market price has risen by 8 cents, and sellers pay 2 cents of the tax because after sending the tax to the government, they are receiving 2 cents less per gallon of gasoline sold. Expressed in percentage terms, consumers pay 80 percent of the tax, and sellers pay 20 percent of the tax.

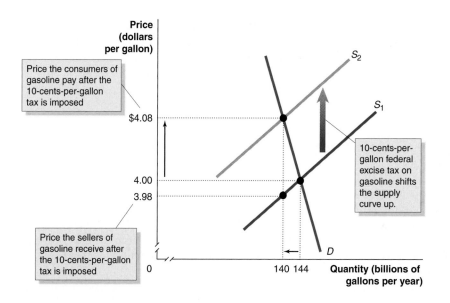

Figure 4-11

The Incidence of a Tax on Gasoline

With no tax on gasoline, the price would be $4.00 per gallon, and 144 billion gallons of gasoline would be sold each year. A 10-cents-per-gallon excise tax shifts up the supply curve from S_1 to S_2, raises the price consumers pay from $4.00 to $4.08, and lowers the price producers receive from $4.00 to $3.98. Therefore, consumers pay 8 cents of the 10-cents-per-gallon tax on gasoline, and producers pay 2 cents.

Solved Problem | 4-4

When Do Consumers Pay All of a Sales Tax Increase?

Briefly explain whether you agree with the following statement: "If the federal government raises the sales tax on gasoline by $0.25, then the price of gasoline will rise by $0.25. Consumers can't get by without gasoline, so they have to pay the whole amount of any increase in the sales tax." Illustrate your answer with a graph.

SOLVING THE PROBLEM:

Step 1: **Review the chapter material.** This problem is about tax incidence, so you may want to review the section "Tax Incidence: Who Actually Pays a Tax?" which begins on page 116.

Step 2: **Draw a graph like Figure 4-11 to illustrate the circumstances when consumers will pay all of an increase in a sales tax.**

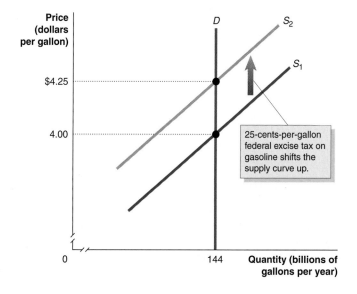

Step 3: **Use the graph to evaluate the statement.** The graph shows that consumers will pay all of an increase in a sales tax only if the demand curve is a vertical line. It is very unlikely that the demand for gasoline looks like this because we expect that for every good, an increase in price will cause a decrease in the quantity demanded. Because the demand curve for gasoline is not a vertical line, the statement is incorrect.

>> End Solved Problem 4-4　　　　　　**YOUR TURN:** For more practice, do related problem 4.5 on page 130 at the end of the chapter.

Does It Matter Whether the Tax Is on Buyers or Sellers? We have already seen the important distinction between the true burden of a tax and whether buyers or sellers are legally required to pay a tax. We can reinforce this point by noting explicitly that the incidence of a tax does *not* depend on whether a tax is collected from the buyers of a good or from the sellers. Figure 4-12 illustrates this point by showing the effect on equilibrium in the market for gasoline if a 10-cents-per-gallon tax is imposed on buyers rather than on sellers. That is, we are now assuming that instead of sellers having to collect the 10-cents-per-gallon tax at the pump, buyers are responsible for keeping track of how many gallons of gasoline they purchase and sending the tax to the government. (Of course, it would be very difficult for buyers to keep track of their purchases or for the government to check whether they were paying all of the tax they owed. That is why the government collects the tax on gasoline from sellers.)

Figure 4-12 is similar to Figure 4-11 except that it shows the gasoline tax being imposed on buyers rather than sellers. In Figure 4-12, the supply curve does not shift because nothing has happened to change the willingness of sellers to change the quantity of gasoline they supply. The demand curve has shifted, however, because consumers now have to pay a 10-cent tax on every gallon of gasoline they buy. Therefore, at every quantity, they are willing to pay a price 10 cents less than they would have without the tax. We indicate this in the figure by shifting the demand curve down by 10 cents, from D_1 to D_2. Once the tax has been imposed and the demand curve has shifted down, the new equilibrium quantity of gasoline is 140 billion gallons, which is exactly the same as in Figure 4-11.

The new equilibrium price after the tax is imposed appears to be different in Figure 4-12 than in Figure 4-11, but if we include the tax, buyers will pay and sellers will receive the same price in both figures. To see this, notice that in Figure 4-11, buyers paid sellers a price of $4.08 per gallon. In Figure 4-12, they pay sellers only $3.98, but they must also pay the government a tax of 10 cents per gallon. So, the total price buyers pay remains

Figure 4-12

The Incidence of a Tax on Gasoline Paid by Buyers

With no tax on gasoline, the demand curve is D_1. If a 10-cents-per-gallon tax is imposed that consumers are responsible for paying, the demand curve shifts down by the amount of the tax, from D_1 to D_2. In the new equilibrium, consumers pay a price of $4.08 per gallon, including the tax. Producers receive $3.98 per gallon. This is the same result we saw when producers were responsible for paying the tax.

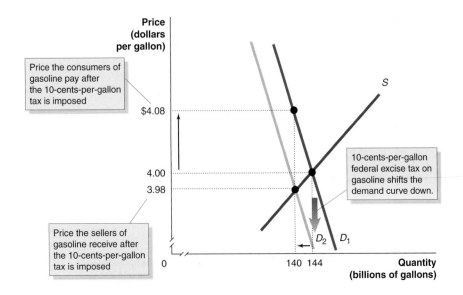

$4.08 per gallon. In Figure 4-11, sellers receive $4.08 per gallon from buyers, but after they pay the tax of 10 cents per gallon, they are left with $3.98, which is the same amount they receive in Figure 4-12.

Making the Connection | Is the Burden of the Social Security Tax Really Shared Equally between Workers and Firms?

Everyone who receives a paycheck has several different taxes withheld from it by their employers, who forward these taxes directly to the government. In fact, many people are shocked after getting their first job, when they discover the gap between their gross pay and their net pay after taxes have been deducted. The largest tax many people of low or moderate income pay is the FICA, which stands for the Federal Insurance Contributions Act. The FICA funds the Social Security and Medicare programs, which provide income and health care to the elderly and disabled. The FICA is sometimes referred to as the *payroll tax*. When Congress passed the FICA, it wanted

employers and workers to equally share the burden of the tax. Currently, the FICA is 15.3 percent of wages, with 7.65 percent paid by workers by being withheld from their paychecks and the other 7.65 percent paid by employers.

But does requiring workers and employers to each pay half the tax mean that the burden of the tax is also shared equally? Our discussion in this chapter shows us that the answer is no. In the

How much FICA do you think this employee pays?

labor market, employers are buyers, and workers are sellers. As we saw in the example of federal taxes on gasoline, whether the tax is collected from buyers or from sellers does not affect the incidence of the tax. Most economists believe, in fact, that the burden of the FICA falls almost entirely on workers. The following figure, which shows the market for labor, illustrates why.

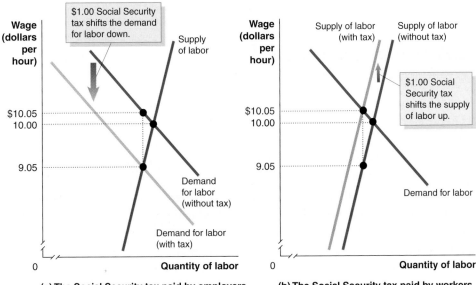

(a) The Social Security tax paid by employers

(b) The Social Security tax paid by workers

In the market for labor, the demand curve reflects the quantity of labor demanded by employers at various wages, and the supply curve reflects the quantity of labor supplied by workers at various wages. The intersection of the demand curve and the supply curve determines the equilibrium wage. In both panels, the equilibrium wage without a Social Security payroll tax is $10 per hour. For simplicity, let's assume that the payroll tax equals $1 per hour of work. In panel (a), we assume that employers must pay the tax. The tax causes the demand for labor curve to shift down by $1 at every quantity of labor because firms now must pay a $1 tax for every hour of labor they hire. We have drawn the supply curve for labor as being very steep because most economists believe the quantity of labor supplied by workers does not change much as the wage rate changes. Workers pay $0.95 of the tax because their wages fall from $10 before the tax to $9.05 after the tax. Firms pay only $0.05 of the tax because the amount they pay for an hour of labor increases from $10 before the tax to $10.05 after the tax. In panel (a), after the tax is imposed, the equilibrium wage declines from $10 per hour to $9.05 per hour. Firms are now paying a total of $10.05 for every hour of work they hire: $9.05 in wages to workers and $1 in tax to the government. In other words, workers have paid $0.95 of the $1 tax, and firms have paid only $0.05.

Panel (b) shows that this result is exactly the same if the tax is imposed on workers rather than on firms. In this case, the tax causes the supply curve for labor to shift up by $1 at every quantity of labor because workers must now pay a tax of $1 for every hour they work. After the tax is imposed, the equilibrium wage increases to $10.05 per hour. But workers receive only $9.05 after they have paid the $1.00 tax. Once again, workers have paid $0.95 of the $1 tax, and firms have paid only $0.05.

Although the figure presents a simplified analysis, it reflects the conclusion of most economists who have studied the incidence of the FICA: Even though Congress requires half the tax to be paid by employers and the other half to be paid by workers, in fact, the burden of the tax falls almost entirely on workers. This conclusion would not be changed even if Congress revised the law to require either employers or workers to pay all of the tax. The forces of demand and supply working in the labor market, and not Congress, determine the incidence of the tax.

YOUR TURN: Test your understanding by doing related problem 4.6 on page 130 at the end of this chapter.

>> Continued from page 99

Economics in YOUR Life!

At the beginning of the chapter, we posed the following question: If you have two job offers in different cities, one with rent control and one without, will you be more likely to find an affordable apartment in the city with rent control? In answering the question, this chapter has shown that although rent control can keep rents lower than they might otherwise be, it can also lead to a permanent shortage of apartments. You may have to search for a long time to find a suitable apartment, and landlords may even ask you to give them payments "under the table," which would make your actual rent higher than the controlled rent. Finding an apartment in a city without rent control should be much easier, although the rent may be higher.

Conclusion

The model of demand and supply introduced in Chapter 3 showed that markets free from government intervention eliminate surpluses and shortages and do a good job of responding to the wants of consumers. We have seen in this chapter that both consumers and firms sometimes try to use the government to change market outcomes in their favor. The concepts of consumer and producer surplus and deadweight loss allow us to measure the benefits consumers and producers receive from competitive market equilibrium. They also allow us to measure the effects of government price floors and price ceilings and the economic impact of taxes.

Read *An Inside Look at Policy* on page 122 for a discussion of the debate over rent control in Los Angeles.

Is Rent Control a Lifeline or Stranglehold?

LOS ANGELES TIMES, JANUARY 14, 2007

The Landlords: Two Sides of a Coin

With apologies to David Letterman, the Top Five reasons why landlords hate rent control are:

No. 1. As private citizens, they believe they shouldn't be forced to do the government's job of providing low-cost housing.

No. 2. In few sectors of private enterprise does a city tell a business how much it may charge.

No. 3. Rent-control buildings sell for less, even in high-rolling realty days.

No. 4. Capping what they may collect in rents translates to capping what they can spend on maintenance and repair—and then they get dinged for lousy upkeep.

No. 5: It's virtually impossible to evict undesirable tenants from a rent-controlled building; owners of buildings not under rent control can boot them out for nearly any reason. . . .

Some Westside owners [in Los Angeles], in particular, complain that longtime renters get a lifetime break, even when they easily can afford market rates. Rent-control laws do not require financial-means testing, so professionals, for example, could still be living in rent-controlled units they secured when they were struggling students. Also, some renters secretly sublet their cheap units for market rate, flouting the terms of their contracts, landlords say. . . .

In an identical unit in the building, a recent tenant was paying about $900 a month while charging $1,000 for one of the bedrooms she rented out on the side, Lambert [a Santa Monica landlord of a rent-controlled building] said.

Selling rent-controlled buildings is no cakewalk, either, said Bruce Bernard, who has bought and sold scores of such buildings in Los Angeles. He recently got his asking price of $6.5 million for a 42-unit building in Hollywood that was not under rent control. One mile away, he also recently sold a 20-unit rent-controlled building with similar amenities for $2.3 million, which was $1.1 million less than his listing price.

More dramatically, Lambert got zero offers on his 15-unit rent-controlled building listed for $890,000 just before the 1994 Northridge earthquake. The temblor shoved the building off the foundation, resulting in all of the tenants vacating the red-tagged structure. Despite $500,000 in needed repairs and not a penny of rent coming in, Lambert quickly sold the building after it was legally rent decontrolled—for $950,000. "It was worth more with all that damage and no rent control than the day before the quake, when it had paying tenants. What does that tell you?"

Hard as it is to sell rent-controlled units for a market-rate profit, owners of those buildings face more urgent daily concerns: covering rising insurance, taxes, upkeep, water, plumbing, landscaping and other costs with 3% or 4% annual rent increases. The result often is that repairs are not made in a timely fashion. . . .

The Rent Stabilization Ordinance allows owners to "pass through" half of the costs of capital improvements to tenants. For example, when an owner replaces a roof for $20,000, he or she may divide half of that cost by the number of units in the building and charge the tenants of each unit up to $55 per month—spread out over multiple years—to cover the cost of the repair.

Even so, Stephens [a landlord near the Hollywood Bowl] said, "some times you get killed" economically. Landlords complain that some renters, hip to the strict Rent Escrow Account Program—which allows them to pay the city up to 50% of their rent and landlords nothing while units with health or safety violations are being brought up to code—deliberately ruin buildings to avoid paying full rent.

Attorney Harold Greenberg, who owns buildings and represents landlords, recalled a tenant who took a sledgehammer to the walls of his apartment, then reported the damage to the city, getting a rent discount while repairs were underway.

Bennett said he fixed a broken pole in the parking lot of one of his buildings and tenants subsequently rammed their cars into it five more times. Bennett finally closed the lot.

"We pay for repairs and pay for the inspections," said Jim Clarke, manager of government relations for the Apartment Assn. of Greater Los Angeles. "We've become the housing department's cash cow." . . .

Key Points in the Article

The article discusses the effects of rent-control laws in the Los Angeles market. Los Angeles, like New York City, which we discussed in the chapter opener, places limits on the rents that landlords can charge some tenants. The purpose of rent-control laws is to ensure that low-income people can find affordable housing. As the article and the chapter explain, rent controls impose substantial costs on landlords, which, in turn, may also harm renters.

Analyzing the News

a The law in Los Angeles does not require that tenants in rent-controlled apartments prove they have low incomes, so some rent-controlled apartments are rented to people with high incomes. In other words, there is nothing in the law to guarantee that rent-controlled apartments go to the intended beneficiaries of the law. A rent-control law may actually increase the rent some tenants pay. The figure in Solved Problem 4-3 on page 112 shows that the rent-control laws create a shortage of apartments and that the resulting black market rent is often higher than the rent without rent-control laws. That is why the Santa Monica tenant in the article was able to charge $1,000 to rent a single room of her rent-controlled apartment when she paid just $900 to rent the entire apartment.

b Not surprisingly, rent-control laws reduce the price for which a landlord can sell a rent-controlled apartment complex. Clearly, this hurts the landlord, but it can also harm renters. The lower selling price for rent-controlled apartment complexes makes building those complexes less profitable. If developers can't make a profit building rent-controlled apartment complexes, then they won't build them. Over time, the number of rent-controlled complexes should decrease as old complexes become run down and developers lack the incentive to build new ones. The supply of rent-controlled apartments should decrease, making the apartment shortage worse. The figure below shows the effect of the decrease in rent-controlled apartment complexes as a shift of the supply curve to the left, from S_1 to S_2. This shift causes the shortage of apartments to increase from $(Q_1 - Q_2)$ to $(Q_1 - Q_3)$. In addition, the black market rent also increases from Black Market$_1$ to Black Market$_2$.

c Rent-control laws also limit the ability of landlords to raise rents to pay for repairs. Indeed, as the article indicates, some of the laws are written in a way that actually gives tenants an incentive to purposely damage the apartment complex. Both the limit on recovering repair costs and the incentives for tenants to damage the property increase the costs of running rent-controlled apartment complexes. These costs can cause the supply curve in this market to shift even further to the left and make the effects we described in part b even larger.

Thinking Critically About Policy

1. The article describes the significant costs associated with rent-control laws. Despite these costs, rent-control laws are very popular with tenants and local politicians. Why would some tenants support rent-control laws? Do all tenants in the market gain from rent-control laws?

2. Economists are critical of rent-control laws for several reasons. One reason is that the laws create a deadweight loss. The magnitude of this deadweight loss depends on the slopes of the demand and supply curves. Look at the figure for Solved Problem 4-3 on page 112. The deadweight loss equals $B + C$, which is the yellow area. What causes the deadweight loss? What would the supply curve have to look like for the deadweight loss to equal zero?

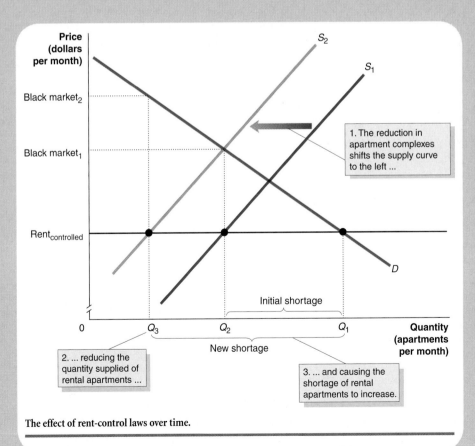

The effect of rent-control laws over time.

123

Key Terms

4.1 LEARNING OBJECTIVE   4.1 | Distinguish between the concepts of consumer surplus and producer surplus, pages 100–105.

Consumer Surplus and Producer Surplus

Summary

Although most prices are determined by demand and supply in markets, the government sometimes imposes *price ceilings* and *price floors*. A **price ceiling** is a legally determined maximum price that sellers may charge. A **price floor** is a legally determined minimum price that sellers may receive. Economists analyze the effects of price ceilings and price floors using *consumer surplus* and *producer surplus*. **Marginal benefit** is the additional benefit to a consumer from consuming one more unit of a good or service. The demand curve is also a marginal benefit curve. **Consumer surplus** is the difference between the highest price a consumer is willing to pay for a product and the price the consumer actually pays. The total amount of consumer surplus in a market is equal to the area below the demand curve and above the market price. **Marginal cost** is the additional cost to a firm of producing one more unit of a good or service. The supply curve is also a marginal cost curve. **Producer surplus** is the difference between the lowest price a firm is willing to accept and the price it actually receives. The total amount of producer surplus in a market is equal to the area above the supply curve and below the market price.

myeconlab Visit www.myeconlab.com to complete these exercises *Get Ahead of the Curve* online and get instant feedback.

Review Questions

1.1 What is marginal benefit? Why is the demand curve referred to as a marginal benefit curve?

1.2 What is marginal cost? Why is the supply curve referred to as a marginal cost curve?

1.3 What is consumer surplus? How does consumer surplus change as the equilibrium price of a good rises or falls?

1.4 What is producer surplus? How does producer surplus change as the equilibrium price of a good rises or falls?

Problems and Applications

1.5 Suppose that a frost in Florida reduces the size of the orange crop, which causes the supply curve for oranges to shift to the left. Briefly explain whether each of the following will increase or decrease. Use demand and supply to illustrate your answers.
a. Consumer surplus
b. Producer surplus

1.6 A student makes the following argument: "When a market is in equilibrium, there is no consumer surplus. We know this because in equilibrium, the market price is equal to the price consumers are willing to pay for the good." Briefly explain whether you agree with the student's argument.

1.7 The following graph illustrates the market for a breast cancer–fighting drug, without which breast cancer patients cannot survive. What is the consumer surplus in this market? How does it differ from the consumer surplus in the markets you have studied up to this point?

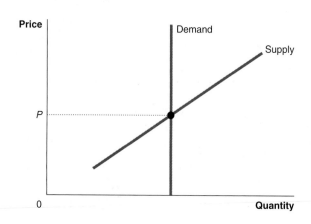

1.8 (Related to the *Making the Connection* on page 102) The *Making the Connection* states that the value of the area representing consumer surplus from satellite television is $2 billion. Use the information from the graph in the *Making the Connection* to show how this value was calculated. (For a review of how to calculate the area of a triangle, see the appendix to Chapter 1.)

1.9 The graph in the next column shows the market for tickets to a concert that will be held in a local arena that seats 15,000 people. What is the producer surplus in this market? How does it differ from the producer surplus in the markets you have studied up to this point?

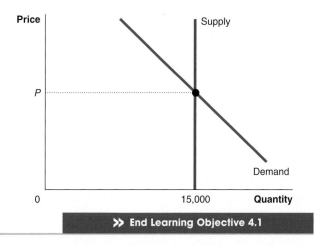

» **End Learning Objective 4.1**

4.2 LEARNING OBJECTIVE   4.2 | Understand the concept of economic efficiency, **pages 105–107.**

The Efficiency of Competitive Markets

Summary

Equilibrium in a competitive market is **economically efficient**. **Economic surplus** is the sum of consumer surplus and producer surplus. Economic efficiency is a market outcome in which the marginal benefit to consumers from the last unit produced is equal to the marginal cost of production and where the sum of consumer surplus and producer surplus is at a maximum. When the market price is above or below the equilibrium price, there is a reduction in economic surplus. The reduction in economic surplus resulting from a market not being in competitive equilibrium is called the **deadweight loss**.

myeconlab Visit www.myeconlab.com to complete these exercises *Get Ahead of the Curve* online and get instant feedback.

Review Questions

2.1 Define economic surplus and deadweight loss?

2.2 What is economic efficiency? Why do economists define efficiency in this way?

Problems and Applications

2.3 Suppose you were assigned the task of coming up with a single number that would allow someone to compare the economic activity in one country to that in another country. How might such a number be related to economic efficiency and consumer and producer surplus?

2.4 Briefly explain whether you agree with the following statement: "If at the current quantity marginal benefit is greater than marginal cost, there will be a deadweight loss in the market. However, there is no deadweight loss when marginal cost is greater than marginal benefit."

2.5 Briefly explain whether you agree with the following statement: "If consumer surplus in a market increases, producer surplus must decrease."

2.6 Does an increase in economic surplus in a market always mean that economic efficiency in the market has increased? Briefly explain.

2.7 Using the graph below, explain why economic surplus would be smaller if Q_1 or Q_3 were the quantity produced than if Q_2 is the quantity produced.

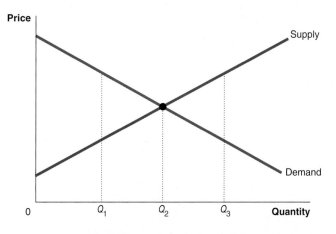

» **End Learning Objective 4.2**

Government Intervention in the Market: Price Floors and Price Ceilings

Summary

Producers or consumers who are dissatisfied with the market outcome can attempt to convince the government to impose price floors or price ceilings. Price floors usually increase producer surplus, decrease consumer surplus, and cause a deadweight loss. Price ceilings usually increase consumer surplus, reduce producer surplus, and cause a deadweight loss. The results of the government imposing price ceilings and price floors are that some people win, some people lose, and a loss of economic efficiency occurs. Price ceilings and price floors can lead to a **black market**, where buying and selling takes place at prices that violate government price regulations. Positive analysis is concerned with what is, and normative analysis is concerned with what should be. Positive analysis shows that price ceilings and price floors cause deadweight losses. Whether these policies are desirable or undesirable, though, is a normative question.

Review Questions

3.1 Why do some consumers tend to favor price controls while others tend to oppose them?

3.2 Do producers tend to favor price floors or price ceilings? Why?

3.3 What is a black market? Under what circumstances do black markets arise?

3.4 Can economic analysis provide a final answer to the question of whether the government should intervene in markets by imposing price ceilings and price floors? Why or why not?

Problems and Applications

3.5 The graph in the next column shows the market for apples. Assume the government has imposed a price floor of $10 per crate.
  a. How many crates of apples will be sold after the price floor has been imposed?
  b. Will there be a shortage or a surplus? If there is a shortage or a surplus, how large will it be?
  c. Will apple producers benefit from the price floor? If so, explain how they will benefit.

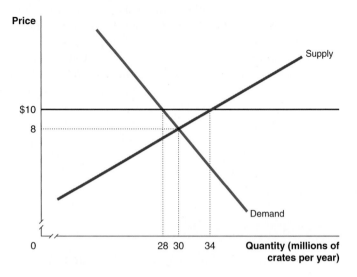

3.6 Use the information on the kumquat market in the table to answer the following questions.

PRICE (PER CRATE)	QUANTITY DEMANDED (MILLIONS OF CRATES PER YEAR)	QUANTITY SUPPLIED (MILLIONS OF CRATES PER YEAR)
$10	120	20
15	110	60
20	100	100
25	90	140
30	80	180
35	70	220

  a. What are the equilibrium price and quantity? How much revenue do kumquat producers receive when the market is in equilibrium? Draw a graph showing the market equilibrium and the area representing the revenue received by kumquat producers.
  b. Suppose the federal government decides to impose a price floor of $30 per crate. Now how many crates of kumquats will consumers purchase? How much revenue will kumquat producers receive? Assume that the government does not purchase any surplus kumquats. On your graph from question (a), show the price floor, the change in the quantity of kumquats purchased, and the revenue received by kumquat producers after the price floor is imposed.
  c. Suppose the government imposes a price floor of $30 per crate and purchases any surplus kumquats from producers. Now how much revenue will kumquat producers receive? How much will the

government spend purchasing surplus kumquats? On your graph from question (a), show the area representing the amount the government spends to purchase the surplus kumquats.

3.7 Suppose that the government sets a price floor for milk that is above the competitive equilibrium price.

a. Draw a graph showing this situation. Be sure your graph shows the competitive equilibrium price, the price floor, the quantity that would be sold in competitive equilibrium, and the quantity that is sold with the price floor.

b. Compare the economic surplus in this market when there is a price floor and when there is no price floor.

3.8 During 2007, the Venezuelan government allowed consumers to buy only a limited quantity of sugar. The government also imposed a ceiling on the price of sugar. As a result, both the quantity of sugar consumed and the market price of sugar were below the competitive equilibrium price and quantity. Draw a graph to illustrate this situation. On your graph, be sure to indicate the areas representing consumer surplus, producer surplus, and deadweight loss.

3.9 Refer again to question 3.8. An article in the *New York Times* contained the following (Hugo Chávez is the president of Venezuela):

> José Vielma Mora, the chief of Seniat, the government's tax agency, oversaw a raid this month on a warehouse here where officials seized about 165 tons of sugar. Mr. Vielma said the raid exposed hoarding by vendors who were unwilling to sell the sugar at official prices. He and other officials in Mr. Chávez's government have repeatedly blamed the shortages on producers, intermediaries and grocers.

Do you agree that the shortages in the Venezuelan sugar market are the fault of "producers, intermediaries and grocers"? Briefly explain.

Source: Simon Romero, "Chavez Threatens to Jail Price Control Violators," *New York Times*, February 17, 2007.

3.10 To drive a taxi legally in New York City, you must have a medallion issued by the city government. City officials have issued only 12,187 medallions. Let's assume this puts an absolute limit on the number of taxi rides that can be supplied in New York City on any day because no one breaks the law by driving a taxi without a medallion. Let's also assume that each taxi can provide 6 trips per day. In that case, the supply of taxi rides is fixed at 73,122 (or 6 rides per taxi × 12,187 taxis). We show this in the following graph, with a vertical line at this quantity. *Assume that there are no government controls on the prices that drivers can charge for rides.* Use the graph to answer the following questions.

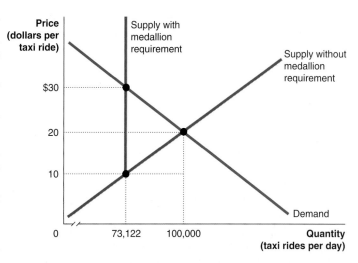

a. What would the equilibrium price and quantity be in this market if there were no medallion requirement?

b. What are the price and quantity with the medallion requirement?

c. Indicate on the graph the areas representing consumer surplus and producer surplus if there were no medallion requirement.

d. Indicate on the graph the areas representing consumer surplus, producer surplus, and deadweight loss with the medallion requirement.

3.11 If the goal of the federal government's farm program is to raise the incomes of poor family farmers, is the current system of price floors and subsidy payments based on the number of acres farmed a good way to reach the goal? Briefly explain. What other ways might the federal government attempt to reach its goals?

3.12 **(Related to the *Making the Connection* on page 109)** Some economists studying the effects of the minimum wage law have found that it tends to reduce the employment of black teenagers relative to white teenagers. Does the graph in the *Making the Connection* on page 109 help you understand why black teenagers may have been disproportionately affected by the minimum wage? Briefly explain.

3.13 **(Related to the *Chapter Opener* on page 98)** Suppose the competitive equilibrium rent for a standard two-bedroom apartment in Lawrence is $600. Now suppose the city council passes a rent-control law imposing a price ceiling of $500. Use a demand and supply graph to illustrate the impact of the rent-control law. Suppose that shortly after the law is passed, a large employer in the area announces that it will close a plant in Lawrence and lay off 5,000 workers. Show on your graph how this will affect the market for rental property in Lawrence.

3.14 **(Related to *Solved Problem 4-3* on page 112)** Use the information on the market for apartments in Bay City in the table on the next page to answer the following questions.

RENT	QUANTITY DEMANDED	QUANTITY SUPPLIED
$500	375,000	225,000
600	350,000	250,000
700	325,000	275,000
800	300,000	300,000
900	275,000	325,000
1,000	250,000	350,000

a. In the absence of rent control, what is the equilibrium rent and what is the equilibrium quantity of apartments rented? Draw a demand and supply graph of the market for apartments to illustrate your answer. In equilibrium, will there be any renters who are unable to find an apartment to rent or any landlords who are unable to find a renter for an apartment?

b. Suppose the government sets a ceiling on rents of $600 per month. What is the quantity of apartments demanded, and what is the quantity of apartments supplied?

c. Assume that all landlords abide by the law. Use a demand and supply graph to illustrate the impact of this price ceiling on the market for apartments. Be sure to indicate on your graph each of the following: (i) the area representing consumer surplus after the price ceiling has been imposed, (ii) the area representing producer surplus after the price ceiling has been imposed, and (iii) the area representing the deadweight loss after the ceiling has been imposed.

d. Assume that the quantity of apartments supplied is the same as you determined in (b). But now assume that landlords ignore the law and rent this quantity of apartments for the highest rent they can get. Briefly explain what this rent will be.

3.15 **(Related to the *Making the Connection* on page 113)** Joel Waldfogel argues that there may be a deadweight loss to holiday gift giving. An article in the *Wall Street Journal* suggests that retail stores might be better off if the tradition of holiday gift giving ended: "In theory, smoother sales throughout the year would be better for retailers, enabling them to avoid the extra costs of planning and stocking up for the holidays." Owners of many stores disagree, however. The owner of a store in New York City was quoted in the article as arguing: "Christmas is the lifeblood of the retail business. It's a time of year when people don't have a choice. They *have* to spend." Do you believe the efficiency of the economy would be improved if the tradition of holiday gift giving ended? Briefly explain your reasoning.

Source: Mark Whitehouse, "How Christmas Brings Out the Grinch in Economists," *Wall Street Journal*, December 23, 2006, p. A1.

3.16 **(Related to the *Don't Let This Happen to You!* on page 111)** Briefly explain whether you agree or disagree with the following statement: "If there is a shortage of a good, it must be scarce, but there is not a shortage of every scarce good."

3.17 A student makes the following argument:

> A price floor reduces the amount of a product that consumers buy because it keeps the price above the competitive market equilibrium. A price ceiling, on the other hand, increases the amount of a product that consumers buy because it keeps the price below the competitive market equilibrium.

Do you agree with the student's reasoning? Use a demand and supply graph to illustrate your answer.

3.18 An advocate of medical care system reform makes the following argument:

> The 15,000 kidneys that are transplanted in the United States each year are received free from organ donors. Despite this, because of hospital and doctor's fees, the average price of a kidney transplant is $250,000. As a result, only rich people or people with very good health insurance can afford these transplants. The government should put a ceiling of $100,000 on the price of kidney transplants. That way, middle-income people will be able to afford them, the demand for kidney transplants will increase, and more kidney transplants will take place.

Do you agree with the advocate's reasoning? Use a demand and supply graph to illustrate your answer.

3.19 **(Related to the *Chapter Opener* on page 98)** The cities of Peabody and Woburn are five miles apart. Woburn enacts a rent-control law that puts a ceiling on rents well below their competitive market value. Predict the impact of this law on the competitive equilibrium rent in Peabody, which does not have a rent-control law. Illustrate your answer with a demand and supply graph.

3.20 **(Related to the *Chapter Opener* on page 98)** Rent controls were first imposed in New York City in the early 1940s, during a housing shortage brought on by World War II. Why do you think that, once established, rent controls continued in New York City for many decades?

3.21 **(Related to the *Chapter Opener* on page 98)** The competitive equilibrium rent in the city of Lowell is currently $1,000 per month. The government decides to enact rent control and to establish a price ceiling for apartments of $750 per month. Briefly explain whether rent control is likely to make each of the following people better or worse off.

a. Someone currently renting an apartment in Lowell

b. Someone who will be moving to Lowell next year and who intends to rent an apartment

c. A landlord who intends to abide by the rent-control law

d. A landlord who intends to ignore the law and illegally charge the highest rent possible for his apartments

3.22 (Related to the *Chapter Opener* on page 98) The following is from an article in the *New York Times*:

> Imagine finding the perfect apartment, only to learn that the landlord is denying you the place because you are on a blacklist of supposedly high-risk renters. Nothing is wrong with your credit rating, but your name showed up on the list because a private screening service found it in housing court records about a dispute you had with a previous landlord—a dispute that was resolved in your favor.

Is it more likely that a "blacklist" of "high-risk" tenants will exist in a city with rent control or one without rent control? Briefly explain.

Source: Motoko Rich, "A Blacklist of Renters," *New York Times*, April 8, 2004.

3.23 (Related to *Solved Problem 4-3* on page 112) Suppose that initially the gasoline market is in equilibrium, at a price of $3.00 per gallon and a quantity of 45 million gallons per month. Then a war in the Middle East disrupts imports of oil into the United States, shifting the supply curve for gasoline from S_1 to S_2. The price of gasoline begins to rise, and consumers protest. The federal government responds by setting a price ceiling of $3.00 per gallon. Use the graph to answer the following questions.

a. If there were no price ceiling, what would be the equilibrium price of gasoline, the quantity of

gasoline demanded, and the quantity of gasoline supplied? Now assume that the price ceiling is imposed and that there is no black market in gasoline. What are the price of gasoline, the quantity of gasoline demanded, and the quantity of gasoline supplied? How large is the shortage of gasoline?

b. Assume that the price ceiling is imposed and there is no black market in gasoline. Show on the graph the areas representing consumer surplus, producer surplus, and deadweight loss.

c. Now assume that there is a black market and the price of gasoline rises to the maximum that consumers are willing to pay for the amount supplied by producers at $3.00 per gallon. Show on the graph the areas representing producer surplus, consumer surplus, and deadweight loss.

d. Are consumers made better off with the price ceiling than without it? Briefly explain.

3.24 In the United States, Amazon.com, BarnesandNoble.com, and many other retailers sell books, DVDs, and music CDs for less than the price marked on the package. In Japan, retailers are not allowed to discount prices in this way. Who benefits and who loses from this Japanese law?

3.25 An editorial in *Economist* discusses the fact that in most countries—including the United States—it is illegal for individuals to buy or sell body parts, such as kidneys.

a. Draw a demand and supply graph for the market for kidneys. Show on your graph the legal maximum price of zero and indicate the quantity of kidneys supplied at this price. (Hint: Because we know that some kidneys are donated, the quantity supplied will not be zero.)

b. The editorial argues that buying and selling kidneys should be legalized:

> With proper regulation, a kidney market would be a big improvement over the current sorry state of affairs. Sellers could be checked for disease and drug use, and cared for after operations. . . . Buyers would get better kidneys, faster. Both sellers and buyers would do better than in the illegal market, where much of the money goes to middlemen.

Do you agree with this argument? Should the government treat kidneys like other goods and allow the market to determine the price?

Source: "Psst, Wanna Buy a Kidney?" *Economist*, November 18, 2006, p. 15.

>> End Learning Objective 4.3

4.4 LEARNING OBJECTIVE   4.4 | Analyze the economic impact of taxes, **pages 115–120.**

The Economic Impact of Taxes

Summary

Most taxes result in a loss of consumer surplus, a loss of producer surplus, and a deadweight loss. The true burden of a tax is not just the amount paid to government by consumers and producers but also includes the deadweight loss. The deadweight loss from a tax is the excess burden of the tax. **Tax incidence** is the actual division of the burden of a tax. In most cases, consumers and firms share the burden of a tax levied on a good or service.

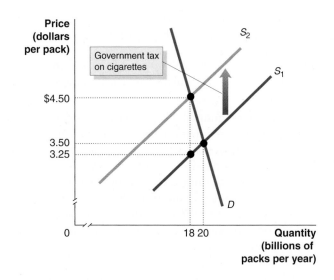

myeconlab Visit www.myeconlab.com to complete these exercises
Get Ahead of the Curve online and get instant feedback.

Review Questions

4.1   What is meant by tax incidence?

4.2   Does it matter whether buyers or sellers are legally responsible for paying a tax? Briefly explain.

Problems and Applications

4.3   Suppose the current equilibrium price of cheese pizzas is $10, and 10 million pizzas are sold per month. After the federal government imposes a $0.50 per pizza tax, the equilibrium price of pizzas rises to $10.40, and the equilibrium quantity falls to 9 million. Illustrate this situation with a demand and supply graph. Be sure your graph shows the equilibrium price before and after the tax, the equilibrium quantity before and after the tax, and the areas representing consumer surplus after the tax, producer surplus after the tax, tax revenue collected by the government, and deadweight loss.

4.4   Use the graph of the market for cigarettes in the next column to answer the following questions.
   a. According to the graph, how much is the government tax on cigarettes?
   b. What price do producers receive after paying the tax?
   c. How much tax revenue does the government collect?

4.5   (Related to *Solved Problem 4-4* on page 117) Suppose the federal government decides to levy a sales tax on pizza of $1.00 per pie. Briefly explain whether you agree with the following statement by a representative of the pizza industry:

   The pizza industry is very competitive. As a result, pizza sellers will have to pay the whole tax because they are unable to pass any of it on to consumers in the form of higher prices. Therefore, a sales tax of $1.00 per pie will result in pizza sellers receiving $1.00 less on each pie sold, after paying the tax.

   Illustrate your answer with a graph.

4.6   (Related to the *Making the Connection* on page 119) If the price consumers pay and the price sellers receive are not affected by whether consumers or sellers collect a tax on a good or service, why does the government usually require sellers and not consumers to collect a tax?

>> End Learning Objective 4.4

Appendix

Quantitative Demand and Supply Analysis

Graphs help us understand economic change *qualitatively*. For instance, a demand and supply graph can tell us that if household incomes rise, the demand curve for a normal good will shift to the right, and its price will rise. Often, though, economists, business managers, and policymakers want to know more than the qualitative direction of change; they want a *quantitative estimate* of the size of the change.

In Chapter 4, we carried out a qualitative analysis of rent controls. We saw that imposing rent controls involves a trade-off: Renters as a group gain, but landlords lose, and the market for apartments becomes less efficient, as shown by the deadweight loss. To better evaluate rent controls, we need to know more than just that these gains and losses exist; we need to know how large they are. A quantitative analysis of rent controls will tell us how large the gains and losses are.

Use **quantitative** demand and supply **analysis**.

Demand and Supply Equations

The first step in a quantitative analysis is to supplement our use of demand and supply curves with demand and supply *equations*. We noted briefly in Chapter 3 that economists often statistically estimate equations for demand curves. Supply curves can also be statistically estimated. For example, suppose that economists have estimated that the demand for apartments in New York City is:

$$Q^D = 3,000,000 - 1,000P,$$

and the supply of apartments is:

$$Q^S = -450,000 + 1,300P.$$

We have used Q^D for the quantity of apartments demanded per month, Q^S for the quantity of apartments supplied per month, and P for the apartment rent in dollars per month. In reality, both the quantity of apartments demanded and the quantity of apartments supplied will depend on more than just the rental price of apartments in New York City. For instance, the demand for apartments in New York City will also depend on the average incomes of families in the New York area and on the rents of apartments in surrounding cities. For simplicity, we will ignore these other factors.

With no government intervention, we know that at competitive market equilibrium, the quantity demanded must equal the quantity supplied, or:

$$Q^D = Q^S.$$

We can use this equation, which is called an *equilibrium condition*, to solve for the equilibrium monthly apartment rent by setting the demand equation equal to the supply equation:

$$3,000,000 - 1,000P = -450,000 + 1,300P$$

$$3,450,000 = 2,300P$$

$$P = \frac{3,450,000}{2,300} = \$1,500.$$

Figure 4A-1

Graphing Supply and Demand Equations

After statistically estimating supply and demand equations, we can use the equations to draw supply and demand curves. In this case, the equilibrium rent for apartments is $1,500 per month, and the equilibrium quantity of apartments rented is 1,500,000. The supply equation tells us that at a rent of $346, the quantity of apartments supplied will be zero. The demand equation tells us that at a rent of $3,000, the quantity of apartments demanded will be zero. The areas representing consumer surplus and producer surplus are also indicated on the graph.

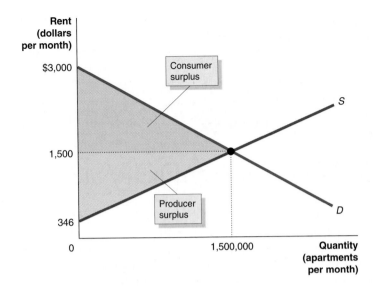

We can then substitute this price back into either the supply equation or the demand equation to find the equilibrium quantity of apartments rented:

$$Q^D = 3,000,000 - 1,000P = 3,000,000 - 1,000(1,500) = 1,500,000$$

$$Q^S = -450,000 + 1,300P = -450,000 + 1,300(1,500) = 1,500,000.$$

Figure 4A-1 illustrates the information from these equations in a graph. The figure shows the values for rent when the quantity supplied is zero and when the quantity demanded is zero. These values can be calculated from the demand equation and the supply equation by setting Q^D and Q^S equal to zero and solving for price:

$$Q^D = 0 = 3,000,000 - 1,000P$$

$$P = \frac{3,000,000}{1,000} = \$3,000$$

and:

$$Q^S = 0 = -450,000 + 1,300P$$

$$P = \frac{-450,000}{-1,300} = \$346.15.$$

Calculating Consumer Surplus and Producer Surplus

Figure 4A-1 shows consumer surplus and producer surplus in this market. Recall that the sum of consumer surplus and producer surplus equals the net benefit that renters and landlords receive from participating in the market for apartments. We can use the values from the demand and supply equations to calculate the value of consumer surplus and producer surplus. Remember that consumer surplus is the area below the demand curve and above the line representing market price. Notice that this area forms a right triangle because the demand curve is a straight line—it is *linear*. As we noted in the appendix to Chapter 1, the area of a triangle is equal to ½ multiplied by the base of the triangle multiplied by the height of the triangle. In this case, the area is:

$$½ \times (1,500,000) \times (3,000 - 1,500) = \$1,125,000,000.$$

So, this calculation tells us that the consumer surplus in the market for rental apartments in New York City would be about $1.125 billion.

We can calculate producer surplus in a similar way. Remember that producer surplus is the area above the supply curve and below the line representing market price. Because our supply curve is also a straight line, producer surplus on the figure is equal to the area of the right triangle:

$$\frac{1}{2} \times 1,500,000 \times (1,500 - 346) = \$865,500,000.$$

This calculation tells us that the producer surplus in the market for rental apartments in New York City is about $865 million.

We can use this same type of analysis to measure the impact of rent control on consumer surplus, producer surplus, and economic efficiency. For instance, suppose the city imposes a rent ceiling of $1,000 per month. Figure 4A-2 can help guide us as we measure the impact.

First, we can calculate the quantity of apartments that will actually be rented by substituting the rent ceiling of $1,000 into the supply equation:

$$Q^S = -450,000 + (1,300 \times 1,000) = 850,000.$$

We also need to know the price on the demand curve when the quantity of apartments is 850,000. We can do this by substituting 850,000 for quantity in the demand equation and solving for price:

$$850,000 = 3,000,000 - 1,000P$$

$$P = \frac{-2,150,000}{-1,000} = \$2,150.$$

Compared with its value in competitive equilibrium, consumer surplus has been reduced by a value equal to the area of the yellow triangle *B* but increased by a value equal to the area of the blue rectangle *A*. The area of the yellow triangle *B* is:

$$\frac{1}{2} \times (1,500,000 - 850,000) \times (2,150 - 1,500) = \$211,250,000,$$

and the area of the blue rectangle *A* is base multiplied by height, or:

$$(\$1,500 - \$1,000) \times (850,000) = \$425,000,000.$$

The value of consumer surplus in competitive equilibrium was $1,125,000,000. As a result of the rent ceiling, it will be increased to:

$$(\$1,125,000,000 + \$425,000,000) - \$211,250,000 = \$1,338,750,000.$$

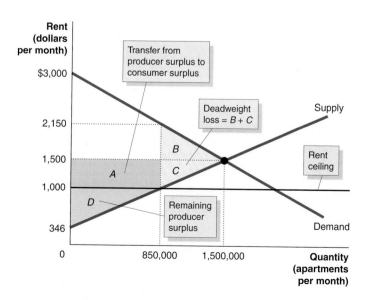

Figure 4A-2

Calculating the Economic Effect of Rent Controls

Once we have estimated equations for the demand and supply of rental housing, a diagram can guide our numeric estimates of the economic effects of rent control. Consumer surplus falls by an amount equal to the area of the yellow triangle *B* and increases by an amount equal to the area of the blue rectangle *A*. The difference between the values of these two areas is $213,750,000. Producer surplus falls by an amount equal to the area of the blue rectangle *A* plus the area of the yellow triangle *C*. The value of these two areas is $587,500,000. The remaining producer surplus is equal to the area of triangle *D*, or $278,000,000. Deadweight loss is equal to the area of triangle *B* plus the area of triangle *C*, or $373,750,000.

Compared with its value in competitive equilibrium, producer surplus has been reduced by a value equal to the area of the yellow triangle C plus a value equal to the area of the blue rectangle. The area of the yellow triangle C is:

$$\frac{1}{2} \times (1,500,000 - 850,000) \times (1,500 - 1,000) = \$162,500,000.$$

We have already calculated the area of the blue rectangle A as \$425,000,000. The value of producer surplus in competitive equilibrium was \$865,500,000. As a result of the rent ceiling, it will be reduced to:

$$\$865,500,000 - \$162,500,000 - \$425,000,000 = \$278,000,000.$$

The loss of economic efficiency, as measured by the deadweight loss, is equal to the value represented by the areas of the yellow triangles B and C, or:

$$\$211,250,000 + \$162,500,000 = \$373,750,000.$$

The following table summarizes the results of the analysis (the values are in millions of dollars).

CONSUMER SURPLUS		PRODUCER SURPLUS		DEADWEIGHT LOSS	
COMPETITIVE EQUILIBRIUM	RENT CONTROL	COMPETITIVE EQUILIBRIUM	RENT CONTROL	COMPETITIVE EQUILIBRIUM	RENT CONTROL
\$1,125	\$1,338.75	\$865.50	\$278	\$0	\$373.75

Qualitatively, we know that imposing rent controls will make consumers better off, make landlords worse off, and decrease economic efficiency. The advantage of the analysis we have just gone through is that it puts dollar values on the qualitative results. We can now see how much consumers have gained, how much landlords have lost, and how great the decline in economic efficiency has been. Sometimes the quantitative results can be surprising. Notice, for instance, that after the imposition of rent control, the deadweight loss is actually greater than the remaining producer surplus.

Economists often study issues where the qualitative results of actions are apparent, even to non-economists. You don't have to be an economist to understand who wins and loses from rent control or that if a company cuts the price of its product, its sales will increase. Business managers, policymakers, and the general public do, however, need economists to measure quantitatively the effects of different actions—including policies such as rent control—so that they can better assess the results of these actions.

LEARNING OBJECTIVE   Use Quantitative Demand and Supply Analysis, **pages 131–134.**

Review Questions

4A.1 In a linear demand equation, what economic information is conveyed by the intercept on the price axis?

4A.2 Suppose you were assigned the task of choosing a price that maximized economic surplus in a market. What price would you choose? Why?

4A.3 Consumer surplus is used as a measure of a consumer's net benefit from purchasing a good or service. Explain why consumer surplus is a measure of net benefit.

4A.4 Why would economists use the term *deadweight loss* to describe the impact on consumer and producer surplus from a price control?

Problems and Applications

4A.5 Suppose that you have been hired to analyze the impact on employment from the imposition of a minimum wage in the labor market. Further suppose that you estimate the supply and demand functions for labor, where L stands for the quantity of labor (measured in thousands of workers) and W stands for the wage rate (measured in dollars per hour):

Demand: $L^D = 100 - 4W$
Supply: $L^S = 6W$

First, calculate the free-market equilibrium wage and quantity of labor. Now suppose the proposed minimum wage is \$12. How large will the surplus of labor in this market be?

4A.6 The following graphs illustrate the markets for two different types of labor. Suppose an identical minimum wage is imposed in both markets. In which market will the minimum wage have the largest impact on employment? Why?

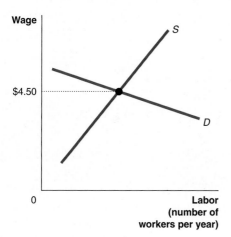

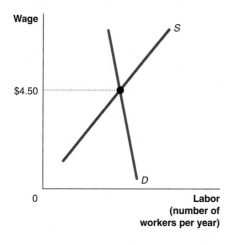

4A.7 Suppose that you are the vice president of operations of a manufacturing firm that sells an industrial lubricant in a competitive market. Further suppose that your economist gives you the following supply and demand functions:

Demand: $Q^D = 45 - 2P$
Supply: $Q^S = -15 + P$

What is the consumer surplus in this market? What is the producer surplus?

4A.8 The following graph shows a market in which a price floor of $3.00 per unit has been imposed. Calculate the values of each of the following.
  a. The deadweight loss
  b. The transfer of producer surplus to consumers or the transfer of consumer surplus to producers
  c. Producer surplus after the price floor is imposed
  d. Consumer surplus after the price floor is imposed

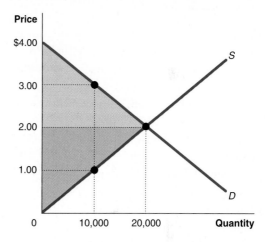

4A.9 Construct a table like the one in this appendix on page 134, but assume that the rent ceiling is $1,200 rather than $1,000.

>> End Appendix Learning Objective

Chapter 5

Externalities, Environmental Policy, and Public Goods

Economic Policy and the Environment

Pollution is a part of economic life. Consumers create air pollution by burning gasoline to power their cars and natural gas to heat their homes. Firms create air pollution when they produce electricity, pesticides, or plastics, among other products. Utilities produce sulfur dioxide when they burn coal to generate electricity. Sulfur dioxide contributes to acid rain, which can damage trees, crops, and buildings. The burning of fossil fuels generates carbon dioxide and other greenhouse gases that can increase global warming.

How should government policy deal with the problem of pollution? Can economic analysis help in formulating more efficient pollution policies? In the past, Congress frequently employed policies that ordered firms to use particular methods to reduce pollution. But many economists are critical of this approach—known as *command and control*—because some companies are able to reduce their emissions much more inexpensively if they are allowed to choose the method. To deal with reducing sulfur dioxide emissions in the most efficient way, economists recommended, and Congress adopted, a *market-based approach* called *tradable emissions allowances*.

Under this system, which went into operation in 1995, the federal government gives utility companies allowances to produce a target amount of sulfur dioxide emissions. Utilities are free to buy and sell allowances, although they must end up with allowances equal to the amount of sulfur dioxide they wish to emit: one allowance for every ton of sulfur dioxide emitted. Utilities that initially lack sufficient allowances either must reduce the amount of sulfur dioxide they emit or buy allowances from other utilities that are polluting less.

For example, Duke Energy generates electricity using coal-burning plants, which emit sulfur dioxide. Because Duke Energy already burns low-sulfur coal, reducing emissions of sulfur dioxide even further would be expensive. Many electric utilities in the Midwest, however, burn high-sulfur coal, and their emissions can be reduced greatly by installing anti-pollution devices known as "scrubbers." As a result, these utilities can drastically reduce their emissions and still have allowances left that they can sell to utilities like Duke Energy. According to the manager in charge of environmental compliance at the company, reducing emissions of sulfur dioxide would cost Duke Energy about $300 per ton. A Midwestern utility could reduce emissions for only about

$100 per ton. These utilities were willing to sell allowances to Duke Energy for $200 each. As the manager put it, "They would make $100, and Duke would save $100." Not only would the utilities gain, but sulfur dioxide emissions would be reduced at a lower total cost to the economy.

Some economists have advocated a similar program of tradable permits to reduce emissions of carbon dioxide from burning fossil fuels. Other economists have endorsed a carbon tax, which is a tax on energy sources that emit carbon dioxide. With a government carbon tax, the generation of power by burning gasoline, natural gas, coal, or other carbon-based fuels would be taxed. As we will see in this chapter, economic analysis can play a significant role in shaping environmental policies.

AN INSIDE LOOK AT POLICY on **page 164** discusses how tradable emissions permits are also being used to reduce emissions of carbon dioxide, one of the gases suspected of contributing to global warming.

Sources: Jeffrey Ball, "New Consensus: In Climate Controversy, Industry Cedes Ground," *Wall Street Journal*, January 23, 2007, p. A1; and Daniel Altman, "Just How Far Can Trading of Emissions Be Extended?" *New York Times*, May 31, 2002.

LEARNING Objectives

After studying this chapter, you should be able to:

5.1 Identify examples of positive and negative **externalities** and use graphs to show how externalities affect **economic efficiency**, page 138.

5.2 Discuss the **Coase theorem** and explain how private bargaining can lead to economic efficiency in a market with an externality, page 141.

5.3 Analyze **government policies** to achieve economic efficiency in a market with an externality, page 147.

5.4 Explain how goods can be categorized on the basis of whether they are **rival or excludable**, and use graphs to illustrate the efficient quantities of **public goods** and **common resources**, page 152.

Economics in YOUR Life!

What's the "Best" Level of Pollution?

Carbon taxes and carbon trading are alternative approaches for achieving the goal of reducing carbon dioxide emissions. But how do we know the "best" level of carbon emissions? If carbon dioxide emissions hurt the environment, should the government take action to eliminate them completely? As you read the chapter, see if you can answer these questions. You can check your answers against those we provide at the end of the chapter. **>> Continued on page 162**

Externality A benefit or cost that affects someone who is not directly involved in the production or consumption of a good or service.

P
ollution is just one example of an *externality*. An **externality** is a benefit or cost that affects someone who is not directly involved in the production or consumption of a good or service. In the case of air pollution, there is a *negative externality* because, for example, people with asthma may bear a cost even though they were not involved in the buying or selling of the electricity that caused the pollution. *Positive externalities* are also possible. For instance, medical research can provide a positive externality because people who are not directly involved in producing it or paying for it can benefit. A competitive market usually does a good job of producing the economically efficient amount of a good or service. This may not be true, though, if there is an externality in the market. When there is a negative externality, the market may produce a quantity of the good that is greater than the efficient amount. When there is a positive externality, the market may produce a quantity that is less than the efficient amount. In Chapter 4, we saw that government interventions in the economy—such as price floors on agricultural products or price ceilings on rents—can reduce economic efficiency. But when there are externalities, government intervention may actually increase economic efficiency and enhance the well-being of society. The way in which government intervenes is important, however. As the example of the program to reduce acid rain by reducing sulfur dioxide emissions shows, economists can help policymakers ensure that government programs are as efficient as possible.

In this chapter, we explore how best to deal with the problem of pollution and other externalities. We also look at *public goods*, which are goods that may not be produced at all unless the government produces them.

5.1 | Identify examples of positive and negative externalities and use graphs to show how externalities affect economic efficiency.

Externalities and Economic Efficiency

When you consume a Big Mac, only you benefit, but when you consume a college education, other people also benefit. College-educated people are less likely to commit crimes and, by being better-informed voters, more likely to contribute to better government policies. So, although you capture most of the benefits of your college education, you do not capture all of them.

When you buy a Big Mac, the price you pay covers all McDonald's costs of producing the Big Mac. When you buy electricity from a utility that burns coal and generates acid rain, the price you pay for the electricity does not cover the cost of the damage caused by the acid rain.

So, there is a *positive externality* in the production of college educations because people who do not pay for college educations will nonetheless benefit from them. There is a *negative externality* in the generation of electricity because, for example, people with homes on a lake from which fish and wildlife have disappeared because of acid rain have incurred a cost, even though they might not have bought their electricity from the polluting utility.

The Effect of Externalities

Private cost The cost borne by the producer of a good or service.

Social cost The total cost of producing a good or service, including both the private cost and any external cost.

Externalities interfere with the *economic efficiency* of a market equilibrium. We saw in Chapter 4 that a competitive market achieves economic efficiency by maximizing the sum of consumer surplus and producer surplus. *But that result holds only if there are no externalities in production or consumption.* An externality causes a difference between the *private cost* of production and the *social cost*, or the *private benefit* from consumption and the *social benefit*. The **private cost** is the cost borne by the producer of a good or service. The **social cost** is the private cost plus any external cost resulting from production,

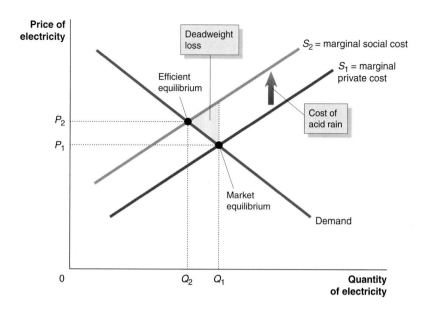

Figure 5-1

The Effect of Pollution on Economic Efficiency

Because utilities do not bear the cost of acid rain, they produce electricity beyond the economically efficient level. Supply curve S_1 represents just the marginal private cost that the utility has to pay. Supply curve S_2 represents the marginal social cost, which includes the costs to those affected by acid rain. The figure shows that if the supply curve were S_2, rather than S_1, market equilibrium would occur at a price of P_2 and a quantity of Q_2, the economically efficient level of output. But when the supply curve is S_1, the market equilibrium occurs at a price of P_1 and a quantity of Q_1 where there is a deadweight loss equal to the area of the yellow triangle. Because of the deadweight loss, this equilibrium is not efficient.

such as the cost of pollution. Unless there is an externality, the private cost and the social cost are equal. The **private benefit** is the benefit received by the consumer of a good or service. The **social benefit** is the private benefit plus any external benefit, such as the benefit to others resulting from your college education. Unless there is an externality, the private benefit and the social benefit are equal.

How a Negative Externality in Production Reduces Economic Efficiency

Consider first how a negative externality in production affects economic efficiency. In Chapters 3 and 4, we assumed that the producer of a good or service must bear all the costs of production. We now know that this observation is not always true. In producing electricity, some private costs are borne by the utility, but some external costs of acid rain are borne by farmers, fishermen, and the general public. The social cost of producing electricity is the sum of the private cost plus the external cost. Figure 5-1 shows the effect on the market for electricity of a negative externality in production.

S_1 is the market supply curve and represents only the private costs that utilities have to bear in generating electricity. As we saw in Chapter 4, firms will supply an additional unit of a good or service only if they receive a price equal to the additional cost of producing that unit, so a supply curve represents the *marginal cost* of producing a good or service. If utilities also had to bear the cost of acid rain, the supply curve would be S_2, which represents the true marginal social cost of generating electricity. The equilibrium with a price P_2 and quantity Q_2 is efficient. The equilibrium with a price P_1 and quantity Q_1 is not efficient. To see why, remember from Chapter 4 that an equilibrium is economically efficient if economic surplus—which is the sum of consumer surplus plus producer surplus—is at a maximum. When economic surplus is at a maximum, the net benefit to society from the production of the good or service is at a maximum. With an equilibrium quantity of Q_2, economic surplus is at a maximum, so this equilibrium is efficient. But with an equilibrium quantity of Q_1, economic surplus is reduced by the deadweight loss, shown in Figure 5-1 by the yellow triangle, and the equilibrium is not efficient. The deadweight loss occurs because the supply curve is above the demand curve for the production of the units of electricity between Q_2 and Q_1. That is, the additional cost—including the external cost—of producing these units is greater than the marginal benefit to consumers, as represented by the demand curve. In other words, because of the cost of the acid rain, economic efficiency would be improved if less electricity were produced.

We can conclude the following: *When there is a negative externality in producing a good or service, too much of the good or service will be produced at market equilibrium.*

Private benefit The benefit received by the consumer of a good or service.

Social benefit The total benefit from consuming a good or service, including both the private benefit and any external benefit.

Figure 5-2

The Effect of a Positive Externality on Efficiency

People who do not consume college educations can still benefit from them. As a result, the marginal social benefit from a college education is greater than the marginal private benefit seen by college students. Because only the marginal private benefit is represented in the market demand curve D_1, the quantity of college educations produced, Q_1, is too low. If the market demand curve were D_2 instead of D_1, the level of college educations produced would be Q_2, which is the efficient level. At the market equilibrium of Q_1, there is a deadweight loss equal to the area of the yellow triangle.

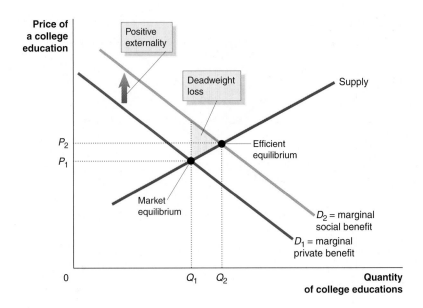

How a Positive Externality in Consumption Reduces Economic Efficiency

We have seen that a negative externality interferes with achieving economic efficiency. The same holds true for a positive externality. In Chapters 3 and 4, we assumed that the demand curve represents all the benefits that come from consuming a good. But we have seen that a college education generates benefits that are not captured by the student receiving the education and so is not represented in the market demand curve for college education. Figure 5-2 shows the effect of a positive externality in consumption on the market for a college education.

If students receiving a college education could capture all its benefits, the demand curve would be D_2, which represents the marginal social benefits. The actual demand curve is D_1, however, which represents only the marginal private benefits received by students. The efficient equilibrium would come at price P_2 and quantity Q_2. At this equilibrium, economic surplus is maximized. The market equilibrium, at price P_1 and quantity Q_1, will not be efficient because the demand curve is above the supply curve for production of the units between Q_1 and Q_2. That is, the marginal benefit—including the external benefit—for producing these units is greater than the marginal cost. As a result, there is a deadweight loss equal to the area of the yellow triangle. Because of the positive externality, economic efficiency would be improved if more college educations were produced. We can conclude the following: *When there is a positive externality in consuming a good or service, too little of the good or service will be produced at market equilibrium.*

Externalities May Result in Market Failure

Market failure A situation in which the market fails to produce the efficient level of output.

We have seen that because of externalities, the efficient level of output may not occur in either the market for electricity or the market for college educations. These are examples of **market failure**: situations in which the market fails to produce the efficient level of output. Later, we will discuss possible solutions to problems of externalities. But first we need to consider why externalities occur.

What Causes Externalities?

Property rights The rights individuals or businesses have to the exclusive use of their property, including the right to buy or sell it.

We saw in Chapter 2 that governments need to guarantee *property rights* for a market system to function well. **Property rights** refers to the rights individuals or businesses have to the exclusive use of their property, including the right to buy or sell it.

Property can be tangible, physical property, such as a store or factory. Property can also be intangible, such as the right to an idea. Most of the time, the U.S. government and the governments of other high-income countries do a good job of enforcing property rights, but in certain situations, property rights do not exist or cannot be legally enforced.

Consider the following situation: Lee owns land that includes a lake. A paper company wants to lease some of Lee's land to build a pulp and paper mill. The paper mill will discharge pollutants into Lee's lake. Because Lee owns the lake, he can charge the paper company the cost of cleaning up the pollutants. The result is that the cost of the pollution is a private cost to the paper company and is included in the price of the paper it sells. There is no externality, the efficient level of paper is produced, and there is no market failure.

Now suppose that the paper company builds its paper mill on privately owned land on the banks of a lake that is owned by the state. In the absence of any government regulations, the company will be free to discharge pollutants into the lake. The cost of the pollution will be external to the company because it doesn't have to pay the cost of cleaning it up. More than the economically efficient level of paper will be produced, and a market failure will occur. Or, suppose that Lee owns the lake, but the pollution is caused by acid rain generated by an electric utility hundreds of miles away. The law does not allow Lee to charge the utility for the damage caused by the acid rain. Even though someone is damaging Lee's property, the law does not allow him to enforce his property rights in this situation. Once again, there is an externality, and the market failure will result in too much electricity being produced.

Similarly, if you buy a house, the government will protect your right to exclusive use of that house. No one else can use the house without your permission. Because of your property rights in the house, your private benefit from the house and the social benefit are the same. When you buy a college education, however, other people are, in effect, able to benefit from your college education. You have no property right that will enable you to prevent them from benefiting or to charge them for the benefits they receive. As a result, there is a positive externality, and the market failure will result in too few college educations being supplied.

We can conclude the following: *Externalities and market failures result from incomplete property rights or from the difficulty of enforcing property rights in certain situations.*

5.2 | Discuss the Coase theorem and explain how private bargaining can lead to economic efficiency in a market with an externality.

Private Solutions to Externalities: The Coase Theorem

As noted at the beginning of this chapter, government intervention may actually increase economic efficiency and enhance the well-being of society when externalities are present. It is also possible, however, for people to find private solutions to the problem of externalities.

Can the market cure market failure? In an important article written in 1960, Ronald Coase of the University of Chicago, winner of the 1991 Nobel Prize in Economics, argued that under some circumstances, private solutions to the problem of externalities will occur. To understand Coase's argument, it is important to recognize that completely eliminating an externality usually is not economically efficient. Consider pollution, for example. There is, in fact, an *economically efficient level of pollution reduction*. At first, this seems paradoxical. Pollution is bad, and you might think the efficient amount of a bad thing is zero. But it isn't zero.

The Economically Efficient Level of Pollution Reduction

Chapter 1 introduced the important idea that the optimal decision is to continue any activity up to the point where the marginal benefit equals the marginal cost. This applies to reducing pollution just as much as to other activities. As sulfur dioxide emissions—or any other type of pollution—decline, society benefits: Fewer trees die, fewer buildings are damaged, and fewer people suffer breathing problems. But a key point is that the additional benefit—that is, the *marginal benefit*—received from eliminating another ton of sulfur dioxide declines as sulfur dioxide emissions are reduced. To see why this is true, consider what happens with no reduction in sulfur dioxide emissions. In this situation, many smoggy days will occur in the cities of the Midwest and Northeast. Even healthy people may experience breathing problems. As sulfur dioxide emissions are reduced, the number of smoggy days will fall, and healthy people will no longer experience breathing problems. Eventually, if emissions of sulfur dioxide fall to low levels, even people with asthma will no longer be affected. Further reductions in sulfur dioxide will have little additional benefit. The same will be true of the other benefits from reducing sulfur dioxide emissions: As the reductions increase, the additional benefits from fewer buildings and trees being damaged and lakes polluted will decline.

Making
the
Connection

The Clean Air Act: How a Government Policy Reduced Infant Mortality

The following bar graphs show that tremendous progress has been made in the United States in reducing air pollution since Congress passed the Clean Air Act in 1970: Total emissions of the six main air pollutants have fallen by more than half. Over the same period, real U.S. gross domestic product—which measures the value, corrected for inflation, of all the final goods and services produced in the country—almost doubled, energy consumption increased by half, and the number of miles traveled by all vehicles almost doubled.

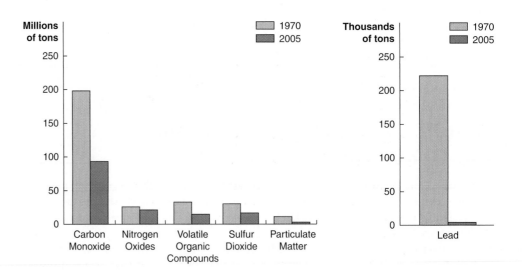

As we have seen, when levels of pollution are high, the marginal benefit of reducing pollution also is high. We would expect, then, that the benefit of reducing air pollution in 1970 was much higher than the benefit from a proportional reduction in air pollution would be today, when the level of pollution is much lower. Kenneth Y. Chay of the University of California, Berkeley, and Michael Greenstone of MIT have shown that the benefits from the air pollution reductions that occurred in the period immediately after passage of the Clean Air Act were indeed high. Chay and Greenstone argue that the exposure of pregnant women to high levels of air pollution can be damaging to their unborn fetuses, possibly by retarding lung functioning. This damage would increase the chance that the infant would die in the first weeks after being born. In the two years following passage of the Clean Air Act, there was a sharp reduction in air pollution and also a reduction in infant mortality. The decline in infant mortality was mainly due to a reduction in deaths within one month of birth. Of course, other factors also may have been responsible for the decline in infant mortality, but Chay and Greenstone use statistical analysis to isolate the effect of the decline in air pollution. They conclude that "1,300 fewer infants died in 1972 than would have in the absence of the Clean Air Act."

Source: Kenneth Y. Chay and Michael Greenstone, "Air Quality, Infant Mortality, and the Clean Air Act of 1970," National Bureau of Economic Research working paper 10053, October 2003.

YOUR TURN: Test your understanding by doing related problem 2.8 on page 168 at the end of this chapter.

What about the marginal cost to electric utilities of reducing pollution? To reduce sulfur dioxide emissions, utilities have to switch from burning high-sulfur coal to burning more costly fuel, or they have to install pollution control devices, such as scrubbers. As the level of pollution falls, further reductions become increasingly costly. Reducing emissions or other types of pollution to very low levels can require complex and expensive new technologies. For example, Arthur Fraas of the federal Office of Management and Budget and Vincent Munley of Lehigh University have shown that the marginal cost of removing 97 percent of pollutants from municipal wastewater is more than twice as high as the marginal cost of removing 95 percent.

The *net benefit* to society from reducing pollution is equal to the difference between the benefit of reducing pollution and the cost. To maximize the net benefit to society, sulfur dioxide emissions—or any other type of pollution—should be reduced up to the point where the marginal benefit from another ton of reduction is equal to the marginal cost. Figure 5-3 illustrates this point.

In Figure 5-3, we measure *reductions* in sulfur dioxide emissions on the horizontal axis. We measure the marginal benefit and marginal cost in dollars from eliminating another ton of sulfur dioxide emissions on the vertical axis. As reductions in pollution increase, the marginal benefit declines and the marginal cost increases. The economically efficient amount of pollution reduction occurs where the marginal benefit equals the marginal cost. The figure shows that in this case, the economically efficient reduction of sulfur dioxide emissions is 8.5 million tons per year, which is the amount of reduction Congress decided should occur by 2010. At that level of emission reduction, the marginal benefit and the marginal cost of the last ton of sulfur dioxide emissions eliminated are both $200 per ton. Suppose instead that the emissions target were only 7.0 million tons. The figure shows that, at that level of reduction, the last ton of reduction has added $250 to the benefits received by society, but it has added only $175 to the costs of utilities. There has been a net benefit to society from this ton of pollution reduction of $75. In fact, the figure shows a net benefit to society from pollution reduction for every ton from 7.0 million to 8.5 million. Only when sulfur dioxide emissions are reduced by 8.5 million tons per year will marginal benefit fall enough and marginal cost rise enough that the two are equal.

Now suppose Congress had set the target for sulfur dioxide emissions reduction at 10 million tons per year. The figure shows that the marginal benefit at that level of reduction has fallen to only $150 per ton and the marginal cost has risen to $225 per ton. The last ton of reduction has actually *reduced* the net benefit to society by $75 per ton. In fact, every ton of reduction beyond 8.5 million reduces the net benefit to society.

To summarize: If the marginal benefit of reducing sulfur dioxide emissions is greater than the marginal cost, further reductions will make society better off. But if the

Figure 5-3

The Marginal Benefit from Pollution Reduction Should Equal the Marginal Cost

If the reduction of sulfur dioxide emissions is at 7.0 million tons per year, the marginal benefit of $250 per ton is greater than the marginal cost of $175 per ton. Further reductions in emissions will increase the net benefit to society. If the reduction of sulfur dioxide emissions is at 10.0 million tons, the marginal cost of $225 per ton is greater than the marginal benefit of $150 per ton. An increase in sulfur dioxide emissions will increase the net benefit to society. Only when the reduction is at 8.5 million tons is the marginal benefit equal to the marginal cost. This level is the economically efficient level of pollution reduction.

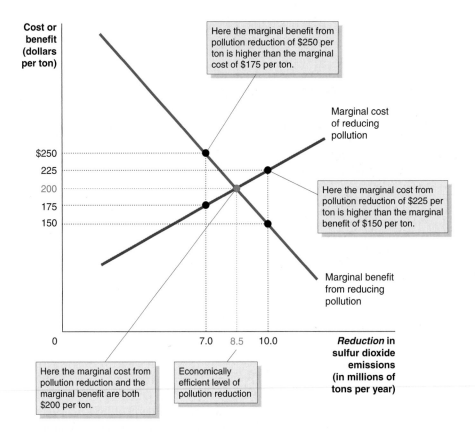

marginal cost of reducing sulfur dioxide emissions is greater than the marginal benefit, reducing sulfur dioxide emissions will actually make society worse off.

The Basis for Private Solutions to Externalities

In arguing that private solutions to the problem of externalities were possible, Ronald Coase emphasized that when more than the optimal level of pollution is occurring, the benefits from reducing the pollution to the optimal level are greater than the costs. Figure 5-4 illustrates this point.

Don't Let This Happen to **YOU!**

Remember That It's the *Net* Benefit That Counts

Why would we not want to *completely* eliminate anything unpleasant? As long as any person suffers any unpleasant consequences from air pollution, the marginal benefit of reducing air pollution will be positive. So, removing every particle of air pollution results in the largest *total* benefit to society. But removing every particle of air pollution is not optimal for the same reason that it is not optimal to remove every particle of dirt or dust from a room when cleaning it. The cost of cleaning your room is not just the price of the cleaning products but also the opportunity cost of your time. The more time you devote to cleaning your

room, the less time you have available for other activities. As you devote more and more additional hours to cleaning your room, the alternative activities you have to give up are likely to increase in value, raising the opportunity cost of cleaning: Cleaning instead of watching TV may not be too costly, but cleaning instead of eating any meals or getting any sleep is very costly. Optimally, you should eliminate dirt in your room up to the point where the marginal benefit of the last dirt removed equals the marginal cost of removing it. Society should take the same approach to air pollution. The result is the largest *net* benefit to society.

YOUR TURN: Test your understanding by doing related problem 2.6 on page 167 at the end of this chapter.

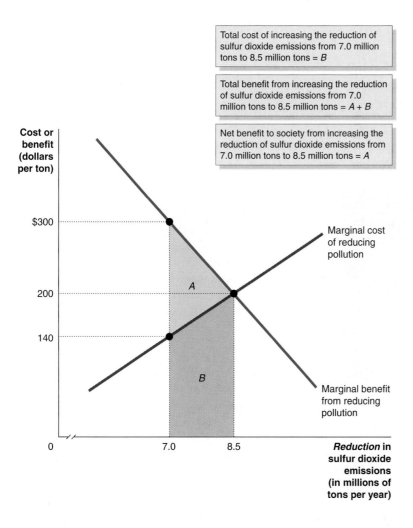

Total cost of increasing the reduction of sulfur dioxide emissions from 7.0 million tons to 8.5 million tons = B

Total benefit from increasing the reduction of sulfur dioxide emissions from 7.0 million tons to 8.5 million tons = A + B

Net benefit to society from increasing the reduction of sulfur dioxide emissions from 7.0 million tons to 8.5 million tons = A

Figure 5-4

The Benefits of Reducing Pollution to the Optimal Level Are Greater Than the Costs

Increasing the reduction in sulfur dioxide emissions from 7.0 million tons to 8.5 million tons results in total benefits equal to the sum of the areas *A* and *B* under the marginal benefits curve. The total cost of this decrease in pollution is equal to the area *B* under the marginal cost curve. The total benefits are greater than the total costs by an amount equal to the area of triangle *A*. Because the total benefits from reducing pollution are greater than the total costs, it's possible for those receiving the benefits to arrive at a private agreement with polluters to pay them to reduce pollution.

The marginal benefit curve shows the additional benefit from each reduction in a ton of sulfur dioxide emissions. The area under the marginal benefit curve between the two emission levels is the *total* benefit received from reducing emissions from one level to another. For instance, in Figure 5-4, the total benefit from increasing the reduction in sulfur dioxide emissions from 7.0 million tons to 8.5 million tons is the sum of the areas of *A* and *B*. The marginal cost curve shows the additional cost from each reduction in a ton of emissions. The *total* cost of reducing emissions from one level to another is the area under the marginal cost curve between the two emissions levels. The total cost from increasing the reduction in emissions from 7.0 million tons to 8.5 million tons is the area *B*. The net benefit from reducing emissions is the difference between the total cost and the total benefit, which is equal to the area of triangle *A*.

In Figure 5-4, the benefits from further reductions in sulfur dioxide emissions are much greater than the costs. In the appendix to Chapter 1, we reviewed the formula for calculating the area of a triangle, which is ½ × base × height, and the formula for the area of a rectangle, which is base × height. Using these formulas, we can calculate the value of the total benefits from the reduction in emissions and the value of the total costs. The value of the benefits (*A* + *B*) is $375 million. The value of the costs (*B*) is $255 million. If the people who would benefit from a reduction in pollution could get together, they could offer to pay the electric utilities $255 million to reduce the pollution to the optimal level. After making the payment, they would still be left with a net benefit of $120 million. In other words, a private agreement to reduce pollution to the optimal level is possible, without any need for government intervention.

Making
the
Connection

The Fable of the Bees

Apple trees must be pollinated by bees to bear fruit. Bees need the nectar from apple trees (or other plants) to produce honey.

In a famous article published in the early 1950s, the British economist James Meade, winner of the 1977 Nobel Prize in Economics, argued that there were positive externalities in both apple growing and beekeeping. The more apple trees growers planted, the more honey would be produced in the hives of local beekeepers. And the more hives beekeepers kept, the larger the apple crops in neighboring apple orchards. Meade assumed that beekeepers were not being compensated by apple grow-

ers for the pollination services they were providing to apple growers and that apple growers were not being compensated by beekeepers for the use of their nectar in honey making. Therefore, he concluded that unless the government intervened, the market would not supply enough apple trees and beehives.

Steven Cheung of the University of Washington showed, however, that government intervention was not necessary because beekeepers and apple growers had long since arrived at private agreements. In fact, in Washington State, farmers with fruit orchards had been renting beehives to pollinate their trees since at least World War I. According to Cheung, "Pollination contracts usually include stipulations regarding the number and strength of the [bee] colonies, the rental fee per hive, the time of delivery and removal of hives, the protection of bees from pesticide sprays, and the strategic placing of hives."

Some apple growers and beekeepers make private arrangements to arrive at an economically efficient outcome.

Today, honeybees pollinate more than $14 billion worth of crops annually. Many beekeepers travel from state to state, renting out their bees to farmers. Increasing demand for almonds has expanded the crop in California until it now stretches for 300 miles across 580,000 acres. Currently, more than one million beehives are required to pollinate the California almond crop. Beehives are shipped into the state in February and March to pollinate the almond trees, and then they are shipped to Oregon and Washington to pollinate the cherry, pear, and apple orchards in those states during April and May.

Sources: J. E. Meade, "External Economies and Diseconomies in a Competitive Situation," *Economic Journal*, Vol. 62, March 1952, pp. 54–67; Steven N. S. Cheung, "The Fable of the Bees: An Economic Investigation," *Journal of Law and Economics*, Vol. 16, 1973, pp. 11–33; and Alexei Barrionuevo, "Honey Bees Vanish, Leaving Keepers in Peril," *New York Times*, February 27, 2007.

YOUR TURN: Test your understanding by doing related problem 2.9 on page 168 at the end of this chapter.

Do Property Rights Matter?

In discussing the bargaining between the electric utilities and the people suffering the effects of the utlities' pollution, we assumed that the electric utilities were not legally liable for the damage they were causing. In other words, the victims of pollution could not legally enforce the right of their property not to be damaged, so they would have to pay the utilities to reduce the pollution. But would it make any difference if the utilities were legally liable for the damages? Surprisingly, as Coase was the first to point out, it does not matter for the amount of pollution reduction. The only difference would be that now the electric utilities would have to pay the victims of pollution for the right to pollute rather than the victims having to pay the utilities. Because the marginal benefits and marginal costs of pollution reduction would not change, the bargaining would still result in the efficient level of pollution reduction—in this case, 8.5 million tons.

In the absence of the utilities being legally liable, the victims of pollution have an incentive to pay the utilities to reduce pollution up to the point where the marginal benefit of the last ton of reduction is equal to the marginal cost. If the utilities are legally liable, they have an incentive to pay the victims of pollution to allow them to pollute up to the same point.

The Problem of Transactions Costs

Unfortunately, there are frequently practical difficulties in the way of a private solution to the problem of externalities. In cases of pollution, for example, there are often both many polluters and many people suffering from the negative effects of pollution. Bringing together all those suffering from pollution with all those causing the pollution and negotiating an agreement often fails due to *transactions costs*. **Transactions costs** are the costs in time and other resources that parties incur in the process of agreeing to and carrying out an exchange of goods or services. In this case, the transactions costs would include the time and other costs of negotiating an agreement, drawing up a binding contract, purchasing insurance, and monitoring the agreement. Unfortunately, when many people are involved, the transactions costs are often higher than the net benefits from reducing the externality. Thus, the cost of transacting ends up exceeding the gain from the transaction. In such cases, a private solution to an externality problem is not feasible.

Transactions costs The costs in time and other resources that parties incur in the process of agreeing to and carrying out an exchange of goods or services.

The Coase Theorem

Coase's argument that private solutions to the problem of externalities are possible is summed up in the **Coase theorem**: If transactions costs are low, private bargaining will result in an efficient solution to the problem of externalities. We have seen the basis for the Coase theorem in the preceding example of pollution by electric utilities: Because the benefits from reducing an externality are often greater than the costs, private bargaining can arrive at an efficient outcome. But we have also seen that this outcome will occur only if transactions costs are low, and in the case of pollution, they usually are not. In general, private bargaining is most likely to reach an efficient outcome if the number of parties bargaining is small.

In practice, we must add a couple of other qualifications to the Coase theorem. In addition to low transactions costs, private solutions to the problem of externalities will occur only if all parties to the agreement have full information about the costs and benefits associated with the externality, and all parties must be willing to accept a reasonable agreement. For example, if those suffering from the effects of pollution do not have information on the costs of reducing pollution, it is unlikely that the parties can reach an agreement. Unreasonable demands can also hinder an agreement. For instance, in the example of pollution by electric utilities, we saw that the total benefit of reducing sulfur dioxide emissions was $375 million. Even if transactions costs are very low, if the utilities insist on being paid more than $375 million to reduce emissions, no agreement will be reached because the amount paid exceeds the value of the reduction to those suffering from the emissions.

Coase theorem The argument of economist Ronald Coase that if transactions costs are low, private bargaining will result in an efficient solution to the problem of externalities.

5.3 | Analyze government policies to achieve economic efficiency in a market with an externality.

5.3 LEARNING OBJECTIVE

Government Policies to Deal with Externalities

When private solutions to externalities are not feasible, how should the government intervene? The first economist to analyze market failure systematically was A. C. Pigou, a British economist at Cambridge University. Pigou argued that to deal with a negative externality in production, the government should impose a tax equal to the cost of the externality. The effect of such a tax is shown in Figure 5-5, which reproduces the negative externality from acid rain shown in Figure 5-1.

By imposing a tax equal to the cost of acid rain on the production of electricity, the government will cause electric utilities to *internalize* the externality. As a consequence, the cost of the acid rain will become a private cost borne by the utilities, and

Figure 5-5

When There Is a Negative Externality, a Tax Can Bring about the Efficient Level of Output

Because utilities do not bear the cost of acid rain, they produce electricity beyond the economically efficient level. If the government imposes a tax equal to the cost of acid rain, the utilities will internalize the externality. As a consequence, the supply curve will shift up from S_1 to S_2. The market equilibrium quantity changes from Q_1, where an inefficiently high level of electricity is produced, to Q_2, the economically efficient equilibrium quantity. The price of electricity will rise from P_1—which does not include the cost of acid rain—to P_2—which does include the cost.

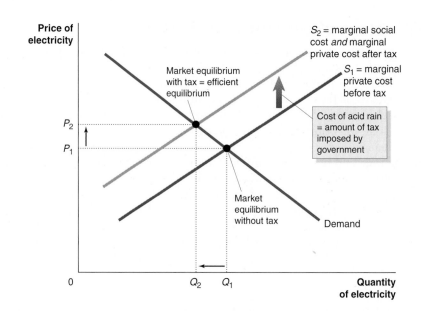

the supply curve for electricity will shift from S_1 to S_2. The result will be a decrease in the equilibrium output of electricity from Q_1 to the efficient level, Q_2. The price of electricity will rise from P_1—which does not include the cost of acid rain—to P_2— which does include the cost.

Solved Problem | **5-3**

Using a Tax to Deal with a Negative Externality

Companies that produce toilet paper bleach the paper to make it white. Some paper plants discharge the bleach into rivers and lakes, causing substantial environmental damage. Suppose the following graph illustrates the situation in the toilet paper market.

Explain how the federal government can use a tax on toilet paper to bring about the efficient level of production. What should the value of the tax be?

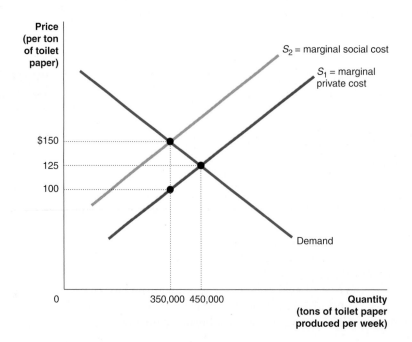

SOLVING THE PROBLEM:

Step 1: **Review the chapter material.** This problem is about the government using a tax to deal with a negative externality in production, so you may want to review the section "Government Policies to Deal with Externalities," which begins on page 147.

Step 2: **Use the information from the graph to determine the necessary tax.** The efficient level of toilet paper production will occur where the marginal social benefit from consuming toilet paper, as represented by the demand curve, is equal to the marginal social cost of production. The graph shows that this will occur at a price of $150 per ton and production of 350,000 tons. In the absence of government intervention, the price will be $125 per ton, and production will be 450,000 tons. It is tempting—but incorrect!—to think that the government could bring about the efficient level of production by imposing a per-ton tax equal to the difference between the price when production is at its optimal level and the current market price. But this would be a tax of only $25. The graph shows that at the optimal level of production, the difference between the marginal private cost and the marginal social cost is $50. Therefore, a tax of $50 per ton is required to shift the supply curve up from S_1 to S_2.

YOUR TURN: For more practice, do related problem 3.8 on page 169 at the end of this chapter.

>> **End Solved Problem 5-3**

Pigou also argued that the government can deal with a positive externality in consumption by giving consumers a subsidy, or payment, equal to the value of the externality. The effect of the subsidy is shown in Figure 5-6, which reproduces the positive externality from college education shown in Figure 5-2.

By paying college students a subsidy equal to the external benefit from a college education, the government will cause students to *internalize* the externality. That is, the external benefit from a college education will become a private benefit received by college students, and the demand curve for college educations will shift from D_1 to D_2. The equilibrium number of college educations supplied will increase from Q_1 to the efficient level, Q_2. In fact, the government does heavily subsidize college educations. All states have government-operated universities that charge tuitions well below the cost of providing the education. The state and federal governments also provide students with grants and low-interest loans that subsidize college educations. The economic justification for these programs is that college educations provide an external benefit to society.

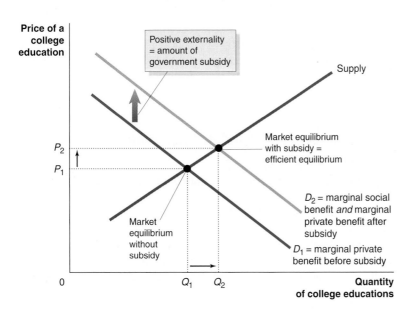

Figure 5-6

When There Is a Positive Externality, a Subsidy Can Bring about the Efficient Level of Output

People who do not consume college educations can benefit from them. As a result, the social benefit from a college education is greater than the private benefit seen by college students. If the government pays a subsidy equal to the external benefit, students will internalize the externality. The subsidy will cause the demand curve to shift up, from D_1 to D_2. The result will be that market equilibrium quantity shifts from Q_1, where an inefficiently low level of college educations is supplied, to Q_2, the economically efficient equilibrium quantity.

Pigovian taxes and subsidies
Government taxes and subsidies intended to bring about an efficient level of output in the presence of externalities.

Because A. C. Pigou was the first economist to propose using government taxes and subsidies to deal with externalities, they are sometimes referred to as **Pigovian taxes and subsidies**. Note that a Pigovian tax eliminates deadweight loss and improves economic efficiency. This situation is the opposite of the one we saw in Chapter 4, in which we discussed how most taxes reduce consumer surplus and producer surplus and create a deadweight loss. In fact, one reason that economists support Pigovian taxes as a way to deal with negative externalities is that the government can use the revenues raised by Pigovian taxes to lower other taxes that reduce economic efficiency.

Command and Control versus Tradable Emissions Allowances

Although the federal government has sometimes used taxes and subsidies to deal with externalities, in dealing with pollution, it has traditionally used a *command and control approach* with firms that pollute. A **command and control approach** to reducing pollution involves the government imposing quantitative limits on the amount of pollution firms are allowed to generate or requiring firms to install specific pollution control devices. For example, in 1983, the federal government required auto manufacturers such as Ford and General Motors to install catalytic converters to reduce auto emissions on all new automobiles.

Command and control approach An approach that involves the government imposing quantitative limits on the amount of pollution firms are allowed to emit or requiring firms to install specific pollution control devices.

Congress could have used direct pollution controls to deal with the problem of acid rain. To achieve its objective of a reduction of 8.5 million tons per year in sulfur dioxide emissions by 2010, it could have required every utility to reduce sulfur dioxide emissions by the same specified amount. However, this approach would not have been an economically efficient solution to the problem. As we saw at the beginning of this chapter, utilities can have very different costs of reducing sulfur dioxide emissions. Some utilities, like Duke Energy, that already use low-sulfur coal can reduce emissions further only at a high cost. Other utilities, particularly those in the Midwest, are able to reduce emissions at a lower cost.

Congress decided to use a market-based approach to reducing sulfur dioxide emissions by setting up a system of tradable emissions allowances. The federal government gave utilities allowances equal to the total amount of allowable sulfur dioxide emissions. The utilities were then free to buy and sell the allowances. An active market where the allowances can be bought and sold is conducted on the Chicago Mercantile Exchange. Utilities that could reduce emissions at low cost did so and sold their allowances. Utilities that could only reduce emissions at high cost bought allowances. Using tradable emissions allowances to reduce acid rain has been a great success and has made it possible for utilities to meet Congress's emissions goal at a much lower cost than expected. As Figure 5-7 shows, just before Congress enacted the allowances program in 1990, the Edison Electrical Institute estimated that the cost to utilities of complying with the program would be $7.4 billion by 2010. By 1994, the federal government's General Accounting Office estimated that the cost would be less than $2 billion. In practice, the cost appears likely to be almost 90 percent less than the initial estimate, or only about $870 *million.*

Are Tradable Emissions Allowances Licenses to Pollute?

Some environmentalists have criticized tradable emissions allowances, labeling them "licenses to pollute." They argue that just as the government does not issue licenses to rob banks or to drive drunk, it should not issue licenses to pollute. But this criticism ignores one of the central lessons of economics: Resources are scarce, and trade-offs exist. Resources that are spent reducing one type of pollution are not available to reduce other types of pollution or for any other use. Because reducing acid rain using tradable emissions allowances cost utilities $870 million, rather than $7.4 billion, as originally estimated, society saved more than $6.5 billion.

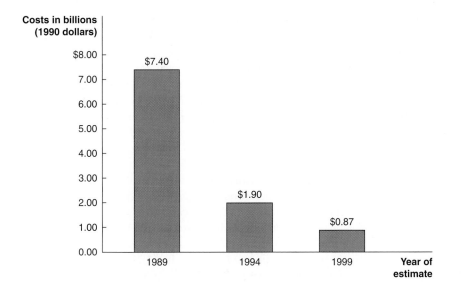

Figure 5-7

Estimated Cost of the Acid Rain Program in 2010

The Edison Electric Institute estimated in 1989 that the program to reduce acid rain pollution would cost utilities a total of $7.4 billion by 2010. The system of tradable emissions allowances used in the program resulted in the bulk of the reduction in pollution being carried out by the utilities that could do it at the lowest cost. As a result, the program is likely to cost $870 million, which is almost 90 percent less than the original estimate. (*Note:* To correct for the effect of inflation, the costs are measured in dollars of 1990 purchasing power.)
Source: Environmental Protection Agency, *Progress Report on the EPA Acid Rain Program*, November 1999, Figure 2.

Making the Connection | Can Tradable Permits Reduce Global Warming?

In the past 25 years, the global surface temperature has increased about three-quarters of 1 degree Fahrenheit (or four-tenths of 1 degree Centigrade) compared with the average for the previous 30 years. The following graph shows changes in temperature over the years since 1880.

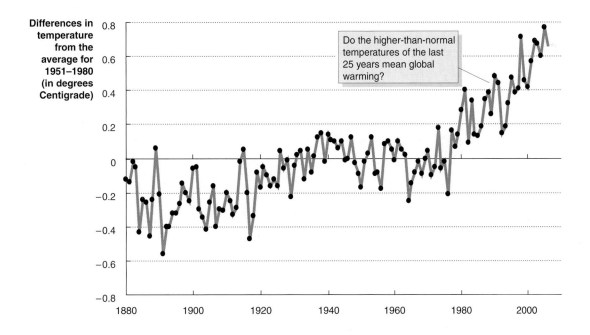

Global temperatures have gone through many periods of warming and cooling. In fact, the below-normal temperatures that prevailed before 1970 led some scientists to predict the eventual arrival of a new ice age. Nevertheless, many scientists are convinced that the recent warming is not part of the natural fluctuations in temperature but is instead due to the burning of fossil fuels, such as coal, natural gas, and petroleum. Burning these fuels releases CO_2 (carbon dioxide), which accumulates in the atmosphere as a "greenhouse gas." Greenhouse gases cause some of the heat released from the earth to be reflected back, increasing temperatures.

If greenhouse gases continue to accumulate in the atmosphere, according to some estimates, global temperatures could increase by 3 degrees Fahrenheit or more during the next 100 years. Such increases in temperature could lead to significant changes in climate, which might result in more storms and flooding as well as other problems. By 1995, a number of nations had concluded that the threat of global warming was significant enough to take steps toward reducing emissions of CO_2 and other greenhouse gases. The result was the 1997 Kyoto Treaty, which, if accepted, would have required the high-income countries to reduce their CO_2 emissions by more than 5 percent compared with their 1990 levels. However, President George W. Bush was not willing to commit the United States to the treaty. He argued that the costs to the United States of complying with the treaty were too high, particularly because some scientists were still skeptical that CO_2 emissions actually were causing the increase in temperature. Even scientists who believed that CO_2 emissions contribute to rising temperatures were skeptical that the Kyoto Treaty would have much effect on global warming. President Bush also argued that developing countries should be included in any agreement. Some developing countries, such as China and India, are experiencing rapid economic growth, which in turn has led to rapid increases in CO_2 emissions. European countries that ratified the Kyoto Treaty have had difficulty fulfilling their commitments to reduce CO_2 emissions to the levels indicated by the treaty. Of the larger European countries, only Great Britain, where emissions have declined by more than 15 percent since 1990, seems likely to succeed in fulfilling its commitments by 2012.

The mechanism by which reductions in CO_2 emissions would occur has also been in dispute. The United States has favored a global system of tradable emission permits for CO_2 that would be similar to the system for sulfur dioxide discussed earlier in this chapter. As we have seen, this type of system has the potential to reduce CO_2 emissions at a lower cost. Most European countries, however, have been reluctant to fully accept such a system, preferring instead to require that each country reduce emissions by a specified amount. In recent years, though, support has grown in Europe for using tradable allowances, and an active market in these allowances has developed under the European Union Greenhouse Gas Emission Trading Scheme, which began operation in 2005. It seems unlikely that the debate over the costs and benefits of reducing CO_2 emissions will be resolved any time soon.

Sources: Juliet Eilperin and Steven Mufson, "Tax on Carbon Emissions Gains Support," *Washington Post*, April 1, 2007, p. A05; United Nations Framework Convention on Climate Change, *National Greenhouse Gas Inventory Data for the Period 1990–2004*, October 19, 2006; and (for data in the graph) NASA, Goddard Institute for Space Studies, http://data.giss.nasa.gov/gistemp/graphs/.

YOUR TURN: Test your understanding by doing related problem 3.11 on page 169 at the end of this chapter.

5.4 LEARNING OBJECTIVE

5.4 | Explain how goods can be categorized on the basis of whether they are rival or excludable, and use graphs to illustrate the efficient quantities of public goods and common resources.

Four Categories of Goods

We can explore further the question of when the market is likely to succeed in supplying the efficient quantity of a good by noting that goods differ on the basis of whether their consumption is *rival* and *excludable*. **Rivalry** occurs when one person's consuming a unit of a good means no one else can consume it. If you consume a Big Mac, for example, no one else can consume it. **Excludability** means that anyone who does not pay for a good cannot consume it. If you don't pay for a Big Mac, for example, MacDonald's can exclude you from consuming it. The consumption of a Big Mac is rival and excludable. The consumption of some goods, however, can be either *nonrival or nonexcludable*. Nonrival means that one person's consumption does not interfere with another person's consumption. Nonexcludable means that it is impossible to exclude others from

Rivalry The situation that occurs when one person's consuming a unit of a good means no one else can consume it.

Excludability The situation in which anyone who does not pay for a good cannot consume it.

	Excludable	Nonexcludable
Rival	**Private Goods** *Examples:* Big Macs Running shoes	**Common Resources** *Examples:* Tuna in the ocean Public pasture land
Nonrival	**Quasi-Public Goods** *Examples:* Cable TV Toll road	**Public Goods** *Examples:* National defense Court system

Figure 5-8

Four Categories of Goods

Goods and services can be divided into four categories on the basis of whether people can be excluded from consuming them and whether they are rival in consumption. A good or service is rival in consumption if it can be consumed by only one person at the same time.

consuming the good, whether they have paid for it or not. Figure 5-8 shows four possible categories into which goods can fall.

We next consider each of the four categories:

1 *Private goods.* A good that is both rival and excludable is a **private good**. Food, clothing, haircuts, and many other goods and services fall into this category. One person's consuming a unit of these goods precludes other people from consuming that unit, and anyone who does not buy these goods can't consume them. Although we didn't state it explicitly, when we analyzed the demand and supply for goods and services in Chapter 3, we assumed that the goods and services were all private goods.

2 *Public goods.* A **public good** is both nonrivalrous and nonexcludable. Public goods are often, although not always, supplied by a government rather than by private firms. The classic example of a public good is national defense. Your consuming national defense does not interfere with your neighbor's consuming it, so consumption is nonrivalrous. You also cannot be excluded from consuming it, whether you pay for it or not. No private firm would be willing to supply national defense because everyone can consume national defense without paying for it. The behavior of consumers in this situation is referred to as *free riding*. **Free riding** involves individuals benefiting from a good—in this case, the provision of national defense—without paying for it.

3 *Quasi-public goods.* Some goods are excludable but not rival. An example is cable television. People who do not pay for cable television do not receive it, but one person's watching it doesn't affect other people's watching it. The same is true of a toll road. Anyone who doesn't pay the toll doesn't get on the road, but one person using the road doesn't interfere with someone else using the road (unless so many people are using the road that it becomes congested). Goods that fall into this category are called *quasi-public goods.*

4 *Common resources.* If a good is rival but not excludable, it is a **common resource**. Forest land in many poor countries is a common resource. If one person cuts down a tree, no one else can use the tree. But if no one has a property right to the forest, no one can be excluded from using it. As we will discuss in more detail later, people often overuse common resources.

Private good A good that is both rival and excludable.

Public good A good that is both nonrivalrous and nonexcludable.

Free riding Benefiting from a good without paying for it.

Common resource A good that is rival but not excludable.

Making the Connection | Should the Government Run the Health Care System?

In many countries, such as Canada, Japan, the United Kingdom, and France, the government either supplies health care directly by operating hospitals and employing doctors and nurses, or pays for most health care expenses even if hospitals are not government owned and doctors are not government employees. In the United States, the federal government supplies health care to veterans of the armed forces through the Veterans Administration (VA) system and pays for the health care of people over age 65 under the Medicare program. The federal government also contributes to the Medicaid program under which state governments pay for health care for some poor people. Most medium and large-size firms provide health insurance as a fringe benefit to their employees. About 88 percent of individuals who have private health insurance receive it as part of a benefits package from their employers. Those individuals not covered by health insurance plans and not eligible for government aid must pay for their own health care bills out of pocket, just as they pay their other bills, or receive charity care. The chart shows that in 2007, government spending on Medicare, Medicaid, and other government health care programs was about 46 percent of total health care spending.

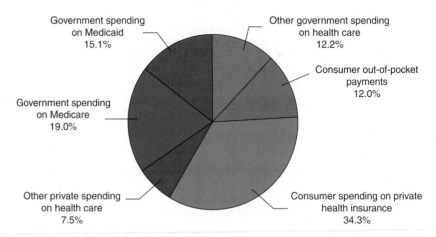

Source: John A. Poisal, et al., *Health Spending Projections through 2017*, Washington, DC: National Health Statistics Group, Centers for Medicare & Medicaid Services, U.S. Department of Health and Human Services.

What should be the government's role in health care? Is health care a public good that government should supply—or, at least, pay for? Is it a private good, like food, clothing, or television sets, that private firms should supply and consumers should pay for without government aid? Should private firms supply most health care, subject to some government regulation? Economists differ in their answers to these questions because the delivery of health care involves a number of complex issues. But we can consider briefly some of the most important points. We have seen that a public good is both nonrivalrous and nonexcludable. In this sense, health care does not qualify as a public good. More than one person cannot simultaneously consume the same surgical operation, for example. And someone who will not pay for an operation can be excluded from consuming it. (Most states require hospitals to treat patients who are too poor to pay for treatment, and many doctors will treat poor people at a reduced price. But because there is nothing in the nature of health care that keeps people who do not pay for it from being excluded from consuming it, health care does not fit the definition of a public good.)

There are aspects of the delivery of health care that have convinced some economists that government intervention is justified, however. For example, consuming certain types of health care generates positive externalities. In particular, being vaccinated against a communicable disease, such as influenza or chicken pox, not only reduces the chance that the person vaccinated will catch the disease but also reduces the probability that an epidemic of the disease will occur. Therefore, the market may supply an inefficiently small quantity of vaccinations unless vaccinations receive a government subsidy. Information problems can also be important in the market for private health insurance. Consumers as buyers of health insurance often know much more about the state of their health than do the companies selling health insurance. This information problem may raise costs to insurance companies when the pool of people being insured is small, making insurance companies less willing to offer health insurance to consumers the companies suspect may file too many claims. Economists debate how important information problems are in health care markets and whether government intervention is required to reduce them. We will consider this question further in Chapter 17, when we discuss the economics of information.

Many economists believe that market-based solutions are the best approach to improving the health care system. Currently, the U.S. health care system is a world leader in innovation in medical technology and prescription drugs. The market-oriented approach to reforming health care starts with the goal of preserving incentives for U.S. firms to continue with innovations in medical screening equipment, surgical procedures, and prescription drugs. Presently, markets are delivering inaccurate signals to consumers because when buying health care, unlike when buying most other goods and services, consumers pay a price well *below* the true cost of providing the service. Consumers usually pay less than the true cost of medical treatment because a third party—typically, an insurance company—often pays most of the bill. For example, consumers who have health insurance provided by their employers usually pay only a small amount—perhaps $20—for a visit to a doctor's office, when the true cost of the visit might be $80 or $90. The result is that consumers demand a larger quantity of health care services than they would if they paid a price that better represented the cost of providing the services. Doctors and other health care providers also have a reduced incentive to control costs because they know that an insurance company will pick up most of the bill.

Under current tax laws, individuals do not pay taxes on health insurance benefits they receive from their employers, and this encourages them to want very generous coverage that reduces incentives to control costs. But individuals get no tax break for buying insurance on their own or for out-of-pocket medical spending. Some economists have proposed making the tax treatment of health insurance and health spending more uniform, a change that could, potentially, significantly reduce spending on health care without reducing the effectiveness of the health care received. Such tax law changes would make it more likely that company-provided health insurance would focus on large medical bills—such as those resulting from hospitalizations—while consumers would pay prices closer to the costs of providing routine medical care.

Because health care is so important to consumers and because health care spending looms so large in the U.S. economy, the role of the government in the health care system is likely to be the subject of intense debate for some time to come.

Source: To read more on the role of the government in the market for health care, see Sherman Folland, Allen C. Goodman, and Miron Stano, *The Economics of Health and Health Care*, 5th ed., Upper Saddle River, NJ: Prentice Hall, 2007, Chapter 19; and John F. Coogan, R. Glenn Hubbard, and Daniel P. Kessler, *Healthy, Wealthy, and Wise: Five Steps to a Better Health Care System*, Washington, DC: The AEI Press, 2005.

YOUR TURN: Test your understanding by doing related problem 4.9 on page 171 at the end of this chapter.

We discussed the demand and supply for private goods in Chapter 3. For the remainder of this chapter, we focus on the categories of public goods and common resources. To determine the optimal quantity of a public good, we have to modify the demand and supply analysis of Chapter 3 to take into account that a public good is both nonrivalrous and nonexcludable.

The Demand for a Public Good

We can determine the market demand curve for a good or service by adding up the quantity of the good demanded by each consumer at each price. To keep things simple, let's take the case of a market with only two consumers. Figure 5-9 shows that the market demand curve for hamburgers depends on the individual demand curves of Jill and Joe.

At a price of $4.00, Jill demands 2 hamburgers per week and Joe demands 4. Adding horizontally, the combination of a price of $4.00 per hamburger and a quantity demanded of 6 hamburgers will be a point on the market demand curve for hamburgers. Similarly, adding horizontally at a price of $1.50, we have a price of $1.50 and a quantity demanded of 11 as another point on the market demand curve. A consumer's demand curve for a good represents the marginal benefit the consumer receives from the good, so when we add together the consumers' demand curves, we not only have the

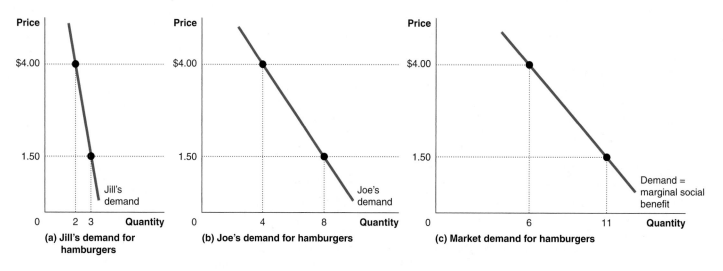

Figure 5-9 | Constructing the Market Demand Curve for a Private Good

The market demand curve for private goods is determined by adding horizontally the quantity of the good demanded at each price by each consumer. For instance, in panel (a), Jill demands 2 hamburgers when the price is $4.00, and in panel (b), Joe demands 4 hamburgers when the price is $4.00. So, a quantity of 6 hamburgers and a price of $4.00 is a point on the market demand curve in panel (c).

market demand curve but also the marginal social benefit curve for this good, assuming that there is no externality in consumption.

How can we find the demand curve or marginal social benefit curve for a public good? Once again, for simplicity, assume that Jill and Joe are the only consumers. Unlike with a private good, where Jill and Joe can end up consuming different quantities, with a public good, they will consume *the same quantity*. Suppose that Jill owns a service station on an isolated rural road, and Joe owns a car dealership next door. These are the only two businesses around for miles. Both Jill and Joe are afraid that unless they hire a security guard at night, their businesses may be burgled. Like national defense, the services of a security guard are in this case a public good: Once hired, the guard will be able to protect both businesses, so the good is nonrival. It also will not be possible to exclude either business from being protected, so the good is nonexcludable.

To arrive at a demand curve for a public good, we don't add quantities at each price, as with a private good. Instead, we add the price each consumer is willing to pay for each quantity of the public good. This value represents the total dollar amount consumers as a group would be willing to pay for that quantity of the public good. Put another way, to find the demand curve, or marginal social benefit curve, for a private good, we add the demand curves of individual consumers horizontally, while for public goods, we add individual demand curves vertically. Figure 5-10 shows how the marginal social benefit curve for security guard services depends on the individual demand curves of Jill and Joe.

The figure shows that Jill is willing to pay $8 per hour for the guard to provide 10 hours of protection per night. Joe would suffer a greater loss from a burglary, so he is willing to pay $10 per hour for the same amount of protection. Adding the dollar amount that each is willing to pay gives us a price of $18 per hour and a quantity of 10 hours as a point on the marginal social benefit curve for security guard services. Because Jill is willing to spend $4 per hour for 15 hours of guard services and Joe is willing to pay $5, a price of $9 per hour and a quantity of 15 hours is also a point on the marginal social benefit curve for security guard services.

The Optimal Quantity of a Public Good

We know that to achieve economic efficiency, a good or service should be produced up to the point where the sum of consumer surplus and producer surplus is maximized, or, alternatively, where the marginal social cost equals the marginal social benefit. Therefore,

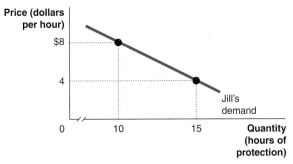

(a) Jill's demand for security guard services

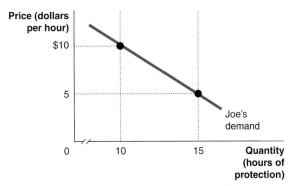

(b) Joe's demand for security guard services

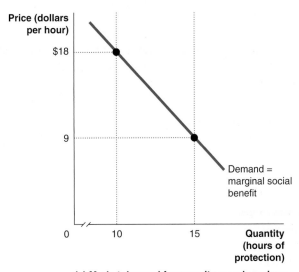

(c) Market demand for security guard services

Figure 5-10

Constructing the Market Demand Curve for a Public Good

To find the demand curve for a public good, we add up the price at which each consumer is willing to purchase each quantity of the good. In panel (a), Jill is willing to pay $8 per hour for a security guard to provide 10 hours of protection. In panel (b), Joe is willing to pay $10 for that level of protection. Therefore, in panel (c), the price of $18 per hour and the quantity of 10 hours will be a point on the market demand curve for security guard services.

the optimal quantity of security guard services—or any other public good—will occur where the marginal social benefit curve intersects the supply curve. As with private goods, in the absence of an externality in production, the supply curve represents the marginal social cost of supplying the good. Figure 5-11 shows that the optimal quantity of security guard services supplied is 15 hours, at a price of $9 per hour.

Will the market provide the economically efficient quantity of security guard services? One difficulty is that the individual preferences of consumers, as shown by their demand curves, are not revealed in this market. This difficulty does not arise with private goods because consumers must reveal their preferences in order to purchase private goods. If the market price of Big Macs is $4.00, Joe either reveals he is willing to pay that much by buying it, or he does without it. In our example, neither Jill nor Joe can be excluded from consuming the services provided by a security guard once either hires one, and, therefore, neither has an incentive to reveal her or his preferences. In this case, though, with only two consumers, it is likely that private

Figure 5-11

The Optimal Quantity of a Public Good

The optimal quantity of a public good is produced where the sum of consumer surplus and producer surplus is maximized, which occurs where the demand curve intersects the supply curve. In this case, the optimal quantity of security guard services is 15 hours at a price of $9 per hour.

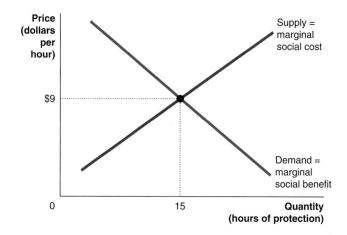

bargaining will result in an efficient quantity of the public good. This outcome is not likely for a public good—such as national defense—that is supplied by the government to millions of consumers.

Governments sometimes use *cost–benefit analysis* to determine what quantity of a public good should be supplied. For example, before building a dam on a river, the federal government will attempt to weigh the costs against the benefits. The costs include the opportunity cost of other projects the government cannot carry out if it builds the dam. The benefits include improved flood control or new recreational opportunities on the lake formed by the dam. However, for many public goods, including national defense, the government does not use a formal cost–benefit analysis. Instead, the quantity of national defense supplied is determined by a political process involving Congress and the president. Even here, of course, Congress and the president realize that trade-offs are involved: The more resources used for national defense, the fewer resources available for other public goods or for private goods.

Solved Problem | 5-4

Determining the Optimal Level of Public Goods

Suppose, once again, that Jill and Joe run isolated businesses that are next door to each other and in need of the services of a security guard. Their demand schedules for security guard services are as follows:

JOE	
PRICE (DOLLARS PER HOUR)	QUANTITY (HOURS OF PROTECTION)
$20	0
18	1
16	2
14	3
12	4
10	5
8	6
6	7
4	8
2	9

JILL	
PRICE (DOLLARS PER HOUR)	QUANTITY (HOURS OF PROTECTION)
$20	1
18	2
16	3
14	4
12	5
10	6
8	7
6	8
4	9
2	10

The supply schedule for security guard services is as follows:

PRICE (DOLLARS PER HOUR)	QUANTITY (HOURS OF PROTECTION)
$8	1
10	2
12	3
14	4
16	5
18	6
20	7
22	8
24	9

a. Draw a graph that shows the optimal level of security guard services. Be sure to label the curves on the graph.

b. Briefly explain why 8 hours of security guard protection is not an optimal quantity.

SOLVING THE PROBLEM:

Step 1: **Review the chapter material.** This problem is about the determination of the optimal level of public goods, so you may want to review the section "The Optimal Quantity of a Public Good," which begins on page 156.

Step 2: **Begin by deriving the demand curve or marginal social benefit curve for security guard services.** To calculate the marginal social benefit of guard services, we need to add the prices that Jill and Joe are willing to pay at each quantity:

DEMAND OR MARGINAL SOCIAL BENEFIT	
PRICE (DOLLARS PER HOUR)	QUANTITY (HOURS OF PROTECTION)
$38	1
34	2
30	3
26	4
22	5
18	6
14	7
10	8
6	9

Step 3: **Answer question (a) by plotting the demand (marginal social benefit) and supply (marginal social cost) curves.** The graph shows that the optimal level of security guard services is 6 hours.

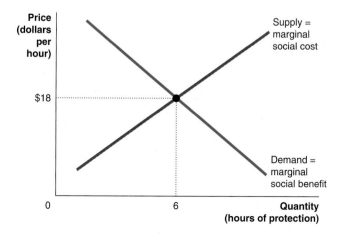

Step 4: **Answer question (b) by explaining why 8 hours of security guard protection is not an optimal quantity.** For each hour beyond 6, the supply curve is above the demand curve. Therefore, the marginal social benefit received will be less than the marginal social cost of supplying these hours. This results in a deadweight loss and a reduction in economic surplus.

YOUR TURN: For more practice, do related problem 4.4 on page 170 at the end of this chapter.

>> End Solved Problem 5-5

Common Resources

In England during the Middle Ages, each village had an area of pasture, known as a *commons*, on which any family in the village was allowed to graze its cows or sheep without charge. Of course, the grass one family's cow ate was not available for another family's cow, so consumption was rival. But every family in the village had the right to use the commons, so it was nonexcludable. Without some type of restraint on usage, the commons would end up overgrazed. To see why, consider the economic incentives facing a family that was thinking of buying another cow and grazing it on the commons. The family would gain the benefits from increased milk production, but adding another cow to the commons would create a negative externality by reducing the amount of grass available for the cows of other families. Because this family—and the other families in the village—did not take this negative externality into account when deciding whether to add another cow to the commons, too many cows would be added. The grass on the commons would eventually be depleted, and no family's cow would get enough to eat.

Tragedy of the commons The tendency for a common resource to be overused.

The Tragedy of the Commons The tendency for a common resource to be overused is called the **tragedy of the commons**. A modern example is the forests in many poor countries. When a family chops down a tree in a public forest, it takes into account the benefits of gaining firewood or wood for building, but it does not take into account the costs of deforestation. Haiti, for example, was once heavily forested. Today, 80 percent of the country's forests have been cut down, primarily to be burned to create charcoal, which is used for heating and cooking. Because the mountains no longer have tree roots to hold the soil, heavy rains lead to devastating floods. The following is from a newspaper account of tree cutting in Haiti:

> "No Tree Cutting" signs hang over the park entrance, but without money and manpower, there is no way to enforce that. Loggers make nightly journeys, hacking away at trees until they fall. The next day, they're on a truck out. Days later, they've been chopped up, burned and packaged in white bags offered for sale by soot-covered women. "This is the only way I can feed my four kids," said Vena Verone, one of the vendors. "I've heard about the floods and deforestation that caused them, but there's nothing I can do about that."

Figure 5-12 shows that with a common resource such as wood from a forest, the efficient level of use, Q_2, is determined by the intersection of the demand curve—which represents the marginal social benefit received by consumers—and S_2, which represents the marginal social cost of cutting the wood. As in our discussion of negative externalities, the social cost is equal to the private cost of cutting the wood plus the external cost. In this case, the external cost represents the fact that the more wood each person cuts, the less wood there is available for others, and the greater the deforestation, which increases the chances of floods. Because each individual tree cutter ignores the external cost, the equilibrium quantity of wood cut is Q_1, which is greater than the efficient quantity. At the equilibrium level of output, there is a deadweight loss, as shown in Figure 5-12 by the yellow triangle.

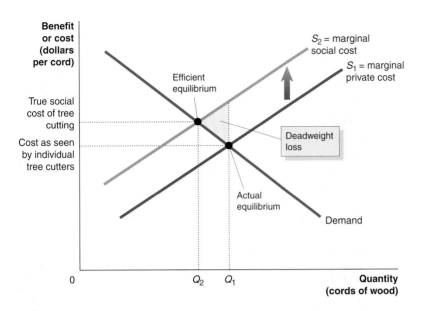

Figure 5-12

Overuse of a Common Resource

For a common resource such as wood from a forest, the efficient level of use, Q_2, is determined by the intersection of the demand curve—which represents the marginal benefit received by consumers—and S_2, which represents the marginal social cost of cutting the wood. Because each individual tree cutter ignores the external cost, the equilibrium quantity of wood cut is Q_1, which is greater than the efficient quantity. At the equilibrium level of output, there is a deadweight loss, as shown by the yellow triangle.

Is There a Way Out of the Tragedy of the Commons? Notice that our discussion of the tragedy of the commons is very similar to our earlier discussion of negative externalities. The source of the tragedy of the commons is the same as the source of negative externalities: lack of clearly defined and enforced property rights. For instance, suppose that instead of being held as a collective resource, a piece of pastureland is owned by one person. That person will take into account the effect of adding another cow on the food available to cows already using the pasture. As a result, the optimal number of cows will be placed on the pasture. Over the years, most of the commons lands in England were converted to private property. Most of the forest land in Haiti and other developing countries is actually the property of the government. The failure of the government to protect the forests against trespassers or convert them to private property is the key to their overuse.

Should these fishermen have unlimited access to the ocean?

In some situations, though, enforcing property rights is not feasible. An example is the oceans. Because no country owns the oceans beyond its own coastal waters, the fish and other resources of the ocean will remain a common resource. In situations in which enforcing property rights is not feasible, two types of solutions to the tragedy of the commons are possible. If the geographic area involved is limited and the number of people involved is small, access to the commons can be restricted through community norms and laws. If the geographic area or the number of people involved is large, legal restrictions on access to the commons are required. As an example of the first type of solution, the tragedy of the commons was avoided in the Middle Ages by traditional limits on the number of animals each family was allowed to put on the common pasture. Although these traditions were not formal laws, they were usually enforced adequately by social pressure.

With the second type of solution, the government imposes restrictions on access to the common resources. These restrictions can take several different forms, of which taxes, quotas, and tradable permits are the most common. By setting a tax equal to the external cost, governments can ensure that the efficient quantity of a resource is used. Quotas, or legal limits, on the quantity of the resource that can be taken during a given time period have been used in the United States to limit access to pools of oil when the pool is beneath property owned by many different persons. The governments of Canada, New Zealand, and Iceland have used a system of tradable permits to restrict access to ocean fisheries. Under this system, a total allowable catch (TAC) limits the number of fish that fishermen can catch during a season. The fishermen are then assigned permits called Individual Transferable Quotas (ITQs) that are equal to the total allowable catch. This system operates like the tradable emissions allowances described earlier in this chapter. The fishermen are free to use the ITQs or to sell them, which ensures that the fishermen with the lowest costs use the ITQs. The use of ITQs has sometimes proven controversial, which has limited their use in managing fisheries along the coastal United States. Critics argue that allowing trading of ITQs can result in their concentration in the hands of a relatively few large commercial fishing firms. Such a concentration may, though, be economically efficient if these firms have lower costs than smaller, family-based firms.

Economics in YOUR Life!

>> Continued from page 137

At the beginning of the chapter, we asked you to think about what the "best" level of carbon emissions is. Conceptually, this is a straightforward question to answer: The correct level of carbon emissions is the level for which the marginal benefit of reducing carbon emissions exactly equals the marginal cost of reducing carbon emissions. In practice, however, this is a very difficult question to answer. Scientists disagree about how much carbon emissions are contributing to the damage from climate change. In addition, the cost of reducing carbon emissions depends on the method of reduction used. As a result, neither the marginal cost curve nor the marginal benefit curve for reducing carbon emissions is known with certainty. This uncertainty makes it difficult for policymakers to determine the correct level of carbon emissions and is the source of much of the current debate. In any case, economists agree that the total cost of *completely* eliminating carbon emissions are much greater than the total benefits.

Conclusion

In Chapter 4, we saw that government intervention in the economy can reduce economic efficiency. In this chapter, however, we have seen that the government has an indispensable role to play in the economy when the absence of well-defined and enforceable property rights keeps the market from operating efficiently. For instance, because no one has a property right for clean air, in the absence of government intervention, firms will produce too great a quantity of products that generate air pollution. We have also seen that public goods are nonrivalrous and nonexcludable and are, therefore, often supplied directly by the government.

Read *An Inside Look at Policy*, which begins on the following page, to learn about problems with carbon trading.

FINANCIAL TIMES, FEBRUARY 7, 2007

Next Carbon Trading Phase Promises to Clean Up Anomalies

When the European Union launched its scheme to trade carbon emission rights to combat climate change, it probably did not envisage that it might eventually provide an incentive to pollute.

But that is exactly what has happened. Just over two years into a scheme that was launched in 2005 as the first of its kind in the world, the price for a permit to emit one tonne of carbon dioxide has plummeted to a record low of just €1.50 ($1.94) a tonne—a fraction of the peak €30 level hit last April.

Chris Rogers, utility analyst at JPMorgan, says that at current prices it is far cheaper for utilities to burn coal—and buy the emissions permits that allow them to pollute—than it is for them to buy cleaner fuels such as natural gas. He estimates that a utility can buy coal that is €10 per megawatt hour cheaper than gas. "There is no economic incentive for users to import less coal than they did last year," he says.

But the scheme was set up to encourage utilities and large industrial consumers of energy to switch from heavy polluting energies such as coal to cleaner fuels such as gas.

Companies were given a set level of permits. If they wanted or needed to pollute more, they had to buy more on the market. If a company was cleaner than envisaged, it could sell excess permits. However, too many emission permits were issued and the low prices have defeated the scheme's original purpose. As a result, coal imports into Europe have been rising, with the UK last year importing record volumes of coal. . . .

The incentive to pollute in the EU, however, changes next year [in 2008] when phase two of the emissions trading scheme starts. In the second phase, the EU will issue fewer permits. Phase one permits cannot be carried over to phase two. As a result, carbon prices for phase two are a lot higher. The December 2008 carbon price is €15 a tonne.

Traders still fear there could be downward pressure on 2008 carbon prices as the second phase allows permits earned from clean energy projects in the developing world—officially called certified emission reductions— to be exchanged for the EU permits.

Louis Redshaw, head of environmental markets at Barclays Capital, said there would be a limit to the amount of CERs that can be converted into EU permits, which varies between each EU member. Mr Redshaw said that by 2009 there would be more carbon schemes, including schemes in

Japan and Canada, where CERs could be exchanged. "When we start getting into 2009, 2010, the EU scheme will not be the only one around and therefore CERs will go to the market that offers the best price. So we may not see so many come into the EU," he said. He said the diminishing potential dilution effect of CERs was reflected in the pricing of phase two, where prices for 2009 trade at a premium to 2008.

The December 2009 carbon price is quoted at €15.50, 2010 at €16.00, 2011 at €16.50 and 2012 at €17.

There is a premium for prices for 2011 and onwards because of the inclusion of the aviation sector in four years' time. In spite of the performance of EU emissions prices in phase one, investors and analysts are confident there will be a phase three of the scheme.

"Neither the Kyoto agenda nor the EU scheme will disappear at the end of 2012 . . . enough people are now involved that there is sure to be a further market of some kind," said Paul Newman, managing director of Icap Energy. "In any case, discontinuing the market in five years' time would be like turning off the ventilator just as the patient is starting to get better."

Source: Kevin Morrison, "Next Carbon Trading Phase Promises to Clean Up Anomalies," *Financial Times*, February 7, 2007, p. 38. Reprinted with permission.

Key Points in the Article

Carbon trading is a relatively straightforward idea. The government determines how much carbon dioxide utilities and firms can emit and issues a corresponding quantity of permits. The government then forces firms to pay for the right to emit carbon dioxide, which gives firms an incentive to reduce carbon emissions. European governments hoped that carbon trading would lead firms to switch from energy sources with high carbon content, like coal, to energy sources with low carbon content, like natural gas. Some practical problems with setting up a carbon trading scheme have resulted in the system not working the way European governments had expected.

Analyzing the News

(a) The goal of the carbon trading program was to raise the price of energy sources such as coal that emit more carbon dioxide than energy sources such as natural gas. If the price of coal goes up and the prices of permits to emit carbon dioxide are high, then utilities and firms will switch from coal to natural gas. As a result, carbon dioxide emissions will decline. Unfortunately, the European Union issued so many carbon permits that it was cheaper for firms to buy permits and continue to burn coal than to switch to natural gas.

(b) The European Union issued the carbon permits in phases. The problems with the program all deal with the first-phase carbon permits. To rectify the problems, the European Union has issued fewer carbon permits for phase two of the program. This reduction in the supply of permits has caused the price to rise from €1.50 a ton for phase one permits to €15 a ton for phase two permits. Figure 1 shows that this is exactly what economic theory predicts. The reduction in the number of permits available causes the supply curve to shift to the left. At the old price of €1.50, there would be a shortage equal to $(Q_1 - Q_2)$, which leads firms to bid up the price of carbon emission permits. The higher price provides an economic incentive for utilities and other firms to reduce the amount of carbon dioxide they emit.

(c) The carbon trading program in Europe does not cover all industries. Airlines were initially exempted from having to purchase permits, but that is going to change in 2011. As a result, the current price of carbon permits for the years 2011 and 2012 is higher than the permits for 2008. Figure 2 shows that this is exactly what an economist would expect. As more firms compete for the fixed supply of carbon permits, the price of those carbon permits rises. To avoid paying for the higher-priced permits, some utilities and firms will reduce the amount of carbon dioxide they emit.

Thinking Critically
About Policy

1. The article points out some of the difficulties with carbon trading programs. Due to these difficulties, the initial phase of the carbon trading program in Europe did not provide a strong incentive to switch from coal to natural gas. As a result, it is likely that firms used too much coal. Would a carbon tax result in similar difficulties?

2. The government raises no revenue from tradable permits, because it gives the permits to firms at no charge. Because tradable permits raise no government revenue—which might be used to reduce other taxes that result in deadweight losses—some economists and policymakers favor carbon taxes over carbon trading. What is an alternative means of allocating the initial carbon permits that would raise revenue for the government?

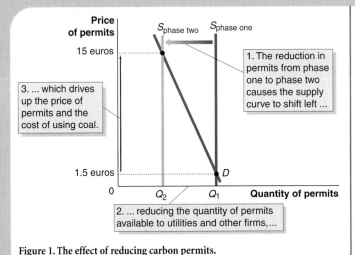

Figure 1. The effect of reducing carbon permits.

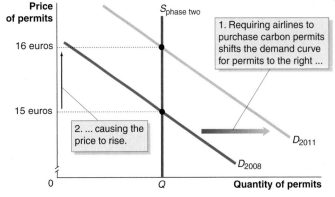

Figure 2. The effect of requiring more firms to purchase permits.

Key Terms

5.1 LEARNING OBJECTIVE   5.1 | Identify examples of positive and negative externalities and use graphs to show how externalities affect economic efficiency, **pages 138–141.**

Externalities and Economic Efficiency

Summary

An **externality** is a benefit or cost to parties who are not involved in a transaction. Pollution and other externalities in production cause a difference between the **private cost** borne by the producer of a good or services and the **social cost**, which includes any external cost, such as the cost of pollution. An externality in consumption causes a difference between the **private benefit** received by the consumer and the **social benefit**, which includes any external benefit. If externalities exist in production or consumption, the market will not produce the optimal level of a good or service. This outcome is referred to as **market failure**. Externalities arise when property rights do not exist or cannot be legally enforced. **Property rights** are the rights individuals or businesses have to the exclusive use of their property, including the right to buy or sell it.

myeconlab   Visit www.myeconlab.com to complete these exercises
Get Ahead of the Curve online and get instant feedback.

Review Questions

1.1 What is an externality? Give an example of a positive externality and give an example of a negative externality.

1.2 When will the private cost of producing a good differ from the social cost? Give an example. When will the private benefit from consuming a good differ from the social benefit? Give an example.

1.3 What is economic efficiency? How do externalities affect the economic efficiency of a market equilibrium?

1.4 What is market failure? When is market failure likely to arise?

1.5 Briefly discuss the relationship between property rights and the existence of externalities.

Problems and Applications

1.6 The chapter states that your consuming a Big Mac does not create an externality. But suppose you arrive at your favorite McDonald's at lunchtime and get in a long line to be served. By the time you reach the counter, there are 10 people in line behind you. Because you decided to have a Big Mac for lunch—instead of, say, a pizza—each of those 10 people must wait in line an additional 2 minutes. Or suppose that after a lifetime of consuming Big Macs, you develop heart disease. Because you are now over age 65, the government must pay most of your medical bills through the Medicare system. Is it still correct to say that your consuming a Big Mac created no externalities? Might there be a justification here for the government to intervene in the market for Big Macs? Explain.

1.7 The chapter discusses the cases of consumption generating a positive externality and production generating a negative externality. Is it possible for consumption to generate a negative externality? If so, give an example. Is it possible for production to generate a positive externality? If so, give an example.

1.8 In a recent study at a large state university, students were randomly assigned roommates. Researchers found that, on average, males assigned to roommates who reported drinking alcohol in the year before entering college had GPAs one-quarter point lower than those assigned to non-drinking roommates. For males who drank frequently before college, being assigned to a roommate who also drank frequently before college reduced their GPAs by two-thirds of a point. Draw a graph showing the price of alcohol and the quantity of alcohol consumption on college campuses. Include in the graph the private and social cost of drinking. Label any deadweight loss that arises in this market.

Source: Michael Kremer and Dan M. Levy, "Peer Effects and Alcohol Use Among College Students," National Bureau of Economic Research working paper 9876, July 2003.

1.9 Tom and Jacob are college students. Each of them will probably get married later and have two or three children. Each knows that if he studies more in college, he'll get a better job and earn more than if he doesn't study. Earning more means the ability to spend more on their future families—things like orthodontia, nice clothes, admission to an expensive college, and travel. Tom thinks about the potential benefits to his potential children when he decides how much studying to do. Jacob doesn't.
   a. What type of externality arises from studying?
   b. Draw a graph showing this externality, contrasting the responses of Tom and Jacob. Who studies more? Who acts more efficiently? Why?

1.10 For several years, *The Sopranos* television series was available only on the HBO cable network. The series was a hit and attracted more viewers than many programs available on the broadcast networks NBC, CBS, ABC, and Fox. But Chris Albrecht, the chair of HBO, found that he was unable to use the popularity of *The Sopranos* to increase the number of subscribers to HBO. To receive HBO, cable viewers usually had to pay for a "premium package" that included not just HBO but other services, like Showtime, that were owned by other companies. As Albrecht put it, "That means we're just part of everything else. First the consumer is asked to pay $60 for the basic cable service and then it's another $40 for the platinum package, and they're selling Showtime and Starz in with us." Is there an externality involved here? If so, is it an externality in production or consumption, and is it positive or negative? If there is an externality, discuss possible solutions.

Source: Excerpt from Bill Carter, "Cable Conquered, What's Next for 'The Sopranos'?" *New York Times*, October 7, 2002. Copyright © 2002 by The New York Times Co. Reprinted with permission.

1.11 A columnist for the *Wall Street Journal* observes: "No one collects money from those who benefit from the flood control a wetland provides, or the nutrient recycling a forest does. . . . In a nutshell, market failures help drive habitat loss." What does the columnist mean by *market failures*? What does she mean by *habitat loss*? Explain why she believes one is causing the other. Illustrate your argument with a graph showing the market for land to be used for development.

Source: Sharon Begley, "Furry Math? Market Has Failed to Capture True Value of Nature," *Wall Street Journal*, August 9, 2002, p. B1.

>> **End Learning Objective 5.1**

5.2 LEARNING OBJECTIVE   5.2 | Discuss the Coase theorem and explain how private bargaining can lead to economic efficiency in a market with an externality, **pages 141–147.**

Private Solutions to Externalities: The Coase Theorem

Summary

Externalities and market failures result from incomplete property rights or from the difficulty of enforcing property rights in certain situations. When an externality exists, and the efficient quantity of a good is not being produced, the total cost of reducing the externality is usually less than the total benefit. According to the **Coase theorem**, if **transactions costs** are low, private bargaining will result in an efficient solution to the problem of externalities.

myeconlab Visit www.myeconlab.com to complete these exercises *Get Ahead of the Curve* online and get instant feedback.

Review Questions

2.1 What do economists mean by "an economically efficient level of pollution"?

2.2 What is the Coase theorem? What are transactions costs? When are we likely to see private solutions to the problem of externalities?

Problems and Applications

2.3 Is it ever possible for an *increase* in pollution to make society better off? Briefly explain using a graph like Figure 5-3 on page 144.

2.4 If the marginal cost of reducing a certain type of pollution is zero, should all of that pollution be eliminated? Briefly explain.

2.5 Discuss the factors that determine the marginal cost of reducing crime. Discuss the factors that determine the marginal benefit of reducing crime. Would it be economically efficient to reduce the amount of crime to zero? Briefly explain.

2.6 **(Related to the** *Don't Let This Happen to You!* **on page 144)** Briefly explain whether you agree or disagree with the following statement: "Sulfur dioxide emissions cause acid rain and breathing difficulties for people with respiratory problems. The total benefit to society is greatest if we completely eliminate sulfur dioxide emissions. Therefore, the economically efficient level of emissions is zero."

2.7 In discussing cleaning up oil spills, Gary Shigenka of the National Oceanographic and Atmospheric Agency observed, "The first 90% of any cleanup comes easy. But the tradeoffs for the remaining bits are brutal." He estimates that the last 1 percent of oil removed can cost seven times as much as the first 99 percent. Why should it be any more costly to clean up the last 1 percent of an oil spill than to clean up the first 1 percent? What trade-offs do you think Shigenka was referring to?

Source: Keith Johnson and Gautam Naik, "For Spain, Exxon Valdez Offers Some Surprising Lessons," *Wall Street Journal*, November 22, 2002.

2.8 (Related to the *Making the Connection* on page 142) In the first years following the passage of the Clean Air Act in 1970, air pollution declined sharply and there were important health benefits, including a decline in infant mortality. Should the government take action to reduce air pollution further? How should government go about deciding this question?

2.9 (Related to the *Making the Connection* on page 146) We know that owners of apple orchards and owners of beehives are able to negotiate private agreements. Is it likely that as a result of these private agreements the market supplies the efficient quantities of apple trees and beehives? Are there any real-world difficulties that might stand in the way of achieving this efficient outcome?

>> **End Learning Objective 5.2**

5.3 LEARNING OBJECTIVE   5.3 | Analyze government policies to achieve economic efficiency in a market with an externality, **pages 147–152.**

Government Policies to Deal with Externalities

Summary

When private solutions to externalities are unworkable, the government sometimes intervenes. One way to deal with a negative externality in production is to impose a tax equal to the cost of the externality. The tax causes the producer of the good to internalize the externality. The government can deal with a positive externality in consumption by giving consumers a subsidy, or payment, equal to the value of the externality. Government taxes and subsidies intended to bring about an efficient level of output in the presence of externalities are called **Pigovian taxes and subsidies**. Although the federal government has sometimes used subsidies and taxes to deal with externalities, in dealing with pollution, it has more often used a command and control approach. A **command and control approach** involves the government imposing quantitative limits on the amount of pollution allowed or requiring firms to install specific pollution control devices. Direct pollution controls of this type are not economically efficient, however. As a result, Congress decided to use a system of tradable emissions allowances to reduce sulfur dioxide emissions.

myeconlab Visit www.myeconlab.com to complete these exercises *Get Ahead of the Curve* online and get instant feedback.

Review Questions

3.1 What is a Pigovian tax? At what level must a Pigovian tax be set to achieve efficiency?

3.2 Why do most economists prefer tradable emissions allowances rather than the command and control approach to pollution?

Problems and Applications

3.3 Why does the government subsidize the purchase of college educations but not the purchase of hamburgers?

3.4 Writing in the *New York Times*, Michael Lewis argues: "Good new technologies are a bit like good new roads: Their social benefits far exceed what any one person or company can get paid for creating them." Does this observation justify the government subsidizing the production of new technologies? If so, how might the government do this?

Source: Michael Lewis, "In Defense of the Boom," *New York Times*, October 27, 2002.

3.5 In 2007, Governor Deval Patrick of Massachusetts proposed that criminals would have to pay a "safety fee" to the government. The size of the fee would be based on the seriousness of the crime (that is, the fee would be larger for more serious crimes).
  a. Is there an economically efficient amount of crime? Briefly explain.
  b. Briefly explain whether the "safety fee" is a Pigovian tax of the type discussed in this chapter.

Source: Michael Levenson, "Patrick Proposes New Fee on Criminals," *Boston Globe*, January 14, 2007.

3.6 We saw in this chapter that market failure occurs when firms ignore the costs generated by pollution in deciding how much to produce. Government intervention is usually necessary to bring about a more efficient level of production. Before 1989, the Communist governments of Eastern Europe directly controlled the production of most goods and were free to choose how much of each good would be produced and what production process would be used. When these Communist governments collapsed, it was revealed that the countries of Eastern Europe suffered from very high levels of pollution, much higher than had existed in the United States and other high-income countries even before there was government anti-pollution legislation. Discuss reasons why the nonmarket Communist system generated more pollution than market economies.

3.7 Bjorn Lomborg, director of the Environmental Assessment Institute in Denmark, argued in a column in the *New York Times*: "Traditionally, the developed nations of the West have shown a greater concern for environmental sustainability, while the third world countries have a stronger desire for economic development." Recall the definition of *normal good* given in Chapter 3. Is environmental protection a normal good? If so, is there any connection between this fact and Lomborg's observation? Briefly explain. How do the marginal cost and marginal benefit of environmental protection change with economic development?

Source: Bjorn Lomborg, "The Environmentalists Are Wrong," *New York Times*, August 26, 2002.

3.8 **(Related to *Solved Problem 5-3* on page 148)** The fumes from dry cleaners can contribute to air pollution. Suppose the following graph illustrates the situation in the dry cleaning market.

a. Explain how a government can use a tax on dry cleaning to bring about the efficient level of production. What should the value of the tax be?

b. How large is the deadweight loss (in dollars) from excessive dry cleaning, according to the figure?

3.9 The graph in the next column illustrates the situation in the dry cleaning market. In contrast to problem 3.8, the marginal social cost of the pollution rises as the quantity of items cleaned per week increases.

In addition, there are two demand curves, one for a smaller city, D_S, the other for a larger city, D_L.

a. Explain why the marginal social cost curve has a different slope than the marginal private cost curve.

b. What tax per item cleaned will achieve economic efficiency in the smaller city? In the larger city? Explain why the efficient tax is different in the two cities.

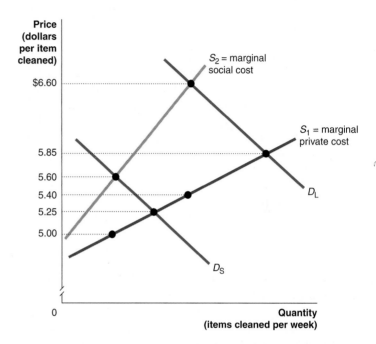

3.10 **(Related to the *Chapter Opener* on page 136)** Anyone can purchase sulfur dioxide emissions allowances on the Chicago Mercantile Exchange. Several environmental groups have raised money to buy allowances. As part of their fund-raising, these groups have urged contributors to buy the allowances as gifts. As one newspaper story put it, "For the environmentalist in your life, here's a gift that is sold by the ton, fits in an envelope and will last forever." What would be the impact of environmental groups buying emission allowances on the total amount of sulfur dioxide pollution in the United States? What would be the impact on the price of the emission allowances?

Source: Randall Edwards, "Dear Santa: Please Bring Me Sulfur Dioxide for Christmas," *Columbus (Ohio) Dispatch*, December 19, 1999.

3.11 **(Related to the *Making the Connection* on page 151)** As discussed in the chapter, a system of tradable permits was very successful in efficiently reducing emissions of sulfur dioxide in the United States. Why have some economists proposed a similar system of tradable permits to reduce carbon dioxide emissions? Briefly discuss similarities and differences between the problem of reducing sulfur dioxide emissions and the problem of reducing carbon dioxide emissions.

>> End Learning Objective 5.3

5.4 LEARNING OBJECTIVE   5.4 | Explain how goods can be categorized on the basis of whether they are rival or excludable and use graphs to illustrate the efficient quantities of public goods and common resources, **pages 152–162.**

Four Categories of Goods

Summary

There are four categories of goods: private goods, public goods, quasi-public goods, and common resources. **Private goods** are both rival and excludable. **Rivalry** means that when one person consumes a unit of a good, no one else can consume that unit. **Excludability** means that anyone who does not pay for a good cannot consume it. **Public goods** are both nonrivalrous and nonexcludable. Private firms are usually not willing to supply public goods because of free riding. **Free riding** involves benefiting from a good without paying for it. **Quasi-public goods** are excludable but not rival. **Common resources** are rival but not excludable. The **tragedy of the commons** refers to the tendency for a common resource to be overused. The tragedy of the commons results from a lack of clearly defined and enforced property rights. We find the market demand curve for a private good by adding the quantity of the good demanded by each consumer at each price. We find the demand curve for a public good by adding vertically the price each consumer would be willing to pay for each quantity of the good. The optimal quantity of a public good occurs where the demand curve intersects the curve representing the marginal cost of supplying the good.

myeconlab Visit www.myeconlab.com to complete these exercises
Get Ahead of the Curve online and get instant feedback.

Review Questions

4.1 Define rivalry and excludability and use these terms to discuss the four categories of goods.

4.2 What is a public good? What is free riding? How is free riding related to the tendency of a public good to create market failure?

4.3 What is the tragedy of the commons? How can it be avoided?

Problems and Applications

4.4 (Related to *Solved Problem 5-4* on page 158) Suppose that Jill and Joe are the only two people in the small town of Andover. Andover has land available to build a park of no more than 9 acres. Jill and Joe's demand schedules for the park are as follows:

JOE	
PRICE PER ACRE	NUMBER OF ACRES
$10	0
9	1
8	2
7	3
6	4
5	5
4	6
3	7
2	8
1	9

JILL	
PRICE PER ACRE	NUMBER OF ACRES
$15	0
14	1
13	2
12	3
11	4
10	5
9	6
8	7
7	8
6	9

The supply curve is as follows:

PRICE	NUMBER OF ACRES
$11	1
13	2
15	3
17	4
19	5
21	6
23	7
25	8
27	9

a. Draw a graph showing the optimal size of the park. Be sure to label the curves on the graph.

b. Briefly explain why a park of 2 acres is not optimal.

4.5 Commercial whaling has been described as a modern example of the tragedy of the commons. Briefly explain whether you agree or disagree.

4.6 According to an article in the *Wall Street Journal*, economist Paul Romer of Stanford University has argued: "The market mechanism and property rights are excellent at conserving scarce resources and putting them to the most profitable use. . . . They aren't so good at encouraging the production and distribution of new ideas, which are critical to progress." What characteristics of the production and distribution of new ideas might make it difficult for the market to produce the optimal amount?

Source: David Wessel, "Precepts from Professor Summers," *Wall Street Journal*, October 17, 2002.

4.7 The more frequently bacteria are exposed to antibiotics, the more quickly the bacteria will develop resistance to the antibiotics. A columnist for the *Wall Street Journal* observes:

> Each parent will press a pediatrician for a drug if there's any chance it will cure a child. Yet if every parent and pediatrician does the same, they will speed the evolution of drug-resistant microbes. And what drug company will enlist its marketers to prod doctors to prescribe its antibiotics less?

Briefly discuss in what sense antibiotics can be considered a common resource.

Source: David Wessel, "Losing the Race with Bugs: Bacteria Beats New Drugs," *Wall Street Journal*, April 25, 2002.

4.8 Put each of these goods or services into one of the boxes in Figure 5-8 on page 153. That is, categorize them as private goods, public goods, quasi-public goods, or common resources.
a. A television broadcast of the World Series
b. Home mail delivery
c. Education in a public school
d. Education in a private school
e. Hiking in a park surrounded by a fence
f. Hiking in a park not surrounded by a fence
g. An apple

4.9 (Related to the *Making the Connection* on page 153) Explain whether you agree or disagree with the following statement: "Providing health care is obviously a public good. If one person becomes ill and doesn't receive treatment, that person may infect many other people. If many people become ill, then the output of the economy will be negatively affected. Therefore, providing health care is a public good that should be supplied by the government."

>> **End Learning Objective 5.4**

Chapter 6

Elasticity: The Responsiveness of Demand and Supply

Do People Care about the Prices of Books?

Some observers have been predicting for years that the printed book will be replaced with the electronic book. The printed book is still holding its own, however. In 2008, U.S. consumers spent $57.5 billion to buy 3.2 billion copies of new printed books. By contrast, although thousands of books were available in electronic format, total sales amounted to only a few million dollars.

While the printed book lives on, book publishers face a problem unique to the industry: Unlike most retailers, bookstores have the right to return unsold books. For example, when a local supermarket orders shampoo, apple juice, or dog food, it knows that if it has overestimated consumer demand, it will be stuck with the unsold items. By contrast, to give bookstores an incentive to order more books, publishers have given the stores the right to return unsold copies. On average, bookstores return 35 percent of books to publishers.

The high return rate of books means that publishers have to be very careful when deciding how many copies of a book to print and ship to bookstores. In 2007, Scholastic, the largest publisher of children's books in the world, published the final installment of the hugely popular Harry Potter series. Barnes & Noble bookstores have a special membership program that gives customers a 20 percent discount on most hardcover books. But on *Harry Potter and the Deathly Hallows*, Barnes & Noble offered a 40 percent discount. The company was willing to accept a small profit on each book in hopes of selling a very large quantity. Scholastic could not simply print all the books ordered by bookstores like Barnes & Noble because it feared that the bookstores might overestimate the quantity of books actually demanded by consumers. Executives at Scholastic knew that the number of copies of the book demanded by consumers would depend in part on the price of the book. But how responsive are consumers to changes in book prices? Will a lower price significantly increase sales? Publishers debate this point.

For example, Stephen Rubin, president and publisher of Doubleday, has made the following argument about book prices: "I am just convinced that there is no difference between $22 and $23. Let's face it. If you want a book in translation from a Czech writer, you are going to buy the book—price is not a factor if it is a book that you really want." On the other hand, Barnes & Noble's program of discounting books for members will be effective only if consumers are sufficiently responsive to lower prices for books. As Bill Armstrong, an industry analyst, put it: "[Barnes & Noble's discount program] will only be a success if these lower prices produce greater unit volume enough to offset the lower price per book." **AN INSIDE LOOK** on **page 198** discusses the effectiveness of Borders bookstores' Borders Rewards program.

Sources: Henry Sanderson, "Barnes & Noble Disappoints Investors with Outlook," *Wall Street Journal*, March 5, 2007; and data on book sales from U.S. Census Bureau, *The 2008 Statistical Abstract*.

Economics in YOUR Life!

How Much Do Book Prices Matter to You?

We have just seen that there is a debate in the publishing industry about how responsive consumers are to changes in book prices. Barnes & Noble was willing to reduce the price of *Harry Potter and the Deathly Hallows* because it believed doing so would significantly increase sales. Some book executives, like Stephen Rubin of Doubleday, seem to think that prices do not matter. What factors would make you more or less sensitive to price when purchasing a book? Is Barnes & Noble's strategy likely to succeed? As you read the chapter, see if can answer these questions. You can check your answers against those we provide at the end of the chapter. **>> Continued on page 196**

W hether you are managing a publishing company, bookstore, or coffee shop, you need to know how an increase or decrease in the price of your products will affect the quantity consumers are willing to buy. We saw in Chapter 3 that cutting the price of a good increases the quantity demanded and that raising the price reduces the quantity demanded. But the critical question is this: *How much* will the quantity demanded change as a result of a price increase or decrease? Economists use the concept of **elasticity** to measure how one economic variable—such as the quantity demanded—responds to changes in another economic variable—such as the price. For example, the responsiveness of the quantity demanded of a good to changes in its price is called the *price elasticity of demand*. Knowing the price elasticity of demand allows you to compute the effect of a price change on the quantity demanded.

We also saw in Chapter 3 that the quantity of a good that consumers demand depends not just on the price of the good but also on consumer income and on the prices of related goods. As a manager, you would also be interested in measuring the responsiveness of demand to these other factors. As we will see, we can use the concept of elasticity here as well. We also are interested in the responsiveness of the quantity supplied of a good to changes in its price, which is called the *price elasticity of supply*.

Elasticity is an important concept not just for business managers but for policymakers as well. If the government wants to discourage teenage smoking, it can raise the price of cigarettes by increasing the tax on them. If we know the price elasticity of demand for cigarettes, we can calculate how many fewer cigarettes will be demanded at a higher price. In this chapter, we will also see how policymakers use the concept of elasticity.

Elasticity A measure of how much one economic variable responds to changes in another economic variable.

6.1 | Define the price elasticity of demand and understand how to measure it.

The Price Elasticity of Demand and Its Measurement

We know from the law of demand that when the price of a product falls, the quantity demanded of the product increases. But the law of demand tells firms only that the demand curves for their products slope downward. More useful is a measure of the responsiveness of the quantity demanded to a change in price. This measure is called the **price elasticity of demand**.

Measuring the Price Elasticity of Demand

Price elasticity of demand The responsiveness of the quantity demanded to a change in price, measured by dividing the percentage change in the quantity demanded of a product by the percentage change in the product's price.

We might measure the price elasticity of demand by using the slope of the demand curve because the slope of the demand curve tells us how much quantity changes as price changes. Using the slope of the demand curve to measure price elasticity has a drawback, however: The measurement of slope is sensitive to the units chosen for quantity and price. For example, suppose a $1 decrease in the price of *Harry Potter and the Deathly Hallows* leads to an increase in the quantity demanded from 10.1 million books to 10.2 million books. The change in quantity is 0.1 million books, and the change in price is −$1, so the slope is 0.1/−1 = −0.1. But if we measure price in cents, rather than dollars, the slope is 0.1/−100 = −0.001. If we measure price in dollars and books in thousands, instead of millions, the slope is 100/−1 = −100. Clearly, the value we compute for the slope can change dramatically, depending on the units we use for quantity and price.

To avoid this confusion over units, economists use *percentage changes* when measuring the price elasticity of demand. Percentage changes are not dependent on units. (For a review of calculating percentage changes, see the appendix to Chapter 1.) No matter what units we use to measure the quantity of wheat, 10 percent more wheat is 10 percent more wheat. Therefore, the price elasticity of demand is measured by dividing the percentage change in the quantity demanded by the percentage change in the price. Or:

$$\text{Price elasticity of demand} = \frac{\text{Percentage change in quantity demanded}}{\text{Percentage change in price}}.$$

It's important to remember that *the price elasticity of demand is not the same as the slope of the demand curve.*

If we calculate the price elasticity of demand for a price cut, the percentage change in price will be negative, and the percentage change in quantity demanded will be positive. Similarly, if we calculate the price elasticity of demand for a price increase, the percentage change in price will be positive, and the percentage change in quantity will be negative. Therefore, the price elasticity of demand is always negative. In comparing elasticities, though, we are usually interested in their relative size. So, we often drop the minus sign and compare their *absolute values*. In other words, although −3 is actually a smaller number than −2, a price elasticity of −3 is larger than a price elasticity of −2.

Elastic Demand and Inelastic Demand

If the quantity demanded is responsive to changes in price, the percentage change in quantity demanded will be *greater* than the percentage change in price, and the price elasticity of demand will be greater than 1 in absolute value. In this case, demand is **elastic**. For example, if a 10 percent fall in the price of bagels results in a 20 percent increase in the quantity of bagels demanded, then:

$$\text{Price elasticity of demand} = \frac{20\%}{-10\%} = -2,$$

and we can conclude that the price of bagels is elastic.

When the quantity demanded is not very responsive to price, however, the percentage change in quantity demanded will be *less* than the percentage change in price, and the price elasticity of demand will be less than 1 in absolute value. In this case, demand is **inelastic**. For example, if a 10 percent fall in the price of wheat results in a 5 percent increase in the quantity of wheat demanded, then:

$$\text{Price elasticity of demand} = \frac{5\%}{-10\%} = -0.5,$$

and we can conclude that the demand for wheat is inelastic.

In the special case in which the percentage change in the quantity demanded is equal to the percentage change in price, the price elasticity of demand equals −1 (or 1 in absolute value). In this case, demand is **unit elastic**.

An Example of Computing Price Elasticities

Suppose you own a small bookstore and you are trying to decide whether to cut the price you are charging for a new John Grisham mystery novel. You are currently at point *A* in Figure 6-1: selling 16 copies of the novel per day at a price of $30 per copy. How many more copies you will sell by cutting the price to $20 depends on the price elasticity of demand for this novel. Let's consider two possibilities: If D_1 is the demand curve for this novel in your store, your sales will increase to 28 copies per day, point *B*. But if D_2 is your demand curve, your sales will increase only to 20 copies per day, point *C*. We might expect—correctly, as we will see—that between these points, demand curve D_1 is *elastic*, and demand curve D_2 is *inelastic*.

To confirm that D_1 is elastic between these points and that D_2 is inelastic, we need to calculate the price elasticity of demand for each curve. In calculating price elasticity between two points on a demand curve, though, we run into a problem because we get

Elastic demand Demand is elastic when the percentage change in quantity demanded is *greater* than the percentage change in price, so the price elasticity is *greater* than 1 in absolute value.

Inelastic demand Demand is inelastic when the percentage change in quantity demanded is *less* than the percentage change in price, so the price elasticity is *less* than 1 in absolute value.

Unit-elastic demand Demand is unit elastic when the percentage change in quantity demanded is *equal to* the percentage change in price, so the price elasticity is equal to 1 in absolute value.

Figure 6-1

Elastic and Inelastic Demand Curves

Along D_1, cutting the price from \$30 to \$20 increases the number of copies sold from 16 per day to 28 per day, so demand is elastic between point A and point B. Along D_2, cutting the price from \$30 to \$20 increases the number of copies sold from 16 per day to only 20 per day, so demand is inelastic between point A and point C.

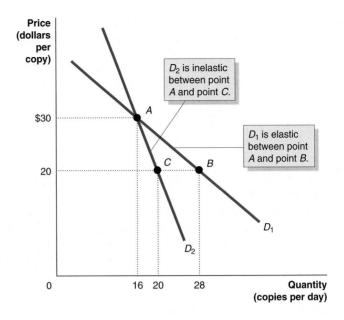

a different value for price increases than for price decreases. For example, suppose we calculate the price elasticity for D_2 as the price is cut from \$30 to \$20. This reduction is a 33 percent price cut that increases the quantity demanded from 16 books to 20 books, or by 25 percent. Therefore, the price elasticity of demand between points A and C is $25/-33 = -0.8$. Now let's calculate the price elasticity for D_2 as the price is *increased* from \$20 to \$30. This is a 50 percent price increase that decreases the quantity demanded from 20 books to 16 books, or by 20 percent. So, now our measure of the price elasticity of demand between points A and C is $-20/50 = -0.4$. It can be confusing to have different values for the price elasticity of demand between the same two points on the same demand curve.

The Midpoint Formula

We can use the *midpoint formula* to ensure that we have only one value of the price elasticity of demand between the same two points on a demand curve. The midpoint formula uses the *average* of the initial and final quantities and the initial and final prices. If Q_1 and P_1 are the initial quantity and price and Q_2 and P_2 are the final quantity and price, the midpoint formula is:

$$\text{Price elasticity of demand} = \frac{(Q_2 - Q_1)}{\left(\dfrac{Q_1 + Q_2}{2}\right)} \div \frac{(P_2 - P_1)}{\left(\dfrac{P_1 + P_2}{2}\right)}.$$

The midpoint formula may seem challenging at first, but the numerator is just the change in quantity divided by the average of the initial and final quantities, and the denominator is just the change in price divided by the average of the initial and final prices.

Let's apply the formula to calculating the price elasticity of D_2 in Figure 6-1. Between point A and point C on D_2, the change in quantity is 4, and the average of the two quantities is 18. Therefore, there is a 22.2 percent change in quantity. The change in price is $-\$10$, and the average of the two prices is \$25. Therefore, there is a -40 percent change in price. So, the price elasticity of demand is $22.2/-40.0 = -0.6$. Notice these three results from calculating the price elasticity of demand using the midpoint formula: First, as we suspected from examining Figure 6-1, demand curve D_2 is inelastic between points A and C. Second, our value for the price elasticity calculated using the midpoint formula is between the two values we calculated earlier. Third, the midpoint formula will give us the same value whether we are moving from the higher price to the lower price or from the lower price to the higher price.

We can also use the midpoint formula to calculate the elasticity of demand between point A and point B on D_1. In this case, there is a 54.5 percent change in quantity and a −40 percent change in price. So, the elasticity of demand is 54.5/−40.0 = −1.4. Once again, as we suspected, demand curve D_1 is price elastic between points A and B.

Solved Problem | 6-1

Calculating the Price Elasticity of Demand

Scholastic Corporation's suggested retail price for *Harry Potter and the Deathly Hallows* is $35. Suppose you own a small bookstore, and you believe that if you keep the price of the book at $35, you will be able to sell 40 copies per day. You are considering cutting the price to $25. The graph below shows two possible increases in the quantity sold as a result of your price cut. Use the information in the graph to calculate the price elasticity between these two prices on each of the demand curves. Use the midpoint formula in your calculations. State whether each demand curve is elastic or inelastic between these two prices.

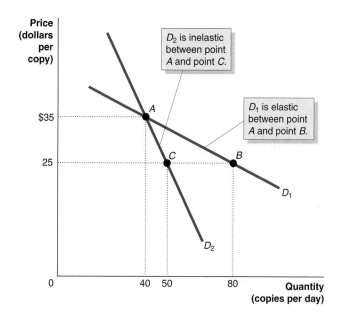

SOLVING THE PROBLEM:

Step 1: **Review the chapter material.** This problem requires calculating the price elasticity of demand, so you may want to review the material in the section "The Midpoint Formula," which begins on page 176.

Step 2: **As the first step in using the midpoint formula, calculate the average quantity and the average price for demand curve D_1.**

$$\text{Average quantity} = \frac{40 + 80}{2} = 60$$

$$\text{Average price} = \frac{\$35 + \$25}{2} = \$30$$

Step 3: **Now calculate the percentage change in the quantity demanded and the percentage change in price for demand curve D_1.**

$$\text{Percentage change in quantity demanded} = \frac{80 - 40}{60} \times 100 = 66.7\%$$

$$\text{Percentage change in price} = \frac{\$25 - \$35}{\$30} \times 100 = -33.3\%$$

Step 4: **Divide the percentage change in the quantity demanded by the percentage change in price to arrive at the price elasticity for demand curve D_1.**

$$\text{Price elasticity of demand} = \frac{66.7\%}{-33.3\%} = -2$$

Because the elasticity is greater than 1 in absolute value, D_1 is price *elastic* between these two prices.

Step 5: **Calculate the price elasticity of demand curve D_2 between these two prices.**

$$\text{Percentage change in quantity demanded} = \frac{50 - 40}{45} \times 100 = 22.2\%$$

$$\text{Percentage change in price} = \frac{\$25 - \$35}{\$30} \times 100 = -33.3\%$$

$$\text{Price elasticity of demand} = \frac{22.2\%}{-33.3\%} = -0.7$$

Because the elasticity is less than 1 in absolute value, D_2 is price *inelastic* between these two prices.

>> End Solved Problem 6-1

YOUR TURN: For more practice, do related problem 1.6 on page 200 at the end of this chapter.

When Demand Curves Intersect, the Flatter Curve Is More Elastic

Remember that elasticity is not the same thing as slope. While slope is calculated using changes in quantity and price, elasticity is calculated using percentage changes. But it *is* true that if two demand curves intersect, the one with the smaller slope (in absolute value)—the flatter demand curve—is more elastic, and the one with the larger slope (in absolute value)—the steeper demand curve—is less elastic. In Figure 6-1, demand curve D_1 is more elastic than demand curve D_2.

Polar Cases of Perfectly Elastic and Perfectly Inelastic Demand

Perfectly inelastic demand The case where the quantity demanded is completely unresponsive to price, and the price elasticity of demand equals zero.

Although they do not occur frequently, you should be aware of the extreme, or polar, cases of price elasticity. If a demand curve is a vertical line, it is **perfectly inelastic**. In this case, the quantity demanded is completely unresponsive to price, and the price elasticity of demand equals zero. However much price may increase or decrease, the quantity remains the same. For only a very few products will the quantity demanded be completely unresponsive to the price, making the demand curve a vertical line. The drug insulin is an example. Diabetics must take a certain amount of insulin each day. If the price of insulin declines, it will not affect the required dose and thus will not increase the quantity demanded. Similarly, a price increase will not affect the required dose or decrease the quantity demanded. (Of course, some diabetics will not be able to afford insulin at a higher price. If so, even in this case, the demand curve may not be completely vertical and, therefore, not perfectly inelastic.)

Perfectly elastic demand The case where the quantity demanded is infinitely responsive to price, and the price elasticity of demand equals infinity.

If a demand curve is a horizontal line, it is **perfectly elastic**. In this case, the quantity demanded would be infinitely responsive to price, and the price elasticity of demand equals infinity. If a demand curve is perfectly elastic, an increase in price causes the quantity demanded to fall to zero. Once again, perfectly elastic demand curves are rare, and it is important not to confuse *elastic* with *perfectly elastic*. Table 6-1 summarizes the different price elasticities of demand.

IF DEMAND IS...	THEN THE ABSOLUTE VALUE OF PRICE ELASTICITY IS
elastic	greater than 1
inelastic	less than 1
unit elastic	equal to 1
perfectly elastic	equal to infinity
perfectly inelastic	equal to 0

TABLE 6-1

Summary of the Price Elasticities of Demand

(Note that the percentage increases shown in the boxes in the graphs were calculated using the midpoint formula on page 176.)

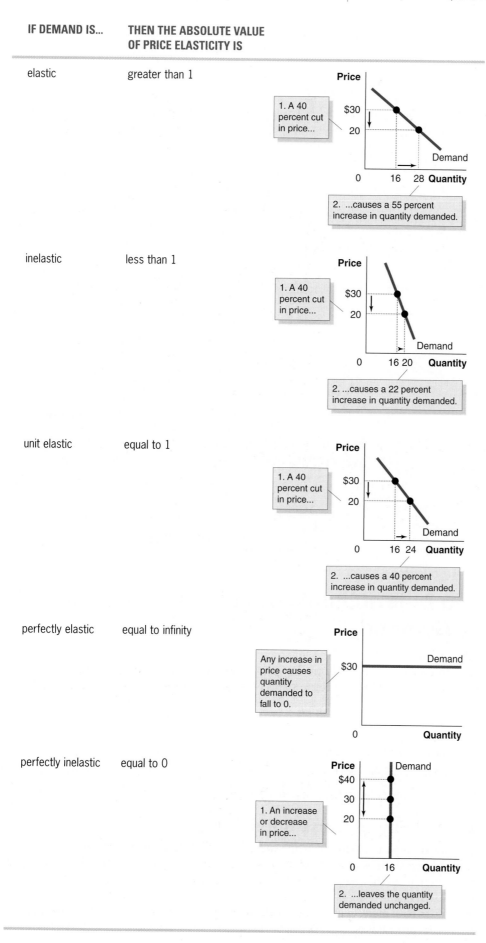

Don't Let This Happen to **YOU!**

Don't Confuse Inelastic with *Perfectly* Inelastic

You may be tempted to simplify the concept of elasticity by assuming that any demand curve described as being inelastic is *perfectly* inelastic. You should never assume this because perfectly inelastic demand curves are rare. For example, consider the following problem: "Use a demand and supply graph to show how a decrease in supply affects the equilibrium quantity of gasoline. Assume that the demand for gasoline is inelastic." The following graph would be an *incorrect* answer to this problem.

The demand for gasoline is inelastic, but it is not *perfectly* inelastic. When the price of gasoline rises, the quantity demanded falls. So, the graph that would be the correct answer to this problem would show a normal downward-sloping demand curve rather than a vertical demand curve.

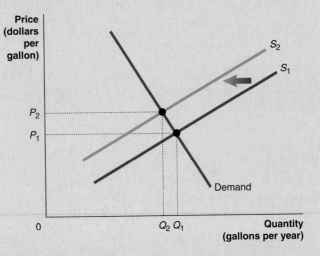

YOUR TURN: Test your understanding by doing related problem 1.11 on page 201 at the end of this chapter.

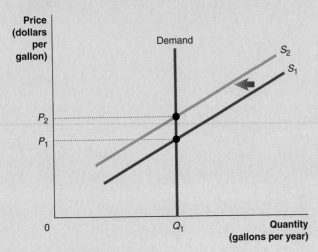

6.2 LEARNING OBJECTIVE

6.2 | Understand the determinants of the price elasticity of demand.

The Determinants of the Price Elasticity of Demand

We have seen that the demand for some products may be elastic, while the demand for other products may be inelastic. In this section, we examine why price elasticities differ among products. The key determinants of the price elasticity of demand are as follows:

*   Availability of close substitutes

*   Passage of time

*   Necessities versus luxuries

*   Definition of the market

*   Share of the good in the consumer's budget

Availability of Close Substitutes

The availability of substitutes is the most important determinant of price elasticity of demand because how consumers react to a change in the price of a product depends on what alternatives they have. When the price of gasoline rises, consumers have few alternatives, so the quantity demanded falls only a little. But if Domino's raises the price of pizza, consumers have many alternatives, so the quantity demanded is likely to fall quite a lot. In fact, a key constraint on a firm's pricing policies is how many close substitutes exist for its product. In general, *if a product has more substitutes available, it will have more elastic demand. If a product has fewer substitutes available, it will have less elastic demand.*

Passage of Time

It usually takes consumers some time to adjust their buying habits when prices change. If the price of chicken falls, for example, it takes a while before consumers decide to change from eating chicken for dinner once per week to eating it twice per week. If the price of gasoline increases, it also takes a while for consumers to decide to shift toward buying more fuel-efficient cars to reduce the quantity of gasoline they buy. *The more time that passes, the more elastic the demand for a product becomes.*

Luxuries versus Necessities

Goods that are luxuries usually have more elastic demand curves than goods that are necessities. For example, the demand for milk is inelastic because milk is a necessity, and the quantity that people buy is not very dependent on its price. Tickets to a concert are a luxury, so the demand for concert tickets is much more elastic than the demand for milk. *The demand curve for a luxury is more elastic than the demand curve for a necessity.*

Definition of the Market

In a narrowly defined market, consumers have more substitutes available. If the price of Kellogg's Raisin Bran rises, many consumers will start buying another brand of raisin bran. If the prices of all brands of raisin bran rise, the responsiveness of consumers will be lower. If the prices of all breakfast cereals rise, the responsiveness of consumers will be even lower. *The more narrowly we define a market, the more elastic demand will be.*

| Making the Connection | **The Price Elasticity of Demand for Breakfast Cereal** |

What happens when the price of raisin bran increases?

MIT economist Jerry Hausman has estimated the price elasticity of demand for breakfast cereal. He divided breakfast cereals into three categories: children's cereals, such as Trix and Froot Loops; adult cereals, such as Special K and Grape-Nuts; and family cereals, such as Corn Flakes and Raisin Bran. Some of the results of his estimates are given in the following table.

CEREAL	PRICE ELASTICITY OF DEMAND
Post Raisin Bran	−2.5
All family breakfast cereals	−1.8
All types of breakfast cereals	−0.9

Source: Jerry A. Hausman, "The Price Elasticity of Demand for Breakfast Cereal," in Timothy F. Bresnahan and Robert J. Gordon, eds., *The Economics of New Goods*, Chicago: University of Chicago Press, 1997. Used with permission of The University of Chicago Press.

Just as we would expect, the price elasticity for a particular brand of raisin bran was larger in absolute value than the elasticity for all family cereals, and the elasticity for all family cereals was larger than the elasticity for all types of breakfast cereals. If Post increases the price of its Raisin Bran by 10 percent, sales will decline by 25 percent, as many consumers switch to another brand of raisin bran. If the prices of all family breakfast cereals rise by 10 percent, sales will decline by 18 percent, as consumers switch to child or adult cereals. In both of these cases, demand is elastic. But if the prices of all types of breakfast cereals rise by 10 percent, sales will decline by only 9 percent. Demand for all breakfast cereals is inelastic.

Source: Jerry A. Hausman, "Valuation of New Goods under Perfect and Imperfect Competition," in Timothy F. Bresnahan and Robert J. Gordon, eds., *The Economics of New Goods*, Chicago: University of Chicago Press, 1997.

YOUR TURN: Test your understanding by doing related problem 2.4 on page 202 at the end of this chapter.

Share of a Good in a Consumer's Budget

Goods that take only a small fraction of a consumer's budget tend to have less elastic demand than goods that take a large fraction. For example, most people buy salt infrequently and in relatively small quantities. The share of the average consumer's budget that is spent on salt is very low. As a result, even a doubling of the price of salt is likely to result in only a small decline in the quantity of salt demanded. "Big-ticket items," such as houses, cars, and furniture, take up a larger share in the average consumer's budget. Increases in the prices of these goods are likely to result in significant declines in quantity demanded. In general, *the demand for a good will be more elastic the larger the share of the good in the average consumer's budget.*

Is the Demand for Books Perfectly Inelastic?

At the beginning of the chapter we quoted Stephen Rubin, publisher of Doubleday, as saying, "I am just convinced that there is no difference between $22 and $23. . . . Price is not a factor if it is a book that you really want." Taken literally, Rubin seems to be arguing that the demand for books is perfectly inelastic because only when demand is perfectly inelastic is price "not a factor." It's unlikely that this is what he means because if demand were really perfectly inelastic, he could charge $200 or $2,000 instead of charging $23 and still sell the same number of books. It is more likely he is arguing that demand is inelastic, so that even though he will sell fewer books at a price of $23 than at a price of $22, the decline in sales will be small.

Notice also that the book he mentions is a "translation from a Czech writer." Specialized books of this type will have relatively few substitutes (although a consumer can buy a used copy or borrow a copy from the library). A cut in price is unlikely to attract many new customers, and an increase in price is unlikely to cause many existing customers to not buy. This lack of substitutes is the main factor that makes demand inelastic. The situation may be different for light fiction written by popular novelists, like John Grisham, Stephen King, or Dean Koontz. Many consumers see books written by these authors as close substitutes. Someone looking for a "good read" on an airplane trip or at the beach may switch from Stephen King to Dean Koontz if the price of the Stephen King book is significantly higher.

6.3 LEARNING OBJECTIVE

6.3 | Understand the relationship between the price elasticity of demand and total revenue.

The Relationship between Price Elasticity of Demand and Total Revenue

Total revenue The total amount of funds received by a seller of a good or service, calculated by multiplying price per unit by the number of units sold.

A firm is interested in price elasticity because it allows the firm to calculate how changes in price will affect its **total revenue**, which is the total amount of funds it receives from selling a good or service. Total revenue is calculated by multiplying price per unit by the number of units sold. When demand is inelastic, price and total revenue move in the same direction: An increase in price raises total revenue, and a decrease in price reduces total revenue. When demand is elastic, price and total revenue move inversely: An increase in price reduces total revenue, and a decrease in price raises total revenue.

To understand the relationship between price elasticity and total revenue, consider Figure 6-2. Panel (a) shows a demand curve for a John Grisham novel (as in Figure 6-1 on page 176). This demand curve is inelastic between point *A* and point *B*. The total revenue received by a bookseller at point *A* equals the price of $30 multiplied by the 16 copies sold, or $480. This amount equals the areas of the rectangles *C* and *D* in the figure because together the rectangles have a height of $30 and a base of 16 copies. Because this demand curve is inelastic between point *A* and point *B* (it was demand curve D_2 in Figure 6-1), cutting the price to $20 (point *B*) reduces total revenue. The new total revenue is shown by the areas of rectangles *D* and *E*, and it is equal to $20 multiplied by 20 copies, or $400. Total revenue falls because the increase in the quantity demanded is not large enough to make up for the

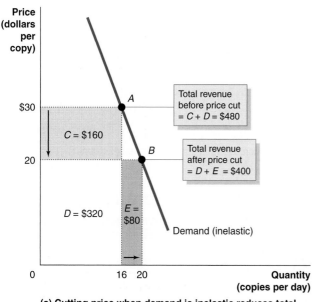

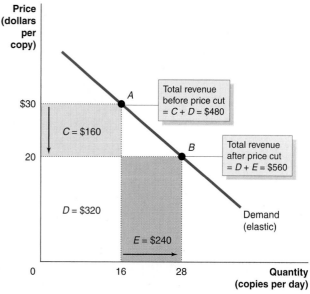

(a) Cutting price when demand is inelastic reduces total revenue.

(b) Cutting price when demand is elastic increases total revenue.

Figure 6-2 | The Relationship between Price Elasticity and Total Revenue

When demand is inelastic, a cut in price will decrease total revenue. In panel (a), at point A, the price is $30, 16 copies are sold, and total revenue received by the bookseller equals $30 × 16 copies, or $480. At point B, cutting price to $20 increases the quantity demanded to 20 copies, but the fall in price more than offsets the increase in quantity. As a result, revenue falls to $20 × 20 copies, or $400. When demand is elastic, a cut in price will increase total revenue. In panel (b), at point A, the area of rectangles C and D is still equal to $480. But at point B, the area of rectangles D and E is equal to $20 × 28 copies, or $560. In this case, the increase in the quantity demanded is large enough to offset the fall in price, so total revenue increases.

decrease in price. As a result, the $80 increase in revenue gained as a result of the price cut—dark-green rectangle E—is less than the $160 in revenue lost—light-green rectangle C.

Panel (b) of Figure 6-2 shows a demand curve that is elastic between point A and point B (it was demand curve D_1 in Figure 6-1). In this case, cutting the price increases total revenue. At point A, the areas of rectangles C and D are still equal to $480, but at point B, the areas of rectangles D and E are equal to $20 multiplied by 28 copies, or $560. Here, total revenue rises because the increase in the quantity demanded is large enough to offset the lower price. As a result, the $240 increase in revenue gained as a result of the price cut—dark-green rectangle E—is greater than the $160 in revenue lost—light-green rectangle C.

The third, less common, possibility is that demand is unit elastic. In that case, a change in price is exactly offset by a proportional change in quantity demanded, leaving revenue unaffected. Therefore, when demand is unit elastic, neither a decrease in price nor an increase in price affects revenue. Table 6-2 summarizes the relationship between price elasticity and revenue.

Elasticity and Revenue with a Linear Demand Curve

Along most demand curves, elasticity is not constant at every point. For example, a straight-line, or linear, demand curve for DVDs is shown in panel (a) of Figure 6-3. The numbers from the table are plotted in the graphs. The demand curve shows that when the price falls by $1, consumers always respond by buying 2 more DVDs per month. When the price is high and the quantity demanded is low, demand is elastic. This is true because a $1 fall in price is a smaller percentage change when the price is high, and an increase of 2 DVDs is a larger percentage change when the quantity of DVDs is small. By similar reasoning, we can see why demand is inelastic when the price is low and the quantity demanded is high.

Panel (a) in Figure 6-3 shows that when price is between $8 and $4 and quantity is between 0 and 6, demand is elastic. Panel (b) shows that over this same range, total revenue will increase as price falls. For example, in panel (a), as price falls from $7 to $6,

TABLE 6-2

The Relationship between Price Elasticity and Revenue

IF DEMAND IS...	THEN...	BECAUSE...
elastic	an increase in price reduces revenue	the decrease in quantity demanded is proportionally *greater* than the increase in price.
elastic	a decrease in price increases revenue	the increase in quantity demanded is proportionally *greater* than the decrease in price.
inelastic	an increase in price increases revenue	the decrease in quantity demanded is proportionally *smaller* than the increase in price.
inelastic	a decrease in price reduces revenue	the increase in quantity demanded is proportionally *smaller* than the decrease in price.
unit elastic	an increase in price does not affect revenue	the decrease in quantity demanded is proportionally *the same as* the increase in price.
unit elastic	a decrease in price does not affect revenue	the increase in quantity demanded is proportionally *the same as* the decrease in price.

quantity demand increases from 2 to 4, and in panel (b), total revenue increases from $14 to $24. Similarly, when price is between $4 and zero and quantity is between 8 and 16, demand is inelastic. Over this same range, total revenue will decrease as price falls. For example, as price falls from $3 to $2 and quantity increases from 10 to 12, total revenue decreases from $30 to $24.

Solved Problem | **6-3**

Price and Revenue Don't Always Move in the Same Direction

Briefly explain whether you agree or disagree with the following statement: "The only way to increase the revenue from selling a product is to increase the product's price."

SOLVING THE PROBLEM:

Step 1:   **Review the chapter material.** This problem deals with the effect of a price change on a firm's revenue, so you may want to review the section "The Relationship between Price Elasticity and Total Revenue," which begins on page 182.

Step 2:   **Analyze the statement.** We have seen that a price increase will increase revenue only if demand is inelastic. In Figure 6-3, for example, increasing the rental price of DVDs from $1 to $2 *increases* revenue from $14 to $24 because demand is inelastic along this portion of the demand curve. But increasing the price from $5 to $6 *decreases* revenue from $30 to $24 because demand is elastic along this portion of the demand curve. If the price is currently $5, increasing revenue would require a price *cut*, not a price increase. As this example shows, the statement is incorrect and you should disagree with it.

>> **End Solved Problem 6-3**

YOUR TURN: For more practice, do related problem 3.6 on page 203 at the end of this chapter.

Price	Quantity Demanded	Total Revenue
$8	0	$0
7	2	14
6	4	24
5	6	30
4	8	32
3	10	30
2	12	24
1	14	14
0	16	0

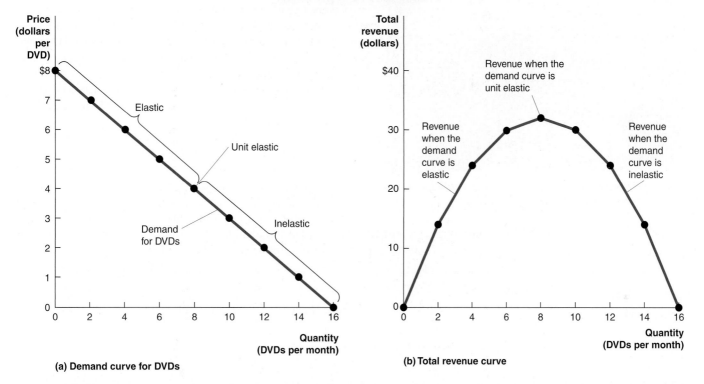

Figure 6-3 | Elasticity Is Not Constant Along a Linear Demand Curve

The data from the table are plotted in the graphs. Panel (a) shows that as we move down the demand curve for DVDs, the price elasticity of demand declines. In other words, at higher prices, demand is elastic, and at lower prices, demand is inelastic. Panel (b) shows that as the quantity of DVDs sold increases from zero, revenue will increase until it reaches a maximum of $32 when 8 DVDs are sold. As sales increase beyond 8 DVDs, revenue falls because demand is inelastic on this portion of the demand curve.

Estimating Price Elasticity of Demand

To estimate the price elasticity of demand, economists need to know the demand curve for a product. To calculate the price elasticity of demand for new products, firms often rely on market experiments. With market experiments, firms try different prices and observe the change in quantity demanded that results.

Making the Connection | **Determining the Price Elasticity of Demand for DVDs by Market Experiment**

DVDs were a relatively new product in 2001. The movie studios producing them were unsure of the price elasticity of the demand curves they were facing, so they experimented with different prices to help determine the price elasticity.

Following are four films and the prices for DVDs and VHS tapes that the studios suggested stores such as Blockbuster Video charge for them:

FILM	DVD PRICE	VHS PRICE
Rugrats in Paris	$22.46	$22.99
The Mummy Returns	26.98	22.98
Miss Congeniality	16.69	22.98
The Perfect Storm	24.98	22.99

When DVDs were first introduced, the movie studios were uncertain about their price elasticity of demand.

VHS tapes had been on the market for many years, and the studios had determined their pricing strategies, given their estimates of the price elasticity of demand. As a result, the prices of VHS tapes were usually very similar; for these four films, the prices were almost identical. The prices of DVDs were much less standardized because the studios were unsure of their price elasticities. Tom Adams, the head of Adams Market Research, a company that does research on the home video market, summed up the situation: "The studios have different views of the market, so they are setting different suggested retail prices, and the stores are discounting those prices to different degrees."

After several years of market experiments, the movie studios had more accurate estimates of the price elasticity of DVDs, and the prices of most DVDs became similar. For instance, in 2007, nearly all newly released DVDs had a list price of about $29, which was often discounted to about $17 when they were sold online or in discount department stores, such as Wal-Mart. When Blu-ray DVDs were introduced, the studios apparently felt confident that they understood their price elasticity, because in 2008 most newly released films had list prices of either $34.99 or $35.99.

Sources: Geraldine Fabrikant, "Sale of DVDs Are Challenging Movie Rental Business," *New York Times*, April 16, 2001; prices from Amazon.com.

YOUR TURN: Test your understanding by doing related problem 3.12 on page 204 at the end of this chapter.

6.4 LEARNING OBJECTIVE

6.4 | Define the cross-price elasticity of demand and the income elasticity of demand, and understand their determinants and how they are measured.

Other Demand Elasticities

Elasticity is an important concept in economics because it allows us to quantify the responsiveness of one economic variable to changes in another economic variable. In addition to price elasticity, two other demand elasticities are important: *cross-price elasticity of demand* and *income elasticity of demand*.

Cross-Price Elasticity of Demand

Cross-price elasticity of demand
The percentage change in quantity demanded of one good divided by the percentage change in the price of another good.

Suppose you work at Apple and you need to predict the effect of an increase in the price of Microsoft's Zune on the quantity of iPods demanded, holding other factors constant. You can do this by calculating the **cross-price elasticity of demand**, which is the percentage change in the quantity of iPods demanded divided by the percentage change in the price of Zunes—or, in general:

$$\text{Cross-price elasticity of demand} = \frac{\text{Percentage change in quantity demanded of one good}}{\text{Percentage change in price of another good}}.$$

IF THE PRODUCTS ARE . . .	THEN THE CROSS-PRICE ELASTICITY OF DEMAND WILL BE . . .	EXAMPLE
substitutes	positive	Two brands of digital music players
complements	negative	Digital music players and song downloads from online music stores
unrelated	zero	Digital music players and peanut butter

TABLE 6-3

Summary of Cross-Price Elasticity of Demand

The cross-price elasticity of demand is positive or negative, depending on whether the two products are substitutes or complements. Recall that substitutes are products that can be used for the same purpose, such as two brands of digital music players. Complements are products that are used together, such as digital music players and song downloads from online music sites. An increase in the price of a substitute will lead to an increase in quantity demanded, so the cross-price elasticity of demand will be positive. An increase in the price of a complement will lead to a decrease in the quantity demanded, so the cross-price elasticity of demand will be negative. Of course, if the two products are unrelated—such as digital music players and peanut butter—the cross-price elasticity of demand will be zero. Table 6-3 summarizes the key points concerning the cross-price elasticity of demand.

Cross-price elasticity of demand is important to firm managers because it allows them to measure whether products sold by other firms are close substitutes for their products. For example, Amazon.com and Barnesandnoble.com are the leading online booksellers. We might predict that if Amazon raises the price of a new John Grisham novel, many consumers will buy it from Barnesandnoble.com instead. But Jeff Bezos, Amazon's chief executive officer, has argued that because of Amazon's reputation for good customer service and because more customers are familiar with the site, ordering a book from Barnesandnoble.com is not a good substitute for ordering a book from Amazon. In effect, Bezos is arguing that the cross-price elasticity between Amazon's books and Barnesandnoble.com's books is low. Economists Judith Chevalier of Yale University and Austan Goolsbee of the University of Chicago used data on prices and quantities of books sold on these Web sites to estimate the cross-price elasticity. They found that the cross-price elasticity of demand between books at Amazon and books at Barnesandnoble.com was 3.5. This estimate means that if Amazon raises its prices by 10 percent, the quantity of books demanded on Barnesandnoble.com will increase by 35 percent. This result indicates that, contrary to Jeff Bezos's argument, consumers do consider books sold on the two Web sites to be close substitutes.

Income Elasticity of Demand

The **income elasticity of demand** measures the responsiveness of quantity demanded to changes in income. It is calculated as follows:

$$\text{Income elasticity of demand} = \frac{\text{Percentage change in quantity demanded}}{\text{Percentage change in income}}.$$

Income elasticity of demand
A measure of the responsiveness of quantity demanded to changes in income, measured by the percentage change in quantity demanded divided by the percentage change in income.

As we saw in Chapter 3, if the quantity demanded of a good increases as income increases, then the good is a *normal good*. Normal goods are often further subdivided into *luxury goods* and *necessity goods*. A good is a luxury if the quantity demanded is very responsive to changes in income, so that a 10 percent increase in income results in more than a 10 percent increase in quantity demanded. Expensive jewelry and vacation homes are examples of luxuries. A good is a necessity if the quantity demanded is not very responsive to changes in income, so that a 10 percent increase in income results in less than a 10 percent increase in quantity demanded. Food and clothing are examples of

TABLE 6-4

Summary of Income Elasticity of Demand

IF THE INCOME ELASTICITY OF DEMAND IS . . .	THEN THE GOOD IS . . .	EXAMPLE
positive but less than 1	normal and a necessity	Milk
positive and greater than 1	normal and a luxury	Caviar
negative	inferior	High-fat meat

necessities. A good is *inferior* if the quantity demanded falls when income increases. Ground beef with a high fat content is an example of an inferior good. We should note that normal goods, inferior goods, necessities, and luxuries are just labels economists use for goods with different income elasticities; they are not intended to be value judgments about the worth of these goods.

Because most goods are normal goods, during periods of economic expansion, when consumer income is rising, most firms can expect—holding other factors constant—that the quantity demanded of their products will increase. Sellers of luxuries can expect particularly large increases. During the late 1990s, rapid increases in income resulted in large increases in demand for luxuries, such as meals in expensive restaurants, luxury apartments, and high-performance automobiles. During recessions, falling consumer income can cause firms to experience increases in demand for inferior goods. For example, the demand for bus trips increases as consumers cut back on air travel, and supermarkets find the demand for hamburger increases relative to the demand for steak. Table 6-4 summarizes the key points about the income elasticity of demand.

Making the Connection | Price Elasticity, Cross-Price Elasticity, and Income Elasticity in the Market for Alcoholic Beverages

Many public policy issues are related to the consumption of alcoholic beverages. These issues include underage drinking, drunk driving, and the possible beneficial effects of red wine in lowering the risk of heart disease. X. M. Gao, an economist who works at American Express, and two colleagues have estimated statistically the following elasticities. (*Spirits* refers to all beverages that contain alcohol, other than beer and wine.)

Price elasticity of demand for beer	−0.23
Cross-price elasticity of demand between beer and wine	0.31
Cross-price elasticity of demand between beer and spirits	0.15
Income elasticity of demand for beer	−0.09
Income elasticity of demand for wine	5.03
Income elasticity of demand for spirits	1.21

The demand for beer is inelastic. A 10 percent increase in the price of beer will result in a 2.3 percent decline in the quantity of beer demanded. Not surprisingly, both wine and spirits are substitutes for beer. A 10 percent increase in the price of wine will result in a 3.1 percent *increase* in the quantity of beer demanded. A 10 percent increase in income will result in a little less than a 1 percent *decline* in the quantity of beer demanded. So, beer is an inferior good. Both wine and spirits are categorized as luxuries because their income elasticities are greater than 1.

Source: X. M. Gao, Eric J. Wailes, and Gail L. Cramer, "A Microeconometric Model Analysis of U.S. Consumer Demand for Alcoholic Beverages," *Applied Economics*, January 1995.

YOUR TURN: Test your understanding by doing related problem 4.8 on page 205 at the end of this chapter.

Using Elasticity to Analyze the Disappearing Family Farm

The concepts of price elasticity and income elasticity can help us understand many economic issues. For example, some people are concerned that the family farm is becoming an endangered species in the United States. Although food production continues to grow rapidly, the number of farms and the number of farmers continue to dwindle. In 1950, the United States was home to more than 5 million farms, and more than 23 million people lived on farms. By 2006, fewer than 2 million farms remained, and fewer than 3 million people lived on them. In Chapter 4, we discussed several federal government programs designed to slow the movement of people out of farming. Many of these programs have been aimed at helping small, family-operated farms, but rapid growth in farm production, combined with low price and income elasticities for most food products, has made family farming difficult in the United States.

Productivity measures the ability of firms to produce goods and services with a given amount of economic inputs, such as workers, machines, and land. Productivity has grown very rapidly in U.S. agriculture. In 1950, the average U.S. wheat farmer harvested about 17 bushels from each acre of wheat planted. By 2006, because of the development of superior strains of wheat and improvements in farming techniques, the average American wheat farmer harvested 42 bushels per acre. So, even though the total number of acres devoted to growing wheat declined from about 62 million to about 50 million, total wheat production rose from about 1.0 billion bushels to about 2.1 billion.

Unfortunately for U.S. farmers, this increase in wheat production resulted in a substantial decline in wheat prices. Two key factors explain this decline in wheat prices: (1) The demand for wheat is inelastic and (2) the income elasticity of demand for wheat is low. Even though the U.S. population has increased greatly since 1950 and the income of the average American is much higher than it was in 1950, the demand for wheat has increased only moderately. For all of the additional wheat to be sold, the price has had to decline. Because the demand for wheat is inelastic, the price decline has been substantial. Figure 6-4 illustrates these points.

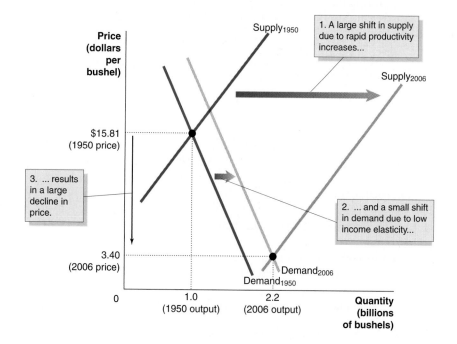

Figure 6-4

Elasticity and the Disappearing Farm

In 1950, U.S. farmers produced 1.0 billion bushels of wheat at a price of $15.81 per bushel. Over the next 50 years, rapid increases in farm productivity caused a large shift to the right in the supply curve for wheat. The income elasticity of demand for wheat is low, so the demand for wheat increased relatively little over this period. Because the demand for wheat is also inelastic, the large shift in the supply curve and the small shift in the demand curve resulted in a sharp decline in the price of wheat, from $15.81 per bushel in 1950 to $3.40 per bushel in 2006.

A large shift in supply, a small shift in demand, and an inelastic demand curve combined to drive down the price of wheat from $15.81 per bushel in 1950 to $3.40 per bushel in 2006. (The 1950 price is measured in terms of prices in 2006, to adjust for the general increase in prices since 1950.) With low prices, only the most efficiently run farms have been able to remain profitable. Smaller, family-run farms have found it difficult to survive, and many of these farms have disappeared. The markets for most food products are similar to the market for wheat. They are characterized by rapid output growth and low income and price elasticities. The result is the paradox of American farming: ever more abundant and cheaper food, supplied by fewer and fewer farms. American consumers have benefited, but most family farmers have not.

Solved Problem | 6-5

Using Price Elasticity to Analyze Policy toward Illegal Drugs

An ongoing policy debate concerns whether to legalize the use of drugs such as marijuana and cocaine. Some researchers estimate that legalizing cocaine would cause its price to fall by as much as 95 percent. Proponents of legalization argue that legalizing drug use would lower crime rates by eliminating the main reason for the murderous gang wars that plague many big cities and by reducing the incentive for drug addicts to commit robberies and burglaries. Opponents of legalization argue that lower drug prices would lead more people to use drugs.

a. Suppose the price elasticity of demand for cocaine is −2. If legalization causes the price of cocaine to fall by 95 percent, what will be the percentage increase in the quantity of cocaine demanded?

b. If the price elasticity is −0.02, what will be the percentage increase in the quantity demanded?

c. Discuss how the size of the price elasticity of demand for cocaine is relevant to the debate over its legalization.

SOLVING THE PROBLEM:

Step 1: **Review the chapter material.** This problem deals with applications of the price elasticity of demand formula, so you may want to review the section "Measuring the Price Elasticity of Demand," which begins on page 174.

Step 2: **Answer question (a) using the formula for the price elasticity of demand.**

$$\text{Price elasticity of demand} = \frac{\text{Percentage change in quantity demanded}}{\text{Percentage change in price}}.$$

We can plug into this formula the values we are given for the price elasticity and the percentage change in price:

$$-2 = \frac{\text{Percentage change in quantity demanded}}{-95\%}.$$

Or, rearranging:

$$\text{Percentage change in quantity demanded} = -2 \times -95\% = 190\%$$

Step 3: **Use the same method to answer question (b).** We only need to substitute −0.02 for −2 as the price elasticity of demand:

$$\text{Percentage change in quantity demanded} = -0.02 \times -95\% = 1.9\%$$

Step 4: **Answer question (c) by discussing how the size of the price elasticity of demand for cocaine helps us to understand the effects of legalization.** Clearly, the higher the absolute value of the price elasticity of demand for cocaine, the greater the increase in cocaine use that would result from legalization. If the price elasticity is as high as in question (a), legalization will lead to a large increase in use. If, however, the price elasticity is as low as in question (b), legalization will lead to only a small increase in use.

EXTRA CREDIT: One estimate puts the price elasticity at −0.28, which suggests that even a large fall in the price of cocaine might lead to only a moderate increase in cocaine use. However, even a moderate increase in cocaine use would have costs. Some studies have shown that cocaine users are more likely to commit crimes, to abuse their children, to have higher medical expenses, and to be less productive workers. Moreover, many people object to the use of cocaine and other narcotics on moral grounds and would oppose legalization even if it led to no increase in use. Ultimately, whether the use of cocaine and other drugs should be legalized is a normative issue. Economics can contribute to the discussion but cannot decide the issue.

Source for estimate of price elasticity of cocaine: Henry Saffer and Frank Chaloupka, "The Demand for Illicit Drugs," *Economic Inquiry*, Vol. 37, No. 3, July 1999, pp. 401–411.

YOUR TURN: For more practice, do related problems 5.2 and 5.3 on page 206 at the end of this chapter.

>> **End Solved Problem 6-5**

6.6 LEARNING OBJECTIVE

6.6 | Define the price elasticity of supply and understand its main determinants and how it is measured.

The Price Elasticity of Supply and Its Measurement

We can use the concept of elasticity to measure the responsiveness of firms to a change in price just as we used it to measure the responsiveness of consumers. We know from the law of supply that when the price of a product increases, the quantity supplied increases. To measure how much quantity supplied increases when price increases, we use the *price elasticity of supply*.

Measuring the Price Elasticity of Supply

Just as with the price elasticity of demand, we calculate the **price elasticity of supply** using percentage changes:

$$\text{Price elasticity of supply} = \frac{\text{Percentage change in quantity supplied}}{\text{Percentage change in price}}.$$

Notice that because supply curves are upward sloping, the price elasticity of supply will be a positive number. We categorize the price elasticity of supply the same way we categorized the price elasticity of demand: If the price elasticity of supply is less than 1, then supply is *inelastic*. For example, the price elasticity of supply of gasoline from U.S. oil refineries is about 0.20, and so it is inelastic. A 10 percent increase in the price of gasoline will result in only a 2 percent increase in the quantity supplied. If the price elasticity of supply is greater than 1, then supply is *elastic*. If the price elasticity of supply is equal to 1, then supply is *unit elastic*. As with other elasticity calculations, when we calculate the price elasticity of supply, we hold the values of other factors constant.

Price elasticity of supply
The responsiveness of the quantity supplied to a change in price, measured by dividing the percentage change in the quantity supplied of a product by the percentage change in the product's price.

Determinants of the Price Elasticity of Supply

Whether supply is elastic or inelastic depends on the ability and willingness of firms to alter the quantity they produce as price increases. Often, firms have difficulty increasing the quantity of the product they supply during any short period of time. For example, a pizza parlor cannot produce more pizzas on any one night than is possible using the ingredients on hand. Within a day or two it can buy more ingredients, and within a few months it can hire more cooks and install additional ovens. As a result, the supply curve for pizza and most other products will be inelastic if we measure it over a short period of time, but increasingly elastic the longer the period of time over which we measure it. Products that require resources that are themselves in fixed supply are an exception to this rule. For example, a French winery may rely on a particular variety of grape. If all the land on which that grape can be grown is already planted in vineyards, then the supply of that wine will be inelastic even over a long period.

Making the Connection | Why Are Oil Prices So Unstable?

Bringing oil to market is a long process. Oil companies hire geologists to locate fields for exploratory oil well drilling. If an exploratory well indicates that significant amounts of oil are present, the company begins full-scale development of the field. The process from exploration to pumping significant amounts of oil can take years. Because it takes so long to bring additional quantities of oil to market, the price elasticity of supply for oil is very low. Substitutes are limited for oil-based products—such as gasoline—so the price elasticity of demand for oil is also low.

As the following graph shows, the combination of inelastic supply and inelastic demand results in shifts in supply causing large changes in price. In the graph, a reduction in supply that shifts the market supply curve from S_1 to S_2 causes the equilibrium quantity of oil to fall only by 5 percent, from 80 million barrels per day to 76 million, but the equilibrium price rises by 40 percent, from $80 per barrel to $120 per barrel.

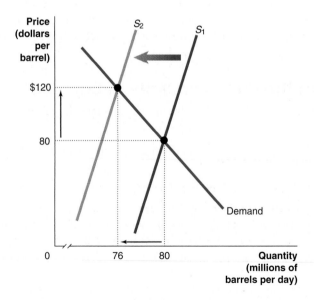

The world oil market is heavily influenced by the Organization of Petroleum Exporting Countries (OPEC). OPEC has 11 members, including Saudi Arabia, Kuwait, and other Arab countries, as well as Iran, Venezuela, Nigeria, and Indonesia. Together these countries own 75 percent of the world's proven oil reserves. Periodically, OPEC has attempted to force up the price of oil by reducing the quantity of oil its members supply. As we will discuss further in Chapter 13, since the 1970s, the attempts by OPEC to reduce the quantity of oil on world markets have been successful only sporadically: Periods during which OPEC members cooperate and reduce supply alternate with periods in which the members fail to cooperate and supply increases. As a result, the supply curve for oil shifts fairly frequently. Combined with the low price elasticities of oil supply and demand, these shifts in supply have caused the price of oil to fluctuate significantly over the past 30 years, from as low as $11 per barrel to more than $130 per barrel.

Over longer periods of time, higher oil prices also lead to greater increases in the quantity supplied; in other words, the price elasticity of supply for oil increases. This increase happens because higher prices increase the economic incentive to explore for oil and to recover oil from more costly sources, such as under the oceans, in the Arctic, or at greater depths in the earth. When supply is more elastic, a given shift in supply results in a smaller increase in price. This effect is illustrated in the following graph. Compared with the preceding graph, the same decrease in supply increases the equilibrium price to $100 per barrel rather than $120 per barrel (and also causes a smaller decrease in the equilibrium quantity).

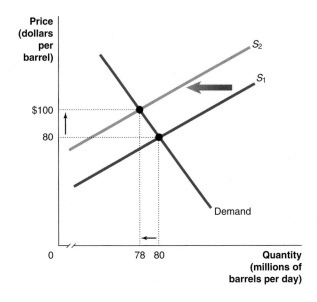

YOUR TURN: Test your understanding by doing related problem 6.3 on page 206 at the end of this chapter.

Polar Cases of Perfectly Elastic and Perfectly Inelastic Supply

Although it occurs infrequently, it is possible for supply to fall into one of the polar cases of price elasticity. If a supply curve is a vertical line, it is *perfectly inelastic.* In this case, the quantity supplied is completely unresponsive to price, and the price elasticity of supply equals zero. However much price may increase or decrease, the quantity remains the same. Over a brief period of time, the supply of some goods and services may be perfectly inelastic. For example, a parking lot may have only a fixed number of parking spaces. If demand increases, the price to park in the lot may rise, but no more spaces will become available. Of course, if demand increases permanently, over a longer period of time, the owner of the lot may buy more land to add additional spaces.

If a supply curve is a horizontal line, it is *perfectly elastic*. In this case, the quantity supplied is infinitely responsive to price, and the price elasticity of supply equals infinity. If a supply curve is perfectly elastic, a very small increase in price causes a very large increase in quantity supplied. Just as with demand curves, it is important not to confuse a supply curve being elastic with its being perfectly elastic and not to confuse a supply curve being inelastic with its being perfectly inelastic. Table 6-5 summarizes the different price elasticities of supply.

Using Price Elasticity of Supply to Predict Changes in Price

Figure 6-5 illustrates the important point that, when demand increases, the amount that price increases depends on the price elasticity of supply. The figure shows the demand and supply for parking spaces at a beach resort. In panel (a), on a typical summer weekend, equilibrium occurs at point *A*, where Demand (typical) intersects a supply curve that is inelastic. The increase in demand for parking spaces on the Fourth of July shifts the demand curve to the right, moving the equilibrium to point *B*. Because the supply curve is inelastic, the increase in demand results in a large increase in price—from $2.00 per hour to $4.00—but only a small increase in the quantity of spaces supplied—from 1,200 to 1,400.

In panel (b), supply is elastic, perhaps because the resort has vacant land that can be used for parking during periods of high demand. As a result, the shift in equilibrium from point *A* to point *B* results in a smaller increase in price and a larger increase in the quantity supplied. An increase in price from $2.00 per hour to $2.50 is sufficient to increase the quantity of parking supplied from 1,200 to 2,100. Knowing the price elasticity of supply makes it possible to predict more accurately how much price will change following an increase or a decrease in demand.

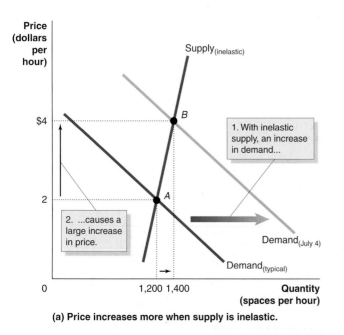

(a) Price increases more when supply is inelastic.

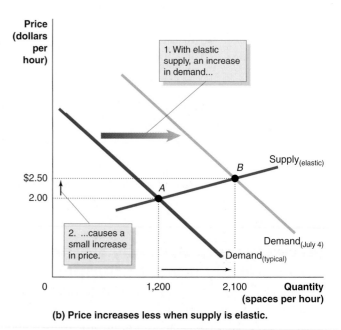

(b) Price increases less when supply is elastic.

Figure 6-5 | Changes in Price Depend on the Price Elasticity of Supply

In panel (a), Demand (typical) represents the typical demand for parking spaces on a summer weekend at a beach resort. Demand (July 4) represents demand on the Fourth of July. Because supply is inelastic, the shift in equilibrium from point *A* to point *B* results in a large increase in price—from $2.00 per hour to $4.00—but only a small increase in the quantity of spaces supplied—from 1,200 to 1,400. In panel

(b), supply is elastic. As a result, the shift in equilibrium from point *A* to point *B* results in a smaller increase in price and a larger increase in the quantity supplied. An increase in price from $2.00 per hour to $2.50 is sufficient to increase the quantity of parking supplied from 1,200 to 2,100.

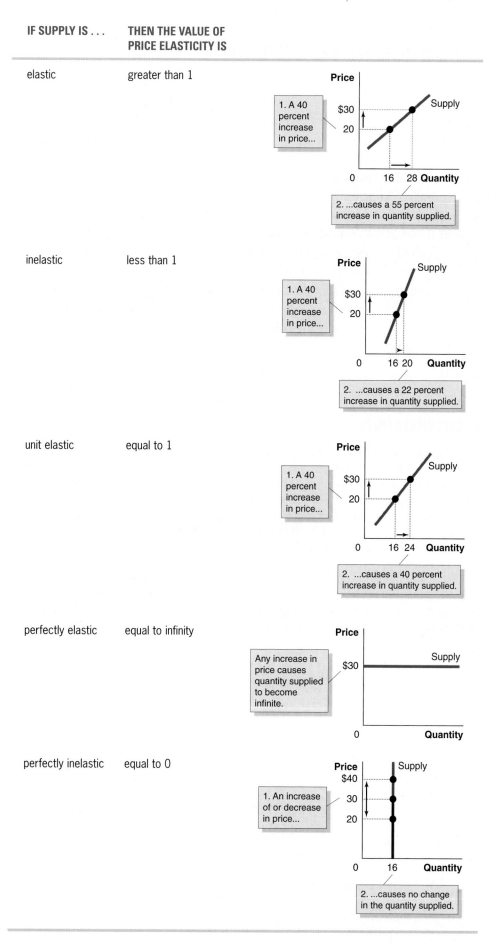

IF SUPPLY IS . . .	THEN THE VALUE OF PRICE ELASTICITY IS
elastic	greater than 1
inelastic	less than 1
unit elastic	equal to 1
perfectly elastic	equal to infinity
perfectly inelastic	equal to 0

TABLE 6-5

Summary of the Price Elasticities of Supply

(Note that the percentage increases shown in the boxes in the graphs were calculated using the midpoint formula on page 176.)

1. A 40 percent increase in price...

2. ...causes a 55 percent increase in quantity supplied.

1. A 40 percent increase in price...

2. ...causes a 22 percent increase in quantity supplied.

1. A 40 percent increase in price...

2. ...causes a 40 percent increase in quantity supplied.

Any increase in price causes quantity supplied to become infinite.

1. An increase of or decrease in price...

2. ...causes no change in the quantity supplied.

>> Continued from page 173

Economics in YOUR Life!

At the beginning of the chapter, we asked you to think about two questions: What factors would make you more or less sensitive to price when purchasing a book? and Is Barnes & Noble's strategy of heavily discounting copies of *Harry Potter and the Deathly Hallows* in hopes of selling a very large quantity likely to succeed? If you have never read any Harry Potter books, you are probably not a fan of the series and are unlikely to purchase the book at any price. If you read all the earlier books in the series as soon as they came out, you are very likely to consider purchasing the book even at a high price. However, if you usually wait to purchase inexpensive paperback editions of books you like to read, you are more likely to purchase the hardcover book when Barnes & Noble discounts it. The answer to the second question depends on the prevalence of this last type of consumer. The more price-conscious consumers there are in the market, the more responsive to price the quantity demanded for the hardcover version will be, and the more likely it is for Barnes & Noble's revenue to increase in response to the drop in price.

Conclusion

In this chapter, we have explored the important concept of elasticity. Table 6-6 summarizes the various elasticities we discussed in this chapter. Computing elasticities is important in economics because it allows us to measure how one variable changes in response to changes in another variable. For example, by calculating the price elasticity of demand for its product, a firm can make a quantitative estimate of the effect of a price change on the revenue it receives. Similarly, by calculating the price elasticity of demand for cigarettes, the government can better estimate the effect of an increase in cigarette taxes on smoking.

Before going further in analyzing how firms decide on the prices to charge and the quantities to produce, we need to look at how firms are organized. We do this in the next chapter. Read *An Inside Look* on page 198 to use the concept of elasticity to analyze the Borders bookstores' Borders Rewards program.

PRICE ELASTICITY OF DEMAND

TABLE 6-6

Summary of Elasticities

Formula: $\dfrac{\text{Percentage change in quantity demanded}}{\text{Percentage change in price}}$

Midpoint Formula: $\dfrac{(Q_2 - Q_1)}{\left(\dfrac{Q_1 + Q_2}{2}\right)} \div \dfrac{(P_2 - P_1)}{\left(\dfrac{P_1 + P_2}{2}\right)}$

	ABSOLUTE VALUE OF PRICE ELASTICITY	EFFECT ON TOTAL REVENUE OF AN INCREASE IN PRICE
Elastic	Greater than 1	Total revenue falls
Inelastic	Less than 1	Total revenue rises
Unit elastic	Equal to 1	Total revenue unchanged

CROSS-PRICE ELASTICITY OF DEMAND

Formula: $\dfrac{\text{Percentage change in quantity demanded of one good}}{\text{Percentage change in price of another good}}$

TYPES OF PRODUCTS	VALUE OF CROSS-PRICE ELASTICITY
Substitutes	Positive
Complements	Negative
Unrelated	Zero

INCOME ELASTICITY OF DEMAND

Formula: $\dfrac{\text{Percentage change in quantity demanded}}{\text{Percentage change in income}}$

TYPES OF PRODUCTS	VALUE OF INCOME ELASTICITY
Normal and a necessity	Positive but less than 1
Normal and a luxury	Positive and greater than 1
Inferior	Negative

PRICE ELASTICITY OF SUPPLY

Formula: $\dfrac{\text{Percentage change in quantity supplied}}{\text{Percentage change in price}}$

	VALUE OF PRICE ELASTICITY
Elastic	Greater than 1
Inelastic	Less than 1
Unit elastic	Equal to 1

WALL STREET JOURNAL, MARCH 28, 2007

Borders Slashes Buyer Rewards, Cuts Discounts

The nation's second-largest book retailer, Borders Group Inc., has decided there can be too much of a good thing when it comes to its free membership-rewards program.

Less than a week after it reported disappointing fourth-quarter and annual results, Borders said that it is phasing out its popular Holiday Savings Rewards and Personal Shopping Days benefits and replacing them with a simpler, less-generous promotion called Borders Bucks.

The move will dramatically alter a program that has been a tremendous hit with consumers. Since the launch of the Borders Rewards membership club in February 2006, nearly 17 million people have signed up, and Borders continues to add an estimated 150,000 new customers each week. Borders' announcement comes at a time when many reward programs—including those from credit-card companies and airlines' frequent-flier plans—are tightening eligibility rules or becoming stingier with benefits.

Under the new Borders plan, each time customers reach $150 in purchases at Borders superstores or Waldenbooks stores, they will receive $5 in Borders Bucks at the beginning of the following month. They can then use that $5 until the end of that month, at which point the offer expires. Users will be contacted by e-mail and urged to print out a $5 coupon, although those who forget will be able to use their $5 credit by presenting their Borders Rewards card in stores. Customers will be able to earn Borders Bucks online after Borders opens its own Web site next year. . . .

But, under the old plan, discounts could be much deeper. Members were given Personal Shopping Days, which enabled those who had spent $50 in a month to apply a 10% discount on all purchases made on a specific day in the following month. Gift cards were the exception. Customers also received a credit equal to 5% of their store purchases made through Nov. 14 in a special Holiday Savings account. That credit could then be used on purchases made from Nov. 15 through Jan. 31. The only caveat was that customers had to have at least $10 in their account—which meant they had to have spent a minimum of $200 to qualify.

A big downside for Borders was that the company had to absorb all of the Holiday Savings account spending during its fourth quarter, a period when shoppers would have been in the stores anyway buying gifts. Under the new program, the impact on the company will be more regulated by enabling customers to claim their Borders Bucks year-round.

George Jones, the retailer's CEO, foreshadowed the changes to the program in January when he told investors that he intended to "make modifications in the program going forward." Earlier this month, Borders cited the "customer redemption of Borders Rewards benefits" as one of the reasons that gross margins as a percentage of sales decreased 3% in the fourth quarter.

In addition, Mr. Tam [Borders' chief marketing officer] said that Borders will now add special savings promotions to make up for the difference between the old and new programs. Although he declined to be specific, he said the retailer will be launching what it calls Bonus Rewards Events for all members. This could include days when discounts can be applied to all purchases, something previously available only to customers who had spent $50 in the prior month. Borders will also continue to send out weekly coupons via its e-mail newsletter.

Some customers weren't impressed. "Why bother?" asked Ron Goodenow, a market research consultant and writer in Northborough, Mass. "I find that on a lot of things that I'm interested in like music and DVDs that their prices are higher than the competition." The five dollars, he says, won't mean anything to him. "It's gratuitous considering how much they've hyped the program."

A spokeswoman for Borders said she believes that based on the retailer's market research, most customers will be happy with the changes.

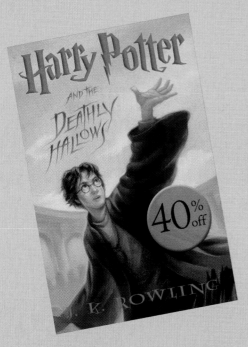

Key Points in the Article

Many retailers have programs that provide repeat buyers with price discounts. From a firm's point of view, whether a discount program is a good idea depends on how customers respond—that is, it depends on the price elasticity of demand. The Borders Rewards program reduces the price of books, but if the lower prices cause enough additional books to be sold, then total revenue will rise. This is why firms offer discount programs: They believe the programs raise total profits. However, not all discount programs increase total profits, and Borders recently changed its discount program for this reason.

Analyzing the News

(a) The Borders Rewards program is immensely popular, as indicated by the 17 million customers who signed up for the program during 2006. Will the Borders Rewards program increase the firm's revenue? Figure 1 shows the effect of a decrease in price on the quantity of books sold, and Figure 2 shows the effect on total revenue. A decrease in price will increase total revenue only if the firm is operating on the elastic region of the demand curve. Even if the firm starts off on the elastic region, it could cut prices so much that total revenue declines. That is exactly what Figure 2 shows.

(b) The old Borders Rewards program had several features designed to ensure that customers bought enough items to make the program profitable. First, customers who spent $50 in a month would receive a 10 percent discount on a specific day the following month. Second, those who spent at least $200 before November 14 received a special credit good for purchases at Borders through the holiday season. By imposing minimum purchase requirements on customers before they could qualify for discounts, Borders hoped that the Rewards program would increase sales enough to make the program profitable. Unfortunately, most of the credits were good during the holiday season, when customers were in the stores anyway, already purchasing books. The Rewards program gave customers discounts on books that they would probaby have bought anyway and did not lead customers to purchase many additional books.

In other words, the price discounts applied when the demand for books was relatively inelastic.

(c) In response to these problems, Borders has substantially changed its discount program. Customers will no longer receive the large holiday discounts. This means that the bulk of the discounts will no longer occur when the demand is relatively inelastic. However, this is no guarantee of success because the discounts offered in the new program may be too small, and too few customers may purchase the discounted books.

Thinking Critically

1. The purpose of discount programs is to increase sales and profits. However, a firm's competitors often have discount programs as well. Suppose Borders and Barnes & Noble both institute discount programs at the same time. Will revenue at Borders necessarily increase, even if Borders is currently on the elastic region of the demand curve?

2. The Internet has made it easy for consumers to buy books online. As a result, many traditional booksellers like Barnes & Noble and Borders (starting in 2008), along with Amazon, sell books on their Web sites. What effect has the Internet had on the demand curve for the books Borders sells in its (non-Internet) stores?

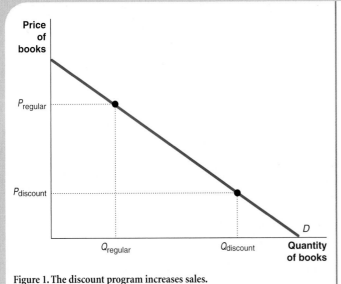

Figure 1. The discount program increases sales.

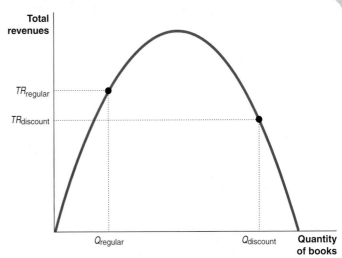

Figure 2. The discount program may not increase total revenues.

Key Terms

Cross-price elasticity
of demand, p. 186

Elastic demand, p. 175

Elasticity, p. 174

Income elasticity of demand,
p. 187

Inelastic demand, p. 175

Perfectly elastic demand, p. 178

Perfectly inelastic demand, p. 178

Price elasticity of demand, p. 174

Price elasticity of supply, p. 191

Total revenue, p. 182

Unit-elastic demand, p. 175

6.1 LEARNING OBJECTIVE   6.1 | Define the price elasticity of demand and understand how to measure it,
pages 174–180.

The Price Elasticity of Demand and Its Measurement

Summary

Elasticity measures how much one economic variable responds to changes in another economic variable. The **price elasticity of demand** measures how responsive quantity demanded is to changes in price. The price elasticity of demand is equal to the percentage change in quantity demanded divided by the percentage change in price. If the quantity demanded changes more than proportionally when price changes, the price elasticity of demand is greater than 1 in absolute value, and demand is **elastic**. If the quantity demanded changes less than proportionally when price changes, the price elasticity of demand is less than 1 in absolute value, and demand is **inelastic**. If the quantity demanded changes proportionally when price changes, the price elasticity of demand is equal to 1 in absolute value, and demand is **unit elastic**. **Perfectly inelastic demand curves** are vertical lines, and **perfectly elastic** demand curves are horizontal lines. Relatively few products have perfectly elastic or perfectly inelastic demand curves.

myeconlab Visit www.myeconlab.com to complete these exercises
Get Ahead of the Curve online and get instant feedback.

Review Questions

1.1 Write the formula for the price elasticity of demand. Why isn't elasticity just measured by the slope of the demand curve?

1.2 If a 10 percent increase in the price of Cap'n Crunch cereal causes a 25 percent reduction in the number of boxes of cereal demanded, what is the price elasticity of demand for Cap'n Crunch cereal? Is demand for Cap'n Crunch elastic or inelastic?

1.3 What is the midpoint method for calculating price elasticity of demand? How else can you calculate the

price elasticity of demand? What is the advantage of the midpoint method?

1.4 Draw a graph of a perfectly inelastic demand curve. Think of a product that would have a perfectly inelastic demand curve. Explain why demand for this product would be perfectly inelastic.

Problems and Applications

1.5 Suppose the following table gives data on the price of rye and the number of bushels of rye sold in 2008 and 2009.

YEAR	PRICE (DOLLARS PER BUSHEL)	QUANTITY (BUSHELS)
2008	$3.00	8 million
2009	2.00	12 million

a. Calculate the change in the quantity of rye demanded divided by the change in the price of rye. Measure the quantity of rye in bushels.

b. Calculate the change in the quantity of rye demanded divided by the change in the price of rye, but this time measure the quantity of rye in millions of bushels. Compare your answer to the one you computed in a.

c. Finally, assuming that the demand curve for rye did not shift between 2008 and 2009, use the information in the table to calculate the price elasticity of demand for rye. Use the midpoint formula in your calculation. Compare the value for the price elasticity of demand to the values you calculated in a and b.

1.6 **(Related to *Solved Problem 6-1* on page 177)** You own a hot dog stand that you set up outside the student union every day at lunch time. Currently, you are selling hot dogs for a price of $3, and you sell 30 hot dogs a day. You are considering cutting the price to $2. The following graph shows two possible increases in the quantity sold as a result of your price cut. Use the information in the graph to calculate the price elasticity between these two prices on each of the demand curves. Use the midpoint formula to calculate the price elasticities.

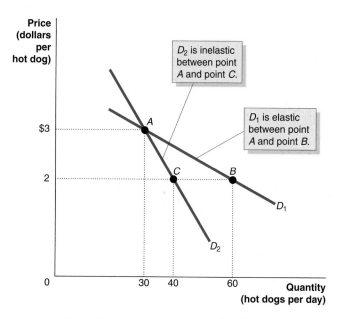

1.7 In fall 2006, Pace University in New York raised its annual tuition from $24,751 to $29,454. Freshman enrollment declined from 1,469 in fall 2005 to 1,131 in fall 2006. Assuming that the demand curve for places in the freshmen class at Pace did not shift between 2005 and 2006, use this information to calculate the price elasticity of demand. Use the midpoint formula in your calculation. Is the demand for places in Pace's freshmen class elastic or inelastic? Did the total amount of tuition Pace received from its freshman class rise or fall in 2006 compared with 2005?

Source: Karen W. Arenson, "At Universities, Plum Post at Top Is Now Shaky," *New York Times*, January 9, 2007.

1.8 Consider the following excerpt from a newspaper story on increases in college tuition:

> Facing stiff competition, Hendrix College, a small liberal arts institution in Conway, Ark., decided two years ago to bolster its academic offerings, promising students at least three hands-on experiences outside

the classroom, including research, internships and service projects. It also raised tuition and fees 29 percent, to $21,636. . . . As a result, 409 students enrolled in the freshman class this year, a 37 percent increase. "What worked was the buzz," said J. Timothy Cloyd, the Hendrix president. "Students saw that they were going to get an experience that had value, and the price positioning conveyed to them the value of the experience."

Does this excerpt provide enough information to calculate the price elasticity of demand for places in Hendrix College's freshman class? Briefly explain.

Source: Jonathan D. Glater and Alan Finder, "In New Twist on Tuition Game, Popularity Rises with the Price," *New York Times*, December 12, 2006.

1.9 In summer 2007, Sony decided to cut the price of its PlayStation 3 video game console from $600 to $500. One industry analyst forecast that the price cut would increase sales from 80,000 units per month to 120,000 units per month. Assuming the analyst's forecast is correct, use the midpoint formula to calculate the price elasticity of demand for PlayStation 3.

Source: "Sony Cuts Price on PlayStation 3 by $100," *New York Times*, July 9, 2007.

1.10 In 1916, the Ford Motor Company sold 500,000 Model T Fords at a price of $440 each. Henry Ford believed that he could increase sales of the Model T by 1,000 cars for every dollar he cut the price. Use this information to calculate the price elasticity of demand for Model T Fords. Use the midpoint formula in your calculation.

1.11 **(Related to the *Don't Let This Happen to You!* on page 180)** The publisher of a magazine gives his staff the following information:

Current price	$2.00 per issue
Current sales	150,000 copies per month
Current total costs	$450,000 per month

He tells the staff, "Our costs are currently $150,000 more than our revenues each month. I propose to eliminate this problem by raising the price of the magazine to $3.00 per issue. This will result in our revenue being exactly equal to our cost." Do you agree with the publisher's analysis? Explain. (*Hint:* Remember that a firm's revenue is equal to the price of the product multiplied by the quantity sold.)

>> End Learning Objective 6.1

6.2 LEARNING OBJECTIVE 6.2 | Understand the determinants of the price elasticity of demand, **pages 180–182.**

The Determinants of the Price Elasticity of Demand

Summary

The main determinants of the price elasticity of demand for a product are the availability of close substitutes, the passage of time, whether the good is a necessity or a luxury, how narrowly the market for the good is defined, and the share of the good in the consumer's budget.

 Visit www.myeconlab.com to complete these exercises *Get Ahead of the Curve* online and get instant feedback.

Review Questions

2.1 Is the demand for most agricultural products elastic or inelastic? Why?

2.2 What are the key determinants of the price elasticity of demand for a product? Which determinant is the most important?

Problems and Applications

2.3 Briefly explain whether the demand for each of the following products is likely to be elastic or inelastic.

a. Milk
b. Frozen cheese pizza
c. Cola
d. Prescription medicine

2.4 (Related to the *Making the Connection* on page 181) A study of the price elasticities of products sold in supermarkets contained the following data:

PRODUCT	PRICE ELASTICITY OF DEMAND
Soft drinks	–3.18
Canned soup	–1.62
Cheese	–0.72
Toothpaste	–0.45

a. For which products is the demand inelastic? Discuss reasons why the demand for each product is either elastic or inelastic.
b. Use the information in the table to predict the change in the quantity demanded for each product following a 10 percent price increase.

Source: Stephen J. Hoch, Byung-do Kim, Alan L. Montgomery, and Peter E. Rossi, "Determinants of Store-Level Price Elasticity," *Journal of Marketing Research*, Vol. 32, February 1995, pp. 17–29.

>> End Learning Objective 6.2

6.3 LEARNING OBJECTIVE 6.3 | Understand the relationship between the price elasticity of demand and total revenue, **pages 182–186.**

The Relationship between Price Elasticity of Demand and Total Revenue

Summary

Total revenue is the total amount of funds received by a seller of a good or service. When demand is inelastic, a decrease in price reduces total revenue, and an increase in price increases total revenue. When demand is elastic, a decrease in price increases total revenue, and an increase in price decreases total revenue. When demand is unit elastic, an increase or a decrease in price leaves total revenue unchanged.

 Visit www.myeconlab.com to complete these exercises *Get Ahead of the Curve* online and get instant feedback.

Review Questions

3.1 If the demand for orange juice is inelastic, will an increase in the price of orange juice increase or decrease the revenue received by orange juice sellers?

3.2 The price of organic apples falls and apple growers find that their revenue increases. Is the demand for organic apples elastic or inelastic?

Problems and Applications

3.3 A newspaper story on the effect of higher milk prices on the market for ice cream contained the following: "As a result [of the increase in milk prices], retail prices for ice cream are up 4 percent from last year. . . . And ice cream consumption is down 3 percent." Given this information, compute the price elasticity of demand for ice cream. Will the revenue received by ice cream suppliers have increased or decreased following the price increase? Briefly explain.

Source: John Curran, "Ice Cream, They Scream: Milk Fat Costs Drive Up Ice Cream Prices," Associated Press, July 23, 2001.

3.4 Use the following graph for Yolanda's Frozen Yogurt Stand to answer the questions that follow.

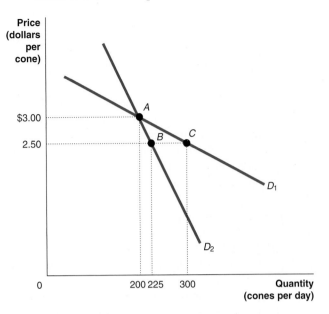

a. Use the midpoint formula to calculate the price elasticity of demand for D_1 between point A and point C and the price elasticity of demand for D_2 between point A and point B. Which demand curve is more elastic, D_1 or D_2? Briefly explain.

b. Suppose Yolanda is initially selling 200 cones per day at a price of $3.00 per cone. If she cuts her price to $2.50 per cone and her demand curve is D_1, what will be the change in her revenue? What will be the change in her revenue if her demand curve is D_2?

3.5 An article in the *Wall Street Journal* noted the following:

Instead of relying on a full-coach, round-trip unrestricted fare of about $2,000 between Cleveland and Los Angeles . . . Continental [Airlines] since June has offered a $716 unrestricted fare in that market. . . . Through October, the test resulted in about the same revenue that Continental thinks it would have collected with its higher fare.

What is the value of the price elasticity of demand on this airline route? Is Continental likely to be better off charging the low fare or the high fare? Briefly explain.

Source: Scott McCartney, "Airlines Try Cutting Business Fares, Find They Don't Lose Revenue," *Wall Street Journal*, November 22, 2002.

3.6 (Related to *Solved Problem 6-3* on page 184) Briefly explain whether you agree or disagree with Manager 2's reasoning:

Manager 1: "The only way we can increase the revenue we receive from selling our frozen pizzas is by cutting the price."

Manager 2: "Cutting the price of a product never increases the amount of revenue you receive. If we want to increase revenue, we have to increase price."

3.7 (Related to the *Chapter Opener* on page 172) Consider the following description of a pricing decision by academic book publishers:

A publisher may have issued a monograph several years ago, when both costs and book prices were lower, and priced it at $14.95. The book is still selling reasonably well and would continue to do so at $19.95. Why not, then, raise the price? The only danger is miscalculation: By raising the price you may reduce sales to the point where you make less money overall, even while making more per copy.

Assume that the situation described in the last sentence happens. What does this tell us about the price elasticity of demand for that book? Briefly explain.

Source: Beth Luey, *Handbook for Academic Authors*, 4th ed., Cambridge, UK: Cambridge University Press, 2002, p. 250.

3.8 Each summer, the city of Bethlehem, Pennsylvania, holds Musikfest, an outdoor music festival. The city had been charging $7 per day to park in city parking lots. One year it raised the fee to $10 per day. According to an article in a local newspaper, "Fewer parkers used city lots, but this year's parking rate increase [from $7 to $10] gave the [parking] authority record [parking] lot revenues for the annual festival." Use the information in the following table to calculate the price elasticity of demand for parking spaces in Bethlehem city parking lots during Musikfest; use the midpoint price elasticity of demand formula. Assume that nothing happened to shift the demand curve for parking places. Be sure to state whether demand is elastic or inelastic.

MUSIKFEST PARKING RATE REVENUE		
YEAR	RATE	REVENUE
1999	$10	$83,760
1998	7	77,791

Source: Matt Assad, "Grinch Alive and Well in Bethlehem Parking Authority," (*Allentown, Pennsylvania*) *Morning Call*, September 29, 1999, page B4.

3.9 An article about the newspaper industry that appeared in the *Wall Street Journal* noted the following: "Declining circulation hasn't stopped Knight Ridder papers from raising subscription prices. Such increases, while boosting revenue per copy, almost always trigger a readership decline."

a. What is a newspaper's "circulation"?

b. To what is "revenue per copy" equal?

c. Why would a newspaper's management increase its subscription price if the result was a decline in the quantity of newspapers sold?

Source: Patricia Callahan and Kevin Helliker, "Subscriptions Fall, but Knight Ridder Lifts Advertising Rates," *Wall Street Journal*, June 18, 2001.

3.10 (Related to the *Chapter Opener* on page 172) Look again at the quote from Stephen Rubin of Doubleday at the beginning of this chapter. Doubleday is selling John Grisham's book *The Innocent Man* at a price of $28.95.

    a. Assume that the demand for this book is perfectly inelastic. Draw a demand curve showing the effect on the quantity demanded of raising the price from $28.95 to $39.95. Assume that sales are 500,000 at a price of $28.95. What is the change in revenue as a result of the price change?

    b. Now assume that the price elasticity of demand is −2. Draw another demand curve showing the effect of raising the price from $28.95 to $39.95. Be sure to show the quantity demanded at each price. Now what is the change in revenue as a result of the price change?

3.11 The Delaware River Joint Toll Bridge Commission increased the toll on the bridges on Route 22 and Interstate 78 from New Jersey to Pennsylvania from $0.50 to $1.00. Use the information in the table to answer the questions. (Assume that nothing other than the toll change occurred during the months that would affect consumer demand.)

NUMBER OF VEHICLES CROSSING THE BRIDGE			
MONTH	TOLL	ROUTE 22 BRIDGE	INTERSTATE 78 BRIDGE
November	$0.50	519,337	728,022
December	1.00	433,691	656,257

    a. Calculate the price elasticity of demand for each bridge, using the midpoint formula.

    b. How much total revenue did the commission collect from these bridges in November? How much did it collect in December? Relate your answer to your answer in part a.

Source: Garrett Therolf, "Frugal Drivers Flood Free Bridge," (*Allentown, Pennsylvania*) *Morning Call,* January 20, 2003.

3.12 (Related to the *Making the Connection* on page 185) Suppose you check out the prices of two products on Amazon.com: Conventional DVD players and Blu-ray DVD players. For which type of players would you expect manufacturers to be offering similar players at about the same prices and for which type of players would you expect prices to be more spread out? Briefly explain.

>> **End Learning Objective 6.3**

6.4 LEARNING OBJECTIVE   6.4 | Define the cross-price elasticity of demand and the income elasticity of demand, and understand their determinants and how they are measured, **pages 186–188.**

Other Demand Elasticities

Summary

Other important demand elasticities are the **cross-price elasticity of demand**, which is equal to the percentage change in quantity demanded of one good divided by the percentage change in the price of another good, and the **income elasticity of demand**, which is equal to the percentage change in the quantity demanded divided by the percentage change in income.

 Visit www.myeconlab.com to complete these exercises *Get Ahead of the Curve* online and get instant feedback.

Review Questions

4.1 Define the cross-price elasticity of demand. What does it mean if the cross-price elasticity of demand is negative? What does it mean if the cross-price elasticity of demand is positive?

4.2 Define the income elasticity of demand. Use income elasticity to distinguish a normal good from an inferior good. Is it possible to tell from the income elasticity of demand whether a product is a luxury good or a necessity good?

Problems and Applications

4.3 In spring 2002, lettuce prices doubled, from about $1.50 per head to about $3.00. The reaction of one consumer was quoted in a newspaper article: "I will not buy [lettuce] when it's $3 a head," she said, adding that other green vegetables can fill in for lettuce. "If bread were $5 a loaf we'd still have to buy it. But lettuce is not that important in our family."

a. For this consumer's household, which product has the higher price elasticity of demand: bread or lettuce? Briefly explain.

b. Is the cross-price elasticity of demand between lettuce and other green vegetables positive or negative for this consumer? Briefly explain.

Source: Justin Bachman, "Sorry, Romaine Only," Associated Press, March 29, 2002.

4.4 In the following graph, the demand for hot dog buns has shifted outward because the price of hot dogs has fallen from $2.20 to $1.80 per package. Calculate the cross-price elasticity of demand between hot dogs and hot dog buns.

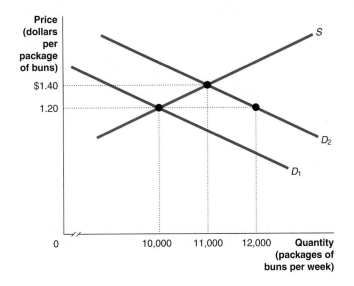

4.5 Are the cross-price elasticities of demand between the following pairs of products likely to be positive or negative? Briefly explain.
a. Pepsi and Coca-Cola
b. French fries and ketchup
c. Steak and chicken
d. Blu-ray players and Blu-ray DVDs

4.6 After World War II, the Japanese government intervened in the economy to provide aid to certain industries that it believed would be most important in the recovery from war. One of the requirements for receiving government aid was that an industry had to be producing a good with a high income elasticity of demand. Why do you think the Japanese government made this a requirement?

4.7 Rank the following four goods from lowest income elasticity of demand to highest income elasticity of demand. Briefly explain your ranking.
a. Bread
b. Pepsi
c. Mercedes-Benz automobiles
d. Personal computers

4.8 **(Related to the *Making the Connection* on page 188)** Is the cross-price elasticity of demand between wine and spirits likely to be positive or negative? Can you think of reasons why the income elasticity of demand for wine is so much higher than the income elasticity of demand for spirits?

>> **End Learning Objective 6.4**

6.5 LEARNING OBJECTIVE   6.5 | Use price elasticity and income elasticity to analyze economic issues, pages 189–191.

Using Elasticity to Analyze the Disappearing Family Farm

Summary

Price elasticity and income elasticity can be used to analyze many economic issues. One example is the disappearance of the family farm in the United States. Because the income elasticity of demand for food is low, the demand for food has not increased proportionally as incomes in the United States have grown. As farmers have become more productive, they have increased the supply of most foods. Because the price elasticity of demand for food is low, increasing supply has resulted in continually falling food prices.

 Visit www.myeconlab.com to complete these exercises
Get Ahead of the Curve online and get instant feedback.

Review Question

5.1 The demand for agricultural products is inelastic, and the income elasticity of demand for agricultural products is low. How do these facts help explain the disappearing family farm?

Problems and Applications

5.2 (Related to *Solved Problem 6-5* on page 190) According to a study by the U.S. Centers for Disease Control and Prevention, the price elasticity of demand for cigarettes is −0.25. Americans purchase about 480 billion cigarettes each year.
   a. If the federal tax on cigarettes were increased enough to raise the price of cigarettes by 50 percent, what would be the effect on the quantity of cigarettes demanded?
   b. Is raising the tax on cigarettes a more effective way to reduce smoking if the demand for cigarettes is elastic or if it is inelastic? Briefly explain.

   Source: "Response to Increases in Cigarette Prices by Race/Ethnicity, Income, and Age Groups—United States, 1976–1993," *Morbidity and Mortality Weekly Report*, July 31, 1998.

5.3 (Related to *Solved Problem 6-5* on page 190) The price elasticity of demand for cocaine has been estimated at −0.28. Suppose that a successful war on illegal drugs reduces the supply of cocaine in the United States enough to result in a 20 percent increase in its price. What will be the percentage reduction in the quantity of cocaine demanded?

   Source: Henry Saffer and Frank Chaloupka, "The Demand for Illicit Drugs," *Economic Inquiry*, Vol. 37, No. 3, July 1999, pp. 401–411.

5.4 The price elasticity of demand for most agricultural products is quite low. What effect is this likely to have on how much the prices of these products change from year to year? Illustrate your answer with a demand and supply graph.

5.5 The head of the United Kumquat Growers Association makes the following statement:

> The federal government is considering implementing a price floor in the market for kumquats. The government will not be able to buy any surplus kumquats produced at the price floor or to pay us any other subsidy. Because the demand for kumquats is elastic, I believe this program will make us worse off, and I say we should oppose it.

Explain whether you agree or disagree with this reasoning.

5.6 Review the concept of economic efficiency from Chapter 4 before answering the following question: Will there be a greater loss of economic efficiency from a price ceiling when demand is elastic or inelastic? Illustrate your answer with a demand and supply graph.

>> **End Learning Objective 6.5**

6.6 LEARNING OBJECTIVE   6.6 | Define the price elasticity of supply and understand its main determinants and how it is measured, **pages 191–195.**

The Price Elasticity of Supply and Its Measurement

Summary

The **price elasticity of supply** is equal to the percentage change in quantity supplied divided by the percentage change in price. The supply curves for most goods are inelastic over a short period of time, but they become increasingly elastic over longer periods of time. Perfectly inelastic demand curves are vertical lines, and perfectly elastic supply curves are horizontal lines. Relatively few products have perfectly elastic or perfectly inelastic supply curves.

myeconlab Visit www.myeconlab.com to complete these exercises *Get Ahead of the Curve* online and get instant feedback.

Review Questions

6.1 Write the formula for the price elasticity of supply. If an increase of 10 percent in the price of frozen pizzas results in a 9 percent increase in the quantity of frozen pizzas supplied, what is the price elasticity of supply for frozen pizzas? Is the supply of pizzas elastic or inelastic?

6.2 What is the main determinant of the price elasticity of supply?

Problems and Applications

6.3 (Related to the *Making the Connection* on page 192) Suppose the demand for oil declines. Will the equilibrium price of oil decline more if the supply of oil is elastic or if it is inelastic? Illustrate your answer with a demand and supply graph.

6.4 Use the midpoint formula for calculating elasticity to calculate the price elasticity of supply between point *A* and point *B* for each panel of Figure 6-5 on page 194.

6.5 Briefly explain whether you agree with the following statement: "The longer the period of time following an increase in the demand for apples, the greater the increase in the equilibrium quantity of apples and the smaller the increase in the equilibrium price."

6.6 On most days, the price of a rose is $1, and 8,000 roses are purchased. On Valentine's Day, the price of a rose jumps to $2, and 30,000 roses are purchased.
   a. Draw a demand and supply diagram that shows why the price jumps.

   b. Based on this information, what do we know about the price elasticity of demand for roses? What do we know about the price elasticity of supply for roses? Calculate values for the price elasticity of demand and the price elasticity of supply or explain why you can't calculate these values.

>> **End Learning Objective 6.6**

Chapter 7

Firms, the **Stock Market,** and **Corporate Governance**

Google: From Dorm Room to Wall Street

There could be no question that Google was cool. The world's most widely used Internet search engine, Google had become the essence of cool as a way to research information stored on Web sites. Founded in 1998 by Larry Page and Sergey Brin, Google grew quickly. By 2008, Google employed 17,000 people and earned $16.6 billion in revenue. Google's founders had transformed the Internet search engine and brought value to users through a combination of intellect, technology, and the talents of many employees. Google's key advantage over competitors such as A9 and Ask Jeeves was its search algorithms that allowed users to easily find the Web sites most relevant to a subject. Google had other advantages as well, such as its automatic foreign-language translation. Google had become so dominant that other major Web sites, such as AOL and Yahoo, were using it as their search engine. Google has also succeeded in expanding into foreign markets. In China, Google has been successful even though it remains in a struggle for market share with the local Chinese firm Baidu.com.

And Google was hot. In 2004, Google sold part of the firm to outside investors by offering stock—and partial ownership—to the public. This stock offering vaulted Larry Page and Sergey Brin to the ranks of the super-rich. Google's stock offering also gained significant press attention, as the firm bypassed conventional financial practice and used an automated online auction to help set the share price and determine who should receive stock. The offering's size grabbed attention, too: It was the most anticipated stock sale since the 1995 launch of Netscape, a deal that sparked the late-1990s Internet gold rush on Wall Street.

As Google grew larger, it was less the informal organization put together by the founders and more a complex organization with greater need for management and funds to grow. Indeed, Google's offering of stock to outside investors provided the firm with a major inflow of funds for growth.

Once a firm grows very large, its owners often do not continue to manage it. Large corporations are owned by millions of individual investors who have purchased the firms' stock. With ownership so dispersed, the top managers who actually run a firm have the opportunity to make decisions that are in the managers' best interests but that may not be in the best interests of the stockholders who own the firm.

Against this backdrop, Google faced significant costs associated with selling stock to the public. High-profile corporate accounting scandals in 2001 and 2002 at major U.S. firms, such as Enron, WorldCom, and Tyco, led to the passage of stronger—and more costly—securities regulation under the Sarbanes-Oxley Act, enacted by Congress in 2002. Google's growth prospects and the health of the financial system were intertwined. **AN INSIDE LOOK** on **page 226** discusses the compensation Google pays its top executives.

LEARNING Objectives

After studying this chapter, you should be able to:

7.1 Categorize the major **types of firms** in the United States, page 210.

7.2 Describe the typical **management structure** of corporations and understand the concepts of **separation of ownership from control** and the **principal–agent problem**, page 212.

7.3 Explain how firms obtain the **funds** they need to **operate** and **expand**, page 214.

7.4 Understand the information provided in corporations' **financial statements**, page 219.

7.5 Understand the role of government in **corporate governance**, page 221.

APPENDIX Understand the concept of **present value** and the information contained on a firm's **income statement** and **balance sheet**, page 233.

Economics in YOUR Life!

Is It Risky to Own Stock?

Although stockholders legally own corporations, managers often have a great deal of freedom in deciding how corporations are run. As a result, managers can make decisions, such as spending money on large corporate headquarters or decorating their offices with expensive paintings, that are in their interests but not in the interests of the shareholders. If managers make decisions that waste money and lower the profits of a firm, the price of the firm's stock will fall, which hurts the investors who own the stock. Suppose you own stock in a corporation, such as Google. Why is it difficult to get the managers to act in your interest rather than in their own? Given this problem, should you ever take on the risk of buying stock? As you read the chapter, see if you can answer these questions. You can check your answers against those we provide at the end of the chapter.

>> **Continued on page 225**

I n this chapter, we look at the firm: how it is organized, how it raises funds, and the information it provides to investors. As we have already discussed, firms in a market system are responsible for organizing the factors of production to produce goods and services. Firms are the vehicles entrepreneurs use to earn profits. To succeed, entrepreneurs must meet consumer wants by producing new or better goods and services or by finding ways of producing existing goods and services at a lower cost so they can be sold at a lower price. Entrepreneurs also need access to sufficient funds, and they must be able to efficiently organize production. As the typical firm in many industries has become larger during the past 100 years, the task of efficiently organizing production has become more difficult. Toward the end of this chapter, we look at why a series of corporate scandals occurred beginning in 2002 and at the steps firms and the government have taken to avoid similar problems in the future.

7.1 | Categorize the major types of firms in the United States.

Types of Firms

Sole proprietorship A firm owned by a single individual and not organized as a corporation.

Partnership A firm owned jointly by two or more persons and not organized as a corporation.

Corporation A legal form of business that provides owners with protection from losing more than their investment should the business fail.

In studying a market economy, it is important to understand the basics of how firms operate. In the United States, there are three legal categories of firms: *sole proprietorships, partnerships,* and *corporations.* A **sole proprietorship** is a firm owned by a single individual. Although most sole proprietorships are small, some are quite large in terms of sales, number of persons employed, and profits earned. **Partnerships** are firms owned jointly by two or more—sometimes many—persons. Most law and accounting firms are partnerships. The famous Lloyd's of London insurance company is a partnership. Although some partnerships, such as Lloyd's, can be quite large, most large firms are organized as *corporations.* A **corporation** is a legal form of business that provides owners with protection from losing more than their investment should the business fail.

Who Is Liable? Limited and Unlimited Liability

Asset Anything of value owned by a person or a firm.

A key distinction among the three types of firms is that the owners of sole proprietorships and partnerships have unlimited liability. Unlimited liability means there is no legal distinction between the personal assets of the owners of the firm and the assets of the firm. An **asset** is anything of value owned by a person or a firm. If a sole proprietorship or a partnership owes a lot of money to the firm's suppliers or employees, the suppliers and employees have a legal right to sue the firm for payment, even if this requires the firm's owners to sell some of their personal assets, such as stocks or bonds. In other words, with sole proprietorships and partnerships, the owners are not legally distinct from the firms they own.

It may seem only fair that the owners of a firm be responsible for a firm's debts. But early in the nineteenth century, it became clear to many state legislatures in the United States that unlimited liability was a significant problem for any firm that was attempting to raise funds from large numbers of investors. An investor might be interested in making a relatively small investment in a firm but be unwilling to become a partner in the firm for fear of placing at risk all of his or her personal assets if the firm were to fail. To get around this problem, state legislatures began to pass *general incorporation laws,* which allowed firms to be organized as corporations. Under the corporate form of business, the owners of a firm have **limited liability**, which means that if the firm fails, the owners can never lose more than the amount they had invested in the firm. The personal assets of the owners of the firm are not affected by the failure of the firm. In fact, in the eyes of the law, a corporation is a legal "person" separate from its owners. Limited

Limited liability The legal provision that shields owners of a corporation from losing more than they have invested in the firm.

	SOLE PROPRIETORSHIP	PARTNERSHIP	CORPORATION
ADVANTAGES	• Control by owner • No layers of management	• Ability to share work • Ability to share risks	• Limited personal liability • Greater ability to raise funds
DISADVANTAGES	• Unlimited personal liability • Limited ability to raise funds	• Unlimited personal liability • Limited ability to raise funds	• Costly to organize • Possible double taxation of income

TABLE 7-1

Differences among Business Organizations

liability has made it possible for corporations to raise funds by issuing shares of stock to large numbers of investors. For example, if you buy a share of Google stock, you are a part owner of the firm, but even if Google were to go bankrupt, you would not be personally responsible for any of Google's debts. Therefore, you could not lose more than the amount you paid for the stock.

Corporate organizations also have some disadvantages. In the United States, corporate profits are taxed twice—once at the corporate level and again when investors receive a share of corporate profits. Corporations generally are larger than sole proprietorships and partnerships and therefore more difficult to organize and run. Table 7-1 reviews the advantages and disadvantages of different forms of business organization.

Making the Connection | What's in a "Name"? Lloyd's of London Learns about Unlimited Liability the Hard Way

The world-famous insurance company Lloyd's of London got its start in Edward Lloyd's coffeehouse in London in the late 1600s. Ship owners would come to the coffeehouse looking for someone to insure (or "underwrite") their ships and cargos in exchange for a flat fee (or "premium"). The customers of the coffeehouse, themselves merchants or ship owners, who agreed to insure ships or cargos would have to make payment from their personal funds if an insured ship was lost at sea. By the late 1700s, the system had become more formal: Each underwriter would recruit investors, known as "Names," and use the funds raised to back insurance policies sold to a wide variety of clients. In the twentieth century, Lloyd's became famous for some of its unusual insurance policies. It issued a policy insuring the legs of Betty Grable, a 1940s movie star. One man bought an insurance policy against seeing a ghost.

By the late 1980s, 34,000 persons around the world had invested in Lloyd's as Names. A series of disasters in the late 1980s and early 1990s—including the *Exxon Valdez* oil spill in Alaska, Hurricane Hugo in South Carolina, and an earthquake in San Francisco—resulted in huge payments on insurance policies written by Lloyd's. In 1989, Lloyd's lost $3.85 billion. In 1990, it lost an additional $4.4 billion. It then became clear to many of the Names that Lloyd's was not a corporation and that the Names did not have the limited liability enjoyed by corporate shareholders. On the contrary, the Names were personally responsible for paying the losses on the insurance policies. Many Names lost far more than they had invested. Some investors, such as Charles Schwab, the discount stockbroker, were wealthy enough to sustain their losses, but others were less fortunate. One California investor ended up living in poverty after having to sell his $1 million house to pay his share of the losses. Another Name, Sir Richard Fitch, a British admiral, committed suicide after most of his wealth was wiped out. As many as 30 Names may have committed suicide as a result of their losses.

By 2008, only 1,100 Names—undoubtedly sadder but wiser—remained as investors in Lloyd's. New rules have allowed insurance companies to underwrite

Investors in Lloyd's of London lost billions of dollars during the 1980s and 1990s.

Lloyd's policies for the first time. Today, Names provide only about 20 percent of Lloyd's funds.

Sources: "The Rip van Winkle of Risk," *Economist*, January 4, 2007; Charles Fleming, "The Master of Disaster Is Trying to Avoid One," *Wall Street Journal*, November 17, 2003; and "Lloyd's of London: Insuring for the Future," *Economist*, September 16, 2004.

YOUR TURN: Test your understanding by doing related problem 1.4 and 1.5 on page 228 at the end of this chapter.

Corporations Earn the Majority of Revenue and Profits

Figure 7-1 gives basic statistics on the three types of business organizations. Panel (a) shows that almost three-quarters of all firms are sole proprietorships. Panels (b) and (c) show that although only 19 percent of all firms are corporations, corporations account for the majority of revenue and profits earned by all firms. *Profit* is the difference between revenue and the total cost to a firm of producing the goods and services it offers for sale.

There are more than 5 million corporations in the United States, but only 30,000 have annual revenues of more than $50 million. We can think of these 30,000 firms—including Microsoft, General Electric, and Google—as representing "big business." These large firms earn almost 85 percent of the total profits of all corporations in the United States.

7.2 LEARNING OBJECTIVE

7.2 | Describe the typical management structure of corporations and understand the concepts of separation of ownership from control and the principal–agent problem.

The Structure of Corporations and the Principal–Agent Problem

Corporate governance The way in which a corporation is structured and the effect a corporation's structure has on the firm's behavior.

Because large corporations account for most sales and profits in the economy, it is important to know how they are managed. Most large corporations have a similar management structure. The way in which a corporation is structured and the effect a corporation's structure has on the firm's behavior is referred to as **corporate governance**.

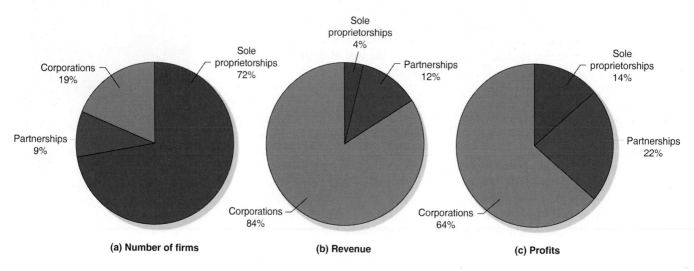

Figure 7-1 | Business Organizations: Sole Proprietorships, Partnerships, and Corporations

The three types of firms in the United States are sole proprietorships, partnerships, and corporations. Panel (a) shows that only 19 percent of all firms are corporations.

Yet, as panels (b) and (c) show, corporations account for a majority of the total revenue and profits earned by all firms.
Source: U.S. Census Bureau, *The 2008 Statistical Abstract of the United States.*

Corporate Structure and Corporate Governance

Corporations are legally owned by their *shareholders*, the owners of the corporation's stock. Unlike family businesses, a corporation's shareholders, although they are the firm's owners, do not manage the firm directly. Instead, they elect a *board of directors* to represent their interests. The board of directors appoints a *chief executive officer* (CEO) to run the day-to-day operations of the corporation. Sometimes the board of directors also appoints other members of *top management*, such as the *chief financial officer* (CFO). At other times, the CEO appoints other members of top management. Members of top management, including the CEO and CFO, often serve on the board of directors. Members of management serving on the board of directors are referred to as *inside directors*. Members of the board of directors who do not have a direct management role in the firm are referred to as *outside directors*. The outside directors are intended to act as checks on the decisions of top managers, but the distinction between an outside director and an inside director is not always clear. For example, the CEO of a firm that sells a good or service to a large corporation may sit on the board of directors of that corporation. Although an outside director, this person may be reluctant to displease the top managers because the top managers have the power to stop purchasing from his firm. In some instances, top managers have effectively controlled their firms' boards of directors.

Unlike founder-dominated businesses, the top management of large corporations does not generally own a large share of the firm's stock, so large corporations have a **separation of ownership from control**. Although the shareholders actually own the firm, top management controls the day-to-day operations of the firm. Because top managers do not own the entire firm, they may have an incentive to decrease the firm's profits by spending money to purchase private jets or schedule management meetings at luxurious resorts. Economists refer to the conflict between the interests of shareholders and the interests of top management as a **principal–agent problem**. This problem occurs when agents—in this case, a firm's top management—pursue their own interests rather than the interests of the principal who hired them—in this case, the shareholders of the corporation. To reduce the impact of the principal–agent problem, many boards of directors in the 1990s began to tie the salaries of top managers to the profits of the firm or to the price of the firm's stock. They hoped this would give top managers an incentive to make the firm as profitable as possible, thereby benefiting its shareholders.

Separation of ownership from control A situation in a corporation in which the top management, rather than the shareholders, control day-to-day operations.

Principal–agent problem A problem caused by an agent pursuing his own interests rather than the interests of the principal who hired him.

Solved Problem | **7-2**

Does the Principal–Agent Problem Apply to the Relationship between Managers and Workers?

Briefly explain whether you agree or disagree with the following argument:

> The principal–agent problem applies not just to the relationship between shareholders and top managers. It also applies to the relationship between managers and workers. Just as shareholders have trouble monitoring whether top managers are earning as much profit as possible, managers have trouble monitoring whether workers are working as hard as possible.

SOLVING THE PROBLEM:

Step 1: **Review the chapter material.** This problem concerns the principal–agent problem, so you may want to review the section "Corporate Structure and Corporate Governance," which is on this page.

Step 2: **Evaluate the argument.** You should agree with the argument. A corporation's shareholders have difficulty monitoring the activities of top managers. In practice, they attempt to do so indirectly through the corporation's board of directors. But the firm's top managers may influence—or even control—the firm's board of directors. Even if top managers do not control a board of directors, it may be difficult for the board to know whether actions managers take—say, opening a branch office in Paris—will increase the profitability of the firm or just increase the enjoyment of the top managers.

To answer the problem, we must extend this analysis to the relationship between managers and workers: Managers would like workers to work as hard as possible. Workers would often rather not work hard, particularly if they do not see a direct financial reward for doing so. Managers can have trouble monitoring whether workers are working hard or goofing off. Is that worker in his cubicle diligently staring at a computer screen because he is hard at work on a report or because he is surfing the Web for sports scores or writing a long e-mail to his girlfriend? So, the principal–agent problem does apply to the relationship between managers and workers.

EXTRA CREDIT: Boards of directors try to reduce the principal–agent problem by designing compensation policies for top managers that give them financial incentives to increase profits. Similarly, managers try to reduce the principal–agent problem by designing compensation policies that give workers an incentive to work harder. For example, some manufacturers pay factory workers on the basis of how much they produce rather than on the basis of how many hours they work.

YOUR TURN: For more practice, do related problems 2.4 and 2.5 on page 229 at the end of this chapter.

>> **End Solved Problem 7-2**

7.3 LEARNING OBJECTIVE

7.3 | Explain how firms obtain the funds they need to operate and expand.

How Firms Raise Funds

Owners and managers of firms try to earn a profit. To earn a profit, a firm must raise funds to pay for its operations, including paying its employees and buying machines. Indeed, a central challenge for anyone running a firm, whether that person is a sole proprietor or a top manager of a large corporation, is raising the funds needed to operate and expand the business. Suppose you decide to open an online trading service using $100,000 you have saved in a bank. You use the $100,000 to rent a building for your firm, to buy computers, and to pay other start-up expenses. Your firm is a great success, and you decide to expand by moving to a larger building and buying more computers. As the owner of a small business, you can obtain the funds for this expansion in three ways:

1 If you are making a profit, you could reinvest the profits back into your firm. Profits that are reinvested in a firm rather than taken out of a firm and paid to the firm's owners are *retained earnings*.

2 You could obtain funds by taking on one or more partners who invest in the firm. This arrangement would increase the firm's *financial capital*.

3 Finally, you could borrow the funds from relatives, friends, or a bank.

The managers of a large firm have some additional ways to raise funds, as we will see in the next section.

Sources of External Funds

Unless firms rely on retained earnings, they have to obtain the *external funds* they need from others who have funds available to invest. It is the role of an economy's *financial system* to transfer funds from savers to borrowers—directly through financial markets or indirectly through financial intermediaries such as banks.

Firms can raise external funds in two ways. The first relies on financial intermediaries such as banks and is called **indirect finance**. If you put $1,000 in a checking account or a savings account, or if you buy a $1,000 certificate of deposit (CD), the bank will loan most of those funds to borrowers. The bank will combine your funds with those of other depositors and, for example, make a $100,000 loan to a local business. Small businesses rely heavily on bank loans as their primary source of external funds.

The second way for firms to acquire external funds is through *financial markets*. Raising funds in these markets, such as the New York Stock Exchange on Wall Street in New York, is called **direct finance**. Direct finance usually takes the form of the borrower selling the lender a *financial security*. A financial security is a document—sometimes in electronic form—that states the terms under which the funds have passed from the buyer of the security—who is lending funds—to the borrower. *Bonds* and *stocks* are the two main types of financial securities. Typically, only large corporations are able to sell bonds and stocks on financial markets. Investors are generally unwilling to buy securities issued by small and medium-sized firms because the investors lack sufficient information on the financial health of smaller firms.

Indirect finance A flow of funds from savers to borrowers through financial intermediaries such as banks. Intermediaries raise funds from savers to lend to firms (and other borrowers).

Direct finance A flow of funds from savers to firms through financial markets, such as the New York Stock Exchange.

Bonds Bonds are financial securities that represent promises to repay a fixed amount of funds. When General Electric (GE) sells a bond to raise funds, it promises to pay the purchaser of the bond an interest payment each year for the term of the bond, as well as a final payment of the amount of the loan, or the *principal*, at the end of the term. GE may need to raise many millions of dollars to build a factory, but each individual bond has a principal, or *face value*, of $1,000, which is the amount each bond purchaser is lending GE. So, GE must sell many bonds to raise all the funds it needs. Suppose GE promises it will pay interest of $60 per year to anyone who will buy one of its bonds. The interest payments on a bond are referred to as **coupon payments**. The **interest rate** is the cost of borrowing funds, usually expressed as a percentage of the amount borrowed. If we express the coupon as a percentage of the face value of the bond, we find the interest rate on the bond, called the *coupon rate*. In this case, the interest rate is:

Bond A financial security that represents a promise to repay a fixed amount of funds.

Coupon payment An interest payment on a bond.

Interest rate The cost of borrowing funds, usually expressed as a percentage of the amount borrowed.

$$\frac{\$60}{\$1,000} = 0.06, \text{ or } 6\%.$$

Many bonds that corporations issue have terms, or *maturities*, of 30 years. For example, if you bought a bond from GE, GE would pay you $60 per year for 30 years, and at the end of the thirtieth year, GE would pay you back the $1,000 principal.

Stocks When you buy a newly issued bond from a firm, you are lending funds to that firm. When you buy **stock** issued by a firm, you are actually buying part ownership of the firm. When a corporation sells stock, it is doing the same thing the owner of a small business does when she takes on a partner: The firm is increasing its financial capital by bringing additional owners into the firm. Any individual shareholder usually owns only a small fraction of the total shares of stock issued by a corporation.

Stock A financial security that represents partial ownership of a firm.

A shareholder is entitled to a share of the corporation's profits, if there are any. Corporations generally keep some of their profits—known as retained earnings—to finance future expansion. The remaining profits are paid to shareholders as **dividends**. If investors expect the firm to earn economic profits on its retained earnings, the firm's share price will rise, providing a *capital gain* for investors. If a corporation is unable to

Dividends Payments by a corporation to its shareholders.

make a profit, it usually does not pay a dividend. Under the law, corporations must make payments on any debt they have before making payments to their owners. That is, a corporation must make promised payments to bondholders before it may make any dividend payments to shareholders. In addition, when firms sell stock, they acquire from investors an open-ended commitment of funds to the firm. Therefore, unlike bonds, stocks do not have a maturity date, so the firm is not obliged to return the investor's funds at any particular date.

Stock and Bond Markets Provide Capital— and Information

The original purchasers of stocks and bonds may resell them to other investors. In fact, most of the buying and selling of stocks and bonds that takes place each day is investors reselling existing stocks and bonds to each other rather than corporations selling new stocks and bonds to investors. The buyers and sellers of stocks and bonds together make up the *stock and bond markets*. There is no single place where stocks and bonds are bought and sold. Some trading of stocks and bonds takes place in buildings known as *exchanges*, such as the New York Stock Exchange or Tokyo Stock Exchange. In the United States, the stocks and bonds of the largest corporations are traded on the New York Stock Exchange. The development of computer technology has spread the trading of stocks and bonds outside exchanges to *securities dealers* linked by computers. These dealers comprise the *over-the-counter market*. The stocks of many computer and other high-technology firms—including Apple, Google, and Microsoft—are traded in the most important of the over-the-counter markets, the *National Association of Securities Dealers Automated Quotation* system, which is referred to by its acronym, Nasdaq.

Don't Let This Happen to **YOU!**

When Google Shares Change Hands, Google Doesn't Get the Money

Google is a popular investment, with investors buying and selling shares often as their views about the firm's valuation shift. That's great for Google, right? Think of all that money flowing into Google's coffers as shares change hands and the stock price goes up. *Wrong.* Google raises funds in a primary market, but shares change hands in a secondary market. Those trades don't put money into Google's hands, but they do give important information to the firm's managers. Let's see why.

Primary markets are those in which newly issued claims are sold to initial buyers by the issuer. Businesses can raise funds in a primary financial market in two ways—by borrowing (selling bonds) or by selling shares of stock— which result in different types of claims on the borrowing firm's future income. Although you hear about the stock market fluctuations each night on the evening news, bonds actually account for more of the funds raised by borrowers. In mid-2007, the value of bonds in the United States was about $27 trillion compared to $15 trillion for stocks, or equities.

In *secondary markets*, stocks and bonds that have already been issued are sold by one investor to another. If Google sells shares to the public, it is turning to a primary market for new funds. Once Google shares are issued, investors trade the shares in the secondary market. The founders of Google do not receive any new funds when Google shares are traded on secondary markets. The initial seller of a stock or bond raises funds from a lender only in the primary market. Secondary markets convey information to firms' managers and to investors by determining the price of financial instruments. For example, a major increase in Google's stock price conveys the market's good feelings about the firm, and the firm may decide to raise funds to expand. Hence, secondary markets are valuable sources of information for corporations that are considering raising funds.

Primary and secondary markets are both important, but they play different roles. As an investor, you principally trade stocks and bonds in a secondary market. As a corporate manager, you may help decide how to raise new funds to expand the firm where you work.

YOUR TURN: Test your understanding by doing related problem 3.10 on page 230 at the end of this chapter.

Shares of stock represent claims on the profits of the firms that issue them. Therefore, as the fortunes of the firms change and they earn more or less profit, the prices of the stock the firms have issued should also change. Similarly, bonds represent claims to receive coupon payments and one final payment of principal. Therefore, a particular bond that was issued in the past may have its price go up or down, depending on whether the coupon payments being offered on newly issued bonds are higher or lower than on existing bonds. If you hold a bond with a coupon of $80 per year, and newly issued bonds have coupons of $100 per year, the price of your bond will fall because it is less attractive to investors. The price of a bond will be affected by changes in investors' perceptions of the issuing firm's ability to make the coupon payments. For example, if investors begin to believe that a firm may soon go out of business and stop making coupon payments to its bondholders, the price of the firm's bonds will fall to very low levels.

Changes in the value of a firm's stocks and bonds offer important information for a firm's managers, as well as for investors. An increase in the stock price means that investors are more optimistic about the firm's profit prospects, and the firm's managers may wish to expand the firm's operations as a result. By contrast, a decrease in the firm's stock price indicates that investors are less optimistic about the firms' profit prospects, so management may want to shrink the firm's operations. Likewise, changes in the value of the firm's bonds imply changes in the cost of external funds to finance the firm's investment in research and development or in new factories. A higher bond price indicates a lower cost of new external funds, while a lower bond price indicates a higher cost of new external funds.

Making the Connection | Following Abercrombie & Fitch's Stock Price in the Financial Pages

If you read the stock listings in your local paper or the *Wall Street Journal*, you will notice that newspapers manage to pack into a small space a lot of information about what happened to stocks during the previous day's trading. The figure on the next page reproduces a small portion of the listings from the *Wall Street Journal* from May 1, 2008, for stocks listed on the New York Stock Exchange. The listings provide information on the buying and selling of the stock of five firms during the previous day. Let's focus on the highlighted listing for Abercrombie & Fitch, the clothing store, and examine the information in each column:

- The first column gives the name of the company.

- The second column gives the firm's "ticker" symbol (ANF), which you may have seen scrolling along the bottom of the screen on cable financial news channels.

- The third column (Open) gives the price (in dollars) of the stock at the time that trading began, which is 9:30 A.M. on the New York Stock Exchange. Abercrombie & Fitch had opened for trading the previous day at a price of $74.25.

- The fourth column (High) and the fifth column (Low) give the highest price and the lowest price the stock sold for during the previous day.

- The sixth column (Close) gives the price the stock sold for the last time it was traded before the close of trading on the previous day (4:30 P.M.), which in this case was $74.91.

- The seventh column (Net Chg) gives the amount by which the closing price changed from the closing price the day before. In this case, the price of Abercrombie & Fitch's stock had risen by $0.81 per share from its closing price the day before. Changes in Abercrombie & Fitch's stock price give the firm's managers a signal that they may want to expand or contract the firm's operations.

- The eighth column (% Chg) gives the change in the price in percentage terms rather than in dollar terms.

- The ninth column (Vol) gives the number of shares of stock traded on the previous day.

- The tenth column (52 Week High) and the eleventh column (52 Week Low) give the highest price the stock has sold for and the lowest price the stock has sold for during the previous year. These numbers tell how *volatile* the stock price is—that is, how much it fluctuates over the course of the year.

- The twelfth column (Div) gives the dividend expressed in dollars. In this case, .70 means that Abercrombie paid a dividend of $0.70 per share.

- The thirteenth column (Yield) gives the *dividend yield*, which is calculated by dividing the dividend by the *closing price* of the stock—that is, the price at which Abercrombie's stock last sold before the close of trading on the previous day.

- The fourteenth column (PE) gives the *P-E ratio* (or *price-earnings ratio*), which is calculated by dividing the price of the firm's stock by its earnings per share. (Remember that because firms retain some earnings, earnings per share is not necessarily the same as dividends per share.) Abercrombie's P-E ratio was 14, meaning that its price per share was 14 times its earnings per share. You would have to pay $14 to buy $1 of Abercrombie & Fitch's earnings.

- The final column (Year-To-Date % Chg) gives the percentage change in the price of the stock from the beginning of the year to the previous day. In this case, the price of Abercrombie's stock had fallen by 6.3 percent since the beginning of 2008.

	Symbol	Open	High	Low	Close	Net Chg	%Chg	Vol	52 Week High	52 Week Low	Div	Yield	PE	Year-To-Date %Chg
ABB LTD ADS	ABB	30.44	31.19	30.20	31.04	0.37	1.21	4,694,962	32.1	19.46	...	...	17	7.8
ABBOTT LABORATORIES	ABT	52.58	53.95	52.50	53.57	0.82	1.55	11,571,468	61.1	49.58	1.44	2.7	22	-4.6
ABERCROMBIE & FITCH CO.	ANF	74.25	75.64	73.02	74.91	0.60	0.81	2,073,480	85.8	66.05	0.70	0.9	14	-6.3
ABITIBI-BOWATER INC.	ABY	9.65	9.94	9.29	9.71	-0.16	-1.62	819,303	51.5	4.70	...	...	...	-52.9
ACADIA REALTY TRUST SBI	AKR	26.05	26.08	25.52	25.85	0.21	0.82	382,985	29.0	21.17	0.84	3.2	20	0.9

YOUR TURN: Test your understanding by doing related problem 3.11 on page 230 at the end of this chapter.

7.4 | Understand the information provided in corporations' financial statements.

Using Financial Statements to Evaluate a Corporation

To raise funds, a firm's managers must persuade financial intermediaries or buyers of its bonds or stock that it will be profitable. Before a firm can sell new issues of stock or bonds, it must first provide investors and financial regulators with information about its finances. To borrow from a bank or another financial intermediary, the firm must disclose financial information to the lender as well.

In most high-income countries, government agencies require firms that want to sell securities in financial markets to disclose specific financial information to the public. In the United States, the Securities and Exchange Commission requires publicly owned firms to report their performance in financial statements prepared using standard accounting methods, often referred to as *generally accepted accounting principles*. Such disclosure reduces information costs, but it doesn't eliminate them—for two reasons. First, some firms may be too young to have much information for potential investors to evaluate. Second, managers may try to present the required information in the best possible light so that investors will overvalue their securities.

Private firms also collect information on business borrowers and sell the information to lenders and investors. As long as the information-gathering firm does a good job, lenders and investors purchasing the information will be better able to judge the quality of borrowing firms. Firms specializing in information—including Moody's Investors Service, Standard & Poor's Corporation, Value Line, and Dun & Bradstreet—collect information from businesses and sell it to subscribers. Buyers include individual investors, libraries, and financial intermediaries. You can find some of these publications in your college library or through online information services.

Making the Connection

A Bull in China's Financial Shop

Prospects for Sichuan Changhong Electric Co., manufacturer of plasma televisions and liquid crystal displays, looked excellent in 2008, with rapidly growing output, employment, and profits earned from trade in the world economy. And Changhong was not alone. In the 2000s, the Chinese economy was sizzling. China's output grew by 11.4 percent during 2007, dominated by an astonishing 24 percent growth in investment in plant and equipment. The Chinese economic juggernaut caught the attention of the global business community—and charged onto the U.S. political stage, as China's growth fueled concerns about job losses in the United States.

Yet at the same time, many economists and financial commentators worried that the Chinese expansion—which was fueling rising living standards in a rapidly developing economy with 1.3 billion people—would come to an end. Indeed, the debate seemed to be over whether China's boom would have a "soft landing" (with gradually declining growth) or a "hard landing" (possibly leading to an economic financial crisis).

Why the debate? Although China's saving rate was estimated to be a very high 40 percent of gross domestic product (GDP)—double or triple the rate in most other countries—the financial system was doing a poor job of allocating capital. Excessive expansion in office construction and factories was fueled less by careful

Will China's weak financial system derail economic growth?

financial analysis than by the directions of national and local government officials trying to encourage growth. With nonperforming loans—where the borrower cannot make promised payments to lenders—at unheard-of levels, China's banks were in financial trouble. Worse still, they continued to lend to weak, politically connected borrowers.

China's prospects for long-term economic growth depend importantly on a better-developed financial system to generate information for borrowers and lenders. Many economists have urged Chinese officials to improve accounting transparency and information disclosure so that stock and bond markets can flourish. In the absence of well-functioning financial markets, banks are crucial allocators of capital. There, too, information disclosure and less government direction of lending will help oil the Chinese growth machine in the long run.

Chinese firms, like Changhong, may well play a major role on the world's economic stage. But China's creaky financial system needs repair if Chinese firms are to grow rapidly enough to raise the standard of living for Chinese workers over the long run.

YOUR TURN: Test your understanding by doing related problem 4.7 on page 231 at the end of this chapter.

What kind of information do investors and firm managers need? A firm must answer three basic questions: What to produce? How to produce it? and What price to charge? To answer these questions, a firm's managers need two pieces of information: The first is the firm's revenues and costs, and the second is the value of the property and other assets the firm owns and the firm's debts, or other **liabilities**, that it owes to other persons and firms. Potential investors in the firm also need this information to decide whether to buy the firm's stocks or bonds. Managers and investors find this information in the firm's *financial statements*, principally its income statement and balance sheet, which we discuss next.

Liability Anything owed by a person or a firm.

The Income Statement

Income statement A financial statement that sums up a firm's revenues, costs, and profit over a period of time.

A firm's **income statement** sums up its revenues, costs, and profit over a period of time. Corporations issue annual income statements, although the 12-month *fiscal year* covered may be different from the calendar year to represent the seasonal pattern of the business better. We explore income statements in greater detail in the appendix to this chapter.

Accounting profit A firm's net income measured by revenue minus operating expenses and taxes paid.

Getting to Accounting Profit An income statement shows a firm's revenue, costs, and profit for the firm's fiscal year. To determine profitability, the income statement starts with the firm's revenue and subtracts its operating expenses and taxes paid. The remainder, *net income*, is the **accounting profit** of the firm.

Opportunity cost The highest-valued alternative that must be given up to engage in an activity.

Explicit cost A cost that involves spending money.

Implicit cost A nonmonetary opportunity cost.

. . . And Economic Profit Accounting profit provides information on a firm's current net income measured according to accepted accounting standards. Accounting profit is not, however, the ideal measure of a firm's profits because it neglects some of the firm's costs. By taking into account all costs, *economic profit* provides a better indication than accounting profit of how successful a firm is. Firms making an economic profit will remain in business and may even expand. Firms making an *economic loss* are unlikely to remain in business in the long run. To understand how economic profit is calculated, remember that economists always measure cost as *opportunity cost*. The **opportunity cost** of any activity is the highest-valued alternative that must be given up to engage in that activity. Costs are either *explicit* or *implicit*. When a firm spends money, an **explicit cost** results. If a firm incurs an opportunity cost but does not spend money, an **implicit cost** results. For example, firms incur an explicit labor cost when they pay wages to employees. Firms have many other explicit costs as well, such as the cost of the electricity used to light their buildings or the costs of advertising or insurance.

Some costs are implicit, however. The most important of these is the opportunity cost to investors of the funds they have invested in the firm. Economists refer to the minimum amount that investors must earn on the funds they invest in a firm, expressed as a percentage of the amount invested, as a *normal rate of return*. If a firm fails to provide investors with at least a normal rate of return, it will not be able to remain in business over the long run because investors will not continue to invest their funds in the firm. For example, Bethlehem Steel was once the second-leading producer of steel in the United States and a very profitable firm with stock that sold for more than $50 per share. By 2002, investors became convinced that the firm's uncompetitive labor costs in world markets meant that the firm would never be able to provide investors with a normal rate of return. Many investors expected that the firm would eventually have to declare bankruptcy, and as a result, the price of Bethlehem Steel's stock plummeted to $1 per share. Shortly thereafter, the firm declared bankruptcy, and its remaining assets were sold off to a competing steel firm. The return (in dollars) that investors require to continue investing in a firm is a true cost to the firm and should be subtracted from the firm's revenues to calculate its profits.

The necessary rate of return that investors must receive to continue investing in a firm varies from firm to firm. If the investment is risky—as would be the case with a biotechnology start-up—investors may require a high rate of return to compensate them for the risk. Investors in firms in more established industries, such as electric utilities, may require lower rates of return. The exact rate of return investors require to invest in any particular firm is difficult to calculate, which also makes it difficult for an accountant to include the return as a cost on an income statement. Firms have other implicit costs besides the return investors require that can also be difficult to calculate. As a result, the rules of accounting generally require that accounts include only explicit costs in the firm's financial records. *Economic costs* include both explicit costs *and* implicit costs. **Economic profit** is equal to a firm's revenues minus all of its costs, implicit and explicit. Because accounting profit excludes some implicit costs, it is larger than economic profit.

Economic profit A firm's revenues minus all of its implicit and explicit costs.

The Balance Sheet

A firm's **balance sheet** sums up its financial position on a particular day, usually the end of a quarter or year. Recall that an asset is anything of value that a firm owns, and a liability is a debt or obligation owed by a firm. Subtracting the value of a firm's liabilities from the value of its assets leaves its *net worth*. We can think of the net worth as what the firm's owners would be left with if the firm were closed, its assets were sold, and its liabilities were paid off. Investors can determine a firm's net worth by inspecting its balance sheet. We analyze a balance sheet in detail in the appendix to this chapter, which begins on page 233.

Balance sheet A financial statement that sums up a firm's financial position on a particular day, usually the end of a quarter or year.

7.5 | Understand the role of government in corporate governance.

7.5 LEARNING OBJECTIVE

Corporate Governance Policy

A firm's financial statements provide important information on the firm's ability to add value for investors and the economy. Accurate and easy-to-understand financial statements are inputs for decisions by the firm's managers and investors. Indeed, the information in accounting statements helps guide resource allocation in the economy.

Firms disclose financial statements in periodic filings to the federal government and in *annual reports* to shareholders. An investor is more likely to buy a firm's stock if the firm's income statement shows a large after-tax profit and if its balance sheet shows a large net worth. The top management of a firm has at least two reasons to attract investors and keep the firm's stock price high. First, a higher stock price increases the funds the firm can raise when it sells a given amount of stock. Second, to reduce the principal–agent problem, boards of directors often tie the salaries of top managers to the firm's stock price or to the profitability of the firm.

Top managers clearly have an incentive to maximize the profits reported on the income statement and the net worth reported on the balance sheet. If top managers make good decisions, the firm's profits will be high, and the firm's assets will be large relative to its liabilities. The business scandals that came to light in 2002 revealed, however, that some top managers have inflated profits and hidden liabilities that should have been listed on their balance sheets.

At Enron, an energy trading firm, CFO Andrew Fastow was accused of creating partnerships that were supposedly independent of Enron but in fact were owned by the firm. He was accused of transferring large amounts of Enron's debts to these partnerships, which reduced the liabilities on Enron's balance sheet, thereby increasing the firm's net worth. Fastow's deception made Enron more attractive to investors, increasing its stock price—and Fastow's compensation. In 2001, however, Enron was forced into bankruptcy. The firm's shareholders lost billions of dollars, and many employees lost their jobs. In 2004, Fastow pleaded guilty to conspiracy and was sentenced to 10 years in federal prison. Enron's CEO, Kenneth Lay, was found guilty of securities fraud in 2006 but died prior to being sentenced.

At WorldCom, a telecommunications firm, David Myers, the firm's controller, pleaded guilty to falsifying "WorldCom's books, to reduce WorldCom's reported actual costs and therefore increase WorldCom's reported earnings." Myers's actions caused WorldCom's income statement to overstate the firm's profits by more than $10 billion. WorldCom CEO Bernard Ebbers is serving a 25-year prison sentence for fraud. The scandals at Enron and WorldCom were the largest cases of corporate fraud in U.S. history.

How was it possible for corporations such as Enron and WorldCom to falsify their financial statements? The federal government regulates how financial statements are prepared, but this regulation cannot by itself guarantee the accuracy of the statements. All firms that issue stock to the public have certified public accountants *audit* their financial statements. The accountants are employees of accounting firms, *not* of the firms being audited. The audits are intended to provide investors with an independent opinion as to whether a firm's financial statements fairly represent the true financial condition of the firm. Unfortunately, as the Enron and WorldCom scandals revealed, top managers who are determined to deceive investors about the true financial condition of their firms can also deceive outside auditors.

The private sector's response to the corporate scandals was almost immediate. In addition to the reexamination of corporate governance practices at many corporations, the New York Stock Exchange and the Nasdaq put forth initiatives to ensure the accuracy and accessibility of information.

To guard against future scandals, new federal legislation was enacted in 2002. The landmark *Sarbanes-Oxley Act of 2002* requires that corporate directors have a certain level of expertise with financial information and mandates that CEOs personally certify the accuracy of financial statements. The Sarbanes-Oxley Act also requires that financial analysts and auditors disclose whether any conflicts of interest might exist that would limit their independence in evaluating a firm's financial condition. The purpose of this provision is to ensure that analysts and auditors are acting in the best interests of shareholders. The act promotes management accountability by specifying the responsibilities of corporate officers and by increasing penalties, including long jail sentences, for managers who do not meet their responsibilities.

Perhaps the most noticeable corporate governance reform under the Sarbanes-Oxley Act is the creation of the Public Company Accounting Oversight Board, a national board that oversees the auditing of public companies' financial reports. The board's mission is to promote the independence of auditors to ensure that they disclose accurate information. On balance, most observers acknowledge that the Sarbanes-Oxley Act brought back confidence in the U.S. corporate governance system, though questions remain for the future about whether the act may chill legitimate business risk-taking by diverting management attention from the core business toward regulatory compliance. And the high accounting costs of implementing Sarbanes-Oxley are borne by all shareholders.

By 2008, it had become clear that Sarbanes-Oxley had raised the costs to firms of issuing stocks and bonds in the United States. Section 404 of Sarbanes-Oxley is intended to reassure investors that accounting "errors"—whether from fraud, mistakes, or omissions—will be minimized by requiring firms to maintain effective controls over financial reporting. Many economists believe, though, that the rules for implementing Section 404 set forth by the Securities and Exchange Commission and the Public Company Accounting Oversight Board have turned out to be much more costly to firms than anticipated and that these costs may exceed the benefits of the regulations. As a result, the share of new issues of stocks and bonds being listed on the New York Stock Exchange or Nasdaq has declined relative to listings on foreign stock markets, such as the London Stock Exchange. Some economists, though, are skeptical that the decline in the share of new listings on the New York Stock Exchange and Nasdaq is due to the effects of Sarbanes-Oxley. These economists argue that as other global exchanges become more mature, they are naturally able to attract new listings from local firms. Therefore, in this view, the declining fraction of foreign firms willing to list new issues on the New York Stock Exchange or Nasdaq is not an indication that the burden of U.S. regulations is too heavy.

Outside the United States, the European Commission and Japan have also tightened corporate governance rules. The challenge of ensuring the accurate reporting of firms' economic profits without excessively raising firms' costs is a global one.

Solved Problem | 7-5

What Makes a Good Board of Directors?

Western Digital Corporation makes computer hard drives. *BusinessWeek* magazine published the following analysis by Standard & Poor's Equity Research Services of Western Digital's corporate governance:

> Overall, we view Western Digital's corporate-governance policies favorably and believe the company compares well in this regard relative to peers. We see the following factors as positives: the board is controlled by a supermajority (greater than 67%) of independent outsiders; the nominating and compensation committees are comprised solely of independent outside directors; all directors with more than one year of service own stock. . . .

a. What is an "independent outsider" on a board of directors?

b. Why is it good for a firm to have a large majority of independent outsiders on the board of directors?

c. Why would it be good for a firm to have the auditing and compensation committees composed of outsiders?

d. Why would it be good for a firm if its directors own the firm's stock?

Source: Jawahar Hingorani, "Western Digital: A Drive Buy," *BusinessWeek*, January 9, 2007.

SOLVING THE PROBLEM:

Step 1: **Review the chapter material.** The context of this problem is the business scandals of 2002 and the underlying principal–agent problem that arises because of the separation of ownership from control in large corporations, so you may want to review the section "Corporate Governance Policy," which begins on page 221.

Step 2: **Answer question (a) by defining "independent outsiders."** *Insiders* are members of top management who also serve on the board of directors. *Outsiders* are members of the board of directors who are not otherwise employed by the firm. *Independent outsiders* are outsiders who have no business connections with the firm.

Step 3: **Answer question (b) by explaining why it is good for a firm to have a large majority of independent outsiders on the board of directors.** Having members of top management on the board of directors provides the board with information about the firm that only top managers possess. Having too many insiders on a board, however, means that top managers may end up controlling the board rather than the other way around. A corporation's board of directors is supposed to provide the monitoring and control of top managers that shareholders cannot provide directly. This is most likely to happen when a larger majority of the board of directors consists of independent outsiders.

Step 4: **Answer question (c) by explaining why it may be good for a firm to have the auditing and compensation committees composed of outsiders.** The auditing committee is responsible for ensuring that the firm's financial statements are accurate, and the compensation committee is responsible for setting the pay of top management. It is of vital importance to a firm that these activities be carried out in an honest and impartial way. Having these two important committees composed exclusively of independent outside members increases the chances that the committees will act in the best interests of the shareholders rather than in the best interests of top management.

Step 5: **Answer question (d) by explaining why it may be good for a firm to have directors owning the firm's stock.** When directors own the firm's stock, they will then share with other stockholders the desire to see the firm maximize profits. The directors will be more likely to insist that top managers take actions to increase profits rather than to pursue other objectives that may be in the interests of the managers but not the stockholders. Of course, when directors own the firm's stock the directors may be tempted not to object if top managers take steps to improperly inflate the firm's profits, as happened during the business scandals of 2002. On balance, though, most economists believe that it improves corporate governance when a firm's directors own the firm's stock.

YOUR TURN: For more practice, do related problems 5.3 and 5.4 on page 232 at the end of this chapter.

>> **End Solved Problem 7-5**

Economics in YOUR Life!

>> Continued from page 209

At the beginning of the chapter, we asked you to consider two questions: Why is it difficult to get the managers of a firm to act in your interest rather than in their own? and Given this problem, should you ever take on the risk of buying stock? The reason managers may not act in shareholders' interest is that in large corporations, there is separation of ownership from control: The shareholders own the firm, but the top managers actually control it. This results in the principal–agent problem discussed in the chapter. The principal–agent problem clearly adds to the risk you would face by buying stock rather than doing something safe with your money, such as putting it in the bank. But the rewards to owning stock can also be substantial, potentially earning you far more over the long run than a bank account will. Buying the stock of well-known firms, such as Google, that are closely followed by Wall Street investment analysts helps to reduce the principal–agent problem. It is less likely that the managers of these firms will take actions that are clearly not in the best interests of shareholders because the managers' actions are difficult to conceal. Buying the stock of large, well-known firms certainly does not completely eliminate the risk from principal–agent problems, however. Enron, WorldCom, and some of the other firms that were involved in the scandals discussed in this chapter were all well known and closely followed by Wall Street analysts, but the misbehavior of their managers went undetected, at least for awhile.

Conclusion

In a market system, firms make independent decisions about which goods and services to produce, how to produce them, and what prices to charge. In modern high-income countries, such as the United States, large corporations account for a majority of the sales and profits earned by firms. Generally, the managers of these corporations do a good job of representing the interests of stockholders, while providing the goods and services demanded by consumers. As the business scandals of 2002 showed, however, some top managers enriched themselves at the expense of stockholders and consumers by manipulating financial statements. Passage of the Sarbanes-Oxley Act of 2002 and other new government regulations have helped restore investor and management confidence in firms' financial statements. However, economists debate whether the benefits from these regulations are greater than their costs.

An Inside Look on the next page discusses the compensation Google pays its top executives.

Executive Compensation at Google

ASSOCIATED PRESS, APRIL 4, 2007

Google CEO, Co-Founders Get $1 Salary

The trio of billionaires who run Google Inc. collected less than $600,000 in combined compensation last year while they raked in big jackpots by selling some of their holdings in the online search leader.

The total amount that Google paid its chief executive, Eric Schmidt, and co-founders Larry Page and Sergey Brin during 2006 would have been less than $5,200 if not for personal security and transportation costs, according to documents filed Wednesday with the Securities and Exchange Commission.

Schmidt's package totaled $557,466, including $532,755 for personal security. Page's pay totaled $38,519, with most of the money covering personal transportation, logistics and security. Brin's 2006 pay consisted solely of a $1 salary and $1,723 bonus. Google paid the same salary and holiday bonus to Schmidt and Page.

The Associated Press bases its executive pay totals on salary, bonus, incentives, perks, above-market returns on deferred compensation and the estimated value of stock options and awards granted during the year.

Schmidt, Page and Brin have refused to take anything more than a token paycheck for the past three years to promote the egalitarian spirit championed by the Mountain View-based company.

It's a sacrifice that the three executives can afford to make because Google's high-flying stock has elevated them into the ranks of the world's richest people. Meanwhile, hundreds of Google's early employees have become millionaires.

As of March 1, Page, 34, owned 29.2 million Google shares currently worth $13.8 billion while Brin, 33, held 28.6 million shares worth about $13.5 billion. Schmidt, 51, owns 10.7 million shares currently worth $5 billion. The three men have been converting some of their holdings into cash by regularly selling some of their stockholdings since the company went public in August 2004.

Last year, Brin, Page and Schmidt made more than $2 billion combined from their Google stock sales, according to data compiled from SEC filings by Thomson Financial. Brin sold 1.99 million shares for a total windfall of $788 million last year while Page pocketed $666 million by selling 1.72 million shares. Schmidt cashed out 1.39 million shares during 2006 for a total $580 million.

Google's stock price rose by 11 percent last year, a gain that lagged the Standard & Poor's 500 index—a blue-chip bellwether that the company joined during 2006. The S&P 500 rose by 13.6 percent last year.

Since its IPO, Google shares have surged to a more than fivefold increase, a meteoric performance that has created more than $120 billion in shareholder wealth. Google shares fell $1.58 Wednesday to close at $471.02 on the Nasdaq Stock Market.

The rapid run-up in Google's stock has been driven by its search engine, which has become synonymous with looking things up on the Internet. The search engine also propels a lucrative online advertising network that enabled Google to turn a 2006 profit of $3.1 billion, more than doubling its earnings from the previous year. The robust growth has enabled Google to add more than 8,000 workers during the past three years. At the end of 2006, Google had 10,674 employees—all of whom were eligible for the same holiday bonus paid to Schmidt, Page and Brin.

Google's brain trust has already agreed to settle for a $1 salary again this year, rejecting an opportunity for a raise, according to the SEC filing.

Source: Michael Liedtke, "Google CEO, Co-Founders Get $1 Salary," *Associated Press*, April 4, 2007. Reprinted by permission of Associated Press via Reprint Management Services.

Key Points in the Article

The article discusses how Google CEO Eric Schmidt and the firm's co-founders Sergey Brin and Larry Page are compensated. Google is different from most large corporations in that most of the compensation for the CEO comes in the form of stock. The figure tracks the performance of Google's stock. Prior to August 2004, when Google had its initial public offering (IPO), Eric Schmidt and the co-founders agreed to cut their salaries to $1 a year plus some fringe benefits and stock in the company. Essentially, they bet that the price of the stock would rise. This turned out to be a good bet. Google's IPO was in August 2004. The price opened at $100 per share and closed at $104.06 that day. Google's stock has performed very well since the initial offering, and on April 4, 2007 (the date of the article) the price closed at $471.02 per share. As a result, the CEO and co-founders of Google have become billionaires.

The chapter discusses the principal–agent problem facing modern corporations. In large corporations, the executives of a firm are not usually the owners of the firm. In this situation, executives (especially the CEO) can take actions that are in their own interests rather than the interests of the shareholders. For example, the executives could use their influence to obtain large base salaries that are not sensitive to the firm's stock price. This reduces the executives' incentive to perform well. After all, the executives have large salaries, regardless of whether the firm does well.

Analyzing the News

ⓐ At Google, the CEO actually has a low base salary. Eric Schmidt earns a salary of $1 per year. He receives other compensation in the form of bonuses and compensation for security. Schmidt's combined compensation package was only $557,466, which is much less than those of most executives at similar firms.

ⓑ Instead of having a large base salary, most of Eric Schmidt's income comes from the sale of Google stock that he owned at the time Google went public or has received since then. He owns 10.7 million shares of Google stocks, making him a major shareholder in the firm. For each $1 increase in the stock price, Schmidt's wealth increases by $10.7 million. This is a strong incentive for him to take actions that will increase the stock price. This is good news to other Google shareholders, because Schmidt's income is tied to increases in the value of Google's stock. It seems Google has significantly reduced the principal–agent problem.

Thinking Critically

1. Compensating executives with stock, or equity, is a way to solve the principal–agent problem, but the practice is not without flaws. Critics of equity compensation point out that it can create incentives for executives to take actions not in the best interests of other shareholders and may have contributed to the corporate scandals discussed in the chapter. How could equity compensation contribute to these scandals?

2. An executive at Google who knew that Google was about to announce a larger than expected profit could have earned a bundle quickly by buying Google stock at $470 per share and then selling it at a higher price a day or so later. Such insider trading is illegal, however. Do you think that insider trading should be illegal? Are there benefits to other investors or to the economy as a whole associated with such trading? Are there problems associated with such trading?

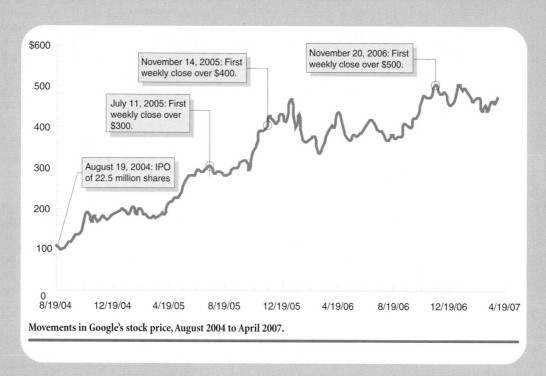

Movements in Google's stock price, August 2004 to April 2007.

Key Terms

Accounting profit, p. 220

Asset, p. 210

Balance sheet, p. 221

Bond, p. 215

Corporate governance, p. 212

Corporation, p. 210

Coupon payment, p. 215

Direct finance, p. 215

Dividends, p. 215

Economic profit, p. 221

Explicit cost, p. 220

Implicit cost, p. 220

Income statement, p. 220

Indirect finance, p. 215

Interest rate, p. 215

Liability, p. 220

Limited liability, p. 210

Opportunity cost, p. 220

Partnership, p. 210

Principal–agent problem, p. 213

Separation of ownership from control, p. 213

Sole proprietorship, p. 210

Stock, p. 215

7.1 LEARNING OBJECTIVE   7.1 | Categorize the major types of firms in the United States, **pages 210–212.**

Types of Firms

Summary

There are three types of firms: A **sole proprietorship** is a firm owned by a single individual and not organized as a corporation. A **partnership** is a firm owned jointly by two or more persons and not organized as a corporation. A **Corporation** is a legal form of business that provides the owners with limited liability. An **asset** is anything of value owned by a person or a firm. The owners of sole proprietorships and partners have unlimited liability, which means there is no legal distinction between the personal assets of the owners of the business and the assets of the business. The owners of corporations have **limited liability**, which means they can never lose more than their investment in the firm. Although only 20 percent of firms are corporations, they account for the majority of revenue and profit earned by all firms.

 Visit www.myeconlab.com to complete these exercises online and get instant feedback.

Review Questions

1.1 What are the three major types of firms in the United States? Briefly discuss the most important characteristics of each type.

1.2 What is limited liability? Why does the government grant limited liability to the owners of corporations?

Problems and Applications

1.3 Suppose that shortly after graduating from college, you decide to start your own business. Will you be likely to organize the business as a sole proprietorship, a partnership, or a corporation? Explain your reasoning.

1.4 (Related to the *Making the Connection* on page 211) Evaluate the following argument:

> I would like to invest in the stock market, but I think that buying shares of stock in a corporation is too risky. Suppose I buy $10,000 of General Motors stock, and the company ends up going bankrupt. Because as a stockholder, I'm part owner of the company, I might be responsible for paying hundreds of thousands of dollars of the company's debts.

1.5 (Related to the *Making the Connection* on page 211) In an article in the *New York Times*, sociologist Dalton Conley proposed the *elimination* of limited liability for corporate shareholders. Do you think that corporations should be granted limited liability? What are the benefits of limited liability? What is its downside? Would you be more willing to buy bonds from a corporation with limited liability? Would you be more willing to buy the stock of a corporation with limited liability?

Source: Dalton Conley, "Reward but No Risk," *New York Times*, May 10, 2003.

>> End Learning Objective 7.1

7.2 | Describe the typical management structure of corporations and understand the concepts of separation of ownership from control and the principal–agent problem, **pages 212–214.**

The Structure of Corporations and the Principal–Agent Problem

Summary

Corporate governance refers to the way in which a corporation is structured and the impact a corporation's structure has on the firm's behavior. Most corporations have a similar management structure: The shareholders elect a board of directors that appoints the corporation's top managers, such as the chief executive officer (CEO). Because the top management often does not own a large fraction of the stock in the corporation, large corporations have a **separation of ownership from control**. Because top managers have less incentive to increase the corporation's profits than to increase their own salaries and their own enjoyment, corporations can suffer from a **principal–agent problem**. A principal–agent problem exists when the principals—in this case, the shareholders of the corporation—have difficulty in getting the agent—the corporation's top management—to carry out their wishes.

Review Questions

2.1 What do we mean by the separation of ownership from control in large corporations?

2.2 How is the separation of ownership from control related to the principal–agent problem?

Problems and Applications

2.3 The principal–agent problem arises almost everywhere in the business world—but it also crops up even closer to home. Discuss the principal–agent problem that exists in the college classroom. Who is the principal? Who is the agent? What is the problem between this principal and this agent?

2.4 (Related to *Solved Problem 7-2* on page 213) Briefly explain whether you agree or disagree with the following argument: "The separation of ownership from control in large corporations and the principal–agent problem means that top managers can work short days, take long vacations, and otherwise slack off."

2.5 (Related to *Solved Problem 7-2* on page 213) An economic consultant gives the board of directors of a firm the following advice:

> You can increase the profitability of the firm if you change your method of compensating top management. Instead of paying your top management a straight salary, you should pay them a salary plus give them the right to buy the firm's stock in the future at a price above the stock's current market price.

Explain the consultant's reasoning. To what difficulties might this compensation scheme lead?

2.6 The following is from an article in the *New York Times*: "In theory, boards [of directors] design pay packages to attract and inspire good chief executives and to align their interests with those of shareholders. . . . But what kind of pay packages are appropriate at companies still run by the founding family?" The article quotes one expert as arguing: "There is little or no justification for treating an owner-manager in exactly the same way as a standard CEO." What does the article mean by saying that pay packages should "align [chief executives'] interests with those of shareholders"? What kind of pay packages would achieve this objective? Do you agree that an "owner-manager" should have a pay package different from that of a CEO who is not a member of the family that started the firm? Briefly explain.

Source: Diana B. Henriques, "What's Fair Pay for Running the Family Store?" *New York Times*, January 12, 2003.

>> End Learning Objective 7.2

7.3 | Explain how firms obtain the funds they need to operate and expand, **pages 214–218.**

How Firms Raise Funds

Summary

Firms rely on retained earnings—which are profits retained by the firm and not paid out to the firm's owners—or on using the savings of households for the funds they need to operate and expand. With **direct finance**, the savings of households flow directly to businesses when investors buy **stocks** and **bonds** in financial markets. With **indirect finance**, savings flow indirectly to businesses when households deposit money in saving and checking accounts in banks and the banks lend these funds to businesses. Federal, state, and local governments also sell bonds in financial markets and households also borrow funds from banks. When a firm sells a bond, it is borrowing money from the buyer of the bond. The firm makes a **coupon payment** to the buyer of the bond. The **interest rate** is the cost of borrowing funds, usually expressed as a percentage of the amount borrowed. When a firm sells stock, it is selling part ownership of the firm to the buyer of the stock. **Dividends** are payments by a corporation to its shareholders. The original purchasers of stocks and bonds may resell them in stock and bond markets, such as the New York Stock Exchange.

 Visit www.myeconlab.com to complete these exercises online and get instant feedback.

Review Questions

3.1 What is the difference between direct finance and indirect finance? If you borrow money from a bank to buy a new car, are you using direct finance or indirect finance?

3.2 Why is a bond considered to be a loan but a share of stock is not? Why do corporations issue both bonds and shares of stock?

3.3 How do the stock and bond markets provide information to businesses? Why do stock and bond prices change over time?

Problems and Applications

3.4 Suppose that a firm in which you have invested is losing money. Would you rather own the firm's stock or the firm's bonds? Explain.

3.5 Suppose you originally invested in a firm when it was small and unprofitable. Now the firm has grown considerably and is large and profitable. Would you be better off if you had bought the firm's stock or the firm's bonds? Explain.

3.6 If you deposit $20,000 in a savings account at a bank, you might earn 3 percent interest per year. Someone who borrows $20,000 from a bank to buy a new car might have to pay an interest rate of 8 percent per year on the loan. Knowing this, why don't you just lend your money directly to the car buyer, cutting out the bank?

3.7 (Related to the *Chapter Opener* on page 208) When Google's owners wanted to raise funds for expansion in 2004, they decided to sell stock in their company rather than borrow the money. Why do some companies fund their expansion by borrowing, while others fund expansion by issuing new stock?

3.8 (Related to the *Chapter Opener* on page 208) What impact would the following events be likely to have on the price of Google's stock?
a. A competitor launches a search engine that's just as good as Google's.
b. The corporate income tax is abolished.
c. Google's board of directors becomes dominated by close friends and relatives of its top management.
d. The price of wireless Internet connections unexpectedly drops, so more and more people use the Internet.
e. Google announces a huge profit of $1 billion, but everybody anticipated that Google would earn a huge profit of $1 billion.

3.9 In 2005, the French government began issuing bonds with 50-year maturities. Would this bond be purchased only by very young investors who expect to still be alive when the bond matures? Briefly explain.

3.10 (Related to the *Don't Let This Happen to You!* on page 216) Briefly explain whether you agree or disagree with the following statement: "The total value of the shares of Microsoft stock traded on the Nasdaq last week was $250 million, so the firm actually received more revenue from stock sales than from selling software."

3.11 (Related to the *Making the Connection* on page 217) Loans from banks are the most important external source of funds to businesses because most businesses are too small to borrow in financial markets by issuing stocks or bonds. Most investors are reluctant to buy the stocks or bonds of small businesses because of the difficulty of gathering accurate information on the financial strength and profitability of the businesses. Nevertheless, news about the stock market is included in nearly every network news program and is often the lead story in the business section of most newspapers. Is there a contradiction here? Why is the average viewer of TV news or the average reader of a newspaper interested in the fluctuations in prices in the stock market?

>> End Learning Objective 7.3

Using Financial Statements to Evaluate a Corporation

Summary

A firm's **income statement** sums up its revenues, costs, and profit over a period of time. A firm's **balance sheet** sums up its financial position on a particular day, usually the end of a quarter or year. A balance sheet records a firm's assets and liabilities. A **liability** is anything owed by a person or a firm. Firms report their **accounting profit** on their income statements. Accounting profit does not always include all of a firm's **opportunity cost**. **Explicit cost** is a cost that involves spending money. **Implicit cost** is a nonmonetary opportunity cost. Because accounting profit excludes some implicit costs, it is larger than **economic profit**.

 Visit www.myeconlab.com to complete these exercises *Get Ahead of the Curve* online and get instant feedback.

Review Questions

4.1 What is the difference between a firm's assets and its liabilities? Give an example of an asset and an example of a liability.

4.2 What is the difference between a firm's balance sheet and a firm's income statement?

Problems and Applications

4.3 Paolo currently has $100,000 invested in bonds that earn him 10 percent interest per year. He wants to open a pizza restaurant and is considering either selling the bonds and using the $100,000 to start his restaurant or borrowing the $100,000 from a bank, which would charge him an annual interest rate of 7 percent. He finally decides to sell the bonds and not take out the bank loan. He reasons, "Because I already have the $100,000 invested in the bonds, I don't have

to pay anything to use the money. If I take out the bank loan, I have to pay interest, so my costs of producing pizza will be higher if I take out the loan than if I sell the bonds." What do you think of Paolo's reasoning?

4.4 Paolo and Alfredo are twins who both want to open pizza restaurants. Because their parents always liked Alfredo best, they buy two pizza ovens and give both to him. Unfortunately, Paolo must buy his own pizza ovens. Does Alfredo have lower cost of producing pizza than Paolo does because Alfredo received his pizza ovens as a gift while Paolo had to pay for his? Briefly explain.

4.5 Dane decides to give up a job earning $100,000 per year as a corporate lawyer and converts the duplex that he owns into a UFO museum. (He had been renting out the duplex for $20,000 a year.) His direct expenses include $50,000 per year paid to his assistants and $10,000 per year for utilities. Fans flock to the museum to see his collection of extraterrestrial paraphernalia, which he could easily sell on eBay for $1,000,000. Over the course of the year, the museum brings in revenues of $100,000.

a. How much is Dane's accounting profit for the year?

b. Is Dane earning an economic profit? Explain.

4.6 The Securities and Exchange Commission requires that every firm that wishes to issue stock and bonds to the public make available its balance sheet and income statement. Briefly explain how information useful to investors can be found in these financial statements.

4.7 (Related to the *Making the Connection* on page 219) The Making the Connection on China argues that "In the absence of well-functioning financial markets, banks are crucial allocators of capital." What is the difference between a financial market and a bank? What is an "allocator of capital"? How do banks allocate capital?

>> End Learning Objective 7.4

Corporate Governance Policy

Summary

Because their compensation often rises with the profitability of the corporation, top managers have an incentive to overstate the profits reported on their firm's income statements. During 2002, it became clear that the

top managers of several large corporations had done this, even though intentionally falsifying financial statements is illegal. The *Sarbanes-Oxley Act* of 2002 and greater scrutiny of financial statements have helped to restore investor and management confidence in firms' financial statements.

Review Questions

5.1 What is the Sarbanes-Oxley Act? Why was it passed?

5.2 Why are some policymakers and business owners concerned about the Sarbanes-Oxley Act?

Problems and Applications

5.3 (Related to *Solved Problem 7-5* on page 223) When Buford Yates, director of accounting at WorldCom, pleaded guilty to fraud, he stated in federal court that top managers at WorldCom ordered him to make certain adjustments to the firm's financial statements:

> I came to believe that the adjustments I was being directed to make in World-Com's financial statements had no justification and contravened generally accepted accounting principles. I concluded that the purpose of these adjustments was to incorrectly inflate World-Com's reported earnings.

What are "generally accepted accounting principles"? How would the "adjustments" Yates was ordered to make benefit top managers at WorldCom? Would these adjustments also benefit WorldCom's stockholders? Briefly explain.

Source: Devlin Barrett, "Ex-WorldCom Exec Pleads Guilty," Associated Press, October 8, 2002.

5.4 (Related to *Solved Problem 7-5* on page 223) In 2002, *BusinessWeek* listed Apple Computer as having one of the worst boards of directors:

> Founder Steve Jobs owns just two shares in the company.... The CEO of Micro Warehouse, which accounted for nearly 2.9% of Apple's net sales in 2001, sits on the compensation committee.... There is an interlocking directorship—with Gap CEO Mickey Drexler and Jobs sitting on each other's boards.

Why might investors be concerned that a top manager like Steve Jobs owns only two shares in the firm? Why might investors be concerned if a member of the board of directors also has a business relationship with the firm? What is an "interlocking directorship"? Why is it a bad thing?

Source: "The Best Boards and the Worst Boards," *BusinessWeek*, October 7, 2002, p. 107.

5.5 The following is from a *BusinessWeek* editorial:

> Welcome to the revolution. After years of paying lip service to reform, Enron Corp. and the ensuing wave of business scandal has finally produced a dramatic change in corporate governance.... Investors are rewarding companies with good governance and punishing those without it.

How are investors able to reward or punish firms? What impact will these rewards and punishments have on boards of directors and top managers?

Source: "Boardrooms Are Starting to Wake Up," *BusinessWeek*, October 7, 2002, p. 107.

5.6 An article in *BusinessWeek* stated that the Allstate Corporation, a large insurance company, would now require a simple majority vote, rather than a two-thirds majority vote, to elect members to its board of directors and to remove directors in between annual meetings when elections are held. The article also stated that the price of Allstate's stock rose following the announcement. Briefly discuss whether there may have been a possible connection between these changes in Allstate's corporate governance and the increase in the firm's stock price.

Source: "Allstate Announces Changes to Governance," *BusinessWeek*, February 20, 2007.

5.7 According to a survey in 2007, 78 percent of corporate executives responding believed that the costs of complying with the Sarbanes-Oxley Act outweighed the benefits. The total costs of compliance were about $2.92 million per company. Is it possible to put a dollar value on the benefits to complying with Sarbanes-Oxley? Which groups are likely to receive the most benefits from Sarbanes-Oxley: investors, corporations, or some other group?

Source: Kara Scannell, "Costs to Comply with Sarbanes-Oxley Decline Again," *Wall Street Journal*, May 16, 2007, p. C7.

>> End Learning Objective 7.5

Appendix
Tools to Analyze Firms' Financial Information

Understand the concept of present value and the information contained on a firm's income statement and balance sheet.

As we saw in the chapter, modern business organizations are not just "black boxes" transforming inputs into output. Most business revenues and profits are earned by large corporations. Unlike founder-dominated firms, the typical large corporation is run by managers who generally do not own a controlling interest in the firm. Large firms raise funds from outside investors, and outside investors seek information on firms and the assurance that the managers of firms will act in the interests of the investors.

This chapter showed how corporations raise funds by issuing stocks and bonds. This appendix provides more detail to support that discussion. We begin by analyzing *present value* as a key concept in determining the prices of financial securities. We then provide greater information on *financial statements* issued by corporations, using Google as an example.

Using Present Value to Make Investment Decisions

Firms raise funds by selling equity (stock) and debt (bonds and loans) to investors and lenders. If you own shares of stock or a bond, you will receive payments in the form of dividends or coupons over a number of years. Most people value funds they already have more highly than funds they will not receive until some time in the future. For example, you would probably not trade $1,000 you already have for $1,000 you will not receive for one year. The longer you have to wait to receive a payment, the less value it will have for you. One thousand dollars you will not receive for two years is worth less to you than $1,000 you will receive after one year. The value you give today to money you will receive in the future is called the future payment's **present value**. The present value of $1,000 you will receive in one year will be less than $1,000.

Present value The value in today's dollars of funds to be paid or received in the future.

Why is this true? Why is the $1,000 you will not receive for one year less valuable to you than the $1,000 you already have? The most important reason is that if you have $1,000 today, you can use that $1,000 today. You can buy goods and services with the money and receive enjoyment from them. The $1,000 you receive in one year does not have direct use to you now.

Also, prices will likely rise during the year you are waiting to receive your $1,000. So, when you finally do receive the $1,000 in one year, you will not be able to buy as much with it as you could with $1,000 today. Finally, there is some risk that you will not receive the $1,000 in one year. The risk may be very great if an unreliable friend borrows $1,000 from you and vaguely promises to pay you back in one year. The risk may be very small if you lend money to the federal government by buying a United States Treasury bond. In either case, though, there is at least some risk that you will not receive the funds promised.

When someone lends money, the lender expects to be paid back both the amount of the loan and some additional interest. Say that you decide that you are willing to lend your $1,000 today if you are paid back $1,100 one year from now. In this case, you are charging $100/$1,000 = 0.10, or 10 percent interest on the funds you have loaned. Economists would say that you value $1,000 today as equivalent to the $1,100 to be received one year in the future.

Notice that $1,100 can be written as $1,000 (1 + 0.10). That is, the value of money received in the future is equal to the value of money in the present multiplied by 1 plus the interest rate, with the interest rate expressed as a decimal. Or:

$$\$1,100 = 1,000 \ (1 + 0.10).$$

Notice, also, that if we divide both sides by (1 + 0.10), we can rewrite this formula as:

$$\$1,000 = \frac{\$1,100}{(1 + 0.10)}.$$

The rewritten formula states that the present value is equal to the future value to be received in one year divided by one plus the interest rate. This formula is important because you can use it to convert any amount to be received in one year into its present value. Writing the formula generally, we have:

$$\text{Present Value} = \frac{\text{Future Value}_1}{(1 + i)}.$$

The present value of funds to be received in one year—Future Value$_1$—can be calculated by dividing the amount of those funds to be received by 1 plus the interest rate. With an interest rate of 10 percent, the present value of $1,000,000 to be received one year from now is:

$$\frac{\$1,000,000}{(1 + 0.10)} = \$909,090.91.$$

This method is a very useful way of calculating the value today of funds that won't be received for one year. But financial securities such as stocks and bonds involve promises to pay funds over many years. Therefore, it would be even more useful if we could expand this formula to calculate the present value of funds to be received more than one year in the future.

This expansion is easy to do. Go back to the original example where we assumed you were willing to loan out your $1,000 for one year, provided that you received 10 percent interest. Suppose you are asked to lend the funds for two years and that you are promised 10 percent interest per year for each year of the loan. That is, you are lending $1,000, which at 10 percent interest will grow to $1,100 after one year, and you are agreeing to loan that $1,100 out for a second year at 10 percent interest. So, after two years, you will be paid back $1,100 (1 + 0.10), or $1,210. Or:

$$\$1,210 = \$1,000 \ (1 + 0.10)(1 + 0.10),$$

or:

$$\$1,210 = \$1,000 \ (1 + 0.10)^2.$$

This formula can also be rewritten as:

$$\$1,000 = \frac{\$1,210}{(1 + 0.10)^2}.$$

To put this formula in words, the $1,210 you receive two years from now has a present value equal to $1,210 divided by the quantity 1 plus the interest rate squared. If you were to agree to lend out your $1,000 for three years at 10 percent interest, you would receive:

$$\$1,331 = \$1,000 \ (1 + 0.10)^3.$$

Notice, again, that:

$$\$1,000 = \frac{\$1,331}{(1 + 0.10)^3}.$$

You can probably see a pattern here. We can generalize the concept to say that the present value of funds to be received n years in the future—whether n is 1, 20, or 85 does not matter—equals the amount of the funds to be received divided by the quantity 1 plus the interest rate raised to the nth power. For instance, with an interest rate of 10 percent, the value of $1,000,000 to be received 25 years in the future is:

$$\text{Present Value} = \frac{\$1,000,000}{(1 + 0.10)^{25}} = \$92,296.$$

Or, more generally:

$$\text{Present Value} = \frac{\text{Future Value}_n}{(1 + i)^n},$$

where Future Value$_n$ represents funds that will be received in n years.

Solved Problem | 7A-1

How to Receive Your Contest Winnings

Suppose you win a contest and are given the choice of the following prizes:

Prize 1: $50,000 to be received right away, with four additional payments of $50,000 to be received each year for the next four years

Prize 2: $175,000 to be received right away

Explain which prize you would choose and the basis for your decision.

SOLVING THE PROBLEM:

Step 1: **Review the material.** This problem involves applying the concept of present value, so you may want to review the section "Using Present Value to Make Investment Decisions," which begins on page 233.

Step 2: **Explain the basis for choosing the prize.** Unless you need immediate cash, you should choose the prize with the highest present value.

Step 3: **Calculate the present value of each prize.** Prize 2 consists of one payment of $175,000 received right away, so its present value is $175,000. Prize 1 consists of five payments spread out over time. To find the present value of the prize, we must find the present value of each of these payments and add them together. To calculate present value, we must use an interest rate. Let's assume an interest rate of 10 percent. In that case, the present value of Prize 1 is:

$$\$50,000 + \frac{\$50,000}{(1 + 0.10)} + \frac{\$50,000}{(1 + 0.10)^2} + \frac{\$50,000}{(1 + 0.10)^3} + \frac{\$50,000}{(1 + 0.10)^4} =$$

$$\$50,000 + \$45,454.55 + \$41,322.31 + \$37,565.74 + \$34,150.67 = \$208,493.$$

Step 4: **State your conclusion.** Prize 1 has the greater present value, so you should choose it rather than Prize 2.

YOUR TURN: For more practice, do related problems 7A.6, 7A.8, 7A.9, and 7A.10 on pages 240–241 at the end of this appendix.

>> End Solved Problem 7A-1

Using Present Value to Calculate Bond Prices

Anyone who buys a financial asset, such as shares of stock or a bond, is really buying a promise to receive certain payments—dividends in the case of shares of stock or coupons in the case of a bond. The price investors are willing to pay for a financial asset should be equal to the value of the payments they will receive as a result of owning the asset. Because most of the coupon or dividend payments will be received in the future, it is their present value that matters. Put another way, we have the following important idea: *The price of a financial asset should be equal to the present value of the payments to be received from owning that asset.*

Let's consider an example. Suppose that in 1980, General Electric issued a bond with an $80 coupon that will mature in 2010. It is now 2008, and that bond has been bought and sold by investors many times. You are considering buying it. If you buy the bond, you will receive two years of coupon payments plus a final payment of the bond's principal or face value of $1,000. Suppose, once again, that you need an interest rate of 10 percent to invest your funds. If the bond has a coupon of $80, the present value of the payments you receive from owning the bond—and, therefore, the present value of the bond—will be:

$$\text{Present Value} = \frac{\$80}{(1+0.10)} + \frac{\$80}{(1+0.10)^2} + \frac{\$1,000}{(1+0.10)^2} = \$965.29.$$

That is, the present value of the bond will equal the present value of the three payments you will receive during the two years you own the bond. You should, therefore, be willing to pay $965.29 to own this bond and have the right to receive these payments from GE. This process of calculating present values of future payments is used to determine bond prices, with one qualification. The relevant interest rate used by investors in the bond market to calculate the present value and, therefore, the price of an existing bond is usually the coupon rate on comparable newly issued bonds. Therefore, the general formula for the price of a bond is:

$$\text{Bond Price} = \frac{\text{Coupon}_1}{(1+i)} + \frac{\text{Coupon}_2}{(1+i)^2} + \cdots + \frac{\text{Coupon}_n}{(1+i)^n} + \frac{\text{Face Value}}{(1+i)^n},$$

where Coupon_1 is the coupon payment to be received after one year, Coupon_2 is the coupon payment to be received after two years, up to Coupon_n, which is the coupon payment received in the year the bond matures. The ellipsis takes the place of the coupon payments—if any—received between the second year and the year the bond matures. Face Value is the face value of the bond, to be received when the bond matures. The interest rate on comparable newly issued bonds is i.

Using Present Value to Calculate Stock Prices

When you own a firm's stock, you are legally entitled to your share of the firm's profits. Remember that the profits a firm pays out to its shareholders are referred to as dividends. The price of a share of stock should be equal to the present value of the dividends investors expect to receive as a result of owning that stock. Therefore, the general formula for the price of a stock is:

$$\text{Stock Price} = \frac{\text{Dividend}_1}{(1+i)} + \frac{\text{Dividend}_2}{(1+i)^2} + \cdots$$

Notice that this formula looks very similar to the one we used to calculate the price of a bond, with a couple of important differences. First, unlike a bond, stock has no maturity date, so we have to calculate the present value of an infinite number of dividend payments. At first, it may seem that the stock's price must be infinite as well, but remember that dollars you don't receive for many years are worth very little today. For instance, a dividend payment of $10 that will be received 40 years in the future is worth only a little more than $0.20 today at a 10 percent interest rate. The second difference between the stock price formula and the bond price formula is that whereas the coupon payments you receive from owning the bond are known with certainty—they are written on the bond and cannot be changed—you don't know for sure what the dividend payments from owning a stock will be. How large a dividend payment you will receive depends on how profitable the company will be in the future.

Although it is possible to forecast the future profitability of a company, this cannot be done with perfect accuracy. To emphasize this point, some economists rewrite the basic stock price formula by adding a superscript e to each Dividend term to emphasize that these are *expected* dividend payments. Because the future profitability of companies is often very difficult to forecast, it is not surprising that differences of opinion exist over what the price of a particular stock should be. Some investors will be very optimistic about the future profitability of a company and will, therefore, believe that the company's stock should have a high price. Other investors might be very pessimistic and believe that the company's stock should have a low price.

A Simple Formula for Calculating Stock Prices

It is possible to simplify the formula for determining the price of a stock, if we assume that dividends will grow at a constant rate:

$$\text{Stock Price} = \frac{\text{Dividend}}{(i - \text{Growth Rate})}.$$

In this equation, Dividend is the dividend expected to be received one year from now, and Growth Rate is the rate at which those dividends are expected to grow. If a company pays a dividend of $1 per share to be received one year from now and Growth Rate is 10 percent, the company is expected to pay a dividend of $1.10 the following year, $1.21 the year after that, and so on.

Now suppose that IBM pays a dividend of $5 per share, the consensus of investors is that these dividends will increase at a rate of 5 percent per year for the indefinite future, and the interest rate is 10 percent. Then the price of IBM's stock should be:

$$\text{Stock Price} = \frac{\$5.00}{(0.10 - 0.05)} = \$100.00.$$

Particularly during the years 1999 and 2000, there was much discussion of whether the high prices of many Internet stocks—such as the stock of Amazon.com—were justified, given that many of these companies had not made any profit yet and so had not paid any dividends. Is there any way that a rational investor would pay a high price for the stock of a company currently not earning profits? The formula for determining stock prices shows that it is possible, provided that the investor's assumptions are optimistic enough! For example, during 1999, one stock analyst predicted that Amazon.com would soon be earning $10 per share of stock. That is, Amazon.com's total earnings divided by the number of shares of its stock outstanding would be $10. Suppose Amazon.com pays out that $10 in dividends and that the $10 will grow rapidly over the years, by, say, 7 percent per year. Then our formula indicates that the price of Amazon.com stock should be:

$$\text{Stock Price} = \frac{\$10.00}{(\$0.10 - 0.07)} = \$333.33.$$

If you are sufficiently optimistic about the future prospects of a company, a high stock price can be justified even if the company is not currently earning a profit. But investors in growth stocks must be careful. Suppose investors believe that growth prospects for Amazon are only 4 percent per year instead of 7 percent because the firm turns out not to be as profitable as initially believed. Then our formula indicates that the price of Amazon.com stock should be:

$$\text{Stock Price} = \frac{\$10.00}{(\$0.10 - 0.04)} = \$166.67.$$

This price is only half the price assuming a more optimistic growth rate. Hence investors use information about a firm's profitability and growth prospects to determine what the firm is worth.

Going Deeper into Financial Statements

Corporations disclose substantial information about their business operations and financial position to actual and potential investors. Some of this information meets the demands of participants in financial markets and of information-collection agencies, such as Moody's Investors Service, which develops credit ratings that help investors judge how risky corporate bonds are. Other information meets the requirements of the U.S. Securities and Exchange Commission.

Key sources of information about a corporation's profitability and financial position are its principal financial statements—the *income statement* and the *balance sheet*. These important information sources were first introduced in the chapter. Here we go into more detail, using recent data for Google as an example.

Analyzing Income Statements

As discussed in the chapter, a firm's income statement summarizes its revenues, costs, and profit over a period of time. Figure 7A-1 shows Google's income statement for 2006.

Google's income statement presents the results of the company's operations during the year. Listed first are the revenues it earned, largely from selling advertising on its Web site, from January 1, 2006, to December 31, 2006: $10,605 million. Listed next are Google's operating expenses, the most important of which is its *cost of revenue*—which is commonly known as *cost of sales* or *cost of goods sold*: $4,225 million. Cost of revenue is the direct cost of producing the products sold, including in this case the salaries of the computer programmers Google hires to write the software for its Web site. Google also has substantial costs for researching and developing its products ($1,229 million) and for advertising and marketing them ($850 million). General and administrative expenses ($752 million) include costs such as the salaries of top managers.

The difference between a firm's revenue and its costs is its profit. "Profit" shows up in several forms on an income statement. A firm's *operating income* is the difference between its revenue and its operating expenses. Most corporations, including Google, also have investments, such as government and corporate bonds, that normally generate some income for them. In this case, Google earned $461 million on its investments, which increased its *income before taxes* to $4,010 million. The federal government taxes the profits of corporations. During 2006, Google paid $934 million—or about 23 percent

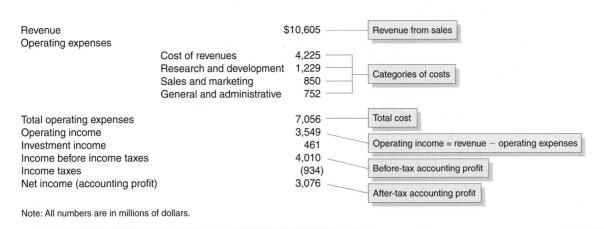

Note: All numbers are in millions of dollars.

Figure 7A-1 | Google's Income Statement for 2006

Google's income statement shows the company's revenue, costs, and profit for 2006. The difference between its revenue ($10,605 million) and its operating expenses ($7,056 million) is its operating income ($3,549 million). Most corporations also have investments, such as government or corporate bonds, that generate some income for them. In this case, Google earned $461 million, giving the firm an income before taxes

of $4,010 million. After paying taxes of $934 million, Google was left with a net income, or accounting profit, of $3,076 million for the year.

Source: Google's Income Statement for 2006. Google Inc., "Consolidated Statements of Income," February 1, 2007. Used with permission of Google, Inc.

of its profits—in taxes. *Net income* after taxes was $3,076 million. The net income that firms report on their income statements is referred to as their after-tax *accounting profit*.

Analyzing Balance Sheets

As discussed in the chapter, whereas a firm's income statement reports a firm's activities for a period of time, a firm's balance sheet summarizes its financial position on a particular day, usually the end of a quarter or year. To understand how a balance sheet is organized, first recall that an asset is anything of value that the firm owns, and a liability is a debt or an obligation that the firm owes. Subtracting the value of a firm's liabilities from the value of its assets leaves its *net worth*. Because a corporation's stockholders are its owners, net worth is often listed as **stockholders' equity** on a balance sheet. Using these definitions, we can state the balance sheet equation (also called the basic accounting equation) as follows:

Assets – Liabilities = Stockholders' Equity,

or:

Assets = Liabilities + Stockholders' Equity.

This formula tells us that the value of a firm's assets must equal the value of its liabilities plus the value of stockholders' equity. An important accounting rule dating back to the beginning of modern bookkeeping in fifteenth-century Italy holds that balance sheets should list assets on the left side and liabilities and net worth, or stockholders' equity, on the right side. Notice that this means that *the value of the left side of the balance sheet must always equal the value of the right side.* Figure 7A-2 shows Google's balance sheet as of December 31, 2006.

A couple of the entries on the asset side of the balance sheet may be unfamiliar: *Current assets* are assets that the firm could convert into cash quickly, such as the balance in its checking account or its accounts receivable, which is money currently owed to the firm for products that have been delivered but not yet paid for. *Goodwill* represents the difference between the purchase price of a company and the market value of its assets. It represents the ability of a business to earn an economic profit from its assets. For example, if you buy a restaurant that is located on a busy intersection and you employ a chef with a reputation for preparing delicious food, you may pay more than the market value of the tables, chairs, ovens, and other assets. This additional amount you pay will be entered on the asset side of your balance sheet as goodwill.

Current liabilities are short-term debts such as accounts payable, which is money owed to suppliers for goods received but not yet paid for, or bank loans that will be paid back in less than one year. Long-term bank loans and the value of outstanding corporate bonds are *long-term liabilities*.

Stockholders' equity The difference between the value of a corporation's assets and the value of its liabilities; also known as net worth.

ASSETS		LIABILITIES AND STOCKHOLDERS' EQUITY	
Current Assets	$13,040	Current Liabilities	$1,305
Property and Equipment	2,395	Long-term liabilities	129
Investments	1,032	Total Liabilities	1,434
Goodwill	1,545	Stockholders' Equity	17,040
Other long-term assets	461		
Total Assets	18,473	Total liabilites and stockholders' equity	18,473

Figure 7A-2 | Google's Balance Sheet as of December 31, 2006

Corporations list their assets on the left of their balance sheets and their liabilities on the right. The difference between the value of the firm's assets and the value of its liabilities equals the net worth of the firm, or stockholders' equity. Stockholders' equity is listed on the right side of the balance sheet. Therefore, the value of the left side of the balance sheet must always equal the value of the right side.

Note: All numbers are in millions of dollars.

Source: Google's Balance Sheet as of December 31, 2006, Google, Inc., "Consolidated Balance Sheets," February 1, 2007. Used with permission of Google, Inc.

Key Terms

LEARNING OBJECTIVE   Understand the concept of present value and the information contained on a firm's income statement and balance sheet, **pages 233–239.**

 Visit www.myeconlab.com to complete these exercises online and get instant feedback.

Review Questions

7A.1 Why is money you receive at some future date worth less than money you receive today? If the interest rate rises, what effect does this have on the present value of payments you receive in the future?

7A.2 Give the formula for calculating the present value of a bond that will pay a coupon of $100 per year for 10 years and that has a face value of $1,000.

7A.3 Compare the formula for calculating the present value of the payments you will receive from owning a bond to the formula for calculating the present value of the payments you will receive from owning a stock. What are the key similarities? What are the key differences?

7A.4 How is operating income calculated? How does operating income differ from net income? How does net income differ from accounting profit?

7A.5 What's the key difference between a firm's income statement and its balance sheet? What is listed on the left side of a balance sheet? What is listed on the right side?

Problems and Applications

7A.6 (Related to *Solved Problem 7A-1* on page 235) If the interest rate is 10 percent, what is the present value of a bond that matures in two years, pays $85 one year from now, and pays $1,085 two years from now?

7A.7 The following is from an Associated Press story on the contract of baseball star Carlos Beltran:

> Beltran's contract calls for his $11 million signing bonus to be paid in four installments: $5 million upon approval and $2 million each this June 15, 2005, and on Jan. 15, 2006, and Jan. 15, 2007. He gets a $10 million salary this year, $12 million in each of the following two seasons and

$18.5 million in each of the final four seasons, with $8.5 million deferred annually from 2008–11. The players' association calculated the present day value of the contract at $115,726,946, using a 6 percent discount rate (the prime rate [which is the interest rate banks charge on loans to their best customers] plus 1 percent, rounded to the nearest whole number). For purposes of baseball's luxury tax, which currently uses a 3.62 percent discount rate, the contract is valued at $116,695,898.

Briefly explain why the present value of Beltran's contract is lower if a higher interest is used to make the calculation than if a lower interest rate is used.

Source: "Like Pedro, Beltran Gets Suite on Road," Associated Press, January 18, 2005.

7A.8 (Related to *Solved Problem 7A-1* on page 235) Before the 2007 season, the Seattle Mariners baseball team signed catcher Kenji Johjima to a contract that would pay him the following amounts: an immediate $1 million signing bonus, $5.1 million for the 2007 season, $5.2 million for the 2008 season, and $5.2 million for the 2009 season. Assume that he receives each of his three seasonal salaries as a lump sum payment at the end of the season and that he receives his 2007 salary one year after he signed the contract.

a. Some newspaper reports described Johjima as having signed a "$16.5 million contract" with the Mariners. Do you agree that $16.5 million was the value of this contract? Briefly explain.

b. What was the present value of Johjima's contract at the time he signed it (assuming an interest rate of 10 percent)?

c. If you use an interest rate of 5 percent, what was the present value of Johjima's contract?

7A.9 (Related to *Solved Problem 7A-1* on page 235) A winner of the Pennsylvania Lottery was given the choice of receiving $18 million at once or $1,440,000 per year for 25 years.

a. If the winner had opted for the 25 annual payments, how much in total would she have received?

b. At an interest rate of 10 percent, what would be the present value of the 25 payments?

c. At an interest rate of 5 percent, what would be the present value of the 25 payments?

d. What interest rate would make the present value of the 25 payments equal to the one payment of $18 million? (This question is difficult and requires the use of a financial calculator or a spreadsheet. *Hint:* If you are familiar with the Excel spreadsheet program, use the RATE function. Questions (b) and (c) can be answered by using the Excel NPV—Net Present Value—function.)

7A.10 (Related to *Solved Problem 7A-1* on page 235) Before the start of the 2000 baseball season, the New York Mets decided they didn't want Bobby Bonilla playing for them any longer. But Bonilla had a contract with the Mets for the 2000 season that would have obliged the Mets to pay him $5.9 million. When the Mets released Bonilla, he agreed to take the following payments in lieu of the $5.9 million the Mets would have paid him in the year 2000: He will receive 25 equal payments of $1,193,248.20 each July 1 from 2011 to 2035. If you were Bobby Bonilla, which would you rather have had, the lump sum $5.9 million or the 25 payments beginning in 2011? Explain the basis for your decision.

7A.11 Suppose that eLake, an online auction site, is paying a dividend of $2 per share. You expect this dividend to grow 2 percent per year, and the interest rate is 10 percent. What is the most you would be willing to pay for a share of stock in eLake? If the interest rate is 5 percent, what is the most you would be willing to pay? When interest rates in the economy decline, would you expect stock prices in general to rise or fall? Explain.

7A.12 Suppose you buy the bond of a large corporation at a time when the inflation rate is very low. If the inflation rate increases during the time you hold the bond, what is likely to happen to the price of the bond?

7A.13 Use the information in the following table for calendar year 2006 to prepare the McDonald's Corporation's income statement. Be sure to include entries for operating income and net income.

Revenue from company restaurants	$16,083 million
Revenue from franchised restaurants	5,503 million
Cost of operating company-owned restaurants	13,542 million
Income taxes	1,293 million
Interest expense	402 million
General and administrative cost	2,338 million
Cost of restaurant leases	1,060 million
Other operating costs	67 million

Source: McDonald's Corporation, *Annual Report, 2006*, February 26, 2007.

7A.14 Use the information in the following table on the financial situation of Starbucks Corporation as of December 31, 2006, to prepare the firm's balance sheet. Be sure to include an entry for stockholders' equity.

Current assets	$1,530 million
Current liabilities	1,936 million
Property and equipment	2,288 million
Long-term liabilities	50 million
Goodwill	161 million
Other assets	187 million

Source: Starbucks Corporation, *Annual Report, 2006*.

7A.15 The *current ratio* is equal to a firm's current assets divided by its current liabilities. Use the information in Figure 7A-2 on page 239 to calculate Google's current ratio on December 31, 2006. Investors generally prefer that a firm's current ratio be greater than 1.5. What problems might a firm encounter if the value of its current assets is low relative to the value of its current liabilities?

>> End Appendix Learning Objective

Comparative Advantage, and the **Gains** from **International Trade**

Is Using Trade Policy to Help U.S. Industries a Good Idea?

Trade is, simply, the act of buying or selling. Is there a difference between trade that takes place within a country and international trade? Within the United States, domestic trade makes it possible for consumers in Ohio to eat salmon caught in Alaska or for consumers in Montana to drive cars built in Michigan or Kentucky. Similarly, international trade makes it possible for consumers in the United States to drink wine from France or use HD-DVD players from Japan. But one significant difference between domestic trade and international trade is that international trade is more controversial. At one time, nearly all the televisions, shoes, clothing, and toys consumed in the United States were also produced in the United States. Today, these goods are produced mainly by firms in other countries. This shift has benefited U.S. consumers because foreign-made goods have lower prices than the U.S.-made goods they have replaced. But at the same time, many U.S. firms that produced these goods have gone out of business, and their workers have had to find other jobs. Not surprisingly, opinion polls show that many Americans favor reducing international trade because they believe doing so would preserve jobs in the United States.

But do restrictions on trade actually preserve jobs? In fact, restrictions on trade may preserve jobs in particular industries, but only at the cost of reducing jobs in other industries. Consider, for example, U.S. policy on imports of sugar and imports of sugar-based ethanol. Ethanol is made from corn or sugar and can be used as a substitute for gasoline as a fuel in automobiles. Sugar is a better base for ethanol than corn because it ferments more quickly and is therefore cheaper to produce. In Brazil, ethanol is made from sugar, but in the United States, ethanol is made from corn. As a result, Brazilian ethanol costs just 80 cents a gallon, about half the cost of ethanol produced in the United States using corn. The Brazilian makers of ethanol would like to ship this cheap fuel to the United States, but the U.S. government has imposed a 54-cent-per-gallon tariff on imported ethanol. The tariff, combined with the cost of transporting the ethanol to the United States, effectively prices Brazilian ethanol out of the market.

The tariff helps U.S. firms that produce corn-based ethanol and U.S. farmers who grown corn, but it effectively increases fuel costs for many U.S. firms. The higher fuel costs make the products these firms produce more expensive, reducing sales and employment in the industries affected.

In addition to the tariff on sugar-based ethanol, Congress has also enacted a sugar quota, which limits the quantity of raw sugar allowed into the United States. Several countries around the world can produce sugar at lower costs than can U.S. sugar producers. As a result, the *world price* of sugar, which is the price at which sugar can be bought on the world market, is too low for U.S. sugar companies to cover their costs. The sugar quota allows U.S. companies to sell sugar domestically for a price that is about three times as high as the world price. Without the sugar quota, competition from foreign sugar producers would drive many U.S. producers out of business. But the United States also has a large candy industry, which uses many tons of sugar. The high price of sugar has led many U.S. candy firms to relocate their operations to other countries where the price of sugar is much lower. Life Savers, Star Brite mints, and Cherry Balls are a few of the candies no longer manufactured in the United States.

Should the United States have a tariff on imports of sugar-based ethanol and a quota on imports of raw sugar? The tariff and the quota create winners—U.S. producers of corn-based ethanol, U.S. sugar companies, and U.S. corn farmers—and losers—U.S. companies that use sugar, their employees, and U.S. consumers who must pay higher prices for goods that contain sugar and who are not able to buy low-priced sugar-based ethanol as an alternative to gasoline. In this chapter, we will explore who wins and who loses from international trade and review the political debate over whether international trade should be restricted. **AN INSIDE LOOK AT POLICY** on **page 268** discusses a recent trade agreement between the United States and South Korea.

Economics in YOUR Life!

Why Haven't You Heard of the Sugar Quota?

Politicians often support restrictions on trade to convince people to vote for them. The workers in the industries protected by tariffs and quotas are likely to vote for these politicians because the workers think trade restrictions will protect their jobs. But most people are not workers in industries protected from foreign competition by trade restrictions. We have seen that the sugar quota protects U.S. sugar companies and the people who work for them, but this amounts to only a few thousand people. Millions of consumers, though, have to pay higher prices for soft drinks, bakery goods, and candy because of the sugar quota. How, then, have sugar companies convinced Congress to enact the sugar quota and why have very few people even heard of the quota? As you read the chapter, see if can answer this question. You can check your answers against those we provide at the end of the chapter. >> Continued on page 267

Markets for internationally traded goods and services can be analyzed using the tools of demand and supply that we developed in Chapter 3. We saw in Chapter 2 that trade in general—whether within a country or between countries—is based on the principle of comparative advantage. In this chapter, we look more closely at the role of comparative advantage in international trade. We also use the concepts of consumer surplus, producer surplus, and deadweight loss from Chapter 4 to analyze government policies, such as the sugar quota, that interfere with trade. With this background, we can return to the political debate over whether the United States benefits from international trade. We begin by looking at how large a role international trade plays in the U.S. economy.

8.1 LEARNING OBJECTIVE

8.1 | Discuss the role of international trade in the U.S. economy.

The United States in the International Economy

International trade has grown tremendously over the past 50 years. The increase in trade is the result of the falling costs of shipping products around the world, the spread of inexpensive and reliable communications, and changes in government policies. Firms can use large container ships to send their products across the oceans at low cost. Businesspeople today can travel to Europe or Asia using fast, inexpensive, and reliable air transportation. The Internet allows managers to communicate instantaneously and at a very low cost with customers and suppliers around the world. These and other improvements in transportation and communication have created a global marketplace that earlier generations of businesspeople could only dream of.

Tariff A tax imposed by a government on imports.

Imports Goods and services bought domestically but produced in other countries.

Exports Goods and services produced domestically but sold to other countries.

In addition, over the past 50 years, many governments have changed policies to facilitate international trade. For example, tariff rates have fallen. A **tariff** is a tax imposed by a government on *imports* of a good into a country. **Imports** are goods and services bought domestically but produced in other countries. In the 1930s, the United States charged an average tariff rate above 50 percent. Today, the rate is less than 2 percent. In North America, most tariffs between Canada, Mexico, and the United States were eliminated following the passage of the North American Free Trade Agreement (NAFTA) in 1994. Twenty-seven countries in Europe have formed the European Union, which has eliminated all tariffs among member countries, greatly increasing both imports and **exports**, which are goods and services produced domestically but sold to other countries.

The Importance of Trade to the U.S. Economy

U.S. consumers buy increasing quantities of goods and services produced in other countries. At the same time, U.S. businesses sell increasing quantities of goods and services to consumers in other countries. Figure 8-1 shows that since 1950, both exports and imports have been steadily increasing as a fraction of U.S. gross domestic product (GDP). Recall that GDP is the value of all the goods and services produced in a country during a year. In 1950, exports and imports were both about 4 percent of GDP. In 2007, exports were about 12 percent of GDP, and imports were about 17 percent.

Not all sectors of the U.S. economy are affected equally by international trade. For example, although it's difficult to import or export some services, such as haircuts or appendectomies, a large percentage of U.S. agricultural production is exported. Each year, the United States exports about 50 percent of the wheat crop, 40 percent of the rice crop, and 20 percent of the corn crop.

Many U.S. manufacturing industries also depend on trade. About 20 percent of U.S. manufacturing jobs depend directly or indirectly on exports. In some industries, such as computers, the products these workers make are directly exported. In other industries, such as steel, the products are used to make other products, such as bulldozers or

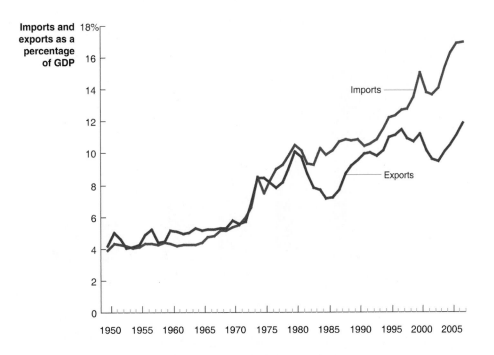

Figure 8-1

International Trade Is of Increasing Importance to the United States

Exports and imports of goods and services as a percentage of total production—measured by GDP—show the importance of international trade to an economy. Since 1950, both imports and exports have been steadily rising as a fraction of the U.S. GDP.
Source: U.S. Department of Commerce, Bureau of Economic Analysis.

machine tools, that are then exported. In all, about two-thirds of U.S. manufacturing industries depend on exports for at least 10 percent of jobs.

U.S. International Trade in a World Context

The United States is the largest exporter in the world, as Figure 8-2 illustrates. Six of the other seven leading exporting countries are also high-income countries. Although China is still a relatively low-income country, the rapid growth of the Chinese economy over the past 20 years has resulted in its becoming the third largest exporter.

International trade remains less important to the United States than it is to most other countries. Figure 8-3 shows that imports and exports remain smaller fractions of GDP in the United States than in other countries. In some smaller countries, like Belgium, imports and exports make up more than half of GDP. Japan is the only high-income country that is less dependent on international trade than is the United States.

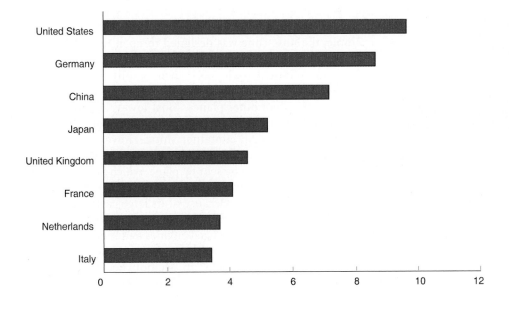

Figure 8-2

The Eight Leading Exporting Countries

The United States is the leading exporting country, accounting for about 10 percent of total world exports. The values are the shares of total world exports of merchandise and commercial services.
Source: World Trade Organization, *International Trade Statistics*, 2007.

Figure 8-3

International Trade as a Percentage of GDP

International trade is still less important to the United States than to most other countries, with the exception of Japan.
Source: Organization for Economic Cooperation and Development.

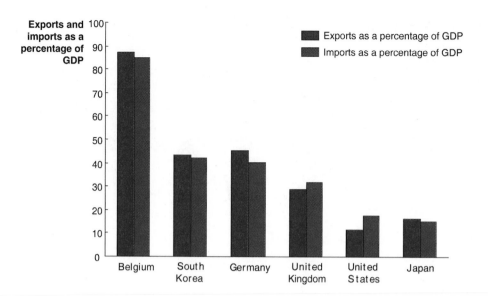

Making the Connection

How Expanding International Trade Has Helped Boeing

The Boeing 747 jumbo jet was a wonder of modern technology when it was introduced in 1970. With a much wider body than existing passenger planes, the 747 had two aisles, with as many as 10 seats per row, and could carry more than 500 passengers. Many early models had a second level with a passenger lounge, complete with a piano. Its range of more than 5,000 miles made it a truly intercontinental plane.

By the late 1990s, however, Boeing, which is based in Chicago and assembles the 747 outside of Seattle, Washington, was experiencing declining sales for the plane. Planes with newer technology were being introduced, and rising prices for jet fuel led some airlines to conclude that jumbo jets were too costly to operate. The decline in passenger travel after September 11, 2001, appeared to be the last nail in the 747's coffin. An executive for Airbus, a European firm that is Boeing's main competitor, boasted, "The 747 is on its last legs. It doesn't have any legs to stand on. Boeing is trying to breathe life into a 1960s-era design. There is only so much you can do with a plane." But in the past few years, the 747 has gone through an unexpected revival, spurred largely by recent growth in international trade. In the 1960s, Boeing's managers made the important decision that the 747 be designed to serve as both a cargo plane and a passenger plane. For example, the nose cone was designed to open to make loading cargo easier.

As international trade has grown rapidly in the past few years, so has the demand for the 747 because the plane has larger cargo capacity than other planes. Most low-value goods being shipped long distances—for instance, from China to Europe— are still sent by sea on container ships. However, high-value goods—such as computers, televisions, and some food products— are increasingly likely to be sent by plane, which is a much faster and safer method of shipping. Air freight shipments have been growing at the rapid rate of 6 percent per year. Because of its large carrying capacity, currently about 60 percent of all air freight worldwide is carried on 747s. The latest model, the 747-400, has new, technologically advanced engines and redesigned wings. It has a maximum speed of 675 miles per hour and has a range of more than 7,500 miles—enough to fly nonstop from Los Angeles to Melbourne, Australia. The increased fuel efficiency of the new engines has reduced operating costs. In 2006,

Rapid growth of international trade has spurred demand for the 747 because it has a larger cargo capacity than other planes.

Boeing received orders for 67 airplanes worth $16.75 billion. That's good news for Boeing's 120,000 employees in the United States.

Sources: Leslie Wayne, "Boeing Not Afraid to Say 'Sold Out,' " *New York Times*, November 28, 2006; Leslie Wayne, "Far from Extinct," *New York Times*, December 7, 2006; and Leslie Wayne, "Still Flying High," *New York Times*, December 25, 2006.

YOUR TURN: Test your understanding by doing related problem 1.4 on page 270 at the end of this chapter.

8.2 | Understand the difference between comparative advantage and absolute advantage in international trade.

Comparative Advantage in International Trade

Why have businesses around the world increasingly looked for markets in other countries? Why have consumers increasingly purchased goods and services made in other countries? People trade for one reason: Trade makes them better off. Whenever a buyer and seller agree to a sale, they must both believe they are better off; otherwise, there would be no sale. This outcome must hold whether the buyer and seller live in the same city or in different countries. As we will see, governments are more likely to interfere with international trade than they are with domestic trade, but the reasons for the interference are more political than economic.

A Brief Review of Comparative Advantage

In Chapter 2, we discussed the key economic concept of *comparative advantage*. **Comparative advantage** is the ability of an individual, a firm, or a country to produce a good or service at a lower opportunity cost than competitors. Recall that **opportunity cost** is the highest-valued alternative that must be given up to engage in an activity. People, firms, and countries specialize in economic activities in which they have a comparative advantage. In trading, we benefit from the comparative advantage of other people (or firms or countries), and others benefit from our comparative advantage.

A good way to think of comparative advantage is to recall the example in Chapter 2 of you and your neighbor picking fruit. Your neighbor is better at picking both apples and cherries than you are. Why, then, doesn't your neighbor pick both types of fruit? Because the opportunity cost to your neighbor of picking her own apples is very high: She is a particularly skilled cherry picker, and every hour spent picking apples is an hour taken away from picking cherries. You can pick apples at a much lower opportunity cost than your neighbor, so you have a comparative advantage in picking apples. Your neighbor can pick cherries at a much lower opportunity cost than you can, so she has a comparative advantage in picking cherries. Your neighbor is better off specializing in picking cherries, and you are better off specializing in picking apples. You can then trade some of your apples for some of your neighbor's cherries, and both of you will end up with more of each fruit.

Comparative Advantage in International Trade

The principle of comparative advantage can explain why people pursue different occupations. It can also explain why countries produce different goods and services. International trade involves many countries importing and exporting many different goods and services. Countries are better off if they specialize in producing the goods for which they have a comparative advantage. They can then trade for the goods for which other countries have a comparative advantage.

We can illustrate why specializing on the basis of comparative advantage makes countries better off with a simple example involving just two countries and two products.

Comparative advantage The ability of an individual, a firm, or a country to produce a good or service at a lower opportunity cost than competitors.

Opportunity cost The highest-valued alternative that must be given up to engage in an activity.

TABLE 8-1

An Example of Japanese Workers Being More Productive Than American Workers

	OUTPUT PER HOUR OF WORK	
	CELL PHONES	DIGITAL MUSIC PLAYERS
JAPAN	12	6
UNITED STATES	2	4

Absolute advantage The ability to produce more of a good or service than competitors when using the same amount of resources.

Suppose the United States and Japan produce only cell phones and digital music players, like Apple's iPod. Assume that each country uses only labor to produce each good, and that Japanese and U.S. cell phones and digital music players are exactly the same. Table 8-1 shows how much each country can produce of each good with one hour of labor.

Notice that Japanese workers are more productive than U.S. workers in making both goods. In one hour of work, Japanese workers can make six times as many cell phones and one and one-half times as many digital music players as U.S. workers. Japan has an *absolute advantage* over the United States in producing both goods. **Absolute advantage** is the ability to produce more of a good or service than competitors when using the same amount of resources. In this case, Japan can produce more of both goods using the same amount of labor as the United States.

It might seem at first that Japan has nothing to gain from trading with the United States because it has an absolute advantage in producing both goods. However, Japan should specialize and produce only cell phones and obtain the digital music players it needs by exporting cell phones to the United States in exchange for digital music players. The reason that Japan benefits from trade is that although it has an *absolute advantage* in the production of both goods, it has a *comparative advantage* only in the production of cell phones. The United States has a comparative advantage in the production of digital music players.

If it seems contrary to common sense that Japan should import digital music players from the United States even though Japan can produce more players per hour of work, think about the opportunity cost to each country of producing each good. If Japan wants to produce more digital music players, it has to switch labor away from cell phone production. Every hour of labor switched from producing cell phones to producing digital music players increases digital music player production by 6 and reduces cell phone production by 12. Japan has to give up 12 cell phones for every 6 digital music players it produces. Therefore, the opportunity cost to Japan of producing one more digital music player is 12/6, or 2 cell phones.

If the United States switches one hour of labor from cell phones to digital music players, production of cell phones falls by 2, and production of digital music players rises by 4. Therefore, the opportunity cost to the United States of producing one more digital music player is 2/4, or 0.5 cell phone. The United States has a lower opportunity cost of producing digital music players and, therefore, has a comparative advantage in making this product. By similar reasoning, we can see that Japan has a comparative advantage in producing cell phones. Table 8-2 summarizes the opportunity each country faces in producing these goods.

TABLE 8-2

The Opportunity Costs of Producing Cell Phones and Digital Music Players

The table shows the opportunity cost each country faces in producing cell phones and digital music players. For example, the entry in the first row and second column shows that Japan must give up 2 cell phones for every digital music player it produces.

	OPPORTUNITY COSTS	
	CELL PHONES	DIGITAL MUSIC PLAYERS
JAPAN	0.5 digital music player	2 cell phones
UNITED STATES	2 digital music players	0.5 cell phone

How Countries Gain from International Trade

Can Japan really gain from producing only cell phones and trading with the United States for digital music players? To see that it can, assume at first that Japan and the United States do not trade with each other. A situation in which a country does not trade with other countries is called **autarky**. Assume that in autarky each country has 1,000 hours of labor available to produce the two goods, and each country produces the quantities of the two goods shown in Table 8-3. Because there is no trade, these quantities also represent consumption of the two goods in each country.

Autarky A situation in which a country does not trade with other countries.

Increasing Consumption through Trade

Suppose now that Japan and the United States begin to trade with each other. The **terms of trade** is the ratio at which a country can trade its exports for imports from other countries. For simplicity, let's assume that the terms of trade end up with Japan and the United States being willing to trade one cell phone for one digital music player.

Terms of trade The ratio at which a country can trade its exports for imports from other countries.

Once trade has begun, the United States and Japan can exchange digital music players for cell phones or cell phones for digital music players. For example, if Japan specializes by using all 1,000 available hours of labor to produce cell phones, it will be able to produce 12,000. It then could export 1,500 cell phones to the United States in exchange for 1,500 digital music players. (Remember: We are assuming that the terms of trade are one cell phone for one digital music player.) Japan ends up with 10,500 cell phones and 1,500 digital music players. Compared with the situation before trade, Japan has the same number of digital music players but 1,500 more cell phones. If the United States specializes in producing digital music players, it will be able to produce 4,000. It could then export 1,500 digital music players to Japan in exchange for 1,500 cell phones. The United States ends up with 2,500 digital music players and 1,500 cell phones. Compared with the situation before trade, the United States has the same number of cell phones but 1,500 more digital music players. Trade has allowed both countries to increase the quantities of goods consumed. Table 8-4 summarizes the gains from trade for the United States and Japan.

By trading, Japan and the United States are able to consume more than they could without trade. This outcome is possible because world production of both goods increases after trade. (Remember that, in this example, our "world" consists of just the United States and Japan.)

Why does total production of cell phones and digital music players increase when the United States specializes in producing digital music players and Japan specializes in producing cell phones? A domestic analogy helps to answer this question: If a company shifts production from an old factory to a more efficient modern factory, its output will increase. In effect, the same thing happens in our example. Producing digital music players in Japan and cell phones in the United States is inefficient. Shifting production to the more efficient country—the one with the comparative advantage—increases total production. The key point is this: *Countries gain from specializing in producing goods in which they have a comparative advantage and trading for goods in which other countries have a comparative advantage.*

	PRODUCTION AND CONSUMPTION	
	CELL PHONES	DIGITAL MUSIC PLAYERS
JAPAN	9,000	1,500
UNITED STATES	1,500	1,000

TABLE 8-3

Production without Trade

TABLE 8-4

The Gains from Trade for Japan and the United States

WITHOUT TRADE

Production and Consumption

	CELL PHONES	MP3 PLAYERS
Japan	9,000	1,500
United States	1,500	1,000

WITH TRADE

	Production with Trade		Trade		Consumption with Trade	
	CELL PHONES	MP3 PLAYERS	CELL PHONES	MP3 PLAYERS	CELL PHONES	MP3 PLAYERS
Japan	12,000	0	Export 1,500	Import 1,500	10,500	1,500
United States	0	4,000	Import 1,500	Export 1,500	1,500	2,500

With trade, the United States and Japan specialize in the good they have a comparative advantage in producing . . .

. . . and export some of that good in exchange for the good the other country has a comparative advantage in producing.

GAINS FROM TRADE

Increased Consumption

| Japan | 1,500 Cell Phones |
| United States | 1,500 MP3 Players |

The increased consumption made possible by trade represents the gains from trade.

Solved Problem | 8-3

The Gains from Trade

The first discussion of comparative advantage appears in *On the Principles of Political Economy and Taxation,* a book written by David Ricardo in 1817. Ricardo provided a famous example of the gains from trade, using wine and cloth production in Portugal and England. The following table is adapted from Ricardo's example, with cloth measured in sheets and wine measured in kegs.

OUTPUT PER YEAR OF LABOR		
	CLOTH	WINE
PORTUGAL	100	150
ENGLAND	90	60

a. Explain which country has an absolute advantage in the production of each good.

b. Explain which country has a comparative advantage in the production of each good.

c. Suppose that Portugal and England currently do not trade with each other. Each country has 1,000 workers, so each has 1,000 years of labor time to use producing cloth and wine, and the countries are currently producing the amounts of each good shown in the table:

	CLOTH	WINE
PORTUGAL	18,000	123,000
ENGLAND	63,000	18,000

Show that Portugal and England can both gain from trade. Assume that the terms of trade are that one sheet of cloth can be traded for one keg of wine.

SOLVING THE PROBLEM:

Step 1: **Review the chapter material.** This problem is about absolute and comparative advantage and the gains from trade, so you may want to review the section "Comparative Advantage in International Trade," which begins on page 247, and the section "How Countries Gain from International Trade," which begins on page 249.

Step 2: **Answer question (a) by determining which country has an absolute advantage.** Remember that a country has an absolute advantage over another country when it can produce more of a good using the same resources. The first table in the problem shows that Portugal can produce more cloth *and* more wine with one year's worth of labor than can England. Thus, Portugal has an absolute advantage in the production of both goods and, therefore, England does not have an absolute advantage in the production of either good.

Step 3: **Answer question (b) by determining which country has a comparative advantage.** A country has a comparative advantage when it can produce a good at a lower opportunity cost. To produce 100 sheets of cloth, Portugal must give up 150 kegs of wine. Therefore, the opportunity cost to Portugal of producing one sheet of cloth is 150/100, or 1.5 kegs of wine. England has to give up 60 kegs of wine to produce 90 sheets of cloth, so its opportunity cost of producing one sheet of cloth is 60/90, or 0.67 keg of wine. The opportunity costs of producing wine can be calculated in the same way. The following table shows the opportunity cost to Portugal and England of producing each good.

OPPORTUNITY COSTS

	CLOTH	WINE
PORTUGAL	1.5 kegs of wine	0.67 sheets of cloth
ENGLAND	0.67 keg of wine	1.5 sheets of cloth

Portugal has a comparative advantage in wine because its opportunity cost is lower. England has a comparative advantage in cloth because its opportunity cost is lower.

Step 4: **Answer question (c) by showing that both countries can benefit from trade.** By now it should be clear that both countries will be better off if they specialize where they have a comparative advantage and trade for the other product. The following table is very similar to Table 8-4 and shows one example of trade making both countries better off. (To test your understanding, construct another example.)

WITHOUT TRADE

	PRODUCTION AND CONSUMPTION	
	CLOTH	WINE
PORTUGAL	18,000	123,000
ENGLAND	63,000	18,000

WITH TRADE

	PRODUCTION WITH TRADE		TRADE		CONSUMPTION WITH TRADE	
	CLOTH	WINE	CLOTH	WINE	CLOTH	WINE
PORTUGAL	0	150,000	Import 18,000	Export 18,000	18,000	132,000
ENGLAND	90,000	0	Export 18,000	Import 18,000	72,000	18,000

GAINS FROM TRADE

	INCREASED CONSUMPTION
PORTUGAL	9,000 wine
ENGLAND	9,000 cloth

YOUR TURN: For more practice, do related problems 3.4 and 3.5 on page 272 at the end of this chapter.

>> **End Solved Problem 8-3**

Why Don't We See Complete Specialization?

In our example of two countries producing only two products, each country specializes in producing one of the goods. In the real world, many goods and services are produced in more than one country. For example, the United States and Japan both produce automobiles. We do not see complete specialization in the real world for three main reasons:

- *Not all goods and services are traded internationally.* Even if, for example, Japan had a comparative advantage in the production of medical services, it would be difficult for Japan to specialize in producing medical services and then export them. There is no easy way for U.S. patients who need appendectomies to receive them from surgeons in Japan.

- *Production of most goods involves increasing opportunity costs.* Recall from Chapter 2 that production of most goods involves increasing opportunity costs. As a result, when the United States devotes more workers to producing digital music players, the opportunity cost of producing more digital music players will increase. At some point, the opportunity cost of producing digital music players in the United States may rise to the level of the opportunity cost of producing digital music players in Japan. When that happens, international trade will no longer push the United States further toward complete specialization. The same will be true of Japan: Increasing opportunity cost will cause Japan to stop short of complete specialization in producing cell phones.

- *Tastes for products differ.* Most products are *differentiated*. Cell phones, digital music players, cars, and televisions—to name just a few products—come with a wide variety of features. When buying automobiles, some people look for reliability and good gasoline mileage, others look for room to carry seven passengers, and still others want styling and high performance. So, some car buyers prefer Toyota Prius hybrids, some prefer Chevy Suburbans, and others prefer BMWs. As a result, Japan, the United States, and Germany may each have a comparative advantage in producing different types of automobiles.

Does Anyone Lose as a Result of International Trade?

In our cell phone and digital music player example, consumption increases in both the United States and Japan as a result of trade. Everyone gains, and no one loses. Or do they? In our example, we referred repeatedly to "Japan" or the "United States" producing cell phones or digital music players. But countries do not produce goods—firms do. In a

---

Don't Let This Happen to **YOU!**

Remember That Trade Creates Both Winners and Losers

The following statement is from a Federal Reserve publication: "Trade is a win–win situation for all countries that participate." Statements like this are sometimes taken to mean that there are no losers from international trade. But notice that the statement refers to *countries*, not individuals. When countries participate in trade, they make their consumers better off by increasing the quantity of goods and services available to them. As we have seen, however, expanding trade eliminates the jobs of workers employed at companies that are less efficient than foreign companies. Trade also creates new jobs at companies that export to foreign markets. It may be difficult, though, for workers who

lose their jobs because of trade to easily find others. That is why in the United States, the federal government uses the Trade Adjustment Assistance program to provide funds for workers who have lost their jobs due to international trade. These funds can be used for retraining, for searching for new jobs, or for relocating to areas where new jobs are available. This program—and similar programs in other countries—recognizes that there are losers from international trade as well as winners.

Source: Quote from Federal Reserve Bank of Dallas Web site, *International Trade and the Economy,* www.dallasfed.org/educate/everyday/ev7.html.

YOUR TURN: Test your understanding by doing related problem 3.12 on page 272 at the end of this chapter.

world without trade, there would be cell phone and digital music player firms in both Japan and the United States. In a world with trade, there would only be Japanese cell phone firms and U.S. digital music player firms. Japanese digital music player firms and U.S. cell phone firms would close. Overall, total employment will not change and production will increase as a result of trade. Nevertheless, the owners of Japanese digital music player firms, the owners of U.S. cell phone firms, and the people who work for them are worse off as a result of trade. The losers from trade are likely to do their best to convince the Japanese and U.S. governments to interfere with trade by barring imports of the competing products from the other country or by imposing high tariffs on them.

Where Does Comparative Advantage Come From?

Among the main sources of comparative advantage are the following:

- *Climate and natural resources.* This source of comparative advantage is the most obvious. Because of geology, Saudi Arabia has a comparative advantage in the production of oil. Because of climate and soil conditions, Costa Rica has a comparative advantage in the production of bananas, and the United States has a comparative advantage in the production of wheat.

- *Relative abundance of labor and capital.* Some countries, such as the United States, have many highly skilled workers and a great deal of machinery. Other countries, such as China, have many unskilled workers and relatively little machinery. As a result, the United States has a comparative advantage in the production of goods that require highly skilled workers or sophisticated machinery to manufacture, such as aircraft, semiconductors, and computer software. China has a comparative advantage in the production of goods that require unskilled workers and small amounts of simple machinery, such as children's toys.

- *Technology.* Broadly defined, *technology* is the process firms use to turn inputs into goods and services. At any given time, firms in different countries do not all have access to the same technologies. In part, this difference is the result of past investments countries have made in supporting higher education or in providing support for research and development. Some countries are strong in *product technologies*, which involve the ability to develop new products. For example, firms in the United States have pioneered the development of such products as televisions, digital computers, airliners, and many prescription drugs. Other countries are strong in *process technologies*, which involve the ability to improve the processes used to make existing products. For example, firms in Japan, such as Toyota and Nissan, have succeeded by greatly improving the processes for designing and manufacturing automobiles.

- *External economies.* It is difficult to explain the location of some industries on the basis of climate, natural resources, the relative abundance of labor and capital, or technology. For example, why does Southern California have a comparative advantage in making movies or Switzerland in making watches or New York in providing financial services? The answer is that once an industry becomes established in an area, firms that locate in that area gain advantages over firms located elsewhere. The advantages include the availability of skilled workers, the opportunity to interact with other firms in the same industry, and being close to suppliers. These advantages result in lower costs to firms located in the area. Because these lower costs result from increases in the size of the industry in an area, economists refer to them as **external economies**.

External economies Reductions in a firm's costs that result from an increase in the size of an industry.

Making the Connection | Why Is Dalton, Georgia, the Carpet-Making Capital of the World?

Factories within a 65-mile radius of Dalton, Georgia account for 80 percent of U.S. carpet production and more than half of world carpet production. Carpet production is highly automated and relies primarily on synthetic fibers. Dalton, a small city located in rural northwest Georgia, would not seem to have any advantages in carpet production. In fact, the location of the carpet industry in Dalton was a historical accident.

In the early 1900s, Catherine Evans Whitener started making bedspreads using a method called "tufting," in which she sewed cotton yarn through the fabric and then cut the ends of the yarn so it would fluff up. These bedspreads became very popular. By the 1930s, the process was mechanized and was then applied to carpets. In the early years, the industry used cotton grown in Georgia, but today synthetic fibers, such as nylon and olefin, have largely replaced cotton and wool in carpet manufacturing.

More than 170 carpet factories are now located in the Dalton area. Supporting the carpet industry are local yarn manufacturers, machinery suppliers, and maintenance firms. Dye plants have opened solely to supply the carpet industry. Printing shops have opened, solely to print tags and labels for carpets. Box factories have opened to produce cartons designed specifically for shipping carpets. The local workforce has developed highly specialized skills for running and maintaining the carpet-making machinery.

Because Catherine Evans Whitener started making bedspreads by hand in Dalton, Georgia, 100 years ago, a multibillion-dollar carpet industry is now located there.

A company establishing a carpet factory outside the Dalton area is unable to use the suppliers or the skilled workers available to factories in Dalton. As a result, carpet factories located outside Dalton may have higher costs than factories located in Dalton. Although there is no particular reason why the carpet industry should have originally located in Dalton, external economies gave the area a comparative advantage in carpet making once it began to grow there.

YOUR TURN: Test your understanding by doing related problem 3.13 on page 272 at the end of this chapter.

Comparative Advantage Over Time: The Rise and Fall—and Rise—of the U.S. Consumer Electronics Industry

A country may develop a comparative advantage in the production of a good, and then, as time passes and circumstances change, the country may lose its comparative advantage in producing that good and develop a comparative advantage in producing other goods. For several decades, the United States had a comparative advantage in the production of consumer electronic goods, such as televisions, radios, and stereos. The comparative advantage of the United States in these products was based on having developed most of the underlying technology, having the most modern factories, and having a skilled and experienced workforce. Gradually, however, other countries, particularly Japan, gained access to the technology, built modern factories, and developed skilled workforces. As mentioned earlier, Japanese firms have excelled in process technologies, which involve the ability to improve the processes used to make existing products. By the 1970s and 1980s, Japanese firms were able to produce many consumer electronic goods more cheaply and with higher quality than could U.S. firms. Japanese firms Sony, Panasonic, and Pioneer replaced U.S. firms Magnavox, Zenith, and RCA as world leaders in consumer electronics.

By 2008, however, as the technology underlying consumer electronics evolved, comparative advantage had shifted again, and several U.S. firms surged ahead of their Japanese competitors. For example, Apple Computer had developed the iPod and iPhone; Linksys, a division of Cisco Systems, took the lead in home wireless networking technology; and Kodak developed digital cameras with EasyShare software that made it easy to organize, enhance, and share digital pictures. As pictures and music converted to digital data, process technologies became less important than the ability to design and develop new products. These new consumer electronics products required skills similar to those in computer design and software writing, where the United States had long maintained a comparative advantage.

Once a country has lost its comparative advantage in producing a good, its income will be higher and its economy will be more efficient if it switches from producing the good to importing it, as the United States did when it switched from producing televisions to importing them. As we will see in the next section, however, there is often political pressure on governments to attempt to preserve industries that have lost their comparative advantage.

8.4 | Analyze the economic effects of government policies that restrict international trade.

8.4 LEARNING OBJECTIVE

Government Policies That Restrict International Trade

Free trade, or trade between countries that is without government restrictions, makes consumers better off. We can expand on this idea by using the concepts of consumer surplus and producer surplus from Chapter 4. Figure 8-4 shows the market for the biofuel ethanol in the United States, assuming autarky, where the United States does not trade with other countries. The equilibrium price of ethanol is $2.00 per gallon, and the equilibrium quantity is 6.0 billion gallons per year. The blue area represents consumer surplus, and the red area represents producer surplus.

Now suppose that the United States begins importing ethanol from Brazil and other countries that produce lower-priced sugar-based ethanol and that ethanol is selling in those countries for $1.00 per gallon. Because the world market for ethanol is large, we will assume that the United States can buy as much ethanol as it wants without causing

Free trade Trade between countries that is without government restrictions.

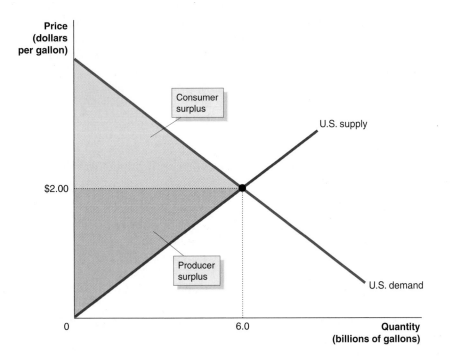

Figure 8-4

The U.S. Market for Ethanol under Autarky

This figure shows the market for ethanol in the United States, assuming autarky, where the United States does not trade with other countries. The equilibrium price of ethanol is $2.00 per gallon, and the equilibrium quantity is 6.0 billion gallons per year. The blue area represents consumer surplus, and the red area represents producer surplus.

Figure 8-5

The Effect of Imports on the U.S. Ethanol Market

When imports are allowed into the United States, the price of ethanol falls from $2.00 to $1.00. U.S. consumers increase their purchases from 6.0 billion gallons to 9.0 billion gallons. Equilibrium moves from point *F* to point *G*. U.S. producers reduce the quantity of ethanol they supply from 6.0 billion gallons to 3.0 billion gallons. Imports equal 6.0 billion gallons, which is the difference between U.S. consumption and U.S. production. Consumer surplus equals the areas *A*, *B*, *C*, and *D*. Producer surplus equals the area *E*.

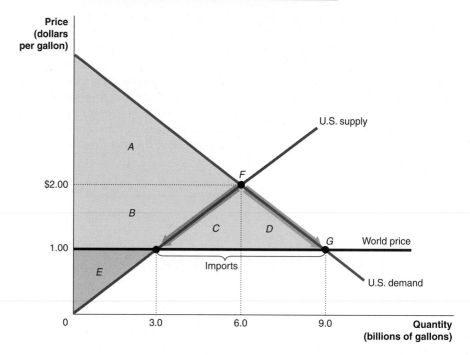

	Under Autarky	With Imports
Consumer Surplus	A	A + B + C + D
Producer Surplus	B + E	E
Economic Surplus	A + B + E	A + B + C + D + E

the *world price* of $1.00 per gallon to rise. Therefore, once imports of ethanol are permitted into the United States, U.S. firms will not be able to sell ethanol at prices higher than the world price of $1.00, and the U.S. price will become equal to the world price.

Figure 8-5 shows the result of allowing imports of ethanol into the United States. With the price lowered from $2.00 to $1.00, U.S. consumers increase their purchases from 6.0 billion gallons to 9.0 billion gallons. Equilibrium moves from point *F* to point *G*. In the new equilibrium, U.S. producers have reduced the quantity of ethanol they supply from 6.0 billion gallons to 3.0 billion gallons. Imports will equal 6.0 billion gallons, which is the difference between U.S. consumption and U.S. production.

Under autarky, consumer surplus would be area *A* in Figure 8-5. With imports, the reduction in price increases consumer surplus, so it is now equal to the sum of areas *A*, *B*, *C*, and *D*. Although the lower price increases consumer surplus, it reduces producer surplus. Under autarky, producer surplus was equal to the sum of the areas *B* and *E*. With imports, producer surplus is equal to only area *E*. Recall that economic surplus equals the sum of consumer surplus and producer surplus. Moving from autarky to allowing imports increases economic surplus in the United States by an amount equal to the sum of areas *C* and *D*.

We can conclude that international trade helps consumers but hurts firms that are less efficient than foreign competitors. As a result, these firms and their workers are often strong supporters of government policies that restrict trade. These policies usually take one of two forms:

- Tariffs

- Quotas and voluntary export restraints

Tariffs

The most common interferences with trade are *tariffs*, which are taxes imposed by a government on goods imported into a country. Like any other tax, a tariff increases the cost of selling a good. Figure 8-6 shows the impact of a tariff of $0.50 per gallon on ethanol

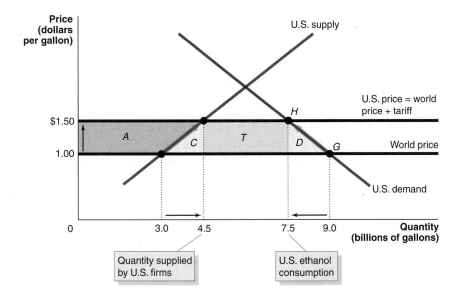

Loss of Consumer Surplus	=	Increase in Producer Surplus	+	Government Tariff Revenue	+	Deadweight Loss
A + C + T + D		A		T		C + D

Figure 8-6

The Effects of a Tariff on Ethanol

Without a tariff on ethanol, U.S. producers will sell 3.0 billion gallons of ethanol, U.S. consumers will purchase 9.0 billion gallons, and imports will be 6.0 billion gallons. The U.S. price will equal the world price of $1.00 per gallon. The $0.50-per-gallon tariff raises the price of ethanol in the United States to $1.50 per gallon, and U.S. producers increase the quantity they supply to 4.5 billion gallons. U.S. consumers reduce their purchases to 7.5 billion gallons. Equilibrium moves from point *G* to point *H*. The ethanol tariff causes a loss of consumer surplus equal to the area *A* + *C* + *T* + *D*. The area *A* is the increase in producer surplus due to the higher price. The area *T* is the government's tariff revenue. The areas *C* and *D* represent deadweight loss.

imports into the United States. The $0.50 tariff raises the price of ethanol in the United States from the world price of $1.00 per gallon to $1.50 per gallon. At this higher price, U.S. ethanol producers increase the quantity they supply from 3.0 billion gallons to 4.5 billion gallons. U.S. consumers, though, cut back their purchases of ethanol from 9.0 billion gallons to 7.5 billion gallons. Imports decline from 6.0 billion gallons (9 billion − 6 billion) to 3.0 billion (7.5 billion − 4.5 billion). Equilibrium moves from point *G* to point *H*.

By raising the price of ethanol from $1.00 to $1.50, the tariff reduces consumer surplus by the sum of areas *A*, *T*, *C*, and *D*. Area *A* is the increase in producer surplus from the higher price. The government collects tariff revenue equal to the tariff of $0.50 per gallon multiplied by the 3.0 billion gallons imported. Area *T* represents the government's tariff revenue. Areas *C* and *D* represent losses to U.S. consumers that are not captured by anyone. They are deadweight loss and represent the decline in economic efficiency resulting from the ethanol tariff. Area *C* shows the effect on U.S. consumers of being forced to buy from U.S. producers who are less efficient than foreign producers, and area *D* shows the effect of U.S. consumers buying less ethanol than they would have at the world price. As a result of the tariff, economic surplus has been reduced by the sum of areas *C* and *D*. Recall from Chapter 4 that deadweight loss represents a loss of economic efficiency.

We can conclude that the tariff succeeds in helping U.S. ethanol producers but hurts U.S. consumers and the efficiency of the U.S. economy.

Quotas and Voluntary Export Restraints

A **quota** is a numeric limit on the quantity of a good that can be imported, and it has an effect similar to a tariff. A quota is imposed by the government of the importing country. A **voluntary export restraint (VER)** is an agreement negotiated between two countries that places a numeric limit on the quantity of a good that can be imported by one country from the other country. In the early 1980s, the United States and Japan negotiated a VER that limited the quantity of automobiles the United States would import from Japan. The Japanese government agreed to the VER primarily because it was afraid

Quota A numeric limit imposed by a government on the quantity of a good that can be imported into the country.

Voluntary export restraint (VER) An agreement negotiated between two countries that places a numeric limit on the quantity of a good that can be imported by one country from the other country.

that if it did not, the United States would impose a tariff or quota on imports of Japanese automobiles. Quotas and VERs have similar economic effects.

The main purpose of most tariffs and quotas is to reduce the foreign competition that domestic firms face. We saw an example of this at the beginning of this chapter when we discussed the sugar quota, which Congress imposed to protect U.S. sugar producers. Figure 8-7 shows the actual statistics for the U.S. sugar market in 2006. The effect of a quota is very similar to the effect of a tariff. By limiting imports, a quota forces the domestic price of a good above the world price. In this case, the sugar quota limits sugar imports to 3.5 billion pounds (shown by the bracket in Figure 8-7), forcing the U.S. price of sugar up to $0.22 per pound, or $0.10 higher than the world price. The U.S. price is above the world price because the quota keeps foreign sugar producers from selling the additional sugar in the United States that would drive the price down to the world price. At a price of $0.22 cents per pound, U.S. producers increased the quantity of sugar they supply from 5.9 billion pounds to 18.0 billion pounds, and U.S. consumers cut back their purchases of sugar from 23.1 billion pounds to 21.5 billion pounds. Equilibrium moves from point *E* to point *F*.

Measuring the Economic Effect of the Sugar Quota

Once again, we can use the concepts of consumer surplus, producer surplus, and deadweight loss to measure the economic impact of the sugar quota. Without a sugar quota, the world price of $0.12 per pound would also be the U.S. price. In Figure 8-7, consumer surplus equals the area above the $0.12 price line and below the demand curve. The sugar quota causes the U.S. price to rise to $0.22 and reduces consumer surplus by the area $A + B + C + D$. Without a sugar quota, producer surplus received by U.S. sugar producers would be equal to the area below the $0.12 price line and above the supply

Figure 8-7

The Economic Effect of the U.S. Sugar Quota

Without a sugar quota, U.S. sugar producers would have sold 5.9 billion pounds of sugar, U.S. consumers would have purchased 23.1 billion pounds of sugar, and imports would have been 17.2 billion pounds. The U.S. price would have equaled the world price of $0.12 per pound. Because the sugar quota limits imports to 3.5 billion pounds (the bracket in the graph), the price of sugar in the United States rises to $0.22 per pound, and U.S. producers increase the quantity of sugar they supply to 18.0 billion pounds. U.S. consumers reduce their sugar purchases to 21.5 billion pounds. Equilibrium moves from point *E* to point *F*. The sugar quota causes a loss of consumer surplus equal to the area $A + B + C + D$. The area *A* is the gain to U.S. sugar producers. The area *B* is the gain to foreign sugar producers. The areas *C* and *D* represent deadweight loss. The total loss to U.S. consumers in 2006 was $2.24 billion.

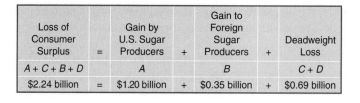

Loss of Consumer Surplus	=	Gain by U.S. Sugar Producers	+	Gain to Foreign Sugar Producers	+	Deadweight Loss
$A + C + B + D$	=	A	+	B	+	$C + D$
$2.24 billion	=	$1.20 billion	+	$0.35 billion	+	$0.69 billion

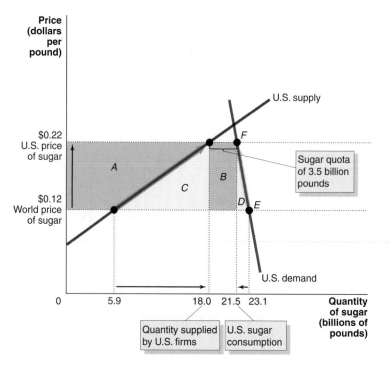

curve. The higher U.S. price resulting from the sugar quota increases the producer surplus of U.S. sugar producers by an amount equal to area *A*.

A foreign producer must have a license from the U.S. government to import sugar under the quota system. Therefore, a foreign sugar producer that is lucky enough to have an import license also benefits from the quota because it is able to sell sugar on the U.S. market at $0.22 per pound instead of $0.12 per pound. The gain to foreign sugar producers is area *B*. Areas *A* and *B* represent transfers from U.S. consumers of sugar to U.S. and foreign producers of sugar. Areas *C* and *D* represent losses to U.S. consumers that are not captured by anyone. They are deadweight losses and represent the decline in economic efficiency resulting from the sugar quota. Area *C* shows the effect of U.S. consumers being forced to buy from U.S. producers that are less efficient than foreign producers, and area *D* shows the effect of U.S. consumers buying less sugar than they would have at the world price.

Figure 8-7 provides enough information to calculate the dollar value of each of the four areas. The results of these calculations are shown in the table in the figure. The total loss to consumers from the sugar quota was $2.24 billion in 2006. About 53 percent of the loss to consumers, or $1.20 billion, was gained by U.S. sugar producers as increased producer surplus. About 16 percent, or $0.35 billion, was gained by foreign sugar producers as increased producer surplus, and about 31 percent, or $0.69 billion, was a deadweight loss to the U.S. economy. The U.S. International Trade Commission estimates that eliminating the sugar quota would result in the loss of about 3,000 jobs in the U.S. sugar industry. The cost to U.S. consumers of saving these jobs is equal to $2.24 billion/3,000, or about $750,000 per job. In fact, this cost is an underestimate because eliminating the sugar quota would result in new jobs being created, particularly in the candy industry. As we saw at the beginning of this chapter, U.S. candy companies have been moving factories to other countries to escape the impact of the sugar quota.

Solved Problem | 8-4

Measuring the Economic Effect of a Quota

Suppose that the United States currently both produces and imports apples. The U.S. government then decides to restrict international trade in apples by imposing a quota that allows imports of only 4 million boxes of apples into the United States each year. The figure shows the results of imposing the quota.

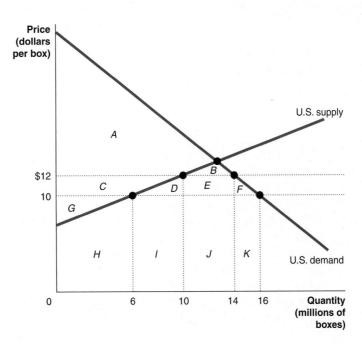

Fill in the following table, using the prices, quantities, and letters in the figure:

	WITHOUT QUOTA	WITH QUOTA
World price of apples	_____	_____
U.S. price of apples	_____	_____
Quantity supplied by U.S. firms	_____	_____
Quantity demanded by U.S. consumers	_____	_____
Quantity imported	_____	_____
Area of consumer surplus	_____	_____
Area of producer surplus	_____	_____
Area of deadweight loss	_____	_____

SOLVING THE PROBLEM:

Step 1: **Review the chapter material.** This problem is about measuring the economic effects of a quota, so you may want to review the section "Quotas and Voluntary Export Restraints," which begins on page 257, and "Measuring the Economic Effect of the Sugar Quota," which begins on page 258.

Step 2: **Fill in the table.** After studying Figure 8-7, you should be able to fill in the table. Remember that consumer surplus is the area below the demand curve and above the market price.

	WITHOUT QUOTA	WITH QUOTA
World price of apples	$10	$10
U.S. price of apples	$10	$12
Quantity supplied by U.S. firms	6 million boxes	10 million boxes
Quantity demanded by U.S. consumers	16 million boxes	14 million boxes
Quantity imported	10 million boxes	4 million boxes
Area of consumer surplus	$A + B + C + D + E + F$	$A + B$
Area of domestic producer surplus	G	$G + C$
Area of deadweight loss	No deadweight loss	$D + F$

>> **End Solved Problem 8-4**   **YOUR TURN:** For more practice, do related problem 4.14 on page 274 at the end of this chapter.

The High Cost of Preserving Jobs with Tariffs and Quotas

The sugar quota is not alone in imposing a high cost on U.S. consumers to save jobs at U.S. firms. Table 8-5 shows, for several industries, the cost tariffs and quotas impose on U.S. consumers per year for each job saved.

Many countries besides the United States also use tariffs and quotas to try to protect jobs. Table 8-6 shows the cost to Japanese consumers per year for each job saved as a result of tariffs and quotas in the listed industries. Note the staggering cost of $51 million for each job saved that is imposed on Japanese consumers by the Japanese government's restrictions on imports of rice.

Just as the sugar quota costs jobs in the candy industry, other tariffs and quotas cost jobs outside the industries immediately affected. For example, in 1991, the United States imposed tariffs on flat-panel displays used in laptop computers. This was good news for U.S. producers of these displays but bad news for companies producing laptop computers. Toshiba, Sharp, and Apple all closed their U.S. laptop production facilities and moved production overseas. In fact, whenever one industry receives tariff or quota protection, jobs are lost in other domestic industries.

PRODUCT	NUMBER OF JOBS SAVED	COST TO CONSUMERS PER YEAR FOR EACH JOB SAVED
Benzenoid chemicals	216	$1,376,435
Luggage	226	1,285,078
Softwood lumber	605	1,044,271
Dairy products	2,378	685,323
Frozen orange juice	609	635,103
Ball bearings	146	603,368
Machine tools	1,556	479,452
Women's handbags	773	263,535
Canned tuna	390	257,640

TABLE 8-5

Preserving U.S. Jobs with Tariffs and Quotas Is Expensive

Source: Federal Reserve Bank of Dallas, *2002 Annual Report*, Exhibit 11.

Gains from Unilateral Elimination of Tariffs and Quotas

Some politicians argue that eliminating U.S. tariffs and quotas would help the U.S. economy only if other countries eliminated their tariffs and quotas in exchange. It is easier to gain political support for reducing or eliminating tariffs or quotas if it is done as part of an agreement with other countries that involves their eliminating some of their tariffs or quotas. But as the example of the sugar quota shows, *the U.S. economy would gain from the elimination of tariffs and quotas even if other countries do not reduce their tariffs and quotas.*

Other Barriers to Trade

In addition to tariffs and quotas, governments sometimes erect other barriers to trade. For example, all governments require that imports meet certain health and safety requirements. Sometimes, however, governments use these requirements to shield domestic firms from foreign competition. This can be true when a government imposes stricter health and safety requirements on imported goods than on goods produced by domestic firms.

PRODUCT	COST TO CONSUMERS PER YEAR FOR EACH JOB SAVED
Rice	$51,233,000
Natural gas	27,987,000
Gasoline	6,329,000
Paper	3,813,000
Beef, pork, and poultry	1,933,000
Cosmetics	1,778,000
Radio and television sets	915,000

TABLE 8-6

Preserving Japanese Jobs with Tariffs and Quotas Is Also Expensive

Source: Yoko Sazabami, Shujiro Urata, and Hiroki Kawai, *Measuring the Cost of Protection in Japan*, Washington, DC: Institute for International Economics, 1995. Used with permission.

Many governments also restrict imports of certain products on national security grounds. The argument is that in time of war, a country should not be dependent on imports of critical war materials. Once again, these restrictions are sometimes used more to protect domestic companies from competition than to protect national security. For example, for years, the U.S. government would buy military uniforms only from U.S. manufacturers, even though uniforms are not a critical war material.

8.5 LEARNING OBJECTIVE

8.5 | Evaluate the arguments over trade policy and globalization.

The Argument over Trade Policies and Globalization

The argument over whether the U.S. government should regulate international trade dates back to the early days of the country. One particularly controversial attempt to restrict trade took place during the Great Depression of the 1930s. At that time, the United States and other countries attempted to help domestic firms by raising tariffs on foreign imports. The United States started the process by passing the Smoot-Hawley Tariff in 1930, which raised average tariff rates to more than 50 percent. As other countries retaliated by raising their tariffs, international trade collapsed.

By the end of World War II in 1945, government officials in the United States and Europe were looking for a way to reduce tariffs and revive international trade. To help achieve this goal, they set up the General Agreement on Tariffs and Trade (GATT) in 1948. Countries that joined GATT agreed not to impose new tariffs or import quotas. In addition, a series of *multilateral negotiations*, called *trade rounds*, took place, in which countries agreed to reduce tariffs from the very high levels of the 1930s.

In the 1940s, most international trade was in goods, and the GATT agreement covered only goods. In the following decades, trade in services and in products incorporating *intellectual property*, such as software programs and movies, grew in importance. Many GATT members pressed for a new agreement that would cover services and intellectual property, as well as goods. A new agreement was negotiated, and in January 1995, GATT was replaced by the **World Trade Organization (WTO)**, headquartered in Geneva, Switzerland. More than 130 countries are currently members of the WTO.

World Trade Organization (WTO) An international organization that oversees international trade agreements.

Why Do Some People Oppose the World Trade Organization?

During the years immediately after World War II, many low-income, or developing, countries erected high tariffs and restricted investment by foreign companies. When these policies failed to produce much economic growth, many of these countries decided during the 1980s to become more open to foreign trade and investment. This process became known as **globalization**. Most developing countries joined the WTO and began to follow its policies.

During the 1990s, opposition to globalization began to increase. In 1999, this opposition took a violent turn at a meeting of the WTO in Seattle, Washington. The purpose of the meeting was to plan a new round of negotiations aimed at further reductions in trade barriers. A large number of protestors assembled in Seattle to meet the WTO delegates. Protests started peacefully but quickly became violent. Protesters looted stores and burned cars, and many delegates were unable to leave their hotel rooms.

Why would attempts to reduce trade barriers with the objective of increasing income around the world cause such a furious reaction? The opposition to the WTO comes from three sources. First, some opponents are specifically against the globalization process that began in the 1980s and became widespread in the 1990s. Second, other opponents have the same motivation as the supporters of tariffs in the 1930s—to erect trade barriers to protect domestic firms from foreign competition. Third, some critics of the WTO support globalization in principle but believe that the WTO favors

Globalization The process of countries becoming more open to foreign trade and investment.

the interests of the high-income countries at the expense of the low-income countries. Let's look more closely at the sources of opposition to the WTO.

Anti-Globalization Many of the protestors in Seattle distrust globalization. Some believe that free trade and foreign investment destroy the distinctive cultures of many countries. As developing countries began to open their economies to imports from the United States and other high-income countries, these imports of food, clothing, movies, and other goods began to replace the equivalent local products. So, a teenager in Thailand might be sitting in a McDonald's restaurant, wearing Levi's jeans and a Ralph Lauren shirt, listening to a recording by U2 on his iPod, before going to the local movie theater to watch *Spider-Man 3*. Globalization has increased the variety of products available to consumers in developing countries, but some people argue that this is too high a price to pay for what they see as damage to local cultures.

Globalization has also allowed multinational corporations to relocate factories from high-income countries to low-income countries. These new factories in Indonesia, Malaysia, Pakistan, and other countries pay much lower wages than are paid in the United States, Europe, and Japan and often do not meet the environmental or safety regulations that are imposed in high-income countries. Some factories use child labor, which is illegal in high-income countries. Some people have argued that firms with factories in developing countries should pay workers wages as high as those paid in the high-income countries. They also believe these firms should follow the health, safety, and environmental regulations that exist in the high-income countries.

The governments of most developing countries have resisted these proposals. They argue that when the currently rich countries were poor, they also lacked environmental or safety standards, and their workers were paid low wages. They argue that it is easier for rich countries to afford high wages and environmental and safety regulations than it is for poor countries. They also point out that many jobs that seem very poorly paid by high-income country standards are often better than the alternatives available to workers in low-income countries.

Making the Connection | The Unintended Consequences of Banning Goods Made with Child Labor

In many developing countries, such as Indonesia, Thailand, and Peru, children as young as seven or eight work 10 or more hours a day. Reports of very young workers laboring long hours, producing goods for export, have upset many people in high-income countries. In the United States, boycotts have been organized against stores that stock goods made in developing countries with child labor. Many people assume that if child workers in developing countries weren't working in factories making clothing, toys, and other products, they would be in school, as are children in high-income countries.

In fact, children in developing countries usually have few good alternatives to work. Schooling is frequently available for only a few months each year, and even children who attend school rarely do so for more than a few years. Poor families are often unable to afford even the small costs of sending their children to school. Families may even rely on the earnings of very young children

Would eliminating child labor in developing countries be a good thing?

to survive, as poor families once did in the United States, Europe, and Japan. There is substantial evidence that as incomes begin to rise in poor countries, families rely less on child labor. The United States eventually outlawed child labor, but not until 1938. In developing countries where child labor is common today, jobs producing export goods are usually better paying and less hazardous than the alternatives.

As preparations began in France for the 1998 World Cup, there were protests that Baden Sports—the main supplier of soccer balls—was purchasing the balls from suppliers in Pakistan that used child workers. France decided to ban all use of soccer balls made by child workers. Bowing to this pressure, Baden Sports moved production from Pakistan, where the balls were hand-stitched by child workers, to China, where the balls were machine-stitched by adult workers in factories. There was some criticism of the boycott of hand-stitched soccer balls at the time. In a broad study of child labor, three economists argued:

> Of the array of possible employment in which impoverished children might engage, soccer ball stitching is probably one of the most benign. . . . [In Pakistan] children generally work alongside other family members in the home or in small workshops. . . . Nor are the children exposed to toxic chemicals, hazardous tools or brutal working conditions. Rather, the only serious criticism concerns the length of the typical child stitcher's work-day and the impact on formal education.

In fact, the alternatives to soccer ball stitching for child workers in Pakistan turned out to be extremely grim. According to Keith Maskus, an economist at the University of Colorado and the World Bank, a "large proportion" of the children who lost their jobs stitching soccer balls ended up begging or in prostitution.

Sources: Drusilla K. Brown, Alan V. Deardorff, and Robert M. Stern, "U.S. Trade and Other Policy Options to Deter Foreign Exploitation of Child Labor," in Magnus Blomstrom and Linda S. Goldberg, eds., *Topics in Empirical International Economics: A Festschrift in Honor of Bob Lipsey*, Chicago: University of Chicago Press, 2001; Tomas Larsson, *The Race to the Top: The Real Story of Globalization*, Washington, DC: Cato Institute, 2001, p. 48; and Eric V. Edmonds and Nina Pavcnik, "Child Labor in the Global Economy," *Journal of Economic Perspectives*, Vol. 19, No. 1, Winter 2005, pp. 199–220.

YOUR TURN: Test your understanding by doing related problem 5.5 on page 275 at the end of this chapter.

———

"Old-Fashioned" Protectionism The anti-globalization argument against free trade and the WTO is relatively new. Another argument against free trade, called *protectionism*, has been around for centuries. **Protectionism** is the use of trade barriers to shield domestic firms from foreign competition. For as long as international trade has existed, governments have attempted to restrict it to protect domestic firms. As we saw with the analysis of the sugar quota, protectionism causes losses to consumers and eliminates jobs in the domestic industries that use the protected product. In addition, by reducing the ability of countries to produce according to comparative advantage, protectionism reduces incomes.

Why, then, does protectionism attract support? Protectionism is usually justified on the basis of one of the following arguments:

Protectionism The use of trade barriers to shield domestic firms from foreign competition.

- *Saving jobs.* Supporters of protectionism argue that free trade reduces employment by driving domestic firms out of business. It is true that when more-efficient foreign firms drive less-efficient domestic firms out of business, jobs are lost, but jobs are also lost when more-efficient domestic firms drive less-efficient domestic firms out of business. These job losses are rarely permanent. In the U.S. economy, jobs are lost and new jobs are created continually. No economic study has ever found a long-term connection between the total number of jobs available and the level of tariff protection for domestic industries. In addition, trade restrictions destroy jobs in some industries at the same time that they preserve jobs in others. The U.S. sugar quota may have saved jobs in the U.S. sugar industry, but, as we saw at the beginning of this chapter, it also has destroyed jobs in the U.S. candy industry.

- *Protecting high wages.* Some people worry that firms in high-income countries will have to start paying much lower wages to compete with firms in developing countries.

This fear is misplaced, however, because free trade actually raises living standards by increasing economic efficiency. When a country practices protectionism and produces goods and services it could obtain more inexpensively from other countries, it reduces its standard of living. The United States could ban imports of coffee and begin growing it domestically. But this would entail a very high opportunity cost because coffee could only be grown in the continental United States in greenhouses and would require large amounts of labor and equipment. The coffee would have to sell for a very high price to cover these costs. Suppose the United States did ban coffee imports: Eliminating the ban at some future time would eliminate the jobs of U.S. coffee workers, but the standard of living in the United States would rise as coffee prices declined and labor, machinery, and other resources moved out of coffee production and into production of goods and services for which the United States has a comparative advantage.

- *Protecting infant industries.* It is possible that firms in a country may have a comparative advantage in producing a good, but because the country begins production of the good later than other countries, its firms initially have higher costs. In producing some goods and services, substantial "learning by doing" occurs. As workers and firms produce more of the good or service, they gain experience and become more productive. Over time, costs and prices will fall. As the firms in the "infant industry" gain experience, their costs will fall, and they will be able to compete successfully with foreign producers. Under free trade, however, they may not get the chance. The established foreign producers can sell the product at a lower price and drive domestic producers out of business before they gain enough experience to compete. To economists, this is the most persuasive of the protectionist arguments. It has a significant drawback, however. Tariffs used to protect an infant industry eliminate the need for the firms in the industry to become productive enough to compete with foreign firms. After World War II, the governments of many developing countries used the "infant industry" argument to justify high tariff rates. Unfortunately, most of their infant industries never grew up, and they continued for years as inefficient drains on their economies.

- *Protecting national security.* As already discussed, a country should not rely on other countries for goods that are critical to its military defense. For example, the United States would probably not want to import all its jet fighter engines from China. The definition of which goods are critical to military defense is a slippery one, however. In fact, it is rare for an industry to ask for protection without raising the issue of national security, even if its products have mainly nonmilitary uses.

Dumping

In recent years, the United States has extended protection to some domestic industries by using a provision in the WTO agreement that allows governments to impose tariffs in the case of *dumping*. **Dumping** is selling a product for a price below its cost of production. Although allowable under the WTO agreement, using tariffs to offset the effects of dumping is very controversial.

Dumping Selling a product for a price below its cost of production.

In practice, it is difficult to determine whether foreign companies are dumping goods because the true production costs of a good are not easy for foreign governments to calculate. As a result, the WTO allows countries to determine that dumping has occurred if a product is exported for a lower price than it sells for on the home market. There is a problem with this approach, however. Often there are good business reasons for a firm to sell a product for different prices to different consumers. For example, the airlines charge business travelers higher ticket prices than leisure travelers. Firms also use "loss leaders"—products that are sold below cost, or even given away free—when introducing a new product or, in the case of retailing, to attract customers who will also buy full-price products. For example, when Sun Microsystems attempted to establish StarOffice as a competitor to Microsoft Office, Sun gave the software away free on its Web site. During the Christmas season, Wal-Mart sometimes offers toys at prices below what they pay to buy them from manufacturers. It's unclear why these normal business practices should be unacceptable when used in international trade.

Positive versus Normative Analysis (Once Again)

Economists emphasize the burden on the economy imposed by tariffs, quotas, and other government restrictions on free trade. Does it follow that these interferences are bad? Remember from Chapter 1 the distinction between *positive analysis* and *normative analysis*. Positive analysis concerns what *is*. Normative analysis concerns what *ought to be*. Measuring the impact of the sugar quota on the U.S. economy is an example of positive analysis. Asserting that the sugar quota is bad public policy and should be eliminated is normative analysis. The sugar quota—like all other interferences with trade—makes some people better off and some people worse off, and it reduces total income and consumption. Whether increasing the profits of U.S. sugar companies and the number of workers they employ justifies the costs imposed on consumers and the reduction in economic efficiency is a normative question.

Most economists do not support interferences with trade, such as the sugar quota. Few people become economists if they don't believe that markets should usually be as free as possible. But the opposite view is certainly intellectually respectable. It is possible for someone to understand the costs of tariffs and quotas but still believe that tariffs and quotas are a good idea, perhaps because they believe unrestricted free trade would cause too much disruption to the economy.

The success of industries in getting the government to erect barriers to foreign competition depends partly on some members of the public knowing full well the costs of trade barriers but supporting them anyway. However, two other factors are also at work:

1 The costs tariffs and quotas impose on consumers are large in total but relatively small per person. For example, the sugar quota imposes a total burden of about $2.24 billion per year on consumers. Spread across 300 million Americans, the burden is only about $7.50 per person: too little for most people to worry about, even if they know the burden exists.

2 The jobs lost to foreign competition are easy to identify, but the jobs created by foreign trade are less easy to identify.

In other words, the industries that benefit from tariffs and quotas benefit a lot—the sugar quota increases the profits of U.S. sugar producers by more than $1 billion—whereas each consumer loses relatively little. This concentration of benefits and widely spread burdens makes it easy to understand why members of Congress receive strong pressure from some industries to enact tariffs and quotas and relatively little pressure from the general public to reduce them.

Making the Connection | Trade Policy in the New Administration

During the 2008 presidential election, Barack Obama, the Democratic nominee, argued that some existing trade agreements, such as the North American Free Trade Agreement (NAFTA), which went into effect in 1994, were flawed. NAFTA eliminated most tariffs on products shipped between the United States, Canada, and Mexico. Supporters of NAFTA argue that the treaty had made it possible for each of these countries to better pursue its comparative advantage. For example, before NAFTA, the Mexican government had used tariffs to protect its domestic automobile industry, but that industry was much less efficient than the U.S. automobile industry. When tariffs were removed, Mexican consumers could take advantage of the efficiency of the U.S. industry, and U.S. exports of motor vehicles to Mexico soared.

Similarly, Canadian consumers could take advantage of lower-priced U.S. beef, and U.S. consumers could take advantage of lower-priced Canadian lumber. As we would expect, expanding trade increased consumption in all three countries. Some early opponents of NAFTA argued that it would lead to a loss of jobs in the United States. Although employment in some industries did decline following the passage of NAFTA, overall employment in the United States increased by more than 23 million between the time NAFTA took effect and 2008.

Obama argued, though, that NAFTA and other trade agreements, such as the Central American Free Trade Agreement, were flawed because they failed to require that U.S. trading partners enact labor regulations and environmental protections similar to those in the United States. In some countries, workers are denied the right to join unions and sometimes work in unsafe conditions. Obama pledged that as president he would "use trade agreements to spread good labor and environmental standards around the world." It is unclear how willing the Mexican and Canadian governments might be to renegotiate NAFTA, or whether other U.S. trading partners would be willing to rewrite their labor and environmental laws in order to reach trade agreements with the United States. The new Obama administration is also expected to push for additional government payments to workers who lose their jobs as a result of competition from foreign firms. Like most presidents before him, Barack Obama will have to balance the efficiency gains from freer trade against the disruptive effects of trade, which often make agreements such as NAFTA politically unpopular.

Source: "The More Things Change," *Economist*, October 23, 2008.

This Emyco shoe factory in Mexico produces shoes, boots, and sandals for the Mexican and U.S. markets. During the 2008 presidential campaign, Barack Obama proposed renegotiating NAFTA with the governments of Mexico and Canada.

YOUR TURN: Test your understanding by doing related problem 5.7 on page 276 at the end of this chapter.

Economics in YOUR Life!

>> Continued from page 243

At the beginning of the chapter, we asked you to consider how sugar companies have convinced Congress to enact the sugar quota and why relatively few people have heard of this quota. In the chapter, we saw that the sugar quota costs U.S. consumers more than $2 billion per year as a result of higher sugar prices and has led several U.S. candy makers to eliminate domestic jobs and move their facilities to other countries. This might seem to increase the mystery of why Congress has enacted the sugar quota, especially because it saves relatively few jobs in the U.S. sugar industry. We have also seen, though, that *per person*, the burden of the sugar quota is small—only about $7.50 per person per year. Not many people will take the trouble of writing a letter to their member of Congress or otherwise make their views known in the hope of saving $7.50 per year. In fact, few people will even spend the time to become aware that the quota exists. So, if before you read this chapter you had never heard of the sugar quota, you are certainly not alone.

Conclusion

There are few issues economists agree upon more than the economic benefits of free trade. However, there are few political issues as controversial as government policy toward trade. Many people who would be reluctant to see the government interfere with domestic trade are quite willing to see it interfere with international trade. The damage high tariffs inflicted on the world economy during the 1930s shows what can happen when governments around the world abandon free trade. Whether future episodes of that type can be avoided is by no means certain.

Read *An Inside Look at Policy* on the next page for a discussion of how eliminating tariffs on cars and other goods benefits the United States and South Korea.

The United States and South Korea Reach a Trade Deal

NEW YORK TIMES, APRIL 3, 2007

U.S. and South Korea Agree to Sweeping Trade Deal

United States and South Korean negotiators struck the world's largest bilateral free trade agreement on Monday, giving the United States a badly needed lift to its trade policy at home and South Korea a chance to reinvigorate its export economy. . . .

If ratified, the trade deal would eliminate tariffs on more than 90 percent of the product categories traded between the countries. South Korea agreed to lift trade barriers to important American products like cars and beef, while the United States agreed to allow Seoul to continue to subsidize South Korean rice. . . .

As South Korean workers and farmers protested in the streets—on Sunday, one man even set himself on fire—negotiators haggled to the end early Monday.

(a) The breakthrough came when both sides compromised on the most delicate deal-breaking issues. Washington dropped its demand that the South Korean government stop protecting its politically powerful rice farmers, and Seoul agreed to resume imports of American beef, halted three years ago over fears of mad cow disease, if, as expected, the World Organization on Animal Health declares United States meat safe in a ruling next month.

South Korea also agreed to phase out the 40 percent tariff on American beef over 15 years. It will remove an 8 percent duty on cars and revise a domestic vehicle tax system that United States officials say discriminates against American cars with bigger engines.

The United States will eliminate the 2.5 percent tariff on South Korean cars with engines smaller than 3,000 cubic centimeters; phase out the 25 percent duty on trucks over the course of 10 years; and remove tariffs, which average 8.9 percent, on 61 percent of South Korean textiles. . . .

The deal is the biggest of its kind for the United States since the North American Free Trade Agreement in 1994 with Canada and Mexico. It is Washington's first bilateral trade pact with a major Asian economy.

(b) Studies have estimated that the accord would add $20 billion to bilateral trade, estimated last year at $78 billion. Potential gains to the United States economy range from $17 billion to $43 billion, according to Usha C. H. Haley, director of the Global Business Center at the University of New Haven. South Korea's exports to the United States are expected to rise in the first year by 12 percent.

Analysts doubt that the deal will provide an immediate lift to American car manufacturers. Only 5,000 American cars were sold here last year, while South Korean automakers sold 800,000 vehicles in the United States. The gap accounted for 80 percent of the $13 billion United States trade deficit with South Korea last year.

American officials hope that the deal will placate American cattle farmers, who are struggling to recapture global market share after an outbreak of mad cow disease in late 2003. Before the import ban, South Korea was the world's third-largest consumer of American beef, importing $800 million a year.

Consumers in both countries are the deal's biggest winners. Hyundai cars and Samsung flat-panel TV sets, as well as Korean-made clothing, will become significantly cheaper in the United States.

American beef and oranges, as well as Ford cars and Toyota vehicles built in the United States, will be more affordable in South Korea. South Korean TV networks will be able to broadcast more American movies and TV series like "CSI," which already command a huge following here, after Seoul eases a cap on foreign content to 80 percent of total airtime from 75 percent.

(c) The deal entails heavy political costs for South Korea, which can expect the loss of tens of thousands of farming jobs. Up to 2 trillion won ($2.2 billion) in agricultural revenue will be lost as cheap American corn, soybeans and processed foods come in, according to studies by South Korean economists. . . .

Key Points in the Article

The article discusses a recent trade agreement negotiated between the United States and South Korea that will reduce restrictions on trade between the two countries. Agreements such as this one to expand trade between two countries are known as *bilateral agreements*. The trade agreements worked out by the World Trade Organization are *multilateral agreements*. Neither Congress nor the South Korean National Assembly has yet ratified the agreement. However, if the legislatures do ratify the agreement, a free-trade zone covering the world's largest and eleventh-largest economies would be created.

Analyzing the News

ⓐ In this chapter, we have seen that expanding trade raises living standards by increasing consumption and economic efficiency. Reducing tariffs on trade between South Korea and the United States will aid consumers in both countries. The figure shows the U.S. market following the elimination of the tariff on South Korean cars. (For simplicity, we assume that there are no remaining U.S. tariffs on cars.) The price of cars in the United States falls from P_1 to P_2, and equilibrium in the U.S. car market moves from point E to point F. U.S. consumption of cars increases from Q_3 to Q_4, the quantity of cars supplied by U.S. car makers declines from Q_2 to Q_1, and imports increase from $Q_3 - Q_2$ to $Q_4 - Q_1$. Consumer surplus increases by the sum of areas A, B, C, and D. Area A represents a transfer from producer surplus under the tariff to consumer surplus. Areas C and D represent the conversion of deadweight loss to consumer surplus. Area B represents a conversion of government tariff revenue to consumer surplus. Eliminating the tariff reduces the cost to South Korean car producers of selling their product in the United States. U.S. consumers purchase a larger quantity of South Korean cars at a lower price.

ⓑ The figure shows that eliminating the tariff on cars also eliminates the revenue the U.S. government had been collecting from this tariff. In high-income countries, such as the United States, governments receive most of their revenue from taxes on personal and corporate income. For example, tariff revenue in the United States for 2006 amounted to only about 1 percent of all revenue received by the federal government, but governments in low-income countries often have difficulty collecting income taxes, so they rely heavily on tariffs for revenue. In these countries, the government's need for revenue can pose a serious barrier to expanding international trade by reducing tariffs because governments have difficulty replacing the revenues lost from tariff reductions. This was also true in the United States early in its history. In 1800, tariffs brought in 90 percent of all federal government revenue. As late as the 1950s, tariffs accounted for 14 percent of federal revenues.

ⓒ Trade benefits the entire economy but can create losses for certain groups in the economy. While South Korean consumers will gain from less expensive food, agricultural interests in South Korea will be hurt. These interests are likely to lobby against ratification of the agreement.

Thinking Critically About Policy

1. Tariffs on South Korean car and textile imports save jobs for Americans working in those industries. Do you support these tariffs? Why or why not?
2. In which goods mentioned in the article does the United States have a comparative advantage? In which does South Korea have a comparative advantage? Explain your reasoning.

Increase in Consumer Surplus	=	Decrease in Producer Surplus	+	Decrease in Government Tariff Revenue	+	Decrease in Deadweight Loss
$A + C + B + D$		A		B		$C + D$

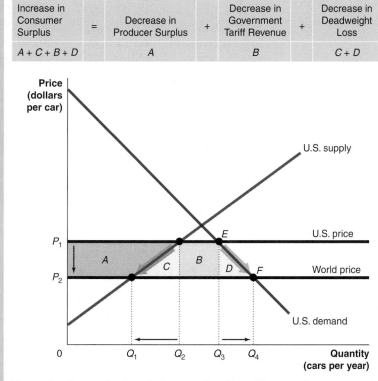

The market for cars in the United States after the tariff on South Korean cars is eliminated.

Key Terms

Absolute advantage, p. 248

Autarky, p. 249

Comparative advantage, p. 247

Dumping, p. 266

Exports, p. 244

External economies, p. 253

Free trade, p. 255

Globalization, p. 262

Imports, p. 244

Opportunity cost, p. 247

Protectionism, p. 264

Quota, p. 257

Tariff, p. 244

Terms of trade, p. 249

Voluntary export restraint (VER), p. 257

World Trade Organization (WTO), p. 262

8.1 LEARNING OBJECTIVE   8.1 | Discuss the role of international trade in the U.S. economy, **pages 244–247.**

The United States in the International Economy

Summary

International trade has been increasing in recent decades, in part because of reductions in *tariffs* and other barriers to trade. A **tariff** is a tax imposed by a government on imports. The quantity of goods and services the United States imports and exports has been continually increasing. **Imports** are goods and services bought domestically but produced in other countries. **Exports** are goods and services produced domestically but sold to other countries. Today, the United States is the leading exporting country in the world, and about 20 percent of U.S. manufacturing jobs depend on exports.

myeconlab Visit www.myeconlab.com to complete these exercises *Get Ahead of the Curve* online and get instant feedback.

Review Questions

1.1 Briefly explain whether you agree or disagree with the following statement: "International trade is more important to the U.S. economy than to most other economies."

Problems and Applications

1.2 If the United States were to stop trading goods and services with other countries, which U.S. industries would be likely to see their sales decline the most? Briefly explain.

1.3 Briefly explain whether you agree with the following statement: "Japan has always been much more heavily involved in international trade than are most other nations. In fact, today Japan exports a larger fraction of its GDP than do Germany, Great Britain, or the United States."

1.4 (Related to the *Making the Connection* on page 246) Some politicians in the United States believe that European governments unfairly help Airbus, Boeing's main competitor, by subsidizing, or making payments, to Airbus. Suppose that the U.S. Congress passes legislation forbidding U.S. airlines from buying planes from Airbus or any other non-U.S. aircraft firm. Would this legislation be likely to actually help Boeing? Briefly explain.

>> End Learning Objective 8.1

8.2 LEARNING OBJECTIVE   8.2 | Understand the difference between comparative advantage and absolute advantage in international trade, **pages 247–248.**

Comparative Advantage in International Trade

Summary

Comparative advantage is the ability of an individual, a business, or a country to produce a good or service at the lowest **opportunity cost**. **Absolute advantage** is the ability to produce more of a good or service than competitors when using the same amount of resources. Countries trade on the basis of comparative advantage, not on the basis of absolute advantage.

 myeconlab Visit www.myeconlab.com to complete these exercises *Get Ahead of the Curve* online and get instant feedback.

Review Questions

2.1 A World Trade Organization publication calls comparative advantage "arguably the single most powerful insight in economics." What is comparative advantage? What makes it such a powerful insight?

Source: World Trade Organization, *Trading into the Future*, April 1999.

2.2 What is the difference between absolute advantage and comparative advantage? Will a country always be an exporter of a good where it has an absolute advantage in production?

Problems and Applications

2.3 Why do the goods that countries import and export change over time? Use the concept of comparative advantage in your answer.

2.4 Briefly explain whether you agree with the following argument: "Unfortunately, Bolivia does not have a comparative advantage with respect to the United States in the production of any good or service." (*Hint:* You do not need any specific information about the economies of Bolivia or the United States to be able to answer this question.)

2.5 In 1987, an economic study showed that, on average, workers in the Japanese consumer electronics industry produced less output per hour than did U.S. workers producing the same goods. Despite this fact, Japan exported large quantities of consumer electronics to the United States. Briefly explain how this is possible.

Source: Study cited in Douglas A. Irwin, *Free Trade under Fire*, Princeton, NJ: Princeton University Press, 2002, p. 27.

2.6 Patrick J. Buchanan, a former presidential candidate, argues in his book on the global economy that there is a flaw in David Ricardo's theory of comparative advantage:

> Classical free trade theory fails the test of common sense. According to Ricardo's law of comparative advantage ... if America makes better computers and textiles than China does, but our advantage in computers is greater than our advantage in textiles, we should (1) focus on computers, (2) let China make textiles, and (3) trade U.S. computers for Chinese textiles. . . .
>
> The doctrine begs a question. If Americans are more efficient than Chinese in making clothes . . . why surrender the more efficient American industry? Why shift to a reliance on a Chinese textile industry that will take years to catch up to where American factories are today?

Do you agree with Buchanan's argument? Briefly explain.

Source: Patrick J. Buchanan, *The Great Betrayal: How American Sovereignty and Social Justice Are Being Sacrificed to the Gods of the Global Economy*, Boston: Little, Brown, 1998, p. 66.

>> End Learning Objective 8.2

8.3 LEARNING OBJECTIVE   8.3 | Explain how countries gain from international trade, **pages 249–255.**

How Countries Gain from International Trade

Summary

Autarky is a situation in which a country does not trade with other countries. The **terms of trade** is the ratio at which a country can trade its exports for imports from other countries. When a country specializes in producing goods where it has a comparative advantage and trades for the other goods it needs, the country will have a higher level of income and consumption. We do not see complete specialization in production for three reasons: Not all goods and services are traded internationally, production of most goods involves increasing opportunity costs, and tastes for products differ across countries. Although the population of a country as a whole benefits from trade, companies—and their workers—that are unable to compete with lower-cost foreign producers lose. Among the main sources of comparative advantage are climate and natural resources, relative abundance of labor and capital, technology, and *external economies*. **External economies** are reductions in a firm's cost that result from an increase in the size of an industry. A country may develop a comparative advantage in the production of a good, and then as time passes and circumstances change, the country may lose its comparative advantage in producing that good and develop a comparative advantage in producing other goods.

myeconlab Visit www.myeconlab.com to complete these exercises
Get Ahead of the Curve online and get instant feedback.

Review Questions

3.1 Briefly explain how international trade increases a country's consumption.

3.2 What is meant by a country specializing in the production of a good? Is it typical for countries to be completely specialized? Briefly explain.

3.3 What are the main sources of comparative advantage?

Problems and Applications

3.4 (Related to *Solved Problem 8-3* on page 250) The following table shows the hourly output per worker in two industries in Chile and Argentina.

	OUTPUT PER HOUR OF WORK	
	HATS	BEER
CHILE	8	6
ARGENTINA	1	2

a. Explain which country has an absolute advantage in the production of hats and which country has an absolute advantage in the production of beer.

b. Explain which country has a comparative advantage in the production of hats and which country has a comparative advantage in the production of beer.

c. Suppose that Chile and Argentina currently do not trade with each other. Each has 1,000 hours of labor to use producing hats and beer, and the countries are currently producing the amounts of each good shown in the following table.

	HATS	BEER
CHILE	7,200	600
ARGENTINA	600	800

Using this information, give a numeric example of how Chile and Argentina can both gain from trade. Assume that after trading begins, one hat can be exchanged for one barrel of beer.

3.5 (Related to *Solved Problem 8-3* on page 250) A political commentator makes the following statement:

> The idea that international trade should be based on the comparative advantage of each country is fine for rich countries like the United States and Japan. Rich countries have educated workers and large quantities of machinery and equipment. These advantages allow them to produce every product more efficiently than poor countries can. Poor countries like Kenya and Bolivia have nothing to gain from international trade based on comparative advantage.

Do you agree with this argument? Briefly explain.

3.6 Demonstrate how the opportunity costs of producing cell phones and digital music players in Japan and the United States were calculated in Table 8-2 on page 248.

3.7 Briefly explain whether you agree or disagree with the following statement: "Most countries exhaust their comparative advantage in producing a good or service before they reach complete specialization."

3.8 Is free trade likely to benefit a large, populous country more than a small country with fewer people? Briefly explain.

3.9 A Federal Reserve publication offers the following observation: "Too many U.S. citizens associate free trade with job losses rather than opportunities and a higher standard of living." Do you agree? Briefly explain.

Source: Surya Sen and Dan Wassmann, *The Great Trade Debate: From Rhetoric to Reality*, Federal Reserve Bank of Chicago, January 1999.

3.10 Hal Varian, an economist at the University of California, Berkeley, has made two observations about international trade:

a. Trade allows a country "to produce more with less."

b. There is little doubt who wins [from trade] in the long run: consumers.

Briefly explain whether you agree with either or both of these observations.

Source: Hal R. Varian, "The Mixed Bag of Productivity," *New York Times*, October 23, 2003.

3.11 In a recent public opinion poll, 41 percent of people responding believed that free trade hurts the U.S. economy, while only 28 percent believed that it helps the economy. (The remaining people were uncertain of the effects of free trade.) What is "free trade"? Do you believe it helps or hurts the economy? (Be sure to define what you mean by "helps" or "hurts.") Why do you think that more Americans appear to believe that free trade hurts the economy than believe that it helps the economy?

Source: Matthew Benjamin, "Americans Souring on Free Trade Amid Optimism About Economy," *Bloomberg News*, January 19, 2007.

3.12 (Related to the *Don't Let This Happen to You!* on page 252) Briefly explain whether you agree or disagree with the following statement: "I can't believe that anyone opposes expanding international trade. After all, when international trade expands, everyone wins."

3.13 (Related to the *Making the Connection* on page 253) Explain why there are advantages to a movie studio operating in southern California, rather than in, say, Florida.

>> **End Learning Objective 8.3**

8.4 | Analyze the economic effects of government policies that restrict international trade, **pages 255–262.**

Government Policies That Restrict International Trade

Summary

Free trade is trade between countries without government restrictions. Government policies that interfere with trade usually take the form of: *tariffs, quotas,* or *voluntary export restraints* (VERs). A **tariff** is a tax imposed by a government on imports. A **quota** is a numeric limit imposed by a government on the quantity of a good that can be imported into the country. A **voluntary export restraint (VER)** is an agreement negotiated between two countries that places a numeric limit on the quantity of a good that can be imported by one country from the other country. The federal government's sugar quota costs U.S. consumers $2.24 billion per year, or about $750,000 per year for each job saved in the sugar industry. Saving jobs by using tariffs and quotas is often very expensive.

myeconlab Visit www.myeconlab.com to complete these exercises
Get Ahead of the Curve online and get instant feedback.

Review Questions

4.1 What is a tariff? What is a quota? Give an example of a non-tariff barrier to trade.

4.2 Who gains and who loses when a country imposes a tariff or a quota on imports of a good?

Problems and Applications

4.3 An editorial in *BusinessWeek* argued the following:

> [President] Bush needs to send a pure and clear signal that the U.S. supports free trade on its merits. . . . That means resisting any further protectionist demands by lawmakers. It could even mean unilaterally reducing tariffs or taking down trade barriers rather than erecting new ones. Such moves would benefit U.S. consumers while giving a needed boost to struggling economies overseas.

What does the editorial mean by "protectionist demands"? How would the unilateral elimination of U.S. trade barriers benefit both U.S. consumers and economies overseas?

Source: "The Threat of Protectionism," *BusinessWeek*, June 3, 2002.

4.4 Political commentator B. Bruce-Biggs once wrote the following in the *Wall Street Journal*: "This is not to say that the case for international free trade is invalid; it is just irrelevant. It is an 'if only everybody . . .'

argument. . . . In the real world almost everybody sees benefits in economic nationalism." What do you think he means by "economic nationalism"? Do you agree that a country benefits from free trade only if every other country also practices free trade? Briefly explain.

Source: B. Bruce-Biggs, "The Coming Overthrow of Free Trade," *Wall Street Journal*, February 24, 1983, p. 28.

4.5 Two U.S. senators make the following argument against allowing free trade: "Fewer and fewer Americans support our government's trade policy. They see a shrinking middle class, lost jobs and exploding trade deficits. Yet supporters of free trade continue to push for more of the same—more job-killing trade agreements. . . ." Do you agree with these senators that reducing barriers to trade reduces the number of jobs available to workers in the United States? Briefly explain.

Source: Byron Dorgan and Sherrod Brown, "How Free Trade Hurts," *Washington Post*, December 23, 2006, p. A21.

4.6 The United States produces beef and also imports beef from other countries.
   a. Draw a graph showing the supply and demand for beef in the United States. Assume that the United States can import as much as it wants at the world price of beef without causing the world price of beef to increase. Be sure to indicate on the graph the quantity of beef imported.
   b. Now show on your graph the effect of the United States imposing a tariff on beef. Be sure to indicate on your graph the quantity of beef sold by U.S. producers before and after the tariff is imposed, the quantity of beef imported before and after the tariff, and the price of beef in the United States before and after the tariff.
   c. Discuss who benefits and who loses when the United States imposes a tariff on beef.

4.7 **(Related to the *Chapter Opener* on page 242)** Which industries are affected unfavorably by the sugar quota and by the tariff on imports of sugar-based ethanol? Are any industries (other than the sugar industry) affected favorably by the sugar quota and the tariff on imports of sugar-based ethanol? (*Hint:* Think about what sugar is used for and whether substitutes exist for these uses and what the substitutes are for sugar-based ethanol.)

4.8 When Congress was considering a bill to impose quotas on imports of textiles, shoes, and other products, Milton Friedman, a Nobel Prize–winning economist, made the following comment: "The consumer will be forced to spend several extra dollars to subsidize the producers [of these goods] by one dollar. A straight handout would be far cheaper." Why would a quota result in consumers paying much more than domestic producers receive? Where do the other dollars go? What does Friedman mean by a "straight handout"? Why would this be cheaper than a quota?

Source: Milton Friedman, "Free Trade," *Newsweek*, August 27, 1970.

4.9 The United States has about 9,000 rice farmers. In 2006, these rice farmers received $780 million in subsidy payments from the U.S. government (or nearly $87,000 per farmer). These payments result in U.S. farmers producing much more rice than they otherwise would, a substantial amount of which is exported. According to an article in the *Wall Street Journal*, Kpalagim Mome, a farmer in the African country of Ghana, can no longer find buyers in Ghana for his rice:

> "We can't sell our rice anymore. It gets worse every year," Mr. Mome says. . . . Years of economic hardship have driven three of his brothers to walk and hitchhike 2,000 miles across the Sahara to reach the Mediterranean and Europe. His sister plans to leave next year. Mr. Mome's plight is repeated throughout farm communities in Africa and elsewhere in the developing world.

Why would subsidies paid by the U.S. government to U.S. rice farmers reduce the incomes of rice farmers in Africa?

Source: Juliane von Reppert-Bismarck, "How Trade Barriers Keep Africans Adrift," *Wall Street Journal*, December 27, 2006.

4.10 An economic analysis of a proposal to impose a quota on steel imports into the United States indicated that the quota would save 3,700 jobs in the steel industry but cost about 35,000 jobs in other U.S. industries. Why would a quota on steel imports cause employment to fall in other industries? Which other industries are likely to be most affected?

Source: Study cited in Douglas A. Irwin, *Free Trade Under Fire*, Princeton, NJ: Princeton University Press, 2002, p. 82.

4.11 A student makes the following argument:

> Tariffs on imports of foreign goods into the United States will cause the foreign companies to add the amount of the tariff to the prices they charge in the United States for those goods. Instead of putting a tariff on imported goods, we should ban importing them. Banning imported goods is better than putting tariffs on them because U.S. producers benefit from the reduced competition and U.S. consumers don't have to pay the higher prices caused by tariffs.

Briefly explain whether you agree with the student's reasoning.

4.12 Suppose China decides to pay large subsidies to any Chinese company that exports goods or services to the United States. As a result, these companies are able to sell products in the United States at far below their cost of production. In addition, China decides to bar all imports from the United States. The dollars that the United States pays to import Chinese goods are left in banks in China. Will this strategy raise or lower the standard of living in China? Will it raise or lower the standard of living in the United States? Briefly explain. Be sure to provide a definition of "standard of living" in your answer.

4.13 (Related to the *Chapter Opener* on page 242) According to an editorial in the *New York Times*, because of the sugar quota, "Sugar growers in this country, long protected from global competition, have had a great run at the expense of just about everyone else—refineries, candy manufacturers, other food companies, individual consumers and farmers in the developing world." Briefly explain how each group mentioned in this editorial is affected by the sugar quota.

Source: "America's Sugar Daddies," *New York Times*, November 29, 2003.

4.14 (Related to *Solved Problem 8-4* on page 259) Suppose that the United States currently both produces kumquats and imports them. The U.S. government then decides to restrict international trade in kumquats by imposing a quota that allows imports of only six million pounds of kumquats into the United States each year. The figure shows the results of imposing the quota.

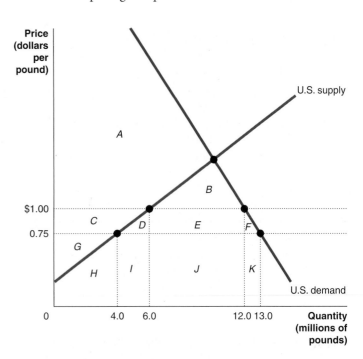

Fill in the table on the following page using the letters in the figure:

	WITHOUT QUOTA	WITH QUOTA
World price of kumquats	_____	_____
U.S. price of kumquats	_____	_____
Quantity supplied by U.S. firms	_____	_____
Quantity demanded	_____	_____
Quantity imported	_____	_____
Area of consumer surplus	_____	_____
Area of domestic producer surplus	_____	_____
Area of deadweight loss	_____	_____

>> End Learning Objective 8.4

8.5 LEARNING OBJECTIVE   8.5 | Evaluate the arguments over trade policy and globalization, **pages 262–267.**

The Argument over Trade Policies and Globalization

Summary

The **World Trade Organization (WTO)** is an international organization that enforces international trade agreements. The WTO has promoted **globalization**, the process of countries becoming more open to foreign trade and investment. Some critics of the WTO argue that globalization has damaged local cultures around the world. Other critics oppose the WTO because they believe in **protectionism**, which is the use of trade barriers to shield domestic firms from foreign competition. The WTO allows countries to use tariffs in cases of **dumping**, when an imported product is sold for a price below its cost of production. Economists can point out the burden imposed on the economy by tariffs, quotas, and other government interferences with free trade. But whether these policies should be used is a normative decision.

myeconlab Visit www.myeconlab.com to complete these exercises
Get Ahead of the Curve online and get instant feedback.

Review Questions

5.1 What events led to the General Agreement on Tariffs and Trade? Why did the World Trade Organization eventually replace GATT?

5.2 What is globalization? Why are some people opposed to globalization?

5.3 What is protectionism? Who benefits and who loses from protectionist policies? What are the main arguments people use to justify protectionism?

5.4 What is dumping? Who benefits and who loses from dumping? What problems arise when implementing anti-dumping laws?

Problems and Applications

5.5 (Related to the *Making the Connection* on page 263) The following excerpt is from a newspaper story on President Bill Clinton's proposals for changes in the World Trade Organization. The story was published just before the 1999 World Trade Organization meeting in Seattle that ended in rioting:

> [President Clinton] suggested that a working group on labor be created within the WTO to develop core labor standards that would become "part of every trade agreement. And ultimately I would favor a system in which sanctions would come for violating any provision of a trade agreement. . . ." But the new U.S. stand is sure to meet massive resistance from developing countries, which make up more than 100 of the 135 countries in the WTO. They are not interested in adopting tougher U.S. labor standards.

What did President Clinton mean by "core labor standards"? Why would developing countries resist adopting these standards?

5.6 Steven Landsburg, an economist at the University of Rochester, wrote the following in an article in the *New York Times*:

> Free trade is not only about the right of American consumers to buy at the cheapest possible price; it's also about the right of foreign producers to earn a living. Steelworkers in West Virginia struggle hard to make ends meet. So do steelworkers in South Korea. To protect one at the expense of the other, solely because of where they happened to be born, is a moral outrage.

How does the U.S. government protect steelworkers in West Virginia at the expense of steelworkers in South Korea? Is Landsburg making a positive or a normative statement? A few days later, Tom Redburn published an article disagreeing with Landsburg:

> It is not some evil character flaw to care more about the welfare of people nearby

than about that of those far away—it's human nature. And it is morally—and economically—defensible. . . . A society that ignores the consequences of economic disruption on those among its citizens who come out at the short end of the stick is not only heartless, it also undermines its own cohesion and adaptability.

Which of the two arguments do you find most convincing?

Sources: Steven E. Landsburg, "Who Cares if the Playing Field Is Level?" *New York Times*, June 13, 2001; and Tom Redburn, "Economic View: Of Politics, Free Markets, and Tending to Society," *New York Times*, June 17, 2001.

5.7 **(Related to the *Making the Connection* on page 266)** An article in the *Economist* magazine argues that:

> Mr. Obama has said he will seek to "renegotiate" the North American Free-Trade Agreement (NAFTA) with Canada and Mexico. This alarms Mexican officials. . . . But Mr. Obama adopted this stance because voters worry about the loss of manufacturing jobs. . . .

Why would voters who worry about the loss of manufacturing jobs like to see the United States renegotiate NAFTA? Why would the prospect of renegotiating NAFTA alarm Mexican officials?

Source: "The More Things Change," *Economist*, October 23, 2008.

5.8 The following appeared in an article in *BusinessWeek* that argued against free trade: "The U.S. is currently in a precarious position. In addition to geopolitical threats, we face a severe economic shock. We have already lost trillions of dollars and millions of jobs to foreigners." If a country engages in free trade, is the total number of jobs in the country likely to decline? Briefly explain.

Source: Vladimir Masch, "A Radical Plan to Manage Globalization," *BusinessWeek*, February 14, 2007.

>> End Learning Objective 8.5

Appendix

Multinational Firms

Understand why firms operate in more than one country.

Most large corporations are multinational. **Multinational enterprises** are firms that conduct operations in more than one country—as opposed to simply trading with other countries. For example, the U.S. firm General Electric employs more than 300,000 people in more than 100 countries. Toyota Motor Corporation of Japan has invested more than $10 billion in factories and other facilities in the United States and assembles more than a million cars and trucks in North American factories. (Almost two-thirds of the cars and trucks Toyota sells in the United States are assembled in North American factories.) The Nestlé Company is headquartered in the small city of Vevey, Switzerland, but it produces and sells food products in practically every country in the world. It has more than 500 factories worldwide, employing about 260,000 people.

Multinational enterprise A firm that conducts operations in more than one country.

Table 8A-1 shows the top 25 multinational corporations, ranked by the value of their revenues in 2007. Large corporations based in the United States generally established multinational operations earlier than did firms based in other countries. Today, 5 of the 10 largest multinational corporations in the world are based in the United States. The table shows that large corporations in the motor vehicle, banking, insurance, and petroleum refining industries are most likely to have extensive multinational operations.

A Brief History of Multinational Enterprises

From at least 2500 B.C., companies have traded over long distances. Well-developed systems of long-distance trade existed in the eastern Mediterranean by 1500 B.C. By the Middle Ages, a number of multinational firms had been established in Europe. For example, the Medici bank was based in Florence, Italy, but had branches in France, Switzerland, and England. Some multinational companies founded during these years still exist. The Austrian freight forwarding firm Gebrueder Weiss, which had offices in several countries in the fourteenth century, continues to operate today. Before the twentieth century, multinational firms were still relatively rare, however.

In the late nineteenth and early twentieth centuries, a few large U.S. corporations began to expand their operations beyond the domestic market. Two key technological innovations made it possible for these firms to coordinate operations on several continents. The first innovation was the successful completion of the transatlantic cable in 1866, which made possible instant communication by telegraph between the United States and Europe. The second innovation was the development of more efficient steam engines, which reduced the cost and increased the speed of long ocean voyages. U.S. firms such as Standard Oil, the Singer Sewing Machine Company, and the American Tobacco Company took advantage of these innovations to establish factories and distribution networks around the world. When firms build or buy facilities in foreign countries, they are engaging in **foreign direct investment**. When individuals or firms buy stocks or bonds issued in another country, they are engaging in **foreign portfolio investment**. In the early twentieth century, most U.S. firms expanded abroad through foreign direct investment because the stock and bond markets in other countries were often too poorly developed to make foreign portfolio investment practical.

Foreign direct investment The purchase or building by a domestic firm of a facility in a foreign country.

Foreign portfolio investment The purchase by an individual or a firm of stocks or bonds issued in another country.

TABLE 8A-1

Top 25 Multinational Corporations, 2007

RANK	CORPORATION	HOME COUNTRY	INDUSTRY
1	Wal-Mart Stores	United States	Retailing
2	Exxon Mobil	United States	Petroleum refining
3	Royal Dutch Shell	The Netherlands/ United Kingdom	Petroleum refining
4	BP	Great Britain	Petroleum refining
5	Toyota Motor	Japan	Motor vehicles
6	Chevron	United States	Petroleum refining
7	ING Group	The Netherlands	Insurance
8	Total	France	Petroleum refining
9	General Motors	United States	Motor vehicles
10	ConocoPhillips	United States	Petroleum refining
11	Daimler	Germany	Motor vehicles
12	General Electric	United States	Diversified Financials
13	Ford Motor	United States	Motor vehicles
14	Fortis	Belgium	Banking
15	AXA	France	Insurance
16	Sinopec	China	Petroleum refining
17	Citigroup	United States	Banking
18	Volkswagen	Germany	Motor vehicles
19	Dexia Group	Belgium	Banking
20	HSBC Holdings	Great Britain	Banking
21	BNP Paribas	France	Banking
22	Allianz	Germany	Insurance
23	Crédit Agricole	France	Banking
24	State Grid	China	Power generation
25	China National Petroleum	China	Petroleum refining

Note: Corporations are ranked by their revenue.

Source: "Fortune Global 500," *Fortune*, May 5, 2008. © 2008 Time Inc. All rights reserved. Reprinted by permission.

Strategic Factors in Moving from Domestic to Foreign Markets

Today, most large U.S. corporations have established factories and other facilities overseas. Corporations expand their operations outside the United States when they expect to increase their profitability by doing so. Firms might expect to increase their profits through overseas operations for five main reasons:

- ***To avoid tariffs or the threat of tariffs.*** As we saw in this chapter, tariffs are taxes imposed by countries on imports from other countries. Sometimes firms establish factories in other countries to avoid having to pay tariffs. At other times, a firm establishes a factory in a country to which it is exporting because it fears the other country's government will impose a tariff or some other restriction on its product. Governments often are less concerned about domestic production by foreign-owned companies than they are about imports. As we also saw in this chapter, government restrictions on imports frequently result from a fear that imports will cause job losses in domestic industries. For example, in the 1970s and 1980s, many Americans feared that imports of Japanese automobiles would reduce employment in the U.S. automobile industry. Members of Congress threatened to increase tariffs or impose quotas on imports of Japanese automobiles. In fact, beginning in 1981, a voluntary export restraint reduced imports of Japanese automobiles. In response to this political pressure, the Japanese automobile companies established assembly plants in the United States. Now that a majority of Japanese automobiles sold in the United States are also assembled in the United States by U.S. workers, the Japanese share of the U.S. automobile market is a less heated political issue than it was during the 1970s and 1980s.

- *To gain access to raw materials.* Some U.S. firms have expanded abroad to secure supplies of raw materials. U.S. oil firms—beginning with Standard Oil in the late nineteenth century—have had extensive overseas operations aimed at discovering, recovering, and refining crude oil. In early 2001, one of Standard Oil's successor firms, ChevronTexaco, headquartered in San Francisco, opened its largest oil field in Kazakstan, in the former Soviet Union. ChevronTexaco also constructed a 990-mile pipeline to bring the oil from this field on the Caspian Sea across Russia to a port on the Black Sea.

- *To gain access to low-cost labor.* In the past 20 years, some U.S. firms have located factories or other facilities in countries such as China, India, Malaysia, and El Salvador to take advantage of the lower wages paid to workers in those countries. Most economists believe that this *outsourcing* ultimately improves the efficiency of the economy and raises the consumption of U.S. households, but it can also disrupt the lives of U.S. workers who lose their jobs. For this reason, outsourcing has caused political controversy.

- *To minimize exchange-rate risk.* The exchange rate tells us how many units of foreign currency are received in exchange for a unit of domestic currency. Fluctuations in exchange rates can reduce the profits of a firm that exports goods to other countries. The J. M. Smucker Company, headquartered in Orrville, Ohio, ships jams, ice cream toppings, peanut butter, and other products to more than 70 other countries. Suppose Smucker's has contracted to sell 200,000 cases of jam to a British importer. The British importer will be paying for the shipment in British currency, the pound (the symbol for the pound is £). The importer will pay Smucker's £21 million in 60 days. It is currently possible to exchange $1 for £0.7, so Smucker's expects to receive $30 million (£21 million/£0.70 per dollar) in 60 days. But if the value of the pound falls against the dollar during the next 60 days, the amount Smucker's receives in dollars could be significantly reduced. For example, if the value of the pound falls to £0.80 per $1, then Smucker's will receive only $26.25 million (£21 million/£0.80 per dollar).

  Firms like Smucker's that have extensive international operations are exposed to significant risk to their profits from fluctuations in the values of international currencies. This risk is known as *exchange-rate risk*. If Smucker's began producing jam in Britain, it would reduce its exposure to exchange-rate risk.

- *To respond to industry competition.* In some instances, companies expand overseas as a competitive response to an industry rival. The worldwide competition for markets between Pepsi and Coke is an example of this kind of expansion. Coke began expanding overseas before World War II, and by the 1970s it was earning more from its foreign sales than from its sales in the United States. It became clear to Pepsi's management that the firm needed to compete with Coke in foreign as well as domestic markets. In 1972, Pepsi had a major success when it signed an agreement with the Soviet Union to become the first foreign product sold in that country. Coke and Pepsi continue to compete vigorously in many countries, with their shares of the market often fluctuating significantly.

Many U.S. jobs require technical training and pay higher wages.

Making the Connection	**Have Multinational Corporations Reduced Employment and Lowered Wages in the United States?**

During the 1990s, some U.S. corporations responded to the greater economic openness of many poorer countries by relocating manufacturing operations to those countries. For example, most U.S. toy firms, such as Mattel, now produce nearly all their toys in factories in China. Most U.S. clothing manufacturers now produce the bulk of their goods in factories in Central America or Asia. These firms have reduced their production costs by paying much lower wages in their overseas factories than they were paying in the United States. The workers who lost their jobs in U.S. factories have often experienced periods of unemployment and have sometimes had to accept lower wages when they find new jobs. Towns and cities where factories closed have also been hurt by losses of tax revenues to support schools and other local services.

Most economists, however, do not believe that relocating jobs abroad has reduced either total employment in the United States or the average wage paid to U.S. workers. The overall level of employment in the United States in the long run is not affected by job losses in particular industries, however painful the losses may be to those experiencing them. The U.S. economy creates more than 2 million additional new jobs during a typical year. Nearly all workers who lose jobs at one firm eventually find new ones at other firms.

Competition from low-wage foreign workers has not reduced the average wages of U.S. workers. Wages are determined by the ability of workers to produce goods and services. This ability depends in part on the workers' education and training and in part on the machinery and equipment available to them. American workers have high wages because, on average, they are well trained and because of the quantity and quality of the machinery and equipment they work with. Low-wage foreign workers are generally less well trained and work with smaller amounts of machinery and equipment than do American workers.

Beginning in the 1990s and continuing through the 2000s, the gap in the United States between the wages of skilled workers and the wages of unskilled workers increased. It has been suggested that competition from low-wage foreign workers forced unskilled U.S. workers to accept lower wages to keep their jobs. To a small extent, the increase in the wage gap in the United States may have been due to this cause. But careful economic studies have shown that most of the increase in the wage gap is due to developments within the U.S. economy—such as the increasing number of jobs that require technical training—that have resulted in higher pay to skilled workers rather than to competition from low-wage foreign workers.

YOUR TURN: Test your understanding by doing related problem 8A.12 on page 282 at the end of this appendix.

Most U.S. firms have followed similar steps in expanding their operations overseas: Newly established firms usually begin by selling only within the United States. If successful in the domestic market, they begin to export. They initially use foreign firms to market and distribute their products. If sales are good in these foreign markets, U.S. firms establish their own overseas marketing and distribution networks. Finally, firms establish their own production facilities in these foreign countries. Since World War II, many U.S. firms have switched from building their own production facilities to a strategy of acquiring local firms that were already producing the good. Some firms have first licensed production to local firms, later acquiring the firms. U.S.-based Colgate-Palmolive, for example, typically has entered a foreign market first by licensing a foreign soap manufacturer to produce its brands, while keeping control over marketing and distribution. Typically, Colgate-Palmolive has eventually acquired ownership of the foreign firm.

Challenges to U.S. Firms in Foreign Markets

It seems obvious that any successful firm will want to expand into foreign markets. After all, it is always better to have more customers than fewer customers. In fact, however, expanding into foreign markets can often be quite difficult, and the additional costs incurred may end up being greater than the additional revenue gained. One problem encountered by U.S. firms is differences in tastes between U.S. and foreign consumers. Although products like Coke seem to appeal to consumers everywhere in the world, other products run into problems because of cultural differences among countries. For example, Singapore banned Janet Jackson's album *All for You* because, according to a government spokesman, its "sexually explicit lyrics" were "not acceptable to our society." In 2002, eBay closed its online auction site in Japan. Although eBay is successful selling collectibles in the United States, many Japanese consumers do not like to buy used goods. In 2006, Wal-Mart announced it would sell its 85 stores in Germany, taking a loss of $1 billion. German consumers were not as receptive as U.S. consumers are to buying groceries, clothes, consumer electronics, and other products in one very large store.

Some U.S. companies have had difficulty adapting their employment practices to deal with the differences between U.S. and foreign labor markets. Many countries have much stronger labor unions than does the United States, and many foreign governments regulate labor markets much more than does the U.S. government. For example, government regulations in most European countries make it much more difficult than it is in the United States to lay off workers.

Competitive Advantages of U.S. Firms

Some U.S. firms have successful foreign operations because of the strength of their brand names. Many producers of soft drinks and many fast food restaurants can be found in nearly every foreign country, but Coca-Cola and McDonald's have such strong name recognition that their appeal extends around the world. Other firms have developed a significant technological edge over foreign rivals. Microsoft, the software giant, and Hewlett-Packard, the computer and printer firm, are examples. Some U.S. firms, such as Dell Computer and Boeing, have advantages over foreign manufacturers based on having developed the most efficient and low-cost way of producing a good.

A U.S. firm's global competitive advantage changes over time. This change is illustrated dramatically by the experience of U.S. semiconductor firms. The semiconductor industry originated in the United States, with the invention of the transistor at Bell Telephone Laboratories in 1947. U.S. predominance in the industry was enhanced further in 1959, with the invention of the integrated circuit, which contains multiple transistors on a single silicon chip. Through 1980, U.S. firms held between 60 and 80 percent of the global market for semiconductors. Beginning in the 1970s, the Japanese government moved to establish a strong domestic semiconductor industry by subsidizing domestic firms and by limiting imports of semiconductors from the United States. The Japanese policy was very successful with respect to DRAM—dynamic random access memory—the most basic chip. By the mid-1980s, Japanese firms dominated the global market, and nearly all U.S. chipmakers had abandoned DRAM manufacture. Many observers predicted the collapse of the U.S. semiconductor industry. Even Intel Corporation, the most successful U.S. semiconductor firm, appeared to be close to bankruptcy.

From this low point, U.S. semiconductor firms rebounded to regain global predominance by the 1990s. The key to the rebound of U.S. firms was the decreasing demand for simple memory chips and the increasing demand for two products: microprocessors—such as Intel's Pentium 4 chip used in personal computers—and ASICs—application-specific integrated circuits—which are used in many electronic products. In manufacturing microprocessors and ASICs, a firm's ability to rapidly design and develop new products is more important than using low-cost production processes. U.S. firms, such as Intel, have proven to be much better at designing and rapidly bringing to market advanced microprocessors and ASICs than have competing firms in Japan, South Korea, and elsewhere.

Key Terms

Foreign direct investment,
p. 277

Foreign portfolio investment,
p. 277

Multinational enterprise,
p. 277

LEARNING OBJECTIVE   Understand the reasons why firms operate in more than one country, **pages 277–281.**

 Visit www.myeconlab.com to complete these exercises
Get Ahead of the Curve online and get instant feedback.

Review Questions

8A.1 When did large U.S. corporations first begin to operate internationally? What key technological changes made it easier for U.S. corporations to operate overseas?

8A.2 What is the difference between foreign direct investment and foreign portfolio investment? Is the Camry assembly plant that Toyota operates in Kentucky an example of foreign direct investment or foreign portfolio investment?

8A.3 What are the five main reasons firms expand their operations overseas? Which of these reasons explains why U.S.-based oil companies have extensive overseas operations?

8A.4 What are the main reasons U.S. firms succeed overseas?

Problems and Applications

8A.5 Suppose it is 1850 and you are operating a large factory manufacturing cotton cloth. You are considering expanding your operations overseas. What technical problems are you likely to encounter in coordinating your overseas and domestic operations?

8A.6 The Ford Motor Company and the International Harvester Company were two of the first U.S. firms to establish extensive manufacturing operations overseas. Why might a producer of automobiles and a producer of farm machinery find it particularly advantageous to manufacture their products in countries in which they have substantial sales?

8A.7 Why might many U.S. firms that were expanding their operations overseas after World War II have been more likely to acquire an existing firm in the market they were entering rather than build new facilities there?

8A.8 Would a firm based in the United States ever produce a good in another country if it cost less to produce it in the United States and ship it to the other country? Explain.

8A.9 Is expanding a firm's operations internationally really any different than expanding within a nation? For example, if a firm is based in Texas, what's the difference between it expanding operations to Mexico, Canada, Singapore, or Germany rather than to North Carolina or Pennsylvania?

8A.10 Is expanding a firm's operations internationally really any different than expanding into a new product market? For example, is Whirlpool's expanding into Europe different than Whirlpool's expanding by making a new line of appliances, such as humidifiers?

8A.11 If you ran a successful U.S. firm like Wal-Mart, IBM, or Hershey's, into which countries would you first expand? Why?

8A.12 (Related to the *Making the Connection* on page 280) Suppose that the U.S. government wanted to help those textile workers who have lost their jobs as U.S. clothing manufacturers have moved to Central America and Asia. To do this, the government imposes a tariff on imported textiles. What would be the effects of this policy on employment in the U.S. textile industry? Would the policy increase total employment in the United States? What would happen to employment in U.S. industries other than the textile industry?

>> End Appendix Learning Objective

Chapter 9

Consumer Choice and **Behavioral Economics**

Can Jay-Z Get You to Drink Cherry Coke?

Coca-Cola hired rapper Shawn "Jay-Z" Carter to appear in television commercials as part of the marketing campaign to relaunch Cherry Coke. Why would the Coca-Cola Company hire Jay-Z? Lucia James, of the consulting firm Agenda, explains: "Jay-Z brings a sense of genuine hip-hop authenticity to the brands. . . . There's reassurance that [the brands] won't appear like an out-of-touch uncle trying to act cool." Over the years, Coca-Cola has used other celebrities, including LeBron James, Lance Armstrong, Paula Abdul, and Ray Charles, to advertise its products. Coca-Cola is not alone in using celebrity endorsements. From Britney Spears and Sean "P. Diddy" Combs endorsing Pepsi to Michael Jordan endorsing Nike basketball shoes to Oprah Winfrey endorsing Pontiac cars, celebrities appear constantly in television, magazine, and online advertising. What do firms hope to gain from celebrity endorsements? The obvious answer is that firms expect that celebrity advertising will increase sales of their products. But why should consumers buy more of a

product just because a celebrity endorses it? In this chapter, we will examine how consumers make decisions about which products to buy. Firms must understand consumer behavior to determine whether strategies such as using celebrities in their advertising are likely to be effective.

Coca-Cola has been a leader in innovative advertising, including the use of celebrity endorsements. Coca-Cola was founded in Atlanta, Georgia, in 1886 by John Styth Pemberton. After Asa G. Candler bought the company in 1891, Coke began to be sold nationally, first primarily in drugstore soda fountains. The firm's advertising in magazines, newspapers, billboards, and calendars featured pictures of attractive young women drinking Coke—instead of emphasizing the taste or other qualities of the cola.

By the 1910s, Coca-Cola had moved from using unnamed women in its advertising to using movie stars. The attempt to associate Coke with

celebrities in the minds of consumers continued through the following decades. From the 1950s on, Coke's television commercials often featured popular singers or sports figures of the time, including the Supremes, the Moody Blues, and football star "Mean" Joe Greene.

Firms' attempts to distinguish their products in the minds of consumers from the products of rival firms will be an important theme in several of the following chapters. Advertising is one way in which firms try to distinguish their products. **AN INSIDE LOOK** on **page 310** discusses whether Elizabeth Arden made a good decision in hiring Mariah Carey to endorse its products.

Source: Kenneth Hein, "Cherry Coke Gets Fresh Jay-Z Remix," *Brandweek*, January 29, 2007, p. 4.

Economics in YOUR Life!

Do You Make Consistent Decisions?

Economists generally assume that people make decisions in a rational, consistent way. But are people actually as consistent as economists assume? Consider the following situation: You bought a concert ticket for $75, which is the most you were willing to pay. While you are in line to enter the concert hall, someone offers you $90 for the ticket. Would you sell the ticket? Would an economist think it is rational to sell the ticket? As you read the chapter, see if you can answer these questions. You can check your answers against those we provide at the end of the chapter. >> Continued on page 308

W e begin this chapter by exploring how consumers make decisions. In Chapter 1, we saw that economists usually assume that people act in a rational, self-interested way. In explaining consumer behavior, this means economists believe consumers make choices that will leave them as satisfied as possible, given their *tastes*, their *incomes*, and the *prices* of the goods and services available to them. We will see how the downward-sloping demand curves we encountered in Chapters 3 through 5 result from the economic model of consumer behavior. We will also see that in certain situations, knowing the best decision to make can be difficult. In these cases, economic reasoning provides a powerful tool for consumers to improve their decision making. Finally, we will see that *experimental economics* has shown that factors such as social pressure and notions of fairness can affect consumer behavior. We will look at how businesses take these factors into account when setting prices. In the appendix to this chapter, we extend the analysis by using indifference curves and budget lines to understand consumer behavior.

9.1 | Define utility and explain how consumers choose goods and services to maximize their utility.

Utility and Consumer Decision Making

We saw in Chapter 3 that the model of demand and supply is a powerful tool for analyzing how prices and quantities are determined. We also saw that, according to the *law of demand*, whenever the price of a good falls, the quantity demanded increases. In this section, we will show how the economic model of consumer behavior leads to the law of demand.

The Economic Model of Consumer Behavior in a Nutshell

Imagine walking through a shopping mall, trying to decide how to spend your clothing budget. If you had an unlimited budget, your decision would be easy: Just buy as much of everything as you want. Given that you have a limited budget, what do you do? Economists assume that consumers act so as to make themselves as well off as possible. Therefore, you should choose the one combination of clothes that makes you as well off as possible from among those combinations that you can afford. Stated more generally, the economic model of consumer behavior predicts that consumers will choose to buy the combination of goods and services that makes them as well off as possible from among all the combinations that their budgets allow them to buy.

This prediction may seem obvious and not particularly useful. But as we explore the implication of this prediction, we will see that it leads to conclusions that are both useful and not obvious.

Utility

Ultimately, how well off you are from consuming a particular combination of goods and services depends on your tastes, or preferences. There is an old saying—"There's no accounting for tastes"—and economists don't try to. If you buy Cherry Coke instead of Pepsi, even though Pepsi has a lower price, you must receive more enjoyment or satisfaction from drinking Cherry Coke. Economists refer to the enjoyment or satisfaction people receive from consuming goods and services as **utility**. So we can say that the goal of a consumer is to spend available income so as to maximize utility. But utility is a difficult concept to measure because there is no way of knowing exactly how much enjoyment or satisfaction someone receives from consuming a product. Similarly, it is not possible to compare utility across consumers. There is no way of knowing for sure whether Jill receives more or less satisfaction than Jack from drinking a bottle of Cherry Coke.

Utility The enjoyment or satisfaction people receive from consuming goods and services.

Two hundred years ago, economists hoped to measure utility in units called "utils." The util would be an objective measure in the same way that temperature is: If it is 70 degrees in New York and 70 degrees in Los Angeles, it is just as warm in both cities. These economists wanted to say that if Jack's utility from eating a hamburger is 10 utils and Jill's utility is 5 utils, then Jack receives exactly twice the satisfaction from eating a hamburger that Jill does. In fact, it is *not* possible to measure utility across people. It turns out that none of the important conclusions of the economic model of consumer behavior depend on utility being directly measurable (a point we demonstrate in the appendix to this chapter). Nevertheless, the economic model of consumer behavior is easier to understand if we assume that utility is something directly measurable, like temperature.

The Principle of Diminishing Marginal Utility

To make the model of consumer behavior more concrete, let's see how a consumer makes decisions in a case involving just two products: pepperoni pizza and Coke. To begin, consider how the utility you receive from consuming a good changes with the amount of the good you consume. For example, suppose that you have just arrived at a Super Bowl party where the hosts are serving pepperoni pizza, and you are very hungry. In this situation, you are likely to receive quite a lot of enjoyment, or utility, from consuming the first slice of pizza. Suppose this satisfaction is measurable and is equal to 20 units of utility, or *utils*. After eating the first slice, you decide to have a second slice. Because you are no longer as hungry, the satisfaction you receive from eating the second slice of pizza is less than the satisfaction you received from eating the first slice. Consuming the second slice increases your utility by only an *additional* 16 utils, which raises your *total* utility from eating the two slices to 36 utils. If you continue eating slices, each additional slice gives you less and less additional satisfaction.

The table in Figure 9-1 shows the relationship between the number of slices of pizza you consume while watching the Super Bowl and the amount of utility you receive. The second column in the table shows the total utility you receive from eating a particular number of slices. The third column shows the additional utility, or **marginal utility** (*MU*), you receive from consuming one additional slice. (Remember that in economics, "marginal" means additional.) For example, as you increase your consumption from 2 slices to 3 slices, your total utility increases from 36 to 46, so your marginal utility from consuming the third slice is 10 utils. As the table shows, by the time you eat the fifth slice of pizza that evening, your marginal utility is very low: only 2 utils. If you were to eat a sixth slice, you would become slightly nauseated, and your marginal utility would actually be a *negative* 3 utils.

> **Marginal utility** (*MU*) The change in total utility a person receives from consuming one additional unit of a good or service.

Figure 9-1 also plots the numbers from the table as graphs. Panel (a) shows how your total utility rises as you eat the first five slices of pizza and then falls as you eat the sixth slice. Panel (b) shows how your marginal utility declines with each additional slice you eat and finally becomes negative when you eat the sixth slice. The height of the marginal utility line at any quantity of pizza in panel (b) represents the change in utility as a result of consuming that additional slice. For example, the change in utility as a result of consuming 4 slices instead of 3 is 6 utils, so the height of the marginal utility line in panel (b) is 6 utils.

The relationship illustrated in Figure 9-1 between consuming additional units of a product during a period of time and the marginal utility received from consuming each additional unit is referred to as the **law of diminishing marginal utility**. For nearly every good or service, the more you consume during a period of time, the less you increase your total satisfaction from each additional unit you consume.

> **Law of diminishing marginal utility** The principle that consumers experience diminishing additional satisfaction as they consume more of a good or service during a given period of time.

The Rule of Equal Marginal Utility per Dollar Spent

The key challenge for consumers is to decide how to allocate their limited incomes among all the products they wish to buy. Every consumer has to make trade-offs: If you have $100 to spend on entertainment for the month, then the more DVDs you buy, the

Figure 9-1

Total and Marginal Utility from Eating Pizza on Super Bowl Sunday

The table shows that for the first 5 slices of pizza, the more you eat, the more your total satisfaction or utility increases. If you eat a sixth slice, you start to feel ill from eating too much pizza, and your total utility falls. Each additional slice increases your utility by less than the previous slice, so your marginal utility from each slice is less than the one before. Panel (a) shows your total utility rising as you eat the first 5 slices and falling with the sixth slice. Panel (b) shows your marginal utility falling with each additional slice you eat and becoming negative with the sixth slice. The height of the marginal utility line at any quantity of pizza in panel (b) represents the change in utility as a result of consuming that additional slice. For example, the change in utility as a result of consuming 4 slices instead of 3 is 6 utils, so the height of the marginal utility line in panel (b) for the fourth slice is 6 utils.

Number of Slices	Total Utility from Eating Pizza	Marginal Utility from the Last Slice Eaten
0	0	--
1	20	20
2	36	16
3	46	10
4	52	6
5	54	2
6	51	-3

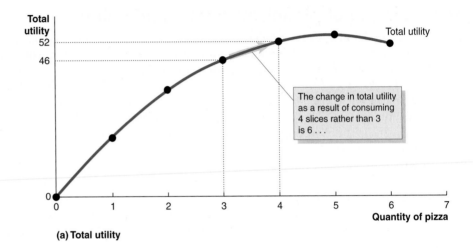

The change in total utility as a result of consuming 4 slices rather than 3 is 6 . . .

(a) Total utility

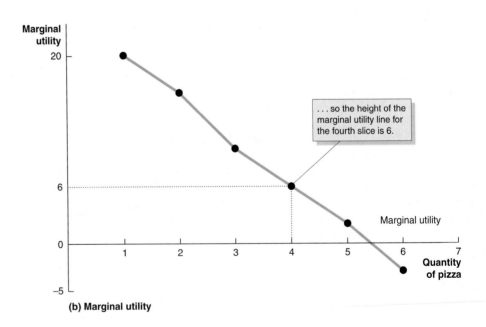

. . . so the height of the marginal utility line for the fourth slice is 6.

(b) Marginal utility

fewer movies you can see in the theater. Economists refer to the limited amount of income you have available to spend on goods and services as your **budget constraint.** The principle of diminishing marginal utility helps us understand how consumers can best spend their limited incomes on the products available to them.

Budget constraint The limited amount of income available to consumers to spend on goods and services.

Suppose you attend a Super Bowl party at a restaurant, and you have $10 to spend on refreshments. Pizza is selling for $2 per slice, and Coke is selling for $1 per cup. Table 9-1 shows the relationship between the amount of pizza you eat, the amount of Coke you drink, and the amount of satisfaction, or utility, you receive. The values for pizza are repeated from the table in Figure 9-1. The values for Coke also follow the principle of diminishing marginal utility.

How many slices of pizza and how many cups of Coke do you buy if you want to maximize your utility? If you did not have a budget constraint, you would buy 5 slices of pizza and 5 cups of Coke because that would give you total utility of 107 (54 + 53), which is the maximum utility you can achieve. Eating another slice of pizza or drinking another cup of Coke during the evening would lower your utility. Unfortunately, you do have a budget constraint: You have only $10 to spend. To buy 5 slices of pizza (at $2 per slice) and 5 cups of Coke (at $1 per cup), you would need $15.

To select the best way to spend your $10, remember this key economic principle: *Optimal decisions are made at the margin.* That is, most of the time, economic decision makers—consumers, firms, and the government—are faced with decisions about whether to do a little more of one thing or a little more of an alternative. In this case, you are choosing to consume a little more pizza or a little more Coke. BMW chooses to manufacture more roadsters or more SUVs in its South Carolina factory. Congress and the president choose to spend more for research on heart disease or more for research on breast cancer. Every economic decision maker faces a budget constraint, and every economic decision maker faces trade-offs.

The key to making the best consumption decision is to maximize utility by following the *rule of equal marginal utility per dollar spent.* As you decide how to spend your income, you should buy pizza and Coke up to the point where the last slice of pizza purchased and the last cup of Coke purchased give you equal increases in utility *per dollar.* By doing this, you will have maximized your total utility.

It is important to remember that to follow this rule, you must equalize your marginal utility per dollar spent, *not* your marginal utility from each good. Buying season tickets for your favorite NFL team or for the opera or buying a BMW may give you a lot more satisfaction than drinking a cup of Coke, but the NFL tickets may well give you less

TABLE 9-1 | **Total Utility and Marginal Utility from Eating Pizza and Drinking Coke**

NUMBER OF SLICES OF PIZZA	TOTAL UTILITY FROM EATING PIZZA	MARGINAL UTILITY FROM THE LAST SLICE	NUMBER OF CUPS OF COKE	TOTAL UTILITY FROM DRINKING COKE	MARGINAL UTILITY FROM THE LAST CUP
0	0	—	0	0	—
1	20	20	1	20	20
2	36	16	2	35	15
3	46	10	3	45	10
4	52	6	4	50	5
5	54	2	5	53	3
6	51	−3	6	52	−1

TABLE 9-2 | Converting Marginal Utility to Marginal Utility per Dollar

(1) SLICES OF PIZZA	(2) MARGINAL UTILITY (MU_{Pizza})	(3) MARGINAL UTILITY PER DOLLAR $\left(\dfrac{MU_{pizza}}{P_{pizza}}\right)$	(4) CUPS OF COKE	(5) MARGINAL UTILITY (MU_{COKE})	(6) MARGINAL UTILITY PER DOLLAR $\left(\dfrac{MU_{Coke}}{P_{Coke}}\right)$
1	20	10	1	20	20
2	16	8	2	15	15
3	10	5	3	10	10
4	6	3	4	5	5
5	2	1	5	3	3
6	−3	−1.5	6	−1	−1

satisfaction *per dollar* spent. To decide how many slices of pizza and how many cups of Coke to buy, you must convert the values for marginal utility in Table 9-1 into marginal utility per dollar. You can do this by dividing marginal utility by the price of each good, as shown in Table 9-2.

In column (3), we calculate marginal utility per dollar spent on pizza. Because the price of pizza is $2 per slice, the marginal utility per dollar from eating one slice of pizza equals 20 divided by $2, or 10 utils per dollar. Similarly, we show in column (6) that because the price of Coke is $1 per cup, the marginal utility per dollar from drinking 1 cup of Coke equals 20 divided by $1, or 20 utils per dollar. To maximize the total utility you receive, you must make sure that the utility per dollar of pizza for the last slice of pizza is equal to the utility per dollar of Coke for the last cup of Coke. Table 9-2 shows that there are three combinations of slices of pizza and cups of Coke where marginal utility per dollar is equalized. Table 9-3 lists the combinations, the total amount of money needed to buy each combination, and the total utility received from consuming each combination.

If you buy 4 slices of pizza, the last slice gives you 3 utils per dollar. If you buy 5 cups of Coke, the last cup also gives you 3 utils per dollar, so you have equalized your marginal utility per dollar. Unfortunately, as the third column in the table shows, to buy 4 slices and 5 cups, you would need $13, and you have only $10. You could also equalize your marginal utility per dollar by buying 1 slice and 3 cups, but that would cost just $5, leaving you with $5 to spend. Only when you buy 3 slices and 4 cups have you equalized your marginal utility per dollar and spent neither more nor less than the $10 available.

TABLE 9-3 | Equalizing Marginal Utility per Dollar Spent

COMBINATIONS OF PIZZA AND COKE WITH EQUAL MARGINAL UTILITIES PER DOLLAR	MARGINAL UTILITY PER DOLLAR (MARGINAL UTILITY/PRICE)	TOTAL SPENDING	TOTAL UTILITY
1 slice of pizza and 3 cups of Coke	10	$2 + $3 = $5	20 + 45 = 65
3 slices of pizza and 4 cups of Coke	5	$6 + $4 = $10	46 + 50 = 96
4 slices of pizza and 5 cups of Coke	3	$8 + $5 = $13	52 + 53 = 105

We can summarize the two conditions for maximizing utility:

$$1 \quad \frac{MU_{Pizza}}{P_{Pizza}} = \frac{MU_{Coke}}{P_{Coke}}$$

2 Spending on pizza + Spending on Coke = Amount available to be spent

The first condition shows that the marginal utility per dollar spent must be the same for both goods. The second condition is the budget constraint, which states that total spending on both goods must equal the amount available to be spent. Of course, these conditions for maximizing utility apply not just to pizza and Coke but to any two pairs of goods.

Solved Problem | 9-1

Finding the Optimal Level of Consumption

The following table shows Lee's utility from consuming ice cream cones and cans of Lime Fizz soda.

NUMBER OF ICE CREAM CONES	TOTAL UTILITY FROM ICE CREAM CONES	MARGINAL UTILITY FROM LAST CONE	NUMBER OF CANS OF LIME FIZZ	TOTAL UTILITY FROM CANS OF LIME FIZZ	MARGINAL UTILITY FROM LAST CAN
0	0	—	0	0	—
1	30	30	1	40	40
2	55	25	2	75	35
3	75	20	3	101	26
4	90	15	4	119	18
5	100	10	5	134	15
6	105	5	6	141	7

a. Ed inspects this table and concludes, "Lee's optimal choice would be to consume 4 ice cream cones and 5 cans of Lime Fizz because with that combination, his marginal utility from ice cream cones is equal to his marginal utility from Lime Fizz." Do you agree with Ed's reasoning? Briefly explain.

b. Suppose that Lee has an unlimited budget to spend on ice cream cones and cans of Lime Fizz. Under these circumstances, how many ice cream cones and how many cans of Lime Fizz will he consume?

c. Suppose that Lee has $7 per week to spend on ice cream cones and Lime Fizz. The price of an ice cream cone is $2, and the price of a can of Lime Fizz is $1. If Lee wants to maximize his utility, how many ice cream cones and how many cans of Lime Fizz should he buy?

SOLVING THE PROBLEM:

Step 1: Review the chapter material. This problem involves finding the optimal consumption of two goods, so you may want to review the section "The Rule of Equal Marginal Utility per Dollar Spent," which begins on page 287.

Step 2: Answer question (a) by analyzing Ed's reasoning. Ed's reasoning is incorrect. To maximize utility, Lee needs to equalize marginal utility per dollar for the two goods.

Step 3: Answer question (b) by determining how Lee would maximize utility with an unlimited budget. With an unlimited budget, consumers maximize utility by continuing to buy each good as long as their utility is increasing. In this case, Lee will maximize utility by buying 6 ice cream cones and 6 cans of Lime Fizz.

Step 4: Answer question (c) by determining Lee's optimal combination of ice cream cones and cans of Lime Fizz. Lee will maximize his utility if he spends his $7 per week so that the marginal utility of ice cream cones divided by the price of ice cream cones is equal to the marginal utility of Lime Fizz divided by the price of Lime Fizz. We can use the following table to solve this part of the problem:

| | ICE CREAM CONES | | CANS OF LIME FIZZ | |
QUANTITY	MU	$\frac{MU}{P}$	MU	$\frac{MU}{P}$
1	30	15	40	40
2	25	12.5	35	35
3	20	10	26	26
4	15	7.5	18	18
5	10	5	15	15
6	5	2.5	7	7

Lee will maximize his utility by buying 1 ice cream cone and 5 cans of Lime Fizz. At this combination, the marginal utility of each good divided by its price equals 15. He has also spent all of his $7.

YOUR TURN: For more practice, do related problems 1.7 and 1.8 on pages 312–313 at the end of this chapter.

>> **End Solved Problem 9-1**

What if the Rule of Equal Marginal Utility per Dollar Does Not Hold?

The idea of getting the maximum utility by equalizing the ratio of marginal utility to price for the goods you are buying can be difficult to grasp, so it is worth thinking about in another way. Suppose that instead of buying 3 slices of pizza and 4 cups of Coke, you buy 4 slices and 2 cups. Four slices and 2 cups cost $10, so you would meet your budget constraint by spending all the money available to you, but would you have gotten the maximum amount of utility? No, you wouldn't have. From the information in Table 9-1, we can list the additional utility per dollar you are getting from the last slice and the last cup and the total utility from consuming 4 slices and 2 cups:

Marginal utility per dollar for the fourth slice of pizza = 3 utils per dollar

Marginal utility per dollar for the second cup of Coke = 15 utils per dollar

Total utility from 4 slices of pizza and 2 cups of Coke = 87 utils

Obviously, the marginal utilities per dollar are not equal. The last cup of Coke gave you considerably more satisfaction per dollar than did the last slice of pizza. You could raise your total utility by buying less pizza and more Coke. Buying 1 less slice of pizza frees up $2 that will allow you to buy 2 more cups of Coke. Eating 1 less slice of pizza reduces your utility by 6 utils, but drinking 2 additional cups of Coke raises your utility by 15 utils (make sure you see this), for a net increase of 9. You end up equalizing your marginal utility per dollar (5 utils per dollar for both the last slice and the last cup) and raising your total utility from 87 utils to 96 utils.

Don't Let This Happen to **YOU!**

Equalize Marginal Utilities *per Dollar*

Consider the information in the following table, which gives Harry's utility from buying CDs and DVDs.

HARRY'S UTILITY FROM BUYING CDS AND DVDS

QUANTITY OF CDs	TOTAL UTILITY FROM CDs	MARGINAL UTILITY FROM LAST CD	QUANTITY OF DVDs	TOTAL UTILITY FROM DVDs	MARGINAL UTILITY FROM LAST DVD
0	0	—	0	0	—
1	50	50	1	60	60
2	85	35	2	105	45
3	110	25	3	145	40
4	130	20	4	175	30
5	140	10	5	195	20
6	145	5	6	210	15

Can you determine from this information the optimal combination of CDs and DVDs for Harry? It is very tempting to say that Harry should buy 4 CDs and 5 DVDs because his marginal utility from CDs is equal to his marginal utility from DVDs with that combination. In fact, we can't be sure this is the best combination because we are lacking some critical information: Harry's budget constraint—how much he has available to spend on CDs and DVDs—and the prices of CDs and DVDs.

Let's say that Harry has $100 to spend this month, the price of CDs is $10, and the price of DVDs is $20. Using the information from the first table, we can now calculate Harry's marginal utility per dollar for both goods, as shown in the following table.

HARRY'S MARGINAL UTILITY AND MARGINAL UTILITY PER DOLLAR FROM BUYING CDS AND DVDS

QUANTITYOF CDs	MARGINAL UTILITY FROM LAST CD (MU_{CD})	MARGINAL UTILITY PER DOLLAR $\left(\dfrac{MU_{CD}}{P_{CD}}\right)$	QUANTITY OF DVDs	MARGINAL UTILITY FROM LAST DVD (MU_{DVD})	MARGINAL UTILITY PER DOLLAR $\left(\dfrac{MU_{DVD}}{P_{DVD}}\right)$
1	50	5	1	60	3
2	35	3.5	2	45	2.25
3	25	2.5	3	40	2
4	20	2	4	30	1.5
5	10	1	5	20	1
6	5	0.5	6	15	0.75

Harry's marginal utility per dollar is the same for two combinations of CDs and DVDs, as shown in the following table.

COMBINATIONS OF CDs AND DVDs WITH EQUAL MARGINAL UTILITIES PER DOLLAR	MARGINAL UTILITY PER DOLLAR (MARGINAL UTILITY/PRICE)	TOTAL SPENDING	TOTAL UTILITY
5 CDs and 5 DVDs	1	$50 + $100 = $150	140 + 195 = 335
4 CDs and 3 DVDs	2	$40 + $60 = $100	130 + 145 = 275

Unfortunately, 5 CDs and 5 DVDs would cost Harry $150, and he has only $100. The best Harry can do is to buy 4 CDs and 3 DVDs. This combination provides him with the maximum amount of utility attainable, given his budget constraint.

The key point, which we also saw in Solved Problem 9-1, is that consumers maximize their utility when they equalize marginal utility *per dollar* for every good they buy, not when they equalize marginal utility.

YOUR TURN: Test your understanding by doing related problem 1.10 on page 313 at the end of this chapter.

The Income Effect and Substitution Effect of a Price Change

We can use the rule of equal marginal utility per dollar to analyze how consumers adjust their buying decisions when a price changes. Suppose you are back at the restaurant for the Super Bowl party, but this time the price of pizza is $1.50 per slice, rather than $2. You still have $10 to spend on pizza and Coke.

Income effect The change in the quantity demanded of a good that results from the effect of a change in price on consumer purchasing power, holding all other factors constant.

When the price of pizza was $2 per slice and the price of Coke was $1 per cup, your optimal choice was to consume 3 slices of pizza and 4 cups of Coke. The fall in the price of pizza to $1.50 per slice has two effects on the quantity of pizza you consume: the *income effect* and the *substitution effect*. First, consider the income effect. When the price of a good falls, you have more purchasing power. In our example, 3 slices of pizza and 4 cups of Coke now cost a total of only $8.50 instead of $10.00. An increase in purchasing power is essentially the same thing as an increase in income. The change in the quantity of pizza you will demand because of this increase in purchasing power—holding all other factors constant— is the **income effect** of the price change. Recall from Chapter 3 that if a product is a *normal good*, a consumer increases the quantity demanded as the consumer's income rises, but if a product is an *inferior good*, a consumer decreases the quantity demanded as the consumer's income rises. So, if we assume that for you pizza is a normal good, the income effect of a fall in price causes you to consume more pizza. If pizza had been an inferior good for you, the income effect of a fall in the price would have caused you to consume less pizza.

Substitution effect The change in the quantity demanded of a good that results from a change in price making the good more or less expensive relative to other goods, holding constant the effect of the price change on consumer purchasing power.

The second effect of the price change is the substitution effect. When the price of pizza falls, pizza becomes cheaper *relative* to Coke, and the marginal utility per dollar for each slice of pizza you consume increases. If we hold constant the effect of the price change on your purchasing power and just focus on the effect of the price being lower relative to the price of the other good, we have isolated the **substitution effect** of the price change. The lower price of pizza relative to the price of Coke has lowered the *opportunity cost* to you of consuming pizza because now you have to give up less Coke to consume the same quantity of pizza. Therefore, the substitution effect from the fall in the price of pizza relative to the price of Coke will cause you to eat more pizza and drink less Coke. In this case, both the income effect and the substitution effect of the fall in price cause you to eat more pizza. If the price of pizza had risen, both the income effect and the substitution effect would have caused you to eat less pizza. Table 9-4 summarizes the effect of a price change on the quantity demanded.

We can use Table 9-5 to determine the effect of the fall in the price of pizza on your optimal consumption. Table 9-5 has the same information as Table 9-2, with one change: The marginal utility per dollar from eating pizza has been changed to reflect the new lower price of $1.50 per slice. Examining the table, we can see that the fall in the price of pizza will result in your eating 1 more slice of pizza, so your optimal consumption now becomes 4 slices of pizza and 4 cups of Coke. You will be spending all of your $10, and the last dollar you spend on pizza will provide you with about the same marginal utility per dollar as the last dollar you spend on Coke. You will not be receiving

TABLE 9-4

Income Effect and Substitution Effect of a Price Change

		INCOME EFFECT		SUBSTITUTION EFFECT
PRICE DECREASE	Increases the consumer's purchasing power, which . . .	. . . if a normal good, causes the quantity demanded to increase.	. . . if an inferior good, causes the quantity demanded to decrease.	Lowers the opportunity cost of consuming the good, which causes the quantity of the good demanded to increase.
PRICE INCREASE	Decreases the consumer's purchasing power, which . . .	. . . if a normal good, causes the quantity demanded to decrease.	. . . if an inferior good, causes the quantity demanded to increase.	Raises the opportunity cost of consuming the good, which causes the quantity of the good demanded to decrease.

TABLE 9-5 | Adjusting Optimal Consumption to a Lower Price of Pizza

NUMBER OF SLICES OF PIZZA	MARGINAL UTILITY FROM LAST SLICE (MU_{PIZZA})	MARGINAL UTILITY PER DOLLAR $\left(\dfrac{MU_{Pizza}}{P_{Pizza}}\right)$	NUMBER OF CUPS OF COKE	MARGINAL UTILITY FROM LAST CUP (MU_{COKE})	MARGINAL UTILITY PER DOLLAR $\left(\dfrac{MU_{Coke}}{P_{Coke}}\right)$
1	20	13.33	1	20	20
2	16	10.67	2	15	15
3	10	6.67	3	10	10
4	6	4	4	5	5
5	2	1.33	5	3	3
6	–3	—	6	–1	—

exactly the same marginal utility per dollar spent on the two products. As Table 9-5 shows, the last slice of pizza gives you 4 utils per dollar, and the last cup of Coke gives you 5 utils per dollar. But this is as close as you can come to equalizing marginal utility per dollar for the two products, unless you can buy a fraction of a slice of pizza or a fraction of a cup of Coke.

9.2 | Use the concept of utility to explain the law of demand.

Where Demand Curves Come From

We saw in Chapter 3 that, according to the *law of demand*, whenever the price of a product falls, the quantity demanded increases. Now that we have covered the concepts of total utility, marginal utility, and the budget constraint, we can look more closely at why the law of demand holds.

In our example of optimal consumption of pizza and Coke at the Super Bowl party, we found the following:

Price of pizza = $2 per slice ⇒ Quantity of pizza demanded = 3 slices

Price of pizza = $1.50 per slice ⇒ Quantity of pizza demanded = 4 slices

In panel (a) of Figure 9-2, we plot the two points showing the optimal number of pizza slices you choose to consume at each price. In panel (b) of Figure 9-2, we draw a line connecting the two points. This downward-sloping line represents your demand curve for pizza. We could find more points on the line by changing the price of pizza and using the information in Table 9-2 to find the new optimal number of slices of pizza you would demand at each price.

To this point in this chapter, we have been looking at an individual demand curve. As we saw in Chapter 3, however, economists are typically interested in market demand curves. We can construct the market demand curve from the individual demand curves for all the consumers in the market. To keep things simple, let's assume that there are only three consumers in the market for pizza: you, David, and Sharon. The table in Figure 9-3 shows the individual demand schedules for the three consumers. Because consumers differ in their incomes and their preferences for products, we would not expect every consumer to demand the same quantity of a given product at each price. The final column gives the market demand, which is simply the sum of the quantities demanded by each of the three consumers at each price. For example, at a price of $1.50 per slice, your quantity demanded is 4 slices, David's quantity demanded is 6 slices, and Sharon's quantity demanded is 5 slices. So, at a price of $1.50, a quantity of 15 slices is demanded in the market. The graphs in the figure show that we can obtain the market demand curve by adding horizontally the individual demand curves.

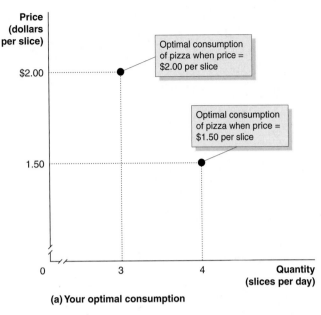

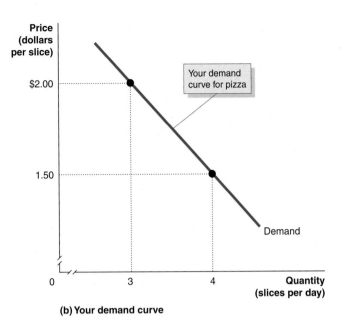

(a) Your optimal consumption

(b) Your demand curve

Figure 9-2 | Deriving the Demand Curve for Pizza

A consumer responds optimally to a fall in the price of a product by consuming more of that product. In panel (a), the price of pizza falls from $2 per slice to $1.50, and the

optimal quantity of slices consumed rises from 3 to 4. When we graph this result in panel (b), we have the consumer's demand curve.

	Quantity (slices per day)			
Price (dollars per slice)	You	David	Sharon	Market
$2.50	2	4	1	7
2.00	3	5	3	11
1.50	4	6	5	15
1.00	5	7	7	19
0.50	6	8	9	23

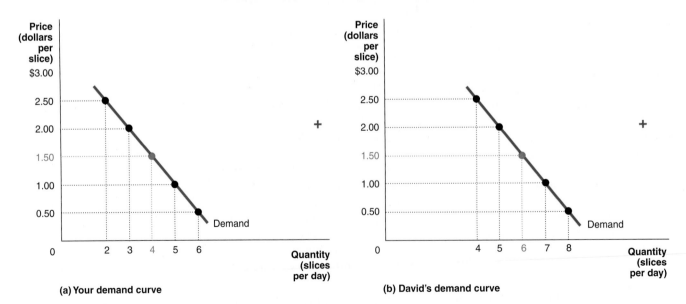

(a) Your demand curve

(b) David's demand curve

Figure 9-3 | Deriving the Market Demand Curve from Individual Demand Curves

The table shows that the total quantity demanded in a market is the sum of the quantities demanded by each buyer. We can find the market demand curve by adding horizontally the individual demand curves in parts (a), (b), and (c). For instance, at a

price of $1.50, your quantity demanded is 4 slices, David's quantity demanded is 6 slices, and Sharon's quantity demanded is 5 slices. Therefore, part (d) shows a price of $1.50, and a quantity demanded of 15 is a point on the market demand curve.

Remember that according to the law of demand, market demand curves always slope downward. We now know that this is true because the income and substitution effects of a fall in price cause consumers to increase the quantity of the good they demand. There is a complicating factor, however. As we discussed earlier, only for normal goods will the income effect result in consumers increasing the quantity of the good they demand when the price falls. If the good is an inferior good, then the income effect leads consumers to *decrease* the quantity of the good they demand. The substitution effect, on the other hand, results in consumers increasing the quantity they demand of both normal and inferior goods when the price falls. So, when the price of an inferior good falls, the income and substitution effects work in opposite directions: The income effect causes consumers to decrease the quantity of the good they demand, whereas the substitution effect causes consumers to increase the quantity of the good they demand. Is it possible, then, that consumers might actually buy less of a good when the price falls? If this happened, the demand curve would be upward sloping.

For a market demand curve to be upward sloping, the good would have to be an inferior good, and the income effect would have to be larger than the substitution effect. Goods that have both of these characteristics are called *Giffen goods*. Although we can conceive of there being Giffen goods, none has ever been discovered because for all actual goods, the substitution effect is larger than the income effect. Therefore, even for an inferior good, a fall in price leads to an increase in quantity demanded, and a rise in price leads to a decrease in the quantity demanded.

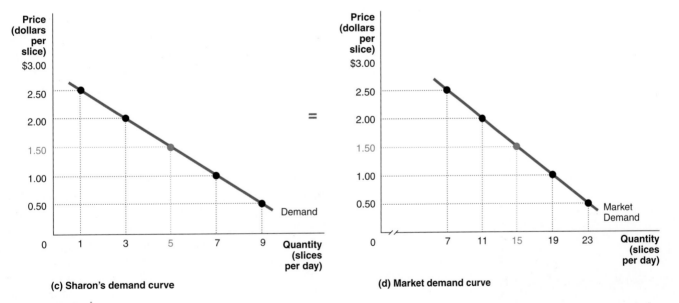

(c) Sharon's demand curve

(d) Market demand curve

Figure 9-3 | Continued

9.3 │ Explain how social influences can affect consumption choices.

Social Influences on Decision Making

Sociologists and anthropologists have argued that social factors such as culture, customs, and religion are very important in explaining the choices consumers make. Economists have traditionally seen such factors as being relatively unimportant, if they take them into consideration at all. Recently, however, some economists have begun to study how social factors influence consumer choice.

For example, people seem to receive more utility from consuming goods they believe are popular. As the economists Gary Becker and Kevin Murphy put it:

> The utility from drugs, crime, going bowling, owning a Rolex watch, voting Democratic, dressing informally at work, or keeping a neat lawn depends on whether friends and neighbors take drugs, commit crimes, go bowling, own Rolex watches, vote Democratic, dress informally, or keep their lawns neat.

This reasoning can help to explain why one restaurant is packed, while another restaurant that serves essentially the same food and has a similar décor has many fewer customers. Consumers decide which restaurant to go to partly on the basis of food and décor but also on the basis of the restaurant's popularity. People receive utility from being seen eating at a popular restaurant because they believe it makes them appear knowledgeable and fashionable. Whenever consumption takes place publicly, many consumers base their purchasing decisions on what other consumers are buying. Examples of public consumption include eating in restaurants, attending sporting events, wearing clothes or jewelry, and driving cars. In all these cases, the decision to buy a product depends partly on the characteristics of the product and partly on how many other people are buying the product.

The Effects of Celebrity Endorsements

In many cases, it is not just the number of people who use a product that makes it desirable but the types of people who use it. If consumers believe that movie stars or professional athletes use a product, demand for the product will often increase. This may be partly because consumers believe public figures are particularly knowledgeable about products: "Tiger Woods knows more about cars than I do, so I'll buy the same car he drives." But many consumers also feel more fashionable and closer to famous people if they use the same products these people do. These considerations help to explain why companies are willing to pay millions of dollars to have celebrities endorse their products. As we saw at the beginning of this chapter, Coke has been using celebrities in its advertising for decades.

Making
the
Connection

Why Do Firms Pay Tiger Woods to Endorse Their Products?

Tiger Woods may be the best golfer who's ever lived. In his first five years as a professional, he won 27 tournaments on the Professional Golfers' Association (PGA) tour. When he won the Masters in 2001, he became the first golfer ever to win all four major professional golf championships in the same year. In late 2006 and early 2007, Tiger seemed hotter than ever when he won seven straight tournaments on the PGA tour. Even though Tiger Woods is a great golfer, should consumers care what products he uses? A number of major companies apparently believe consumers do care. The General Motors, Nike, Titleist, American Express, and Rolex companies collectively pay him more than $50 million per year to endorse their products.

There seems little doubt that consumers care what products Tiger uses, but *why* do they care? It might be that they believe Tiger has better information than they do about the products he endorses. The average weekend golfer might believe that if Tiger

In 2007, Tiger Woods earned $11 million from playing golf and $100 million from product endorsements.

endorses Titleist golf clubs, maybe Titleist clubs are better than other golf clubs. But it seems more likely that people buy products associated with Tiger Woods or other celebrities because using these products makes them feel closer to the celebrity endorser or because it makes them appear to be fashionable.

YOUR TURN: Test your understanding by doing related problem 3.9 on page 315 at the end of this chapter.

Network Externalities

Technology can play a role in explaining why consumers buy products that many other consumers are already buying. There is a **network externality** in the consumption of a product if the usefulness of the product increases with the number of consumers who use it. For example, if you owned the only cell phone in the world, it would not be very useful. The usefulness of cell phones increases with the number of people who own them. Similarly, your willingness to buy an iPod depends in part on the number of other people who own iPods. The more people who own iPods, the more music that will be available to download and the more useful an iPod is to you.

Some economists have suggested the possibility that network externalities may have a significant downside because they might result in consumers buying products that contain inferior technologies. This outcome could occur because network externalities can create significant *switching costs* to changing products: When a product becomes established, consumers may find it too costly to switch to a new product that contains a better technology. The selection of products may be *path dependent*. This means that because of switching costs, the technology that was first available may have advantages over better technologies that were developed later. In other words, the path along which the economy has developed in the past is important.

One example of path dependency and the use of an inferior technology is the QWERTY order of the letters along the top row of most computer keyboards. This order became widely used when manual typewriters were developed in the late nineteenth century. The metal keys on manual typewriters would stick together if a user typed too fast, and the QWERTY keyboard was designed to slow down typists and minimize the problem of the keys sticking together. With computers, the problem that QWERTY was developed to solve no longer exists, so keyboards could be changed easily to have letters in a more efficient layout. But because the overwhelming majority of people have learned to use keyboards with the QWERTY layout, there might be significant costs to them if they had to switch, even if a new layout ultimately made them faster typists.

Other products that supposedly embodied inferior technologies are VHS video recorders—supposedly inferior to Sony Betamax recorders—and the Windows computer operating system—supposedly inferior to the Macintosh operating system. Some economists have argued that because of path dependence and switching costs, network externalities can result in *market failures*. As we saw in Chapter 5, a market failure is a situation in which the market fails to produce the efficient level of output. If network externalities result in market failure, government intervention in these markets might improve economic efficiency. Many economists are skeptical, however, that network externalities really do lead to consumers being locked into products with inferior technologies. In particular, economists Stan Leibowitz of the University of Texas, Dallas, and Stephen Margolis of North Carolina State University have argued that in practice, the gains from using a superior technology are larger than the losses due to switching costs. After carefully studying the cases of the QWERTY keyboard, VHS video recorders, and the Windows computer operating system, they have concluded that there is no good evidence that the alternative technologies were actually superior. The implications of network externalities for economic efficiency remain controversial among economists.

Network externality The situation where the usefulness of a product increases with the number of consumers who use it.

Does Fairness Matter?

If people were only interested in making themselves as well off as possible in a material sense, they would not be concerned with fairness. There is a great deal of evidence, however, that people like to be treated fairly and that they usually attempt to treat others fairly, even if doing so makes them worse off financially. Tipping servers in restaurants is an example. Diners in restaurants typically add 15 percent to their food bills as tips to their servers. Tips are not *required*, but most people see it as very unfair not to tip, unless the service has been exceptionally bad. You could argue that people leave tips not to be fair but because they are afraid that if they don't leave a tip, the next time they visit the restaurant they will receive poor service. Studies have shown, however, that most people leave tips at restaurants even while on vacation or in other circumstances where they are unlikely to visit the restaurant again.

There are many other examples where people willingly part with money when they are not required to do so and when they receive nothing material in return. The most obvious example is making donations to charity. Apparently, donating money to charity or leaving tips in restaurants that they will never visit again gives people more utility than they would receive from keeping the money and spending it on themselves.

A Test of Fairness in the Economic Laboratory: The Ultimatum Game Experiment Economists have used experiments to increase their understanding of the role that fairness plays in consumer decision making. Experimental economics has been widely used during the past two decades, and a number of experimental economics laboratories exist in the United States and Europe. Economists Maurice Allais, Reinhard Selten, and Vernon Smith were awarded the Nobel Prize in Economics in part because of their contributions to experimental economics. Experiments make it possible to focus on a single aspect of consumer behavior. The *ultimatum game*, first popularized by Werner Güth of the Max Planck Institute of Economics, is an experiment that tests whether fairness is important in consumer decision making. Various economists have conducted the ultimatum game experiment under slightly different conditions, but with generally the same result. In this game, a group of volunteers—often college students—are divided into pairs. One member of each pair is the "allocator," and the other member of the pair is the "recipient."

Each pair is given an amount of money, say $20. The allocator decides how much of the $20 each member of the pair will get. There are no restrictions on how the allocator divides up the money. He or she could keep it all, give it all to the recipient, or anything in between. The recipient must then decide whether to accept the allocation or reject it. If the recipient decides to accept the allocation, each member of the pair gets to keep his or her share. If the recipient decides to reject the allocation, both members of the pair receive nothing.

If neither the allocator nor the recipient cared about fairness, optimal play in the ultimatum game is straightforward: The allocator should propose a division of the money in which the allocator receives $19.99 and the recipient receives $0.01. The allocator has maximized his or her gain. The recipient should accept the division because the alternative is to reject the division and receive nothing at all: Even a penny is better than nothing.

In fact, when the ultimatum game experiment is carried out, both allocators and recipients act as if fairness is important. Allocators usually offer recipients at least a 40 percent share of the money, and recipients almost always reject offers of less than a 10 percent share. Why do allocators offer recipients more than a negligible amount? It might be that allocators do not care about fairness but fear that recipients do care and will reject offers they consider unfair. This possibility was tested in an experiment known as the *dictator game* carried out by Daniel Kahneman (a psychologist who shared the Nobel Prize in Economics), Jack Knetsch, and Richard Thaler, using students at Cornell University. In this experiment, the allocators were given only two possible divisions of $20: either $18 for themselves and $2 for the recipient or an even division of $10 for themselves and $10 for the recipient. One important difference from the ultimatum game was that *the recipient was not allowed to reject the division*. Of the 161 allocators, 122 chose the even division of the $20. Because there was no possibility of the $18/$2 split being rejected, the allocators must have chosen the even split because they valued acting fairly.

Why would recipients in the ultimatum game ever reject any division of the money in which they receive even a very small amount, given that even a small amount of money is better than nothing? Apparently, most people value fairness enough that they will refuse to participate in transactions they consider unfair, even if they are worse off financially as a result.

Business Implications of Fairness If consumers value fairness, how does that affect firms? One consequence is that firms will sometimes not raise prices of goods and services, even when there is a large increase in demand, because they are afraid their customers will consider the price increases unfair and may buy elsewhere.

For example, the Broadway play *The Producers* was extremely popular during its first year in production. Even though ticket prices were an average of $75, on most nights, many more people wanted to buy tickets at that price than could be accommodated in the St. James Theater, where the play was running. Figure 9-4 illustrates this situation.

Notice that the supply curve in Figure 9-4 is a vertical line, which indicates that the capacity of the St. James Theater is fixed at 1,644 seats. At a price of $75 per ticket, there was a shortage of more than 400 tickets. Why didn't the theater raise ticket prices to $125, where the quantity supplied would equal the quantity demanded?

Let's look at two other examples in which it seems that businesses could increase their profits by raising prices. First, each year, many more people would like to buy tickets to see the Super Bowl than there are tickets for them to buy at the price the National Football League charges. Why doesn't the National Football League raise prices? Second, at popular restaurants, there are often long lines of people waiting to be served. Some of the people will wait hours to be served, and some won't be served at all before the restaurant closes. Why doesn't the restaurant raise prices high enough to eliminate the lines?

In each of these cases, it appears that a firm could increase its profits by raising prices. The seller would be selling the same quantity—of seats in a theater or a football

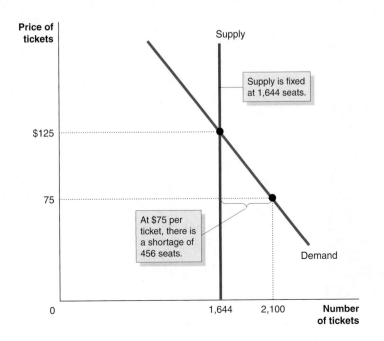

Figure 9-4

The Market for Tickets to *The Producers*

The St. James Theater could have raised prices for the Broadway musical *The Producers* to $125 per ticket and still sold all of the 1,644 tickets available. Instead, the theater kept the price of tickets at $75, even though the result was a shortage of more than 400 seats. Is it possible that this strategy maximized profits?

stadium or meals in a restaurant—at a higher price, so profits should increase. Economists have provided two explanations why firms sometimes do not raise prices in these situations. Gary Becker, winner of the Nobel Prize in Economics, has suggested that the products involved—theatrical plays, football games, rock concerts, or restaurant meals—are all products that buyers consume together with other buyers. In those situations, the amount consumers wish to buy may be related to how much of the product other people are consuming. People like to consume, and be seen consuming, a popular product. In this case, a popular restaurant that increased its prices enough to eliminate lines might find that it had also eliminated its popularity.

Daniel Kahneman, Jack Knetsch, and Richard Thaler have offered another explanation for why firms don't always raise prices when doing so would seem to increase their profits. In surveys of consumers, these researchers found that most people considered it fair for firms to raise their prices following an increase in costs but unfair to raise prices following an increase in demand. For example, Kahneman, Knetsch, and Thaler conducted a survey in which people were asked their opinion of the following situation: "A hardware store has been selling snow shovels for $15. The morning after a large snowstorm, the store raises the price to $20." Eighty-two percent of those surveyed responded that they considered the hardware store's actions to be unfair. Kahneman, Knetsch, and Thaler have concluded that firms may sometimes not raise their prices even when the quantity demanded of their product is greater than the quantity supplied out of fear that in the long run, they will lose customers who believe the price increases were unfair.

These explanations share the same basic idea: Sometimes firms will give up some profits in the short run to keep their customers happy and increase their profits in the long run.

Making the Connection | Professor Krueger Goes to the Super Bowl

Economist Alan Krueger of Princeton University has studied the question of why the National Football League does not charge a price for Super Bowl tickets that is high enough to make the quantity of tickets demanded equal to the quantity of tickets available. The prices may seem high—$400 for the best seats, $325 for the rest—but the quantity demanded still greatly exceeds the quantity supplied. Most Super Bowl tickets are allocated to the two teams playing in the game or to the league's corporate sponsors. To give ordinary fans a chance to attend the game, in 2001, the NFL set aside 500 pairs of tickets. They held a lottery for the opportunity to buy these tickets, and more than 36,000 people applied. Some fans were willing to pay as much as $5,000 to buy a ticket from ticket scalpers. (Scalpers buy tickets at their face value and then resell them at much higher prices, even though in Florida, where the 2001 Super Bowl was held, ticket scalping is illegal.)

Why didn't the NFL simply raise the price of tickets to clear the market? Krueger decided to survey football fans attending the game to see if their views could help explain this puzzle. Krueger's survey provides support for the Kahneman, Knetsch, and Thaler explanation of why companies do not always raise prices when the quantity demanded is greater than the quantity supplied. When asked whether it would "be fair for the NFL to raise the [price of tickets] to $1,500 if that is still less than the amount most people are willing to pay for tickets," 92 percent of the fans surveyed answered "no." Even 83 percent of the fans who had paid more than $1,500 for their tickets answered "no." Krueger concluded

Should the NFL raise the price of Super Bowl tickets?

that whatever the NFL might gain in the short run from raising ticket prices, it would more than lose in the long run by alienating football fans.

Source: Alan B. Krueger, "Supply and Demand: An Economist Goes to the Super Bowl," *Milken Institute Review*, Second Quarter 2001.

YOUR TURN: Test your understanding by doing related problems 3.11 and 3.12 on page 315 at the end of this chapter.

9.4 LEARNING OBJECTIVE

9.4 | Describe the behavioral economics approach to understanding decision making.

Behavioral Economics: Do People Make Their Choices Rationally?

When economists say that consumers and firms are behaving "rationally," they mean that consumers and firms are taking actions that are appropriate to reach their goals, given the information available to them. In recent years, some economists have begun studying situations in which people do not appear to be making choices that are economically rational. This new area of economics is called **behavioral economics**. Why might consumers or businesses not act rationally? The most obvious reason would be that they do not realize that their actions are inconsistent with their goals. As we discussed in Chapter 1, one of the objectives of economics is to suggest ways to make better decisions. In this section, we discuss ways in which consumers can improve their decisions by avoiding some common pitfalls.

Behavioral economics The study of situations in which people make choices that do not appear to be economically rational.

Consumers commonly commit the following three mistakes when making decisions:

- They take into account monetary costs but ignore nonmonetary opportunity costs.

- They fail to ignore sunk costs.

- They are overly optimistic about their future behavior.

Ignoring Nonmonetary Opportunity Costs

Remember from Chapter 2 that the **opportunity cost** of any activity is the highest-valued alternative that must be given up to engage in that activity. For example, if you own something you could sell, using it yourself involves an opportunity cost. It is often difficult for people to think of opportunity costs in these terms.

Opportunity cost The highest-valued alternative that must be given up to engage in an activity.

Consider the following example: Some of the fans at the 2001 Super Bowl participated in a lottery run by the National Football League that allowed the winners to purchase tickets at their face value, which was either $325 or $400, depending on where in the stadium the seats were located. Alan Krueger surveyed the lottery winners, asking them two questions:

Question 1: If you had not won the lottery, would you have been willing to pay $3,000 for your ticket?
Question 2: If after winning your ticket (and before arriving in Florida for the Super Bowl) someone had offered you $3,000 for your ticket, would you have sold it?

In answer to the first question, 94 percent said that if they had not won the lottery, they would not have paid $3,000 for a ticket. In answer to the second question, 92 percent said they would not have sold their ticket for $3,000. But these answers are contradictory! If someone offers you $3,000 for your ticket, then by using the ticket rather than selling it, you incur an opportunity cost of $3,000. There really is a $3,000 cost involved in using that ticket, even though you do not pay $3,000 in cash. The alternatives of either paying $3,000 or not receiving $3,000 amount to exactly the same thing.

Endowment effect The tendency of people to be unwilling to sell a good they already own even if they are offered a price that is greater than the price they would be willing to pay to buy the good if they didn't already own it.

If the ticket is really not worth $3,000 to you, you should sell it. If it is worth $3,000 to you, you should be willing to pay $3,000 in cash to buy it. Not being willing to sell a ticket you already own for $3,000, while at the same time not being willing to buy a ticket for $3,000 if you didn't already own one is inconsistent behavior. The inconsistency comes from a failure to take into account nonmonetary opportunity costs. Behavioral economists believe this inconsistency is caused by the **endowment effect**, which is the tendency of people to be unwilling to sell a good they already own even if they are offered a price that is greater than the price they would be willing to pay to buy the good if they didn't already own it.

The failure to take into account opportunity costs is a very common error in decision making. Suppose, for example, that a friend is in a hurry to have his room cleaned—it's the Friday before parents' weekend—and he offers you $50 to do it for him. You turn him down and spend the time cleaning your own room, even though you know somebody down the hall who would be willing to clean your room for $20. Leave aside complicating details—the guy who asked you to clean his room is a real slob, or you don't want the person who offered to clean your room for $20 to go through your stuff—and you should see the point we are making. The opportunity cost of cleaning your own room is $50—the amount your friend offered to pay you to clean his room. It is inconsistent to turn down an offer from someone else to clean your room for $20 when you are doing it for yourself at a cost of $50. The key point here is this: *Nonmonetary opportunity costs are just as real as monetary costs and should be taken into account when making decisions.*

Business Implications of Consumers Ignoring Nonmonetary Opportunity Costs

Behavioral economist Richard Thaler has studied several examples of how businesses make use of consumers' failure to take into account opportunity costs. Whenever you buy something with a credit card, the credit card company charges the merchant a fee to process the bill. Credit card companies generally do not allow stores to charge higher prices to customers who use credit cards. A bill was introduced in Congress that would have made it illegal for credit card companies to enforce this rule. The credit card industry was afraid that if this law passed, credit card usage would drop because stores might begin charging a fee to credit card users. They attempted to have the law amended so that stores would be allowed to give a cash discount to people not using credit cards but would not be allowed to charge a fee to people using credit cards. There really is no difference in terms of opportunity cost between being charged a fee and not receiving a discount. The credit card industry was relying on the fact that *not* receiving a discount is a nonmonetary opportunity cost—and, therefore, likely to be ignored by consumers—but a fee is a monetary cost that people do take into account.

Film processing companies provide another example. Many of these companies have a policy of printing every picture on a roll of film, even if the picture is very fuzzy. Customers are allowed to ask for refunds on pictures they don't like. Once again, the companies are relying on the fact that passing up a refund once you have already paid for a picture is a nonmonetary opportunity cost rather than a direct monetary cost. In fact, customers rarely ask for refunds.

Making	Why Do Hilton Hotels and other
the	**Firms Hide Their Prices?**
Connection	

Economists recently began to use ideas from behavioral economics to understand a puzzling aspect of how some businesses price their products. David Laibson of Harvard University and Xavier Gabaix of New York University note that some products consist of a "base good" and "add-ons." For instance, to use a printer, you buy the printer itself—the base good—and replacement ink cartridges—the add-on. Typically, firms compete on the price of the base good but do their best to hide the prices of the add-ons. Because consumers sometimes spend more on the add-ons than on the base good, it may seem surprising that firms are able to successfully hide the prices of add-ons. For instance, over the life of a printer, consumers spend, on average, 10 times the price of the printer in buying ink cartridges. Yet one survey indicates that only 3 percent of consumers know the true cost of using a printer, including the cost of the ink cartridges. Similarly, many consumers are unaware of the add-on charges from using a checking account, such as ATM fees, returned check charges, and minimum balance fees. Many consumers making a hotel reservation are unaware of the hotel's charges for Internet access, for food from minibars, for breakfast at the hotel restaurant, or for local phone calls.

How are firms able to hide the prices of add-ons? Why doesn't competition lead some firms to offer lower-priced add-ons and advertise that their competitors' add-ons are higher priced? Laibson and Gabaix explain this puzzle by arguing that there are two types of consumers: sophisticated consumers, who pay attention to prices of add-ons, and myopic consumers, who ignore the prices of add-ons. It turns out that using advertising to convert myopic consumers into sophisticated consumers is not a profitable strategy. Consider the following example: Suppose that Hilton Hotels charges $80 per night for a room and the typical myopic consumer also spends $20 per night on local phone calls, food from the minibar, high-priced breakfasts, and other add-ons. Could a competing hotel, such as Marriott, attract Hilton's customers by advertising that Marriott's add-ons were more fairly priced than Hilton's? Laibson and Gabaix argue that this strategy would not work because its main effect would be to turn myopic consumers into sophisticated consumers. Once Hilton's customers become sophisticated, they will avoid the add-on fees, by, for instance, using their cell phones rather than the hotel phones to make calls or by eating breakfast in nearby restaurants rather than in the hotel. According to Laibson and Gabaix, Marriott's advertising campaign, "hurts Hilton—which sells fewer add-ons—but helps Hilton's customers, who are taught to substitute away from add-ons." But these sophisticated consumers are no more likely to switch from Hilton to Marriott than they were before Marriott incurred the cost of its advertising campaign. Exposing a competitor's hidden costs, say Laibson and Gabaix, "is good for the consumer and bad for both firms. Neither firm has an incentive to do it." As a result, many consumers remain unaware of the true prices of some of the products they purchase.

Some hotels hide what they charge for room service and Internet access.

Sources: Christopher Shay, "The Hidden-Fee Economy," *New York Times*, December 10, 2006; and Xavier Gabaix and David Laibson, "Shrouded Attributes, Consumer Myopia, and Information Suppression in Competitive Markets," *Quarterly Journal of Economics*, Vol. 121, No. 2, May 2006, pp. 351–397.

YOUR TURN: Test your understanding by doing related problem 4.10 on page 316 at the end of this chapter.

Failing to Ignore Sunk Costs

A **sunk cost** is a cost that has already been paid and cannot be recovered. Once you have paid money and can't get it back, you should ignore that money in any later decisions you make. Consider the following two situations:

Situation 1: You bought a ticket to a play for $75. The ticket is nonrefundable and must be used on Tuesday night, which is the only night the play will be performed. On Monday, a friend calls and invites you to a local comedy club to see a comedian you both like who is appearing only on Tuesday night. Your friend offers to pay the cost of going to the club.

Situation 2: It's Monday night, and you are about to buy a ticket for the Tuesday night performance of the same play as in situation 1. As you are leaving to buy the ticket, your friend calls and invites you to the comedy club.

Sunk cost A cost that has already been paid and cannot be recovered.

Would your decision to go to the play or to the comedy club be different in situation 1 than in situation 2? Most people would say that in situation 1, they would go to the play, because otherwise they would lose the $75 they had paid for the ticket. In fact, though, the $75 is "lost" no matter what you do because the ticket is not refundable. The only real issue for you to decide is whether you would prefer to see the play or prefer to go with your friend to the comedy club. If you would prefer to go to the club, the fact that you have already paid $75 for the ticket to the play is irrelevant. Your decision should be the same in situation 1 and situation 2.

Psychologists Daniel Kahneman and Amos Tversky explored the tendency of consumers to not ignore sunk costs by asking two samples of people the following questions:

Question 1: One sample of people was asked the following question: "Imagine that you have decided to see a play and have paid the admission price of $10 per ticket. As you enter the theater, you discover that you have lost the ticket. The seat was not marked, and the ticket cannot be recovered. Would you pay $10 for another ticket?" Of those asked, 46 percent answered "yes," and 54 percent answered "no."

Question 2: A different sample of people was asked the following question: "Imagine that you have decided to see a play where admission is $10 per ticket. As you enter the theater, you discover that you have lost a $10 bill. Would you still pay $10 for a ticket to the play?" Of those asked, 88 percent answered "yes," and 12 percent answered "no."

The situations presented in the two questions are actually the same and should have received the same fraction of yes and no responses. Many people, though, have trouble seeing that in question 1, when deciding whether to see the play, they should ignore the $10 already paid for a ticket because it is a sunk cost.

Being Unrealistic about Future Behavior

Studies have shown that a majority of adults in the United States are overweight. Why do many people choose to eat too much? One possibility is that they receive more utility from eating too much than they would from being thin. A more likely explanation, however, is that many people eat a lot today because they expect to eat less tomorrow. But they never do eat less, and so they end up overweight. (Of course, some people also suffer from medical problems that lead to weight gain.) Similarly, some people continue smoking today because they expect to be able to give it up sometime in the future. Unfortunately, for many people that time never comes, and they suffer the health consequences of prolonged smoking. In both these cases, people are overvaluing the utility from current choices—eating chocolate cake or smoking—and undervaluing the utility to be received in the future from being thin or not getting lung cancer.

Economists who have studied this question argue that many people have preferences that are not consistent over time. In the long run, you would like to be thin or give up smoking or achieve some other goal, but each day, you make decisions (such as to eat too much or to smoke) that are not consistent with this long-run goal. If you are unrealistic about your future behavior, you underestimate the costs of choices—like overeating or smoking—that you make today. A key way of avoiding this problem is to be realistic about your future behavior.

Making | **Why Don't Students Study More?**
the | Government statistics show that students who do well in col-
Connection | lege earn at least $10,000 more per year than students who
fail to graduate or who graduate with low grades. So, over the course of a career of 40 years or more, students who do well in college will have earned

upwards of $400,000 more than students who failed to graduate or who received low grades. Most colleges advise that students study at least two hours outside of class for every hour they spend in class. Surveys show that students often ignore this advice.

If the payoff to studying is so high, why don't students study more?

If the opportunity cost of not studying is so high, why do many students choose to study relatively little? Some students have work or family commitments that limit the amount of time they can study. But many other students study less than they would if they were more realistic about their future behavior. On any given night, a student has to choose between studying and other activities—like watching television, going to the movies, or going to a party—that may seem to provide higher utility in the short run. Many students choose one of these activities over studying because they expect to study tomorrow or the next day, but tomorrow they face the same choices and make similar decisions. As a result, they do not study enough to meet their long-run goal of graduating with high grades. If they were more realistic about their future behavior, they would not make the mistake of overvaluing the utility from activities like watching television or partying because they would realize that those activities can endanger their long-run goal of graduating with honors.

YOUR TURN: Test your understanding by doing related problem 4.13 on page 316 at the end of this chapter.

Solved Problem | **9-4**

How Do You Get People to Save More of Their Income?

An article in the *New York Times* states the following:

> When it comes to saving for retirement, Americans . . . know they do not put away enough. . . . But ask them to save more in their [retirement] plans and they balk. A buck in the hand is irresistibly spent. Try a different approach. Ask them to commit now to increasing their savings in the future, make the increase coincide with the next raise, and they cheerfully sign up.

Why would people refuse to increase their savings now but agree to increase their savings in the future?

Source: Louis Uchitelle, "Why It Takes Psychology to Make People Save," *New York Times*, January 13, 2002.

SOLVING THE PROBLEM:

Step 1: **Review the chapter material.** This problem is about how people are not always realistic about their future behavior, so you may want to review the section "Being Unrealistic about Future Behavior," which begins on page 306.

Step 2: **Use your understanding of consumer decision making to show that this plan may work.** We have seen that many people are unrealistic about their future behavior. They spend money today that they should be saving for retirement, partly because they expect to increase their saving in the future. A savings plan that gets people to commit today to saving in the future takes advantage of people's optimism about their future behavior. They agree to save more in the future because they expect to be doing that anyway. In fact, without being part of a plan that automatically saves their next raise, they probably would not have increased their savings.

YOUR TURN: For more practice, do related problems 4.11 and 4.12 on page 316 at the end of this chapter.

>> **End Solved Problem 9-2**

Taking into account nonmonetary opportunity costs, ignoring sunk costs, and being more realistic about future behavior are three ways in which consumers are able to improve the decisions they make.

Economics in YOUR Life!

>> **Continued from page 285**

At the beginning of the chapter, we asked you to consider a situation in which you had paid $75 for a concert ticket, which is the most you would be willing to pay. Just before you enter the concert hall, someone offers you $90 for the ticket. We posed two questions: Would you sell the ticket? and Would an economist think it is rational to sell the ticket? If you answered that you would sell, then your answer is rational in the sense in which economists use the term. The cost of going to see the concert is what you have to give up for the ticket. Initially, the cost was just $75—the dollar price of the ticket. This amount was also the most you were willing to pay. However, once someone offers you $90 for the ticket, the cost of seeing the concert rises to $90. The reason the cost of the concert is now $90 is that once you turn down an offer of $90 for the ticket you have incurred a nonmonetary opportunity cost of $90 if you use the ticket yourself. The endowment effect explains why some people would not sell the ticket. People seem to value things that they have more than things that they do not have. Therefore, a concert ticket you already own may be worth more to you than a concert ticket you have yet to purchase. Behavioral economists study situations like this where people make choices that do not appear to be economically rational.

Conclusion

In a market system, consumers are in the driver's seat. Goods are produced only if consumers want them to be. Therefore, how consumers make their decisions is an important area for economists to study, a fact that was highlighted when Daniel Kahneman—whose research was mentioned several times in this chapter—shared the Nobel Prize in Economics. Economists expect that consumers will spend their incomes so that the last dollar spent on each good provides them with equal additional amounts of satisfaction, or utility. In practice, there are significant social influences on consumer decision making, particularly when a good or service is consumed in public. Fairness also seems to be an important consideration for most consumers. Finally, many consumers could improve the decisions they make if they would take into account nonmonetary opportunity costs and ignore sunk costs.

In this chapter, we studied consumers' choices. In the next several chapters, we will study firms' choices. Before moving on to the next chapter, read *An Inside Look* on the next page for a discussion of whether Elizabeth Arden made a good decision in hiring Mariah Carey to endorse its products.

Can Mariah Carey Get You to Buy Elizabeth Arden Perfume?

WOMEN'S WEAR DAILY, APRIL 7, 2006

Mariah Signs Scent Deal with Arden

NEW YORK - The celebrity fragrance craze has a new player—Mariah Carey.

The Grammy Award-winning singer has signed with Elizabeth Arden to develop and market her own line of fragrance products, the first of which are to be launched in spring 2007 in what the company described as "prestige department stores."

ⓐ Financial terms of the deal, announced on Thursday, were not disclosed. However, industry experts have speculated that such agreements often include an up-front payout of $1 million to $2 million, and 1 to 3 percent of fragrance sales after the scent is on the counter.

Carey, whose projects include a self-branded line sold by costume jewelry retailer Claire's, will be involved with all aspects of the fragrance's development, Arden said in a statement. "I've already been involved with the team at Elizabeth Arden in the early stages of the creative process," Carey said.

The deal further amps up the significance of celebrities in the beauty world—particularly in the fragrance arena. Coty is arguably the most entrenched, with Jennifer Lopez, Sarah Jessica Parker, Kimora Lee Simmons, David and Victoria Beckham, Mary-Kate and Ashley Olsen, Shania Twain and the "Desperate Housewives" in its stable.

ⓑ Arden's deal with Britney Spears, signed in March 2004, has yielded two top-five hits: Curious Britney Spears and Fantasy Britney Spears. Arden has had teen queen Hilary Duff under contract for beauty products since September (the first fruits of that deal have not yet been released), and it signed Catherine Zeta-Jones in February 2002 to be the face of its core Elizabeth Arden brand. In addition, NASCAR star Jeff Gordon has been the face of its Halston Z-14 brand since May 2004, and the original celebrity fragrance maven, Elizabeth Taylor, is also part of the company's constellation.

"Mariah has immense popularity with a very diverse consumer base—from teenagers to grandmothers," Ron Rolleston, executive vice president of global marketing for Elizabeth Arden, said in an interview. "She is global in terms of her appeal, which spans generations and cultures, which we believe will translate well into sales when the fragrance is launched. . . . She has already met with the four major fragrance houses that we work with, and has very definite ideas." Rolleston noted that Federated Department Stores, Belk and Dillard's are stores that would be likely to carry the scent.

Part of the reason retailers applaud the category is that many of the celebrities are drawing lapsed department store consumers back into the beauty department. "In Mariah, Arden has someone who is a proven hit-maker and an undervalued asset," said Steve Stoute—managing partner of Carol's Daughter and chairman and chief creative officer, Translation—who has brokered celebrity endorsement deals. "Her music has always been bigger than her personality, and she not only appeals to a younger consumer, she has a consumer who has grown up with her. I believe that Arden has her at the right time. I just hope that they have the bandwidth to market all of these celebrity brands.

Key Points in the Article

This article discusses how firms benefit from using celebrity endorsements in their advertising. Elizabeth Arden clearly believes that hiring Mariah Carey to endorse a new line of fragrances will pay off financially. The firm believes that because Carey is a popular celebrity, some of that popularity will rub off on the new fragrance products. Essentially, the firm is betting that a large number of consumers will see Carey's endorsement and purchase the fragrance because of that endorsement. Consumers may purchase the fragrance to be like Mariah Carey or just to signal that they are like Mariah Carey. However, celebrity endorsements come with risks. Mary-Kate and Ashley Olsen were dropped from the "Got Milk?" campaign after Mary-Kate was reportedly hospitalized for an eating disorder. In addition, Slim-Fast dropped Whoopi Goldberg from its advertisements after she made critical and vulgar comments about President George W. Bush. Once a firm hires a celebrity, consumers associate the product with the celebrity. This association can be a good or a bad thing depending on the celebrity's actions.

Analyzing the News

ⓐ Elizabeth Arden is giving Mariah Carey a large up-front payment and a significant part of the revenues from the fragrance sales. The firm is willing to hire Carey because it believes doing so will increase its profits. Her endorsement could lead to higher prices or a greater quantity sold, but the firm's profits will increase only if its increase in revenue is greater than the required payments to Carey.

We saw in Chapter 3 that when consumers' taste for a product increases, the demand curve will shift to the right, and when consumers' taste for a product decreases, the demand curve for the product will shift to the left. When a firm hires a celebrity to endorse its products, it is hoping to increase consumers' taste for its product. The figure shows that if the endorsement is successful, the demand curve for Elizabeth Arden fragrances shifts from D_1 to D_2. The increase in demand allows the firm to sell more fragrance bottles at every price. For example, at a price of P_1 it could sell Q_1 bottles without the endorsement but Q_2 fragrances with the endorsement.

ⓑ Elizabeth Arden's experience with celebrity endorsements has been very positive. The firm has used many celebrity endorsements in the past and the collaboration with Britney Spears produced two very successful fragrances. Therefore, the firm's experience suggests that celebrity endorsements can increase sales.

Thinking Critically

1. Celebrity endorsements may be rewarding to firms, but they can also be risky. Elizabeth Arden has committed a significant amount of money to hiring Mariah Carey and developing the fragrances that she will endorse. What do you think would happen to the demand curve for these fragrances if Mariah Carey gets involved in an embarrassing scandal?

2. Celebrity endorsements are also expensive. Should a firm whose celebrity endorser was just arrested make its decision about whether or not to cancel its ad campaign based on the amount it has already spent on making the ads? Briefly explain.

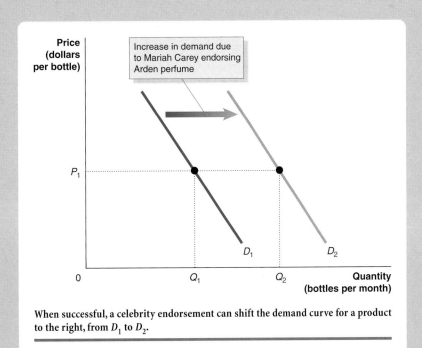

When successful, a celebrity endorsement can shift the demand curve for a product to the right, from D_1 to D_2.

Key Terms

Behavioral economics, p. 303

Budget constraint, p. 289

Endowment effect, p. 304

Income effect, p. 294

Law of diminishing marginal utility, p. 287

Marginal utility (*MU*), p. 287

Network externality, p. 299

Opportunity cost, p. 303

Substitution effect, p. 294

Sunk cost, p. 305

Utility, p. 286

9.1 LEARNING OBJECTIVE 9.1 | Define utility and explain how consumers choose goods and services to maximize their utility, **pages 286–295.**

Utility and Consumer Decision Making

Summary

Utility is the enjoyment or satisfaction that people receive from consuming goods and services. The goal of a consumer is to spend available income so as to maximize utility. **Marginal utility** is the change in total utility a person receives from consuming one additional unit of a good or service. The **law of diminishing marginal utility** states that consumers receive diminishing additional satisfaction as they consume more of a good or service during a given period of time. The **budget constraint** is the amount of income consumers have available to spend on goods and services. To maximize utility, consumers should make sure they spend their income so that the last dollar spent on each product gives them the same marginal utility. The **income effect** is the change in the quantity demanded of a good that results from the effect of a change in the price on consumer purchasing power. The **substitution effect** is the change in the quantity demanded of a good that results from a change in price making the good more or less expensive relative to other goods, holding constant the effect of the price change on consumer purchasing power.

myeconlab Visit www.myeconlab.com to complete these exercises *Get Ahead of the Curve* online and get instant feedback.

Review Questions

1.1 What is the economic definition of utility? Is utility measurable?

1.2 What is the definition of marginal utility? What is the law of diminishing marginal utility? Why is marginal utility more useful than total utility in consumer decision making?

1.3 What is meant by a consumer's budget constraint? What is the rule of equal marginal utility per dollar spent?

Problems and Applications

1.4 Does the law of diminishing marginal utility hold true in every situation? Is it possible to think of goods for which consuming additional units will result in increasing marginal utility?

1.5 If consumers should allocate their income so that the last dollar spent on every product gives them the same amount of additional utility, how should they decide the amount of their income to save?

1.6 You have six hours to study for two exams tomorrow. The relationship between hours of study and test scores is shown in the following table.

ECONOMICS		PSYCHOLOGY	
HOURS	SCORE	HOURS	SCORE
0	54	0	54
1	62	1	60
2	69	2	65
3	75	3	69
4	80	4	72
5	84	5	74
6	87	6	75

a. Use the rule for determining optimal purchases to decide how many hours you should study each subject. Treat each point on an exam like 1 unit of utility and assume that you are equally interested in doing well in economics and psychology.

b. Now suppose that you are a psychology major, and that you value each point you earn on a psychology exam as being worth three times as much as each point you earn on an economics exam. Now how many hours will you study each subject?

1.7 (Related to *Solved Problem 9-1* on page 291) Joe has $16 to spend on Twinkies and Ho-Hos. Twinkies have a price of $1 per pack, and Ho-Hos have a price of $2 per pack. Use the information in the graphs on the following page to determine the number of Twinkies packs and the number of Ho-Hos packs Joe should buy to maximize his utility. Briefly explain your reasoning.

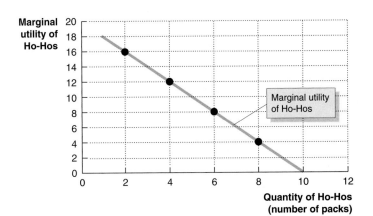

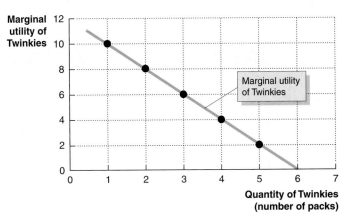

1.8 **(Related to *Solved Problem 9-1* on page 291)** Joe has $55 to spend on apples and oranges. Given the information in the following table, is Joe maximizing utility? Briefly explain.

PRODUCT	PRICE	QUANTITY	TOTAL UTILITY	MARGINAL UTILITY OF LAST UNIT
Apples	$0.50	50	1,000	20
Oranges	$0.75	40	500	30

1.9 Suppose the price of a bag of Frito's corn chips declines from $0.69 to $0.59. Which is likely to be larger: the income effect or the substitution effect? Briefly explain.

1.10 **(Related to the *Don't Let This Happen to You!* on page 293)** Mary is buying corn chips and soda. She has four bags of corn chips and five bottles of soda in her shopping cart. The marginal utility of the fourth bag of corn chips is 10, and the marginal utility of the fifth bottle of soda is also 10. Is Mary maximizing utility? Briefly explain.

1.11 When the price of pizza falls in the Super Bowl example on pages 289–291, both the income and the substitution effect cause you to want to consume more pizza. If pizza were an inferior good, how would the analysis be changed? In this case, is it possible that a lower price of pizza might lead you to buy less pizza? Briefly explain.

>> End Learning Objective 9.1

9.2 LEARNING OBJECTIVE   9.2 | Use the concept of utility to explain the law of demand, **pages 295–297.**

Where Demand Curves Come From

Summary

When the price of a good declines, the ratio of the marginal utility to price rises. This leads consumers to buy more of that good. As a result, whenever the price of a product falls, the quantity demanded increases. We saw in Chapter 3 that this is known as the *law of demand*. The market demand curve can be constructed from the individual demand curves for all the consumers in the market.

 Visit www.myeconlab.com to complete these exercises *Get Ahead of the Curve* online and get instant feedback.

Review Questions

2.1 Explain how a downward-sloping demand curve results from consumers adjusting their consumption choices to changes in price.

2.2 What would need to be true for a demand curve to be upward sloping?

Problems and Applications

2.3 Considering only the income effect, if the price of an inferior good declines, would a consumer want to buy a larger quantity or a smaller quantity of the good? Does this mean that the demand curves for inferior goods should slope upward? Briefly explain.

2.4 The chapter states that "when the price of an inferior good falls, the income and substitution effects work in opposite directions." Explain what this statement means.

2.5 Suppose the market for ice cream cones is made up of three consumers: Josh, Curt, and Tim. Use the information in the following table to construct the market demand curve for ice cream cones. Show the information in a table and in a graph.

	JOSH	CURT	TIM
PRICE	QUANTITY DEMANDED (CONES PER WEEK)	QUANTITY DEMANDED (CONES PER WEEK)	QUANTITY DEMANDED (CONES PER WEEK)
$1.75	2	1	0
1.50	4	3	2
1.25	6	4	3
1.00	7	6	4
0.75	9	7	5

2.6 Suppose the wage you are being paid increases. Is there an income and substitution effect involved? If so, what is being substituted for what?

>> **End Learning Objective 9.2**

9.3 LEARNING OBJECTIVE   9.3 | Explain how social influences can affect consumption choices, **pages 298–303.**

Social Influences on Decision Making

Summary

Social factors can have an influence on consumption. For example, the amount of utility people receive from consuming a good often depends on how many other people they know who also consume the good. There is a **network externality** in the consumption of a product if the usefulness of the product increases with the number of consumers who use it. There is also evidence that people like to be treated fairly and that they usually attempt to treat others fairly, even if doing so makes them worse off financially. This result has been demonstrated in laboratory experiments, such as the ultimatum game. When firms set prices, they take into account consumers' preference for fairness. For example, hardware stores often do not increase the price of snow shovels to take advantage of a temporary increase in demand following a snowstorm.

 Visit www.myeconlab.com to complete these exercises *Get Ahead of the Curve* online and get instant feedback.

Review Questions

3.1 In which of the following situations are social influences on consumer decision making likely to be greater: choosing a restaurant for dinner or choosing a brand of toothpaste to buy? Briefly explain.

3.2 Why do consumers pay attention to celebrity endorsements of products?

3.3 What are network externalities? For what types of products are network externalities likely to be important? What is path dependence?

3.4 What is the ultimatum game? What insight does it provide into consumer decision making?

3.5 How does the fact that consumers apparently value fairness affect the decisions that businesses make?

Problems and Applications

3.6 Which of the following products are most likely to have significant network externalities? Explain.
   a. Fax machines
   b. Dog food
   c. Board games
   d. Conventional (CRT) television sets
   e. Plasma television sets

3.7 Linux is a computer operating system that is an alternative to Microsoft's Windows system. According to a newspaper article:

> The dominance of the Windows operating system, which runs 95 per cent of the world's PCs, is coming under greater attack in Asia than in any other part of the world, analysts say. Linux for PCs sold three times as many copies in Asia as in the US last year. . . . "In emerging markets such as India and China, where PC growth rates are the highest, Linux's momentum seems to be accelerating," said Robert Stimson, a Bank of America analyst in San Francisco.

If network externalities are important in choosing a computer operating system, why might Linux be more successful in Asia than in the United States?

Source: "Gates Blitzes Asia to Stem Linux Threat," *New Zealand Herald*, June 29, 2004.

3.8 (Related to the *Chapter Opener* on page 284) Think of some firms that don't use celebrities to endorse their products. Why do some firms, like Coca-Cola, use celebrity endorsers, while other firms don't?

3.9 (Related to the *Making the Connection* on page 298) Tiger Woods is a professional golfer who knows more about golfing and golf related products than most consumers. However, this is not necessarily the case for Buicks, Rolexes, and American Express products. Consider the model of utility maximizing behavior described in this chapter. For Buick's use of Tiger Woods as a celebrity endorser to make economic sense, then how must Woods's endorsement affect the marginal utility that at least some consumers receive from driving Buicks? What will this do to the demand curve for Buicks?

3.10 An article in the *New York Times* published during the 2002 Winter Olympics held in Utah indicated that many businesses raised prices during the two-week event. The article described one incident as follows:

> Susanne and Heather McDonald, sisters from the northwest Wyoming town of Moose, said a friend was having sushi at a restaurant in Park City, where skiing events are held, and the waiter was adding $3 for every side dish until the man identified himself as a local resident. "Then he got them for free," Susanne McDonald said.

When setting the price for a meal, why would it matter to the restaurant whether the customer was a local resident?

Source: Michael Janofsky, "Olympic Boom Leaves Visitors Feeling Busted," *New York Times*, February 19, 2002.

3.11 (Related to the *Making the Connection* on page 302) Suppose the rock band U2 can sell out a concert at Madison Square Garden with tickets priced at $45. U2's manager estimates that they could still sell out the Garden at $85 per ticket. Why might U2 and their manager want to keep ticket prices at $45?

3.12 (Related to the *Making the Connection* on page 302) Suppose that *Spider-Man 4* comes out, and hundreds of people arrive at a theater and discover that the movie is already sold out. Meanwhile, the theater is also showing a boring movie in its third week of release in a mostly empty theater. Why would this firm charge the same $7.50 for a ticket to either movie, when the quantity of tickets demanded is much greater than the quantity supplied for one movie, and the quantity of tickets demanded is much less than the quantity supplied for the other?

>> **End Learning Objective 9.3**

9.4 LEARNING OBJECTIVE   9.4 | Describe the behavioral economics approach to understanding decision making, **pages 303–308.**

Behavioral Economics: Do People Make Their Choices Rationally?

Summary

Behavioral economics is the study of situations in which people act in ways that are not economically rational. **Opportunity cost** is the highest-value alternative that must be given up to engage in an activity. People would improve their decision making if they took into account nonmonetary opportunity costs. People sometimes ignore nonmonetary opportunity costs because of the *endowment effect.* The **endowment effect** is the tendency of people to be unwilling to sell something they already own even if they are offered a price that is greater than the price they would be willing to pay to buy the good if they didn't already own it. People would also improve their decision making if they ignored *sunk costs.* A **sunk cost** is a cost that has already been paid and cannot be recovered. Finally, people would improve their decision making if they were more realistic about their future behavior.

 Visit www.myeconlab.com to complete these exercises online and get instant feedback.

Review Questions

4.1 What does it mean to be economically rational?

4.2 Define behavioral economics and give an example of three common mistakes that consumers often make.

Problems and Applications

4.3 Suppose your little brother tells you on Tuesday that one of his friends offered him $20 for his Albert Pujols rookie baseball card, but your brother decided not to sell the card. On Wednesday, your brother loses the card. Your parents feel sorry for him and give him $20 to make up the loss. Instead of buying another

Albert Pujols card with the money (which we will assume he could have done), your brother uses the money to go to the movies. Explain your brother's actions by using the concepts in this chapter.

4.4 Economist Richard Thaler has argued that the behavior of professional football teams during the college draft is an example of the endowment effect. Professional football teams take turns drafting eligible college players. Suppose that the New England Patriots now have a turn to pick, and the best college player not yet drafted is a quarterback. Suppose also that the Patriots already have a great quarterback and don't need another one. What should they do? Their optimal choice would appear to be to draft the quarterback and then trade him to another team that needs a quarterback. The Patriots could then receive in return a player from the other team who plays a position for which the Patriots need help. In fact, teams very rarely draft a college player and immediately trade him. Explain how the endowment effect could be involved here. (*Hint:* Consider the potential reaction of a team's fans to the team drafting a star college player and immediately trading him.)

Source: Richard Thaler, *Quasi Rational Economics*, New York: Russell Sage, 1991, p. 10.

4.5 Oldies 93 has a promotion in which it announces that a local gas station will sell gasoline at 93 cents per gallon beginning in 30 minutes. Jack hops in his car and drives to the station to fill up his half-empty tank. He pays only $9.30 for 10 gallons instead of the going price of $19.30. Did Jack save $10.00? Is the radio station doing its listeners a favor by offering this promotion? Briefly explain.

4.6 You have tickets to see Bruce Springsteen in concert at a stadium 50 miles away. A severe thunderstorm on the night of the concert makes driving hazardous. Will your decision to attend the concert be different if you paid $70 for the tickets than if you received the tickets for free? Explain your answer.

4.7 Rob Neyer is a baseball writer for ESPN.com. He described attending a Red Sox game at Fenway Park in Boston and having a seat in the sun on a hot, humid day: "Granted, I could have moved under the overhang and enjoyed today's contest from a nice, cool, shady seat. But when you paid forty-five dollars for a ticket in the fourth row, it's tough to move back to the twenty-fourth [row]." Evaluate Neyer's reasoning.

Source: Rob Neyer, *Feeding the Green Monster*, New York: iPublish.com, 2001, p. 50.

4.8 After owning a used car for two years, you start having problems with it. You take it into the shop, and a mechanic tells you that repairs will cost $4,000. What factors will you take into account in deciding whether to have the repairs done or to junk the car and buy another one? Will the price you paid for the car be one of those factors? Briefly explain.

4.9 The following excerpt is from a letter sent to a financial advice columnist: "My wife and I are trying to decide how to invest a $250,000 windfall. She wants to pay off our $114,000 mortgage, but I'm not eager to do that because we refinanced only nine months ago, paying $3,000 in fees and costs." Briefly discuss what effect the $3,000 refinancing cost should have on this couple's investment decision.

Source: Liz Pulliam, *Los Angeles Times* advice column, March 24, 2004.

4.10 **(Related to the *Making the Connection* on page 304)** Consumers tend to ignore the prices of "add-on" goods like ATM fees for checking accounts. Does this mean that if the government were to ban ATM fees that consumers would benefit?

4.11 **(Related to *Solved Problem 9-4* on page 307)** In an article in the *Quarterly Journal of Economics*, Ted O'Donoghue and Matthew Rabin make the following observation: "People have self-control problems caused by a tendency to pursue immediate gratification in a way that their 'long-run selves' do not appreciate." What do they mean by a person's "long-run self"? Give two examples of people pursuing immediate gratification that their long-run selves would not appreciate.

Source: Ted O'Donoghue and Matthew Rabin, "Choice and Procrastination," *Quarterly Journal of Economics*, February 2001, pp. 125–126.

4.12 **(Related to *Solved Problem 9-4* on page 307)** Data from health clubs show that members who choose a contract with a flat monthly fee over $70 attend, on average, 4.8 times per month. They pay a price per expected visit of more than $14, even though a $10-per-visit fee is also available. Why would these consumers choose a monthly contract when they lose money on it?

4.13 **(Related to the *Making the Connection* on page 306)** Briefly explain whether you agree or disagree with the following statement: "If people were more realistic about their future behavior, the demand curve for potato chips would shift to the left."

>> **End Learning Objective 9.4**

Appendix

Using Indifference Curves and Budget Lines to Understand Consumer Behavior

Use indifference curves and budget lines to understand consumer behavior.

Consumer Preferences

In this chapter, we analyzed consumer behavior, using the assumption that satisfaction, or *utility*, is measurable in utils. Although this assumption made our analysis easier to understand, it is unrealistic. Instead, we can use the more realistic assumption that consumers are able to *rank* different combinations of goods and services in terms of how much utility they provide. In other words, a consumer is able to determine whether he or she prefers 2 slices of pizza and 1 can of Coke or 1 slice of pizza and 2 cans of Coke, even if the consumer is unsure exactly how much utility he or she would receive from consuming these goods. This approach has the advantage that it allows us to actually draw a map of a consumer's preferences.

To begin with, suppose that a consumer is presented with the following alternatives, or *consumption bundles:*

CONSUMPTION BUNDLE A	CONSUMPTION BUNDLE B
2 slices of pizza and 1 can of Coke	1 slice of pizza and 2 cans of Coke

We assume that the consumer will always be able to decide which of the following is true:

- The consumer prefers bundle A to bundle B.

- The consumer prefers bundle B to bundle A.

- The consumer is indifferent between bundle A and bundle B; that is, the consumer receives equal utility from the two bundles.

For consistency, we also assume that the consumer's preferences are *transitive.* For example, if a consumer prefers pepperoni pizza to mushroom pizza and prefers mushroom pizza to anchovy pizza, the consumer must prefer pepperoni pizza to anchovy pizza.

Indifference Curves

Given the assumptions in the preceding section, we can draw a map of a consumer's preferences by using indifference curves. An **indifference curve** shows combinations of consumption bundles that give the consumer the same utility. In reality, consumers choose among consumption bundles containing many goods and services, but to make

Indifference curve A curve that shows the combinations of consumption bundles that give the consumer the same utility.

Figure 9A-1

Plotting Dave's Preferences for Pizza and Coke

Every possible combination of pizza and Coke will have an indifference curve passing through it, although in the graph we show just four of Dave's indifference curves. Dave is indifferent among all the consumption bundles that are on the same indifference curve. So, he is indifferent among bundles E, B, and F because they all lie on indifference curve I_3. Moving to the upper right in the graph increases the quantities of both goods available for Dave to consume. Therefore, the further to the upper right the indifference curve is, the greater the utility Dave receives.

Consumption Bundle	Slices of Pizza	Cans of Coke
A	1	2
B	3	4
C	4	5
D	1	6
E	2	8
F	5	2

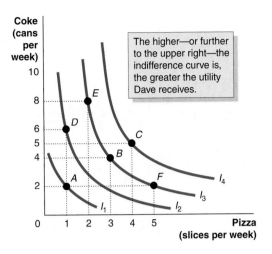

The higher—or further to the upper right the indifference curve is, the greater the utility Dave receives.

the discussion easier to follow, we will assume that only two goods are involved. Nothing important would change if we expanded the discussion to include many goods instead of just two.

The table in Figure 9A-1 gives Dave's preferences for pizza and Coke. The graph plots the information from the table. Every possible combination of pizza and Coke will have an indifference curve passing through it, although in the figure we have shown only four of Dave's indifference curves. Dave is indifferent among all the consumption bundles that are on the same indifference curve. So, he is indifferent among bundles E, B, and F because they all lie on indifference curve I_3. Even though Dave has 4 fewer cans of Coke with bundle B than with bundle E, the additional slice of pizza he has in bundle B means he has the same amount of utility at both points.

Even without looking at Dave's indifference curves, we know he will prefer consumption bundle D to consumption bundle A because in D he receives the same quantity of pizza as in A but 4 additional cans of Coke. But we need to know Dave's preferences, as shown by his indifference curves, to know how he will rank bundle B and bundle D. Bundle D contains more Coke but less pizza than bundle B, so Dave's ranking will depend on how much pizza he would be willing to give up to receive more Coke. The higher the indifference curve—that is, the further to the upper right on the graph—the greater the amounts of both goods that are available for Dave to consume and the greater his utility. In other words, Dave receives more utility from the consumption bundles on indifference curve I_2 than from the consumption bundles on indifference curve I_1, more utility from the bundles on I_3 than from the bundles on I_2, and so on.

The Slope of an Indifference Curve

Marginal rate of substitution (*MRS*) The slope of an indifference curve, which represents the rate at which a consumer would be willing to trade off one good for another.

Remember that the slope of a curve is the ratio of the change in the variable on the vertical axis to the change in the variable on the horizontal axis. Along an indifference curve, the slope tells us the rate at which the consumer is willing to trade off one product for another while keeping the consumer's utility constant. The slope of an indifference curve is referred to as the **marginal rate of substitution (*MRS*)**.

We expect that the *MRS* will change as we move down an indifference curve. In Figure 9A-1, at a point like E on indifference curve I_3, Dave's indifference curve is relatively steep. As we move down the curve, it becomes less steep until it becomes relatively flat at a point like F. This is the usual shape of indifference curves: They are bowed in, or convex. A consumption bundle like E contains a lot of Coke and not much pizza. We would expect that Dave could give up a significant quantity of Coke for a smaller quantity of additional pizza and still have the same level of utility. Thus, the *MRS* will be high. As we move down the indifference curve, Dave moves to bundles, like B and F, that have more pizza and less Coke. As a result, Dave is willing to trade less Coke for pizza, and the *MRS* declines.

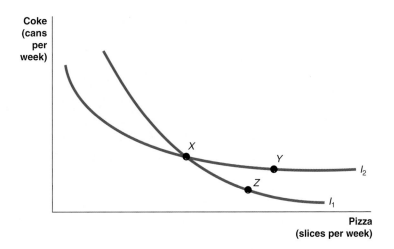

Indifference Curves Cannot Cross

Because bundle X and bundle Z are both on indifference curve I_1, Dave must be indifferent between them. Similarly, because bundle X and bundle Y are on indifference curve I_2, Dave must be indifferent between them. The assumption of transitivity means that Dave should also be indifferent between bundle Z and bundle Y. We know that this is not true, however, because bundle Y contains more pizza and more Coke than bundle Z. So Dave will definitely prefer bundle Y to bundle Z, which violates the assumption of transitivity. *Therefore, none of Dave's indifference curves can cross.*

Can Indifference Curves Ever Cross?

Remember that we assume that consumers have transitive preferences. That is, if Dave prefers consumption bundle X to consumption bundle Y and he prefers consumption bundle Y to consumption bundle Z, he must prefer bundle X to bundle Z. If indifference curves cross, this assumption is violated. To understand why, look at Figure 9A-2, which shows two of Dave's indifference curves crossing.

Because bundle X and bundle Z are both on indifference curve I_1, Dave must be indifferent between them. Similarly, because bundle X and bundle Y are on indifference curve I_2, Dave must be indifferent between them. The assumption of transitivity means that Dave should also be indifferent between bundle Z and bundle Y. We know that this is not true, however, because bundle Y contains more pizza and more Coke than bundle Z. So, Dave will definitely prefer bundle Y to bundle Z, which violates the assumption of transitivity. Therefore, none of Dave's indifference curves can cross.

The Budget Constraint

Remember that a consumer's *budget constraint* is the amount of income he or she has available to spend on goods and services. Suppose that Dave has $10 per week to spend on pizza and Coke. The table in Figure 9A-3 shows the combinations that he can afford to buy if the price of pizza is $2 per slice and the price of Coke is $1 per can. As you can see, all the points lie on a straight line. This line represents Dave's budget constraint. The line intersects the vertical axis at the maximum number of cans of Coke Dave can afford to buy with $10, which is consumption bundle G. The line intersects the horizontal axis at the maximum number of slices of pizza Dave can afford to buy with $10, which is consumption bundle L. As he moves down his budget constraint from bundle G, he gives up 2 cans of Coke for every slice of pizza he buys.

Any consumption bundle along the line or inside the line is *affordable* for Dave because he has the income to buy those combinations of pizza and Coke. Any bundle that lies outside the line is *unaffordable* because those bundles cost more than the income Dave has available to spend.

The slope of the budget constraint is constant because the budget constraint is a straight line. The slope of the line equals the change in the number of cans of Coke divided by the change in the number of slices of pizza. In this case, moving down the budget constraint from one point to another point, the change in the number of cans of Coke equals −2, and the change in the number of slices of pizza equals 1, so the slope equals −2/1, or −2. Notice that with the price of pizza equal to $2 per slice and the price of Coke equal to $1 per can, the slope of the budget constraint is equal to the ratio of the price of pizza to the price of Coke (multiplied by −1). In fact, this

Figure 9A-3

Dave's budget constraint shows the combinations of slices of pizza and cans of Coke he can buy with $10. The price of Coke is $1 per can, so if he spends all of his $10 on Coke, he can buy 10 cans (bundle *G*). The price of pizza is $2 per slice, so if he spends all of his $10 on pizza, he can buy 5 slices (bundle *L*). As he moves down his budget constraint from bundle *G*, he gives up 2 cans of Coke for every slice of pizza he buys. Any consumption bundles along the line or inside the line are affordable. Any bundles that lie outside the line are unaffordable.

Combinations of Pizza and Coke Dave Can Buy with $10			
Consumption Bundle	Slices of Pizza	Cans of Coke	Total Spending
G	0	10	$10.00
H	1	8	10.00
I	2	6	10.00
J	3	4	10.00
K	4	2	10.00
L	5	0	10.00

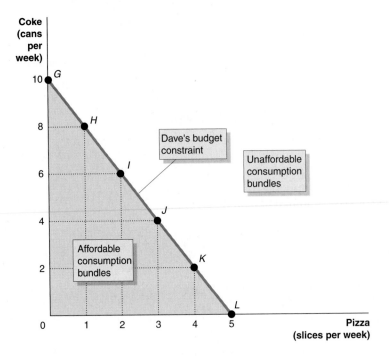

result will always hold: *The slope of the budget constraint is equal to the ratio of the price of the good on the horizontal axis divided by the price of the good on the vertical axis, multiplied by −1.*

Choosing the Optimal Consumption of Pizza and Coke

Dave would like to be on the highest possible indifference curve because higher indifference curves represent more pizza and more Coke. But Dave can only buy the bundles that lie on or inside his budget constraint. In other words, *to maximize utility, a consumer needs to be on the highest indifference curve, given his budget constraint.*

Figure 9A-4 plots the consumption bundles from Figure 9A-1 along with the budget constraint from Figure 9A-3. The figure also shows the indifference curves that pass through each consumption bundle. In Figure 9A-4, the highest indifference curve shown is I_4. Unfortunately, Dave lacks the income to purchase consumption bundles—like *C*—that lie on I_4. He has the income to purchase bundles like *A* and *D*, but he can do better. If he consumes bundle *B*, he will be on the highest indifference curve he can reach, given his budget constraint of $10. The resulting combination of 3 slices of pizza and 4 cans of Coke represents optimal consumption of pizza and Coke, given Dave's preferences and given his budget constraint. Notice that at point *B*, Dave's budget constraint just touches—or is *tangent* to— I_3. In fact, bundle *B* is the only bundle on I_3 that Dave is able to purchase for $10.

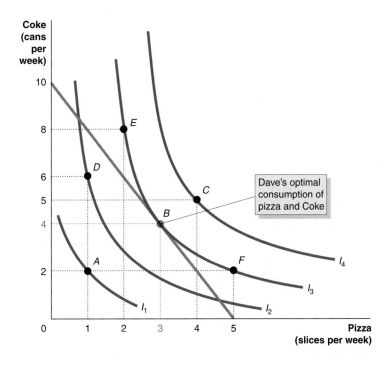

Figure 9A-4

Finding Optimal Consumption

Dave would like to be on the highest possible indifference curve, but he cannot reach indifference curves like I_4 that are outside his budget constraint. Dave's optimal combination of slices of pizza and cans of Coke comes at point B, where his budget constraint just touches—or is *tangent* to—the highest indifference curve he can reach. At point B, he buys 3 slices of pizza and 4 cans of Coke.

Making the Connection | Dell Determines the Optimal Mix of Products

Consumers have different preferences, which helps explain why many firms offer products with a variety of characteristics. For example, Dell sells laptop computers with different screen sizes, processor speeds, hard drive sizes, graphics cards, and so on. We can use the model of consumer choice to analyze a simplified version of the situation Dell faces in deciding which features to offer consumers.

Assume that consumers have $1,000 each to spend on laptops and that they are concerned with only two laptop characteristics: screen size and processor speed. Because larger screens and faster processors increase Dell's cost of producing laptops, consumers face a trade-off: The larger the screen, the slower the processor speed. Consumers in panel (a) of the figure prefer screen size to processor speed. For this group, the point of tangency between a typical consumer's indifference curve and the budget constraint shows an optimal choice of a 17-inch screen and a 1.5-gigahertz processor. Consumers in panel (b) prefer processor speed to screen size. For this group, the point of tangency between a typical consumer's indifference curve and the budget constraint shows an optimal choice of a 12-inch screen and 3.0-gigahertz processor.

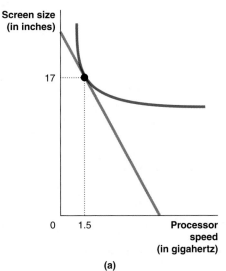

(a)

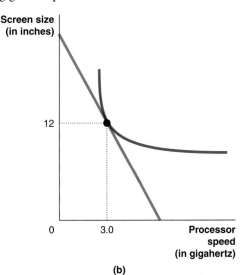

(b)

Companies like Dell use surveys and other means to gather information about consumer preferences. With knowledge of consumers' preferences and data on the costs of producing different laptop components, Dell can determine the mix of components to offer consumers.

YOUR TURN: Test your understanding by doing related problem 9A.8 on page 330 at the end of this chapter.

How a Price Change Affects Optimal Consumption

Suppose the price of pizza falls from $2 per slice to $1 per slice. How will this affect Dave's decision about which combination of pizza and Coke is optimal? First, notice what happens to Dave's budget constraint when the price of pizza falls. As Figure 9A-5 shows, when the price of pizza is $2 per slice, the maximum number of slices Dave can buy is 5. After the price of pizza falls to $1 per slice, Dave can buy a maximum of 10 slices. His budget constraint rotates outward from point *A* to point *B* to represent this. (Notice that the fall in the price of pizza does not affect the maximum number of cans of Coke Dave can buy with his $10.)

When his budget constraint rotates outward, Dave is able to purchase consumption bundles that were previously unaffordable. Figure 9A-6 shows that the combination of 3 slices of pizza and 4 cans of Coke was optimal when the price of pizza was $2 per slice, but the combination of 7 slices of pizza and 3 cans of Coke is optimal when the price of pizza falls to $1. The lower price of pizza causes Dave to consume more pizza and less Coke and to end up on a higher indifference curve.

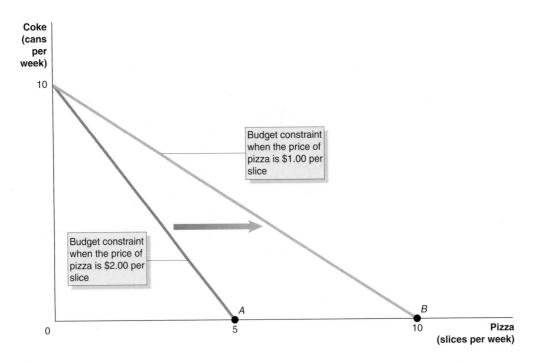

Figure 9A-5 | How a Price Decrease Affects the Budget Constraint

A fall in the price of pizza from $2 per slice to $1 per slice increases the maximum number of slices Dave can buy with $10 from 5 to 10. The budget constraint rotates outward from point *A* to point *B* to show this.

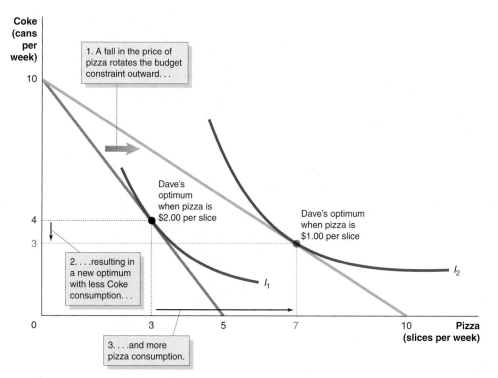

Coke (cans per week)

1. A fall in the price of pizza rotates the budget constraint outward. . .

Dave's optimum when pizza is $2.00 per slice

Dave's optimum when pizza is $1.00 per slice

2. . . .resulting in a new optimum with less Coke consumption. . .

I_1

I_2

3. . . .and more pizza consumption.

Pizza (slices per week)

Figure 9A-6

How a Price Change Affects Optimal Consumption

A fall in the price of pizza results in Dave consuming less Coke and more pizza.

1. A fall in the price of pizza rotates the budget constraint outward because Dave can now buy more pizza with his $10.
2. In the new optimum on indifference curve I_2, Dave changes the quantities he consumes of both goods. His consumption of Coke falls from 4 cans to 3 cans.
3. In the new optimum, Dave's consumption of pizza increases from 3 slices to 7 slices.

Solved Problem | **9A-1**

When Does a Price Change Make a Consumer Better Off?

Dave has $300 to spend each month on DVDs and CDs. DVDs and CDs both currently have a price of $10, and Dave is maximizing his utility by buying 20 DVDs and 10 CDs. Suppose Dave still has $300 to spend, but the price of CDs rises to $20, while the price of DVDs drops to $5. Is Dave better or worse off than he was before the price change? Use a budget constraint–indifference curve graph to illustrate your answer.

SOLVING THE PROBLEM:

Step 1: **Review the chapter material.** This problem concerns the effect of price changes on optimal consumption, so you may want to review the section "How a Price Change Affects Optimal Consumption," which begins on page 322.

Step 2: **Answer the problem by drawing the appropriate graph.** We begin by drawing the budget constraint, indifference curve, and point of optimal consumption for the original prices:

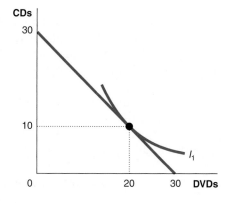

CDs

30

10

I_1

0   20   30   DVDs

Now draw a graph that shows the results of the price changes. Notice that in this problem, the prices of *both* goods change. However, you can determine the position of the new budget constraint by calculating the maximum quantity of DVDs and CDs Dave can buy after the price changes. You should also note that after the price changes, Dave can still buy his original optimal consumption bundle—20 DVDs and 10 CDs—by spending all of his $300, so his new budget constraint must pass through this point.

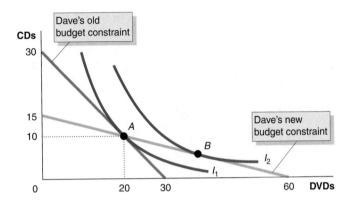

At the new prices, Dave can buy a maximum of 60 DVDs or 15 CDs. Both his old and his new budget constraints pass through the consumption bundle at point *A*. This consumption bundle is no longer optimal, however, because with the new prices, it is possible for him to reach an indifference curve that is higher than I_1. We can draw in the new highest indifference curve he can reach—I_2—and show the new optimal consumption bundle—point *B*.

Because Dave can now reach a higher indifference curve, we can conclude that he is better off as a result of the price change.

YOUR TURN: For more practice, do related problem 9A.10 on page 330 at the end of this appendix.

>> End Solved Problem 9A-1

Deriving the Demand Curve

The change in Dave's optimal consumption of pizza as the price changes explains why demand curves slope downward. Dave adjusted his consumption of pizza as follows:

Price of pizza = $2 per slice $\Rightarrow$ Quantity of pizza demanded = 3 slices

Price of pizza = $1 per slice $\Rightarrow$ Quantity of pizza demanded = 7 slices

In panel (a) of Figure 9A-7, we plot the two points of optimal consumption. In panel (b) of Figure 9A-7, we draw a line connecting the points. This downward-sloping line is Dave's demand curve for pizza. We could find more points on the demand curve by changing the price of pizza and finding the new optimal number of slices of pizza Dave would demand.

Remember that according to the law of demand, demand curves always slope downward. We have just shown that the law of demand results from the optimal adjustment by consumers to changes in prices. A fall in the price of a good will rotate *outward* the budget constraint and make it possible for a consumer to reach higher indifference curves. As a result, the consumer will increase the quantity of the good demanded. An increase in price will rotate *inward* the budget constraint and force the

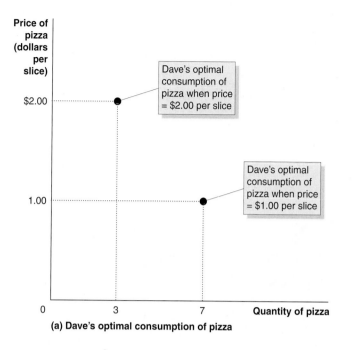

Price of pizza (dollars per slice)

Dave's optimal consumption of pizza when price = $2.00 per slice

Dave's optimal consumption of pizza when price = $1.00 per slice

(a) Dave's optimal consumption of pizza

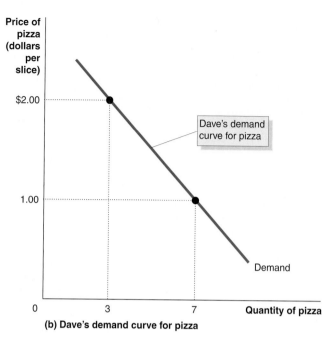

Price of pizza (dollars per slice)

Dave's demand curve for pizza

Demand

(b) Dave's demand curve for pizza

Figure 9A-7 | Deriving a Demand Curve

Dave responds optimally to the fall in the price of a product by consuming more of that product. In panel (a), the price of pizza falls from $2 per slice to $1, and the optimal quantity of slices consumed rises from 3 to 7. When we graph this result in panel (b), we have Dave's demand curve for pizza.

consumer to a lower indifference curve. As a result, the consumer will decrease the quantity of the good demanded.

The Income Effect and the Substitution Effect of a Price Change

We saw in this chapter that a price change has two effects on the quantity of a good consumed: the *income effect* and the *substitution effect*. The income effect is the change in the quantity demanded of a good that results from the effect of a change in price on consumer purchasing power, holding all other factors constant. The substitution effect is the change in the quantity demanded of a good that results from a change in price making the good more or less expensive relative to other goods, holding constant the effect of the price change on consumer purchasing power. We can use indifference curves and budget constraints to analyze these two effects more exactly.

Figure 9A-8 illustrates the same situation as Figure 9A-7: The price of pizza has fallen from $2 per slice to $1 per slice, and Dave's budget constraint has rotated outward. As before, Dave's optimal consumption of pizza increases from 3 slices (point *A* in Figure 9A-8) per week to 7 slices per week (point *C*). We can think of this movement from point *A* to point *C* as taking place in two steps: The movement from point *A* to point *B* represents the substitution effect, and the movement from point *B* to point *C* represents the income effect. To isolate the substitution effect, we have to hold constant the effect of the price change on Dave's income. We do this by changing the price of pizza relative to the price of Coke *but at the same time holding his utility constant by keeping Dave on the same indifference curve*. In Figure 9A-8, in moving from point *A* to point *B*, Dave remains on indifference curve I_1. Point *A* is a point of tangency between I_1 and Dave's original budget constraint. Point *B* is a point of tangency

Figure 9A-8

Income and Substitution Effects of a Price Change

Following a decline in the price of pizza, Dave's optimal consumption of pizza increases from 3 slices (point *A*) per week to 7 slices per week (point *C*). We can think of this movement from point *A* to point *C* as taking place in two steps: The movement from point *A* to point *B* along indifference curve I_1 represents the substitution effect, and the movement from point *B* to point *C* represents the income effect. Dave increases his consumption of pizza from 3 slices per week to 5 slices per week because of the substitution effect of a fall in the price of pizza and from 5 slices per week to 7 slices per week because of the income effect.

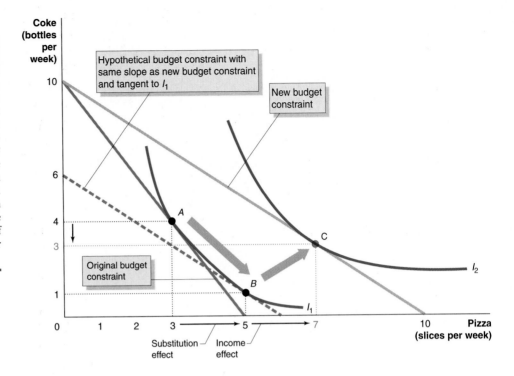

between I_1 and a new, *hypothetical* budget constraint that has a slope equal to the new ratio of the price of pizza to the price of Coke. At point *B*, Dave has increased his consumption of pizza from 3 slices to 5 slices. Because we are still on indifference curve I_1, we know that this increase is Dave's response only to the change in the relative price of pizza and, therefore, that the increase represents the substitution effect of the fall in the price of pizza.

At point *B*, Dave has not spent all his income. Remember that the fall in the price of pizza has increased Dave's purchasing power. In Figure 9A-8, we illustrate the additional pizza Dave consumes because of the income effect of increased purchasing power by the movement from point *B* to point *C*. Notice that in moving from point *B* to point *C*, the price of pizza relative to the price of Coke is constant because the slope of the new budget constraint is the same as the slope of the hypothetical budget constraint that is tangent to I_1 at point *B*.

We can conclude that Dave increases his consumption of pizza from 3 slices per week to 5 slices per week because of the substitution effect of a fall in the price of pizza and from 5 slices per week to 7 slices per week because of the income effect. Recall from our discussion of income and substitution effects in this chapter that the income effect of a price decline causes consumers to buy more of a normal good and less of an inferior good. Because the income effect causes Dave to increase his consumption of pizza, pizza must be a normal good for him.

How a Change in Income Affects Optimal Consumption

Suppose that the price of pizza remains at $2 per slice, but the income Dave has to spend on pizza and Coke increases from $10 to $20. Figure 9A-9 shows how this affects his budget constraint. With an income of $10, Dave could buy a maximum of 5 slices of pizza or 10 cans of Coke. With an income of $20, he can buy 10 slices of pizza or 20 cans of Coke. The additional income allows Dave to increase his consumption of both pizza and Coke and to move to a higher indifference curve. Figure 9A-10 shows Dave's new optimum. Dave is able to increase his consumption of pizza from 3 slices per week to 7 and his consumption of Coke from 4 cans per week to 6.

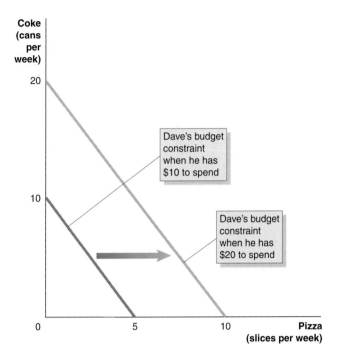

Figure 9A-9

How a Change in Income Affects the Budget Constraint

When the income Dave has to spend on pizza and Coke increases from \$10 to \$20, his budget constraint shifts outward. With \$10, Dave could buy a maximum of 5 slices of pizza or 10 cans of Coke. With \$20, he can buy a maximum of 10 slices of pizza or 20 cans of Coke.

The Slope of the Indifference Curve, the Slope of the Budget Line, and the Rule of Equal Marginal Utility per Dollar Spent

In this chapter, we saw that consumers maximize utility when they consume each good up to the point where the marginal utility per dollar spent is the same for every good. This condition seems different from the one we stated earlier in this appendix that to

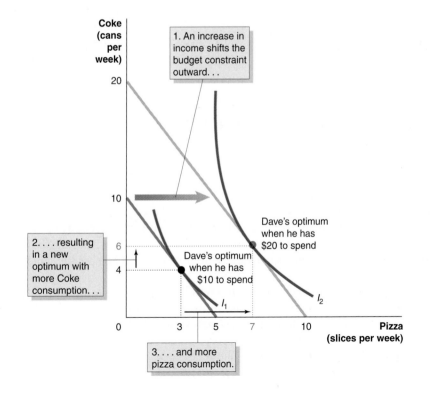

Figure 9A-10

How a Change in Income Affects Optimal Consumption

An increase in income leads Dave to consume more Coke and more pizza.
1. An increase in income shifts Dave's budget constraint outward because he can now buy more of both goods.
2. In the new optimum on indifference curve I_2, Dave changes the quantities he consumes of both goods. His consumption of Coke increases from 4 cans to 6 cans.
3. In the new optimum, Dave's consumption of pizza increases from 3 slices to 7 slices.

Figure 9A-11

At the Optimum Point, the Slopes of the Indifference Curve and Budget Constraint Are the Same

At the point of optimal consumption, the marginal rate of substitution is equal to the ratio of the price of the product on the horizontal axis to the price of the product on the vertical axis.

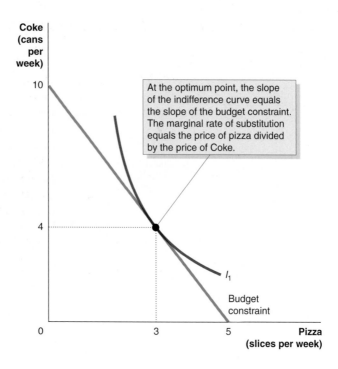

At the optimum point, the slope of the indifference curve equals the slope of the budget constraint. The marginal rate of substitution equals the price of pizza divided by the price of Coke.

maximize utility, a consumer needs to be on the highest indifference curve, given his budget constraint. In fact, though, the two conditions are equivalent. To see this, begin by looking at Figure 9A-11, which again combines Dave's indifference curve and budget constraint. Remember that at the point of optimal consumption, the indifference curve and the budget constraint are tangent, so they have the same slope. Therefore: *At the point of optimal consumption, the marginal rate of substitution* (MRS) *is equal to the ratio of the price of the product on the horizontal axis to the price of the product on the vertical axis.*

The slope of the indifference curve tells us the rate at which a consumer is *willing* to trade off one good for the other. The slope of the budget constraint tells us the rate at which a consumer is *able* to trade off one good for the other. Only at the point of optimal consumption is the rate at which a consumer is willing to trade off one good for the other equal to the rate at which he can trade off one good for the other.

The Rule of Equal Marginal Utility per Dollar Spent Revisited

Recall from this chapter the *rule of equal marginal utility per dollar*, which states that to maximize utility, consumers should spend their income so that the last dollar spent on each product gives them the same marginal utility. We can use our indifference curve and budget constraint analysis to see why this rule holds. When we move from one point on an indifference curve to another, we end up with more of one product and less of the other product but the same amount of utility. For example, as Dave moves down an indifference curve, he consumes less Coke and more pizza, but he has the same amount of utility.

Remember that marginal utility (*MU*) tells us how much additional utility a consumer gains (or loses) from consuming more (or less) of a good. So when Dave consumes less Coke by moving down an indifference curve, he loses utility equal to:

$$-\text{Change in the quantity of Coke} \times MU_{Coke}$$

but he consumes more pizza, so he gains utility equal to:

$$\text{Change in the quantity of pizza} \times MU_{Pizza}.$$

We know that the gain in utility from the additional pizza is equal to the loss from the smaller quantity of Coke because Dave's total utility remains the same along an indifference curve. Therefore we can write:

$$-(\text{Change in the quantity of Coke} \times MU_{Coke}) = (\text{Change in the quantity of pizza} \times MU_{Pizza}).$$

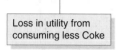

Loss in utility from consuming less Coke

Gain in utility from consuming more pizza

If we rearrange terms, we have:

$$\frac{-\text{Change in the quantity of Coke}}{\text{Change in the quantity of pizza}} = \frac{MU_{Pizza}}{MU_{Coke}}$$

because the

$$\frac{-\text{Change in the quantity of Coke}}{\text{Change in the quantity of pizza}}$$

is the slope of the indifference curve, or the marginal rate of substitution, we can write:

$$\frac{-\text{Change in the quantity of Coke}}{\text{Change in the quantity of pizza}} = MRS = \frac{MU_{Pizza}}{MU_{Coke}}.$$

The slope of Dave's budget constraint equals the price of pizza divided by the price of Coke. At the point of optimal consumption, the slope of the indifference curve is equal to the slope of the budget line. Therefore:

$$\frac{MU_{Pizza}}{MU_{Coke}} = \frac{P_{Pizza}}{P_{Coke}}.$$

We can rewrite this to show that at the point of optimal consumption:

$$\frac{MU_{Pizza}}{P_{Pizza}} = \frac{MU_{Coke}}{P_{Coke}}.$$

This last expression is the rule of equal marginal utility per dollar that we first developed in this chapter. So we have shown how this rule follows from the indifference curve and budget constraint approach to analyzing consumer choice.

Key Terms

Indifference curve, p. 317

Marginal rate of substitution (MRS), p. 318

Review Questions

9A.1 What are the two assumptions economists make about consumer preferences?

9A.2 What is an indifference curve? What is a budget constraint?

9A.3 How do consumers choose the optimal consumption bundle?

Problems and Applications

9A.4 Jacob receives an allowance of $5 per week. He spends all his allowance on ice cream cones and cans of Lemon Fizz soda.

   a. If the price of ice cream cones is $0.50 per cone and the price of Lemon Fizz is $1 per can, draw a graph showing Jacob's budget constraint. Be sure to indicate on the graph the maximum number of ice cream cones and the maximum number of cans of Lemon Fizz that Jacob can buy.

   b. Jacob buys 8 cones and 1 can of Lemon Fizz. Draw an indifference curve representing Jacob's choice, assuming that he has chosen the optimal combination.

   c. Suppose that the price of ice cream cones rises to $1 per cone. Draw in Jacob's new budget constraint and his new optimal consumption of ice cream cones and Lemon Fizz.

9A.5 Suppose that Jacob's allowance in problem 9A.4 climbs from $5 per week to $10 per week.

   a. Show how the increased allowance alters Jacob's budget constraint.

   b. Draw a set of indifference curves showing how Jacob's choice of cones and Lemon Fizz changes when his allowance increases. Assume that both goods are normal.

   c. Draw a set of indifference curves showing how Jacob's choice of cones and Lemon Fizz changes when his allowance increases. Assume that Lemon Fizz is normal but cones are inferior.

9A.6 Suppose that Calvin considers Pepsi and Coke to be perfect substitutes. They taste the same to him, and he gets exactly the same amount of enjoyment from drinking a can of Pepsi or a can of Coke.

   a. Will Calvin's indifference curves showing his trade-off between Pepsi and Coke have the same curvature as the indifference curves drawn in the figures in this appendix? Briefly explain.

   b. How will Calvin decide whether to buy Pepsi or to buy Coke?

9A.7 In the following budget constraint–indifference curve graph, Nikki has $200 to spend on blouses and skirts.

   a. What is the price of blouses? What is the price of skirts?

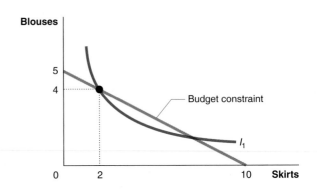

   b. Is Nikki making the optimum choice if she buys 4 blouses and 2 skirts? Explain how you know this.

9A.8 **(Related to the *Making the Connection* on page 321)** Marilou and Hunter both purchase milk and doughnuts at the same Quik Mart. They have different tastes for milk and doughnuts and different incomes. They both buy some milk and some doughnuts, but they buy considerably different quantities of the two goods. Can we conclude that their marginal rate of substitution between milk and doughnuts is the same? Draw a graph showing their budget constraints and indifference curves and explain.

9A.9 Sunsweet decides that prune juice has a bad image problem, so it launches a slick advertising campaign to convince young people that prune juice is very hip. They hire Eminem, Ludacris, and Trick Daddy to tout their product. The campaign works! Prune juice sales soar, even though Sunsweet hasn't cut the price. Draw a budget constraint and indifference curve diagram with Sunsweet Prune Juice on one axis and other drinks on the other axis and show how the celebrity endorsements have changed things.

9A.10 **(Related to *Solved Problem 9A-1* on page 323)** Dave has $300 to spend each month on

DVDs and CDs. DVDs and CDs both currently have a price of $10, and Dave is maximizing his utility by buying 20 DVDs and 10 CDs. Suppose Dave still has $300 to spend, but the price of DVDs rises to $12, while the price of CDs drops to $6. Is Dave better or worse off than he was before the price change? Use a budget constraint–indifference curve graph to illustrate your answer.

>> End Appendix Learning Objective

Chapter 10

Technology, Production, and **Costs**

Sony Uses a Cost Curve to Determine the Price of Radios

In consumer electronics, rapid technological change leads to new products and lower cost ways of manufacturing existing products. How do firms take costs into account when setting prices? This is an important question that we will explore in the next few chapters and it is a question that Sony Corporation, the Japanese electronics giant, must answer every day. Sony manufactures televisions, computers, satellite systems, semiconductors, telephones, and flat-screen televisions, among other products.

Like most firms, Sony started small. Its early success resulted from the vision and energy of two young entrepreneurs, Akio Morita and Masaru Ibuka.

In 1953, Sony purchased a license that allowed it to use transistor technology developed in the United States at Western Electric's Bell Laboratories.

Sony used the technology to develop a transistor radio that was small enough to fit in a shirt pocket and far smaller than any other radio then available. In 1955, Akio Morita, Sony's chairman, arrived in New York, hoping to convince one of the U.S. department store chains to carry the Sony radios.

Morita offered to sell one department store chain 5,000 radios at a price of $29.95 each. If the chain wanted more than 5,000 radios, the price would change. As Morita described it later:

I sat down and drew a curve that looked something like a lopsided letter U. The price for five thousand would be our regular price. That would be the beginning of the curve. For ten thousand there would be a discount, and that was at the bottom of the curve. For thirty thousand the price would begin to climb. For fifty thousand the price per unit would be higher than for five thousand, and for one hundred thousand units the price per unit would have to be much higher than for the first five thousand.

Why would the prices Morita offered the department store follow a U shape? Because Sony's cost per unit, or *average cost*, of manufacturing the radios would have the same shape. Curves that show the relationship between the level of output and per-unit cost are called *average total cost curves*. Average total cost curves typically have the U shape of Morita's curve. As we explore the relationship between production and costs in this chapter, we will see why average total cost curves have this shape.

Today, Sony is one of the largest electronics firms in the world, but more than 50 years ago, when it was a small, struggling company, Akio Morita used a simple economic tool—the average cost curve—to help make an important business decision. Every day, in companies large and small, managers use economic tools to make decisions. **AN INSIDE LOOK** on **page 354** discusses the effect of lower manufacturing costs on the prices of flat-panel televisions.

Source: Akio Morita, with Edwin M. Reingold and Mitsuko Shimomura, *Made in Japan: Akio Morita and Sony*, New York: Signet Books, 1986, p. 94.

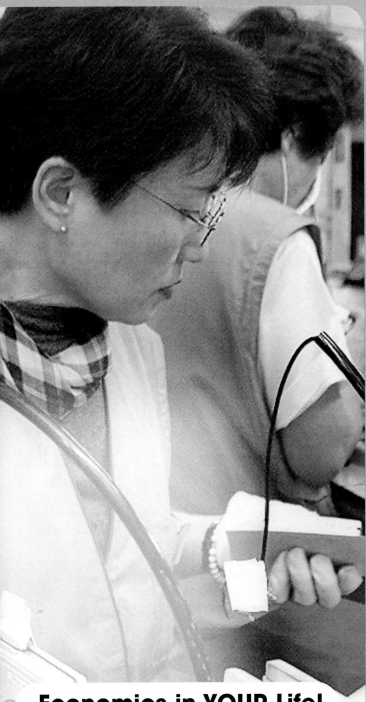

LEARNING Objectives

After studying this chapter, you should be able to:

10.1 Define **technology** and give examples of **technological change**, page 334.

10.2 Distinguish between the economic **short run** and the economic **long run**, page 335.

10.3 Understand the relationship between the **marginal product of labor** and the **average product of labor**, page 339.

10.4 Explain and illustrate the relationship between **marginal cost** and **average total cost**, page 342.

10.5 **Graph** average total cost, average variable cost, average fixed cost, and marginal cost, page 346.

10.6 Understand how firms use the **long-run average cost curve** in their planning, page 346.

APPENDIX Use **isoquants** and **isocost lines** to understand production and cost, page 364.

Economics in YOUR Life!

Using Cost Concepts in Your Own Business

Suppose that you have the opportunity to open a store selling recliners. You learn that you can purchase the recliners from the manufacturer for $300 each. Bob's Big Chairs is an existing store that is the same size as your new store will be. Bob's sells the same recliners you plan to sell and also buys them from the manufacturer for $300 each. Your plan is to sell the recliners for a price of $500. After studying how Bob's is operated, you find that they are selling more recliners per month than you expect to be able to sell and that they are selling them for $450. You wonder how Bob's makes a profit at the lower price. Are there any reasons to expect that because Bob's sells more recliners per month, its costs will be lower than your store's costs? You can check your answer against the one we provide at the end of the chapter. **>> Continued on page 352**

In Chapter 9, we looked behind the demand curve to better understand consumer decision making. In this chapter, we look behind the supply curve to better understand firm decision making. Earlier chapters showed that supply curves are upward sloping because marginal cost increases as firms increase the quantity of a good that they supply. In this chapter, we look more closely at why this is true. In the appendix to this chapter, we extend the analysis by using isoquants and isocost lines to understand the relationship between production and costs. Once we have a good understanding of production and cost, we can proceed in the following chapters to understand how firms decide what level of output to produce and what price to charge.

10.1 | Define technology and give examples of technological change.

Technology: An Economic Definition

The basic activity of a firm is to use *inputs*, such as workers, machines, and natural resources, to produce *outputs* of goods and services. A pizza parlor, for example, uses inputs such as pizza dough, pizza sauce, cooks, and ovens to produce pizza. A firm's **technology** is the processes it uses to turn inputs into outputs of goods and services. Notice that this economic definition of technology is broader than the everyday definition. When we use the word *technology* in everyday language, we usually refer only to the development of new products. In the economic sense, a firm's technology depends on many factors, such as the skill of its managers, the training of its workers, and the speed and efficiency of its machinery and equipment. The technology of pizza production, for example, includes not only the capacity of the pizza ovens and how quickly they bake the pizza but also how quickly the cooks can prepare the pizza for baking, how well the manager motivates the workers, and how well the manager has arranged the facilities to allow the cooks to quickly prepare the pizzas and get them in the ovens.

Technology The processes a firm uses to turn inputs into outputs of goods and services.

Whenever a firm experiences positive **technological change**, it is able to produce more output using the same inputs or the same output using fewer inputs. Positive technological change can come from many sources. The firm's managers may rearrange the factory floor or the layout of a retail store, thereby increasing production and sales. The firm's workers may go through a training program. The firm may install faster or more reliable machinery or equipment. It is also possible for a firm to experience negative technological change. If a firm hires less-skilled workers or if a hurricane damages its facilities, the quantity of output it can produce from a given quantity of inputs may decline.

Technological change A change in the ability of a firm to produce a given level of output with a given quantity of inputs.

Making the Connection

Improving Inventory Control at Wal-Mart

Inventories are goods that have been produced but not yet sold. For a retailer such as Wal-Mart, inventories at any point in time include the goods on the store shelves as well as goods in warehouses. Inventories are an input into Wal-Mart's output of goods sold to consumers. Having money tied up in holding inventories is costly, so firms have an incentive to hold as few inventories as possible and to *turn over* their inventories as rapidly as possible by ensuring that goods do not remain on the shelves long. Holding too few inventories, however, results in *stockouts*—that is, sales being lost because the goods consumers want to buy are not on the shelf.

Improvements in inventory control meet the economic definition of positive technological change because they allow firms to produce the same output with fewer inputs. In recent years, many firms have adopted *just-in-time* inventory systems in which firms accept shipments from suppliers as close as possible to the time they will be needed. The just-in-time system was pioneered by Toyota, which used it to reduce the inventories of parts in its automobile assembly plants. Wal-Mart has been a pioneer in using similar inventory control systems in its stores.

Better inventory controls have helped reduce firms' costs.

Wal-Mart actively manages its *supply chain*, which stretches from the manufacturers of the goods it sells to its retail stores. Entrepreneur Sam Walton, the company founder, built a series of distribution centers spread across the country to supply goods to the retail stores. As goods are sold in the stores, this *point-of-sale* information is sent electronically to the firm's distribution centers to help managers determine what products will be shipped to each store. Depending on a store's location relative to a distribution center, managers can use Wal-Mart's trucks to ship goods overnight. This distribution system allows Wal-Mart to minimize its inventory holdings without running the risk of many stockouts. Because Wal-Mart sells 15 percent to 25 percent of all the toothpaste, disposable diapers, dog food, and many other products sold in the United States, it has been able to involve many manufacturers closely in its supply chain. For example, a company such as Procter & Gamble, which is one of the world's largest manufacturers of toothpaste, laundry detergent, toilet paper, and other products, receives Wal-Mart's point-of-sale and inventory information electronically. Procter & Gamble uses that information to help determine its production schedules and the quantities it should ship to Wal-Mart's distribution centers.

Technological change has been a key to Wal-Mart's becoming one of the largest firms in the world, with 2.1 million employees and revenue of more than $379 billion in 2007.

YOUR TURN: Test your understanding by doing related problem 1.5 on page 356 at the end of this chapter.

10.2 | Distinguish between the economic short run and the economic long run.

The Short Run and the Long Run in Economics

When firms analyze the relationship between their level of production and their costs, they separate the time period involved into the short run and the long run. In the **short run**, at least one of the firm's inputs is fixed. In particular, in the short run, the firm's technology and the size of its physical plant—its factory, store, or office—are both fixed, while the number of workers the firm hires is variable. In the **long run**, the firm is able to vary all its inputs and can adopt new technology and increase or decrease the size of its physical plant. Of course, the actual length of calendar time in the short run will be different from firm to firm. A pizza parlor may be able to increase its physical plant by adding another pizza oven and some tables and chairs in just a few weeks. BMW, in contrast, may take more than a year to increase the capacity of one of its automobile assembly plants by installing new equipment.

Short run The period of time during which at least one of a firm's inputs is fixed.

Long run The period of time in which a firm can vary all its inputs, adopt new technology, and increase or decrease the size of its physical plant.

The Difference between Fixed Costs and Variable Costs

Total cost is the cost of all the inputs a firm uses in production. We have just seen that in the short run, some inputs are fixed and others are variable. The costs of the fixed inputs are *fixed costs*, and the costs of the variable inputs are *variable costs*. We can also think of **variable costs** as the costs that change as output changes. Similarly, **fixed costs** are costs that remain constant as output changes. A typical firm's variable costs include its labor costs, raw material costs, and costs of electricity and other utilities. Typical fixed costs include lease payments for factory or retail space, payments for fire insurance, and payments for newspaper and television advertising. All of a firm's costs are either fixed or variable, so we can state the following:

Total cost The cost of all the inputs a firm uses in production.

Variable costs Costs that change as output changes.

Fixed costs Costs that remain constant as output changes.

$$\text{Total Cost} = \text{Fixed Cost} + \text{Variable Cost}$$

or, using symbols:

$$TC = FC + VC.$$

Publishers consider the salaries of editors to be a fixed cost.

Making the Connection | Fixed Costs in the Publishing Industry

An editor at Cambridge University Press gives the following estimates of the annual fixed cost for a medium-size academic book publisher.

COST	AMOUNT
Salaries and benefits	$437,500
Rent	75,000
Utilities	20,000
Supplies	6,000
Postage	4,000
Travel	8,000
Subscriptions, etc.	4,000
Miscellaneous	5,000
Total	$559,500

Academic book publishers hire editors, designers, and production and marketing managers who help prepare books for publication. Because these employees work on several books simultaneously, the number of people the company hires does not go up and down with the quantity of books the company publishes during any particular year. Publishing companies therefore consider the salaries and benefits of people in these job categories as fixed costs.

In contrast, for a company that *prints* books, the quantity of workers varies with the quantity of books printed. The wages and benefits of the workers operating the printing presses, for example, would be a variable cost.

The other costs listed in the preceding table are typical of fixed costs at many firms.

Source: Beth Luey, *Handbook for Academic Authors*, 4th ed., Cambridge, UK: Cambridge University Press, 2002, p. 244.

YOUR TURN: Test your understanding by doing related problems 2.3, 2.4, and 2.5 on page 357 at the end of this chapter.

Implicit Costs versus Explicit Costs

Opportunity cost The highest-valued alternative that must be given up to engage in an activity.

Explicit cost A cost that involves spending money.

Implicit cost A nonmonetary opportunity cost.

It is important to remember that economists always measure costs as *opportunity costs*. The **opportunity cost** of any activity is the highest-valued alternative that must be given up to engage in that activity. As we saw in Chapter 7, costs are either *explicit* or *implicit*. When a firm spends money, it incurs an **explicit cost**. When a firm experiences a non-monetary opportunity cost, it incurs an **implicit cost**.

For example, suppose that Jill Johnson owns a pizza restaurant. In operating her store, Jill has explicit costs, such as the wages she pays her workers and the payments she makes for rent and electricity. But some of Jill's most important costs are implicit. Before opening her own restaurant, Jill earned a salary of $30,000 per year managing a restaurant for someone else. To start her restaurant, Jill quit her job, withdrew $50,000 from her bank account—where it earned her interest of $3,000 per year—and used the funds to equip her restaurant with tables, chairs, a cash register, and other equipment. To open her own business, Jill had to give up the $30,000 salary and the $3,000 in interest. This $33,000 is an implicit cost because it does not represent payments that Jill has to make. All the same, giving up this $33,000 per year is a real cost to Jill. In addition, during the course of the year, the $50,000 worth of tables, chairs, and other physical capital in Jill's store will lose some of its value due partly to wear and tear and partly to better furniture, cash registers, and so forth becoming available. *Economic depreciation* is the difference between what Jill paid for her capital at the beginning of the year and what she could sell the capital for at the end of the year. If Jill could sell the capital for $40,000 at the end of the year, then the $10,000 in economic depreciation represents another implicit cost.

Pizza dough, tomato sauce, and other ingredients	$20,000	
Wages	48,000	
Interest payments on loan to buy pizza ovens	10,000	
Electricity	6,000	
Lease payment for store	24,000	
Foregone salary	30,000	
Foregone interest	3,000	
Economic depreciation	10,000	
Total	$151,000	

TABLE 10-1

Jill Johnson's Costs per Year

(Note that the whole $50,000 she spent on the capital is not a cost because she still has the equipment at the end of the year, although it is now worth only $40,000.)

Table 10-1 lists Jill's costs. The entries in red are explicit costs, and the entries in blue are implicit costs. As we saw in Chapter 7, the rules of accounting generally require that only explicit costs be used for purposes of keeping the company's financial records and for paying taxes. Therefore, explicit costs are sometimes called *accounting costs*. *Economic costs* include both accounting costs and implicit costs.

The Production Function

Let's look at the relationship between the level of production and costs in the short run for Jill Johnson's restaurant. To keep things simpler than in the more realistic situation in Table 10-1, let's assume that Jill uses only labor—workers—and one type of capital—pizza ovens—to produce a single good: pizzas. Many firms use more than two inputs and produce more than one good, but it is easier to understand the relationship between output and cost by focusing on the case of a firm using only two inputs and producing only one good. In the short run, Jill doesn't have time to build a larger restaurant, install additional pizza ovens, or redesign the layout of her restaurant. So, in the short run, she can increase or decrease the quantity of pizzas she produces only by increasing or decreasing the quantity of workers she employs.

The first three columns of Table 10-2 show the relationship between the quantity of workers and ovens Jill uses each week and the quantity of pizzas she can produce. The relationship between the inputs employed by a firm and the maximum output it can

TABLE 10-2 | **Short-Run Production and Cost at Jill Johnson's Restaurant**

QUANTITY OF WORKERS	QUANTITY OF PIZZA OVENS	QUANTITY OF PIZZAS PER WEEK	COST OF PIZZA OVENS (FIXED COST)	COST OF WORKERS (VARIABLE COST)	TOTAL COST OF PIZZAS	COST PER PIZZA (AVERAGE TOTAL COST)
0	2	0	$800	$0	$800	—
1	2	200	800	650	1,450	$7.25
2	2	450	800	1,300	2,100	4.67
3	2	550	800	1,950	2,750	5.00
4	2	600	800	2,600	3,400	5.67
5	2	625	800	3,250	4,050	6.48
6	2	640	800	3,900	4,700	7.34

Production function The relationship between the inputs employed by a firm and the maximum output it can produce with those inputs.

produce with those inputs is called the firm's **production function**. Because a firm's technology is the processes it uses to turn inputs into output, the production function represents the firm's technology. In this case, Table 10-2 shows Jill's *short-run* production function because we are assuming that the time period is too short for Jill to increase or decrease the quantity of ovens she is using.

A First Look at the Relationship between Production and Cost

Table 10-2 gives us information on Jill's costs. We can determine the total cost of producing a given quantity of pizzas if we know how many workers and ovens are required to produce that quantity of pizzas and what Jill has to pay for those workers and pizzas. Suppose Jill has taken out a bank loan to buy two pizza ovens. The cost of the loan is $800 per week. Therefore, her fixed costs are $800 per week. If Jill pays $650 per week to each worker, her variable costs depend on how many workers she hires. In the short run, Jill can increase the quantity of pizzas she produces only by hiring more workers. The table shows that if she hires 1 worker, she produces 200 pizzas during the week; if she hires 2 workers, she produces 450 pizzas; and so on. For a particular week, Jill's total cost of producing pizzas is equal to the $800 she pays on the loan for the ovens plus the amount she pays to hire workers. If Jill decides to hire 4 workers and produce 600 pizzas, her total cost is $3,400: $800 to lease the ovens and $2,600 to hire the workers. Her cost per pizza is equal to her total cost of producing pizzas divided by the quantity of pizzas produced. If she produces 600 pizzas at a total cost of $3,400, her cost per pizza, or *average total cost*, is $3,400/600 = $5.67. A firm's **average total cost** is always equal to its total cost divided by the quantity of output produced.

Average total cost Total cost divided by the quantity of output produced.

Panel (a) of Figure 10-1 uses the numbers in the next-to-last column of Table 10-2 to graph Jill's total cost. Panel (b) uses the numbers in the last column to graph her average

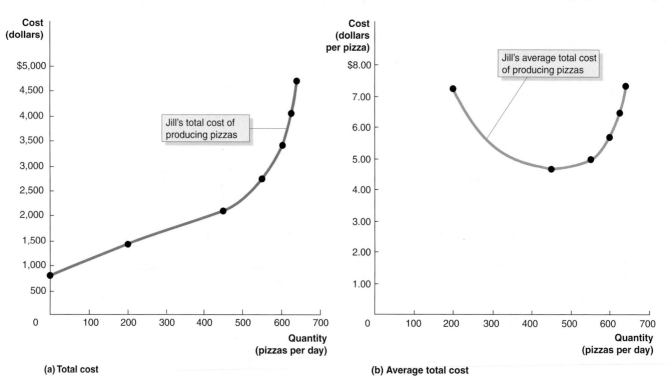

(a) Total cost

(b) Average total cost

Figure 10-1 | Graphing Total Cost and Average Total Cost at Jill Johnson's Restaurant

We can use the information from Table 10-2 to graph the relationship between the quantity of pizzas Jill produces and her total cost and average total cost. Panel (a) shows that total cost increases as the level of production increases. In panel (b), we see that the average total cost is roughly U-shaped: As production increases from low levels, average cost falls before rising at higher levels of production. To understand why average cost has this shape, we must look more closely at the technology of producing pizzas, as shown by the production function.

total cost. Notice in panel (b) that Jill's average cost has roughly the same U shape as the average cost curve we saw Akio Morita calculate for Sony transistor radios at the beginning of this chapter. As production increases from low levels, average cost falls. Average cost then becomes fairly flat, before rising at higher levels of production. To understand why average cost has this U shape, we first need to look more closely at the technology of producing pizzas, as shown by the production function for Jill's restaurant. Then we need to look at how this technology determines the relationship between production and cost.

10.3 | Understand the relationship between the marginal product of labor and the average product of labor.

The Marginal Product of Labor and the Average Product of Labor

To better understand the choices Jill faces, given the technology available to her, think first about what happens if she hires only one worker. That one worker will have to perform several different activities, including taking orders from customers, baking the pizzas, bringing the pizzas to the customers' tables, and ringing up sales on the cash register. If Jill hires two workers, some of these activities can be divided up: One worker could take the orders and ring up the sales, and one worker could bake the pizzas. With this division of tasks, Jill will find that hiring two workers actually allows her to produce more than twice as many pizzas as she could produce with just one worker.

The additional output a firm produces as a result of hiring one more worker is called the **marginal product of labor**. We can calculate the marginal product of labor by determining how much total output increases as each additional worker is hired. We do this for Jill's restaurant in Table 10-3.

When Jill hires only 1 worker, she produces 200 pizzas per week. When she hires 2 workers, she produces 450 pizzas per week. Hiring the second worker increases her production by 250 pizzas per week. So, the marginal product of labor for 1 worker is 200 pizzas. For 2 workers, the marginal product of labor rises to 250 pizzas. This increase in marginal product results from the *division of labor* and from *specialization*. By dividing the tasks to be performed—the division of labor—Jill reduces the time workers lose moving from one activity to the next. She also allows them to become more specialized at their tasks. For example, a worker who concentrates on baking pizzas will become skilled at doing so quickly and efficiently.

Marginal product of labor The additional output a firm produces as a result of hiring one more worker.

The Law of Diminishing Returns

In the short run, the quantity of pizza ovens Jill leases is fixed, so as she hires more workers, the marginal product of labor eventually begins to decline. This happens because at some point, Jill uses up all the gains from the division of labor and from specialization

QUANTITY OF WORKERS	QUANTITY OF PIZZA OVENS	QUANTITY OF PIZZAS	MARGINAL PRODUCT OF LABOR
0	2	0	—
1	2	200	200
2	2	450	250
3	2	550	100
4	2	600	50
5	2	625	25
6	2	640	15

TABLE 10-3

The Marginal Product of Labor at Jill Johnson's Restaurant

Law of diminishing returns The principle that, at some point, adding more of a variable input, such as labor, to the same amount of a fixed input, such as capital, will cause the marginal product of the variable input to decline.

and starts to experience the effects of the **law of diminishing returns**. This law states that adding more of a variable input, such as labor, to the same amount of a fixed input, such as capital, will eventually cause the marginal product of the variable input to decline. For Jill, the marginal product of labor begins to decline when she hires the third worker. Hiring three workers raises the quantity of pizzas she produces from 450 per week to 550. But the increase in the quantity of pizzas—100—is less than the increase when she hired the second worker—250.

If Jill kept adding more and more workers to the same quantity of pizza ovens, eventually workers would begin to get in each other's way, and the marginal product of labor would actually become negative. When the marginal product is negative, the level of total output declines. No firm would actually hire so many workers as to experience a negative marginal product of labor and falling total output.

Graphing Production

Panel (a) in Figure 10-2 shows the relationship between the quantity of workers Jill hires and her total output of pizzas, using the numbers from Table 10-3. Panel (b) shows the marginal product of labor. In panel (a), output increases as more workers are hired, but the increase in output does not occur at a constant rate. Because of specialization and the division of labor, output at first increases at an increasing rate, with each additional worker hired causing production to increase by a *greater* amount than did the hiring of the previous worker. But after the second worker has been hired, hiring more workers while keeping the quantity of ovens constant results in diminishing returns. When the point of diminishing returns is reached, production increases at a decreasing rate. Each additional worker hired after the second worker causes production to increase by a *smaller* amount than did the hiring of the previous worker. In panel (b), the marginal product of labor curve rises initially because of the effects of specialization and division of labor, and then it falls due to the effects of diminishing returns.

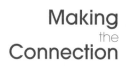

Making the **Connection**

Adam Smith's Famous Account of the Division of Labor in a Pin Factory

In *The Wealth of Nations*, Adam Smith uses production in a pin factory as an example of the gains in output resulting from the division of labor. The following is an excerpt from his account of how pin making was divided into a series of tasks:

> One man draws out the wire, another straightens it, a third cuts it, a fourth points it, a fifth grinds it at the top for receiving the head; to make the head requires two or three distinct operations; to put it on is a [distinct operation], to whiten the pins is another; it is even a trade by itself to put them into the paper; and the important business of making a pin is, in this manner, divided into eighteen distinct operations.

Because the labor of pin making was divided up in this way, the average worker was able to produce about 4,800 pins per day. Smith speculated that a single worker using the pin-making machinery alone would make only about 20 pins per day. This lesson from more than 225 years ago, showing the tremendous gains from division of labor and specialization, remains relevant to most business situations today.

Source: Adam Smith, *An Inquiry into the Nature and Causes of the Wealth of Nations*, Vol. I, Oxford, UK: Oxford University Press edition, 1976, pp. 14–15.

YOUR TURN: Test your understanding by doing related problem 3.6 on page 358 at the end of this chapter.

The gains from division of labor and specialization are as important to firms today as they were in the eighteenth century, when Adam Smith first discussed them.

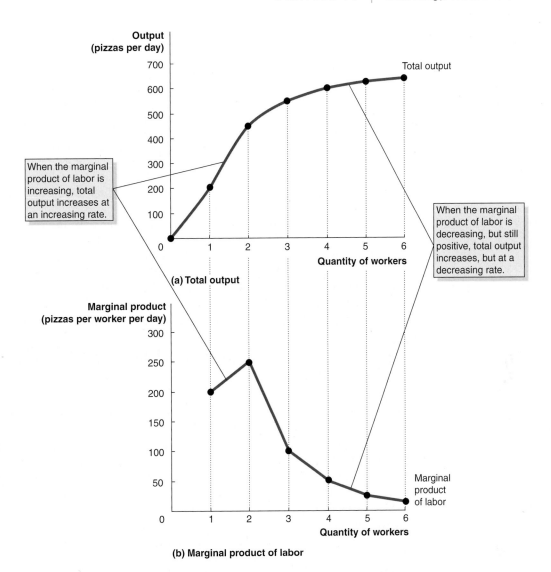

Figure 10-2 | Total Output and the Marginal Product of Labor

In panel (a), output increases as more workers are hired, but the increase in output does not occur at a constant rate. Because of specialization and the division of labor, output at first increases at an increasing rate, with each additional worker hired causing production to increase by a *greater* amount than did the hiring of the previous worker. After the third worker has been hired, hiring more workers while keeping the number of pizza ovens constant results in diminishing returns. When the point of diminishing returns is reached, production increases at a decreasing rate. Each additional worker hired after the third worker causes production to increase by a *smaller* amount than did the hiring of the previous worker. In panel (b), the *marginal product of labor* is the additional output produced as a result of hiring one more worker. The marginal product of labor rises initially because of the effects of specialization and division of labor, and then it falls due to the effects of diminishing returns.

The Relationship between Marginal and Average Product

The marginal product of labor tells us how much total output changes as the quantity of workers hired changes. We can also calculate how many pizzas workers produce on average. The **average product of labor** is the total output produced by a firm divided by the quantity of workers. For example, using the numbers in Table 10-3, if Jill hires 4 workers to produce 600 pizzas, the average product of labor is 600/4 = 150.

We can state the relationship between the marginal and average products of labor this way: *The average product of labor is the average of the marginal products of labor.* For example, the numbers from Table 10-3 show that the marginal product of the first worker Jill hires is 200, the marginal product of the second worker is 250, and the

Average product of labor The total output produced by a firm divided by the quantity of workers.

marginal product of the third worker is 100. Therefore, the average product of labor for three workers is 183.3:

$$183.3 = (200 + 250 + 100) / 3$$

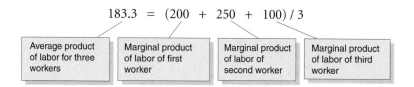

| Average product of labor for three workers | Marginal product of labor of first worker | Marginal product of labor of second worker | Marginal product of labor of third worker |

By taking the average of the marginal products of the first three workers, we have the average product of the three workers.

Whenever the marginal product of labor is greater than the average product of labor, the average product of labor must be increasing. This statement is true for the same reason that a person 6 feet, 2 inches tall entering a room where the average height is 5 feet, 9 inches raises the average height of people in the room. Whenever the marginal product of labor is less than the average product of labor, the average product of labor must be decreasing. The marginal product of labor equals the average product of labor for the quantity of workers where the average product of labor is at its maximum.

An Example of Marginal and Average Values: College Grades

The relationship between the marginal product of labor and the average product of labor is the same as the relationship between the marginal and average values of any variable. To see this more clearly, think about the familiar relationship between a student's grade point average (GPA) in one semester and his overall, or cumulative, GPA. The table in Figure 10-3 shows Paul's college grades for each semester, beginning with fall 2005. The graph in Figure 10-3 plots the grades from the table. Just as each additional worker hired adds to a firm's total production, each additional semester adds to Paul's total grade points. We can calculate what each individual worker hired adds to total production (marginal product), and we can calculate the average production of the workers hired so far (average product).

Similarly, we can calculate the GPA Paul earns in a particular semester (his "marginal GPA"), and we can calculate his cumulative GPA for all the semesters he has completed so far (his "average GPA"). As the table shows, Paul gets off to a weak start in the fall semester of his freshman year, earning only a 1.50 GPA. In each subsequent semester through the fall of his junior year, his GPA for the semester increases from the previous semester—raising his cumulative GPA. As the graph shows, however, his cumulative GPA does not increase as rapidly as his semester-by-semester GPA because his cumulative GPA is held back by the low GPAs of his first few semesters. Notice that in Paul's junior year, even though his semester GPA declines from fall to spring, his cumulative GPA rises. Only in the fall of his senior year, when his semester GPA drops below his cumulative GPA, does his cumulative GPA decline.

10.4 LEARNING OBJECTIVE

10.4 | Explain and illustrate the relationship between marginal cost and average total cost.

The Relationship between Short-Run Production and Short-Run Cost

We have seen that technology determines the values of the marginal product of labor and the average product of labor. In turn, the marginal and average products of labor affect the firm's costs. Keep in mind that the relationships we are discussing are *short-run* relationships: We are assuming that the time period is too short for the firm to change its technology or the size of its physical plant.

	Semester GPA (Marginal) GPA	Cumulative GPA (Average) GPA
Freshman Year		
Fall	1.50	1.50
Spring	2.00	1.75
Sophomore Year		
Fall	2.20	1.90
Spring	3.00	2.18
Junior Year		
Fall	3.20	2.38
Spring	3.00	2.48
Senior Year		
Fall	2.40	2.47
Spring	2.00	2.41

Average GPA continues to rise, although marginal GPA falls.

With the marginal GPA below the average, the average GPA falls.

Figure 10-3

Marginal and Average GPAs

The relationship between marginal and average values for a variable can be illustrated using GPAs. We can calculate the GPA Paul earns in a particular semester (his "marginal GPA"), and we can calculate his cumulative GPA for all the semesters he has completed so far (his "average GPA"). Paul's GPA is only 1.50 in the fall semester of his freshman year. In each following semester through fall of his junior year, his GPA for the semester increases—raising his cumulative GPA. In Paul's junior year, even though his semester GPA declines from fall to spring, his cumulative GPA rises. Only in the fall of his senior year, when his semester GPA drops below his cumulative GPA, does his cumulative GPA decline.

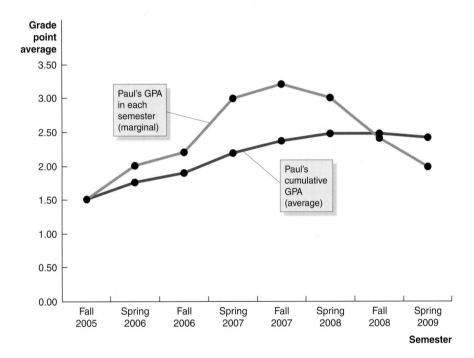

Paul's GPA in each semester (marginal)

Paul's cumulative GPA (average)

At the beginning of this chapter, we saw how Akio Morita used an average total cost curve to determine the price of radios. The average total cost curve Morita used and the average total cost curve in Figure 10-1 for Jill Johnson's restaurant both have a U shape. As we will soon see, the U shape of the average total cost curve is determined by the shape of the curve that shows the relationship between *marginal cost* and the level of production.

Marginal Cost

As we saw in Chapter 1, one of the key ideas in economics is that optimal decisions are made at the margin. Consumers, firms, and government officials usually make decisions about doing a little more or a little less. As Jill Johnson considers whether to hire additional workers to produce additional pizzas, she needs to consider how much she will add to her total cost by producing the additional pizzas. **Marginal cost** is the change in a firm's total cost from producing one more unit of a good or service. We can calculate marginal cost for a particular increase in output by dividing the change in cost by the

Marginal cost The change in a firm's total cost from producing one more unit of a good or service.

change in output. We can express this idea mathematically (remembering that the Greek letter delta, Δ, means "change in"):

$$MC = \frac{\Delta TC}{\Delta Q}.$$

In the table in Figure 10-4, we use this equation to calculate Jill's marginal cost of producing pizzas.

Why Are the Marginal and Average Cost Curves U-Shaped?

Notice in the graph in Figure 10-4 that Jill's marginal cost of producing pizzas declines at first and then increases, giving the marginal cost curve a U shape. The table in Figure 10-4 also shows the marginal product of labor. This table helps us see the important relationship between the marginal product of labor and the marginal cost of production: The marginal product of labor is *rising* for the first two workers, but the marginal cost of the pizzas produced by these workers is *falling*. The marginal product of labor is *falling* for the last four workers, but the marginal cost of pizzas produced by these workers is *rising*. To summarize this point: *When the marginal product of labor is rising, the marginal cost of output is falling. When the marginal product of labor is falling, the marginal cost of production is rising.*

Figure 10-4

Jill Johnson's Marginal Cost and Average Total Cost of Producing Pizzas

We can use the information in the table to calculate Jill's marginal cost and average total cost of producing pizzas. For the first two workers hired, the marginal product of labor is increasing. This increase causes the marginal cost of production to fall. For the last four workers hired, the marginal product of labor is falling. This causes the marginal cost of production to increase. Therefore, the marginal cost curve falls and then rises—that is, has a U shape—because the marginal product of labor rises and then falls. As long as marginal cost is below average total cost, average total cost will be falling. When marginal cost is above average total cost, average total cost will be rising. The relationship between marginal cost and average total cost explains why the average total cost curve also has a U shape.

Quantity of Workers	Quantity of Ovens	Marginal Product of Labor	Total Cost of Pizzas	Marginal Cost of Pizzas	Average Total Cost of Pizzas
0	0	—	$800	—	—
1	200	200	1,450	$3.25	$7.25
2	450	250	2,100	2.60	4.67
3	550	100	2,750	6.50	5.00
4	600	50	3,400	13.00	5.67
5	625	25	4,050	26.00	6.48
6	640	15	4,700	43.33	7.34

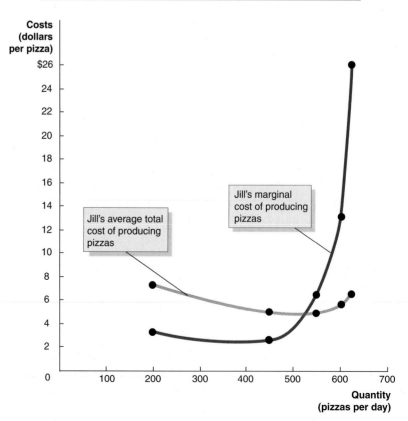

One way to understand why this point is true is first to notice that the only additional cost to Jill from producing more pizzas is the additional wages she pays to hire more workers. She pays each new worker the same $650 per week. So the marginal cost of the additional pizzas each worker makes depends on that worker's additional output, or marginal product. As long as the additional output from each new worker is rising, the marginal cost of that output is falling. When the additional output from each new worker is falling, the marginal cost of that output is rising. *We can conclude that the marginal cost of production falls and then rises—forming a U shape—because the marginal product of labor rises and then falls.*

The relationship between marginal cost and average total cost follows the usual relationship between marginal and average values. As long as marginal cost is below average total cost, average total cost falls. When marginal cost is above average total cost, average total cost rises. Marginal cost equals average total cost when average total cost is at its lowest point. Therefore, the average total cost curve has a U shape because the marginal cost curve has a U shape.

Solved Problem | 10-4

The Relationship between Marginal Cost and Average Cost

Is Jill Johnson right or wrong when she says the following? "I am currently producing 10,000 pizzas per month at a total cost of $500.00. If I produce 10,001 pizzas, my total cost will rise to $500.11. Therefore, my marginal cost of producing pizzas must be increasing." Draw a graph to illustrate your answer.

SOLVING THE PROBLEM:

Step 1: **Review the chapter material.** This problem requires understanding the relationship between marginal and average cost, so you may want to review the section "Why Are the Marginal and Average Cost Curves U-Shaped?" which begins on page 344.

Step 2: **Calculate average total cost and marginal cost.** Average total cost is total cost divided by total output. In this case, average total cost is $500.11/10,001 = $0.05. Marginal cost is the change in total cost divided by the change in output. In this case, marginal cost is $0.11/1 = $0.11.

Step 3: **Use the relationship between marginal cost and average total cost to answer the question.** When marginal cost is greater than average total cost, marginal cost must be increasing. You have shown in step 2 that marginal cost is greater than average total cost. Therefore, Jill is right: Her marginal cost of producing pizzas must be increasing.

Step 4: **Draw the graph.**

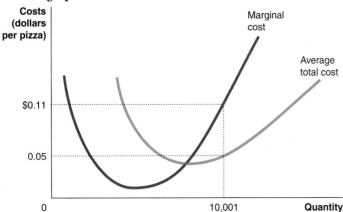

YOUR TURN: For more practice, do related problems 4.5 and 4.6 on page 359 at the end of this chapter.

>> End Solved Problem 10-4

10.5 | Graph average total cost, average variable cost, average fixed cost, and marginal cost.

Graphing Cost Curves

Average fixed cost Fixed cost divided by the quantity of output produced.

Average variable cost Variable cost divided by the quantity of output produced.

We have seen that we calculate average total cost by dividing total cost by the quantity of output produced. Similarly, we can calculate **average fixed cost** by dividing fixed cost by the quantity of output produced. And we can calculate **average variable cost** by dividing variable cost by the quantity of output produced. Or, mathematically, with Q being the level of output, we have:

$$\text{Average total cost} = ATC = \frac{TC}{Q}$$

$$\text{Average fixed cost} = AFC = \frac{FC}{Q}$$

$$\text{Average variable cost} = AVC = \frac{VC}{Q}.$$

Finally, notice that average total cost is the sum of average fixed cost plus average variable cost:

$$ATC = AFC + AVC.$$

The only fixed cost Jill incurs in operating her restaurant is the $800 per week she pays on the bank loan for her pizza ovens. Her variable costs are the wages she pays her workers. The table and graph in Figure 10-5 show Jill's costs.

We will use graphs like the one in Figure 10-5 in the next several chapters to analyze how firms decide the level of output to produce and the price to charge. Before going further, be sure you understand the following three key facts about Figure 10-5:

1 The marginal cost (MC), average total cost (ATC), and average variable cost (AVC) curves are all U-shaped, and the marginal cost curve intersects the average variable cost and average total cost curves at their minimum points. When marginal cost is less than either average variable cost or average total cost, it causes them to decrease. When marginal cost is above average variable cost or average total cost, it causes them to increase. Therefore, when marginal cost equals average variable cost or average total cost, they must be at their minimum points.

2 As output increases, average fixed cost gets smaller and smaller. This happens because in calculating average fixed cost, we are dividing something that gets larger and larger—output—into something that remains constant—fixed cost. Firms often refer to this process of lowering average fixed cost by selling more output as "spreading the overhead." By "overhead" they mean fixed costs.

3 As output increases, the difference between average total cost and average variable cost decreases. This happens because the difference between average total cost and average variable cost is average fixed cost, which gets smaller as output increases.

10.6 | Understand how firms use the long-run average cost curve in their planning.

Costs in the Long Run

The distinction between fixed cost and variable cost that we just discussed applies to the short run but *not* to the long run. For example, in the short run, Jill Johnson has fixed costs of $800 per week because she signed a loan agreement with a bank when she bought her pizza ovens. In the long run, the cost of purchasing more pizza ovens becomes variable because Jill can choose whether to expand her business by buying

Quantity of Workers	Quantity of Ovens	Quantity of Pizzas	Cost of Ovens (Fixed Cost)	Cost of Workers (Variable Cost)	Total Cost of Pizzas	ATC	AFC	AVC	MC
0	2	0	$800	$0	$800	—	—	—	—
1	2	200	800	650	1,450	$7.25	$4.00	$3.25	$3.25
2	2	450	800	1,300	2,100	4.67	1.78	2.89	2.60
3	2	550	800	1,950	2,750	5.00	1.45	3.55	6.50
4	2	600	800	2,600	3,400	5.67	1.33	4.33	13.00
5	2	625	800	3,250	4,050	6.48	1.28	5.2	26.00
6	2	640	800	3,900	4,700	7.34	1.25	6.09	43.33

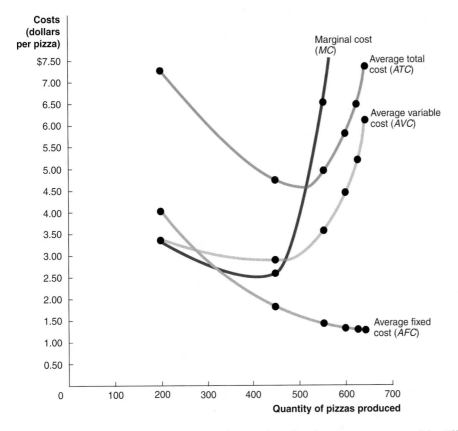

Figure 10-5

Costs at Jill Johnson's Restaurant

Jill's costs of making pizzas are shown in the table and plotted in the graph. Notice three important facts about the graph: (1) The marginal cost (*MC*), average total cost (*ATC*), and average variable cost (*AVC*) curves are all U-shaped, and the marginal cost curve intersects both the average variable cost curve and average total cost curve at their minimum points. (2) As output increases, average fixed cost (*AFC*) gets smaller and smaller. (3) As output increases, the difference between average total cost and average variable cost decreases. Make sure you can explain why each of these three facts is true. You should spend time becoming familiar with this graph because it is one of the most important graphs in microeconomics.

more ovens. The same would be true of any other fixed costs a company like Jill's might have. Once a company has purchased a fire insurance policy, the cost of the policy is fixed. But when the policy expires, the company must decide whether to renew it, and the cost becomes variable. The important point here is this: *In the long run, all costs are variable. There are no fixed costs in the long run.* In other words, in the long run, total cost equals variable cost, and average total cost equals average variable cost.

Managers of successful firms simultaneously consider how they can most profitably run their current store, factory, or office and also whether in the long run they would be more profitable if they became larger or, possibly, smaller. Jill must consider how to run her current restaurant, which has only two pizza ovens, and she must also plan what to do when her current bank loan is paid off and the lease on her store ends. Should she buy more pizza ovens? Should she lease a larger restaurant?

Economies of Scale

Short-run average cost curves represent the costs a firm faces when some input, such as the quantity of machines it uses, is fixed. The **long-run average cost curve** shows the lowest cost at which a firm is able to produce a given level of output in the long run, when no inputs are fixed. Many firms experience **economies of scale**, which means the firm's

Long-run average cost curve A curve showing the lowest cost at which a firm is able to produce a given quantity of output in the long run, when no inputs are fixed.

Economies of scale The situation when a firm's long-run average costs fall as it increases output.

Figure 10-6

The Relationship between Short-Run Average Cost and Long-Run Average Cost

If a small bookstore expects to sell only 1,000 books per month, then it will be able to sell that quantity of books at the lowest average cost of $22 per book if it builds the small store represented by the *ATC* curve on the left of the figure. A larger bookstore will be able to sell 20,000 books per month at a lower cost of $18 per book. A bookstore selling 20,000 books per month and a bookstore selling 40,000 books per month will experience constant returns to scale and have the same average cost. A bookstore selling 20,000 books per month will have reached minimum efficient scale. Very large bookstores will experience diseconomies of scale, and their average costs will rise as sales increase beyond 40,000 books per month.

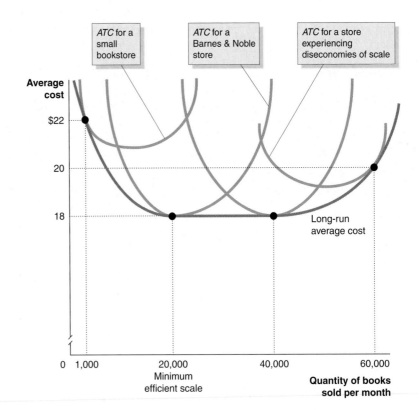

long-run average costs fall as it increases the quantity of output it produces. We can see the effects of economies of scale in Figure 10-6, which shows the relationship between short-run and long-run average cost curves. Managers can use long-run average cost curves for planning because they show the effect on cost of expanding output by, for example, building a larger factory or store.

Long-Run Average Total Cost Curves for Bookstores

Figure 10-6 shows long-run average cost in the retail bookstore industry. If a small bookstore expects to sell only 1,000 books per month, then it will be able to sell that quantity of books at the lowest average cost of $22 per book if it builds the small store represented by the *ATC* curve on the left of the figure. A much larger bookstore, such as one run by a national chain like Barnes & Noble, will be able to sell 20,000 books per month at a lower average cost of $18 per book. This decline in average cost from $22 to $18 represents the economies of scale that exist in bookselling. Why would the larger bookstore have lower average costs? One important reason is that the Barnes & Noble store is selling 20 times as many books per month as the small store but might need only six times as many workers. This saving in labor cost would reduce Barnes & Noble's average cost of selling books.

Firms may experience economies of scale for several reasons. First, as in the case of Barnes & Noble, the firm's technology may make it possible to increase production with a smaller proportional increase in at least one input. Second, both workers and managers can become more specialized, enabling them to become more productive, as output expands. Third, large firms, like Barnes & Noble, Wal-Mart, and General Motors, may be able to purchase inputs at lower costs than smaller competitors. In fact, as Wal-Mart expanded, its bargaining power with its suppliers increased, and its average costs fell. Finally, as a firm expands, it may be able to borrow money more inexpensively, thereby lowering its costs.

Economies of scale do not continue forever. The long-run average cost curve in most industries has a flat segment that often stretches over a substantial range of output. As Figure 10-6 shows, a bookstore selling 20,000 books per month and a bookstore selling 40,000 books per month have the same average cost. Over this range of output, firms in the industry experience **constant returns to scale**. As these firms increase their output, they have to increase their inputs, such as the size of the store and the quantity of

Constant returns to scale The situation when a firm's long-run average costs remain unchanged as it increases output.

workers, proportionally. The level of output at which all economies of scale are exhausted is known as **minimum efficient scale**. A bookstore selling 20,000 books per month has reached minimum efficient scale.

Very large bookstores experience increasing average costs as managers begin to have difficulty coordinating the operation of the store. Figure 10-6 shows that for sales above 40,000 books per month, firms in the industry experience **diseconomies of scale**. Toyota ran into diseconomies of scale in assembling automobiles. The firm found that as it expanded production at its Georgetown, Kentucky, plant and its plants in China, its managers had difficulty keeping costs from rising. The president of Toyota's Georgetown plant was quoted as saying, "Demand for . . . high volumes saps your energy. Over a period of time, it eroded our focus . . . [and] thinned out the expertise and knowledge we painstakingly built up over the years." One analysis of the problems Toyota faced in expanding production concluded: "It is the kind of paradox many highly successful companies face: Getting bigger doesn't always mean getting better."

Minimum efficient scale The level of output at which all economies of scale are exhausted.

Diseconomies of scale The situation when a firm's long-run average costs rise as the firm increases output.

Solved Problem | 10-6

Using Long-Run Average Cost Curves to Understand Business Strategy

In fall 2002, Motorola and Siemens were each manufacturing both mobile phone handsets and wireless infrastructure—the base stations needed to operate a wireless communications network. The firms discussed the following arrangement: Motorola would give Siemens its wireless infrastructure business in exchange for Siemens giving Motorola its mobile phone handsets business. The main factor motivating the trade was the hope of taking advantage of economies of scale in each business. Use long-run average total cost curves to explain why this trade might make sense for Motorola and Siemens.

SOLVING THE PROBLEM:

Step 1: **Review the chapter material.** This problem is about the long-run average cost curve, so you may want to review the material in the section "Costs in the Long Run," which begins on page 346.

Step 2: **Draw long-run average cost graphs for Motorola and Siemens.** The question does not provide us with the details of the quantity of each product each firm is producing before the trade or the firms' average costs of production. If economies of scale were an important reason for the trade, we can assume that Motorola and Siemens were not yet at minimum efficient scale in the wireless infrastructure and phone handset businesses. Therefore, we can draw the following graphs:

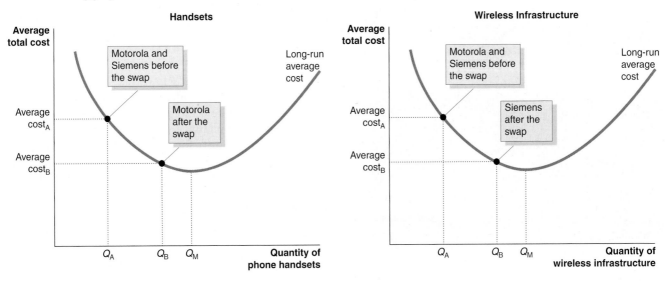

Step 3: **Explain the curves in the graphs.** Before the proposed trade, Motorola and Siemens are producing both products at less than the minimum efficient scale, which is Q_M in both graphs. After the trade, Motorola's production of handsets will increase, moving it from Q_A to Q_B in the first graph. This increase in production will allow it to take advantage of economies of scale and reduce its average cost from Average Cost$_A$ to Average Cost$_B$. Similarly, production of wireless infrastructure by Siemens will increase from Q_A to Q_B, lowering its average cost from Average Cost$_A$ to Average Cost$_B$. As drawn, the graphs show that both firms will still be short of minimum efficient scale after the trade, although their average costs will have fallen.

EXTRA CREDIT: These were new technologies at the time Motorola and Siemens discussed the trade. As a result, companies making these products were only beginning to understand how large minimum efficient scale was. To survive in the industry, the managements of both companies wanted to lower their costs by taking advantage of economies of scale. As one industry analyst put it: "Motorola and Siemens may be driven by the conviction that they have little choice. Most observers believe consolidation in both the [wireless] networking and handset areas is inevitable."

Source for quote: Ray Hegarty, *Rumored Motorola–Siemens Business Unit Swap? A Compelling M&A Story*, www.thefeature.com.

YOUR TURN: For more practice, do related problems 6.4, 6.5, 6.6, and 6.7 on pages 361 and 362 at the end of this chapter.

>> **End Solved Problem 10-6**

Over time, most firms in an industry will build factories or stores that are at least as large as the minimum efficient scale but not so large that diseconomies of scale occur. In the bookstore industry, stores will sell between 20,000 and 40,000 books per month. However, firms often do not know the exact shape of their long-run average cost curves. As a result, they may mistakenly build factories or stores that are either too large or too small.

Making
the
Connection | **The Colossal River Rouge: Diseconomies of Scale at Ford Motor Company**

When Henry Ford started the Ford Motor Company in 1903, automobile companies produced cars in small workshops, using highly skilled workers. Ford introduced two new ideas that allowed him to take advantage of economies of scale. First, Ford used identical—or, interchangeable—parts so that unskilled workers could assemble the cars. Second, instead of having groups of workers moving from one stationary automobile to the next, he had the workers remain stationary while the automobiles moved along an assembly line. Ford built a large factory at Highland Park, outside Detroit, where he used these ideas to produce the famous Model T at an average cost well below what his competitors could match using older production methods in smaller factories.

Ford believed that he could produce automobiles at an even lower average cost by building a still larger plant along the River Rouge. Unfortunately, Ford's River Rouge plant was too large and suffered from diseconomies of scale. Ford's managers had great difficulty coordinating the production of automobiles in such a large plant. The following description of the River Rouge comes from a biography of Ford by Allan Nevins and Frank Ernest Hill:

A total of 93 separate structures stood on the [River Rouge] site. . . . Railroad trackage covered 93 miles, conveyors 27 [miles]. About 75,000 men worked in the great plant. A force of 5000 did

Is it possible for a factory to be too big?

nothing but keep it clean, wearing out 5000 mops and 3000 brooms a month, and using 86 tons of soap on the floors, walls, and 330 acres of windows. The Rouge was an industrial city, immense, concentrated, packed with power. . . . By its very massiveness and complexity, it denied men at the top contact with and understanding of those beneath, and gave those beneath a sense of being lost in inexorable immensity and power.

Beginning in 1927, Ford produced the Model A—its only car model at that time—at the River Rouge plant. Ford failed to achieve economies of scale and actually *lost money* on each of the four Model A body styles.

Ford could not raise the price of the Model A to make it profitable because at a higher price, the car could not compete with similar models produced by competitors such as General Motors and Chrysler. He eventually reduced the cost of making the Model A by constructing smaller factories spread out across the country. These smaller factories produced the Model A at a lower average cost than was possible at the River Rouge plant.

Source for quote: Allan Nevins and Frank Ernest Hill, *Ford: Expansion and Challenge, 1915–1933*, New York: Scribner, 1957, pp. 293, 295.

YOUR TURN: Test your understanding by doing related problem 6.8 on page 362 at the end of this chapter.

Don't Let This Happen to **YOU!**

Don't Confuse Diminishing Returns with Diseconomies of Scale

The concepts of diminishing returns and diseconomies of scale may seem similar, but, in fact, they are unrelated. Diminishing returns applies only to the short run, when at least one of the firm's inputs, such as the quantity of machinery it uses, is fixed. The law of diminishing returns

tells us that in the short run, hiring more workers will, at some point, result in less additional output. Diminishing returns explains why marginal cost curves eventually slope upward. Diseconomies of scale apply only in the long run, when the firm is free to vary all its inputs, can adopt new technology, and can vary the amount of machinery it uses and the size of its facility. Diseconomies of scale explain why long-run average cost curves eventually slope upward.

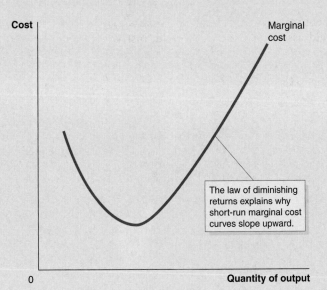

The law of diminishing returns explains why short-run marginal cost curves slope upward.

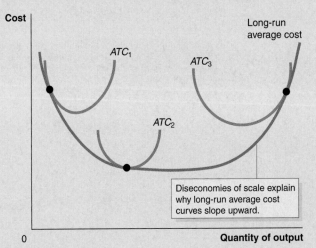

Diseconomies of scale explain why long-run average cost curves slope upward.

YOUR TURN: Test your understanding by doing related problem 6.10 on page 362 at the end of this chapter.

Economics in YOUR Life!

>> Continued from page 333

At the beginning of the chapter, we asked you to consider a situation in which you are about to open a store to sell recliners. Both you and a competing store, Bob's Big Chairs, can buy recliners from the manufacturer for $300 each. But because Bob's sells more recliners per month than you expect to be able to, his costs per recliner are lower than yours. We asked you to think about why this might be true. In this chapter, we have seen that firms often experience declining average costs as the quantity they sell increases. One significant reason Bob's average cost might be lower than yours has to do with fixed costs. Because your stores are the same size, you may be paying about the same amount to lease the store space. You may also be paying about the same amounts for utilities, insurance, and advertising. All these are fixed costs because they do not change as the quantity of recliners you sell changes. Because Bob's fixed costs are the same as yours, but he is selling more recliners, his average fixed costs are lower than yours, and, therefore, so are his average total costs. With lower average total costs, he can sell his recliners for a lower price than you do and still make a profit.

Conclusion

In this chapter, we discussed the relationship between a firm's technology, production, and costs. In the discussion, we encountered a number of definitions of costs. Because we will use these definitions in later chapters, it is useful to bring them together in Table 10-4 for you to review.

We have seen the important relationship between a firm's level of production and its costs. Just as this information was vital to Akio Morita in deciding which price to charge for his transistor radios, so it remains vital today to all firms as they attempt to decide the optimal level of production and the optimal prices to charge for their products. We will explore this point further in Chapter 11. Before moving on to that chapter, read *An Inside Look* on pages 354–355 to see how we can use long-run average cost curves to understand the effect of lower costs of production on the pricing of flat-panel TVs.

TERM	DEFINITION	SYMBOLS AND EQUATIONS
Total cost	The cost of all the inputs used by a firm, or fixed cost plus variable cost	TC
Fixed cost	Costs that remain constant when a firm's level of output changes	FC
Variable cost	Costs that change when the firm's level of output changes	VC
Marginal cost	Increase in total cost resulting from producing another unit of output	$MC = \dfrac{\Delta TC}{\Delta Q}$
Average total cost	Total cost divided by the quantity of output produced	$ATC = \dfrac{TC}{Q}$
Average fixed cost	Fixed cost divided by the quantity of output produced	$AFC = \dfrac{FC}{Q}$
Average variable cost	Variable cost divided by the quantity of output produced	$AVC = \dfrac{VC}{Q}$
Implicit cost	A nonmonetary opportunity cost	—
Explicit cost	A cost that involves spending money	—

TABLE 10-4

A Summary of Definitions of Cost

WALL STREET JOURNAL, APRIL 15, 2006

Flat-Panel TVs, Long Touted, Finally Are Becoming the Norm

After years as the Next Big Thing in consumer electronics, flat-panel TVs are finally becoming the mainstream standard. . . .

Last year, flat-screen TVs for the first time accounted for the majority of TVs bought in Japan, Hong Kong and Singapore. That crossover will happen this year or next in the U.S. and most European countries, industry watchers say, and at least one company has already stopped shipping tube TVs in the U.S. "It's happening faster than the most optimistic targets," says Ross Young, president of DisplaySearch, an Austin, Texas, market-research firm.

World-wide, sales this year of liquid-crystal display and plasma flat-panel TVs are on track to total about 44 million units, valued at as much as $54 billion, out of an overall market of 185 million TVs, according to market research firms. In the U.S., sales are expected to reach between 12 million and 14 million flat-panel TVs, or roughly half of all TVs sold. Last year, world-wide sales of flat-panel TVs totaled 25 million units.

Consumers like the thin form and light weight of flat-panel TVs, but until recently, many considered them too expensive. Two years ago, a 30-inch, LCD-TV cost $3,500 to $4,000. Since then, more than a dozen factories producing critical glass and screen components have opened, which has pushed down manufacturing costs, allowing for lower prices.

Competition between LCD and plasma technologies is pushing down prices, too. Plasma models use electricity to light individual points of gas on a screen; in LCDs, a layer of liquid crystal filters a bright light. LCD beat plasma about 15 years ago as the flat-panel of choice in notebook computers. From there, plasma developers jumped to big size screens, where they have since been most cost effective, while technical challenges long limited the size of LCDs. . . .

Increased production is likely to help prices continue to fall throughout the year. Seven new factories are under construction in Asia that will make LCD panels 40 inches or larger, and three new factories for plasma screens are under construction. Several are being optimized for screens that are 50 inches or larger. By late next year, prices of 40-inch models will be closing in on $1,000 as production ramps up. . . .

Japan's Matsushita Electric Industrial Co., maker of Panasonic products, has stopped shipping tube TVs altogether to the U.S., where it expects to sell about 1.5 million plasma-screen TVs this year. Just two years ago, it sold one million tube TVs and 150,000 plasma models in the U.S. Flat-panel TVs of all types have become an easier sell as popular television shows such as "CSI" and "Lost" adopt the widescreen, high-definition look of movies. The U.S. and several other countries are shifting their broadcast systems to digital signals that promise to broaden the availability of HDTV content. Higher-definition DVDs that are emerging this year may also fuel demand. . . .

To meet demand, manufacturers are in a mad dash to build new factories, or change existing ones, to accommodate flat-panel TVs. In one week last month, Sony, LG Electronics Co. and China's Changhong Group announced new factories in Eastern Europe to assemble flat-panel models for the European market. Just this week, Sony and Samsung Electronics Co. said they would expand their LCD-panel joint venture by spending $2 billion on what, for the moment, will be the industry's largest factory. Hitachi Corp. a week earlier said it's considering building factories to quadruple its annual output of LCD-TVs to more than five million annually. . . .

Key Points in the Article

This article illustrates how several firms are racing to expand production of flat-panel televisions. The article discusses long-run decisions firms make, such as what plant size to build. It also discusses how the costs of inputs into flat-panel televisions have been declining. Lower costs of production have resulted in sharply lower prices of flat-panel televisions.

Analyzing the News

(a) As more factories open to produce components to make flat-panel televisions, the price of the components should fall. As a result, the marginal and average cost of producing flat-panel televisions should decline. In Figure 1, we see that more factories producing components for flat-panel TVs increases the supply of components from S_1 to S_2. The increased supply

causes the price of components to fall from P_1 to P_2, while the quantity of components sold increases from Q_1 to Q_2.

Because these components are inputs in production of flat-panel TVs, as the price of components falls, the costs of producing flat-panel TVs also fall. This is seen in Figure 2, where the marginal cost curve of TVs falls from MC_1 to MC_2 and the average cost curve falls from ATC_1 to ATC_2.

Falling costs, make it possible for firms like Sony to sell TVs at lower prices and still cover their costs. You can see in Figure 2 that prior to the decrease in input prices a firm would need to receive ATC_1 dollars per TV to cover the cost of producing Q_1 TVs. After the reduction in input prices, the average cost of producing Q_1 TVs falls to ATC_2 dollars and the firm is able to cover its costs at lower prices.

(b) Increased production moves a firm further to the right on its cost curve. For goods like flat-panel TVs, fixed costs tend to be high relative to marginal costs, because the factories that produce the televisions are expensive to build. So, average cost will decline over large ranges of output, which makes it possible for Sony and other manufacturers to offer the televisions for sale at lower prices.

(c) Firms use the long-run average cost curve when choosing what size

manufacturing plant to build. The long-run average cost curve shows the minimum cost of producing at each output level. Choosing the best point to be on the long-run average cost curve requires firms to forecast future sales. In this case, firms are expecting continuing rapid increases in demand for flat-panel televisions and are building increasingly larger plants. They are expecting that economies of scale will make the average costs of production in the larger plants lower than the average costs of production in smaller plants. But as the example of Ford's River Rouge plant discussed on pages 350–351 shows, when a new industry is rapidly expanding, it is not unusual for at least one firm to build a plant that is too large and to begin experiencing diseconomies of scale. With diseconomies of scale, the average cost of production in a larger plant is actually *higher* than in a smaller plant.

Thinking Critically

1. Suppose you are a manager at Sony and you are asked to determine what size manufacturing plants for flat-panel televisions the firm should be planning to build. What information would you need to gather in order to determine the optimal sized plant?

2. Use the concepts from this chapter to explain why the long-run supply of flat-panel TVs is more elastic than the short-run supply of flat-panel TVs.

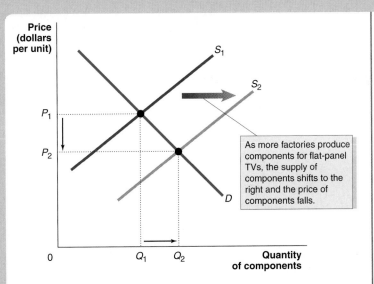

Figure 1. An increased supply of flat-panel televisions components leads to a lower price.

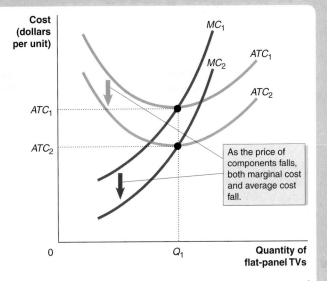

Figure 2. Lower input prices reduce the marginal and average costs of producing flat-panel televisions.

Key Terms

Average fixed cost, p. 346

Average product of labor, p. 341

Average total cost, p. 338

Average variable cost, p. 346

Constant returns to scale, p. 348

Diseconomies of scale, p. 349

Economies of scale, p. 347

Explicit cost, p. 336

Fixed costs, p. 335

Implicit cost, p. 336

Law of diminishing returns, p. 340

Long run, p. 335

Long-run average cost curve, p. 347

Marginal cost, p. 343

Marginal product of labor, p. 339

Minimum efficient scale, p. 349

Opportunity cost, p. 336

Production function, p. 338

Short run, p. 335

Technological change, p. 334

Technology, p. 334

Total cost, p. 335

Variable costs, p. 335

10.1 LEARNING OBJECTIVE   10.1 | Define technology and give examples of technological change, **pages 334–335.**

Technology: An Economic Definition

Summary

The basic activity of a firm is to use inputs, such as workers, machines, and natural resources, to produce goods and services. The firm's **technology** is the processes it uses to turn inputs into goods and services. **Technological change** refers to a change in the ability of a firm to produce a given level of output with a given quantity of inputs.

 Visit www.myeconlab.com to complete these exercises online and get instant feedback.

Review Questions

1.1 What is the difference between technology and technological change?

1.2 Is it possible for technological change to be negative? If so, give an example.

Problems and Applications

1.3 Briefly explain whether you agree with the following observation: "Technological change refers only to the introduction of new products, so it is not relevant to the operations of most firms."

1.4 Which of the following are examples of a firm experiencing positive technological change?
   a. A firm is able to cut each worker's wage rate by 10 percent and still produce the same level of output.
   b. A training program makes a firm's workers more productive.
   c. An exercise program makes a firm's workers more healthy and productive.
   d. A firm cuts its workforce and is able to maintain its initial level of output.
   e. A firm rearranges the layout of its factory and finds that by using its initial set of inputs, it can produce exactly as much as before.

1.5 (Related to the *Making the Connection* on page 334) The Seven-Eleven chain of convenience stores in Japan reorganized its system for supplying its stores with food. This lead to a sharp reduction in the number of trucks the company had to use, while increasing the amount of fresh food on store shelves. Someone discussing Seven-Eleven's new system argues "This is not an example of technological change because it did not require the use of new machinery or equipment." Briefly explain whether you agree with this argument.

> **>> End Learning Objective 10.1**

10.2 LEARNING OBJECTIVE   10.2 | Distinguish between the economic short run and the economic long run, **pages 335–339.**

The Short Run and the Long Run in Economics

Summary

In the **short run**, a firm's technology and the size of its factory, store, or office are fixed. In the **long run**, a firm is able to adopt new technology and to increase or decrease the size of its physical plant. **Total cost** is the cost of all the inputs a firm uses in production. Variable costs are costs that change as output changes. Fixed costs are costs that remain constant as output changes. Opportunity cost is the highest-valued alternative that must be given up to engage in an activity. An explicit cost is a cost that involves spending money. An implicit cost is a nonmonetary opportunity cost. The relationship between the inputs employed by a firm and the maximum output it can produce with those inputs is called the firm's **production function**.

Review Questions

2.1 What is the difference between the short run and the long run? Is the amount of time that separates the short run from the long run the same for every firm?

2.2 What are implicit costs? How are they different from explicit costs?

Problems and Applications

2.3 (Related to the *Making the Connection* on page 336) Many firms consider their wage costs to be variable costs. Why do publishers usually consider their wage and salary costs to be fixed costs? Are the costs of utilities always fixed, always variable, or can they be both? Briefly explain?

2.4 (Related to the *Making the Connection* on page 336) For Jill Johnson's pizza restaurant, explain whether each of the following is a fixed cost or a variable cost.
 a. The payment she makes on her fire insurance policy
 b. The payment she makes to buy pizza dough
 c. The wages she pays her workers
 d. The lease payment she makes to her landlord who owns the building where her store is located
 e. The $300-per-month payment she makes to her local newspaper for running her weekly advertisements

2.5 (Related to the *Making the Connection* on page 336) The *Statistical Abstract of the United States* is published each year by the U.S. Census Bureau. It provides a summary of business, economic, social, and political statistics. It is available for free online and a printed copy can also be purchased from the U.S. Government Printing Office for $35.00. Because government documents are not copyrighted anyone can print copies of the *Statistical Abstract* and

sell them. Each year, one or two companies typically will print and sell copies for a significantly lower price than the Government Printing Office does. The copies of the *Statistical Abstract* that these companies sell are usually identical to those sold by the government, except for having different covers. How can these companies sell the same book for a lower price than the government and still cover their costs?

2.6 Suppose Jill Johnson operates her pizza restaurant in a building she owns in the center of the city. Similar buildings in the neighborhood rent for $4,000 per month. Jill is considering selling her building and renting space in the suburbs for $3,000 per month. Jill decides not to make the move. She reasons, "I would like to have a restaurant in the suburbs, but I pay no rent for my restaurant now, and I don't want to see my costs rise by $3,000 per month." What do you think of Jill's reasoning?

2.7 When the DuPont chemical company first attempted to enter the paint business, it was not successful. According to a company report, in one year it "lost nearly $500,000 in actual cash in addition to an expected return on investment of nearly $500,000, which made a total loss of income to the company of nearly a million." Why did this report include as part of the company's loss the amount it had expected to earn—but didn't—on its investment in manufacturing paint?

Source: Alfred D. Chandler, Jr., Thomas K. McCraw, and Richard Tedlow, *Management Past and Present*, Cincinnati: South-Western, 2000, pp. 3–92.

2.8 An account of Benjamin Franklin's life notes that he started his career as a printer and publisher of the newspaper the *Pennsylvania Gazette*. He also opened a store where he sold stationery, books, and food. According to this account, "He could without expense apprise the public of items on hand by advertisements in his *Gazette*." Is the author correct that Franklin did not incur a cost when he used space in his newspaper to run advertisements for his store? Briefly explain.

Source: Richard Tedlow, "Benjamin Franklin and the Definition of American Values," in Alfred D. Chandler, Jr., Thomas K. McCaw, and Richard S. Tedlow, *Management Past and Present: A Casebook on the History of American Business*, Cincinnati: South-Western College Publishing, 2000.

>> **End Learning Objective 10.2**

10.3 LEARNING OBJECTIVE   10.3 | Understand the relationship between the marginal product of labor and the average product of labor, **pages 339–342.**

The Marginal Product of Labor and the Average Product of Labor

Summary

The **marginal product of labor** is the additional output produced by a firm as a result of hiring one more worker. Specialization and division of labor cause the marginal

product of labor to rise for the first few workers hired. Eventually, the **law of diminishing returns** causes the marginal product of labor to decline. The **average product of labor** is the total amount of output produced by a firm divided by the quantity of workers hired. When the marginal product of labor is greater than the average product of labor, the average product of labor increases. When the marginal product of labor is less than the average product of labor, the average product of labor decreases.

 Visit www.myeconlab.com to complete these exercises
Get Ahead of the Curve online and get instant feedback.

Review Questions

3.1 Draw a graph showing the usual relationship between the marginal product of labor and the average product of labor. Why do the marginal product of labor and the average product of labor have the shapes you drew?

3.2 What is the law of diminishing returns? Does it apply in the long run?

Problems and Applications

3.3 Fill in the missing values in the following table.

QUANTITY OF WORKERS	TOTAL OUTPUT	MARGINAL PRODUCT OF LABOR	AVERAGE PRODUCT OF LABOR
0	0		
1	400		
2	900		
3	1,500		
4	1,900		
5	2,200		
6	2,400		
7	2,300		

3.4 Use the numbers from problem 3.3 to draw one graph showing how total output increases with the quantity of workers hired and a second graph showing the marginal product of labor and the average product of labor.

3.5 A student looks at the data in Table 10-3 on page 339 and draws this conclusion: "The marginal product of labor is increasing for the first two workers hired, and then it declines for the next four workers. I guess each of the first two workers must have been hard workers. Then Jill must have had to settle for increasingly poor workers." Do you agree with the student's analysis? Briefly explain.

3.6 (Related to the *Making the Connection* on page 340) Briefly explain whether you agree or disagree with the following argument: Adam Smith's idea of the gains to firms from the division of labor makes a lot of sense when the good being manufactured is something complex like automobiles or computers, but it doesn't apply in the manufacturing of less complex goods or in other sectors of the economy, such as retail sales.

3.7 Sally looks at her college transcript and says to Sam, "How is this possible? My grade point average for this semester's courses is higher than my grade point average for last semester's courses, but my cumulative grade point average still went down from last semester to this semester." Explain to Sally how this is possible.

3.8 Is it possible for a firm to experience a technological change that would increase the marginal product of labor while leaving the average product of labor unchanged? Explain.

>> **End Learning Objective 10.3**

10.4 LEARNING OBJECTIVE   10.4 | Explain and illustrate the relationship between marginal cost and average total cost, **pages 342–345.**

The Relationship between Short-Run Production and Short-Run Cost

Summary

The **marginal cost** of production is the increase in total cost resulting from producing another unit of output. The marginal cost curve has a U shape because when the marginal product of labor is rising, the marginal cost of output is falling. When the marginal product of labor is falling, the marginal cost of output is rising. When marginal cost is less than average total cost, average total cost falls. When marginal cost is greater than average total cost, average total cost rises.

 Visit www.myeconlab.com to complete these exercises
Get Ahead of the Curve online and get instant feedback.

Review Questions

4.1 If the marginal product of labor is rising, is the marginal cost of production rising or falling? Briefly explain.

4.2 Explain why the marginal cost curve intersects the average total cost curve at the level of output where average total cost is at a minimum.

Problems and Applications

4.3 Is it possible for average total cost to be decreasing over a range of output where marginal cost is increasing? Briefly explain.

4.4 Suppose a firm has no fixed costs, so all of its costs are variable, even in the short run.

   a. If the firm's marginal costs are continually increasing (that is, marginal cost is increasing from the first unit of output produced) will the firm's average total cost curve have a U shape?

   b. If the firm's marginal costs are $5 at every level of output, what shape will the firm's average total cost have?

4.5 (Related to *Solved Problem 10-4* on page 345) Is Jill Johnson right or wrong when she says the following: "Currently, I am producing 20,000 pizzas per month at a total cost of $750.00. If I produce 20,001 pizzas, my total cost will rise to $750.02. Therefore, my marginal cost of producing pizzas must be increasing." Illustrate your answer with a graph.

4.6 (Related to *Solved Problem 10-4* on page 345) The following problem is somewhat advanced. Using symbols, we can write that the marginal product of labor is equal to $\Delta Q/\Delta L$. Marginal cost is equal to $\Delta TC/\Delta Q$. Because fixed costs by definition don't change, marginal cost is also equal to $\Delta VC/\Delta Q$. If Jill Johnson's only variable cost is labor cost, then her variable cost is just the wage multiplied by the quantity of workers hired, or wL.

   a. If the wage Jill pays is constant, then what is ΔVC in terms of w and L?

   b. Use your answer to question (a) and the expressions given above for the marginal product of labor and the marginal cost of output to find an expression for marginal cost, $\Delta TC/\Delta Q$, in terms of the wage, w, and the marginal product of labor, $\Delta Q/\Delta L$.

   c. Use your answer to question (b) to determine Jill's marginal cost of producing pizzas if the wage is $750 per week and the marginal product of labor is 150. If the wage falls to $600 per week and the marginal product of labor is unchanged, what happens to Jill's marginal cost? If the wage is unchanged at $750 per week and the marginal product rises to 250, what happens to Jill's marginal cost?

>> **End Learning Objective 10.4**

10.5 LEARNING OBJECTIVE | 10.5 | Graph average total cost, average variable cost, average fixed cost, and marginal cost, **page 346.**

Graphing Cost Curves

Summary

Average fixed cost is equal to fixed cost divided by the level of output. **Average variable cost** is equal to variable cost divided by the level of output. Figure 10-5 on page 347 shows the relationship among marginal cost, average total cost, average variable cost, and average fixed cost. It is one of the most important graphs in microeconomics.

myeconlab Visit www.myeconlab.com to complete these exercises online and get instant feedback.

Review Questions

5.1 As the level of output increases, what happens to the value of average fixed cost?

5.2 As the level of output increases, what happens to the difference between the value of average total cost and average variable cost?

Problems and Applications

5.3 Suppose the total cost of producing 10,000 tennis balls is $30,000, and the fixed cost is $10,000.

   a. What is the variable cost?

   b. When output is 10,000, what are the average variable cost and the average fixed cost?

   c. Assuming that the cost curves have the usual shape, is the dollar difference between the average total cost and the average variable cost greater when the output is 10,000 tennis balls or when the output is 30,000 tennis balls? Explain.

5.4 One description of the costs of operating a railroad makes the following observation: "The fixed . . . expenses which attach to the operation of railroads . . . are in the nature of a tax upon the business of the road; the smaller the [amount of] business, the larger the tax." Briefly explain why fixed costs are like a tax. In what sense is this tax smaller when the amount of business is larger?

Source for quote: Alfred D. Chandler, Jr., Thomas K. McCraw, and Richard Tedlow, *Management Past and Present*, Cincinnati: South-Western, 2000, pp. 2–27.

5.5 In the ancient world, a book could be produced either on a scroll or as a codex, which was made of folded sheets glued together, something like a modern book. One scholar has estimated the following variable costs (in Greek drachmas) of the two methods:

	SCROLL	CODEX
Cost of writing (wage of a scribe)	11.33 drachmas	11.33 drachmas
Cost of paper	16.50 drachmas	9.25 drachmas

Another scholar points out that a significant fixed cost was involved in producing a codex:

> In order to copy a codex . . . the amount of text and the layout of each page had to be carefully calculated in advance to determine the exact number of sheets . . . needed. No doubt, this is more time-consuming and calls for more experimentation than the production of a scroll would. But for the next copy, these calculations would be used again.

a. Suppose that the fixed cost of preparing a codex was 58 drachmas and that there was no similar fixed cost for a scroll. Would an ancient book publisher who intended to sell 5 copies of a book be likely to publish it as a scroll or as a codex? What if he intended to sell 10 copies? Briefly explain.

b. Although most books were published as scrolls in the first century A.D., by the third century, most were published as codices. Considering only the factors mentioned in this problem, explain why this change may have taken place.

Sources: T. C. Skeat, "The Length of the Standard Papyrus Roll and the Cost-Advantage of the Codex," *Zeitschrift fur Papyrologie and Epigraphik*, 1982, p. 175; and David Trobisch, *The First Edition of the New Testament*, New York: Oxford University Press, 2000, p. 73.

5.6 Use the information in the following graph to find the values for the following at an output level of 1,000.
a. Marginal cost
b. Total cost
c. Variable cost
d. Fixed cost

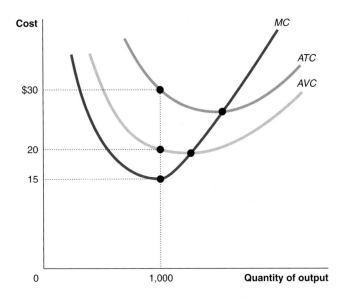

5.7 List the errors in the following graph. Carefully explain why the curves drawn this way are wrong. In other words, why can't these curves be as they are shown in the graph?

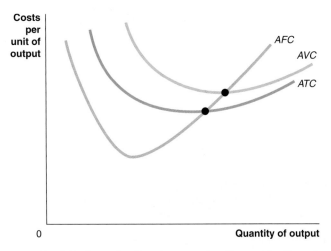

5.8 Explain how the listed events (a–d) would affect the following at Ford Motor Company:
  i. Marginal cost
  ii. Average variable cost
  iii. Average fixed cost
  iv. Average total cost

a. Ford signs a new contract with the United Automobile Workers union that requires the company to pay higher wages.

b. The federal government starts to levy a $1,500-per-vehicle tax on sport-utility vehicles.

c. Ford decides to give its senior executives a one-time $100,000 bonus.

d. Ford decides to increase the amount it spends on designing new car models.

>> End Learning Objective 10.5

10.6 | Understand how firms use the long-run average cost curve in their planning,
pages 346–353.

Costs in the Long Run

Summary

The **long-run average cost curve** shows the lowest cost at which a firm is able to produce a given level of output in the long run. For many firms, the long-run average cost curve falls as output expands because of **economies of scale**. **Minimum efficient scale** is the level of output at which all economies of scale have been exhausted. After economies of scale have been exhausted, firms experience **constant returns to scale**, where their long-run average cost curve is flat. At high levels of output, the long-run average cost curve turns up as the firm experiences **diseconomies of scale**.

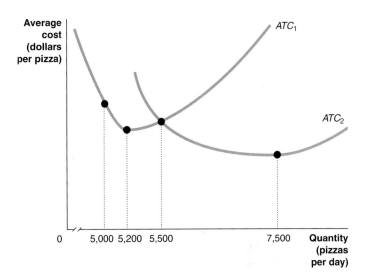

> Visit www.myeconlab.com to complete these exercises
> online and get instant feedback.

Review Questions

6.1 What is the difference between total cost and variable cost in the long run?

6.2 What is minimum efficient scale? What is likely to happen in the long run to firms that do not reach minimum efficient scale?

6.3 What are economies of scale? What are diseconomies of scale? What is the main reason that firms eventually encounter diseconomies of scale as they keep increasing the size of their store or factory?

Problems and Applications

6.4 (Related to *Solved Problem 10-6* on page 349) Suppose that Jill Johnson has to choose between building a smaller restaurant and a larger restaurant. In the following graph, the relationship between costs and output for the smaller restaurant is represented by the curve ATC_1, and the relationship between costs and output for the larger restaurant is represented by the curve ATC_2.
  a. If Jill expects to produce 5,100 pizzas per week, should she build a smaller restaurant or a larger restaurant? Briefly explain.
  b. If Jill expects to produce 6,000 pizzas per week, should she build a smaller restaurant or a larger restaurant? Briefly explain.
  c. A student asks, "If the average cost of producing pizzas is lower in the larger restaurant when Jill produces 7,500 pizzas per week, why isn't it also lower when Jill produces 5,200 pizzas per week?" Give a brief answer to the student's question.

6.5 (Related to *Solved Problem 10-6* on page 349) Consider the following description of U.S. manufacturing in the late nineteenth century:

> When . . . Standard Oil . . . reorganized its refinery capacity in 1883 and concentrated almost two-fifths of the nation's refinery production in three huge refineries, the unit cost dropped from 1.5 cents a gallon to 0.5 cents. A comparable concentration of two-fifths of the nation's output of textiles or shoes in three plants would have been impossible, and in any case would have brought huge diseconomies of scale and consequently higher prices.

  a. Use this information to draw a long-run average cost curve for an oil-refining firm and a long-run average cost curve for a firm manufacturing shoes.
  b. Is it likely that there were more oil refineries or more shoe factories in the United States in the late nineteenth century? Briefly explain.
  c. Why would concentrating two-fifths of total shoe output in three factories have led to higher shoe prices?

Source: Alfred D. Chandler, Jr., Thomas K. McCraw, and Richard Tedlow, *Management Past and Present*, Cincinnati: South-Western, 2000, pp. 4–53.

6.6 (Related to *Solved Problem 10-6* on page 349) The company eToys sold toys on the Internet. In 1999, the total value of the company was about $7.7 billion, but by early 2001, the company was in deep financial trouble, and it eventually closed. One of the company's key mistakes was the decision in

2000 to build a large distribution center from which it would ship toys throughout the United States. The following description of this decision appeared in an article in the *Wall Street Journal*:

> [eToys built] a giant automated distribution center in Virginia. . . . Although many analysts agreed that the costly move was a sound decision for the long run . . . [the] decision meant eToys needed to generate much higher sales to justify its costs. . . . Despite a spiffy TV ad campaign and an expanded line of goods, there weren't enough customers.

What does the author mean when she says that eToys "needed to generate much higher sales to justify its costs"? Use a graph like Figure 10-6 to illustrate your answer.

Source: Lisa Bannon, "The eToys Saga: Costs Kept Rising but Sales Slowed," *Wall Street Journal*, January 22, 2001.

6.7 (Related to *Solved Problem 10-6* on page 349) In 2003, Time Warner and the Walt Disney Company discussed merging their news operations. Time Warner owns the Cable News Network (CNN), and Disney owns ABC News. After analyzing the situation, the companies decided that a combined news operation would have higher average costs than either CNN or ABC News had separately. Use a long-run average cost curve graph to illustrate why the companies did not merge their news operations.

Source: Martin Peers and Joe Flint, "AOL Calls Off CNN–ABC Deal, Seeing Operating Difficulties," *Wall Street Journal*, February 14, 2003.

6.8 (Related to the *Making the Connection* on page 350) Suppose that Henry Ford had continued to experience increasing returns to scale, no matter how large an automobile factory he built. Discuss what the implications of this would have been for the automobile industry.

6.9 One scholar has made the following comment on the publishing industry: "If publishers were able to determine exactly what sells a book, they all would feature fewer titles and produce them in larger numbers." What must be true about the costs of publishing books for this statement to be correct? Briefly explain.

Source: David Trobisch, *The First Edition of the New Testament*, New York: Oxford University Press, 2000, p. 75.

6.10 (Related to the *Don't Let This Happen to You!* on page 351) Explain whether you agree or disagree with the following statement: "Henry Ford expected to be able to produce cars at a lower average cost at his River Rouge plant. Unfortunately, because of diminishing returns, his costs were actually higher."

6.11 (Related to the *Chapter Opener* on page 332) Review the discussion at the beginning of the chapter of Akio Morita selling transistor radios in the United States. Suppose that Morita became convinced that Sony would be able to sell more than 75,000 transistor radios each year in the United States. What steps would he have taken?

6.12 TIAA-CREF is a retirement system for people who work at colleges and universities. For some years, TIAA-CREF also sold long-term care insurance before deciding to sell that business to MetLife, a large insurance company. TIAA-CREF's chairman and chief executive officer explained the decision this way:

> In recent years, the long-term care insurance market has experienced significant consolidation. A few large insurance companies now own most of the business. MetLife has 428,000 policies, for example—nearly 10 times the number we have—and can achieve economies of scale that we can't. Over time, we would have had difficulty holding down premium rates.

Briefly explain what economies of scale have to do with the premiums (that is, the prices buyers have to pay for insurance policies) that insurance companies can charge for their policies.

Source: "Long-Term Care Sale in Best Interest of Policyholders," *Advance*, Spring 2004, p. 6.

6.13 According to one account of the problems DuPont had in entering the paint business, "the du Ponts had assumed that large volume would bring profits through lowering unit costs." In fact, according to one company report, "The more paint and varnish we sold, the more money we lost." Draw an average cost curve graph showing the relationship between paint output and average cost as DuPont expected it to be. Draw another graph that explains the result that the more paint the company sold, the more money it lost.

Source: Alfred D. Chandler, Jr., Thomas K. McCraw, and Richard Tedlow, *Management Past and Present*, Cincinnati: South-Western, 2000, pp. 3–88.

6.14 According to a study of chicken processing plants by the U.S. Department of Agriculture, the largest plants have average costs that are 20 percent lower than the smallest plants. The report concludes, "These cost differentials are consistent with the near-disappearance of small plants." Briefly explain the reasoning behind this conclusion.

Source: Michael Ollinger, James MacDonald, and Milton Madison, *Structural Change in U.S. Chicken and Turkey Slaughter*, Agricultural Economic Report No. 787, Economic Research Service, U.S. Department of Agriculture.

6.15 Michael Korda was for many years editor-in-chief at the Simon & Schuster book publishing company. He has described how during the 1980s many publishing companies merged together to form larger firms. He claims that publishers hoped to take advantage of economies of scale. But, he concludes, "sheer size did not make publishing necessarily more profitable, and most of these big publishing monoliths would continue to disappoint their corporate owners in terms of earnings." On the basis of this information, draw a long-run average cost curve for a publishing firm that reflects the economies of scale expected to result from the mergers. Draw another long-run average cost curve that reflects the actual results experienced by the new larger publishing firms.

Source: Michael Korda, *Making the List: A Cultural History of the American Bestseller, 1900–1999*, New York: Barnes & Noble Books, 2001, p. 166.

>> End Learning Objective 10.6

Appendix

Using Isoquants and Isocosts to Understand Production and Cost

Use isoquants and isocost lines to understand production and cost.

Isoquants

In this chapter, we studied the important relationship between a firm's level of production and its costs. In this appendix, we will look more closely at how firms choose the combination of inputs to produce a given level of output. Firms usually have a choice of how they will produce their output. For example, Jill Johnson is able to produce 5,000 pizzas per week using 10 workers and 2 ovens or using 6 workers and 3 ovens. We will see that firms search for the *cost-minimizing* combination of inputs that will allow them to produce a given level of output. The cost-minimizing combination of inputs depends on two factors: technology—which determines how much output a firm receives from employing a given quantity of inputs—and input prices—which determine the total cost of each combination of inputs.

An Isoquant Graph

We begin by graphing the levels of output that Jill can produce using different combinations of two inputs: labor—the quantity of workers she hires per week—and capital—the quantity of ovens she uses per week. In reality, of course, Jill uses more than just these two inputs to produce pizzas, but nothing important would change if we expanded the discussion to include many inputs instead of just two. Figure 10A-1 measures capital along the vertical axis and labor along the horizontal axis. The curves in the graph are **isoquants**, which show all the combinations of two inputs, in this case capital and labor, that will produce the same level of output.

> **Isoquant** A curve that shows all the combinations of two inputs, such as capital and labor, that will produce the same level of output.

The isoquant labeled $Q = 5,000$ shows all the combinations of workers and ovens that enable Jill to produce that quantity of pizzas per week. For example, at point *A*, she produces 5,000 pizzas using 6 workers and 3 ovens, and at point *B*, she produces the same output using 10 workers and 2 ovens. With more workers and ovens, she can move to a higher isoquant. For example, with 12 workers and 4 ovens, she can produce at point *C* on the isoquant $Q = 10,000$. With even more workers and ovens, she could move to the isoquant $Q = 13,000$. The higher the isoquant—that is, the further to the upper right on the graph—the more output the firm produces. Although we have shown only three isoquants in this graph, there are, in fact, an infinite number of isoquants—one for every level of output.

The Slope of an Isoquant

Remember that the slope of a curve is the ratio of the change in the variable on the vertical axis to the change in the variable on the horizontal axis. Along an isoquant, the slope tells us the rate at which a firm is able to substitute one input for another while

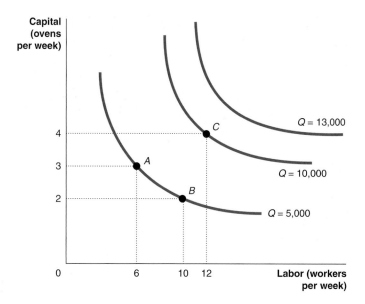

Figure 10A-1

Isoquants

Isoquants show all the combinations of two inputs, in this case capital and labor, that will produce the same level of output. For example, the isoquant labeled $Q = 5,000$ shows all the combinations of ovens and workers that enable Jill to produce that quantity of pizzas per week. At point A, she produces 5,000 pizzas using 3 ovens and 6 workers, and at point B, she produces the same output using 2 ovens and 10 workers. With more ovens and workers, she can move to a higher isoquant. For example, with 4 ovens and 12 workers, she can produce at point C on the isoquant $Q = 10,000$. With even more ovens and workers, she could move to the isoquant $Q = 13,000$.

keeping the level of output constant. The slope of an isoquant is called the **marginal rate of technical substitution** (*MRTS*).

We expect that the *MRTS* will change as we move down an isoquant. In Figure 10A-1, at a point like A on isoquant $Q = 5,000$, the isoquant is relatively steep. As we move down the curve, it becomes less steep at a point like B. This shape is the usual one for isoquants: They are bowed in, or convex. The reason isoquants have this shape is that as we move down the curve, we continue to substitute labor for capital. As the firm produces the same quantity of output using less capital, the additional labor it needs increases because of diminishing returns. Remember from the chapter that, as a consequence of diminishing returns, for a given decline in capital, increasing amounts of labor are necessary to produce the same level of output. Because the *MRTS* is equal to the change in capital divided by the change in labor, it will become smaller (in absolute value) as we move down an isoquant.

Marginal rate of technical substitution (*MRTS*) The slope of an isoquant, or the rate at which a firm is able to substitute one input for another while keeping the level of output constant.

Isocost Lines

Any firm wants to produce a given quantity of output at the lowest possible cost. We can show the relationship between the quantity of inputs used and the firm's total cost by using an *isocost* line. An **isocost line** shows all the combinations of two inputs, such as capital and labor, that have the same total cost.

Isocost line All the combinations of two inputs, such as capital and labor, that have the same total cost.

Graphing the Isocost Line

Suppose Jill has $6,000 per week to spend on capital and labor. Suppose, to simplify the analysis, that Jill can rent pizza ovens by the week. The table in Figure 10A-2 shows the combinations of capital and labor available to her if the rental price of ovens is $1,000 per week and the wage rate is $500 per week. The graph uses the data in the table to construct an isocost line. The isocost line intersects the vertical axis at the maximum number of ovens Jill can rent per week, which is shown by point A. The line intersects the horizontal axis at the maximum number of workers Jill can hire per week, which is point G. As Jill moves down the isocost line from point A, she gives up renting 1 oven for every 2 workers she hires. Any combination of inputs along the line or inside the line can be purchased with $6,000. Any combination that lies outside the line cannot be purchased because it would have a total cost to Jill of more than $6,000.

The Slope and Position of the Isocost Line

The slope of the isocost line is constant and equals the change in the quantity of ovens divided by the change in the quantity of workers. In this case, in moving from any point on the isocost line to any other point, the change in the quantity of ovens equals −1, and

Figure 10A-2

An Isocost Line

The isocost line shows the combinations of inputs with a total cost of $6,000. The rental price of ovens is $1,000 per week, so if Jill spends the whole $6,000 on ovens, she can rent 6 ovens (point *A*). The wage rate is $500 per week, so if Jill spends the whole $6,000 on workers, she can hire 12 workers. As she moves down the isocost line, she gives up renting 1 oven for every 2 workers she hires. Any combinations of inputs along the line or inside the line can be purchased with $6,000. Any combinations that lie outside the line cannot be purchased with $6,000.

Combinations of Workers and Ovens with a Total Cost of $6,000			
Point	Ovens	Workers	Total Cost
A	6	0	(6 x $1,000) + (0 x $500) = $6,000
B	5	2	(5 x $1,000) + (2 x $500) = 6,000
C	4	4	(4 x $1,000) + (4 x $500) = 6,000
D	3	6	(3 x $1,000) + (6 x $500) = 6,000
E	2	8	(2 x $1,000) + (8 x $500) = 6,000
F	1	10	(1 x $1,000) + (10 x $500) = 6,000
G	0	12	(0 x $1,000) + (12 x $500) = 6,000

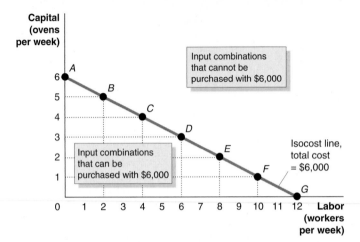

the change in the quantity of workers equals 2, so the slope equals $-1/2$. Notice that with a rental price of ovens of $1,000 per week and a wage rate for labor of $500 per week, the slope of the isocost line is equal to the ratio of the wage rate divided by the rental price of capital, multiplied by -1: $-\$500/\$1,000 = -1/2$. In fact, this result will always hold, whatever inputs are involved and whatever their prices may be: *The slope of the isocost line is equal to the ratio of the price of the input on the horizontal axis divided by the price of the input on the vertical axis, multiplied by -1.*

The position of the isocost line depends on the level of total cost. Higher levels of total cost shift the isocost line outward, and lower levels of total cost shift the isocost line inward. This can be seen in Figure 10A-3, which shows isocost lines for total

Figure 10A-3

The Position of the Isocost Line

The position of the isocost line depends on the level of total cost. As total cost increases from $3,000 to $6,000 to $9,000 per week, the isocost line shifts outward. For each isocost line shown, the rental price of ovens is $1,000 per week, and the wage rate is $500 per week.

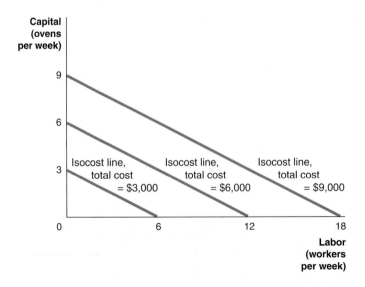

costs of $3,000, $6,000, and $9,000. We have shown only three isocost lines in the graph, but there are, in fact, an infinite number of isocost lines—one for every level of total cost.

Choosing the Cost-Minimizing Combination of Capital and Labor

Suppose Jill wants to produce 5,000 pizzas per week. Figure 10A-1 shows that there are many combinations of ovens and workers that will allow Jill to produce this level of output. There is only one combination of ovens and workers, however, that will allow her to produce 5,000 pizzas *at the lowest total cost.* Figure 10A-4 shows the isoquant Q = 5,000 along with three isocost lines. Point B is the lowest-cost combination of inputs shown in the graph, but this combination of 1 oven and 4 workers will produce fewer than the 5,000 pizzas needed. Points C and D are combinations of ovens and workers that will produce 5,000 pizzas, but their total cost is $9,000. The combination of 3 ovens and 6 workers at point A produces 5,000 pizzas at the lowest total cost of $6,000.

The graph shows that moving to an isocost line with a total cost of less than $6,000 would mean producing fewer than 5,000 pizzas. Being at any point along the isoquant Q = 5,000 other than point A would increase total cost above $6,000. In fact, the combination of inputs at point A is the only one on isoquant Q = 5,000 that has a total cost of $6,000. All other input combinations on this isoquant have higher total costs. Notice also that at point A, the isoquant and the isocost lines are tangent, so the slope of the isoquant is equal to the slope of the isocost line at that point.

Different Input Price Ratios Lead to Different Input Choices

Jill's cost-minimizing choice of 3 ovens and 6 workers is determined jointly by the technology available to her—as represented by her firm's isoquants—and by input prices—as represented by her firm's isocost lines. If the technology of making pizzas changes, perhaps because new ovens are developed, her isoquants will be affected, and her choice of inputs may change. If her isoquants remain unchanged but input

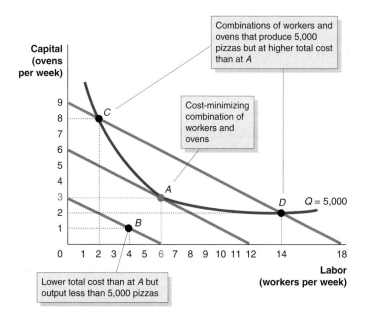

Figure 10A-4

Choosing Capital and Labor to Minimize Total Cost

Jill wants to produce 5,000 pizzas per week at the lowest total cost. Point B is the lowest-cost combination of inputs shown in the graph, but this combination of 1 oven and 4 workers will produce fewer than the 5,000 pizzas needed. Points C and D are combinations of ovens and workers that will produce 5,000 pizzas, but their total cost is $9,000. The combination of 3 ovens and 6 workers at point A produces 5,000 pizzas at the lowest total cost of $6,000.

Figure 10A-5

Changing Input Prices Affects the Cost-Minimizing Input Choice

As the graph shows, the input combination at point *A*, which was optimal for Jill, is not optimal for a businessperson in China. Using the input combination at point *A* would cost businesspeople in China more than $6,000. Instead, the Chinese isocost line is tangent to the isoquant at point *B*, where the input combination is 2 ovens and 10 workers. Because ovens cost more in China but workers cost less, a Chinese firm will use fewer ovens and more workers than a U.S. firm, even if it has the same technology as the U.S. firm.

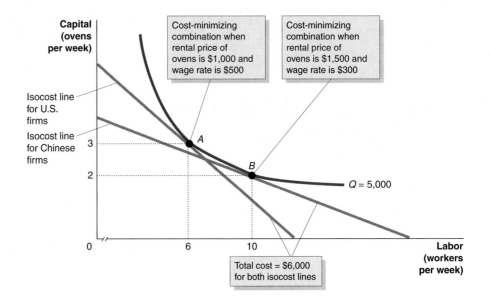

prices change, then her choice of inputs may also change. This fact can explain why firms in different countries that face different input prices may produce the same good using different combinations of capital and labor, even though they have the same technology available.

For example, suppose that in China, pizza ovens are higher priced and labor is lower priced than in the United States. In our example, Jill Johnson pays $1,000 per week to rent pizza ovens and $500 per week to hire workers. Suppose a businessperson in China must pay a price of $1,500 per week to rent the identical pizza ovens but can hire Chinese workers who are as productive as U.S. workers at a wage of $300 per week. Figure 10A-5 shows how the cost-minimizing input combination for the businessperson in China differs from Jill's.

Remember that the slope of the isocost line equals the wage rate divided by the rental price of capital, multiplied by −1. The slope of the isocost line that Jill and other U.S. firms face is −$500/$1,000, or −1/2. Firms in China, however, face an isocost line with a slope of −$300/$1,500, or −1/5. As the graph shows, the input combination at point *A*, which was optimal for Jill, is not optimal for a firm in China. Using the input combination at point *A* would cost a firm in China more than $6,000. Instead, the Chinese isocost line is tangent to the isoquant at point *B*, where the input combination is 2 ovens and 10 workers. This result makes sense: Because ovens cost more in China, but workers cost less, a Chinese firm will use fewer ovens and more workers than a U.S. firm, even if it has the same technology as the U.S. firm.

Making the **Connection** | **The Changing Input Mix in Walt Disney Film Animation**

The inputs used to make feature-length animated films have changed dramatically in the past 15 years. Prior to the early 1990s, the Walt Disney Company dominated the market for animated films. Disney's films were produced using hundreds of animators drawing most of the film by hand. Each film would contain as many as 170,000 individual drawings. Then, two developments dramatically affected how animated films are produced. First, in 1994, Disney had a huge hit with *The Lion King*, which cost only $50 million but earned the company more than $1 billion in profit. As a result of this success, Disney and other film studios began to produce more animated films, increasing the demand for animators and more than doubling their salaries. The second development came in 1995, when Pixar Animation Studios released the film *Toy Story*. This was the first successful feature-length film produced using computers, with no hand-drawn animation. In the following years, technological advance continued to reduce the cost of the computers and software necessary to produce an animated film.

As a result of these two developments, the price of capital—computers and software—fell relative to the price of labor—animators. As the figure shows, the change in the price of computers relative to animators changed the slope of the isocost line and resulted in film studios now producing animated films using many more computers and many fewer animators than in the early 1990s.

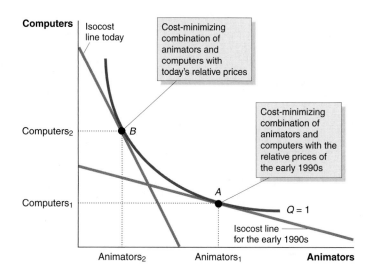

Source: Bruce Orwall, "Disney Delivers 'Lilo and Stitch' on Competition-Driven Budget," *Wall Street Journal*, June 18, 2002, p. A1.

YOUR TURN: Test your understanding by doing related problem 10A.8 on page 374 at the end of this chapter.

Another Look at Cost Minimization

In Chapter 9, we saw that consumers maximize utility when they consume each good up to the point where the marginal utility per dollar spent is the same for every good. We can derive a very similar cost-minimization rule for firms. Remember that at the point of cost minimization, the isoquant and the isocost line are tangent, so they have the same slope. Therefore, *at the point of cost minimization, the marginal rate of technical substitution (MRTS) is equal to the wage rate divided by the rental price of capital*.

The slope of the isoquant tells us the rate at which a firm is able to substitute labor for capital, *given existing technology*. The slope of the isocost line tells us the rate at which a firm is able to substitute labor for capital, *given current input prices*. Only at the point of cost minimization are these two rates the same.

When we move from one point on an isoquant to another, we end up using more of one input and less of the other input, but the level of output remains the same. For example, as Jill moves down an isoquant, she uses fewer ovens and more workers but produces the same quantity of pizzas. In this chapter, we defined the *marginal product of labor* (MP_L) as the additional output produced by a firm as a result of hiring one more worker. Similarly, we can define the *marginal product of capital* (MP_K) as the additional output produced by a firm as a result of using one more machine. So, when Jill uses fewer ovens by moving down an isoquant, she loses output equal to:

$$-\text{Change in the quantity of ovens} \times MP_K.$$

But she uses more workers, so she gains output equal to:

$$\text{Change in the quantity of workers} \times MP_L.$$

We know that the gain in output from the additional workers is equal to the loss from the smaller quantity of ovens because total output remains the same along an isoquant. Therefore, we can write:

$$-\text{Change in the quantity of ovens} \times MP_K = \text{Change in the quantity of workers} \times MP_L.$$

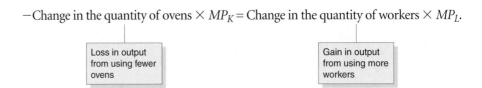

Loss in output from using fewer ovens

Gain in output from using more workers

If we rearrange terms, we have the following:

$$\frac{-\text{Change in the quantity of ovens}}{\text{Change in the quantity of workers}} = \frac{MP_L}{MP_K}.$$

Because the

$$\frac{-\text{Change in the quantity of ovens}}{\text{Change in the quantity of workers}}$$

is the slope of the isoquant, or the marginal rate of technical substitution (*MRTS*), we can write:

$$\frac{-\text{Change in the quantity of ovens}}{\text{Change in the quantity of workers}} = MRTS = \frac{MP_L}{MP_K}.$$

The slope of the isocost line equals the wage rate (*w*) divided by the rental price of capital (*r*). At the point of cost minimization, the slope of the isoquant is equal to the slope of the isocost line. Therefore:

$$\frac{MP_L}{MP_K} = \frac{w}{r}.$$

We can rewrite this to show that at the point of cost minimization:

$$\frac{MP_L}{w} = \frac{MP_K}{r}.$$

This last expression tells us that to minimize cost, a firm should hire inputs up to the point where the last dollar spent on each input results in the same increase in output. If this equality did not hold, a firm could lower its costs by using more of one input and less of the other. For example, if the left-hand side of the equation were greater than the right-hand side, a firm could rent fewer ovens, hire more workers, and produce the same output at lower cost.

Solved Problem | 10A-1

Determining the Optimal Combination of Inputs

Consider the information in the following table for Jill Johnson's restaurant:

Marginal product of capital	3,000 pizzas
Marginal product of labor	1,200 pizzas
Wage rate	$300 per week
Rental price of ovens	$600 per week

Briefly explain whether Jill is minimizing costs. If she is not minimizing costs, explain whether she should rent more ovens and hire fewer workers or rent fewer ovens and hire more workers.

SOLVING THE PROBLEM:

Step 1: **Review the chapter material.** This problem is about determining the optimal choice of inputs by comparing the ratios of the marginal products of inputs to their prices, so you may want to review the section "Another Look at Cost Minimization," which begins on page 369.

Step 2: **Compute the ratios of marginal product to input price to determine whether Jill is minimizing costs.** If Jill is minimizing costs, the following relationship should hold:

$$\frac{MP_L}{w} = \frac{MP_K}{r}.$$

In this case, we have:

$$MP_L = 1,200$$
$$MP_K = 3,000$$
$$w = \$300$$
$$r = \$600.$$

So:

$$\frac{MP_L}{w} = \frac{1,200}{\$300} = 4 \text{ pizzas per dollar, and } \frac{MP_K}{r} = \frac{3,000}{\$600} = 5 \text{ pizzas per dollar.}$$

Because the two ratios are not equal, Jill is not minimizing cost.

Step 3: **Determine how Jill should change the mix of inputs she uses.** Jill produces more pizzas per dollar from the last oven than from the last worker. This indicates that she has too many workers and too few ovens. Therefore, to minimize cost, Jill should use more ovens and hire fewer workers.

YOUR TURN: For more practice, do related problems 10A.6 and 10A.7 on page 374 at the end of this appendix.

>> **End Solved Problem 10A-1**

Making
the
Connection

Do National Football League Teams Behave Efficiently?

In the National Football League (NFL), the "salary cap" is the maximum amount each team can spend each year on salaries for football players. Each year's salary cap results from negotiations between the league and the union representing the players. To achieve efficiency, an NFL team should distribute salaries among players so as to maximize the level of output—in this case, winning football games—given the constant level of cost represented by the salary cap. (Notice that maximizing the level of output for a given level of cost is equivalent to minimizing cost for a given level of output. To see why, think about the situation where an isocost line is tangent to an isoquant. At the point of tangency, the firm has simultaneously minimized the cost of producing the level of output represented by the isoquant and maximized the output produced at the level of cost represented by the isocost line.) In distributing salaries, teams should equalize the marginal productivity of players as represented by their contribution to winning games to the salaries paid. Just as a firm may not use a machine that has a very high marginal product if its rental price is very high, a football team may not want to hire a superstar player if the salary the team would need to pay is too high.

Are the Detroit Lions paying too much to Calvin Johnson?

Economists Cade Massey, of Duke University, and Richard Thaler, of the University of Chicago, have analyzed whether NFL teams distribute their salaries efficiently. NFL teams obtain their players either by signing free agents—who are players whose contracts with other teams have expired—or by signing players chosen in the annual draft of eligible college players. The college draft consists of seven rounds, with the teams with the worst records the previous year choosing first. Massey and Thaler find that, in fact, NFL teams do not allocate salaries efficiently. In particular, the players chosen with the first few picks of the first round of the draft tend to be paid salaries that are much higher relative to their marginal products than is true for players taken later in the first round. A typical team with a high draft pick would increase its ability to win football games at the constant cost represented by the salary cap if it traded for lower draft picks. Why do NFL teams apparently make the error of not efficiently distributing salaries? Massey and Thaler argue that managers of NFL teams tend to be overconfident in their ability to forecast how well a college player is likely to perform in the NFL.

Managers of NFL teams are not alone in suffering from overconfidence. Studies have shown that, in general, people tend to overestimate their ability to forecast an uncertain outcome. Because NFL teams tend to overestimate the future marginal productivity of high draft picks, they pay them salaries that are inefficiently high when compared to salaries other draft picks receive.

This example shows that the concepts developed in this chapter provide powerful tools for analyzing whether firms are operating efficiently.

Source: Cade Massey and Richard Thaler, "Overconfidence versus Market Efficiency in the National Football League," Working Paper 11270, Cambridge, MA: National Bureau of Economic Research, April 2005.

YOUR TURN: Test your understanding by doing related problem 10A.14 on page 375 at the end of this chapter.

The Expansion Path

We can use isoquants and isocost lines to examine what happens as a firm expands its level of output. Figure 10A-6 shows three isoquants for a firm that produces bookcases. The isocost lines are drawn, assuming that the machines used in producing bookcases can be rented for $100 per day and the wage rate is $25 per day. The point where each isoquant is tangent to an isocost line determines the cost-minimizing combination of capital and labor for producing that level of output. For example, 10 machines and 40 workers

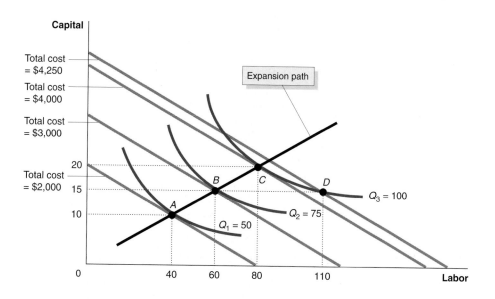

Figure 10A-6

The Expansion Path

The tangency points *A*, *B*, and *C* lie along the firm's expansion path, which is a curve that shows the cost-minimizing combination of inputs for every level of output. In the short run, when the quantity of machines is fixed, the firm can expand output from 75 bookcases per day to 100 bookcases per day at the lowest cost only by moving from point *B* to point *D* and increasing the number of workers from 80 to 110. In the long run, when it can increase the quantity of machines it uses, the firm can move from point *D* to point *C*, thereby reducing its total costs of producing 100 bookcases per day from $4,250 to $4,000.

is the cost-minimizing combination of inputs for producing 50 bookcases per day. The cost-minimizing points *A*, *B*, and *C* lie along the firm's **expansion path**, which is a curve that shows the cost-minimizing combination of inputs for every level of output.

An important point to note is that the expansion path represents the least-cost combination of inputs to produce a given level of output *in the long run*, when the firm is able to vary the levels of all of its inputs. We know, though, that in the short run, at least one input is fixed. We can use Figure 10A-6 to show that as the firm expands in the short run, its costs will be higher than in the long run. For example, suppose that the firm is currently at point *B*, using 15 machines and 60 workers to produce 75 bookcases per day. The firm wants to expand its output to 100 bookcases per day, but in the short run, it is unable to increase the quantity of machines it uses. Therefore, to expand output, it must hire more workers. The figure shows that in the short run, to produce 100 bookcases per day using 15 machines, the lowest costs it can attain are at point *D*, where it employs 110 workers. With a rental price of machines of $100 per day and a wage rate of $25 per day, in the short run, the firm will have total costs of $4,250 to produce 100 bookcases per day. In the long run, though, the firm can increase the number of machines it uses from 15 to 20 and reduce the number of workers from 110 to 80. This change allows it to move from point *D* to point *C* on its expansion path and to lower its total costs of producing 100 bookcases per day from $4,250 to $4,000. The firm's minimum total costs of production are lower in the long run than in the short run.

Expansion path A curve that shows a firm's cost-minimizing combination of inputs for every level of output.

Key Terms

Expansion path, p. 373

Isocost line, p. 365

Isoquant, p. 364

Marginal rate of technical substitution (*MRTS*), p. 365

Review Questions

10A.1 What is an isoquant? What is the slope of an isoquant?

10A.2 What is an isocost line? What is the slope of an isocost line?

10A.3 How do firms choose the optimal combination of inputs?

Problems and Applications

10A.4 Draw an isoquant–isocost line graph to illustrate the following situation: Jill Johnson can rent pizza ovens for $400 per week and hire workers for $200 per week. She is currently using 5 ovens and 10 workers to produce 20,000 pizzas per week and has total costs of $4,000. Make sure to label your graph showing the cost-minimizing input combination and the maximum quantity of labor and capital she can use with total costs of $4,000.

10A.5 Use the following graph to answer the questions.

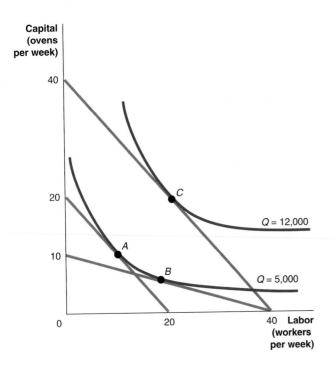

a. If the wage rate and the rental price of machines are both $100 and total cost is $2,000, is the cost-minimizing point *A*, *B*, or *C*? Briefly explain.

b. If the wage rate is $25, the rental price of machines is $100, and total cost is $1,000, is the cost-minimizing point *A*, *B*, or *C*? Briefly explain.

c. If the wage rate and the rental price of machines are both $100 and total cost is $4,000, is the cost-minimizing point *A*, *B*, or *C*? Briefly explain.

10A.6 (Related to *Solved Problem 10A-1* on page 371) Consider the information in the following table for Jill Johnson's restaurant.

Marginal product of capital	4,000
Marginal product of labor	100
Wage rate	$10
Rental price of pizza ovens	$500

Briefly explain whether Jill is minimizing costs. If she is not minimizing costs, explain whether she should rent more ovens and hire fewer workers or rent fewer ovens and hire more workers.

10A.7 (Related to *Solved Problem 10A-1* on page 371) Draw an isoquant–isocost line graph to illustrate the following situation: Jill Johnson can

rent pizza ovens for $200 per week and hire workers for $100 per week. Currently, she is using 5 ovens and 10 workers to produce 20,000 pizzas per week and has total costs of $2,000. Jill's marginal rate of technical substitution (*MRTS*) equals −1. Explain why this means that she's not minimizing costs and what she could do to minimize costs.

10A.8 (Related to the *Making the Connection on page 368*) During the eighteenth century, the American colonies had much more land per farmer than did Europe, with the result that the price of labor in the colonies was much higher relative to the price of land than was true in Europe. Assume that Europe and the colonies had access to the same technology for producing food. Use an isoquant-isocost line graph to illustrate why the combination of land and labor used in producing food in the colonies would have been different than the combination used to produce food in Europe.

10A.9 Draw an isoquant–isocost line graph to illustrate the following situation and the change that occurs: Jill Johnson can rent pizza ovens for $2,000 per week and hire workers for $1,000 per week. Currently, she is using 5 ovens and 10 workers to produce 20,000 pizzas per week and has total costs of $20,000. Then Jill reorganizes the way things are done in her business and achieves positive technological change.

10A.10 Use the following graph to answer the following questions about Jill Johnson's isoquant curve.

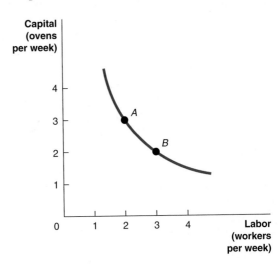

a. Which combination of inputs yields more output: combination *A* (3 ovens and 2 workers) or combination *B* (2 ovens and 3 workers)?

b. What will determine whether Jill selects *A*, *B*, or some other point along this isoquant curve?

c. Is the marginal rate of technical substitution (*MRTS*) greater at point *A* or point *B*?

10A.11 Draw an isoquant–isocost line graph to illustrate the following situation: Jill Johnson can rent pizza ovens for $2,000 per week and hire workers for $1,000 per week. She can minimize the cost of producing 20,000 pizzas per week by using 5 ovens and 10 workers, at a total cost of $20,000. She can minimize the cost of producing 45,000 pizzas per week by using 10 ovens and 20 workers, at a total cost of $40,000. And she can minimize the cost of producing 60,000 pizzas per week by using 15 ovens and 30 workers, at a total cost of $60,000. Now draw Jill's long-run average cost curve and discuss its economies and diseconomies of scale.

10A.12 In Brazil, a grove of oranges is picked using 20 workers, ladders, and baskets. In Florida, a grove of oranges is picked using 1 worker and a machine that shakes the oranges off the trees and scoops up the fallen oranges. Using an isoquant–isocost line graph, illustrate why these two different methods are used to pick the same number of oranges per day in these two locations.

10A.13 Jill Johnson is minimizing the costs of producing pizzas. The rental price of one of her ovens is $2,000 per week, and the wage rate is $600 per week. The marginal product of capital in her business is 12,000 pizzas. What must be the marginal product of her workers?

10A.14 (Related to the *Making the Connection* on page 372) If Massey and Thaler are correct, then should the team that has the first pick in the draft keep the pick or trade it to another team for a lower pick? Explain.

>> **End Appendix Learning Objective**

Chapter 11

Firms in Perfectly Competitive Markets

Perfect Competition in the Market for Organic Apples

The market for organically grown food has expanded rapidly in the United States. As recently as 15 years ago, organic food was sold primarily in small health food stores. By the 2000s, sales of organic foods were growing at a rate of more than 20 percent per year, and organic foods were available in nearly every supermarket. In 2002, the U.S. Department of Agriculture (USDA) established standards for organic food labeling. The standards were intended to protect consumers from false and misleading claims and to make it easier for U.S. farmers to export to foreign countries whose governments also require organic food labeling. According to the USDA, a firm can label and advertise food as "organic" only if that food is "produced without using most conventional pesticides; fertilizers made with synthetic ingredients or sewage sludge; bioengineering; or ionizing radiation."

Organically grown apples became popular with consumers during the late 1990s. Farmers growing apples organically use only organic fertilizers and control insects with sprays made from soil compounds. These growing methods add about 15 percent to the cost of growing apples. The Yakima Valley of Washington State is particularly suited to growing apples organically because of the absence of certain insects. In 1997, Yakima Valley apple farmers were able to sell organically grown apples for a price 50 percent higher than the price of regular apples, more than offsetting the higher costs of organic growing methods. This price difference made organically grown apples considerably more profitable than apples grown using traditional methods.

Between 1997 and 2001, many apple farmers switched from traditional to organic growing methods, increasing production of organically grown apples from 1.2 million boxes per year to more than 3 million boxes. The additional supply of organically grown apples forced down prices and made them no more profitable than apples grown using traditional methods.

As one farmer in the Yakima Valley put it, "It's like anything else in agriculture. If people see an economic opportunity, usually it only lasts for a few years." **AN INSIDE LOOK** on **page 402** discusses how an organic farmer in South Dakota responds to large firms like Wal-Mart entering the market for organic foods.

What the organic apple farmers in the Yakima Valley experienced is not unique to agriculture. Throughout the economy, entrepreneurs are continually introducing new products, which—when successful—enable them to earn economic profits in the short run. But in the long run, competition among firms force prices to the level where they just cover the costs of production. This process of competition is at the heart of the market system and is the focus of this chapter.

Sources: Lydia Oberholtzer, Carolyn Dimitri, and Catherine Greene, "Price Premiums Hold on as U.S. Organic Produce Market Expands," Agricultural Economic Report No. VGS-308-01, Economic Research Service, U.S. Department of Agriculture, May 2005; Emily Green, "Study Gives Nod to Organic Apples, but It's Crunch Time for All State Growers," Seattle Times, April 19, 2001; quote from farmer from All Things Considered, National Public Radio, www.npr.org, April 18, 2001.

Economics in YOUR Life!

Are You an Entrepreneur?

Were you an entrepreneur during your high school years? Perhaps you didn't have your own store, but you may have worked as a babysitter, or perhaps you mowed lawns for families in your neighborhood. While you may not think of these jobs as being small businesses, that is exactly what they are. How did you decide what price to charge for your services? You may have wanted to charge $25 per hour to babysit or mow lawns, but you probably charged much less. As you read the chapter, think about the competitive situation you faced as a teenaged entrepreneur and try to determine why the prices received by most people who babysit and mow lawns are so low. You can check your answers against those we provide at the end of the chapter. >> **Continued on page 401**

Organic apple growing is an example of a *perfectly competitive* industry. Firms in perfectly competitive industries are unable to control the prices of the products they sell and are unable to earn an economic profit in the long run. There are two main reasons for this result: Firms in these industries sell identical products, and it is easy for new firms to enter these industries. Studying how perfectly competitive industries operate is the best way to understand how markets answer the fundamental economic questions discussed in Chapter 1:

- What goods and services will be produced?

- How will the goods and services be produced?

- Who will receive the goods and services produced?

In fact, though, most industries are not perfectly competitive. In most industries, firms do *not* produce identical products, and in some industries, it may be difficult for new firms to enter. There are thousands of industries in the United States. Although in some ways each industry is unique, industries share enough similarities that economists group them into four market structures. In particular, any industry has three key characteristics:

- The number of firms in the industry

- The similarity of the good or service produced by the firms in the industry

- The ease with which new firms can enter the industry

Economists use these characteristics to classify industries into the four market structures listed in Table 11-1.

Many industries, including restaurants, hardware stores, and other retailers, have a large number of firms selling products that are differentiated, rather than identical, and fall into the category of *monopolistic competition*. Some industries, such as computers and automobiles, have only a few firms and are *oligopolies*. Finally, a few industries, such as the delivery of first-class mail by the U.S. Postal Service, have only one firm and are *monopolies*. After discussing perfect competition in this chapter, we will devote a chapter to each of these other market structures.

TABLE 11-1 | The Four Market Structures

CHARACTERISTIC	MARKET STRUCTURE			
	PERFECT COMPETITION	MONOPOLISTIC COMPETITION	OLIGOPOLY	MONOPOLY
Number of firms	Many	Many	Few	One
Type of product	Identical	Differentiated	Identical or differentiated	Unique
Ease of entry	High	High	Low	Entry blocked
Examples of industries	• Wheat • Apples	• Selling DVDs • Restaurants	• Manufacturing computers • Manufacturing automobiles	• First-class mail delivery • Tap water

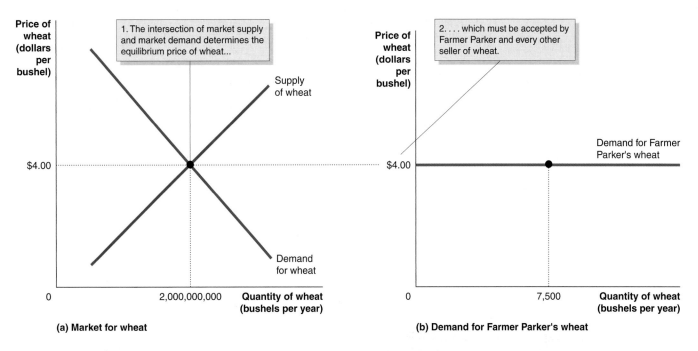

Figure 11-2 | The Market Demand for Wheat versus the Demand for One Farmer's Wheat

In a perfectly competitive market, price is determined by the intersection of market demand and market supply. In panel (a), the demand and supply curves for wheat intersect at a price of $4 per bushel. An individual wheat farmer like Farmer Parker has no ability to affect the market price for wheat. Therefore, as panel (b) shows, the demand curve for Farmer Parker's wheat is a horizontal line. To understand this figure, it is important to notice that the scales on the horizontal axes in the two panels are very different. In panel (a), the equilibrium quantity of wheat is 2 *billion* bushels, and in panel (b), Farmer Parker is producing only 7,500 bushels of wheat.

demand curve in panel (a) is the *market demand curve for wheat* and has the normal downward slope we are familiar with from the market demand curves in Chapter 3. Panel (b) of Figure 11-2 shows the demand curve for Farmer Parker's wheat, which is a horizontal line. By viewing these graphs side by side, you can see that the price Farmer Parker receives for his wheat in panel (b) is determined by the interaction of all sellers and all buyers of wheat in the wheat market in panel (a). Keep in mind, however, that the scales on the horizontal axes in the two panels are very different. In panel (a), the equilibrium quantity of wheat is 2 *billion* bushels. In panel (b), Farmer Parker is producing only 7,500 bushels, or less than 0.0004 percent of market output. We need to use different scales in the two panels so we can display both of them on one page. Keep in mind the key point: Farmer Parker's output of wheat is very small relative to the total market output.

11.2 | Explain how a firm maximizes profits in a perfectly competitive market.

How a Firm Maximizes Profit in a Perfectly Competitive Market

We have seen that Farmer Parker cannot control the price of his wheat. In this situation, how does he decide how much wheat to produce? We assume that Farmer Parker's objective is to maximize profits. This is a reasonable assumption for most firms, most of the time. Remember that **profit** is the difference between total revenue (*TR*) and total cost (*TC*):

Profit Total revenue minus total cost.

$$\text{Profit} = TR - TC.$$

To maximize his profit, Farmer Parker should produce the quantity of wheat where the difference between the total revenue he receives and his total cost is as large as possible.

TABLE 11-2

Farmer Parker's Revenue from Wheat Farming

NUMBER OF BUSHELS (Q)	MARKET PRICE (PER BUSHEL) (P)	TOTAL REVENUE (TR)	AVERAGE REVENUE (AR)	MARGINAL REVENUE (MR)
0	$4	$0	—	—
1	4	4	$4	$4
2	4	8	4	4
3	4	12	4	4
4	4	16	4	4
5	4	20	4	4
6	4	24	4	4
7	4	28	4	4
8	4	32	4	4
9	4	36	4	4
10	4	40	4	4

Revenue for a Firm in a Perfectly Competitive Market

To understand how Farmer Parker maximizes profits, let's first consider his revenue. To keep the numbers simple, we will assume that he owns a very small farm and produces at most 10 bushels of wheat per year. Table 11-2 shows the revenue Farmer Parker will earn from selling various quantities of wheat if the market price for wheat is $4.

The third column in Table 11-2 shows that Farmer Parker's *total revenue* rises by $4 for every additional bushel he sells because he can sell as many bushels as he wants at the market price of $4 per bushel. The fourth and fifth columns in the table show Farmer Parker's *average revenue* and *marginal revenue* from selling wheat. His **average revenue** (*AR*) is his total revenue divided by the quantity of bushels he sells. For example, if he sells 5 bushels for a total of $20, his average revenue is $20/5 = $4. Notice that his average revenue is also equal to the market price of $4. In fact, for any level of output, a firm's average revenue is always equal to the market price. One way to see this is to note that total revenue equals price times quantity ($TR = P \times Q$), and average revenue equals total revenue divided by quantity ($AR = TR/Q$). So, $AR = TR/Q = (P \times Q)/Q = P$.

Farmer Parker's **marginal revenue** (*MR*) is the change in his total revenue from selling one more bushel:

$$\text{Marginal Revenue} = \frac{\text{Change in total revenue}}{\text{Change in quantity}}, \text{ or } MR = \frac{\Delta TR}{\Delta Q}.$$

Because for each additional bushel sold he always adds $4 to his total revenue, his marginal revenue is $4. Farmer Parker's marginal revenue is $4 per bushel because he is selling wheat in a perfectly competitive market and can sell as much as he wants at the market price. In fact, Farmer Parker's marginal revenue and average revenue are both equal to the market price. This is an important point: *For a firm in a perfectly competitive market, price is equal to both average revenue and marginal revenue.*

Determining the Profit-Maximizing Level of Output

To determine how Farmer Parker can maximize profit, we have to consider his costs as well as his revenue. A wheat farmer has many costs, including seed, fertilizer, and the wages of farm workers. In Table 11-3, we bring together the revenue data from Table 11-1 with cost data for Farmer Parker's farm. Recall from Chapter 10 that a firm's *marginal cost* is the increase in total cost resulting from producing another unit of output.

Average revenue (AR) Total revenue divided by the quantity of the product sold.

Marginal revenue (MR) Change in total revenue from selling one more unit of a product.

QUANTITY (BUSHELS) (Q)	TOTAL REVENUE (TR)	TOTAL COST (TC)	PROFIT ($TR-TC$)	MARGINAL REVENUE (MR)	MARGINAL COST (MC)
0	$0.00	$1.00	–$1.00	—	—
1	4.00	4.00	0.00	$4.00	$3.00
2	8.00	6.00	2.00	4.00	2.00
3	12.00	7.50	4.50	4.00	1.50
4	16.00	9.50	6.50	4.00	2.00
5	20.00	12.00	8.00	4.00	2.50
6	24.00	15.00	9.00	4.00	3.00
7	28.00	19.50	8.50	4.00	4.50
8	32.00	25.50	6.50	4.00	6.00
9	36.00	32.50	3.50	4.00	7.00
10	40.00	40.50	–0.50	4.00	8.00

TABLE 11-3

Farmer Parker's Profits from Wheat Farming

We calculate profit in the fourth column by subtracting total cost in the third column from total revenue in the second column. The fourth column shows that as long as Farmer Parker produces between 2 and 9 bushels of wheat, he will earn a profit. His maximum profit is $9.00, which he will earn by producing 6 bushels of wheat. Because Farmer Parker wants to maximize his profits, we would expect him to produce 6 bushels of wheat. Producing more than 6 bushels reduces his profit. For example, if he produces 7 bushels of wheat, his profit will decline from $9.00 to $8.50. The values for marginal cost given in the last column of the table help us understand why Farmer Parker's profits will decline if he produces more than 6 bushels of wheat. After the sixth bushel of wheat, rising marginal cost causes Farmer Parker's profits to fall.

In fact, comparing the marginal cost and marginal revenue at each level of output is an alternative method of calculating Farmer Parker's profits. We illustrate the two methods of calculating profits in Figure 11-3 on the next page. We show the total revenue and total cost approach in panel (a) and the marginal revenue and marginal cost approach in panel (b). Total revenue is a straight line on the graph in panel (a) because total revenue increases at a constant rate of $4 for each additional bushel sold. Farmer Parker's profits are maximized when the vertical distance between the line representing total revenue and the total cost curve is as large as possible. Just as we saw in Table 11-3, this occurs at an output of 6 bushels.

The last two columns of Table 11-3 provide information on the marginal revenue (MR) Farmer Parker receives from selling another bushel of wheat and his marginal cost (MC) of producing another bushel of wheat. Panel (b) is a graph of Farmer Parker's marginal revenue and marginal cost. Because marginal revenue is always equal to $4, it is a horizontal line at the market price. We have already seen that the demand curve for a perfectly competitive firm is also a horizontal line at the market price. *Therefore, the marginal revenue curve for a perfectly competitive firm is the same as its demand curve.* Farmer Parker's marginal cost of producing wheat first falls and then rises, following the usual pattern we discussed in Chapter 10.

We know from panel (a) that profit is at a maximum at 6 bushels of wheat. In panel (b), profit is also at a maximum at 6 bushels of wheat. To understand why profit is maximized at the level of output where marginal revenue equals marginal cost, remember a key economic principle that we discussed in Chapter 1: *Optimal decisions are made at the margin.* Firms use this principle to decide the quantity of a good to produce. For example, in deciding how much wheat to produce, Farmer Parker needs

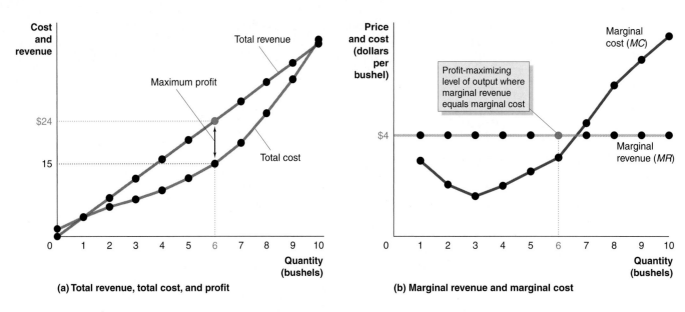

Figure 11-3 | The Profit-Maximizing Level of Output

In panel (a), Farmer Parker maximizes his profit where the vertical distance between total revenue and total cost is the largest. This happens at an output of 6 bushels. Panel (b) shows that Farmer Parker's marginal revenue (*MR*) is equal to a constant $4 per bushel. Farmer Parker maximizes profits by producing wheat up to the point where the marginal revenue of the last bushel produced is equal to its marginal cost, or *MR = MC*.

In this case, at no level of output does marginal revenue exactly equal marginal cost. The closest Farmer Parker can come is to produce 6 bushels of wheat. He will not want to continue to produce once marginal cost is greater than marginal revenue because that would reduce his profits. Panels (a) and (b) show alternative ways of thinking about how Farmer Parker can determine the profit-maximizing quantity of wheat to produce.

to compare the marginal revenue he earns from selling another bushel of wheat to the marginal cost of producing that bushel. The difference between the marginal revenue and the marginal cost is the additional profit (or loss) from producing one more bushel. As long as marginal revenue is greater than marginal cost, Farmer Parker's profits are increasing, and he will want to expand production. For example, he will not stop producing at 5 bushels of wheat because producing and selling the sixth bushel adds $4 to his revenue but only $3 to his cost, so his profit increases by $1. He wants to continue producing until the marginal revenue he receives from selling another bushel is equal to the marginal cost of producing it. At that level of output, he will make no *additional* profit by selling another bushel, so he will have maximized his profits.

By inspecting the table, we can see that at no level of output does marginal revenue exactly equal marginal cost. The closest Farmer Parker can come is to produce 6 bushels of wheat. He will not want to continue to produce once marginal cost is greater than marginal revenue because that would reduce his profits. For example, the seventh bushel of wheat adds $4.50 to his cost but only $4.00 to his revenue, so producing the seventh bushel *reduces* his profit by $0.50.

From the information in Table 11-3 and Figure 11-3, we can draw the following conclusions:

1 The profit-maximizing level of output is where the difference between total revenue and total cost is the greatest.

2 The profit-maximizing level of output is also where marginal revenue equals marginal cost, or *MR = MC*.

Both these conclusions are true for any firm, whether or not it is in a perfectly competitive industry. We can draw one other conclusion about profit maximization that is true only of firms in perfectly competitive industries: For a firm in a perfectly competitive industry, price is equal to marginal revenue, or *P = MR*. So, we can restate the *MR = MC* condition as *P = MC*.

Illustrating Profit or Loss on the Cost Curve Graph

We have seen that profit is the difference between total revenue and total cost. We can also express profit in terms of *average total cost* (*ATC*). This allows us to show profit on the cost curve graph we developed in Chapter 10.

To begin, we need to work through the several steps necessary to determine the relationship between profit and average total cost. Because profit is equal to total revenue minus total cost (*TC*) and total revenue is price times quantity, we can write the following:

$$\text{Profit} = (P \times Q) - TC.$$

If we divide both sides of this equation by Q, we have:

$$\frac{\text{Profit}}{Q} = \frac{(P \times Q)}{Q} - \frac{TC}{Q},$$

or:

$$\frac{\text{Profit}}{Q} = P - ATC,$$

because TC/Q equals ATC. This equation tells us that profit per unit (or average profit) equals price minus average total cost. Finally, we obtain the expression for the relationship between total profit and average total cost by multiplying again by Q:

$$\text{Profit} = (P - ATC) \times Q.$$

This expression tells us that a firm's total profit is equal to the quantity produced multiplied by the difference between price and average total cost.

Showing a Profit on the Graph

Figure 11-4 shows the relationship between a firm's average total cost and its marginal cost that we discussed in Chapter 10. In this figure, we also show the firm's marginal revenue curve (which is the same as its demand curve) and the area representing total profit. Using the relationship between profit and average total cost that we just determined, we can say that the area representing total profit has a height equal to ($P - ATC$) and a base equal to Q. This area is shown by the green-shaded rectangle.

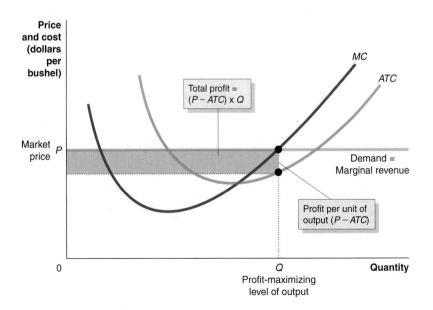

Figure 11-4

The Area of Maximum Profit

A firm maximizes profit at the level of output at which marginal revenue equals marginal cost. The difference between price and average total cost equals profit per unit of output. Total profit equals profit per unit multiplied by the number of units produced. Total profit is represented by the area of the green-shaded rectangle, which has a height equal to ($P - ATC$) and a width equal to Q.

Solved Problem | 11-3

Determining Profit-Maximizing Price and Quantity

Suppose that Andy sells basketballs in the perfectly competitive basketball market. His output per day and his costs are as follows:

OUTPUT PER DAY	TOTAL COST
0	$10.00
1	15.00
2	17.50
3	22.50
4	30.00
5	40.00
6	52.50
7	67.50
8	85.00
9	105.00

a. If the current equilibrium price in the basketball market is $12.50, to maximize profits, how many basketballs will Andy produce, what price will he charge, and how much profit (or loss) will he make? Draw a graph to illustrate your answer. Your graph should be labeled clearly and should include Andy's demand, ATC, AVC, MC, and MR curves; the price he is charging; the quantity he is producing; and the area representing his profit (or loss).

b. Suppose the equilibrium price of basketballs falls to $5.00. Now how many basketballs will Andy produce, what price will he charge, and how much profit (or loss) will he make? Draw a graph to illustrate this situation, using the instructions in question (a).

SOLVING THE PROBLEM:

Step 1: **Review the chapter material.** This problem is about using cost curve graphs to analyze perfectly competitive firms, so you may want to review the section "Illustrating Profit or Loss on the Cost Curve Graph," which begins on page 385.

Step 2: **Calculate Andy's marginal cost, average total cost, and average variable cost.** To maximize profits, Andy will produce the level of output where marginal revenue is equal to marginal cost. We can calculate marginal cost from the information given in the table. We can also calculate average total cost and average variable cost in order to draw the required graph. Average total cost (ATC) equals total cost (TC) divided by the level of output (Q). Average variable cost (AVC) equals variable cost (VC) divided by output (Q). To calculate variable cost, recall that total cost equals variable cost plus fixed cost. When output equals zero, total cost equals fixed cost. In this case, fixed cost equals $10.00.

OUTPUT PER DAY (Q)	TOTAL COST (TC)	FIXED COST (FC)	VARIABLE COST (VC)	AVERAGE TOTAL COST (ATC)	AVERAGE VARIABLE COST (AVC)	MARGINAL COST (MC)
0	$10.00	$10.00	$0.00	—	—	—
1	15.00	10.00	5.00	$15.00	$5.00	$5.00
2	17.50	10.00	7.50	8.75	3.75	2.50
3	22.50	10.00	12.50	7.50	4.17	5.00
4	30.00	10.00	20.00	7.50	5.00	7.50
5	40.00	10.00	30.00	8.00	6.00	10.00
6	52.50	10.00	42.50	8.75	7.08	12.50
7	67.50	10.00	57.50	9.64	8.21	15.00
8	85.00	10.00	75.00	10.63	9.38	17.50
9	105.00	10.00	95.00	11.67	10.56	20.00

Step 3: **Use the information from the table in step 2 to calculate how many basket-balls Andy will produce, what price he will charge, and how much profit he will earn if the market price of basketballs is $12.50.** Andy's marginal revenue is equal to the market price of $12.50. Marginal revenue equals marginal cost when Andy produces 6 basketballs per day. So, Andy will produce 6 basketballs per day and charge a price of $12.50 per basketball. Andy's profits are equal to his total revenue minus his total costs. His total revenue equals the 6 basketballs he sells multiplied by the $12.50 price, or $75.00. So, his profits equal $75.00 − $52.50 = $22.50.

Step 4: **Use the information from the table in step 2 to illustrate your answer to question (a) with a graph.**

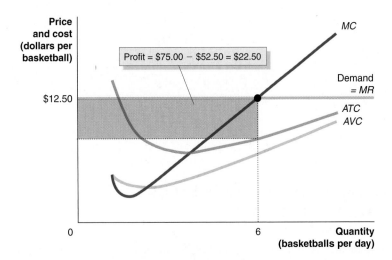

Step 5: **Calculate how many basketballs Andy will produce, what price he will charge, and how much profit he will earn when the market price of basketballs is $5.00.** Referring to the table in step 2, we can see that marginal revenue equals marginal cost when Andy produces 3 basketballs per day. He charges the market price of $5.00 per basketball. His total revenue is only $15.00, while his total costs are $22.50, so he will have a loss of $7.50. (Can we be sure that Andy will continue to produce even though he is operating at a loss? We answer this question in the next section.)

Step 6: **Illustrate your answer to question (b) with a graph.**

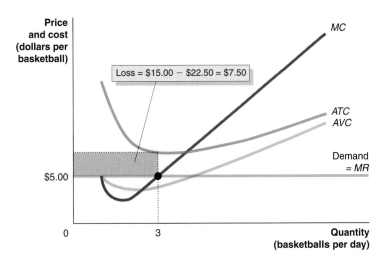

YOUR TURN: For more practice, do related problems 3.3 and 3.4 on page 406 at the end of this chapter.

>> End Solved Problem 11-3

Don't Let This Happen to **YOU!**

Remember That Firms Maximize Total Profit, Not Profit per Unit

A student examines the following graph and argues, "I believe that a firm will want to produce at Q_1, not Q_2. At Q_1, the distance between price and average total cost is the greatest. Therefore, at Q_1, the firm will be maximizing its profits per unit." Briefly explain whether you agree with the student's argument.

The student's argument is incorrect because firms are interested in maximizing their *total* profits and not their profits per unit. We know that profits are not maximized at Q_1 because at that level of output, marginal revenue is greater than marginal cost. A firm can always increase its profits by producing any unit that adds more to its revenue than it does to its costs. Only when the firm has expanded production to Q_2 will it have produced every unit for which marginal revenue is greater than marginal cost. At that point, it will have maximized profit.

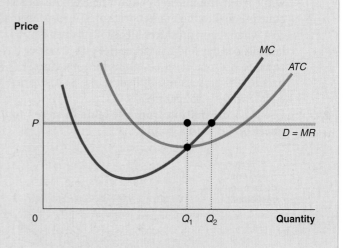

YOUR TURN: Test your understanding by doing related problem 3.5 on page 406 at the end of this chapter.

Illustrating When a Firm Is Breaking Even or Operating at a Loss

We have already seen that to maximize profits, a firm produces the level of output where marginal revenue equals marginal cost. But will the firm actually make a profit at that level of output? It depends on the relationship of price to average total cost. There are three possibilities:

1. $P > ATC$, which means the firm makes a profit.
2. $P = ATC$, which means the firm *breaks even* (its total cost equals its total revenue).
3. $P < ATC$, which means the firm experiences losses.

Figure 11-4 shows the first possibility, where the firm makes a profit. Panels (a) and (b) of Figure 11-5 show the situations where a firm experiences losses or breaks

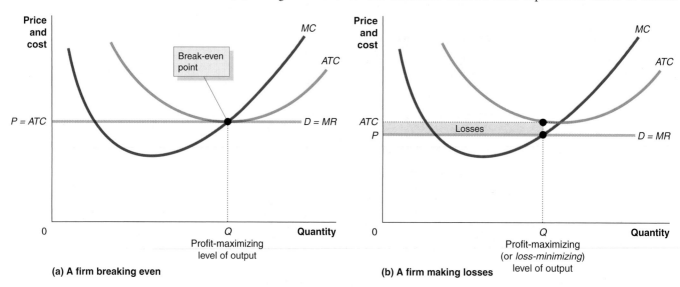

(a) A firm breaking even

(b) A firm making losses

Figure 11-5 | A Firm Breaking Even and a Firm Experiencing Losses

In panel (a), price equals average total cost, and the firm breaks even because its total revenue will be equal to its total cost. In this situation, the firm makes zero economic profit. In panel (b), price is below average total cost, and the firm experiences a loss.

The loss is represented by the area of the red-shaded rectangle, which has a height equal to $(ATC - P)$ and a width equal to Q.

even. In panel (a) of Figure 11-5, at the level of output at which $MR = MC$, price is equal to average total cost. Therefore, total revenue is equal to total cost, and the firm will break even, making zero economic profit. In panel (b), at the level of output at which $MR = MC$, price is less than average total cost. Therefore, total revenue is less than total cost, and the firm has losses. In this case, maximizing profits amounts to *minimizing* losses.

Making the Connection

Losing Money in the Medical Screening Industry

In a market system, a good or service becomes available to consumers only if an entrepreneur brings the product to market. Thousands of new businesses open every week in the United States. Each new business represents an entrepreneur risking his or her funds trying to earn a profit by offering a good or service to consumers. Of course, there are no guarantees of success, and many new businesses experience losses rather than earn the profits their owners hoped for.

In the early 2000s, technological advance reduced the price of computed tomography (CT) scanning equipment. For years, doctors and hospitals have prescribed CT scans to diagnose patients showing symptoms of heart disease, cancer, and other disorders. The declining price of CT scanning equipment convinced many entrepreneurs that it would be profitable to offer preventive body scans to apparently healthy people. The idea was that the scans would provide early detection of diseases before the customers had begun experiencing symptoms. Unfortunately, the new firms offering this service ran into several difficulties: First, because the CT scan was a voluntary procedure, it was not covered under most medical insurance plans. Second, very few consumers used the service more than once, so there was almost no repeat business. Finally, as with any other medical test, some false positives occurred, where the scan appeared to detect a problem that did not actually exist. Negative publicity from people who had expensive additional—and unnecessary—medical procedures as a result of false-positive CT scans also hurt these new businesses.

As a result of these difficulties, the demand for CT scans was less than most of these entrepreneurs had expected, and the new businesses operated at a loss. For example, the owner of California HeartScan would have broken even if the market price had been $495 per heart scan, but it suffered losses because the actual market price was only $250. The following graphs show the owner's situation.

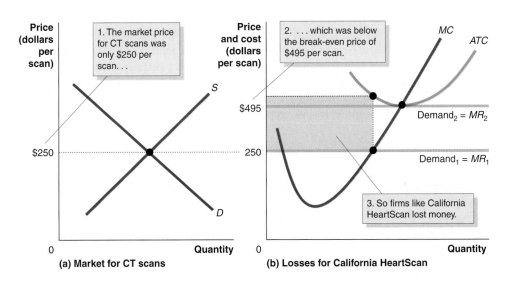

(a) Market for CT scans

(b) Losses for California HeartScan

Why didn't California HeartScan and other medical clinics just raise the price to the level they needed to break even? We have already seen that any firm that tries to raise the price it charges above the market price loses customers to competing firms. By fall 2003, many scanning businesses began to close. Most of the entrepreneurs who had started these businesses lost their investments.

Source: Patricia Callahan, "Scanning for Trouble," *Wall Street Journal*, September 11, 2003, p. B1.

YOUR TURN: Test your understanding by doing related problem 3.8 on page 406 at the end of this chapter.

11.4 | Explain why firms may shut down temporarily.

Deciding Whether to Produce or to Shut Down in the Short Run

In panel (b) of Figure 11-5, we assumed that the firm would continue to produce, even though it was operating at a loss. In fact, in the short run, a firm suffering losses has two choices:

1 Continue to produce

2 Stop production by shutting down temporarily

In many cases, a firm experiencing losses will consider stopping production temporarily. Even during a temporary shutdown, however, a firm must still pay its fixed costs. For example, if the firm has signed a lease for its building, the landlord will expect to receive a monthly rent payment, even if the firm is not producing anything that month. Therefore, if a firm does not produce, it will suffer a loss equal to its fixed costs. This loss is the maximum the firm will accept. If, by producing, the firm would lose an amount greater than its fixed costs, it will shut down.

A firm will be able to reduce its loss below the amount of its total fixed cost by continuing to produce, provided the total revenue it receives is greater than its variable cost. A firm can use the revenue over and above variable cost to cover part of its fixed cost. In this case, the firm will have a smaller loss by continuing to produce than if it shut down.

Sunk cost A cost that has already been paid and that cannot be recovered.

In analyzing the firm's decision to shut down, we are assuming that its fixed costs are *sunk costs*. Remember from Chapter 9 that a **sunk cost** is a cost that has already been paid and cannot be recovered. We assume, as is usually the case, that the firm cannot recover its fixed costs by shutting down. For example, if a farmer has taken out a loan to buy land, the farmer is legally required to make the monthly loan payment whether he grows any wheat that season or not. The farmer has to spend those funds and cannot get them back, so the farmer should treat his sunk costs as irrelevant to his decision making. For any firm, whether total revenue is greater or less than *variable costs* is the key to deciding whether to shut down. As long as a firm's total revenue is greater than its variable costs, it should continue to produce no matter how large or small its fixed costs are.

Making
the
Connection

When to Close a Laundry

An article in the *Wall Street Journal* describes what happened to Robert Kjelgaard when he quit his job writing software code at Microsoft and bought a laundry by paying the previous owner $80,000. For this payment, he received 76 washers and dryers and the existing lease on the building. The lease had six years remaining and required a monthly payment of $3,300. Unfortunately, Mr. Kjelgaard had difficulty operating the laundry at a profit. His explicit costs were $4,000 per month more than his revenue.

He tried but failed to sell the laundry. As he told a reporter, "It's hard to sell a business that's losing money." He considered closing the laundry, but as a sole proprietor, he would be responsible for the remainder of the lease. At $3,300 per month for six years, he would be responsible for paying almost $200,000 out of his personal savings. Closing the laundry would still seem to be the better choice because his $3,300 per month in sunk costs were less than the $4,000 per month plus the opportunity cost of his time, which he was losing from operating the laundry.

He finally decided to reorganize his business and hire a professional manager. This change allowed him to return to Microsoft and still reduce his losses to $2,000 per month. Because this amount was less than the $3,300 per month he would lose by shutting down, it made sense for him to continue to operate the laundry. But he was still suffering losses and, according to the article, his wife was "counting the days until the lease runs out."

Source: G. Pascal Zachary, "How a Success at Microsoft Washed Out at a Laundry," *Wall Street Journal*, May 30, 1995.

YOUR TURN: Test your understanding by doing related problems 4.5 and 4.6 on page 407 at the end of this chapter.

Keeping a business open even when suffering losses can sometimes be the best decision for an entrepreneur in the short run.

One option not available to a firm with losses in a perfectly competitive market is to raise its price. If the firm did raise its price, it would lose all its customers, and its sales would drop to zero. For example, in a recent year, the price of wheat in the United States was $3.16 per bushel. At that price, the typical U.S. wheat farmer lost $9,500. At a price of about $4.25 per bushel, the typical wheat farmer would have broken even. But any wheat farmer who tried to raise his price to $4.25 per bushel would have seen his sales quickly disappear because buyers could purchase all the wheat they wanted at $3.16 per bushel from the thousands of other wheat farmers.

The Supply Curve of a Firm in the Short Run

Remember that the supply curve for a firm tells us how many units of a product the firm is willing to sell at any given price. Notice that the marginal cost curve for a firm in a perfectly competitive market tells us the same thing. The firm will produce at the level of output where $MR = MC$. Because price equals marginal revenue for a firm in a perfectly competitive market, the firm will produce where $P = MC$. For any given price, we can determine from the marginal cost curve the quantity of output the firm will supply. *Therefore, a perfectly competitive firm's marginal cost curve also is its supply curve.* There is, however, an important qualification to this. We have seen that if a firm is experiencing losses, it will shut down if its total revenue is less than its variable cost:

$$\text{Total revenue} < \text{Variable cost,}$$

or, in symbols:

$$P \times Q < VC.$$

If we divide both sides by Q, we have the result that the firm will shut down if:

$$P < AVC.$$

If the price drops below average variable cost, the firm will have a smaller loss if it shuts down and produces no output. *So, the firm's marginal cost curve is its supply curve only for prices at or above average variable cost.* The red line in Figure 11-6 shows the supply curve for the firm in the short run.

Recall that the marginal cost curve intersects the average variable cost where the average variable cost curve is at its minimum point. Therefore, the firm's supply curve is its marginal cost curve above the minimum point of the average variable cost curve. For prices below minimum average variable cost (P_{MIN}), the firm will shut down, and its output will fall to zero. The minimum point on the average variable cost curve is called the **shutdown point** and occurs in Figure 11-6 at output level Q_{SD}.

Shutdown point The minimum point on a firm's average variable cost curve; if the price falls below this point, the firm shuts down production in the short run.

Figure 11-6

The Firm's Short-Run Supply Curve

The firm will produce at the level of output at which $MR = MC$. Because price equals marginal revenue for a firm in a perfectly competitive market, the firm will produce where $P = MC$. For any given price, we can determine the quantity of output the firm will supply from the marginal cost curve. In other words, the marginal cost curve is the firm's supply curve. But remember that the firm will shut down if the price falls below average variable cost. The marginal cost curve crosses the average variable cost at the firm's shutdown point. This point occurs at output level Q_{SD}. For prices below P_{MIN}, the supply curve is a vertical line along the price axis, which shows that the firm will supply zero output at those prices. The red line in the figure is the firm's short-run supply curve.

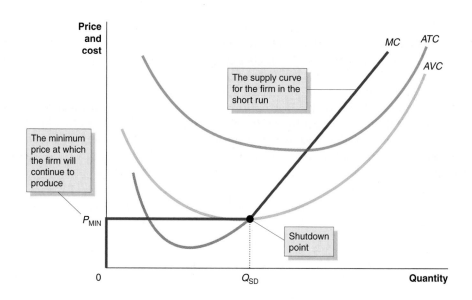

The Market Supply Curve in a Perfectly Competitive Industry

We saw in Chapter 9 that the market demand curve is determined by adding up the quantity demanded by each consumer in the market at each price. Similarly, the market supply curve is determined by adding up the quantity supplied by each firm in the market at each price. Each firm's marginal cost curve tells us how much that firm will supply at each price. So, the market supply curve can be derived directly from the marginal cost curves of the firms in the market. Panel (a) of Figure 11-7 shows the marginal cost curve for one wheat farmer. At a price of $4, this wheat farmer supplies 8,000 bushels of wheat.

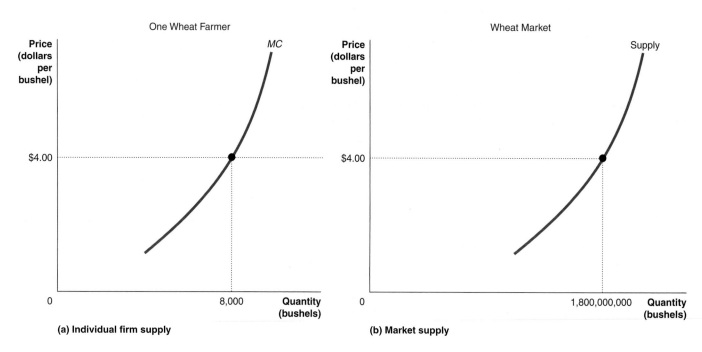

Figure 11-7 | Firm Supply and Market Supply

We can derive the market supply curve by adding up the quantity that each firm in the market is willing to supply at each price. In panel (a), one wheat farmer is willing to supply 8,000 bushels of wheat at a price of $4 per bushel. If every wheat farmer supplies the same amount of wheat at this price and if there are 225,000 wheat farmers, the total amount of wheat supplied at a price of $4 will equal 8,000 bushels per farmer × 225,000 farmers = 1.8 billion bushels of wheat. This is one point on the market supply curve for wheat shown in panel (b). We can find the other points on the market supply curve by seeing how much wheat each farmer is willing to supply at each price.

If every wheat farmer supplies the same amount of wheat at this price and if there are 225,000 wheat farmers, the total amount of wheat supplied at a price of $4 will be:

8,000 bushels per farmer × 225,000 farmers = 1.8 billion bushels of wheat.

Panel (b) shows a price of $4 and a quantity of 1.8 billion bushels as a point on the market supply curve for wheat. In reality, of course, not all wheat farms are alike. Some wheat farms supply more at the market price than the typical farm; other wheat farms supply less. The key point is that we can derive the market supply curve by adding up the quantity that each firm in the market is willing to supply at each price.

11.5 LEARNING OBJECTIVE

11.5 | Explain how entry and exit ensure that perfectly competitive firms earn zero economic profit in the long run.

"If Everyone Can Do It, You Can't Make Money at It": The Entry and Exit of Firms in the Long Run

In the long run, unless a firm can cover all its costs, it will shut down and exit the industry. In a market system, firms continually enter and exit industries. In this section, we will see how profits and losses provide signals to firms that lead to entry and exit.

Economic Profit and the Entry or Exit Decision

To begin, let's look more closely at how economists characterize the profits earned by the owners of a firm. Suppose Anne Moreno decides to start her own business. After considering her interests and preparing a business plan, she decides to start an organic apple farm rather than open a restaurant or gift shop. After 10 years of effort, Anne has saved $100,000 and borrowed another $900,000 from a bank. With these funds, she has bought the land, apple trees, and farm equipment necessary to start her organic apple business. As we saw in Chapter 10, when someone invests her own funds in her firm, the opportunity cost to the firm is the return the funds would have earned in their best alternative use. If Farmer Moreno could have earned a 10 percent return on her $100,000 in savings in their best alternative use—which might have been, for example, to buy a small restaurant—then her apple business incurs a $10,000 opportunity cost. We can also think of this $10,000 as being the minimum amount that Farmer Moreno needs to earn on her $100,000 investment in her farm to remain in the industry in the long run.

Table 11-4 lists Farmer Moreno's costs. In addition to her explicit costs, we assume that she has two implicit costs: the $10,000, which represents the opportunity cost of the

TABLE 11-4

Farmer Moreno's Costs per Year

EXPLICIT COSTS	
Water	$10,000
Wages	$15,000
Organic fertilizer	$10,000
Electricity	$5,000
Payment on bank loan	$45,000
IMPLICIT COSTS	
Foregone salary	$30,000
Opportunity cost of the $100,000 she has invested in her farm	$10,000
Total cost	$125,000

Economic profit A firm's revenues minus all its costs, implicit and explicit.

funds she invested in her farm, and the $30,000 salary she could have earned managing someone else's farm instead of her own. Her total costs are $125,000. If the market price of organic apples is $15 per box and Farmer Moreno sells 10,000 boxes, her total revenue will be $150,000 and her economic profit will be $25,000 (total revenue of $150,000 minus total costs of $125,000). Recall from Chapter 7 that **economic profit** equals a firm's revenues minus all of its costs, implicit and explicit. So, Farmer Moreno is covering the $10,000 opportunity cost of the funds invested in her firm, and she is also earning an additional $25,000 in economic profit.

Economic Profit Leads to Entry of New Firms Unfortunately, Farmer Moreno is unlikely to earn an economic profit for very long. Suppose other apple farmers are just breaking even by growing apples using conventional methods. In that case, they will have an incentive to convert to organic growing methods so they can begin earning an economic profit. Remember that the more firms there are in an industry, the further to the right the market supply curve is. Panel (a) of Figure 11-8 shows that more farmers entering the market for organically grown apples will cause the market supply curve to shift to the right. Farmers will continue entering the market until the market supply curve has shifted from S1 to S2.

With the supply curve at S_2, the market price will have fallen to $10 per box. Panel (b) shows the effect on Farmer Moreno, whom we assume has the same costs as other organic apple farmers. As the market price falls from $15 to $10 per box, Farmer Moreno's demand curve shifts down, from D_1 to D_2. In the new equilibrium, Farmer Moreno is selling 8,000 boxes at a price of $10 per box. She and the other organic apple growers are no longer earning any economic profit. They are just breaking even, and the return on their investment is just covering the opportunity cost of these funds. New farmers will stop entering the market for organic apples because the rate of return is no better than they can earn elsewhere.

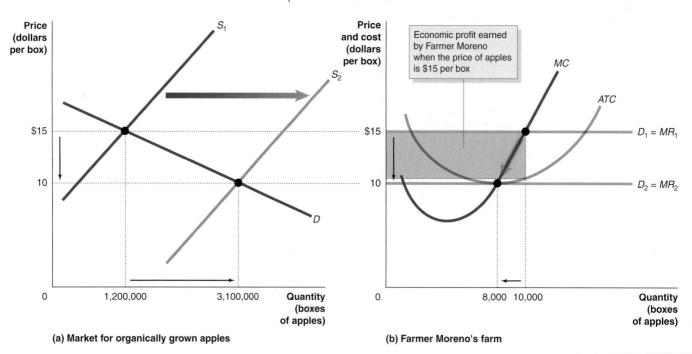

(a) Market for organically grown apples

(b) Farmer Moreno's farm

Figure 11-8 | The Effect of Entry on Economic Profits

We assume that Farmer Moreno's costs are the same as the costs of other organic apple growers. Initially, she and other producers of organically grown apples are able to charge $15 per box and earn an economic profit. Farmer Moreno's economic profit is represented by the area of the green box. Panel (a) shows that as other farmers begin to grow apples using organic methods, the market supply curve shifts to the right, from S_1 to S_2, and the market price drops to $10 per box. Panel (b) shows that

the falling price causes Farmer Moreno's demand curve to shift down from D_1 to D_2, and she reduces her output from 10,000 boxes to 8,000. At the new market price of $10 per box, organic apple growers are just breaking even: Their total revenue is equal to their total cost, and their economic profit is zero. Notice the difference in scale between the graph in panel (a) and the graph in panel (b).

Will Farmer Moreno continue to grow organic apples even though she is just breaking even? She will because growing organic apples earns her as high a return on her investment as she could earn elsewhere. It may seem strange that new firms will continue to enter a market until all economic profits are eliminated and that established firms remain in a market despite not earning any economic profit. It only seems strange because we are used to thinking in terms of accounting profits, rather than *economic* profits. Remember that accounting rules generally require that only explicit costs be included on a firm's financial statements. The opportunity cost of the funds Farmer Moreno invested in her firm—$10,000—and her foregone salary—$30,000—are economic costs, but neither is an accounting cost. So, although an accountant would see Farmer Moreno as earning a profit of $40,000, an economist would see her as just breaking even. Farmer Moreno must pay attention to her accounting profit when preparing her financial statements and when paying her income tax. But because economic profit takes into account all her costs, it gives a truer indication of the financial health of her farm.

Economic Losses Lead to Exit of Firms Suppose some consumers decide there are no important benefits from eating organically grown apples and they switch back to buying conventionally grown apples. Panel (a) of Figure 11-9 shows that the demand curve for organically grown apples will shift to the left, from D_1 to D_2, and the market price will fall from $10 per box to $7. Panel (b) shows that as the price falls, a typical organic apple farmer, like Anne Moreno, will move down her marginal cost curve to a lower level of output. At the lower level of output and lower price, she will be suffering an **economic loss** because she will not cover all her costs. As long as price is above average variable cost, she will continue to produce in the short run, even when suffering losses. But in the long run, firms will exit an industry if they are unable to cover all their costs. In this case, some organic apple growers will switch back to growing apples using conventional methods.

Economic loss The situation in which a firm's total revenue is less than its total cost, including all implicit costs.

Panel (c) of Figure 11-9 shows that firms exiting the organic apple industry will cause the market supply curve to shift to the left. Firms will continue to exit, and the supply curve will continue to shift to the left until the price has risen back to $10 and the market supply curve is at S_2. Panel (d) shows that when the price is back to $10, the remaining firms in the industry will be breaking even.

Long-Run Equilibrium in a Perfectly Competitive Market

We have seen that economic profits attract firms to enter an industry. The entry of firms forces down the market price until the typical firm is breaking even. Economic losses cause firms to exit an industry. The exit of firms forces up the equilibrium market price until the typical firm is breaking even. This process of entry and exit results in *long-run competitive equilibrium*. In **long-run competitive equilibrium**, entry and exit have resulted in the typical firm breaking even. The *long-run equilibrium market price* is at a level equal to the minimum point on the typical firm's average total cost curve.

Long-run competitive equilibrium The situation in which the entry and exit of firms has resulted in the typical firm breaking even.

The long run in the organic apple market is three to four years, which is the amount of time it takes farmers to convert from conventional growing methods to organic growing methods. As discussed at the beginning of this chapter, only during the years from 1997 to 2001 was it possible for organic apple farmers to earn economic profits. By 2002, the entry of new firms had eliminated economic profits in the industry.

Firms in perfectly competitive markets are in a constant struggle to stay one step ahead of their competitors. They are always looking for new ways to provide a product, such as growing apples organically. It is possible for firms to find ways to earn an economic profit for a while, but to repeat the quote from a Yakima Valley organic apple farmer at the beginning of this chapter, "It's like anything else in agriculture. If people see an economic opportunity, usually it only lasts for a few years." This observation is not restricted to agriculture. In any perfectly competitive market, an opportunity to make economic profits never lasts long. As Sharon Oster, an economist at Yale University, has put it, "If everyone can do it, you can't make money at it."

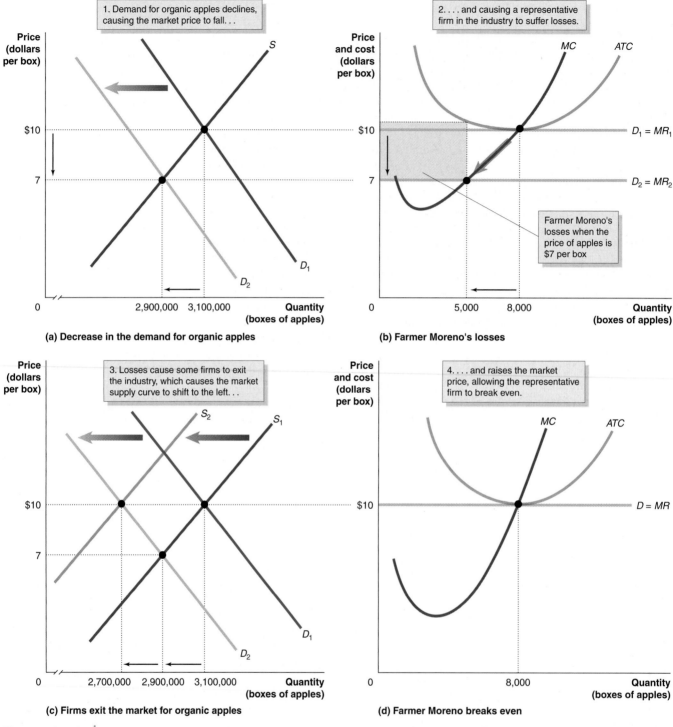

Figure 11-9 | The Effect of Exit on Economic Losses

When the price of apples is $10 per box, Farmer Moreno and other producers of organically grown apples are breaking even. A total quantity of 3,100,000 boxes is sold in the market. Farmer Moreno sells 8,000 boxes. Panel (a) shows a decline in the demand for organically grown apples from D_1 to D_2 that reduces the market price to $7 per box. Panel (b) shows that the falling price causes Farmer Moreno's demand curve to shift down from D_1 to D_2 and her output to fall from 8,000 to 5,000 boxes. At a market

price of $7 per box, farmers have economic losses, represented by the area of the red box. As a result, some farmers will exit the market, which shifts the market supply curve to the left. Panel (c) shows that exit continues until the supply curve has shifted from S_1 to S_2 and the market price has risen from $7 back to $10. Panel (d) shows that with the price back at $10, Farmer Moreno will break even. In the new market equilibrium, total production of organic apples has fallen from 3,100,000 to 2,700,000 boxes.

The Long-Run Supply Curve in a Perfectly Competitive Market

If the typical organic apple grower breaks even at a price of $10 per box, in the long run, the market price will always return to this level. If an increase in demand causes the market price to rise above $10, farmers will be earning economic profits. This profit will attract additional farmers into the market, and the market supply curve will shift to the right until the price is back to $10. Panel (a) in Figure 11-10 illustrates the long-run effect of an increase in demand. An increase in demand from D_1 to D_2 causes the market price to temporarily rise from $10 per box to $15. At this price, farmers are making economic profits growing organic apples, but these profits attract entry of new farmers' organic apples. The result is an increase in supply from S_1 to S_2, which forces the price back down to $10 per box and eliminates the economic profits.

Similarly, if a decrease in demand causes the market price to fall below $10, farmers will experience economic losses. These losses will cause some farmers to exit the market, the supply curve will shift to the left, and the price will return to $10. Panel (b) in Figure 11-10 illustrates the long-run effect of a decrease in demand. A decrease in demand from D_1 to D_2 causes the market price to fall temporarily from $10 per box to $7. At this price, farmers are suffering economic losses growing organic apples, but these losses cause some farmers to exit the market for organic apples. The result is a decrease in supply from S_1 to S_2, which forces the price back up to $10 per box and eliminates the losses.

The **long-run supply curve** shows the relationship in the long run between market price and the quantity supplied. In the long run, the price in the organic apple market will be $10 per box, no matter how many boxes of apples are produced. So, as Figure 11-10 shows, the long-run supply curve (S_{LR}) for organic apples is a horizontal line at a price of $10. Remember that the reason the price returns to $10 in the long run is that this is the price at which the typical firm in the industry just breaks even. The typical firm breaks even at this

Long-run supply curve A curve that shows the relationship in the long run between market price and the quantity supplied.

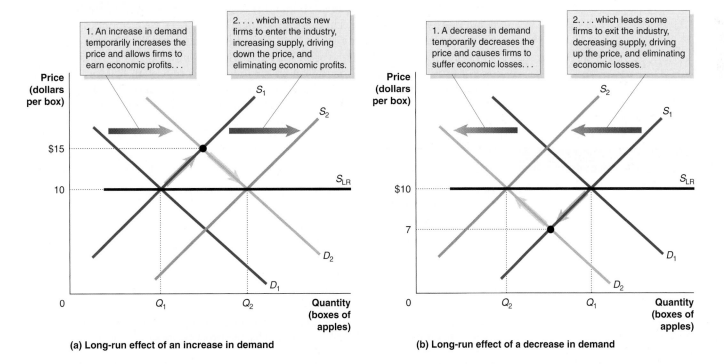

(a) Long-run effect of an increase in demand

(b) Long-run effect of a decrease in demand

Figure 11-10 | The Long-Run Supply Curve in a Perfectly Competitive Industry

Panel (a) shows that an increase in demand for organic apples will lead to a temporary increase in price from $10 to $15 per box, as the market demand curve shifts to the right, from D_1 to D_2. The entry of new firms shifts the market supply curve to the right, from S_1 to S_2, which will cause the price to fall back to its long-run level of $10. Panel (b) shows that a decrease in demand will lead to a temporary decrease in price from $10 to $7 per box, as the market demand curve shifts to the left, from D_1 to D_2. The exit of firms shifts the market supply curve to the left, from S_1 to S_2, which causes the price to rise back to its long-run level of $10. The long-run supply curve (S_{LR}) shows the relationship between market price and the quantity supplied in the long run. In this case, the long-run supply curve is a horizontal line.

price because it is at the minimum point on the firm's average total cost curve. We can draw the important conclusion that *in the long run, a perfectly competitive market will supply whatever amount of a good consumers demand at a price determined by the minimum point on the typical firm's average total cost curve.*

Because the position of the long-run supply curve is determined by the minimum point on the typical firm's average total cost curve, anything that raises or lowers the costs of the typical firm in the long run will cause the long-run supply curve to shift. For example, if a disease infects apple trees and the costs of treating the disease adds $2 per box to the cost of producing apples, the long-run supply curve will shift up by $2.

Increasing-Cost and Decreasing-Cost Industries

Any industry in which the typical firm's average costs do not change as the industry expands production will have a horizontal long-run supply curve, like the one in Figure 11-10. Industries, like the apple industry, where this holds true are called *constant-cost industries*. It's possible, however, for the typical firm's average costs to change as an industry expands.

For example, if an input used in producing a good is available in only limited quantities, the cost of the input will rise as the industry expands. If only a limited amount of land is available on which to grow the grapes to make a certain variety of wine, an increase in demand for wine made from these grapes will result in competition for the land and will drive up its price. As a result, more of the wine will be produced in the long run only if the price rises to cover the higher average costs of the typical firm. In this case, the long-run supply curve will slope upward. Industries with upward-sloping long-run supply curves are called *increasing-cost industries*.

Finally, in some cases, the typical firm's costs may fall as the industry expands. Suppose that someone invents a new microwave that uses as an input a specialized memory chip that is currently produced only in small quantities. If demand for the microwave increases, firms that produce microwaves will increase their orders for the memory chip. We saw in Chapter 10 that if there are economies of scale in producing a good, its average cost will decline as output increases. If there are economies of scale in producing this memory chip, the average cost of producing it will fall, and competition will result in its price falling as well. This price decline, in turn, will lower the average cost of producing the new microwave. In the long run, competition will force the price of the microwave to fall to the level of the new lower average cost of the typical firm. In this case, the long-run supply curve will slope downward. Industries with downward-sloping long-run supply curves are called *decreasing-cost industries*.

11.6 | Explain how perfect competition leads to economic efficiency.

Perfect Competition and Efficiency

Notice how powerful consumers are in a market system. If consumers want more organic apples, the market will supply them. This happens not because a government bureaucrat in Washington, DC, or an official in an apple growers' association gives orders. The additional apples are produced because an increase in demand results in higher prices and a higher rate of return on investments in organic growing techniques. Apple growers, trying to get the highest possible return on their investment, begin to switch from using conventional growing methods to using organic growing methods. If consumers lose their taste for organic apples and demand falls, the process works in reverse.

Making the Connection | **The Decline of Apple Production in New York State**

Although New York State is second only to Washington State in production of apples, its production has been declining during the past 20 years. The decline has been particularly steep in counties close to New York City. In 1985, there were more than 11,000 acres of apple orchards in Ulster County, which is 75 miles north of New York City. Today, fewer than 5,000 acres remain. As it became difficult for apple growers in the county to compete with lower-cost producers elsewhere, the resources these entrepreneurs were using to produce apples—particularly land— became more valuable in other uses. Many farmers sold their land to housing developers. As one apple farmer put it, "Over the last ten years or so, [apple] prices have been stagnant or going down. I didn't see a return on the money, and I didn't want to continue."

In a market system, entrepreneurs will not continue to employ economic resources to produce a good or service unless consumers are willing to pay a price at least high enough for them to break even. Consumers were not willing to pay a high enough price for apples for many New York State apple growers to break even on their investments. As a result, resources left apple production in that state.

Sources: Lisa W. Foderaro, "Where Apples Don't Pay, Developers Will," *New York Times*, June 23, 2001; and USDA, *2002 Census of Agriculture, Volume 1, Chapter 2*, New York County Level Data, Table 31.

When apple growers in New York State stopped breaking even, many sold their land to housing developers.

YOUR TURN: Test your understanding by doing related problem 6.7 on page 409 at the end of this chapter.

Productive Efficiency

In the market system, consumers get as many apples as they want, produced at the lowest average cost possible. The forces of competition will drive the market price to the minimum average cost of the typical firm. **Productive efficiency** refers to the situation in which a good or service is produced at the lowest possible cost. As we have seen, perfect competition results in productive efficiency.

The managers of every firm strive to earn an economic profit by reducing costs. But in a perfectly competitive market, other firms quickly copy ways of reducing costs, so that in the long run, only the consumer benefits from cost reductions.

Productive efficiency The situation in which a good or service is produced at the lowest possible cost.

Solved Problem | 11-6

How Productive Efficiency Benefits Consumers

Writing in the *New York Times* on the technology boom of the late 1990s, Michael Lewis argues "The sad truth, for investors, seems to be that most of the benefits of new technologies are passed right through to consumers free of charge."

a. What do you think Lewis means by the benefits of new technology being "passed right through to consumers free of charge"? Use a graph like Figure 11-8 on page 394 to illustrate your answer.

b. Explain why this result is a "sad truth" for investors.

SOLVING THE PROBLEM:

Step 1: **Review the chapter material.** This problem is about perfect competition and efficiency, so you may want to review the section "Perfect Competition and Efficiency," which begins on page 398.

Step 2: **Use the concepts from this chapter to explain what Lewis means.** By "new technologies," Lewis means new products—like cell phones or plasma television sets—or lower-cost ways of producing existing products. In either case, new technologies will allow firms to earn economic profits for a while, but these profits will lead new firms to enter the market in the long run.

Step 3: **Use a graph like Figure 11-8 to illustrate why the benefits of new technologies are "passed right through to consumers free of charge."** Figure 11-8 shows the situation in which a firm is making economic profits in the short run but has these profits eliminated by entry in the long run. We can draw a similar graph to analyze what happens in the long run in the market for plasma televisions:

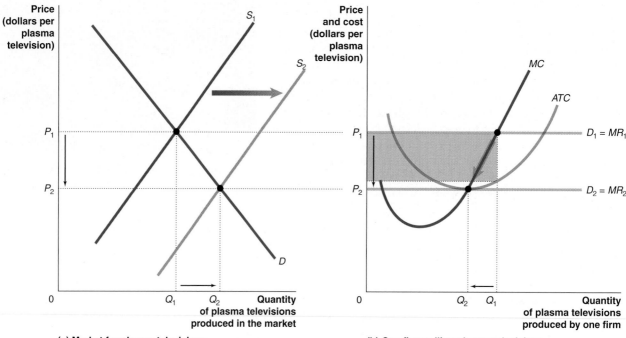

(a) Market for plasma televisions

(b) One firm selling plasma televisions

When plasma televisions were first introduced, prices were high, and only a few firms were in the market. Panel (a) shows that the initial equilibrium price in the market for plasma televisions is P_1. Panel (b) shows that at this price, the typical firm in the industry is earning an economic profit, which is shown by the green-shaded box. The economic profit attracts new firms into the industry. This entry shifts the market supply curve from S_1 to S_2 in panel (a) and lowers the equilibrium price from P_1 to P_2. Panel (b) shows that at the new market price, P_2, the typical firm is breaking even. Therefore, plasma televisions are being produced at the lowest possible cost, and productive efficiency is achieved. Consumers receive the new technology "free of charge" in the sense that they only have to pay a price equal to the lowest possible cost of production.

Step 4: **Answer question (b) by explaining why the result in question (a) is a "sad truth" for investors.** We have seen in answering question (a) that in the long run, firms only break even on their investment in producing high-technology goods. That result implies that investors in these firms are also unlikely to earn an economic profit in the long run.

EXTRA CREDIT: Lewis is using a key result from this chapter: In the long run, entry of new firms competes away economic profits. We should notice that, strictly speaking, the high-technology industries Lewis is discussing are not perfectly competitive. Cell phones or plasma televisions, for instance, are not identical, and each cell phone company produces a quantity large enough to affect the market price. However, as we will see in Chapter 12, these deviations from perfect competition do not change the important conclusion that the entry of new firms benefits consumers by forcing prices down to the level of average cost. In fact, the price of plasma televisions dropped by more than 75 percent within five years of their first becoming widely available.

Source: Michael Lewis, "In Defense of the Boom," *New York Times*, October 27, 2002.

YOUR TURN: For more practice, do related problems 6.4, 6.5, and 6.6 on page 409 at the end of this chapter.

>> **End Solved Problem 11-6**

Allocative Efficiency

Not only do perfectly competitive firms produce goods and services at the lowest possible cost, they also produce the goods and services that consumers value most. Firms will produce a good up to the point where the marginal cost of producing another unit is equal to the marginal benefit consumers receive from consuming that unit. In other words, firms will supply all those goods that provide consumers with a marginal benefit at least as great as the marginal cost of producing them. We know this is true because:

1 The price of a good represents the marginal benefit consumers receive from consuming the last unit of the good sold.

2 Perfectly competitive firms produce up to the point where the price of the good equals the marginal cost of producing the last unit.

3 Therefore, firms produce up to the point where the last unit provides a marginal benefit to consumers equal to the marginal cost of producing it.

These statements are another way of saying that entrepreneurs in a market system efficiently *allocate* labor, machinery, and other inputs to produce the goods and services that best satisfy consumer wants. In this sense, perfect competition achieves **allocative efficiency**. As we will explore in the next few chapters, many goods and services sold in the U.S. economy are not produced in perfectly competitive markets. Nevertheless, productive efficiency and allocative efficiency are useful benchmarks against which to compare the actual performance of the economy.

Allocative efficiency A state of the economy in which production represents consumer preferences; in particular, every good or service is produced up to the point where the last unit provides a marginal benefit to consumers equal to the marginal cost of producing it.

Economics in YOUR Life!

>> Continued from page 377

At the beginning of the chapter, we asked you to think about why you can charge only a relatively low price for performing services such as babysitting or lawn mowing. In the chapter, we saw that firms selling products in competitive markets are unable to charge prices higher than those being charged by competing firms. The market for babysitting and lawn mowing is very competitive. In most neighborhoods, there are a lot of teenagers willing to supply these services. The price you can charge for babysitting may not be worth your while at age 20 but is enough to cover the opportunity cost of a 14-year-old eager to enter the market. (Or, as we put it in Table 11-1 on page 378, the ease of entry into babysitting and lawn mowing is high.) So, in your career as a teenage entrepreneur, you may have become familiar with one of the lessons of this chapter: A firm in a competitive market has no control over price.

Conclusion

The competitive forces of the market impose relentless pressure on firms to produce new and better goods and services at the lowest possible cost. Firms that fail to adequately anticipate changes in consumer tastes or that fail to adopt the latest and most efficient technology do not survive in the long run. In the nineteenth century, the biologist Charles Darwin developed a theory of evolution based on the idea of the "survival of the fittest." Only those plants and animals that are best able to adapt to the demands of their environment are able to survive. Darwin first realized the important role that the struggle for existence plays in the natural world after reading early nineteenth-century economists' descriptions of the role it plays in the economic world. Just as "survival of the fittest" is the rule in nature, so it is in the economic world.

At the start of this chapter, we saw that there are four market structures: perfect competition, monopolistic competition, oligopoly, and monopoly. Now that we have studied perfect competition, in the following chapters we move on to the other three market structures. Before turning to those chapters, read *An Inside Look* on the next page to learn how firms are rushing to enter the market for organic snacks.

Why Are Organic Farmers Worried about Wal-Mart?

BUSINESSWEEK, MARCH 29, 2006

Wal-Mart's Organic Offensive

Richard DeWilde has a long history with organic farming. His grandfather, Nick Hoogshagen, adopted the organic approach five decades ago on his farm in South Dakota, well before it became popular with consumers and fueled the popularity of retailers like Whole Foods Market.

Now, DeWilde, 57 is a working farmer himself, carrying on the family tradition of avoiding pesticides and other chemicals that can contaminate food in favor of a more natural approach. He's co-owner of Harmony Valley Farm, which grows Swiss chard, parsnips, turnips, and kale on 100 acres in the southwestern corner of Wisconsin. So you might think that DeWilde would be overjoyed at the news that Wal-Mart has finally come around to his grandfather's philosophy. The juggernaut retailer said recently that it plans to double its offering of organic product, including produce, dairy, and dry goods.

But DeWilde isn't thrilled. Instead, he's dismayed at the prospect of Wal-Mart becoming a player in the organic market. He fears that the company will use its market strength to drive down prices and hurt U.S. farmers. "Wal-Mart has the reputation of beating up on its suppliers," says DeWilde. "I certainly don't see 'selling at a lower price' as an opportunity."

He's hardly the only one. Many farmers who have benefited from the strong demand and healthy margins for organic goods are fretting that the market's newfound success also brings with it newfound risks. As large companies enter the market, from Kraft and Dean Foods to Wal-Mart, farmers worry that the corporatization of organic foods could have negative consequences.

Large corporations have taken sizable steps into the organic market, even if it isn't always obvious from the brands on store shelves. Silk, the best-selling branded soy milk, is a product from Dean Foods, the $10 billion behemoth that sells the most milk in the country. Cascadian Farms, which makes organic cereal, frozen fruits, and other products, is a brand of cereal giant General Mills. And Kraft owns Boca Burgers. . . .

Organic farmers are straining to meet rising demand, one of the reasons that legislators have been willing to drop certain requirements for organic foods. In the past year, the demand for organic milk outstripped the supply by 10% and created acute shortages. That even prompted organic dairy company Stonyfield Farms to stop producing its fat-free 32-ounce cups of yogurt. Now Stonyfield has resumed its production, but organic milk consumption nationwide is growing 30% annually.

Wal-Mart is making its aggressive move into organics at the same time it's trying to improve its environmental image. Last year, it embarked on a new green policy and has several initiatives to demonstrate how serious it is. The company recently said that it will require that all its wild-caught fresh and frozen fish meet the Marine Stewardship Council's standard for sustainable and well-managed fisheries. Fish accounts for a third of all the chain's seafood sales. . . .

While some farmers are concerned that Wal-Mart may try to squeeze them financially, there could be a more benign impact. Farmers who now use pesticides and other chemicals could turn to organic farming, as they see increased demand. Consider what's happening in California.

Last year, the state showed an increase of 40,000 acres, or 27%, in organic livestock production. The number of acres dedicated to organic vegetable production increased by 5,000 acres, or 12%, according to the California Certified Organic Farmers, an organics trade association. "Strong demand is creating markets here," says Jake Lewin, director of marketing at the organization.

Meanwhile, back in Wisconsin, DeWilde is preparing for warmer weather and the spring planting season. He is worried about how the increasing attention from Wal-Mart and other large companies may change the business of organic foods. Yet he's more convinced than ever of the benefits of the approach his grandfather helped champion. "It's the future of farming," he says.

Source: Pallavi Gogoi, "Wal-Mart's Organic Offensive," *BusinessWeek*, March 29, 2006.

Key Points in the Article

The increasing popularity of organic food has caught the attention of large food producers, such as Dean Foods, which produces Silk, the best-selling brand of soy milk. Wal-Mart, which is the largest seller of groceries in the United States, has also begun to offer more organic foods for sale. Some farmers who supply organic foods are concerned that Wal-Mart may offer lower prices than they have been receiving from supermarkets. Other farmers believe that if Wal-Mart begins selling more organic foods it may increase the popularity of these products and increase the demand for them.

Analyzing the News

ⓐ One of the key points of this chapter is that, ultimately, it is *consumers* who decide which goods will be produced. If consumers increase their demand for organic foods, then firms will redirect workers, machines, and natural resources toward producing those goods. One industry analyst (not quoted in the article) observed, "Organic is a niche, but a very profitable niche. Give consumers what they truly want/need and they will dig deeply into their pockets."

In fact, it is those profits that signal to entrepreneurs that demand for organic foods has increased. We know from the analysis in this chapter, though, that these profits will not persist in the long run. Figure 1 shows that an increase in demand for organic food raises the price from P_1 to P_2, which results in the typical firm earning economic profits.

ⓑ Figure 2 shows the long-run result. The economic profit earned by producing organic foods will attract additional firms to enter the industry. As the article mentions, farmers in California are taking resources out of non-organic farming and putting them into organic farming. The entrance of new firms will eventually cause the market price to fall back to P_1. At a price of P_1, the typical firm is once again breaking even. The increase in consumer demand for organic foods results in the quantity supplied rising in the long run, as new firms enter the industry. In the long run the typical firm in a perfectly competitive industry breaks even, as economic profits are competed away.

Thinking Critically

1. Use a demand and supply graph and a cost curve graph to show what would happen if the government tightened its regulations, making it more difficult for foods to be labeled as "organic."

2. Suppose that farmers who produce organic foods protest to Congress as prices decline. Use a demand and supply graph to show the impact on the market for organic foods if Congress decides to impose a price floor above the equilibrium price. What happens to consumer surplus and producer surplus as a result of the price floor?

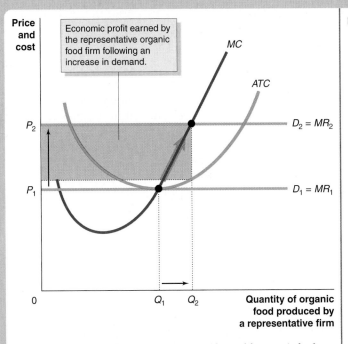

Figure 1. The short-run effects of an increase in demand for organic food.

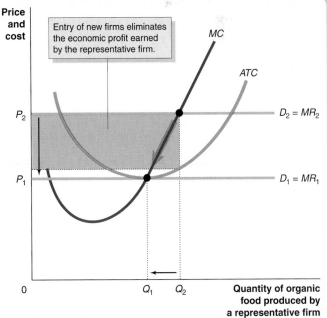

Figure 2. The long-run effects of an increase in demand for organic foods.

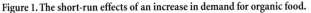

403

Key Terms

Allocative efficiency, p. 401

Average revenue (*AR*), p. 382

Economic loss, p. 395

Economic profit, p. 394

Long-run competitive equilibrium, p. 395

Long-run supply curve, p. 397

Marginal revenue (*MR*), p. 382

Perfectly competitive market, p. 379

Price taker, p. 379

Productive efficiency, p. 399

Profit, p. 381

Shutdown point, p. 391

Sunk cost, p. 390

11.1 LEARNING OBJECTIVE   11.1 | Define a perfectly competitive market and explain why a perfect competitor faces a horizontal demand curve, **pages 379–381.**

Perfectly Competitive Markets

Summary

A **perfectly competitive market** must have many buyers and sellers, firms must be producing identical products, and there must be no barriers to entry of new firms. The demand curve for a good or service produced in a perfectly competitive market is downward sloping, but the demand curve for the output of one firm in a perfectly competitive market is a horizontal line at the market price. Firms in perfectly competitive markets are **price takers** and see their sales drop to zero if they attempt to charge more than the market price.

myeconlab   Visit www.myeconlab.com to complete these exercises *Get Ahead of the Curve* online and get instant feedback.

Review Questions

1.1 What are the three conditions for a market to be perfectly competitive?

1.2 What is a price taker? When are firms likely to be price takers?

1.3 Draw a graph showing the market demand and supply for corn and the demand for the corn produced by one corn farmer. Be sure to indicate the market price and the price received by the corn farmer.

Problems and Applications

1.4 Explain whether each of the following is a perfectly competitive market. For each market that is not perfectly competitive, explain why it is not.
   a. Corn farming
   b. Retail bookselling
   c. Automobile manufacturing
   d. New home construction

1.5 Why are consumers usually price takers when they buy most goods and services, while relatively few firms are price takers?

1.6 **(Related to the *Don't Let This Happen to You!* on page 380)** Explain whether you agree or disagree with the following remark:

> According to the model of perfectly competitive markets, the demand for wheat should be a horizontal line. But this can't be true: When the price of wheat rises, the quantity of wheat demanded falls, and when the price of wheat falls, the quantity of wheat demanded rises. Therefore, the demand for wheat is not a horizontal line.

1.7 The financial writer Andrew Tobias has described an incident when he was a student at the Harvard Business School: Each student in the class was given large amounts of information about a particular firm and asked to determine a pricing strategy for the firm. Most of the students spent hours preparing their answers and came to class carrying many sheets of paper with their calculations. Tobias came up with the correct answer after just a few minutes and without having made any calculations. When his professor called on him in class for an answer, Tobias stated, "The case said the XYZ Company was in a very competitive industry . . . and the case said that the company had all the business it could handle." Given this information, what price do you think Tobias argued the company should charge? Briefly explain. (Tobias says the class greeted his answer with "thunderous applause.")

Source: Andrew Tobias, *The Only Investment Guide You'll Ever Need*, San Diego: Harcourt, 2005, pp. 6–8.

>> End Learning Objective 11.1

11.2 LEARNING OBJECTIVE   11.2 | Explain how a firm maximizes profits in a perfectly competitive market,
pages 381–384.

How a Firm Maximizes Profit in a Perfectly Competitive Market

Summary

Profit is the difference between total revenue (*TR*) and total cost (*TC*). **Average revenue** (*AR*) is total revenue divided by the quantity of the product sold. A firm maximizes profit by producing the level of output where the difference between revenue and cost is the greatest. This is the same level of output where marginal revenue is equal to marginal cost. **Marginal revenue** is the change in total revenue from selling one more unit.

 Visit www.myeconlab.com to complete these exercises
Get Ahead of the Curve online and get instant feedback.

Review Questions

2.1 Explain why it is true that for a firm in a perfectly competitive market that $P = MR = AR$.

2.2 Explain why it is true that for a firm in a perfectly competitive market, the profit-maximizing condition $MR = MC$ is equivalent to the condition $P = MC$.

Problems and Applications

2.3 A student argues: "To maximize profit, a firm should produce the quantity where the difference between marginal revenue and marginal cost is the greatest. If it produces more than this quantity, then the profit made on each additional unit will be falling." Briefly explain whether you agree with this reasoning.

2.4 Why don't firms maximize revenue rather than profit? If a firm decided to maximize revenue, would it be likely to produce a smaller or a larger quantity than if it were maximizing profit? Briefly explain.

2.5 Refer to Table 11-2 on page 382 and Table 11-3 on page 383. Suppose the price of wheat rises to $6.00 per bushel. How many bushels of wheat will Farmer Parker produce, and how much profit will he make? Briefly explain.

2.6 Refer to Table 11-2 and Table 11-3. Suppose that the marginal cost of wheat is $0.50 higher for every bushel of wheat produced. For example, the marginal cost of producing the eighth bushel of wheat is now $6.50. Assume that the price of wheat remains $4 per bushel. Will this increase in marginal cost change the profit-maximizing level of production for Farmer Parker? Briefly explain. How much profit will Farmer Parker make now?

>> **End Learning Objective 11.2**

11.3 LEARNING OBJECTIVE   11.3 | Use graphs to show a firm's profit or loss, **pages 385–390.**

Illustrating Profit or Loss on the Cost Curve Graph

Summary

From the definitions of profit and average total cost, we can develop the following expression for the relationship between total profit and average total cost: Profit = $(P - ATC) \times Q$. Using this expression, we can determine the area showing profit or loss on a cost-curve graph: The area of profit or loss is a box with a height equal to price minus average total cost (for profit) or average total cost minus price (for loss) and a base equal to the quantity of output.

 Visit www.myeconlab.com to complete these exercises
Get Ahead of the Curve online and get instant feedback.

Review Questions

3.1 Draw a graph showing a firm in a perfectly competitive market that is making a profit. Be sure your graph includes the firm's demand curve, marginal revenue curve, marginal cost curve, average total cost curve, and average variable cost curve and make sure to indicate the area representing the firm's profits.

3.2 Draw a graph showing a firm in a perfectly competitive market that is operating at a loss. Be sure your graph includes the firm's demand curve, marginal revenue curve, marginal cost curve, average total cost curve, and average variable cost curve and make sure to indicate the area representing the firm's losses.

Problems and Applications

3.3 (Related to *Solved Problem 11-3* on page 386) Frances sells earrings in the perfectly competitive earring market. Her output per day and costs are as follows:

OUTPUT PER DAY	TOTAL COST
0	$1.00
1	2.50
2	3.50
3	4.20
4	4.50
5	5.20
6	6.80
7	8.70
8	10.70
9	13.00

a. If the current equilibrium price in the earring market is $1.80, how many earrings will Frances produce, what price will she charge, and how much profit (or loss) will she make? Draw a graph to illustrate your answer. Your graph should be clearly labeled and should include Frances's demand, *ATC*, *AVC*, *MC*, and *MR* curves; the price she is charging; the quantity she is producing; and the area representing her profit (or loss).

b. Suppose the equilibrium price of earrings falls to $1.00. Now how many earrings will Frances produce, what price will she charge, and how much profit (or loss) will she make? Show your work. Draw a graph to illustrate this situation, using the instructions in question (a).

c. Suppose the equilibrium price of earrings falls to $0.25. Now how many earrings will Frances produce, what price will she charge, and how much profit (or loss) will she make?

3.4 (Related to *Solved Problem 11-3* on page 386) Review Solved Problem 11-3 and then answer the following: Suppose the equilibrium price of basketballs falls to $2.50. Now how many basketballs will Andy produce? What price will he charge? How much profit (or loss) will he make?

3.5 (Related to the *Don't Let This Happen to You!* on page 388) A student examines the following

graph and argues, "I believe that a firm will want to produce at Q_1, not Q_2. At Q_1, the distance between price and marginal cost is the greatest. Therefore, at Q_1, the firm will be maximizing its profits." Briefly explain whether you agree with the student's argument.

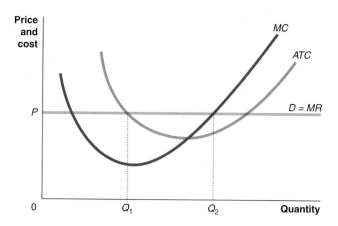

3.6 According to a report in the *Wall Street Journal*, during the fourth quarter of 2003, the profits of British Airways rose to £83 million, from £13 million one year earlier. At the same time, "the average amount the airline makes on each paying passenger fell 0.8%." If profit per passenger fell, how could total profits rise? Illustrate your answer with a graph. Be sure to indicate profit per passenger and total profit on the graph.

Source: Emma Blake, "British Airways Reports Sharp Jump in Net Profits," *Wall Street Journal*, February 9, 2004.

3.7 The following is from an article in the *Los Angeles Times*: "Gerald Lasseigne, a 53-year-old information systems technician in Donaldsonville, La., lost his job last month when steep natural gas prices forced Triad Nitrogen to shut down its fertilizer plant on the banks of the Mississippi River." Draw a graph showing the Triad Nitrogen company earning a profit from its fertilizer plant before the increase in the price of natural gas. Draw a second graph showing why Triad Nitrogen shut down the plant following the increase in the price of natural gas.

Source: Warren Vieth and Aparna Kumar, "Higher Oil Prices Ooze into Economy," *Los Angeles Times*, March 25, 2003, p. C1.

3.8 (Related to the *Making the Connection* on page 389) Suppose the medical screening firms had run an effective advertising campaign which convinced a large number of people that yearly CT scans were critical for good health. How would this have changed the fortunes of these firms? Illustrate your answer with a graph showing the situation for a representative firm in the industry. Be sure your graph includes the firm's demand curve, marginal revenue curve, marginal cost curve, and average total cost curve.

>> **End Learning Objective 11.3**

Deciding Whether to Produce or to Shut Down in the Short Run

Summary

In deciding whether to shut down or produce during a given period, a firm should ignore its *sunk costs*. A **sunk cost** is a cost that has already been paid and that cannot by recovered. In the short run, a firm continues to produce as long as its price is at least equal to its average variable cost. A perfectly competitive firm's **shutdown point** is the minimum point on the firm's average variable cost curve. If price falls below average variable cost, the firm shuts down in the short run. For prices above the shutdown point, a perfectly competitive firm's marginal cost curve is also its supply curve.

 Visit www.myeconlab.com to complete these exercises
Get Ahead of the Curve online and get instant feedback.

Review Questions

4.1 What is the difference between a firm's shutdown point in the short run and in the long run? Why are firms willing to accept losses in the short run but not in the long run?

4.2 What is the relationship between a perfectly competitive firm's marginal cost curve and its supply curve?

Problems and Applications

4.3 Edward Scahill produces table lamps in the perfectly competitive desk lamp market.
a. Fill in the missing values in the table.

OUTPUT PER WEEK	TOTAL COSTS	AFC	AVC	ATC	MC
0	$100				
1	150				
2	175				
3	190				
4	210				
5	240				
6	280				
7	330				
8	390				
9	460				
10	540				

b. Suppose the equilibrium price in the desk lamp market is $50. How many table lamps should Edward produce, and how much profit will he make?
c. If next week the equilibrium price of desk lamps drops to $30, should Edward shut down? Explain.

4.4 The graph represents the situation of a perfectly competitive firm.

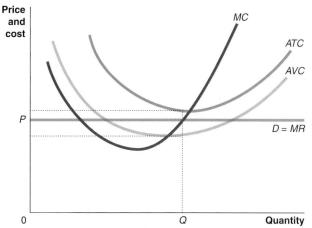

Indicate on the graph the areas that represent the following:
a. Total cost
b. Total revenue
c. Variable cost
d. Profit or loss
   Briefly explain whether the firm will continue to produce in the short run.

4.5 (Related to the *Making the Connection* on page 390) Suppose you decide to open a copy store. You rent store space (signing a one-year lease to do so), and you take out a loan at a local bank and use the money to purchase 10 copiers. Six months later, a large chain opens a copy store two blocks away from yours. As a result, the revenue you receive from your copy store, while sufficient to cover the wages of your employees and the costs of paper and utilities, doesn't cover all your rent and the interest and repayment costs on the loan you took out to purchase the copiers. Should you continue operating your business?

4.6 (Related to the *Making the Connection* on page 390) Club Mediterranee operates 120 Club Med resorts around the world. Following the September 11, 2001, terrorist attacks on the United States, many American tourists were reluctant to travel to foreign resorts. As a result, the prices Club Med could charge visitors to its resorts declined. In November 2001, Club Med decided to temporarily shut down 15 of its resorts. Analyze possible reasons for Club Med's decision. Be sure to discuss the likely relationship between the revenue Club Med received from operating these resorts and the resorts' fixed and variable costs.

Source: Rafer Guzmán, "Club Med Plans to Temporarily Close 15 Resorts," *Wall Street Journal*, November 9, 2001, p. B1.

11.5 LEARNING OBJECTIVE   11.5 | Explain how entry and exit ensure that perfectly competitive firms earn zero economic profit in the long run, **pages 393-398.**

"If Everyone Can Do It, You Can't Make Money at It": The Entry and Exit of Firms in the Long Run

Summary

Economic profit is a firm's revenues minus all its costs, implicit and explicit. **Economic loss** is the situation in which a firm's total revenue is less than its total cost, including all implicit costs. If firms make economic profits in the short run, new firms enter the industry until the market price has fallen enough to wipe out the profits. If firms make economic losses, firms exit the industry until the market price has risen enough to wipe out the losses. **Long-run competitive equilibrium** is the situation in which the entry and exit of firms has resulted in the typical firm breaking even. The **long-run supply curve** shows the relationship between market price and the quantity supplied.

myeconlab Visit www.myeconlab.com to complete these exercises *Get Ahead of the Curve* online and get instant feedback.

Review Questions

5.1   When are firms likely to enter an industry? When are they likely to exit an industry?

5.2   Would a firm earning zero economic profit continue to produce, even in the long run?

5.3   Discuss the shape of the long-run supply curve in a perfectly competitive market. Suppose that a perfectly competitive market is initially at long-run equilibrium and then there is a permanent decrease in the demand for the product. Draw a graph showing how the market adjusts in the long run.

Problems and Applications

5.4   Suppose an assistant professor of economics is earning a salary of $65,000 per year. One day she quits her job, sells $100,000 worth of bonds that had been earning 5 percent per year, and uses the funds to open a bookstore. At the end of the year, she shows an accounting profit of $80,000 on her income tax return. What is her economic profit?

5.5   Suppose that you and your sister both decide to open copy stores. Your parents always liked your sister better than you, so they purchase and give to her free of charge the three copiers she needs to operate her store. You, however, have to rent your copiers for $1,500 per month each. Does your sister have lower costs in operating her copy store than you have in operating your copy store because of this? Explain.

5.6   Consider the following statement: "The products for which demand is the greatest will also be the products that are most profitable to produce." Briefly explain whether you agree with this statement.

5.7   In panel (b) of Figure 11-9 on page 396, Anne Moreno reduces her output from 8,000 to 5,000 boxes of apples when the price falls to $7. At this price and this output level, she is operating at a loss. Why doesn't she just continue charging the original $10 and continue producing 8,000 boxes of apples?

5.8   The following statement appeared in a Congressional analysis of the airline industry: "In lean times, airlines can operate for extended periods of time [while making losses] . . . because revenues will cover a large part of their costs (Pan Am lost money for about a decade before finally closing down)." Why would Pan Am—or any other airline—continue losing money for 10 years rather than shut down immediately? In the statement "revenues will cover a large part of their costs," does it matter if the costs being referred to are fixed costs or variable costs? Briefly explain.
    Source: Joint Economic Committee, Democratic Staff, *Assessing Losses for the Airline Industry and Its Workers in the Aftermath of the Terrorist Attacks*, October 3, 2001.

5.9   A student in a principles of economics course makes the following remark: "The economic model of perfectly competitive markets is fine in theory but not very realistic. It predicts that in the long run, a firm in a perfectly competitive market will earn no profits. No firm in the real world would stay in business if it earned zero profits." Do you agree with this remark?

5.10   Suppose that the laptop computer industry is perfectly competitive and that the firms that assemble laptops do not also make the displays, or screens, for them. Suppose that the laptop display industry is also perfectly competitive. Finally, suppose that because the demand for laptop displays is currently relatively small, firms in the laptop display industry have not been able to take advantage of all the economies of scale in laptop display production. Use a graph of the laptop computer market to illustrate the long-run effects on equilibrium price and quantity in the laptop computer market of a substantial and sustained increase in the demand for laptop computers. Use another graph to show the impact on the cost curves of a typical firm in the laptop computer industry. Briefly explain your graphs. Do your graphs indicate that the laptop computer industry is a constant-cost industry, an increasing-cost industry, or a decreasing-cost industry?

5.11 (Related to the *Chapter Opener* on page 376) If in the long run apple growers who use organic methods of cultivation make no greater rate of return on their investment than apple growers who use conventional methods, why did a significant number of apple growers switch from conventional to organic methods in the first place?

>> End Learning Objective 11.5

11.6 LEARNING OBJECTIVE   11.6 | Explain how perfect competition leads to economic efficiency, **pages 398–401.**

Perfect Competition and Efficiency

Summary

Perfect competition results in **productive efficiency,** which means that goods and services are produced at the lowest possible cost. Perfect competition also results in **allocative efficiency,** which means the goods and services are produced up to the point where the last unit provides a marginal benefit to consumers equal to the marginal cost of producing it.

 Visit www.myeconlab.com to complete these exercises online and get instant feedback.

Review Questions

6.1 What is meant by allocative efficiency? What is meant by productive efficiency? Briefly discuss the difference between these two concepts.

6.2 How does perfect competition lead to allocative and productive efficiency?

Problems and Applications

6.3 The chapter states, "Firms will supply all those goods that provide consumers with a marginal benefit at least as great as the marginal cost of producing them." A student objects to this statement by making the following argument: "I doubt that firms will really do this. After all, firms are in business to make a profit; they don't care about what is best for consumers." Evaluate the student's argument.

6.4 (Related to *Solved Problem 11-6* on page 399) Discuss the following statement: "In a perfectly competitive market, in the long run consumers benefit from reductions in costs, but firms don't." Don't firms also benefit from cost reductions because they are able to earn greater profits?

6.5 (Related to *Solved Problem 11-6* on page 399) Suppose you read the following item in a newspaper article under the headline "Price Gouging Alleged in Pencil Market":

Consumer advocacy groups charged at a press conference yesterday that there is widespread price gouging in the sale of pencils. They released a study showing that whereas the average retail price of pencils was $1.00, the average cost of producing pencils was only $0.50. "Pencils can be produced without complicated machinery or highly skilled workers, so there is no justification for companies charging a price that is twice what it costs them to produce the product. Pencils are too important in the life of every American for us to tolerate this sort of price gouging any longer," said George Grommet, chief spokesperson for the consumer groups. The consumer groups advocate passage of a law that would allow companies selling pencils to charge a price no more than 20 percent greater than their average cost of production.

Do you believe such a law would be advisable in a situation like this? Explain.

6.6 (Related to *Solved Problem 11-6* on page 399) In early 2007, Pioneer and JVC, two Japanese electronics firms, each announced that their profits would be lower than expected because they had been forced to cut prices for LCD and plasma television sets. Given the strong consumer demand for plasma television sets, shouldn't firms have been able to raise prices and increase their profits? Briefly explain.

Source: Hiroyuki Kachi, "Pioneer's Net Rises 74%, JVC Posts Loss," *Wall Street Journal,* February 1, 2007.

6.7 (Related to the *Making the Connection* on page 398) Suppose a nutritionist develops a revolutionary new diet that involves eating 10 apples per day. The new diet becomes wildly popular. What effect is the new diet likely to have on the number of apple orchards within 100 miles of New York City? What effect is the diet likely to have on housing prices in New York City?

>> End Learning Objective 11.6

Monopolistic Competition: The Competitive Model in a More Realistic Setting

Starbucks: Growth through Product Differentiation

Starbucks coffee shops seem to be everywhere—in malls, airports, Barnes & Noble bookstores, and practically everywhere else you can imagine. In 2008, Starbucks decided that they might be in too many places and announced they were closing 600 stores in the United States. Still, that left the company operating 15,000 stores worldwide. More than 44 million people visit a Starbucks each week.

Like many other firms that are currently large, Starbucks started small. In 1971, entrepreneurs Gordon Bowker, Gerald Baldwin, and Zev Siegl opened the first Starbucks in Seattle. About 10 years later, they hired Howard Schultz to manage the firm's retail sales and marketing. Schultz was determined to make the company first a national chain and then a worldwide chain. By 1993, Starbucks was opening stores on the East Coast, and in 1996, it opened its first store outside North America, in Tokyo, Japan. Today, Starbucks has stores in 38 countries. Schultz had achieved his dream and had become

chairman of the board and chief executive officer of the company.

Of course, fresh-brewed coffee has always been widely available in restaurants, diners, and donut shops. What Howard Schultz and the other Starbucks executives realized, however, was that a significant consumer demand existed for coffeehouses where customers could sit, relax, read newspapers, and drink higher-quality coffee than was typically served in diners or donut shops. The espresso-based coffees served at Starbucks were relatively difficult to find elsewhere during the 1990s, as Starbucks expanded nationally.

Still, Starbucks is *not* unique: You probably know of three or more coffeehouses in your neighborhood. The coffeehouse market is competitive because it is inexpensive to open a new store by leasing store space and buying espresso machines. Hundreds of firms in the United States operate coffeehouses. Some firms are large nationwide chains, such as Caribou Coffee and Diedrich Coffee, which have hundreds of stores. Others are regional chains, such as Dunn Brothers Coffee, which operates 65 stores in four states. Still others are small firms that operate only one store.

In Chapter 11, we discussed the situation of firms in perfectly competitive markets. These markets share three key characteristics:

1. There are many firms.
2. All firms sell identical products.
3. There are no barriers to new firms entering the industry.

The market Starbucks competes in shares two of these characteristics: There are many other coffeehouses—with the number increasing all the time—and the barriers to entering the market are very low. But consumers do not view the products sold by coffeehouses as being identical. The coffee at Starbucks, as well as the muffins and other snacks, are not identical to what competing coffeehouses offer. Selling coffee in coffeehouses is not like selling wheat: The products that Starbucks and its competitors sell are *differentiated* rather than identical. So, the coffeehouse market is *monopolistically competitive* rather than perfectly competitive. **AN INSIDE LOOK** on **page 430** explores one of the ways that businesses like Starbucks and Dunkin' Donuts attempt to differentiate themselves from the competition.

LEARNING Objectives

After studying this chapter, you should be able to:

12.1 Explain why a **monopolistically competitive firm** has downward-sloping **demand and marginal revenue curves**, page 412.

12.2 Explain how a monopolistically competitive firm **maximizes profits** in the **short run**, page 415.

12.3 Analyze the situation of a monopolistically competitive firm in the **long run**, page 417.

12.4 Compare the **efficiency** of monopolistic competition and perfect competition, page 423.

12.5 Define **marketing** and explain how firms use it to differentiate their products, page 425.

12.6 Identify the **key factors** that determine a **firm's success**, page 427.

Economics in YOUR Life!

Opening Your Own Restaurant

After you graduate, you plan to realize your dream of opening your own Italian restaurant. You are confident that many people will enjoy the pasta prepared with your grandmother's secret sauce. Although your hometown already has three Italian restaurants, you are convinced that you can enter this market and make a profit.

You have many choices to make in operating your restaurant. Will it be "family style," with sturdy but inexpensive furniture, where families with small—and noisy!—children will feel welcome, or will it be more elegant, with nice furniture, tablecloths, and candles? Will you offer a full menu or concentrate on just pasta dishes that use your grandmother's secret sauce? These and other choices you make will distinguish your restaurant from other competing restaurants. What's likely to happen in the restaurant market in your hometown after you open? How successful are you likely to be? See if you can answer these questions as you read this chapter. You can check your answers against those we provide at the end of the chapter. **>> Continued on page 429**

Monopolistic competition A market structure in which barriers to entry are low and many firms compete by selling similar, but not identical, products.

Many markets in the U.S. economy are similar to the coffeehouse market: They have many buyers and sellers, and the barriers to entry are low, but the goods and services offered for sale are differentiated rather than identical. Examples of these markets include consumer electronics stores, restaurants, movie theaters, supermarkets, and manufacturers of men's and women's clothing. In fact, the majority of the firms you patronize are competing in **monopolistically competitive** markets.

In Chapter 11, we saw how perfect competition benefits consumers and results in economic efficiency. Will these same desirable outcomes also hold for monopolistically competitive markets? This question, which we explore in this chapter, is important because monopolistically competitive markets are so common.

12.1 LEARNING OBJECTIVE

12.1 | Explain why a monopolistically competitive firm has downward-sloping demand and marginal revenue curves.

Demand and Marginal Revenue for a Firm in a Monopolistically Competitive Market

If the Starbucks coffeehouse located one mile from your house raises the price for a caffè latte from $3.00 to $3.25, it will lose some, but not all, of its customers. Some customers will switch to buying their coffee at another store, but other customers will be willing to pay the higher price for a variety of reasons: This store may be closer to them, or they may prefer Starbucks caffè lattes to similar coffees at competing stores. Because changing the price affects the quantity of caffè lattes sold, a Starbucks store will face a downward-sloping demand curve rather than the horizontal demand curve that a wheat farmer faces.

The Demand Curve for a Monopolistically Competitive Firm

Figure 12-1 shows how a change in price affects the quantity of caffè lattes Starbucks sells. The increase in the price from $3.00 to $3.25 decreases the quantity of caffè lattes sold from 3,000 per week to 2,400 per week.

Figure 12-1

The Downward-Sloping Demand for Caffè Lattes at a Starbucks

If a Starbucks increases the price of caffè lattes, it will lose some, but not all, of its customers. In this case, raising the price from $3.00 to $3.25 reduces the quantity of caffè lattes sold from 3,000 to 2,400. Therefore, unlike a perfect competitor, a Starbucks store faces a downward-sloping demand curve.

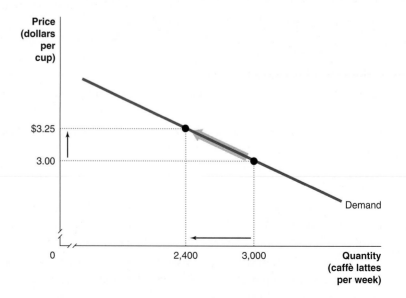

Marginal Revenue for a Firm with a Downward-Sloping Demand Curve

Recall from Chapter 11 that for a firm in a perfectly competitive market, the demand curve and the marginal revenue curve are the same. A perfectly competitive firm faces a horizontal demand curve and does not have to cut the price to sell a larger quantity. A monopolistically competitive firm, however, must cut the price to sell more, so its marginal revenue curve will slope downward and will be below its demand curve.

The data in Table 12-1 illustrate this point. To keep the numbers simple, let's assume that your local Starbucks coffeehouse is very small and sells at most 10 caffè lattes per week. If Starbucks charges a price of $6.00 or more, all of its potential customers will buy their coffee somewhere else. If it charges $5.50, it will sell 1 caffè latte per week. For each additional $0.50 Starbucks reduces the price, it increases the number of caffè lattes it sells by 1. The third column in the table shows how the firm's *total revenue* changes as it sells more caffè lattes. The fourth column shows the firm's revenue per unit, or its *average revenue*. Average revenue is equal to total revenue divided by quantity. Because total revenue equals price multiplied by quantity, dividing by quantity leaves just price. Therefore, *average revenue is always equal to price*. This result will be true for firms selling in any of the four market structures we discussed in Chapter 11.

The last column shows the firm's marginal revenue, or the amount that total revenue changes as the firm sells 1 more caffè latte. For a perfectly competitive firm, the additional revenue received from selling 1 more unit is just equal to the price. That will not be true for Starbucks because to sell another caffè latte, it has to reduce the price. When the firm cuts the price by $0.50, one good thing and one bad thing happen:

- **The good thing.** It sells one more caffè latte; we can call this the *output effect.*

- **The bad thing.** It receives $0.50 less for each caffè latte that it could have sold at the higher price; we can call this the *price effect.*

Figure 12-2 illustrates what happens when the firm cuts the price from $3.50 to $3.00. Selling the sixth caffè latte adds the $3.00 price to the firm's revenue; this is the output effect. But Starbucks now receives a price of $3.00, rather than $3.50, on the first 5 caffè lattes sold; this is the price effect. As a result of the price effect, the firm's revenue

TABLE 12-1

Demand and Marginal Revenue at a Starbucks

CAFFÈ LATTES SOLD PER WEEK (Q)	PRICE (P)	TOTAL REVENUE ($TR = P \times Q$)	AVERAGE REVENUE $\left(AR = \dfrac{TR}{Q} \right)$	MARGINAL REVENUE $\left(MR = \dfrac{\Delta TR}{\Delta Q} \right)$
0	$6.00	$0.00	—	—
1	5.50	5.50	$5.50	$5.50
2	5.00	10.00	5.00	4.50
3	4.50	13.50	4.50	3.50
4	4.00	16.00	4.00	2.50
5	3.50	17.50	3.50	1.50
6	3.00	18.00	3.00	0.50
7	2.50	17.50	2.50	−0.50
8	2.00	16.00	2.00	−1.50
9	1.50	13.50	1.50	−2.50
10	1.00	10.00	1.00	−3.50

Figure 12-2

How a Price Cut Affects a Firm's Revenue

If the local Starbucks reduces the price of a caffè latte from $3.50 to $3.00, the number of caffè lattes it sells per week will increase from 5 to 6. Its marginal revenue from selling the sixth caffè latte will be $0.50, which is equal to the $3.00 additional revenue from selling 1 more caffè latte (the area of the green box) minus the $2.50 loss in revenue from selling the first 5 caffè lattes for $0.50 less each (the area of the red box).

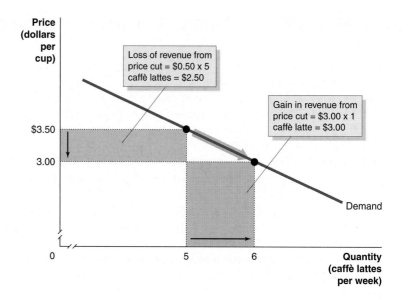

on these 5 caffè lattes is $2.50 less than it would have been if the price had remained at $3.50. So, the firm has gained $3.00 in revenue on the sixth caffè latte and lost $2.50 in revenue on the first 5 caffè lattes, for a net change in revenue of $0.50. Marginal revenue is the change in total revenue from selling one more unit. Therefore, the marginal revenue of the sixth caffè latte is $0.50. Notice that the marginal revenue of the sixth unit is far below its price of $3.00. In fact, for each additional caffè latte Starbucks sells, marginal revenue will be less than price. There is an important general point: *Every firm that has the ability to affect the price of the good or service it sells will have a marginal revenue curve that is below its demand curve.* Only firms in perfectly competitive markets, which can sell as many units as they want at the market price, have marginal revenue curves that are the same as their demand curves.

Figure 12-3 shows the relationship between the demand curve and the marginal revenue curve for the local Starbucks. Notice that after the sixth caffè latte, marginal

Figure 12-3

The Demand and Marginal Revenue Curves for a Monopolistically Competitive Firm

Any firm that has the ability to affect the price of the product it sells will have a marginal revenue curve that is below its demand curve. We plot the data from Table 12-1 to create the demand and marginal revenue curves. After the sixth caffè latte, marginal revenue becomes negative because the additional revenue received from selling 1 more caffè latte is smaller than the revenue lost from receiving a lower price on the caffè lattes that could have been sold at the original price.

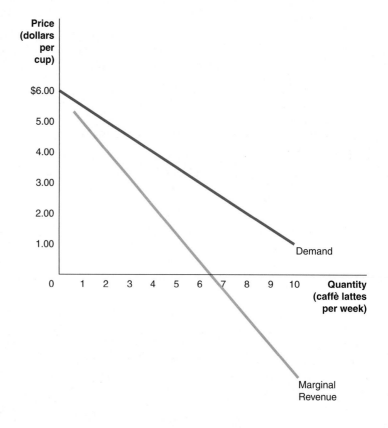

revenue becomes negative. Marginal revenue is negative because the additional revenue received from selling 1 more caffè latte is smaller than the revenue lost from receiving a lower price on the caffè lattes that could have been sold at the original price.

12.2 | Explain how a monopolistically competitive firm maximizes profits in the short run.

How a Monopolistically Competitive Firm Maximizes Profits in the Short Run

All firms use the same approach to maximize profits: They produce where marginal revenue is equal to marginal cost. For the local Starbucks, this means selling the quantity of caffè lattes for which the last caffè latte sold adds the same amount to the firm's revenue as to its costs. To begin our discussion of how monopolistically competitive firms maximize profits, let's consider the situation the local Starbucks faces in the short run. Recall from Chapter 10 that in the short run, at least one factor of production is fixed and there is not enough time for new firms to enter the market. A Starbucks has many costs, including the cost of purchasing the ingredients for its caffè lattes and other coffees, the electricity it uses, and the wages of its employees. Recall that a firm's *marginal cost* is the increase in total cost resulting from producing another unit of output. We have seen that for many firms, marginal cost has a U shape. We will assume that the Starbucks marginal cost has this usual shape.

In the table in Figure 12-4, we bring together the revenue data from Table 12-1 with the cost data for Starbucks. The graphs in Figure 12-4 plot the data from the table. In panel (a), we see how Starbucks can determine its profit-maximizing quantity and price. As long as the marginal cost of selling one more caffè latte is less than the marginal revenue, the firm should sell additional caffè lattes. For example, increasing the quantity of caffè lattes sold from 3 per week to 4 per week increases marginal cost by $1.00 but increases marginal revenue by $2.50. So, the firm's profits are increased by $1.50 as a result of selling the fourth caffè latte.

As Starbucks sells more caffè lattes, rising marginal cost eventually equals marginal revenue, and the firm sells the profit-maximizing quantity of caffè lattes. Marginal cost equals marginal revenue with the fifth caffè latte, which adds $1.50 to the firm's costs and $1.50 to its revenues—point *A* in panel (a) of Figure 12-4. The demand curve tells us the price at which the firm is able to sell 5 caffè lattes per week. In Figure 12-4, if we draw a vertical line from 5 caffè lattes up to the demand curve, we can see that the price at which the firm can sell 5 caffè lattes per week is $3.50 (point *B*). We can conclude that for Starbucks the profit-maximizing quantity is 5 caffè lattes, and its profit-maximizing price is $3.50. If the firm sells more than 5 caffè lattes per week, its profits fall. For example, selling a sixth caffè latte adds $2.00 to its costs and only $0.50 to its revenues. So, its profit would fall from $5.00 to $3.50.

Panel (b) adds the average total cost curve for Starbucks. The panel shows that the average total cost of selling 5 caffè lattes is $2.50. Recall from Chapter 11 that:

$$\text{Profit} = (P - ATC) \times Q.$$

In this case, profit = ($3.50 − $2.50) × 5 = $5.00. The green box in panel (b) shows the amount of profit. The box has a base equal to Q and a height equal to $(P - ATC)$, so its area equals profit.

Notice that, unlike a perfectly competitive firm, which produces where $P = MC$, a monopolistically competitive firm produces where $P > MC$. In this case, Starbucks is charging a price of $3.50, although marginal cost is $1.50. For the perfectly competitive firm, price equals marginal revenue, $P = MR$. Therefore, to fulfill the $MR = MC$ condition for profit maximization, a perfectly competitive firm will produce where $P = MC$. Because $P > MR$ for a monopolistically competitive firm—which results from the marginal revenue curve being below the demand curve—a monopolistically competitive firm will maximize profits where $P > MC$.

Caffè Lattes Sold per Week (Q)	Price (P)	Total Revenue (TR)	Marginal Revenue (MR)	Total Cost (TC)	Marginal Cost (MC)	Average Total Cost (ATC)	Profit
0	$6.00	$0.00	–	$5.00	–	–	–$5.00
1	5.50	5.50	$5.50	8.00	$3.00	$8.00	–2.50
2	5.00	10.00	4.50	9.50	1.50	4.75	0.50
3	4.50	13.50	3.50	10.00	0.50	3.33	3.50
4	4.00	16.00	2.50	11.00	1.00	2.75	5.00
5	3.50	17.50	1.50	12.50	1.50	2.50	5.00
6	3.00	18.00	0.50	14.50	2.00	2.42	3.50
7	2.50	17.50	–0.50	17.00	2.50	2.43	0.50
8	2.00	16.00	–1.50	20.00	3.00	2.50	–4.00
9	1.50	13.50	–2.50	23.50	3.50	2.61	–10.00
10	1.00	10.00	–3.50	27.50	4.00	2.75	–17.50

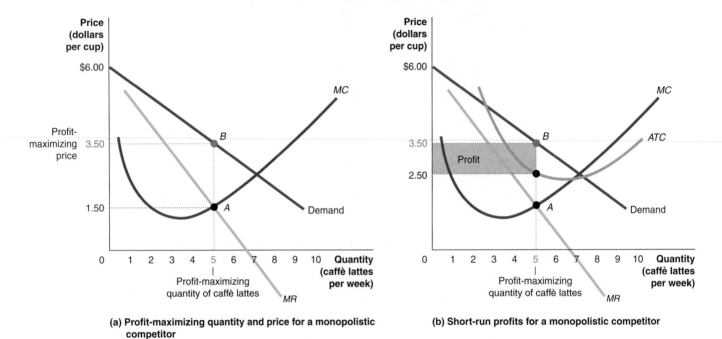

(a) Profit-maximizing quantity and price for a monopolistic competitor

(b) Short-run profits for a monopolistic competitor

Figure 12-4 | Maximizing Profit in a Monopolistically Competitive Market

To maximize profit, a Starbucks coffeehouse wants to sell caffè lattes up to the point where the marginal revenue from selling the last caffè latte is just equal to the marginal cost. As the table shows, this happens with the fifth caffè latte—point A in panel (a)—which adds $1.50 to the firm's costs and $1.50 to its revenues. The firm then uses the demand curve to find the price that will lead consumers to buy this quantity of caffè lattes (point B). In panel (b), the green box represents the firm's profits. The box has a height equal to $1.00, which is the price of $3.50 minus the average total cost of $2.50, and a base equal to the quantity of 5 caffè lattes. So, this Starbucks profit equals $1 × 5 = $5.00.

Solved Problem | **12-2**

How Not to Maximize Profits at a Publishing Company

In an article in the *New York Times*, Virginia Postrel states that when deciding the "question of whether printing another copy of a given, already published book, is a profitable thing to do," managers at publishing firms begin by calculating the cost of printing one additional copy. But these managers "often fall prey to the mistake of adding up every expense associated with a book, including the overhead like rent and editors' salaries, and then dividing by the number of copies." Will the process described in the previous sentence give an accurate estimate of marginal cost? If you were a manager at a publishing firm, how would you determine whether producing one more copy of a book will increase your profits?

SOLVING THE PROBLEM:

Step 1: **Review the chapter material.** This problem is about how monopolistically competitive firms maximize profits, so you may want to review the section "How a Monopolistically Competitive Firm Maximizes Profits in the Short Run," which begins on page 415.

Step 2: **Analyze the costs described in the problem.** We have seen that to maximize profits, firms should produce up to the point where marginal revenue equals marginal cost. Marginal cost is the increase in total cost that results from producing another unit of output. Rent and editors' salaries are part of a publishing company's fixed costs because they do not change as the company increases its output of books. Therefore, managers at publishing companies should not include them in calculating marginal cost.

Step 3: **Explain how a manager at a publishing firm should decide whether to publish one more copy of a book.** To determine whether producing one more copy of a book will increase your profits, you need to compare the marginal revenue received from selling the book with the marginal cost of producing it. If the marginal revenue is greater than the marginal cost, producing the book will increase your profits.

Source: Virginia Postrel, "Often, Basic Concepts in Economics Are Taken for Granted," *New York Times*, January 3, 2002.

YOUR TURN: For more practice, do related problem 2.9 on pages 433–434 at the end of this chapter.

>> **End Solved Problem 12-2**

12.3 | Analyze the situation of a monopolistically competitive firm in the long run.

What Happens to Profits in the Long Run?

Remember that a firm makes an economic profit when its total revenue is greater than all of its costs, including the opportunity cost of the funds invested in the firm by its owners. Because cost curves include the owners' opportunity costs, the Starbucks coffeehouse represented in Figure 12-4 is making an economic profit. This economic profit gives entrepreneurs an incentive to enter this market and establish new firms. If a Starbucks is earning economic profit selling caffè lattes, new coffeehouses are likely to open in the same area.

How Does the Entry of New Firms Affect the Profits of Existing Firms?

As new coffeehouses open near the local Starbucks, the firm's demand curve will shift to the left. The demand curve will shift because Starbucks will sell fewer caffè lattes at each price when there are additional coffeehouses in the area selling similar drinks. The demand curve will also become more elastic because consumers have additional coffeehouses from which to buy coffee, so Starbucks will lose more sales if it raises its prices. Figure 12-5 shows how the demand curve for the local Starbucks shifts as new firms enter its market.

In panel (a) of Figure 12-5, the short-run demand curve shows the relationship between the price of caffè lattes and the quantity of caffè lattes Starbucks sells per week before the entry of new firms. With this demand curve, Starbucks can charge a price above average total cost—shown as point *A* in panel (a)—and make a profit. But this profit attracts additional coffeehouses to the area and shifts the demand curve for the Starbucks caffè lattes to the left. As long as Starbucks is making an economic profit, there is an incentive for additional coffeehouses to open in the area, and the demand curve will

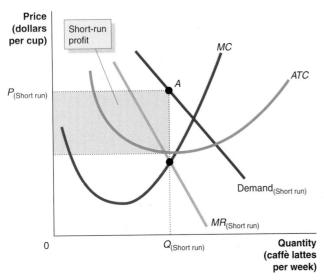

(a) A monopolistic competitor may earn a short-run profit

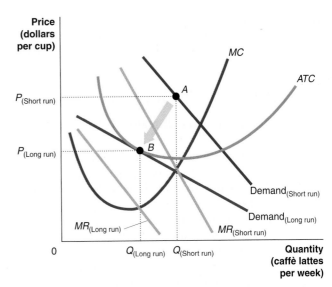

(b) A monopolistic competitor's profits are eliminated in the long run

Figure 12-5 | How Entry of New Firms Eliminates Profits

In the short run—panel (a)—the local Starbucks faces the demand and marginal revenue curves labeled "Short run." With this demand curve, Starbucks can charge a price above average total cost (point A) and make a profit, shown by the green rectangle. But this profit attracts new firms to enter the market, which shifts the demand and marginal revenue curves to the ones labeled "Long run" in panel (b). Because price is now equal to average total cost (point B), Starbucks breaks even and no longer earns an economic profit.

continue shifting to the left. As panel (b) shows, eventually the demand curve will have shifted to the point where it is just touching—or tangent to—the average cost curve.

In the long run, at the point at which the demand curve is tangent to the average cost curve, price is equal to average total cost (point B), the firm is breaking even, and it no longer earns an economic profit. In the long run, the demand curve is also more elastic because the more coffeehouses there are in the area, the more sales Starbucks will lose to other coffeehouses if it raises its price.

Of course, it is possible that a monopolistically competitive firm will suffer economic losses in the short run. As a consequence, the owners of the firm will not be covering the opportunity cost of their investment. We expect that, in the long run, firms will exit an industry if they are suffering economic losses. If firms exit, the demand curve for the output of a remaining firm will shift to the right. This process will continue until the representative firm in the industry is able to charge a price equal to its average cost and break even. Therefore, in the long run, monopolistically competitive firms will experience neither economic profits nor economic losses. Table 12-2 summarizes the short run and the long run for a monopolistically competitive firm.

Don't Let This Happen to **YOU!**

Don't Confuse Zero Economic Profit with Zero Accounting Profit

Remember that economists count the opportunity cost of the owner's investment in a firm as a cost. For example, suppose you invest $200,000 opening a pizza parlor, and the return you could earn on those funds each year in a similar investment—such as opening a sandwich shop—is 10 percent. Therefore, the annual opportunity cost of investing the funds in your own business is 10 percent of $200,000, or $20,000. This

$20,000 is part of your profit in the accounting sense, and you would have to pay taxes on it. But in an economic sense, the $20,000 is a cost. In long-run equilibrium, we would expect that entry of new firms would keep you from earning more than 10 percent on your investment. So, you would end up breaking even and earning zero economic profit, even though you were earning an accounting profit of $20,000.

YOUR TURN: Test your understanding by doing related problem 3.4 on page 435 at the end of this chapter.

TABLE 12-2 | The Short Run and the Long Run for a Monopolistically Competitive Firm

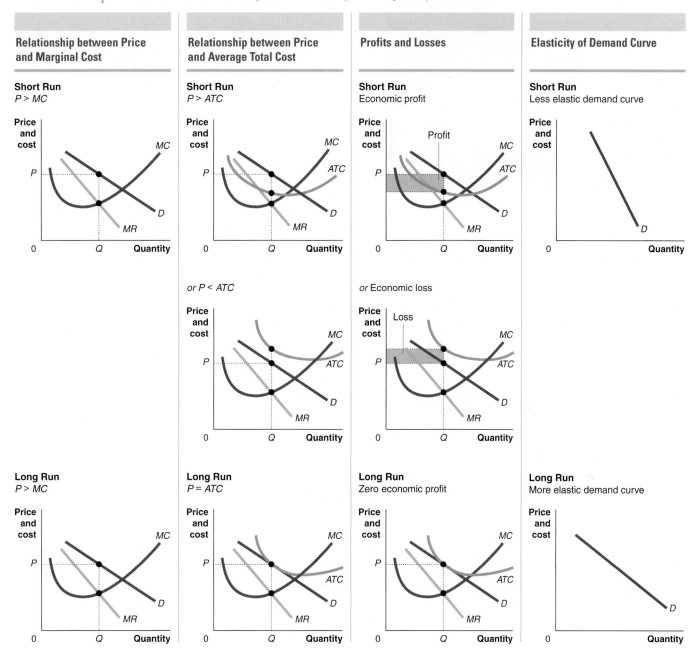

Relationship between Price and Marginal Cost	Relationship between Price and Average Total Cost	Profits and Losses	Elasticity of Demand Curve
Short Run $P > MC$	**Short Run** $P > ATC$	**Short Run** Economic profit	**Short Run** Less elastic demand curve
	or $P < ATC$	**or** Economic loss	
Long Run $P > MC$	**Long Run** $P = ATC$	**Long Run** Zero economic profit	**Long Run** More elastic demand curve

Making the Connection

The Rise and Fall of Apple's Macintosh Computer

In 1983, there were more than 15 firms selling personal computers nationally, as well as many smaller firms in local markets selling computers assembled from purchased components. None of these personal computers operated using the current system of clicking on icons with a mouse. Instead, users had to type in commands to call up word processing, spreadsheet, and other software programs. This awkward system required users to memorize many commands or constantly consult computer manuals. In January 1984, Apple Computer introduced the Macintosh, which used a mouse and could be operated by clicking on icons. The average cost of producing Macintoshes was about $500. Apple sold them for prices between $2,500 and $3,000. This price was more than twice that

Macintosh lost its differentiation, but still has a loyal—if relatively small—following.

of comparable personal computers sold by IBM and other companies, but the Macintosh was so easy to use that it was able to achieve a 15 percent share of the market. Apple had successfully introduced a personal computer that was strongly differentiated from its competitors. One journalist covering the computer industry has gone so far as to call the Macintosh "the most important consumer product of the last half of the twentieth century."

Microsoft produced the operating system known as MS-DOS (for Microsoft disk operating system), which most non-Apple computers used. The financial success of the Macintosh led Microsoft to develop an operating system that would also use a mouse and icons. In 1992, Microsoft introduced the operating system Windows 3.1, which succeeded in reproducing many of the key features of the Macintosh. By August 1995, when Microsoft introduced Windows 95, non-Apple computers had become as easy to use as Macintosh computers. By that time, most personal computers operated in a way very similar to the Macintosh, and Apple was no longer able to charge prices that were significantly above those that its competitors charged. The Macintosh had lost its differentiation. Although the Macintosh (now known as the iMac) continues to have a loyal following, and experienced strong sales growth in 2007 and 2008, in part because of the popularity of the iPod, today the Mac has only a 6 percent share of the personal computer market.

Source for quote: Steven Levy, *Insanely Great: The Life and Times of Macintosh, the Computer that Changed Everything*, New York: Viking, 1994, p. 7.

YOUR TURN: Test your understanding by doing related problem 3.5 on page 435 at the end of this chapter.

Solved Problem | 12-3

The Short Run and the Long Run for the Macintosh

Use the information in *Making the Connection* on page 419 to draw a graph that shows changes in the market for Macintosh computers between 1984 and 1995.

SOLVING THE PROBLEM:

Step 1: **Review the chapter material.** This problem is about how the entry of new firms affected the market for the Macintosh, so you may want to review the section "How Does the Entry of New Firms Affect the Profits of Existing Firms?" which begins on page 417.

Step 2: **Draw the graph.** The *Making the Connection* about Apple indicates that in 1984, when the Macintosh was first introduced, its differentiation from other computers allowed Apple to make a substantial economic profit. In 1995, the release of Windows 95 meant that non-Macintosh computers were as easy to use as Macintosh computers. Apple's product differentiation was eliminated, as was its ability to earn economic profits. The change over time in Apple's situation is shown in the following graph, which combines panels (a) and (b) from Figure 12-5 in one graph.

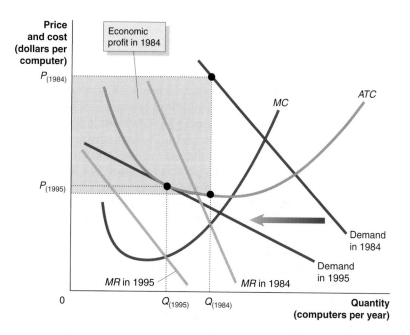

Between 1984 and 1995, Microsoft's development of the Windows operating system eliminated Macintosh's product differentiation. The demand curve for Macintosh shifted to the left and became more elastic throughout the relevant range of prices.

EXTRA CREDIT: Note that this analysis is simplified. The Macintosh of 1995 was a different—and better—computer than the Macintosh of 1984. Apple has made changes to the Macintosh, such as the introduction of the colorful iMac computer in 1999, that have sometimes led to increases in sales. The great success of the Apple iPod has also lead some consumers to switch to Apple computers. But the Macintosh has never been able to regain the high demand and premium prices it enjoyed from the mid-1980s to the early 1990s.

YOUR TURN: For more practice, do related problem 3.6 on page 435 at the end of this chapter.

>> End Solved Problem 12-3

Is Zero Economic Profit Inevitable in the Long Run?

The economic analysis of the long run shows the effects of market forces over time. In the case of Starbucks, the effect of market forces is to eliminate the economic profit earned by a monopolistically competitive firm. Owners of monopolistically competitive firms, of course, do not have to passively accept this long-run result. The key to earning economic profits is either to sell a differentiated product or to find a way of producing an existing product at a lower cost. If a monopolistically competitive firm selling a differentiated product is earning profits, these profits will attract the entry of additional firms, and the entry of those firms will eventually eliminate the firm's profits. If a firm introduces new technology that allows it to sell a good or service at a lower cost, competing firms will eventually be able to duplicate that technology and eliminate the firm's profits. *But this result holds only if the firm stands still and fails to find new ways of differentiating its product or fails to find new ways of lowering the cost of producing its product.* Firms continually struggle to find new ways of differentiating their products as they try to stay one step ahead of other firms that are attempting to copy their success. As new coffeehouses enter the area served by the Starbucks coffeehouse, the owners can expect to see their economic profits competed away, unless they can find ways to differentiate their product.

In 2008, Howard Schultz, the chairman of Starbucks, was well aware of this fact. In opening thousands of coffeehouses worldwide, he worried that Starbucks had made the customer experience less distinctive and easier for competitors to copy. Starbucks has used various strategies to differentiate itself from competing coffeehouses. Competitors have found it difficult to duplicate the European espresso bar atmosphere of Starbucks, with its large, comfortable chairs; music playing; and groups of friends dropping in and out during the day. Most importantly, Starbucks has continued to be very responsive to its customers' preferences. As one observer put it, "How many retailers could put up with 'I'll have a grande low-fat triple-shot half-caf white-chocolate mocha, extra hot, easy on the whipped cream. And I'm in a rush'?" But Howard Schultz was worried. In a memo sent to employees, he wrote, "Over the past ten years, in order to achieve the growth, development, and scale necessary to go from less than 1,000 stores to 13,000 stores . . . we have had to make a series of decisions that . . . have led to the watering down of the Starbucks experience." Starbucks has begun serving breakfast sandwiches and installing drive-through windows that make its stores appear similar to other fast-food restaurants. Although at one time Starbucks had been able to maintain greater control over the operations of its coffeehouses, because unlike many of its competitors, all of its coffeehouses were company owned, it now has thousands of *franchises*. A franchise is a business with the legal right to sell a good or service in a particular area. When a firm uses franchises, local businesspeople are able to buy and run the stores in their area. This makes it easier for a firm to finance its expansion but forces the firm to give up some control over its stores.

Starbucks experienced great success during the 1990s and the early 2000s, but history shows that in the long run competitors will be able to duplicate most of what it does. In the face of that competition, it will be very difficult for Starbucks to continue earning economic profits. In fact, as mentioned at the beginning of this chapter, in 2008, Starbucks announced plans to close 600 unprofitable stores in the United States. As Howard Schultz put it "I have said for 20 years that our success is not an entitlement and now it's proving to be a reality."

The owner of a competitive firm is in a position similar to that of Ebenezer Scrooge in Charles Dickens's *A Christmas Carol*. When the Ghost of Christmas Yet to Come shows Scrooge visions of his own death, he asks the ghost, "Are these the shadows of the things that Will be, or are they shadows of things that May be, only?" The shadow of the end of their profits haunts owners of every firm. Firms try to avoid losing profits by reducing costs, by improving their products, or by convincing consumers their products are indeed different from what competitors offer. To stay one step ahead of its competitors, a firm has to offer consumers goods or services that they perceive to have greater *value* than those offered by competing firms. Value can take the form of product differentiation that makes the good or service more suited to consumers' preferences, or it can take the form of a lower price.

Making the Connection | Staying One Step Ahead of the Competition: Eugène Schueller and L'Oréal

Today, L'Oréal, with headquarters in the Paris suburb of Clichy, is the largest seller of perfumes, cosmetics, and hair care products in the world. In addition to L'Oréal, its brands include Lancôme, Maybelline, Soft Sheen/Carson, Garnier, Redken, Ralph Lauren, and Matrix. Like most other large firms, L'Oréal was started by an entrepreneur with an idea. Eugène Schueller was a French chemist who experimented in the evenings trying to find a safe and reliable hair coloring for women. In 1907, he founded the firm that became L'Oréal and began selling his hair coloring preparations to Paris hair salons. Schueller was able to take advantage of changes in fashion. In the early twentieth century, women began to cut their hair much shorter than had been typical in the nineteenth century, and it had become socially acceptable to spend time and money styling it. The number of hair salons in Europe and the United States increased rapidly. By the 1920s and 1930s, the international popularity of Hollywood films, many starring "platinum blonde bombshells" such as Jean Harlow, made it fashionable for women to color their hair. By the late 1920s, L'Oréal was selling its products throughout Europe, the United States, and Japan.

Perfumes, cosmetics, and hair coloring are all products that should be easy for rival firms to duplicate. We would expect, then, that the economic profits L'Oréal earned in its early years would have been competed away in the long run through the entry of new firms. In fact, though, the firm has remained profitable through the decades, following a strategy of developing new products, improving existing products, and expanding into new markets. For example, when French workers first received paid holidays during the

Unlike many monopolistically competitive firms, L'Oréal has earned economic profits for a very long time.

1930s, L'Oréal moved quickly to dominate the new market for suntan lotion. Today, the firm's SoftSheen brand is experiencing rapid sales increases in Africa. When L'Oréal launched a new line of men's skin-care products, including shaving cream, one analyst observed that at L'Oréal, "brands don't stay at home serving the same old clientele. They get spruced up, put in a new set of traveling clothes, and sent abroad to meet new customers." L'Oréal has maintained its ability to innovate by spending more on research and development than do competing firms. The firm has a research staff of more than 1,000.

One reason L'Oréal has been able to follow a focused strategy is that the firm has had only three chairmen in its nearly century of existence: founder Eugène Schueller, François Dalle, and Lindsay Owen-Jones, who became chairman in 1988. Owen-Jones has described the firm's strategy: "Each brand is positioned on a very precise [market] segment, which overlaps as little as possible with the others." The story of L'Oréal shows that it is possible for a firm to stay one step ahead of the competition, but it takes top management committed to an entrepreneurial spirit of continually developing new products.

Source for quotes: Richard Tomlinson, "L'Oréal's Global Makeover," *Fortune*, September 30, 2002.

YOUR TURN: Test your understanding by doing related problem 3.9 on page 436 at the end of this chapter.

12.4 | Compare the efficiency of monopolistic competition and perfect competition.

12.4 LEARNING OBJECTIVE

Comparing Perfect Competition and Monopolistic Competition

We have seen that monopolistic competition and perfect competition share the characteristic that in long-run equilibrium, firms earn zero economic profits. As Figure 12-6 shows, however, there are two important differences between long-run equilibrium in the two markets:

- Monopolistically competitive firms charge a price greater than marginal cost.

- Monopolistically competitive firms do not produce at minimum average total cost.

Excess Capacity under Monopolistic Competition

Recall that a firm in a perfectly competitive market faces a perfectly elastic demand curve that is also its marginal revenue curve. Therefore, the firm maximizes profit by producing where price equals marginal cost. As panel (a) of Figure 12-6 shows, in

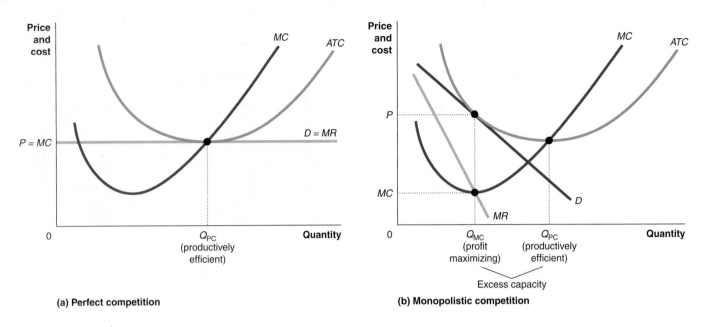

(a) Perfect competition

(b) Monopolistic competition

Figure 12-6 │ Comparing Long-Run Equilibrium under Perfect Competition and Monopolistic Competition

In panel (a), the perfectly competitive firm in long-run equilibrium produces at Q_{PC}, where price equals marginal cost, and average total cost is at a minimum. The perfectly competitive firm is both allocatively efficient and productively efficient. In panel (b), the monopolistically competitive firm produces at Q_{MC}, where price is greater than marginal cost, and average total cost is not at a minimum. As a result, the monopolistically competitive firm is neither allocatively efficient nor productively efficient. The monopolistically competitive firm has excess capacity equal to the difference between its profit-maximizing level of output and the productively efficient level of output.

long-run equilibrium, a perfectly competitive firm produces at the minimum point of its average total cost curve.

Panel (b) of Figure 12-6 shows that the profit-maximizing level of output for a monopolistically competitive firm comes at a level of output where price is greater than marginal cost and the firm is not at the minimum point of its average total cost curve. A monopolistically competitive firm has *excess capacity*: If it increased its output, it could produce at a lower average cost.

Is Monopolistic Competition Inefficient?

In Chapter 11, we discussed *productive efficiency* and *allocative efficiency*. Productive efficiency refers to the situation where a good is produced at the lowest possible cost. Allocative efficiency refers to the situation where every good or service is produced up to the point where the last unit provides a marginal benefit to consumers equal to the marginal cost of producing it. For productive efficiency to hold, firms must produce at the minimum point of average total cost. For allocative efficiency to hold, firms must charge a price equal to marginal cost. In a perfectly competitive market, both productive efficiency and allocative efficiency are achieved, but in a monopolistically competitive market, neither is achieved. Does it matter? Economists have debated whether monopolistically competitive markets being neither productively nor allocatively efficient results in a significant loss of well-being to society in these markets compared with perfectly competitive markets.

How Consumers Benefit from Monopolistic Competition

Looking again at Figure 12-6, you can see that the only difference between the monopolistically competitive firm and the perfectly competitive firm is that the demand curve for the monopolistically competitive firm slopes downward, whereas the demand curve for the perfectly competitive firm is a horizontal line. The demand curve for the monopolistically competitive firm slopes downward because the good or service the firm is selling is differentiated from the goods or services being sold by competing firms. The perfectly competitive firm is selling a good or service identical to those being sold by its competitors. A key point to remember is that *firms differentiate their products to appeal to consumers.* When Starbucks coffeehouses begin offering new flavors of coffee, when Blockbuster stores begin carrying more Blu-ray DVDs and fewer regular DVDs, when General Mills introduces Apple-Cinnamon Cheerios, or when PepsiCo introduces caffeine-free Diet Pepsi, they are all attempting to attract and retain consumers through product differentiation. The success of these product differentiation strategies indicates that some consumers find these products preferable to the alternatives. Consumers, therefore, are better off than they would have been had these companies not differentiated their products.

We can conclude that consumers face a trade-off when buying the product of a monopolistically competitive firm: They are paying a price that is greater than marginal cost, and the product is not being produced at minimum average cost, but they benefit from being able to purchase a product that is differentiated and more closely suited to their tastes.

| Making the Connection | **Abercrombie & Fitch: Can the Product Be Too Differentiated?** |

Business managers often refer to differentiating their products as finding a "market niche." The larger the niche you have, the greater the potential profit but the more likely that other firms will be able to compete against you. Too small a niche, however, may reduce competition— but also reduce profits. Some analysts believe that the market niche chosen by the managers of the Abercrombie & Fitch clothing stores is too small. The chief executive, Mike Jeffries, argues that his store's target customer is an "18-to-22 [year old] college guy who has a good body and is aspirational." He admits that this is a narrow niche: "If I exclude people—absolutely. Delighted to do so."

Did Abercrombie and Fitch narrow its target market too much?

But is A&F excluding too many people? One analyst argues "they've . . . pushed a lot of people out of the brand." A&F's sales results seemed to indicate that this analyst may be correct. Managers of retail stores closely monitor "same-store sales," which measures how much sales have increased in the same stores from one year to the next. To offset the effects of inflation—or general increases in prices in the economy—same-store sales need to increase at least 2 percent to 3 percent each year. A firm whose strategy of product differentiation succeeds will experience increases in same-store sales of at least 5 percent to 6 percent each year. For several years in the early 2000s, A&F's 350 stores experienced *negative* same-store results. Although sales increased from 2004 through early 2006, negative changes in same-store sales returned in late 2006 and continued sporadically through mid-2008. A&F may have gone too far in narrowing its market niche.

Sources: James Covert, "Retail Sales Slide Fuels Concern," *Wall Street Journal*, May 11, 2007; and Shelly Branch, "Maybe Sex Doesn't Sell, A&F Is Discovering," *Wall Street Journal*, December 12, 2003.

YOUR TURN: Test your understanding by doing related problem 4.6 on page 437 at the end of this chapter.

12.5 | Define marketing and explain how firms use it to differentiate their products.

How Marketing Differentiates Products

Firms can differentiate their products through marketing. **Marketing** refers to all the activities necessary for a firm to sell a product to a consumer. Marketing includes activities such as determining which product to produce, designing the product, advertising the product, deciding how to distribute the product—for example, in retail stores or

Marketing All the activities necessary for a firm to sell a product to a consumer.

through a Web site—and monitoring how changes in consumer tastes are affecting the market for the product. Peter F. Drucker, a leading business strategist, describes marketing as follows: "It is the whole business seen from the point of view of its final result, that is, from the consumer's point of view. . . . True marketing . . . does not ask, 'What do we want to sell?' It asks, 'What does the consumer want to buy?' "

As we have seen, for monopolistically competitive firms to earn economic profits and to defend those profits from competitors, they must differentiate their products. Firms use two marketing tools to differentiate their products: brand management and advertising.

Brand Management

Brand management The actions of a firm intended to maintain the differentiation of a product over time.

Once a firm has succeeded in differentiating its product, it must try to maintain that differentiation over time through **brand management**. As we have seen, whenever a firm successfully introduces a new product or a significantly different version of an old product, it earns economic profits in the short run. But the success of the firm inspires competitors to copy the new or improved product and, in the long run, the firm's economic profits will be competed away. Firms use brand management to postpone the time when they will no longer be able to earn economic profits.

Advertising

An innovative advertising campaign can make even long-established and familiar products, such as Coke or McDonald's Big Mac hamburgers, seem more desirable than competing products. When a firm advertises a product, it is trying to shift the demand curve for the product to the right and to make it more inelastic. If the firm is successful, it will sell more of the product at every price, and it will be able to increase the price it charges without losing as many customers. Of course, advertising also increases a firm's costs. If the increase in revenue that results from the advertising is greater than the increase in costs, the firm's profits will rise.

Needless to say, advertising campaigns are not always successful. In 1957, the Ford Motor Company introduced a new car, the Edsel, designed to compete with the Buick from General Motors. Ford set up a new division of the company to produce the Edsel in five different models and hired the advertising firm of Foote, Cone & Belding to direct a massive advertising campaign. Among other things, Ford purchased an hour of prime television time on the CBS network to broadcast *The Edsel Show*, hosted by Frank Sinatra, Bing Crosby, and Louis Armstrong, three of the biggest stars of the 1950s. Ford set a sales goal of 200,000 cars during the first year of production. Unfortunately, most of the car-buying public found the styling of the Edsel, with its oversized headlights and elaborate front grill, unappealing. First-year sales were only about 63,000 cars. During the same period, General Motors sold more than 230,000 Buicks. Ford decided to shift its advertising account for the Edsel from Foote, Cone & Belding to Kenyon & Eckhardt. Despite a revised advertising campaign, sales of the Edsel remained very low. Ford sold fewer than 45,000 Edsels during the car's second year of production. In November 1959, after only two years in production, Ford stopped making the Edsel. Even one of the largest advertising campaigns in history had failed to make the Edsel successful.

Defending a Brand Name

Once a firm has established a successful brand name, it has a strong incentive to defend it. A firm can apply for a *trademark*, which grants legal protection against other firms using its product's name.

One threat to a trademarked name is the possibility that it will become so widely used for a type of product that it will no longer be associated with the product of a specific company. Courts in the United States have ruled that when this happens, a firm is no longer entitled to legal protection of the brand name. For example, "aspirin," "escalator," and "thermos" were originally all brand names of the products of particular firms, but each became so widely used to refer to a type of product that none remains a legally protected brand name. Firms spend substantial amounts of money trying to make sure that this does not happen to them. Coca-Cola, for example, employs workers to travel around the country stopping at restaurants and asking to be served a "Coke" with their meal. If the restaurant serves Pepsi or some other cola, rather than Coke, Coca-Cola's legal department sends the restaurant a letter reminding that "Coke" is a trademarked name and not a generic name for any cola. Similarly, Xerox Corporation spends money on advertising to remind the public that "Xerox" is not a generic term for making photocopies.

Legally enforcing trademarks can be difficult. Estimates are that each year, U.S. firms lose hundreds of billions of dollars in sales worldwide as a result of unauthorized use of their trademarked brand names. U.S. firms often find it difficult to enforce their trademarks in the courts of some foreign countries, although recent international agreements have increased the legal protections for trademarks.

Firms that sell their products through franchises rather than through company-owned stores encounter the problem that if a franchisee does not run his or her business well, the firm's brand may be damaged. Automobile firms send "roadmen" to visit their dealers to make sure the dealerships are clean and well maintained and that the service departments employ competent mechanics and are well equipped with spare parts. Similarly, McDonald's sends employees from corporate headquarters to visit McDonald's franchises to make sure the bathrooms are clean and the French fries are hot.

12.6 | Identify the key factors that determine a firm's success.   **12.6 LEARNING** OBJECTIVE

What Makes a Firm Successful?

A firm's owners and managers control some of the factors that make a firm successful and allow it to earn economic profits. The most important of these are the firm's ability to differentiate its product and to produce its product at a lower average cost than competing firms. A firm that successfully does these things creates *value* for its customers. Consumers will buy a product if they believe it meets a need not met by competing products or if its price is below that of competitors.

Some factors that affect a firm's profitability are not directly under the firm's control. Certain factors will affect all the firms in a market. For example, rising prices for jet fuel will reduce the profitability of all airlines. If consumers decide that they would rather watch pay-for-view movies delivered to their homes by cable or satellite than buy DVDs, the profitability of all stores selling DVDs will be reduced.

Sheer chance also plays a role in business, as it does in all other aspects of life. A struggling McDonald's franchise may see profits increase dramatically after the county unexpectedly decides to build a new road nearby. Many businesses in New York City, including restaurants, hotels, and theaters, experienced a marked drop in customers and profits following the September 11, 2001, terrorist attacks. Figure 12-7 illustrates the important point that factors within the firm's control and factors outside the firm's control interact to determine the firm's profitability.

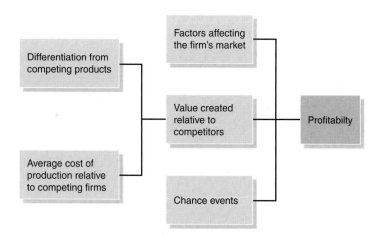

Figure 12-7

What Makes a Firm Successful?

The factors under a firm's control—the ability to differentiate its product and the ability to produce it at lower cost—combine with the factors beyond its control to determine the firm's profitability.

Source: Adapted from Figure 11.3 in David Besanko, David Dranove, Mark Shanley, and Scott Schaefer, *The Economics of Strategy*, 4th ed., New York: Wiley, 2007.

Although not first to market, Bic ultimately was more successful than the firm that pioneered ballpoint pens.

Making the Connection

Is Being the First Firm in the Market a Key to Success?

Some business analysts argue that the first firm to enter a market can have important *first-mover advantages.* By being the first to sell a particular good, a firm may find its name closely associated with the good in the public's mind, as, for instance, Amazon is closely associated with ordering books online or eBay is associated with online auctions. This close association may make it more difficult for new firms to enter the market and compete against the first mover.

Surprisingly, though, recent research has shown that the first firm to enter a market often does *not* have a long-lived advantage over later entrants. Consider, for instance, the market for pens. Until the 1940s, the only pens available were fountain pens that had to be refilled frequently from an ink bottle and used ink that dried slowly and smeared easily. In October 1945, entrepreneur Milton Reynolds introduced the first ballpoint pen, which never needed to be refilled. When it went on sale at Gimbel's department store in New York City, it was an instant success. Although the pen had a price of $12.00—the equivalent of about $135.00 at today's prices—hundreds of thousands were sold, and Milton Reynolds became a millionaire. Unfortunately, it didn't last. Although Reynolds had guaranteed that his pen would write for two years—later raised to five years—in fact, the pen often leaked and frequently stopped writing after only limited use. Sales began to collapse, the flood of pens returned under the company's guarantee wiped out its profits, and within a few years, Reynolds International Pen Company stopped selling pens in the United States. By the late 1960s, firms such as Bic selling inexpensive—but reliable—ballpoint pens dominated the market.

What happened to the Reynolds International Pen Company turns out to be more the rule than the exception. For example, Apple's iPod was not the first digital music player to appear on the U.S. market. Both Seahan's MPMan and Diamond's PMP300 were released in the United States in 1998, three years before the iPod. Similarly, although Hewlett-Packard currently dominates the market for laser printers, with a market share of more than 50 percent, it did not invent the laser printer. Xerox invented the laser printer, and IBM sold the first commercial laser printers. Nor was Procter & Gamble the first firm to sell disposable diapers when it introduced Pampers in 1961. Microsoft's Internet Explorer was not the first Web browser: Before Internet Explorer, there was Netscape; before Netscape, there was Mosaic; and before Mosaic, there were several other Web browsers that for a time looked as if they might dominate the market. In all these cases, the firms that were first to introduce a product ultimately lost out to latecomers who did a better job of providing consumers with products that were more reliable, less expensive, more convenient, or otherwise provided greater value.

Sources: Steven P. Schnaars, *Managing Imitation Strategies: How Later Entrants Seize Markets from Pioneers*, New York: The Free Press, 1994; and Gerard J. Tellis and Peter N. Golder, *Will and Vision: How Latecomers Grow to Dominate Markets*, Los Angeles: Figueroa Press, 2002.

YOUR TURN: Test your understanding by doing related problem 6.6 on page 438 at the end of this chapter.

Economics in YOUR Life!

>> Continued from page 411

At the beginning of the chapter, we asked you to think about how successful you are likely to be in opening an Italian restaurant in your hometown. As you learned in this chapter, if your restaurant is successful, other people are likely to open competing restaurants, and all your economic profits will eventually disappear. This occurs because economic profits attract entry of new firms into a market. The new restaurants will sell Italian food, but it won't be exactly like your Italian food—after all, they don't have your grandmother's secret recipe! Each restaurant will have its own ideas on how best to appeal to people who like Italian food. Unless your food is so different from the food competing restaurants offer that your consumers will continue to pay higher prices for your food, you probably won't earn an economic profit in the long run.

In a monopolistically competitive market, free entry will lead to zero economic profits in the long run. But competition will also lead firms to offer somewhat different versions of the same product; for example, two Italian restaurants will rarely be exactly alike.

Conclusion

In this chapter, we have applied many of the ideas about competition we developed in Chapter 11 to the more common market structure of monopolistic competition. We have seen that these ideas apply to monopolistically competitive markets, just as they do to perfectly competitive markets. At the end of Chapter 11, we concluded that "The competitive forces of the market impose relentless pressure on firms to produce new and better goods and services at the lowest possible cost. Firms that fail to adequately anticipate changes in consumer tastes or that fail to adopt the latest and most efficient production technology do not survive in the long run." These conclusions are as true for coffeehouses and firms in other monopolistically competitive markets as they are for wheat farmers or apple growers.

In Chapter 13 and Chapter 14, we discuss the remaining market structures: oligopoly and monopoly. Before moving on to those chapters, read *An Inside Look* on the next page for a discussion of how Starbucks and Dunkin' Donuts each try to differentiate their product and services.

Can Dunkin' Donuts Really Compete with Starbucks?

WALL STREET JOURNAL, APRIL 8, 2006

Brewing Battle: Dunkin' Donuts Tries to Go Upscale, but Not too Far

Dunkin' Donuts last year paid dozens of faithful customers in Phoenix, Chicago and Charlotte, N.C., $100 a week to buy coffee at Starbucks instead. At the same time, the no-frills coffee chain paid Starbucks customers to make the opposite switch.

When it later debriefed the two groups, Dunkin' says it found them so polarized that company researchers dubbed them "tribes"—each of whom loathed the very things that made the other tribe loyal to their coffee shop. Dunkin' fans viewed Starbucks as pretentious and trendy, while Starbucks loyalists saw Dunkin' as austere and unoriginal.

"I don't get it," one Dunkin' regular told researchers after visiting Starbucks. "If I want to sit on a couch, I stay at home."

Bridging some of that divide—but not too much—is key to Dunkin' Donuts' ambitious plan to expand its largely Eastern coffee chain into a national powerhouse that's as synonymous with coffee as Starbucks Corp., the nation's largest coffee chain. Armed with fresh capital from December's $2.43 billion private-equity buyout of Dunkin' Brands Inc., Dunkin' plans to remake its nearly 5,000 U.S. stores over the next three years and have triple that number in less than 15 years. . . .

While executives of Canton, Mass.-based Dunkin' insist they aren't trying to emulate their Seattle rival, Dunkin's store makeovers include some similarities to Starbucks. A prototype Dunkin' store in Euclid, Ohio, outside Cleveland, features rounded granite-style coffee bars where workers make espresso drinks face-to-face with customers. Open-air pastry cases brim with yogurt parfaits and fresh fruit while a carefully orchestrated pop-music soundtrack is piped throughout. . . .

Yet Dunkin' built itself on serving simple fare to working-class customers. Inching upscale without alienating that base is proving tricky. There will be no couches in the new stores. And Dunkin' renamed a new hot sandwich a "stuffed melt" after customers complained that calling it a "panini" was too fancy.

Some customers "have remarked along the lines of 'You're trying to be somebody else,'" says Ryan Humphrey, who oversees Dunkin' franchisees in the Cleveland area. Regina Lewis, the chain's vice president, consumer and brand insights, says, "We're walking that line. The thing about the Dunkin' tribe is, they see through the hype."

Anne Saunders, Starbucks senior vice president, global brand, says Starbucks doesn't focus on Dunkin' Donuts as a competitor. While competitors may use elements of its strategy, they can't recreate Starbucks' "unique and differentiated concept," she says. . . .

Company researchers set out to determine whether Dunkin' could draw consumers in new cities, and how to lure customers from fast-food chains, coffee houses and convenience stores. "Consumers love environments," Mr. Luther (Dunkin's Chief Executive) says. "We have to move our environment where the customer is."

Early research showed customers wanted nicer stores, but revealed a potential problem: the loyal Dunkin' tribe was bewildered and turned off by the atmosphere at Starbucks. They groused that crowds of laptop users made it difficult to find a seat, Dunkin' says. They didn't like Starbucks' "tall," "grande" and "venti" lingo for small, medium and large coffees. And, Dunkin' says, they couldn't understand why anyone would pay as much as $4 for a cup of coffee. . . .

Dunkin' researchers concluded that it wasn't income that set the two tribes apart, as much as an ideal: Dunkin' tribe members wanted to be part of a crowd, while members of the Starbucks tribe had a desire to stand out as individuals. "The Starbucks tribe, they seek out things to make them feel more important," Ms. Lewis says. Members of the Dunkin' Donuts tribe "don't need to be any more important than they are." . . .

Key Points in the Article

This article discusses an attempt by Dunkin' Donuts to appeal to some of Starbucks' customers. As we have seen in this chapter, when a firm successfully differentiates its product, its competitors do their best to copy it. Starbucks has experienced great success by reinventing the coffeehouse. But the article notes that many Starbucks customers see Dunkin' Donuts stores as "austere and unoriginal." As Dunkin' Donuts begins to expand nationwide, it is redesigning its stores to make them more like Starbucks. As this chapter has shown, once consumers show they want a particular good or service, firms will compete to offer it to them.

Analyzing the News

ⓐ Currently, upscale coffeehouses like Starbucks are earning an economic profit. This would suggest that an existing firm could be represented by point A in the figure selling Q_1 cups of coffee and charging a price of P_1 dollars. The profit-maximizing quantity is found at the point where the marginal revenue curve MR_1 intersects the marginal cost curve MC. The price is determined by the demand curve. The firm is earning economic profits equal to the shaded area. The economic profits earned by coffeehouses like Starbucks explains why as Dunkin' Donuts expands nationwide, it has been building stores that are more upscale than its older stores.

ⓑ Dunkin' Donuts is trying to capture the feel of a Starbucks' store in order to attract customers who may like some of the elements of Starbucks, but who may also like some of the elements of Dunkin' Donuts. Dunkin' Donuts will never attract loyal Starbucks' customers, but they do hope to attract customers who like some features about Starbucks but who may prefer a different environment and food selection. As the figure shows, new entrants in a market will take some demand away from current firms in the market. This causes the demand curve to shift to the left from demand curve D_1 to demand curve D_2. The marginal revenue curve also shifts to the left (from MR_1 to MR_2).

The profit-maximizing level of output is now Q_2, where the new marginal revenue curve intersects the marginal cost curve, MC. The new profit maximizing price is P_2. Notice that at this point the demand curve D_2 is tangent to the average total cost curve ATC and the firm is earning zero profits. At equilibrium, all firms in the market will earn zero profits. This is shown as point E in the figure.

ⓒ This section illustrates why product differentiation is important in a market. While customers at Dunkin' Donuts and Starbucks are looking for similar products—coffee and food—there are important differences between the customers that cause them to shop at one coffee shop over another. Those who are in the Starbucks tribe or the Dunkin' Donuts tribe are unlikely to go to another coffee shop. There may, however, be a third tribe looking for a home.

Thinking Critically

1. Suppose the government required a license to open a coffeehouse and that the number of licenses was limited. How would this new requirement affect the equilibrium market price and quantity in the coffeehouse market? Who would gain from this requirement, and who would lose?

2. Suppose that the number of people in the Dunkin' Donuts tribe increases as people begin to prefer donuts with their coffee rather than couches. How would Starbucks likely respond to this change in tastes?

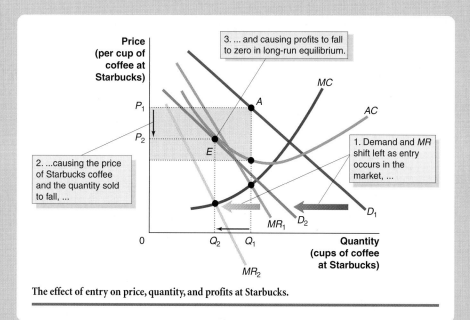

The effect of entry on price, quantity, and profits at Starbucks.

Key Terms

Brand management, p. 426   Monopolistic competition, p. 412

Marketing, p. 425

12.1 LEARNING OBJECTIVE   12.1 | Explain why a monopolistically competitive firm has downward-sloping
demand and marginal revenue curves, **pages 412–415.**

Demand and Marginal Revenue for a Firm in a Monopolistically Competitive Market

Summary

A firm competing in a **monopolistically competitive** market sells a differentiated product. Therefore, unlike a firm in a perfectly competitive market, it faces a downward-sloping demand curve. When a monopolistically competitive firm cuts the price of its product, it sells more units but must accept a lower price on the units it could have sold at the higher price. As a result, its marginal revenue curve is downward sloping. Every firm that has the ability to affect the price of the good or service it sells will have a marginal revenue curve that is below its demand curve.

 Visit www.myeconlab.com to complete these exercises
Get Ahead of the Curve online and get instant feedback.

Review Questions

1.1 What are the most important differences between perfectly competitive markets and monopolistically competitive markets? Give two examples of products sold in perfectly competitive markets and two examples of products sold in monopolistically competitive markets.

1.2 Why does the local McDonald's face a downward-sloping demand curve for Big Macs? If it raises the price it charges for Big Macs above the prices charged by other McDonald's stores, won't it lose all its customers?

1.3 Explain the differences between total revenue, average revenue, and marginal revenue.

Problems and Applications

1.4 Complete the following table:

DVDS RENTED PER WEEK (Q)	PRICE (P)	TOTAL REVENUE (TR = P × Q)	AVERAGE REVENUE (AR = TR/Q)	MARGINAL REVENUE (MR = ΔTR/ΔQ)
0	$8.00			
1	7.50			
2	7.00			
3	6.50			
4	6.00			
5	5.50			
6	5.00			
7	4.50			
8	4.00			

1.5 A student makes the following argument:

> When a firm sells another unit of a good, the additional revenue the firm receives is equal to the price: If the price is $10, then the additional revenue is also $10. Therefore, this chapter is incorrect when it says that marginal revenue is less than price for a monopolistically competitive firm.

Briefly explain whether you agree with this argument.

1.6 There are many wheat farms in the world, but there are also many Starbucks coffeehouses. Why, then, does a Starbucks coffeehouse face a downward-sloping demand curve when a wheat farmer faces a horizontal demand curve?

1.7 Is it possible for marginal revenue to be negative for a firm selling in a perfectly competitive market? Would a firm selling in a monopolistically competitive market ever produce where marginal revenue is negative?

>> End Learning Objective 12.1

How a Monopolistically Competitive Firm Maximizes Profits in the Short Run

Summary

A monopolistically competitive firm maximizes profits at the level of output where marginal revenue equals marginal cost. Price equals marginal revenue for a perfectly competitive firm, but price is greater than marginal revenue for a monopolistically competitive firm. Therefore, unlike a perfectly competitive firm, which produces where $P = MC$, a monopolistically competitive firm produces where $P > MC$.

myeconlab Visit www.myeconlab.com to complete these exercises *Get Ahead of the Curve* online and get instant feedback.

Review Questions

2.1 Sally runs a McDonald's franchise. She is selling 350 Big Macs per week at a price of $3.25. If she lowers the price to $3.20, she will sell 351 Big Macs. What is the marginal revenue of the 351st Big Mac?

2.2 Sam runs a Hollywood Video store. Sam is currently renting 3,525 DVDs per week. If instead of renting 3,525 DVDs, he rents 3,526 DVDs, he will add $2.95 to his costs and $2.75 to his revenues. What will be the effect on his profits of renting 3,526 DVDs instead of 3,525 DVDs?

2.3 Should a monopolistically competitive firm take into account its fixed costs when deciding how much to produce? Briefly explain.

Problems and Applications

2.4 If Daniel sells 350 Big Macs at a price of $3.25, and his average cost of producing 350 Big Macs is $3.00, what is his profit?

2.5 Alicia manages a Hollywood Video store and has the following information on demand and costs:

DVDS RENTED PER WEEK (*Q*)	PRICE (*P*)	TOTAL COST (*TC*)
0	$6.00	$3.00
1	5.50	7.00
2	5.00	10.00
3	4.50	12.50
4	4.00	14.50
5	3.50	16.00
6	3.00	17.00
7	2.50	18.50
8	2.00	21.00

a. To maximize profit, how many DVDs should Alicia rent, what price should she charge, and how much profit will she make?

b. What is the marginal revenue received by renting the profit-maximizing DVD? What is the marginal cost of renting the profit-maximizing DVD?

2.6 A trucking company investigates the relationship between the gas mileage of its trucks and the average speed at which the trucks are driven on the highway. The company finds the relationship shown in the following graph:

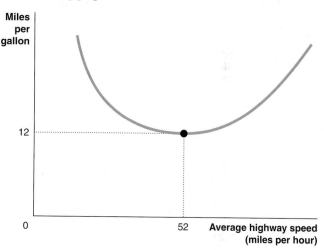

Will the firm maximize profits if it instructs its drivers to maintain an average speed of 52 miles per hour? Briefly explain.

2.7 The following is from an article in the *Wall Street Journal*: "Krispy Kreme Doughnuts Inc. reported its profit fell 56% in its second quarter despite an 11% increase in revenue." Briefly explain how it is possible for a firm's revenue to increase at the same time its profits decrease.

Source: "Krispy Kreme's Net Falls 56%; Company Cuts Sales Forecast," *Wall Street Journal*, August 26, 2004.

2.8 During 2003, General Motors cut the prices of most of its car models. As a result, GM earned a profit of only $184 per car, compared to the profit of $555 per car it had earned in 2002. Does the decline in GM's profits per car indicate that cutting prices was not a profit-maximizing strategy? Briefly explain.

Source: Karen Lundergaard and Sholnn Freeman, "Detroit's Challenge: Weaning Buyers from Years of Deals," *Wall Street Journal*, January 6, 2004.

2.9 **(Related to *Solved Problem 12-2* on page 416)** William Germano is vice president and publishing director at the Routledge publishing company. He has given the following description of how a publisher might deal with an unexpected increase in the cost of publishing a book:

> It's often asked why the publisher can't simply raise the price [if costs increase]. . . . It's likely that the editor [is already] . . . charging as much as the market will bear. . . . In other words, you might be willing to pay $50.00 for a . . . book on the Brooklyn Bridge, but if . . . production costs [increase] by 25 percent, you might think $62.50 is too much to pay, though that would be what the publisher needs to charge. And indeed the publisher may determine that $50.00 is this book's ceiling—the most you would pay before deciding to rent a movie instead.

According to what you have learned in this chapter, how do firms adjust the price of a good when there is an increase in cost? Use a graph to illustrate your answer. Does the model of monopolistic competition seem to fit Germano's description? If a publisher does not raise the price of a book following an increase in its production cost, what will be the result?

Source: William Germano, *Getting It Published: A Guide to Scholars and Anyone Else Serious about Serious Books*, Chicago: University of Chicago Press, 2001, pp. 110–111.

2.10 The following excerpt is from an article in the *Wall Street Journal*:

> [Amazon.com], whose sales stagnated last year, increased revenue [this quarter] by 21 percent, to $806 million. . . . It attributed the increase to its price-cutting strategy: discounting books that cost more than $15 each and offering free shipping on orders of at least $49.

a. If Amazon.com's revenue increased after it cut the price of books, what must be true about the price elasticity of demand for ordering books online?

b. Suppose that before the price cut, Amazon.com was not selling the profit-maximizing quantity of books, but after the price cut, it was. Draw a graph that shows Amazon.com's situation before and after the price cut. (For simplicity, assume that Amazon charges the same price for all books.) Be sure your graph includes the price Amazon was charging and the quantity of books it was selling before the price cut; the price and quantity after the price cut; Amazon's demand, marginal revenue, average total cost, and marginal cost curves; and the areas representing Amazon's profits before and after the price cut.

Source: Saul Hansell, "Citing Its Price Strategy, Amazon Pares Loss," *Wall Street Journal*, July 24, 2002.

2.11 In 1916, the Ford Motor Company produced 500,000 Model T Fords at a price of $440 each. The company made a profit of $60 million that year. Henry Ford told a newspaper reporter that he intended to reduce the price of the Model T to $360, and he expected to sell 800,000 cars at that price. Ford said, "Less profit on each car, but more cars, more employment of labor, and in the end we get all the total profit we ought to make."

a. Did Ford expect the total revenue he received from selling Model Ts to rise or fall following the price cut?

b. Use the information given above to calculate the price elasticity of demand for Model Ts. Use the midpoint formula to make your calculation. See Chapter 6, page 176, if you need a refresher on the midpoint formula.

c. What would the average total cost of producing 800,000 Model Ts have to be for Ford to make as much profit selling 800,000 Model Ts as it made selling 500,000 Model Ts? Is this smaller or larger than the average total cost of producing 500,000 Model Ts?

d. Assume that Ford would make the same total profit when selling 800,000 cars as when selling 500,000 cars. Was Henry Ford correct in saying he would make less profit per car when selling 800,000 cars than when selling 500,000 cars?

> **» End Learning Objective 12.2**

12.3 LEARNING OBJECTIVE   12.3 | Analyze the situation of a monopolistically competitive firm in the long run, pages 417–423.

What Happens to Profits in the Long Run?

Summary

If a monopolistically competitive firm is earning economic profits in the short run, entry of new firms will eliminate those profits in the long run. If a monopolistically competitive firm is suffering economic losses in the short run, exit of existing firms will eliminate those losses in the long run. Monopolistically competitive firms continually struggle to find new ways of differentiating their products as they try to stay one step ahead of other firms that are attempting to copy their success.

Review Questions

3.1 What effect does the entry of new firms have on the economic profits of existing firms?

3.2 What is the difference between zero accounting profit and zero economic profit.

Problems and Applications

3.3 Use this graph to answer the questions that follow.

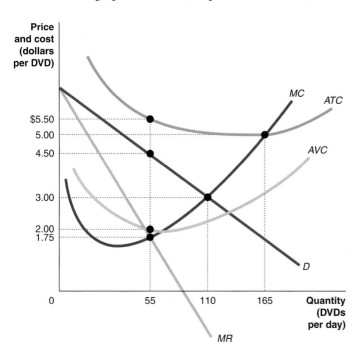

a. If the owner of this video store wants to maximize profits, how many DVDs should she rent per day, and what rental price should she charge? Briefly explain your answer.

b. How much economic profit (or loss) is she making? Briefly explain.

c. Is the owner likely to continue renting this number of DVDs in the long run? Briefly explain.

3.4 **(Related to the *Don't Let This Happen to You!* on page 418)** A student remarks:

> If firms in a monopolistically competitive industry are earning economic profits, new firms will enter the industry. Eventually, the representative firm will find its demand curve has shifted to the left until it is just tangent to its average cost curve and it is earning zero profit. Because firms are earning zero profit at that point, some firms will leave the industry and the representative firm will

find its demand curve will shift to the right. In long-run equilibrium, price will be above average total cost by just enough so that each firm is just breaking even.

Briefly explain whether you agree with this analysis.

3.5 **(Related to the *Making the Connection* on page 419)** Writing in the *Wall Street Journal*, Walter Mossberg argues:

> But the new popularity of the [Macintosh computer] is also partly due to the fact that it can now run Windows along with Apple's superior Mac OS X operating system. That means that if there's a program you need that comes only in a Windows version, you can run it on any current Mac model, speedily and with all its features.

If it is an advantage to Apple that the Macintosh can now run Windows as well as the Mac operating system, would Apple be even better off if it abandoned its own operating system and installed only Windows on the computers it sells?

Source: Walter S. Mossberg, "Fusion Is the Latest Way for Macs to Run Windows. PC Software," *Wall Street Journal*, August 2, 2007.

3.6 **(Related to *Solved Problem 12-3* on page 420)** Michael Porter, an economist at Harvard Business School, argues that firms in the U.S. commercial-printing industry have been "investing heavily in the same new equipment, running their presses faster, and reducing crew sizes. But the resulting major productivity gains are being captured by customers and equipment suppliers, not retained in superior profitability." How would consumers gain from these productivity increases? Why haven't the productivity increases made the printing firms more profitable?

Source: Michael E. Porter, "What Is Strategy?" *Harvard Business Review*, November–December 1996, p. 63.

3.7 Michael Korda was, for many years, editor-in-chief at the Simon & Schuster book publishing company. He has written about the many books that have become bestsellers by promising to give readers financial advice that will make them wealthy, by, for example, buying and selling real estate. Korda is very skeptical about the usefulness of the advice in these books because "I have yet to meet anybody who got rich by buying a book, though quite a few people got rich by writing one." On the basis of the analysis in this chapter, discuss why it may be very difficult to become rich by following the advice found in a book.

Source: Michael Korda, *Making the List: A Cultural History of the American Bestseller, 1900–1999*, New York: Barnes & Noble Books, 2001, p. 168.

3.8 **(Related to the *Chapter Opener* on page 410)** According to an article in *Fortune* magazine, "The big question for [Starbucks' chairman] Howard Schultz is whether Starbucks can keep it up. There are those on Wall Street who say that Starbucks' game is almost over." What do you think the article means by "Starbucks' game is almost over"? Why would some people on Wall Street be making this prediction about a firm that was making substantial economic profits at the time the article was written?

Source: Andy Serwer, "Hot Starbucks to Go," *Fortune*, January 12, 2004.

3.9 (Related to the *Making the Connection* on page 422) L'Oréal devotes significant resources to developing new products and differentiating its products from those of its competitors. Suppose it did not do that. What would be the effect on its profits in the short run? What would be the effect on its profits in the long run?

>> **End Learning Objective 12.3**

12.4 LEARNING OBJECTIVE   12.4 | Compare the efficiency of monopolistic competition and perfect competition, pages 423–425.

Comparing Perfect Competition and Monopolistic Competition

Summary

Perfectly competitive firms produce where price equals marginal cost and at minimum average total cost. Perfectly competitive firms achieve both allocative and productive efficiency. Monopolistically competitive firms produce where price is greater than marginal cost and above minimum average total cost. Monopolistically competitive firms do not achieve either allocative or productive efficiency. Consumers face a trade-off when buying the product of a monopolistically competitive firm: They are paying a price that is greater than marginal cost, and the product is not being produced at minimum average cost, but they benefit from being able to purchase a product that is differentiated and more closely suited to their tastes.

myeconlab Visit www.myeconlab.com to complete these exercises
Get Ahead of the Curve online and get instant feedback.

Review Questions

4.1 What are the differences between the long-run equilibrium of a perfectly competitive firm and the long-run equilibrium of a monopolistically competitive firm?

4.2 Does the fact that monopolistically competitive markets are not allocatively or productively efficient mean that there is a significant loss in economic well-being to society in these markets? In your answer, be sure to define what you mean by "economic well-being."

Problems and Applications

4.3 A student asks the following question:

I can understand why a perfectly competitive firm will not earn profits in the long run because a perfectly competitive firm charges a price equal to marginal cost. But a monopolistically competitive firm can charge a price greater than marginal cost,

so why can't it continue to earn profits in the long run?

How would you answer this question?

4.4 Consider the following graph.

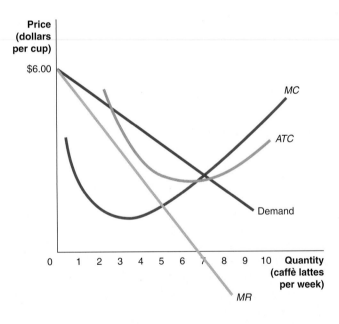

a. Is it possible to say whether this firm is a perfectly competitive firm or a monopolistically competitive firm? If so, explain how you are able to say this.

b. Does the graph show a short-run equilibrium or a long-run equilibrium? Briefly explain.

c. What quantity on the graph represents long-run equilibrium if the firm were perfectly competitive?

4.5 Before the fall of Communism, most basic consumer products in Eastern Europe and the Soviet Union were standardized. For example, government-run stores would offer for sale only one type of bar soap or one type of toothpaste. Soviet economists often argued that this system of standardizing basic consumer products avoided the waste associated with the differentiated goods and services produced in

Western Europe and the United States. Do you agree with this argument?

4.6 **(Related to the *Making the Connection* on page 425)** Juicy Couture has been successful in selling women's clothing using an unusual strategy. According to an article in the *Wall Street Journal* the key to the firm's strategy is to "Limit distribution to maintain the brand's exclusive cachet, even if that means sacrificing sales, a brand-management technique once used only for high-end luxury brands." In 2006, Juicy clothes were sold in only four department stores: Neiman Marcus, Saks, Bloomingdale's, and Nordstrom. Although Juicy was originally known mainly for the fashion tracksuits it sold, "Juicy Couture doesn't just make tracksuits favored by celebrities any more. With its edgy contemporary sportswear and accessories, it has become a lifestyle brand for women, men and kids with estimated annual sales of more than $300 million, up from $47 million in 2002. . . . "

a. Why would limiting the number of stores your product was sold in be a successful strategy for a clothing firm? What would be likely to happen to Juicy's sales if it began to sell its clothes at Wal-Mart and similar stores?

b. Compared with the situation Apple Computer faced during the mid 1980s, is Juicy more or less likely to be able to maintain its product differentiation over a long period of time?

Source: Rachel Dodes, "From Track Suits to Fast Track," *Wall Street Journal*, September 13, 2006.

>> **End Learning Objective 12.4**

12.5 LEARNING OBJECTIVE 12.5 | Define marketing and explain how firms use it to differentiate their products, pages 425–427.

How Marketing Differentiates Products

Summary

Marketing refers to all the activities necessary for a firm to sell a product to a consumer. Firms use two marketing tools to differentiate their products: brand management and advertising. **Brand management** refers to the actions of a firm intended to maintain the differentiation of a product over time. When a firm has established a successful brand name, it has a strong incentive to defend it. A firm can apply for a *trademark*, which grants legal protection against other firms using its product's name.

myeconlab Visit www.myeconlab.com to complete these exercises *Get Ahead of the Curve* online and get instant feedback.

Review Questions

5.1 Define marketing. Is marketing just another name for advertising?

5.2 Why are many companies so concerned about brand management?

Problems and Applications

5.3 Draw a graph that shows the impact on a firm's profits when it increases spending on advertising and the increased advertising has *no* effect on the demand for the firm's product.

5.4 A skeptic says, "Marketing research and brand management are redundant. If a company wants to find out what customers want, it should simply look at what they're already buying." Do you agree with this comment? Explain.

5.5 The National Football League (NFL) has a trademark on the name "Super Bowl" for its championship game. Advertisers can only use the words Super Bowl in their advertising if they pay the NFL a fee. Many companies attempt to get around this trademark by using the phrase "the big game" in their advertising. For example, just before the Super Bowl is to be played a consumer electronics store might have an advertisement with the phrase "Watch the big game on a new HD TV." In 2007, the National Football League indicated that it might attempt legal action to have the phrase "the big game" included in its Super Bowl trademark.

a. Why does the government allow firms to trademark their products?

b. Would consumers gain or lose if the NFL were allowed to trademark the phrase "the big game"? Briefly explain.

5.6 Some companies have done a poor job protecting their products' images. For example, Hormel's Spam brand name is widely ridiculed and has escaped from the company's control in cyberspace. Think of other cases where companies have failed to protect their brand names. What can they do about it now? Should they re-brand their products?

>> **End Learning Objective 12.5**

12.6 LEARNING OBJECTIVE   12.6 | Identify the key factors that determine a firm's success, **pages 427–428.**

What Makes a Firm Successful?

Summary

A firm's owners and managers control some of the factors that determine the profitability of the firm. Other factors affect all the firms in the market or are the result of chance, so they are not under the control of the firm's owners. The interactions between factors the firm controls and factors it does not control determine its profitability.

myeconlab Visit www.myeconlab.com to complete these exercises
Get Ahead of the Curve online and get instant feedback.

Review Questions

6.1 What are the key factors that determine the profitability of a firm in a monopolistically competitive market?

6.2 How might a monopolistically competitive firm continually earn economic profit greater than zero?

Problems and Applications

6.3 According to an article in the *Wall Street Journal*:

> In early January last year, after a disappointing Christmas season and amid worries about competition from discount retailers, Zale Corp. decided to shake things up: The self-proclaimed jeweler to Middle America was going to chase upscale customers. . . . The move was a disaster. The Irving, Texas, retailer lost many of its traditional customers without winning the new ones it coveted.

Why would a firm like Zale abandon one market niche for another market niche? We know that in this case the move was not successful. Can you think of other cases where it has been successful?

Source: Ann Zimmerman and Kris Hudson, "Chasing Upscale Customers Tarnishes Mass-Market Jeweler," *Wall Street Journal*, June 26, 2006. p. A1.

6.4 7-Eleven, Inc., operates more than 20,000 convenience stores worldwide. Edward Moneypenny, 7-Eleven's chief financial officer, was asked to name the biggest risk the company faced. He replied, "I would say that the biggest risk that 7-Eleven faces, like all retailers, is competition . . . because that is something that you've got to be aware of in this business." In what sense is competition a "risk" to a business? Why would a company in the retail business need to be particularly aware of competition?

Source: Company Report, CEO Interview: Edward Moneypenny—7-Eleven, Inc., The Wall Street Transcript Corporation.

6.5 In 2006, Wal-Mart closed its stores in South Korea and Germany. According to an article in the *New York Times*:

> Wal-Mart's most successful markets, like Mexico, are those in which it started big. There, the company bought the country's largest and best-run retail chain, Cifra, and has never looked back. This year, Wal-Mart is spending more than $1 billion in Mexico to open 120 new stores.

What advantages does Wal-Mart gain from buying large retail chains, as it did in Mexico, rather than small chains, as it did in its unsuccessful attempts to enter the South Korean and German markets?

Source: Mark Landler and Michael Barbaro, "Wal-Mart Finds That Its Formula Doesn't Fit Every Culture," *New York Times*, August 2, 2006.

6.6 **(Related to the *Making the Connection* on page 428)** A firm that is first to the market with a new product frequently discovers that there are design flaws or problems with the product that were not anticipated. For example, the ballpoint pens made by the Reynolds International Pen Company often leaked. What effect do these problems have on the innovating firm and how do these unexpected problems open up possibilities for other firms to enter the market?

>> **End Learning Objective 12.6**

Chapter 13

Oligopoly: Firms in Less Competitive Markets

Competing with Wal-Mart

Many of the largest corporations in the United States began as small businesses. In 1975, Bill Gates and Paul Allen founded the Microsoft Corporation in Albuquerque, New Mexico, with themselves as the only employees. Michael Dell started the Dell computer company in 1984 from his dorm room at the University of Texas. Sam Walton, founder of Wal-Mart, bought his first store in 1945 with $20,000 borrowed from his father-in-law. Eventually, Wal-Mart would become the largest company in the world. Today, Wal-Mart employs nearly 2.1 million people, which is four times as many as McDonald's, the second largest employer.

When each of these firms was founded, their industries included many more firms than they do now. Today, in the software and computer industries, fewer than 10 firms account for the great majority of sales. Wal-Mart accounts for a large share of several segments of retail sales. In 2008, Wal-Mart was the leading seller of groceries in the United States. It sells more than 25 percent of all the disposable diapers, toothpaste, dog food, and photographic film sold in

the United States. It is also the leading seller of CDs and DVDs, with market shares of 15 to 20 percent. More than 93 percent of U.S. families shop at Wal-Mart at least once per year.

An industry with only a few firms is an *oligopoly*. In an oligopoly, a firm's profitability depends on its interactions with other firms. In these industries, firms must develop *business strategies*, which involve not just deciding what price to charge and how many units to produce but also how much to advertise, which new technologies to adopt, how to manage relations with suppliers, and which new markets to enter.

A key part of Sam Walton's business strategy for Wal-Mart involved placing stores in small towns, where the main competition was from small, locally owned stores. By buying in bulk directly from manufacturers, Walton was able to lower costs, which enabled him to charge lower prices than his competitors. As early as the 1970s, Wal-Mart also made large investments in information technology (IT). Unlike most of its competitors, which had to count unsold goods by hand to find out how many were left in inventory, Wal-Mart had a computerized system for tracking goods. To aid this system, Wal-Mart insisted in the early 1980s that its suppliers use UPC barcodes on

products. This helped spread the use of barcodes to nearly every product sold in the United States. Today, Wal-Mart is pioneering the use of radio frequency identification (RFID) tracking tags that may ultimately replace barcodes. With this system, employees will no longer have to manually scan barcodes. Instead, a radio signal will automatically record the arrival of a product in the warehouse, its shipment to a Wal-Mart store, and its purchase by the consumer. By 2007, many of Wal-Mart's largest suppliers had implemented RFID systems.

In recent years, Wal-Mart has been criticized for several practices, including selling goods produced in foreign factories by low-paid workers, paying low wages to its own workers, providing limited health care benefits, and driving smaller competitors into bankruptcy. As a result, Wal-Mart has run into some difficulty getting local government approvals to open new stores. Wal-Mart's competitors, however, continue to search for ways to successfully compete. **AN INSIDE LOOK** on **page 462** discusses Target's attempts to compete with Wal-Mart in the market for generic prescription drugs.

Source: "The Bulldozer of Bentonville Slows," *Economist*, February 15, 2007.

LEARNING Objectives

After studying this chapter, you should be able to:

13.1 Show how **barriers to entry** explain the existence of **oligopolies**, page 442.

13.2 Use **game theory** to analyze the strategies of oligopolistic firms, page 445.

13.3 Use **sequential games** to analyze business strategies, page 454.

13.4 Use the **five competitive forces model** to analyze competition in an industry, page 457.

Economics in YOUR Life!

Why Can't You Find a Cheap PlayStation 3?

It's the end of finals, and you and your roommate decide to treat yourselves to a PlayStation 3 game system—provided that you can find one that has a relatively low price. First you check Amazon.com and find a price of $499.99. Then you check Best Buy, but the price is also $499.99. Then you check Target; $499.99 again! Finally, you check Wal-Mart, and you find a lower price: $499.*82*, a whopping discount of $0.17. Why isn't one of these big retailers willing to charge a lower price? What happened to price competition? As you read the chapter, see if you can answer these questions. You can check your answers against those we provide at the end of the chapter. **>> Continued on page 461**

Oligopoly A market structure in which a small number of interdependent firms compete.

I n Chapters 11 and 12, we studied perfectly competitive and monopolistically competitive industries. Our analysis focused on the determination of a firm's profit-maximizing price and quantity. We concluded that firms maximize profit by producing where marginal revenue equals marginal cost. To determine marginal revenue and marginal cost, we used graphs that included the firm's demand, marginal revenue, and marginal cost curves. In this chapter, we will study **oligopoly**, a market structure in which a small number of interdependent firms compete. In analyzing oligopoly, we cannot rely on the same types of graphs we used in analyzing perfect competition and monopolistic competition—for two reasons.

First, we need to use economic models that allow us to analyze the more complex business strategies of large oligopoly firms. Second, even in determining the profit-maximizing price and output of an oligopoly firm, demand curves and cost curves are not as useful as in the cases of perfect competition and monopolistic competition. We are able to draw the demand curves for competitive firms by assuming that the prices these firms charge have no impact on the prices other firms in their industries charge. This assumption is realistic when each firm is small relative to the market. It is not a realistic assumption, however, for firms that are as large relative to their markets as Microsoft, Dell, or Wal-Mart.

When large firms cut their prices, their rivals in the industry often—but not always—respond by also cutting their prices. Because we don't know for sure how other firms will respond to a price change, we don't know the quantity an oligopolist will sell at a particular price. In other words, it is difficult to know what an oligopolist's demand curve will look like. As we have seen, a firm's marginal revenue curve depends on its demand curve. If we don't know what an oligopolist's demand curve looks like, we also don't know what its marginal revenue curve looks like. Not knowing marginal revenue, we can't calculate the profit-maximizing level of output and the profit-maximizing price the way we did for competitive firms.

The approach we use to analyze competition among oligopolists is called *game theory*. Game theory can be used to analyze any situation in which groups or individuals interact. In the context of economic analysis, game theory is the study of the decisions of firms in industries where the profits of each firm depend on its interactions with other firms. It has been applied to strategies for nuclear war, for international trade negotiations, and for political campaigns, among many other examples. In this chapter, we use game theory to analyze the business strategies of large firms.

13.1 LEARNING OBJECTIVE

13.1 | Show how barriers to entry explain the existence of oligopolies.

Oligopoly and Barriers to Entry

Oligopolies are industries with only a few firms. This market structure lies between the competitive industries we studied in Chapters 11 and 12, which have many firms, and the monopolies we will study in Chapter 14, which have only a single firm. One measure of the extent of competition in an industry is the *concentration ratio*. Every five years, the U.S. Bureau of the Census publishes four-firm concentration ratios that state the fraction of each industry's sales accounted for by its four largest firms. Most economists believe that a four-firm concentration ratio of greater than 40 percent indicates that an industry is an oligopoly.

The concentration ratio has some flaws as a measure of the extent of competition in an industry. For example, concentration ratios do not include sales in the United States by foreign firms. In addition, concentration ratios are calculated for the national market, even though the competition in some industries, such as restaurants or college bookstores, is mainly local. Finally, competition sometimes exists between firms in different industries. For example, Wal-Mart is included in the discount department stores industry but also competes with firms in the supermarket industry and the retail toy store industry. As we will see in Chapter 14, some economists prefer another measure of competition, known as the *Herfindahl-Hirschman Index*. Despite their shortcomings, concentration ratios can be useful in providing a general idea of the extent of competition in an industry.

Table 13-1 lists examples of oligopolies in manufacturing and retail trade. Notice that the "Discount Department Stores" industry that includes Wal-Mart is highly concentrated. Wal-Mart also operates Sam's Club stores, which are in the highly concentrated "Warehouse Clubs and Supercenters" industry.

Barriers to Entry

Why do oligopolies exist? Why aren't there many more firms in the discount department store industry, the beer industry, or the automobile industry? Recall that new firms will enter industries where existing firms are earning economic profits. But new firms often have difficulty entering an oligopoly. Anything that keeps new firms from entering an industry in which firms are earning economic profits is called a **barrier to entry**. Three barriers to entry are economies of scale, ownership of a key input, and government-imposed barriers.

Economies of Scale The most important barrier to entry is economies of scale. Chapter 10 stated that **economies of scale** exist when a firm's long-run average costs fall as it increases output. The greater the economies of scale, the fewer the number of firms that will be in the industry. Figure 13-1 illustrates this point.

If economies of scale are relatively unimportant in the industry, the typical firm's long-run average cost curve (*LRAC*) will reach a minimum at a level of output (Q_1 in Figure 13-1) that is a small fraction of total industry sales. The industry will have room for a large number of firms and will be competitive. If economies of scale are significant, the typical firm will not reach the minimum point on its long-run average cost curve (Q_2 in Figure 13-1) until it has produced a large fraction of industry sales. Then the industry will have room for only a few firms and will be an oligopoly.

Barrier to entry Anything that keeps new firms from entering an industry in which firms are earning economic profits.

Economies of scale The situation when a firm's long-run average costs fall as it increases output.

RETAIL TRADE		MANUFACTURING	
INDUSTRY	**FOUR-FIRM CONCENTRATION RATIO**	**INDUSTRY**	**FOUR-FIRM CONCENTRATION RATIO**
Discount Department Stores	95%	Cigarettes	95%
Warehouse Clubs and Supercenters	92%	Beer	91%
Hobby, Toy, and Game Stores	72%	Aircraft	81%
Athletic Footwear Stores	71%	Breakfast Cereal	78%
College Bookstores	70%	Automobiles	76%
Radio, Television, and Other Electronic Stores	69%	Computers	76%
Pharmacies and Drugstores	53%	Dog and Cat Food	64%

TABLE 13-1

Examples of Oligopolies in Retail Trade and Manufacturing

Source: U.S. Census Bureau, *Concentration Ratios, 2002*, May 2006; and U.S. Census Bureau, *Establishment and Firm Size, 2002*, November 2005.

Figure 13-1

Economies of Scale Help Determine the Extent of Competition in an Industry

An industry will be competitive if the minimum point on the typical firm's long-run average cost curve ($LRAC_1$) occurs at a level of output that is a small fraction of total industry sales, like Q_1. The industry will be an oligopoly if the minimum point comes at a level of output that is a large fraction of industry sales, like Q_2.

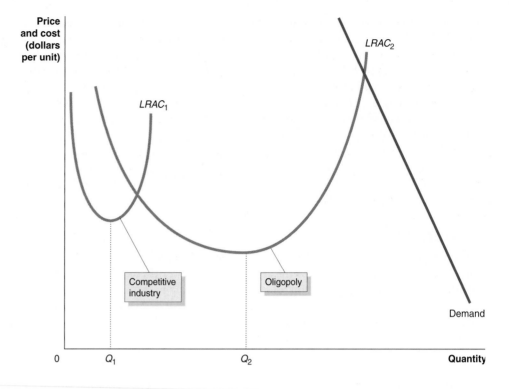

Economies of scale can explain why there is much more competition in the restaurant industry than in the discount department store industry. Because very large restaurants do not have lower average costs than smaller restaurants, the restaurant industry has room for many firms. In contrast, large discount department stores, such as Wal-Mart, have much lower average costs than small discount department stores, for the reasons we discussed in the chapter opener. As a result, just four firms—Wal-Mart, Target, Kmart, and Costco—account for about 95 percent of all sales in this industry.

Ownership of a Key Input If production of a good requires a particular input, then control of that input can be a barrier to entry. For many years, the Aluminum Company of America (Alcoa) controlled most of the world's supply of high-quality bauxite, the mineral needed to produce aluminum. The only way other companies could enter the industry to compete with Alcoa was to recycle aluminum. The De Beers Company of South Africa was able to block competition in the diamond market by controlling the output of most of the world's diamond mines. Until the 1990s, Ocean Spray had very little competition in the market for fresh and frozen cranberries because it controlled almost the entire supply of cranberries. Even today, it controls about 80 percent of the cranberry crop.

Government-Imposed Barriers Firms sometimes try to have the government impose barriers to entry. Many large firms employ *lobbyists* to convince state legislators and members of Congress to pass laws favorable to the economic interests of the firms. There are tens of thousands of lobbyists in Washington, DC, alone. Top lobbyists command annual salaries of $300,000 or more, which indicates the value firms place on their activities. Examples of government-imposed barriers to entry are patents, licensing requirements, and barriers to international trade. A **patent** gives a firm the exclusive right to a new product for a period of 20 years from the date the product is invented. Governments use patents to encourage firms to carry out research and development of new and better products and better ways of producing existing products. Output and living standards increase faster when firms devote resources to research and development, but a firm that spends money to develop a new product may not earn much profit if other firms can copy the product. For example, the pharmaceutical company Merck spends more than $3 billion per year to develop new prescription drugs. If rival companies could freely produce these new drugs as soon as Merck developed them, most of the firm's investment would be wasted. Because

Patent The exclusive right to a product for a period of 20 years from the date the product is invented.

Merck can patent a new drug, the firm can charge higher prices during the years the patent is in force and make an economic profit on its successful innovation.

The government also restricts competition through *occupational licensing*. The United States currently has about 500 occupational licensing laws. For example, doctors and dentists in every state need licenses to practice. The justification for the laws is to protect the public from incompetent practitioners, but by restricting the number of people who can enter the licensed professions, the laws also raise prices. Studies have shown that states that make it harder to earn a dentist's license have prices for dental services that are about 15 percent higher than in other states. Similarly, states that require a license for out-of-state firms to sell contact lenses have higher prices for contact lenses. When state licenses are required for occupations like hair braiding, which was done several years ago in California, restricting competition is the main result.

Government also imposes barriers to entering some industries by imposing tariffs and quotas on foreign competition. As we saw in Chapter 8, a *tariff* is a tax on imports, and a *quota* limits the quantity of a good that can be imported into a country. A quota on foreign sugar imports severely limits competition in the U.S. sugar market. As a result, U.S. sugar companies can charge prices that are more than twice as high as those charged by companies outside the United States.

In summary, to earn economic profits, all firms would like to charge a price well above average cost, but earning economic profits attracts new firms to enter the industry. Eventually, the increased competition forces price down to average cost, and firms just break even. In an oligopoly, barriers to entry prevent—or at least slow down—entry, which allows firms to earn economic profits over a longer period.

13.2 | Use game theory to analyze the strategies of oligopolistic firms.

Using Game Theory to Analyze Oligopoly

As we noted at the beginning of the chapter, economists analyze oligopolies using *game theory*, which was developed during the 1940s by the mathematician John von Neumann and the economist Oskar Morgenstern. **Game theory** is the study of how people make decisions in situations in which attaining their goals depends on their interactions with others. In oligopolies, the interactions among firms are crucial in determining profitability because the firms are large relative to the market.

In all games—whether poker, chess, or Monopoly—the interactions among the players are crucial in determining the outcome. In addition, games share three key characteristics:

1 *Rules* that determine what actions are allowable

2 *Strategies* that players employ to attain their objectives in the game

3 *Payoffs* that are the results of the interaction among the players' strategies

In business situations, the rules of the "game" include not just laws that a firm must obey but also other matters beyond a firm's control—at least in the short run—such as its production function. A **business strategy** is a set of actions that a firm takes to achieve a goal, such as maximizing profits. The *payoffs* are the profits earned as a result of a firm's strategies interacting with the strategies of the other firms. The best way to understand the game theory approach is to look at an example.

Game theory The study of how people make decisions in situations in which attaining their goals depends on their interactions with others; in economics, the study of the decisions of firms in industries where the profits of each firm depend on its interactions with other firms.

Business strategy Actions taken by a firm to achieve a goal, such as maximizing profits.

A Duopoly Game: Price Competition between Two Firms

In this simple example, we use game theory to analyze price competition in a *duopoly*—an oligopoly with two firms. Suppose that an isolated town in Alaska has only two stores: Wal-Mart and Target. Both stores sell the new Sony PlayStation 3. For simplicity, let's assume that no other stores stock PlayStation 3 and that consumers in the town can't

Figure 13-2

A Duopoly Game

Wal-Mart's profits are in blue, and Target's profits are in red. Wal-Mart and Target would each make profits of $10,000 per month on sales of PlayStation 3 if they both charged $600. However, each store manager has an incentive to undercut the other by charging a lower price. If both charge $400, they would each make a profit of only $7,500 per month.

Payoff matrix A table that shows the payoffs that each firm earns from every combination of strategies by the firms.

Collusion An agreement among firms to charge the same price or otherwise not to compete.

Dominant strategy A strategy that is the best for a firm, no matter what strategies other firms use.

Nash equilibrium A situation in which each firm chooses the best strategy, given the strategies chosen by other firms.

buy it on the Internet or through mail-order catalogs. The manager of each store decides whether to charge $400 or $600 for the PlayStation. Which price will be more profitable depends on the price the other store charges. The decision regarding what price to charge is an example of a business strategy. In Figure 13-2, we organize the possible outcomes that result from the actions of the two firms into a *payoff matrix*. A **payoff matrix** is a table that shows the payoffs that each firm earns from every combination of strategies by the firms.

Wal-Mart's profits are shown in blue, and Target's profits are shown in red. If Wal-Mart and Target both charge $600 for the PlayStation, each store will make a profit of $10,000 per month from sales of the game console. If Wal-Mart charges the lower price of $400, while Target charges $600, Wal-Mart will gain many of Target's customers. Wal-Mart's profits will be $15,000, and Target's will be only $5,000. Similarly, if Wal-Mart charges $600, while Target is charging $400, Wal-Mart's profits will be only $5,000, while Target's profits will be $15,000. If both stores charge $400, each will earn profits of $7,500 per month.

Clearly, the stores will be better off if they both charge $600 for the PlayStation. But will they both charge this price? One possibility is that the manager of the Wal-Mart and the manager of the Target will get together and *collude* by agreeing to charge the higher price. **Collusion** is an agreement among firms to charge the same price or otherwise not to compete. Unfortunately, for Wal-Mart and Target—but fortunately for their customers—collusion is against the law in the United States. The government can fine companies that collude and send the managers involved to jail.

The manager of the Wal-Mart store legally can't discuss his pricing decision with the manager of the Target store, so he has to predict what the other manager will do. Suppose the Wal-Mart manager is convinced that the Target manager will charge $600 for the PlayStation. In this case, the Wal-Mart manager will definitely charge $400 because that will increase his profit from $10,000 to $15,000. But suppose instead the Wal-Mart manager is convinced that the Target manager will charge $400. Then the Wal-Mart manager also definitely will charge $400 because that will increase his profit from $5,000 to $7,500. In fact, whichever price the Target manager decides to charge, the Wal-Mart manager is better off charging $400. So, we know that the Wal-Mart manager will choose a price of $400 for the PlayStation.

Now consider the situation of the Target manager. The Target manager is in the identical position to the Wal-Mart manager, so we can expect her to make the same decision to charge $400 for the PlayStation. In this situation, each manager has a *dominant strategy*. A **dominant strategy** is the best strategy for a firm, no matter what strategies other firms use. The result is an equilibrium where both managers charge $400 for the PlayStation. This situation is an equilibrium because each manager is maximizing profits, *given the price chosen by the other manager*. In other words, neither firm can increase its profits by changing its price, given the price chosen by the other firm. An equilibrium where each firm chooses the best strategy, given the strategies chosen by other firms, is called a **Nash equilibrium**, named after Nobel laureate John Nash of Princeton University, a pioneer in the development of game theory.

Making the Connection	### A Beautiful Mind: Game Theory Goes to the Movies

John Nash is the most celebrated game theorist in the world, partly because of his achievements and partly because of his dramatic life. In 1948, at the age of 20, Nash received bachelor's and master's degrees in mathematics from the Carnegie Institute of Technology (now known as Carnegie Mellon University). Two years later, he received a Ph.D. from Princeton for his 27-page dissertation on game theory. It was in this dissertation that he first discussed the concept that became known as the *Nash equilibrium.* Nash appeared to be on his way to a brilliant academic career until he developed schizophrenia in the 1950s. He spent decades in and out of mental hospitals. During these years, he roamed the Princeton campus, covering blackboards in unused classrooms with indecipherable writings. He became known as the "Phantom of Fine Hall." In the 1970s, Nash gradually began to recover. In 1994, he shared the Nobel Prize in Economics with John Harsanyi of the University of California, Berkeley, and Reinhard Selten of Rheinische Friedrich–Wilhelms Universität, Germany, for his work on game theory.

In the film A Beautiful Mind, *Russell Crowe played John Nash, winner of the Nobel Prize in Economics.*

In 1998, Sylvia Nasar of the *New York Times* wrote a biography of Nash, titled *A Beautiful Mind.* Three years later, the book was adapted into an award-winning film starring Russell Crowe. Unfortunately, the (fictitious) scene in the film that shows Nash discovering the idea of Nash equilibrium misstates the concept. In the scene, Nash is in a bar with several friends when four women with brown hair and one with blonde hair walk in. Nash and all of his friends prefer the blonde to the brunettes. One of Nash's friends points out that if they all compete for the blonde, they are unlikely to get her. In competing for the blonde, they will also insult the brunettes, with the result that none of them will end up with a date. Nash then gets a sudden insight. He suggests that they ignore the blonde and each approach one of the brunettes. That is the only way, he argues, that each of them will end up with a date.

Nash immediately claims that this is also an economic insight. He points out that Adam Smith had argued that the best result comes from everyone in the group doing what's best for himself. Nash argues, however, "The best result comes from everyone in the group doing what's best for himself *and* the group." But this is not an accurate description of the Nash equilibrium. As we have seen, in a Nash equilibrium, each player uses a strategy that will make him as well off as possible, *given the strategies of the other players.* The bar situation would not be a Nash equilibrium. Once the other men have chosen a brunette, each man will have an incentive to switch from the brunette he initially chose to the blonde.

YOUR TURN: Test your understanding by doing related problem 2.11 on page 466 at the end of this chapter.

Don't Let This Happen to **YOU!**

Don't Misunderstand Why Each Manager Ends Up Charging a Price of $400

It is tempting to think that the Wal-Mart manager and the Target manager would each charge $400 rather than $600 for the PlayStation because each is afraid that the other manager will charge $400. In fact, fear of being undercut by the other firm's charging a lower price is not the key to understanding each manager's pricing strategy. Notice that charging $400 is the most profitable strategy for each

manager, no matter which price the other manager decides to charge. For example, even if the Wal-Mart manager somehow knew for sure that the Target manager intended to charge $600, he would still charge $400 because his profits would be $15,000 instead of $10,000. The Target manager is in the same situation. That is why charging $400 is a dominant strategy for both managers.

YOUR TURN: Test your understanding by doing related problem 2.15 on page 467 at the end of the chapter.

Firm Behavior and the Prisoners' Dilemma

Cooperative equilibrium An equilibrium in a game in which players cooperate to increase their mutual payoff.

Noncooperative equilibrium An equilibrium in a game in which players do not cooperate but pursue their own self-interest.

Prisoners' dilemma A game in which pursuing dominant strategies results in noncooperation that leaves everyone worse off.

Notice that the equilibrium in Figure 13-2 is not very satisfactory for either firm. The firms earn $7,500 profit each month by charging $400, but they could have earned $10,000 profit if they had both charged $600. By "cooperating" and charging the higher price, they would have achieved a *cooperative equilibrium*. In a **cooperative equilibrium**, players cooperate to increase their mutual payoff. We have seen, though, that the outcome of this game is likely to be a **noncooperative equilibrium**, in which each firm pursues its own self-interest.

A situation like this, in which pursuing dominant strategies results in noncooperation that leaves everyone worse off, is called a **prisoners' dilemma**. The game gets its name from the problem faced by two suspects the police arrest for a crime. If the police lack other evidence, they may separate the suspects and offer each a reduced prison sentence in exchange for confessing to the crime and testifying against the other criminal. Because each suspect has a dominant strategy to confess to the crime, they will both confess and serve a jail term, even though they would have gone free if they had both remained silent.

Solved Problem | 13-2

Is Advertising a Prisoners' Dilemma for Coca-Cola and Pepsi?

Coca-Cola and Pepsi both advertise aggressively, but would they be better off if they didn't? Their commercials are not designed to convey new information about the products. Instead, they are designed to capture each other's customers. Construct a payoff matrix using the following hypothetical information:

- If neither firm advertises, Coca-Cola and Pepsi both earn profits of $750 million per year.

- If both firms advertise, Coca-Cola and Pepsi both earn profits of $500 million per year.

- If Coca-Cola advertises and Pepsi doesn't, Coca-Cola earns profits of $900 million and Pepsi earns profits of $400 million.

- If Pepsi advertises and Coca-Cola doesn't, Pepsi earns profits of $900 million and Coca-Cola earns profits of $400 million.

  a. If Coca-Cola wants to maximize profit, will it advertise? Briefly explain.

  b. If Pepsi wants to maximize profit, will it advertise? Briefly explain.

  c. Is there a Nash equilibrium to this advertising game? If so, what is it?

SOLVING THE PROBLEM:

Step 1: **Review the chapter material.** This problem uses payoff matrixes to analyze a business situation, so you may want to review the section "A Duopoly Game: Price Competition between Two Firms," which begins on page 445.

Step 2: **Construct the payoff matrix.**

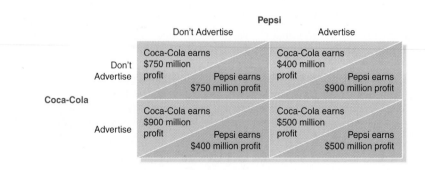

Step 3: **Answer question (a) by showing that Coca-Cola has a dominant strategy of advertising.** If Pepsi doesn't advertise, then Coca-Cola will make $900 million if it advertises but only $750 million if it doesn't. If Pepsi advertises, then Coca-Cola will make $500 million if it advertises but only $400 million if it doesn't. Therefore, advertising is a dominant strategy for Coca-Cola.

Step 4: **Answer question (b) by showing that Pepsi has a dominant strategy of advertising.** Pepsi is in the same position as Coca-Cola, so it also has a dominant strategy of advertising.

Step 5: **Answer question (c) by showing that there is a Nash equilibrium for this game.** Both firms advertising is a Nash equilibrium. Given that Pepsi is advertising, Coca-Cola's best strategy is to advertise. Given that Coca-Cola is advertising, Pepsi's best strategy is to advertise. Therefore, advertising is the optimal decision for both firms, *given the decision by the other firm.*

EXTRA CREDIT: This is another example of the prisoners' dilemma game. Coca-Cola and Pepsi would be more profitable if they both refrained from advertising, thereby saving the enormous expense of television and radio commercials and newspaper and magazine ads. Each firm's dominant strategy is to advertise, however, so they end up in an equilibrium where both advertise, and their profits are reduced.

YOUR TURN: For more practice, do related problems 2.12, 2.13, and 2.14 on pages 466–467 at the end of this chapter.

>> End Solved Problem 13-2

Making the Connection | **Is There a Dominant Strategy for Bidding on eBay?**

An auction is a game in which bidders compete to buy a product. The payoff in winning an auction is equal to the difference between the subjective value you place on the product being auctioned and the amount of the winning bid. On the online auction site eBay, more than 200 million items valued at more than $10 billion are auctioned each year.

eBay is run as a *second-price auction*, where the winning bidder pays the price of the second-highest bidder. If the high bidder on a DVD of *Spider-Man 3* bids $15, and the second bidder bids $10, the high bidder wins the auction and pays $15. It may seem that your best strategy when bidding on eBay is to place a bid well below the subjective value you place on the item in the hope of winning it at a low price. In fact, bidders on eBay have a dominant strategy of entering a bid equal to the maximum value they place on the item. For instance, suppose you are looking for a present for your parents' anniversary. They are Rolling Stones fans, and someone is auctioning a pair of Stones concert tickets. If the maximum value you place on the tickets is $200, that should be your bid. To see why, consider the results of strategies of bidding more or less than $200.

There are two possible outcomes of the auction: Either someone else bids more than you do, or you are the high bidder. First, suppose you bid $200 but someone else bids more than you do. If you had bid less than

On eBay, bidding the maximum value you place on an item is a dominant strategy.

$200, you would still have lost. If you had bid more than $200, you might have been the high bidder, but because your bid would be for more than the value you place on the tickets, you would have a negative payoff. Second, suppose you bid $200 and you are the high bidder. If you had bid less than $200, you would have run the risk of losing the tickets to someone whose bid you would have beaten by bidding $200. You would be worse off than if you had bid $200 and won. If you had bid more than $200, you would not have affected the price you ended up paying—which, remember, is equal to the amount bid by the second-highest bidder. Therefore, a strategy of bidding $200—the maximum value you place on the tickets—dominates bidding more or less than $200.

Even though making your first bid your highest bid is a dominant strategy on eBay, many bidders don't use it. After an auction is over, a link leads to a Web page showing all the bids. In many auctions, the same bidder bids several times, showing that the bidder had not understood his or her dominant strategy.

YOUR TURN: Test your understanding by doing related problem 2.16 on page 467 at the end of this chapter.

Can Firms Escape the Prisoners' Dilemma?

Although the prisoners' dilemma game seems to show that cooperative behavior always breaks down, we know it doesn't. People often cooperate to achieve their goals, and firms find ways to cooperate by not competing on price. The reason the basic prisoners' dilemma story is not always applicable is that it assumes the game will be played only once. Most business situations, however, are repeated over and over. Each month, the Target and Wal-Mart managers will decide again what price they will charge for PlayStation 3. In the language of game theory, the managers are playing a *repeated game.* In a repeated game, the losses from not cooperating are greater than in a game played once, and players can also employ *retaliation strategies* against those who don't cooperate. As a result, we are more likely to see cooperative behavior.

Figure 13-2 on page 446 shows that Wal-Mart and Target are earning $2,500 less per month by both charging $400 instead of $600 for the PlayStation 3. Every month that passes with both stores charging $400 increases the total amount lost: Two years of charging $400 will cause each store to lose $60,000 in profit. This lost profit increases the incentive for the store managers to cooperate by *implicitly* colluding. Remember that *explicit* collusion—such as the managers meeting and agreeing to charge $600—is illegal. But if the managers can find a way to signal each other that they will charge $600, they may be within the law.

Suppose, for example, that Wal-Mart and Target both advertise that they will match the lowest price offered by any competitor—in our simple example, they are each other's only competitor. These advertisements are signals to each other that they intend to charge $600 for the PlayStation. The signal is clear because each store knows that if it charges $400, the other store will automatically retaliate by also lowering its price to $400. The offer to match prices is a good *enforcement mechanism* because it guarantees that if either store fails to cooperate and charges the lower price, the competing store will automatically punish that store by also charging the lower price. As Figure 13-3 shows, the stores have changed the payoff matrix they face.

With the original payoff matrix (a), there is no matching offer, and each store makes more profit if it charges $400 when the other charges $600. The matching offer changes the payoff matrix to (b). Now the stores can charge $600 and receive a profit of $10,000 per month, or they can charge $400 and receive a profit of $7,500 per month. The equilibrium shifts from the prisoners' dilemma result of both stores charging the low price and receiving low profits to a result where both stores charge the high price and receive high profits. An offer to match competitors' prices might seem to benefit consumers, but game theory shows that it actually may hurt consumers by helping to keep prices high.

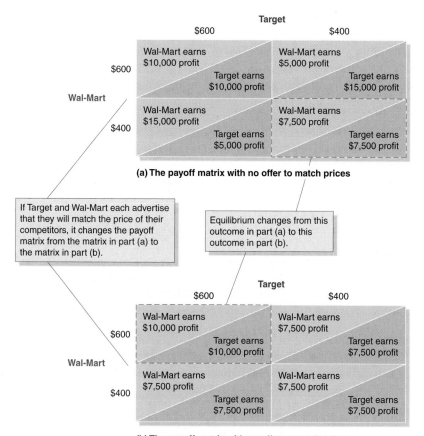

(a) The payoff matrix with no offer to match prices

If Target and Wal-Mart each advertise that they will match the price of their competitors, it changes the payoff matrix from the matrix in part (a) to the matrix in part (b).

Equilibrium changes from this outcome in part (a) to this outcome in part (b).

(b) The payoff matrix with an offer to match prices

Figure 13-3

Changing the Payoff Matrix in a Repeated Game

Wal-Mart and Target can change the payoff matrix by advertising that they will match their competitor's price. This retaliation strategy provides a signal that one store charging a lower price will be met automatically by the other store charging a lower price. In payoff matrix (a), there is no matching offer, and each store benefits if it charges $400 when the other charges $600. In payoff matrix (b), with the matching offer, the companies have only two choices: They can charge $600 and receive a profit of $10,000 per month, or they can charge $400 and receive a profit of $7,500 per month. The equilibrium shifts from the prisoners' dilemma result of both stores charging the low price and receiving low profits to both stores charging the high price and receiving high profits.

One form of implicit collusion occurs as a result of *price leadership*. With **price leadership**, one firm takes the lead in announcing a price change, which is then matched by the other firms in the industry. For example, through the 1970s, General Motors would announce a price change at the beginning of a model year and Ford and Chrysler would match GM's price change. In some cases, such as the airline industry, firms have attempted to act as price leaders, but failed when other firms in the industry declined to cooperate.

Price leadership A form of implicit collusion where one firm in an oligopoly announces a price change, which is matched by the other firms in the industry.

Making the Connection | American Airlines and Northwest Airlines Fail to Cooperate on a Price Increase

Coordinating prices is easier in some industries than in others. Fixed costs in the airline industry are very large, and marginal costs are very small. The marginal cost of flying one more passenger from New York to Chicago is no more than a few dollars: the cost of another snack served and a small amount of additional jet fuel. As a result, airlines often engage in last-minute price cutting to fill the remaining empty seats on a flight. Even a low-price ticket will increase marginal revenue more than marginal cost. As with other oligopolies, if all airlines cut prices, industry profits will decline. Airlines therefore continually adjust their prices while at the same time monitoring their rivals' prices and retaliating against them either for cutting prices or failing to go along with price increases.

The airlines have trouble raising the price this business traveler pays for a ticket.

Consider the following fairly typical events from the spring of 2002. American Airlines decided to raise some of its ticket prices in a roundabout way. Business travelers are usually willing to pay higher prices for airline tickets than are leisure travelers. Business travelers also often must make their flight plans only a few days before they leave. Airlines take advantage of this fact by requiring 10- to 14-day advance reservations to get a fully discounted ticket. A smaller discount is available with a 3-day advance reservation. This smaller discount is aimed at business travelers. American decided to increase to 7 days the advance purchase requirement for the business travel discount. Because many business travelers cannot make their reservations that far in advance, they would have to buy full-fare tickets.

Continental Airlines matched American's change, but the other airlines refused to go along. They hoped that by not matching American's price increase, they would gain some of its customers. American then retaliated by offering very low $99 one-way tickets in 10 markets where Northwest Airlines, United Airlines, Delta Air Lines, and US Airways offered nonstop service. American did not offer the $99 fares in the markets where Continental offered nonstop service. An airline industry consultant observed that "American is trying to slap the hands of people who wouldn't go along with its increase."

Northwest immediately responded by offering $99 fares in 20 markets where American offers nonstop service. American retaliated by offering the low fare in 10 additional markets served by Northwest. Northwest then further retaliated by offering the low fare in a total of 160 markets served by American. After several days of very low fares and lost profits, American and Northwest restored their normal fares, and American went back to a 3-day advance reservation requirement for discounted business-travel tickets.

Did American's aggressive retaliation make it easier for airlines to agree on ticket price increases in the future? Apparently not. A few weeks later, Continental raised its prices for round-trip discounted tickets by $20. Every airline but Northwest matched the price increase. Rather than lose customers to Northwest, Continental and the other airlines rolled back the price increase.

Sources: Scott McCartney, "Airfare Wars Show Why Deals Arrive and Depart," *Wall Street Journal*, March 19, 2002; and Scott McCartney, "Airlines Drop $20 Fare Increase after Northwest Fails to Join In," *Wall Street Journal*, April 16, 2002.

YOUR TURN: Test your understanding by doing related problems 2.18, 2.19, and 2.20 on pages 467–468 at the end of this chapter.

Cartels: The Case of OPEC

In the United States, firms cannot legally meet to agree on what prices to charge and how much to produce. But suppose they could. Would this be enough to guarantee that their collusion would be successful? The example of the Organization of Petroleum Exporting Countries (OPEC) indicates that the answer to this question is "no." OPEC has 11 members, including Saudi Arabia, Kuwait, and other Arab countries, as well as Iran, Venezuela, Nigeria, and Indonesia. Together, these countries own 75 percent of the world's proven oil reserves, although they pump a smaller share of the total oil sold each year. OPEC operates as a **cartel**, which is a group of firms that collude to restrict output to increase prices and profits. The members of OPEC meet periodically and agree on quotas, quantities of oil that each country agrees to produce. The quotas are intended to reduce oil production well below the competitive level, to force up the price of oil, and to increase the profits of member countries.

Figure 13-4 shows oil prices from 1972 to mid-2008. The blue line shows the price of a barrel of oil in each year. Prices in general have risen since 1972, which has reduced the amount of goods and services that consumers can purchase with a dollar. The red line corrects for general price increases by measuring oil prices in terms of the dollar's purchasing power in 2008. Although political unrest in the Middle East and other factors also affect the price of oil, the figure shows that OPEC had considerable success in raising the price of oil during the mid-1970s and early 1980s. Oil prices, which had been below $3 per barrel in 1972, rose to more than $39 per barrel in 1980, which was almost

Cartel A group of firms that collude by agreeing to restrict output to increase prices and profits.

Figure 13-4

Oil Prices, 1972–mid-2008

The blue line shows the price of a barrel of oil in each year. The red line measures the price of a barrel of oil in terms of the purchasing power of the dollar in 2008. By reducing oil production, the Organization of Petroleum Exporting Countries (OPEC) was able to raise the world price of oil in the mid-1970s and early 1980s. Sustaining high prices has been difficult over the long run, however, because members often exceed their output quotas.
Source: Federal Reserve Bank of St. Louis.

$100 measured in dollars of 2008 purchasing power. The figure also shows that OPEC has had difficulty sustaining the high prices of 1980 in later years, although beginning in 2004, oil prices rose, in part due to increasing demand from China and India.

Game theory helps us understand why oil prices have fluctuated. If every member of OPEC cooperates and produces the low output level dictated by its quota, prices will be high, and the cartel will earn large profits. Once the price has been driven up, however, each member has an incentive to stop cooperating and to earn even higher profits by increasing output beyond its quota. But if no country sticks to its quota, total oil output will increase, and profits will decline. In other words, OPEC is caught in a prisoners' dilemma.

If the members of OPEC always exceeded their production quotas, the cartel would have no effect on world oil prices. In fact, the members of OPEC periodically meet and assign new quotas that, at least for a while, enable them to restrict output enough to raise prices. OPEC's occasional success at behaving as a cartel can be explained by two factors. First, the members of OPEC are participating in a repeated game. As we have seen, this increases the likelihood of a cooperative outcome. Second, Saudi Arabia has far larger oil reserves than any other member of OPEC. Therefore, it has the most to gain from high oil prices and a greater incentive to cooperate. To see this, consider the payoff matrix shown in Figure 13-5. To keep things simple, let's assume that OPEC has only two members:

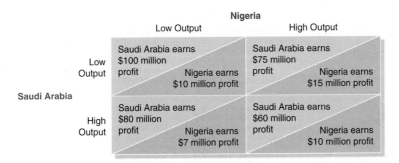

Figure 13-5 | The OPEC Cartel with Unequal Members

Because Saudi Arabia can produce so much more oil than Nigeria, its output decisions have a much larger effect on the price of oil. In the figure, "low output" corresponds to cooperating with the OPEC-assigned output quota, and "high output" corresponds to producing at maximum capacity. Saudi Arabia has a dominant strategy to cooperate and produce a low output. Nigeria, however, has a dominant strategy not to cooperate and produce a high output. Therefore, the equilibrium of this game will occur with Saudi Arabia producing a low output and Nigeria producing a high output.

Saudi Arabia and Nigeria. In Figure 13-5, "low output" corresponds to cooperating with the OPEC-assigned output quota, and "high output" corresponds to producing at maximum capacity. The payoff matrix shows the profits received per day by each country.

We can see that Saudi Arabia has a strong incentive to cooperate and maintain its low output quota. By keeping output low, Saudi Arabia can by itself significantly raise the world price of oil, increasing its own profits as well as those of other members of OPEC. Therefore, Saudi Arabia has a dominant strategy of cooperating with the quota and producing a low output. Nigeria, however, cannot by itself have much effect on the price of oil. Therefore, Nigeria has a dominant strategy of not cooperating and producing a high output. The equilibrium of this game will occur with Saudi Arabia producing a low output and Nigeria producing a high output. In fact, OPEC often operates in just this way. Saudi Arabia will cooperate with the quota, while the other 10 members produce at capacity. Because this is a repeated game, however, Saudi Arabia will occasionally produce more oil than its quota to intentionally drive down the price and retaliate against the other members for not cooperating.

13.3 LEARNING OBJECTIVE

13.3 | Use sequential games to analyze business strategies.

Sequential Games and Business Strategy

We have been analyzing games in which both players move simultaneously. In many business situations, however, one firm will act first, and then other firms will respond. These situations can be analyzed using *sequential games*. We will use sequential games to analyze two business strategies: deterring entry and bargaining between firms. To keep things simple, we consider situations that involve only two firms.

Deterring Entry

We saw earlier that barriers to entry are a key to firms continuing to earn economic profits. Can firms create barriers to deter new firms from entering an industry? Some recent research in game theory has focused on this question. To take a simple example, suppose a town in South Dakota currently has no discount department stores. Executives at Wal-Mart decide to enter the market and are considering what size store to build. To break even by covering the opportunity cost of the funds involved, the store must provide a minimum rate of return of 15 percent on the firm's investment. If Wal-Mart builds a small store in the town, it will earn economic profits by receiving a return of 30 percent. If Wal-Mart builds a large store, its costs will be somewhat higher, and it will receive a return of only 22 percent.

It seems clear that Wal-Mart should build the small store, but the executives are worried that Target may also build a store in this market. If Wal-Mart builds a small store and Target enters the market, both firms will earn an 18 percent return on their investment in this market. If Wal-Mart builds a large store and Target enters, the stores will have to cut prices, and the firms will each earn only 10 percent return on their investments, which is below the 15 percent return necessary for either firm to break even.

We can analyze a sequential game by using a *decision tree*, like the one shown in Figure 13-6. The boxes in the figure represent *decision nodes*, which are points when the firms must make the decisions contained in the boxes. At the left, Wal-Mart makes the initial decision of what size store to build, and then Target responds by either entering the market or not. The decisions made are shown beside the arrows. The *terminal nodes* at the right side of the figure show the resulting rates of return.

Let's start with Wal-Mart's initial decision. If Wal-Mart builds a large store, then the arrow directs us to the upper red decision node for Target. If Target decides to enter, it will earn only a 10 percent rate of return on its investment, which represents an economic loss because it is below the opportunity cost of the funds involved. If Target doesn't enter, Wal-Mart will earn 22 percent, and Target will not earn anything in this

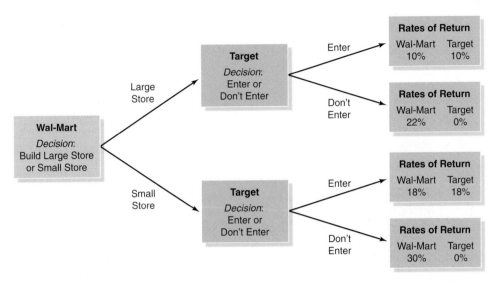

Figure 13-6

The Decision Tree for an Entry Game

Wal-Mart earns its highest return if it builds a small store and Target doesn't enter the market. If Wal-Mart builds a small store, Target will enter because it will earn economic profit by receiving an 18 percent return on its investment. Therefore, the best decision for Wal-Mart is to build a large store to deter Target's entry. Once Wal-Mart has built a large store, Target knows that if it enters this market, it will earn only 10 percent on its investment, which represents an economic loss, so it won't enter the market.

market. Wal-Mart executives can conclude that if they build a large store, Target will not enter, and Wal-Mart will earn 22 percent on its investment.

If Wal-Mart decides to build a small store, then the arrow directs us to the lower red decision node for Target. If Target decides to enter, it will earn an 18 percent rate of return. If it doesn't enter, Wal-Mart will earn 30 percent, and Target will not earn anything in this market. Wal-Mart executives can conclude that if they build a small store, Target will enter, and Wal-Mart will earn 18 percent on its investment.

This analysis should lead Wal-Mart executives to conclude that they can build a small store and earn 18 percent—because Target will enter—or they can build a large store and earn 22 percent by deterring Target's entry.

Solved Problem | 13-3

Is Deterring Entry Always a Good Idea?

Whether deterring entry makes sense depends on how costly it is to the firm doing the deterring. Use the following decision tree to decide whether Wal-Mart should deter Target from entering this market. Assume that each firm must earn a 15 percent return on its investment to break even.

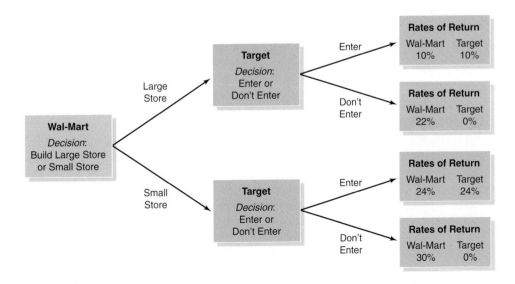

SOLVING THE PROBLEM:

Step 1:   **Review the chapter material.** This problem is about sequential games, so you may want to review the section "Deterring Entry," which begins on page 454.

Step 2:   **Determine how Target will respond to Wal-Mart's decision.** If Wal-Mart builds a large store, Target will not enter this market because the return on its investment represents an economic loss. If Wal-Mart builds a small store, Target will enter because it will earn a return that represents an economic profit.

Step 3:   **Given how Target will react, determine which strategy maximizes profits for Wal-Mart.** If Wal-Mart builds the large store, it will have deterred Target's entry, and the rate of return on its investment will be 22 percent. If it builds the small store, Target will enter, but Wal-Mart will actually earn a higher return of 24 percent.

Step 4:   **State your conclusion.** Like any other business strategy, deterrence is worth pursuing only if its costs are not too high. In this case, the high cost of building a large store lowers Wal-Mart's economic profits below what it earns by building a small store, even given that Target will enter the market.

>> **End Solved Problem 13-3**

YOUR TURN: For more practice, do related problem 3.3 on page 469 at the end of this chapter.

Bargaining

The success of many firms depends on how well they bargain with other firms. For example, firms often must bargain with their suppliers over the prices they pay for inputs. Suppose that TruImage is a small firm that has developed software that improves how pictures from a digital camera are displayed on computer screens. TruImage currently sells its software only on its Web site and earns profits of $2 million per year. Dell Computer informs TruImage that it is considering installing the software on every new computer Dell sells. Dell expects to sell more computers at a higher price if it can install TruImage's software on its computers. The two firms begin bargaining over what price Dell will pay TruImage for its software.

The decision tree in Figure 13-7 illustrates this bargaining game. At the left, Dell makes the initial decision on what price to offer TruImage for its software, and then TruImage responds by either accepting or rejecting the contract offer. First, suppose that Dell offers TruImage a contract price of $30 per copy for its software. If TruImage accepts this contract, its profits will be $5 million per year, and Dell will earn $10 million in additional profits. If TruImage rejects the contract, its profits will be the $2 million per year it earns selling its software on its Web site, and Dell will earn zero additional profits.

Now, suppose Dell offers TruImage a contract price of $20 per copy. If TruImage accepts this contract, its profits will be $3 million per year, and Dell will earn $15 million in additional profits. If TruImage rejects this contract, its profits will be the $2 million it earns selling its software on its Web site, and Dell will earn zero additional profits. Clearly, for Dell, a contract of $20 per copy is more profitable, while for TruImage, a contract of $30 per copy is more profitable.

Suppose TruImage attempts to obtain a favorable outcome from the bargaining by telling Dell that it will reject a $20-per-copy contract. If Dell believes this threat, then it will offer TruImage a $30-per-copy contract because Dell is better off with the $10 million profit that will result from TruImage's accepting the contract than with the zero profits Dell will earn if TruImage rejects the $20-per-copy contract. This result is a Nash equilibrium because neither firm can increase its profits by changing its choice—*provided that Dell believes TruImage's threat.* But is TruImage's threat credible? Once Dell has offered TruImage the $20 contract, TruImage's choices are to accept the contract and earn $3 million or reject the contract and earn only $2 million. Because rejecting the

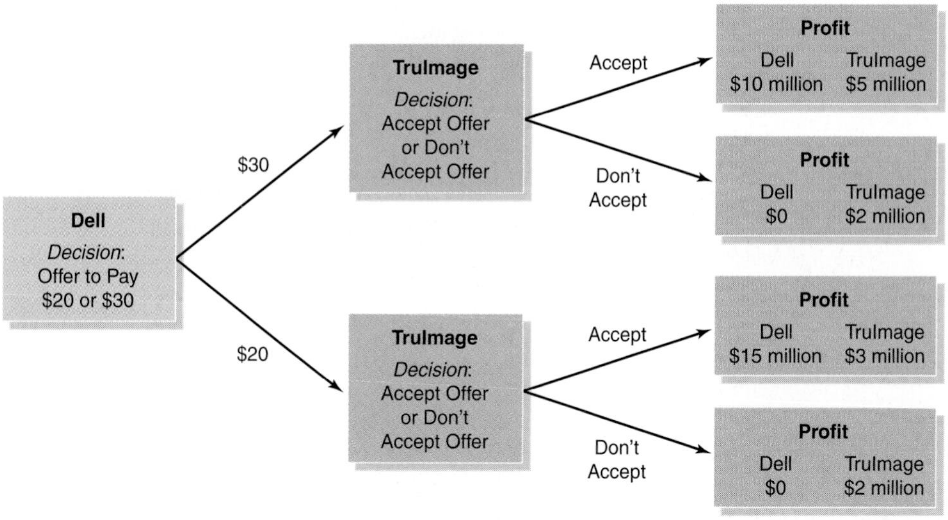

Figure 13-7 | The Decision Tree for a Bargaining Game

Dell earns the highest profit if it offers a contract price of $20 per copy and TruImage accepts the contract. TruImage earns the highest profit if Dell offers it a contract of $30 per copy and it accepts the contract. TruImage may attempt to bargain by threatening to reject a $20-per-copy contract. But Dell knows this threat is not credible because once Dell has offered a $20-per-copy contract, TruImage's profits are higher if it accepts the contract than if it rejects it.

contract reduces TruImage's profits, TruImage's threat to reject the contract is not credible, and Dell should ignore it.

As a result, we would expect Dell to use the strategy of offering TruImage a $20-per-copy contract and TruImage to use the strategy of accepting the contract. Dell will earn additional profits of $15 million per year, and TruImage will earn profits of $3 million per year. This outcome is called a *subgame-perfect equilibrium.* A subgame-perfect equilibrium is a Nash equilibrium in which no player can make himself better off by changing his decision at any decision node. In our simple bargaining game, each player has only one decision to make. As we have seen, Dell's profits are highest if it offers the $20-per-copy contract, and TruImage's profits are highest if it accepts the contract. Typically, in sequential games of this type, there is only one subgame-perfect equilibrium.

Managers use decision trees like those in Figures 13-6 and 13-7 in business planning because they provide a systematic way of thinking through the implications of a strategy and of predicting the reactions of rivals. We can see the benefits of decision trees in the simple examples we considered here. In the first example, Wal-Mart managers can conclude that building a large store is more profitable than building a smaller store. In the second example, Dell managers can conclude that TruImage's threat to reject a $20-per-copy contract is not credible.

13.4 | Use the five competitive forces model to analyze competition in an industry.

13.4 LEARNING OBJECTIVE

The Five Competitive Forces Model

We have seen that the number of competitors in an industry affects a firm's ability to charge a price above average cost and earn an economic profit. The number of firms is not the only determinant of the level of competition in an industry, however. Michael Porter of Harvard Business School has drawn on the research of a number of economists to develop a model that shows how five competitive forces determine the overall level of competition in an industry. Figure 13-8 illustrates Porter's model.

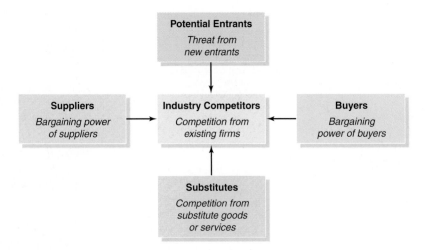

Figure 13-8 | The Five Competitive Forces Model

Michael Porter's model identifies five forces that determine the level of competition in an industry: (1) competition from existing firms, (2) the threat from new entrants, (3) competition from substitute goods or services, (4) the bargaining power of buyers, and (5) the bargaining power of suppliers.

Source: Reprinted with the permission of The Free Press, a Division of Simon & Schuster Adult Publishing Group, from Michael E. Porter, *Competitive Strategy: Techniques for Analyzing Industries and Competitors.* Copyright © 1980, 1998 by The Free Press. All rights reserved.

We now look at each of the five competitive forces: (1) competition from existing firms, (2) the threat from potential entrants, (3) competition from substitute goods or services, (4) the bargaining power of buyers, and (5) the bargaining power of suppliers.

Competition from Existing Firms

We have already seen that competition among firms in an industry can lower prices and profits. To take another example: The Educational Testing Service (ETS) produces the Scholastic Aptitude Test (SAT) and the Graduate Record Exam (GRE). The GRE is taken by students applying to graduate school. In 2007, the Educational Testing Service charged a price of $43 to take the SAT, but $140 to take the GRE. Part of the explanation for these large price differences is that ETS faces competition in the market for tests given to high school seniors applying to college, where the SAT competes with the ACT Assessment, produced by ACT, Inc. But there is no competition for the GRE test. As we saw earlier in this chapter, when there are only a few firms in a market, it is easier for them to implicitly collude and to charge a price close to the monopoly price. In this case, however, competition from a single firm was enough to cause ETS to keep the price of the SAT near the competition level.

Competition in the form of advertising, better customer service, or longer warranties can also reduce profits by raising costs. For example, online booksellers Amazon.com, BarnesandNoble.com, and Buy.com have competed by offering low-cost—or free—shipping, by increasing their customer service staffs, and by building more warehouses to provide faster deliveries. These activities have raised the booksellers' costs and reduced their profits.

The Threat from Potential Entrants

Firms face competition from companies that currently are not in the market but might enter. We have already seen how actions taken to deter entry can reduce profits. In our hypothetical example in the previous section, Wal-Mart built a larger store and earned less profit to deter Target's entry. Business managers often take actions aimed at deterring entry. Some of these actions include advertising to create product loyalty, introducing new products—such as slightly different cereals or toothpastes—to fill market niches, and setting lower prices to keep profits at a level that would make entry less attractive.

Competition from Substitute Goods or Services

Firms are always vulnerable to competitors introducing a new product that fills a consumer need better than their current product does. Consider the encyclopedia business. For decades, many parents bought expensive and bulky encyclopedias for their children attending high school or college. By the 1990s, computer software companies were offering electronic encyclopedias that sold for a small fraction of the price of the printed encyclopedias. Encyclopedia Britannica and the other encyclopedia publishers responded by cutting prices and launching advertising campaigns aimed at showing the superiority of printed encyclopedias. Still, profits continued to decline, and by the end of the 1990s, most printed encyclopedias had disappeared.

The Bargaining Power of Buyers

If buyers have enough bargaining power, they can insist on lower prices, higher-quality products, or additional services. Automobile companies, for example, have significant bargaining power in the tire market, which tends to lower tire prices and limit the profitability of tire manufacturers. Some retailers have significant buying power over their suppliers. For instance, Wal-Mart has required many of its suppliers to alter their distribution systems to accommodate Wal-Mart's need to control the stocks of goods in its stores.

The Bargaining Power of Suppliers

If many firms can supply an input and the input is not specialized, the suppliers are unlikely to have the bargaining power to limit a firm's profits. For instance, suppliers of paper napkins to McDonald's restaurants have very little bargaining power. With only a single or a few suppliers of an input, the purchasing firm may face a high price. During the 1930s and 1940s, for example, the Technicolor Company was the only producer of the cameras and film that studios needed to produce color movies. Technicolor charged the studios high prices to use its cameras, and it had the power to insist that only its technicians could operate the cameras. The only alternative for the movie studios was to make black-and-white movies.

As with other competitive forces, the bargaining power of suppliers can change over time. For instance, when IBM chose Microsoft to supply the operating system for its personal computers, Microsoft was a small company with very limited bargaining power. As Microsoft's Windows operating system became standard in more than 90 percent of personal computers, this large market share increased Microsoft's bargaining power.

Making the Connection	**Is Southwest's Business Strategy More Important Than the Structure of the Airline Industry?**

For years, economists and business strategists believed that market structure was the most important factor in explaining the ability of some firms to continue earning economic profits. For example, most economists argued

Southwest's business strategy allowed it to remain profitable when many other airlines faced heavy losses.

that during the first few decades after World War II, steel companies in the United States earned economic profits because barriers to entry were high, there were few firms in the industry, and competition among firms was low. In contrast, restaurants were seen as less profitable because barriers to entry were low and the industry was intensely competitive. One problem with this approach to analyzing the profitability of firms is that it does not explain how firms in the same industry can have very different levels of profit.

Today, economists and business strategists put greater emphasis on the characteristics of individual firms and the strategies their managements use to continue to earn economic profits. This approach helps explain why Nucor continues to be a profitable steel company while Bethlehem Steel, at one time the second-largest steel producer in the United States, was forced into bankruptcy. It also explains why Dell, which began as a small company run by Michael Dell from his dorm room at the University of Texas, went on to become extremely profitable and an industry leader, while other computer companies have disappeared.

Many economists argue that the best strategy for a company is to identify a segment of the market and then shape the company to fit that segment. This strategy makes it more difficult for rivals to compete in that part of the market. For example, Southwest Airlines concentrates on customers who fly relatively short distances and who want a low-price, no-frills airline flight. Every aspect of the company is focused on this goal. Southwest's planes have no first-class or business sections—only coach seats are available. By flying primarily between midsize cities, Southwest can avoid the delays at the crowded airports near big cities and can keep its planes at the airport gate for only 15 minutes—much less time than other airlines. This lowers its costs by allowing it to keep its planes in the air longer and to offer more flights with fewer planes. Southwest also lowers costs by not serving meals, flying only Boeing 737s to standardize maintenance, not assigning passengers to particular seats, and not checking luggage through to connecting flights.

It is very difficult for the other full-service airlines, such as Delta, American, and United, to compete with Southwest. Because they fly out of larger, more congested airports, those airlines have no hope of turning around their planes at the gate as quickly as Southwest does. Because many of their passengers are flying longer distances—often using connecting flights—they have to serve meals and check luggage through. Many of the other airlines' customers want upgraded seats and service, so those airlines must offer first-class and business-class seats. Even when Delta, American, and United have tried to offer stripped-down service on certain routes in direct competition with Southwest, they have not been successful. Southwest's complete focus on providing low-cost, low-price service has proven very difficult for the other airlines to copy. While other airlines suffered heavy losses in 2003–2004 as fuel prices rose and demand declined as a result of the war in Iraq and the spread of the disease SARS (severe acute respiratory syndrome), Southwest continued to earn profits. In 2008, it remained the leading major airline in on-time arrivals and fewest customer complaints.

Southwest's corporate strategy, rather than the structure of the airline industry, explains why Southwest earns economic profits.

Source: Scott McCartney, "A Report Card on the Nation's Airlines," *Wall Street Journal*, February 6, 2007, p. D1.

YOUR TURN: Test your understanding by doing related problem 4.5 on page 470 at the end of this chapter.

Economics in YOUR Life!

>> Continued from page 441

At the beginning of this chapter, we asked you to consider why the price of the PlayStation 3 game system is almost the same at every large retailer, from Amazon.com to Wal-Mart. Why don't these retailers seem to compete on price for this type of product? In this chapter, we have seen that if big retailers were engaged in a one-time game of pricing PlayStations, they would be in a prisoner's dilemma and probably all charge a low price. However, we have also seen that pricing PlayStations is actually a repeated game because the retailers will be selling the game system in competition over a long period of time. In this situation, it is more likely that a cooperative equilibrium will be arrived at in which the retailers will all charge a high price. This is good news for the profits of the retailers but bad news for consumers! This is one of many insights that game theory provides into the business strategies of oligopolists.

Conclusion

Firms are locked in a never-ending struggle to earn economic profits. As noted in the two preceding chapters, competition erodes economic profits. Even in the oligopolies discussed in this chapter, firms have difficulty earning economic profits in the long run. We have seen that firms attempt to avoid the effects of competition in various ways. For example, they can stake out a secure niche in the market, they can engage in implicit collusion with competing firms, or they can attempt to have the government impose barriers to entry. Read *An Inside Look* on the next page for a discussion of the business strategy Target uses to compete with Wal-Mart in the market for generic prescription drugs.

Can Target Compete with Wal-Mart in the Market for Generic Drugs?

USA TODAY, SEPTEMBER 23, 2006

Target Says It Will Match Wal-Mart's $4 Generic Drug Price

(a) Chain store Target said late Thursday that it will match rival Wal-Mart's $4 price on 150 generic drug prescriptions in the Tampa Bay area. Target's brief press release didn't say whether it would keep pace with Wal-Mart's plan to take the lower prices nationwide, but it did say it has a "long-standing practice to be price competitive with Wal-Mart."

Wal-Mart, the nation's third-largest seller of prescription drugs, said earlier Thursday that it will offer the $4 price on about 150 generic drugs to the insured and uninsured alike, starting immediately in the Tampa area, and will take the program statewide by January.

"We intend to take it nationwide (b) next year," says Bill Simon, Wal-Mart's executive vice president of the Professional Services Division. For uninsured consumers, the $4 price for some generics is below what they would pay at most pharmacy counters and is less than typical $10 to $15 co-payments on generics offered by many insurance plans.

Wal-Mart's move could save modest amounts for some consumers. It may also draw more customers to its stores or prompt a price war with other pharmacies. Savings could be less than $1 per prescription to more than $20, depending on the drug and pharmacy where customers shop, according to information from Wal-Mart and prices of other retailers posted at MyFloridarx.com, a state-run website.

That could draw more customers to Wal-Mart, already the largest seller of groceries and toys, possibly forcing other chain drugstores to cut their prices, says Ed Kaplan of the Segal Co., a benefits consulting firm. "Customers who take five or seven medications a month and can save $10 on each might switch," says Kaplan.

The move caused share prices for generic drug and pharmacy companies to drop Thursday.

Wal-Mart says the $4 for 30-day (c) supply price would save customers $7.98 a month for blood-pressure drug Lisinopril, $3.85 for diabetes drug metformin and 80 cents for blood-pressure drug atenolol.

Simon says the $4 generics are not expected to be a "loss leader," meaning Wal-Mart doesn't expect to lose money on the drugs in hopes of attracting more customers to buy other products. That's because the drugs offered are longtime generics that have multiple manufacturers and they are already inexpensive on the wholesale market. Large companies such as Wal-Mart can often buy in bulk for less than the $4 cost.

Wal-Mart's press release said 291 drugs will be covered, a total that includes different dosage strengths of the same drugs. When the differing dosage strengths are taken out, the list includes fewer than 150 products, including treatments for high blood pressure, infection and diabetes, along with some vitamins and painkiller ibuprofen. That's a fraction of the estimated 2,100 generic products available.

"This is a much narrower list than they're giving the impression it is," says drug-industry expert Stephen Schondelmeyer at the University of Minnesota. Simon says the drugs chosen for the list represent 20% of the prescriptions Wal-Mart currently fills and cover a wide range of medical needs. More products may be added, he says.

The move comes as Wal-Mart works to counter critics who say the firm doesn't make health insurance affordable for many of its workers. "Providing low-cost drugs is a good thing. But not providing affordable health care to workers is not a good thing. Why can't Wal-Mart address the serious health care crisis in its own stores?" says Chris Kofinis, with Wake-UpWalmart.com.

Some praised Wal-Mart's move. "That's a great price for a 30-day supply of drugs and will be a tremendous boon for seniors," says Devon Herrick, economist at the National Center for Policy Analysis.

Source: Julie Appley, "Target Says It Will Match Wal-Mart's $4 Generic Drug Price," *USA Today,* September 23, 2006. Reprinted by permission of *USA Today.*

Key Points in the Article

This article illustrates Target's plan to match Wal-Mart's low price on generic prescription drugs. As we have seen in this chapter, when a market is an oligopoly, there are only a few firms. So, each firm must take into account the actions of its competitors. When a competitor changes the price it charges, the other firms in the industry must decide how to react. In this case, Target determined that its profits would be higher by matching Wal-Mart's price.

Analyzing the News

Ⓐ In an oligopoly market, a firm's profits depend not only on the price it chooses, but on the price its rivals choose. In this case, Target had to choose how to respond to Wal-Mart's pricing decision. From Target's action, we can assume that it believes its profits will be higher with a low price, given that Wal-Mart is charging a low price. The figure is helpful in analyzing whether Wal-Mart can profitably sell generic

drugs at a price of $4. In both panel (a) and panel (b), the rate of return by Wal-Mart is higher when it offers generics at $4 regardless of what Target does. So, Wal-Mart has a dominant strategy of charging $4.

Target faces the choice of whether to match this price. In panel (a), if Target matches the price it earns an 8 percent return, while if it does not match the price it will earn a return of 0 percent. Target prefers the 8 percent return and will choose to match Wal-Mart's $4 generic drug price.

But suppose that Target determines that given its competitive position relative to Wal-Mart the situation is actually that shown in panel (b). Wal-Mart still has a dominant strategy of charging $4 for generic prescription, but now Target faces the choice of a 3 percent return if it matches Wal-Mart's price, or a 5 percent return if it does not match Wal-Mart's price. In this case, Target would be better off not matching the $4 generic price.

Ⓑ Larger stores sometimes cut the price of a product even if this means they will take a loss on sales of the product, if the store manager believes the low price will attract new customers. If low prescription prices attract more customers to Wal-Mart stores, we would expect that Wal-Mart would earn additional profits from the other goods those customers purchased while in Wal-Mart.

Ⓒ As mentioned in the chapter opener, Wal-Mart is facing increased criticism over its corporate policies. Just as Wal-Mart has to decide how to respond to the market behavior of its rivals, such as pricing, it must also decide how to respond to the behavior of its critics.

Thinking Critically

1. Suppose that you manage a small pharmacy in a local town. How will you decide whether to match the lower generic drug prices of Wal-Mart and Target?

2. Suppose that Congress passes legislation that places a price floor on generic drugs. Who would likely gain from such a law? Who would likely lose? Use a graph to show changes in producer surplus and consumer surplus.

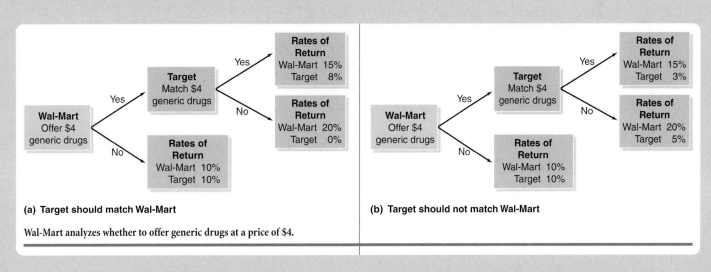

(a) Target should match Wal-Mart

(b) Target should not match Wal-Mart

Wal-Mart analyzes whether to offer generic drugs at a price of $4.

Key Terms

Barrier to entry, p. 443

Business strategy, p. 445

Cartel, p. 452

Collusion, p. 446

Cooperative equilibrium, p. 448

Dominant strategy, p. 446

Economies of scale, p. 443

Game theory, p. 445

Nash equilibrium, p. 446

Noncooperative equilibrium, p. 448

Oligopoly, p. 442

Patent, p. 444

Payoff matrix, p. 446

Price leadership, p. 451

Prisoners' dilemma, p. 448

13.1 LEARNING OBJECTIVE   13.1 | Show how barriers to entry explain the existence of oligopolies, **pages 442–445.**

Oligopoly and Barriers to Entry

Summary

An **oligopoly** is a market structure in which a small number of interdependent firms compete. **Barriers to entry** keep new firms from entering an industry. The three most important barriers to entry are economies of scale, ownership of a key input or raw material, and government barriers. Economies of scale are the most important barrier to entry. **Economies of scale** exist when a firm's long-run average costs fall as it increases output. Government barriers include patents, licensing, and barriers to international trade. A **patent** is the exclusive right to a product for a period of 20 years from the date the product is invented.

 Visit www.myeconlab.com to complete these exercises online and get instant feedback.

Review Questions

1.1 What is an oligopoly? Give three examples of oligopolistic industries in the United States.

1.2 What do barriers to entry have to do with the extent of competition, or lack thereof, in an industry? What are the most important barriers to entry?

1.3 Give an example of a government-imposed barrier to entry. Why would the government be willing to erect barriers to entering an industry?

Problems and Applications

1.4 Michael Porter has argued, "The intensity of competition in an industry is neither a matter of coincidence nor bad luck. Rather, competition in an industry is rooted in its underlying economic structure." What does Porter mean by "economic structure"? What factors, other than economic structure, might be expected to determine the intensity of competition in an industry?

Source: Michael Porter, *Competitive Strategy: Techniques for Analyzing Industries and Competitors*, New York: The Free Press, 1980, p. 3.

1.5 "Less-than-truckload" trucking companies include goods from several shippers in their highway trailers. According to an article in the *Wall Street Journal*: "Unlike [the truckload industry, which is] a fiercely

competitive business it is relatively easy to enter, less-than-truckload companies face a higher entry barrier due to the cost of an extensive network of terminals to consolidate shipments." Would you expect truckload companies or less-than-truckload companies to charge higher prices to ship freight? Which companies are likely to earn economic profits? Briefly explain.

Source: Daniel Machalaba, "Yellow Freight to Raise Rates 4.9% on Bet about Lower Inventory Costs," *Wall Street Journal*, July 5, 2001.

1.6 Thomas McCraw, a professor at Harvard Business School, has written the following: "Throughout American history, entrepreneurs have tried, sometimes desperately, to create big businesses out of naturally small-scale operations. It has not worked." What advantage would entrepreneurs expect to gain from creating "big businesses"? Why would entrepreneurs fail to create big businesses with "naturally small-scale operations"? Illustrate your answer with a graph showing long-run average costs.

Source: Thomas K. McCraw, ed., *Creating Modern Capitalism*, Cambridge, MA: Harvard University Press, 1997, p. 323.

1.7 The graph below illustrates the average total cost curves for two automobile manufacturing firms: Little Auto and Big Auto. Under which of the following

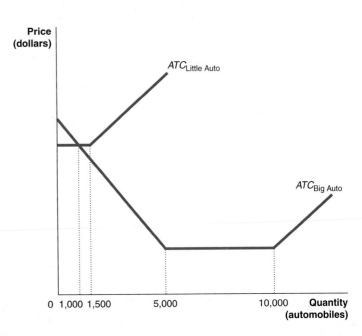

conditions would you expect to see the market composed of firms like Little Auto, and under which conditions would you expect to see the market dominated by firms like Big Auto?

    a. When the market demand curve intersects the quantity axis at less than 1,000 units

    b. When the market demand curve intersects the quantity axis at more than 1,000 units but less than 10,000 units

    c. When the market demand curve intersects the quantity axis at more than 10,000 units

1.8 The following graph contains two long-run average cost curves. Briefly explain which cost curve would most likely be associated with an oligopoly and which would most likely be associated with a perfectly competitive industry.

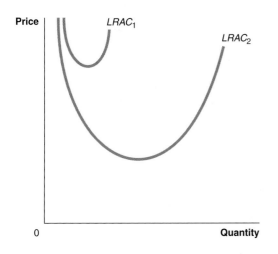

1.9 Alfred Chandler, who was a professor at Harvard Business School, observed, "Imagine the diseconomies of scale—the great increase in unit costs—that would result from placing close to one-fourth of the world's production of shoes, or textiles, or lumber into three factories or mills!" The shoe, textiles, and lumber industries are very competitive, with many firms producing each of these products. Briefly explain whether Chandler's observation helps us explain why.

Source: Alfred D. Chandler, Jr., "The Emergence of Managerial Capitalism," in Alfred D. Chandler, Jr., and Richard S. Tedlow, *The Coming of Managerial Capitalism*, New York: Irwin, 1985, p. 406.

1.10 A historical account of the development of the cotton textile industry in England argues the following:

> The cotton textile industry was shaped by ruthless competition. Rapid growth in demand, low barriers to entry, frequent technological innovations, and a high rate of firm bankruptcy all combined to form an environment in which . . . oligopolistic competition became almost impossible.

Explain how each of the factors described here would contribute to making the cotton textile industry competitive rather than oligopolistic.

Source: Thomas K. McCraw, ed., *Creating Modern Capitalism*, Cambridge, MA: Harvard University Press, pp. 61–62.

>> **End Learning Objective 13.1**

13.2 LEARNING OBJECTIVE   13.2 | Use game theory to analyze the strategies of oligopolistic firms, **pages 445–454.**

Using Game Theory to Analyze Oligopoly

Summary

Because an oligopoly has only a few firms, interactions among those firms are particularly important. **Game theory** is the study of how people make decisions in situations in which attaining their goals depends on their interactions with others; in economics, it is the study of the decisions of firms in industries where the profits of each firm depend on its interactions with other firms. A **business strategy** refers to actions taken by a firm to achieve a goal, such as maximizing profits. Oligopoly games can be illustrated with a **payoff matrix**, which is a table that shows the payoffs that each firm earns from every combination of strategies by the firms. One possible outcome in oligopoly is **collusion**, which is an agreement among firms to charge the same price or otherwise not to compete. A **cartel** is a group of firms that collude by agreeing to restrict output to increase prices and profits. In a **cooperative equilibrium**, firms cooperate to increase their mutual payoff. In a **noncooperative equilibrium**, firms do not cooperate but pursue their own self-interest. A **dominant strategy** is a strategy that is the best for a firm, no matter what strategies other firms use. A **Nash equilibrium** is a situation in which each firm chooses the best strategy, given the strategies chosen by other firms. A situation in which pursuing dominant strategies results in noncooperation that leaves everyone worse off is called a **prisoners' dilemma**. Because many business situations are repeated games, firms may end up implicitly colluding to keep prices high. With **price leadership**, one firm takes the lead in announcing a price change, which is then matched by the other firms in the industry.

Visit www.myeconlab.com to complete these exercises online and get instant feedback.

Review Questions

2.1 Give brief definitions of the following concepts.
   a. Game theory
   b. Cooperative equilibrium
   c. Noncooperative equilibrium
   d. Dominant strategy
   e. Nash equilibrium

2.2 Why do economists refer to the methodology for analyzing oligopolies as game theory?

2.3 Why do economists refer to the pricing strategies of oligopoly firms as a prisoners' dilemma game?

2.4 What is the difference between explicit collusion and implicit collusion? Give an example of each.

2.5 How is the prisoners' dilemma result changed in a repeated game?

Problems and Applications

2.6 Bob and Tom are two criminals who have been arrested for burglary. The police put Tom and Bob in separate cells. They offer to let Bob go free if he confesses to the crime and testifies against Tom. Bob also is told that he will serve a 15-year sentence if he remains silent while Tom confesses. If he confesses and Tom also confesses, they will each serve a 10-year sentence. Separately, the police make the same offer to Tom. Assume that if Bob and Tom both remain silent, the police have only enough evidence to convict them of a lesser crime, and they will both serve 3-year sentences.
   a. Use the information provided to write a payoff matrix for Bob and Tom.
   b. Does Bob have a dominant strategy? If so, what is it?
   c. Does Tom have a dominant strategy? If so, what is it?
   d. What sentences do Bob and Tom serve? How might they have avoided this outcome?

2.7 Explain how collusion makes firms better off. Given the incentives to collude, briefly explain why every industry doesn't become a cartel.

2.8 Under "early decision" college admission plans, students apply to a college in the fall and, if they are accepted, they must enroll in that college. According to an article in *BusinessWeek*, Yale president Richard Levin argues that early decision plans put too much pressure on students to decide early in their senior years which college they wish to attend. Levin has proposed abolishing early decision plans. But the author of the article is doubtful that this will succeed because "as long as some big-name schools offer early admissions, the others feel they must, too, or lose out on the best talent." Do you agree with this conclusion? How can game theory help us analyze this situation?

2.9 Baseball players who hit the most home runs *relative to other players* usually receive the highest pay. Beginning in the mid-1990s, the typical baseball player became significantly stronger and more muscular. As one baseball announcer put it, "The players of 20 years ago look like stick figures compared with the players of today." As a result, the average number of home runs hit each year increased dramatically. Some of the increased strength that baseball players gained came from more weight training and better conditioning and diet. As some players admitted, though, some of the increased strength came from taking steroids and other illegal drugs. Taking steroids can significantly increase the risk of developing cancer and other medical problems.
   a. In these circumstances, are baseball players in a prisoners' dilemma? Carefully explain.
   b. Suppose that Major League Baseball begins testing players for steroids and firing players who are caught using them (or other illegal muscle-building drugs). Will this testing make baseball players as a group better off or worse off? Briefly explain.

2.10 Soldiers in battle may face a prisoners' dilemma. If all soldiers stand and fight, the chance that the soldiers, as a unit, will survive is maximized. If there is a significant chance that the soldiers will lose the battle, an individual soldier may maximize his chance of survival by running away while the other soldiers hold off the enemy by fighting. If all soldiers run away, however, many of them are likely to be killed or captured by the enemy because no one is left to hold off the enemy. In ancient times, the Roman army practiced "decimation." If a unit of soldiers was guilty of running away during a battle or committing other cowardly acts, all would be lined up, and every tenth soldier would be killed by being run through with a sword. No attempt was made to distinguish between soldiers in the unit who had fought well and those who had been cowardly. Briefly explain under what condition the Roman system of decimation was likely to have solved the prisoners' dilemma of soldiers running away in battle.

2.11 (Related to the *Making the Connection* on page 447) Convert the scene from the bar into a game. There are two players John and Steve. They each have the same possible strategies: "approach the blonde" or "approach the brunette." Think of the payoffs in the matrices as measures of utility. Choose payoffs so that there is no Nash equilibrium.

2.12 (Related to *Solved Problem 13-2* on page 448) Would a ban on advertising beer on television be likely to increase or decrease the profits of beer companies? Briefly explain.

2.13 (Related to *Solved Problem 13-2* on page 448) Beginning in 2003, the U.S. government spent billions of dollars rebuilding the infrastructure damaged by the war in Iraq. Much of the work was carried out by construction and engineering firms that had to bid for the business. Suppose, hypothetically, that only two companies—Bechtel and Halliburton—enter the bidding and that each firm is deciding whether to bid either $4 billion or $5 billion. (Remember that in this type of bidding, the winning bid is the *low* bid because the bid represents the amount the government will have to pay to have the work done.) Each firm will have costs of $2.5 billion to do the work. If they both make the same bid, they will both be hired and will split the work and the profits. If one makes a low bid and one makes a high bid, only the low bidder will be hired, and it will receive all the profits. The result is the following payoff matrix.

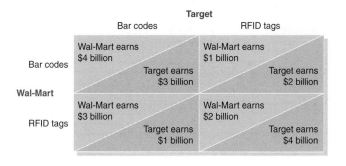

a. Is there a Nash equilibrium in this game? Briefly explain.

b. How might the situation be changed if the two companies expect to be bidding on many similar projects in future years?

2.14 (Related to *Solved Problem 13-2* on page 448 and the *Chapter Opener* on page 440) Suppose that Wal-Mart and Target are independently deciding whether to stick with bar codes or switch to RFID tags to monitor the flow of products. Because many suppliers sell to both Wal-Mart and Target, it is much less costly for suppliers to use one system or the other rather than to use both. The following payoff matrix shows the profits per year for each company resulting from the interaction of their strategies.

a. Briefly explain whether Wal-Mart has a dominant strategy.

b. Briefly explain whether Target has a dominant strategy.

c. Briefly explain whether there is a Nash equilibrium in this game.

2.15 (Related to the *Don't Let This Happen to You!* on page 447) A student argues, "The prisoners' dilemma game is unrealistic. Each player's strategy is based on the assumption that the other player won't cooperate. But if each player assumes that the other player *will* cooperate, the 'dilemma' disappears." Briefly explain whether you agree with this argument.

2.16 (Related to the *Making the Connection* on page 449) We made the argument that a bidder on an eBay auction has a dominant strategy of bidding only once, with that bid being the maximum the bidder would be willing to pay.

a. Is it possible that a bidder might receive useful information during the auction, particularly from the dollar amounts other bidders are bidding? If so, how does that change a bidder's optimal strategy?

b. Many people recommend the practice of "sniping," or placing your bid at the last second before the auction ends. Is there connection between sniping and your answer to part a?

2.17 Consider two oligopolistic industries. In the first industry, firms always match price changes by any other firm in the industry. In the second industry, firms always ignore price changes by any other firm. In which industry are firms likely to charge higher prices? Briefly explain.

2.18 (Related to the *Making the Connection* on page 451) Airlines often find themselves in price wars. Consider the following game: Northwest and Continental are the only two airlines flying the route from Houston to Omaha. Each firm has two strategies: charge a high price or charge a low price.

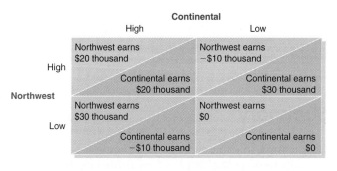

a. What (if any) is the dominant strategy for each firm?

b. Is this game a prisoner's dilemma?

c. How could repeated playing of the game change the strategy each firm uses?

2.19 (Related to the *Making the Connection* on page 451) Consider the following two excerpts from articles in the *Wall Street Journal*:

[From February 2003] An attempt by major airlines to raise fares $20 per round-trip ticket fell apart over the weekend as Northwest Airlines, the fourth-largest carrier, refused to go along. . . . By yesterday morning, all airlines had rolled back prices.

[From August 2003] Northwest Airlines triggered a major round of discounting last week when it launched a fare sale for late summer and early fall travel—setting off a chain reaction in the industry. During the course of one day, airlines cut fares on nearly 35,881 routes.

Briefly explain why airlines might be more likely to match price cuts than price increases.

Sources: Scott McCartney and Susan Carey, "Airlines' Move to Raise Fares Falls Apart as Northwest Balks," *Wall Street Journal*, February 18, 2003; and Eleena De Lisser, "Fall Travel Deals Arrive Early," *Wall Street Journal*, August 14, 2003.

2.20 (Related to the *Making the Connection* on page 451) Until the late 1990s, airlines would post proposed changes in ticket prices on computer reservations systems several days before the new ticket prices went into effect. Then the federal government took action to end the practice. Now airlines can only post prices on their reservations systems for tickets that are immediately available for sale. Why would the federal government object to the old system of posting prices before they went into effect?

Source: Scott McCartney, "Airfare Wars Show Why Deals Arrive and Depart," *Wall Street Journal*, March 19, 2002.

2.21 Finding dominant strategies is often a very effective way of analyzing a game. Consider the following game: Microsoft and Apple are the two firms in the

market for operating systems. Each firm has two strategies: charge a high price or charge a low price.

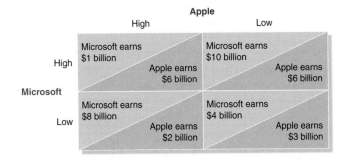

a. What (if any) is the dominant strategy for each firm?
b. Is there a Nash equilibrium? Briefly explain.

2.22 One day in October 2006, oil prices dropped 93 cents per barrel, to their lowest level in almost one year. As an article in the *Wall Street Journal* noted: "The drop Wednesday came even as the Organization of Petroleum Exporting Countries said it will cut global production by one million barrels a day to boost prices, Nigerian oil minister and OPEC president Edmund Daukoru said." Why would oil prices drop at the same time that OPEC was announcing a cut in production. Shouldn't lower production lead to higher prices?

Source: Worth Civils, "Stocks Decline Amid Fed Minutes, Alcoa Earnings, Lower Oil Prices," *Wall Street Journal*, October 11, 2006.

2.23 In 2007, some countries that export natural gas discussed forming a cartel, modeled on the OPEC oil cartel. The head of Libya's energy sector was quoted as saying: "We are trying to strengthen the cooperation among gas producers to avoid harmful competition."
a. What is a cartel?
b. What is "harmful competition"? Is competition typically harmful to consumers?
c. What factors would help the cartel succeed? What factors would reduce the cartel's chances for success?

Source: Ayesha Daya and James Herron, "Gas Exporters to Study Cartel," *Wall Street Journal*, April 10, 2007, p. A6.

> **>> End Learning Objective 13.2**

13.3 LEARNING OBJECTIVE 13.3 | Use sequential games to analyze business strategies, **pages 454–457.**

Sequential Games and Business Strategy

Summary

Recent work in game theory has focused on actions firms can take to deter the entry of new firms into an industry. Deterring entry can be analyzed using a sequential game, where first one firm makes a decision and then another firm reacts to that decision. Sequential games can be illustrated using decision trees.

 Visit www.myeconlab.com to complete these exercises *Get Ahead of the Curve* online and get instant feedback.

Review Questions

3.1 What is a sequential game?

3.2 How are decision trees used to analyze sequential games?

Problems and Applications

3.3 **(Related to *Solved Problem 13-3* on page 455)** Bradford is a small town that currently has no fast-food restaurants. McDonald's and Burger King are both considering entering this market. Burger King will wait until McDonald's has made its decision before deciding whether to enter. Use the following decision tree to decide the optimal strategy for each company. Does your answer depend on the rate of return that owners of fast-food restaurants must earn on their investments in order to break even? Briefly explain.

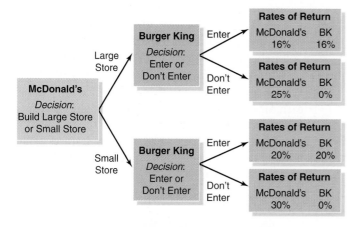

3.4 Suppose that in the situation shown in Figure 13-7 on page 457, TruImage's profits are $1.5 million if the firm accepts Dell's contract offer of $20 per copy. Now will Dell offer TruImage a contract of $20 per copy or a contract of $30 per copy? Briefly explain.

3.5 Refer to Figure 13-5 on page 453. Consider the entries in the row of the payoff matrix that correspond to Saudi Arabia choosing "low output." Suppose the numbers change so that Nigeria's profit is $15 million when Nigeria chooses "low output" and $10 million when it chooses "high output."

  a. Create the payoff matrix for this new situation, assuming that Saudi Arabia and Nigeria choose their output levels simultaneously. Is there a Nash equilibrium to this game? If so, what is it?

  b. Now draw the decision tree for this situation, (using the values from the payoff matrix you created in part a), assuming that Saudi Arabia and Nigeria make their decisions sequentially: First Saudi Arabia chooses its output level, and then Nigeria responds by choosing its output level. Is there a Nash equilibrium to this game? If so, what is it?

  c. Compare your answers to parts a and b. Briefly explain the reason for any differences in the outcomes of these two games.

>> **End Learning Objective 13.3**

13.4 LEARNING OBJECTIVE   13.4 | Use the five competitive forces model to analyze competition in an industry, pages 457–460.

The Five Competitive Forces Model

Summary

Michael Porter of Harvard Business School argues that the state of competition in an industry is determined by five competitive forces: the degree of competition among existing firms, the threat from new entrants, competition from substitute goods or services, the bargaining power of buyers, and the bargaining power of suppliers.

myeconlab Visit www.myeconlab.com to complete these exercises *Get Ahead of the Curve* online and get instant feedback.

Review Questions

4.1 List the competitive forces in the five competitive forces model.

4.2 Does the strength of each of the five competitive forces remain constant over time? Briefly explain.

Problems and Applications

4.3 Michael Porter has argued that in many industries, "strategies converge and competition becomes a series of races down identical paths that no one can win." Briefly explain whether firms in these industries likely will earn economic profits.

Source: Michael E. Porter, "What Is Strategy?" *Harvard Business Review*, November–December 1996, p. 64.

4.4 According to an article in the *Wall Street Journal*:

> The big car makers are pushing a wide array of new technology into production, responding to relentless competitive pressure, rising energy prices and consumer demand for better safety. Once, side-curtain airbags were rare. Now they're becoming standard equipment on a growing number of vehicles. Car makers

are racing to deploy fuel-saving technologies such as cylinder shutdown (variously known as "active fuel management" or "multi-displacement system"), six-speed transmissions and, of course, various kinds of gas-electric hybrid drives.

a. What does the article mean by "relentless competitive pressure"? Which of the five competitive forces is being referred to?

b. In the long run, will the car maker who first successfully incorporates these new technologies in its cars earn economic profits? Which group is likely to benefit the most from these innovations: the car companies or consumers?

Source: Joseph B. White, "Ford, GM Eye Shift in Buying Habits," *Wall Street Journal*, May 22, 2006.

4.5 **(Related to *Making the Connection* on page 459)** An article in the *Wall Street Journal* argues, "Finally, American [Airlines] has figured out what Southwest Airlines and others have known for some time: There is a cost to complexity." What does the author mean by a "cost to complexity"? How does Southwest Airlines avoid this cost?

Source: Scott McCartney, "Large Carriers Are Beginning to Discover the Benefits of Simplicity," *Wall Street Journal*, August 15, 2002, p. D4.

4.6 In early 2004, Yahoo was set to challenge Google as the leading online search engine. According to an article in the *Wall Street Journal*, Yahoo's strategy was "not simply to match what Google does now but to add features its rival can't easily match." The article quoted a senior vice president at Yahoo as stating, "We're not going to beat the competition by being the competition." Briefly explain what the Yahoo executive means by "being the competition." Briefly discuss whether the strategy of "being the competition" ever makes sense.

Source: Mylene Mangalindan, "Yahoo Gets Set to Give Google a Run for Its Money," *Wall Street Journal*, January 6, 2004.

4.7 The following is from an article in the *Wall Street Journal*:

As U.S. car makers continue to offer generous cash discounts and cut-rate financing to woo buyers, top Japanese manufacturers are taking a different pricing approach that seems to be working: Hold sticker prices steady but pack cars with alluring new features.

What happens to the profit a car company makes on each car sold if it cuts the price while holding the car's features constant? What happens to the company's profit per car if the company adds new features while holding the price constant? Briefly discuss how a car company might decide which of these strategies to use.

Source: Todd Zaun, "Japanese Battle U.S. Discounts with Extras," *Wall Street Journal*, January 6, 2004.

>> **End Learning Objective 13.4**

Chapter 14

Monopoly and Antitrust Policy

Time Warner Rules Manhattan

Today most people can hardly imagine life without cable television. In fact, almost 80 percent of U.S. homes have cable television: a larger fraction than have clothes dryers, dishwashers, air conditioning, or personal computers. The first cable systems were established in the 1940s in cities that were too small to support broadcast stations. Those systems consisted of large antennas set up on hills to receive broadcasts from television stations within range. The signals were then transmitted by cable to individual houses.

The cable industry grew slowly because the technology did not exist to rebroadcast the signals of distant stations, so cable systems offered just a few channels. By 1970, only about 7 percent of households had cable television. In addition, the Federal Communications Commission (FCC)—the U.S. government agency that regulates the television industry—placed restrictions on both rebroadcasting the signals of distant stations and the fees that could be charged for "premium channels" that would show movies or sporting events. In the

late 1970s, two key developments occurred: First, satellite relay technology made it feasible for local cable systems to receive signals relayed by satellite from distant broadcast stations. Second, Congress loosened regulations on rebroadcasting distant stations and premium channels. The result of these developments was the growth of both "superstations," which are local broadcast stations in large cities—such as New York, Chicago, and Atlanta—whose programming is sent by satellite to cable systems around the country, and premium channels, such as Home Box Office (HBO).

One of the most successful of the superstations was WTBS, started by Atlanta entrepreneur Robert Edward "Ted" Turner III. Turner went on to found the Turner Broadcasting System (TBS), which included the Cable News Network (CNN), the first 24-hour news network. In 2001, Turner was involved in the largest merger of entertainment companies in history, when AOL Time Warner was formed. The company—now known as Time Warner—was made up of leading firms from four segments of the entertainment industry: Warner Brothers (movie making), *Time* (magazine publishing), TBS (cable television),

and AOL (Internet). Today, Time Warner operates cable systems in 22 states through Time Warner Cable.

A firm needs a license from the city government to enter a local cable television market. If you live in Manhattan and you want cable television, you have to purchase it from Time Warner Cable. Other cable companies could ask the New York City government for licenses to compete against Time Warner Cable in Manhattan, but none have. This is not an unusual situation for a cable television system: Of the nearly 9,000 markets for cable television in the United States, fewer than 400 have competing cable systems.

As the only provider of cable TV in Manhattan, Time Warner has a *monopoly*. Few firms in the United States are monopolies because in a market system, whenever a firm earns economic profits, other firms will enter its market. Therefore, it is very difficult for a firm to remain the only provider of a good or service. In this chapter, we will develop an economic model of monopoly that can help us analyze how such firms affect the economy. **AN INSIDE LOOK AT POLICY** on **page 496** explores how legislation in California is lowering barriers to entry in the cable TV market.

LEARNING Objectives

After studying this chapter, you should be able to:

14.1 Define **monopoly**, page 474.

14.2 Explain the four main **reasons monopolies arise**, page 475.

14.3 Explain how a monopoly chooses **price** and **output**, page 481.

14.4 Use a graph to illustrate how a monopoly affects **economic efficiency**, page 485.

14.5 Discuss **government policies** toward monopoly, page 488.

Economics in YOUR Life!

Why Can't I Watch the NFL Network?

Are you a fan of the National Football League? Would you like to see more NFL-related programming on television? If so, you're not alone. The NFL felt there was so much demand for more football programming that it began its own football network, the NFL Network.

Unfortunately for many football fans, the NFL Network is not available to most households with cable television. Why are some of the largest cable TV systems unwilling to include the NFL Network in their channel lineups? Why are some systems requiring customers who want the NFL Network to upgrade to more expensive channel packages or digital service? As you read this chapter, see if you can answer these questions. You can check your answers against those we provide at the end of the chapter. **≫ Continued on page 495**

Although few firms are monopolies, the economic model of monopoly can still be quite useful. As we saw in Chapter 11, even though perfectly competitive markets are rare, this market model provides a benchmark for how a firm acts in the most competitive situation possible: when it is in an industry with many firms that all supply the same product. Monopoly provides a benchmark for the other extreme, where a firm is the only one in its market and, therefore, faces no competition from other firms supplying its product. The monopoly model is also useful in analyzing situations in which firms agree to *collude*, or not compete, and act together as if they were a monopoly. As we will discuss in this chapter, collusion is illegal in the United States, but it occasionally happens.

Monopolies also pose a dilemma for the government. Should the government allow monopolies to exist? Are there circumstances in which the government should actually promote the existence of monopolies? Should the government regulate the prices monopolies charge? If so, will such price regulation increase economic efficiency? In this chapter, we will explore these public policy issues.

14.1 | Define monopoly.

Is Any Firm Ever Really a Monopoly?

Monopoly A firm that is the only seller of a good or service that does not have a close substitute.

A **monopoly** is a firm that is the only seller of a good or service that does not have a close substitute. Because substitutes of some kind exist for just about every product, can any firm really be a monopoly? The answer is "yes," provided that the substitutes are not "close" substitutes. But how do we decide whether a substitute is a close substitute? A narrow definition of monopoly that some economists use is that a firm has a monopoly if it can ignore the actions of all other firms. In other words, other firms must not be producing close substitutes if the monopolist can ignore the other firms' prices. For example, candles are a substitute for electric lights, but your local electric company can ignore candle prices because however low the price of candles falls, almost no customers will give up using electric lights and switch to candles. Therefore, your local electric company is clearly a monopoly.

Many economists, however, use a broader definition of monopoly. For example, suppose Joe Santos owns the only pizza parlor in a small town. (We will consider later the question of *why* a market may have only a single firm.) Does Joe have a monopoly? Substitutes for pizzas certainly exist. If the price of pizza is too high, people will switch to hamburgers or fried chicken or some other food instead. People do not have to eat at Joe's or starve. Joe is in competition with the local McDonald's and Kentucky Fried Chicken, among other firms. So, Joe does not meet the narrow definition of a monopoly. But many economists would still argue that it is useful to think of Joe as having a monopoly.

Although hamburgers and fried chicken are substitutes for pizza, competition from firms selling them is not enough to keep Joe from earning economic profits. We saw in Chapter 11 that when firms earn economic profits, we can expect new firms to enter the industry, and in the long run, the economic profits are competed away. Joe's profits will not be competed away as long as he is the *only* seller of pizza. Using the broader definition, Joe has a monopoly because there are no other firms selling a substitute close enough that his economic profits are competed away in the long run.

Making the Connection | Is Xbox 360 a Close Substitute for PlayStation 3?

In the early 2000s, Microsoft's Xbox and Sony's PlayStation 2 (PS2) were the best-selling video game consoles. When the two companies began work on the next generation of consoles, they had important decisions to make. In developing the Xbox, Microsoft had decided to include a hard disk and a version of the Windows computer operating system. As a result, the cost of producing the Xbox was much higher than the cost to Sony of producing the PlayStation 2. Microsoft was not concerned by the higher production cost because it believed it would be able to charge a higher price for Xbox than Sony charged for PlayStation 2. Unfortunately for Microsoft, consumers considered the Sony PS2 a close substitute for the Xbox. Microsoft was forced to charge the same price for the Xbox that Sony charged for the PS2. So, while Sony was able to make a substantial profit at that price, Microsoft initially lost money on the Xbox because of its higher costs.

In developing the next generation of video game consoles, both companies hoped to produce devices that could serve as multipurpose home-entertainment systems. To achieve this goal, the new systems needed to play DVDs as well as games. Sony developed a new type of DVD called Blu-ray. Blu-ray DVDs can store five times as much data as conventional DVDs and can play back high-definition (HD) video. Sony's decision to give the new PlayStation 3 (PS3) the capability to play Blu-ray DVDs was risky in two ways: First,

To many gamers, PlayStation 3 is a close substitute for Xbox.

it raised the cost of producing the consoles. Second, because there is a competing second-generation standard for DVDs, called HD-DVD, the PlayStation 3 would not be capable of playing all available second-generation DVDs, thereby reducing its appeal to some consumers. Microsoft decided to sell its Xbox 360 with only the capability of playing older-format DVDs, while making available an add-on component that would play HD-DVDs.

At first it appeared that Microsoft may have made the better decision. Consumers seemed to consider the PS3 and the Xbox to be close substitutes. In that case, the PS3's higher price was a significant problem for Sony. By 2008, however, it became clear that Sony's gamble had paid off when film studios decided to stop producing HD-DVDs and release films only in the Blu-ray format, causing PS3 sales to surpass X-Box 360 sales.

Sources: Stephen H, Wildstrom, "PlayStation 3: It's Got Game," *BusinessWeek*, December 4, 2006; and Nick Wingfield and Yukari Iwatani Kane, "Sony PlayStation3 Revival Lifts Results," *Wall Street Journal*, May 15, 2008.

YOUR TURN: Test your understanding by doing related problem 1.7 on page 498 at the end of this chapter.

14.2 | Explain the four main reasons monopolies arise.

14.2 LEARNING OBJECTIVE

Where Do Monopolies Come From?

Because monopolies do not face competition, every firm would like to have a monopoly. But to have a monopoly, barriers to entering the market must be so high that no other firms can enter. *Barriers to entry* may be high enough to keep out competing firms for four main reasons:

1 Government blocks the entry of more than one firm into a market.

2 One firm has control of a key resource necessary to produce a good.

3 There are important *network externalities* in supplying the good or service.

4 Economies of scale are so large that one firm has a *natural monopoly*.

Entry Blocked by Government Action

As we will discuss later in this chapter, governments ordinarily try to promote competition in markets, but sometimes governments take action to block entry into a market. In the United States, government blocks entry in two main ways:

1 By granting a *patent* or *copyright* to an individual or firm, giving it the exclusive right to produce a product.

2 By granting a firm a *public franchise*, making it the exclusive legal provider of a good or service.

Patent The exclusive right to a product for a period of 20 years from the date the product is invented.

Patents and Copyrights The U.S. government grants patents to firms that develop new products or new ways of making existing products. A **patent** gives a firm the exclusive right to a new product for a period of 20 years from the date the product is invented. Because Microsoft has a patent on the Windows operating system, other firms cannot sell their own versions of Windows. The government grants patents to encourage firms to spend money on the research and development necessary to create new products. If other firms could have freely copied Windows, Microsoft is unlikely to have spent the money necessary to develop it. Sometimes firms are able to maintain a monopoly in the production of a good without patent protection, provided that they can keep secret how the product is made.

Patent protection is of vital importance to pharmaceutical firms as they develop new prescription drugs. Pharmaceutical firms start research and development work on a new prescription drug an average of 12 years before the drug is available for sale. A firm applies for a patent about 10 years before it begins to sell the product. The average 10-year delay between the government granting a patent and the firm actually selling the drug is due to the federal Food and Drug Administration's requirements that the firm demonstrate that the drug is both safe and effective. Therefore, during the period before the drug can be sold, the firm will have substantial costs to develop and test the drug. If the drug does not make it successfully to market, the firm will have a substantial loss.

Once a drug is available for sale, the profits the firm earns from the drug will increase throughout the period of patent protection—which is usually about 10 years—as the drug becomes more widely known to doctors and patients. After the patent has expired, other firms are free to legally produce chemically identical drugs called *generic drugs*. Gradually, competition from generic drugs will eliminate the profits the original firm had been earning. For example, when patent protection expired for Glucophage, a diabetes drug manufactured by Bristol-Myers Squibb, sales of the drug declined by more than $1.5 billion in the first year due to competition from 12 generic versions of the drug produced by other firms. When the patent expired on Prozac, an antidepressant drug manufactured by Eli Lilly, sales dropped by more than 80 percent. Most economic profits from selling a prescription drug are eliminated 20 years after the drug is first offered for sale.

At one time, the Ecke family had a monopoly on growing poinsettias, but many new firms entered the industry.

Making the Connection

The End of the Christmas Plant Monopoly

In December, the poinsettia plant seems to be almost everywhere, decorating stores, restaurants, and houses. Although it may seem strange that anyone can have a monopoly on the production of a plant, for many years the Paul Ecke Ranch in Encinitas, California, had a monopoly on poinsettias.

The poinsettia is a wildflower native to Mexico. It was almost unknown in the United States before Albert Ecke, a German immigrant, began selling it in the early twentieth century at his flower stand in Hollywood, California. Unlike almost every other flowering plant, the poinsettia blossoms in the winter. This timing, along with the plant's striking red and green colors, makes the Poinsettia ideal for Christmas decorating.

Albert Ecke's son, Paul, discovered that by grafting together two varieties of poinsettias, it was possible to have multiple branches grow from one stem. The result was a plant that had more leaves and was much more colorful than conventional poinsettias. Paul Ecke did not attempt to patent his new technique for growing poinsettias. But because the Ecke family kept the technique secret for decades, it was able to maintain a monopoly on the commercial production of the plants. Unfortunately for the Ecke family—but fortunately for consumers—a university researcher discovered the technique and published it in an academic journal.

New firms quickly entered the industry, and the price of poinsettias plummeted. Soon consumers could purchase them for as little as three for $10. At those prices, the Ecke's firm was unable to earn economic profits. Eventually, Paul Ecke III, the owner of the firm, decided to sell off more than half the firm's land to fund new state-of-the-art greenhouses and research into new varieties of plants that he hoped would earn the firm economic profits once again. One of the firm's new products was a variety of white poinsettias that could be spray-painted in different colors and sold for $10 or more—double the price of plain poinsettias.

Sources: Bart Ziegler, "What Color Is Your Poinsettia?" *Wall Street Journal*, December 14, 2006; Cynthia Crossen, "Holiday's Ubiquitous Houseplant," *Wall Street Journal*, December 19, 2000; and Mike Freeman and David E. Graham, "Ecke Ranch Plans to Sell Most of Its Remaining Land," *San Diego Union-Tribune*, December 11, 2003.

YOUR TURN: Test your understanding by doing related problem 2.9 on page 499 at the end of this chapter.

Just as the government grants a new product patent protection, books, films, and software receive **copyright** protection. U.S. law grants the creator of a book, film, or piece of music the exclusive right to use the creation during the creator's lifetime. The creator's heirs retain this exclusive right for 70 years after the creator's death. In effect, copyrights create monopolies for the copyrighted items. Without copyrights, individuals and firms would be less likely to invest in creating new books, films, and software.

Copyright A government-granted exclusive right to produce and sell a creation.

Public Franchises In some cases, the government grants a firm a **public franchise** that allows it to be the only legal provider of a good or service. For example, state and local governments often designate one company as the sole provider of electricity, natural gas, or water.

Occasionally, the government may decide to provide certain services directly to consumers through a *public enterprise*. This is much more common in Europe than in the United States. For example, the governments in most European countries own the railroad systems. In the United States, many city governments provide water and sewage service themselves rather than rely on private firms.

Public franchise A designation by the government that a firm is the only legal provider of a good or service.

Control of a Key Resource

Another way for a firm to become a monopoly is by controlling a key resource. This happens infrequently because most resources, including raw materials such as oil or iron ore, are widely available from a variety of suppliers. There are, however, a few prominent examples of monopolies based on control of a key resource, such as the Aluminum Company of America (Alcoa) and the International Nickel Company of Canada.

For many years until the 1940s, Alcoa either owned or had long-term contracts to buy nearly all of the available bauxite, the mineral needed to produce aluminum. Without access to bauxite, competing firms had to use recycled aluminum, which limited the amount of aluminum they could produce. Similarly, the International Nickel Company of Canada controlled more than 90 percent of available nickel supplies. Competition in the nickel market increased when the Petsamo nickel fields in northern Russia were developed after World War II.

In the United States, a key resource for a professional sports team is a large stadium. The teams that make up the major professional sports leagues—Major League Baseball, the National Football League, and the National Basketball Association—usually have long-term leases with the stadiums in major cities. Control of these stadiums is a major barrier to new professional baseball, football, or basketball leagues forming.

Making the Connection | Are Diamond Profits Forever? The De Beers Diamond Monopoly

The most famous monopoly based on control of a raw material is the De Beers diamond mining and marketing company of South Africa. Before the 1860s, diamonds were extremely rare. Only a few pounds of diamonds were produced each year, primarily from Brazil and India. Then in 1870,

De Beers promoted the sentimental value of diamonds as a way to maintain its position in the diamond market.

enormous deposits of diamonds were discovered along the Orange River in South Africa. It became possible to produce thousands of pounds of diamonds per year, and the owners of the new mines feared that the price of diamonds would plummet. To avoid financial disaster, the mine owners decided in 1888 to merge and form De Beers Consolidated Mines, Ltd.

De Beers became one of the most profitable and longest-lived monopolies in history. The company has carefully controlled the supply of diamonds to keep prices high. As new diamond deposits were discovered in Russia and Zaire, De Beers was able to maintain prices by buying most of the new supplies.

Because diamonds are rarely destroyed, De Beers has always worried about competition from the resale of stones. Heavily promoting diamond engagement and wedding rings with the slogan "A Diamond Is Forever" was a way around this problem. Because engagement and wedding rings have great sentimental value, they are seldom resold, even by the heirs of the original recipients. De Beers advertising has been successful even in some countries, such as Japan, that have had no custom of giving diamond engagement rings. As the populations in De Beers's key markets age, its advertising in recent years has focused on middle-aged men presenting diamond rings to their wives as symbols of financial success and continuing love and on professional women buying "right-hand rings" for themselves.

In the past few years, competition has finally come to the diamond business. By 2000, De Beers directly controlled only about 40 percent of world diamond production. The company became concerned about the amount it was spending to buy diamonds from other sources to keep them off the market. It decided to adopt a strategy of differentiating its diamonds by relying on its name recognition. Each De Beers diamond is now marked with a microscopic brand—a "Forevermark"—to reassure consumers of its high quality. Other firms, such as BHP Billiton, which owns mines in northern Canada, have followed suit by branding their diamonds. Sellers of Canadian diamonds stress that they are "mined under ethical, environmentally friendly conditions," as opposed to "blood diamonds," which are supposedly "mined under armed force in war-torn African countries and exported to finance military campaigns." Whether consumers will pay attention to brands on diamonds remains to be seen, although through 2007, the branding strategy had helped De Beers maintain its 40 percent share of the diamond market.

Sources: Edward Jay Epstein, "Have You Ever Tried to Sell a Diamond?" *Atlantic Monthly*, February 1982; Donna J. Bergenstock, Mary E. Deily, and Larry W. Taylor, "A Cartel's Response to Cheating: An Empirical Investigation of the De Beers Diamond Empire," *Southern Economic Journal*, Vol. 73, No. 1, July 2006, pp. 173–189; Bernard Simon, "Adding Brand Names to Nameless Stones," *New York Times*, June 27, 2002; Blythe Yee, "Ads Remind Women They Have Two Hands," *Wall Street Journal*, August 14, 2003; quote in last paragraph from Joel Baglole, "Political Correctness by the Carat," *Wall Street Journal*, April 17, 2003.

YOUR TURN: Test your understanding by doing related problem 2.10 on page 499 at the end of this chapter.

Network Externalities

Network externalities The situation where the usefulness of a product increases with the number of consumers who use it.

There are **network externalities** in the consumption of a product if the usefulness of the product increases with the number of people who use it. If you owned the only cell phone in the world, for example, it would not be very valuable. The more cell phones there are in use, the more valuable they become to consumers.

Some economists argue that network externalities can serve as barriers to entry. For example, in the early 1980s, Microsoft gained an advantage over other software companies by developing MS-DOS, the operating system for the first IBM personal computers. Because IBM sold more computers than any other company, software developers wrote many application programs for MS-DOS. The more people who used MS-DOS–based programs, the greater the usefulness to a consumer of using an MS-DOS–based program. Today, Windows, the program Microsoft developed to succeed MS-DOS, has a 95 percent share in the market for personal computer operating systems (although

Windows has a much lower share in the market for operating systems for servers). If another firm introduced a competing operating system, some economists argue that relatively few people would use it initially, and few applications would run on it, which would limit the operating system's value to other consumers.

eBay was the first Internet site to attract a significant number of people to its online auctions. Once a large number of people began to use eBay to buy and sell collectibles, antiques, and many other products, it became a more valuable place to buy and sell. Yahoo.com, Amazon.com, and other Internet sites eventually started online auctions, but they found it difficult to attract buyers and sellers. On eBay, a buyer expects to find more sellers, and a seller expects to find more potential buyers than on Amazon or other auction sites.

As these examples show, network externalities can set off a *virtuous cycle*: If a firm can attract enough customers initially, it can attract additional customers because its product's value has been increased by more people using it, which attracts even more customers, and so on. With products such as computer operating systems and online auctions, it might be difficult for new firms to enter the market and compete away the profits being earned by the first firm in the market.

Economists engage in considerable debate, however, about the extent to which network externalities are important barriers to entry in the business world. Some economists argue that the dominant positions of Microsoft and eBay reflect the efficiency of those firms in offering products that satisfy consumer preferences more than the effects of network externalities. In this view, the advantages existing firms gain from network externalities would not be enough to protect them from competing firms offering better products. In other words, a firm entering the operating system market with a program better than Windows or a firm offering an Internet auction site better than eBay would be successful despite the effects of network externalities. (We discussed this point in more detail in Chapter 9.)

Natural Monopoly

We saw in Chapter 10 that economies of scale exist when a firm's long-run average costs fall as it increases the quantity of output it produces. A **natural monopoly** occurs when economies of scale are so large that one firm can supply the entire market at a lower average total cost than two or more firms. In that case, there is really "room" in the market for only one firm.

Figure 14-1 shows the average total cost curve for a firm producing electricity and the total demand for electricity in the firm's market. Notice that the average total cost

Natural monopoly A situation in which economies of scale are so large that one firm can supply the entire market at a lower average total cost than can two or more firms.

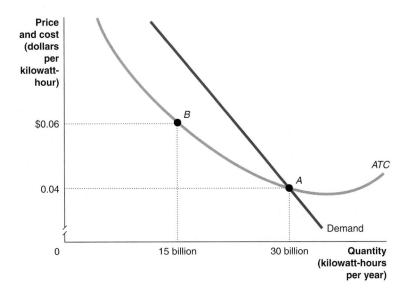

Figure 14-1

Average Total Cost Curve for a Natural Monopoly

With a natural monopoly, the average total cost curve is still falling when it crosses the demand curve (point A). If only one firm is producing electric power in the market and it produces where average cost intersects the demand curve, average total cost will equal $0.04 per kilowatt-hour of electricity produced. If the market is divided between two firms, each producing 15 billion kilowatt-hours, the average cost of producing electricity rises to $0.06 per kilowatt-hour (point B). In this case, if one firm expands production, it can move down the average total cost curve, lower its price, and drive the other firm out of business.

curve is still falling when it crosses the demand curve at point *A*. If the firm is a monopoly and produces 30 billion kilowatt-hours of electricity per year, its average total cost of production will be $0.04 per kilowatt-hour. Suppose instead that two firms are in the market, each producing half of the market output, or 15 billion kilowatt-hours per year. Assume that each firm has the same average total cost curve. The figure shows that producing 15 billion kilowatt-hours would move each firm back up its average cost curve so that the average cost of producing electricity would rise to $0.06 per kilowatt-hour (point *B*). In this case, if one of the firms expands production, it will move down the average total cost curve. With lower average costs, it will be able to offer electricity at a lower price than the other firm can. Eventually, the other firm will be driven out of business, and the remaining firm will have a monopoly. Because a monopoly would develop automatically—or *naturally*—in this market, it is a natural monopoly.

Natural monopolies are most likely to occur in markets where fixed costs are very large relative to variable costs. For example, a firm that produces electricity must make a substantial investment in machinery and equipment necessary to generate the electricity and in wires and cables necessary to distribute it. Once the initial investment has been made, however, the marginal cost of producing another kilowatt-hour of electricity is relatively small.

Solved Problem | 14-2

Is the "Proxy Business" a Natural Monopoly?

A corporation is owned by its shareholders, who elect members of the corporation's board of directors and who also vote on particularly important issues of corporate policy. The shareholders of large corporations are spread around the country, and relatively few of them are present at the annual meetings at which elections take place. Before each meeting, corporations must provide shareholders with annual reports and forms that allow them to vote by mail. Voting by mail is referred to as "proxy voting." People who work on Wall Street refer to providing annual reports and ballots to shareholders as the "proxy business." Currently, one company, Broadridge, controls almost all of the proxy business.

According to the *Wall Street Journal*, Don Kittell of the Securities Industry Association has explained Broadridge's virtual monopoly by arguing that, "The economies of scale and the efficiencies achieved by Broadridge handling all the brokerage business—rather than multiple companies—resulted in savings to [corporations]."

a. Assuming that Kittell is correct, draw a graph showing the market for handling proxy materials. Be sure that the graph contains the demand for proxy materials and Broadridge's average total cost curve. Explain why cost savings result from having the proxy business handled by a single firm.

b. According to a spokesperson for Broadridge, the proxy business produces a profit rate of about 7 percent, which is lower than the profit rate the company receives from any of its other businesses. Does this information support or undermine Kittell's analysis? Explain.

SOLVING THE PROBLEM:

Step 1: **Review the chapter material.** This problem is about natural monopoly, so you may want to review the section "Natural Monopoly," which begins on page 479.

Step 2: **Answer question (a) by drawing a natural monopoly graph and discussing the potential cost savings in this industry.** Kittell describes a situation of natural monopoly. Otherwise, the entry of another firm into the market would not raise average cost. Draw a natural monopoly graph, like the one in Figure 14-1:

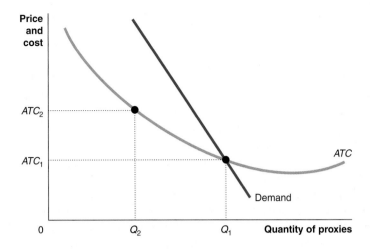

Make sure your average total cost curve is still declining when it crosses the demand curve. If one firm can supply Q_1 proxies at an average total cost of ATC_1, then dividing the business equally between two firms each supplying Q_2 proxies would raise average total cost to ATC_2.

Step 3: **Answer question (b) by discussing the implications of Broadridge's low profit rate in the proxy business.** If Broadridge earns a low profit rate on its investment in this business even though it has a monopoly, Kittell probably is correct that the proxy business is a natural monopoly.

EXTRA CREDIT: Keep in mind that competition is not good for its own sake. It is good because it can lead to lower costs, lower prices, and better products. In certain markets, however, cost conditions are such that competition is likely to lead to higher costs and higher prices. These markets are natural monopolies that are best served by one firm.

Source: Phyllis Plitch, "Competition Remains Issue in Proxy-Mailing Costs," *Wall Street Journal*, January 16, 2002.

YOUR TURN: For more practice, do related problem 2.11 on page 499 at the end of this chapter.

>> **End Solved Problem 14-2**

14.3 | Explain how a monopoly chooses price and output.

How Does a Monopoly Choose Price and Output?

Like every other firm, a monopoly maximizes profit by producing where marginal revenue equals marginal cost. A monopoly differs from other firms in that *a monopoly's demand curve is the same as the demand curve for the product.* We emphasized in Chapter 11 that the market demand curve for wheat was very different from the demand curve for the wheat produced by any one farmer. If, however, one farmer had a monopoly on wheat production, the two demand curves would be exactly the same.

Marginal Revenue Once Again

Recall from Chapter 11 that firms in perfectly competitive markets—such as a farmer in the wheat market—face horizontal demand curves. They are *price takers.* All other firms, including monopolies, are *price makers.* If price makers raise their prices, they will lose some, but not all, of their customers. Therefore, they face a downward-sloping demand curve and a downward-sloping marginal revenue curve as well. Let's review why a firm's marginal revenue curve slopes downward if its demand curve slopes downward.

Remember that when a firm cuts the price of a product, one good thing happens, and one bad thing happens:

- **The good thing.** It sells more units of the product.
- **The bad thing.** It receives less revenue from each unit than it would have received at the higher price.

For example, consider the table in Figure 14-2, which shows the demand curve for Time Warner Cable's basic cable package. For simplicity, we assume that the market has only 10 potential subscribers instead of the millions it actually has. If Time Warner charges a price of $60 per month, it won't have any subscribers. If it charges a price of $57, it sells 1 subscription. At $54, it sells 2, and so on. Time Warner's total revenue is equal to the number of subscriptions sold per month multiplied by the price. The firm's average revenue—or revenue per subscription sold—is equal to its total revenue divided by the quantity of subscriptions sold. Time Warner is particularly interested in marginal revenue because marginal revenue tells the firm how much revenue will increase if it cuts the price to sell one more subscription.

Notice that Time Warner's marginal revenue is less than the price for every subscription sold after the first subscription. To see why, think about what happens if Time Warner cuts the price of its basic cable package from $42 to $39, which increases its subscriptions sold from 6 to 7. Time Warner increases its revenue by the $39 it receives for the seventh subscription. But it also loses revenue of $3 per subscription on the first 6 subscriptions because it could have sold them at the old price of $42. So, its marginal

Figure 14-2

Calculating a Monopoly's Revenue

Time Warner Cable faces a downward-sloping demand curve for subscriptions to basic cable. To sell more subscriptions, it must cut the price. When this happens, it gains the revenue from selling more subscriptions but loses revenue from selling at a lower price the subscriptions that it could have sold at a higher price. The firm's marginal revenue is the change in revenue from selling another subscription. We can calculate marginal revenue by subtracting the revenue lost as a result of a price cut from the revenue gained. The table shows that Time Warner's marginal revenue is less than the price for every subscription sold after the first subscription. Therefore, Time Warner's marginal revenue curve will be below its demand curve.

Subscribers per Month (Q)	Price (P)	Total Revenue (TR = P x Q)	Average Revenue (AR = TR/Q)	Marginal Revenue (MR = ΔTR/ΔQ)
0	$60	$0	–	–
1	57	57	$57	$57
2	54	108	54	51
3	51	153	51	45
4	48	192	48	39
5	45	225	45	33
6	42	252	42	27
7	39	273	39	21
8	36	288	36	15
9	33	297	33	9
10	30	300	30	3

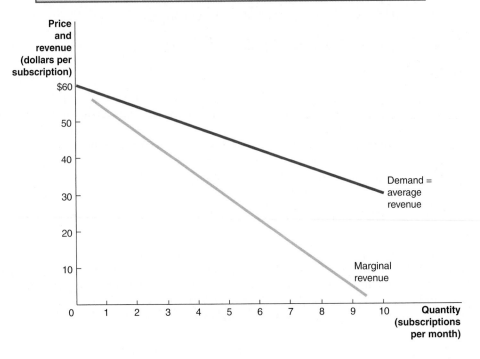

revenue on the seventh subscription is $39 − $18 = $21, which is the value shown in the table. The graph in Figure 14-2 plots Time Warner's demand and marginal revenue curves, based on the information given in the table.

Profit Maximization for a Monopolist

Figure 14-3 shows how Time Warner combines the information on demand and marginal revenue with information on average and marginal costs to decide how many subscriptions to sell and what price to charge. We assume that the firm's marginal cost and average total cost curves have the usual U shapes we encountered in Chapters 10 and 11. In panel (a), we see how Time Warner can calculate its profit-maximizing quantity and price. As long as the marginal cost of selling one more subscription is less than the marginal revenue, the firm should sell additional subscriptions because it is adding to its profits. As Time Warner sells more cable subscriptions, rising marginal cost will eventually equal marginal revenue, and the firm will be selling the profit-maximizing quantity of subscriptions. This happens with the sixth subscription, which adds $27 to the firm's costs and $27 to its revenues (point A in panel (a) of Figure 14-3). The demand curve tells us that Time Warner can sell 6 subscriptions for a price of $42 per month. We can conclude that Time Warner's profit-maximizing quantity of subscriptions is 6 and its profit-maximizing price is $42.

Panel (b) shows that the average total cost of 6 subscriptions is $30 and that Time Warner can sell 6 subscriptions at a price of $42 per month (point B on the demand curve). Time Warner is making a profit of $12 per subscription—the price of $42 minus the average cost of $30. Its total profit is $72 (6 subscriptions × $12 profit per subscription), which is shown by the area of the green-shaded rectangle in the figure. We could also have calculated Time Warner's total profit as the difference between its total revenue and its total cost. Its total revenue from selling 6 subscriptions is $252. Its total cost equals its average cost multiplied by the number of subscriptions sold, or $30 × 6 = $180. So, its profit is $252 − $180 = $72.

It's important to note that even though Time Warner is earning economic profits, new firms will *not* enter the market. Because Time Warner has a monopoly, it will not face competition from other cable operators. Therefore, if other factors remain unchanged, Time Warner will be able to continue to earn economic profits, even in the long run.

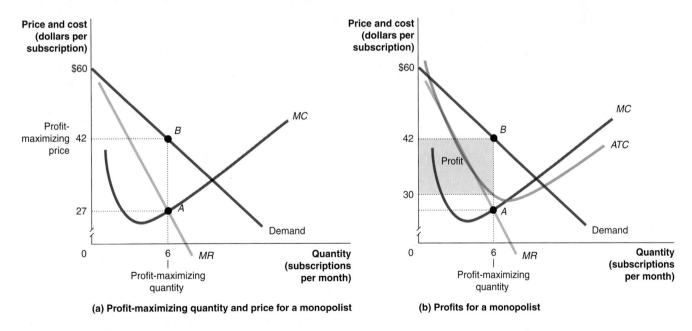

Figure 14-3 | Profit-Maximizing Price and Output for a Monopoly

Panel (a) shows that to maximize profit, Time Warner should sell subscriptions up to the point that the marginal revenue from selling the last subscription equals its marginal cost (point A). In this case, the marginal revenue from selling the sixth subscription and the marginal cost are both $27. Time Warner maximizes profit by

selling 6 subscriptions per month and charging a price of $42 (point B). In panel (b), the green box represents Time Warner's profits. The box has a height equal to $12, which is the price of $42 minus the average total cost of $30, and a base equal to the quantity of 6 cable subscriptions. Time Warner's profit equals $12 × 6 = $72.

Solved Problem | 14-3

Finding the Profit-Maximizing Price and Output for a Monopolist

Suppose that Comcast has a cable monopoly in Philadelphia. The following table gives Comcast's demand and costs per month for subscriptions to basic cable (for simplicity, we once again keep the number of subscribers artificially small).

PRICE	QUANTITY	TOTAL REVENUE	MARGINAL REVENUE $(MR = \Delta TR/\Delta Q)$	TOTAL COST	MARGINAL COST $(MC = \Delta TC/\Delta Q)$
$17	3			$56	
16	4			63	
15	5			71	
14	6			80	
13	7			90	
12	8			101	

a. Fill in the missing values in the table.

b. If Comcast wants to maximize profits, what price should it charge and how many cable subscriptions per month should it sell? How much profit will Comcast make? Briefly explain.

c. Suppose the local government imposes a $2.50 per month tax on cable companies. Now what price should Comcast charge, how many subscriptions should it sell, and what will its profits be?

SOLVING THE PROBLEM:

Step 1: **Review the chapter material.** This problem is about finding the profit-maximizing quantity and price for a monopolist, so you may want to review the section "Profit Maximization for a Monopolist," which begins on page 483.

Step 2: **Answer question (a) by filling in the missing values in the table.** Remember that to calculate marginal revenue and marginal cost, you must divide the change in total revenue or total cost by the change in quantity.

PRICE	QUANTITY	TOTAL REVENUE	MARGINAL REVENUE $(MR = \Delta TR/\Delta Q)$	TOTAL COST	MARGINAL COST $(MC = \Delta TC/\Delta Q)$
$17	3	$51	—	$56	—
16	4	64	$13	63	$7
15	5	75	11	71	8
14	6	84	9	80	9
13	7	91	7	90	10
12	8	96	5	101	11

We don't have enough information from the table to fill in the values for marginal revenue or marginal cost in the first row.

Step 3: **Answer question (b) by determining the profit-maximizing quantity and price.** We know that Comcast will maximize profits by selling subscriptions up to the point where marginal cost equals marginal revenue. In this case, that means selling 6 subscriptions per month. From the information in the first two columns, we know Comcast can sell 6 subscriptions at a price of $14 each. Comcast's profits are equal to the difference between its total revenue and its total cost: Profit = $84 − $80 = $4 per month.

Step 4: **Answer question (c) by analyzing the impact of the tax.** This tax is a fixed cost to Comcast because it is a flat $2.50, no matter how many subscriptions it sells. Because the tax has no impact on Comcast's marginal revenue or marginal cost, the profit-maximizing level of output has not changed. So, Comcast will still sell 6 subscriptions per month at a price of $14, but its profits will fall by the amount of the tax from $4.00 per month to $1.50.

YOUR TURN: For more practice, do related problems 3.3 and 3.4 on page 500 at the end of this chapter.

>> **End Solved Problem 14-3**

14.4 | Use a graph to illustrate how a monopoly affects economic efficiency.

14.4 LEARNING OBJECTIVE

Does Monopoly Reduce Economic Efficiency?

We saw in Chapter 11 that a perfectly competitive market is economically efficient. How would economic efficiency be affected if instead of being perfectly competitive, a market were a monopoly? In Chapter 4, we developed the idea of *economic surplus*. Economic surplus provides a way of characterizing the economic efficiency of a perfectly competitive market: *Equilibrium in a perfectly competitive market results in the greatest amount of economic surplus, or total benefit to society, from the production of a good or service.* What happens to economic surplus under a monopoly? We can begin the analysis by considering the hypothetical case of what would happen if the market for television sets begins as perfectly competitive and then becomes a monopoly. (In reality, the market for television sets is not perfectly competitive, but assuming that it is simplifies our analysis.)

Comparing Monopoly and Perfect Competition

Panel (a) in Figure 14-4 illustrates the situation if the market for televisions is perfectly competitive. Price and quantity are determined by the intersection of the demand and supply curves. Remember that none of the individual firms in a perfectly competitive industry has any control over price. Each firm must accept the price determined by the market. Panel (b) shows what happens if the television industry becomes a monopoly. We know that the monopoly will maximize profits by producing where marginal revenue equals marginal cost. To do this, the monopoly reduces the quantity of televisions

Don't Let This Happen to **YOU!**

Don't Assume That Charging a Higher Price Is Always More Profitable for a Monopolist

In answering question (c) of Solved Problem 14-3, it's tempting to argue that Comcast should increase its price to make up for the tax. After all, Comcast is a monopolist, so why can't it just pass along the tax to its customers? The reason it can't is that Comcast, like any other monopolist, must pay attention to demand. Comcast is not interested in charging high prices for the sake of charging high prices; it is interested in maximizing profits. Charging a price of $1,000 for a basic cable subscription sounds nice, but if no one will buy at that price, Comcast would hardly be maximizing profits.

To look at it another way, before the tax is imposed, Comcast has already determined $14 is the price that will maximize its profits. After the tax is imposed, it must determine whether $14 is still the profit-maximizing price. Because the tax has not affected Comcast's marginal revenue or marginal cost (or had any effect on consumer demand), $14 is still the profit-maximizing price, and Comcast should continue to charge it. The tax reduces Comcast's profits but doesn't cause it to increase the price of cable subscriptions.

YOUR TURN: Test your understanding by doing related problems 3.7 and 3.8 on page 500 at the end of this chapter.

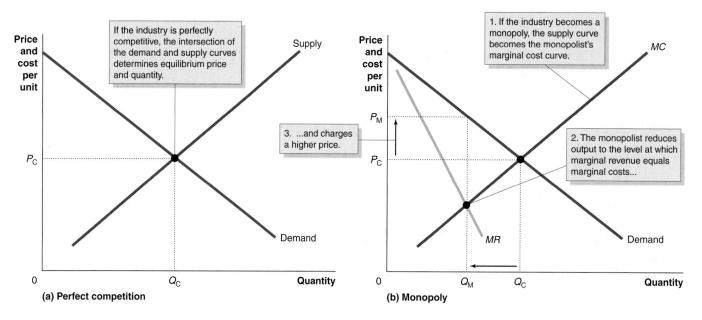

Figure 14-4 | What Happens If a Perfectly Competitive Industry Becomes a Monopoly?

In panel (a), the market for television sets is perfectly competitive, and price and quantity are determined by the intersection of the demand and supply curves. In panel (b), the perfectly competitive television industry became a monopoly. As a result, the equilibrium quantity falls, and the equilibrium price rises.

1. The industry supply curve becomes the monopolist's marginal cost curve.
2. The monopolist reduces output to where marginal revenue equals marginal cost, Q_M.
3. The monopolist raises the price from P_C to P_M.

that would have been produced if the industry were perfectly competitive and increases the price. Panel (b) illustrates an important conclusion: *A monopoly will produce less and charge a higher price than would a perfectly competitive industry producing the same good.*

Measuring the Efficiency Losses from Monopoly

Figure 14-5 uses panel (b) from Figure 14-4 to illustrate how monopoly affects consumers, producers, and the efficiency of the economy. Recall from Chapter 4 that *consumer surplus* measures the net benefit received by consumers from purchasing a good or service. We measure consumer surplus as the area below the demand curve and above the market price. The higher the price, the smaller the consumer surplus. Because a monopoly raises the market price, it reduces consumer surplus. In Figure 14-5, the loss of consumer surplus is equal to rectangle *A* plus triangle *B*. Remember that *producer surplus* measures the net benefit to producers from selling a good or service. We measure producer surplus as the area above the supply curve and below the market price. The increase in price due to monopoly increases producer surplus by an amount equal to rectangle *A* and reduces it by an amount equal to triangle *C*. Because rectangle *A* is larger than triangle *C*, we know that a monopoly increases producer surplus compared with perfect competition.

Economic surplus is equal to the sum of consumer surplus plus producer surplus. By increasing price and reducing the quantity produced, the monopolist has reduced economic surplus by an amount equal to the areas of triangles *B* and *C*. This reduction in economic surplus is called *deadweight loss* and represents the loss of economic efficiency due to monopoly.

The best way to understand how a monopoly causes a loss of economic efficiency is to recall that price is equal to marginal cost in a perfectly competitive market. As a result, a consumer in a perfectly competitive market is always able to buy a good if she is willing to pay a price equal to the marginal cost of producing it. As Figure 14-5 shows, the monopolist stops producing at a point where the price is well above marginal cost. Consumers are unable to buy some units of the good for which they would be willing to pay a price greater

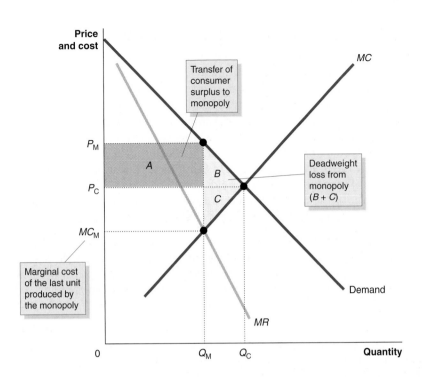

Figure 14-5

The Inefficiency of Monopoly

A monopoly charges a higher price, P_M, and produces a smaller quantity, Q_M, than a perfectly competitive industry, which charges a price of P_C and produces at Q_C. The higher price reduces consumer surplus by the area equal to the rectangle A and the triangle B. Some of the reduction in consumer surplus is captured by the monopoly as producer surplus, and some becomes deadweight loss, which is the area equal to triangles B and C.

than the marginal cost of producing them. Why doesn't the monopolist produce this additional output? Because the monopolist's profits are greater if it restricts output and forces up the price. A monopoly produces the profit-maximizing level of output but fails to produce the efficient level of output from the point of view of society.

We can summarize the effects of monopoly as follows:

1 Monopoly causes a reduction in consumer surplus.

2 Monopoly causes an increase in producer surplus.

3 Monopoly causes a deadweight loss, which represents a reduction in economic efficiency.

How Large Are the Efficiency Losses Due to Monopoly?

We know that there are relatively few monopolies, so the loss of economic efficiency due to monopoly must be small. Many firms, though, have **market power**, which is the ability of a firm to charge a price greater than marginal cost. The analysis we just completed shows that some loss of economic efficiency will occur whenever a firm has market power and can charge a price greater than marginal cost, even if the firm is not a monopoly. The only firms that do *not* have market power are firms in perfectly competitive markets, who must charge a price equal to marginal cost. Because few markets are perfectly competitive, *some loss of economic efficiency occurs in the market for nearly every good or service.*

Is the total loss of economic efficiency due to market power large or small? It is possible to put a dollar value on the loss of economic efficiency by estimating for every industry the size of the deadweight loss triangle, as in Figure 14-5. The first economist to do this was Arnold Harberger of the University of Chicago. His estimates—largely confirmed by later researchers—indicated that the total loss of economic efficiency in the U.S. economy due to market power is small. According to his estimates, if every industry in the economy were perfectly competitive, so that price were equal to marginal cost in every market, the gain in economic efficiency would equal less than 1 percent of the value of total production in the United States, or about $450 per person.

The loss of economic efficiency is this small primarily because true monopolies are very rare. In most industries, competition keeps price much closer to marginal cost than would be the case in a monopoly. The closer price is to marginal cost, the smaller the size of the deadweight loss.

Market power The ability of a firm to charge a price greater than marginal cost.

Market Power and Technological Change

Some economists have raised the possibility that the economy may actually benefit from firms having market power. This argument is most closely identified with Joseph Schumpeter, an Austrian economist who spent many years as a professor of economics at Harvard. Schumpeter argued that economic progress depended on technological change in the form of new products. For example, the replacement of horse-drawn carriages by automobiles, the replacement of ice boxes by refrigerators, and the replacement of mechanical calculators by electronic computers all represent technological changes that significantly raised living standards. In Schumpeter's view, new products unleash a "gale of creative destruction" that drives older products—and, often, the firms that produced them—out of the market. Schumpeter was unconcerned that firms with market power would charge higher prices than perfectly competitive firms:

> It is not that kind of [price] competition which counts but the competition from the new commodity, the new technology, the new source of supply, the new type of organization . . . competition which commands a decisive cost or quality advantage and which strikes not at the margins of the profits and outputs of the existing firms but at their foundations and their very lives.

Economists who support Schumpeter's view argue that the introduction of new products requires firms to spend funds on research and development. It is possible for firms to raise this money by borrowing from investors or from banks. But investors and banks are usually skeptical of ideas for new products that have not yet passed the test of consumer acceptance in the market. As a result, firms are often forced to rely on their profits to finance the research and development needed for new products. Because firms with market power are more likely to earn economic profits than are perfectly competitive firms, they are also more likely to carry out research and development and introduce new products. In this view, the higher prices firms with market power charge are unimportant compared with the benefits from the new products these firms introduce to the market.

Some economists disagree with Schumpeter's views. These economists point to the number of new products developed by smaller firms, including, for example, Steve Jobs and Steve Wozniak inventing the first Apple computer in Wozniak's garage, and Larry Page and Sergey Brin inventing the Google search engine as graduate students at Stanford. As we will see in the next section, government policymakers continue to struggle with the issue of whether, on balance, large firms with market power are good or bad for the economy.

14.5 LEARNING OBJECTIVE

14.5 | Discuss government policies toward monopoly.

Government Policy toward Monopoly

Collusion An agreement among firms to charge the same price or otherwise not to compete.

Because monopolies reduce consumer surplus and economic efficiency, most governments have policies that regulate their behavior. Recall from Chapter 13 that **collusion** refers to an agreement among firms to charge the same price or otherwise not to compete. In the United States, government policies with respect to monopolies and collusion are embodied in the *antitrust laws*. These laws make illegal any attempts to form a monopoly or to collude. Governments also regulate firms that are natural monopolies, often by controlling the prices they charge.

Antitrust Laws and Antitrust Enforcement

The first important law regulating monopolies in the United States was the Sherman Act, which Congress passed in 1890 to promote competition and prevent the formation of monopolies. Section 1 of the Sherman Act outlaws "every contract, combination in the form of trust or otherwise, or conspiracy in restraint of trade." Section 2 states that "every person who shall monopolize, or attempt to monopolize, or combine or conspire

with any other person or persons, to monopolize any part of the trade or commerce . . .
shall be deemed guilty of a felony."

The Sherman Act targeted firms in several industries that had combined together
during the 1870s and 1880s to form "trusts." In a trust, the firms were operated independently but gave voting control to a board of trustees. The board enforced collusive agreements for the firms to charge the same price and not to compete for each other's customers. The most notorious of the trusts was the Standard Oil Trust, organized by John
D. Rockefeller. After the Sherman Act was passed, trusts disappeared, but the term
antitrust laws has lived on to refer to the laws aimed at eliminating collusion and promoting competition among firms.

Antitrust laws Laws aimed at eliminating collusion and promoting competition among firms.

The Sherman Act prohibited trusts and collusive agreements, but it left several loopholes. For example, it was not clear whether it would be legal for two or more firms to
merge to form a new, larger firm that would have substantial market power. A series of
Supreme Court decisions interpreted the Sherman Act narrowly, and the result was a
wave of mergers at the turn of the twentieth century. Included in these mergers was the
U.S. Steel Corporation, which was formed from dozens of smaller companies. U.S. Steel,
organized by J. P. Morgan, was the first billion-dollar corporation, and it controlled two-
thirds of steel production in the United States. The Sherman Act also left unclear
whether any business practices short of outright collusion were illegal.

To address the loopholes in the Sherman Act, in 1914, Congress passed the Clayton
Act and the Federal Trade Commission Act. Under the Clayton Act, a merger was illegal
if its effect was "substantially to lessen competition, or to tend to create a monopoly."
The Federal Trade Commission Act set up the Federal Trade Commission (FTC), which
was given the power to police unfair business practices. The FTC has brought lawsuits
against firms employing a variety of business practices, including deceptive advertising.
In setting up the FTC, however, Congress divided the authority to police mergers.
Currently, both the Antitrust Division of the U.S. Department of Justice and the FTC are
responsible for merger policy. Table 14-1 lists the most important U.S. antitrust laws and
the purpose of each.

Mergers: The Trade-off between Market Power and Efficiency

The federal government regulates business mergers because it knows that if firms gain
market power by merging, they may use that market power to raise prices and reduce
output. As a result, the government is most concerned with **horizontal mergers**, or
mergers between firms in the same industry. Horizontal mergers are more likely to
increase market power than **vertical mergers**, which are mergers between firms at different stages of the production of a good. An example of a vertical merger would be a
merger between a company making personal computers and a company making computer hard drives.

Horizontal merger A merger between firms in the same industry.

Vertical merger A merger between firms at different stages of production of a good.

LAW	DATE	PURPOSE
Sherman Act	1890	Prohibited "restraint of trade," including price fixing and collusion. Also outlawed monopolization.
Clayton Act	1914	Prohibited firms from buying stock in competitors and from having directors serve on the boards of competing firms.
Federal Trade Commission Act	1914	Established the Federal Trade Commission (FTC) to help administer antitrust laws.
Robinson–Patman Act	1936	Prohibited charging buyers different prices if the result would reduce competition.
Cellar–Kefauver Act	1950	Toughened restrictions on mergers by prohibiting any mergers that would reduce competition.

TABLE 14-1
Important U.S. Antitrust Laws

Regulating horizontal mergers can be complicated by two factors. First, the "market" that firms are in is not always clear. For example, if Hershey Foods wants to merge with Mars, Inc., maker of M&Ms, Snickers, and other candies, what is the relevant market? If the government looks just at the candy market, the newly merged company would have more than 70 percent of the market, a level at which the government would likely oppose the merger. What if the government looks at the broader market for "snacks"? In this market, Hershey and Mars compete with makers of potato chips, pretzels, peanuts, and, perhaps, even producers of fresh fruit. Of course, if the government looked at the very broad market for "food," then both Hershey and Mars have very small market shares, and there would be no reason to oppose their merger. In practice, the government defines the relevant market on the basis of whether there are close substitutes for the products being made by the merging firms. In this case, potato chips and the other snack foods mentioned are not close substitutes for candy. So, the government would consider the candy market to be the relevant market and would oppose the merger on the grounds that the new firm would have too much market power.

The second factor that complicates merger policy is the possibility that the newly merged firm might be more efficient than the merging firms were individually. For example, one firm might have an excellent product but a poor distribution system for getting the product into the hands of consumers. A competing firm might have built a great distribution system but have an inferior product. Allowing these firms to merge might be good for both the firms and consumers. Or, two competing firms might each have an extensive system of warehouses that are only half full, but if the firms merged, they could consolidate their warehouses and significantly reduce their costs.

An example of the government dealing with the issue of greater efficiency versus reduced competition occurred in early 2000, when Time Warner—which owns cable systems with more than 20 million subscribers—and America Online (AOL)—which was the country's largest Internet service provider (ISP), with more than 26 million subscribers—announced plans to merge. The firms argued that the merger would speed the development of high-speed (or "broadband") Internet access and would lead to more rapid growth of services such as interactive television. Some competing firms complained that the new firm created by the merger would have excessive market power. In particular, other ISPs were worried that they would be denied access to the cable systems owned by Time Warner. After more than a year of study, the FTC finally approved the merger, subject to certain conditions. One key condition was that Time Warner was required to allow AOL's competitors to offer their services over Time Warner's high-speed cable lines before AOL would be permitted to offer its services over those lines.

Most of the mergers that come under scrutiny by the Department of Justice and the FTC are between large firms. For simplicity, let's consider a case where all the firms in a perfectly competitive industry want to merge to form a monopoly. As we saw in Figure 14-5, as a result of this merger, prices will rise and output will fall, leading to a decline in consumer surplus and economic efficiency. But what if the larger, newly merged firm actually is more efficient than the smaller firms had been? Figure 14-6 shows a possible result.

If costs are unaffected by the merger, we get the same result as in Figure 14-5: Price rises from P_C to P_M, quantity falls from Q_C to Q_M, consumer surplus is lower, and a loss of economic efficiency results. If the monopoly has lower costs than the competitive firms, it is possible for price to decline and quantity to increase. In Figure 14-6, to find the new profit-maximizing quantity, note where MR crosses MC after the merger. This new profit-maximizing quantity is Q_{Merge}. The demand curve shows that the monopolist can sell this quantity at a price of P_{Merge}. Therefore, the price declines after the merger from P_C to P_{Merge} and quantity increases from Q_C to Q_{Merge}. We have the following seemingly paradoxical result: *Although the newly merged firm has a great deal of market power, because it is more efficient, consumers are better off and economic efficiency is improved.* Of course, sometimes a merged firm will be more efficient and have lower costs, and other times it won't. Even if a merged firm is more efficient and has lower costs, that may not offset the increased market power of the firm enough to increase consumer surplus and economic efficiency.

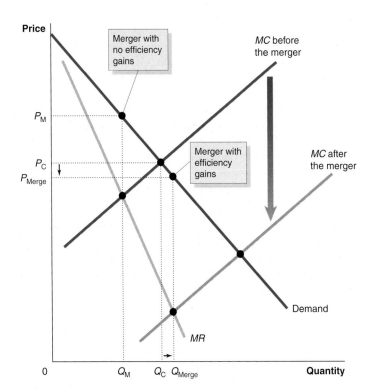

Figure 14-6

A Merger That Makes Consumers Better Off

This figure shows the result of all the firms in a perfectly competitive industry merging to form a monopoly. If costs are unaffected by the merger, the result is the same as in Figure 14-5 on page 487: Price rises from P_C to P_M, quantity falls from Q_C to Q_M, consumer surplus declines, and a loss of economic efficiency results. If, however, the monopoly has lower costs than the perfectly competitive firms, as shown by the marginal cost curve shifting to MC after the merger, it is possible that the price will actually decline from P_C to P_{Merge} and output will increase from Q_C to Q_{Merge} following the merger.

As you might expect, whenever large firms propose a merger, they claim that the newly merged firm will be more efficient and have lower costs. They realize that without these claims, it is unlikely their merger will be approved. It is up to the Department of Justice and the FTC, along with the court system, to evaluate the merits of these claims.

The Department of Justice and Federal Trade Commission Merger Guidelines

For many years after the passage of the Sherman Antitrust Act in 1890, lawyers from the Department of Justice enforced the antitrust laws. They rarely considered economic arguments, such as the possibility that consumers might be made better off by a merger if economic efficiency were significantly improved. This began to change in 1965, when Donald Turner became the first Ph.D. economist to head the Antitrust Division of the Department of Justice. Under Turner and his successors, economic analysis shaped antitrust policy. In 1973, the Economics Section of the Antitrust Division was established and staffed with economists who evaluate the economic consequences of proposed mergers.

Economists played a major role in the development of merger guidelines by the Department of Justice and the FTC in 1982. The guidelines made it easier for firms considering a merger to understand whether the government was likely to allow the merger or to oppose it. The guidelines have three main parts:

1 Market definition

2 Measure of concentration

3 Merger standards

Market Definition A market consists of all firms making products that consumers view as close substitutes. We can identify close substitutes by looking at the effect of a price increase. If our definition of a market is too narrow, a price increase will cause firms to experience a significant decline in sales—and profits—as consumers switch to buying close substitutes.

Identifying the relevant market involved in a proposed merger begins with a narrow definition of the industry. For the hypothetical merger of Hershey Foods and Mars, Inc., discussed previously in this chapter, we might start with the candy industry. If all firms in the candy industry increased price by 5 percent, would their profits increase or decrease? If profits would increase, the market is defined as being just these firms. If profits would decrease, we would try a broader definition—say, by adding in potato chips and other snacks. Would a price increase of 5 percent by all firms in the broader market raise profits? If profits increase, the relevant market has been identified. If profits decrease, we consider a broader definition. We continue this procedure until a market has been identified.

Measure of Concentration A market is *concentrated* if a relatively small number of firms have a large share of total sales in the market. A merger between firms in a market that is already highly concentrated is very likely to increase market power. A merger between firms in an industry that has a very low concentration is unlikely to increase market power and can be ignored. The guidelines use the *Herfindahl-Hirschman Index (HHI)* of concentration, which squares the market shares of each firm in the industry and adds up the values of the squares. The following are some examples of calculating a Herfindahl-Hirschman Index:

- 1 firm, with 100% market share (a monopoly):

$$HHI = 100^2 = 10,000$$

- 2 firms, each with a 50% market share:

$$HHI = 50^2 + 50^2 = 5,000$$

- 4 firms, with market shares of 30%, 30%, 20%, and 20%:

$$HHI = 30^2 + 30^2 + 20^2 + 20^2 = 2,600$$

- 10 firms, each with market shares of 10%:

$$HHI = 10\,(10^2) = 1,000$$

Merger Standards The Department of Justice and the FTC use the HHI calculation for a market to evaluate proposed horizontal mergers according to these standards:

- *Post-merger HHI below 1,000.* These markets are not concentrated, so mergers in them are not challenged.

- *Post-merger HHI between 1,000 and 1,800.* These markets are moderately concentrated. Mergers that raise the HHI by less than 100 probably will not be challenged. Mergers that raise the HHI by more than 100 may be challenged.

- *Post-merger HHI above 1,800.* These markets are highly concentrated. Mergers that increase the HHI by less than 50 points will not be challenged. Mergers that increase the HHI by 50 to 100 points may be challenged. Mergers that increase the HHI by more than 100 points will be challenged.

Increases in economic efficiency will be taken into account and can lead to approval of a merger that otherwise would be opposed, but the burden of showing that the efficiencies exist lies with the merging firms:

> The merging firms must substantiate efficiency claims so that the [Department of Justice and the FTC] can verify by reasonable means the likelihood and magnitude of each asserted efficiency. . . . Efficiency claims will not be considered if they are vague or speculative or otherwise cannot be verified by reasonable means.

Making the Connection

Should the Government Prevent Banks from Becoming Too Big?

For many years, state and federal regulations kept banks small. Until the 1990s, federal regulations required a bank to operate in only a single state. This restriction on interstate banking meant that there were no nationwide banks. As recently as the 1980s, some states—including Illinois and Texas—did not allow banks to have branches. So, if a bank opened in Chicago, it could not have branches in other cities in Illinois. Today, these regulations have been repealed, and banks are free to have as many branches as they choose and can operate nationwide. Many economists believe that the old regulations on banks reduced economic efficiency. If there are significant economies of scale in banking, then keeping banks artificially small by not allowing them to operate in more than one state will drive up their average cost of providing banking services. As a result, consumers will have to pay higher interest rates on loans and will receive lower interest rates on deposits.

The elimination of government regulations on nationwide banking and on branch banking led to a sharp decline in the number of banks. In the early 1980s, there were 14,500 banks in the United States; today there are fewer than 7,500. Smaller, less efficient banks were acquired by larger banks or went out of business, and some large banks merged with other large banks. There is, however, still one limit on the size of banks. In 1994, when Congress removed restrictions on interstate banking, it wrote into the law a restriction that no bank mergers would be allowed if they resulted in one bank having more than 10 percent of all bank deposits. This provision was included because some smaller, community-based banks were afraid that they would be unable to compete against large, nationwide banks.

The Top-Five U.S. Banks by Domestic Deposits, Through Sept. 30 of Each Year

2006	Dometic deposits, in billions	Percentage of all U.S. deposits	1994	Dometic deposits, in billions	Percentage of all U.S. deposits
Bank of America	$584.33	9.0%	Bank of America	$125.59	4.0%
J.P. Morgan Chase	447.30	6.9	NationsBank	87.44	2.8
Wachovia/Golden West Financial*	375.61	5.8	Chemical Banking	66.86	2.1
Wells Fargo	295.14	4.6	Banc One	64.74	2.1
Citigroup	226.26	3.5	First Union	52.54	1.7

Note: Deposit share information is based on FDIC quarterly reports. The Federal Reserve, which approves acquisitions, uses a slightly different definition of deposits.
* Figures are combined to reflect merger that took place October 1, 2006.
Source: FDIC call reports

As the chart shows, at the time the government removed restrictions on interstate banking, no bank was near the 10 percent limit. But by the end of 2006, Bank of America had 9 percent of all U.S. deposits and was considering mergers that would have brought its share above 10 percent. Bank of America Chairman and Chief Executive Kenneth D. Lewis began to push for Congress to remove the 10 percent limit. He argued that because other countries did not have limits on the size of banks, foreign banks were able to take advantage of economies of scale beyond what was possible for U.S. banks. In a position paper, Bank of America argued, "In time, the mega-foreign banks will be positioned to acquire the largest U.S. banks." Many community banks, though, remained opposed to lifting the 10 percent limit. Some consumer groups also argued that very large banks would have enough market power to raise interest rates on loans and lower interest rates on deposits because they would have less competition. Members of Congress considering the possibility of changing the law had to face the usual question raised by antitrust policy: Will a potential increase in monopoly power made possible by lifting the 10-percent limit be offset by gains in economic efficiency?

Source: Valerie Bauerlein and Damian Paletta, "Bank of America Quietly Targets Barrier to Growth," *Wall Street Journal*, January 16, 2007, p. A1.

YOUR TURN: Test your understanding by doing related problem 5.16 on page 504 at the end of this chapter.

Regulating Natural Monopolies

If a firm is a natural monopoly, competition from other firms will not play its usual role of forcing price down to the level where the company earns zero economic profit. As a result, local or state *regulatory commissions* usually set the prices for natural monopolies, such as firms selling natural gas or electricity. What price should these commissions set? Recall from Chapter 11 that economic efficiency requires the last unit of a good or service produced to provide an additional benefit to consumers equal to the additional cost of producing it. We can measure the additional benefit consumers receive from the last unit by the price and the additional cost to the monopoly of producing the last unit by marginal cost. Therefore, to achieve economic efficiency, regulators should require that the monopoly charge a price equal to its marginal cost. There is, however, an important drawback to doing so, which is illustrated in Figure 14-7. This figure shows the situation of a typical regulated natural monopoly.

Remember that with a natural monopoly, the average total cost curve is still falling when it crosses the demand curve. If unregulated, the monopoly will charge a price equal to P_M and produce Q_M. To achieve economic efficiency, regulators should require the monopoly to charge a price equal to P_E. The monopoly will then produce Q_E. But here is the drawback: P_E is less than average total cost, so the monopoly will be suffering a loss, shown by the area of the red-shaded rectangle. In the long run, the owners of the monopoly will not continue in business if they are experiencing losses. Realizing this, most regulators will set the regulated price, P_R, equal to the level of average total cost at which the demand curve intersects the *ATC* curve. At that price, the owners of the monopoly are able to break even on their investment by producing the quantity Q_R.

Figure 14-7

Regulating a Natural Monopoly

A natural monopoly that is not subject to government regulation will charge a price equal to P_M and produce Q_M. If government regulators want to achieve economic efficiency, they will set the regulated price equal to P_E, and the monopoly will produce Q_E. Unfortunately, P_E is below average cost, and the monopoly will suffer a loss, shown by the shaded rectangle. Because the monopoly will not continue to produce in the long run if it suffers a loss, government regulators set a price equal to average cost, which is P_R in the figure.

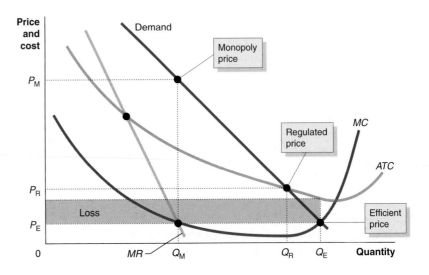

Economics in YOUR Life

>> Continued from page 473

At the beginning of the chapter, we asked why many cable systems won't carry the NFL Network. You might think that the cable systems would want to televise one of the most popular sports in the nation. In most cities, a customer of a cable system can't switch to a competing cable system, so many areas cable systems can be the sole source of many programs. (Although some consumers have the option of switching to satellite television.) As a result, a cable system can increase its profits by, for example, not offering popular programming such as the NFL Network as part of its normal programming package, requiring instead that consumers upgrade to digital programming at a higher price.

Conclusion

The more intense the level of competition among firms, the better a market works. In this chapter, we have seen that with monopoly—where competition is entirely absent—price is higher, output is lower, and consumer surplus and economic efficiency decline compared with perfect competition. Fortunately, true monopolies are rare. Even though most firms resemble monopolies in being able to charge a price above marginal cost, most markets have enough competition to keep the efficiency losses from market power quite low.

We've seen that barriers to entry are an important source of market power. Read *An Inside Look at Policy* on the next page for a discussion of how legislation in California is lowering barriers to entry into the cable TV market.

As Barriers Fall, Will Cable TV Competition Rise?

WALL STREET JOURNAL, SEPTEMBER 28, 2006

Cable Guys

In an era of partisan nastiness and gridlock, the California legislature did something on Aug. 31 that was shockingly harmonious, reasonable and beneficial to consumers. Both parties voted overwhelmingly to allow competition into a sector—cable television—where prices have been elevated and service depressed by the most pernicious monopoly in America.

When Gov. Arnold Schwarzenegger signs the bill, as expected, companies that want a statewide video franchise can go straight to the Public Utility Commission and get approval to operate within 44 days. In the past, in California, as in other states, cable companies had to make separate deals with America's 33,760 municipal units—a process that can take years....

The effect was to create cable monopolies that often infuriated captive customers. According to a 2004 study by the Government Accountability Office, "cable subscribers in about 2% of all markets have the opportunity to choose between two or more wire-based operators." As cable rates rose in the 1980s, the federal government tried to fix the market with more regulation. That attempt, of course, failed. For the five years ending January 2004, the Federal Communications Commission reports that average cable rates increased 7.8% annually, compared with a 2.1% increase in the Consumer Price Index.

Very quietly, things are changing. Seven states, comprising about one-third of the U.S. population, have now passed video franchise laws, which will not only lower monthly subscriber costs but also create new technology jobs—10,000 in California alone, according to one estimate—as Verizon and AT&T, along with cable overbuilders like RCN, jump in with both feet. To bring high-quality video to the home over a technology called Internet protocol, the telcos will make major investments to drive the fiber—which carries the data—much more deeply into their networks. Broadband service will improve; state and local governments will still get their franchise fees. All that will end is a monopoly that drives consumers nuts....

With a national election coming up, you would expect Congress to get on the bandwagon and embrace a version of the state bills, killing the monopoly and taking the credit. Instead, federal legislation is slowed down by measures promoting "net neutrality"—the concept that telecom companies should be barred from asking content providers, like Amazon, to pay extra for higher-speed service the telcos develop—the way that an airline asks more for a first-class seat....

How much will consumers save? A 2004 study by the GAO looked at six markets with cable competition and found that rates were 15% to 41% below similar markets with no competition. Annual savings for U.S. households through competition will total $8 billion, says the Phoenix Center for Advanced Legal and Economic Public Policy.

In Texas, where a statewide franchising law went into effect last year, a study by the American Consumer Institute surveyed consumers and found that 22% switched cable providers and saved an average of $22.30 per month. Subscribers who stayed with incumbent providers saved $26.83 per month because of the downward pressure on prices. Verizon rolled out a service in Keller, Plano and Lewisville, charging $43.95 a month for 180 video and music channels. "Shortly thereafter," writes the Heartland Institute's Steven Titch, Charter, the erstwhile monopoly cable provider, "began offering a bundle of 240 channels and fast Internet service for $50 a month, compared to $68.99 Charter had been charging for the TV package alone." Savings in Texas this year alone will total $599 million, according to the Phoenix Center. Yale Braunstein, an economist at the University of California at Berkeley, estimates that Californians will save between $692 million and $1 billion a year.

Yes, Americans can choose satellite TV, but, for reasons of convenience and service, many find it an inadequate substitute. There's a reason that cable families far outnumber satellite families. "Overall customer satisfaction among satellite subscribers has declined," says Steve Kirkeby, senior director of telecommunication research for J.D. Power and Associates....

Key Points in the Article

This article discusses a change in regulatory policy toward cable television in California. The change should make it easier for new cable firms to enter the market. As a result, prices for cable TV should fall, and we should see more firms offering cable TV in California cities. This article indicates that an increase in quantity and a decrease in price occurs as policy makes entry into the cable TV market easier.

Analyzing the News

a In California, the state government's requirement that a cable provider buy a franchise in each jurisdiction was a barrier to entry because of the high cost of franchises. By allowing firms a statewide license, California has made it easier for them to enter the cable TV market in a given jurisdiction, making competition more likely. In fact, the relative lack of competition in many local cable television markets was partly the result of technology—laying more than one set of cables to an individual home would be very expensive—and partly the result of government regulations, which often allowed only one firm to be in the market.

b Entry, of course, will reduce the economic profit existing firms earn. The figure illustrates what happens as entry occurs and the market becomes competitive. For simplicity, we assume that the marginal cost of providing cable services is constant, so the marginal cost curve is a horizontal line. Notice that output increases from Q_M to Q_C, and price falls from P_M to P_C. You can also see that consumer surplus increases from areas $A + E$ to areas $A + E + B + C + D$, and the deadweight loss in the market (area D) disappears and becomes consumer surplus. In this figure, what were profits to the monopoly (areas $B + C$) are redistributed to consumers as consumer surplus. Economic profits fall to zero.

c One of the benefits of competition is that firms compete not just by cutting prices, but also by improving the services they offer. Here, we see cable systems competing by providing more services and channels to their customers.

Thinking Critically
About Policy

1. What is the most a firm would be willing to spend to remain the sole provider of cable television in a market?
2. Even with a statewide franchise, what might prevent new cable TV firms from entering local markets?

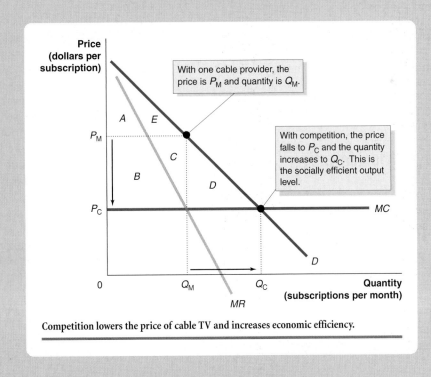

With one cable provider, the price is P_M and quantity is Q_M.

With competition, the price falls to P_C and the quantity increases to Q_C. This is the socially efficient output level.

Competition lowers the price of cable TV and increases economic efficiency.

Key Terms

14.1 LEARNING OBJECTIVE   14.1 | Define monopoly, **pages 474–475.**

Is Any Firm Ever Really a Monopoly?

Summary

A **monopoly** exists only in the rare situation in which a firm is producing a good or service for which there are no close substitutes. A narrow definition of monopoly that some economists use is that a firm has a monopoly if it can ignore the actions of all other firms. Many economists favor a broader definition of monopoly. Under the broader definition, a firm has a monopoly if no other firms are selling a substitute close enough that the firm's economic profits are competed away in the long run.

myeconlab Visit www.myeconlab.com to complete these exercises
Get Ahead of the Curve online and get instant feedback.

Review Questions

1.1 What is a monopoly? Can a firm be a monopoly if close substitutes for its product exist?

1.2 If you own the only hardware store in a small town, do you have a monopoly?

Problems and Applications

1.3 Is "monopoly" a good name for the game *Monopoly*? What aspects of the game involve monopoly? Explain briefly, using the definition of monopoly.

1.4 (Related to the *Chapter Opener* on page 472) Some observers say that changes in the past few years have eroded the monopoly power of local cable TV companies, even though no other cable firms have entered their markets. What are these changes? Do these "monopoly" firms still have monopoly power?

1.5 Are there any products for which there are no substitutes? Are these the only products for which it would be possible to have a monopoly? Briefly explain.

1.6 An economist argues, "No firm can remain a monopoly for long in the face of technological change." Do you agree?

1.7 (Related to the *Making the Connection* on page 474) Microsoft thought that the initial Xbox was sufficiently different from PS2 that it could charge a significantly higher price for the Xbox than Sony could charge for PS2. As it turns out, Microsoft was wrong. Draw the average total cost and marginal cost curves for Microsoft's Xbox. Now draw the demand curve Microsoft thought would exist for Xbox and the demand curve that actually existed. Why were the two demand curves different? Show on your graph the profits Microsoft would earn with each demand curve.

>> End Learning Objective 14.1

14.2 LEARNING OBJECTIVE   14.2 | Explain the four main reasons monopolies arise, **pages 475–481.**

Where Do Monopolies Come From?

Summary

To have a monopoly, barriers to entering the market must be so high that no other firms can enter. Barriers to entry may be high enough to keep out competing firms for four main reasons: (1) government blocks the entry of more than one firm into a market by issuing a **patent**, which is the exclusive right to a product for 20 years, or a **copyright**, which is the

exclusive right to produce and sell a creation, or giving a firm a **public franchise**, which is the right to be the only legal provider of a good or service (2) one firm has control of a key raw material necessary to produce a good, (3) there are important *network externalities* in supplying the good or service, or (4) economies of scale are so large that one firm has a *natural monopoly*. **Network externalities** refer to the situation where the usefulness of a product increases with the number of consumers who use it. A **natural monopoly** is a situation in which economies of scale are so large that one firm can supply the entire market at a lower average cost than two or more firms.

myeconlab Visit www.myeconlab.com to complete these exercises
Get Ahead of the Curve online and get instant feedback.

Review Questions

2.1 What are the four most important ways a firm becomes a monopoly?

2.2 If patents reduce competition, why does the federal government grant them?

2.3 What is a public franchise? Are all public franchises natural monopolies?

2.4 What is "natural" about a natural monopoly?

Problems and Applications

2.5 The U.S. Postal Service (USPS) is a monopoly because the federal government has blocked entry into the market for delivering first-class mail. Is it also a natural monopoly? How can we tell? What would happen if the law preventing competition in this market were removed?

2.6 Patents are granted for 20 years, but pharmaceutical companies can't use their patent-guaranteed monopoly powers for anywhere near this long because it takes several years to acquire FDA approval of drugs. Should the life of drug patents be extended to 20 years *after* FDA approval? What would be the costs and benefits of this extension?

2.7 Just as a new product or a new method of making a product receives patent protection from the government, books, articles, and essays receive copyright protection. Under U.S. law, authors have the exclusive right to their writings during their lifetimes—unless they sell this right, as most authors do to their

publishers—and their heirs retain this exclusive right for 50 years after their death. The historian Thomas Macaulay once described the copyright law as "a tax on readers to give a bounty to authors." In what sense does the existence of the copyright law impose a tax on readers? What "bounty" do copyright laws give authors? Discuss whether the government would be doing readers a favor by abolishing the copyright law.

Source of quote: Thomas Mallon, *Stolen Words: The Classic Book on Plagiarism*, San Diego: Harcourt, 2001 (original ed. 1989), p. 59.

2.8 The German company Koenig & Bauer has 90 percent of the world market for presses that print currency. Discuss the factors that would make it difficult for new companies to enter this market.

2.9 (Related to the *Making the Connection* on page 476) Would the Ecke's have been better off if they had patented their process for growing poinsettias? Briefly explain.

2.10 (Related to the *Making the Connection* on page 477) Why was De Beers worried that people might resell their old diamonds? How did De Beers attempt to convince consumers that used diamonds were not good substitutes for new diamonds? How did De Beers' strategy affect the demand curve for new diamonds? How were De Beers' profits affected?

2.11 (Related to *Solved Problem 14-2* on page 480) Suppose that the quantity demanded per day for a product is 90 when the price is $35. The following table shows costs for a firm with a monopoly in this market:

QUANTITY (PER DAY)	TOTAL COST
30	$1,200
40	1,400
50	2,250
60	3,000

Briefly explain whether this firm has a natural monopoly in this market.

>> **End Learning Objective 14.2**

14.3 LEARNING OBJECTIVE 14.3 | Explain how a monopoly chooses price and output, **pages 481–485.**

How Does a Monopoly Choose Price and Output?

Summary

Monopolists face downward-sloping demand and marginal revenue curves and, like all other firms, maximize profit by producing where marginal revenue equals marginal cost.

Unlike a perfect competitor, a monopolist that earns economic profits does not face the entry of new firms into the market. Therefore, a monopolist can earn economic profits, even in the long run.

Review Questions

3.1 What is the relationship between a monopolist's demand curve and the market demand curve? What is the relationship between a monopolist's demand curve and its marginal revenue curve?

3.2 Draw a graph that shows a monopolist that is earning a profit. Be sure your graph includes the monopolist's demand, marginal revenue, average total cost, and marginal cost curves. Be sure to indicate the profit-maximizing level of output and price.

Problems and Applications

3.3 (Related to *Solved Problem 14-3* on page 484) Ed Scahill has acquired a monopoly on the production of baseballs (don't ask how), and faces the demand and cost situation given in the following table:

PRICE	QUANTITY (PER WEEK)	TOTAL REVENUE	MARGINAL REVENUE	TOTAL COST	MARGINAL COST
$20	15,000			$330,000	
19	20,000			365,000	
18	25,000			405,000	
17	30,000			450,000	
16	35,000			500,000	
15	40,000			555,000	

    a. Fill in the remaining values in the table.

    b. If Ed wants to maximize profits, what price should he charge and how many baseballs should he sell? How much profit will he make?

    c. Suppose the government imposes a tax of $50,000 per week on baseball production. Now what price should Ed charge, how many baseballs should he sell, and what will his profits be?

3.4 (Related to *Solved Problem 14-3* on page 484) Use the information in Solved Problem 14-3 to answer the following questions.

    a. What will Comcast do if the tax is $6.00 per month instead of $2.50? (*Hint:* Will its decision be different in the long run than in the short run?)

    b. Suppose that the flat per-month tax is replaced with a tax on the firm of $0.50 per cable subscriber. Now how many subscriptions should Comcast sell if it wants to maximize profit? What

price does it charge? What are its profits? (Assume that Comcast will sell only the quantities listed in the table.)

3.5 Before inexpensive pocket calculators were developed, many science and engineering students used slide rules to make numeric calculations. Slide rules are no longer produced, which means nothing prevents you from establishing a monopoly in the slide rule market. Draw a graph showing the situation your slide rule firm would be in. Be sure to include on your graph your demand, marginal revenue, average total cost, and marginal cost curves. Indicate the price you would charge and the quantity you would produce. Are you likely to make a profit or a loss? Show this area on your graph.

3.6 Does a monopolist have a supply curve? Briefly explain. (*Hint:* Look again at the definition of a supply curve in Chapter 3 and consider whether this applies to a monopolist.)

3.7 (Related to the *Don't Let This Happen to You!* on page 485) A student argues, "If a monopolist finds a way of producing a good at lower cost, he will not lower his price. Because he is a monopolist, he will keep the price and the quantity the same and just increase his profit." Do you agree? Use a graph to illustrate your answer.

3.8 (Related to the *Don't Let This Happen to You!* on page 485) Discuss whether you agree or disagree with the following statement: "A monopolist maximizes profit by charging the highest price at which it can sell any of the good at all."

3.9 When home builders construct a new housing development, they usually sell the rights to lay cable to a single cable television company. As a result, anyone buying a home in that development is not able to choose between competing cable companies. Some cities have begun to ban such exclusive agreements. Williams Township, Pennsylvania, decided to allow any cable company to lay cable in the utility trenches of new housing developments. The head of the township board of supervisors argued, "What I would like to see and do is give the consumers a choice. If there's no choice, then the price [of cable] is at the whim of the provider." In a situation in which the consumers in a housing development have only one cable company available, is the price really at the whim of the company? Would a company in this situation be likely to charge, say, $500 per month for basic cable services? Briefly explain why or why not.

Source: Sam Kennedy, "Williams Township May Ban Exclusive Cable Provider Pacts," (*Allentown, Pennsylvania*) *Morning Call*, November 5, 2004, p. D1.

3.10 Will a monopoly that maximizes profit also be maximizing revenue? Will it be maximizing production? Briefly explain.

>> End Learning Objective 14.3

Does Monopoly Reduce Economic Efficiency?

Summary

Compared with a perfectly competitive industry, a monopoly charges a higher price and produces less, which reduces consumer surplus and economic efficiency. Some loss of economic efficiency will occur whenever firms have **market power** and can charge a price greater than marginal cost. The total loss of economic efficiency in the U.S. economy due to market power is small, however, because true monopolies are very rare. In most industries, competition will keep price much closer to marginal cost than would be the case in a monopoly.

myeconlab Visit www.myeconlab.com to complete these exercises
Get Ahead of the Curve online and get instant feedback.

Review Questions

4.1 Suppose that a perfectly competitive industry becomes a monopoly. Describe the effects of this change on consumer surplus, producer surplus, and deadweight loss.

4.2 Explain why market power leads to a deadweight loss. Is the total deadweight loss from market power for the economy large or small?

Problems and Applications

4.3 Review Figure 14-5 on page 487 on the inefficiency of monopoly. Will the deadweight loss due to monopoly be larger if the demand is elastic or if it is inelastic? Briefly explain.

4.4 Economist Harvey Leibenstein argued that the loss of economic efficiency in industries that are not perfectly competitive has been understated. He argues that when competition is weak, firms are under less pressure to adopt the best techniques or to hold down their costs. He refers to this effect as "x-inefficiency." If x-inefficiency causes a firm's marginal costs to rise, show that the deadweight loss in Figure 14-5 understates the true deadweight loss caused by a monopoly.

4.5 In most cities, the city owns the water system that provides water to homes and businesses. Some cities charge a flat monthly fee, while other cities charge by the gallon. Which method of pricing is more likely to result in economic efficiency in the water market? Be sure to refer to the definition of economic efficiency in your answer. Why do you think the same method of pricing isn't used by all cities?

4.6 Review the concept of externalities on page 138 in Chapter 5. If a market is a monopoly, will a negative externality in production always lead to production beyond the level of economic efficiency? Use a graph to illustrate your answer.

>> End Learning Objective 14.4

Government Policy toward Monopoly

Summary

Because monopolies reduce consumer surplus and economic efficiency, most governments regulate monopolies. Firms that are not monopolies have an incentive to avoid competition by **colluding**, or agreeing to charge the same price, or otherwise not to compete. In the United States, **antitrust laws** are aimed at deterring monopoly, eliminating collusion, and promoting competition among firms. The Antitrust Division of the U.S. Department of Justice and the Federal Trade Commission share responsibility for enforcing the antitrust laws including regulating mergers between firms. A **horizontal merger** is a merger between firms in the same industry. A **vertical merger** is a merger between firms at different stages of production of a good. Local governments regulate the prices charged by natural monopolies.

myeconlab Visit www.myeconlab.com to complete these exercises
Get Ahead of the Curve online and get instant feedback.

Review Questions

5.1 What is the purpose of the antitrust laws? Who is in charge of enforcing them?

5.2 What is the difference between a horizontal merger and a vertical merger? Which type of merger is more likely to increase the market power of a newly merged firm?

5.3 Why would it be economically efficient to require a natural monopoly to charge a price equal to marginal cost? Why do most regulatory agencies require natural monopolies to charge a price equal to average cost instead?

Problems and Applications

5.4 Use the following graph for a monopoly to answer the questions.

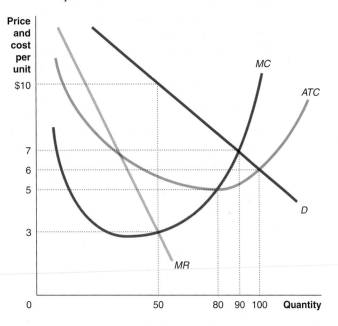

a. What quantity will the monopoly produce, and what price will the monopoly charge?

b. Suppose the monopoly is regulated. If the regulatory agency wants to achieve economic efficiency, what price should it require the monopoly to charge? How much output will the monopoly produce at this price? Will the monopoly make a profit if it charges this price? Briefly explain.

5.5 Use the following graph for a monopoly to answer the questions.

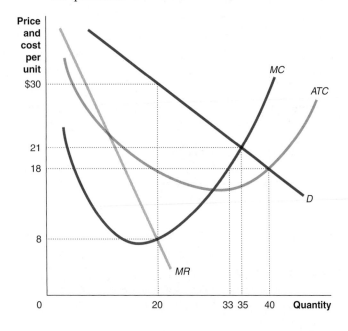

a. What quantity will the monopoly produce, and what price will the monopoly charge?

b. Suppose the government decides to regulate this monopoly and imposes a price ceiling of $18 (in other words, the monopoly can charge less than $18 but can't charge more). Now what quantity will the monopoly produce, and what price will the monopoly charge? Will every consumer who is willing to pay this price be able to buy the product? Briefly explain.

5.6 The following is from an article in the *New York Times*: "United Airlines and US Airways announced today that they had called off their proposed merger after the Justice Department threatened to file a lawsuit to block the $4.2 billion deal, calling it anticompetitive." Why would the Justice Department care if two airlines merge? What is "anticompetitive" about two airlines merging?

Source: Kenneth N. Gilpin and Jack Lynch, "United and US Airways Call Off Merger after U.S. Opposes It," *New York Times*, July 27, 2001.

5.7 A marketing textbook observes, "Pricing actions that violate laws can land executives in jail." Why would executives be thrown in jail because of the prices they charge? Which laws are they likely to have violated?

Source: David W. Cravens, *Strategic Marketing*, 5th ed., Boston: Irwin McGraw-Hill, 1997, p. 343.

5.8 Draw a graph like Figure 14-6 on page 491. On your graph, show producer surplus and consumer surplus before a merger and consumer surplus and producer surplus after a merger.

5.9 The following phone call took place in February 1982 between Robert Crandall, the chief executive officer of American Airlines, and Howard Putnam, the chief executive officer of Braniff Airways. Although Crandall didn't know it, Putnam was recording the call:

> *Crandall:* I think it's dumb . . . to sit here and pound the (obscenity) out of each other and neither one of us making a (obscenity) dime . . .
>
> *Putnam:* Do you have a suggestion for me?
>
> *Crandall:* Yes, I have a suggestion for you. Raise your . . . fares 20 percent. I'll raise mine the next morning.
>
> *Putnam:* Robert, we . . .
>
> *Crandall:* You'll make more money and I will, too.
>
> *Putnam:* We can't talk about pricing.
>
> *Crandall:* Oh (obscenity), Howard. We can talk about any . . . thing we want to talk about.

Who had a better understanding of antitrust law, Crandall or Putnam? Briefly explain.

Source: Mark Potts, "American Airlines Charged with Seeking a Monopoly," *Washington Post*, February 24, 1983; "Blunt Talk on the Phone," *New York Times*, February 24, 1983; and Thomas Petzinger Jr., *Hard Landing: The Epic Contest for Power and Profits that Plunged the Airline Industry into Chaos*, New York: Random House, 1995, pp. 149–150.

5.10 Look again at the section "The Department of Justice and Federal Trade Commission Merger Guidelines," which begins on page 491. Evaluate the following situations.

a. A market initially has 20 firms, each with a 5 percent market share. Of the firms, 4 propose to merge, leaving a total of 17 firms in the industry. Are the Department of Justice and the Federal Trade Commission likely to oppose the merger? Briefly explain.

b. A market initially has 5 firms, each with a 20 percent market share. Of the firms, 2 propose to merge, leaving a total of 4 firms in the industry. Are the Department of Justice and the Federal Trade Commission likely to oppose the merger? Briefly explain.

5.11 In 2007, Sirius Satellite Radio and XM Satellite Radio, the only two satellite radio firms, announced that they would attempt to merge. Maurice McKenzie, an analyst for Signal Hill investment bank, was quoted in the *Wall Street Journal* as arguing, "We believe that governmental approval could hinge on the market definition surrounding radio competition, which we expect to be narrowly defined to include terrestrial and satellite radio operators. . . . " What is a "terrestrial" radio operator? Why would government approval depend on how it defines the relevant market? What other firms—apart from terrestrial radio operators—might the government consider competitors to a newly merged Sirius-XM firm?

Source: "Analysts Like Sirius-XM Merger, but Note Regulatory Difficulties," *Wall Street Journal*, February 20, 2007.

5.12 In a column in the *Wall Street Journal*, David Henderson, an economist at the Hoover Institution, argued that it was possible to judge whether the proposed merger between Sirius and XM would make consumers better or worse off by looking at how owners of "free," or broadcast, radio stations reacted:

> Look at what the "free" broadcasters are saying about the XM-Sirius merger. As this newspaper recently reported, "The radio industry has loudly opposed the deal since it was announced, and broadcasters cite satellite-radio operators as major competitors in securities filings." Traditional radio broadcasters understand that they are competing with satellite radio. And they oppose the merger.

Why would "free" radio broadcasters oppose the merger? If the newly merged Sirius-XM charged higher prices, wouldn't that be good news to "free" radio broadcasters? Does the reaction of the "free" radio broadcasters indicate that consumers would be made better or worse off by the Sirius-XM merger?

Source: David R. Henderson, "Sirius Business," *Wall Street Journal*, February 28, 2007.

5.13 Industrial gases are used in the electronics industry. For example, nitrogen trifluoride is used for cleaning semiconductor wafers. The following table shows the market shares for the companies in this industry.

COMPANY	MARKET SHARE
Air Products	29%
Air Liquide	22
BOC Gases	21
Nippon Sanso	17
Praxzir	8
Other	3

In 2000, Air Products discussed a merger with BOC Gases. Use the information in the section "The Department of Justice and Federal Trade Commission Merger Guidelines" that begins on page 491 to predict whether the Department of Justice and the Federal Trade Commission opposed this merger. Assume that "Other" in the table consists of three firms, each of which has a 1 percent share of the market.

Source for market share data: Dan Shope, "Air Products Turns a Corner," (*Allentown, Pennsylvania*) *Morning Call*, July 29, 2001.

5.14 The following table gives the market shares of the companies in the U.S. carbonated soft drink industry.

COMPANY	MARKET SHARE
Coca-Cola	37%
PepsiCo	35
Cadbury Schweppes	17
Other	11

Use the information in the section "The Department of Justice and Federal Trade Commission Merger Guidelines," which begins on page 491 to predict whether the Department of Justice and the Federal Trade Commission would be likely to approve a merger between any two of the first three companies listed. Does your answer depend on how many companies are included in the "Other" category? Briefly explain.

Source: Pepsico, *Annual Report, 2003.*

5.15 According to a column in the *New York Times* by Austan Goolsbee of the University of Chicago, the French National Assembly approved a bill:

> . . . that would require Apple Computer to crack open the software codes of its iTunes music store and let the files work on players other than the iPod. . . . If the French gave away the codes, Apple would lose much of its rationale for improving iTunes.

a. Why would Apple no longer want to improve iTunes if its software codes were no longer secret?

b. Why would the French government believe it was a good idea to require Apple to make the codes public?

Source: Austan Goolsbee, "In iTunes War, France Has Met the Enemy. Perhaps It Is France," *New York Times*, April 27, 2006.

5.16 **(Related to the *Making the Connection* on page 493)** Bank of America has attempted to convince Congress to eliminate the rule that banks may not merge if the newly merged bank would have more than a 10 percent share of U.S. deposits. In 2007, Bank of America was expanding its banking activities by, among other things, offering checking accounts and credit cards to illegal immigrants and other people who lacked Social Security numbers. An article in the *Wall Street Journal* observed:

> Unorthodox initiatives like the new credit-card program may be crucial to Bank of America's long-term success. In the past the bank, which operates in 31 states and the District of Columbia, grew mostly by buying up other banks. Now, however, it is bumping up against a regulatory cap that bars any U.S. bank from an acquisition that would give it more than 10% of the nation's total bank deposits. That means Bank of America's only way to grow domestically is to sell more products to existing customers and to attract new ones.

Should the government take this information into account in evaluating the policy of limiting mergers among large banks? The *Wall Street Journal* article also notes, "Illegal immigrants have typically relied on loan sharks and neighborhood finance shops [which charge very high interest rates] for credit." Should the government consider this additional piece of information when formulating policy on bank mergers?

Source: Miriam Jordan and Valerie Bauerlein, "Bank of America Casts Wider Net for Hispanics," *Wall Street Journal*, February 13, 2007, p. A1.

>> End Learning Objective 14.5

Chapter 15

Pricing Strategy

Getting into Walt Disney World: One Price Does Not Fit All

When you visit Walt Disney World in Florida, your age, home address, and occupation can determine how much you pay for admission. In the summer of 2008, the price for a one-day ticket for an adult was $75.62. The same ticket for a child, aged three to nine, was $63.90. Children under three were free. Florida residents paid $68.05. Florida residents who were also members of Auto Club South paid $63.90. Active members of the military paid $71. Why does Disney charge so many different prices for the same product?

In previous chapters, we assumed that firms charge all consumers the same price for a given product. In reality, many firms charge customers different prices, based on differences in their willingness to pay for the product. Firms often face complicated pricing problems. For example, the Walt Disney Company faces the problem of determining the profit-maximizing prices to charge different groups of consumers for admission to its Disneyland and Walt Disney World theme parks.

The Walt Disney Company was founded in 1923 by Walt Disney and his brother Roy O. Disney. Several times, the Disney brothers risked financial ruin by investing most of the company's funds in innovative entertainment ideas. In 1927, they released *Steamboat Willie* starring Mickey Mouse, the first cartoon to feature synchronized sound. The profits from *Steamboat Willie* and other short cartoons helped finance production of *Snow White and the Seven Dwarfs*. Released in 1937, this was the first full-length Technicolor cartoon.

In the early 1950s, Walt Disney began to believe there was a market for theme parks. At that time, amusement parks—like Coney Island in New York—were usually collections of unrelated rides, such as roller coasters and Ferris wheels. The parks often had rowdy reputations and appealed more to teenagers and young adults than to families with children. Disney believed that a theme park, with attractions that emphasized storytelling over thrills, would be more attractive to families than were amusement parks. Disney had trouble raising the funds necessary to build his new park, however, because it was so strikingly different from existing parks. Disney hired an economist to evaluate the feasibility of the park. Managers of existing parks gave this advice to the economist: "Tell your boss to save his money. Tell him to stick to what he knows and leave the amusement business to people who know it." Eventually, Disney convinced the ABC television network to provide funding in exchange for his providing them with a weekly television program.

When Disneyland opened in Anaheim, California, in July 1955, the Disney company had to set ticket prices. Should the company charge for entry into the park—which most amusements parks did not—and also charge for each ride within the park? Disney decided to charge a low price—$1 for adults and $0.50 for children—for admission into the park and also to charge for tickets to the rides. This system of separate charges for admission and for the rides continued until the early 1980s, when Disney decided to switch to a very different pricing strategy. Today, there is a high price for admission to Disneyland and Walt Disney World, but once a customer is in the park, the rides are free. Why did Disney change its pricing strategy? In this chapter, we will study some common pricing strategies, and we will see how Disney and other firms use these strategies to increase their profits. **AN INSIDE LOOK** on **page 526** discusses how colleges also charge different prices to different students.

Sources: Harrison Price, *Walt's Revolution! By the Numbers*, Ripley Entertainment, Inc., 2004, p. 31; and Bruce Gordon and David Mumford, *Disneyland: The Nickel Tour*, Santa Clarita, CA: Camphor Tree Publishers, 2000, pp. 174–175.

LEARNING Objectives

After studying this chapter, you should be able to:

15.1 Define the **law of one price** and explain the role of **arbitrage**, page 508.

15.2 Explain how a firm can increase its profits through **price discrimination**, page 510.

15.3 Explain how some firms increase their profits through the use of **odd pricing, cost-plus pricing**, and **two-part tariffs**, page 519.

Economics in YOUR Life!

Why So Many Prices to See a Movie?

Think about the movie theaters in your area. How much do you, as a student, pay to get into a theater? Would your parents pay the same amount? What about your grandparents? How about your little brother or sister? Is the price the same at night as in the afternoon? Why do you suppose movie theaters charge different prices to different groups of consumers?

    If you buy popcorn at the movie theater, you pay the same price as everyone else. Why do you suppose people in certain age groups get a discount on movie admission but not on movie popcorn? As you read the chapter, see if you can answer these questions. You can check your answers against those we provide at the end of the chapter. **>> Continued on page 525**

I n previous chapters, we saw that entrepreneurs continually seek out economic profit. Pricing strategies are one way firms can attempt to increase their economic profit. One of these strategies is called *price discrimination*. It involves firms setting different prices for the same good or service, as Disney does when setting admission prices at Disney World. In Chapter 14, we analyzed the situation of a monopolist who sets a single price for its product. In this chapter, we will see how a firm can increase its profits by charging a higher price to consumers who value the good more and a lower price to consumers who value the good less.

We will also analyze the widely used strategies of *odd pricing* and *cost-plus pricing*. Finally, we will analyze situations in which firms are able to charge consumers one price for the right to buy a good and a second price for each unit of the good purchased. The ability of Disney to charge for admission to Disney World and also to charge for each ride is an example of this situation, which economists call a *two-part tariff*.

15.1 LEARNING OBJECTIVE

15.1 | Define the law of one price and explain the role of arbitrage.

Pricing Strategy, the Law of One Price, and Arbitrage

We saw in the opening to this chapter that sometimes firms can increase their profits by charging different prices for the same good. In fact, many firms rely on economic analysis to practice *price discrimination* by charging higher prices to some customers and lower prices to others. Firms use technology to gather information on the preferences of consumers and their responsiveness to changes in prices. Managers use the information to rapidly adjust the prices of their goods and services. This practice of rapidly adjusting prices, called *yield management*, has been particularly important to airlines and hotels. There are limits, though, to the ability of firms to charge different prices for the same product. The key limit is the possibility in some circumstances that consumers who can buy a good at a low price will resell it to consumers who would otherwise have to buy at a high price.

Arbitrage

According to the *law of one price*, identical products should sell for the same price everywhere. Let's explore why the law of one price usually holds true. Suppose that a Sony PlayStation Portable (PSP) handheld video game player sells for $249 in stores in Atlanta and for $199 in stores in San Francisco. Anyone who lives in San Francisco could buy PSPs for $199 and resell them for $249 in Atlanta. They could sell them on eBay or ship them to someone they know in Atlanta who could sell them in local flea markets. Buying a product in one market at a low price and reselling it in another market at a high price is referred to as *arbitrage*. The profits received from engaging in arbitrage are referred to as *arbitrage profits*.

As the supply of PSPs in Atlanta increases, the price of PSPs in Atlanta will decline, and as the supply of PSPs in San Francisco decreases, the price of PSPs in San Francisco will rise. Eventually the arbitrage process will eliminate most, but not all, of the price difference. Some price difference will remain because sellers must pay to list PSPs on eBay and to ship them to Atlanta. The costs of carrying out a transaction—by, for example, listing items on eBay and shipping them across the country—are called **transactions costs**. The law of one price holds exactly *only if transactions costs are zero*. As we will soon see, in cases in which it is impossible to resell a product, the law of one price will not hold, and firms will be able to price discriminate. Apart from this important qualification, we expect that arbitrage will result in a product selling for the same price everywhere.

Transactions costs The costs in time and other resources that parties incur in the process of agreeing to and carrying out an exchange of goods or services.

Solved Problem | 15-1

Is Arbitrage Just a Rip-off?

People are often suspicious of arbitrage. Buying something at a low price and reselling it at a high price exploits the person buying at the high price. Or does it? Is this view correct? If so, do the auctions on eBay serve any useful economic purpose?

SOLVING THE PROBLEM:

Step 1: **Review the chapter material.** This problem is about arbitrage, so you may want to review the section "Arbitrage," which begins on page 508. If necessary, also review the discussion of the benefits from trade in Chapters 2 and 8.

Step 2: **Use the discussion of arbitrage and the discussion in earlier chapters of the benefits from trade to answer the questions.** Many of the goods on eBay have been bought at a low price and are being resold at a higher price. In fact, some people supplement their incomes by buying collectibles and other goods at garage sales and reselling them on eBay. Does eBay serve a useful economic purpose? Economists would say that it does. Consider the case of Lou, who buys collectible movie posters and resells them on eBay. Suppose Lou buys a *Spider-Man 3* poster at a garage sale for $30 and resells it on eBay for $60. Both the person who sold to Lou at the garage sale and the person who bought from him on eBay must have been made better off by the deals *or they would not have made them.* Lou has performed the useful service of locating the poster and making it available for sale on eBay. In carrying out this service, Lou has incurred costs, including the opportunity cost of his time spent searching garage sales, the opportunity cost of the funds he has tied up in posters he has purchased but not yet sold, and the cost of the fees eBay charges him. It is easy to sell goods on eBay, so over time, competition among Lou and other movie poster dealers should cause the difference between the prices of posters sold at garage sales and the prices on eBay to shrink until they are equal to the dealers' costs of reselling the posters.

YOUR TURN: For more practice, do related problems 1.5 and 1.6 on page 528 at the end of this chapter.

>> End Solved Problem 15-1

Why Don't All Firms Charge the Same Price?

The law of one price may appear to be violated even where transactions costs are zero and a product can be resold. For example, different Internet Web sites may sell what seem to be identical products for different prices. We can resolve this apparent contradiction if we look more closely at what "product" an Internet Web site—or other business—actually offers for sale.

Suppose you want to buy a copy of the book *Harry Potter and the Deathly Hallows*. You use mySimon.com or some other search engine to compare the book's price at various Web sites. You get the results shown in Table 15-1.

Would you automatically buy the book from one of the last two sites listed rather than from Amazon.com or BarnesandNoble.com? We can think about why you might not. Consider what product is being offered for sale. Amazon.com is not just offering *Harry Potter and the Deathly Hallows*; it is offering *Harry Potter and the Deathly Hallows* delivered quickly to your home, well packaged so it's not damaged in the mail, and charged to your credit card using a secure method that keeps your credit card number safe from computer hackers. As we discussed in Chapter 12, firms differentiate the products they sell in many ways. One way is by providing faster and more reliable delivery than competitors.

TABLE 15-1

Which Internet Bookseller Would You Buy From?

PRODUCT: *HARRY POTTER AND THE DEATHLY HALLOWS*	
COMPANY	PRICE
Amazon.com	$18.89
BarnesandNoble.com	18.89
WaitForeverForYourOrder.com	17.50
JustStartedinBusinessLastWednesday.com	16.75

Amazon.com and BarnesandNoble.com have built reputations for fast and reliable service. New Internet booksellers who lack that reputation will have to differentiate their products on the basis of price, as the two fictitious firms listed in the table have done. So, the difference in the prices of products offered on Web sites does *not* violate the law of one price. A book Amazon.com offers for sale is not the same product as a book JustStartedinBusinessLastWednesday.com offers for sale.

15.2 LEARNING OBJECTIVE

15.2 | Explain how a firm can increase its profits through price discrimination.

Price Discrimination: Charging Different Prices for the Same Product

Price discrimination Charging different prices to different customers for the same product when the price differences are not due to differences in cost.

We saw at the beginning of this chapter that the Walt Disney Company charges different prices for the same product: admission to Disney World. Charging different prices to different customers for the same good or service when the price differences are not due to differences in cost is called **price discrimination**. But doesn't price discrimination

---

Don't Let This Happen to **YOU!**

Don't Confuse Price Discrimination with Other Types of Discrimination

Don't confuse price discrimination with discrimination based on race or gender. Discriminating on the basis of arbitrary characteristics, like race or gender, is illegal under the civil rights laws. Price discrimination is legal because it involves charging people different prices on the basis of their willingness to pay rather than on the basis of arbitrary characteristics. There is a gray area, however, when companies charge different prices on the basis of race or gender. For example, insurance companies usually charge women lower prices than men for automobile insurance. The courts have ruled that this is not illegal discrimination under the civil rights laws because women, on average, have better driving records than men. Because the costs of insuring men are higher than the costs of insuring women, insurance companies are allowed to charge them higher prices. Notice that this is not actually price discrimination as we have defined it here. Price discrimination involves charging different prices for the same product *where the price differences are not due to differences in cost*.

Insurance companies have been less successful in defending the practice of charging black people higher life insurance prices than white people. The insurance companies had claimed that this practice, which continued into the 1960s, was based on the shorter average life span of black people. Even though most insurance companies stopped the practice in the 1960s for new policies, most companies continued to collect the higher prices on policies that were already in effect. When this became widely known, several state insurance commissions launched investigations. Eventually, most companies reimbursed policyholders for the higher prices and paid substantial fines to the government. MetLife, the largest publicly held life insurance company in the United States, paid $250 million to settle a lawsuit by policyholders and to pay fines imposed by the New York State Insurance Department.

YOUR TURN: Test your understanding by doing related problem 2.18 on page 531 at the end of this chapter.

contradict the law of one price? Why doesn't the possibility of arbitrage profits lead people to buy at the low price and resell at the high price?

The Requirements for Successful Price Discrimination

A successful strategy of price discrimination has three requirements:

1 A firm must possess market power.

2 Some consumers must have a greater willingness to pay for the product than other consumers, and the firm must be able to know what prices customers are willing to pay.

3 The firm must be able to divide up—or *segment*—the market for the product so that consumers who buy the product at a low price are not able to resell it at a high price. In other words, price discrimination will not work if arbitrage is possible.

Note that a firm selling in a perfectly competitive market cannot practice price discrimination because it can only charge the market price. But because most firms do not sell in perfectly competitive markets, they have market power and can set the price of the good they sell. Many firms may also be able to determine that some customers have a greater willingness to pay for the product than others. However, the third requirement—that markets be segmented so that customers buying at a low price will not be able to resell the product—can be difficult to fulfill. For example, some people really love Big Macs and would be willing to pay $10 rather than do without one. Other people would not be willing to pay a penny more than $1 for one. Even if McDonald's could identify differences in the willingness of its customers to pay for Big Macs, it would not be able to charge them different prices. Suppose McDonald's knows that Joe is willing to pay $10, whereas Jill will pay only $1. If McDonald's tries to charge Joe $10, he will just have Jill buy his Big Mac for him.

Only firms that can keep consumers from reselling a product are able to practice price discrimination. Because buyers cannot resell the product, the law of one price does not hold. For example, movie theaters know that many people are willing to pay more to see a movie at night than during the afternoon. As a result, theaters usually charge higher prices for tickets to night showings than for tickets to afternoon showings. They keep these markets separate by making the tickets to afternoon showings a different color or by having the time printed on them, and by having a ticket taker examine the tickets. That makes it difficult for someone to buy a lower-priced ticket in the afternoon and use the ticket to gain admission to an evening showing.

Figure 15-1 illustrates how the owners of movie theaters use price discrimination to increase their profits. The marginal cost to the movie theater owner from another person attending a showing is very small: a little more wear on a theater seat and a few more kernels of popcorn to be swept from the floor. In previous chapters, we assumed that marginal cost has a U shape. In Figure 15-1, we assume for simplicity that marginal cost is a constant $0.50, shown as a horizontal line. Panel (a) shows the demand for afternoon showings. In this segment of its market, the theater should maximize profit by selling the number of tickets for which marginal revenue equals marginal cost, or 450 tickets. We know from the demand curve that the theater can sell 450 tickets at a price of $4.50 per ticket. Panel (b) shows the demand for night showings. Notice that charging $4.50 per ticket would *not* be profit maximizing in this market. At a price of $4.50, the theater sells 850 tickets, which is 225 more tickets than the profit-maximizing number of 625. By charging $4.50 for tickets to afternoon showings and $6.75 for tickets to night showings, the theater has maximized profits.

Figure 15-1 also illustrates another important point about price discrimination: When firms can price discriminate, they will charge customers who are less sensitive to price—those whose demand for the product is *less elastic*—a higher price and charge customers who are more sensitive to price—those whose demand is *more elastic*—a lower price. In this case, the demand for tickets to night showings is less elastic, so the price charged is higher, and the demand for tickets to afternoon showings is more elastic, so the price charged is lower.

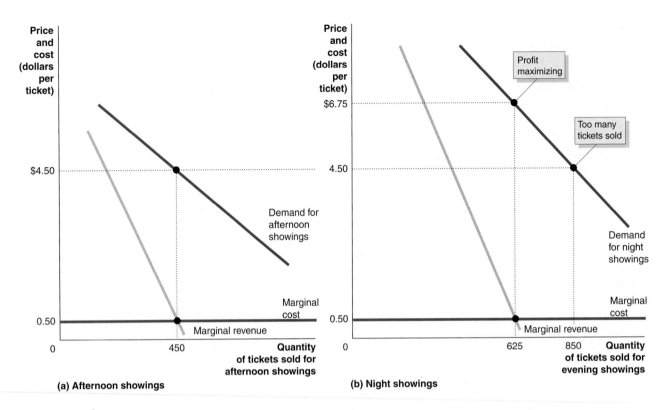

Figure 15-1 | Price Discrimination by a Movie Theater

Fewer people want to go to the movies in the afternoon than in the evening. In panel (a), the profit-maximizing price for a ticket to an afternoon showing is $4.50. Charging this same price for night showings would not be profit maximizing, as panel

(b) shows. At a price of $4.50, 850 tickets would be sold to night showings, which is more than the profit-maximizing number of 625 tickets. To maximize profits, the theater should charge $6.75 for tickets to night showings.

Solved Problem | 15-2

How Dell Computer Uses Price Discrimination to Increase Profits

According to an article in the *Wall Street Journal*, "On Dell's Web site recently, the same Optiplex business desktop PC priced at $1,498 for education customers was offered at $1,426 on a page devoted to health-care customers." Why

would Dell charge different prices for the same computer, depending on whether the buyer is an education customer or a health-care customer? Draw a graph to illustrate your answer.

SOLVING THE PROBLEM:

Step 1: Review the chapter material. This problem is about using price discrimination to increase profits, so you may want to review the section "Price Discrimination: Charging Different Prices for the Same Product," which begins on page 510.

Step 2: Explain why charging different prices to education customers and health care customers will increase Dell's profits. It makes sense for Dell to charge different prices if education customers have a different price elasticity of demand than do health-care customers. In that case, Dell will charge the market segment with the less elastic demand a higher price and the market segment with the more elastic demand a lower price. Because education customers are being charged the higher price, they must have a less elastic demand than health-care customers.

Step 3: **Draw a graph to illustrate your answer.** Your graph should look like the one below, where we have chosen hypothetical quantities to illustrate the ideas. As in the case of movie theaters, you can assume for simplicity that the marginal cost is constant; in the graph we assume that marginal cost is $400.

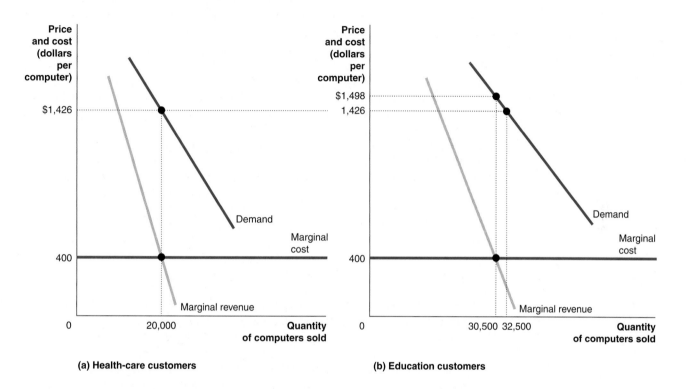

(a) Health-care customers

(b) Education customers

The graph shows that in the health-care customers segment of the market, marginal revenue equals marginal cost at 20,000 computers sold. Therefore, Dell should charge a price of $1,426 to maximize profits. But if Dell also charged $1,426 in the education customers segment of the market, it would sell 32,500 computers, which is more than the profit-maximizing quantity. By charging $1,498 to education customers, Dell will sell 30,500 computers, the profit-maximizing quantity. We have shown that Dell maximizes its profits by charging education customers a higher price than health-care customers. Notice that although the demand curve in panel (a) is more elastic, it is also steeper. This reminds us of the important point from Chapter 5 that elasticity is different from slope.

Source: David Bank and Gary McWilliams, "Picking a Big Fight with Dell, H-P Cuts PC Profits Razor-Thin," *Wall Street Journal*, May 12, 2004.

YOUR TURN: For more practice, do problem 2.12 on page 530 at the end of this chapter.　　**>> End Solved Problem 15-2**

Airlines: The Kings of Price Discrimination

Airline seats are a perishable product. Once a plane has taken off from Chicago for Los Angeles, any seat that has not been sold on that particular flight will never be sold. In addition, the marginal cost of flying one additional passenger is low. This situation gives airlines a strong incentive to manage prices so that as many seats as possible are filled on each flight.

Airlines divide their customers into two main categories: business travelers and leisure travelers. Business travelers often have inflexible schedules, can't commit until the last minute to traveling on a particular day, and, most importantly, are not very sensitive to changes in price. The opposite is true for leisure travelers: They are flexible about when they travel, willing to buy their tickets well in advance, and sensitive to changes in price. Based on what we discussed earlier in this chapter, you can see that airlines will maximize profits by charging business travelers higher ticket prices than leisure travelers, but they need to determine who is a business traveler and who is a leisure traveler. Some airlines do this by requiring people who want to buy a ticket at the leisure price to buy 14 days in advance and to stay at their destination over a Saturday night. Anyone unable to meet these requirements must pay a much higher price. Because business travelers often cannot make their plans 14 days in advance of their flight and don't want to stay over a weekend, they end up paying the higher ticket price. The gap between leisure fares and business fares is often very substantial. For example, in April 2007, the price of a leisure-fare ticket between New York and San Francisco on United Airlines was $308. The price of a business-fare ticket was $1,198.

The airlines go well beyond a single leisure fare and a single business fare in their pricing strategies. Although they ordinarily charge high prices for tickets sold only a few days in advance, they are willing to reduce prices for seats that they expect will not be sold at existing prices. Since the late 1980s, airlines have employed economists and mathematicians to construct computer models of the market for airline tickets. To calculate a suggested price each day for each seat, these models take into account factors that affect the demand for tickets, such as the season of the year, the length of the route, the day of the week, and whether the flight typically attracts primarily business or leisure travelers. This practice of continually adjusting prices to take into account fluctuations in demand is called *yield management.*

Since the late 1990s, Internet sites such as Priceline.com have helped the airlines to implement yield management. On Priceline.com, buyers commit to paying a price of their choosing for a ticket on a particular day and agree that they will fly at any time on that day. This gives airlines the opportunity to fill seats that otherwise would have gone empty, particularly on late night or early morning flights, even though the price may be well below the normal leisure fare. In 2001, several airlines combined to form the Internet site Orbitz, which became another means of filling seats at discount prices. In fact, in the past few years, the chance that you paid the same price for your airline ticket as the person sitting next to you has become quite small. Figure 15-2 shows an actual

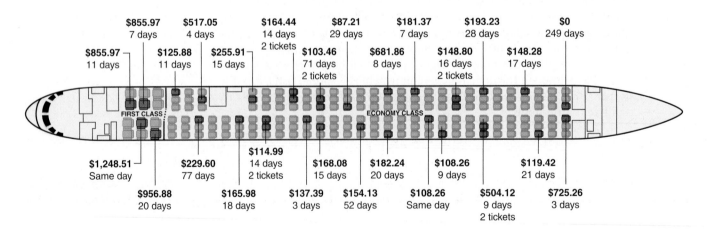

Figure 15-2 | **33 Customers and 27 Different Prices**

To fill as many seats on a flight as possible, airlines charge many different ticket prices. The 33 passengers on this United Airlines flight from Chicago to Los Angeles paid 27 different prices for their tickets, including one passenger who used frequent flyer miles to obtain a free ticket. The first number in the figure is the price paid for the ticket; the second number is the number of days in advance that the ticket was purchased.

Source: Matthew L. Wald, "So, How Much Did You Pay for Your Ticket?" *New York Times,* April 12, 1998. Used with permission of New York Times Agency.

United Airlines flight from Chicago to Los Angeles. The 33 passengers on the flight paid 27 different prices for their tickets, including one passenger who used frequent flyer miles to obtain a free ticket.

Making the Connection | How Colleges Use Yield Management

Some colleges use yield management techniques to determine financial aid.

Traditionally, colleges have based financial aid decisions only on the incomes of prospective students. In recent years, however, many colleges have started using yield management techniques, first developed for the airlines, to determine the amount of financial aid they offer different students. Colleges typically use a name like "financial aid engineering" or "student enrollment management" rather than "yield management" to describe what they are doing. There is an important difference between the airlines and colleges: Colleges are interested not just in maximizing the revenue they receive from student tuition but also in increasing the academic quality of the students who enroll.

The "price" of a college education equals the tuition charged minus any financial aid received. When colleges use yield management techniques, they increase financial aid offers to students likely to be more price sensitive, and they reduce financial aid offers to students likely to be less price sensitive. As Stanford economist Caroline Hoxby puts it, "Universities are trying to find the people whose decisions will be changed by these [financial aid] grants." Some of the factors colleges use to judge how sensitive to price students are likely to be include whether they applied for early admission, whether they came for an on-campus interview, their intended major, their home state, and the level of their family's income. Focusing on one of these factors, William F. Elliot, vice president for enrollment management at Carnegie Mellon University, advises, "If finances are a concern, you shouldn't be applying any place [for] early decision" because you are less likely to receive a large financial aid offer.

Many students (and their parents) are critical of colleges that use yield management techniques in allocating financial aid. Some colleges, such as those in the Ivy League, have large enough endowments to meet all of their students' financial aid needs, so they don't practice yield management. Less well-endowed colleges defend the practice on the grounds that it allows them to recruit the best students at a lower cost in financial aid.

Sources: Jane J. Kim and Anjali Athavaley, "Colleges Seek to Address Affordability," *Wall Street Journal*, May 3, 2007; and Albert B. Crenshaw, "Price Wars on Campus: Colleges Use Discounts to Draw Best Mix of Top Students, Paying Customers," *Washington Post*, October 15, 2002; and Steve Stecklow, "Expensive Lesson: Colleges Manipulate Financial-Aid Offers, *Wall Street Journal*, April 1, 1996.

YOUR TURN: Test your understanding by doing related problem 2.14 on page 530 at the end of this chapter.

Perfect Price Discrimination

If a firm knew every consumer's willingness to pay—and could keep consumers who bought a product at a low price from reselling it—the firm could charge every consumer a different price. In this case of *perfect price discrimination*—also known as *first-degree price discrimination*—each consumer would have to pay a price equal to the consumer's willingness to pay and, therefore, would receive no consumer surplus. To see why, remember that consumer surplus is the difference between the highest price a consumer is willing to pay for a product and the price the consumer actually pays. But if the price the consumer pays is the maximum the consumer would be willing to pay, there is no consumer surplus.

Figure 15-3 shows the effects of perfect price discrimination. To simplify the discussion, we assume that the firm is a monopoly and that it has constant marginal and average costs. Panel (a) should be familiar from Chapter 14. It shows the case of a monopolist who cannot price discriminate and, therefore, can charge only a single price for its product. The monopolist maximizes profits by producing the level of output where marginal revenue equals marginal cost. Recall that the economically efficient level of output occurs where price is equal to marginal cost, which is the level of output in a perfectly competitive market. Because the monopolist produces where price is greater than marginal cost, it causes a loss of economic efficiency equal to the area of the deadweight loss triangle in the figure.

Panel (b) shows the situation of a monopolist practicing perfect price discrimination. Because the firm can now charge each consumer the maximum the consumer is willing to pay, its marginal revenue from selling one more unit is equal to the price of that unit. Therefore, the monopolist's marginal revenue curve becomes equal to its demand curve, and the firm will continue to produce up to the point where price is equal to marginal cost. It may seem like a paradox, but the ability to perfectly price discriminate causes the monopolist to produce the efficient level of output. By doing so, it converts into profits what in panel (a) had been consumer surplus *and* what had been deadweight loss. In both panel (a) and panel (b), the profit shown is also producer surplus.

Even though the result in panel (b) is more economically efficient than the result in panel (a), consumers clearly are worse off because the amount of consumer surplus has been reduced to zero. We probably will never see a case of perfect price discrimination in the real world because firms typically do not know how much each consumer is willing to pay and therefore cannot charge each consumer a different price. Still, this extreme case helps us to see the two key results of price discrimination:

1 Profits increase.

2 Consumer surplus decreases.

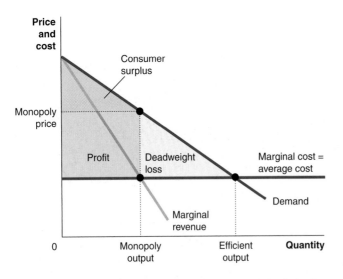

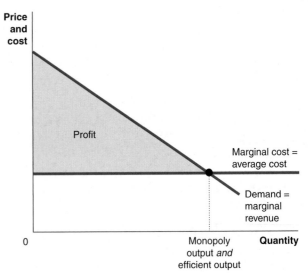

(a) A monopolist who cannot practice price discrimination   (b) A monopolist practicing perfect price discrimination

Figure 15-3 | Perfect Price Discrimination

Panel (a) shows the case of a monopolist who cannot price discriminate and, therefore, can charge only a single price for its product. The graph, like those in Chapter 14, shows that to maximize profits, the monopolist will produce the level of output where marginal revenue equals marginal cost. The resulting profit is shown by the area of the green rectangle. Given the monopoly price, the amount of consumer surplus in this market is shown by the area of the blue triangle. The economically efficient level of output occurs where price equals marginal cost. Because the monopolist stops production at a level of output where price is above marginal cost, there is a deadweight loss equal to the area of the yellow triangle. In panel (b), the monopolist is able to perfectly price discriminate by charging a different price to each consumer. The result is to convert both the consumer surplus *and* the deadweight loss from panel (a) into profit.

With perfect price discrimination, economic efficiency is improved. Can we also say that this will be the case if price discrimination is less than perfect? Often, less-than-perfect price discrimination will improve economic efficiency. But under certain circumstances, it may actually reduce economic efficiency, so we can't draw a general conclusion.

Price Discrimination across Time

Firms are sometimes able to engage in price discrimination over time. With this strategy, firms charge a higher price for a product when it is first introduced and a lower price later. Some consumers are *early adopters* who will pay a high price to be among the first to own certain new products. This pattern helps explain why DVD players, digital cameras, and flat-screen plasma televisions all sold for very high prices when they were first introduced. After the demand of the early adopters was satisfied, the companies reduced prices to attract more price-sensitive customers. For example, the price of DVD players dropped by 95 percent within five years of their introduction. Some of the price reductions over time for these products was also due to falling costs as companies took advantage of economies of scale, but some represented price discrimination across time.

Book publishers routinely use price discrimination across time to increase profits. Hardcover editions of novels have much higher prices and are published months before paperback editions. For example, the hardcover edition of Stephen King's novel *Lisey's Story* was published in October 2006 at a price of $28. The paperback edition was published in June 2007 for $9.99. Although this difference in price might seem to reflect the higher costs of hardcover books, in fact, it does not. The marginal cost of printing another copy of the hardcover is about $1.50. The marginal cost of printing another copy of the paperback edition is only slightly less, about $1.25. So, the difference in price between the hardcover and paperback is driven primarily by differences in demand. Stephen King's most devoted fans want to read his next book at the earliest possible moment and are not too sensitive to price. Many casual readers are also interested in King's books but will read something else if the price is too high.

As Figure 15-4 shows, a publisher will maximize profits by segmenting the market—in this case across time—and by charging a higher price to the less elastic market segment and a lower price to the more elastic segment. (This example is similar to our earlier analysis of movie tickets in Figure 15-1 on page 512.) If the publisher had skipped the hardcover and issued only the paperback version at a price of $9.99 when the book was first published in October, its revenue would have dropped by the number of readers who bought the hardcover multiplied by the difference between the price of the hardcover and the price of the paperback, or $500,000 \times (\$28 - 9.99) = \$9,005,000$.

Can Price Discrimination Be Illegal?

In Chapter 14, we saw that Congress has passed *antitrust laws* to promote competition. Price discrimination may be illegal if its effect is to reduce competition in an industry. In 1936, Congress passed the Robinson–Patman Act, which outlawed price discrimination that reduced competition, but which also contained language that could be interpreted as making illegal *all* price discrimination not based on differences in cost. In the 1960s, the Federal Trade Commission sued the Borden company under this act because Borden was selling the same evaporated milk for two different prices. Cans with the Borden label were sold for a high price, and cans sold to supermarkets to be repackaged as the supermarkets' private brands were sold for a much lower price. The courts ultimately ruled that Borden had not violated the law because the price differences increased, rather than reduced, competition in the market

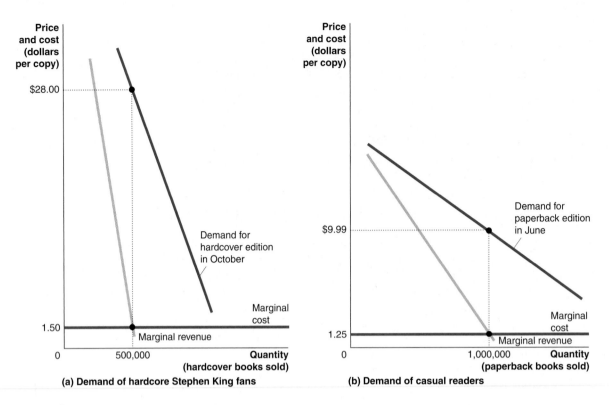

(a) Demand of hardcore Stephen King fans

(b) Demand of casual readers

Figure 15-4 | Price Discrimination across Time

Publishers issue most novels in hardcover at high prices to satisfy the demand of the novelists' most devoted fans. Later, they publish paperback editions at much lower prices to capture sales from casual readers. In panel (a), with a marginal cost of $1.50 per copy for a hardcover, the profit-maximizing level of output is 500,000 copies,

which can be sold at a price of $28. In panel (b), the more elastic demand of casual readers and the slightly lower marginal cost result in a profit-maximizing output of 1,000,000 for the paperback edition, which can be sold at a price of $9.99.

for evaporated milk. In recent years, the courts have interpreted Robinson–Patman narrowly, allowing firms to use the types of price discrimination described in this chapter.

Why does renting only a few movies get you better service on Netflix?

Making the Connection

Price Discrimination with a Twist at Netflix

Price discrimination usually refers to charging different prices to different consumers for the same good or service. But price discrimination can also involve charging the same price for goods or services of different quality. Netflix, an online DVD rental service, has apparently engaged in this second form of price discrimination. According to a newspaper story, "Netflix customers who pay the same price for the same service are often treated differently, depending on their rental patterns." Netflix subscribers pay a fixed monthly fee to rent a given number of DVDs. For instance, in 2008, Netflix was charging $16.99 per month to rent three DVDs at a time. After a subscriber returns a DVD, Netflix mails that subscriber a new DVD. Subscribers can rent an unlimited number of DVDs per month, although they can have no more than three at any one time. Netflix has become very popular, with more than seven million subscribers by 2008.

But does every Netflix subscriber receive service of the same quality? In particular, does every subscriber have an equal chance of receiving the latest movie released on DVD? Apparently not. Although Netflix does not emphasize it in its advertising, subscribers who rent the fewest movies per month have the best chance of receiving the latest releases and will typically receive their DVDs faster. According to Netflix's Terms of Use (the "fine print" that most subscribers don't read):

> In determining priority for shipping and inventory allocation, we may utilize many different factors. . . . For example, if all other factors are the same, we give priority to those members who receive the fewest DVDs through our service. . . . Also . . . [the service you experience] may be different from the service we provide to other members on the same membership plan.

One Netflix subscriber was quoted in a newspaper article as saying, "Sometimes it would be two or three months before I got [a movie] once it came out on DVD. The longer I was a customer, the worse it got."

Why would Netflix provide better service to subscribers who rent only a few DVDs per month and poorer service to subscribers who rent many DVDs per month? Subscribers who rent many DVDs per month are likely to have less elastic demand—they really like watching movies—than subscribers who rent only a few DVDs per month. As we have seen in this chapter, firms can increase their profits by charging higher prices to consumers with less elastic demand and lower prices to consumers with more elastic demand. But this strategy works only if firms have a way of reliably separating consumers into groups on the basis of how elastic their demand is. When they first subscribe, Netflix has no way of separating their consumers on the basis of how elastic their demand is, so it has to charge the same price to everyone. But after a few months of observing a subscriber's pattern of rentals, Netflix has enough information to determine whether the subscriber's demand is more or less elastic. By reducing the level of service to subscribers with less elastic demand, Netflix is, in effect, raising the price these consumers pay relative to consumers who receive better service. In effect, Netflix is engaging in price discrimination and increasing its profits over what they would be if every subscriber received the same service at the same price.

Sources: Alina Tugend, "Getting Movies from a Store or a Mailbox (or Just a Box)," *New York Times*, August 5, 2006; and "Netflix Critics Slam 'Throttling,'" Associated Press, February 10, 2006.

YOUR TURN: Test your understanding by doing related problem 2.17 on page 531 at the end of this chapter.

15.3 LEARNING OBJECTIVE

15.3 | Explain how some firms increase their profits through the use of odd pricing, cost-plus pricing, and two-part tariffs.

Other Pricing Strategies

In addition to price discrimination, firms use many different pricing strategies, depending on the nature of their products, the level of competition in their markets, and the characteristics of their customers. In this section, we consider three important strategies: odd pricing, cost-plus pricing, and two-part tariffs.

Odd Pricing: Why Is the Price $2.99 Instead of $3.00?

Many firms use what is called *odd pricing*—for example, charging $4.95 instead of $5.00, or $199 instead of $200. Surveys show that 80 percent to 90 percent of the products sold in supermarkets have prices ending in "9" or "5" rather than "0." Odd pricing has a long history. In the early nineteenth century, most goods in the United States were sold in general stores and did not have fixed prices. Instead, prices were often determined by haggling, much as prices of new cars are often determined today by haggling on dealers' lots. Later in the nineteenth century, when most products began to sell for a fixed price, odd pricing became popular.

Different explanations have been given for the origin of odd pricing. One explanation is that it began because goods imported from Great Britain had a reputation for high quality. When the prices of British goods in British currency—the pound—were translated into U.S. dollars, the result was an odd price. Because customers connected odd prices with high-quality goods, even sellers of domestic goods charged odd prices. Another explanation is that odd pricing began as an attempt to guard against employee theft. An odd price forced an employee to give the customer change, which reduced the likelihood that the employee would simply pocket the customer's money without recording the sale.

Whatever the origins of odd pricing, why do firms still use it today? The most obvious answer is that an odd price, say $9.99, seems somehow significantly—more than a penny—cheaper than $10.00. But do consumers really have this illusion? To find out, three market researchers conducted a study. We saw in Chapter 3 that demand curves can be estimated statistically. If consumers have the illusion that $9.99 is significantly cheaper than $10.00, they will demand a greater quantity of goods at $9.99—and other odd prices—than the estimated demand curve predicts. The researchers surveyed consumers about their willingness to purchase six different products—ranging from a block of cheese to an electric blender—at a series of prices. Ten of the prices were either odd cent prices—99 cents or 95 cents—or odd dollar prices—$95 or $99. Nine of these 10 odd prices resulted in an odd-price effect, with the quantity demanded being greater than predicted using the estimated demand curve. The study was not conclusive because it relied on surveys rather than on observing actual purchasing behavior and because it used only a small group of products, but it does provide some evidence that using odd prices makes economic sense.

Why Do Firms Use Cost-Plus Pricing?

Many firms use *cost-plus pricing*, which involves adding a percentage *markup* to average cost. With this pricing strategy, the firm first calculates average cost at a particular level of production, usually equal to the firm's expected sales. It then increases average cost by a percentage amount, say 30 percent, to arrive at the price. For example, if average cost is $100 and the percentage markup is 30 percent, the price will be $130. In a firm selling multiple products, the markup is intended to cover all costs, including those that the firm cannot assign to any particular product. Most firms have costs that are difficult to assign to one particular product. For example, the work performed by the employees in McDonald's accounting and finance departments applies to all of McDonald's products and can't be assigned directly to Big Macs or Happy Meals.

Making the Connection | Cost-Plus Pricing in the Publishing Industry

Book publishing companies incur substantial costs for editing, designing, marketing, and warehousing books. These costs are difficult to assign directly to any particular book. Most publishers arrive at a price for a book by applying a markup to their production costs, which are usually divided into plant costs and manufacturing costs. Plant costs include typesetting the manuscript and preparing graphics or artwork for printing. Manufacturing costs include the costs of printing, paper, and binding the book.

Consider the following example for the hypothetical new book by Adam Smith, *How to Succeed at Economics without Really Trying*. We will assume that the book is 250 pages long, the publisher expects to sell 5,000 copies, and plant and manufacturing costs are as given in the following table:

PLANT COST

	Typesetting	$3,500
	Other plant costs	2,000

MANUFACTURING COST

	Printing	$5,750
	Paper	6,250
	Binding	5,000

TOTAL PRODUCTION COST

		$22,500

With total production cost of $22,500 and production of 5,000 books, the per-unit production cost is $22,500/5,000 = $4.50. Many publishers multiply the unit production cost number by 7 or 8 to arrive at the retail price they will charge customers in bookstores. In this case, multiplying by 7 results in a price of $31.50 for the book. The markup seems quite high, but publishers typically sell books to bookstores at a 40 percent discount. Although a customer in a bookstore will pay $31.50 for the book—or less, of course, if it is purchased from a bookseller that discounts the retail price—the publisher receives only $18.90. The difference between the $18.90 received from the bookstore and the $4.50 production cost equals the cost of editing, marketing, warehousing, and all other costs, including the opportunity cost of the investment in the firm by its owners, plus any economic profit received by the owners.

Source: Beth Luey, *Handbook for Academic Authors*, 4th ed., New York: Cambridge University Press, 2002.

YOUR TURN: Test your understanding by doing related problem 3.8 on page 532 at the end of this chapter.

A difficulty that firms face when using cost-plus pricing should be obvious to you. In this chapter, as in the previous four chapters, we have emphasized that firms maximize profit by producing the quantity where marginal revenue equals marginal cost and charging a price that will cause consumers to buy this quantity. The cost-plus approach doesn't appear to maximize profits unless the cost-plus price turns out to be the same as the price that will cause the quantity sold to be where marginal revenue is equal to marginal cost. Economists have two views of cost-plus pricing. One is that cost-plus pricing is simply a mistake that firms should avoid. The other view is that cost-plus pricing is a good way to come close to the profit-maximizing price when either marginal revenue or marginal cost is difficult to calculate.

Small firms often like cost-plus pricing because it is easy to use. Unfortunately, these firms can fall into the trap of mechanically applying a cost-plus pricing rule, which can result in charging prices that do not maximize profits. The most obvious problems with cost-plus pricing are that it ignores demand and focuses on average cost rather than marginal cost. If the firm's marginal cost is significantly different from its average cost at its current level of production, cost-plus pricing is unlikely to maximize profits.

Despite these problems, cost-plus pricing is used by some large firms, such as General Motors, that clearly have the knowledge and resources to devise a better method of pricing if cost-plus pricing fails to maximize profits. Economists conclude that cost-plus pricing may be the best way to determine the optimal price in two situations:

1 When marginal cost and average cost are roughly equal

2 When the firm has difficulty estimating its demand curve

In fact, most large firms that use cost-plus pricing do not just mechanically apply a markup to their estimate of average cost. Instead, they adjust the markup to reflect their best estimate of current demand. At General Motors, for example, a pricing policy committee adjusts prices to reflect its views of the current state of competition in the industry and the current state of the economy. If competition is strong in a weak economy, the pricing committee may decide to set price significantly below the cost-plus price—perhaps by offering buyers a rebate.

In general, firms that take demand into account will charge lower markups on products that are more price elastic and higher markups on products that are less elastic. Supermarkets, where cost-plus pricing is widely used, have markups in the 5 percent to 10 percent range for products with more elastic demand, such as soft drinks and breakfast cereals, and markups in the 50 percent range for products with less elastic demand, such as fresh fruits and vegetables.

Pricing with Two-Part Tariffs

Some firms can require consumers to pay an initial fee for the right to buy their product and an additional fee for each unit of the product purchased. For example, many golf and tennis clubs require members to buy an annual membership in addition to paying a fee each time they use the tennis court or golf course. Sam's Club requires consumers to pay a membership fee before shopping at its stores. Cellular phone companies charge a monthly fee and then have a per-minute charge after a certain number of minutes have been used. Economists refer to this situation as a **two-part tariff**.

Two-part tariff A situation in which consumers pay one price (or tariff) for the right to buy as much of a related good as they want at a second price.

The Walt Disney Company is in a position to use a two-part tariff by charging consumers for admission to Walt Disney World or Disneyland and also charging them to use the rides in the parks. As mentioned at the beginning of this chapter, at one time, the admission price to Disneyland was low, but people had to purchase tickets to go on the rides. Today, you must pay a high price for admission to Disneyland or Disney World, but the rides are free once you're in the park. Figure 15-5 helps us understand which of these pricing strategies is more profitable for Disney. The numbers in the figure are simplified to make the calculations easier.

Once visitors are inside the park, Disney is in the position of a monopolist—no other firm is operating rides in Disney World. So, we can draw panel (a) in Figure 15-5 to represent the market for rides at Disney World. This graph looks like the standard monopoly graph from Chapter 14. (Note that the marginal cost of another rider is quite low. We can assume that it is a constant $2 and equal to the average cost.) It seems obvious—but it will turn out to be wrong!—that Disney should determine the profit-maximizing quantity of ride tickets by setting marginal revenue equal to marginal cost. In this case, that would lead to 20,000 ride tickets sold per day at a price of $26 per ride. Disney's profit from selling *ride tickets* is shown by the area of the light-green rectangle, *B*. It equals the difference between the $26 price and the average cost of $2, multiplied by the 20,000 tickets sold, or ($26 − $2) × 20,000 = $480,000. Disney also has a second source of profit from selling *admission tickets* to the park. Given the $26 price for ride tickets, what price would Disney be able to charge for admission tickets?

Let's assume the following for simplicity: The only reason people want admission to Disney World is to go on the rides, all consumers have the same individual demand curve for rides, and Disney knows what this demand curve is. This last assumption allows Disney to be able to practice perfect price discrimination. More realistic assumptions would make the outcome of the analysis somewhat different but would not affect

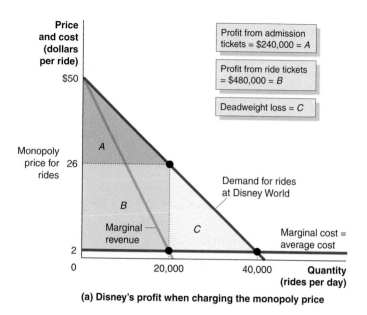

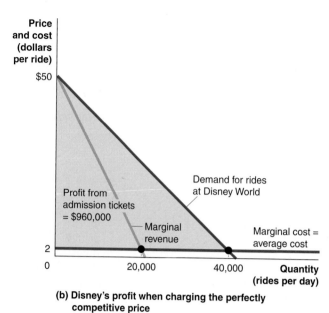

Figure 15-5 | A Two-Part Tariff at Disney World

In panel (a), Disney charges the monopoly price of $26 per ride ticket and sells 20,000 ride tickets. Its profit from *ride tickets* is shown by the area of the light-green rectangle, B, $480,000. If Disney is in the position of knowing every consumer's willingness to pay, it can also charge a price for *admission tickets* that would result in the total amount paid for admission tickets being equal to total consumer surplus from the rides. Total consumer surplus from the rides equals the area of the dark-green triangle, A, or $240,000. So, when charging the monopoly price, Disney's total profit equals $480,000 + $240,000, or $720,000. In panel (b), Disney charges the perfectly competitive price of $2, where marginal revenue equals marginal cost, and sells 40,000 ride tickets. At the lower ride ticket price, Disney can charge a higher price for admission tickets, which will increase its total profits from operating the park to the area of the light-green triangle, or $960,000.

the main point of how Disney uses a two-part tariff to increase its profits. With these assumptions, we can use the concept of consumer surplus to calculate the maximum total amount consumers would be willing to pay for admission. Remember that consumer surplus is equal to the area below the demand curve and above the price line, shown by the dark-green triangle, A, in panel (a). The area represents the benefit to buyers from consuming the product. In this case, consumers would not be willing to pay more for admission to the park than the consumer surplus they receive from the rides. In panel (a) of Figure 15-5, the total consumer surplus when Disney charges a price of $26 per ride is $240,000. (This number is easy to calculate if you remember that the formula for the area of a triangle is ½ × base × height, or ½ × 20,000 × $24.) Disney can set the price of admission tickets so that the *total* amount spent by buyers would be $240,000. In other words, Disney can set the price of admission to capture the entire consumer surplus from the rides. So, Disney's total profit from Disney World would be the $240,000 it receives from admission tickets plus the $480,000 in profit from the rides, or $720,000 per day.

Is this the most profit Disney can earn from selling admission tickets and ride tickets? The answer is "no." The key to seeing why is to notice that *the lower the price Disney charges for ride tickets, the higher the price it can charge for admission tickets.* Lower-priced ride tickets increase consumer surplus from the rides and, therefore, increase the willingness of buyers to pay a higher price for admission tickets. In panel (b) of Figure 15-5, we assume that Disney acts as it would in a perfectly competitive market and charges a price for ride tickets that is equal to marginal cost, or $2. Charging this price increases consumer surplus—*and* the maximum total amount that Disney can charge for admission tickets—from $240,000 to $960,000. (Once again, we use the formula for the area of a triangle to calculate the light-green area in panel (b): ½ × 40,000 × 48 × $960,000.) Disney's profits from the rides will decline to

TABLE 15-2		MONOPOLY PRICE FOR RIDES	COMPETITIVE PRICE FOR RIDES
Disney's Profits per Day from Different Pricing Strategies	PROFITS FROM ADMISSION TICKETS	$240,000	$960,000
	PROFITS FROM RIDE TICKETS	480,000	0
	TOTAL PROFIT	720,000	960,000

zero because it is now charging a price equal to average cost, *but its total profit from Disney World will rise from $720,000 per day to $960,000.* Table 15-2 summarizes this result.

What is the source of Disney's increased profit from charging a price equal to marginal cost? The answer is that Disney has converted what was deadweight loss when the monopoly price was charged—the area of triangle *C* in panel (a)—into consumer surplus. It then turns this consumer surplus into profit by increasing the price of admission tickets.

It is important to note the following about the outcome of a firm using an optimal two-part tariff:

1 Because price equals marginal cost at the level of output supplied, the outcome is economically efficient.

2 All of consumer surplus is transformed into profit.

Notice that, in effect, Disney is practicing perfect price discrimination. As we noted in our discussion of perfect price discrimination on page 515, Disney's use of a two-part tariff has increased the amount of the product—in this case, rides at Disney World—consumers are able to purchase, but has eliminated consumer surplus. Although it may seem paradoxical, consumer surplus was actually higher when consumers were being charged the monopoly price for the rides. The solution to the paradox is that although consumers pay a lower price for the rides when Disney employs a two-part tariff, the overall amount they pay to be at Disney World increases.

Disney actually does follow the profit-maximizing strategy of charging a high price for admission to the park and a very low price—zero—for the rides. It seems that Disney could increase its profits by raising the price for the rides from zero to the marginal cost of the rides. But the marginal cost is so low that it would not be worth the expense of printing ride tickets and hiring additional workers to sell the tickets and collect them at each ride. Finally, note that because the demand curves of Disney's customers are not all the same, and because Disney does not actually know precisely what these demand curves are, Disney is not able to convert all of consumer surplus into profit.

The rides at Disney World are free—once you have paid to get into the park.

Economics in YOUR Life!

>> Continued from page 507

At the beginning of the chapter, we asked you to think about what you pay for a movie ticket and what people in other age groups pay. A movie theater will try to charge different prices to different consumers based on their willingness to pay. If you have two otherwise identical people, one a student and one not, you might assume that the student has less income, and thus a lower willingness to pay, than the non-student, and the movie theater would like to charge the student a lower price. The movie theater employee can ask to see a student ID to ensure that the theater is giving the discount to a student.

But why don't theaters practice price discrimination at the concession stand? It is likely that a student will also have a lower willingness to pay for popcorn, and the theater can check for a student ID at the time of purchase, but unlike the case of the entry ticket, the theater would have a hard time preventing the student from giving the popcorn to a non-student once inside the theater. Since it is easier to limit resale in movie admissions, we often see different prices for different groups. Since it is difficult to limit resale of popcorn and other movie concessions, all groups will typically pay the same price.

Conclusion

Firms in perfectly competitive industries must sell their products at the market price. For firms in other industries—which means, of course, the vast majority of firms—pricing is an important part of the strategy used to maximize profits. We have seen in this chapter, for example, that if firms can successfully segment their customers into different groups on the basis of willingness to pay, they can increase their profits by charging different segments different prices.

Read *An Inside Look* on the next page for a discussion of why colleges do not charge all students the same tuition.

College Tuition: One Price Does Not Fit All

WALL STREET JOURNAL, OCTOBER 11, 2006

Amid Rising Costs and Criticism, Some Colleges Cut Back Merit Aid

As colleges and universities consider whether to join Harvard and Princeton in abandoning early-admissions programs, some are also trying to roll back another popular recruiting tool: merit aid.

Colleges offer merit aid, which is typically awarded on the basis of grades, class rank and test scores, to students who ordinarily wouldn't qualify for financial help. Because merit aid can be a deciding factor in these students' choice of schools, it has become a major weapon in the bidding wars among colleges for high achievers who can help boost their national rankings. . . .

But the cost of such programs has mounted as their use has expanded and tuition has risen. Meanwhile, criticism has grown that they disproportionately benefit students from wealthier communities with better school systems, siphoning resources away from lower-income students with greater financial need. In some cases, students who qualify for neither need- nor merit-based aid end up paying even more to cover a college's costs. As a result, a small but growing number of schools and university systems are trying to reduce their merit offerings. The University of Florida recently slashed the value of its four-year scholarships for in-state scholars who qualified under the National Merit program by 79% to a total of $5,000. . . .

Allegheny College, in Meadville, Pa., where annual tuition and fees total about $28,300, gave its $15,000-a-year merit scholarships to 15% of this year's freshmen, down from about 33% three years ago. To free up funding for more need-based aid, Rhode Island's Providence College scuttled its smaller merit scholarships and raised the eligibility requirements for its larger ones: A grade-point average of about 3.7 on a 4.0 scale used to be good enough; now it takes around a 3.83. Providence's merit scholarships can run as high as full tuition, which is $26,780 this year. . . .

Efforts to cut back on merit aid also risk setting off a backlash from middle- and upper-income families who don't qualify for need-based aid but are finding the rising cost of a college to be a daunting stretch. "Family income isn't keeping pace with the things driving higher-education costs," says Jim Scannell, a partner at Scannell & Kurz Inc., a Pittsford, N.Y., consulting firm that works with colleges on enrollment issues.

Some high-achieving applicants target schools that have merit-aid programs, hoping to win a tuition break. With tuition and fees at many private schools surpassing $40,000 a year, small private liberal-arts colleges that lack the cachet of the Ivy League but whose tuitions far exceed those of state colleges could have the most to lose from any cutbacks in merit aid. . . .

Many institutions have no intention of cutting back on merit aid. Baylor University, a Baptist college in Waco, Texas, recently increased the value of the merit awards it gives to all incoming freshmen who score at least 1,300 points out of a possible 1,600 on SAT reading and math exams. The awards, which rise in value in tandem with a student's SAT scores, range from $2,000 to $4,000 a year. . . .

For some smaller schools, merit aid is less about boosting rankings than adding revenue by swelling enrollment. In most cases, students are still paying substantial sums for tuition even after receiving a scholarship. "I think in many cases it's misleading to call it merit aid," says Michael McPherson, president of the Spencer Foundation, a Chicago-based educational research group. "It's 'get 'em in the door' aid."

At private Wilkes University, Wilkes Barre, Pa., where tuition and fees are about $23,000 a year, only 81 of this year's 580 incoming freshmen didn't get merit aid. To land a scholarship, which starts at $6,000 a year, students have to have graduated in the top half of their high-school class and to have scored a combined total of at least a 900 on the SAT reading and math exams, not much above average. . . .

Although families with earnings of $100,000 or more might qualify for need-based aid, depending on factors such as how many college-aged children they have, college administrators say many such families usually don't bother to apply for need-based aid because they presume they won't get it. . . .

Source: Robert Tomsho, "Amid Rising Costs and Criticism, Some Colleges Cut Back Merit Aid," *Wall Street Journal*, October 11, 2006.

Key Points in the Article

This article highlights a change in the scholarships offered by universities and colleges. In particular, colleges are reducing merit aid and increasing the amount of need-based financial aid. Because many students receive scholarships and other types of aid, they pay a variety of actual tuition prices, which may be very different from the posted tuition price.

Analyzing the News

(a) High-achieving students are typically offered admission by a number of different universities, many of which are good substitutes for each other. As a result, talented high school seniors would have a relatively elastic demand for attending any particular college. Consumers with more elastic demands tend to pay lower prices for goods.

(b) Need-based aid can be thought of as a form of price discrimination, separating the market into high-income students (with high demand) and low-income students (with low demand). Panel (a) in the figure below shows two demand curves for college education: one for high-income students and the other for low-income students. Notice that for any quantity, high-income students have a higher willingness to pay for education. So for Q_1 of each type of student to be enrolled, the school could charge P_1 dollars to high-income students but only P_2 dollars to low-income students. Need-based aid makes it possible to charge a lower price to low-income students without changing the tuition price charged to high-income students. You can see in panel (a) that if the school had to charge P_1 to both types of students, it would still enroll Q_1 high-income students but only Q_2 low-income students, so it would not maximize revenue.

(c) An additional student adds very little to the cost of running a college or university. As a result, offering merit aid is usually not the difference between a student paying full tuition or reduced tuition; it is the difference between a student enrolling and paying some tuition or not enrolling and paying $0 to the school. Panel (b) in the figure below shows the demand curve for enrollment at a school. Notice that in this example as the price drops from P_1 to P_2, there is a large increase in quantity, from Q_1 to Q_2 students. If the demand for education at a particular college is elastic, as it likely is, tuition revenues will increase as the school lowers its price. At the higher price, P_1, with Q_1 students, revenue is shown as areas $A + B$. If tuition drops, revenue at price P_2 with Q_2 students will be areas $B + C$. The school will be better off if the increased revenue from additional students is (area C) greater than the lost revenue from the lower price now charged to the original Q_1 students (area A). In this example, area C is greater than area A, so the college's revenues increase when it cuts its tuition.

Thinking Critically

1. If lowering the tuition to some students increases a university's revenue, why don't universities just lower the tuition for everyone?

2. If customers with less elastic demands will pay more for a product when firms can price discriminate, would you expect to see freshmen or seniors pay higher tuition at your college? How might a college charge different classes different levels of tuition?

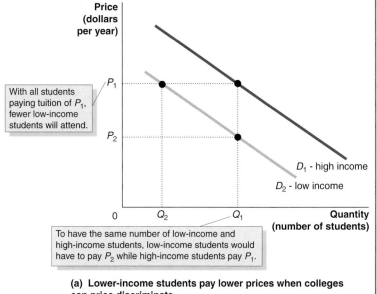

With all students paying tuition of P_1, fewer low-income students will attend.

To have the same number of low-income and high-income students, low-income students would have to pay P_2 while high-income students pay P_1.

(a) Lower-income students pay lower prices when colleges can price discriminate.

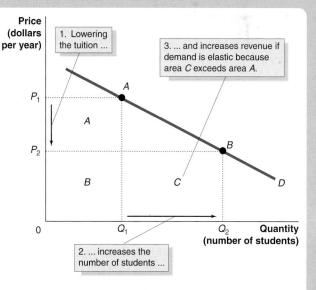

1. Lowering the tuition ...

3. ... and increases revenue if demand is elastic because area C exceeds area A.

2. ... increases the number of students ...

(b) Demand and revenue at different tuition prices.

College tuition strategies.

Key Terms

Price discrimination, p. 510   Two-part tariff, p. 522

Transactions costs, p. 508

15.1 LEARNING OBJECTIVE   15.1 | Define the law of one price and explain the role of arbitrage, **pages 508–510.**

Pricing Strategy, the Law of One Price, and Arbitrage

Summary

According to the *law of one price*, identical products should sell for the same price everywhere. If a product sells for different prices, it will be possible to make a profit through *arbitrage*: buying a product at a low price and reselling it at a high price. The law of one price will hold as long as arbitrage is possible. Arbitrage is sometimes blocked by high **transactions costs**, which are the costs in time and other resources incurred to carry out an exchange, or because the product cannot be resold. Another apparent exception to the law of one price occurs when companies offset the higher price they charge for a product by providing superior or more reliable service to customers.

myeconlab Visit www.myeconlab.com to complete these exercises *Get Ahead of the Curve* online and get instant feedback.

Review Questions

1.1 What is the law of one price? What is arbitrage?

1.2 Does a product always have to sell for the same price everywhere? Briefly explain.

Problems and Applications

1.3 A newspaper article contains the following description:

> For years, shoppers from New York City have played a game of retail arbitrage, traveling to the many malls in northern New Jersey, a state where there is no tax on clothing and shoes. Even accounting for tolls, gas and time, shoppers could save money by visiting the Westfield Garden State Plaza and other malls here, escaping the 8.375 percent sales tax they must pay in New York City on clothing and shoes that cost more than $110 per item.

Does this article use the word *arbitrage* correctly? Briefly explain.

Source: Ken Belson and Nate Schweber, "Sales Tax Cut in City May Dim Allure of Stores Across Hudson," *New York Times*, January 18, 2007.

1.4 The following table contains the actual prices charged by four Web sites for a DVD of the movie *Borat* in March 2007.

Amazon.com	$15.99
Wal-Mart	$15.87
DeepDiscount	$17.21
CDUniverse	$22.19

Briefly explain whether the information in this table contradicts the law of one price.

1.5 (Related to *Solved Problem 15-1* on page 509) Suppose California has many apple trees, and the price of apples there is low. Nevada has few apple trees, and the price of apples there is high. Abner buys low-priced California apples and ships them to Nevada, where he resells them at a high price. Is Abner exploiting Nevada consumers by doing this? Is he likely to earn economic profits in the long run? Briefly explain.

1.6 (Related to *Solved Problem 15-1* on page 509) Suspicions of arbitrage have a long history. For example, Valerian of Cimiez, a Catholic bishop who lived during the fifth century, wrote, "When something is bought cheaply only so it can be retailed dearly, doing business always means cheating." What might Valerian think of eBay? Do you agree with his conclusion? Explain.

Source for quote: Michael McCormick, *The Origins of the European Economy: Communications and Commerce, A.D. 300–900*, New York: Cambridge University Press, 2001, p. 85.

>> End Learning Objective 15.1

Price Discrimination: Charging Different Prices for the Same Product

Summary

Price discrimination occurs if a firm charges different prices for the same product when the price differences are not due to differences in cost. Three requirements must be met for a firm to successfully price discriminate: (1) A firm must possess market power. (2) Some consumers must have a greater willingness to pay for the product than other consumers, and firms must be able to know what customers are willing to pay. (3) Firms must be able to divide up—or segment—the market for the product so that consumers who buy the product at a low price cannot resell it a high price. In the case of *perfect price discrimination*, each consumer pays a price equal to the consumer's willingness to pay.

Review Questions

2.1   What is price discrimination? Under what circumstances can a firm successfully practice price discrimination?

2.2   During a particular week, America West charged $218 for a round-trip ticket on a flight from New York to San Francisco, provided that the ticket was purchased at least 10 days in advance and the ticket buyer was willing to stay over a Saturday night. If the buyer did not meet these conditions, the price for the ticket was $1,361. Why does America West use this pricing strategy?

2.3   What is yield management? Give an example of a firm using yield management to increase profits.

2.4   What is perfect price discrimination? Is it likely to ever occur? Explain. Is perfect price discrimination economically efficient? Explain.

2.5   Is it possible to price discriminate across time? Briefly explain.

Problems and Applications

2.6   An article on the AMC movie theater chain contained the following:

In July, [AMC] announced plans to offer steeply discounted movie tickets to shows on Friday, Saturday and Sunday mornings. "Seventy-five percent of the revenue comes from the weekend," Mr. Brown [AMC's CEO] said. His recent initiatives

are attempts to address the question: "Is there a way with price that you can create opportunity, a new market?"

Why would it be profitable for AMC to sell "steeply discounted" movie tickets for movies being shown on weekend mornings? Wouldn't the firm's revenues be higher if it charged the regular—higher—price for these showings? Briefly explain.

Source: Kate Kelly, "Box-Office Bounty Stirs Theater Deals," *Wall Street Journal,* August 10, 2006, p. C1.

2.7   According to an article in the *Wall Street Journal,* the average price of Ford Explorers sold in Dallas, Texas, was $30,142. During the same period, the average price of identically equipped Explorers in Oklahoma was only $27,939. Briefly explain whether this is an example of price discrimination.

Source: Karen Lundegaard, "How to Buy Your Next Car: First, Get a Plane Ticket," *Wall Street Journal,* April 30, 2002.

2.8   An article on how prices in South Bend, Indiana, rise during Notre Dame home football games contained the following:

[Notre Dame football fan Anthony] Gallis ended up reserving a suite at a Hampton Inn and Suites in South Bend, which normally goes for $129 a night, for $400 a night, with a three-night minimum. "It's just insane," says the 42-year-old owner of a State Farm Insurance agency back in Pennsylvania. . . . Indeed, rates for many of the 4,015 hotel rooms in the South Bend area are skyrocketing. Two weeks before the start of the season, the Comfort Suites here was asking $245 a night, with a two-night minimum, for the Penn State weekend. That's up from $109 a night on non-football weekends. For the Sept. 16 game against the University of Michigan, the South Bend Marriott is charging $649 a night for a double room. That's more than the price of a room at the Waldorf-Astoria Hotel in New York. The Marriott's regular weekend price is $149 a night.

Is this an example of price discrimination? Briefly explain.

Source: Ilan Brat, "Notre Dame Football Introduces Its Fans to Inflationary Spiral, *Wall Street Journal,* September 7, 2006, p. A1.

2.9   Political columnist Michael Kinsley writes, "The infuriating [airline] rules about Saturday night stayovers and so on are a crude alternative to administering truth serum and asking, 'So how much are you really willing to pay?'" Would a truth serum—or some other way of knowing how much people would be willing to pay for an airline ticket—really be all the airlines need to price discriminate? Briefly explain.

Source: Michael Kinsley, "Consuming Gets More Complicated," *Slate*, November 21, 2001.

2.10 In a column in the *Wall Street Journal*, Walter Mossberg offered the following opinion:

> There's a sucker in the software business today, and if you're in an average family with a couple of PCs, that sucker is you. . . . Families constitute the only significant customer group not getting a discount on [Microsoft] Office when upgrading multiple PCs. Big corporations, organizations and government agencies get a discount, called a "site license." College students get a discount. Small and medium-size businesses get a discount. But not families.

Why might Microsoft charge families a higher price for Office than it charges the other groups Mossberg mentions?

Source: Walter Mossberg, "Microsoft Should Offer Families a Deal with Its Office Program," *Wall Street Journal*, July 18, 2002.

2.11 According to an article in the *Economist*, "The PS3 [PlayStation 3] is available in two configurations, costing $500 and $600 in America, and ¥50,000 ($425) and ¥60,000 ($510) in Japan." Based on this information, does Sony consider the demand of U.S. consumers for the PS3 to be more elastic or less elastic than the demand of Japanese consumers? Briefly explain.

Source: "Playing a Long Game," *Economist*, November 16, 2006.

2.12 **(Related to *Solved Problem 15-2* on page 512)** Use the graphs at the bottom of the page to answer the following questions.
   a. If the firm wants to maximize profits, what price will it charge in Market 1, and what quantity will it sell?
   b. If the firm wants to maximize profits, what price will it charge in Market 2, and what quantity will it sell?

2.13 When a firm offers a rebate on a product, the buyer normally has to fill out a form and mail it in to receive a rebate check in the mail. A financial columnist argues:

> When a manufacturer offers a rebate, you needn't be too suspicious. The manufacturer wants to lower the price temporarily (to move an old product or combat a competitor's new low price), but doesn't have faith that the retailer will pass on the savings.

But suppose that a manufacturer wants to engage in price discrimination. Would offering rebates be a way of doing this? Briefly explain.

Source: Carol Vinzant, "The Great Rebate Scam," *Slate*, June 10, 2003.

2.14 **(Related to the *Making the Connection* on page 515)** Assume that the marginal cost of admitting one more student is constant for every university. Also assume that the demand for places in the freshmen class is downward sloping at every university. Now suppose that the public becomes upset that universities charge different prices to different students. Responding to these concerns, the federal government requires universities to charge the same price to each student. Who would gain and who would lose?

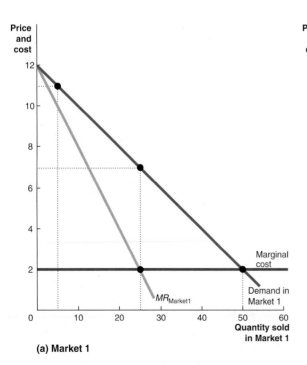

(a) Market 1

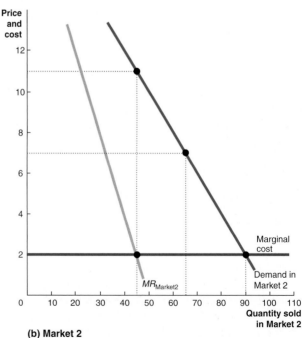

(b) Market 2

2.15 (Related to the *Chapter Opener* on page 506) Why does Walt Disney World charge a lower admission price for children aged 3 to 9 than for adults? Why does it categorize a 10-year-old as an adult for this purpose? Why does it admit children under 3 for free? Why does it charge residents of Florida a lower price than residents of other states?

2.16 Are supermarket coupons a form of price discrimination? Briefly explain why or why not.

2.17 (Related to the *Making the Connection* on page 518) Netflix offers subscriptions. Some have a higher price and allow more—or unlimited—movies to be rented per month. Others have a lower price and allow fewer movies to be rented per month. Is Netflix practicing price discrimination by offering these different subscriptions? Briefly explain.

2.18 (Related to the *Don't Let This Happen to You!* on page 510) Beginning in 2002, a state law in California made it illegal for businesses to charge men and women different prices for dry cleaning, laundry, tailoring, or hair grooming. The state legislator who proposed the law did so after a dry cleaner charged her more to have her shirts dry-cleaned than to have her husband's shirts dry-cleaned: "They charged me $1.50 for each of his, and he wears an extra large. They charged $3.50 for each of mine, and I wear a small." According to a newspaper article, "the dry cleaning proprietor told her that the price difference stemmed from the need for hand ironing her shirts because automatic presses are not made to handle small-sized women's garments."

a. Was the dry cleaner practicing price discrimination, as defined in this chapter? Briefly explain.
b. Do you support laws like this one? Briefly explain.

Source: Harry Brooks, "Law Mandates Equality in Dry Cleaning, Hair Styling," *North County (California) Times*, October 7, 2001.

2.19 Eric Orkin, the president of Opus 2 Revenue Technologies, Inc., which sells yield management systems to hotels, argues, "The price-sensitive person gets what he wants as long as he's willing to have some flexibility." Why would a yield management system for hotels result in lower prices for "price-sensitive" customers than the alternative of charging one price for all customers? Why would a price-sensitive person need to be "flexible" to receive a lower price?

Source: Neal Templin, "Property Report: Your Room Costs $250 . . . No! $200 . . . No . . . ," *Wall Street Journal*, May 5, 1999.

2.20 Draw a graph that shows producer surplus, consumer surplus, and deadweight loss (if any) in a market where the seller practices perfect price discrimination. Profit-maximizing firms select an output at which marginal cost equals marginal revenue. Where is the marginal revenue curve in this graph?

>> **End Learning Objective 15.2**

15.3 LEARNING OBJECTIVE | 15.3 | Explain how some firms increase their profits through the use of odd pricing, cost-plus pricing, and two-part tariffs, **pages 519–524.**

Other Pricing Strategies

Summary

In addition to price discrimination, firms also use odd pricing, cost-plus pricing, and two-part tariffs as pricing strategies. Firms use *odd pricing*—for example, charging $1.99 rather than $2.00—because consumers tend to buy more at odd prices than would be predicted from estimated demand curves. With *cost-plus pricing*, firms set the price for a product by adding a percentage markup to average cost. Cost-plus pricing may be a good way to come close to the profit-maximizing price when marginal revenue or marginal cost is difficult to measure. Some firms can require consumers to pay an initial fee for the right to buy their product and an additional fee for each unit of the product purchased. Economists refer to this situation as a **two-part tariff**. Sam's Club, cell phone companies, and many golf and tennis clubs use two-part tariffs in pricing their products.

 Visit www.myeconlab.com to complete these exercises online and get instant feedback.

Review Questions

3.1 What is odd pricing?

3.2 What is cost-plus pricing? Is using cost-plus pricing consistent with a firm maximizing profits?

3.3 Give an example of a firm using a two-part tariff as part of its pricing strategy.

3.4 Why did the Walt Disney Company switch from charging for admission to Disneyland and charging for the rides to charging for admission and *not* charging for the rides?

Problems and Applications

3.5 One leading explanation for odd pricing is that it allows firms to trick buyers into the illusion that they're paying less than they really are. If this is true, in what types of markets and among what groups of consumers would you be mostly likely to find odd pricing? Should the government ban this practice and force companies to round up their prices to the nearest dollar?

3.6 Emerson Electric Company of St. Louis makes industrial equipment. Jerry Bernstein, the director of its price improvement team, describes how the company previously determined the prices of its products: "You developed a product, worked at the costs, and said, 'I need to make X [profit],' and you marked it up accordingly." Using this approach, Emerson arrived at a cost of $2,650 for a compact sensor used in pharmaceutical factories. In recent years, Emerson has moved away from a policy of cost-plus pricing, so it ended up charging $3,150, rather than $2,650, for the sensor. Discuss the factors that would lead Emerson to charge a price higher than the cost-plus price.

Source: Timothy Aeppel, "Amid Weak Inflation, Firms Turn Creative to Boost Prices," *Wall Street Journal*, September 18, 2002.

3.7 An article in the *Wall Street Journal* gives the following explanation of how products were traditionally priced at Parker-Hannifin Corporation:

> For as long as anyone at the 89-year-old company could recall, Parker used the same simple formula to determine prices of its 800,000 parts—from heat-resistant seals for jet engines to steel valves that hoist buckets on cherry pickers. Company managers would calculate how much it cost to make and deliver each product and add a flat percentage on top, usually aiming for about 35%. Many managers liked the method because it was straightforward. . . .

Is it likely that this system of pricing maximized the firm's profits? Briefly explain.

Source: Timothy Aeppel, "Changing the Formula: Seeking Perfect Prices, CEO Tears Up the Rules," *Wall Street Journal*, March 27, 2007, p. A1.

3.8 **(Related to the *Making the Connection* on page 520)** Would you expect a publishing company to use a strict cost-plus pricing system for all of its books? How might you find some indication whether a publishing company actually was using cost-pull pricing for all of its books?

3.9 Some professional sports teams charge fans a one-time lump sum for a "personal seat license." The personal seat license allows a fan the right to buy season tickets each year. No one without a personal seat license can buy season tickets. After the original purchase from the team, the personal seat licenses usually can be bought and sold by fans—whoever owns the seat license in a given year can buy season tickets—but the team does not earn any additional revenue from this buying and selling. Suppose a new sports stadium has been built, and the team is trying to decide on the price to charge for season tickets.

    a. Will the team make more profit from the combination of selling personal seat licenses and season tickets if it keeps the prices of the season tickets low or if it charges the monopoly price? Briefly explain.

    b. After the first year, is the team's strategy for pricing season tickets likely to change?

    c. Will it make a difference in the team's pricing strategy for season tickets if all the personal seat licenses are sold in the first year?

3.10 During the nineteenth century, the U.S. Congress encouraged railroad companies to build transcontinental railways across the Great Plains by giving them land grants. At that time, the federal government owned most of the land on the Great Plains. The land grants consisted of the land on which the railway was built and alternating sections of 1 square mile each on either side of the railway to a distance of 6 to 40 miles, depending on the location. The railroad companies were free to sell this land to farmers or anyone else who wanted to buy it. The process of selling the land took decades. Some economic historians have argued that the railroad companies charged lower prices to ship freight because they owned so much land along the tracks. Briefly explain the reasoning of these economic historians.

3.11 Thomas Kinnaman, an economist at Bucknell University, has analyzed the pricing of garbage collection:

> Setting the appropriate fee for garbage collection can be tricky when there are both fixed and marginal costs of garbage collection. . . . A curbside price set equal to the average total cost of collection would have high garbage generators partially subsidizing the fixed costs of low garbage generators. For example, if the time that a truck idles outside a one-can household and a two-can household is the same, and the fees are set to cover the total cost of garbage collection, then the two-can household paying twice that of the one-can household has subsidized a portion of the collection costs of the one-can household.

Briefly explain how a city might solve this pricing problem by using a two-part tariff in setting the garbage collection fees households are charged.

Source: Thomas C. Kinnaman, "Examining the Justification for Residential Recycling," *Journal of Economic Perspectives*, Vol. 20, No. 4, Fall 2006, p. 224.

>> **End Learning Objective 15.3**

Chapter 16

The **Markets** for **Labor** and **Other Factors** of **Production**

Why Are the Chicago Cubs Paying Alfonso Soriano $18 Million per Year?

Few businesses arouse in their customers the level of passion that sports teams do. Unlike most other industries, the sports industry has an entire section devoted to it in most newspapers. Jerry Jones made a fortune in the oil and gas exploration business in Oklahoma, but few people knew who he was until he bought the Dallas Cowboys football team. Of course, the best-known people in sports are not the owners of teams but some of their employees—the players.

Sports fans admire the skills of star athletes, but many are also fascinated by their high salaries. How is it, fans often wonder, that some athletes are paid salaries in the millions of dollars "just for playing a game"? Many baseball fans also wonder why a few teams, such as the New York Yankees, Boston Red Sox, and Chicago Cubs, are able to pay higher salaries than other teams. For example, before the 2007 baseball season, the Chicago Cubs signed Alfonso Soriano to a contract worth an average of $18 million per season. This represented a significant raise from the $10 million the Washington Nationals, his previous team, had paid him the year before.

The University of Illinois, Chicago pays professors on its faculty an average salary of $80,000. Why are the Cubs willing to pay a baseball player so much more than the University of Illinois, Chicago is willing to pay a professor?

The key to answering these questions is to understand that wages are determined in the labor market by the demand and supply of labor, just as the price of apples is determined by the demand and supply of apples and the price of DVDs is determined by the demand and supply of DVDs. In Chapter 3, we developed a model for analyzing the demand and supply of goods and services. We will use some of the same concepts in this chapter to analyze the demand and supply of labor and other factors of production. But there are important ways in which the markets for factors of production are not like markets for goods. The most obvious difference is that in factor markets, firms are demanders, and households are suppliers.

Another difference between the labor market and the markets for goods and services is that concepts of fairness arise more frequently in labor markets. When an athlete like Alfonso Soriano signs a contract for millions of dollars, people often wonder "Why should someone playing a game get paid so much more than teachers, nurses, and other people doing

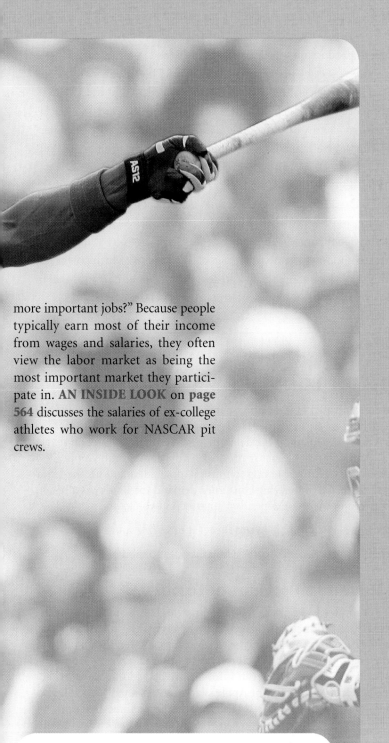

more important jobs?" Because people typically earn most of their income from wages and salaries, they often view the labor market as being the most important market they participate in. **AN INSIDE LOOK** on **page 564** discusses the salaries of ex-college athletes who work for NASCAR pit crews.

LEARNING Objectives

After studying this chapter, you should be able to:

16.1 Explain how firms choose the **profit-maximizing quantity of labor** to employ, page 536.

16.2 Explain how people choose the quantity of **labor** to **supply**, page 540.

16.3 Explain how **equilibrium wages** are determined in labor markets, page 543.

16.4 Use demand and supply analysis to explain how **compensating differentials**, **discrimination**, and **labor unions** cause wages to differ, page 548.

16.5 Discuss the role **personnel economics** can play in helping firms deal with human resources issues, page 557.

16.6 Show how equilibrium prices are determined in the markets for **capital** and **natural resources**, page 560.

Economics in YOUR Life!

Why Is It So Hard to Get a Raise?

Imagine that you have worked for a local sandwich shop for over a year and are preparing to ask for a raise. You might tell the manager that you are a good employee, with a good attitude and work ethic. You might also explain that you have learned more about your job and are now able to make sandwiches quicker, track inventory more accurately, and work the cash register more effectively than when you were first hired. Will this be enough to convince your manager to give you a raise? How can you convince your manager that you are worth more money than you are currently being paid? As you read this chapter, see if you can answer these questions. You can check your answers against those we provide at the end of the chapter. >> Continued on page 563

Factors of production Labor, capital, natural resources, and other inputs used to produce goods and services.

Firms use **factors of production**—such as labor, capital, and natural resources—to produce goods and services. For example, the Chicago Cubs use labor (baseball players), capital (Wrigley Field), and natural resources (the land on which Wrigley Field sits) to produce baseball games. In this chapter, we will explore how firms choose the profit-maximizing quantity of labor and other factors of production. The interaction between firm demand for labor and household supply of labor determines the equilibrium wage rate.

Because there are many different types of labor, there are many different labor markets. The equilibrium wage in the market for baseball players is much higher than the equilibrium wage in the market for college professors. We will explore why this is true. We will also explore how factors such as discrimination, unions, and compensation for dangerous or unpleasant jobs help explain differences among wages. We will then look at *personnel economics*, which is concerned with how firms can use economic analysis to design their employee compensation plans. Finally, we will analyze the markets for other factors of production.

16.1 LEARNING OBJECTIVE

16.1 │ Explain how firms choose the profit-maximizing quantity of labor to employ.

The Demand for Labor

Up until now we have concentrated on consumer demand for final goods and services. The demand for labor is different from the demand for final goods and services because it is a *derived demand*. A **derived demand** is the demand for a factor of production that is based on the demand for the good the factor produces. You demand an Apple iPod because of the utility you receive from listening to music. Apple's demand for the labor to make iPods is derived from the underlying consumer demand for iPods. As a result, we can say that Apple's demand for labor depends primarily on two factors:

Derived demand The demand for a factor of production that is derived from the demand for the good the factor produces.

1   The additional iPods Apple will be able to produce if it hires one more worker

2   The additional revenue Apple receives from selling the additional iPods

The Marginal Revenue Product of Labor

Consider the following example. To keep the main point clear, let's assume that in the short run, Apple can increase production of iPods only by increasing the quantity of labor it employs. The table in Figure 16-1 shows the relationship between the quantity of workers Apple hires, the quantity of iPods it produces, the additional revenue from selling the additional iPods, and the additional profit from hiring each additional worker.

For simplicity, we are keeping the scale of Apple's factory very small. We will also assume that Apple is a perfect competitor both in the market for selling digital music players and in the market for hiring labor. This means that Apple is a *price taker* in both markets. Although this is not realistic, the basic analysis would not change if we assumed that Apple can affect the price of digital music players and the wage paid to workers. Given these assumptions, suppose that Apple can sell as many iPods as it wants at a price of $200 and can hire as many workers as it wants at a wage of $600 per week. Remember from Chapter 10 that the additional output a firm produces as a result of hiring one more worker is called the **marginal product of labor**. In the table, we calculate the marginal product of labor as the change in total output as each additional worker is hired. As we saw in Chapter 10, because of *the law of diminishing returns*, the marginal product of labor declines as a firm hires more workers.

Marginal product of labor The additional output a firm produces as a result of hiring one more worker.

When deciding how many workers to hire, a firm is not interested in how much *output* will increase as it hires another worker but in how much *revenue* will increase as it hires another worker. In other words, what matters is how much the firm's revenue will rise when it sells the additional output it can produce by hiring one more worker.

Number of Workers	Output of iPods per Week	Marginal Product of Labor (iPods per week)	Product Price	Marginal Revenue Product of Labor (dollars per week)	Wage (dollars per week)	Additional Profit from Hiring One More Worker (dollars per week)
L	Q	MP	P	MRP = P x MP	W	MRP – W
0	0	—	$200	—	$600	—
1	6	6	200	$1,200	600	$600
2	11	5	200	1,000	600	400
3	15	4	200	800	600	200
4	18	3	200	600	600	0
5	20	2	200	400	600	–200
6	21	1	200	200	600	–400

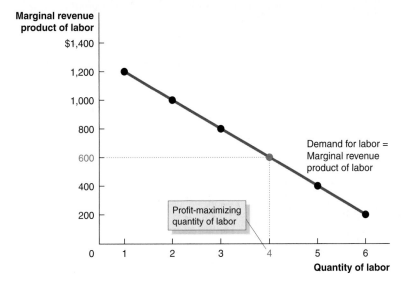

Figure 16-1

The Marginal Revenue Product of Labor and the Demand for Labor

The marginal revenue product of labor equals the marginal product of labor multiplied by the price of the good. The marginal revenue product curve slopes downward because diminishing returns cause the marginal product of labor to decline as more workers are hired. A firm maximizes profits by hiring workers up to the point where the wage equals the marginal revenue product of labor. The marginal revenue product of labor curve is the firm's demand curve for labor because it tells the firm the profit-maximizing quantity of workers to hire at each wage. For example, using the demand curve shown in this figure, if the wage is $600, the firm will hire 4 workers.

We can calculate this amount by multiplying the additional output produced by the product price. This amount is called the **marginal revenue product of labor** (*MRP*). For example, consider what happens if Apple increases the number of workers hired from 2 to 3. The table in Figure 16-1 shows that hiring the third worker allows Apple to increase its weekly output of iPods from 11 to 15, so the marginal product of labor is 4 iPods. The price of the iPods is $200, so the marginal revenue product of the third worker is 4 × $200, or $800. In other words, Apple adds $800 to its revenue as a result of hiring the third worker. In the graph, we plot the values of the marginal revenue product of labor at each quantity of labor.

To decide how many workers to hire, Apple must compare the additional revenue it earns from hiring another worker to the increase in its costs from paying that worker. The difference between the additional revenue and the additional cost is the additional profit (or loss) from hiring one more worker. This additional profit is shown in the last column of the table in Figure 16-1 and is calculated by subtracting the wage from the marginal revenue product of labor. As long as the marginal revenue product of labor is greater than the wage, Apple's profits are increasing, and it should continue to hire more workers. When the marginal revenue product of labor is less than the wage, Apple's profits are falling, and it should hire fewer workers. When the marginal revenue product of labor is equal to the wage, Apple has maximized its profits by hiring the optimal number of workers. The values in the table show that Apple should hire 4 workers. If the company hires a fifth worker, the marginal revenue product of $400 will be less than the wage of $600, and its profits will fall by $200. Table 16-1 summarizes the relationship between the marginal revenue product of labor and the wage.

Marginal revenue product of labor (*MRP*) The change in a firm's revenue as a result of hiring one more worker.

TABLE 16-1

The Relationship between the Marginal Revenue Product of Labor and the Wage

WHEN . . .	THEN THE FIRM . . .
MRP > W,	should hire more workers to increase profits.
MRP < W,	should hire fewer workers to increase profits.
MRP = W,	is hiring the optimal number of workers and is maximizing profits.

We can see from Figure 16-1 that if Apple has to pay a wage of $600 per week, it should hire 4 workers. If the wage were to rise to $1,000, then applying the rule that profits are maximized where the marginal revenue product of labor equals the wage, Apple should hire only 2 workers. Similarly, if the wage is only $400 per week, Apple should hire 5 workers. In fact, the marginal revenue product curve tells a firm how many workers it should hire at any wage rate. In other words, *the marginal revenue product of labor curve is the demand curve for labor.*

Solved Problem | 16-1

Hiring Decisions by a Firm That Is a Price Maker

We have assumed that Apple can sell as many iPods as it wants without having to cut the price. Recall from Chapter 11 that this is the case for firms in perfectly competitive markets. These firms are *price takers*. Suppose instead that a firm has market power and is a *price maker*, so that to increase sales, it must reduce the price.

Suppose Apple faces the situation shown in the following table. Fill in the blanks and then determine the profit-maximizing number of workers for Apple to hire. Briefly explain why hiring this number of workers is profit maximizing.

(1) QUANTITY OF LABOR	(2) OUTPUT OF iPODS PER WEEK	(3) MARGINAL PRODUCT OF LABOR	(4) PRODUCT PRICE	(5) TOTAL REVENUE	(6) MARGINAL REVENUE PRODUCT OF LABOR	(7) WAGE	(8) ADDITIONAL PROFIT FROM HIRING ONE ADDITIONAL WORKER
0	0	—	$200		—	$500	—
1	6	6	180			500	
2	11	5	160			500	
3	15	4	140			500	
4	18	3	120			500	
5	20	2	100			500	
6	21	1	80			500	

SOLVING THE PROBLEM:

Step 1: **Review the chapter material.** This problem is about determining the profit-maximizing quantity of labor for a firm to hire, so you may want to review the section "The Demand for Labor," which begins on page 536.

Step 2: **Fill in the blanks in the table.** As Apple hires more workers, it sells more iPods and earns more revenue. You can calculate how revenue increases by multiplying the number of iPods produced—shown in column 2—by the price—shown in column 4. Then you can calculate the marginal revenue product of labor as the change in revenue as each additional worker is hired. (Notice that in this case marginal revenue product is *not* calculated by multiplying the marginal product by the product price. Because Apple is a price maker, its marginal revenue from selling additional iPods is less than the price of iPods.) Finally, you can calculate the additional profit from hiring one more worker by subtracting the wage—shown in column 7—from each worker's marginal revenue product.

(1) QUANTITY OF LABOR	(2) OUTPUT OF iPODS PER WEEK	(3) MARGINAL PRODUCT OF LABOR	(4) PRODUCT PRICE	(5) TOTAL REVENUE	(6) MARGINAL REVENUE PRODUCT OF LABOR	(7) WAGE	(8) ADDITIONAL PROFIT FROM HIRING ONE ADDITIONAL WORKER
0	0	—	$200	$0	—	$500	—
1	6	6	180	1,080	$1,080	500	$580
2	11	5	160	1,760	680	500	180
3	15	4	140	2,100	340	500	−160
4	18	3	120	2,160	60	500	−440
5	20	2	100	2,000	−160	500	−660
6	21	1	80	1,680	−320	500	−820

Step 3: **Use the information in the table to determine the profit-maximizing quantity of workers to hire.** To determine the profit-maximizing quantity of workers to hire, you need to compare the marginal revenue product of labor with the wage. Column 8 does this by subtracting the wage from the marginal revenue product. As long as the values in column 8 are positive, the firm should continue to hire workers. The marginal revenue product of the second worker is $680, and the wage is $500, so column 8 shows that hiring the second worker will add $180 to Apple's profits. The marginal revenue product of the third worker is $340, and the wage is $500, so hiring the third worker would reduce Apple's profits by $160. Therefore, Apple will maximize profits by hiring 2 workers.

YOUR TURN: For more practice, do problem 1.5 on page 566 at the end of this chapter.   **>> End Solved Problem 16-1**

The Market Demand Curve for Labor

We can determine the market demand curve for labor in the same way we determine a market demand curve for a good. We saw in Chapter 9 that the market demand curve for a good is determined by adding up the quantity of the good demanded by each consumer at each price. Similarly, the market demand curve for labor is determined by adding up the quantity of labor demanded by each firm at each wage, holding constant all other variables that might affect the willingness of firms to hire workers.

Factors That Shift the Market Demand Curve for Labor

In constructing the demand curve for labor, we held constant all variables that would affect the willingness of firms to demand labor—except for the wage. An increase or a decrease in the wage causes *an increase or a decrease in the quantity of labor demanded*, which we show by a movement along the demand curve. If any variable other than the wage changes, the result is *an increase or a decrease in the demand for labor*, which we show by a shift of the demand curve. The five most important variables that cause the labor demand curve to shift are the following:

- *Increases in human capital.* **Human capital** represents the accumulated training and skills that workers possess. For example, a worker with a college education generally has more skills and is more productive than a worker who has only a high school diploma. If workers become more educated and are therefore able to produce more

Human capital The accumulated training and skills that workers possess.

output per day, the demand for their services will increase, shifting the labor demand curve to the right.

- *Changes in technology.* As new and better machinery and equipment are developed, workers become more productive. This effect causes the labor demand curve to shift to the right over time.

- *Changes in the price of the product.* The marginal revenue product of labor depends on the price a firm receives for its output. A higher price increases the marginal revenue product and shifts the labor demand curve to the right. A lower price shifts the labor demand curve to the left.

- *Changes in the quantity of other inputs.* Workers are able to produce more if they have more machinery and other inputs available to them. The marginal product of labor in the United States is higher than the marginal product of labor in other countries in large part because U.S. firms provide workers with more machinery and equipment. Over time, workers in the United States have had increasing amounts of other inputs available to them, and that has increased their productivity and caused the demand for labor to shift to the right.

- *Changes in the number of firms in the market.* If new firms enter the market, the demand for labor will shift to the right. If firms exit the market, the demand for labor will shift to the left. This effect is similar to that which increasing or decreasing the number of consumers in a market has on the demand for a good.

16.2 LEARNING OBJECTIVE

16.2 │ Explain how people choose the quantity of labor to supply.

The Supply of Labor

Having discussed the demand for labor, we can now consider the supply of labor. Of the many trade-offs each of us faces in life, one of the most important is how to divide up the 24 hours in the day between labor and leisure. Every hour spent watching television, walking on the beach, or in other forms of leisure is one less hour spent working. Because in devoting an hour to leisure, we give up an hour's earnings from working, the *opportunity cost* of leisure is the wage. The higher the wage we could earn working, the higher the opportunity cost of leisure. Therefore, as the wage increases, we tend to take less leisure and work more. This relationship explains why the labor supply curve for most people is upward sloping, as Figure 16-2 shows.

Figure 16-2

The Labor Supply Curve

As the wage increases, the opportunity cost of leisure increases, causing individuals to supply a greater quantity of labor. Therefore, the labor supply curve is upward sloping.

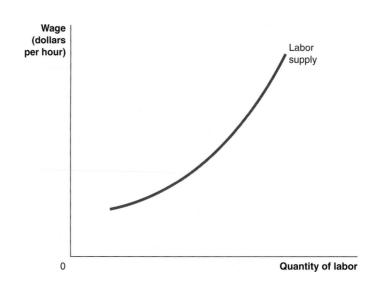

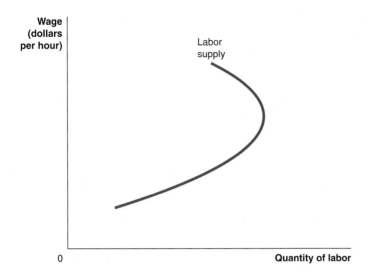

Figure 16-3

A Backward-Bending Labor Supply Curve

As the wage rises, a greater quantity of labor is usually supplied. As the wage climbs above a certain level, the individual is able to afford more leisure even though the opportunity cost of leisure is high. The result may be a smaller quantity of labor supplied.

Although we normally expect the labor supply curve for an individual to be upward sloping, it is possible that at very high wage levels, the supply curve of an individual might be *backward bending*, so that higher wages actually result in a *smaller* quantity of labor supplied, as shown in Figure 16-3. To understand why, recall the definitions of the *substitution effect* and the *income effect*, which we introduced in Chapter 3 and discussed more fully in Chapter 9. The substitution effect of a price change refers to the fact that an increase in price makes a good more expensive *relative* to other goods. In the case of a wage change, the substitution effect refers to the fact that an increase in the wage raises the opportunity cost of leisure and causes a worker to devote *more* time to working and less time to leisure.

The income effect of a price change refers to the change in the quantity demanded of a good that results from changes in consumer purchasing power as a result of a price change. An increase in the wage will clearly increase a consumer's purchasing power for any given number of hours worked. For a normal good, the income effect leads to a larger quantity demanded. Because leisure is a normal good, the income effect of a wage increase will cause a worker to devote *less* time to working and more time to leisure. So, the substitution effect of a wage increase causes a worker to supply a larger quantity of labor, but the income effect causes a worker to supply a smaller quantity of labor. Whether a worker supplies more or less labor following a wage increase depends on whether the substitution effect is larger than the income effect. Figure 16-3 shows the typical case of the substitution effect being larger than the income effect at low levels of wages—so the worker supplies a larger quantity of labor as the wage rises—and the income effect being larger than the substitution effect at high levels of wages—so the worker supplies a smaller quantity of labor as the wage rises. For example, suppose an attorney has become quite successful and can charge clients very high fees. Or suppose a rock band has become very popular and receives a large payment for every concert it performs. In these cases, there is a high opportunity cost for the lawyer to turn down another client to take a longer vacation or for the band to turn down another concert. But because their incomes are already very high, they may decide to give up additional income for more leisure. For the lawyer or the rock band, the income effect is larger than the substitution effect, and a higher wage causes them to supply *less* labor.

The Market Supply Curve of Labor

We can determine the market supply curve of labor in the same way we determine a market supply curve of a good. We saw in Chapter 11 that the market supply curve of a good is determined by adding up the quantity of the good supplied by each firm at each price. Similarly, the market supply curve of labor is determined by adding up the quantity of labor supplied by each worker at each wage, holding constant all other variables that might affect the willingness of workers to supply labor.

Factors That Shift the Market Supply Curve of Labor

In constructing the market supply curve of labor, we hold constant all other variables that would affect the willingness of workers to supply labor, except the wage. If any of these other variables change, the market supply curve will shift. The following are the three most important variables that cause the market supply curve of labor to shift:

- *Increases in population.* As the population grows because of natural increase and immigration, the supply curve of labor shifts to the right. The effects of immigration on labor supply are largest in the markets for unskilled workers. In some large cities in the United States, for example, the majority of taxi drivers and workers in hotels and restaurants are immigrants. Some supporters of reducing immigration argue that wages in these jobs have been depressed by the increased supply of labor from immigrants.

- *Changing demographics.* *Demographics* refers to the composition of the population. The more people who are between the ages of 16 and 65, the greater the quantity of labor supplied. During the 1970s and 1980s, the U.S. labor force grew particularly rapidly as members of the baby boom generation—born between 1946 and 1964—first began working. In contrast, a low birth rate in Japan has resulted in an aging population. The number of working-age people in Japan actually began to decline during the 1990s, causing the labor supply curve to shift to the left.

  A related demographic issue is the changing role of women in the labor force. In 1900, only 21 percent of women in the United States were in the labor force. By 1950, this had risen to 30 percent, and today, it is 60 percent. This increase in the *labor force participation* of women has significantly increased the supply of labor in the United States.

- *Changing alternatives.* The labor supply in any particular labor market depends, in part, on the opportunities available in other labor markets. For example, the telecommunications industry bust in 2001 reduced the opportunities for optical engineers. Many workers left this market—causing the labor supply curve to shift to the left—and entered other markets, causing the labor supply curves to shift to the right in those markets. People who have lost jobs or who have low incomes are eligible for unemployment insurance and other payments from the government. The more generous these payments are, the less pressure unemployed workers have to quickly find another job. In many European countries, it is much easier than in the United States for unemployed workers to receive a greater replacement of their wage income from government payments. In one case that received widespread publicity, an unemployed German banker received payments of $2,400 per month from the German government to help pay for his apartment in Miami Beach in a gated community with a swimming pool and sauna. The banker's psychiatrist reportedly argued that the banker needed to remain in sunny Florida because the overcast weather in his hometown in Germany might worsen his depression. Although cases like this are extreme, many economists believe generous unemployment benefits help explain the higher unemployment rates experienced in Europe. For example, in the 10 years from 1997 to 2006, the average of the unemployment rates in the United Kingdom, France, Germany, Italy, and Spain was 9 percent, while in the United States, the unemployment rate averaged just under 5 percent. There have been proposals in some European countries to reduce the size of these government payments in the hope of increasing the labor supply.

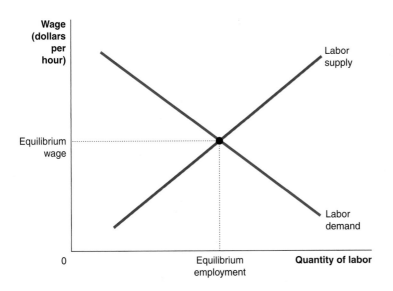

Figure 16-4

Equilibrium in the Labor Market

As in other markets, equilibrium in the labor market occurs where the demand curve for labor and the supply curve of labor intersect.

16.3 | Explain how equilibrium wages are determined in labor markets.

16.3 LEARNING OBJECTIVE

Equilibrium in the Labor Market

In Figure 16-4, we bring labor demand and labor supply together to determine equilibrium in the labor market. We can use demand and supply to analyze changes in the equilibrium wage and the level of employment for the entire labor market, or we can use it to analyze markets for different types of labor, such as baseball players or college professors.

The Effect on Equilibrium Wages of a Shift in Labor Demand

In many labor markets, increases over time in labor productivity will cause the demand for labor to increase. As Figure 16-5 shows, if labor supply is unchanged, an increase in labor demand will increase both the equilibrium wage and the number of workers employed.

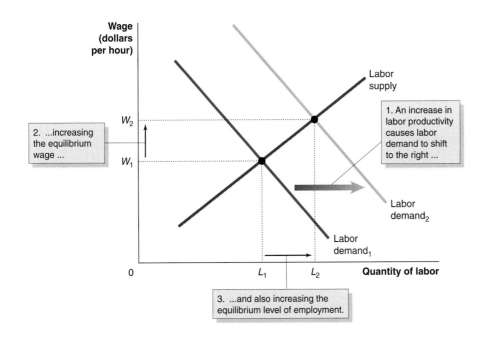

Figure 16-5

The Effect of an Increase in Labor Demand

Increases in labor demand will cause the equilibrium wage and the equilibrium level of employment to rise.

1. If the productivity of workers rises, the marginal revenue product increases, causing the labor demand curve to shift to the right.
2. The equilibrium wage rises from W_1 to W_2.
3. The equilibrium level of employment rises from L_1 to L_2.

Making
the
Connection

Will Your Future Income Depend on Which Courses You Take in College?

Most people realize the value of a college education. As the following chart shows, in 2007, full-time workers ages 25 and over with a college degree earned more per week than other workers; for example, they earned 2.5 times as much as high school dropouts.

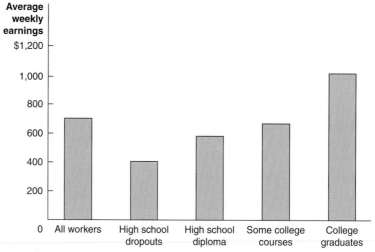

Source: U.S. Bureau of Labor Statistics, "Usual Weekly Earnings of Wage and Salary Workers," April 18, 2007.

Why do college graduates earn more than others? The obvious answer would seem to be that a college education provides skills that increase productivity. Some economists, though, advocate an alternative explanation, known as the *signaling hypothesis,* first proposed by Nobel laureate A. Michael Spence of Stanford University. This hypothesis is based on the idea that job applicants will always have more information than will potential employers about how productive the applicants are likely to be. Although employers attempt through job interviews and background checks to distinguish "good workers" from "bad workers," they are always looking for more information.

According to the signaling hypothesis, employers see a college education as a signal that workers possess certain desirable characteristics: self-discipline, the ability to meet deadlines, and the ability to make a sustained effort. Even if these characteristics are not related to the specifics of a particular job, employers value them because they usually lead to success in any activity. People generally believe that college graduates possess these characteristics, so employers often require a college degree for their best-paying jobs. In this view, the signal that a college education sends about a person's inherent characteristics—which the person presumably already possessed *before* entering college—is much more important than any skills the person may have learned in college. Or, as a college math professor of one of the authors put it (only half-jokingly), "The purpose of college is to show employers that you can succeed at something that's boring and hard."

Recently, though, several economic studies have provided evidence that the higher incomes of college graduates are due to their greater productivity rather than the signal that a college degree sends to employers. Orley Ashenfelter and Cecilia Rouse of Princeton University studied the relationship between schooling and income among 700 pairs of identical twins. Identical twins have identical genes, so differences in their inherent abilities should be relatively small. Therefore, if they have different numbers of years in school, differences in their earnings should be mainly due to the effect of schooling on their productivity. Ashenfelter and Rouse found that identical twins had returns of about 9 percent per additional year of schooling, enough to account for most of the gap in income between high school graduates and college graduates.

Daniel Hamermesh and Stephen G. Donald of the University of Texas have studied the determinants of the earnings of college graduates 5 to 25 years after graduation. They collected extensive information on each person in their study, including the person's SAT scores, rank in high school class, grades in every college course taken, and college major. Hamermesh and Donald discovered that, holding constant all other factors, business and engineering majors earned more than graduates with other majors. They also discovered a large impact on future earnings of taking science and math courses: "A student who takes 15 credits of upper-division science and math courses and obtains a B average in them will earn about 10 percent more than an otherwise identical student in the same major . . . who takes no upper-division classes in these areas." This result held even after adjusting for a student's SAT score. The study by Hamermesh and Donald contradicts the signaling hypothesis because if the signaling hypothesis is correct, the choice of courses taken in college should be of minor importance compared with the signal workers send to employers just by having completed college.

Sources: Orley Ashenfelter and Cecilia Rouse, "Income, Schooling, and Ability: Evidence from a New Sample of Identical Twins," *Quarterly Journal of Economics*, Vol. 113, No. 1 (February 1998), pp. 253–284; Daniel S. Hamermesh and Stephen G. Donald, "The Effect of College Curriculum on Earnings: Accounting for Non-Ignorable Non-Response Bias," National Bureau of Economic Research working paper 10809, September 2004.

YOUR TURN: Test your understanding by doing related problem 3.3 on page 568 at the end of this chapter.

The Effect on Equilibrium Wages of a Shift in Labor Supply

What is the effect on the equilibrium wage of an increase in labor supply due to population growth? As Figure 16-6 shows, if labor demand is unchanged, an increase in labor supply will decrease the equilibrium wage but increase the number of workers employed.

Whether the wage rises in a market depends on whether demand increases faster than supply. For example, after the success of Walt Disney's animated film *The Lion King* in 1994, most movie studios increased production of animated films, increasing the

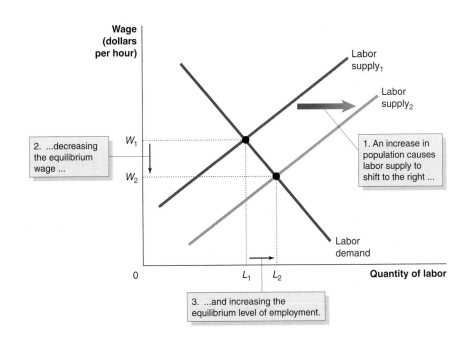

Figure 16-6

The Effect of an Increase in Labor Supply

Increases in labor supply will cause the equilibrium wage to fall but the equilibrium level of employment to rise.

1. As population increases, the labor supply curve shifts to the right.
2. The equilibrium wage falls from W_1 to W_2.
3. The equilibrium level of employment increases from L_1 to L_2.

demand for animators much faster than the supply of animators was increasing. The annual salary for a top animator rose from about $125,000 in 1994 to $550,000 in 1999. These high salaries led more people with artistic ability to choose to get training as film animators, causing the supply of animators to increase after 1999. Several of the animated films released between 1999 and 2001 failed to earn profits, which caused some companies to stop making these films, thereby decreasing the demand for animators. The decrease in demand for animators and the increase in supply caused the salaries of top animators to fall from $550,000 in 1999 to $225,000 in 2002.

The flower industry is one of many industries in the United States that rely on immigrant workers.

Making the Connection | Immigration and Wages, Then and Now

Between 1900 and the outbreak of World War I in 1914, about 13.4 million immigrants arrived in the United States. Relative to the U.S. population—which was about 76 million in 1900—this was the largest wave of immigration in the history of the world. Many commentators at the time predicted that this great increase in the U.S. labor supply would cause a sharp fall in wages. Figure 16-6 shows that this is a reasonable prediction of the effect of an increase in labor supply on the equilibrium wage, *but only if the demand for labor remains unchanged*. In fact, the demand for labor increased rapidly during these years as technological progress, such as electrification and the development of mass-production techniques, increased the productivity of labor.

As a result, the demand for labor shifted to the right faster than the supply of labor, and wages rose. The following figure shows the situation in manufacturing. Both demand and supply increased, but because the shift in demand was greater than the shift in supply, average hourly earnings rose from less than $0.18 in 1900 to $0.22 in 1914, or by almost 25 percent. (The data for both years use 1914 prices to correct for the effects of inflation.) During the same years, employment in manufacturing rose from about 5.5 million workers to almost 9 million.

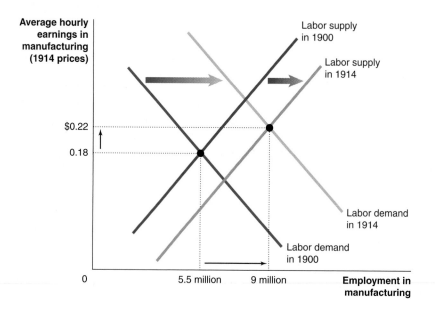

In 2007, the economics of immigration was once again in the forefront during the debate over a proposal by President George W. Bush to revise the immigration laws. President Bush proposed allowing the approximately 12 million illegal immigrants in the United States to enter a process that would allow them to become legal permanent residents. He also proposed strengthening security at the country's borders to reduce future illegal immigration. The figure below shows estimates by the Pew Hispanic Center indicating that illegal immigrants had become a substantial part of the labor supply in a number of industries.

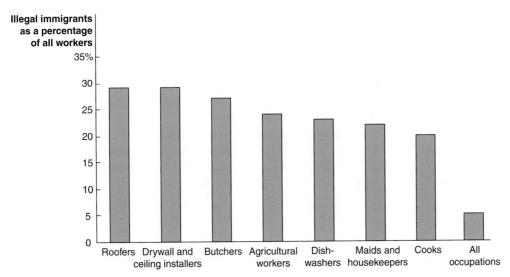

Source: Jeffrey S. Passel, "The Size and Characteristics of the Unauthorized Migrant Population in the U.S.," Pew Hispanic Center Research Report, March 7, 2006, Table 1, p. 12.

Economists have debated the impact of illegal immigrants on the wages of unskilled workers. As the figure indicates, illegal immigrants have substantially increased the supply of labor in some occupations. Some economists argue that illegal immigration may have significantly contributed to the distribution of income becoming more unequal in recent years. Illegal immigration increases income inequality if the supply of illegal workers reduces the wages of low-income workers relative to high-income workers. Claudia Goldin and Lawrence Katz, economists at Harvard University, have recently estimated that immigration—both legal and illegal—can explain only about 10 percent of the increase in the gap between the wages of college-educated workers and the wages of high school–educated workers during the years between 1980 and 2005. George Borjas, of Harvard, Jeffrey Grogger, of the University of Chicago, and Gordon Hanson, of the University of California, San Diego, find a significant impact of immigration on the employment opportunities of African Americans. They find that if as a result of immigration there is a 10 percent increase in the supply of labor with a particular skill, the wages of African Americans with that skill fall by 4 percent, the employment rate of African Americans falls by 3.5 percentage points, and the fraction of African Americans in jail increases by 1 percentage point.

The economic impact of immigration is certain to remain a hotly debated issue for the foreseeable future.

Source: U.S. Department of Commerce, *Historical Statistics of the United States*, Washington, DC: USGPO, 1976; Jeffrey S. Passel, "The Size and Characteristics of the Unauthorized Migrant Population in the U.S.," Pew Hispanic Center Research Report, March 7, 2006; Claudia Goldin and Lawrence F. Katz, "The Race Between Education and Technology," NBER Working Paper, No. 12984, March 2007; and George J. Borjas, Jeffrey Grogger, and Gordon H. Hanson, "Immigration and African-American Employment Opportunties," NBER Working Paper No. 12518, May 2007.

YOUR TURN: Test your understanding by doing related problems 3.5, 3.6, 3.7, and 3.8 on page 568 at the end of this chapter.

16.4 | Use demand and supply analysis to explain how compensating differentials, discrimination, and labor unions cause wages to differ.

Explaining Differences in Wages

A key conclusion of our discussion of the labor market is that the equilibrium wage equals the marginal revenue product of labor. The more productive workers are and the higher the price workers' output can be sold for, the higher the wages workers will receive. At the beginning of the chapter, we raised the question of why major league baseball players are paid so much more than college professors. We are now ready to use demand and supply analysis to answer this question. Figure 16-7 shows the demand and supply curves for major league baseball players and the demand and supply curves for college professors.

Consider first the marginal revenue product of baseball players, which is the additional revenue a team owner will receive from hiring one more player. Baseball players are hired to produce baseball games that are then sold to fans who pay admission to baseball stadiums and to radio and television stations that broadcast the games. Because a major league baseball team can sell each baseball game for a large amount, the marginal revenue product of baseball players is high. The supply of people with the ability to play major league baseball is also very limited. As a result, the average annual salary of the 750 major league baseball players is about $2,700,000.

The marginal revenue product of college professors is much lower than for baseball players. College professors are hired to produce college educations that are then sold to students and their parents. Although one year's college tuition is quite high at many colleges, hiring one more professor allows a college to admit at most a few more students. So, the marginal revenue product of a college professor is much lower than the marginal revenue product of a baseball player. There are also many more people who possess the skills to be a college professor than possess the skills to be a major league baseball player. As a result, the country's 663,000 college professors are paid an average salary of about $73,000.

This still leaves unanswered the question raised at the beginning of this chapter: Why are the Chicago Cubs willing to pay Alfonso Soriano more than the Washington Nationals were? Soriano's marginal product—which we can think of as the extra games a

Figure 16-7

The marginal revenue product of baseball players is very high, and the supply of people with the ability to play major league baseball is low. The result is that the 750 major league baseball players receive an average wage of $2,700,000. The marginal revenue product of college professors is much lower, and the supply of people with the ability to be college professors is much higher. The result is that the 663,000 college professors in the United States receive an average wage of $73,000, far below that of baseball players.

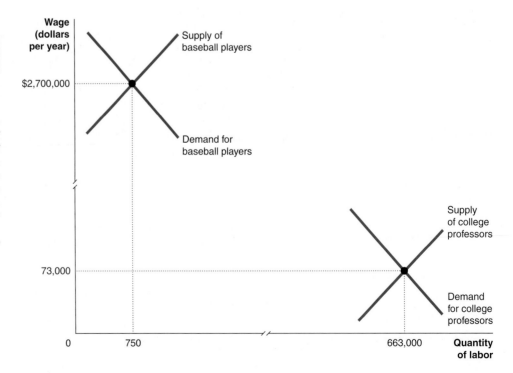

Don't Let This Happen to **YOU!**

Remember That Prices and Wages Are Determined at the Margin

You have probably heard some variation of the following remark: "We could live without baseball, but we can't live without the garbage being hauled away. In a more rational world, garbage collectors would be paid more than baseball players." This remark seems logical: The total value to society of having the garbage hauled away certainly is greater than the total value of baseball games. But wages—like prices—do not depend on total value but on *marginal* value. The *additional* baseball games the Chicago Cubs expect to win by signing Alfonso Soriano will result in millions of dollars in increased revenue. The supply of people with the ability to play major league baseball is very limited. The supply of people with the ability to be trash haulers is much greater. If a trash-hauling firm hires another worker, the *additional* trash-hauling services it can

now offer will bring in a relatively small amount of revenue. The *total* value of baseball games and the *total* value of trash hauling are not relevant in determining the relative salaries of baseball players and garbage collectors.

This point is related to the diamond and water paradox first noted by Adam Smith. On the one hand, water is very valuable—we literally couldn't live without it—but its price is very low. On the other hand, apart from a few industrial uses, diamonds are used only for jewelry, yet their prices are quite high. We resolve the paradox by noting that the price of water is low because the supply is very large and the additional benefit consumers receive from the last gallon purchased is low. The price of diamonds is high because the supply is very small, and the additional benefit consumers receive from the last diamond purchased is high.

YOUR TURN: Test your understanding by doing related problem 4.6 on page 569 at the end of this chapter.

team will win by employing him—should be about the same in Chicago as it was in Washington, DC. But his *marginal revenue product* will be higher in Chicago. Because the population of the Chicago metropolitan area is about twice as large as the population of the Washington metropolitan area, winning more games will result in a greater increase in attendance at Chicago Cubs games than it would at Washington Nationals games. It will also result in a greater increase in viewers for Cubs games on television. Therefore, the Cubs are able to sell the extra wins that Soriano produces for much more than the Washington Nationals can. This difference explains why the Cubs were willing to pay Soriano $18 million per year when he had made "only" $10 million with the Nationals.

Making the Connection | Technology and the Earnings of "Superstars"

The gap between Alfonso Soriano's salary and the salary of the lowest-paid baseball players is much greater than the gap between the salaries paid during the 1950s and 1960s to top players such as Mickey Mantle and Willie Mays and the salaries of the lowest-paid players. Similarly, the gap between the $20 million Julia Roberts is paid to star in a movie and the salary paid to an actor in a minor role is much greater than the gap between the salaries paid during the 1930s and 1940s to stars such as Clark Gable and Cary Grant and the salaries paid to bit players. In fact, in most areas of sports and entertainment, the highest-paid performers—the "superstars"—now have much higher incomes relative to other members of their professions than was true a few decades ago.

The increase in the relative incomes of superstars is mainly due to technological advances. The spread of cable television has increased the number of potential viewers of Cubs games, but many of those viewers will watch only if the Cubs are winning. This increases the value to the Cubs of winning games and, therefore, increases Soriano's marginal revenue product and the salary he can earn.

With DVDs, Internet streaming video, and pay-per-view cable, the value to movie studios of producing a hit movie has risen greatly. Not surprisingly, movie studios have also increased their willingness to pay large salaries to stars like Julia Roberts or Brad Pitt because they think these superstars will significantly raise the chances of a film being successful.

Why does Julia Roberts earn more today relative to the typical actor than stars did in the 1940s?

This process has been going on for a long time. For instance, before the invention of the motion picture, anyone who wanted to see a play had to attend the theater and see a live performance. Limits on the number of people who could see the best actors and actresses perform created an opportunity for many more people to succeed in the acting profession, and the gap between the salaries earned by the best actors and the salaries earned by average actors was relatively small. Today, when a hit movie starring Julia Roberts appears on DVD, millions of people will buy or rent it, and they will not be forced to spend money to see a lesser actress, as their great-great-grandparents might have been.

YOUR TURN: Test your understanding by doing related problems 4.9 and 4.10 on page 569 at the end of this chapter.

────────

Differences in marginal revenue products are the most important factor in explaining differences in wages, but they are not the whole story. To provide a more complete explanation for differences in wages, we must take into account three important aspects of labor markets: compensating differentials, discrimination, and labor unions. We begin with compensating differentials.

Compensating Differentials

Compensating differentials Higher wages that compensate workers for unpleasant aspects of a job.

Suppose Paul runs a video rental store and acquires a reputation for being a bad boss who yells at his workers and is generally unpleasant. Two blocks away, Brendan also runs a video rental store, but Brendan is always very polite to his workers. We would expect in these circumstances that Paul will have to pay a higher wage than Brendan to attract and retain workers. Higher wages that compensate workers for unpleasant aspects of a job are called **compensating differentials**.

If working in a dynamite factory requires the same degree of training and education as working in a semiconductor factory but is much more dangerous, a larger number of workers will want to work making semiconductors than will want to work making dynamite. As a consequence, the wages of dynamite workers will be higher than the wages of semiconductor workers. We can think of the difference in wages as being the price of risk. As each worker decides on his or her willingness to assume risk and decides how much higher the wage must be to compensate for assuming more risk, wages will adjust so that dynamite factories will end up paying wages that are just high enough to compensate workers who choose to work there for the extra risk they assume. Only when workers in dynamite factories have been fully compensated with higher wages for the additional risk they assume will dynamite companies be able to attract enough workers.

One surprising implication of compensating differentials is that *laws protecting the health and safety of workers may not make workers better off*. To see this, suppose that dynamite factories pay wages of $25 per hour, and semiconductor factories pay wages of $20 per hour, with the $5 difference in wages being a compensating differential for the greater risk of working in a dynamite factory. Suppose that the government passes a law regulating the manufacture of dynamite in order to improve safety in dynamite factories. As a result of this law, dynamite factories are no longer any more dangerous than semiconductor factories. Once this happens, the wages in dynamite factories will decline to $20 per hour, the same as in semiconductor factories. Are workers in dynamite factories any better or worse off? Before the law was passed, their wages were $25 per hour, but $5 per hour was a compensating differential for the extra risk they were exposed to. Now their wages are only $20 per hour, but the extra risk has been eliminated. The conclusion seems to be that dynamite workers are no better off as a result of the safety legislation.

This conclusion is only true, though, if the compensating differential actually does compensate workers fully for the additional risk. George Akerlof of the University of California, Berkeley, and William Dickens of the Brookings Institution have argued that the psychological principle known as *cognitive dissonance* might cause workers to underestimate the true risk of their jobs. According to this principle, people prefer to think of themselves as intelligent and rational and tend to reject evidence that seems to contradict this image. Because working in a very hazardous job may seem irrational, workers in such jobs may refuse to believe that the jobs really are hazardous. Akerlof and Dickens present evidence that workers in chemical plants producing benzene and workers in nuclear power plants underestimate the hazards of their jobs. If this is true, the wages of these workers will not be high enough to compensate them fully for the risk they have assumed. So, in this situation, safety legislation may make workers better off.

Discrimination

Table 16-2 shows that in the United States, white males on average earn more than other groups. One possible explanation for this is **economic discrimination**, which involves paying a person a lower wage or excluding a person from an occupation on the basis of an irrelevant characteristic such as race or gender.

If employers discriminate by hiring only white males for high-paying jobs or by paying white males higher wages than other groups working the same jobs, white males would have higher earnings, as Table 16-2 shows. However, excluding groups from certain jobs or paying one group more than another has been illegal in the United States since the passage of the Equal Pay Act of 1963 and the Civil Rights Act of 1964. Nevertheless, it is possible that employers are ignoring the law and practicing economic discrimination.

Most economists believe that only a small amount of the gap between the wages of white males and the wages of other groups is due to discrimination. Instead, most of the gap is explained by three main factors:

1 Differences in education

2 Differences in experience

3 Differing preferences for jobs

Differences in Education Some of the difference between the incomes of whites and the incomes of blacks can be explained by differences in education. Historically, African Americans have had less schooling than whites. Although the gap has closed significantly over the years, 90 percent of adult non-Hispanic white males in 2006 had graduated from high school, but only 82 percent of adult African American males had. Whereas 33 percent of white males had graduated from college, only 18 percent of African American males had. These statistics understate the true gap in education between blacks and whites because many blacks receive a substandard education in inner-city schools. Not surprisingly, studies have shown that differing levels of education can account for a significant part of the gap between the earnings of white and black males.

Economic discrimination Paying a person a lower wage or excluding a person from an occupation on the basis of an irrelevant characteristic such as race or gender.

GROUP	ANNUAL EARNINGS
White males	$48,698
White females	35,822
Black males	34,372
Black females	30,453
Hispanic males	29,072
Hispanic females	25,252

Note: The values are median annual earnings for persons who worked full time, year-round in 2007. Persons of Hispanic origin can be of any race.

Source: U.S. Bureau of the Census, Table PINC-10, Current Population Survey, *Annual Social and Economic Supplement,* March 2008.

TABLE 16-2

Why Do White Males Earn More Than Other Groups?

Differences in Experience Women are much more likely than men to leave their jobs for a period of time after having a child. Women with several children will sometimes have several interruptions in their careers. Some women leave the workforce for several years until their children are of school age. As a result, on average, women with children have less workforce experience than do men of the same age. Because workers with greater experience are, on average, more productive, the difference in levels of experience helps to explain some of the difference in earnings between men and women. One indication of this is that, on average, married women earn about 39 percent less than married men, but women who have never been married—and whose careers are less likely to have been interrupted—earn only about 10 percent less than men who have never been married.

Differing Preferences for Jobs Significant differences exist between the types of jobs held by women and men. As Table 16-3 shows, women are overrepresented in some jobs where average weekly earnings are less than $500 per week, and men are overrepresented in some jobs where weekly earnings are greater than $700 per week.

Although the patterns shown in Table 16-3 could be explained by women being excluded from some occupations, it is likely that they reflect differences in job preferences between men and women. For example, because many women interrupt their careers—at least briefly—when their children are born, they are more likely to take jobs where work experience is less important. Women may also be more likely to take jobs, such as teaching, that allow them to be home in the afternoons when their children return from school.

TABLE 16-3

"Men's Jobs" Often Pay More Than "Women's Jobs"

"WOMEN'S JOBS"			"MEN'S JOBS"		
OCCUPATION	WEEKLY EARNINGS	PERCENTAGE OF WORKERS WHO ARE WOMEN	OCCUPATION	WEEKLY EARNINGS	PERCENTAGE OF WORKERS WHO ARE WOMEN
Preschool and kindergarten teachers	$521	96%	Electricians	$713	2%
Dental assistants	474	95	Firefighters	944	4
Childcare workers	332	93	Aircraft mechanics	919	6
Receptionists	466	92	Aircraft pilots	1,366	6
Hairdressers	416	91	Engineering managers	1,788	10
Teacher assistants	398	91	Aerospace engineers	1,366	11
Nursing aides	388	89	Civil engineers	1,138	13
Maids and housekeeping cleaners	335	87	Computer software engineers	1,401	21
Cashiers	336	75	Chief executives	1,834	24

Note: Earnings are for men and women in the occupation and are "median usual weekly earnings of full-time wage and salary workers."

Source: U.S. Department of Labor, Bureau of Labor Statistics, *Highlights of Women's Earnings in 2005*, Report 995, Table 2, September 2006.

Solved Problem | 16-4

Is "Comparable Worth" Legislation the Answer to Closing the Gap between Men's and Women's Pay?

As we have seen, either because of discrimination or differing preferences, certain jobs are filled primarily by men, and other jobs are filled primarily by women. On average, the "men's jobs" have higher wages than the "women's jobs." Some observers have argued that many "men's jobs" are more highly paid than "women's jobs," despite the jobs being comparable in terms of the education and skills required and the working conditions involved. These observers have argued that the earnings gap between men and women could be closed at least partially if the government required employers to pay the same wages for jobs that have *comparable worth*. Many economists are skeptical of these proposals because they believe allowing markets to determine wages results in a more efficient outcome.

Suppose that electricians are currently being paid a market equilibrium wage of $700 per week, and dental technicians are being paid a market equilibrium wage of $400 per week. Comparable-worth legislation is passed, and a study finds that an electrician and a dental technician have comparable jobs, so employers will now be required to pay workers in both jobs $550 per week. Analyze the effects of this requirement on the market for electricians and on the market for dental technicians. Be sure to use demand and supply graphs.

SOLVING THE PROBLEM:

Step 1: **Review the chapter material.** This problem is about economic discrimination, so you may want to review the section "Discrimination," which begins on page 551.

Step 2: **Draw the graphs.** We saw in Chapter 4 that when the government sets the price in a market, the result is a surplus or a shortage, depending on whether the government-mandated price is above or below the competitive market equilibrium. A wage of $550 per week is below the market wage for electricians and above the market wage for dental technicians. Therefore, we expect the requirement to result in a shortage of electricians and a surplus of dental technicians.

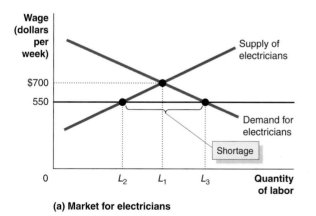

(a) Market for electricians

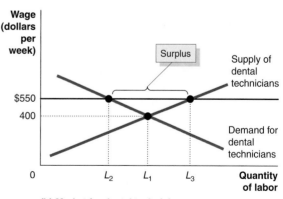

(b) Market for dental technicians

In panel (a), without comparable-worth legislation, the equilibrium wage for electricians is $700, and the equilibrium quantity of electricians hired is L_1. Setting the wage for electricians below equilibrium at $550 reduces the quantity of labor supplied in this occupation from L_1 to L_2 but increases the quantity of labor demanded by employers from L_1 to L_3. The result is a shortage of electricians equal to $L_3 - L_2$, as shown by the bracket in the graph.

In panel (b), without comparable-worth legislation, the equilibrium wage for dental technicians is $400, and the equilibrium quantity of dental technicians hired is L_1. Setting the wage for dental technicians above equilibrium at $550 increases the quantity of labor supplied in this occupation from L_1 to L_3 but reduces the quantity of labor demanded by employers from L_1 to L_2. The result is a surplus of dental technicians equal to $L_3 - L_2$, as shown by the bracket in the graph.

EXTRA CREDIT: Most economists are skeptical of government attempts to set wages and prices, as comparable-worth legislation would require. Supporters of comparable-worth legislation, by contrast, see differences between men's and women's wages as being mainly due to discrimination and are looking to government legislation as a solution.

YOUR TURN: For more practice, do related problems 4.15 and 4.16 on page 570 at the end of this chapter.

>> **End Solved Problem 16-4**

The Difficulty of Measuring Discrimination When two people are paid different wages, discrimination may be the explanation. But differences in productivity or preferences may also be an explanation. Labor economists have attempted to measure what part of differences in wages between blacks and whites and between men and women is due to discrimination and what part is due to other factors. Unfortunately, it is difficult to measure precisely differences in productivity or in worker preferences. As a result, we can't know exactly the extent of economic discrimination in the United States today. Most economists do believe, however, that most of the differences in wages between different groups are due to factors other than discrimination.

Does It Pay to Discriminate? Many economists argue that economic discrimination is no longer a major factor in labor markets in the United States. One reason is that *employers who discriminate pay an economic penalty.* To see why this is true, let's consider a simplified example. Suppose that men and women are equally qualified to be airline pilots and that, initially, airlines do not discriminate. In Figure 16-8, we divide the airlines

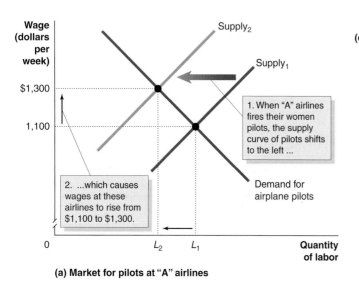

(a) Market for pilots at "A" airlines

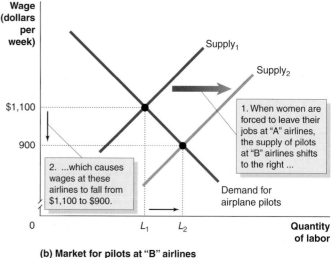

(b) Market for pilots at "B" airlines

Figure 16-8 | Discrimination and Wages

In this hypothetical example, we assume that initially neither "A" airlines nor "B" airlines discriminate. As a result, men and women pilots receive the same wage of $1,100 per week at both groups of airlines. We then assume that "A" airlines discriminates by firing all their women pilots. Panel (a) shows that this reduces the supply of pilots to "A" airlines and raises the wage paid by these airlines from $1,100 to $1,300. Panel (b) shows that this increases the supply of pilots to "B" airlines and lowers the wage paid by these airlines from $1,100 to $900. All the women pilots will end up being employed at the nondiscriminating airlines and will be paid a lower wage than the men who are employed by the discriminating airlines.

into two groups: "A" airlines and "B" airlines. If neither group of airlines discriminates, we would expect them to pay an equal wage of $1,100 per week to both men and women pilots. Now suppose that "A" airlines decide to discriminate and to fire all their women pilots. This action will reduce the supply of pilots to these airlines and, as shown in panel (a), that will force up the wage from $1,100 to $1,300. At the same time, as women fired from the jobs with "A" airlines apply for jobs with "B" airlines, the supply of pilots to "B" airlines will increase, and the equilibrium wage will fall from $1,100 to $900. All the women pilots will end up being employed at the nondiscriminating airlines and be paid a lower wage than the men who are employed by the discriminating airlines.

But this situation cannot persist for two reasons. First, male pilots employed by "B" airlines will also receive the lower wage. This lower wage gives them an incentive to quit their jobs at "B" airlines and apply at "A" airlines, which will shift the labor supply curve for "B" airlines to the left and the labor supply curve for "A" airlines to the right. Second, "A" airlines are paying $1,300 per week to hire pilots who are no more productive than the pilots being paid $900 per week by "B" airlines. As a result, "B" airlines will have lower costs and will be able to charge lower prices. Eventually, "A" airlines will lose their customers to "B" airlines and be driven out of business. The market will have imposed an economic penalty on the discriminating airlines. So, discrimination will not persist, and the wages of men and women pilots will become equal.

Can we conclude from this analysis that competition in markets will eliminate all economic discrimination? Unfortunately, this optimistic conclusion is not completely accurate. We know that until the Civil Rights Act of 1964 was passed, many firms in the United States refused to hire blacks. Even though this practice had persisted for decades, nondiscriminating competitors did not drive these firms out of business. Why not? There were three important factors:

1 **Worker discrimination.** In many cases, white workers refused to work alongside black workers. As a result, some industries—such as the important cotton textile industry in the South—were all white. Because of discrimination by white workers, a businessperson who wanted to use low-cost black labor might need to hire an all-black workforce. Some businesspeople tried this, but because blacks had been excluded from these industries, they often lacked the skills and experience to form an effective workforce.

2 **Customer discrimination.** Some white consumers were unwilling to buy from companies in certain industries if they employed black workers. This was not a significant barrier in manufacturing industries, where customers would not know the race of the workers producing the good. It was, however, a problem for firms in industries in which workers came into direct contact with the public.

3 **Negative feedback loops.** Our analysis in Figure 16-8 assumed that men and women pilots were equally qualified. However, if discrimination makes it difficult for a member of a group to find employment in a particular occupation, his or her incentive to be trained to enter that occupation is reduced. Consider the legal profession as an example. In 1952, future Supreme Court Justice Sandra Day O'Connor graduated third in her class at Stanford University Law School and was an editor of the *Stanford Law Review*, but for some time she was unable to find a job as a lawyer because in those years, many law firms would not hire women. Facing such bleak job prospects, it's not surprising that relatively few women entered law school. As a result, a law firm that did not discriminate would have been unable to act like the nondiscriminating airlines in our example by hiring women lawyers at a lower salary and using this cost advantage to drive discriminating law firms out of business. In this situation, an unfortunate feedback loop was in place: Few women prepared to become lawyers because many law firms discriminated against women, and nondiscriminating law firms were unable to drive discriminating law firms out of business because there were too few women lawyers available.

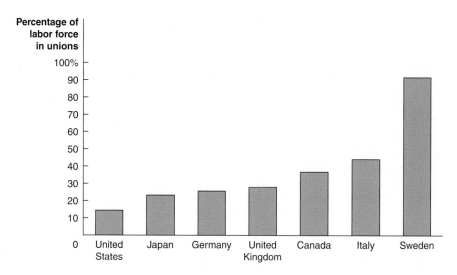

Figure 16-9 | The United States Is Less Unionized Than Most Industrial Countries

In 2008, the percentage of the labor force belonging to unions was lower in the United States than in most other industrial countries.
Source: International Labour Organization.

Most economists agree that the market imposes an economic penalty on firms that discriminate, but because of the factors just discussed, it may take the market a very long time to eliminate discrimination entirely. The passage of the Civil Rights Act of 1964, which outlawed hiring discrimination on the basis of race and sex, greatly sped up the process of reducing economic discrimination in the United States.

Labor Unions

Labor union An organization of employees that has the legal right to bargain with employers about wages and working conditions.

Workers' wages can differ depending on whether the workers are members of labor unions. **Labor unions** are organizations of employees that have the legal right to bargain with employers about wages and working conditions. If a union is unable to reach an agreement with a company, it has the legal right to call a *strike*, which means its members refuse to work until a satisfactory agreement has been reached. As Figure 16-9 shows, a smaller fraction of the U.S. labor force is unionized than in most other industrial countries.

As Table 16-4 shows, in the United States, workers in unions receive higher wages than workers who are not in unions. Do union members earn more than nonunion members because they are in unions? The answer might seem to be "yes," but many union workers are in industries, such as automobile manufacturing, in which their marginal revenue products are high, so their wages would be high even if they were not unionized. Economists who have attempted to estimate statistically the impact of unionization on wages have concluded that being in a union increases a worker's wages about 10 percent, holding constant other factors, such as the industry the worker is in. A

TABLE 16-4

Union Workers Earn More Than Nonunion Workers

	AVERAGE WEEKLY EARNINGS
UNION WORKERS	$863
NONUNION WORKERS	663

Note: "Union workers" includes union members as well as workers who are represented by unions but who are not members of them.
Source: U.S. Bureau of Labor Statistics, *Union Members Summary*, January 25, 2008.

related question is whether unions raise the total amount of wages received by all workers, whether unionized or not. Because the share of national income received by workers has remained roughly constant over many years, most economists do not believe that unions have raised the total amount of wages received by workers.

16.5 | Discuss the role personnel economics can play in helping firms deal with human resources issues.

Personnel Economics

Traditionally, labor economists have focused on issues such as the effects of labor unions on wages or the determinants of changes in average wages over time. They have spent less time analyzing *human resources issues*, which address how firms hire, train, and promote workers and set their wages and benefits. In recent years, some labor economists, including Edward Lazear of Stanford University and William Neilson of Texas A&M University, have begun exploring the application of economic analysis to human resources issues. This new focus has become known as **personnel economics.**

Personnel economics analyzes the link between differences among jobs and differences in the way workers are paid. Jobs have different skill requirements, require more or less interaction with other workers, have to be performed in more or less unpleasant environments, and so on. Firms need to design compensation policies that take into account these differences. Personnel economics also analyzes policies related to other human resources issues, such as promotions, training, and pensions. In this brief overview, we look only at compensation policies.

Personnel economics The application of economic analysis to human resources issues.

Should Workers' Pay Depend on How Much They Work or on How Much They Produce?

One issue personnel economics addresses is when workers should receive *straight-time pay*—a certain wage per hour or salary per week or month—and when they should receive *commission* or *piece-rate pay*—a wage based on how much output they produce.

Suppose, for example, that Anne owns a car dealership and is trying to decide whether to pay her salespeople a salary of $800 per week or a commission of $200 on each car they sell. Figure 16-10 compares the compensation a salesperson would receive under the two systems, according to the number of cars the salesperson sells.

With a straight salary, the salesperson receives $800 per week, no matter how many cars she sells. This outcome is shown by the horizontal line in Figure 16-10. If she receives a commission of $200 per car, her compensation will increase with every car she sells. This outcome is shown by the upward-sloping line. A salesperson who sells fewer than 4 cars per week would earn more by receiving a straight salary of $800 per week. A salesperson who sells more than 4 cars per week would be better off receiving the $200-per-car commission. We can identify two advantages Anne would receive from paying her salespeople commissions rather than salaries: She would attract and retain the most productive employees, and she would provide an incentive to her employees to sell more cars.

Suppose that other car dealerships were all paying salaries of $800 per week. If Anne pays her employees on commission, any of her employees who are unable to sell at least 4 cars per week can improve their pay by going to work for one of her competitors. By the same token, any salespeople at Anne's competitors who can sell more than 4 cars per week can raise their pay by quitting and coming to work for Anne. Over time, Anne will find her least productive employees leaving, while she is able to hire new employees who are more productive.

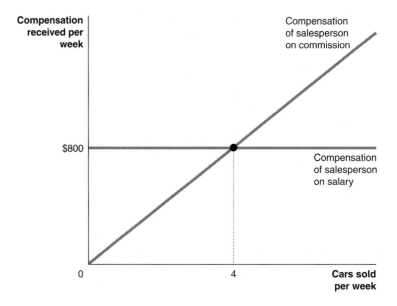

Figure 16-10 | Paying Car Salespeople by Salary or by Commission

This figure compares the compensation a car salesperson receives if she is on a straight salary of $800 per week or if she receives a commission of $200 for each car she sells. With a straight salary, she receives $800 per week, no matter how many cars she sells. This outcome is shown by the horizontal line in the figure. If she receives a commission of $200 per car, her compensation will increase with every car she sells. This outcome is shown by the upward-sloping line. If she sells fewer than 4 cars per week, she would be better off with the $800 salary. If she sells more than 4 cars per week, she would be better off with the $200-per-car commission.

Paying a commission also increases the incentive Anne's salespeople have to sell more cars. If Anne paid a salary, her employees would receive the same amount no matter how few cars they sold. An employee on salary might decide on a particularly hot or cold day that it was less trouble to stay inside the building than to go out on the car lot to greet potential customers. An employee on commission would know that the additional effort expended on selling more cars would be rewarded with additional compensation.

A piece-rate system at Safelite AutoGlass led to increased worker wages and firm profits.

Making the Connection

Raising Pay, Productivity, and Profits at Safelite AutoGlass

Safelite Group, headquartered in Columbus, Ohio, is the parent company of Safelite AutoGlass, the nation's largest installer of auto glass, with 600 repair shops. In the mid-1990s, Safelite shifted from paying its glass installers hourly wages to paying them on the basis of how many windows they installed. Safelite already had in place a computer system that allowed it to track easily how many windows each worker installed per day. To make sure quality did not suffer, Safelite added a rule that if a workmanship-related defect occurred with the installed windshield, the worker would have to install a new windshield and would not be paid for the additional work.

Edward Lazear analyzed data provided by the firm and discovered that under the new piece-rate system, the number of windows installed per worker jumped 44 percent. Lazear estimates that half of this increase was due to increased productivity from workers who continued with the company and half was due to new hires being more productive than the workers they replaced who had left the company. Worker pay rose on average by about 9.9 percent. Ninety-two percent of workers experienced a pay increase, and one-quarter received an increase of at least 28 percent. Safelite's profits also increased as the cost to the company per window installed fell from $44.43 under the hourly wage system to $35.24 under the piece-rate system.

Sociologists sometimes question whether worker productivity can be increased through the use of monetary incentives. The experience of Safelite AutoGlass provides a clear example of workers reacting favorably to the opportunity to increase output in exchange for higher compensation.

Source: Edward P. Lazear, "Performance Pay and Productivity," *American Economic Review*, Vol. 90, No. 5, December 2000, pp. 1346–1361.

YOUR TURN: Test your understanding by doing related problem 5.7 on page 572 at the end of this chapter.

Other Considerations in Setting Compensation Systems

The discussion so far indicates that companies will find it more profitable to use a commission or piece-rate system of compensation rather than a salary system. In fact, many firms continue to pay their workers salaries, which means they are paying their workers on the basis of how long they work rather than on the basis of how much they produce. Firms may choose a salary system for several good reasons:

- *Difficulty in measuring output.* Often it is difficult to attribute output to any particular worker. For example, projects carried out by an engineering firm may involve teams of workers whose individual contributions are difficult to distinguish. On assembly lines, such as those used in the automobile industry, the amount produced by each worker is determined by the speed of the line, which is set by managers rather than by workers. Managers at many firms perform such a wide variety of tasks that measuring their output would be costly, if it could be done at all.

- *Concerns about quality.* If workers are paid on the basis of the number of units produced, they may become less concerned about quality. An office assistant who is paid on the basis of the quantity of letters typed may become careless about how many typos the letters contain. In some cases, there are ways around this problem; for example, the assistant may be required to correct the mistakes on his or her own time without pay.

- *Worker dislike of risk.* Piece-rate or commission systems of compensation increase the risk to workers because sometimes output declines for reasons not connected to the worker's effort. For example, if there is a very snowy winter, few customers may show up at Anne's auto dealership. Through no fault of their own, her salespeople may have great difficulty selling any cars. If they are paid a salary, their income will not be affected, but if they are on commission, their incomes may drop to low levels. The flip side of this is that by paying salaries, Anne assumes a greater risk. During a snowy winter, her payroll expenses will remain high even though her sales are low. With a commission system of compensation, her payroll expenses will decline along with her sales. But owners of firms are typically better able to bear risk than are workers. As a result, some firms may find that workers who would earn more under a commission system will prefer to receive a salary to reduce their risk. In these situations, paying a lower salary may reduce the firm's payroll expenses compared with what they would have been under a commission or piece-rate system.

Personnel economics is a relatively new field, but it holds great potential for helping firms deal more efficiently with human relations issues.

16.6 | Show how equilibrium prices are determined in the markets for capital and natural resources.

The Markets for Capital and Natural Resources

The approach we have used to analyze the market for labor can also be used to analyze the markets for other factors of production. We have seen that the demand for labor is determined by the marginal revenue product of labor because the value to a firm from hiring another worker equals the increase in the firm's revenue from selling the additional output it can produce by hiring the worker. The demand for capital and natural resources is determined in a similar way.

The Market for Capital

Physical capital includes machines, equipment, and buildings. Firms sometimes buy capital, but we will focus on situations in which firms rent capital. A chocolate manufacturer renting a warehouse and an airline leasing a plane are examples of firms renting capital. Like the demand for labor, the demand for capital is a derived demand. When a firm is considering increasing its capital by, for example, employing another machine, the value it receives equals the increase in the firm's revenue from selling the additional output it can produce by employing the machine. The *marginal revenue product of capital* is the change in the firm's revenue as a result of employing one more unit of capital, such as a machine. We have seen that the marginal revenue product of labor curve is the demand curve for labor. Similarly, the marginal revenue product of capital curve is also the demand curve for capital.

Firms producing capital goods face increasing marginal costs, so the supply curve of capital goods is upward sloping, as are the supply curves for other goods and services. Figure 16-11 shows equilibrium in the market for capital. In equilibrium,

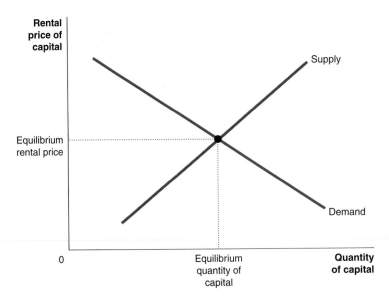

Figure 16-11 | Equilibrium in the Market for Capital

The rental price of capital is determined by equilibrium in the market for capital. In equilibrium, the rental price of capital is equal to the marginal revenue product of capital.

suppliers of capital receive a rental price equal to the marginal revenue product of capital, just as suppliers of labor receive a wage equal to the marginal revenue product of labor.

The Market for Natural Resources

The market for natural resources can be analyzed in the same way as the markets for labor and capital. When a firm is considering employing more natural resources, the value it receives equals the increase in the firm's revenue from selling the additional output it can produce by buying the natural resources. So, the demand for natural resources is also a derived demand. The *marginal revenue product of natural resources* is the change in the firm's revenue as a result of employing one more unit of natural resources, such as a barrel of oil. The marginal revenue product of natural resources curve is also the demand curve for natural resources.

Although the total quantity of most natural resources is ultimately fixed—as the humorist Will Rogers once remarked, "Buy land; They ain't making any more of it"—in many cases, the quantity supplied still responds to the price. For example, although the total quantity of oil deposits in the world is fixed, an increase in the price of oil will result in an increase in the quantity of oil supplied during a particular period. The result, as shown in panel (a) of Figure 16-12, is an upward-sloping supply curve. In some cases, however, the quantity of a natural resource that will be supplied is fixed and will not change as the price changes. The land available at a busy intersection is fixed, for example. In panel (b) of Figure 16-12, we illustrate this situation with a supply curve that is a vertical line, or perfectly inelastic. The price received by a factor of production that is in fixed supply is called an **economic rent** (or **pure rent**) because, in this case, the price of the factor is determined only by demand. For example, if a new highway diverts much of the traffic from a previously busy intersection, the demand

Economic rent (or **pure rent**) The price of a factor of production that is in fixed supply.

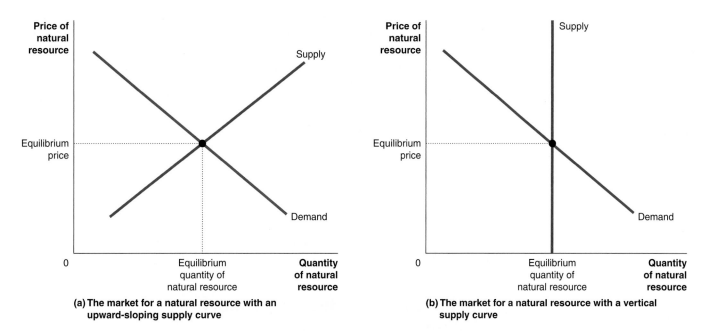

(a) The market for a natural resource with an upward-sloping supply curve

(b) The market for a natural resource with a vertical supply curve

Figure 16-12 | Equilibrium in the Market for Natural Resources

In panel (a), the supply curve of a natural resource is upward sloping. The price of the natural resource is determined by the interaction of demand and supply. In panel (b), the supply curve of the natural resource is a vertical line, indicating that the quantity supplied does not respond to changes in price. In this case, the price of the natural resource is determined only by demand. The price of a factor of production with a vertical supply curve is called an *economic rent* or a *pure rent*.

for the land will decline and the price of the land will fall, but the quantity of the land will not change.

Monopsony

Monopsony The sole buyer of a factor of production.

In Chapter 14, we analyzed the case of *monopoly*, where a firm is the sole *seller* of a good or service. What happens if a firm is the sole *buyer* of a factor of production? This case, which is known as **monopsony**, is comparatively rare. An example is a firm in an isolated town—perhaps a lumber mill in a small town in Washington or Oregon—that is the sole employer of labor in that location. In the nineteenth and early twentieth centuries, some coal mining firms were the sole employers in certain small towns in West Virginia and some pineapple plantations were the sole employers on certain small islands in Hawaii. In these cases, not only would the firm own the mill, mine, or plantation, but it would also own the stores and other businesses in the town. Workers would have the choice of working for the sole employer in the town or moving to another town.

With only one lumber mill in town, the wages of these loggers won't be as high.

We know that a firm with a monopoly in an output market takes advantage of its market power to reduce the quantity supplied to force up the market price and increase its profits. A firm that has a monopsony in a factor market would employ a similar strategy: It would restrict the quantity of the factor demanded to force down the price of the factor and increase profits. A firm with a monopsony in a labor market will hire fewer workers and pay lower wages than would be the case in a competitive market. Because fewer workers are hired than would be true in a competitive market, monopsony results in a deadweight loss. Monopoly and monopsony have similar effects on the economy: In both cases a firm's market power results in a lower equilibrium quantity, a deadweight loss, and a reduction in economic efficiency compared with a competitive market.

In some cases, monopsony in labor markets is offset by worker membership in a labor union. A notable example of this is professional sports. For instance, Major League Baseball (MLB) effectively has a monopsony on employing professional baseball players. (Although independent baseball leagues exist, none of the best players play for these teams, and the teams pay salaries that are a small fraction of those paid by MLB teams.) The monopsony power of the owners of MLB teams is offset by the power of the Major League Baseball Players Association, the union that represents baseball players. Bargaining between the representatives of MLB and the players union has resulted in baseball players being paid something close to what they would be receiving in a competitive market.

The Marginal Productivity Theory of Income Distribution

We have seen that in equilibrium, each factor of production receives a price equal to its marginal revenue product. We can use this fact to explain the distribution of income. Marginal revenue product represents the value of a factor's marginal contribution to producing goods and services. Therefore, individuals will receive income equal to the marginal contributions to production from the factors of production they own, including their labor. The more factors of production an individual owns and the more productive those factors are, the higher the individual's income will be. This approach to explaining the distribution of income is called the **marginal productivity theory of income distribution**. The marginal productivity theory of income distribution was developed by John Bates Clark, who taught at Columbia University in the late nineteenth and early twentieth centuries.

Marginal productivity theory of income distribution The theory that the distribution of income is determined by the marginal productivity of the factors of production that individuals own.

Economics in YOUR Life!

>> Continued from page 535

At the beginning of the chapter, we asked you to imagine that you work at a local sandwich shop and that you plan to ask your manager for a raise. One way to show the manager your worth is to demonstrate how many dollars your work earns for the sandwich shop: your marginal revenue product. You could certainly suggest that as you have become better at your job and have gained new skills that you are a more productive employee, but more importantly, that your productivity results in increased revenue to the sandwich shop. By showing how your employment contributes to higher revenue and profit for the shop, you may be able to convince your manager to raise your pay.

Conclusion

In this chapter, we used the demand and supply model from Chapter 3 to explain why wages differ among workers. The demand for workers depends on their productivity and on the price that firms receive for the output the workers produce. The supply of workers to an occupation depends on the wages and working conditions offered by employers and on the skills required. The demand and supply for labor can also help us analyze such issues as economic discrimination and the impact of labor unions.

Read *An Inside Look* on the next page to see how demand and supply determine the salaries of ex-college athletes who work for NASCAR pit crews.

An Inside **LOOK**

Are Race Car Drivers Athletes? We Don't Know, but the Pit-Crew Members Are

WALL STREET JOURNAL, JUNE 16, 2005

Racing Teams Recruit Athletes and Train Them Hard; The $60,000 Tire Carrier

After Bob Dowens finished playing college football, he turned pro. But not in the NFL—in the National Association for Stock Car Auto Racing.

Once a defensive back at Fairleigh Dickinson University, the 28-year-old Mr. Dowens is now a professional tire carrier in a Nascar pit crew. At Evernham Motorsports, the stock-car racing team for which Mr. Dowens works, pit-crew members practice five days a week. A pit coach studies videos to hone their footwork and hand speed. A trainer has them lift weights and run sprints.

Years ago, mechanics who worked on race cars during the week simply did double duty on Sundays in the pits. Nobody thought about athletic fitness, and beer bellies were OK. The crew was too busy during the week welding and machining to practice pit stops.

Today, teams like Evernham look increasingly for college jocks whose strength and speed can save precious tenths of a second in a race. One of Mr. Dowens's teammates, jack-man Ed Watkins, was a 300-pound offensive lineman at East Carolina University. The Chip Ganassi Racing team's pit crew includes baseball players from Wake Forest University; football players from Wake, the University of Kentucky and the University of North Carolina; and a hockey player from Dartmouth.

Top tire-changers—the guys who air-wrench lug nuts off and on—can make $100,000 a year. The average at Evernham is about $60,000. Mr. Dowens figures he'll be a bit over that, with bonuses, this year.

Big money is what drives the demand for world-class tire-changers. In the 1990s, Nascar's popularity exploded, bringing hundreds of millions of dollars in television and sponsorship revenue into the sport. With more money at stake, competition intensified, and pit stops often affected the outcome of a race. Twenty years ago, pit crews were doing pretty well to change four tires in less than 30 seconds. Today, taking more than 16 seconds can be disastrous.

"These guys are serious athletes," says Evernham's pit coach, Greg Miller, 33. A car going 200 miles per hour covers nearly 300 feet in a second, so a half-second advantage in the pit can put a driver ahead two or three spots. "In our world, two seconds is a lifetime." . . .

That brought Mr. Dowens under the tutelage of Evernham's coach, Mr. Miller. A former fitness trainer with a master's degree in physiology, he thought he could combine his profession with his love of Nascar and joined a team in 1998. At Evernham, Mr. Miller keeps a thick binder with details of every practice and race-day pit stop of the three crews he coaches, with times of each man's tasks, the car's position entering and leaving the pit.

Last year, Mr. Miller got approval to add a full-time strength coach. It started badly: The first running drill left the former East Carolina lineman, Mr. Watkins, with torn tendons in both knees. Now it's paying off. At 5 feet 10 inches, Mr. Dowens weighs 190 pounds, 20 pounds less than in his football days. The 6-foot-3-inch Mr. Watkins is a buff 230. In May, an Evernham crew came in second in a Nascar pit competition. Two weeks later, a different Evernham pit crew took the title and shared $75,000 in bonus money. . . .

On Sunday at the race, the Coca-Cola 600 in Charlotte, fans strolled the pit area seeking autographs and souvenir lug nuts. . . .

On this day Mr. Dowens was carrying for the No. 19 car driven by Jeremy Mayfield. Early in the 600-mile race, Mr. Mayfield's Charger screamed into the pit; 14.32 seconds later, it was gone. On the next stop, a tire changer slipped on an air hose. The time: 15.39. Mr. Miller grimaced.

As the 600-mile race wore on, the pit times edged below 14 seconds. Mr. Dowens was doing well, indexing tires at under seven-tenths of a second. With their car hanging on in a crash-filled race, Mr. Miller shouted, "Need a good one, boys." With 59 laps to go, the car pulled in for four tires and two cans of gas. It was out in 13.95 seconds, a time that helped Mr. Mayfield leap from 14th to ninth. With that momentum, he finished the race in fourth place, tying his best finish this year.

The pit crew did well, too. "We can do better, but no major problems," Mr. Miller said. "All it takes is one to screw up the race."

Source: Neal E. Boudette, "Racing Teams Recruit Athletes and Train Them Hard; The $60,000 Tire Carrier," *Wall Street Journal,* June 16, 2005, p. A1. Copyright © 2005 Dow Jones. Reprinted by permission of Dow Jones via Copyright Clearance.

Key Points in the Article

This article highlights college athletes who have found a career working on pit crews for NASCAR races. Productivity and the value of the output produced are the two key factors that determine the wages of these pit-crew workers.

Analyzing the News

(a) Changes in marginal product will shift the demand for labor. You can see this in the figure as the demand curve shifts to the right from D_1 to D_2. Because labor demand is based on the marginal revenue product of labor, as the marginal product increases, so too will the demand for labor. For race teams, faster pit times would represent an increase in productivity. By hiring athletes, a race team hopes that the speed of its pit stops will fall, which will improve its finishing spot in the race. Holding the value of winning a NASCAR race constant, this would increase the demand for labor.

(b) As NASCAR has become more popular, sponsors are willing to pay more money to place logos on the cars, and prize money for races has increased. Sponsors will pay more money for cars with better finishing positions. If a pit crew can improve the finishing position of a team, the value of the output increases. As the value of the output increases, the value of the marginal product of labor increases, holding productivity constant. This will also increase the demand for labor, as shown in the figure as the demand curve shifts from D_1 to D_2. So, the article indicates that the demand for pit crews has increased for two reasons: pit crews have become more productive and the value of winning a NASCAR race has increased. As labor demand increases, the wages paid to pit-crew workers increases from W_1 to W_2.

(c) How can we measure the value of a pit crew? A quick pit stop allowed Jeremy Mayfield to advance five spots in the field. The additional prize money—not only per race but over the 36-race season—adds a large amount of revenue to the race team. The value of a better pit crew could be measured by the additional prize money and sponsorship money the team receives from higher race finishes.

Thinking Critically

1. Suppose NASCAR loses popularity over the next few years. What do you suppose will happen to the wages offered to pit-crew members?

2. The United Auto Workers labor union and an automotive company, such as Ford or General Motors, will sometimes jointly sponsor a NASCAR race. Why would a labor union want to help a company sell more cars?

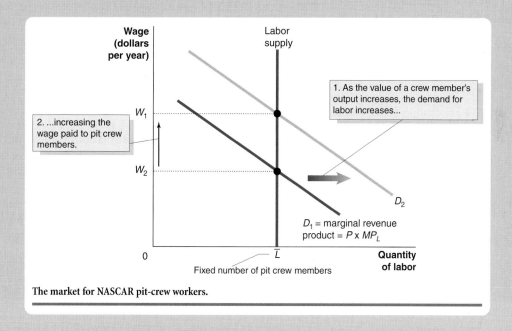

The market for NASCAR pit-crew workers.

Key Terms

Compensating differentials, p. 550

Derived demand, p. 536

Economic discrimination, p. 551

Economic rent (or pure rent), p. 561

Factors of production, p. 536

Human capital, p. 539

Labor union, p. 556

Marginal product of labor, p. 536

Marginal productivity theory of income distribution, p. 563

Marginal revenue product of labor (*MRP*), p. 537

Monopsony, p. 562

Personnel economics, p. 557

16.1 LEARNING OBJECTIVE   16.1 | Explain how firms choose the profit-maximizing quantity of labor to employ, pages 536–540.

The Demand for Labor

Summary

The demand for labor is a **derived demand** because it depends on the demand consumers have for goods and services. The additional output produced by a firm as a result of hiring another worker is called the **marginal product of labor**. The amount by which the firm's revenue will increase as a result of hiring one more worker is called the **marginal revenue product of labor** (*MRP*). A firm's marginal revenue product of labor curve is its demand curve for labor. Firms maximize profit by hiring workers up to the point where the wage is equal to the marginal revenue product of labor. The market demand curve for labor is determined by adding up the quantity of labor demanded by each firm at each wage, holding constant all other variables that might affect the willingness of firms to hire workers. The most important variables that shift the labor demand curve are changes in human capital, technology, the price of the product, the quantity of other inputs, and the number of firms in the market. **Human capital** is the accumulated training and skills that workers possess.

 Visit www.myeconlab.com to complete these exercises
Get Ahead of the Curve online and get instant feedback.

Review Questions

1.1 What is the difference between the marginal product of labor and the marginal revenue product of labor?

1.2 Why is the demand curve for labor downward sloping?

1.3 What are the five most important variables that cause the market demand curve for labor to shift?

Problems and Applications

1.4 Frank Gunter owns an apple orchard. He employs 87 apple pickers and pays them each $8 per hour to pick apples, which he sells for $1.60 per box. If Frank is maximizing profits, what is the marginal revenue product of the last worker he hired? What is that worker's marginal product?

1.5 (Related to *Solved Problem 16-1* on page 538) Fill in the blanks in the following table for Tommy's Televisions:

NUMBER OF WORKERS (*L*)	OUTPUT OF TELEVISIONS PER WEEK (*Q*)	MARGINAL PRODUCT OF LABOR (TELEVISION SETS PER WEEK) (*MP*)	PRODUCT PRICE (*P*)	MARGINAL REVENUE PRODUCT OF LABOR (DOLLARS PER WEEK)	WAGE (DOLLARS PER WEEK) (*W*)	ADDITIONAL PROFIT FROM HIRING ONE MORE WORKER (DOLLARS PER WEEK)
0	0	—	$300	—	$1,800	—
1	8	—	300	—	1,800	—
2	15	—	300	—	1,800	—
3	21	—	300	—	1,800	—
4	26	—	300	—	1,800	—
5	30	—	300	—	1,800	—
6	33	—	300	—	1,800	—

a. From the information in the table, can you determine whether this firm is a price taker or a price maker? Briefly explain.

b. Use the information in the table to draw a graph like Figure 16-1 on page 537 that shows the demand for labor by this firm. Be sure to indicate the profit-maximizing quantity of labor on your graph.

1.6 State whether each of the following events will result in a movement along the market demand curve for labor in electronics factories in Japan or whether it will cause the market demand curve for labor to shift. If the demand curve shifts, indicate whether it will shift to the left or to the right and draw a graph to illustrate the shift.

a. The wage rate declines.

b. The price of televisions declines.

c. Several firms exit the television market in Japan.

d. Japanese high schools introduce new vocational courses in assembling electronic products.

1.7 Under what circumstances would a firm's demand curve for labor be a horizontal line?

>> End Learning Objective 16.1

16.2 LEARNING OBJECTIVE   16.2 | Explain how people choose the quantity of labor to supply, **pages 540–543.**

The Supply of Labor

Summary

As the wage increases, the opportunity cost of leisure increases, causing individuals to supply a greater quantity of labor. Normally, the labor supply curve is upward sloping, but it is possible that at very high wage levels, the supply curve might be backward bending. This outcome occurs when someone with a high income is willing to accept a somewhat lower income in exchange for more leisure. The market labor supply curve is determined by adding up the quantity of labor supplied by each worker at each wage, holding constant all other variables that might affect the willingness of workers to supply labor. The most important variables that shift the labor supply curve are increases in population, changing demographics, and changing alternatives.

myeconlab Visit www.myeconlab.com to complete these exercises
Get Ahead of the Curve online and get instant feedback.

Review Questions

2.1 How can we measure the opportunity cost of leisure? Why is the supply curve of labor usually upward sloping?

2.2 What are the three most important variables that cause the market supply curve of labor to shift?

Problems and Applications

2.3 Daniel had been earning $65 per hour and working 45 hours per week. Then Daniel's wage rose to $75 per hour, and as a result, he now works 40 hours per week.

What can we conclude from this information about the income effect and the substitution effect of a wage change for Daniel?

2.4 Most labor economists believe that many adult males are on the vertical section of their labor supply curves. Explain when and why someone's supply of labor curve would be vertical, using the concepts of income and substitution effects.

Source: Robert Whaples, "Is There Consensus among American Labor Economists: Survey Results on Forty Propositions," *Journal of Labor Research*, Vol. 17, No. 4, Fall 1996.

2.5 Suppose that a large oil field is discovered in Michigan. By imposing a tax on the oil, the state government is able to eliminate the state income tax on wages. What is likely to be the effect on the labor supply curve in Michigan?

2.6 State whether each of the following events will result in a movement along the market supply curve of agricultural labor in the United States or whether it will cause the market supply curve of labor to shift. If the supply curve shifts, indicate whether it will shift to the left or to the right and draw a graph to illustrate the shift.
a. The agricultural wage rate declines.
b. Wages outside of agriculture increase.
c. The law is changed to allow for unlimited immigration into the United States.

>> End Learning Objective 16.2

16.3 LEARNING OBJECTIVE   16.3 | Explain how equilibrium wages are determined in labor markets,

pages 543–547.

Equilibrium in the Labor Market

Summary

The intersection between labor supply and labor demand determines the equilibrium wage and the equilibrium level of employment. If labor supply is unchanged, an increase in labor demand will increase both the equilibrium wage and the number of workers employed. If labor demand is unchanged, an increase in labor supply will lower the equilibrium wage and increase the number of workers employed.

myeconlab Visit www.myeconlab.com to complete these exercises
Get Ahead of the Curve online and get instant feedback.

Review Questions

3.1 If the labor demand curve shifts to the left and the labor supply curve remains unchanged, what will happen to the equilibrium wage and the equilibrium level of employment? Illustrate your answer with a graph.

3.2 If the labor supply curve shifts to the left and the labor demand curve remains unchanged, what will happen to the equilibrium wage and the equilibrium level of employment? Illustrate your answer with a graph.

Problems and Applications

3.3 **(Related to the *Making the Connection* on page 544)** Over time, the gap between the wages of workers with a college degree and the wages of workers without a college degree has been increasing. Shouldn't this gap have increased the incentive for workers to earn a college degree, thereby increasing the supply of college-educated workers, and reducing the size of the gap?

3.4 Reread the discussion on page 545 of changes in the salaries of film animators. Use a graph to illustrate this situation. Make sure your graph has labor demand and supply curves for 1994, 1999, and 2002 and that the equilibrium point for each year is clearly indicated.

3.5 **(Related to the *Making the Connection* on page 546)** Francis Walker served as commissioner general of the U.S. Immigration Service and as first president of the American Economic Association. In 1896, he wrote the following:

> The question today is protecting the American rate of wages, the American standard of living, and the quality of American citizenship from degradation through the tumultuous access of vast throngs of ignorant and brutalized peasantry from the countries of Eastern and Southern Europe.
>
> Why would Walker have feared that immigration to the United States would drive down wages? Did wages, in fact, fall as he predicted? Briefly explain.

Source: Quoted in Julian L. Simon and Rita James Simon, "Do We Really Need All These Immigrants?" in D. N. McCloskey, *Second Thoughts: Myths and Morals of U.S. Economic History*, New York: Oxford University Press, 1993, p. 20.

3.6 **(Related to the *Making the Connection* on page 546)** Suppose the United States had not allowed any immigration between 1900 and 1914. Which groups would have benefited from prohibiting immigration and which groups would have lost?

3.7 **(Related to the *Making the Connection* on page 546)** Former presidential candidate Patrick J. Buchanan has argued, "The U.S. labor supply has grown by more tens of millions in the past twenty-five years than in any other period in history. How could the price of labor *not* fall?" Answer Buchanan's question: If there is an increase in labor supply, does the equilibrium wage have to fall?

Source: Patrick J. Buchanan, *The Great Betrayal: How American Sovereignty and Social Justice Are Being Sacrificed to the Gods of the Global Economy*, Boston: Little, Brown, 1998, p. 16.

3.8 **(Related to the *Making the Connection* on page 546)** According to an article in the *Wall Street Journal*:

> Through the 1990s, U.S.-bound immigration was split between the poor fleeing hunger or oppression and wealthy elites seeking high-paying jobs. Now, more middle-class, middle-skilled emigrants are heading to the U.S.

Most of the "middle-class, middle-skilled emigrants" referred to in the article were legal immigrants to the United States. Suppose that more effective border control measures reduce the number of low-skilled, illegal immigrants to the United States and the fraction of immigrants who are "middle-skilled" increases significantly. What difference would this change make in the economic impact of immigration? Would it be likely to affect the political debate over immigration?

Source: Joel Millman, "Tidy Business: Immigrant Group Puts a New Spin On Cleaning Niche," *Wall Street Journal*, February 16, 2006, p. A1.

3.9 In 541 A.D., an outbreak of bubonic plague hit the Byzantine Empire. Because the plague was spread by flea-infested rats that often lived on ships, ports were hit particularly hard. In some ports, more than 40 percent of the population died. The emperor, Justinian, was concerned that the wages of sailors were rising very rapidly as a result of the plague. In 544 A.D., he placed a ceiling on the wages of sailors. Use a demand and supply graph of the market for sailors to show the effect of the plague on the wages of sailors. Use the same graph to show the effect of Justinian's wage ceiling. Briefly explain what is happening in your graph.

Source: Michael McCormick, *The Origins of the European Economy: Communications and Commerce*, A.D., *300–900*, New York: Cambridge University Press, 2001, p. 109.

>> End Learning Objective 16.3

16.4 LEARNING OBJECTIVE   16.4 | Use demand and supply analysis to explain how compensating differentials, discrimination, and labor unions cause wages to differ, **pages 548–557.**

Explaining Differences in Wages

Summary

The equilibrium wage is determined by the intersection of the labor demand and labor supply curves. Some differences in wages are explained by **compensating differentials**, which are higher wages that compensate workers for unpleasant aspects of a job. Wages can also differ because of **economic discrimination**, which involves paying a person a lower wage or excluding a person from an occupation on the basis of irrelevant characteristics, such as race or gender. **Labor unions** are organizations of employees that have the legal right to bargain with employers about wages and working conditions. Being in a union increases a worker's wages about 10 percent, holding constant other factors, such as the industry in question.

Visit www.myeconlab.com to complete these exercises online and get instant feedback.

Review Questions

4.1 What is a compensating differential? Give an example.

4.2 Define economic discrimination. Is the fact that one group in the population has higher earnings than other groups evidence of economic discrimination? Briefly explain.

4.3 Is the fraction of U.S. workers in labor unions larger or smaller than in other countries?

Problems and Applications

4.4 The journalist Michael Kinsley has argued, "Free-market capitalism . . . works well for almost all by rewarding some people more than others." Discuss whether you agree.

Source: Michael Kinsley, "Curse You, Robert Caro!" *Slate*, November 21, 2002.

4.5 **(Related to the *Chapter Opener* on page 534)** A student remarks, "I don't think the idea of marginal revenue product really helps explain differences in wages. After all, a ticket to a baseball game costs much less than college tuition, yet baseball players are paid much more than college professors." Do you agree with the student's reasoning?

4.6 **(Related to the *Don't Let This Happen to You!* on page 549)** Joe Morgan is a sportscaster and former baseball player. After he stated that he thought the salaries of major league baseball players were justified, a baseball fan wrote the following to ESPN.com columnist, Rob Neyer:

Mr. Neyer,

What are your feelings about Joe Morgan's comment that players are justified in being paid what they're being paid? How is it ok for A-Rod [New York Yankees infielder Alex Rodriguez] to earn $115,000 per GAME while my boss works 80 hour weeks and earns $30,000 per year?

How would you answer this fan's questions?

Source: ESPN.com, August 30, 2002.

4.7 Buster Olney, a columnist for ESPN.com, wonders why baseball teams pay the teams' managers and general managers less than they pay most baseball players:

About two-thirds of the players on the [New York] Mets' roster will make more money than [manager Willie] Randolph; Willie will get somewhere in the neighborhood of half of an average major league salary for 2007. But Randolph's deal is right in line with what other managers are making, and right in the range of what the highest-paid general managers are making. . . . I have a hard time believing that Randolph or general manager Omar Minaya will have less impact on the Mets than left-handed reliever Scott Schoeneweis, who will get paid more than either the manager or GM.

Provide an economic explanation of why baseball managers and general managers are generally paid less than baseball players.

Source: Buster Olney, "Managers Low on Pay Scale," ESPN.com, January 25, 2007.

4.8 In early 2007, Nick Saban agreed to leave his job as head coach of the Miami Dolphins National Football League team to take a job as head football coach at the University of Alabama at a salary of $4 million per year for eight years. Ivan Maisel, a columnist for ESPN.com, wondered whether Saban was worth such a large salary: "Is Saban eight times better than the coach who outmaneuvered Bob Stoops of Oklahoma on Monday night? Boise State paid Chris Petersen $500,000 this season—and he still hasn't lost a game." Might Saban still be a worth a salary of $4 million per year to Alabama even if he is not "eight times better" than a coach being paid $500,000 at another school? In your answer, be sure to refer to the difference between the marginal product of labor and the marginal revenue product of labor.

Source: Ivan Maisel, "Saban Will Find Crowded Pond in Tuscaloosa," ESPN.com, January 3, 2007.

4.9 **(Related to the *Making the Connection* on page 549)** According to Alan Krueger, an economist at Princeton University, the share of concert ticket revenue received by the top 1 percent of all acts rose from 26 percent in 1982 to 56 percent in 2003. Does this information indicate that the top acts in 2003 must have been much better performers relative to other acts than was the case in 1982? If not, can you think of another explanation?

Source: Eduardo Porter, "More Than Ever, It Pays to Be the Top Executive," *New York Times*, May 25, 2007.

4.10 **(Related to the *Making the Connection* on page 549)** Why are there superstar basketball players but no superstar automobile mechanics?

4.11 Tennis stars Venus Williams and Serena Williams do not play for teams. They enter tennis tournaments as individuals. Is the concept of marginal revenue product as important in explaining their earnings as it is in explaining the earnings of major league baseball players? Briefly explain.

4.12 (Related to the *Chapter Opener* on page 534) The number of players on each major league baseball team is determined by negotiation between the players' union and the owners of major league teams. How does this fact affect the explanation given in the text of why baseball players are paid more than college professors? Briefly explain.

4.13 Prior to the early twentieth century, a worker who was injured on the job could collect damages only by suing his employer. To sue successfully, the worker—or his family, if the worker had been killed—had to show that the injury was due to the employer's negligence, that the worker did not know the job was hazardous, and that the worker's own negligence had not contributed to the accident. These lawsuits were difficult for workers to win, and even workers who had been seriously injured on the job often were unable to collect any damages from their employers. Beginning in 1910, most states passed "workers' compensation" laws that required employers to purchase insurance that would compensate workers for injuries suffered on the job. A study by Price Fishback and Shawn Kantor of the University of Arizona shows that after the passage of workers' compensation laws, wages received by workers in the coal and lumber industries fell. Briefly explain why passage of workers' compensation laws would lead to a fall in wages in some industries.

Source: Price V. Fishback and Shawn Everett Kantor, "Did Workers Pay for the Passage of Workers' Compensation Laws?" *Quarterly Journal of Economics*, Vol. 100, No. 3, August 1995, pp. 713–742.

4.14 The following table is similar to Table 16-2 on page 551, except that it includes the earnings of Asian males and females. Does the fact that Asian males are the highest-earning group in the table affect the likelihood that economic discrimination is the best explanation for why earnings differ among the groups listed in the table? Briefly explain your argument.

GROUP	ANNUAL EARNINGS
Asian males	$52,026
White males	48,698
Asian females	40,172
White females	35,822
Black males	34,372
Black females	30,453
Hispanic males	29,072
Hispanic females	25,272

Source: U.S. Bureau of the Census, Current Population Survey, *Annual Social and Economic Supplement*, Table PINC-10, March 2008.

4.15 (Related to *Solved Problem 16-4* on page 553) Use the following graphs to answer the questions.

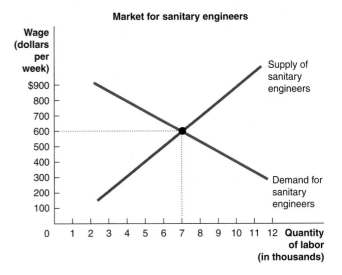

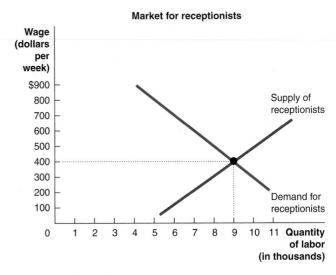

a. What is the equilibrium quantity of sanitary engineers hired, and what is the equilibrium wage?

b. What is the equilibrium quantity of receptionists hired, and what is the equilibrium wage?

c. Briefly discuss why sanitary engineers might earn a higher weekly wage than receptionists.

d. Suppose that comparable-worth legislation is passed and the government requires that sanitary engineers and receptionists must be paid the same wage of $500 per week. Now how many sanitary engineers will be hired and how many receptionists will be hired?

4.16 (Related to *Solved Problem 16-4* on page 553) In most universities, economics professors receive larger salaries than English professors. Suppose that the government requires that from now on, all universities must pay economics professors the same salaries as English professors. Use demand and supply graphs to analyze the effect of this requirement.

4.17 During the 1970s, many women changed their minds about whether they would leave the labor force after marrying and having children or whether they would be in the labor force most of their adult lives. In 1968, the National Longitudinal Survey asked a representative sample of women aged 14 to 24 whether they expected to be in the labor force at age 35. Twenty-nine percent of white women and 59 percent of black women responded that they expected to be in the labor force at that age. In fact, when these women were 35, 60 percent of those who were married and 80 percent of those who were unmarried were in the labor force. In other words, many more women ended up being in the labor force than expected to be when they were of high school and college age. What impact did this fact have on the earnings of these women? Briefly explain.

Source: Claudia Goldin, *Explaining the Gender Gap: An Economic History of American Women*, New York: Oxford University Press, 1990, p. 155.

4.18 In the early twentieth century, black people in the U.S. South were excluded from some occupations, but in jobs such as agriculture that employed both white and black workers, black workers received about the same wages as white workers. Briefly discuss why economic discrimination in the South took this form.

>> **End Learning Objective 16.4**

16.5 LEARNING OBJECTIVE 16.5 | Discuss the role personnel economics can play in helping firms deal with human resources issues, **pages 557–559.**

Personnel Economics

Summary

Personnel economics is the application of economic analysis to human resources issues. One insight of personnel economics is that the productivity of workers often can be increased if firms move from straight-time pay to commission or piece-rate pay.

 Visit www.myeconlab.com to complete these exercises online and get instant feedback.

Review Questions

5.1 What is personnel economics?

5.2 If piece-rate or commission systems of compensating workers have important advantages for firms, why don't more firms use them?

Problems and Applications

5.3 According to a recent economic study, the number of jobs in which firms used bonuses, commission, or piece rates to tie workers' pay to their performance increased from an estimated 30 percent of all jobs in the 1970s to 40 percent in the 1990s. Why would systems that tie workers pay to how much they produce have become increasingly popular with firms? The same study found that these pay systems were more common in higher-paid jobs than in lower-paid jobs. What explains this result?

Source: Thomas Lemieux, W. Bentley MacLeod, and Daniel Parent, "Performance Pay and Wage Inequality," NBER Working Paper No. 13128, May 2007.

5.4 Many companies that pay workers an hourly wage require some minimum level of acceptable output. Suppose a company that has been using this system decides to switch to a piece-rate system under which workers are compensated on the basis of how much output they produce but under which they are also free to choose how much to produce. Is it likely that workers under a piece-rate system will end up choosing to produce less than the minimum output required under the hourly wage system? Briefly explain.

5.5 In most jobs, the harder you work, the more you earn. Some workers would rather work harder and earn more; others would rather work less hard, even though as a result they earn less. Suppose, though, that all workers at a company fall into the "work harder and earn more" group. Suppose, also, that the workers all have the same abilities. In these circumstances, would output per worker be the same under an hourly wage compensation system as under a piece-rate system? Briefly explain.

5.6 For years, the Goodyear Tire & Rubber Company compensated its sales force by paying a salesperson a salary plus a bonus based on the number of tires he or she sold. In early 2002, Goodyear made two changes to this policy: (1) The basis for the bonus was changed from the *quantity* of tires sold to the *revenue* from the tires sold, and (2) salespeople were required to get approval from corporate headquarters in Akron, Ohio, before offering to sell tires to customers at reduced prices. Explain why these changes were likely to increase Goodyear's profits.

Source: Timothy Aeppel, "Amid Weak Inflation, Firms Turn Creative to Boost Prices," *Wall Street Journal*, September 18, 2002.

5.7 (Related to the *Making the Connection* on page 558) What affect did the incentive pay system have on Safelite's marginal cost of installing replacement car windows? If all firms that replace car windows adopted an incentive pay system, what would happen to the price of replacing automobile glass? Who ultimately would benefit?

>> **End Learning Objective 16.5**

16.6 LEARNING OBJECTIVE 16.6 | Show how equilibrium prices are determined in the markets for capital and natural resources, **pages 560–563.**

The Markets for Capital and Natural Resources

Summary

The approach used to analyze the market for labor can also be used to analyze the markets for other factors of production. In equilibrium, the price of capital is equal to the marginal revenue product of capital, and the price of natural resources is equal to the marginal revenue product of natural resources. The price received by a factor that is in fixed supply is called an *economic rent*, or pure rent. A **monopsony** is the sole buyer of a factor of production. According to the **marginal productivity theory of income distribution**, the distribution of income is determined by the marginal productivity of the factors of production individuals own.

myeconlab Visit www.myeconlab.com to complete these exercises *Get Ahead of the Curve* online and get instant feedback.

Review Questions

6.1 In equilibrium, what determines the price of capital? What determines the price of natural resources? What is the marginal productivity theory of income distribution?

6.2 What is an economic rent? What is a monopsony?

Problems and Applications

6.3 Adam operates a pin factory. Suppose Adam faces the situation shown in the following table and the cost of renting a machine is $550 per week.

a. Fill in the blanks in the table and determine the profit-maximizing number of machines for Adam to rent. Briefly explain why renting this number of machines is profit maximizing.
b. Draw Adam's demand curve for capital.

6.4 Many people have predicted, using a model like the one in panel (b) of Figure 16-12 on page 561, that the price of natural resources should rise consistently over time in comparison with the prices of other goods because the demand curve for natural resources is continually shifting to the right while the supply curve must be shifting to the left as natural resources are used up. However, the relative prices of most natural resources have not been increasing. Draw a graph that shows the demand and supply for natural resources that can explain why prices haven't risen even though demand has.

6.5 In 1879, economist Henry George published *Progress and Poverty*, which became one of the best-selling books of the nineteenth century. In this book, George argued that all existing taxes should be replaced with a single tax on land. In Chapter 4, we discussed the concept of tax incidence, or the actual division of the burden of a tax between buyers and sellers in a market. If land is taxed, how will the burden of the tax be divided between the sellers of land and the buyers of land? Illustrate your answer with a graph of the market for land.

6.6 The total amount of oil in the earth is not increasing. Does this mean that in the market for oil, the supply curve is perfectly inelastic? Briefly explain.

6.7 In a competitive labor market, imposing a minimum wage should reduce the equilibrium level of employment. Will this also be true if the labor market is a monopsony? Briefly explain.

NUMBER OF MACHINES	OUTPUT OF PINS (BOXES PER WEEK)	MARGINAL PRODUCT OF CAPITAL	PRODUCT PRICE (DOLLARS PER BOX)	TOTAL REVENUE	MARGINAL REVENUE PRODUCT OF CAPITAL	RENTAL COST PER MACHINE	ADDITIONAL PROFIT FROM RENTING ONE ADDITIONAL MACHINE
0	0	—	$100		—	$550	
1	12		100			550	
2	21		100			550	
3	28		100			550	
4	34		100			550	
5	39		100			550	
6	43		100			550	

>> **End Learning Objective 16.6**

Chapter 17

The Economics of Information

Why Does State Farm Charge Young Men So Much More Than Young Women for Auto Insurance?

In 2008, if you were a 21-year-old male in Denver, Colorado, driving a car of average value an average number of miles per year, you had to pay State Farm Insurance $781 for automobile insurance. If you were a 21-year-old female, you paid only $642. A 35-year-old male paid $457, and a 68-year-old female paid just $326. Was State Farm practicing age and sex discrimination? Was the company practicing price discrimination of the type we discussed in Chapter 15? Actually, State Farm was attempting to match up the prices they charged for automobile insurance with the costs they were likely to incur on each policy. Young males are involved in many more auto accidents than young females, or middle-aged males, so they cost State Farm more to insure.

With corporate headquarters in Bloomington, Illinois, State Farm is the largest automobile insurance company in the United States, insuring one out of five automobiles. State Farm was founded in 1922 by George J. Mecherle. Mecherle had started life as a farmer, but later took a job selling insurance. The company he worked for charged the same price for automobile insurance to people living in the city of Bloomington as it did to farmers living outside town. Mecherle realized that farmers had far fewer accidents than did city drivers. So he started the State Farm Mutual Automobile Insurance Company to offer farmers automobile insurance polices at lower prices.

Mecherle's success highlights the importance to insurance companies of correctly pricing policies. A key difficulty facing insurance companies is that drivers know more about how likely they are to have accidents than do the companies. As a result, insurance companies may charge safe drivers prices that are too high—causing these drivers to buy policies from other companies—and charge risky drivers prices that are too low. The difficulties insurance companies face in pricing their policies are caused by *asymmetric information*, which exists when one party to an economic transaction has less information than the other party. In the market for insurance, asymmetric information leads to two problems: *adverse selection* and *moral hazard*. Adverse selection can result in an insurance company attracting more high-risk drivers than it would like, given the prices of its policies. Moral hazard occurs when people change their behavior *after* purchasing insurance. Whether drivers have an accident depends partly on how safely they drive. If drivers did not have insurance to pay for the repairs needed after accidents, they would be likely to drive more cautiously.

In recent years, insurance companies have changed how they price policies. Insurance companies have always aimed at charging high prices to drivers likely to have more accidents and file more claims and lower prices to safer drivers. Usually, though, companies had divided drivers into just a few categories, based on their ages and driving records. Today, many companies use sophisticated computer models that employ thousands of variables to predict the chance that a driver will have an accident. The result has been an increase in the different prices being charged to drivers. For example, until recently, most companies lumped all drivers aged 21 to 70 into one category. But more sophisticated analysis of accident data shows that more categories would be better. As one executive of an insurance company put it, "Now we know a 22-year-old married woman is not as good a driving risk as a 45-year-old married woman." The differing prices State Farm charges drivers in Denver were the result of implementing the new pricing models.

AN INSIDE LOOK on page 590 examines how insurance companies use credit reports to decide who is likely to be a risky driver.

Sources: Information on State Farm pricing from the Colorado State Department of Regulatory Agencies, Division of Insurance Web site; Denise Trowbridge, "State Farm to Lower Auto Rates," *The Columbus (Ohio) Dispatch*, March 23, 2007, p. 01H; and Christopher Oster, "Auto Insurers Cut Rates—For Some," *Wall Street Journal*, April 22, 2004, p. D1.

Economics in YOUR Life!

Have You Ever Tried to Sell a Car?

The classified sections of newspapers are filled with ads from people trying to sell cars. Many colleges also have online bulletin boards where students can list cars for sale. Some people also list cars for sale on eBay. Car buyers choose between buying from individual sellers or buying from used car dealers. If you have tried to sell a car through a newspaper or an online ad, you have probably had trouble selling at a price as high as car dealers receive.

Why are used car buyers only willing to pay relatively low prices for cars they buy from individual sellers? If you found two seemingly identical cars, one at a local car dealer and the other for sale by an individual on eBay, would you be willing to pay the same amount for the two cars? As you read this chapter, see if you can answer these questions. You can check your answers against those we provide at the end of the chapter. >> Continued on page 589

I
n previous chapters, we assumed that buyers and sellers in a market possess the same amount of information. In the market for insurance, as we have seen, buyers often have more information than sellers. Later in this chapter, we will see that the reverse is often true in financial markets: Firms selling stocks and bonds usually have more information than buyers. In other markets, buyers and sellers may both lack complete information. For example, when an oil company bids for the right to drill on tracts of government land, neither the company nor the government has complete information on how much oil the tracts contain. When telecommunications companies bid in U.S. Federal Communications Commission auctions for licenses to provide mobile phone services, they don't have complete information on how valuable the licenses may be.

In this chapter, we discuss the economics of information and how imperfect information can affect the decisions of both households and firms. After reading this chapter, you will better understand situations such as auctions and the markets for insurance and stocks and bonds, in which the role of imperfect information is particularly important.

17.1 LEARNING OBJECTIVE

17.1 | Define asymmetric information and distinguish between adverse selection and moral hazard.

Asymmetric Information

Asymmetric information A situation in which one party to an economic transaction has less information than the other party.

The difficulty in correctly pricing insurance policies arises from the problem of **asymmetric information**, which occurs when one party to an economic transaction has less information than the other party. As we will see, in some markets, it is difficult to understand the actions of buyers and sellers without understanding the effects of asymmetric information. In fact, guarding against the effects of asymmetric information is a major objective of sellers in the insurance market and of buyers in financial markets. The market for used automobiles was the first in which economists began to carefully study the problem of asymmetric information.

Adverse Selection and the Market for "Lemons"

The study of asymmetric information began with an analysis of the used car market by Nobel laureate George Akerlof, of the University of California, Berkeley. Akerlof pointed out that the seller of a used car will always have more information on the true condition of the car than will potential buyers. A car that has been poorly maintained—by, for instance, not having its oil changed regularly—may have damage that could be difficult to detect even by a trained mechanic.

If potential buyers of used cars know that they will have difficulty separating the good used cars from the bad used cars, or "lemons," they will take this into account in the prices they are willing to pay. Consider the following simple example: Suppose that half of the 2006 Volkswagen Jettas offered for sale have been well maintained and are good, reliable used cars. The other half have been poorly maintained and are lemons that will be unreliable. Suppose that potential buyers of 2006 Jettas would be willing to pay $10,000 for a reliable one but only $5,000 for an unreliable one. The sellers know how well they have maintained their cars and whether they are reliable, but the buyers do not have this information and so have no way of telling the reliable cars from the unreliable ones.

In this situation, buyers will generally offer a price somewhere between the price they would be willing to pay for a good car and the price they would be willing to pay for a lemon. In this case, with a 50–50 chance of buying a good car or a lemon, buyers might offer $7,500, which is halfway between the price they would pay if they knew for certain the car was a good one and the price they would pay if they knew it was a lemon.

Unfortunately for used car buyers, a major glitch arises at this point. From the buyers' perspective, given that they don't know whether any particular car offered for sale is a good car or a lemon, an offer of $7,500 seems reasonable. But the sellers *do* know whether the cars they are offering are good cars or lemons. To a seller of a good car, an offer of $7,500 is $2,500 below the true value of the car, and the seller will be reluctant to sell. But to a seller of a lemon, an offer of $7,500 is $2,500 *above* the true value of the car, and the seller will be quite happy to sell. As sellers of lemons take advantage of knowing more about the cars they are selling than buyers do, the used car market will fall victim to **adverse selection**: Most used cars offered for sale will be lemons. In other words, because of asymmetric information, the market has selected adversely the cars that will be offered for sale. Notice as well that the problem of adverse selection reduces the total quantity of used cars bought and sold in the market because few good cars are offered for sale. From this example we can conclude that information problems reduce economic efficiency in a market.

> **Adverse selection** The situation in which one party to a transaction takes advantage of knowing more than the other party to the transaction.

Reducing Adverse Selection in the Car Market: Warranties and Reputations

There are ways of reducing the adverse selection problem in the used car market. Car manufacturers provide warranties when cars are sold new. These warranties cover the costs of major repairs and can be transferred to a new owner when a car is resold. Warranties give prospective buyers some assurance that they will not be stuck with all the cost of repairs. In addition, used car dealers take steps to assure buyers that the cars they are selling are not lemons. They do this by building a reputation for selling reliable used cars and by offering their own warranties if the manufacturer's warranty has expired or can't be transferred. If a used car dealer can convince buyers that the dealer is selling reliable cars, then, using the numbers from our earlier example, buyers would be willing to pay $10,000 rather than $7,500 for a used Jetta.

Some states have passed "lemon laws" to help reduce information problems in the car market. Most lemon laws have two main provisions:

1 New cars that need several major repairs during the first year or two after the date of the original purchase may be returned to the manufacturer for a full refund.

2 Car manufacturers must indicate whether a used car they are offering for sale was repurchased from the original owner as a lemon.

Although lemon laws are popular with consumers, opposition from manufacturers has resulted in these laws being enacted in fewer than 20 states.

Asymmetric Information in the Market for Insurance

Asymmetric information problems are particularly severe in the market for insurance. Buyers of insurance policies will always know more about the likelihood of the event being insured against happening than will insurance companies. For example, buyers of health insurance policies know more about the state of their health—and, therefore, how likely they are to submit medical bills to the insurance company—than will the insurance company that sells them the policies. Similarly, drivers know more about whether they are reckless drivers, homeowners know more about potential fire hazards in their homes, and so on than do the insurance companies selling them policies. Insurance companies will cover their costs, including the opportunity cost of funds invested in them by their owners, only if they set the prices—or *premiums*—of policies at levels that cover the claims for payment insured people are likely to submit.

Reducing Adverse Selection in the Insurance Market

Adverse selection problems arise because sick people are more likely to want health insurance than are healthy people, reckless drivers are more likely to want automobile insurance than are careful drivers, and people living in homes that are fire hazards are more likely to want fire insurance than are people living in safe homes. If insurance companies have trouble determining who is healthy and who is sick or who is a reckless driver and who is a safe driver, they will end up setting their premiums too low and will fail to cover their costs. To reduce the problem of adverse selection, insurance companies gather as much information as they can on people applying for policies. For example, people applying for individual health insurance policies or life insurance policies usually need to submit their medical records to the insurance company. Insurance companies usually also carry out their own medical examinations. People applying for automobile insurance have their driving record reviewed. Insurance companies charge higher premiums to people who have caused accidents or who have speeding tickets. As we saw in the chapter opener, insurance companies like State Farm will remain profitable only if they succeed in identifying the riskiest drivers so as to charge them higher premiums.

Sometimes the adverse selection problem leads insurance companies simply to refuse to offer insurance policies to certain people at any price. Someone with a terminal or chronic illness, for example, may find it difficult to buy an individual health insurance or life insurance policy. The owner of a home or warehouse in an area that is prone to arson fires may have difficulty getting fire insurance. An alternative to refusing to sell policies to these people would be for insurance companies to charge very high premiums for coverage. This may make the adverse selection problem worse, however. When premiums are very high, only people who are almost certain to make a claim will purchase a policy.

The adverse selection problem can also be reduced if people are automatically covered by insurance. For example, state governments require that every driver buy automobile insurance. This policy reduces the problem of insurance being purchased primarily by bad drivers. As we saw at the beginning of the chapter, however, State Farm and other insurance companies still face the problem of determining the profit-maximizing prices to charge for their policies.

Insurance companies can reduce adverse selection problems in selling health insurance and life insurance by offering *group coverage* to large firms—including colleges and universities—or to alliances of smaller firms. With group coverage, everyone employed by a firm is automatically covered. As long as the group is large enough, the coverage is likely to represent the proportions of healthy and unhealthy people found in the general population. As a result of this *risk pooling*, it is much easier for insurance companies to estimate the average number of claims likely to be filed under a group health insurance or life insurance policy than it would be to predict the number of claims likely to be filed under an individual policy. Because everyone in the group must pay the premium—or have it paid for them by their employer—insurance companies avoid the problem of only sick people buying the insurance. Group coverage that allows healthy people not to participate is still subject to adverse selection problems, however. If healthy people don't participate, the number of claims filed per participating employee is likely to be high. This level of claims may cause the insurance company to raise the price it charges to the firm for the group policy. If the firm then raises the monthly payment required of employees, the higher price will discourage additional numbers of healthy employees from participating.

Making the Connection | Does Adverse Selection Explain Why Some People Do Not Have Health Insurance?

Roughly 47 million people in the United States do not have health insurance. As the chart shows, more than two-thirds of Americans are covered by private health insurance plans—primarily plans provided by firms to their employees—and more than one-quarter of people are covered by government health insurance plans—such as the Medicare program for people over age 65 or the Medicaid program for poor people. But about 16 percent of people are not covered by health insurance. (Note that the percentages in the chart sum to more than 100 because some people are covered by both private health insurance and government health insurance.)

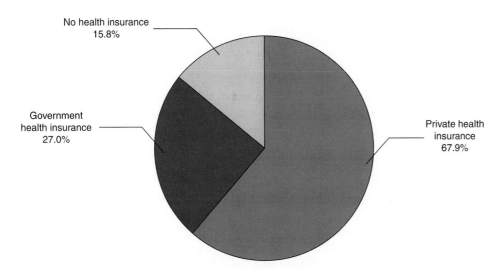

No health insurance
15.8%

Government
health insurance
27.0%

Private health
insurance
67.9%

Source: U.S. Bureau of the Census, *Income, Poverty and Health Insurance in the United States, 2006*, P60–231, Figure 6, August 2007. www.census.gov/prod/2007pubs/p60-233.pdf.

There are a number of reasons people may not have health insurance. Some healthy young adults don't expect to need medical care and so do not want to pay the monthly premiums to buy insurance they don't expect to need. As a result, although 15.8 percent of the total population lacks health insurance, the proportion of people between the ages of 18 and 24 who do not have insurance is almost twice as large, at 29.3 percent. And more than one-quarter of those between the ages of 25 and 34 do not have insurance. Many low-income people qualify for government health insurance through the Medicaid program. But some low-income people either do not take advantage of Medicaid or are not eligible for it. For these people, their low incomes may be the main reason that they do not have insurance. However, only about 20 percent of the uninsured have incomes below the official U.S. poverty line; more than 30 percent of the uninsured have incomes more than three times greater than the poverty line. Kate Bundorf of Stanford University and Mark Pauly of the University of Pennsylvania have estimated that as many as three-quarters of the uninsured can afford to buy health insurance.

Some economists have argued that adverse selection may be an important explanation for the significant percentage of people lacking health insurance in the United States. We have seen that one effect of adverse selection in a market is that the equilibrium quantity of the good or service may be smaller than it would have been if there were no information problems. Because insurance companies are aware of the adverse selection problem, they may sometimes offer health insurance policies at prices higher than young, healthy consumers are willing to pay. Similarly, as we have already seen, insurance companies will sometimes refuse to offer insurance to people with chronic illnesses.

In recent years, state governments may have unintentionally made the adverse selection problem worse by regulating the terms of the policies insurance companies are allowed to offer small firms. These state regulations generally restrict the ability of insurance companies to offer policies that charge higher premiums to employees with existing health conditions. Research by Kosali Ilayperuma Simon of Cornell University indicates that insurance companies responded to the regulations by raising the prices of the policies they offer to small companies. When the companies, in turn, raised the prices their employees have to pay to participate in the health plans, some younger, healthier employees dropped out of the plans and became uninsured.

So, although no one factor provides a complete explanation of why some people in the United States lack health insurance, adverse selection appears to play a significant role.

Sources: M. Kate Bundorf and Mark V. Pauly, "Is Health Insurance Affordable for the Uninsured?" *Journal of Health Economics*, Vol. 25, No. 4, July 2006, pp. 650–673; and Kosali Ilayperuma Simon, "Adverse Selection in Health Insurance Markets? Evidence from State Small-Group Health Insurance Reforms," *Journal of Public Economics*, Vol. 89, Nos. 9–10, September 2005, pp. 1865–1877.

YOUR TURN: Test your understanding by doing related problems 1.11 and 1.12 on page 593 at the end of this chapter.

Moral Hazard

Moral hazard The actions people take after they have entered into a transaction that make the other party to the transaction worse off.

The insurance market is subject to a second consequence of asymmetric information, called *moral hazard*. **Moral hazard** refers to actions people take after they have entered into a transaction that make the other party to the transaction worse off. Moral hazard in the insurance market occurs when people change their behavior after becoming insured. For example, once a firm has taken out a fire insurance policy on a warehouse, it may be a little less careful about avoiding fire hazards. Similarly, someone with health insurance may visit the doctor for treatment of a cold or other minor illness, when he or she would not do so without the insurance.

Insurance companies can take steps to reduce moral hazard problems. For example, a fire insurance company may insist that a firm install a sprinkler system in a warehouse to offset any increased carelessness once the policy is in place, or it may reserve the right to inspect the warehouse periodically to check for fire hazards. Insurance companies also use *deductibles* and *coinsurance* to reduce moral hazard. A deductible requires the holder of the insurance policy to pay a certain dollar amount of a claim. With coinsurance, the insurance company pays only a percentage of any claim. Suppose you have a health insurance policy with a $200 deductible and 20 percent coinsurance, and you have a medical bill of $1,000. You must pay the first $200 of the bill and 20 percent of the remaining $800. Deductibles and coinsurance give the holders of insurance policies incentives to avoid filing claims.

Don't Let This Happen to **YOU!**

Don't Confuse Adverse Selection with Moral Hazard

The two key consequences of asymmetric information are adverse selection and moral hazard. It is easy to get these concepts mixed up. One way to keep the concepts straight is to remember that adverse selection refers to what happens *at the time* of entering into the transaction. An example would be an insurance company that sells a life insurance policy to a terminally ill person because the company lacks full information on the state of the person's

health. Moral hazard refers to what happens *after* entering into the transaction. For example, a nonsmoker buys a life insurance policy and then starts smoking four packs of cigarettes a day. (It may help to remember that *a* comes before *m* in the alphabet just as *a*dverse selection comes before *m*oral hazard.)

YOUR TURN: Test your understanding by doing related problems 1.14 on page 593 and 3.3 on page 594 at the end of this chapter.

17.2 | Apply the concepts of adverse selection and moral hazard to financial markets.

Adverse Selection and Moral Hazard in Financial Markets

Adverse selection and moral hazard pose problems for firms and investors in the markets for stocks and bonds. In Chapter 7, we saw that most firms have to raise funds by borrowing from banks. Asymmetric information is a key reason only large corporations are able to raise funds by selling stocks and bonds. Every firm knows more about its financial situation than does any potential investor. Because investors have trouble distinguishing between well-run and poorly run firms, they are reluctant to buy the stocks and bonds of firms unless a great deal of public information about those firms is available. As a result, this means only firms that are studied closely by investment analysts working for brokerage firms and investment companies can succeed in selling stocks and bonds to investors. The investment analysts state their opinions of the true financial health of firms in reports that are available to the investing public. A great deal of public information about Microsoft is available, and investment analysts follow the firm closely. Not much public information is available about small firms like Anisul's Software Solutions, and no investment analysts follow the firm. As a result, Microsoft can raise funds by selling stocks and bonds, but Anisul's Software Solutions can't.

Investors also worry about moral hazard. Once a firm has sold stocks and bonds, what will it do with the funds it has raised? Of course, investors expect that the firm will use the funds in ways that will make the firm more profitable. But the possibility exists that the firm will use the funds in ways that actually reduce profits, which is obviously not in the best interests of investors. For instance, a firm might use the funds to pay high salaries to the firm's managers or to open an unneeded branch office in Paris, to which the managers can make frequent visits. In the worst case, the firm's managers might actually steal the funds. Once again, the larger the firm is and the more carefully investment analysts follow its activities, the less likely moral hazard is to be a problem. This explains, in part, why investors are willing to buy the stocks and bonds of large firms but not of small firms. Note that we are using a broader definition of moral hazard here than we did when discussing insurance. In this case, moral hazard refers to actions taken by one party to a transaction that are different from what the other party expected at the time of the transaction.

Reducing Adverse Selection and Moral Hazard in Financial Markets

The decline in stock prices that followed the great stock market crash of 1929 wiped out the savings of many investors. Some investors complained that firms had failed to provide them with accurate financial information. Congress responded in 1934 by establishing the *Securities and Exchange Commission (SEC)* to regulate the stock and bond markets. The SEC requires that firms register stocks or bonds they wish to sell with the SEC. The firms must also provide potential investors with a *prospectus* that contains all relevant financial information on the firms. Although investors sometimes complain that a firm's prospectus is difficult to understand, the SEC did succeed in increasing the amount of information available to potential investors. This additional information helped reduce the adverse selection and moral hazard problems in financial markets and increased the number of firms that have been able to raise funds by selling stocks and bonds.

The steep decline in stock prices that occurred from 2000 to 2002 made it clear that information problems still exist in financial markets. During the stock market boom of the late 1990s, many investors became less cautious and more willing to invest in firms about which they had relatively little information. As investors became more focused on stock prices during those years, pressure increased for firms to report that they had earned profits at least as high as investment analysts were forecasting. Firms reporting profits that were lower than analysts had forecast could experience a sharp decline in the price of their stock. As we discussed in Chapter 7, the managers of some firms gave in to the temptation to "cook the books" by falsely reporting that their profits were much higher than they really were. This cheating could not be concealed forever. During 2002, a number of scandals involving the reporting of inflated profits came to light. These scandals served as a reminder to investors of the difficulty of overcoming adverse selection and moral hazard problems in financial markets.

| Making the Connection | Using Government Policy to Reduce Moral Hazard in Investments |

The basic information on the financial condition of a company is contained in its *financial statements*, particularly its income statement and balance sheet. A firm's income statement reports its profits over a period of time, and its balance sheet shows the net value of the firm, based on the value of everything it owns minus the value of everything it owes. (For more on financial statements, see the appendix to Chapter 7.) Investment analysts at brokerage firms and individual investors rely on this information when evaluating firms. All firms that issue stock to the public have their statements *audited* by certified public accountants (CPAs). A CPA is an employee of an accounting firm, *not* of the company being audited. The audit is intended to provide investors with an independent opinion as to whether the company's financial statements reflect the true financial condition of the firm.

Unfortunately, a series of spectacular scandals during 2002 revealed that the financial statements of even some very large firms were not reliable. In July 2002, WorldCom, the second-largest provider of long-distance telephone service in the United States, filed for bankruptcy. In June, WorldCom executives had admitted to misstating more than $3.8 billion in expenses on WorldCom's financial statements. As a result, instead of the profit it initially reported earning during 2001 and the first quarter of 2002, it had actually lost

The government has intervened to increase the confidence of investors in the securities traded on the New York Stock Exchange and in other financial markets.

$1.2 billion. Investors saw the value of the 3 billion shares of stock issued by WorldCom drop to zero. Enron, an energy trading company, had managed to keep much of its debt from being included on its balance sheet. Eventually, it too had to declare bankruptcy. Members of the Rigas family, which controlled Adelphia Communications, one of the largest cable television companies in the United States, were accused of using more than $250 million of the firm's money for personal expenses—a striking example of moral hazard. The firm also filed for bankruptcy, and two Rigas family members were convicted of looting the company and are serving prison terms of 15 to 20 years.

The news that these and other firms had "cooked the books" illustrates the difficulty that moral hazard poses for investors. The management of a firm knows far more about the firm's finances than any outside investor can. If investors believe they cannot rely on the firm's financial statements to represent the true financial condition of the firm, they will be extremely reluctant to invest in the firm. Many observers have argued that a general loss of confidence in the reliability of financial statements was behind the wave of selling that hit U.S. stock markets in the summer of 2002.

To help restore confidence in financial statements, Congress passed and President George W. Bush signed into law the Sarbanes-Oxley Act of 2002, which is aimed at strengthening the country's security laws. The bill authorizes the SEC to set up a government board to oversee the auditing of financial statements. The role of the board was to address the problem of outside auditors who failed to ensure the accuracy of corporate financial statements. Under the provisions of the bill, auditors who willfully violate accounting rules face five-year prison sentences. The bill also requires chief executive officers and chief financial officers to personally certify the accuracy of financial statements. The maximum prison term for violating the securities laws was raised to 25 years.

YOUR TURN: Test your understanding by doing related problem 2.7 on page 594 at the end of this chapter.

17.3 | Apply the concepts of adverse selection and moral hazard to labor markets.

Adverse Selection and Moral Hazard in Labor Markets

We saw in Chapter 7 that economists refer to the conflict between the interests of shareholders and the interests of top management as a **principal–agent problem**. This problem occurs when agents—in this case, a firm's top management—pursue their own interests rather than the interests of the principal—in this case, the shareholders of the corporation—who hired them. There is also the potential for a principal–agent problem between the managers of a firm and its workers. The moral hazard behind the principal–agent problem is that workers, once hired, may shirk their obligations and not work hard.

Principal–agent problem A problem caused by agents pursuing their own interests rather than the interests of the principals who hired them.

Employers can ensure that workers are doing their jobs by closely monitoring them. Telemarketing firms, for example, can monitor their employees electronically to ensure that they make the required number of telephone calls per hour. Not all firms, however, can monitor their employees so closely. Often firms must rely on workers being sufficiently motivated so they do not shirk their responsibilities. One way to motivate workers is to increase the value to them of their current jobs, relative to other jobs they might have. If you consider your current job to be more valuable than the alternatives, you will be reluctant to shirk because you won't want to risk being fired. Firms have several ways to make a worker's job seem more valuable:

- *Efficiency wages.* There is a market for every kind of labor, just as there is a market for every good and service. A firm's demand for labor is determined by how much output workers can produce for the firm—the workers' *productivity*—and by the price the firm receives when it sells the output the workers produce. The supply of labor is determined by the willingness of workers to supply a given amount of work at a particular wage. The equilibrium wage equates the quantity of labor demanded to the quantity of labor supplied. If a firm offers to pay a wage above the equilibrium wage, a worker will consider the job to be valuable and will be less likely to shirk and risk losing the job. An *efficiency wage* is a higher-than-equilibrium wage firms pay to give workers an incentive to work harder.

- *Seniority system.* Many firms use a seniority system under which workers who have been with the firm longer receive higher pay and other benefits, such as the choice of better or more interesting jobs. A worker who early in his career at a firm is fired for shirking will give up the possibility of participating in the benefits of seniority. A seniority system can have an effect similar to that of an efficiency wage in giving workers an incentive to work harder.

- *Profit sharing.* The harder employees work, the more profits a firm makes, but employees don't share in these increased profits if they are paid a fixed wage or salary. Under a profit-sharing plan, employees receive a share of the profits earned by the firm. The harder the employee works, the more profit the firm earns, and the higher the employee's income. Profit sharing increases the incentive of an employee to work hard. One problem with some profit-sharing plans is that they don't increase the incentive very much. For example, suppose you work at a firm with 100 employees, and by working harder, you can increase the firm's profits by $10,000 per year. If each employee shares equally in the increased profits, your income will rise, but only by $100 per year. This increase is probably not enough to compensate you for the additional effort required. In addition, a firm's profits can be affected by many factors, such as a slowdown in the economy, that are unrelated to how hard a particular employee works. So, you might work very hard during a given period and actually see the profits of the firm fall for reasons you can't control. In that case, your hard work would not have increased your income at all.

Solved Problem | 17-3

Changing Workers' Compensation to Reduce Adverse Selection and Moral Hazard

Jill runs a clothing store. She is concerned that her salespeople are not making much effort to be friendly to customers or to persuade them to buy more clothes. Because Jill has to be out of the store most of the day, it isn't easy for her to monitor the activities of her salespeople. Jill is paying her workers an hourly wage, but she is considering switching to paying them on commission: They would be compensated on the basis of how much clothing they sold.

a. What effect would this change have on the types of workers Jill attracts?

b. Briefly explain whether this change is likely to increase Jill's profits.

SOLVING THE PROBLEM:

Step 1: **Review the chapter material.** This problem is about adverse selection and moral hazard in labor markets, so you may want to review the section "Adverse Selection and Moral Hazard in Labor Markets," which begins on page 583.

Step 2: **Use the ideas of adverse selection and moral hazard in labor markets to answer question (a).** When workers are not monitored, they have an incentive to expend as little effort as possible, which is the moral hazard problem in labor markets. When salespeople are paid an hourly wage, their compensation is determined by how many hours they are at work rather than how much they sell. If Jill switches to a system in which compensation depends on how much workers sell, she is likely to attract more workers who have the ability and interest to sell clothes. Workers who don't have much interest in selling clothes are unlikely to stay because their compensation will be reduced. Jill's new compensation scheme will reduce the adverse selection problem she faces when hiring workers.

Step 3: **Answer question (b) by analyzing the effect of the new compensation system on Jill's profits.** Whether Jill's profits rise under the new compensation system depends on whether she is correct that her workers are not making much effort to sell clothes. If she is correct, switching from paying hourly wages to paying commissions is likely to reduce both the adverse selection and moral hazard problems she faces. She will attract people willing to work harder, and she will provide them with an incentive to sell more clothes, so her sales and profits should increase.

>> **End Solved Problem 17-3**

YOUR TURN: For more practice, do related problem 3.4 on page 594 at the end of this chapter.

17.4 | Explain the winner's curse and why it occurs.

The Winner's Curse: When Is It Bad to Win an Auction?

Information problems can occur in auctions. In some auctions, neither the bidder nor the seller has complete information about what is being auctioned. For example, when the government auctions off land for oil drilling, neither the government nor the oil companies bidding in the auctions know with certainty how much oil is in the land. In the 1950s and 1960s, the oil companies that won bids to drill on the North Slope of Alaska and in the Gulf of Mexico did not earn the profits they expected. Three engineers with the Atlantic Richfield oil company argued that this was not due to bad luck but was the result of a general tendency for the winners of auctions, like the ones held for the oil fields, to bid too high. This outcome, called the **winner's curse**, applies to other auctions as well. Knowledge of the winner's curse can make it possible for a savvy firm to win an auction with a high bid that is low enough to be very profitable.

Winner's curse The idea that the winner in certain auctions may have overestimated the value of the good, thus ending up worse off than the losers.

Why were the winning bidders in government auctions of oil fields disappointed with their profits? Three Atlantic Richfield engineers, E. C. Capen, R. V. Clapp, and W. M. Campbell, proposed an explanation. They noted that each firm participating in the auctions used geological data, data on how productive nearby wells had been, and other information to estimate how much oil was likely to be available in each tract of land up for bid. Because of the uncertainty in interpreting the information available, companies made very different bids. Figure 17-1 shows the actual bids made by seven oil companies in 1967 on a tract of land off the Louisiana coast.

Clearly, Company A, with a bid of $32.5 million, was the most optimistic about how much oil the tract contained. Company G, which bid only $3.3 million, was the least optimistic. Who was right? Capen, Clapp, and Campbell argued that as the companies bid on many tracts using the best available information, each company would overestimate the amount of oil in some tracts and underestimate the amount of oil in other tracts. Their mistakes of sometimes being too high would tend to offset their mistakes of sometimes being too low, so *on average their estimates would be correct*. For example, in the case of the tract in Figure 17-1, it was likely that the true amount of oil in the tract was worth about $11.6 million, or the average of the seven bids. The problem for Company A is that it won the auction with a bid of $32.5 million, which was much too

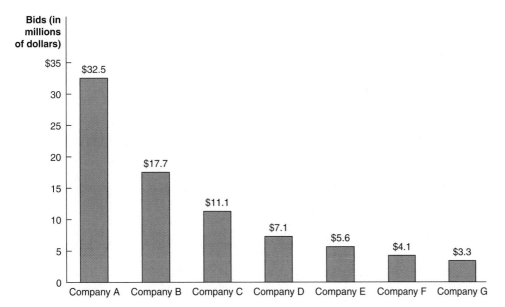

Figure 17-1

Oil Company Bids to Drill off the Louisiana Coast

In 1967, seven oil companies bid to drill on land off the Louisiana coast. Because the amount of oil contained in any particular tract of land up for bid is very uncertain, the bids by oil companies differ widely. The company that has the most optimistic estimate is likely to win the auction. It is also likely to be disappointed in the profits it earns from the tract.
Source: E. C. Capen, R. V. Clapp, and W. M. Campbell, "Competitive Bidding in High-Risk Situations," *Journal of Petroleum Engineering*, June 1971, p. 642.

high given the amount of oil that was likely to actually be in the tract. Capen, Clapp, and Campbell came to two conclusions:

1 "In competitive bidding, the winner tends to be the player who most overestimates true tract value."

2 "He who bids on a parcel what he thinks it is worth will, in the long run, be taken to the cleaners."

These conclusions became known as the *winner's curse* because they indicate that the winner of an auction may end up worse off than the losers. In fact, Capen, Clapp, and Campbell concluded that the oil companies would have made a greater return on their investments if they had taken the funds and put them in a savings account in a bank rather than using them to bid on oil tracts.

<table>
<tr><td>Making
the
Connection</td><td>**Is There a Winner's Curse
in the Marriage Market?**</td></tr>
</table>

In the United States, about 43 percent of all marriages end in divorce. Why the divorce rate is so high is a complicated question. But economics can provide some insight, even if it can't provide a full explanation. Economists have proposed thinking of the interactions of men and women looking for marriage partners as a *marriage market*. Of course, the marriage market is not a typical market in which a good or service is bought and sold for money. But like participants in other markets, the men and women in the marriage market are trying to make themselves as well off as possible, and they are competing against each other to find the best partners.

It's hard to tell how good a marriage partner someone will make until you are actually married to him or her. Like oil companies trying to estimate the amount of oil in a tract of land, men and women use all the information they can to estimate how good a spouse someone will be. But which potential mate are you likely to pursue most strongly? And which potential mate is most likely to find your romantic ardor greater than that of other potential marriage partners? The answer to both questions is the person whose value as a marriage partner you have most greatly overestimated. In other words, if your estimate of how desirable someone is as a marriage partner is much higher than other people's estimates, you have a good chance of marrying that person—but also a good chance of discovering later that your estimate was wrong. The idea of the winner's curse can help explain not only why oil companies can be dissatisfied with the profits from winning oil field auctions but also why many people are apparently dissatisfied with their marriages.

A life of bliss or the winner's curse?

YOUR TURN: Test your understanding by doing related problem 4.7 on page 595 at the end of this chapter.

When Does the Winner's Curse Apply?

Does the winner's curse indicate that the winner of every auction would have been better off losing? No, because the winner's curse applies only to auctions of *common-value* assets—such as oil fields—that would be given the same value by all bidders if they had perfect information. The winner's curse does not apply to auctions of *private-value* assets where the value to each bidder depends on the bidder's own preferences. For example, if you win an auction on eBay for a DVD player, you are not subject to the winner's curse if the DVD player is new and the auction described it completely. You had all the information you needed to evaluate the DVD player, and your bid was based on your preference for a DVD player relative to other things you could have purchased.

Solved Problem | 17-4

Auctions, Available Information, and the Winner's Curse

Suppose that the government has decided to auction off oil fields in Alaska. Suppose, also, that advances in geology have increased the accuracy with which oil companies can pre-dict how much oil will be found in a tract of land. Are these advances likely to increase or decrease the amount of revenue the government receives from the auction?

SOLVING THE PROBLEM:

Step 1: **Review the chapter material.** This problem is about the winner's curse, so you may want to review the section "The Winner's Curse: When Is It Bad to Win an Auction?" which begins on page 585.

Step 2: **Use the information on the winner's curse to answer the problem.** This is an example of a common-value auction where the bidders lack full information about what is being auctioned. We've already seen that oil companies run the risk of the winner's curse when they do not know exactly how much oil is in each tract being auctioned. As shown in Figure 17-1, the winning bidder may significantly overestimate the true amount of oil and end up earning little, if any profit, from its investment.

 If the oil companies knew with certainty how much oil was in each tract, the bids would all be close together and close to the true value of the tract. The amount of revenue received by the government would be lower in this case because the highest bid would be lower. In this problem, however, some uncertainty remains about how much oil is in each tract, so the winner's curse may still arise. Because advances in geology have allowed the companies to make more accurate estimates, the highest bid is likely to be lower than it would have been. Therefore, the advances in geology are likely to *decrease* the amount of revenue the government receives from the auction.

YOUR TURN: For more practice, do related problem 4.5 on page 595 at the end of this chapter.

▶▶ End Solved Problem 17-4

Pacific Telesis Uses the Winner's Curse to Its Own Advantage

In late 1994, the Federal Communications Commission began auctioning 99 licenses that would allow firms to operate wireless communication networks—for mobile phones and similar devices—in specific geographic areas. Pacific Telesis (now part of AT&T) was the local telephone provider in California at that time. It was determined to win the FCC auctions to provide wireless service in California.

 Pacific Telesis hired several economists to help plan its bidding strategy. There was no doubt that the licenses being auctioned were valuable, but given the rapid evolution of the market for mobile phones and other wireless devices, no firm had enough information to determine exactly how valuable. In these circumstances, the Pacific Telesis economists knew that the problem of the winner's curse meant that the firm ran the risk of either overpaying or losing the auction to another firm that would overpay. To avoid this outcome, Pacific Telesis launched a campaign to warn other firms that it was far more knowledgeable about this market than they were and that to win the auction, another firm would have to pay more than the licenses were worth. Pacific Telesis took out full-page ads in newspapers in the cities where the corporate headquarters of

Fear of the winner's curse affected the bidding in auctions for wireless service in California.

their competitors were located. The ads emphasized that Pacific Telesis had significant cost advantages over its rivals in California and that it was determined to win the licenses there. Lyndon Daniels, president of wireless operations at Pacific Telesis, stated in an interview with the *Wall Street Journal*, "If somebody takes California away from us, they'll never make any money." Finally, in an effort to ensure that other firms understood the potential dangers of overbidding, Pacific Telesis hired a prominent economist to give seminars on the winner's curse to the other telecommunications firms.

The strategy Pacific Telesis used proved successful. Most other firms bid very cautiously on the California licenses—at least partly to avoid the winner's curse—and Pacific Telesis won the auctions with relatively low bids. For example, it paid only $437 million—or about $23 per person—for the Los Angeles license. This amount was less than other companies paid for licenses in other U.S. cities where the licenses were thought to be less valuable because of lower incomes, less concentrated populations, and slower population growth than in Los Angeles. Not only had Pacific Telesis avoided the winner's curse, it had used it to help hold down bids from rival companies.

Making the Connection | Want to Make Some Money? Try Auctioning a Jar of Coins

A simple experiment illustrates the winner's curse. Fill a jar with coins. Let a group of people—everyone in your economics class?—inspect the jar. Then auction off the jar: Whoever makes the highest bid gets the jar. The winner will, of course, be the person with the highest estimate of how many coins are in the jar. Just as with oil companies bidding on oil fields, the winner is also likely to have *overestimated* the value of the coins in the jar. Because the high bid is likely to be greater than the value of the coins in the jar, you should end up with a profit—equal to the difference between what the high bidder pays and the value of the coins in the jar.

The highest bidder on this jar of coins could lose money.

Will the winner's curse really apply in this situation? Max Bazerman of Harvard University and William Samuelson of Boston University tested this possibility using MBA students enrolled in economics classes at Boston University. In each of 12 classes, they auctioned off four jars containing either coins or paper clips. The students were told that large paper clips were worth 4 cents and small paper clips were worth 2 cents. They were also told that the winning bidder would receive the value of the jar minus the value of his bid. For example, if the value of the coins or paper clips in a jar was $20, and the high bid for a jar was $15, the winner would receive $5. In addition, they asked students to submit written estimates of the value of the coins in the jars. They offered a $2 prize for the best estimate of each jar.

Although the students didn't know it, each jar contained exactly $8 worth of coins or paper clips. The students' average estimate of the value of the coins or paper clips in the jar was too low—just $5.13. Despite this, the average of the winning bids in the 48 auctions for the jars was $10.01, so on average the high bidders lost $2.01. These MBA students had fallen victim to the winner's curse.

Sources: Richard H. Thaler, *The Winner's Curse: Paradoxes and Anomalies of Economic Life*, New York: The Free Press, 1992, Chapter 5; and Max Bazerman and William Samuelson, "I Won the Auction but Don't Want the Prize," *Journal of Conflict Resolution*, Vol. 27, December 1983, pp. 618–634.

YOUR TURN: Test your understanding by doing related problem 4.10 on page 596 at the end of this chapter.

Economics in YOUR Life!

>> Continued from page 575

At the beginning of the chapter, we asked you to consider why an individual will only be able to sell a used car for a much lower price than a dealer can. The key to the answer is that asymmetric information is a major problem in the used car market. Most buyers are aware that the seller of a used car knows much more about the condition of the car than the buyer does. In fact, most people get their primary information about a car from the seller of the car. The seller has some incentive to overstate the condition of the car: The better the seller makes the car sound, the higher the price the seller can hope to get. When you sell a car as an individual, the buyer is unlikely to ever buy a car from you again or to know anyone who has bought a car from you in the past. So, the buyer knows you don't have much incentive to be honest in the hopes of attracting future buyers. Car dealers, however, are hoping to continue to sell cars to many people, and their need for a good reputation keeps them from too greatly overstating the true condition of the car. So, if you have a good, well-maintained used car for sale, you may have to accept a price considerably below what a used car dealer with a good reputation could sell the car for.

Conclusion

In this chapter, we looked at situations of asymmetric information, where either the buyer or the seller has information not available to the other. We also looked at situations where both the buyer and the seller lack full information, which can lead to outcomes such as the winner's curse. Markets, including financial markets and labor markets, are more efficient when buyers and sellers have full information. Because information problems are significant in many markets, the economics of information is an important area of study.

Read *An Inside Look* on the next page to learn how insurance companies use information on a person's credit to determine premiums.

USA TODAY, JUNE 11, 2007

Your Money: Bad Credit Can Inflate Car Insurance Premiums

(a) You always use your turn signal and observe the speed limit. The only ticket you've ever gotten was for an expired parking meter. You should be eligible for lower car-insurance premiums than that bozo who cut you off this morning is, right? Not necessarily.

If your credit report is blemished, you might not get the lowest insurance rates, despite your spotless driving record. And as a result of a Supreme Court decision last week, your insurer doesn't have to tell you that you're not getting the best rates.

The high court overturned a 9th Circuit Court of Appeals ruling that said the federal Fair Credit Reporting Act requires insurers to notify customers whenever their credit history prevents them from getting the best available rate.

(b) Insurers argued that credit histories are just one of many factors they use to set rates. They also contended that the ruling would have required insurers to send out millions of notices to customers to avoid costly class-action lawsuits.

For about a decade, most insurers have considered a customer's credit history when setting rates, says Joseph Annotti, a spokesman for the Property Casualty Insurers Association of America. Annotti says research has shown that drivers with poor credit are more likely to file insurance claims.

(c) A credit report "is a solid predictor of risk," Annotti says. "People can get tickets taken off their record, DUIs get changed into running a stop sign—there are lots of ways to play with your motor vehicle record. It's less likely for a person who is inherently financial irresponsible to, all of a sudden overnight, change their behavior."

Consumer groups disagree. The insurance industry's contention that people with damaged credit are high-risk drivers is a "pretty disturbing moral hypothesis," says Chi Chi Wu, of the National Consumer Law Center. Many people have poor credit because of divorce, job loss or serious illness, she says. "They're not bad people. They're people who have fallen on hard times."

In addition, credit reports are "notorious for errors," Wu says. Identity theft could also damage an individual's record, she notes.

In November, Oregon voters defeated a measure that would have barred insurers from using credit histories to set auto and home insurance rates. Still, 26 states have adopted a model law that requires insurers to notify consumers that their credit history might affect their rates. The law also bars insurers from refusing to insure someone based solely on the individual's credit history.

The model law also encourages insurers to take into account "extraordinary life events," such as a catastrophic illness or the loss of a spouse, when evaluating a consumer's credit history.

Know Your Score

Consumer groups contend that a notification requirement would encourage people to check their credit reports more frequently. Most consumers aren't aware that their credit histories can affect their insurance rates, says Scott Shorr, a lawyer in Portland, Ore., who represented the plaintiffs in the insurance case.

Now, though, "If you want to know whether there's some inaccuracy in your credit report that's resulting in your paying more for insurance or credit generally, then you're going to have to check your credit report yourself," says Scott Nelson, an attorney for Public Citizen, a consumer-advocacy group.

How to protect yourself:

- When applying for insurance, ask the insurer what factors will be considered in determining your rates. Insurers won't tell you how they weigh them, but the company might tell you the factors it considers when reviewing a potential customer's credit report, Annotti says.

  For example, he says, some insurers are interested only in major credit events, such as foreclosures and bankruptcies. . . .

- Monitor your credit reports regularly for errors. You're entitled to a free copy of a credit report from the three credit-reporting agencies—TransUnion, Equifax and Experian—once a year. . . .

  If you find errors in your credit report, contact the credit agency that issued the report. The agencies are required by law to investigate disputed items.

- Beware of companies that claim they can "repair" your credit report.

Source: Sandra Block, "Your Money: Bad Credit Can Inflate Car Insurance Premiums," *USA Today*, June 11, 2007. Reprinted by permission of *USA Today*.

Key Points in the Article

This article discusses the controversy over insurance companies using credit records to set the policy premiums they charge their customers. Because the buyers of insurance know more about their driving habits and risk-taking than do the sellers of insurance, sellers are looking for some signal that will indicate which buyers are likely to be good risks and which are likely to be bad risks.

Analyzing the News

a In markets where one side of the market has more information than the other, the less informed party will seek ways to gain information. Because credit records can provide information about how responsible a person acts, insurance companies may find it valuable to use credit records to separate consumers who are likely to be safe drivers from those who are more likely to have accidents. Insurance companies are using credit histories both to decide whether or not to offer insurance to a particular applicant,

but also to decide what premiums to charge.

b When a firm uses a credit report to determine whether a person is a good or bad insurance risk, the firm is relying on the statistical correlation between a person's credit history and the likelihood that the person will have an accident. Having bad credit does not cause a person to be a bad driver, but bad credit may be a signal that a person has some unobservable characteristic that results in the person making bad decisions. A person's credit history may be a good signal that reveals to the insurance companies information that is relevant to setting insurance premiums. When insurance companies have better information about the risks they face from different consumers, the companies will be better able to judge the profitability of the policies, and the supply of insurance in the market should increase. You can see the increase in the figure as the supply curve shifts from S_1 to S_2. When this occurs, the market price of insurance falls from P_1 to P_2, and the quantity of insurance sold in the market increases from Q_1 to Q_2.

c How does the information insurance companies obtain from credit histories affect the market for insurance? Suppose that there are only two types of consumers: good risks and bad risks. A good risk will have insurance claims of $100 per year, and

a bad risk will have insurance claims of $5,000 per year. If the insurance company believes that half of its customers are of each type, the expected payout for the insurance company is $2,550 per year, calculated as 0.5($100) + 0.5($5,000). If the company charged that premium, bad risks would happily seek coverage, and good risks would not. Suppose instead that the insurance company could use credit records to identify which customers are likely to be good risks and charge them close to $100 per year, and which are likely to be bad risks and charge them close to $5,000 per year. This would make it less likely that only bad risks would seek insurance. The insurance companies would be more likely to cover their costs (which they must do to stay in business) and encourage drivers who are good risks to purchase insurance.

Thinking Critically
About Policy

1. Suppose states banned the use of credit checks by insurance companies in setting premiums. What would happen to the price and quantity of insurance offered in those states? Who would benefit from this change?

2. What would be the benefits and the costs of states requiring that insurance companies charge all drivers the same premium?

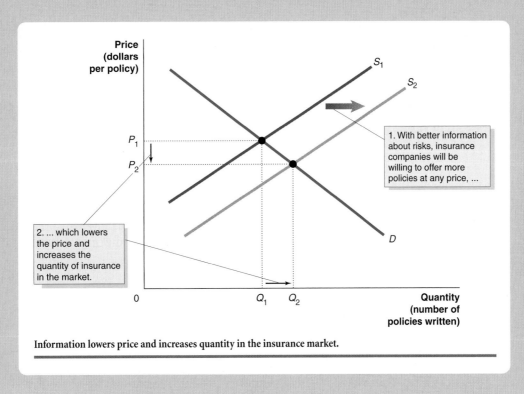

Information lowers price and increases quantity in the insurance market.

591

Key Terms

17.1 LEARNING OBJECTIVE 17.1 | Define asymmetric information and distinguish between adverse selection and moral hazard, **pages 576–580.**

Asymmetric Information

Summary

Asymmetric information is a situation in which one party to an economic transaction has less information than the other party. Asymmetric information can lead to **adverse selection**, which occurs when one party to a transaction takes advantage of knowing more than the other party to the transaction. An example is the "lemons" problem, where adverse selection may lead to only unreliable used cars being offered for sale. Asymmetric information can also lead to **moral hazard**, which refers to actions people take after they have entered into a transaction that make the other party to the transaction worse off. For example, a firm that has taken out a fire insurance policy on a warehouse may be less careful in the future about avoiding fire hazards. Information problems result in the equilibrium quantity in markets being smaller than it would be if these problems did not exist. Therefore, there is a reduction in economic efficiency.

myeconlab Visit www.myeconlab.com to complete these exercises *Get Ahead of the Curve* online and get instant feedback.

Review Questions

1.1 What is asymmetric information? How does asymmetric information show up in the market for used cars?

1.2 What is the difference between adverse selection and moral hazard? Which is a bigger problem for consumers in the market for used cars?

1.3 Briefly discuss how adverse selection and moral hazard affect the market for insurance.

1.4 What methods do insurance companies use to reduce adverse selection and moral hazard?

Problems and Applications

1.5 Suppose you see a 2006 Volkswagen Jetta GLS Turbo Sedan advertised in the campus newspaper for $10,000. If you knew the car was reliable, you would be willing to pay $12,000 for it. If you knew the car was unreliable, you would only be willing to pay $8,000 for it. Under what circumstances should you buy the car?

1.6 Why are there lemon laws for the car market but not for the television market or the toothbrush market?

1.7 Michael Kinsley, a political columnist, observes that, "The idea of insurance is to share the risks of bad outcomes." In what sense does insurance involve sharing risks? How does the problem of adverse selection affect the ability of insurance to provide the benefit of sharing risk?

Source: Michael Kinsley, "Congress on Drugs," *Slate*, August 1, 2002.

1.8 Under the Social Security retirement system, the federal government collects a tax on most people's wage income and makes payments to retired workers above a certain age who are covered by the system. (The age to receive full Social Security retirement benefits varies based on the year the worker was born.) The Social Security retirement system is sometimes referred to as a program of social insurance. Is Social Security an insurance program in the same sense as a group life insurance or health insurance policy that a company provides to its workers? Briefly explain.

1.9 There are 10,000 houses in Lawrence. Suppose that houses cost $100,000, and 5 percent of the houses burn down each year. Which 5 percent of houses will burn down in any particular year is impossible for anyone, including the owners, to predict. There is no fire insurance available to Lawrence residents, so you decide to start an insurance company and begin offering policies. Your policy will pay the purchaser $100,000 if his or her house burns down. You charge a premium of $22,000 per year.

   a. Are the residents of Lawrence likely to buy your policies? Briefly explain.

   b. Now suppose that 5 percent of the owners know with certainty that their houses will burn down and that the other 95 percent of the owners know with certainty that their houses will not burn down. You offer everyone the same insurance policy with the same $22,000 premium. What is your accounting profit likely to be for the year? Assume that you have no explicit costs except for the payments you make to people who bought your policies and had their houses burn down.

   c. Now suppose that people do not know with certainty whether their houses will burn down and that some houses are significantly more likely to burn down than others. Unfortunately, the owners of the houses that are significantly more likely to burn down know it, but you do not. Is it possible for you to restructure the insurance policies you offer—that is, change the terms of how much you pay out and the premium you charge—in order to deal with this problem?

1.10 Every state requires that drivers have an automobile insurance policy that covers any car they own and operate. Some people have such bad driving records that they are unable to find any insurance company willing to sell them a policy. These drivers are placed in an "assigned risk pool." Every insurance company that sells automobile insurance in the state is required to insure some drivers from the assigned risk pool. The state government usually sets the rates these drivers pay for insurance. Why is this system necessary? Why don't insurance companies voluntarily insure these bad drivers and charge them very high rates? Why does the state government have to force insurance companies to insure bad drivers?

1.11 (Related to the *Making the Connection* on page 578) Suppose a large firm allows its employees to choose whether to participate in its health insurance plan. The firm is trying to decide whether to offer a plan with a high deductible, but a low monthly premium, or one with a low deductible, but a high monthly premium. Under which plan is adverse selection likely to be a bigger problem? Briefly explain.

1.12 (Related to the *Making the Connection* on page 578) An editorial in the *Wall Street Journal* argues that regulations imposed by state governments are responsible for making health insurance "so expensive to buy." The editorial singles out "'community rating' (insurers can't price based on differing risk factors such as age) and 'guaranteed issue' (you can wait until you're sick to buy insurance)." What problems do these regulations cause for insurance companies? How might insurance companies respond to these regulations? Do these regulations make consumers better off? The editorial concludes:

> The real scandal in American health insurance isn't that some people lack coverage for this or that treatment, but that tens of millions of Americans risk financial ruin because of [government] policies that make basic insurance difficult or impossible to buy.

Briefly explain whether you agree or disagree with this conclusion.

Source: "Why Can't You Buy Insurance?" *Wall Street Journal*, October 1, 2002.

1.13 (Related to the *Chapter Opener* on page 574) Why have auto insurers like State Farm started collecting more information on drivers and using computer models that employ thousands of variables to predict the chance that a driver will have an accident? Why didn't these firms do this sooner if these differences among drivers always existed?

1.14 (Related to the *Don't Let This Happen to You!* on page 580) Briefly explain whether you agree with the following statement: "The reluctance of healthy young adults to buy medical insurance creates a moral hazard problem for insurance companies."

>> **End Learning Objective 17.1**

17.2 LEARNING OBJECTIVE   17.2 | Apply the concepts of adverse selection and moral hazard to financial markets, **pages 581–583.**

Adverse Selection and Moral Hazard in Financial Markets

Summary

Adverse selection and moral hazard are serious problems in financial markets. When firms sell stocks and bonds, they know much more about their true financial condition than do potential investors. Investors are reluctant to buy stocks and bonds issued by small and medium-sized firms because they lack sufficient information about these firms. Investors also worry about the moral hazard problem of firms misusing the funds they raise through the sale of stocks and bonds. The Securities and Exchange Commission (SEC) has the authority to regulate the stock and bond markets and attempts to reduce adverse selection and moral hazard problems. The scandals of 2002 that involved the top managers in a number of corporations misusing funds and reporting inflated profits indicate the extent of information problems in financial markets.

myeconlab Visit www.myeconlab.com to complete these exercises *Get Ahead of the Curve* online and get instant feedback.

Review Questions

2.1 Explain why asymmetric information makes it difficult for small firms to sell stocks and bonds.

2.2 What is the Securities and Exchange Commission? Why was it founded?

2.3 What additional responsibility did the SEC receive in 2002? Why did Congress and the president decide that the SEC needed to take on this additional responsibility?

Problems and Applications

2.4 In an article in the *New York Times*, Warren Buffett, one of the most successful investors of the past 30 years, wrote, "For many years, I've had little confidence in the earnings reported by corporations." Why might he be suspicious that firms were not reporting their profits accurately?

Source: Warren Buffett, "Who Really Cooks the Books?" *New York Times*, July 24, 2002.

2.5 Many firms provide information about their plans and financial health to investment analysts who have no stake in the firm. Why would firms divulge such secrets?

2.6 After the countries of Eastern Europe converted from Communism to the market system, they tried to set up stock and bond markets. Most of these markets have remained very small, with few firms being able to find buyers for their stocks or bonds. One economist remarked that the reason these financial markets have been unsuccessful is that "the lemons problem has been too great." Explain what the economist meant.

2.7 (Related to the *Making the Connection* on page 582) In 2002, Congress prohibited firms from making loans to members of their boards of directors or to their top managers. Do you think this prohibition is meant to reduce asymmetric information problems? Briefly explain.

>> **End Learning Objective 17.2**

17.3 LEARNING OBJECTIVE | 17.3 | Apply the concepts of adverse selection and moral hazard to labor markets, **pages 583–584.**

Adverse Selection and Moral Hazard in Labor Markets

Summary

The potential for a **principal–agent problem** exists between employers and workers. This problem is caused by agents—workers—pursuing their own interests rather than the interests of the principals who hired them. When workers are not monitored, they may have no incentive to work hard. Employers try to avoid this moral hazard problem by increasing the value to a worker of the worker's current job. Three ways to increase the value of a worker's job are offering efficiency wages, using a seniority system, and offering profit sharing.

myeconlab Visit www.myeconlab.com to complete these exercises *Get Ahead of the Curve* online and get instant feedback.

Review Questions

3.1 What problems can adverse selection and moral hazard cause in labor markets? What steps do firms take to deal with these problems?

3.2 What are efficiency wages? What role can they play in reducing the principal–agent problem?

Problems and Applications

3.3 (Related to the *Don't Let This Happen to You!* on page 580) Briefly explain whether you agree with the following:

From an employer's point of view, the moral hazard problem in labor markets is that the potential employees who don't intend to work hard are the ones who are most eager for you to hire them. The adverse selection problem is that once you have hired a worker, he or she has an incentive to work hard only if monitored.

3.4 (Related to *Solved Problem 17-3* on page 584) What role do tips play in dealing with the principal–agent problem in the market for restaurant servers? Suppose that a law is passed that outlaws tips, so that now restaurant servers just receive a wage, instead of a wage plus tips. Is the total income of servers likely to rise or fall? Briefly explain.

3.5 Colleges and universities grant tenure to many professors, making it virtually impossible to fire them after they've worked there for six or seven years. Analyze this labor market strategy in light of asymmetric information, adverse selection, and moral hazard.

3.6 The going wage for janitors is $6 per hour. The Executive Building decides to pay its janitors $10 per hour. Will this higher wage increase or decrease the firm's profits? Or could it go either way? In your answer, discuss asymmetric information and efficiency wages.

>> **End Learning Objective 17.3**

The Winner's Curse: When Is It Bad to Win an Auction?

Summary

In auctions where bidders do not know the true value of what is being auctioned, the winner, by overestimating the value of what is being bid for, can end up worse off than the losers. This is known as the **winner's curse**, and it occurs in auctions of common-value assets that would be given the same value by all bidders if they had perfect information.

Review Questions

4.1 What is the winner's curse? Is it a problem for the winner of every auction? Briefly explain why or why not.

4.2 Briefly explain whether you agree or disagree with the following statement: "The more information bidders have on the true value of what is being auctioned, the less likely they are to fall victim to the winner's curse."

Problems and Applications

4.3 Suppose you are advising one of the oil companies involved in the oil field bidding shown in Figure 17-1 on page 585. What bidding strategy would you recommend to the company so it could avoid the winner's curse?

4.4 After playing for six years in the major leagues, baseball players are free to sign a contract to play for any team. (Before that time, they are obligated to play for the team that first signed them.) In this situation, players often sign a contract to play for several years with the team that offers them the highest salary. Consider two players: Joe is a minor star who performs at about the same level each year. Sam's performance has been more uneven: Some years, he seems like one of the best players in baseball, but in other years, his performance has not been very good. Suppose Joe signs with the Cleveland Indians and Sam signs with the Cincinnati Reds. Three years later, is Cleveland or Cincinnati likely to be most satisfied that the player they signed played well enough to justify his salary? Briefly explain.

4.5 (Related to *Solved Problem 17-4* on page 587) Suppose that everyone in an auction has perfect information about the value of whatever is being auctioned. Will the winner's curse still apply? Briefly explain.

4.6 A corporate takeover occurs when one firm—or a group of outside investors—buys up a majority of the stock in another firm. The usual aim of a takeover is to take advantage of the efficiencies possible with the newly merged firm or to bring in new management and run the acquired firm more profitably. In either case, the investors taking over the acquired firm are expecting to profit from the takeover. However, studies of corporate takeovers by Richard Roll of UCLA show that although the stockholders of the firm being taken over receive substantial gains—because the acquiring firm or investors bid up the price of the stock of the acquired firm as they try to take it over—the firm or investors carrying out the takeover earn small gains, if any. Relate Roll's finding to the problem of the winner's curse.

Source: Richard Roll, "The Hubris Hypothesis of Corporate Takeovers," *Journal of Business*, Vol. 59, No. 2, Pt. 1, April 1986, pp. 197–216.

4.7 (Related to the *Making the Connection* on page 586) The winner's curse may apply to the marriage market. The winner's curse usually applies in markets with common-value assets but not in markets with private-value assets. Discuss whether it is more accurate to think of the marriage market as a market with common-value assets, private-value assets, or some combination of the two.

4.8 Well-known novelists often auction off the rights to publish their latest books. John Dessauer has described the process:

> Major books are often "auctioned off" among publishers, *i.e.*, literally sold to the highest bidder. . . . The problem is, simply, that most of the auctioned books are not earning [the amounts paid for them]. In fact, very often such books have turned out to be dismal failures whose value was more perceived than real and which benefited from the ability of a plausible agent to sell the big sizzle on a small, tough steak.

Why do publishers who win auctions for books often end up paying more than the book turns out to be worth?

Source: John P. Dessauer, *Book Publishing: What It Is, What It Does*, 2nd ed., New York: Bowker, 1981, pp. 34–35.

4.9 In ancient Rome, the Praetorian Guards were the personal bodyguards of the emperor. The guard was made up of thousands of troops, and occasionally an emperor would lose control over them. In 193 A.D., the Praetorian Guard revolted and murdered Emperor

Pertinax. The guard then decided to auction off the office of emperor. The ancient historian Dio described the situation:

> Then ensued a most disgraceful business and one unworthy of Rome. For, just as if it had been in some market or auction-room, both the City and its entire empire were auctioned off. The sellers were the ones who had slain their emperor, and the would-be buyers were Sulpicianus and Julianus.

Didius Julianus won the auction with a bid that would be the equivalent of more than $1 billion today. Unfortunately, he greatly overestimated the value of becoming emperor in this way. His reign was very short. The general Septimius Severus brought his army from the Danube to Rome, deposed Didius Julianus, and was proclaimed emperor. In the words of the historian Edward Gibbon, Didius Julianus was "beheaded as a common criminal, after having purchased, with an immense treasure, an anxious and precarious reign of only sixty-six days." Does the analysis in this chapter help you understand what happened to Didius Julianus?

Source: Paul Klemperer and Peter Temin, "An Early Example of the 'Winner's Curse' in an Auction," *Journal of Political Economy*, December 2001.

4.10 **(Related to the *Making the Connection* on page 588)** Suppose that a $100 bill is auctioned off instead of a jar containing an unknown number of coins. Will the winner's curse still apply? Briefly explain.

>> **End Learning Objective 17.4**

Chapter 18

Public Choice, Taxes, and the **Distribution** of **Income**

Should the Government Use the Tax System to Reduce Inequality?

Taxes can have a large effect on business decisions. When the federal government cut the tax on dividends—payments corporations make to stockholders—many companies responded in a big way. Before the tax cut, Microsoft, for instance, had never paid a dividend. After the tax cut, in one year alone, Microsoft paid out more than $40 billion in dividends, with Bill Gates, Microsoft's chair and largest shareholder, receiving a $3 billion dividend check. (Gates donated his dividend to the Bill and Melinda Gates Foundation.) Supporters of cutting the tax on dividends argued that corporate profits are taxed once under corporate income tax; if shareholders have to pay taxes on dividends, then the same income is taxed twice. Reducing the tax on dividends reduces this "double taxation." Opponents of cutting the tax pointed out that high-income people are more likely to receive dividends than are low-income people. If high-income people, like Bill Gates, received the largest immediate gain from the tax cut, then the distribution of income would be made more unequal.

How should we evaluate tax laws? Tax laws affect economic incentives and economic activity and can also affect fairness. The questions raised by the debate over the tax cut on dividends are not new. Presidents John F. Kennedy and Ronald Reagan proposed significant cuts in income taxes that they claimed would enhance economic efficiency, while their opponents claimed that the tax cuts rewarded high-income taxpayers.

The debate over the tax system was particularly heated during the 2008 presidential election campaign. Illinois Senator Barack Obama, while running for the Democratic nomination for president, argued that major changes were needed in the U.S. tax system. According to Obama, the tax cut on dividends, as well as other tax cuts enacted during the early 2000s, had increased the burden on individuals with low and moderate incomes, while the burden on the wealthy and on corporations had been reduced, resulting in the highest level of income inequality since 1928. He advocated raising taxes on the wealthy to pay for a system of universal health care. In contrast, Arizona Senator John McCain, while running for the Republican nomination, argued that the individuals with the highest incomes were paying the majority of the federal individual income tax and that many of those individuals were businesspeople who used the tax cuts to fund investments in their firms. McCain doubted that changes in taxes had had much effect on the distribution of income.

Putting aside the particulars of the political debate of 2008, the design of the tax system and the criteria to use in evaluating it are important

LEARNING Objectives

After studying this chapter, you should be able to:

18.1 Define the **public choice model** and explain how it is used to analyze **government decision making**, page 600.

18.2 Understand the **tax system** in the United States, including the principles that governments use to create **tax policy**, page 604.

18.3 Understand the effect of price **elasticity** on **tax incidence**, page 612.

18.4 Discuss the **distribution of income** in the United States and understand the extent of **income mobility**, page 615.

questions. Has the tax code improved economic efficiency? Has the government, through its tax and other policies, had much impact on the distribution of income?

AN INSIDE LOOK AT POLICY on **page 624** examines a speech by Federal Reserve Chairman Ben Bernanke in which he discusses sources of income inequality in the United States.

Sources: Bret Hayworth, "Obama Touts Renewed Role," *Sioux City Journal*, April 1, 2007; and Christopher Cooper and Elizabeth Holmes, "Economy Takes Spotlight," *Wall Street Journal*, July 8, 2008.

Economics in YOUR Life!

How Much Tax Should You Pay?

Government is ever present in your life. Just today, you likely drove on roads that the government paid for. You may attend a public college or university, paid for, at least in part, by government. Where does a government get its money? By taxing citizens. Think of the different taxes you pay. Do you think you pay more than, less than, or just about your fair share in taxes? How do you determine what your fair share is? As you read this chapter, see if you can answer these questions. You can check your answers against those we provide at the end of the chapter. **>> Continued on page 623**

Public choice model A model that applies economic analysis to government decision making.

W e saw in Chapter 2 that the government plays a significant role in helping the market system work efficiently by providing secure rights to private property and an independent court system to enforce contracts among private individuals. We saw in Chapter 5 that the government itself must sometimes supply goods—known as *public goods*—that private firms will not supply. But how does the government decide which policies to adopt? In recent years, economists led by Nobel laureate James Buchanan and Gordon Tullock, both of George Mason University, have developed the **public choice model**, which applies economic analysis to government decision making. In this chapter, we will explore how public choice can help us understand how policymakers make decisions.

We will also discuss the principles that governments use to create tax policy. In particular, we will see how economists identify which taxes are most economically efficient. At the end of the chapter, we discuss the extent to which government policy—including tax policy—affects the distribution of income.

18.1 | Define the public choice model and explain how it is used to analyze government decision making.

Public Choice

So far, we have focused on explaining the actions of households and firms. We assumed that households and firms act to make themselves as well off as possible. In particular, we assumed that households choose the goods they buy to maximize their utility, and that firms choose the quantities and prices of the goods they sell to maximize profits. Because government policy plays an important role in the economy, it is important also to consider how government policymakers—such as Senators, governors, presidents, and state legislators—arrive at their decisions. One of the key insights from the public choice model is that policymakers are no different than consumers or managers of firms: Policymakers are likely to pursue their own self-interest, even if their self-interest conflicts with the public interest. In particular, we expect that public officials will take actions that are likely to result in their being re-elected.

How Do We Know the Public Interest? Models of Voting

It is possible to argue that, in fact, elected officials simply represent the preferences of the voters who elect them. After all, it would seem logical that voters will not re-elect a politician who fails to act in the public interest. A closer look at voting, however, makes it less clear that politicians are simply representing the views of the voters.

The Voting Paradox Many policy decisions involve multiple alternatives. Because the size of the federal budget is limited, policymakers face tradeoffs. To take a simple example, suppose that there is $1 billion available in the budget and Congress must choose whether to spend it on *only one* of three alternatives: 1) Research on breast cancer; 2) Subsidies for mass transit; or 3) Increased border security. Assume that the votes of members of Congress will represent the preferences of their constituents. We might expect that Congress will vote for the alternative favored by a majority of the voters. In fact, though, there are circumstances in which majority voting will fail to result in a consistent decision. For example, suppose there are only three voters and they have the preferences shown at the top of Table 18-1.

In the table, we show the three policy alternatives in the first column. The remaining columns show the voters' rankings of the alternatives. For example, Lena would prefer to see the money spent on cancer research. Her second choice is mass transit, and her third choice is border security. What happens if a series of votes are taken in which each pair

POLICY	LENA	DAVID	KATHLEEN
Cancer research	1st	2nd	3rd
Mass transit	2nd	3rd	1st
Border security	3rd	1st	2nd

VOTES	OUTCOME
Cancer research versus mass transit	Cancer research wins
Mass transit versus border security	Mass transit wins
Border security versus cancer research	Border security wins

TABLE 18-1

The Voting Paradox

of alternatives is considered in turn? The bottom of Table 18-1 shows the results of these votes. If the vote is between spending the money on cancer research and spending the money on mass transit, cancer research wins because Lena and David both prefer spending the money on cancer research to spending the money on mass transit. So, if the votes of members of Congress represent the preferences of voters, we have a clear verdict and the money is spent on cancer research. Suppose, though, that the vote is between spending the money on mass transit and spending the money on border security. Then because Lena and Kathleen prefer spending on mass transit to spending on border security, mass transit wins. Now, finally, suppose the vote is between spending on cancer research and spending on border security. Surprisingly, border security wins because that is what David and Kathleen prefer. The outcome of this vote is surprising because if voters prefer cancer research to mass transit and mass transit to border security, we would expect that *transitivity* would ensure they prefer cancer research to border security. But in this example the collective preferences of the voters turn out not to be transitive, and we do not have a consistent outcome. The failure of majority voting to always result in consistent choices is called the **voting paradox**.

This is an artificial example because we assumed that there were only three alternatives, only three voters, and a simple majority vote determined the outcomes. In fact, though, Nobel laureate Kenneth Arrow of Stanford University has shown mathematically that the failure of majority votes to always represent voters' preferences is a very general result. The **Arrow impossibility theorem** states that no system of voting can be devised that will consistently represent the underlying preferences of voters. This theorem suggests that there is no way through democratic voting to ensure that the preferences of voters are translated into policy choices. In fact, the Arrow impossibility theorem might lead us to expect that voting will lead to shifts in policy that may not be efficient. For instance, which of the three alternatives for spending the $1 billion Congress will actually choose would depend on the order in which the alternatives happened to be voted on, which might be expected to change from one year to the next. So, with respect to economic issues, such as providing funding for public goods, we cannot count on the political process to necessarily result in an efficient outcome. In other words, the "voting market"—as represented by elections—may often do a less efficient job of representing consumer preferences than do markets for goods and services.

The Median Voter Theorem In practice, many political issues are decided by a majority vote. In those cases, what can we say about which voters' preferences the outcome is likely to represent? An important result known as the **median voter theorem** states that the outcome of a majority vote is likely to represent the preferences of the voter who is in the political middle. To take another simplified example, suppose there are five voters and their preferences for spending on breast cancer research are shown in Figure 18-1. Their preferences range from Kathleen, who prefers to spend nothing on breast cancer research—preferring

Voting paradox The failure of majority voting to always result in consistent choices.

Arrow impossibility theorem A mathematical theorem that holds that no system of voting can be devised that will consistently represent the underlying preferences of voters.

Median voter theorem The proposition that the outcome of a majority vote is likely to represent the preferences of the voter who is in the political middle.

Figure 18-1

The Median Voter Theorem

The median voter theorem states that the outcome of a majority vote is likely to represent the preferences of the voter who is in the political middle. In this case, David is in the political middle because two voters want to spend more on breast cancer research than he does and two voters want to spend less. In any vote between a proposal to spend $2 billion and a proposal to spend a different amount, a proposal to spend $2 billion will win.

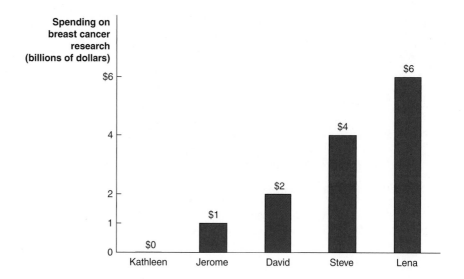

the funds to be spent on other programs or for federal spending to be reduced and taxes lowered— to Lena, who prefers to spend $6 billion.

In this case, David is the median voter because he is in the political middle; two voters would prefer to spend less than David wants to and two would prefer to spend more. To see why the median voter's preferences are likely to prevail, consider first a vote between David's preferred outcome of spending $2 billion and a proposal to spend $6 billion. Because only Lena favors $6 billion and the other voters all prefer spending less, the proposal to spend $2 billion would win four votes to one. Similarly, consider a vote between spending $2 billion and spending $1 billion. Three voters prefer spending more than $1 billion and only two prefer spending $1 billion or less, so the proposal to spend $2 billion will win three votes to two. Only the proposal to spend $2 billion will have the support of a majority when paired with proposals to spend a different amount. Notice also that the amount spent as a result of the voting is less than the amount that would result from taking the simple average of the voter's preferences—$2 billion versus $2.6 billion.

One implication of the median voter theorem is that the political process tends to serve individuals whose preferences are in the middle, but not those individuals whose preferences are far away from the median. There is an important contrast between the political process, which results in collective actions in which everyone is obliged to participate, and the market process in which individuals are free to participate or not. For instance, even though Kathleen would prefer not to spend government funds on breast cancer research, once a majority has voted to spend $2 billion, Kathleen is obliged to go along with the spending—and the taxes required to fund the research. This is in contrast with the market for goods and services where if, for instance, Kathleen disagrees with the majority of consumers who like iPods, she is under no obligation to buy one. Similarly, even though Lena and Steve might prefer to pay significantly higher taxes to fund additional spending on breast cancer research, they are obligated to go along with the lower level of spending the majority approved. If Lena would like to have her iPod gold plated, she can choose to do so, even if the vast majority of consumers would consider such spending a waste of money.

Government Failure?

The voting models we have just looked at indicate that individuals are less likely to see their preferences represented in the outcomes of government policies than in the outcomes of markets. The public choice model goes beyond this observation to question whether the self-interest of policymakers is likely to cause them to take actions that are inconsistent with the preferences of voters, even where those preferences are clear. There are several aspects of how the political process works that might lead to this outcome.

Rent seeking Economists usually focus on analyzing the actions of individuals and firms as they attempt to make themselves better off by interacting in markets. The public choice model shifts the focus to attempts by individuals and firms to engage in **rent seeking**, which is the use of government action to make themselves better off at the expense of others. One of the benefits of the market system is that it channels self-interested behavior in a way that benefits society as a whole. Although Apple developed the iPod to make profits, its actions increased the well-being of millions of consumers. When Microsoft introduced the Zune to compete with the iPod, it also was motivated by the desire for profit, but it further increased consumer well-being by expanding the choice of digital music players available. Rent seeking, in contrast, can benefit a few individuals or firms at the expense of all other individuals and firms. For example, we saw in Chapter 8 that U.S. sugar firms have successfully convinced Congress to impose a quota on imports of sugar. The quota has benefited the owners of U.S. sugar firms and the people who work for them but has reduced consumer surplus, hurt U.S. candy companies and their workers, and reduced economic efficiency.

> **Rent seeking** The attempts by individuals and firms to use government action to make themselves better off at the expense of others.

Because firms can benefit from government intervention in the economy, as the sugar companies benefited from the sugar quota, they are willing to spend resources attempting to secure these interventions. Members of Congress, state legislators, governors, and presidents need funds to finance their election campaigns. So, these policymakers may accept campaign contributions from rent-seeking firms and be willing to introduce *special interest legislation* in their behalf.

Logrolling and Rational Ignorance Two other factors help explain why rent-seeking behavior can sometimes succeed. It may seem puzzling that the sugar quota has been enacted when the number of workers and firms helped by it is so small. Why would members of Congress vote for the sugar quota if they do not have sugar producers in their districts? One possibility is *logrolling*. Logrolling refers to the situation where a member of Congress votes to approve a bill in exchange for favorable votes from other members on other bills. For example, a member of Congress from Texas might vote for the sugar quota, even though none of the member's constituents will benefit from it. In exchange, members of Congress from districts where sugar producers are located will vote for legislation the member of Congress from Texas would like to see passed. This vote trading may result in a majority of Congress supporting legislation that benefits the economic interests of a few, while harming the economic interests of a much larger group.

But if the majority of voters is harmed by rent-seeking legislation, how does it get passed, even given the effects of logrolling? In Chapter 8, we discussed one possible explanation with respect to the sugar quota. Although, collectively, consumer surplus declines by $2.2 billion per year because of the sugar quota, spread across a population of 300 million, the loss per person is only $7.50. Because the loss is so small, most people do not take it into account when deciding how to vote in elections, and many people are not even aware that the sugar quota exists. Other voters may be convinced to support restrictions on trade because the jobs saved by tariffs and quotas are visible and often highly publicized, while the jobs lost because of these restrictions and the reductions in consumer surplus are harder to detect. Because becoming informed on an issue may require time and effort and the economic payoff is often low, some economists argue that many voters are *rationally ignorant* of the effect of rent-seeking legislation. In this view, because voters frequently lack an economic incentive to become informed about pending legislation, the voters' preferences do not act as a constraint on legislators voting for rent-seeking legislation.

Regulatory Capture One way in which the government intervenes in the economy is by establishing a regulatory agency or commission that is given authority over a particular industry or type of product. For example, no firm is allowed to sell prescription drugs in the United States without receiving authorization from the Food and Drug Administration (FDA). Ideally, regulatory agencies will make decisions in the public interest. The FDA should weigh the benefits to patients from quickly approving a new drug against the costs that the agency may overlook potentially dangerous side effects of the drug if approval is too rapid. However, because the firms being regulated are significantly affected by the regulatory agency's actions, the firms have an incentive to try to influence those actions. In extreme cases, this influence may lead the agency to make decisions that are in the best interests of the firms being regulated, even if these actions are not in the public interest. In that case, the agency has been subject to *regulatory capture* by the industry being regulated. Some economists point to the Interstate Commerce Commission (ICC) as an example of regulatory capture. Although it has since been abolished by Congress, for decades the ICC determined the prices that railroads and long-distance trucking firms could charge to haul freight. Congress originally established the ICC to safeguard the interests of consumers, but some economists have argued that for many years the ICC operated to suppress competition, which was in the interests of the railroads and trucking firms. Economists debate the extent to which regulatory capture explains the decision of some government agencies.

In Chapter 5, we saw how the presence of externalities can lead to market failure, which is the situation where the market does not supply the economically efficient quantity of a good or service. Public choice analysis indicates that *government failure* can also occur. For the reasons we have discussed in this section, it is possible that government intervention in the economy may reduce economic efficiency rather than increase it. Economists differ over the extent to which they believe government failure results in serious economic inefficiency in the U.S. economy. Most economists, though, accept the basic argument of the public choice model that policymakers may have incentives to intervene in the economy in ways that do not promote efficiency and that proposals for such intervention should be evaluated with care.

Is Government Regulation Necessary?

The public choice model raises important questions about the effect of government regulation on economic efficiency. But can we conclude that Congress should abolish agencies such as the Food and Drug Administration (FDA), the Environmental Protection Agency (EPA), and the Federal Trade Commission (FTC)? In fact, most economists agree that these agencies can serve a very useful purpose. For instance, in Chapter 5 we discussed how the EPA can help correct the effects of production externalities, such as pollution. Regulatory agencies can also improve economic efficiency in markets where consumers have difficulty obtaining the information needed for informed purchases. For example, consumers have no easy way of detecting bacteria and other contaminants in food or determining whether prescription drugs are safe and effective. The FDA was established in the early twentieth century to monitor the nation's food supply following newspaper accounts of unsanitary practices in many meatpacking plants.

Although government regulation can clearly provide important benefits to consumers, we need to take the costs of regulations into account. Recent estimates indicate that the costs of federal regulations may be several thousand dollars per taxpayer. Economics can help policymakers devise regulations that provide benefits to consumers that exceed their costs.

18.2 LEARNING OBJECTIVE

18.2 | Understand the tax system in the United States, including the principles that governments use to create tax policy.

The Tax System

However the size of government and the types of activities it engages in are determined, government spending has to be financed. The government primarily relies on taxes to raise the revenue it needs. Some taxes, though, such as those on cigarettes or alcohol, are intended more to discourage what society views as undesirable behavior than to raise revenue. These are the most widely used taxes:

- *Individual income taxes.* The federal government, most state governments, and some local governments tax the wages, salaries, and other income of households and the profits of firms. The individual income tax is the largest source of revenue for the federal government. In 2006, the average U.S. taxpayer earned about $57,670 and paid federal personal income taxes of $7,429.

- *Social insurance taxes.* The federal government taxes wages and salaries to raise revenue for the Social Security and Medicare systems. *Social Security* makes payments to retired workers and to the disabled. *Medicare* helps pay the medical expenses of people over age 65. The Social Security and Medicare taxes are often referred to as "payroll taxes." As the U.S. population has aged, payroll taxes have increased. By 2008, 75 percent of taxpayers paid more in payroll taxes than in federal income taxes. The federal government and state governments also tax wages and salaries to raise revenue for the unemployment insurance system, which makes payments to workers who have lost their jobs.

- *Sales taxes.* Most state and local governments tax retail sales of most products. More than half the states exempt food from the sales tax, and a few states also exempt clothing.

- *Property taxes.* Most local governments tax homes, offices, factories, and the land they are built on. In the United States, the property tax is the largest source of funds for public schools.

- *Excise taxes.* The federal government and some state governments levy excise taxes on specific goods, such as gasoline, cigarettes, and beer.

An Overview of the U.S. Tax System

Panels (a) and (b) of Figure 18-2 show the revenue sources of the federal, state, and local governments. Panel (a) shows that the federal government raises almost 80 percent of its revenue from the individual income tax and from social insurance taxes. Corporate

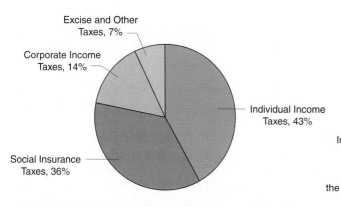

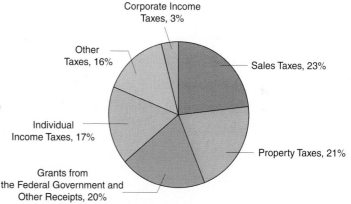

Tax	Amount (billions)	Amount per Person	Percentage of Total Tax Receipts
Individual Income Taxes	$1,163	$3,854	43%
Social Insurance Taxes	954	3,163	36
Corporate Income Taxes	381	1,263	14
Excise and Other Taxes	176	583	7
Total	$2,674	$8,865	100%

Tax	Amount (billions)	Amount per Person	Percentage of Total Tax Receipts
Sales Taxes	$429	$1,423	23%
Property Taxes	390	$1,293	21
Grants from the Federal Government and Other Receipts	378	1,253	20
Individual Income Taxes	320	1,061	17
Other Taxes	305	1,011	16
Corporate Income Taxes	64	212	3
Total	$1,886	$6,253	100%

(a) Sources of federal government revenue, 2007

(b) Sources of state and local government revenue, 2007

Figure 18-2 | Federal, State, and Local Sources of Revenue, 2007

Individual income taxes are the most important source of revenue for the federal government, with social insurance taxes being the second most important source. State and local governments receive the most revenue from sales taxes. State and local governments also receive large transfers from the federal government, in part to help pay for federally mandated programs. Many local governments depend on property taxes to raise most of their tax revenue.

Source: U.S. Department of Commerce, Bureau of Economic Analysis, *National Income and Product Accounts of the United States*, Tables 3.2 and 3.3, June 26, 2008.

income taxes and excise taxes account for much smaller fractions of federal revenues. In 2007, federal revenues of all types amounted to almost $2.7 trillion, or about $8,900 per person. Over the past 40 years, federal revenues as a share of gross domestic product (GDP; the value of all the goods and services produced in the U.S. economy) have remained in a fairly narrow range between 17 and 23 percent.

Panel (b) shows that state and local governments rely on different sources of revenue than does the federal government. In fact, the largest source of revenue for state and local governments is sales taxes. State and local governments also receive large grants from the federal government. These grants are intended in part to pay for programs that the federal government requires states and local governments to carry out. These programs, often called *federal mandates*, include the *Medicaid* program, which provides health care to poor people, and the Temporary Assistance for Needy Families (TANF) program, which provides financial assistance to poor families. Local governments depend heavily on property taxes. Many local school districts, in particular, rely almost entirely on revenues from property taxes.

Progressive and Regressive Taxes

Regressive tax A tax for which people with lower incomes pay a higher percentage of their income in tax than do people with higher incomes.

Progressive tax A tax for which people with lower incomes pay a lower percentage of their income in tax than do people with higher incomes.

Economists often categorize taxes on the basis of how much tax people with different levels of income pay relative to their incomes. A tax is **regressive** if people with lower incomes pay a higher percentage of their income in tax than do people with higher incomes. A tax is **progressive** if people with lower incomes pay a lower percentage of their income in tax than do people with higher incomes. A tax is *proportional* if people with lower incomes pay the same percentage of their income in tax as do people with higher incomes.

The federal income tax is an example of a progressive tax. To see why, we must first consider the important distinction between a tax rate and a tax bracket. A *tax rate* is the percentage of income paid in taxes. A *tax bracket* refers to the income range within which a tax rate applies. Table 18-2 shows the federal income tax brackets and tax rates for single taxpayers in 2008.

We can use Table 18-2 to calculate what Matt, a single taxpayer with an income of $100,000, pays in federal income tax. This example is somewhat simplified because we are ignoring the *exemptions* and *deductions* that taxpayers can use to reduce the amount of income subject to tax. For example, taxpayers are allowed to exclude from taxation a certain amount of income, called the *personal exemption*, that represents very basic living expenses. Ignoring Matt's exemptions and deductions, he will have to make the tax payment to the federal government shown in Table 18-3. Matt's first $8,025 of income is in the 10 percent bracket, so he pays $802.50. His next $24,525 of income is in the 15 percent bracket, so he pays $3,678.75. His next $46,300 of income is in the 25 percent bracket, so he pays $11,575. His last $21,150 of income is in the 28 percent bracket, so he pays $5,922, which brings his total federal income tax bill to $21,978.25.

TABLE 18-2

Federal Income Tax Brackets and Tax Rates for Single Taxpayers, 2008

INCOME	TAX RATE
$0–$8,025	10%
$8,026–$32,550	15
$32,551–$78,850	25
$78,851–$164,550	28
$164,551–$357,700	33
Over $357,700	35

Source: Internal Revenue Service.

ON MATT'S . . .	MATT PAYS TAX OF . . .
first $8,025 of income	$ 802.50
next $24,525 of income	3,678.75
next $46,300 of income	11,575.00
last $21,150 of income	5,922.00
His total federal income tax payment is	$21,978.25

TABLE 18-3

Federal Income Tax Paid on Taxable Income of $100,000

Making the Connection | Which Groups Pay the Most in Federal Taxes?

At the beginning of this chapter, we mentioned the ongoing debate over whether to increase taxes on people with high incomes. To evaluate this debate, it's useful to know how much each income group pays of the total taxes collected by the federal government. The following table shows projections for 2008 by the Tax Policy Center, with taxpayers divided into quintiles from the 20 percent with the lowest income to the 20 percent with the highest income. The last row also shows taxpayers whose incomes put them in the top 1 percent. Column (1) shows the percentage of total income earned by each income group. Column (2) shows the percentage of total federal individual income tax paid by each income group. Column (3) shows the percentage of all federal taxes—including Social Security and Medicare payroll taxes—paid by each income group.

INCOME CATEGORY	PERCENTAGE OF TOTAL INCOME EARNED (1)	PERCENTAGE OF TOTAL FEDERAL INDIVIDUAL INCOME TAXES PAID (2)	PERCENTAGE OF TOTAL FEDERAL TAXES PAID (3)
Lowest 20%	3.7%	−3.2%	0.2%
Second 20%	8.1	−2.7	3.2
Third 20%	13.8	4.7	9.9
Fourth 20%	19.5	13.6	17.3
Highest 20%	55.2	87.5	69.2
Total	100.0%	100.0%	100.0%
Highest 1%	19.3	37.2	27.7

Source: Urban Institute and Brookings Institution, Tax Policy Center, www.taxpolicycenter.org. Used with permission. (Columns do not sum to 100 percent precisely due to rounding.)

The data in column (2) show that more than 87 percent of federal individual income taxes are paid by the 20 percent of taxpayers with the highest incomes. This share is more than their share of total income earned, which is about 55 percent, as shown in column (1). Taxpayers whose incomes put them in the top 1 percent pay more than one-third of the individual income tax. Many individuals in the lowest two quintiles of incomes receive tax credits from the federal government so that they in effect pay negative taxes. Column (3) includes all federal taxes—including the payroll taxes that fund the Social Security and Medicare systems—but does not change the result very much: The 40 percent of taxpayers with the lowest incomes pay only about 3.4 percent of all federal taxes, while the 20 percent with the highest incomes pay almost 70 percent of all federal taxes. Notice, though, that the distribution of all federal taxes is less progressive than the distribution of income taxes. This outcome occurs because the Social Security and Medicare payroll taxes are less progressive than the federal income tax.

The following table shows projections of the taxes paid in 2008, as a fraction of income by each income group. Column (1) shows federal income taxes paid as a fraction of income, and column (2) shows all federal taxes paid as a fraction of income. The table shows that as people's incomes rise, they pay a larger fraction of their income in taxes.

INCOME CATEGORY	FEDERAL INCOME TAXES PAID AS A FRACTION OF INCOME (1)	ALL FEDERAL TAXES PAID AS A FRACTION OF INCOME (2)
Lowest 20%	−8.1%	1.1%
Second 20%	−3.1	8.3
Third 20%	3.3	15.1
Fourth 20%	6.6	18.6
Highest 20%	15.0	26.2
All income categories	9.5%	20.9%
Highest 1%	18.3	30.0

Source: Urban Institute and Brookings Institution, Tax Policy Center, www.taxpolicycenter.org. Used with permission.

We can conclude that the federal individual income tax and all federal taxes taken together are progressive. Whether the federal tax system should be made more or less progressive remains a source of political debate.

YOUR TURN: Test your understanding by doing related problem 2.9 on page 628 at the end of this chapter.

Marginal and Average Income Tax Rates

The fraction of each additional dollar of income that must be paid in taxes is called the **marginal tax rate**. The **average tax rate** is the total tax paid divided by total income. When a tax is progressive, as is the federal income tax, the marginal and average tax rates will differ. For example, in Table 18-3, Matt had a marginal tax rate of 28 percent because that is the rate he paid on the last dollar of his income. But his average tax rate was:

Marginal tax rate The fraction of each additional dollar of income that must be paid in taxes.

Average tax rate Total tax paid divided by total income.

$$\left(\frac{\$21,978.25}{\$100,000}\right) \times 100 = 22.0\%$$

His average tax rate was lower than his marginal tax rate because the first $78,850 of his income was taxed at rates below his marginal rate of 28 percent.

When economists consider a change in tax policy, they generally focus on the marginal tax rate rather than the average tax rate because the marginal tax rate is a better indicator of how a change in a tax will affect people's willingness to work, save, and invest. For example, if Matt is considering working longer hours to raise his income, he will use his marginal tax rate to determine how much extra income he will earn after taxes. He will ignore his average tax rate because it does not reflect the taxes he must pay on the *additional* income he earns. The higher the marginal tax rate, the lower the return he receives from working additional hours and the less likely he is to work those additional hours.

The Corporate Income Tax

The federal government taxes the profits earned by corporations under the *corporate income tax*. Like the individual income tax, the corporate income tax is progressive, with the lowest tax rate being 15 percent and the highest being 35 percent. Unlike the personal income tax, however, where relatively few taxpayers are taxed at the highest rate, most corporations are in the 35 percent tax bracket.

Economists debate the costs and benefits of a separate tax on corporate profits. The corporate income tax ultimately must be paid by a corporation's owners—which are its shareholders—or by its employees, in the form of lower wages, or by its customers, in the form of higher prices. Some economists argue that if the purpose of the corporate income tax is to tax the owners of corporations, it would be better to do so directly by taxing the owners' incomes rather than by taxing the owners indirectly through the corporate income tax. Individual taxpayers already pay income taxes on the dividends and capital gains they receive from owning stock in corporations. As we mentioned in the chapter opener, in effect, the corporate income tax "double taxes" earnings on individual shareholders' investments in corporations. An alternative policy that avoids this double taxation would be for corporations to calculate their total profits each year and send a notice to each shareholder indicating the shareholder's portion of the profits. The shareholder would then be required to include this amount as taxable income on his or her personal income tax. Under another alternative, the federal government could continue to tax corporate income through the corporate income tax but allow individual taxpayers to receive corporate dividends and capital gains tax free. In 2003, Congress enacted a reduction on dividend and capital gains taxes to reduce double taxation.

International Comparison of Corporate Income Taxes

In the past 10 years, several countries have cut corporate income taxes to increase investment spending and growth. Table 18-4 compares corporate income tax rates in several high-income countries. The tax rates given in the table include taxes at all levels of government. So, in the United States, for example, they include taxes imposed on corporate profits by state governments as well as by the federal government. The table shows that several countries, including France, Germany, and Ireland, significantly reduced corporate income tax rates between 2000 and 2007. Ireland, in particular, has been successful in using lower corporate income tax rates to attract foreign corporations to locate facilities there. In recent years, Microsoft, Intel, and Dell have all based some of their operations in Ireland. The table also shows that corporate income tax rates are higher in the United States than in other high-income countries, except Japan.

Evaluating Taxes

We have seen that to raise revenue, governments have available a variety of taxes. In selecting which taxes to use, governments take into account the following goals and principles:

- The goal of economic efficiency
- The ability-to-pay principle
- The horizontal-equity principle
- The benefits-received principle
- The goal of attaining social objectives

The Goal of Economic Efficiency In Chapter 4, we analyzed the effect taxes have on economic efficiency. We briefly review that discussion here. Whenever a government taxes an activity, it raises the cost of engaging in that activity, so less of that activity will occur.

COUNTRY	TAX IN 2000	TAX IN 2007
France	37%	33%
Germany	52	38
Ireland	24	13
Italy	41	37
Japan	42	41
Spain	35	35
Sweden	28	28
United Kingdom	30	31
United States	40	40

TABLE 18-4

Corporate Income Tax Rates around the World

Source: *KPMG's Corporate Tax Rate Survey.*

Figure 18-3

The Efficiency Loss from a Sales Tax

This figure reviews the discussion from Chapter 4 on the efficiency loss from a tax. A sales tax increases the cost of supplying a good, which causes the supply curve to shift up from S_1 to S_2. Without the tax, the equilibrium price of the good is P_1, and the equilibrium quantity is Q_1. After the tax is imposed, the equilibrium price rises to P_2, and the equilibrium quantity falls to Q_2. After paying the tax, producers receive P_3. The government receives tax revenue equal to the green-shaded rectangle. Some consumer surplus and some producer surplus become tax revenue for the government, and some become deadweight loss, shown by the yellow-shaded triangle. The deadweight loss is the *excess burden* of the tax.

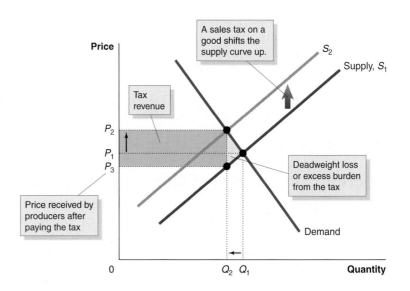

Excess burden The efficiency loss to the economy that results from a tax causing a reduction in the quantity of a good produced; also known as the deadweight loss.

Figure 18-3 uses a demand and supply graph to illustrate this point for a sales tax. As we saw in Chapter 4, a sales tax increases the cost of supplying a good, which causes the supply curve to shift up by the amount of the tax. In the figure, the equilibrium price rises from P_1 to P_2, and the equilibrium quantity falls from Q_1 to Q_2. When a good is taxed, less of it is produced.

The government collects tax revenue equal to the tax per unit multiplied by the number of units sold. The green-shaded rectangle in Figure 18-3 represents the government's tax revenue. Although sellers appear to receive a higher price for the good—P_2—the price they receive after paying the tax falls to P_3. Because the price consumers pay has risen, consumer surplus has fallen. Because the price producers receive has also fallen, producer surplus has fallen. Some of the reduction in consumer surplus and producer surplus becomes tax revenue for the government. The rest of the reduction in consumer surplus and producer surplus is equal to the deadweight loss from the tax and is shown in the figure by the yellow-shaded triangle. The deadweight loss from a tax is known as the **excess burden** of the tax. The excess burden measures the efficiency loss to the economy that results from the tax having reduced the quantity of the good produced. *A tax is efficient if it imposes a small excess burden relative to the tax revenue it raises.*

To improve the economic efficiency of a tax system, economists argue that the government should reduce its reliance on taxes that have a high deadweight loss relative to the revenue raised. The tax on interest earned from savings is an example of a tax with a high deadweight loss because savings often comes from income already taxed once. Therefore, taxing interest earned on savings from income that has already been taxed amounts to double taxation.

There are other examples of significant deadweight losses of taxation. High taxes on work can reduce the number of hours an individual works, as well as how hard the individual works or whether the individual starts a business. In each case, the reduction in the taxed activity—here, work—generates less government revenue, and individuals are worse off because the tax encourages them to change their behavior.

Taxation can have substantial effects on economic efficiency by altering incentives to work, save, or invest. A good illustration of this effect can be seen in the large differences between annual hours worked in Europe and in the United States. It is well known that Europeans now work fewer hours than do Americans. According to a recent analysis by Nobel laureate Edward Prescott of Arizona State University, this difference was not always present. In the early 1970s, when European and U.S. tax rates on income were comparable, European and U.S. hours worked per employee were also comparable. Prescott finds that virtually all of the difference between labor supply in the United States and labor supply in France and Germany since that time is due to differences in their tax systems.

Making the Connection

Should the United States Shift from an Income Tax to a Consumption Tax?

A key issue in recent debates over tax policy is whether the federal government should shift from relying on an income tax to relying on a *consumption tax*. Under the income tax, households pay taxes on all income earned. Under a consumption tax, households pay taxes only on the part of income they spend. Households pay taxes on saved income only if they spend the money at a later time.

To see how a shift from an income tax to a consumption tax can affect the economic incentives individuals face, consider the following example: Suppose a 20-year-old is deciding whether to save a $1,000 bonus paid by her employer. If she saves the $1,000 by putting it in a bank certificate of deposit (CD), the $1,000 *and* the interest she earns will both be taxed under the income tax, but neither will be taxed if the income tax is replaced by a consumption tax. Suppose she earns 6 percent per year on the CD and keeps it until she retires at age 70. With interest compounding tax-free over 50 years, she will have accumulated $18,420 at age 70. Now suppose that under the income tax she is taxed at a rate of 33 percent. As a result, she will only have $670 of her bonus left after paying the tax. In addition, if she saves the money in a CD, her after-tax return each year is only 6 percent × (1 − 0.33) = 4 percent. Now saving her bonus in a CD at age 20 yields only $4,761 at age 70. This big difference in accumulation—$13,659—is the tax burden on saving, a burden that makes saving less attractive.

Would a consumption tax be more efficient than an income tax?

Many economists argue that a taxpayer's well-being is better measured by his or her consumption (how much he or she spends) than by his or her income (how much he or she earns). Taxing consumption may therefore be more appropriate than taxing income. Also, because the income tax taxes interest and other returns to saving, it taxes *future* consumption—which is what current saving is for—more heavily than *present* consumption. That is, under an income tax, current consumption is taxed more favorably than future consumption, reducing households' willingness to save, as in the preceding example.

Some economists oppose a shift from an income tax to a consumption tax because they believe a consumption tax will be more regressive than an income tax. These economists argue that people with very low incomes are able to save little or nothing and so would not be able to benefit from the increased incentives for saving that exist under a consumption tax.

Would a shift to a consumption tax be a radical change in the tax system? For many households, the answer is, perhaps surprisingly, "no." Most taxpayers can already put part of their savings into accounts where the funds deposited and the interest received are not taxed until the funds are withdrawn for retirement spending—for example, 401(k) plans and certain types of Individual Retirement Accounts (IRAs). In effect, individuals whose savings are mainly in these retirement accounts are already paying a consumption tax rather than an income tax. And recent reductions in tax rates on dividends and capital gains—which are both returns to savings—and proposals to expand saving incentives will further increase the role of consumption taxation.

YOUR TURN: Test your understanding by doing related problem 2.11 on page 628 at the end of this chapter.

The administrative burden of a tax represents another example of the deadweight loss of taxation. Individuals spend many hours during the year keeping records for income tax purposes, and they spend many more hours prior to April 15 preparing their tax returns. The opportunity cost of this time is tens of billions of dollars each year and represents an administrative burden of the federal income tax. For corporations, complexity in tax planning arises in many areas. The federal government also has to devote resources to enforcing the tax laws. Although the government collects the revenue from taxation, the resources spent on administrative burdens benefit neither taxpayers nor the government.

Wouldn't tax simplification reduce the administrative burden and the deadweight loss of taxation? Yes. So why is the tax code complicated? In part, complexity arises because the political process has resulted in different types of income being taxed at different rates, requiring rules to limit taxpayers' ability to avoid taxes. In addition, interest groups seek benefits, while the majority of taxpayers, who do not benefit, find it difficult to organize a drive for a simpler tax system.

The Ability-to-Pay Principle The *ability-to-pay principle* holds that when the government raises revenue through taxes, it is fair to expect a greater share of the tax burden to be borne by people who have a greater ability to pay. Usually this principle means raising more taxes from people with high incomes than from people with low incomes, which is sometimes referred to as *vertical equity*. The federal income tax is consistent with the ability-to-pay principle. The sales tax, in contrast, is not consistent with the ability-to-pay principle because low-income people tend to spend a larger fraction of their income than do high-income people. As a result, low-income people will pay a greater fraction of their income in sales taxes than will high-income people.

The Horizontal-Equity Principle The *horizontal-equity principle* states that people in the same economic situation should be treated equally. Although this principle seems desirable, it is not easy to use in practice because it is sometimes difficult to determine whether two people are in the same economic situation. For example, two people with the same income are not necessarily in the same economic situation. Suppose one person does not work but receives an income of $50,000 per year entirely from interest received on bonds and another person receives an income of $50,000 per year from working at two jobs 16 hours a day. In this case, we could argue that the two people are in different economic situations and should not pay the same tax. Although policymakers and economists usually consider horizontal equity when evaluating proposals to change the tax system, it is not a principle that they can follow easily.

The Benefits-Received Principle According to the *benefits-received principle*, those people who receive the benefits from a government program should pay the taxes that support the program. For example, if a city operates a marina used by private boat owners, the government can raise the revenue to operate the marina by levying a tax on the boat owners. Raising the revenue through a general income tax paid both by boat owners and non–boat owners would be inconsistent with the benefits-received principle. Because the government has many programs, however, it would be impractical to identify and tax the beneficiaries of every program.

The Goal of Attaining Social Objectives Taxes are sometimes used to attain social objectives. For example, the government may want to discourage smoking and drinking alcohol. Taxing cigarettes and alcoholic beverages is one way to help achieve this objective. Taxes intended to discourage certain activities are sometimes referred to as "sin taxes."

18.3 LEARNING OBJECTIVE

18.3 | Understand the effect of price elasticity on tax incidence.

Tax Incidence Revisited: The Effect of Price Elasticity

In Chapter 4, we saw the difference between who is legally required to send a tax payment to the government and who actually bears the burden of a tax. Recall that the actual division of the burden of a tax between buyers and sellers in a market is known as **tax incidence**. We can go beyond the basic analysis of tax incidence by considering how the price elasticity of demand and price elasticity of supply affect how the burden of a tax is shared between consumers and firms.

Tax incidence The actual division of the burden of a tax between buyers and sellers in a market.

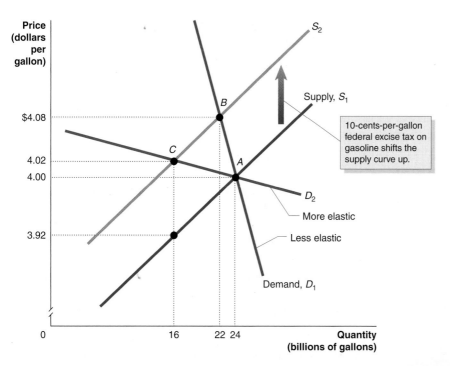

Figure 18-4

The Effect of Elasticity on Tax Incidence

When demand is more elastic than supply, consumers bear less of the burden of a tax. When supply is more elastic than demand, firms bear less of the burden of a tax. D_1 is inelastic between point A and point B, and D_2 is elastic between point A and point C. With demand curve D_1, a 10-cents-per-gallon tax raises the equilibrium price from $4.00 (point A) to $4.08 (point B), so consumers pay 8 cents of the tax, and firms pay 2 cents. With D_2, a 10-cents-per-gallon tax on gasoline raises the equilibrium price only from $4.00 (point A) to $4.02 (point C), so consumers pay 2 cents of the tax. Because in this case producers receive $3.92 per gallon after paying the tax, their share of the tax is 8 cents per gallon.

In Chapter 4, we discussed whether consumers or firms bear the larger share of a 10-cents-per-gallon federal excise tax on gasoline. We saw that consumers paid the majority of the tax. We can expand on this conclusion by stating that consumers of gasoline pay a larger fraction of gasoline taxes than do sellers because the elasticity of demand for gasoline is smaller than the elasticity of supply. In fact, we can draw a general conclusion: *When the demand for a product is less elastic than the supply, consumers pay the majority of the tax on the product. When demand for a product is more elastic than the supply, firms pay the majority of the tax on the product.*

We can see why this conclusion is correct with the aid of Figure 18-4. In Figure 18-4, D_1 is inelastic between points A and B, and D_2 is elastic between points A and C. With demand curve D_1, the 10-cents-per-gallon tax raises the market price of gasoline from $4.00 (point A) to $4.08 (point B) per gallon, so consumers pay 8 cents of the tax, and firms pay 2 cents. With D_2, the market price rises only to $4.02 (point C) per gallon, and consumers pay only 2 cents of the tax. With demand curve D_2, sellers of gasoline receive only $3.92 per gallon after paying the tax. So, the amount they receive per gallon after taxes falls from $4.00 to $3.92 per gallon, and they pay 8 cents of the tax.

Don't Let This Happen to **YOU!**

Remember Not to Confuse Who Pays the Tax with Who Bears the Burden of the Tax

Consider the following statement: "Of course I bear the burden of the sales tax on everything I buy. I can show you my sales receipts with the 6 percent sales tax clearly labeled. The seller doesn't bear that tax. I do."

The statement is incorrect. To understand why it is incorrect, think about what would happen to the price of a product if the sales tax on it were eliminated. Figure 18-4 shows that the price of the product would fall because the supply curve would shift down by the amount of the tax. The equilibrium price, however, would fall by less than the amount of the tax. (If you doubt that this is true, draw the

graph to convince yourself.) So, the gain from eliminating the tax would be received partly by consumers in the form of a lower price but also partly by sellers in the form of a new price that is higher than the amount they received from the old price minus the tax. Therefore, the burden from imposing a sales tax is borne partly by consumers and partly by sellers.

In determining the burden of a tax, what counts is not what is printed on the receipt for a product but what happens to the price of a product as a result of the tax.

YOUR TURN: Test your understanding by doing related problem 3.9 on page 629 at the end of this chapter.

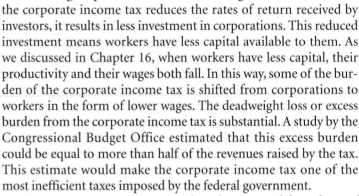

Making
the
Connection

Do Corporations Really Bear the Burden of the Federal Corporate Income Tax?

The incidence of the corporate income tax is one of the most controversial questions in the economics of tax policy. It is straightforward to determine the incidence of the gasoline tax using demand and supply analysis. Determining the incidence of the corporate income tax is more complicated because economists disagree over how corporations respond to the tax.

As a study by the Congressional Budget Office puts it:

> A corporation may write its check to the Internal Revenue Service for payment of the corporate income tax, but the money must come from somewhere: from reduced returns to investors in the company, lower wages to its workers, or higher prices that consumers pay for the products the company produces.

Most economists agree that some of the burden of the corporate income tax is passed on to consumers in the form of higher prices. There is also some agreement that because

Who really bears the burden of the taxes Apple pays?

the corporate income tax reduces the rates of return received by investors, it results in less investment in corporations. This reduced investment means workers have less capital available to them. As we discussed in Chapter 16, when workers have less capital, their productivity and their wages both fall. In this way, some of the burden of the corporate income tax is shifted from corporations to workers in the form of lower wages. The deadweight loss or excess burden from the corporate income tax is substantial. A study by the Congressional Budget Office estimated that this excess burden could be equal to more than half of the revenues raised by the tax. This estimate would make the corporate income tax one of the most inefficient taxes imposed by the federal government.

As a consequence, economists have long argued for reform of the system of double taxing income earned on investments that corporations finance by issuing stock. This income is taxed once by the corporate income tax and again by the individual income tax as profits are distributed to shareholders. Tax rates on dividends and capital gains were reduced in 2003, but whether to reduce double taxation further remains the subject of vigorous political debate.

Source: Congressional Budget Office, "The Incidence of the Corporate Income Tax," CBO paper, March 1996.

YOUR TURN: Test your understanding by doing related problem 3.7 on page 629 at the end of this chapter.

Solved Problem | 18-3

The Effect of Price Elasticity on the Excess Burden of a Tax

Explain whether you agree or disagree with the following statement: "For a given supply curve, the excess burden of a tax will be greater when demand is less elastic than when it is more elastic." Illustrate your answer with a demand and supply graph.

SOLVING THE PROBLEM:

Step 1: **Review the chapter material.** This problem is about both excess burden and tax incidence, so you may want to review the section "Evaluating Taxes," which begins on page 609, and the section "Tax Incidence Revisited: The Effect of Price Elasticity," which begins on page 612.

Step 2: **Draw a graph to illustrate the relationship between tax incidence and excess burden.** Figure 18-4 provides a good example of the type of graph to draw. Be sure to indicate the areas representing excess burden.

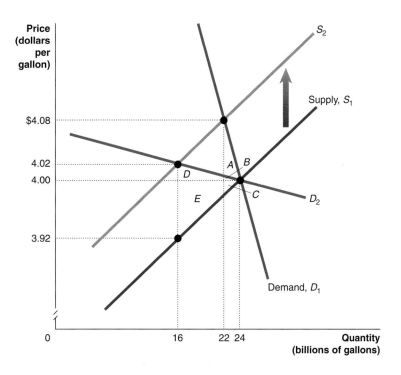

Step 3: **Use the graph to evaluate the statement.** The graph above is the same as Figure 18-4. As we have seen, for a given supply curve, when demand is more elastic, as with demand curve D_2, the fall in equilibrium quantity is greater than when demand is less elastic, as with demand curve D_1. The deadweight loss when demand is less elastic is shown by the area of the triangle made up of A, B, and C. The deadweight loss when demand is more elastic is shown by the area of the triangle made up of B, C, D, and E. The area of the deadweight loss is clearly larger when demand is more elastic than when it is less elastic. Recall that the excess burden of a tax is measured by the deadweight loss. Therefore, when demand is less elastic, the excess burden of a tax is *smaller* than when demand is more elastic. We can conclude that the statement is incorrect.

YOUR TURN: For more practice, do related problems 3.5 and 3.6 on pages 628–629 at the end of this chapter.

>> **End Solved Problem 18-3**

18.4 LEARNING OBJECTIVE

18.4 | Discuss the distribution of income in the United States and understand the extent of income mobility.

Income Distribution and Poverty

In practice, in most economies, some individuals will have very high incomes, and some individuals will have very low incomes. But how unequal is the distribution of income in the United States today? How does this compare with the distribution of income in the United States in the past or with the distribution of income in other countries today? What determines the distribution of income? And, to return to an issue raised at the beginning of this chapter, what impact does the tax system have on the distribution of income? These are questions we will explore in the remainder of this chapter.

TABLE 18-5

The Distribution of Household Income in the United States, 2006

ANNUAL INCOME	PERCENTAGE OF ALL HOUSEHOLDS
$0–$14,999	13.4%
$15,000–$24,999	11.8
$25,000–$34,999	11.5
$35,000–$49,999	14.6
$50,000–$74,999	18.2
$75,000–$99,999	11.3
$100,000 and over	19.1

Source: U.S. Census Bureau, *Income, Poverty, and Health Insurance Coverage in the United States: 2006*, P60–233, Table A-1, August 2007.

Measuring the Income Distribution and Poverty

Tables 18-5 and 18-6 show that the distribution of income clearly is unequal. Table 18-5 shows that while about 13 percent of U.S. households have annual incomes less than $15,000, the top 19 percent of households have incomes greater than $100,000. Table 18-6 divides the population of the United States into five groups, from the 20 percent with the lowest incomes to the 20 percent with the highest incomes. The fraction of total income received by each of the five groups is shown for selected years. Table 18-6 reinforces the fact that income is unequally distributed in the United States. The first row shows that in 2006, the 20 percent of Americans with the lowest incomes received only 3.4 percent of all income, while the 20 percent with the highest incomes received 50.5 percent of all income.

Table 18-6 also shows that over time, there have been some changes in the distribution of income. There was a moderate decline in inequality between 1936 and 1980, followed by some increase in inequality during the years after 1980. We will discuss some reasons for the recent increase in income inequality later in this chapter.

Poverty line A level of annual income equal to three times the amount of money necessary to purchase the minimal quantity of food required for adequate nutrition.

The Poverty Rate in the United States Much of the discussion of the distribution of income focuses on poverty. The federal government has a formal definition of poverty that was first developed in the early 1960s. According to this definition, a family is below the **poverty line** if its annual income is less than three times the amount of money necessary to

TABLE 18-6

How Has the Distribution of Income Changed over Time?

YEAR	LOWEST 20%	SECOND 20%	THIRD 20%	FOURTH 20%	HIGHEST 20%
2006	3.4%	8.6%	14.5%	22.9%	50.5%
1990	3.9	9.6	15.9	24.0	46.6
1980	4.3	10.3	16.9	24.9	43.7
1970	4.1	10.8	17.4	24.5	43.3
1960	3.2	10.6	17.6	24.7	44.0
1950	3.1	10.5	17.3	24.1	45.0
1936	4.1	9.2	14.1	20.9	51.7

Sources: U.S. Census Bureau, *Income, Poverty, and Health Insurance Coverage in the United States: 2006*, P60–233, Table 2, August 2007; U.S. Census Bureau, *Income in the United States, 2002*, P60–221, September 2003; and U.S. Census Bureau, *Historical Statistics of the United States, Colonial Times to 1970*, Washington, DC: U.S. Government Printing Office, 1975.

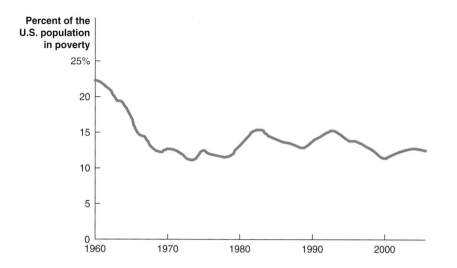

Figure 18-5

Poverty in the United States, 1960–2006

The poverty rate in the United States declined from 22 percent of the population in 1960 to 11 percent in 1973. Over the past 30 years, the poverty rate has fluctuated between 11 percent and 15 percent of the population.
Source: U.S. Census Bureau, *Income, Poverty, and Health Insurance Coverage in the United States: 2006*, P60–233, Table B-1, August 2007.

purchase the minimal quantity of food required for adequate nutrition. In 2006, the poverty line was $20,444 for a family of four with two children. Figure 18-5 shows the **poverty rate**, or the percentage of the U.S. population that was poor during each year between 1960 and 2006. Between 1960 and 1973, the poverty rate declined by half, falling from 22 percent of the population to 11 percent. In the past 30 years, however, the poverty rate has declined very little. In 2006, it was actually slightly greater than it was in 1973.

Different groups in the population have substantially different poverty rates. Table 18-7 shows that while the overall poverty rate in 2006 was 12.3 percent, the rate among women who head a family with no husband present, among black people, and among Hispanic people was about twice as high. The poverty rates for white and Asian people were below average.

Poverty rate The percentage of the population that is poor according to the federal government's definition.

Explaining Income Inequality

The novelists Ernest Hemingway and F. Scott Fitzgerald supposedly once had a conversation about the rich. Fitzgerald said to Hemingway, "You know, the rich are different from you and me." To which Hemingway replied, "Yes. They have more money." Although witty, Hemingway's joke doesn't help answer the question of why the rich have more money. In Chapter 16, we provided one answer to the question when we discussed the *marginal productivity theory of income distribution*. We saw that in equilibrium, each factor of production receives a payment equal to its marginal revenue product. The more factors of production an individual owns, and the more productive those factors are, the higher the individual's income will be.

All people	12.3%
Female head of family, no husband present (all races)	28.3
Blacks	24.3
Hispanics	20.6
Asians	10.3
White, not Hispanic	8.2

TABLE 18-7

Poverty Rates Vary across Groups, 2006

Note: Hispanics can be of any race.

Source: U.S. Census Bureau, *Income, Poverty, and Health Insurance Coverage in the United States: 2006*, P60–233, Table 3, August 2007.

For most people, of course, the most important factor of production they own is their labor. Therefore, the income they earn depends on how productive they are and on the prices of the goods and services their labor helps produce. Baseball player Alfonso Soriano earns $18 million per year because he is a very productive player, and his employer, the Chicago Cubs, can sell tickets and television rights to the baseball games Soriano plays in for a high price. Individuals who help to produce goods and services that can be sold for only a low price earn lower incomes.

Many people own other factors of production as well. For example, many people own capital by owning stock in corporations or by owning shares in mutual funds that buy the stock of corporations. Ownership of capital is not equally distributed, and income earned from capital is more unequally distributed than income earned from labor. Some people supply entrepreneurial skills by starting and managing businesses. Their income is increased by the profits from these businesses.

We saw in Table 18-6 that income inequality has increased somewhat during the past 25 years. Two factors that appear to have contributed to this increase are technological change and expanding international trade. Rapid technological change, particularly the development of information technology, has led to the substitution of computers and other machines for unskilled labor. This substitution has caused a decline in the wages of unskilled workers relative to other workers. Expanding international trade has put U.S. workers in competition with foreign workers to a greater extent than in the past. This competition has caused the wages of unskilled workers to be depressed relative to the wages of other workers. Some economists have also argued that the incomes of low-income workers have been depressed by competition with workers who are in the United States illegally.

Most economists believe that changes in tax laws have not played a major role in recent changes in income inequality. Federal income tax rates have changed dramatically during the years covered in Table 18-6. For example, the top marginal income tax rate was 91 percent in the 1950s, declining to 70 percent in the 1960s and to 28 percent in the 1980s. It then rose to 39.6 percent in the 1990s, before declining to 35 percent in 2003. Because tax rates changed significantly but the distribution of income has changed relatively little, it is unlikely that changes in tax rates have had a large impact on the distribution of income.

Finally, like everything else in life, earning an income is also subject to good and bad fortune. A poor person who becomes a millionaire by winning the state lottery is an obvious example, as is a person whose earning power drastically declines after a debilitating illness or accident. So, we can say that as a group, the people with high incomes are likely to have greater-than-average productivity and own greater-than-average amounts of capital. They are also likely to have experienced good fortune. As a group, poor people are likely to have lower-than-average productivity and own lower-than-average amounts of capital. They are also likely to have been less fortunate.

Showing the Income Distribution with a Lorenz Curve

Lorenz curve A curve that shows the distribution of income by arraying incomes from lowest to highest on the horizontal axis and indicating the cumulative fraction of income earned by each fraction of households on the vertical axis.

Figure 18-6 presents the distribution of income using a *Lorenz curve*. A **Lorenz curve** shows the distribution of income by arraying incomes from lowest to highest on the horizontal axis and indicating the cumulative fraction of income earned by each fraction of households on the vertical axis. If the distribution of income were perfectly equal, a Lorenz curve would be a straight line because the first 20 percent of households would earn 20 percent of total income, the first 40 percent of households would earn 40 percent of total income, and so on. Panel (a) of Figure 18-6 shows a Lorenz curve for the actual distribution of income in the United States in 1980 and another curve for the distribution of income in 2006, using the data in Table 18-6. We know that income was distributed more unequally in 2006 than in 1980 because the Lorenz curve for 2006 is farther away from the line of equal distribution than is the Lorenz curve for 1980.

Panel (b) illustrates how to calculate the *Gini coefficient*, which is one way of summarizing the information provided by a Lorenz curve. The Gini coefficient is equal to

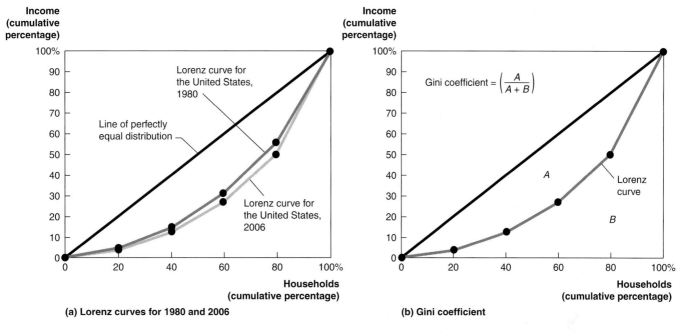

Figure 18-6 | The Lorenz Curve and Gini Coefficient

In panel (a), the Lorenz curves show the distribution of income by arraying incomes from the lowest to the highest on the horizontal axis and indicating the cumulative fraction of income by each fraction of households on the vertical axis. The straight line represents perfect income equality. Because the Lorenz curve for 1980 is closer to the line of perfect equality than the Lorenz curve for 2006, we know that income was more equally distributed in 1980 than in 2006. In panel (b), we show the Gini coefficient, which is equal to the area between the line of perfect income equality and the Lorenz curve—area A—divided by the whole area below the line of perfect equality—area A plus area B. The closer the Gini coefficient is to 1, the more unequal the income distribution.

the area between the line of perfect income equality and the Lorenz curve—area *A* in panel (b)—divided by the whole area below the line of perfect equality—area *A* plus area *B* in panel (b). Or:

$$\text{Gini coefficient} = \left(\frac{A}{A + B} \right).$$

If the income distribution were completely *equal*, the Lorenz curve would be the same as the line of perfect income equality, area *A* would be zero, and the Gini coefficient would be zero. If the income distribution were completely *unequal*, area *B* would be zero, and the Gini coefficient would equal 1. Therefore, the greater the degree of income inequality, the greater the value of the Gini coefficient. In 1980, the Gini coefficient for the United States was 0.403. In 2006, it was 0.470, which tells us again that income inequality increased between 1980 and 2006.

Problems in Measuring Poverty and the Distribution of Income

The measures of poverty and the distribution of income that we have discussed to this point may be misleading for two reasons. First, these measures are snapshots in time that do not take into account *income mobility*. Second, they ignore the effects of government programs meant to reduce poverty.

Income Mobility in the United States We expect to see some income mobility. When you graduate from college, your income will rise as you assume a new job. A family may be below the poverty line one year because the main wage earner is unemployed but may rise well above the poverty line the next year when that wage earner finds a job.

A medical student may have a very low income for several years but a very high income after graduating and establishing a medical practice. It is also true that someone might have a high income one year—perhaps from making a killing on the stock market—and have a much lower income in future years.

Statistics on income mobility are more difficult to collect than statistics on income during a particular year because they involve following the same individuals over a number of years. A study by the U.S. Census Bureau tracked the incomes of the same households for each year from 1996 to 1999. Figure 18-7 shows the results of the study. Each column represents one quintile—or 20 percent—of households, arranged by their incomes in 1996. Reading up the column, we can see where the households that started in that quintile in 1996 ended up in 1999. For example, the bottom quintile (the first column) consists of households with incomes of $16,220 or less in 1996 (all values are measured in 1999 dollars to correct for the effects of inflation). Only 62 percent of these households were still in the bottom quintile in 1999. Only a small number—1.2 percent—had moved all the way to the top quintile, but more than one-third had moved into either the second quintile or the middle quintile. At the other end of the income distribution, of those households in the top income quintile—with incomes of $68,649 or more—in 1996, only two-thirds were still in the top quintile in 1999. Given the relatively short time period involved, this study indicates that there is significant income mobility in the United States over time.

It should be noted that the U.S. economy experienced rapid growth between 1996 and 1999, which may have increased the degree of income mobility. However, an earlier study by Peter Gottschalk of Boston College and Sheldon Danziger of the University of Michigan also provides evidence of significant income mobility. In that study, only 47 percent of those people who were in the lowest 20 percent of incomes in 1968 were still in the lowest bracket in 1991. More than 25 percent had incomes in 1991 that put them in the middle or higher-income brackets. Of those people who were in the highest-income bracket in 1968, only 42 percent were still in the highest bracket in 1991. Almost 8 percent of this group had fallen to the lowest-income bracket.

Another study by the U.S. Census Bureau showed that of the people who were in poverty in 1996, only 50.5 percent remained in poverty in 1999. The same study indicated that of the people who were in poverty at any time during 1996, 51.1 percent were in poverty for four months or less. Only 20.4 percent were in poverty for more than one year.

Figure 18-7

Income Mobility in the United States, 1996–1999

Each column represents one quintile—or 20 percent—of households, arranged by their incomes in 1996. Reading up the column, we can see where the households that started in that quintile in 1996 ended up in 1999. Only 62 percent of the households that were in the bottom quintile of income in 1996 were still in the bottom quintile in 1999. Only 66 percent of the households that were in the top quintile of income in 1996 were still in the top quintile in 1999.

Note: Incomes are in 1999 dollars to correct for the effects of inflation.

Source: U.S. Census Bureau, "Dynamics of Economic Well-Being: Movements in the U.S. Income Distribution, 1996–1999," *Current Population Reports*, P70–95, July 2004.

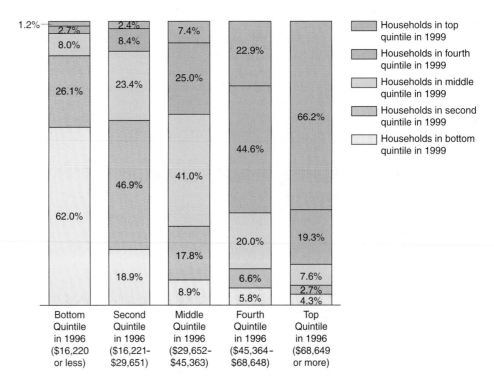

Solved Problem | 18-4

Are Many Individuals Stuck in Poverty?

Evaluate the following statement:

> Government statistics indicate that 12 percent of the population is below the poverty line. The fraction of the population in poverty has never dropped below 10 percent. Therefore, more than 10 percent of the population must cope with very low incomes year after year.

SOLVING THE PROBLEM:

Step 1: **Review the chapter material.** This problem is about income mobility, so you may want to review the section "Income Mobility in the United States," which begins on page 619.

Step 2: **Use the discussion in this chapter to evaluate the statement.** Although it is true that the poverty rate in the United States is never below 10 percent, it is not the same 10 percent of the population that is in poverty each year. This chapter discusses a U.S. Census Bureau study that showed that only about half of the people who were in poverty in 1996 were still in poverty in 1999. Poverty remains a problem in the United States, but fortunately, the number of people who remain in poverty for many years is much smaller than the number who are in poverty during any one year.

YOUR TURN: For more practice, do related problem 4.7 on page 630 at the end of this chapter.

>> **End Solved Problem 18-4**

The Effect of Taxes and Transfers A second reason the conventional statistics on poverty and income distribution may be misleading is that they omit the effects of government programs. Because of government programs, there is a difference between the income people earn and the income they actually have available to spend. The data in Tables 18-5 and 18-6 show the distribution of income before taxes are paid. We have seen that at the federal level, taxes are progressive, meaning people with high incomes pay a larger share of their incomes in taxes than do people with low incomes. Therefore, income remaining after taxes is more equally distributed than is income before taxes. The tables also do not include income from *transfer payments* individuals receive from the government, such as Social Security payments to retired and disabled people. The Social Security system has been very effective in reducing the poverty rate among people older than 65. In 1960, 35 percent of people in the United States over age 65 had incomes below the poverty line. By 2006, only about 9 percent of people over 65 had incomes below the poverty line.

Individuals with low incomes also receive noncash benefits, such as food stamps, free school lunches, and rent subsidies. The *food stamp program* has been a particularly important noncash benefit. Under this program, individuals with low incomes can buy, at a discount, coupons to purchase food in supermarkets. During 2007, more than 26 million people participated in this program at a cost to the federal government of $33.2 billion. Because individuals with low incomes are more likely to receive transfer payments and other benefits from the government than are individuals with high incomes, the distribution of income is more equal if we take these benefits into account. For example, in 2006, 12.3 percent of the U.S. population was below the poverty line using the official definition of income. Taking into account taxes paid and benefits received from government programs raises the incomes of enough people to reduce the poverty rate to 9.0 percent.

Income Distribution and Poverty around the World

How does income inequality in the United States compare with income inequality in other countries? Table 18-8 compares the ratio of total income received by the 20 percent of the population with the lowest incomes and the 20 percent with the highest incomes

TABLE 18-8

Income Inequality around the World

	LOWEST 20%	HIGHEST 20%	RATIO
BOLIVIA	1.5%	63.0%	42.0
PARAGUAY	2.4	61.9	25.8
BRAZIL	2.8	61.1	21.8
CHILE	3.8	60.0	15.8
UNITED STATES	3.4	50.5	14.9
THAILAND	6.3	49.0	7.8
UNITED KINGDOM	6.1	44.0	7.2
IRELAND	7.4	42.0	5.7
FRANCE	7.2	40.2	5.6
CANADA	7.2	39.9	5.5
SOUTH KOREA	7.9	37.5	4.7
GERMANY	8.5	36.9	4.3
NORWAY	9.6	37.2	3.9
JAPAN	10.6	35.7	3.4

Note: Data for most countries are from the early 2000s; U.S. data are from 2006.

Source: Adapted from United Nations, *Human Development Report, 2007/2008*, New York: Palgrave Macmillan, 2007, Table 15.

in several countries. The countries are ranked from most unequal to least unequal. In Bolivia, for example, the highest-income group has 63.0/1.5 = 42.0 times the income of the lowest-income group. In Japan, by contrast, the highest-income group has only 35.7/10.6 = 3.4 times the income of the lowest-income group. As the table shows, poor countries, such as Bolivia and Paraguay, typically have more unequal distributions of income than does the United States. The distribution of income in the United States is more equal than some moderate-income countries, such as Brazil and Chile, but less equal than other moderate-income countries, such as Thailand. The United States has the most unequal distribution of income of any high-income country in the world. Of course, one must be careful with such comparisons because transfer payments are not counted in income. For example, the Social Security and Medicare systems in the United States are much more generous than the corresponding systems in Japan but less generous than those in France and Germany.

Although poverty remains a problem in high-income countries, it is a much larger problem in poor countries. The level of poverty in much of Sub-Saharan Africa, in particular, is a human catastrophe. In 2006, the poverty line in the United States for a family of four was an annual income of $20,444, but economists often use a much lower threshold income of $570 per person per year (or about $1.50 per day) when calculating the rate of poverty in poor countries. As Table 18-9 shows, by this measure, poverty declined from about 20 percent of the world population in 1970 to 7 percent in 2000, the most recent year for which statistics are available. The greatest reduction in poverty has taken place in Asia. In China, the poverty rate dropped spectacularly from 32 percent in 1970 to 3.1 percent in 2000. In south Asia, which includes India, poverty rates dropped from 30.3 percent to 2.5 percent. By contrast, the poverty rate in Sub-Saharan Africa *increased* from 35.1 percent in 1970 to 48.8 percent in 2000. Why has poverty fallen dramatically in Asia but risen in Africa? The key explanation is that the countries of Asia have had higher rates of economic growth than have the countries of Sub-Saharan Africa. Recent economic research demonstrates a positive relationship between economic growth and the incomes of lower-income people.

REGION	PERCENTAGE OF THE POPULATION IN POVERTY	
	1970	2000
World	20.2%	7.0%
East Asia	32.7	2.4
China	32.0	3.1
South Asia	30.3	2.5
Middle East and North Africa	10.7	0.6
Latin America	10.3	4.2
Sub-Saharan Africa	35.1	48.8

TABLE 18-9

Poverty in Sub-Saharan Africa Is Much Greater Than Elsewhere in the World

Source: Xavier Sala-i-Martin, "The World Distribution of Income: Falling Poverty and Convergence, Period," *Quarterly Journal of Economics*, Vol. 121, No. 2 (May 2006), pp. 351–397.

Economics in YOUR Life!

>> Continued from page 599

At the beginning of the chapter, we asked you to think about where government gets the money to provide goods and services and about whether you pay your fair share of taxes. After reading this chapter, you should see that you pay taxes in many different forms. When you work, you pay taxes on your income, both for individual income taxes and social insurance taxes. When you buy gasoline, you pay an excise tax, which, in part, pays for highways. When you buy goods at a local store, you pay state and local sales taxes the government uses to fund education and other services. Whether you are paying your fair share of taxes is a normative question. The U.S. tax system is progressive, so higher-income individuals pay more in taxes than do lower-income individuals. In fact, as we saw in the *Making the Connection* on page 607, people in the lowest 40 percent of the income distribution pay no federal income taxes at all. You may find that you will not pay much in federal income taxes in your first job after college. But as your income grows during your career, so will the percentage of your income you pay in taxes.

Conclusion

The public choice model provides insights into how government decisions are made. The decisions of policymakers will not necessarily reflect the preferences of voters. Attempts by government to intervene in the economy may increase economic efficiency, as we saw in Chapter 5, but also lead to government failure and a reduction in economic efficiency.

A saying attributed to Benjamin Franklin states that "nothing in this world is certain but death and taxes." But which taxes? As we saw at the beginning of this chapter, politicians continue to debate whether the government should use the tax system and other programs to reduce the level of income inequality in the United States. The tax system represents a balance among the objectives of economic efficiency, ability to pay, paying for benefits received, and achieving social objectives. Those favoring government intervention to reduce inequality argue that it is unfair for some people to have much higher incomes than others. Others argue that income inequality largely reflects higher incomes resulting from greater skills and from entrepreneurial ability and that higher taxes reduce work, saving, and investment.

Many economists are skeptical of tax policy proposals to reduce income inequality very significantly. They argue that a market system relies on individuals being willing to work hard and take risks with the promise of high incomes if they are successful. If some of those incomes are taken from them in the name of reducing income inequality, the incentives to work hard and take risks are reduced. Ultimately, whether policies to reduce income inequality should be pursued is a normative question. Economics alone cannot decide the issue.

Read *An Inside Look at Policy* on the next page for a discussion of the views of Federal Reserve Chairman Ben Bernanke on sources of income inequality in the United States.

Balancing Flexible Markets and a Government Safety Net

WASHINGTON POST, FEBRUARY 7, 2007

The Grand Bargainer

With President Bush having finally acknowledged the problem of growing income inequality, and Democratic leaders tripping over each other to do something about it, we desperately need a trustworthy moderator for this national debate.

Now we may have one, in Federal Reserve Chairman Ben Bernanke. In a speech yesterday to the Greater Omaha Chamber of Commerce, the former Princeton University professor cut through all the usual cant of the left and right and drew on the best and latest research to quantify just how much inequality has increased over the past 30 years. He gently, but deftly, dismissed the favorite conservative arguments that the story is not one of greater inequality so much as one of greater mobility. At the same time, Bernanke exposed as myth all those overblown fears about the broad decline in standard of living and the death of the American middle class.

The causes of rising inequality are well known: technological change that has reduced demand for unskilled labor and increased it for skilled labor; increased trade and immigration, which march under the now-tainted banner of globalization; the winner-take-all dynamic of certain labor markets that produces superstar salaries for professional athletes, entertainers and chief executives; and changing "institutional arrangements," from the declining power of unions to deregulation.

Much effort has gone into figuring out the relative importance of these factors, driven in part because how you define the problem often dictates how you craft a solution. Bernanke tends to side with those who credit new technologies, like computers, that have increased the demand—and thus the relative pay—for educated workers. This analysis suggests the answer lies in more education, which appeals to market-oriented conservatives who are anxious to avoid solutions that might throw sand in the gears of globalization. It also appeals to academic economists, who have a natural preference for anything that involves hiring more college professors. . . .

One reason the U.S. economy is the most productive, the most dynamic, the most innovative in the world, Bernanke explained, is that we offer the biggest rewards to skill, effort and ingenuity. We also have an economic framework that not only allows companies and individuals the flexibility to adapt to changes in technology or consumer tastes or competition, but rewards them handsomely when they do.

Bernanke says the flip side of this dynamism has been to generate not only a higher level of inequality, but also a higher level of economic insecurity. Now, he says, the only way to make these politically acceptable is to "put some limits on the downside risks to individuals affected by economic change."

One way to limit those risks, of course, would be to restrict trade, impose new regulations on labor and product markets, or use the tax code to massively redistribute incomes. For Bernanke, the costs in terms of slower growth and higher unemployment would be too high.

The better alternative, he argued, is to preserve the political consensus for open and flexible markets by offering Americans a stronger economic safety net—one that might include more portable and affordable health insurance and pensions, some expansion of income support in the event of a job loss and a big new investment in education and training, from early childhood through adulthood.

Key Points in the Article

This article highlights the political problem of growing income inequality. Most agree that growing income inequality is a problem. Popular solutions to the problem involve limiting trade and using the tax code to redistribute income. Ben Bernanke suggests that the cost of these approaches is too high and that we should instead explore strengthening the economic safety net while investing in education and training. The U.S. economy rewards skill, innovation, and effort. The article suggests that we need to continue to make progress in these areas, while taking steps to reduce the economic insecurity caused by the dynamic nature of the U.S. economy.

Analyzing the News

(a) U.S. politicians of both parties see income inequality in the United States as a growing problem. Some of the concern is the growing gap between the very rich and the simply rich. Some of the concern is the sense that the standard of living of middle-income earners is staying constant, while the upper-income earners are enjoying higher-income and wealth. While many agree on the existence of the problem, as we saw in the chapter, the way to reduce income inequality is far less certain.

(b) Recall from Chapter 16 that a worker is paid the worker's marginal revenue product, or the value of the additional output that the worker produces. Higher-skilled workers will not only be able to produce more output—that is, have a higher marginal product—but will also be able to produce more valuable output. Both higher marginal product and a higher value of output will lead to higher wages.

(c) The government already uses the tax code to redistribute income. The nature of a progressive tax system distributes income by taxing high-income people at higher rates than low-income people. In addition, programs such as the Earned Income Tax Credit give money to lower-income working families with children. The following table shows the distribution of individual income tax payments by adjusted gross income (AGI), range from 1999 to 2004. Since 1999, the share of federal income taxes paid by the bottom 50 percent of the income distribution has fallen while that of top income earners has increased. For 2004, the top 10 percent of tax filers claimed 44.35 percent of AGI and paid 68.19 percent of income taxes. Making the income tax system more progressive would require placing a larger tax burden on those in the top of the income distribution.

The article points out that this may be costly in terms of economic growth.

It should be noted that parts of the tax system are not very progressive at all. For example, in 2007, the payroll tax for Social Security is not paid on labor earnings above $97,500 per year, and the Medicare tax is a constant rate of labor earnings, regardless of income.

Thinking Critically About Policy

1. It is often claimed that recent tax cuts have provided more tax relief for those in the upper ranges of the income distribution than those in the lower ranges. Evaluate this claim in light of the tax shares given in the table.
2. While they may pay little individual income taxes, all low-income families with earned income are subject to the payroll taxes for Social Security and Medicare. Some policymakers have proposed abolishing the payroll taxes and funding Social Security and Medicare by increasing the personal income tax. What potential benefits and drawbacks are there to this proposal?

PERCENTAGE OF FEDERAL INCOME TAX PAID

PERCENTILES BY AGI	1999	2000	2001	2002	2003	2004	2004 SHARE OF AGI EARNED BY TAXPAYERS IN THIS CATEGORY	2004 AGI LEVEL FOR THIS CATEGORY
Top 1%	36.18	37.42	33.89	33.71	34.27	36.89	19.00	$328,049
Top 5	55.45	56.47	53.25	53.80	54.36	57.13	33.45	137,056
Top 10	66.45	67.33	64.89	65.73	65.84	68.19	44.35	99,112
Top 25	83.54	84.01	82.90	83.90	83.88	84.86	66.13	60,041
Top 50	96.00	96.09	96.03	96.50	96.54	96.70	86.58	30,122
Bottom 50	4.00	3.91	3.97	3.50	3.46	3.30	13.42	<30,122

Sources: Gerald Prante, Tax Foundation, *Summary of Latest Federal Individual Income Tax Data*, Fiscal Fact No. 66; National Taxpayers Union, *Who Pays Income Taxes? See Who Pays What*, www.ntu.org/main/page.php?PageID=6; and Internal Revenue Service, *Statistics of Income*, various years.

Key Terms

18.1 LEARNING OBJECTIVE   18.1 | Define the public choice model and explain how it is used to analyze government decision making, **pages 600–604.**

Public Choice

Summary

The **public choice model** applies economic analysis to government decision making. The observation that majority voting may not always result in consistent choices is called the **voting paradox**. The **Arrow impossibility theorem** states that no system of voting can be devised that will consistently represent the underlying preferences of voters. The **median voter theorem** states that the outcome of a majority vote is likely to represent the preferences of the voter who is in the political middle. Individuals and firms sometimes engage in **rent seeking**, which is the use of government action to make themselves better off at the expense of others. Although government intervention can sometimes improve economic efficiency, public choice analysis indicates that *government failure* can also occur reducing economic efficiency.

 Visit www.myeconlab.com to complete these exercises online and get instant feedback.

Review Questions

1.1 What is the public choice model?

1.2 What is the difference between the voting paradox and the Arrow impossibility theorem?

1.3 What is rent seeking and what relation does it have to regulatory capture?

1.4 What is the relationship between market failure and government failure?

Problems and Applications

1.5 Will the preferences shown in the following table lead to a voting paradox? Briefly explain.

POLICY	LENA	DAVID	KATHLEEN
Cancer research	1st	2nd	3rd
Mass transit	2nd	1st	1st
Border security	3rd	3rd	2nd

1.6 Many political observers have noted that Republican presidential candidates tend to emphasize their conservative positions on policy issues while running for their party's nomination, and Democratic presidential candidates tend to emphasize their liberal positions on policy issues while running for their party's nomination. In the general election, though, Republican candidates tend to downplay their conservative positions and Democratic candidates tend to downplay their liberal positions. Can the median voter theorem help explain this pattern? Briefly explain.

1.7 Briefly explain whether you agree with the following argument: "The median voter theorem will be an accurate predicator of the outcomes of elections when a majority of voters have preferences very similar to those of the median voter. When the majority of voters have preferences very different from those of the median voter, then the median voter theorem will not lead to accurate predictions of the outcomes of elections."

1.8 An article in the *Economist* magazine makes the following observation:

> People often complain that it is simplistic for economics to assume that individuals are rational and self-interested. Of course this is a simplification, but it is an enlightening one, and not flatly contradicted in the real world. The corresponding assumption about government—that the state aims to maximize social welfare—is contradicted by the real world about as flatly as you could wish.

What does it mean for the state to "maximize the social welfare"? If policymakers are not attempting to maximize the social welfare, what are they attempting to do?

Source: "The Grabbing Hand," *Economist*, February 11, 1999.

1.9 Is the typical person likely to gather more information when buying a new car or when voting for a member of the House of Representatives? Briefly explain.

1.10 James Buchanan, who is one of the key figures in developing the public choice model, has written that:

"The relevant difference between markets and politics does not lie in the kinds of values/interests that persons pursue, but in the conditions under which they pursue their various interests."

Do you agree with this statement? Are there significant ways in which the business marketplace differs from the political marketplace?

Source: James M. Buchanan, "The Constitution of Economic Policy," *American Economic Review*, Vol. 77, No. 3, June 1987, p. 246.

>> **End Learning Objective 18.1**

18.2 LEARNING OBJECTIVE | 18.2 | Understand the tax system in the United States, including the principles that governments use to create tax policy, **pages 604–612.**

The Tax System

Summary

Governments raise the funds they need through taxes. The most widely used taxes are income taxes, social insurance taxes, sales taxes, property taxes, and excise taxes. Governments take into account several important objectives when deciding which taxes to use: efficiency, ability to pay, horizontal equity, benefits received, and attaining social objectives. A **regressive tax** is a tax for which people with lower incomes pay a higher percentage of their incomes in tax than do people with higher incomes. A **progressive tax** is a tax for which people with lower incomes pay a lower percentage of their incomes in tax than do people with higher incomes. The **marginal tax rate** is the fraction of each additional dollar of income that must be paid in taxes. The **average tax rate** is the total tax paid divided by total income. When analyzing the impact of taxes on how much people are willing to work or save or invest, economists focus on the marginal tax rate rather than the average tax rate. The **excess burden** of a tax is the efficiency loss to the economy that results from a tax causing a reduction in the quantity of a good produced.

 Visit www.myeconlab.com to complete these exercises online and get instant feedback.

Review Questions

2.1 Which type of tax raises the most revenue for the federal government?

2.2 A study showed that, on average, a family in Pennsylvania earning $40,000 per year paid 6 percent of its income in state taxes. A family earning $100,000 paid 5.6 percent of its income in taxes. Are state taxes in Pennsylvania progressive or regressive? Be sure to explain the difference between a progressive tax and a regressive tax.

2.3 What is the difference between a marginal tax rate and an average tax rate? Which is more important in determining the impact of the tax system on economic behavior?

2.4 Briefly discuss each of the principles governments consider when deciding which taxes to use.

Problems and Applications

2.5 Why does the federal government raise more tax revenue from taxes on individuals than from taxes on businesses?

2.6 According to an article in the *New York Times*, "the poor and middle class . . . spend a greater portion of their income on cigarettes than the wealthy do." Assuming that this observation is correct, is a sales tax on cigarettes likely to be regressive or progressive? Be sure to define regressive and progressive taxes in your answer.

Source: David Leonhardt, "How a Tax on Cigarettes Can Help the Taxed," *New York Times*, April 14, 2002.

2.7 Many state governments have begun using lotteries to raise revenue. If we think of a lottery as a type of tax, is a lottery likely to be progressive or regressive? What data would you need to determine whether the burden of a lottery is progressive or regressive?

2.8 Use the information in Table 18-2 on page 606 to calculate the total federal income tax paid, the marginal tax rate, and the average tax rate for people with the following incomes. (For simplicity, assume that these people have no exemptions or deductions from their incomes.)

a. $25,000

b. $125,000

c. $300,000

2.9 (Related to the *Making the Connection* on page 607) The following table shows the distribution of federal taxes in 2000.

INCOME CATEGORY	PERCENTAGE OF FEDERAL INDIVIDUAL INCOME TAXES PAID	PERCENTAGE OF TOTAL FEDERAL TAXES PAID
Lowest 20%	−0.6	0.7
Second 20%	0.5	3.9
Third 20%	6.9	10.2
Fourth 20%	16.3	19.9
Highest 20%	76.6	65.1
Total	**100.0%**	**100.0%**
Highest 1%	29.5	20.1

Source: Department of the Treasury: Office of Tax Analysis Working Paper #85, "U.S. Treasury Distributional Methodology" by Julie-Anne Cronin (September 1999).

Taxes were cut several times under the administration of George W. Bush. The table shows the distribution of federal taxes paid for the year before the first Bush administration tax cut. How did the tax cuts influence the distribution of federal taxes?

2.10 Almost all states levy sales taxes on retail products, but about half of them exempt purchases of food. In addition, virtually all services are exempt from state sales taxes. Evaluate these tax rate differences, using the goals and principles of taxation on pages 609 to 612.

2.11 (Related to the *Making the Connection* on page 611) Suppose the government eliminates the income tax and replaces it with a consumption tax. Think about the effect of this on the market for automobiles. Can you necessarily tell what will happen to the price and quantity of automobiles? Briefly explain.

>> **End Learning Objective 18.2**

18.3 LEARNING OBJECTIVE   18.3 | Understand the effect of price elasticity on tax incidence, **pages 612–615.**

Tax Incidence Revisited: The Effect of Price Elasticity

Summary

Tax incidence is the actual division of the burden of a tax. In most cases, buyers and sellers share the burden of a tax levied on a good or service. When the elasticity of demand for a product is smaller than the elasticity of supply, consumers pay the majority of the tax on the product. When the elasticity of demand for a product is larger than the elasticity of supply, sellers pay the majority of the tax on the product.

 Visit www.myeconlab.com to complete these exercises *Get Ahead of the Curve* online and get instant feedback.

Review Questions

3.1 What is meant by tax incidence?

3.2 Briefly discuss the effect of price elasticity of supply and demand on tax incidence.

Problems and Applications

3.3 According to the 2004 *Economic Report of the President*, "The actual incidence of a tax may have little to do with the legal specification of its incidence." Briefly explain what this statement means and discuss whether you agree or disagree with it.

3.4 According to the 2004 *Economic Report of the President*, "Another crucial principle [of tax incidence] is that

only people can pay taxes. Businesses and other artificial entities cannot pay taxes." Do you agree that businesses cannot pay taxes? Don't businesses pay the federal corporate income tax? Briefly explain.

3.5 (Related to *Solved Problem 18-3* on page 614) Use the following graph of the market for cigarettes to answer the following questions.

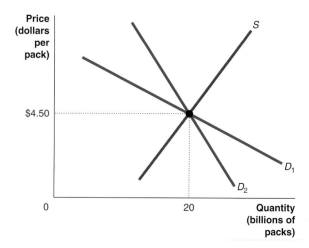

a. If the government imposes a 10-cents-per-pack tax on cigarettes, will the price consumers pay rise more if the demand curve is D_1 or if the demand curve is D_2? Briefly explain.

b. If the government imposes a 10-cents-per-pack tax on cigarettes, will the revenue to the government be greater if the demand curve is D_1 or if the demand curve is D_2? Briefly explain.

c. If the government imposes a 10-cents-per-pack tax on cigarettes, will the excess burden from the tax be greater if the demand curve is D_1 or if the demand curve is D_2? Briefly explain.

3.6 (Related to *Solved Problem 18-3* on page 614) Explain whether you agree or disagree with the following statement: "For a given demand curve, the excess burden of a tax will be greater when supply is less elastic than when it is more elastic." Illustrate your answer with a demand and supply graph.

3.7 (Related to the *Making the Connection* on page 614) Use a demand and supply model for the labor market to show the effect of the corporate income tax on workers. What factors would make the deadweight loss or excess burden from the tax larger or smaller?

3.8 Governments often have multiple objectives in imposing a tax. In each part of this question, use a demand and supply graph to illustrate your answer.

a. If the government wants to minimize the excess burden from excise taxes, should these taxes be imposed on goods that are elastic or goods that are inelastic?

b. Suppose that rather than minimizing excess burden, the government is most interested in maximizing the revenue it receives from the tax. In this situation, should the government impose excise taxes on goods that are elastic or on goods that are inelastic?

c. Suppose that the government wishes to discourage smoking and drinking alcohol. Will a tax be more effective in achieving this objective if the demand for these goods is elastic or if the demand is inelastic?

3.9 (Related to the *Don't Let This Happen to You!* on page 613) Evaluate the following statement: "I just bought a television set that was priced at $300. Because there was a 5 percent sales tax, the total amount I paid was $315. If my state didn't have a sales tax, I would have paid only $300."

>> **End Learning Objective 18.3**

18.4 LEARNING OBJECTIVE   18.4 | Discuss the distribution of income in the United States and understand the extent of income mobility, **pages 615–623.**

Income Distribution and Poverty

Summary

No dramatic changes in the distribution of income have occurred over the past 70 years, although there was some decline in inequality between 1936 and 1980, as well as some increase in inequality between 1980 and today. A **Lorenz curve** shows the distribution of income by arraying incomes from lowest to highest on the horizontal axis and indicating the cumulative fraction of income earned by each fraction of households on the vertical axis. About 12 percent of Americans are below the **poverty line**, which is defined as the annual income equal to three times the amount necessary to purchase the minimal quantity of food required for adequate nutrition. Over time, there has been significant income mobility in the United States. The United States has a more unequal distribution of income than do other high-income countries. **Poverty rates**, the percentage of the population that is poor, have been declining in most countries around the world, with the important exception of Africa. The *marginal productivity theory of income distribution* states that in equilibrium, each factor of production receives a payment equal to its marginal revenue product. The more factors of production an individual owns and the more productive those factors are, the higher the individual's income will be.

myeconlab   Visit www.myeconlab.com to complete these exercises online and get instant feedback.
Get Ahead of the Curve

Review Questions

4.1 Discuss the extent of income inequality in the United States. Has inequality in the distribution of income in the United States increased or decreased over time? Briefly explain.

4.2 Define poverty line and poverty rate. How has the poverty rate changed in the United States since 1960?

4.3 What is a Lorenz curve? What is a Gini coefficient? If a country had a Gini coefficient of 0.48 in 1960 and 0.44 in 2009, would income inequality in the country have increased or decreased?

4.4 Describe the main factors economists believe cause inequality of income.

4.5 Compare the distribution of income in the United States with the distribution of income in other high-income countries.

4.6 Describe the trend in global poverty rates.

Problems and Applications

4.7 (Related to *Solved Problem 18-4* on page 621) Evaluate the following statement: "Policies to redistribute income are desperately needed in the United States. Without such policies, the more than 12 percent of the population that is currently poor has no hope of ever climbing above the poverty line."

4.8 (Related to the *Chapter Opener* on page 598) In his column on MSNBC.com, Robert J. Samuelson wrote, "As for what's caused greater inequality, we're also in the dark. The Reagan and Bush tax cuts are weak explanations, because gains have occurred in pretax incomes. . . . Up to a point, inequality is inevitable and desirable."
   a. What are pretax incomes?
   b. Evaluate Samuelson's argument that tax cuts are unlikely to have been the cause of greater income inequality in the United States.
   c. Do you agree with Samuelson's argument that income inequality may be inevitable and desirable?

   Source: Robert J. Samuelson, "The Rich and the Rest," MSNBC.com, April 18, 2007.

4.9 Use the following Lorenz curve graph to answer the questions.

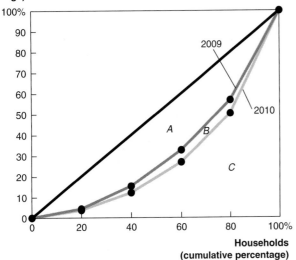

   a. Did the distribution become more equal in 2010 than it was in 2009, or did it become less equal? Briefly explain.
   b. If area $A = 2,150$, area $B = 250$, and area $C = 2,600$, calculate the Gini coefficient for 2009 and the Gini coefficient for 2010.

4.10 Draw a Lorenz curve showing the distribution of income for the five people in the following table.

NAME	ANNUAL EARNINGS
Lena	$70,000
David	60,000
Steve	50,000
Jerome	40,000
Sharon	30,000

4.11 Why do economists often use a lower poverty threshold for poor countries than for high-income countries such as the United States? Is there a difference between *relative* poverty and *absolute* poverty?

4.12 Suppose the Congress and the president decide on a policy of bringing about a perfectly equal distribution of income. What factors might make this policy difficult to achieve? If it were possible to achieve the goal of this policy, would this be desirable?

4.13 If everyone had the same income, would everyone have the same level of well-being?

4.14 Suppose that a country has 20 million households. Ten million are poor households that each have labor market earnings of $20,000 per year, and 10 million are rich households that each have labor market earnings of $80,000 per year. If the government enacted a marginal tax of 10 percent on all labor market earnings above $20,000 and transferred this money to households earning $20,000 or less, would the incomes of the poor rise by $6,000 per year? Explain.

4.15 A U.S. Census Bureau report showed that 46 percent of households living below the poverty line owned their own homes, 76 percent lived in dwellings with air-conditioning, about 75 percent owned cars, and 62 percent had cable or satellite TV reception. All these levels are considerably higher than they were for households below the poverty line a generation ago, but the official poverty rate is virtually unchanged over this period, as Figure 18-5 on page 617 shows. Going back to the official definition of poverty, how could ownership and purchases of these goods by the poor become more common while the poverty rate stayed the same?

4.16 In the speech cited in the *Inside Look* on page 624, Federal Reserve Chairman Ben Bernanke made the following observation: "Although we Americans strive to provide equality of economic opportunity, we do not guarantee equality of economic outcomes, nor should we." Suppose the federal government wanted to "guarantee equality of economic outcomes," how would it do it? If the government succeeded in making the distribution of income completely equal, what would be the benefits and what would be the costs?

   Source: "Remarks by Chairman Ben S. Bernanke Before the Greater Omaha Chamber of Commerce, Omaha, Nebraska," February 6, 2007.

4.17 In an article in the *Wall Street Journal*, Edward Lazear of Stanford University was quoted as saying: "There is some good news . . . most of the inequality reflects an increase in returns to 'investing in skills.'" Why would it be good news if it were true that most of the income inequality in the United States reflected an increase to returns in investing in skills?

Source: Greg Ip and John D. McKinnon, "Bush Reorients Rhetoric, Acknowledges Income Gap," *Wall Street Journal*, March 26, 2007, p. A2.

>> End Learning Objective 18.4

Chapter **19**

GDP: Measuring Total Production and Income

American Airlines Feels the Effects of Fluctuations in GDP

American Airlines has the largest fleet of planes and flies more passengers than any other airline in the world. So, it was bad news for the struggling U.S. airline industry when American announced in spring 2008 that it would stop flying between certain cities, cut back the number of flights on other routes, and, for the first time, charge passengers $15 for each piece of luggage checked. After earning a profit of $504 million during 2007, American reported losing $328 million during the first three months of 2008. American's 85,000 employees faced job losses and the prospect of limited raises.

What caused American's problems during 2008? American was experiencing rising costs and falling ticket sales. This decrease in demand and increase in costs resulted from factors outside of American's control. American was experiencing the effects of the *business cycle*, which refers to the alternating periods of economic expansion and recession that occur in the United States and other industrial

economies. Production and employment increase during expansions and fall during recessions. Although in mid-2008 it was unclear whether the U.S. economy had entered into a full-fledged recession, economic activity had clearly slowed, with the airlines and many other industries experiencing declining demand. In addition, American was suffering from the effects of surging oil prices, which had sharply increased the price of jet fuel.

Although American had made profits in 2006 and 2007, these profits followed several years of losses caused by an economic recession that began in 2001. Airlines are typically hit hard during recessions, as falling incomes cause some leisure travelers to cancel pleasure trips and some firms to cut back on business travel. The recession of 2001 was particularly difficult for airlines because the terrorist attacks of September 11, 2001, made some passengers afraid to travel by air. Increased airport security increased the inconveniences of air travel. So, although the business cycle expansion had begun to increase sales and profits for many firms by 2003, the airlines did not experience a significant revival until 2006.

Whether the general level of economic activity is increasing is not just important to firms like American, as

they decide whether to expand or contract their operations. It is also important to workers hoping for pay increases and to consumers wondering how rapidly prices will be increasing. College students are also affected by the state of the economy at the time they graduate. One recent study found that college students who graduate during a recession have to search longer to find a job and end up accepting jobs that, on average, pay 9 percent less than the jobs accepted by students who graduate during expansions. What's more, students who graduate during recessions will continue to earn less for 8 to 10 years after they graduate. The overall state of the economy is clearly important!

AN INSIDE LOOK on **page 652** discusses the fact that the business cycle does not affect all industries in the same way. For example, some trucking firms experienced slow sales during 2006 while airlines were prospering.

Sources: Susan Carey and Paulo Prada, "American Cuts Flights, Adds Fees as Airlines Face Crisis," *Wall Street Journal*, May 22, 2008, p. A1; Susan Carey and Paulo Prada, "Soaring Fuel Prices Pinch Airlines Harder," *Wall Street Journal*, June 18, 2008, p. B1; and Philip Oreopoulos, Till von Wachter, and Andrew Heisz, "The Short-and-Long-Term Career Effects of Graduating in a Recession," National Bureau of Economic Research Paper 12159, April 2006.

>> Continued on page 651

LEARNING Objectives

After studying this chapter, you should be able to:

19.1 Explain how **total production** is measured, page 635.

19.2 Discuss whether **GDP** is a good **measure** of **well-being**, page 642.

19.3 Discuss the difference between **real GDP** and **nominal GDP**, page 645.

19.4 Become familiar with **other measures** of **total production** and **total income**, page 648.

Economics in YOUR Life!

What's the Best Country for You to Work In?

Suppose that an airline offers you a job after graduation. Because the firm has offices in Canada and China, and because you are fluent in English and Mandarin, you get to choose the country in which you will work and live. Because gross domestic product (GDP) is a measure of an economy's total production of goods and services, one factor in your decision is likely to be the growth rate of GDP in each country. In 2007, the growth rate of GDP was 2.7 percent in Canada and 10.8 percent in China. What effect do these two very different growth rates have on your decision to work and live in one country or the other? If China's much larger growth rate does not necessarily lead you to decide to work and live in China, why not? As you read this chapter, see if you can answer these questions. You can check your answers against those we provide at the end of the chapter.

>> Continued on page 651

Microeconomics The study of how households and firms make choices, how they interact in markets, and how the government attempts to influence their choices.

Macroeconomics The study of the economy as a whole, including topics such as inflation, unemployment, and economic growth.

Business cycle Alternating periods of economic expansion and economic recession.

Expansion The period of a business cycle during which total production and total employment are increasing.

Recession The period of a business cycle during which total production and total employment are decreasing.

Economic growth The ability of an economy to produce increasing quantities of goods and services.

Inflation rate The percentage increase in the price level from one year to the next.

As we saw in Chapter 1, we can divide economics into the subfields of microeconomics and macroeconomics. **Microeconomics** is the study of how households and firms make choices, how they interact in markets, and how the government attempts to influence their choices. **Macroeconomics** is the study of the economy as a whole, including topics such as inflation, unemployment, and economic growth. In microeconomic analysis, economists generally study individual markets, such as the market for personal computers. In macroeconomic analysis, economists study factors that affect many markets at the same time. As we saw in the chapter opener, one important macroeconomic issue is the business cycle. The **business cycle** refers to the alternating periods of expansion and recession that the U.S. economy has experienced since at least the early nineteenth century. A business cycle **expansion** is a period during which total production and total employment are increasing. A business cycle **recession** is a period during which total production and total employment are decreasing. In the following chapters, we will discuss the causes of the business cycle and policies the government may use to reduce its effects.

Another important macroeconomic topic is **economic growth**, which refers to the ability of an economy to produce increasing quantities of goods and services. Economic growth is important because an economy that grows too slowly fails to raise living standards. In many countries in Africa, very little economic growth has occurred in the past 50 years, and many people remain in severe poverty. Macroeconomics analyzes both what determines the rate of economic growth within a country and the reasons growth rates differ so greatly across countries.

Macroeconomics also analyzes what determines the total level of employment in an economy. As we will see, the level of employment is affected significantly by the business cycle, but other factors also help determine the level of employment in the long run. A related issue is why some economies are more successful than others in maintaining high levels of employment over time. Another important macroeconomic issue is what determines the **inflation rate**, or the percentage increase in the average level of prices from one year to the next. As with employment, inflation is affected both by the business cycle and by other long-run factors. Finally, macroeconomics is concerned with the linkages among economies: international trade and international finance.

Macroeconomic analysis provides information that consumers and firms need in order to understand current economic conditions and to help predict future conditions. A family may be reluctant to buy a house if employment in the economy is declining because some family members may be at risk of losing their jobs. Similarly, firms may be reluctant to invest in building new factories or to undertake major new expenditures on information technology if they expect that future sales may be weak. For example, in 2008, Toyota announced that it would not go forward with plans to expand its assembly plants in the United States. The decision was made because macroeconomic forecasts indicated that consumer demand for trucks and SUVs would be weak. Macroeconomic analysis can also aid the federal government in designing policies that help the U.S. economy perform more efficiently.

In this chapter and Chapter 20, we begin our study of macroeconomics by considering how best to measure key macroeconomic variables. As we will see, there are important issues involved in measuring macroeconomic variables. We start by considering measures of total production and total income in an economy.

19.1 | Explain how total production is measured.

Gross Domestic Product Measures Total Production

"GDP News Provides Little Comfort"

"GDP Stayed Sluggish at end of 2007"

"Japan Expects Slower GDP Growth"

"Taiwan sees GDP Growth Surprise"

"Singapore's GDP Shrinks"

These headlines are from articles that appeared in the *Wall Street Journal* in 2008. Why is GDP so often the focus of news stories? In this section, we explore what GDP is and how it is measured. We also explore why knowledge of GDP is important to consumers, firms, and government policymakers.

Measuring Total Production: Gross Domestic Product

Economists measure total production by **gross domestic product (GDP)**. GDP is the market *value* of all *final* goods and services produced in a country during a period of time, typically one year. In the United States, the Bureau of Economic Analysis (BEA) in the Department of Commerce compiles the data needed to calculate GDP. The BEA issues reports on the GDP every three months. GDP is a central concept in macroeconomics, so we need to consider its definition carefully.

Gross domestic product (GDP) The market value of all final goods and services produced in a country during a period of time, typically one year.

GDP Is Measured Using Market Values, Not Quantities The word *value* is important in the definition of GDP. In microeconomics, we measure production in quantity terms: the number of iPods Apple produces, the tons of wheat U.S. farmers grow, or the number of passengers flown by American Airlines. When we measure total production in the economy, we can't just add together the quantities of every good and service because the result would be a meaningless jumble. Tons of wheat would be added to gallons of milk, numbers of plane flights, and so on. Instead, we measure production by taking the *value*, in dollar terms, of all the goods and services produced.

GDP Includes Only the Market Value of Final Goods In measuring GDP, we include only the value of *final goods and services*. A **final good or service** is one that is purchased by its final user and is not included in the production of any other good or service. Examples of final goods are a hamburger purchased by a consumer and a computer purchased by a business. Some goods and services, though, are used in the production of other goods and services. For example, General Motors does not produce tires for its cars and trucks; it buys them from tire companies, such as Goodyear and Michelin. The tires are an **intermediate good**, while a General Motors truck is a final good. In calculating GDP, we include the value of the General Motors truck but not the value of the tire. If we included the value of the tire, we would be *double counting*: The value of the tire would be counted once when the tire company sold it to General Motors, and a second time when General Motors sold the truck, with the tire installed, to a consumer.

Final good or service A good or service purchased by a final user.

Intermediate good or service A good or service that is an input into another good or service, such as a tire on a truck.

GDP Includes Only Current Production GDP includes only production that takes place during the indicated time period. For example, GDP in 2008 includes only the goods and services produced during that year. In particular, GDP does *not* include the value of used goods. If you buy a DVD of *Iron Man* from Amazon.com, the purchase is included in GDP. If six months later you resell that DVD on eBay, that transaction is not included in GDP.

Solved Problem | 19-1

Calculating GDP

Suppose that a very simple economy produces only four goods and services: eye examinations, pizzas, textbooks, and paper. Assume that all the paper in this economy is used in the production of textbooks. Use the information in the following table to compute GDP for the year 2009.

PRODUCTION AND PRICE STATISTICS FOR 2009		
(1) **PRODUCT**	**(2)** **QUANTITY**	**(3)** **PRICE PER UNIT**
Eye examinations	100	$50.00
Pizzas	80	10.00
Textbooks	20	100.00
Paper	2,000	0.10

SOLVING THE PROBLEM:

Step 1: **Review the chapter material.** This problem is about gross domestic product, so you may want to review the section "Measuring Total Production: Gross Domestic Product," which begins on page 635.

Step 2: **Determine which goods and services listed in the table should be included in the calculation of GDP.** GDP is the value of all final goods and services. Therefore, we need to calculate the value of the final goods and services listed in the table. Eye examinations, pizzas, and textbooks are final goods. Paper would also be a final good if, for instance, a consumer bought it to use in a printer. However, here we are assuming that publishers purchase all the paper to use in manufacturing textbooks, so the paper is an intermediate good, and its value is not included in GDP.

Step 3: **Calculate the value of the three final goods and services listed in the table.** Value is equal to the quantity produced multiplied by the price per unit, so we multiply the numbers in column (1) by the numbers in column (2).

PRODUCT	**(1)** QUANTITY	**(2)** PRICE PER UNIT	**(3)** VALUE
Eye examinations	100	$50	$5,000
Pizzas	80	10	800
Textbooks	20	100	2,000

Step 4: **Add the value for each of the three final goods and services to find GDP.** GDP = Value of eye examinations produced + Value of pizzas produced + Value of textbooks produced = $5,000 + $800 + $2,000 = $7,800.

>> **End Solved Problem 19-1**

YOUR TURN: For more practice, do related problem 1.12 on page 655 at the end of this chapter.

Production, Income, and the Circular-Flow Diagram

When we measure the value of total production in the economy by calculating GDP, we are simultaneously measuring the value of total income. To see why the value of total production is equal to the value of total income, consider what happens to the money you spend on a single product. Suppose you buy an Apple iPod for $250 at a Best Buy store. *All* of that $250 must end up as someone's income. Apple and Best Buy will receive some of the $250 as profits, workers at Apple will receive some as wages, the salesperson who sold you the iPod will receive some as salary, the firms that sell parts to Apple will receive some as profits, the workers for these firms will receive some as wages, and so on: Every penny must end up as someone's income. (Note, though, that any sales tax on the iPod will be collected by the store and sent to the government without ending up as anyone's income.) Therefore, if we add up the value of every good and service sold in the economy, we must get a total that is exactly equal to the value of all of the income in the economy.

The circular-flow diagram in Figure 19-1 was introduced in Chapter 2 to illustrate the interaction of firms and households in markets. We use it here to illustrate the flow of spending and money in the economy. Firms sell goods and services to three groups: domestic households, foreign firms and households, and the government. Expenditures

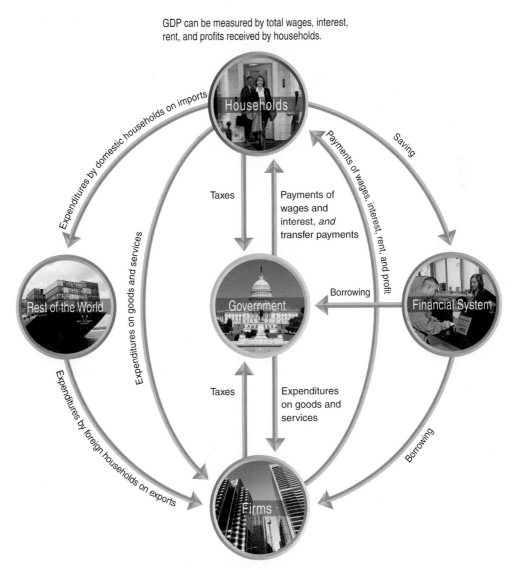

Figure 19-1 | The Circular Flow and the Measurement of GDP

The circular-flow diagram illustrates the flow of spending and money in the economy. Firms sell goods and services to three groups: domestic households, foreign firms and households, and the government. To produce goods and services, firms use factors of production: labor, capital, natural resources, and entrepreneurship. Households supply the factors of production to firms in exchange for income in the form of wages, interest, profit, and rent. Firms make payments of wages and interest to households in exchange for hiring workers and other factors of production. The sum of wages, interest, rent, and profit is total income in the economy. We can measure GDP as the total income received by households. The diagram also shows that households use their income to purchase goods and services, pay taxes, and save. Firms and the government borrow the funds that flow from households into the financial system. We can measure GDP either by calculating the total value of expenditures on final goods and services or by calculating the value of total income.

by foreign firms and households (shown as the "Rest of the World" in the diagram) on domestically produced goods and services are called *exports*. For example, American Airlines sells many tickets to passengers in Europe and Asia. As we note at the bottom of Figure 19-1, we can measure GDP by adding up the total expenditures of these three groups on goods and services.

Firms use the *factors of production*—labor, capital, natural resources, and entrepreneurship—to produce goods and services. Households supply the factors of production to firms in exchange for income. We divide income into four categories: wages, interest, rent, and profit. Firms pay wages to households in exchange for labor services, interest for the use of capital, and rent for natural resources such as land. Profit is the income that remains after a firm has paid wages, interest, and rent. Profit is the return to entrepreneurs for organizing the other factors of production and for bearing the risk of producing and selling goods and services. As Figure 19-1 shows, federal, state, and local governments make payments of wages and interest to households in exchange for hiring workers and other factors of production. Governments also make *transfer payments* to households. **Transfer payments** include Social Security payments to retired and disabled people and unemployment insurance payments to unemployed workers. These payments are not included in GDP because they are not received in exchange for production of a new good or service. The sum of wages, interest, rent, and profit is total income in the economy. As we note at the top of Figure 19-1, we can measure GDP as the total income received by households.

The diagram also allows us to trace the ways that households use their income. Households spend some of their income on goods and services. Some of this spending is on domestically produced goods and services, and some is on foreign-produced goods and services. Spending on foreign-produced goods and services is known as *imports*. Households also use some of their income to pay taxes to the government. (Note that firms also pay taxes to the government.) Some of the income earned by households is not spent on goods and services or paid in taxes but is deposited in checking or savings accounts in banks or is used to buy stocks or bonds. Banks and stock and bond markets make up the *financial system*. The flow of funds from households into the financial system makes it possible for the government and firms to borrow. As we will see, the health of the financial system is of vital importance to an economy. Without the ability to borrow funds through the financial system, firms will have difficulty expanding and adopting new technologies. In fact, as we will discuss in Chapter 21, no country without a well-developed financial system has been able to sustain high levels of economic growth.

The circular-flow diagram shows that we can measure GDP either by calculating the total value of expenditures on final goods and services or by calculating the value of total income. We get the same dollar amount of GDP whichever approach we take.

Components of GDP

The BEA divides its statistics on GDP into four major categories of expenditures. Economists use these categories to understand why GDP fluctuates and to forecast future GDP.

Personal Consumption Expenditures, or "Consumption" Consumption expenditures are made by households and are divided into expenditures on *services*, such as medical care, education, and haircuts; expenditures on *nondurable goods*, such as food and clothing; and expenditures on *durable goods*, such as automobiles and furniture. The spending by households on new houses is not included in consumption. Instead, spending on new houses is included in the investment category, which we discuss next.

Gross Private Domestic Investment, or "Investment" Spending on *gross private domestic investment*, or simply **investment**, is divided into three categories: *Business fixed investment* is spending by firms on new factories, office buildings, and machinery used to produce other goods. *Residential investment* is spending by households and firms on

Transfer payments Payments by the government to individuals for which the government does not receive a new good or service in return.

Consumption Spending by households on goods and services, not including spending on new houses.

Investment Spending by firms on new factories, office buildings, machinery, and additions to inventories, and spending by households on new houses.

Don't Let This Happen to **YOU!**

Remember What Economists Mean by *Investment*

Notice that the definition of *investment* in this chapter is narrower than in everyday use. For example, people often say they are investing in the stock market or in rare coins. As we have seen, economists reserve the word *investment* for purchases of machinery, factories, and houses. Economists don't include purchases of stock or rare coins or deposits in savings accounts in the definition of investment because these activities don't result in the production of new goods.

For example, a share of Microsoft stock represents part ownership of that company. When you buy a share of Microsoft stock, nothing new is produced—there is just a transfer of that small piece of ownership of Microsoft. Similarly, buying a rare coin or putting $1,000 in a savings account does not result in an increase in production. GDP is not affected by any of these activities, so they are not included in the economic definition of investment.

YOUR TURN: Test your understanding by doing related problem 1.8 on page 654 at the end of this chapter.

new single-family and multi-unit houses. *Changes in business inventories* are also included in investment. Inventories are goods that have been produced but not yet sold. If General Motors has $200 million worth of unsold cars at the beginning of the year and $350 million worth of unsold cars at the end of the year, then the firm has spent $150 million on inventory investment during the year.

Government Consumption and Gross Investment, or "Government Purchases"

Government purchases are spending by federal, state, and local governments on goods and services, such as teachers' salaries, highways, and aircraft carriers. Again, government spending on transfer payments is not included in government purchases because it does not result in the production of new goods and services.

Government purchases Spending by federal, state, and local governments on goods and services.

Making the Connection

Spending on Homeland Security

The federal government established the Department of Homeland Security after September 11, 2001, to guard against future terrorist attacks within the United States. Spending by this department is intended to increase the security of the nation's borders and transportation system, identify and arrest terrorists within the United States, and gather intelligence on potential terrorist threats.

Although the Department of Homeland Security has overall responsibility for homeland security, other federal agencies also have increased their spending on related programs. For example, the Department of Health and Human Services increased its spending on research to find new ways to combat the use of biological weapons from $300 million in 2001 to more than $4 billion in 2006. Several other federal agencies, such as the Department of Justice, the Department of Agriculture, and the Department of Transportation, have increased their spending as well. In 2008, the total spending on homeland security by the Department of Homeland Security and other federal agencies was about $50 billion—more than double the amount spent on these activities before 2001.

Because the United States has a federal system of government, responsibility for some homeland security activities lies with state or local authorities. For example, spending to provide security for the Golden Gate Bridge is the responsibility of the state of California and the city of San Francisco. The Department of Homeland Security provides grants to help support this state

Government spending on homeland security more than doubled between 2001 and 2008.

and local spending. Of course, governments at all levels have limited budgets, so at some point, spending more on homeland security requires them to spend less on other programs.

Sources: Congressional Budget Office, *Federal Funding for Homeland Security: An Update*, July 20, 2005; and Executive Office of the President, Office of Management and Budget, *Department of Homeland Security*, February 2008.

YOUR TURN: Test your understanding by doing related problem 1.11 on page 655 at the end of this chapter.

Net exports Exports minus imports.

Net Exports of Goods and Services, or "Net Exports"

Net exports are equal to *exports* minus *imports*. Exports are goods and services produced in the United States but purchased by foreign firms, households, and governments. We add exports to our other categories of expenditures because otherwise we would not be including all spending on new goods and services produced in the United States. For example, if a farmer in South Dakota sells wheat to China, the value of the wheat is included in GDP because it represents production in the United States. Imports are goods and services produced in foreign countries but purchased by U.S. firms, households, and governments. We subtract imports from total expenditures because otherwise we would be including spending that does not result in production of new goods and services in the United States. For example, if U.S. consumers buy $50 billion worth of furniture manufactured in China, that spending is included in consumption expenditures. But the value of those imports is subtracted from GDP because the imports do not represent production in the United States.

An Equation for GDP and Some Actual Values

A simple equation sums up the components of GDP:

$$Y = C + I + G + NX.$$

The equation tells us that GDP (denoted as Y) equals consumption (C) plus investment (I) plus government purchases (G) plus net exports (NX). Figure 19-2 shows the values of the components of GDP for the year 2007. The graph in the figure highlights that

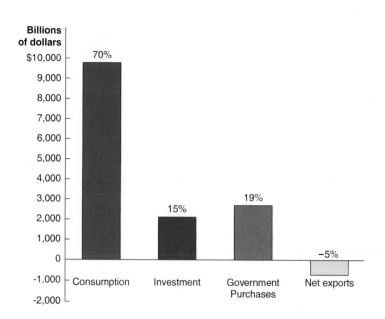

COMPONENTS OF GDP (billions of dollars)		
Consumption		$9,734
Durable goods	$1,078	
Nondurable goods	2,833	
Services	5,823	
Investment		2,125
Business fixed investment	1,482	
Residential construction	641	
Change in business inventories	3	
Government Purchases		2,690
Federal	976	
State and local	1,714	
Net Exports		−708
Exports	1,643	
Imports	2,351	
Total GDP		$13,841

Figure 19-2 | Components of GDP in 2007

Consumption accounts for 70 percent of GDP, far more than any of the other components. In recent years, net exports typically have been negative, which reduces GDP.

consumption is by far the largest component of GDP. The table provides a more detailed breakdown and shows several interesting points:

- Consumer spending on services is greater than the sum of spending on durable and nondurable goods. This greater spending on services reflects the continuing trend in the United States and other high-income countries away from the production of goods and toward the production of services. As the populations of these countries have become, on average, both older and wealthier, their demand for services such as medical care and financial advice has increased faster than their demand for goods.

- Business fixed investment is the largest component of investment. As we will see in later chapters, spending by firms on new factories, computers, and machinery can fluctuate. For example, a decline in business fixed investment played an important role in causing the 2001 recession.

- Purchases made by state and local governments are greater than purchases made by the federal government. Because basic government activities, such as education and law enforcement, occur largely at the state and local levels, state and local government spending is greater than federal government spending.

- Imports are greater than exports, so net exports are negative. We will discuss in Chapter 29 why imports have typically been larger than exports for the U.S. economy.

Measuring GDP by the Value-Added Method

We have seen that GDP can be calculated by adding together all expenditures on final goods and services. An alternative way of calculating GDP is the *value-added method*. **Value added** refers to the additional market value a firm gives to a product and is equal to the difference between the price for which the firm sells a good and the price it paid other firms for intermediate goods. Table 19-1 gives a hypothetical example of the value added by each firm involved in the production of a shirt offered for sale on L.L.Bean's Web site.

> **Value added** The market value a firm adds to a product.

 Suppose a cotton farmer sells $1 of raw cotton to a textile mill. If, for simplicity, we ignore any inputs the farmer may have purchased from other firms—such as cottonseed or fertilizer—then the farmer's value added is $1. The textile mill then weaves the raw cotton into cotton fabric, which it sells to a shirt company for $3. The textile mill's value added ($2) is the difference between the price it paid for the raw cotton ($1) and the price for which it can sell the cotton fabric ($3). Similarly, the shirt company's value added is the difference between the price it paid for the cotton fabric ($3) and the price it receives for the shirt from L.L.Bean ($15). L.L.Bean's value added is the difference between the price it pays for the shirt ($15) and the price for which it can sell the shirt on its Web site ($35). Notice that *the price of the shirt on L.L.Bean's Web site is exactly equal to the sum of the value added by each firm involved in the production of the shirt.* We can

Table 19-1
Calculating Value Added

FIRM	VALUE OF PRODUCT	VALUE ADDED	
Cotton farmer	Value of raw cotton = $1	Value added by cotton farmer	= 1
Textile mill	Value of raw cotton woven into cotton fabric = $3	Value added by cotton textile mill = ($3 – $1)	= 2
Shirt company	Value of cotton fabric made into a shirt = $15	Value added by shirt manufacturer = ($15 – $3)	= 12
L.L.Bean	Value of shirt for sale on L.L.Bean's Web site = $35	Value added by L.L.Bean = ($35 – $15)	= 20
	Total value added		= **$35**

calculate GDP by adding up the market value of every final good and service produced during a particular period. Or, we can arrive at the same value for GDP by adding up the value added of every firm involved in producing those final goods and services.

19.2 | Discuss whether GDP is a good measure of well-being.

Does GDP Measure What We Want It to Measure?

Economists use GDP to measure total production in the economy. For that purpose, we would like GDP to be as comprehensive as possible, not overlooking any significant production that takes place in the economy. Most economists believe that GDP does a good—but not flawless—job of measuring production. GDP is also sometimes used as a measure of well-being. Although it is generally true that the more goods and services people have, the better off they are, we will see that GDP provides only a rough measure of well-being.

Shortcomings in GDP as a Measure of Total Production

When the BEA calculates GDP, it does not include two types of production: production in the home and production in the underground economy.

Household Production With only a couple exceptions, the Bureau of Economic Analysis does not attempt to estimate the value of goods and services that are not bought and sold in markets. If a carpenter makes and sells bookcases, the value of those bookcases will be counted in GDP. If the carpenter makes a bookcase for personal use, it will not be counted in GDP. *Household production* refers to goods and services people produce for themselves. The most important type of household production is the services a homemaker provides to the homemaker's family. If a person has been caring for children, cleaning house, and preparing the family meals, the value of such services is not included in GDP. If the person then decides to work outside the home, enrolls the children in daycare, hires a cleaning service, and begins eating family meals in restaurants, the value of GDP will rise by the amount paid for daycare, cleaning services, and restaurant meals, even though production of these services has not actually increased.

Underground economy Buying and selling of goods and services that is concealed from the government to avoid taxes or regulations or because the goods and services are illegal.

The Underground Economy Individuals and firms sometimes conceal the buying and selling of goods and services, in which case their production isn't counted in GDP. Individuals and firms conceal what they buy and sell for three basic reasons: They are dealing in illegal goods and services, such as drugs or prostitution; they want to avoid paying taxes on the income they earn; or they want to avoid government regulations. This concealed buying and selling is referred to as the **underground economy**. Estimates of the size of the underground economy in the United States vary widely, but it may be as much as 10 percent of measured GDP, or over $1.3 trillion. The underground economy in some low-income countries, such as Zimbabwe or Peru, may be more than half of measured GDP.

Is not counting household production or production in the underground economy a serious shortcoming of GDP? Most economists would answer "no" because the most important use of GDP is to measure changes in how the economy is performing over short periods of time, such as from one year to the next. For this purpose, omitting household production and production in the underground economy doesn't have much effect because there is not likely to be much change in the amounts of these types of production from one year to the next.

We also use GDP statistics to measure how production of goods and services grows over fairly long periods of a decade or more. For this purpose, omitting household production and production in the underground economy may be more important. For example, beginning in the 1970s, the number of women working outside the home increased dramatically. Some of the goods and services—such as childcare and restaurant meals—produced in the following years were not true additions to total production; rather, they were replacing what had been household production.

| Making the Connection | **How the Underground Economy Hurts Developing Countries** |

Although few economists believe the underground economy in the United States amounts to more than 10 percent of measured GDP, the underground economy in some developing countries may be more than 50 percent of measured GDP. In developing countries, the underground economy is often referred to as the *informal sector*, as opposed to the *formal sector* in which output of goods and services is measured. Although it might not seem to matter whether production of goods and services is measured and included in GDP or unmeasured, a large informal sector can be a sign of government policies that are retarding economic growth.

Because firms in the informal sector are acting illegally, they tend to be smaller and have less capital than firms acting legally. The entrepreneurs who start firms in the informal sector may be afraid their firms could someday be closed or confiscated by the government. Therefore, the entrepreneurs limit their investments in these firms. As a consequence, workers in these firms have less machinery and equipment to work with and so can produce fewer goods and services. Entrepreneurs in the informal sector also have to pay the costs of avoiding government authorities. For example, construction firms operating in the informal sector in Brazil have

In some developing countries, more than half the workers may be in the underground economy.

to employ lookouts who can warn workers to hide when government inspectors come around. In many countries, firms in the informal sector have to pay substantial bribes to government officials to remain in business. The informal sector is large in some developing economies because taxes are high and government regulations are extensive. For example, firms in Brazil pay 85 percent of all taxes collected, as compared with 41 percent in the United States. Not surprisingly, about half of all Brazilian workers are employed in the informal sector. In Zimbabwe and Peru, the fraction of workers in the informal sector may be as high as 60 or 70 percent.

Many economists believe taxes in developing countries are so high because these countries are attempting to pay for government sectors that are as large relative to their economies as the government sectors of industrial economies. Government spending in Brazil, for example, is 39 percent of measured GDP, compared to 32 percent in the United States. In the early twentieth century, when the United States was much poorer than it is today, government spending was only about 8 percent of GDP, so the tax burden on U.S. firms was much lower. In countries like Brazil, bringing firms into the formal sector from the informal sector may require reductions in government spending and taxes. In many developing countries, however, voters are reluctant to see government services reduced.

Sources: Mary Anastasia O'Grady, "Why Brazil's Underground Economy Grows and Grows," *Wall Street Journal*, September 10, 2004, p. A13; and "In the Shadows," *Economist*, June 17, 2004.

YOUR TURN: Test your understanding by doing related problem 2.6 on page 656 at the end of this chapter.

Shortcomings of GDP as a Measure of Well-Being

The main purpose of GDP is to measure a country's total production. GDP is also frequently used, though, as a measure of well-being. For example, newspaper and magazine articles often include tables that show for different countries the levels of GDP per person, which is usually referred to as *real GDP per capita*. Real GDP per capita is calculated by dividing the value of real GDP for a country by the country's population. These articles imply that people in the countries with higher levels of real GDP per capita are better off. Although increases in GDP often do lead to increases in the well-being of the population, it is important to be aware that GDP is not a perfect measure of well-being for several reasons.

The Value of Leisure Is Not Included in GDP If an economic consultant decides to retire, GDP will decline even though the consultant may value increased leisure more than the income he or she was earning running a consulting firm. The consultant's well-being has increased, but GDP has decreased. In 1890, the typical American worked 60 hours per week. Today, the typical American works fewer than 40 hours per week. If Americans still worked 60-hour weeks, GDP would be much higher than it is, but the well-being of the typical person would be lower because less time would be available for leisure activities.

GDP Is Not Adjusted for Pollution or Other Negative Effects of Production When a dry cleaner cleans and presses clothes, the value of this service is included in GDP. If chemicals the dry cleaner uses pollute the air or water, GDP is not adjusted to compensate for the costs of the pollution. Similarly, the value of cigarettes produced is included in GDP, with no adjustment made for the costs of the lung cancer that some smokers develop.

We should note, though, that increasing GDP often leads countries to devote more resources to pollution reduction. For example, in the United States between 1970 and 2007, as GDP was steadily increasing, emissions of the six main air pollutants declined by more than 50 percent. Developing countries often have higher levels of pollution than high-income countries because the lower GDPs of the developing countries make them more reluctant to spend resources on pollution reduction. Levels of pollution in China are much higher than in the United States, Japan, or the countries of Western Europe. According to the World Health Organization, 7 of the 10 most polluted cities in the world are in China, but as Chinese GDP continues to rise, it is likely to devote more resources to reducing pollution.

GDP Is Not Adjusted for Changes in Crime and Other Social Problems An increase in crime reduces well-being but may actually increase GDP if it leads to greater spending on police, security guards, and alarm systems. GDP is also not adjusted for changes in divorce rates, drug addiction, or other factors that may affect people's well-being.

GDP Measures the Size of the Pie but Not How the Pie Is Divided Up When a country's GDP increases, the country has more goods and services, but those goods and services may be very unequally distributed. Therefore, GDP may not provide good information about the goods and services consumed by the typical person.

To summarize, we can say that a person's well-being depends on many factors that are not taken into account in calculating GDP. Because GDP is designed to measure total production, it should not be surprising that it does an imperfect job of measuring well-being.

Making the Connection | **Did World War II Bring Prosperity?**

The Great Depression of the 1930s was the worst economic downturn in U.S. history. GDP declined by more than 25 percent between 1929 and 1933 and did not reach its 1929 level again until 1938. The unemployment rate remained at very high levels of 10 percent or more through 1940. Then, in 1941, the United States entered World War II. The following graph shows that GDP rose dramatically during the war years of 1941 to 1945. (The graph shows values for real GDP, which, as we will see in the next section, corrects measures of GDP for changes in the price level.) The unemployment rate also fell to very low levels—below 2 percent.

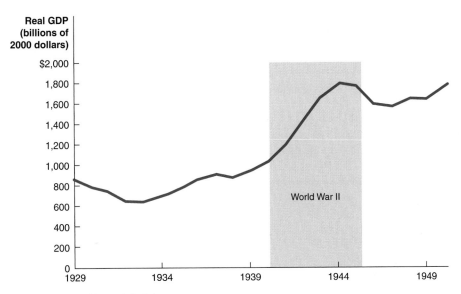

Source: U.S. Bureau of Economic Analysis.

Traditionally, historians have argued that World War II brought prosperity back to the U.S. economy. But did it? Economist Robert Higgs argues that if we look at the well-being of the typical person, the World War II years were anything but prosperous. Higgs points out that increased production of tanks, ships, planes, and munitions account for most of the increase in GDP during those years. Between 1943 and 1945, more than 40 percent of the labor force was either in the military or producing war goods. As a result, between 1939 and 1944, production of consumption goods per person increased only about 2 percent, leaving the quantity of consumption goods available to the typical person in 1944 still below what it had been in 1929. With the end of the war, true prosperity did return to the U.S. economy, and by 1946, production of consumption goods per person had risen by more than 25 percent from what it had been in 1929.

World War II was a period of extraordinary sacrifice and achievement by the "greatest generation." But statistics on GDP may give a misleading indication of whether it was also a period of prosperity.

Sources: Robert Higgs, "Wartime Prosperity? A Reassessment of the U.S. Economy in the 1940s," *Journal of Economic History*, Vol. 52, No. 1, March 1992; and Robert Higgs, "From Central Planning to the Market: The American Transition, 1945–1947," *Journal of Economic History*, Vol. 59, No. 3, September 1999.

YOUR TURN: Test your understanding by doing related problem 2.8 on page 656 at the end of this chapter.

19.3 LEARNING OBJECTIVE

19.3 | Discuss the difference between real GDP and nominal GDP.

Real GDP versus Nominal GDP

Because GDP is measured in value terms, we have to be careful about interpreting changes over time. To see why, consider interpreting an increase in the total value of heavy truck production from $40 billion in 2009 to $44 billion in 2010. Can we be sure—because $44 billion is 10 percent greater than $40 billion—that the number of trucks produced in 2010 was 10 percent greater than the number produced in 2009? We can draw this conclusion only if the average price of trucks did not change between 2009 and 2010. In fact, when GDP increases from one year to the next, the increase is due partly to increases in production of goods and services and partly to increases in prices.

Because we are interested mainly in GDP as a measure of production, we need a way of separating the price changes from the quantity changes.

Calculating Real GDP

Nominal GDP The value of final goods and services evaluated at current-year prices.

Real GDP The value of final goods and services evaluated at base-year prices.

The Bureau of Economic Analysis (BEA) separates price changes from quantity changes by calculating a measure of production called *real GDP*. **Nominal GDP** is calculated by summing the current values of final goods and services. **Real GDP** is calculated by designating a particular year as the *base year* and then using the prices of goods and services in the base year to calculate the value of goods and services in all other years. For instance, if the base year is 2000, real GDP for 2009 would be calculated by using prices of goods and services from 2000. By keeping prices constant, we know that changes in real GDP represent changes in the quantity of goods and services produced in the economy.

Solved Problem | 19-3

Calculating Real GDP

Suppose that a very simple economy produces only the following three final goods and services: eye examinations, pizzas, and textbooks. Use the information in the following table to compute real GDP for the year 2009. Assume that the base year is 2000.

	2000		2009	
PRODUCT	**QUANTITY**	**PRICE**	**QUANTITY**	**PRICE**
Eye examinations	80	$40	100	$50
Pizzas	90	11	80	10
Textbooks	15	90	20	100

SOLVING THE PROBLEM:

Step 1: **Review the chapter material.** This problem is about calculating real GDP, so you may want to review the section "Calculating Real GDP," which begins on this page.

Step 2: **Calculate the value of the three goods and services listed in the table, using the quantities for 2009 and the prices for 2000.** The definition on this page tells us that real GDP is the value of all final goods and services, evaluated at base-year prices. In this case, the base year is 2000, and we are given information on the price of each product in that year.

PRODUCT	2009 QUANTITY	2000 PRICE	VALUE
Eye examinations	100	$40	$4,000
Pizzas	80	11	880
Textbooks	20	90	1,800

Step 3: **Add up the values for the three products to find real GDP.**

Real GDP for 2009 equals the sum of:

Quantity of eye examinations in 2009 × Price of eye exams in 2000 = $4,000

+ Quantity of pizzas produced in 2009 × Price of pizzas in 2000 = $880

+ Quantity of textbooks produced in 2009 × Price of textbooks in 2000 = $1,800

or, $6,680

EXTRA CREDIT: Notice that the quantities of each good produced in 2000 were irrelevant for calculating real GDP in 2009. Notice also that the value of $6,680 for real GDP in 2009 is lower than the value of $7,800 for nominal GDP in 2009 calculated in Solved Problem 19-1.

>> **End Solved Problem 19-3**

YOUR TURN: For more practice, do related problem 3.3 on page 657 at the end of this chapter.

One drawback of calculating real GDP using base-year prices is that, over time, prices may change relative to each other. For example, the price of cell phones may fall relative to the price of milk. Because this change is not reflected in the fixed prices from the base year, the estimate of real GDP is somewhat distorted. The further away the current year is from the base year, the worse the problem becomes. To make the calculation of real GDP more accurate, in 1996, the BEA switched to using *chain-weighted prices*, and it now publishes statistics on real GDP in "chained (2000) dollars."

The details of calculating real GDP using chain-weighted prices are more complicated than we need to discuss here, but the basic idea is straightforward. Starting with the base year, the BEA takes an average of prices in that year and prices in the following year. It then uses this average to calculate real GDP in the year following the base year (currently the year 2000). For the next year—in other words, the year that is two years after the base year—the BEA calculates real GDP by taking an average of prices in that year and the previous year. In this way, prices in each year are "chained" to prices from the previous year, and the distortion from changes in relative prices is minimized.

Holding prices constant means that the *purchasing power* of a dollar remains the same from one year to the next. Ordinarily, the purchasing power of the dollar falls every year, as price increases reduce the amount of goods and services that a dollar can buy.

Comparing Real GDP and Nominal GDP

Real GDP holds prices constant, which makes it a better measure than nominal GDP of changes in the production of goods and services from one year to the next. In fact, growth in the economy is almost always measured as growth in real GDP. If a headline in the *Wall Street Journal* states, "U.S. Economy Grew 4.3% Last Year," the article will report that real GDP increased by 4.3 percent during the previous year.

We describe real GDP as being measured in "base-year dollars." For example, with a base year of 2000, nominal GDP in 2007 was $13,841 billion, and real GDP in 2007 was $11,567 billion in 2000 dollars. Because, on average, prices rise from one year to the next, real GDP is greater than nominal GDP in years before the base year and less than nominal GDP for years after the base year. In the base year, real GDP and nominal GDP are the same because both are calculated for the base year using the same prices and quantities. Figure 19-3 shows movements in nominal GDP and real GDP between 1990 and 2007. In the 1990s, prices were, on average, lower than in 2000, so nominal GDP was lower than real GDP. In 2000, nominal and real GDP were equal. Since 2000, prices have been, on average, higher than in 2000, so nominal GDP is higher than real GDP.

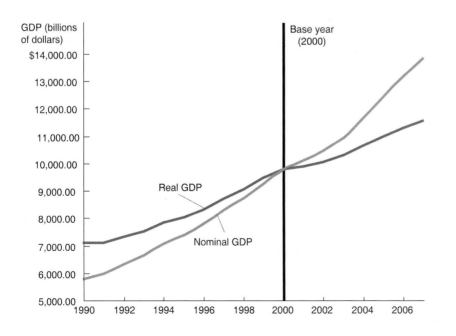

Figure 19-3

Nominal GDP and Real GDP, 1990–2007

Currently, the base year for calculating GDP is 2000. In the 1990s, prices were, on average, lower than in 2000, so nominal GDP was lower than real GDP. In 2000, nominal and real GDP were equal. After 2000, prices have been, on average, higher than in 2000, so nominal GDP is higher than real GDP.

Source: U.S. Bureau of Economic Analysis.

The GDP Deflator

Price level A measure of the average prices of goods and services in the economy.

GDP deflator A measure of the price level, calculated by dividing nominal GDP by real GDP and multiplying by 100.

Economists and policymakers are interested not just in the level of total production, as measured by real GDP, but also in the *price level*. The **price level** measures the average prices of goods and services in the economy. One of the goals of economic policy is a stable price level. We can use values for nominal GDP and real GDP to compute a measure of the price level called the *GDP deflator*. We can calculate the **GDP deflator** using this formula:

$$\text{GDP deflator} = \frac{\text{Nominal GDP}}{\text{Real GDP}} \times 100.$$

To see why the GDP deflator is a measure of the price level, think about what would happen if prices of goods and services rose while production remained the same. In that case, nominal GDP would increase, but real GDP would remain constant, so the GDP deflator would increase. In reality, both prices and production increase each year, but the more prices increase relative to the increase in production, the more nominal GDP increases relative to real GDP, and the higher the value for the GDP deflator. Increases in the GDP deflator allow economists and policymakers to track increases in the price level over time.

Remember that in the base year (currently 2000), nominal GDP is equal to real GDP, so the value of the GDP price deflator will always be 100 in the base year. The following table gives the values for nominal and real GDP for 2006 and 2007.

	2006	2007
NOMINAL GDP	$13,195 billion	$13,841 billion
REAL GDP	$11,319 billion	$11,567 billion

We can use the information from the table to calculate values for the GDP price deflator for 2006 and 2007:

FORMULA	APPLIED TO 2006	APPLIED TO 2007
$\dfrac{\text{GDP}}{\text{Deflator}} = \dfrac{\text{Nominal GDP}}{\text{Real GDP}} \times 100$	$\left(\dfrac{\$13,195 \text{ billion}}{\$11,319 \text{ billion}}\right) \times 100 = 117$	$\left(\dfrac{\$13,841 \text{ billion}}{\$11,567 \text{ billion}}\right) \times 100 = 120$

From these values for the deflator, we can calculate that the price level increased by 2.6 percent between 2006 and 2007:

$$\frac{120 - 117}{117} = 2.6\%.$$

In Chapter 20, we will see that economists and policymakers also rely on another measure of the price level, known as the consumer price index. In addition, we will discuss the strengths and weaknesses of different measures of the price level.

19.4 LEARNING OBJECTIVE | 19.4 | Become familiar with other measures of total production and total income.

Other Measures of Total Production and Total Income

National income accounting refers to the methods the BEA uses to track total production and total income in the economy. The statistical tables containing this information are called the *National Income and Product Accounts (NIPA)*. Every quarter, the BEA releases

NIPA tables containing data on several measures of total production and total income. We have already discussed the most important measure of total production and total income: gross domestic product (GDP). In addition to computing GDP, the BEA computes the following five measures of production and income: gross national product, net national product, national income, personal income, and disposable personal income.

Gross National Product (GNP)

We have seen that GDP is the value of final goods and services produced within the United States. Gross national product (GNP) is the value of final goods and services produced by residents of the United States, even if the production takes place *outside* the United States. U.S. firms have facilities in foreign countries, and foreign firms have facilities in the United States. Ford, for example, has assembly plants in the United Kingdom, and Toyota has assembly plants in the United States. GNP includes foreign production by U.S. firms but excludes U.S. production by foreign firms. For the United States, GNP is almost the same as GDP. For example, in 2007, GDP was $13,841 billion, and GNP was $13,937 billion. This difference is less than three-quarters of 1 percent.

For many years, GNP was the main measure of total production compiled by the federal government and used by economists and policymakers in the United States. However, in many countries other than the United States, a significant percentage of domestic production takes place in foreign-owned facilities. For those countries, GDP is much larger than GNP and is a more accurate measure of the level of production within the country's borders. As a result, many countries and international agencies had long preferred using GDP to using GNP. In 1991, the United States joined those countries in using GDP as its main measure of total production.

Net National Product (NNP)

In producing goods and services, some machinery, equipment, and buildings wear out and have to be replaced. The value of this worn-out machinery, equipment, and buildings is *depreciation*. If we subtract this value from GNP, we are left with net national product (NNP). In the NIPA tables, depreciation is referred to as the *consumption of fixed capital*.

National Income

When a consumer pays sales tax on a product, there is a difference between the amount the consumer has paid for the product and the amount the people who produced the product will receive as income. For instance, suppose you buy a television that is priced at $200. If the sales tax is 6 percent, you will actually pay $212, but the seller will send the $12 in tax directly to the government and it will never show up as anyone's income. Therefore, to calculate the total income actually received by a country's residents, the BEA has to subtract the value of sales taxes from net national product. In the NIPA tables, sales taxes are referred to as *indirect business taxes*. Previously in this chapter, we stressed that the value of total production is equal to the value of total income. This point is not strictly true if by "value of total production" we mean GDP and by "value of total income" we mean national income because national income will always be smaller than GDP. In practice, though, the difference between the value of GDP and value of national income does not matter for most macroeconomic issues.

Personal Income

Personal income is income received by households. To calculate personal income, we subtract the earnings that corporations retain rather than pay to shareholders in the form of dividends. We also add in the payments received by households from the government in the form of *transfer payments* or interest on government bonds.

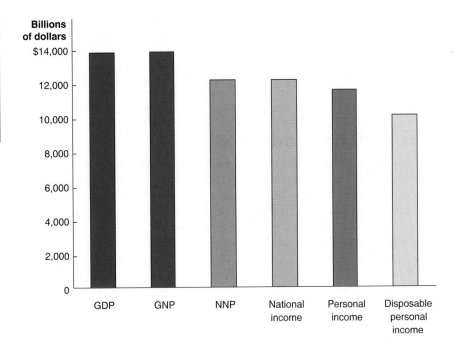

Measure	Billions of dollars
GDP	$13,841
GNP	13,937
NNP	12,251
National Income	12,221
Personal Income	11,660
Disposable Personal Income	10,177

Figure 19-4 | Measures of Total Production and Total Income, 2007

The most important measure of total production and total income is gross domestic product (GDP). As we will see in later chapters, for some purposes, the other measures of total production and total income shown in the figure turn out to be more useful than GDP.

Source: U.S. Bureau of Economic Analysis.

Disposable Personal Income

Disposable personal income is equal to personal income minus personal tax payments, such as the federal personal income tax. It is the best measure of the income households actually have available to spend.

Figure 19-4 shows the values of these measures of total production and total income for the year 2007 in a table and a graph.

The Division of Income

Figure 19-1 on page 637 illustrates the important fact that we can measure GDP in terms of total expenditure or as the total income received by households. GDP calculated as the sum of income payments to households is sometimes referred to as *gross domestic income.* Figure 19-5 shows the division of total income among wages, interest, rent, profit, and certain non-income items. The non-income items are included in gross domestic income because, as we have seen, some of the value of goods and services produced is not directly received by households as income. *Wages* include all compensation received by employees, including fringe benefits such as health insurance. *Interest* is net interest received by households, or the difference between the interest received on savings accounts, government bonds, and other investments and the interest paid on car loans, home mortgages, and other debts. *Rent* is rent received by households. *Profits* include the profits of sole proprietorships, which are usually small businesses, and the profits of corporations. Also included in gross domestic income are indirect business taxes, depreciation, other smaller items, and an allowance for measurement problems called the "statistical discrepancy." The figure shows that the largest component of gross domestic income is wages, which are about three times as large as profits.

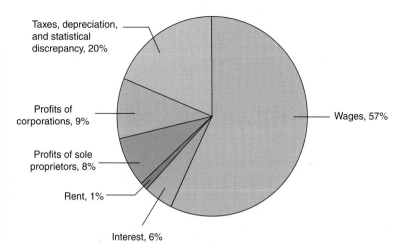

		Billions of dollars
Wages		$7,881
Interest		837
Rent		65
Profit		2,300
Profits of sole proprietors	1,043	
Profits of corporations	1,258	
Taxes, depreciation, and statistical discrepancy		2,757
Total		**$13,841**

Figure 19-5 | The Division of Income

We can measure GDP in terms of total expenditure or as the total income received by households. The largest component of income received by households is wages, which Source: U.S. Bureau of Economic Analysis.

are about three times as large as the profits received by sole proprietors and the profits received by corporations combined.

Economics in YOUR Life!

>> Continued from page 633

At the beginning of the chapter, we posed two questions: What effect should Canada's and China's two very different growth rates of GDP have on your decision to work and live in one country or the other? And if China's much higher growth rate does not necessarily lead you to decide to work and live in China, why not? This chapter has shown that although it is generally true that the more goods and services people have, the better off they are, GDP provides only a rough measure of well-being. That is to say, GDP does not include the value of leisure; nor is it adjusted for pollution and other negative effects of production or crime and other social problems. So, in deciding where to live and work you would need to balance China's much higher growth rate of GDP against these other considerations. You would also need to take into account that although China's *growth rate* is higher than Canada's, Canada's current *level* of real GDP is higher than China's.

Conclusion

In this chapter, we have begun the study of macroeconomics by examining an important concept—how a nation's total production and income can be measured. Understanding GDP is important for understanding the business cycle and the process of long-run economic growth. In the next chapter, we discuss the issues involved in measuring two other key economic variables: the unemployment rate and the inflation rate.

Read *An Inside Look* on the next page for a discussion of why some trucking firms were experiencing slow sales at the same time that the airlines were prospering.

Trucking Industry Depends on the Goods—Not Services—Component of GDP

OMAHA WORLD-HERALD, JANUARY 11, 2007

Economic Slowdown Slams Breaks on Trucking Sector

A sudden, dramatic drop in freight demand has sucked the air out of a trucking sector pumped up by several years of growth.

"For the trucking industry, the first half of this year is likely to be the toughest environment we have seen since the last recession," Bob Costello, chief economist and vice president of the American Trucking Association [ATA], said in a telephone interview Wednesday. That's bad news for the rest of the economy, for which trucking is considered a bellwether. "Trucking sees slowdowns and recovery first," Costello said. "I do anticipate that we will start to recover before the general economy."

The second half of 2007 looks better for trucking, he said. "The general consensus is that 2008 will be a better time for the economy, and I would expect trucking to improve before that," he said. November was the single worst month for for-hire truck tonnage since the last recession, according to the ATA's index. The ATA reported the truck-tonnage index dropped 3.6 percent in November from October and 8.8 percent compared to the same month a year earlier. . . .

Jim Hill at Omaha-based Merit Transportation Co. said the pace of what he termed one of the slowest fourth quarters he has seen in more than 20 years in the trucking business has continued into January. Although he remains optimistic about Merit's corner of the trucking world—refrigerated transportation—Hill said consumer demand is off. . . . Merit delayed by a year the $6 million purchase of 40 tractors and 40 trailers from fall 2006 when demand suddenly deflated. . . .

The factors behind the slowdown are varied, Costello said. "It's really broad-based." Slowdowns in housing and auto markets are easy targets, "but it's more than that," he said.

The portion of the gross national product made up of goods, rather than services, is projected to grow at a slower 1.6 percent rate than the overall economy's 2.3 percent rate, he said.

"We don't haul services. We get more bang for your buck from the goods side of the economy," he said. A persistent driver shortage kept trucking companies from expanding further during the good times, Costello said. . . . With the driver shortage limiting how much firms can transport, a quick change in demand could quickly eat up any excess capacity. . . .

Tonn Ostergard, president and chief executive of Crete Carrier Corp., said the transportation industry has changed greatly since 2000, when trucking first felt the effects of the last recession. Comparisons are difficult because circumstances are different, he said.

Shippers have changed the way they manage transportation, maintaining thinner inventories and building distribution centers closer to their customers for overnight restocking. "We don't see the cycles that we used to see," he said. "They are much more proactive about managing their supply chain. They continually improve on things—their technology, their distribution patterns." More shippers also are responding to fuel prices by moving freight to intermodal rail, he said. . . .

Lincoln-based Crete Carrier is one of the nation's largest privately held trucking companies. Ostergard declined to release revenue figures. "The first 11 days of the new year aren't particularly rebounding, but January is never going to be as solid as other months. By some comparative measurements, January has been just a little below what we would have expected," he said. The company didn't make major changes in the fourth quarter.

"That's what separates well-managed companies from the rest of the pack," he said. "You work a little harder and manage the business a little better. We're working closer with our customers and doing everything we can to be as efficient as possible."

At Merit, Hill sees opportunity in the refrigerated segment, and the private company is projected to grow again in 2007. The company, which was founded in 1999, limited its growth in 2006. . . .

Source: Stacie Hamel, "Economic Slowdown Slams Breaks on Trucking Sector," *Omaha World-Herald*, January 11, 2007. Reprinted by permission.

Key Points in the Article

This article discusses a significant decline in the demand for ground-freight transportation in the last quarter of 2006, which many in the trucking industry anticipated would continue during the first two quarters of 2007. Some in the industry feared that this decline might be the worst that they had seen since the recession of 2001. The article cites several causes for the downturn in the demand for trucking, including the slowdowns in the housing and automobile industries, and the long-term trend toward faster growth in services than in goods. The article also notes that the trucking industry is relatively less cyclical now than it was during the recession in 2001. Since the last recession, shippers have learned to manage inventories much more efficiently.

Analyzing the News

(a) Trucking-industry observers expect that the first two quarters of 2007 will be the worst for the industry since the recession of 2001. The early stages of this slowdown were apparent in November 2006, when the American Trucking Association's (ATA's) truck-tonnage index fell 8.8 percent from a year earlier; this was the worst showing since 2001. As Bob Costello, chief economist and vice president of the ATA explains, this much-anticipated industry slowdown may not bode well for the overall U.S. economy. This is because activity in the trucking industry tends to slow before activity in the overall U.S. economy does.

(b) The reasons for the slowdown are varied; however, three factors seem to have played a particularly significant role. According to the article, the first two factors are slowdowns in the demand for housing and automobiles. As the demand for new residential construction and automobiles declined, so too did the demand for the ground-freight transportation required to get building materials to job sites and automobiles to dealers' lots. The third has been the slowdown in the growth of the goods portion of U.S. GDP. This is obviously a problem for the trucking industry, which ships goods but not services. In fact, the percentage of U.S. GDP composed of goods has fallen consistently since at least 1980. This pattern is shown in the figure below, which shows that goods have fallen from 41 percent of GDP in 1980 to 31 percent in 2006; during this same period, services have increased from 47 percent of GDP to 58 percent.

(c) The trucking industry is less cyclical today than it was during the recession of 2001. According to Tonn Ostergard, president and chief executive of Crete Carrier Corp., this is because shippers, who hire trucking companies, have learned to manage more efficiently their inventories and supply chains—networks of resources involved in moving goods to where they are needed. So, the demand for trucking is no longer as sensitive as it once was to general fluctuations in economic activity.

Thinking Critically

1. Both trucking firms and airlines are in the transportation business, yet while 2006 and 2007 were good years for the airlines, they were poor years for trucking firms. Why did macroeconomic conditions in these years affect these two industries differently?

2. In the past 20 years, exports and imports have both increased as a fraction of GDP. Has this trend been good news or bad news for the trucking industry?

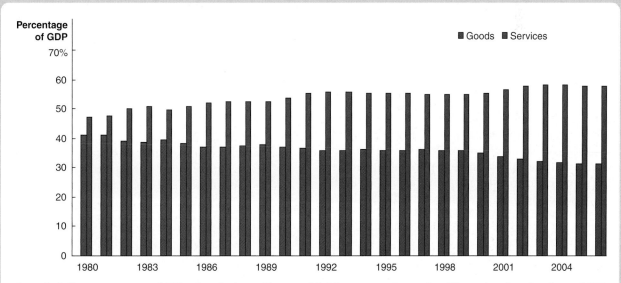

As goods decline as a percentage of GDP, so does the demand for ground-freight transportation services. (The goods and services shares of GDP do not sum to 100 percent because GDP is composed of goods, services, and structures.)

Key Terms

19.1 LEARNING OBJECTIVE   19.1 | Explain how total production is measured, **pages 635–642.**

Gross Domestic Product Measures Total Production

Summary

Economics is divided into the subfields of **microeconomics**—which studies how households and firms make choices—and **macroeconomics**—which studies the economy as a whole. An important macroeconomic issue is the **business cycle**, which refers to alternating periods of economic expansion and economic recession. An **expansion** is a period during which production and employment are increasing. A **recession** is a period during which production and employment are decreasing. Another important macroeconomic topic is **economic growth**, which refers to the ability of the economy to produce increasing quantities of goods and services. Macroeconomics also studies the **inflation rate**, or the percentage increase in the price level from one year to the next. Economists measure total production by **gross domestic product** (**GDP**), which is the value of all *final goods and services* produced in an economy during a period of time. A **final good or service** is purchased by a final user. An **intermediate good or service** is an input into another good or service and is not included in GDP. When we measure the value of total production in the economy by calculating GDP, we are simultaneously measuring the value of total income. GDP is divided into four major categories of expenditures: **consumption, investment, government purchases, and net exports**. Government **transfer payments** are not included in GDP because they are payments to individuals for which the government does not receive a good or service in return. We can also calculate GDP by adding up the **value added** of every firm involved in producing final goods and services.

Review Questions

1.1 Why in microeconomics can we measure production in terms of quantity, but in macroeconomics we measure production in terms of market value?

1.2 If the U.S. Bureau of Economic Analysis added up the values of every good and service sold during the year, would the total be larger or smaller than GDP?

1.3 In the circular flow of expenditure and income, why must the value of total production in an economy equal the value of total income?

1.4 Describe the four major components of expenditures in GDP and write the equation used to represent the relationship between GDP and the four expenditure components.

1.5 What is the difference between the value of a firm's final product and the value added by the firm to the final product?

Problems and Applications

1.6 Is the value of intermediate goods and services produced during the year included in GDP? For example, are computer chips produced and installed on a new PC included in GDP? (Note that this question does not ask whether the computer chips are directly counted in GDP but rather whether their production is included in GDP.)

1.7 Briefly explain whether each of the following transactions represents the purchase of a final good.
   a. The purchase of wheat from a wheat farmer by a bakery
   b. The purchase of an aircraft carrier by the federal government
   c. The purchase of French wine by a U.S. consumer
   d. The purchase of a new machine tool by the Ford Motor Company

1.8 (Related to the *Don't Let This Happen to You!* on page 639) Briefly explain whether you agree or disagree with the following statement: "In years when people buy many shares of stock, investment will be high and, therefore, so will GDP."

1.9 (Related to the *Chapter Opener* on page 632) Which component of GDP will be affected by each of the following transactions involving American

Airlines? If you do not believe any component of GDP will be affected by the transactions, briefly explain why.

a. You purchase a ticket on an American flight to Seattle to visit your uncle.

b. American purchases a new jetliner from Boeing.

c. American purchases new seats to be installed on a jetliner it already owns.

d. American purchases 100 million gallons of jet fuel.

e. A person in France purchases a ticket to fly on an American flight from Paris to New York.

f. The city of Nashville agrees to spend funds to extend one of the runways at Nashville International Airport so that American will be able to land larger jets.

1.10 Is the value of a house built in 2000 and resold in 2009 included in the GDP of 2009? Why or why not? Would the services of the real estate agent who helped sell (or buy) the house in 2009 be counted in GDP for 2009? Why or why not?

1.11 (Related to the *Making the Connection on page 639*) In recent years, the BEA has classified government purchases into consumption expenditures and gross government investment. Would you classify the expenditures for the Department of Homeland Security as government investment or as government consumption? Briefly explain.

1.12 (Related to *Solved Problem 19-1* on page 636) Suppose that a simple economy produces only the following four goods and services: textbooks, hamburgers, shirts, and cotton. Assume that all the cotton is used in the production of shirts. Use the information in the following table to calculate nominal GDP for 2009.

PRODUCTION AND PRICE STATISTICS FOR 2009

PRODUCT	QUANTITY	PRICE
Textbooks	100	$60.00
Hamburgers	100	2.00
Shirts	50	25.00
Cotton	8,000	0.60

1.13 For the total value of expenditures on final goods and services to equal the total value of income generated from producing those final goods and services, all the money that a business receives from the sale of its product must be paid out as income to the owners of the factors of production. How can a business make a profit if it pays out as income all the money it receives?

1.14 How does the value added of a business differ from the profits of a business?

1.15 It is reported that some state-owned firms in the former Soviet Union produced goods and services whose value was less than the value of the raw materials the firms used to produce their goods and services. If so, what would have been the value added of these state-owned firms? Would such a firm be able to survive in a free-market economy?

1.16 An artist buys scrap metal from a local steel mill as a raw material for her metal sculptures. Last year, she bought $5,000 worth of the scrap metal. During the year, she produced 10 metal sculptures that she sold for $800 each to the local art store. The local art store sold all of them to local art collectors at an average price of $1,000 each. For the 10 metal sculptures, what was the total value added of the artist and what was the total value added of the local art store?

>> **End Learning Objective 19.1**

19.2 LEARNING OBJECTIVE   19.2 | Discuss whether GDP is a good measure of well-being, **pages 642–645.**

Does GDP Measure What We Want It to Measure?

Summary

GDP does not include household production, which refers to goods and services people produce for themselves, nor does it include production in the **underground economy**, which consists of concealed buying and selling. The underground economy in some developing countries may be more than half of measured GDP. GDP is not a perfect measure of well-being because it does not include the value of leisure, it is not adjusted for pollution or other negative effects of production, and it is not adjusted for changes in crime and other social problems.

 Visit www.myeconlab.com to complete these exercises online and get instant feedback.

Review Questions

2.1 Why does the size of a country's GDP matter? How does it affect the quality of life of the country's people?

2.2 Why is GDP an imperfect measure of economic well-being? What types of production does GDP not measure? Even if GDP included these types of production, why would it still be an imperfect measure of economic well-being?

Problems and Applications

2.3 Which of the following are likely to increase measured GDP, and which are likely to reduce it?

  a. The fraction of women working outside the home increases.

  b. There is a sharp increase in the crime rate.

  c. Higher tax rates cause some people to hide more of the income they earn.

2.4 What would you expect to happen to household production as unemployment rises during a recession? What would you expect to happen to household production as unemployment falls during an expansion? Would you therefore expect the fluctuation in actual production—GDP plus household production—to be greater or less than the fluctuation in measured GDP?

2.5 Review the definition of real GDP per capita on page 644 before answering the following question. Does the fact that the typical American works less than 40 hours per week today and worked 60 hours per week in 1890 make the difference between the economic well-being of Americans today versus 1890 higher or lower than indicated by the difference in real GDP per capita today versus 1890? Explain.

2.6 **(Related to the** *Making the Connection* **on page 643)** A report of the World Bank, an international organization devoted to increasing economic growth in developing countries, includes the following statement: "Informal economic activities pose a particular measurement problem [in calculating GDP], especially in developing countries, where much economic activity may go unrecorded." What do they mean by "informal economic activities"? Why would these activities make it harder to measure GDP? Why might they make it harder to evaluate the standard of living in developing countries relative to the standard of living in the United States?

Source: The World Bank, *World Development Indicators*, Washington, DC: The World Bank, 2003, p. 189.

2.7 Each year, the United Nations publishes the Human Development Report, which provides information on the standard of living in nearly every country in the world. The report includes data on real GDP per person and also contains a broader measure of the standard of living called the Human Development Index (HDI). The HDI combines data on real GDP per person with data on life expectancy at birth, adult literacy, and school enrollment. The following table shows values for real GDP per person and the HDI for several countries. Prepare one list that ranks countries from highest real GDP per person to lowest and another list that ranks countries from highest HDI to lowest. Briefly discuss possible reasons for any differences in the rankings of countries in your two lists. (All values in the table are for the year 2005.)

COUNTRY	REAL GDP PER PERSON	HDI
Australia	$31,794	0.962
China	6,757	0.777
Greece	23,381	0.926
Iran	7,968	0.759
Norway	41,420	0.968
Singapore	29,663	0.922
South Korea	22,029	0.921
United Arab Emirates	25,514	0.868
United States	41,890	0.951

Source: United Nations Development Programme, *Human Development Report, 2007/2008*, New York: Palgrave Macmillan, 2007.

2.8 **(Related to the** *Making the Connection* **on page 644)** Think about the increase in spending for the Department of Homeland Security and the wars in Afghanistan and Iraq. These all represent government expenditures that have increased GDP. Briefly explain whether you think that these increases in GDP have made the typical person better off.

>> End Learning Objective 19.2

19.3 LEARNING OBJECTIVE   19.3 | Discuss the difference between real GDP and nominal GDP, **pages 645-648.**

Real GDP versus Nominal GDP

Summary

Nominal GDP is the value of final goods and services evaluated at current-year prices. **Real GDP** is the value of final goods and services evaluated at *base-year* prices. By keeping prices constant, we know that changes in real GDP represent changes in the quantity of goods and services produced in the economy. When the **price level**, the average prices of goods and services in the economy, is increasing, real GDP is greater than nominal GDP in years before the base year and less than nominal GDP for years after the base year. The

GDP deflator is a measure of the price level and is calculated by dividing nominal GDP by real GDP and multiplying by 100.

 Visit www.myeconlab.com to complete these exercises Get Ahead of the Curve online and get instant feedback.

Review Questions

3.1 Why does inflation make nominal GDP a poor measure of the increase in total production from one year to the next? How does the U.S. Bureau of Economic

Analysis deal with the problem inflation causes with nominal GDP?

3.2 What is the GDP deflator, and how is it calculated?

Problems and Applications

3.3 **(Related to *Solved Problem 19-3* on page 646)** Suppose the information in the following table is for a simple economy that produces only the following four goods and services: textbooks, hamburgers, shirts, and cotton. Assume that all the cotton is used in the production of shirts.

PRODUCT	2000 STATISTICS		2009 STATISTICS		2010 STATISTICS	
	QUANTITY	PRICE	QUANTITY	PRICE	QUANTITY	PRICE
Textbooks	90	$50.00	100	$60.00	100	$65.00
Hamburgers	75	2.00	100	2.00	120	2.25
Shirts	50	30.00	50	25.00	65	25.00
Cotton	10,000	0.80	8,000	0.60	12,000	0.70

a. Use the information in the table to calculate real GDP for 2009 and 2010, assuming that the base year is 2000.

b. What is the growth rate of real GDP during 2010?

3.4 Assuming that inflation has occurred over time, what is the relationship between nominal GDP and real GDP in each of the following situations?
   a. Years after the base year
   b. In the base year
   c. Years before the base year

3.5 If the quantity of final goods and services produced decreased, could real GDP increase? Could nominal GDP increase? If so, how?

3.6 Use the data in the following table to calculate the GDP deflator for each year (values are in billions of dollars).

	NOMINAL GDP	REAL GDP
2003	$10,961	$10,301
2004	11,686	10,676
2005	12,434	11,003
2006	11,319	13,195
2007	13,841	11,567

Which year from 2004 to 2007 saw the largest percentage increase in the price level, as measured by changes in the GDP deflator? Briefly explain.

>> End Learning Objective 19.3

19.4 LEARNING OBJECTIVE   19.4 | Become familiar with other measures of total production and total income, **pages 648–651.**

Other Measures of Total Production and Total Income

Summary

The most important measure of total production and total income is gross domestic product (GDP). As we will see in later chapters, for some purposes, the other measures of total production and total income shown in Figure 19-4 are actually more useful than GDP. These measures are gross national product (GNP), net national product (NNP), national income, personal income, and disposable personal income.

 Visit www.myeconlab.com to complete these exercises online and get instant feedback.

Review Questions

4.1 Under what circumstances would GDP be a better measure of total production and total income than GNP?

4.2 What are the differences in national income, personal income, and personal disposable income?

Problems and Applications

4.3 Suppose a country has many of its citizens temporarily working in other countries, and many of its firms have facilities in other countries. Furthermore, relatively few citizens of foreign countries are working in this country, and relatively few foreign firms have facilities in this country. In these circumstances, which would you expect to be larger for this country, GDP or GNP? Briefly explain.

4.4 Suppose the amount the federal government collects in personal income taxes increases, while the level of GDP remains the same. What will happen to the values of national income, personal income, and personal disposable income?

4.5 If you were attempting to forecast the level of consumption spending by households, which measure of total production or total income might be most helpful to you in making your forecast? Briefly explain.

4.6 Briefly discuss the accuracy of the following statement: "Corporate profits are much too high: Most corporations make profits equal to 50 percent of the price of the products they sell."

>> End Learning Objective 19.4

Chapter 20

Unemployment and **Inflation**

Alcatel-Lucent Contributes to Unemployment

When we study macroeconomics, we are looking at the big picture: total production, total employment, and the price level. Of course, the big picture is determined by the decisions of millions of individual consumers and firms. Lucent Technologies has been involved in developing many important innovations, including equipment for long-distance television transmission, the transistor, the Unix computer operating system, and Wi-Fi wireless broadband technology.

When total employment in the United States declined during 2001, Lucent contributed to the decline. In 2000, Lucent employed 175,000 workers. It began laying off large numbers of workers during 2001. By 2005,

Lucent employed only 31,500 workers. In December 2006, Lucent merged with the French technology firm Alcatel to form the new firm Alcatel-Lucent. Unfortunately, the new firm continued to have problems. In January 2007, Alcatel-Lucent reported that during the fourth quarter of 2006, its sales had fallen by 16 percent, while its profits were near zero. According to then Chief Executive Patricia Russo, the quarter "proved challenging from a market perspective, driven by a shift in spending from some of our large North American customers and heightened competition in the global wireless market." In the face of this growing competition from communications-technology rivals such as Ericsson of Sweden and Huawei of China, the company could not increase revenue, and so its only option was to reduce costs. Less than one month after the company reported its disappointing earnings, Ms. Russo announced the elimination of 12,500

jobs. Unfortunately, for Russo and Alcatel-Lucent, the bad news just kept on coming. Shortly after reporting that the firm had lost more than $1.5 billion in the second quarter of 2008, Russo announced that she would be stepping down as chief executive at the end of the year.

Alcatel-Lucent's decision to reduce employment will ultimately leave thousands of people out of work. In this chapter, we will focus on measuring changes in unemployment and changes in the price level, or *inflation*. Because unemployment and inflation are both important macroeconomic problems, it is important to understand how they are measured. For an example of a newspaper discussion of newly released government statistics on unemployment, read **AN INSIDE LOOK** on **page 686**.

Sources: Carol Matlock, "The Reasons for Alcatel's 'Shocking' Miss," *BusinessWeek Online*, January 24, 2007; and "Unix's Founding Fathers," *Economist*, June 10, 2004.

Economics in YOUR Life!

Should You Change Your Career Plans if You Graduate During a Recession?

Suppose that you are about to graduate from college with a bachelor's degree in engineering. You plan to seek a job in manufacturing. If the economy is currently in a recession and the unemployment rate is a relatively high 7 percent, should you change your career plans? Should you still try for a job in manufacturing, or should you try to enter another industry or, perhaps, stay in school to get a master's degree? As you read this chapter, see if you can answer these questions. You can check your answers against those we provide at the end of the chapter. **»» Continued on page 685**

U nemployment and inflation are the macroeconomic problems that are most often discussed in the media and during political campaigns. For many members of the general public, the state of the economy is summarized in just two measures: the unemployment rate and the inflation rate. In the 1960s, Arthur Okun, who was chairman of the Council of Economic Advisers during President Lyndon Johnson's administration, coined the term *misery index*, which adds together the inflation rate and the unemployment rate to give a rough measure of the state of the economy. As we will see in later chapters, although inflation and unemployment are important problems, the long-run success of an economy is best judged by its ability to generate high levels of real GDP per person. We devote this chapter to discussing how the government measures the unemployment and inflation rates. In particular, we will look closely at the statistics on unemployment and inflation that the federal government issues each month.

20.1 | Define unemployment rate and labor force participation rate and understand how they are computed.

Measuring the Unemployment Rate and the Labor Force Participation Rate

At 8:30 A.M. on a Friday early in each month, the U.S. Department of Labor reports its estimate of the previous month's unemployment rate. If the unemployment rate is higher or lower than expected, investors are likely to change their views on the health of the economy. The result is seen an hour later, when trading begins on the New York Stock Exchange. Good news about unemployment usually causes stock prices to rise, and bad news causes stock prices to fall. The unemployment rate can also have important political implications. In most presidential elections, the incumbent president is reelected if unemployment is falling early in the election year but is defeated if unemployment is rising. This relationship held true in 2004, when the unemployment rate was lower during the first six months of 2004 than it had been during the last six months of 2003, and incumbent George W. Bush was reelected.

The unemployment rate is a key macroeconomic statistic. But how does the Department of Labor prepare its estimates of the unemployment rate, and how accurate are these estimates? We will explore the answers to these questions in this section.

The Household Survey

Each month, the U.S. Bureau of the Census conducts the *Current Population Survey* (often referred to as the *household survey*) to collect data needed to compute the unemployment rate. The bureau interviews adults in a sample of 60,000 households, chosen to represent the U.S. population, about the employment status of everyone in the household 16 years of age and older. The Department of Labor's Bureau of Labor Statistics (BLS) uses these data to calculate the monthly unemployment rate. People are considered *employed* if they worked during the week before the survey or if they were temporarily away from their job because they were ill, on vacation, on strike, or for other reasons. People are considered *unemployed* if they did not work in the previous week but were available for work and had actively looked for work at some time during the previous four weeks. The **labor force** is the sum of the *employed* and the *unemployed*. The **unemployment rate** is the percentage of the labor force that is unemployed.

People who do not have a job and who are not actively looking for a job are classified by the BLS as *not in the labor force*. People not in the labor force include retirees, homemakers, full-time students, and people on active military service, in prison, or in mental hospitals. Also not in the labor force are people who are available for work and who have actively looked for a job at some point during the previous 12 months but who have not looked during the previous four weeks. Some people have not actively looked

Labor force The sum of employed and unemployed workers in the economy.

Unemployment rate The percentage of the labor force that is unemployed.

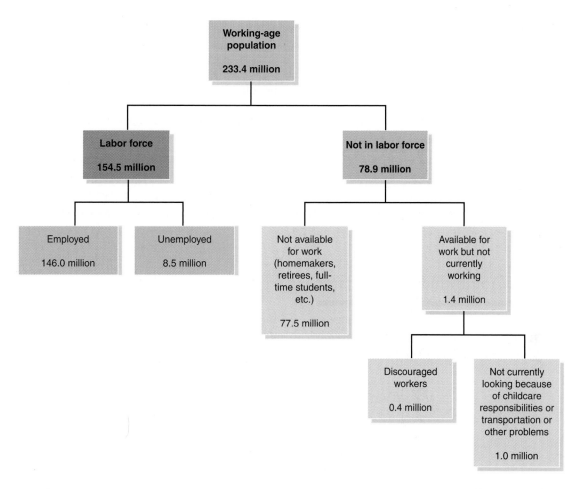

Figure 20-1 | The Employment Status of the Civilian Working-Age Population, May 2008

In May 2008, the working-age population of the United States was 233.4 million. The working-age population is divided into those in the labor force (154.5 million) and those not in the labor force (78.9 million). The labor force is divided into the employed (146.0 million) and the unemployed (8.5 million). Those not in the labor force are divided into those not available for work (77.5 million) and those available

for work (1.4 million). Finally, those available for work but not in the labor force are divided into discouraged workers (0.4 million) and those currently not working for other reasons (1.0 million).

Source: U.S. Department of Labor, *Employment Situation Summary*, May 2008.

for work lately for reasons such as transportation difficulties or childcare responsibilities. Other people who have not actively looked for work are called *discouraged workers.* **Discouraged workers** are available for work but have not looked for a job during the previous four weeks because they believe no jobs are available for them.

Figure 20-1 shows the employment status of the civilian working-age population in May 2008. We can use the information in the figure to calculate two important macroeconomic indicators:

- *The unemployment rate.* The unemployment rate measures the percentage of the labor force that is unemployed:

$$\frac{\text{Number of unemployed}}{\text{Labor force}} \times 100 = \text{Unemployment rate.}$$

Using the numbers from Figure 20-1, we can calculate the unemployment rate for May 2008:

$$\frac{8.5 \text{ million}}{154.5 \text{ million}} \times 100 = 5.5\%.$$

Discouraged workers People who are available for work but have not looked for a job during the previous four weeks because they believe no jobs are available for them.

Labor force participation rate The percentage of the working-age population in the labor force.

- *The labor force participation rate.* The **labor force participation rate** measures the percentage of the working-age population that is in the labor force:

$$\frac{\text{Labor force}}{\text{Working-age population}} \times 100 = \text{Labor force participation rate.}$$

For May 2008, the labor force participation rate was:

$$\frac{154.5 \text{ million}}{233.4 \text{ million}} \times 100 = 66.2\%.$$

Solved Problem | 20-1

What Happens if You Include the Military?

In the BLS household survey, people on active military service are not included in the totals for employment, the labor force, or the working-age population. Suppose people in the military were included in these categories. How would the unemployment rate and the labor force participation rate change?

SOLVING THE PROBLEM:

Step 1: **Review the chapter material.** This problem is about calculating the unemployment rate and the labor force participation rate, so you may want to review the section "Measuring the Unemployment Rate and the Labor Force Participation Rate," which begins on page 660.

Step 2: **Show that including the military decreases the measured unemployment rate.** The unemployment rate is calculated as:

$$\frac{\text{Number of unemployed}}{\text{Labor force}} \times 100.$$

Including people in the military would increase the number of people counted as being in the labor force but would leave unchanged the number of people counted as unemployed. Therefore, the unemployment rate would decrease.

Step 3: **Show that including the military increases the measured labor force participation rate.** The labor force participation rate is calculated as:

$$\frac{\text{Labor force}}{\text{Working-age population}} \times 100.$$

Including people in the military would increase both the number of people in the labor force and the number of people in the working-age population by the same amount. This change would increase the labor force participation rate because adding the same number to both the numerator and the denominator of a fraction that is less than one increases the value of the fraction.

To see why this is true, consider the following simple example. Suppose that 100,000,000 people are in the working-age population and 50,000,000 are in the labor force, not counting people in the military. Suppose that 1,000,000 people are in the military. Then, the labor force participation rate excluding the military is:

$$\frac{50,000,000}{100,000,000} \times 100 = 50\%,$$

and the labor force participation rate including the military is:

$$\frac{51,000,000}{101,000,000} \times 100 = 50.5\%.$$

YOUR TURN: For more practice, do related problem 1.7 on page 688 at the end of this chapter.

>> End Solved Problem 20-1

Problems with Measuring the Unemployment Rate

Although the BLS reports the unemployment rate measured to the tenth of a percentage point, it is not a perfect measure of the current state of joblessness in the economy. One problem that the BLS confronts is distinguishing between the unemployed and people who are not in the labor force. During an economic recession, for example, an increase in discouraged workers usually occurs, as people who have had trouble finding a job stop actively looking. Because these workers are not counted as unemployed, the unemployment rate as measured by the BLS may significantly understate the true degree of joblessness in the economy. The BLS also counts people as being employed if they hold part-time jobs even though they would prefer to hold full-time jobs. In a recession, counting as "employed" a part-time worker who wants to work full time tends to understate the degree of joblessness in the economy and make the employment situation appear better than it is.

Not counting discouraged workers as unemployed and counting people as employed who are working part time, although they would prefer to be working full time, has a substantial effect on the measured unemployment rate. For example, in May 2008, if the BLS counted as unemployed all people who were available for work but not actively looking for a job and all people who were in part-time jobs but wanted full-time jobs, the unemployment rate would have increased from 5.5 percent to 9.7 percent.

There are other measurement problems, however, that cause the measured unemployment rate to *overstate* the true extent of joblessness. These problems arise because the Current Population Survey does not verify the responses of people included in the survey. Some people who claim to be unemployed and actively looking for work may not be actively looking. A person might claim to be actively looking for a job to remain eligible for government payments to the unemployed. In this case, a person who is actually not in the labor force is counted as unemployed. Other people might be employed but engaged in illegal activity—such as drug dealing—or might want to conceal a legitimate job to avoid paying taxes. In these cases, individuals who are actually employed are counted as unemployed. These inaccurate responses to the survey bias the unemployment rate as measured by the BLS toward overstating the true extent of joblessness. We can conclude that, although the unemployment rate provides some useful information about the employment situation in the country, it is far from an exact measure of joblessness in the economy.

Trends in Labor Force Participation

The labor force participation rate is important because it determines the amount of labor that will be available to the economy from a given population. The higher the labor force participation rate, the more labor will be available and the higher a country's levels of GDP and GDP per person. Figure 20-2 highlights two important trends in labor force participation rates of adults aged 20 and over in the United States since 1950—the rising labor force participation rate of adult women and the falling labor force participation rate of adult men.

The labor force participation rate of adult males has fallen from 89 percent in 1948 to 76 percent in 2007. Most of this decline is due to older men retiring earlier and younger men remaining in school longer. There has also been a decline in labor force participation among males who are not in school but who are too young to retire.

Figure 20-2

The labor force participation rate of adult men has declined gradually since 1948, but the labor force participation rate of adult women has increased significantly, leaving the overall labor force participation rate higher today than it was in 1948.
Source: U.S. Bureau of Labor Statistics.

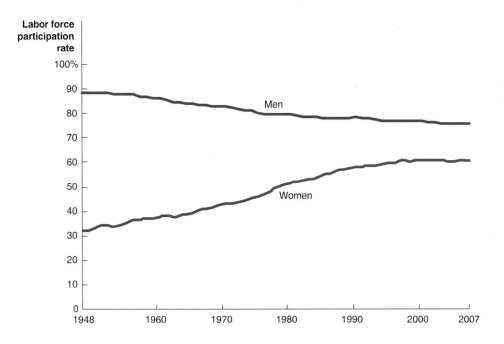

Making the Connection

What Explains the Increase in "Kramers"?

Cosmo Kramer is the name of Jerry Seinfeld's next-door neighbor on the popular television comedy *Seinfeld*. One of the running jokes on the program is Kramer's ability to support himself without apparently ever holding a job. In recent years, there has been an increase in the number of men who seem to be following Kramer's lifestyle. In 1967, only 2.2 percent of men between the ages of 25 and 54 who were not in school did no paid work at all during the year. By 2006, 9.4 percent of men in this age category did not work. The rate of nonworking men is even higher among some groups. For example, about 20 percent of men aged 25 to 54 who lack a high school degree do not have a job and are not looking for one.

Why do more men seem to be adopting Kramer's lifestyle?

More than half of nonworking men receive Social Security Disability Insurance. Under this program, people with disabilities receive cash payments from the federal government and receive medical benefits under the Medicaid program. In 1984, Congress passed legislation that made it easier for people with disabilities that are difficult to verify medically, such as back injuries or mental illnesses, to qualify for disability payments. In addition, the value of disability payments has increased faster than the wages of low-skilled workers. The result is that some men who in the past might have been working or actively looking for work are now being supported by disability payments and are not in the labor force.

An increasing share of nonworking men, however, are not disabled. How do nonworking men who do not receive disability payments support themselves, and how do they spend their time? Most nonworking men live with their parents, wives, or other relatives. Many of these men appear to rely on these other household members for food, clothing, and money. A recent study by Jay Stewart of the Bureau of Labor Statistics shows that most nonworking men are not substituting nonmarket work—such as childcare or housework—for market work. Instead, nonworking men engage in leisure activities, such as sports, watching television, or sleeping during the hours freed up by not working. Stewart concludes that "the average day of a nonworking man looks very much like the average day-off of a man who works full time."

Sources: Alan Krueger, "A Growing Number of Men Are Not Working, So What Are They Doing?" *New York Times*, April 29, 2004, p. C2; and Jay Stewart, "Male Nonworkers: Who Are They and Who Supports Them?" *Demography*, Vol. 43, No. 3, August 2006, pp. 537–552.

YOUR TURN: Test your understanding by doing related problem 1.9 on page 689 at the end of this chapter.

The decline in labor force participation among adult men has been more than offset by a sharp increase in the labor force participation rate for adult women, which rose from 32 percent in 1948 to 61 percent in 2007. As a result, the overall labor force participation rate for adult workers rose from 59 percent in 1948 to 68 percent in 2007. The increase in the labor force participation rate for women has several causes, including changing social attitudes due in part to the women's movement, federal legislation outlawing discrimination, increasing wages for women, and the typical family having fewer children.

Unemployment Rates for Demographic Groups

Different groups in the population can have very different unemployment rates. Figure 20-3 shows unemployment rates for different demographic groups in May 2008, when the unemployment rate for the entire population was 5.5 percent. White adults had an unemployment rate of 4.3 percent. The unemployment rate for black adults was 8.5 percent, or almost twice the rate for white adults. Teenagers have higher unemployment rates than adults. The black teenage unemployment rate of 32.3 percent was the highest for the groups shown.

How Long Are People Typically Unemployed?

The longer a person is unemployed, the greater the hardship. During the Great Depression of the 1930s, some people were unemployed for years at a time. In the modern U.S. economy, the typical unemployed person stays unemployed for a relatively brief period of time. Table 20-1 shows for May 2008 the percentage of the unemployed who had been unemployed for a given period of time. Eighty-two percent of the people

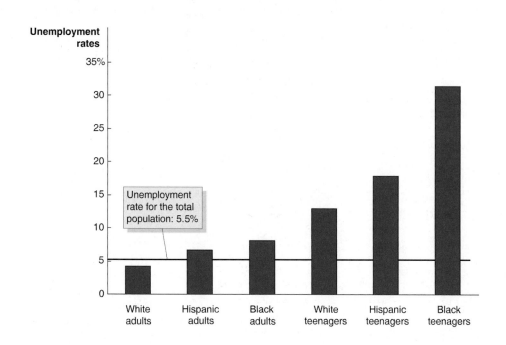

Figure 20-3

Unemployment Rates in the United States by Demographic Group, May 2008

The unemployment rate of black adults is almost twice that of white adults, and the unemployment rate of black teenagers is almost twice that of white teenagers. The adult unemployment rates apply to persons aged 20 and over who are in the labor force. The teenage unemployment rates apply to persons aged 16 to 19 who are in the labor force.
Note: People identified as Hispanic may be of any race.
Source: U.S. Department of Labor, *Employment Situation Summary*, May 2008.

TABLE 20-1

Duration of Unemployment

LENGTH OF TIME UNEMPLOYED	PERCENTAGE OF TOTAL UNEMPLOYED
Less than 5 weeks	38.2%
5 to 14 weeks	29.1
15 to 26 weeks	14.4
27 weeks or more	18.3

Source: U.S. Department of Labor, *Employment Situation Summary*, May 2008.

unemployed in that month had been unemployed for less than six months. Half had been unemployed for eight weeks or less. The important conclusion is that, *except in severe recessions, the typical person who loses a job finds another one or is recalled to a previous job within a few months.*

The Establishment Survey: Another Measure of Employment

In addition to the household survey, the BLS uses the *establishment survey*, sometimes called the *payroll survey*, to measure total employment in the economy. This monthly survey samples about 300,000 business establishments. An establishment is a factory, a store, or an office. A small company typically operates only one establishment, but large companies may operate many establishments. The establishment survey provides information on the total number of persons who are employed *and on a company payroll.* The establishment survey has three drawbacks. First, the survey does not provide information on the number of self-employed persons because they are not on a company payroll. Second, the survey may fail to count some persons employed at newly opened firms that are not included in the survey. Third, the survey provides no information on unemployment. Despite these drawbacks, the establishment survey has the advantage of being determined by actual payrolls rather than by unverified answers, as is the case with the household survey. In recent years, some economists have come to rely more on establishment survey data than on household survey data in analyzing current labor market conditions. Some financial analysts who forecast the future state of the economy to help forecast stock prices have also begun to rely more on establishment survey data than on household survey data.

Table 20-2 shows household survey and establishment survey data for the months of April and May 2008. Notice that the household survey, because it includes the

TABLE 20-2 | **Household and Establishment Survey Data for April and May 2008**

	HOUSEHOLD SURVEY			ESTABLISHMENT SURVEY		
	APRIL	MAY	CHANGE	APRIL	MAY	CHANGE
EMPLOYED	146,331,000	146,046,000	−285,000	137,803,000	137,754,000	−49,000
UNEMPLOYED	7,626,000	8,487,000	+861,000			
LABOR FORCE	153,957,000	154,534,000	+577,000			
UNEMPLOYMENT RATE	5.0%	5.5%	+0.5%			

Source: U.S. Department of Labor, *Employment Situation Summary*, May 2008.

Note: The sum of employed and unemployed may not equal the labor force due to rounding.

self-employed, gives a larger total for employment than does the establishment survey. The household survey provides information on the number of persons unemployed and on the number of persons in the labor force. This information is not available in the establishment survey. In the household survey, employment fell by 285,000 between April and May 2008, while it fell by only 49,000 in the establishment survey. This discrepancy is partly due to the slightly different groups covered by the two surveys and partly to inaccuracies in the surveys.

Job Creation and Job Destruction Over Time

One important fact about employment is not very well known: The U.S. economy creates and destroys millions of jobs every year. In 2006, for example, about 30.8 million jobs were created, and about 29.1 million jobs were destroyed. This degree of job creation and destruction is not surprising in a vibrant market system where new firms are constantly being started, some existing firms are expanding, some existing firms are contracting, and some firms are going out of business. The creation and destruction of jobs results from changes in consumer tastes, technological progress, and the success and failures of entrepreneurs in responding to the opportunities and challenges of shifting consumer tastes and technological change. The volume of job creation and job destruction helps explain why the typical person who loses a job is unemployed for a relatively brief period of time.

When the BLS announces each month the increases or decreases in the number of persons employed and unemployed, these are net *figures.* That is, the change in the number of persons employed is equal to the total number of jobs created minus the number of jobs eliminated. Take, for example, the months from June to September 2007. During that period, 7,249,000 jobs were created, and 7,484,000 were eliminated, for a net decrease of 235,000 jobs. Because the net change is so much smaller than the total job increases and decreases, the net change gives a misleading indication of how dynamic the U.S. job market really is.

The data in Table 20-3 reinforce the idea of how large the volume of job creation and job elimination is over a period as brief as three months. The table shows the number of establishments creating and eliminating jobs during the period from June through September 2007. During these three months, 13 percent of all private sector jobs were either created or destroyed. Fifty-five percent of establishments either eliminated jobs or added new jobs. About 367,000 new establishments opened, creating 1.43 million new jobs, and 359,000 establishments closed, eliminating 1.35 million jobs.

	NUMBER OF ESTABLISHMENTS	NUMBER OF JOBS
ESTABLISHMENTS CREATING JOBS		
Existing establishments	1,519,000	5,821,000
New establishments	367,000	1,428,000
ESTABLISHMENTS ELIMINATING JOBS		
Existing establishments	1,585,000	6,134,000
Closing establishments	359,000	1,350,000

TABLE 20-3

Establishments Creating and Eliminating Jobs, June–September 2007

Source: U.S. Bureau of Labor Statistics, *Business Employment Dynamics: Third Quarter 2007*, May 21, 2008.

20.2 | Identify the three types of unemployment.

Types of Unemployment

Figure 20-4 illustrates that the unemployment rate follows the business cycle, rising during recessions and falling during expansions. Notice, though, that the unemployment rate never falls to zero. To understand why this is true, we need to discuss the three types of unemployment:

- Frictional unemployment
- Structural unemployment
- Cyclical unemployment

Frictional Unemployment and Job Search

Frictional unemployment Short-term unemployment that arises from the process of matching workers with jobs.

Workers have different skills, interests, and abilities, and jobs have different skill requirements, working conditions, and pay levels. As a result, a new worker entering the labor force or a worker who has lost a job probably will not find an acceptable job right away. Most workers spend at least some time engaging in *job search*, just as most firms spend time searching for a new person to fill a job opening. **Frictional unemployment** is short-term unemployment that arises from the process of matching workers with jobs. Some frictional unemployment is unavoidable. As we have seen, the U.S. economy creates and destroys millions of jobs each year. The process of job search takes time, so there will always be some workers who are frictionally unemployed because they are between jobs and in the process of searching for new ones.

Some unemployment is due to seasonal factors, such as weather or fluctuations in demand for some products or services during different times of the year. For example, stores located in beach resort areas reduce their hiring during the winter, and ski resorts reduce their hiring during the summer. Department stores increase their hiring in November and December and reduce their hiring after New Year's Day. In agricultural areas, employment increases during harvest season and declines thereafter. Construction workers experience greater unemployment during the winter than during the summer. *Seasonal unemployment* refers to unemployment due to factors such as weather, variations in tourism, and other calendar-related events. Because seasonal unemployment can make the unemployment rate seem artificially high during some months and artificially low during other months, the BLS reports two unemployment

Figure 20-4

The Annual Unemployment Rate in the United States, 1950–2007

The unemployment rate rises during recessions and falls during expansion. Shaded areas indicate recessions.
Source: U.S. Bureau of Labor Statistics.

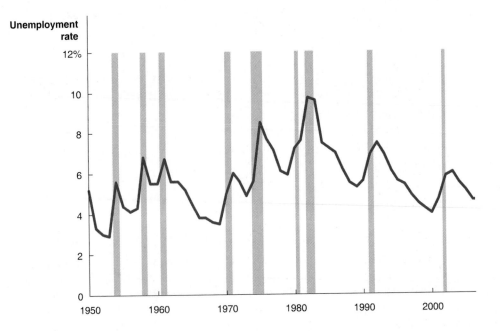

rates each month—one that is *seasonally adjusted* and one that is not seasonally adjusted. The seasonally adjusted data eliminate the effects of seasonal unemployment. Economists and policymakers rely on the seasonally adjusted data as a more accurate measure of the current state of the labor market.

Would eliminating all frictional unemployment be good for the economy? No, because some frictional unemployment actually increases economic efficiency. Frictional unemployment occurs because workers and firms take the time necessary to ensure a good match between the attributes of workers and the characteristics of jobs. By devoting time to job search, workers end up with jobs they find satisfying and in which they can be productive. Of course, having more productive and better-satisfied workers is also in the best interest of firms.

Structural Unemployment

By 2007, computer-generated three-dimensional animation, which was used in movies such as *Shrek* and *Ratatouille*, had become much more popular than traditional hand-drawn two-dimensional animation. Many people who were highly skilled in hand-drawn animation lost their jobs at Walt Disney Pictures, Dreamworks, and other movie studios. To become employed again, many of these people either became skilled in computer-generated animation or found new occupations. In the meantime, they were unemployed. Economists consider these animators *structurally unemployed*. **Structural unemployment** arises from a persistent mismatch between the job skills or attributes of workers and the requirements of jobs. While frictional unemployment is short term, structural unemployment can last for longer periods because workers need time to learn new skills. For example, employment by U.S. steel firms dropped by more than half between the early 1980s and the early 2000s as a result of competition from foreign producers and technological change that substituted machines for workers. Many steelworkers found new jobs in other industries only after lengthy periods of retraining.

Some workers lack even basic skills, such as literacy, or have addictions to drugs or alcohol that make it difficult for them to perform adequately the duties of almost any job. These workers may remain structurally unemployed for years.

Structural unemployment
Unemployment arising from a persistent mismatch between the skills and characteristics of workers and the requirements of jobs.

Cyclical Unemployment

When the economy moves into recession, many firms find their sales falling and cut back on production. As production falls, they start laying off workers. Workers who lose their jobs because of a recession are experiencing **cyclical unemployment**. For example, Freightliner, which is the leading manufacturer of trucks and other commercial vehicles in North America, laid off workers from its heavy truck plants during the recession of 2001. As the economy recovered from the recession, Freightliner began rehiring those workers. The Freightliner workers had experienced cyclical unemployment.

Cyclical unemployment
Unemployment caused by a business cycle recession.

Full Employment

As the economy moves through the expansion phase of the business cycle, cyclical unemployment will eventually drop to zero. The unemployment rate will not be zero, however, because of frictional and structural unemployment. As Figure 20-4 shows, the unemployment rate in the United States is rarely below 4 percent. When the only remaining unemployment is structural and frictional unemployment, the economy is said to be at *full employment*.

Economists consider frictional and structural unemployment as the normal underlying level of unemployment in the economy. The fluctuations around this normal level of unemployment, which we see in Figure 20-4, are mainly due to the changes in the level of cyclical unemployment. This normal level of unemployment, which is the sum of frictional and structural unemployment, is referred to as the **natural rate of unemployment**. Economists disagree on the exact value of the natural rate of unemployment, and there is good reason to believe it varies over time. Currently, most economists estimate the natural rate to be about 5 percent. The natural rate of unemployment is also sometimes called the *full-employment rate of unemployment*.

Natural rate of unemployment
The normal rate of unemployment, consisting of frictional unemployment plus structural unemployment.

Making
the
Connection

How Should We Categorize the Unemployment at Alcatel-Lucent?

We saw at the beginning of this chapter that the technology firm Alcatel-Lucent has experienced sharp declines in employment over the past few years. Was the unemployment caused by the layoffs at Alcatel-Lucent frictional unemployment, structural unemployment, or cyclical unemployment? In answering this question, we should acknowledge that categorizing unemployment as

frictional, structural, or cyclical is useful in understanding the sources of unemployment, but it can be difficult to apply these categories in a particular case. The Bureau of Labor Statistics, for instance, provides estimates of total unemployment but does not classify it as frictional, structural, or cyclical.

Despite these difficulties, we can roughly categorize the unemployment at Alcatel-Lucent. We begin by considering the three basic reasons the layoffs occurred: the long-lived decline in some of the telecommunications products Alcatel-Lucent sells; the recession of 2001 that reduced the demand for the firm's products; and the failure of the firm's managers to compete successfully against other firms in the industry. Each reason corresponds to a category of unemployment. Because the demand for the telecommunications products Alcatel-Lucent sells—particularly products used with fiber-optic cable networks—declined for a significant period, employment at Lucent and competing firms also declined. Between late 2000 and mid-2002, employment in the telecommunications industry declined by more than 500,000. Certain cate-

The people who lost their jobs at Alcatel-Lucent fit into more than one category of unemployment.

gories of employees, such as optical engineers, had difficulty finding new jobs. They were structurally unemployed because they were not able to find new jobs without learning new skills. Some of the decline in Alcatel-Lucent's sales was due to the 2001 recession rather than to long-term problems in the telecommunications industry. So, some of the workers who lost their jobs during that period were cyclically unemployed. Finally, from 2006 to 2008, Alcatel-Lucent had difficulty competing with other communications-technology firms and as a result experienced declining sales, which led to further layoffs. Some workers who lost their jobs at Alcatel-Lucent were able to find new jobs at the firm's competitors after relatively brief job searches. These workers were frictionally unemployed.

YOUR TURN: Test your understanding by doing related problem 2.4 on page 689 at the end of this chapter.

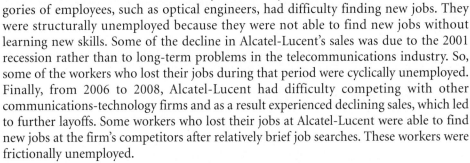

20.3 LEARNING OBJECTIVE   20.3 | Explain what factors determine the unemployment rate.

Explaining Unemployment

We have seen that some unemployment is caused by the business cycle. In later chapters, we will explore the causes of the business cycle, which will help us understand the causes of cyclical unemployment. In this section, we will look at what determines the levels of frictional and structural unemployment.

Government Policies and the Unemployment Rate

Workers search for jobs by sending out resumes, registering with Internet job sites such as Monster.com, and getting job referrals from friends and relatives. Firms fill job openings by advertising in newspapers, participating in job fairs, and recruiting on college campuses. Government policy can aid these private efforts. Governments can help reduce the level of frictional unemployment by pursuing policies that help speed up the process of matching unemployed workers with unfilled jobs. Governments can help reduce structural unemployment through policies that aid the retraining of workers. For example, the federal government's Trade Adjustment Assistance program offers training to workers whose firms laid them off as a result of competition from foreign firms.

Some government policies, however, can add to the level of frictional and structural unemployment. These government policies increase the unemployment rate either by increasing the time workers devote to searching for jobs, by providing disincentives to firms to hire workers, or by keeping wages above their market level.

Unemployment Insurance and Other Payments to the Unemployed Suppose you have been in the labor force for a few years but have just lost your job. You could probably find a low-wage job immediately if you needed to—perhaps at Wal-Mart or McDonald's. But you might decide to search for a better, higher-paying job by sending out resumes and responding to want ads and Internet job postings. Remember from Chapter 1 that the *opportunity cost* of any activity is the highest-valued alternative that you must give up to engage in that activity. In this case, the opportunity cost of continuing to search for a job is the salary you are giving up at the job you could have taken. The longer you search, the greater your chances of finding a better, higher-paying job, but the longer you search, the greater the opportunity cost of the salary you are giving up by not working.

In the United States and most other industrial countries, the unemployed are eligible for *unemployment insurance payments* from the government. In the United States, these payments are equal to about half the average wage. The unemployed spend more time searching for jobs because they receive these payments. This additional time spent searching raises the unemployment rate. Does this mean that the unemployment insurance program is a bad idea? Most economists would say no. Before Congress established the unemployment insurance program at the end of the 1930s, unemployed workers suffered very large declines in their incomes, which led them to greatly reduce their spending. This reduced spending contributed to the severity of recessions. Unemployment insurance helps the unemployed maintain their income and spending, which lessens the personal hardship of being unemployed and also helps reduce the severity of recessions.

International Comparisons In the United States, unemployed workers are typically eligible to receive unemployment insurance payments equal to about half their previous wage for only six months. After that, the opportunity cost of continuing to search for a job rises. In many other high-income countries, such as Canada and most of the countries of Western Europe, workers are eligible to receive unemployment payments for a year or more, and the payments may equal 70 percent to 80 percent of their previous wage. In addition, many of these countries have generous *social insurance programs* that allow unemployed adults to receive some government payments even after their eligibility for unemployment insurance has ended. In the United States, very few government programs make payments to healthy adults, with the exception of the Temporary Assistance for Needy Families program, which allows single parents to receive payments for up to five years. Although there are many reasons unemployment rates may differ across countries, most economists believe that because the opportunity cost of job search is lower in Canada and Western Europe, unemployed workers in those countries search longer for jobs and, therefore, the unemployment rates in those countries tend to be higher than in the United States.

Figure 20-5 shows the average yearly unemployment rate for the 10-year period from 1998 to 2007 for the United States, Canada, Japan, and several Western European countries. The United States and Japan provide unemployment insurance payments for only a short period of time, and their average unemployment rate during these years was lower than for the other countries shown. Many European countries also have laws that make it difficult for companies to fire workers. These laws create a disincentive for firms to hire workers, which also contributes to a higher unemployment rate.

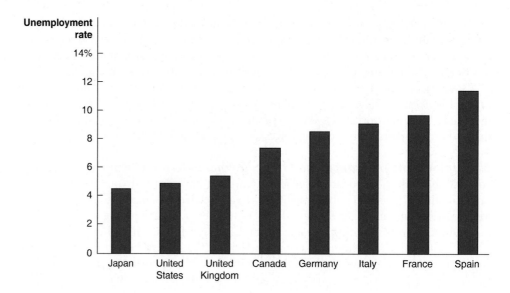

Figure 20-5 | Average Unemployment Rates in the United States, Canada, Japan, and Europe, 1998–2007

The unemployment rate in the United States is usually lower than the unemployment rates in most other high-income countries, partly because the United States has tougher requirements for the unemployed to receive government payments. These requirements raise the costs of searching for a better job and lower the unemployment rate.
Source: Organization for Economic Cooperation and Development.

Minimum Wage Laws In 1938, the federal government enacted a national minimum wage law. At first, the lowest legal wage firms could pay workers was $0.25 per hour. Over the years, Congress gradually has raised the minimum wage; by 2009, it will reach $7.25 per hour. Some states and cities also have minimum wage laws. For example, in 2008, California set its minimum wage at $8.00 per hour, and the minimum wage in San Francisco in 2008 was $9.36 per hour. If the minimum wage is set above the market wage determined by the demand and supply of labor, the quantity of labor supplied will be greater than the quantity of labor demanded. Some workers will be unemployed who would have been employed if there were no minimum wage. As a result, the unemployment rate will be higher than it would be without a minimum wage. Economists agree that the current minimum wage is above the market wage for some workers, but they disagree on the amount of unemployment that has resulted. Because teenagers generally have relatively few job-related skills, they are the group most likely to receive the minimum wage. Studies estimate that a 10 percent increase in the minimum wage reduces teenage employment by about 2 percent. Because teenagers and others receiving the minimum wage are a relatively small part of the labor force, most economists believe that, at its present level, the effect of the minimum wage on the unemployment rate in the United States is fairly small.

Labor Unions

Labor unions are organizations of workers that bargain with employers for higher wages and better working conditions for their members. In unionized industries, the wage is usually above what otherwise would be the market wage. This above-market wage results in employers in unionized industries hiring fewer workers, but does it also increase the overall unemployment rate in the economy? Most economists would say the answer is "no" because only about 9 percent of workers outside the government sector are unionized. Although unions remain strong in a few industries, such as airlines, automobiles, steel, and telecommunications, most industries in the United States are not unionized. The result is that workers who can't find jobs in unionized industries because the wage is above its market level can find jobs in other industries.

Efficiency Wages

Many firms pay higher-than-market wages, not because the government requires them to or because they are unionized, but because they believe doing so will increase their profits. This link may seem like a paradox. Wages are the largest cost for many employers, so paying higher wages seems like a good way for firms to lower profits rather than to increase them. The key to understanding the paradox is that the level of wages can affect the level of worker productivity. Many studies have shown that workers are motivated to work harder by higher wages. An **efficiency wage** is a higher-than-market wage that a firm pays to motivate workers to be more productive. Can't firms ensure that workers work hard by supervising them? In some cases, they can. For example, a telemarketing firm can monitor workers electronically to ensure that they make the required number of phone calls per hour. In many business situations, however, it is much more difficult to monitor workers. Many firms must rely on workers being motivated enough to work hard. In fact, the following is the key to the efficiency wage: By paying a wage above the market wage, a firm raises the costs to workers of losing their jobs because most alternative jobs will pay only the market wage. The increase in productivity that results from paying the high wage can more than offset the cost of the wage, thereby lowering the firm's costs of production.

Efficiency wage A higher-than-market wage that a firm pays to increase worker productivity.

Because the efficiency wage is above the market wage, it results in the quantity of labor supplied being greater than the quantity of labor demanded, just as do minimum wage laws and unions. So, efficiency wages are another reason economies experience some unemployment even when cyclical unemployment is zero.

Making the Connection

Why Does Costco Pay Its Workers So Much More Than Wal-Mart Does?

The concept of efficiency wages raises the possibility that firms might find it more profitable to pay higher wages even when it is possible to pay lower wages. We might expect that a firm would maximize profits by paying the lowest wages at which it was able to attract the number of workers needed. But if low wages significantly reduce worker productivity, then paying higher wages might actually reduce costs and increase profits. Wal-Mart and Costco are competitors in the discount department store industry, but the two companies have taken different approaches to compensating their workers.

Wal-Mart employs more than 1.3 million workers in the United States, more than three times as many as McDonald's, which is the second largest employer. Becoming a sales associate at Wal-Mart is one way to begin a career in retailing that may ultimately lead to a high-paying job. About three-quarters of Wal-Mart's store managers started as hourly workers. But Wal-Mart's hourly workers receive relatively low wages. In 2007, Wal-Mart paid its hourly workers on average about $10.50 per hour. In contrast, the lowest wage that Wal-Mart's rival Costco pays is about $11 per hour, and the average wage is about $17 per hour. Costco's benefits also are more generous, with about 90 percent of its

Costco's relatively high wages and health benefits reduce employee turnover and raise morale and productivity.

employees covered by medical insurance, as opposed to about 50 percent at Wal-Mart.

Why does Costco pay wages so much higher than Wal-Mart pays? Costco's chief executive officer, Jim Sinegal, argues that paying high wages reduces employee turnover and raises morale and productivity: "Paying good wages and keeping your people working for you is very good business. . . . Imagine that you have 120,000 loyal ambassadors out there who are constantly saying good things about Costco. It has to be a significant advantage for you." But it is likely that not all the difference between the wages Costco pays and the wages Wal-Mart pays is due to Costco's employing a strategy of paying efficiency wages. Unlike Wal-Mart, Costco charges a fee of at least $45 per year to shop in its stores. The typical Costco store stocks only about 4,000 items as opposed to the 100,000 items that the average Wal-Mart store stocks. Costco stores also stock more high-priced items, such as jewelry and consumer electronics. As a result, the average income of Costco customers is about $74,000, more than twice as high as the average income of Wal-Mart customers. One observer concludes that Costco pays higher wages than Wal-Mart "because it requires higher-skilled workers to sell higher-end products to its more affluent customers." So, even if Costco were not pursuing a strategy of paying efficiency wages, it is likely it would still have to pay higher wages than Wal-Mart does.

Sources: Alan B. Goldberg and Bill Ritter, "Costco CEO Finds Pro-Worker Means Profitability," ABCNews.com, August 2, 2006; Lori Montgomery, "Maverick CEO Joins Push to Raise Minimum Wage," *Washington Post*, January 30, 2007; and John Tierney, "The Good Goliath," *New York Times*, November 29, 2005.

YOUR TURN: Test your understanding by doing related problem 3.7 on page 690 at the end of this chapter.

20.4 │ Define price level and inflation rate and understand how they are computed.

Measuring Inflation

One of the facts of economic life is that the prices of most goods and services rise over time. As a result, the cost of living continually rises. In 1914, Henry Ford began paying his workers a wage of $5 per day, which was more than twice as much as other automobile manufacturers. Ford's $5-a-day wage provided his workers with a middle class income because prices were so low. In 1914, Ford's Model T, the best-selling car in the country, sold for less than $600, the price of a man's suit was $15, the price of a ticket to a movie theater was $0.15, and the price of a box of Kellogg's Corn Flakes was $0.08. In 2009, with the cost of living being much higher than it was in 1914, the minimum wage law will require firms to pay a wage of at least $7.25 per *hour*, more than Ford's highly paid workers earned in a day.

Knowledge of how the government's employment and unemployment statistics are compiled is important in interpreting them. The same is true of the government's statistics on the cost of living. As we saw in Chapter 19, the **price level** measures the average prices of goods and services in the economy. The **inflation rate** is the percentage increase in the price level from one year to the next. In Chapter 19, we introduced the *GDP deflator* as a measure of the price level. The GDP deflator is the broadest measure we have of the price level because it includes the price of every final good and service. But, for some purposes, it is too broad. For example, if we want to know the impact of inflation on the typical household, the GDP price deflator may be misleading because it includes the prices of products such as large electric generators and machine tools that are included in the investment component of GDP but are not purchased by the typical household. In this chapter, we will focus on measuring the inflation rate by changes in the *consumer price index* because changes in this index come closest to measuring changes in the cost of living as experienced by the typical household. We will also briefly discuss a third measure of inflation: the *producer price index*.

Price level A measure of the average prices of goods and services in the economy.

Inflation rate The percentage increase in the price level from one year to the next.

The Consumer Price Index

To obtain prices of a representative group of goods and services, the BLS surveys 30,000 households nationwide on their spending habits. It uses the results of this survey to construct a *market basket* of 211 types of goods and services purchased by the typical urban

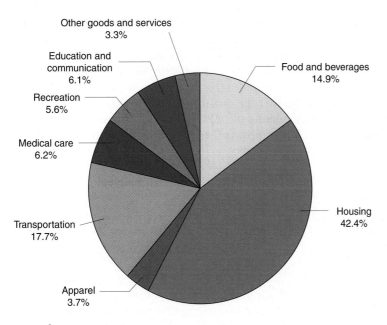

Figure 20-6 | The CPI Market Basket, December 2007

The Bureau of Labor Statistics surveys 30,000 households on their spending habits. The results are used to construct a *market basket* of goods and services purchased by the typical urban family of four. The chart shows these goods and services, grouped into eight broad categories. The percentages represent the expenditure shares of the categories within the market basket. The categories housing, transportation, and food make up about three-quarters of the market basket. Source: U.S. Bureau of Labor Statistics.

family of four. Figure 20-6 shows the goods and services in the market basket, grouped into eight broad categories. Almost three-quarters of the market basket falls into the categories of housing, transportation, and food. Each month, hundreds of BLS employees visit 23,000 stores in 87 cities and record prices of the goods and services in the market basket. Each price in the consumer price index is given a weight equal to the fraction of the typical family's budget spent on that good or service. The **consumer price index (CPI)** is an average of the prices of the goods and services purchased by the typical urban family of four. One year is chosen as the base year, and the value of the CPI is set equal to 100 for that year. In any year other than the base year, the CPI is equal to the ratio of the dollar amount necessary to buy the market basket of goods in that year divided by the dollar amount necessary to buy the market basket of goods in the base year, multiplied by 100. Because the CPI measures the cost to the typical family to buy a representative basket of goods and services, it is sometimes referred to as the *cost-of-living index*.

A simple example can clarify how the CPI is constructed. For purposes of this example, we assume that the market basket has only three products: eye examinations, pizzas, and books:

Consumer price index (CPI)
An average of the prices of the goods and services purchased by the typical urban family of four.

	BASE YEAR (1999)			**2008**		**2009**	
PRODUCT	QUANTITY	PRICE	EXPENDITURES	PRICE	EXPENDITURES (ON BASE-YEAR QUANTITIES)	PRICE	EXPENDITURES (ON BASE-YEAR QUANTITIES)
Eye examinations	1	$50.00	$50.00	$100.00	$100.00	$85.00	$85.00
Pizzas	20	10.00	200.00	15.00	300.00	14.00	280.00
Books	20	25.00	500.00	25.00	500.00	27.50	550.00
Total			$750.00		$900.00		$915.00

Suppose that during the base year of 1999, a survey determines that each month, the typical family purchases 1 eye examination, 20 pizzas, and 20 books. At 1999 prices, the typical family must spend $750.00 to purchase this market basket of goods and services. The CPI for every year after the base year is determined by dividing the amount necessary to purchase the market basket in that year by the amount required in the base year, multiplied by 100. Notice that the quantities of the products purchased in 2008 and 2009 are irrelevant in calculating the CPI because *we are assuming that households buy the same market basket of products each month.* Using the numbers in the table, we can calculate the CPI for 2008 and 2009:

FORMULA	APPLIED TO 2008	APPLIED TO 2009
$\text{CPI} = \dfrac{\text{Expenditures in the current year}}{\text{Expenditures in the base year}} \times 100$	$\left(\dfrac{\$900}{\$750}\right) \times 100 = 120$	$\left(\dfrac{\$915}{\$750}\right) \times 100 = 122$

How do we interpret values such as 120 and 122? The first thing to recognize is that they are *index numbers*, which means they are not measured in dollars or any other units. *The CPI is intended to measure changes in the price level over time.* We can't use the CPI to tell us in an absolute sense how high the price level is, only how much it has changed over time. We measure the inflation rate as the percentage increase in the CPI from one year to the next. For our simple example, the inflation rate in 2009 would be the percentage change in the CPI from 2008 to 2009:

$$\left(\frac{122 - 120}{120}\right) \times 100 = 1.7\%.$$

Because the CPI is designed to measure the cost of living, we can also say that the cost of living increased by 1.7 percent during 2009.

Is the CPI Accurate?

The CPI is the most widely used measure of inflation. Policymakers use the CPI to track the state of the economy. Businesses use it to help set the prices of their products and the wages and salaries of their employees. Each year, the federal government increases the

Don't Let This Happen to **YOU!**

Don't Miscalculate the Inflation Rate

Suppose you are given the data in the following table and are asked to calculate the inflation rate for 2007.

YEAR	CPI
2006	202
2007	207

It is tempting to avoid any calculations and simply to report that the inflation rate in 2007 was 107 percent because 207 is a 107 percent increase from 100. But 107

percent would be the wrong answer. A value for the CPI of 207 in 2007 tells us that the price level in 2007 was 107 percent higher than in the base year, but the inflation rate is the percentage increase in the price level from the previous year, *not* the percentage increase from the base year. The correct calculation of the inflation rate for 2007 is:

$$\left(\frac{207 - 202}{202}\right) \times 100 = 2.5\%.$$

YOUR TURN: Test your understanding by doing related problem 4.3 on page 691 at the end of this chapter.

Social Security payments made to retired workers by a percentage equal to the increase in the CPI during the previous year. In setting alimony and child support payments in divorce cases, judges often order that the payments increase each year by the inflation rate, as measured by the CPI.

It is important that the CPI be as accurate as possible, but there are four biases that make changes in the CPI overstate the true inflation rate:

- **Substitution bias.** In constructing the CPI, the BLS assumes that each month, consumers purchase the same amount of each product in the market basket. In fact, consumers are likely to buy fewer of those products that increase most in price and more of those products that increase least in price (or fall the most in price). For instance, if apple prices rise rapidly during the month while orange prices fall, consumers will reduce their apple purchases and increase their orange purchases. Therefore, the prices of the market basket consumers actually buy will rise less than the prices of the market basket the BLS uses to compute the CPI.

- **Increase in quality bias.** Over time, most products included in the CPI improve in quality: Automobiles become more durable and side air bags become standard equipment, computers become faster and have more memory, dishwashers use less water while getting dishes cleaner, and so on. Increases in the prices of these products partly reflect their improved quality and partly are pure inflation. The BLS attempts to make adjustments so that only the pure inflation part of price increases is included in the CPI. These adjustments are difficult to make, so the recorded price increases overstate the pure inflation in some products.

- **New product bias.** For many years, the BLS updated the market basket of goods used in computing the CPI only every 10 years. That meant that new products introduced between updates were not included in the market basket. For example, the 1987 update took place before cell phones were introduced. Although millions of American households used cell phones by the mid-1990s, they were not included in the CPI until the 1997 update. The prices of many products, such as cell phones, HD-DVD players, and computers, decrease in the years immediately after they are introduced. If the market basket is not updated frequently, these price decreases are not included in the CPI.

- **Outlet bias.** During the mid-1990s, many consumers began to increase their purchases from discount stores such as Sam's Club. By the late 1990s, the Internet began to account for a significant fraction of sales of some products. Because the BLS continued to collect price statistics from traditional full-price retail stores, the CPI was not reflecting the prices some consumers actually paid.

Most economists believe these biases cause changes in the CPI to overstate the true inflation rate by one-half of a percentage point to one percentage point. That is, if the CPI indicates that the inflation rate was 3 percent, it is probably between 2 percent and 2.5 percent. The BLS continues to take steps to reduce the size of the bias. For example, the BLS has reduced the size of the substitution and new product biases by updating the market basket every 2 years rather than every 10 years. The BLS has reduced the size of the outlet bias by conducting a point-of-purchase survey to track where consumers actually make their purchases. Finally, the BLS has used statistical methods to reduce the size of the quality bias. Prior to these changes, the size of the total bias in the CPI was probably greater than 1 percent.

The Producer Price Index

In addition to the GDP deflator and the CPI, the government also computes the **producer price index (PPI)**. Like the CPI, the PPI tracks the prices of a market basket of goods. But, whereas the CPI tracks the prices of goods and services purchased by the typical household, the PPI tracks the prices firms receive for goods and services at all

Producer price index (PPI)
An average of the prices received by producers of goods and services at all stages of the production process.

stages of production. The PPI includes the prices of intermediate goods, such as flour, cotton, yarn, steel, and lumber, and raw materials, such as raw cotton, coal, and crude petroleum. If the prices of these goods rise, the cost to firms of producing final goods and services will rise, which may lead firms to increase the prices of goods and services purchased by consumers. Changes in the PPI therefore can give an early warning of future movements in the CPI.

20.5 LEARNING OBJECTIVE

20.5 | Use price indexes to adjust for the effects of inflation.

Using Price Indexes to Adjust for the Effects of Inflation

The typical college student today is likely to receive a much higher salary than the student's parents did 25 or more years ago, but prices 25 years ago were, on average, much lower than prices today. Put another way, the purchasing power of a dollar was much higher 25 years ago because the prices of most goods and services were much lower. Price indexes such as the CPI give us a way of adjusting for the effects of inflation so that we can compare dollar values from different years. For example, suppose your mother received a salary of $20,000 in 1980. By using the CPI, we can calculate what $20,000 in 1980 is equivalent to in 2007. The consumer price index is 82 for 1980 and 207 for 2007. Because 207/82 = 2.5, we know that, on average, prices were about 2.5 times as high in 2007 as in 1980. We can use this result to inflate a salary of $20,000 received in 1980 to its value in current purchasing power:

$$\text{Value in 2007 dollars} = \text{Value in 1980 dollars} \times \left(\frac{\text{CPI in 2007}}{\text{CPI in 1980}} \right)$$

$$= \$20,000 \times \left(\frac{207}{82} \right) = \$50,488.$$

Our calculation shows that if you are paid a salary of $50,488 today, you will be able to purchase roughly the same amount of goods and services that your mother could have purchased with a salary of $20,000 in 1980. Economic variables that are calculated in current-year prices are referred to as *nominal variables*. The calculation we have just made used a price index to adjust a nominal variable—your mother's salary—for the effects of inflation.

For some purposes, we are interested in tracking changes in an economic variable over time rather than in seeing what its value would be in today's dollars. In that case, to correct for the effects of inflation, we can divide the nominal variable by a price index and multiply by 100 to obtain a *real variable*. The real variable will be measured in dollars of the base year for the price index. Currently, the base year for the CPI is the average of prices in the years 1982 to 1984.

Solved Problem | 20-5

Calculating Real Average Hourly Earnings

In addition to data on employment, the BLS establishment survey gathers data on average hourly earnings of production workers. Production workers are all workers, except for managers and professionals. Average hourly earnings are the wages or salaries earned by these workers per hour. Economists closely follow average hourly earnings because they are a broad measure of the typical worker's income. Use the information in the following table to calculate real average hourly earnings for each year. What was the percentage change in real average hourly earnings between 2006 and 2007?

YEAR	NOMINAL AVERAGE HOURLY EARNINGS	CPI (1982–1984 = 100)
2005	$16.13	195.3
2006	16.76	201.6
2007	17.42	207.3

SOLVING THE PROBLEM:

Step 1: **Review the chapter material.** This problem is about using price indexes to correct for inflation, so you may want to review the section "Using Price Indexes to Adjust for the Effects of Inflation," which begins on page 678.

Step 2: **Calculate real average hourly earnings for each year.** To calculate real average hourly earnings for each year, divide nominal average hourly earnings by the CPI and multiply by 100. For example, real average hourly earnings for 2005 are equal to:

$$\frac{\$16.13}{195.3} \times 100 = \$8.26.$$

These are the results for all the years:

YEAR	NOMINAL AVERAGE HOURLY EARNINGS	CPI (1982–1984 = 100)	REAL AVERAGE HOURLY EARNINGS (1982–1984 DOLLARS)
2005	$16.13	195.3	$8.26
2006	16.76	201.6	8.31
2007	17.42	207.3	8.40

Step 3: **Calculate the percentage change in real average earnings from 2006 to 2007.** This percentage change is equal to:

$$\frac{\$8.40 - \$8.31}{\$8.31} \times 100 = 1.1\%.$$

We can conclude that both nominal average hourly earnings and real average hourly earnings increased between 2006 and 2007.

EXTRA CREDIT: The values we have computed for real average hourly earnings are in 1982–1984 dollars. Because this period is more than 20 years ago, the values are somewhat difficult to interpret. We can convert the earnings to 2007 dollars using the method we used earlier to calculate your mother's salary. But notice that, for purposes of calculating the *change* in the value of real average hourly earnings over time, the base year of the price index doesn't matter. The change from 2006 to 2007 would have still been 1.1 percent, no matter what the base year of the price index. If you don't see that this is true, test it by using the mother's salary method to calculate real average hourly earnings for 2006 and 2007 in 2007 dollars. Then calculate the percentage change. Unless you make an arithmetic error, you should find the answer is still 1.1 percent.

YOUR TURN: For more practice, do related problems 5.3, 5.4, 5.5, and 5.6 on pages 691–692 at the end of this chapter.

>> End Solved Problem 20-5

Falling Real Wages at Alcatel-Lucent

Nominal average hourly earnings are often referred to as the *nominal wage*, and real average hourly earnings are often referred to as the *real wage*. In a multiyear wage contract, a union knows that unless it is able to negotiate increases in nominal wages that are greater than the expected inflation rate, real wages will fall. Before its merger with Alcatel, Lucent Technology and its unionized workers signed a contract that called for nominal wages to increase 16 percent over a period of seven years. If the inflation rate is 3 percent per year over those seven years, the price level will have risen by about 23 percent by the end of the seventh year. With nominal wages rising 16 percent and the price level rising 23 percent, Lucent's workers will have experienced falling real wages.

Both Lucent and its unions realized that the agreement they were signing was likely to lead to falling real wages. The unions accepted the agreement because employment at telecommunications firms had declined sharply. Lucent stated that it might grant further wage increases in the later years of the contract. Lucent probably made this promise because it recognized that if output and employment in the telecommunications industry revived more quickly than expected, the firm would need to pay higher wages to attract and retain good workers.

20.6 LEARNING OBJECTIVE | 20.6 | Distinguish between the nominal interest rate and the real interest rate.

Real versus Nominal Interest Rates

The difference between nominal and real values is important when money is being borrowed and lent. As we saw in Chapter 7, the *interest rate* is the cost of borrowing funds, expressed as a percentage of the amount borrowed. If you lend someone $1,000 for one year and charge an interest rate of 6 percent, the borrower will pay back $1,060, or 6 percent more than the amount you lent. But is $1,060 received one year from now really 6 percent more than $1,000 today? If prices rise during the year, you will not be able to buy as much with $1,060 one year from now as you could with that amount today. Your true return from lending the $1,000 is equal to the percentage change in your purchasing power after taking into account the effects of inflation.

Nominal interest rate The stated interest rate on a loan.

Real interest rate The nominal interest rate minus the inflation rate.

The stated interest rate on a loan is the **nominal interest rate**. The **real interest rate** corrects the nominal interest rate for the effect of inflation on purchasing power. As a simple example, suppose that the only good you purchase is DVDs, and at the beginning of the year, the price of DVDs is $10.00. With $1,000, you can purchase 100 DVDs. If you lend the $1,000 out for one year at an interest rate of 6 percent, you will receive $1,060 at the end of the year. Suppose the inflation rate during the year is 2 percent, so that the price of DVDs has risen to $10.20 by the end of the year. How has your purchasing power increased as a result of making the loan? At the beginning of the year, your $1,000 could purchase 100 DVDs. At the end of the year, your $1,060 can purchase $1,060/$10.20 = 103.92 DVDs. In other words, you can purchase almost 4 percent more DVDs. So, in this case the real interest rate you received from lending was a little less than 4 percent (actually, 3.92 percent). For low rates of inflation, a convenient approximation for the real interest rate is:

$$\text{Real interest rate} = \text{Nominal interest rate} - \text{Inflation rate.}$$

In our example, we can calculate the real interest rate by using this formula as 6 percent − 2 percent = 4 percent, which is close to the actual value of 3.92 percent. If the inflation rate during the year was 4 percent, the real interest rate would be only 2 percent. Holding the nominal interest rate constant, the higher the inflation rate, the lower the real interest rate. Notice that if the inflation rate turns out to be higher than expected, borrowers pay and lenders receive a lower real interest rate than either of them expected. For example, if both you and the person to whom you lent the $1,000 expected the inflation rate to be 2 percent, you both expected the real interest rate on the loan to be 4 percent. If inflation actually turns out to be 4 percent, the real interest rate on the loan will be 2 percent: That's bad news for you but good news for your borrower.

For the economy as a whole, we can measure the nominal interest rate as the interest rate on three-month U.S. Treasury bills. U.S. Treasury bills are short-term loans investors make to the federal government. We can use inflation as measured by changes in the CPI to calculate the real interest rate on Treasury bills. Figure 20-7 shows the nominal and real interest rates for the years 1970 to 2007. Notice that when the inflation rate is low, as it was during the 1990s, the gap between the nominal and real interest rates is small. When the inflation rate is high, as it was during the 1970s, the gap between the nominal and real interest rates becomes large. In fact, a particular nominal interest rate can be associated in different periods with very different real interest rates. For example, during late 1975, the nominal interest rate was about 5.5 percent, but because the inflation rate was 7 percent, the real interest rate was −1.5 percent. In early 1987, the nominal interest rate was also 5.5 percent, but because the inflation rate was only 2 percent, the real interest rate was 3.5 percent.

This example shows that it is impossible to know whether a particular nominal interest rate is "high" or "low." It all depends on the inflation rate. *The real interest rate provides a better measure of the true cost of borrowing and the true return from lending than does the nominal interest rate.* When a firm like Alcatel-Lucent is deciding whether

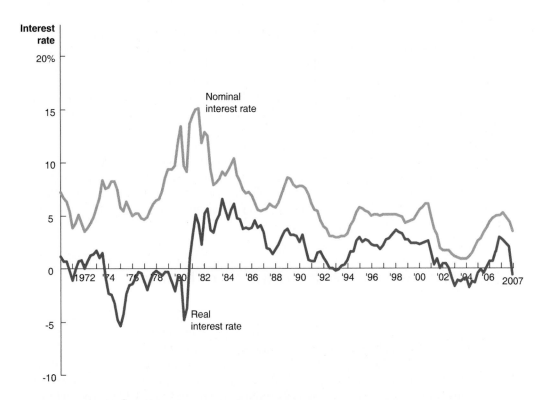

Figure 20-7 | Nominal and Real Interest Rates, 1970–2007

The real interest rate is equal to the nominal interest rate minus the inflation rate. The real interest rate provides a better measure of the true cost of borrowing and the true return on lending than does the nominal interest rate. The nominal interest rate in the figure is the interest rate on three-month U.S. Treasury bills. The inflation rate is measured by changes in the CPI.

Sources: U.S. Federal Reserve Bank of St. Louis; and U.S. Bureau of Labor Statistics.

to borrow the funds to buy an investment good, such as a new factory, it will look at the real interest rate because the real interest rate measures the true cost to the firm of borrowing.

Is it possible for the nominal interest rate to be less than the real interest rate? Yes, but only when the inflation rate is negative. A negative inflation rate is referred to as **deflation** and occurs on the rare occasions when the price level falls. During the years shown in Figure 20-7, the inflation rate as measured by changes in the CPI was never negative.

Deflation A decline in the price level.

20.7 LEARNING OBJECTIVE

20.7 | Discuss the problems that inflation causes.

Does Inflation Impose Costs on the Economy?

Imagine waking up tomorrow morning and finding that every price in the economy has doubled. The prices of food, gasoline, DVDs, computers, houses, and haircuts have all doubled. But suppose that all wages and salaries have also doubled. Will this doubling of prices and wages matter? Think about walking into Best Buy expecting to find an iPod selling for $250. Instead, you find it selling for $500. Will you turn around and walk out? Probably not because your salary has also increased overnight from $30,000 per year to $60,000 per year. So, the purchasing power of your salary has remained the same, and you are just as likely to buy the iPod today as you were yesterday.

This hypothetical situation makes an important point: Nominal incomes generally increase with inflation. Remember from Chapter 19 that we can think of the $250 price of the iPod as representing either the value of the product or the value of all the income generated in producing the product. The two amounts are the same, whether the iPod sells for $250 or $500. When the price of the iPod rises from $250 to $500, that extra $250 ends up as income that goes to the workers at Apple, the salespeople at Best Buy, or the stockholders of Apple, just as the first $250 did.

It's tempting to think that the problem with inflation is that, as prices rise, consumers can no longer afford to buy as many goods and services, but our example shows that this is a fallacy. An expected inflation rate of 10 percent will raise the average price of goods and services by 10 percent, but it will also raise average incomes by 10 percent. Goods and services will be as affordable to the average consumer as they were before the inflation.

Inflation Affects the Distribution of Income

If inflation will not reduce the affordability of goods and services to the average consumer, why do people dislike inflation? One reason is that the argument in the previous section applies to the *average* person but not to every person. Some people will find their incomes rising faster than the rate of inflation, and so their purchasing power will rise. Other people will find their incomes rising slower than the rate of inflation—or not at all—and their purchasing power will fall. People on fixed incomes are particularly likely to be hurt by inflation. If a retired worker receives a pension fixed at $2,000 per month, over time, inflation will reduce the purchasing power of that payment. In that way, inflation can change the distribution of income in a way that strikes many people as being unfair.

The extent to which inflation redistributes income depends in part on whether the inflation is *anticipated*—in which case consumers, workers, and firms can see it coming and can prepare for it—or *unanticipated*—in which case they do not see it coming and do not prepare for it.

The Problem with Anticipated Inflation

Like many of life's other problems, inflation is easier to manage if you see it coming. Suppose that everyone knows that the inflation rate for the next 10 years will be 10 percent per year. Workers know that unless their wages go up by at least 10 percent per year, the real purchasing power of their wages will fall. Businesses will be willing to increase workers' wages enough to compensate for inflation because they know that the prices of the products they sell will increase. Lenders will realize that the loans they make will be paid back with dollars that are losing 10 percent of their value each year, so they will charge a higher interest rate to compensate for this. Borrowers will be willing to pay these higher interest rates because they also know they are paying back these loans with dollars that are losing value. So far, there don't seem to be costs to anticipated inflation.

Even when inflation is perfectly anticipated, however, some individuals will experience a cost. Inevitably, there will be a redistribution of income, as some people's incomes fall behind even an anticipated level of inflation. In addition, firms and consumers have to hold some paper money to facilitate their buying and selling. Anyone holding paper money will find its purchasing power decreasing each year by the rate of inflation. To avoid this cost, workers and firms will try to hold as little paper money as possible, but they will have to hold some. In addition, firms that print catalogs listing the prices of their products will have to reprint them more frequently. Supermarkets and other stores that mark prices on packages or on store shelves will have to devote more time and labor to changing the marked prices. The costs to firms of changing prices are called **menu costs**. Although at moderate levels of anticipated inflation, menu costs are relatively small, at very high levels of inflation, such as are experienced in some developing countries, menu costs and the costs due to paper money losing value can become substantial. Finally, even anticipated inflation acts to raise the taxes paid by investors and raises the cost of capital for business investment. These effects arise because investors are taxed on the nominal payments they receive rather than on the real payments.

Menu costs The costs to firms of changing prices.

Making the Connection	Why a Lower Inflation Rate Is Like a Tax Cut for Alcatel-Lucent's Bondholders

Borrowers and lenders are interested in the real interest rate rather than the nominal interest rate. Therefore, if expected inflation increases, the nominal interest rate will rise, and if expected inflation decreases, the nominal interest rate will fall. Suppose that Alcatel-Lucent sells bonds to investors to raise funds to purchase investment goods. Suppose also that Alcatel-Lucent is willing to pay, and investors are willing to receive, a real interest rate of 4 percent. If the inflation rate is expected to be 2 percent, the nominal interest rate on Alcatel-Lucent's bonds must be 6 percent for the real interest rate to be 4 percent. If the inflation rate is expected to be 6 percent, the nominal rate on the bond must rise to 10 percent for the real interest rate to be 4 percent. The following table summarizes this information, assuming that the bond has a principal, or face value, of $1,000 (see Chapter 7 for a review of bonds).

PRINCIPAL	REAL INTEREST RATE	INFLATION RATE	NOMINAL INTEREST RATE
$1,000	4%	6%	10%
$1,000	4%	2%	6%

With a nominal interest rate of 6 percent, the interest payment (also known as the *coupon payment*) on newly issued bonds is $60. When the nominal interest rate rises to 10 percent, the interest payment on newly issued bonds is $100. Unfortunately for investors, the government taxes the nominal payment on bonds, with no adjustment for inflation. So, even though in this case, the increase in the interest payment from $60 to $100 represents only compensation for inflation, the whole $100 is subject to the income tax. The following table shows the effect of inflation on an investor's real after-tax interest payment, assuming a tax rate of 25 percent.

INFLATION RATE	NOMINAL INTEREST PAYMENT	TAX PAYMENT	AFTER-TAX INTEREST PAYMENT	ADJUSTMENT FOR INFLATION	REAL AFTER-TAX INTEREST PAYMENT
6%	$100	− $25	= $75	− $60	= $15
2%	$60	− $15	= $45	− $20	= $25

The table shows that reducing the inflation rate from 6 percent to 2 percent will increase the real after-tax payment received by investors who purchase a $1,000 Alcatel-Lucent bond from $15 to $25. By raising the after-tax reward to investors, lower inflation rates will increase the incentive for investors to lend funds to firms. The greater the flow of funds to firms, the greater the amount of investment spending that will occur.

YOUR TURN: Test your understanding by doing related problem 7.7 on page 693 at the end of this chapter.

The Problem with Unanticipated Inflation

In any advanced economy—such as the United States—households, workers, and firms routinely enter into contracts that commit them to make or receive certain payments for years in the future. For example, before it merged with Alcatel, Lucent Technologies in 2004 signed a seven-year wage contract with two of its unions. Once signed, this contract committed Lucent to paying a specified wage for the duration of the contract. When people buy homes, they usually borrow most of the amount they need from a bank. These loans, called *mortgage loans*, commit a borrower to make a fixed monthly payment for the length of the loan. Most mortgage loans are for long periods, often as much as 30 years.

To make these long-term commitments, households, workers, and firms must forecast the rate of inflation. If a firm believes the inflation rate over the next three years will be 6 percent per year, signing a three-year contract with a union that calls for wage increases of 8 percent per year may seem reasonable because the firm may be able to raise its prices by at least the rate of inflation each year. If the firm believes that the inflation rate will be only 2 percent over the next three years, paying wage increases of 8 percent may significantly reduce its profits or even force it out of business.

When people borrow money or banks lend money, they must forecast the inflation rate so they can calculate the real rate of interest on a loan. In 1980, banks were charging interest rates of 18 percent or more on mortgage loans. This rate seems very high compared to the roughly 6 percent charged on such loans in 2007, but the inflation rate in 1980 was more than 13 percent and was expected to remain high. In fact, the inflation rate declined unexpectedly during the early 1980s. By 1983, the inflation rate was only about 3 percent. People who borrowed money for 30 years at the high interest rates of 1980 soon found that the real interest rate on their loans was much higher than they expected.

When the actual inflation rate turns out to be very different from the expected inflation rate, some people gain, and other people lose. This outcome seems unfair to most people because they are either winning or losing only because something unanticipated has happened. This apparently unfair redistribution is a key reason why people dislike unanticipated inflation.

Economics in YOUR Life!

≫ Continued from page 659

At the beginning of this chapter, we posed a question: Should you change your career plans if you graduate during a recession when the unemployment rate is high? We have seen in this chapter that the high unemployment rates during a recession, although painful for people who lose their jobs, do not generally last very long. So, on the one hand, if you graduate with an engineering degree and want a job in manufacturing, you may have some difficulty finding one during a recession, but you probably do not need to change your career plans. On the other hand, if you plan at some point to earn a master's degree, you might consider staying in school to ride out the temporary increases in unemployment caused by the recession. You may also want to keep in mind the result of a recent study that college graduates who enter the labor force during a recession typically receive wages that are about 9 percent less than those received by college graduates who enter the labor force during an economic expansion.

Conclusion

Inflation and unemployment are key macroeconomic problems. Presidential elections are often won or lost on the basis of which candidate is able to convince the public that he or she can best deal with these problems. Many economists, however, would argue that, in the long run, maintaining high rates of growth of real GDP per person is the most important macroeconomic concern. Only when real GDP per person is increasing will a country's standard of living increase. We turn in the next chapter to discussing this important issue of economic growth.

Read *An Inside Look* on the next page for an example of a newspaper discussion of newly released government statistics on unemployment.

WALL STREET JOURNAL, FEBRUARY 3, 2007

Jobs Data Signal Growth Is Easing but Still Solid

U.S. employers were more cautious about taking on new workers in January, a hint that economic growth may be easing. But plenty of underlying signs suggest that a strong labor market will continue to lift wages and boost consumer spending in the months ahead.

(a) The Labor Department Friday said nonfarm payrolls rose by 110,000 jobs last month following December's gain of 206,000 jobs. The smaller increase in January—together with a rise in the unemployment rate to 4.6% from 4.5% in December and a tepid 0.2% gain in the typical employee's pay last month—suggests the economy is slowing somewhat after a strong finish to 2006.

But the tone of the report wasn't entirely soft. Revised data showed that employers brought on 80,000 more workers in November and December than initially thought, which means employers have added an average of 170,000 jobs a month since November. . . .

(b) In its annual revision, based on a thorough count of unemployment insurance tax records, the Labor Department said the economy created more than 2.2 million jobs last year, 400,000 more than previously estimated.

That helps explain why consumers seemed so resilient last year despite higher interest rates and a sharp reversal in the housing market, and it bodes well for economic growth this year. "One reason the U.S. economy has weathered this downdraft in housing and autos is that it's been generating a lot of income" for consumers, said Robert Gay, a former senior economist at the Federal Reserve. . . .

(c) White-collar, service-sector workers like Mr. Gay, now a hedge-fund consultant in New York, have been in particular demand. Employment in the category of professional and business services, which includes accountants, consultants and lawyers, grew by 25,000 positions in January. The health-care field added 18,000 workers last month and an average 28,000 positions a month last year.

FairPoint Communications Inc., a Charlotte, N.C., telecommunications company, said it plans to add 600 jobs this year, to "support field operations" and mostly in the accounting, logistics, information-technology and human-resources departments.

Roy Krause, chief executive of Spherion, a staffing firm in Fort Lauderdale, Fla., said, "You're taking out of a lot of companies the 60-year-old middle-management professional that needs to be replaced somehow." He said Spherion's professional placements are running 8% to 10% higher than a year ago, compared with 4% to 5% growth for clerical or industrial placements.

Amid the vigorous labor market, the University of Michigan yesterday said its consumer-sentiment survey rose to 96.9 in January from 91.7 in December, hitting its highest mark in two years. Meanwhile, the Commerce Department said factory orders surged 2.4% in December after a 1.2% gain in November, but underlying trends suggest the manufacturing sector could struggle in the months ahead as it works off stockpiles of unsold goods.

Key Points in the Article

This article discusses a jobs report that the U.S. Department of Labor released for January 2007. Although employment increased by 110,000, the unemployment rate increased slightly. The article also shows that U.S. job growth is not distributed proportionately across all sectors of the economy. For example, although these data are not included in this article, during 2006, while the national unemployment rate averaged 4.6 percent, the unemployment rate in the financial sector averaged less than 3 percent, while the unemployment rate in the construction sector topped 6 percent.

Analyzing the News

(a) On February 2, 2007, the U.S. Department of Labor announced that although the economy added 111,000 new jobs in January, the unemployment rate increased from 4.5 percent to 4.6 percent. This article actually combines information from the establishment survey and the household survey without alerting the reader. The number for the increase in employment is from the establishment survey, while the unemployment rates numbers are from the household survey. Not stated in the article is the fact that employment as measured by the household survey increased by only 31,000. This discrepancy between the measures of changes in employment is not unusual, as we saw in

Table 20-2 in the chapter. Because many economists consider the employment numbers in the establishment survey to be more reliable, they are the ones often reported in the media. But because the establishment survey does not measure unemployment and because there is significant public interest in changes in the unemployment rate, the household survey estimate of the unemployment rate is also reported.

(b) The article also mentions that each year, the Department of Labor revises the initial estimates of changes in employment by using additional sources of information, such as unemployment insurance tax records. Remember that both the establishment survey and the household survey are *surveys* rather than complete counts. It would be impossible for the government to gather information from every household for the household survey or every firm for the establishment survey. Instead, the Labor Department relies on samples of households and samples of firms. After the household survey has been completed each month, the Labor Department does not attempt to gather any more information from households on the labor market status, so the household survey data is never revised. The Labor Department does attempt to gather additional information on the number of workers actually on company payrolls and issues revisions of the payroll survey data as more information becomes available. In the case discussed in the article, the Department of Labor decided that employment had

increased by 400,000 more during 2006 than it had originally estimated.

(c) The jobs that the U.S. economy created between December 2006 and January 2007 were not distributed evenly across all sectors of the economy. In particular, the demand for workers in the information, financial, and education and health sectors was the strongest. This pattern is shown in the figure below, with the unemployment rates in these sectors during 2006 being some of the lowest among all sectors of the economy.

Thinking Critically

1. The figure shows that the unemployment rate in the construction industry in January 2007 was 6.7 percent, which was more than 2 percentage points above the overall unemployment rate. Some economists believed that beginning in 2005, housing construction entered a period of decline that might last for several years. If this assumption was true, how should we characterize unemployment in the construction industry: mainly frictional, mainly structural, mainly cyclical, or some combination of these types?

2. Suppose that you manage a used-book store in a college town. Your employees request a 3 percent wage increase for next year. Meanwhile, you expect inflation to be 4 percent next year. Should you agree to the 3 percent wage increase? Why or why not?

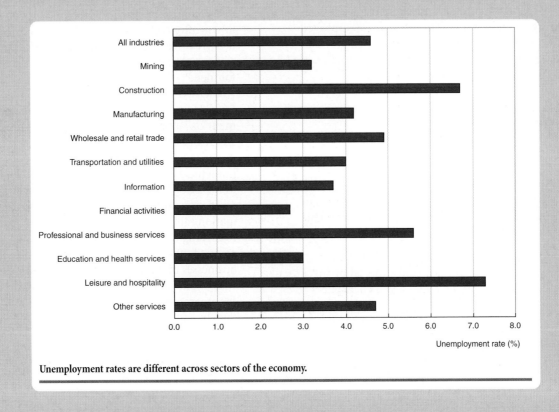

Unemployment rates are different across sectors of the economy.

Key Terms

Consumer price index (CPI), p. 675	Frictional unemployment, p. 668	Natural rate of unemployment, p. 669	Real interest rate, p. 680
Cyclical unemployment, p. 669	Inflation rate, p. 674	Nominal interest rate, p. 680	Structural unemployment, p. 669
Deflation, p. 682	Labor force, p. 660	Price level, p. 674	Unemployment rate, p. 660
Discouraged workers, p. 661	Labor force participation rate, p. 662	Producer price index (PPI), p. 677	
Efficiency wage, p. 673	Menu costs, p. 683		

> **20.1 LEARNING** OBJECTIVE   20.1 | Define unemployment rate and labor force participation rate and understand how they are computed, **pages 660–667.**

Measuring the Unemployment Rate and the Labor Force Participation Rate

Summary

The U.S. Bureau of Labor Statistics uses the results of the monthly household survey to calculate the *unemployment rate* and the *labor force participation rate*. The **labor force** is the total number of people who have jobs plus the number of people who do not have jobs but are actively looking for them. The **unemployment rate** is the percentage of the labor force that is unemployed. **Discouraged workers** are people who are available for work but who are not actively looking for a job. Discouraged workers are not counted as unemployed. The **labor force participation rate** is the percentage of the working-age population in the labor force. Since 1950, the labor force participation rate of women has been rising, while the labor force participation rate of men has been falling. White men and women have below-average unemployment rates. Teenagers and black men and women have above-average unemployment rates. The typical unemployed person finds a new job or returns to his or her previous job within a few months. Each year, millions of jobs are created and destroyed in the United States.

 ⓧ myeconlab   Visit www.myeconlab.com to complete these exercises
Get Ahead of the Curve online and get instant feedback.

Review Questions

1.1 How is the unemployment rate calculated? Which groups tend to have above-average unemployment rates, and which groups tend to have below-average unemployment rates?

1.2 How is the labor force participation rate calculated? In the years since 1950, how have the labor force participation rates of men and women changed?

1.3 What is the difference between the household survey and the establishment survey? Which survey do many economists prefer for measuring changes in employment? Why?

Problems and Applications

1.4 Fill in the missing values in the table of data collected in the household survey for the year 2007.

Working-age population	
Employment	146,047,000
Unemployment	
Unemployment rate	4.6%
Labor force	
Labor force participation rate	66.0%

1.5 (Related to the *Chapter Opener* on page 658) What would be some general reasons a firm would lay off a substantial number of workers?

1.6 Figure 20-2 on page 664 shows that the rapid increases in the labor force participation rate of women slowed down after 1995. Why might this slowdown have occurred? Discuss whether the labor force participation rate for women eventually might be equal to the rate for men.

1.7 (Related to *Solved Problem 20-1* on page 662) Homemakers are not included in the employment or labor force totals compiled in the Bureau of Labor Statistics household survey. They are included in the working-age population totals. Suppose that homemakers were counted as employed and included in the labor force statistics. What would be the impact on the unemployment rate and the labor force participation rate?

1.8 According to the Bureau of Labor Statistics, at the end of April 2008 there were 3.7 million job openings at businesses in the United States. At the same time, there were about 7.6 million people unemployed. Why didn't the unemployed workers accept these job openings, thereby reducing the total number of unemployed by almost 50 percent?

Source: U.S. Bureau of Labor Statistics.

1.9 (Related to the *Making the Connection* on page 664) In recent years, the percentage of men between the ages of 25 and 54 who are not in the labor force has increased. Suppose the federal government enacted a law that required the men between those ages who were not disabled or in school must either be in the labor force or pay a substantial fine. What would happen to measured GDP? What would happen to the measured income of these men? Would these men be better off as a result of this policy?

1.10 Between December 2001 and January 2002, the total number of people employed and the unemployment rate both fell. Briefly explain how this is possible.

1.11 The following appeared in a *BusinessWeek* article:

> [The household survey for January 2002] from the Bureau of Labor Statistics showed that the labor force participation rate—the percentage of people either employed or

actively job-hunting—fell by 0.8 percentage points over the past year, to 66.4%. . . . The sharp decline suggests the published unemployment rate understates the damage to the labor market.

Why would a fall in the labor force participation rate indicate that the unemployment rate is not doing a good job reflecting labor market conditions?

Source: "Climbing Out of the Job Pool," *BusinessWeek*, February 25, 2002, p. 32.

1.12 In an article on the conditions in the labor market, two business reporters remarked that the unemployment rate "typically rises months after the economy rebounds." What do they mean by the phrase "the economy rebounds"? Why would the unemployment rate be rising if the economy is rebounding?

Source: Vince Golle and Terry Barrett, "Hiring Picks Up, Factories Expand," *Bloomberg News*, April 1, 2002.

>> **End Learning Objective 20.1**

20.2 LEARNING OBJECTIVE   20.2 | Identify the three types of unemployment, **pages 668–670.**

Types of Unemployment

Summary

There are three types of unemployment: frictional, structural, and cyclical. **Frictional unemployment** is short-term unemployment that arises from the process of matching workers with jobs. One type of frictional unemployment is *seasonal unemployment*, which refers to unemployment due to factors such as weather, variations in tourism, and other calendar-related events. **Structural unemployment** arises from a persistent mismatch between the job skills or attributes of workers and the requirements of jobs. **Cyclical unemployment** is caused by a business cycle recession. The **natural rate of unemployment** is the normal rate of unemployment, consisting of structural unemployment and frictional unemployment. The natural rate of unemployment is also sometimes called the *full-employment rate of unemployment*.

myeconlab   Visit www.myeconlab.com to complete these exercises
Get Ahead of the Curve online and get instant feedback.

Review Questions

2.1 What is the relationship between frictional unemployment and job search?

2.2 Why isn't the natural rate of unemployment equal to zero?

Problems and Applications

2.3 Macroeconomic conditions affect the decisions firms and families make. Why, for example, might a college student after graduation enter the job market during an economic expansion but apply for graduate school during a recession?

2.4 (Related to the *Making the Connection* on page 670) What advice for finding a job would you give someone who is frictionally unemployed? What advice would you give someone who is structurally unemployed? What advice would you give someone who is cyclically unemployed?

2.5 Recall from Chapter 3 the definitions of normal and inferior goods. During an economic expansion, would you rather be working in an industry that produces a normal good or in an industry that produces an inferior good? Why? During a recession, would you rather be working in an industry that produces a normal good or an inferior good? Why?

2.6 If Congress eliminated the unemployment insurance system, what would be the effect on the level of frictional unemployment? What would be the effect on the level of real GDP? Would well-being in the economy be increased? Briefly explain.

>> **End Learning Objective 20.2**

Explaining Unemployment

Summary

Government policies can reduce the level of frictional and structural unemployment by aiding the search for jobs and the retraining of workers. Some government policies, however, can add to the level of frictional and structural unemployment. Unemployment insurance payments can raise the unemployment rate by extending the time that unemployed workers search for jobs. Government policies have caused the unemployment rates in most other industrial countries to be higher than in the United States. Wages above market levels can also increase unemployment. Wages may be above market levels because of the minimum wage, labor unions, and *efficiency wages*. An **efficiency wage** is a higher-than-market wage paid by a firm to increase worker productivity.

myeconlab   Visit www.myeconlab.com to complete these exercises
Get Ahead of the Curve online and get instant feedback.

Review Questions

3.1 What effect does the payment of government unemployment insurance have on the unemployment rate?

3.2 Discuss the effect of each of the following on the unemployment rate.
   a. The minimum wage law
   b. Labor unions
   c. Efficiency wages

Problems and Applications

3.3 In 2007, Ségolène Royal, who was running unsuccessfully for president of France, proposed that workers who lost their jobs would receive unemployment payments equal to 90 percent of their previous wages during their first year of unemployment. If this proposal were enacted, what would likely be the effect on the unemployment rate in France? Briefly explain.

Source: Alessandra Galloni and David Gauthier-Villars, "France's Royal Introduces Platform Ahead of Election," *Wall Street Journal*, February 12, 2007, p. A.8.

3.4 Discuss the likely impact of each of the following on the unemployment rate.
   a. The length of time workers are eligible to receive unemployment insurance payments doubles.
   b. The minimum wage is abolished.
   c. Most U.S. workers join labor unions.
   d. More companies make information on job openings easily available on Internet job sites.

3.5 Why do you think the minimum wage was set at only $0.25 per hour in 1938? Wouldn't this wage have been well below the equilibrium wage?

3.6 An economic consultant studies the labor policies of a firm where it is difficult to monitor workers and prepares a report in which she recommends that the firm raise employee wages. At a meeting of the firm's managers to discuss the report, one manager makes the following argument: "I think the wages we are paying are fine. As long as enough people are willing to work here at the wages we are currently paying, why should we raise them?" What argument can the economic consultant make to justify her advice that the firm should increase its wages?

3.7 (Related to the *Making the Connection* on page 673) If Wal-Mart adopted Costco's compensation policies, what would likely happen to the number of workers employed by Wal-Mart? Is it likely that consumers would be better off or worse off?

>> **End Learning Objective 20.3**

Measuring Inflation

Summary

The **price level** measures the average prices of goods and services. The **inflation rate** is equal to the percentage change in the price level from one year to the next. The federal government compiles statistics on three different measures of the price level: the consumer price index (CPI), the GDP price deflator, and the producer price index (PPI). The **consumer price index (CPI)** is an average of the prices of goods and services purchased by the typical urban family of four. Changes in the CPI are the best measure of changes in the cost of living as experienced by the typical household. Biases in the construction of the CPI cause changes in it to overstate the true inflation rate by one-half of a percentage point to one percentage point. The **producer price index (PPI)** is an average of prices received by producers of goods and services at all stages of production.

Review Questions

4.1 Briefly describe the three major measures of the price level. Which measure is used most frequently?

4.2 What potential biases exist in calculating the consumer price index? What steps has the Bureau of Labor Statistics taken to reduce the size of the biases?

Problems and Applications

4.3 (Related to the *Don't Let This Happen to You!* on page 676) Briefly explain whether you agree or disagree with the following statement: "I don't believe the government price statistics. The CPI for 2007 was 207, but I know that the inflation rate couldn't have been as high as 107 percent in 2007."

4.4 Briefly explain whether you agree with the following statement: "If changes in the CPI were a more accurate measure of the inflation rate, the federal government would pay less in Social Security payments each year."

4.5 Consider a simple economy that produces only three products. Use the information in the following table to calculate the inflation rate for 2009 as measured by the consumer price index.

		PRICE		
PRODUCT	QUANTITY	BASE YEAR (1999)	2008	2009
Haircuts	2	$10.00	$11.00	$16.20
Hamburgers	10	2.00	2.45	2.40
DVDs	6	15.00	15.00	14.00

4.6 The *Wall Street Journal* publishes an index of the prices of luxury homes in various cities. The base year for the index is January 2000. Here are the indexes for December 2005 and December 2006.

CITY	DECEMBER 2005	DECEMBER 2006
New York	184.6	193.1
Los Angeles	223.9	226.7
Chicago	153.4	157.1
Seattle	147.4	159.1

a. In which city did the prices of luxury homes increase the most during this year?

b. Can you determine on the basis of these numbers which city had the most expensive luxury homes in December 2006? Briefly explain.

Source: "Luxury Home Index," *Wall Street Journal*, December 29, 2006.

>> **End Learning Objective 20.4**

20.5 LEARNING OBJECTIVE 20.5 | Use price indexes to adjust for the effects of inflation, **pages 678–680.**

Using Price Indexes to Adjust for the Effects of Inflation

Summary

Price indexes are designed to measure changes in the price level over time, not the absolute level of prices. To correct for the effects of inflation, we can divide a *nominal variable* by a price index and multiply by 100 to obtain a *real variable*. The real variable will be measured in dollars of the base year for the price index.

Review Questions

5.1 What is the difference between a nominal variable and a real variable?

5.2 Briefly explain how you can use data on nominal wages for 2002 to 2008 and data on the consumer price index for the same years to calculate the real wage for these years.

Problems and Applications

5.3 (Related to *Solved Problem 20-5* on page 678) In 1914, when Henry Ford paid his workers $5 per day for an eight-hour day, the CPI was 10. In 2007, when the average wage in the automobile industry was about $30 per hour, the CPI was 207. Were auto workers in 1914 or auto workers in 2007 paid more in real terms? Be sure to show your calculation.

5.4 (Related to *Solved Problem 20-5* on page 678) Use the information in the following table to determine the percentage changes in the U.S. and French *real* minimum wages between 1956 and 2007.

	UNITED STATES		FRANCE	
YEAR	MINIMUM WAGE (DOLLARS PER HOUR)	CPI	MINIMUM WAGE (EUROS PER HOUR)	CPI
1956	$1.00	27	0.19 euros	10
2007	5.85	207	8.44 euros	116

Does it matter for your answer that you have not been told the base year for the U.S. CPI or the French CPI? Was the percentage increase in the price level greater in the United States or in France during these years?

Sources: John M. Abowd, Francis Kramarz, Thomas Lemieux, and David N. Margolis, "Minimum Wages and Youth Employment in France and the United States," in D. Blanchflower and R. Freeman, eds., *Youth Employment and Joblessness in Advanced Countries*, Chicago: University of Chicago Press, 1999, pp. 427–472 (the value for the minimum wage is given in francs; it was converted to euros at a conversion rate of 1 euro = 6.55957 francs); Insee online data bank, www.insee.fr; U.S. Department of Labor; and U.S. Bureau of Labor Statistics.

5.5 **(Related to *Solved Problem 20-5* on page 678)** The Great Depression was the worst economic disaster in U.S. history in terms of declines in real GDP and increases in the unemployment rate. Use the data in the following table to calculate the percentage decline in real GDP between 1929 and 1933.

YEAR	NOMINAL GDP (BILLIONS OF DOLLARS)	GDP PRICE DEFLATOR (2000 = 100)
1929	103.6	11.9
1933	56.4	8.9

5.6 **(Related to *Solved Problem 20-5* on page 678)** The following table shows the top 10 films of all time through 2007, measured by box office receipts in the United States, as well as several other films farther down the list:

RANK	FILM	TOTAL BOX OFFICE RECEIPTS	YEAR RELEASED	CPI
1	Titanic	$600,779,824	1997	161
2	Star Wars	460,935,655	1977	61
3	Shrek 2	436,471,036	2004	189
4	E.T. the Extra-Terrestrial	434,949,459	1982	97
5	Star Wars: Episode I— The Phantom Menace	431,065,444	1999	167
6	Pirates of the Caribbean: Dead Man's Chest	423,032,628	2006	202
7	Spider-Man	403,706,375	2002	180
8	Star Wars: Episode III— Revenge of the Sith	380,262,555	2005	195
9	Lord of the Rings: The Return of the King	377,019,252	2003	184
10	Spider-Man 2	373,377,893	2004	189
39	Jaws	260,000,000	1975	54
84	Gone with the Wind	198,655,278	1939	14
95	Snow White and the Seven Dwarfs	184,208,842	1937	14
138	The Sound of Music	163,214,286	1965	32
159	One Hundred and One Dalmatians	153,000,000	1961	30

The CPI in 2007 was 207. Use this information and the data in the table to calculate the box office receipts for each film in 2007 dollars. Assume that each film generated all of its box office receipts during the year it was released. Use your results to prepare a new list of the top 10 films based on their earnings in 2007 dollars. (Some of the films, such as the first *Star Wars* film, *Gone with the Wind*, and *Snow White and the Seven Dwarfs*, were re-released several times, so their receipts were actually earned during several different years, but we will ignore that complication.)

Source: IMDb online database, www.imdb.com.

>> End Learning Objective 20.5

20.6 LEARNING OBJECTIVE 20.6 | Distinguish between the nominal interest rate and the real interest rate, pages 680–682.

Real versus Nominal Interest Rates

Summary

The stated interest rate on a loan is the **nominal interest rate**. The **real interest rate** is the nominal interest rate minus the inflation rate. Because it is corrected for the effects of inflation, the real interest rate provides a better measure of the true cost of borrowing and the true return from lending than does the nominal interest rate. The nominal interest rate is always greater than the real interest rate unless the economy experiences *deflation*. **Deflation** is a decline in the price level.

myeconlab Visit www.myeconlab.com to complete these exercises online and get instant feedback. *Get Ahead of the Curve*

Review Questions

6.1 What is the difference between the nominal interest rate and the real interest rate?

6.2 If the inflation is expected to increase, what is likely to happen to the nominal interest rate? Briefly explain.

Problems and Applications

6.3 The following appeared in a newspaper article: "Inflation in the Lehigh Valley during the first quarter of [the year] was less than half the national rate. . . . So, unlike much of the nation, the fear here is deflation—when prices sink so low the CPI drops below zero." Do you agree with the reporter's definition of deflation? Briefly explain.

Source: Dan Shope, "Valley's Inflation Rate Slides." (*Allentown, PA*) *Morning Call*, July 9, 1996.

6.4 Suppose you were borrowing money to buy a car. Which of these situations would you prefer: The interest rate on your car loan is 20 percent and the inflation rate is 19 percent or the interest rate on your car loan is 5 percent and the inflation rate is 2 percent? Briefly explain.

6.5 Describing the situation in England in 1920, the historian Robert Skidelsky wrote the following: "Who would not borrow at 4 per cent a year, with prices going up 4 per cent a *month*?" What was the real interest rate paid by borrowers in this situation? (*Hint:* What is the annual inflation rate, if the monthly inflation rate is 4 percent?)

Source: Robert Skidelsky, *John Maynard Keynes: Volume 2, The Economist as Saviour, 1920–1937*, New York: The Penguin Press, 1992, p. 39, emphasis in original.

6.6 Suppose that the only good you purchase is hamburgers and that at the beginning of the year, the price of hamburgers is $2.00. Suppose you lend $1,000 for one year at an interest rate of 5 percent. At the end of the year, hamburgers cost $2.08. What was the real rate of interest you earned on your loan?

>> End Learning Objective 20.6

20.7 LEARNING OBJECTIVE   20.7 | Discuss the problems that inflation causes, **pages 682–684.**

Does Inflation Impose Costs on the Economy?

Summary

Inflation does not reduce the affordability of goods and services to the average consumer, but it still imposes costs on the economy. When inflation is anticipated, its main costs are that paper money loses some of its value and firms incur *menu costs*. **Menu costs** include the costs of changing prices on products and printing new catalogs. When inflation is unanticipated, the actual inflation rate can turn out to be different from the expected inflation rate. As a result, income is redistributed as some people gain and some people lose.

myeconlab   Visit www.myeconlab.com to complete these exercises
Get Ahead of the Curve online and get instant feedback.

Review Questions

7.1 How can inflation affect the distribution of income?

7.2 Which is a greater problem: anticipated inflation or unanticipated inflation? Why?

Problems and Applications

7.3 What are menu costs? What affect has the Internet had on the size of menu costs?

7.4 Suppose that the inflation rate turns out to be much higher than most people expected. In that case, would you rather have been a borrower or a lender? Briefly explain.

7.5 During the late nineteenth century in the United States, many farmers borrowed heavily to buy land. During most of the period between 1870 and the mid-1890s, the United States experienced mild deflation: The price level declined each year. Many farmers engaged in political protests during these years, and deflation was often a subject of their protests. Explain why farmers would have felt burdened by deflation.

7.6 Suppose James and Frank both retire this year. For income from retirement, James will rely on a pension from his company that pays him a fixed $2,500 per month for as long as he lives. James hasn't saved anything for retirement. Frank has no pension but has saved a considerable amount, which he has invested in certificates of deposit (CDs) at his bank. Currently, Frank's CDs pay him interest of $2,300 per month.

a. Ten years from now, is James or Frank likely to have a higher real income? In your answer, be sure to define real income.

b. Now suppose that instead of being a constant amount, James's pension increases each year by the same percentage as the CPI. For example, if the CPI increases by 5 percent in the first year after James retires, then his pension in the second year equals $2,500 + ($2,500 ×.05) = $2,625. In this case, 10 years from now, is James or Frank likely to have a higher real income?

7.7 (Related to the *Making the Connection* on page 683) Suppose that Alcatel-Lucent and the investors buying the firm's bonds both expect a 2 percent inflation rate for the year. Given that expectation, suppose the nominal interest rate on the bonds is 6 percent and the real interest rate is 4 percent. Suppose that a year after the investors have purchased the bonds, the inflation turns out to be 6 percent, rather than the 2 percent that had been expected. Who gains and who loses from the unexpectedly high inflation rate?

>> End Learning Objective 20.7

Economic Growth, the **Financial System,** and **Business Cycles**

Growth and the Business Cycle at Boeing

On the morning of December 17, 1903, at Kitty Hawk, North Carolina, the Wright Flyer became the first human-piloted, machine-powered, heavier-than-air craft to fly—for all of 12 seconds and a distance of 120 feet. Roughly a century later, on November 10, 2005, the Boeing 777-200LR became the first commercial aircraft to fly nonstop more than halfway around the world—for 22 hours and 42 minutes across 13,422 miles, from Hong Kong eastbound to London. This tremendous advance in aviation technology has been matched by technological progress in many other areas of the economy. In this chapter, we begin to explore how technological change has affected the standard of living in the United States and around the world.

Boeing was established in 1916, when William Boeing incorporated his twin-float seaplane business, which he later named Boeing Airplane Co. Today, Boeing is one of the world's largest

designers and manufacturers of commercial jetliners, military aircraft, satellites, missiles, and defense systems. The company is headquartered in Chicago and employs more than 150,000 people in 70 countries. Boeing's experiences have often mirrored those of the U.S. economy. Two key macroeconomic facts are that in the long run, the U.S. economy has experienced economic growth, and in the short run, the economy has experienced a series of business cycles. Living standards in the United States have increased enormously because, in the long run, growth in the production of goods and services has been faster than growth in population. But the increase in living standards has been interrupted by periods of business cycle recession during which production of goods and services has declined. Boeing has experienced growth over the long run, while also being affected by the business cycle.

For several years up through 2007, Boeing experienced an increase in orders as a result of economic growth in the United States, Europe, and several Asian countries. This growth peaked in 2007 when the firm received a record 1,413 orders for new commercial jets. While benefiting from economic growth, Boeing has been vulnerable to the business

cycle. Firms like Boeing that produce expensive durable goods are particularly likely to experience a decline in demand during a business cycle recession. For example, the U.S. economy experienced a recession in 2001, which, together with the terrorist attacks on September 11, caused orders for Boeing's commercial aircraft to decline by 45 percent. And in 2008, a slowing economy and rising fuel prices left Boeing once again facing the threat of declining orders and profits. In this chapter, we will provide an overview of long-run growth and the business cycle and discuss their importance for individual firms, for consumers, and for the economy as a whole.

For another example of how companies can contribute to, and benefit from, long-run economic growth, read **AN INSIDE LOOK AT POLICY** on **page 722**, where we discuss how China's domestic aviation market, which is the second largest in the world, is struggling because of a shortage of trained workers.

Sources: Lynn Lunsford, "Boeing's Boom Has Wings," *Wall Street Journal*, January 5, 2007, p. A8; Lynn Lunsford, "Ugly in the Air: Boeing's New Plane Gets Gawks and Stares," *Wall Street Journal*, January 8, 2007, p. A1; and James Wallace, "Boeing 777 Stretches Its Wings, Record," *Seattle-Post Intelligencer*, November 11, 2005, p. B2.

LEARNING Objectives

After studying this chapter, you should be able to:

21.1 Discuss the importance of **long-run economic growth**, page 696.

21.2 Discuss the role of the **financial system** in facilitating long-run economic growth, page 703.

21.3 Explain what happens during a **business cycle**, page 712.

Economics in YOUR Life!

If You Spend More, Will the Economy Grow More?

Suppose that, after a full day of unsuccessfully shopping for a pair of jeans, you decide to use the money you would have spent to open a savings account instead. When you return home empty handed, your roommate informs you that your decision to save instead of consume will reduce economic growth because consumption expenditures comprise over two-thirds of gross domestic product. How do you respond to your roommate's assertion? As you read this chapter, see if you can answer this question. You can check your answer against the one we provide at the end of the chapter. **>> Continued on page 721**

A key measure of the success of any economy is its ability to increase production of goods and services faster than the growth in population. Increasing production faster than population growth is the only way that the standard of living of the average person in a country can increase. Unfortunately, many economies around the world are not growing at all or are growing very slowly. In many countries in sub-Saharan Africa, living standards are barely higher, or in some cases are lower, than they were 50 years ago. Most people in these countries live in the same grinding poverty as their ancestors. In the United States and other developed countries, however, living standards are much higher than they were 50 years ago. An important macroeconomic question is why some countries grow much faster than others.

As we will see, one determinant of economic growth is the ability of firms to expand their operations, buy additional equipment, train workers, and adopt new technologies. To carry out these activities, firms must acquire funds from households, either directly through financial markets—such as the stock and bond markets—or indirectly through financial intermediaries—such as banks. Financial markets and financial intermediaries together comprise the *financial system*. In this chapter, we will present an overview of the financial system and see how funds flow from households to firms through the *market for loanable funds*.

Business cycle Alternating periods of economic expansion and economic recession.

Dating back to at least the early nineteenth century, the U.S. economy has experienced periods of expanding production and employment followed by periods of recession during which production and employment decline. As we noted in Chapter 19, these alternating periods of expansion and recession are called the **business cycle**. The business cycle is not uniform: Each period of expansion is not the same length, nor is each period of recession, but every period of expansion in U.S. history has been followed by a period of recession, and every period of recession has been followed by a period of expansion.

In this chapter, we begin the exploration of two key aspects of macroeconomics—the long-run growth that has steadily raised living standards in the United States and the short-run fluctuations of the business cycle.

21.1 | Discuss the importance of long-run economic growth.

Long-Run Economic Growth

Most people in the United States, Western Europe, Japan, and other advanced countries expect that over time, their standard of living will improve. They expect that year after year, firms will introduce new and improved products, new prescription drugs and better surgical techniques will overcome more diseases, and their ability to afford these goods and services will increase. For most people, these are reasonable expectations.

In 1900, the United States was already enjoying the highest standard of living in the world. Yet in that year, only 3 percent of U.S. homes had electricity, and only 15 percent had indoor flush toilets. Diseases such as smallpox, typhus, dysentery, and cholera were still menacing the health of Americans. In 1900, 5,000 of the 45,000 children born in Chicago died before their first birthday. In 1900, there were, of course, no televisions, radios, computers, air-conditioners, or refrigerators. Many homes were heated in the winter by burning coal, which contributed to the severe pollution that fouled the air of most large cities. There were no modern appliances, so most women worked inside the home at least 80 hours per week. The typical American homemaker in 1900 baked a half ton of bread per year.

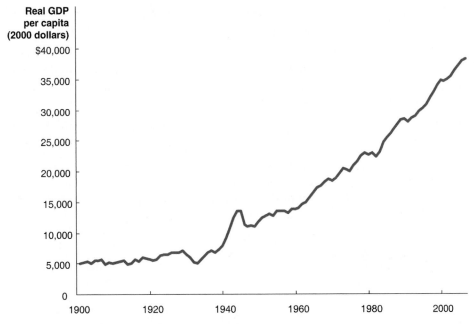

Figure 21-1 | The Growth in Real GDP per Capita, 1900–2007

Measured in 2000 dollars, real GDP per capita in the United States grew from about $4,900 in 1900 to about $38,000 in 2007. The average American in the year 2006 could buy nearly eight times as many goods and services as the average American in the year 1900.

Sources: Louis D. Johnston and Samuel H. Williamson, "The Annual Real and Nominal GDP for the United States, 1790–Present," Economic History Services, April 1, 2006, www.eh.net/hmit/gdp; and U.S. Bureau of Economic Analysis.

The process of **long-run economic growth** brought the typical American from the standard of living of 1900 to the standard of living of today. The best measure of the standard of living is real GDP per person, which is usually referred to as *real GDP per capita*. So, we measure long-run economic growth by increases in real GDP per capita over long periods of time, generally decades or more. We use real GDP rather than nominal GDP to adjust for changes in the price level over time. Figure 21-1 shows the growth in real GDP per capita in the United States from 1900 to 2007. The figure shows that although real GDP per capita fluctuates because of the short-run effects of the business cycle, over the long-run, the trend is strongly upward. It is the upward trend in real GDP per capita that we focus on when discussing long-run economic growth.

The values in Figure 21-1 are measured in prices of the year 2000, so they represent constant amounts of purchasing power. In 1900, real GDP per capita was about $4,900. Over a century later, in 2007, it had risen to about $38,000, which means that the average American in 2007 could purchase nearly eight times as many goods and services as the average American in 1900. Large as it is, this increase in real GDP per capita actually understates the true increase in the standard of living of Americans in 2007 compared with 1900. Many of today's goods and services were not available in 1900. For example, if you lived in 1900 and became ill with a serious infection, you would have been unable to purchase antibiotics to treat your illness—no matter how high your income. You might have died from an illness for which even a very poor person in today's society could receive effective medical treatment. Of course, the quantity of goods and services that a person can buy is not a perfect measure of how happy or contented that person may be. The level of pollution, the level of crime, spiritual well-being, and many other factors ignored in calculating GDP contribute to a person's happiness. Nevertheless, economists rely heavily on comparisons of real GDP per capita because it is the best means of comparing the performance of one economy over time or the performance of different economies at any particular time.

Long-run economic growth The process by which rising productivity increases the average standard of living.

Making
the
Connection | **The Connection between Economic Prosperity and Health**
We can see the direct impact of economic growth on living standards by looking at improvements in health in the high-income countries over the past 100 years. The research of Robert Fogel, winner of the Nobel Prize in Economics, has highlighted the close connection between economic growth, improvements in technology, and improvements in human physiology. One important measure of health is life expectancy at birth. As the following graph shows, in 1900 life expectancy was less than 50 years in the United States, the United Kingdom, and France. Today, life expectancy is about 80 years. Although life expectancies in the lowest-income countries remain very short, some countries that have begun to experience economic growth have seen dramatic increases in life expectancies. For example, life expectancy in India has more than doubled from 27 years in 1900 to 69 years today.

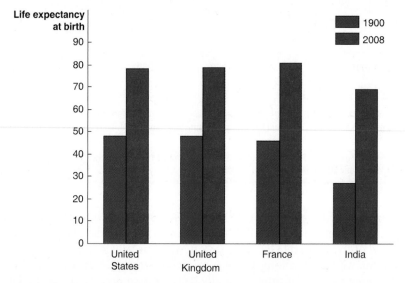

Sources: Robert William Fogel, *The Escape from Hunger and Premature Death, 1700–2100*, New York: Cambridge University Press, 2004, p. 2; and U.S. Central Intelligence Agency, *The 2008 World Factbook*, online version.

Many economists believe there is a link between health and economic growth. In the United States and Western Europe during the nineteenth century, improvements in agricultural technology and rising incomes led to dramatic improvements in the nutrition of the average person. The development of the germ theory of disease and technological progress in the purification of water in the late nineteenth century led to sharp declines in sickness due to waterborne diseases. As people became taller, stronger, and less susceptible to disease, they also became more productive. Today, economists studying economic development have put increasing emphasis on the need for low-income countries to reduce disease and increase nutrition if they are to experience economic growth.

Many researchers believe that the state of human physiology will continue to improve as technology advances. In high-income countries, life expectancy at birth is expected to rise from about 80 years today to about 90 years by the middle of the century. Technological advance will continue to reduce the average number of hours worked per day and the number of years the average person spends in the paid workforce. Individuals spend about 10 hours per day sleeping, eating, and bathing. Their remaining "discretionary hours" are divided between paid work and leisure. The following graph is based on estimates by Robert Fogel that contrast how individuals in the United States will divide their time in 2040 compared with 1880 and 1995.

Not only will technology and economic growth allow people in the near future to live longer lives, but a much smaller fraction of those lives will need to be spent at paid work.

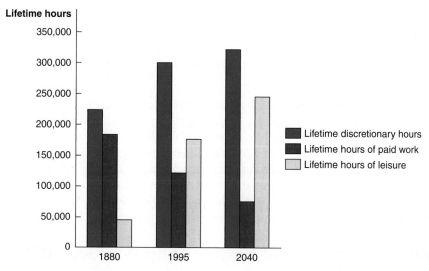

Source: Robert William Fogel, *The Escape from Hunger and Premature Death*, 1700–2100, New York: Cambridge University Press, 2004, p. 71.

YOUR TURN: Test your understanding by doing related problem 1.7 on page 724 at the end of this chapter.

Calculating Growth Rates and the Rule of 70

The growth rate of real GDP or real GDP per capita during a particular year is equal to the percentage change from the previous year. For example, measured in prices of the year 2000, real GDP equaled $11,319 billion in 2007 and rose to $11,567 billion in 2007. We calculate the growth of real GDP in 2007 as:

$$\left(\frac{\$11,567 \text{ billion} - \$11,319 \text{ billion}}{\$11,319 \text{ billion}} \right) \times 100 = 2.2\%.$$

For longer periods of time, we can use the *average annual growth rate*. For example, real GDP in the United States was $1,777 billion in 1950 and $11,567 billion in 2007. To find the average annual growth rate during this 57-year period, we compute the annual growth rate that would result in $1,777 billion increasing to $11,567 billion over 57 years. In this case, the growth rate is 3.3 percent. That is, if $1,777 billion grows at an average rate of 3.3 percent per year, after 57 years it will have grown to $11,567 billion.

For shorter periods of time, we get approximately the same answer by averaging the growth rate for each year. For example, real GDP in the United States grew by 3.1 percent in 2005, 2.9 percent in 2006, and 2.2 percent in 2007. So, the average annual growth rate of real GDP for the period 2005–2007 was 2.7 percent, which is the average of the three annual growth rates:

$$\frac{3.1\% + 2.9\% + 2.2\%}{3} = 2.7\%.$$

When discussing long-run economic growth, we usually shorten "average annual growth rate" to "growth rate."

We can judge how rapidly an economic variable is growing by calculating the number of years it would take to double. For example, if real GDP per capita in a country doubles, say, every 20 years, most people in the country will experience significant increases in their standard of living over the course of their lives. If real GDP per capita doubles only every 100 years, increases in the standard of living will be too slow to notice. One easy way to calculate approximately how many years it will take real GDP per capita to double is to use the *rule of 70*. The formula for the rule of 70 is as follows:

$$\text{Number of years to double} = \frac{70}{\text{Growth rate}}.$$

For example, if real GDP per capita is growing at a rate of 5 percent per year, it will double in 70/5 = 14 years. If real GDP per capita is growing at the rate of 2 percent per year, it will take 70/2 = 35 years to double. These examples illustrate an important point that we will discuss further in Chapter 22: Small differences in growth rates can have large effects on how rapidly the standard of living in a country increases. Finally, notice that the rule of 70 applies not just to growth in real GDP per capita but to growth in any variable. For example, if you invest $1,000 in the stock market, and your investment grows at an average annual rate of 7 percent, your investment will double to $2,000 in 10 years.

What Determines the Rate of Long-Run Growth?

In Chapter 22, we will explore the sources of economic growth in more detail and discuss why growth in the United States and other high-income countries has been so much faster than growth in poorer countries. For now, we will focus on the basic point that *increases in real GDP per capita depend on increases in labor productivity*. **Labor productivity** is the quantity of goods and services that can be produced by one worker or by one hour of work. In analyzing long-run growth, economists usually measure labor productivity as output per hour of work to avoid the effects of fluctuations in the length of the workday and in the fraction of the population employed. If the quantity of goods and services consumed by the average person is to increase, the quantity of goods and services produced per hour of work must also increase. Why in 2007 was the average American able to consume almost eight times as many goods and services as the average American in 1900? Because the average American worker in 2007 was eight times as productive as the average American worker in 1900.

If increases in labor productivity are the key to long-run economic growth, what causes labor productivity to increase? Economists believe two key factors determine labor productivity: the quantity of capital per hour worked and the level of technology. Therefore, economic growth occurs if the quantity of capital per hour worked increases and if technological change occurs.

Increases in Capital per Hour Worked Workers today in high-income countries such as the United States have more physical capital available than workers in low-income countries or workers in the high-income countries of 100 years ago. Recall that **capital** refers to manufactured goods that are used to produce other goods and services. Examples of capital are computers, factory buildings, machine tools, warehouses, and trucks. The total amount of physical capital available in a country is known as the country's *capital stock*.

As the capital stock per hour worked increases, worker productivity increases. A secretary with a personal computer can produce more documents per day than a secretary who has only a typewriter. A worker with a backhoe can excavate more earth than a worker who has only a shovel.

Human capital refers to the accumulated knowledge and skills workers acquire from education and training or from their life experiences. For example, workers with a college education generally have more skills and are more productive than workers who have only a high school degree. Increases in human capital are particularly important in stimulating economic growth.

Technological Change Economic growth depends more on *technological change* than on increases in capital per hour worked. Technology refers to the processes a firm uses to turn inputs into outputs of goods and services. Technological change is an increase in the quantity of output firms can produce using a given quantity of inputs. Technological change can come from many sources. For example, a firm's managers may rearrange a factory floor or the layout of a retail store to increase production and sales. Most technological change, however, is embodied in new machinery, equipment, or software.

Labor productivity The quantity of goods and services that can be produced by one worker or by one hour of work.

Capital Manufactured goods that are used to produce other goods and services.

A very important point is that just accumulating more inputs—such as labor, capital, and natural resources—will not ensure that an economy experiences economic growth unless technological change also occurs. For example, the Soviet Union failed to maintain a high rate of economic growth, even though it continued to increase the quantity of capital available per hour worked, because it experienced relatively little technological change.

In implementing technological change, *entrepreneurs* are of crucial importance. Recall from Chapter 2 that an entrepreneur is someone who operates a business, bringing together the factors of production—labor, capital, and natural resources—to produce goods and services. In a market economy, entrepreneurs make the crucial decisions about whether to introduce new technology to produce better or lower-cost products. Entrepreneurs also decide whether to allocate the firm's resources to research and development that can result in new technologies. One of the difficulties centrally planned economies have in sustaining economic growth is that managers employed by the government are usually much slower to develop and adopt new technologies than entrepreneurs in a market system.

Solved Problem | 21-1

The Role of Technological Change in Growth

Between 1960 and 1995, real GDP per capita in Singapore grew at an average annual rate of 6.2 percent. This very rapid growth rate results in the level of real GDP per capita doubling about every 11.5 years. In 1995, Alywn Young of the University of Chicago published an article in which he argued that Singapore's growth depended more on increases in capital per hour worked, increases in the labor force participation rate, and the transfer of workers from agricultural to nonagricultural jobs than on technological change. If Young's analysis was correct, predict what was likely to happen to Singapore's growth rate in the years after 1995.

SOLVING THE PROBLEM:

Step 1: **Review the chapter material.** This problem is about what determines the rate of long-run growth, so you may want to review the section "What Determines the Rate of Long-Run Growth?" which begins on page 700.

Step 2: **Predict what happened to the growth rate in Singapore after 1995.** As countries begin to develop, they often experience an increase in the labor force participation rate, as workers who are not part of the paid labor force respond to rising wage rates. Many workers also leave the agricultural sector—where output per hour worked is often low—for the nonagricultural sector. These changes increase real GDP per capita, but they are "one-shot" changes that eventually come to an end, as the labor force participation rate and the fraction of the labor force outside agriculture both approach the levels found in high-income countries. Similarly, as we already noted, increases in capital per hour worked cannot sustain high rates of economic growth unless they are accompanied by technological change.

We can conclude that Singapore was unlikely to sustain its high growth rates in the years after 1995. In fact, from 1996 to 2007, the growth of real GDP per capita slowed to an average rate of 2.5 percent per year. Although this growth rate is comparable to those experienced in high-income countries, such as the United States, it leads to a doubling of real GDP per capita only every 28 years rather than every 11.5 years.

Source: Alwyn Young, "The Tyranny of Numbers: Confronting the Statistical Realities of the East Asian Growth Experience," *Quarterly Journal of Economics*, Vol. 110, No. 3, August 1995, pp. 641–680.

YOUR TURN: For more practice, do related problem 1.12 on page 725 at the end of this chapter.   **>> End Solved Problem 21-1**

Finally, an additional requirement for economic growth is that the government provides secure rights to private property. As we saw in Chapter 2, a market system cannot function unless rights to private property are secure. In addition, the government can help the market work and aid economic growth by establishing an independent court system that enforces contracts between private individuals. Many economists would also say the government has a role in facilitating the development of an efficient financial system, as well as systems of education, transportation, and communication. Economist Richard Sylla of New York University has argued that every country that has experienced economic growth first experienced a "financial revolution." For example, before the United States was able to experience significant economic growth in the early nineteenth century, the country's banking and monetary systems were reformed under the guidance of Alexander Hamilton, the first secretary of the treasury. Without supportive government policies, long-run economic growth is unlikely.

Making the Connection | What Explains Rapid Economic Growth in Botswana?

Economic growth in much of sub-Saharan Africa has been very slow. As desperately poor as most of these countries were in 1960, some are even poorer today. The growth rate in one country in this region stands out, however, as being exceptionally rapid. The following graph shows the average annual growth rate in real GDP per capita between 1960 and 2004 for Botswana and the six most populous sub-Saharan countries. Botswana's average annual growth rate over this 44-year period was four times as great as that of Tanzania and South Africa, which were the second-fastest-growing countries in the group. Botswana may seem an unlikely country to experience rapid growth because it has been hard hit by the HIV epidemic. Despite the disruptive effects of the epidemic, growth in real per capita GDP slowed only moderately to 4.7 percent in 2007.

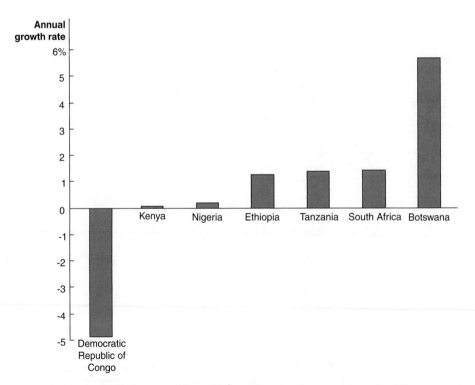

Note: Data for Democratic Republic of Congo are for 1970–2004.

Source: Authors' calculations from data in Alan Heston, Robert Summers, and Bettina Aten, *Penn World Table Version 6.2*, Center for International Comparisons of Production, Income and Prices at the University of Pennsylvania, September 2006.

What explains Botswana's rapid growth rate? Several factors have been important. Botswana avoided the civil wars that plagued other African countries during these years. The country also benefited from earnings from diamond exports. But many economists believe the pro-growth policies of its government are the most important reason for the country's success. Economists Shantayanan Devarajan of the World Bank, William Easterly of New York University, and Howard Pack of the University of Pennsylvania have summarized these policies:

> The government [of Botswana] made it clear it would protect private property rights. It was a "government of cattlemen" who were attuned to commercial interests. . . . The relative political stability and relatively low corruption also made Botswana a favorable location for investment. Botswana's relatively high level of press freedom and democracy (continuing a pre-colonial tradition that held chiefs responsible to tribal members) held the government responsible for any economic policy mistakes.

These policies—protecting private property, avoiding political instability and corruption, and allowing press freedom and democracy—may seem a straightforward recipe for providing an environment in which economic growth can occur. As we will see in Chapter 22, however, in practice, these are policies many countries have difficulty implementing successfully.

Source: Shantayanan Devarajan, William Easterly, and Howard Pack, "Low Investment Is Not the Constraint on African Development," *Economic Development and Cultural Change*, Vol. 51, No. 3, April 2003, pp. 547–571.

YOUR TURN: Test your understanding by doing related problem 1.14 on page 725 at the end of this chapter.

Potential Real GDP

Because economists take a long-run perspective in discussing economic growth, the concept of *potential GDP* is useful. **Potential GDP** is the level of GDP attained when all firms are producing at capacity. The capacity of a firm is *not* the maximum output the firm is capable of producing. A Boeing assembly plant could operate 24 hours per day for 52 weeks per year and would be at its maximum production level. The plant's capacity, however, is measured by its production when operating on normal hours, using a normal workforce. If all firms in the economy were operating at capacity, the level of total production of final goods and services would equal potential GDP. Potential GDP will increase over time as the labor force grows, new factories and office buildings are built, new machinery and equipment are installed, and technological change takes place.

Growth in potential real GDP in the United States is estimated to be about 3.5 percent per year. In other words, each year, the capacity of the economy to produce final goods and services expands by 3.5 percent. The *actual* level of GDP may increase by more or less than 3.5 percent as the economy moves through the business cycle. Figure 21-2 on page 704 shows movements in actual and potential real GDP for the years since 1950. The smooth light blue line represents potential real GDP, and the dark blue line represents actual real GDP.

Potential GDP The level of GDP attained when all firms are producing at capacity.

21.2 | Discuss the role of the financial system in facilitating long-run economic growth.   **21.2 LEARNING** OBJECTIVE

Saving, Investment, and the Financial System

The process of economic growth depends on the ability of firms to expand their operations, buy additional equipment, train workers, and adopt new technologies. Firms can finance some of these activities from *retained earnings*, which are profits that are

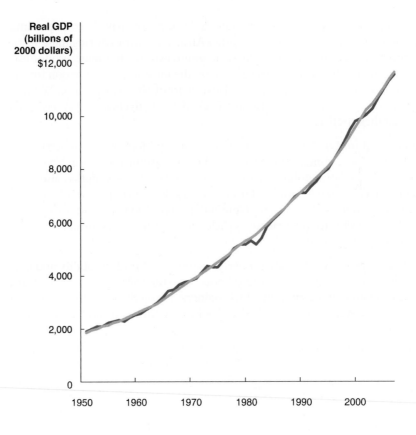

Figure 21-2 | Actual and Potential Real GDP

Potential real GDP increases every year as the labor force and the capital stock grow and technological change occurs. The smooth light blue line represents potential real GDP, and the dark blue line represents actual real GDP. Because of the business cycle, actual real GDP has sometimes been greater than potential real GDP and sometimes less.

Sources: Congressional Budget Office, *Spreadsheets for Selected Estimates and Projections*, January 2008; and U.S. Bureau of Economic Analysis.

reinvested in the firm rather than paid to the firm's owners. For many firms, retained earnings are not sufficient to finance the rapid expansion required in economies experiencing high rates of economic growth. Firms acquire funds from households, either directly through financial markets—such as the stock and bond markets—or indirectly through financial intermediaries—such as banks. Financial markets and financial intermediaries together comprise the **financial system**. Without a well-functioning financial system, economic growth is impossible because firms will be unable to expand and adopt new technologies. As we noted earlier, no country without a well-developed financial system has been able to sustain high levels of economic growth.

Financial system The system of financial markets and financial intermediaries through which firms acquire funds from households.

An Overview of the Financial System

The financial system channels funds from savers to borrowers and channels returns on the borrowed funds back to savers. Recall from Chapter 7 that in **financial markets**, such as the stock market or the bond market, firms raise funds by selling financial securities directly to savers. A financial security is a document—sometimes in electronic form—that states the terms under which funds pass from the buyer of the security—who is lending funds—to the seller. *Stocks* are financial securities that represent partial ownership of a firm. If you buy one share of stock in General Electric, you become one of

Financial markets Markets where financial securities, such as stocks and bonds, are bought and sold.

millions of owners of that firm. *Bonds* are financial securities that represent promises to repay a fixed amount of funds. When General Electric sells a bond, the firm promises to pay the purchaser of the bond an interest payment each year for the term of the bond, as well as a final payment of the amount of the loan.

Financial intermediaries, such as banks, mutual funds, pension funds, and insurance companies, act as go-betweens for borrowers and lenders. In effect, financial intermediaries borrow funds from savers and lend them to borrowers. When you deposit funds in your checking account, you are lending your funds to the bank. The bank may lend your funds (together with the funds of other savers) to an entrepreneur who wants to start a business. Suppose Lena wants to open a laundry. Rather than you lending money directly to Lena's Laundry, the bank acts as a go-between for you and Lena. Intermediaries pool the funds of many small savers to lend to many individual borrowers. The intermediaries pay interest to savers in exchange for the use of savers' funds and earn a profit by lending money to borrowers and charging borrowers a higher rate of interest on the loans. For example, a bank might pay you as a depositor a 3 percent rate of interest, while it lends the money to Lena's Laundry at a 6 percent rate of interest.

Financial intermediaries Firms, such as banks, mutual funds, pension funds, and insurance companies, that borrow funds from savers and lend them to borrowers.

Banks, mutual funds, pension funds, and insurance companies also make investments in stocks and bonds on behalf of savers. For example, *mutual funds* sell shares to savers and then use the funds to buy a portfolio of stocks, bonds, mortgages, and other financial securities. Mutual funds are either closed-end or open-end funds. In closed-end mutual funds, the mutual fund company issues shares that investors may buy and sell in financial markets, like shares of stock issued by corporations. More common are open-end mutual funds, which issue shares that the mutual fund company will buy back—or redeem—at a price that represents the underlying value of the financial securities owned by the fund. Large mutual fund companies, such as Fidelity, Vanguard, and Dreyfus, offer many alternative stock and bond funds. Some funds hold a wide range of stocks or bonds; others specialize in securities issued by a particular industry or sector, such as technology; and others invest as an index fund in a fixed market basket of securities such as shares of the Standard & Poor's 500 firms. Over the past 30 years, the role of mutual funds in the financial system has increased dramatically. By 2008, competition among hundreds of mutual fund firms gave investors thousands of funds from which to choose.

In addition to matching households that have excess funds with firms that want to borrow funds, the financial system provides three key services for savers and borrowers: risk sharing, liquidity, and information. *Risk* is the chance that the value of a financial security will change relative to what you expect. For example, you may buy a share of stock in Google at a price of $450, only to have the price fall to $100. Most individual savers are not gamblers and seek a steady return on their savings rather than erratic swings between high and low earnings. The financial system provides risk sharing by allowing savers to spread their money among many financial investments. For example, you can divide your money among a bank certificate of deposit, individual bonds, and a mutual fund.

Liquidity is the ease with which a financial security can be exchanged for money. The financial system provides the service of liquidity by providing savers with markets in which they can sell their holdings of financial securities. For example, savers can easily sell their holdings of the stocks and bonds issued by large corporations on the major stock and bond markets.

A third service that the financial system provides savers is the collection and communication of *information*, or facts about borrowers and expectations about returns on financial securities. For example, Lena's Laundry may want to borrow $10,000 from you. Finding out what Lena intends to do with the funds and how likely she is to pay you back may be costly and time-consuming. By depositing $10,000 in the bank, you are, in effect, allowing the bank to gather this information for you. Because banks specialize in gathering information on borrowers, they are able to do it faster and at a lower cost than can individual savers. The financial system plays an important role in communicating information. If you read a newspaper headline announcing that an automobile firm has invented a car with an engine that runs on water, how would you determine the effect of this discovery on the firm's profits? Financial markets do that job for you by incorporating information into the prices of stocks, bonds, and other financial securities. In this example, the expectation of higher future profits would boost the prices of the automobile firm's stock and bonds.

The Macroeconomics of Saving and Investment

As we have seen, the funds available to firms through the financial system come from saving. When firms use funds to purchase machinery, factories, and office buildings, they are engaging in investment. In this section, we explore the macroeconomics of saving and investment. A key point we will develop is that *the total value of saving in the economy must equal the total value of investment.* We saw in Chapter 19 that *national income accounting* refers to the methods the Bureau of Economic Analysis uses to keep track of total production and total income in the economy. We can use some relationships from national income accounting to understand why total saving must equal total investment.

We begin with the relationship between GDP (Y) and its components, consumption (C), investment (I), government purchases (G), and net exports (NX):

$$Y = C + I + G + NX.$$

Remember that GDP is a measure of both total production in the economy and total income.

In an *open economy*, there is interaction with other economies in terms of both trading of goods and services and borrowing and lending. All economies today are open economies, although they vary significantly in the extent of their openness. In a *closed economy*, there is no trading or borrowing and lending with other economies. For simplicity, we will develop the relationship between saving and investment for a closed economy. This allows us to focus on the most important points in a simpler framework. We will consider the case of an open economy in Chapter 29.

In a closed economy, net exports are zero, so we can rewrite the relationship between GDP and its components as:

$$Y = C + I + G.$$

If we rearrange this relationship, we have an expression for investment in terms of the other variables:

$$I = Y - C - G.$$

This expression tells us that in a closed economy, investment spending is equal to total income minus consumption spending and minus government purchases.

We can also derive an expression for total saving. *Private saving* is equal to what households retain of their income after purchasing goods and services (C) and paying taxes (T). Households receive income for supplying the factors of production to firms. This portion of household income is equal to Y. Households also receive income from government in the form of *transfer payments* (TR). Recall that transfer payments include Social Security payments and unemployment insurance payments. We can write an expression for private saving ($S_{private}$):

$$S_{private} = Y + TR - C - T.$$

The government also engages in saving. *Public saving* (S_{public}) equals the amount of tax revenue the government retains after paying for government purchases and making transfer payments to households:

$$S_{public} = T - G - TR.$$

So, total saving in the economy (S) is equal to the sum of private saving and public saving:

$$S = S_{\text{private}} + S_{\text{public}},$$

or:

$$S = (Y + TR - C - T) + (T - G - TR),$$

or:

$$S = Y - C - G.$$

The right-hand side of this expression is identical to the expression we derived earlier for investment spending. So, we can conclude that total saving must equal total investment:

$$S = I.$$

When the government spends the same amount that it collects in taxes, there is a *balanced budget*. When the government spends more than it collects in taxes, there is a *budget deficit*. In the case of a deficit, T is less than $G + TR$, which means that public saving is negative. Negative saving is also known as *dissaving*. How can public saving be negative? When the federal government runs a budget deficit, the U.S. Department of the Treasury sells Treasury bonds to borrow the money necessary to fund the gap between taxes and spending. In this case, rather than adding to the total amount of saving available to be borrowed for investment spending, the government is subtracting from it. (Notice that if households borrow more than they save, the total amount of saving will also fall.) With less saving, investment must also be lower. We can conclude that, holding constant all other factors, there is a lower level of investment spending in the economy when there is a budget deficit than when there is a balanced budget.

When the government spends less than it collects in taxes, there is a *budget surplus*. A budget surplus increases public saving and the total level of saving in the economy. A higher level of saving results in a higher level of investment spending. Therefore, holding constant all other factors, there is a higher level of investment spending in the economy when there is a budget surplus than when there is a balanced budget.

The U.S. federal government has experienced dramatic swings in the state of its budget over the past 15 years. In 1992, the federal budget deficit was $297.4 billion. This figure changed to a surplus of $189.5 billion in 2000 and was back to a deficit of $220.6 billion in 2007.

The Market for Loanable Funds

We have seen that the value of total saving must equal the value of total investment, but we have not yet discussed how this equality actually is brought about in the financial system. We can think of the financial system as being composed of many markets through which funds flow from lenders to borrowers: the market for certificates of deposit at banks, the market for stocks, the market for bonds, the market for mutual fund shares, and so on. For simplicity, we can combine these markets into a single market for *loanable funds*. In the model of the **market for loanable funds**, the interaction of borrowers and lenders determines the market interest rate and the quantity of loanable funds exchanged. As we will discuss in Chapter 29, firms can also borrow from savers in other countries. For the remainder of this chapter, we will assume that there are no interactions between households and firms in the United States and those in other countries.

Market for loanable funds The interaction of borrowers and lenders that determines the market interest rate and the quantity of loanable funds exchanged.

Demand and Supply in the Loanable Funds Market
The demand for loanable funds is determined by the willingness of firms to borrow money to engage in new investment projects, such as building new factories or carrying out research and development of new products. In determining whether to borrow funds, firms

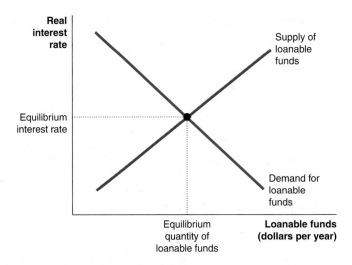

Figure 21-3 | The Market for Loanable Funds

The demand for loanable funds is determined by the willingness of firms to borrow money to engage in new investment projects. The supply of loanable funds is determined by the willingness of households to save and by the extent of government saving or dissaving. Equilibrium in the market for loanable funds determines the real interest rate and the quantity of loanable funds exchanged.

compare the return they expect to make on an investment with the interest rate they must pay to borrow the necessary funds. For example, if Home Depot is considering opening several new stores and expects to earn a return of 15 percent on its investment, the investment will be profitable if it can borrow the funds at an interest rate of 10 percent but will not be profitable if the interest rate is 20 percent. In Figure 21-3, the demand for loanable funds is downward sloping because the lower the interest rate, the more investment projects firms can profitably undertake, and the greater the quantity of loanable funds they will demand.

The supply of loanable funds is determined by the willingness of households to save and by the extent of government saving or dissaving. When households save, they reduce the amount of goods and services they can consume and enjoy today. The willingness of households to save rather than consume their incomes today will be determined in part by the interest rate they receive when they lend their savings. The higher the interest rate, the greater the reward to saving and the larger the amount of funds households will save. Therefore, the supply curve for loanable funds in Figure 21-3 is upward sloping because the higher the interest rate, the greater the quantity of saving supplied.

In Chapter 20, we discussed the distinction between the *nominal interest rate* and the *real interest rate*. The nominal interest rate is the stated interest rate on a loan. The real interest rate corrects the nominal interest rate for the impact of inflation and is equal to the nominal interest rate minus the inflation rate. Because both borrowers and lenders are interested in the real interest rate they will receive or pay, equilibrium in the market for loanable funds determines the real interest rate rather than the nominal interest rate.

Making the Connection | **Ebenezer Scrooge: Accidental Promoter of Economic Growth?**

Ebenezer Scrooge's name has become synonymous with miserliness. Before his reform at the end of Charles Dickens's *A Christmas Carol*, Scrooge is extraordinarily reluctant to spend money. Although he earns a substantial income, he lives in a cold, dark house that he refuses to heat or light properly, and he eats a meager diet of gruel because he refuses to buy more expensive food. Throughout most of the book, Dickens portrays Scrooge's behavior in an unfavorable way. Only at the end of the book, when the reformed Scrooge begins to spend lavishly on himself and others, does Dickens praise his behavior.

As economist Steven Landsburg of the University of Rochester points out, however, economically speaking, it may be the pre-reform Scrooge who is more worthy of praise:

> In this whole world, there is nobody more generous than the miser—the man who *could* deplete the world's resources but chooses not to. The only difference between miserliness and philanthropy is that the philanthropist serves a favored few while the miser spreads his largess far and wide.

Who was better for economic growth: Scrooge the saver or Scrooge the spender?

We can extend Landsburg's discussion to consider whether the actions of the pre-reform Scrooge or the actions of the post-reform Scrooge were more helpful to economic growth. Pre-reform Scrooge spends very little, investing most of his income in the financial markets. These funds became available for firms to borrow to build new factories and to carry out research and development. Post-reform Scrooge spends much more—and saves much less. Funds that he had previously saved are now spent on food for Bob Cratchit's family and on "making merry" at Christmas. In other words, the actions of post-reform Scrooge contributed to more consumption goods being produced and fewer investment goods. We can conclude that Scrooge's reform caused economic growth to slow down—if only by a little. The larger point is, of course, that savers provide the funds that are indispensable for the investment spending that economic growth requires, and the only way to save is to not consume.

Source: Steven E. Landsburg, "What I Like About Scrooge," *Slate*, December 9, 2004.

YOUR TURN: Test your understanding by doing related problem 2.17 on page 727 at the end of this chapter

---

Explaining Movements in Saving, Investment, and Interest Rates

Equilibrium in the market for loanable funds determines the quantity of loanable funds that will flow from lenders to borrowers each period. It also determines the real interest rate that lenders will receive and that borrowers must pay. We draw the demand curve for loanable funds by holding constant all factors, other than the interest rate, that affect the willingness of borrowers to demand funds. We draw the supply curve by holding constant all factors, other than the interest rate, that affect the willingness of lenders to supply funds. A shift in either the demand curve or the supply curve will change the equilibrium interest rate and the equilibrium quantity of loanable funds.

Suppose, for example, that the profitability of new investment increases due to technological change. Firms will increase their demand for loanable funds. Figure 21-4 shows the impact of an increase in demand in the market for loanable funds. As in the markets for goods and services we studied in Chapter 3, an increase in demand in the market for loanable funds shifts the demand curve to the right. In the new equilibrium, the interest rate increases from i_1 to i_2, and the equilibrium quantity of loanable funds increases from L_1 to L_2. Notice that an increase in the quantity of loanable funds means that both the quantity of saving by households and the quantity of investment by firms have increased. Increasing investment increases the capital stock and the quantity of capital per hour worked, helping to increase economic growth.

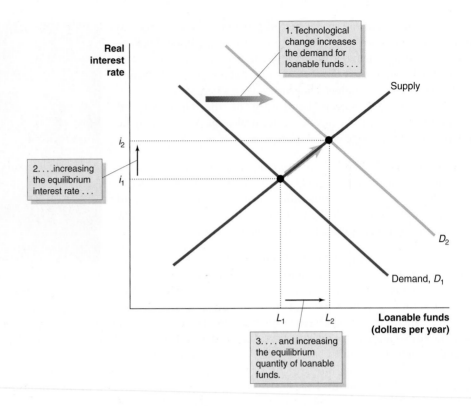

Figure 21-4 | An Increase in the Demand for Loanable Funds

An increase in the demand for loanable funds increases the equilibrium interest rate from i_1 to i_2, and it increases the equilibrium quantity of loanable funds from L_1 to L_2. As a result, saving and investment both increase.

We can also use the market for loanable funds to examine the impact of a government budget deficit. Putting aside the effects of foreign saving—which we will consider in Chapter 29—recall that if the government begins running a budget deficit, it reduces the total amount of saving in the economy. Suppose the government increases spending, which results in a budget deficit. We illustrate the effects of the budget deficit in Figure 21-5 by shifting the supply of loanable funds to the left. In the new equilibrium, the interest rate is higher, and the equilibrium quantity of loanable funds is lower. Running a deficit has reduced the level of total saving in the economy and, by increasing the interest rate, has also reduced the level of investment spending by firms. By borrowing to finance its budget deficit, the government will have *crowded out* some firms that would otherwise have been able to borrow to finance investment. **Crowding out** refers to a decline in investment spending as a result of an increase in government purchases. In Figure 21-5, the decline in investment spending due to crowding out is shown by the movement from L_1 to L_2 on the demand for loanable funds curve. Lower investment spending means that the capital stock and the quantity of capital per hour worked will not increase as much.

A government budget surplus would have the opposite effect of a deficit. A budget surplus increases the total amount of saving in the economy, shifting the supply of loanable funds to the right. In the new equilibrium, the interest rate will be lower, and the quantity of loanable funds will be higher. We can conclude that a budget surplus increases the level of saving and investment.

In practice, however, the impact of government budget deficits and surpluses on the equilibrium interest rate is relatively small. (This finding reflects in part the importance of global saving in determining the interest rate.) For example, a recent study found that increasing government borrowing by an amount equal to 1 percent

Crowding out A decline in private expenditures as a result of an increase in government purchases.

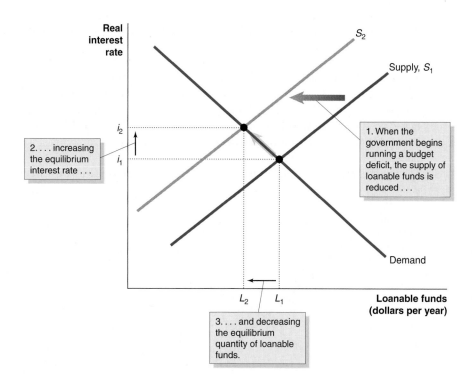

Figure 21-5 | The Effect of a Budget Deficit on the Market for Loanable Funds

When the government begins running a budget deficit, the supply of loanable funds shifts to the left. The equilibrium interest rate increases from i_1 to i_2, and the equilibrium quantity of loanable funds falls from L_1 to L_2. As a result, saving and investment both decline.

of GDP would increase the equilibrium real interest rate by only about three one-hundredths of a percentage point. However, this small effect on interest rates does not imply that we can ignore the effect of deficits on economic growth. Paying off government debt in the future may require higher taxes, which can depress economic growth.

Solved Problem | 21-2

How Would a Consumption Tax Affect Saving, Investment, the Interest Rate, and Economic Growth?

Some economists and policymakers have suggested that the federal government shift from relying on an income tax to relying on a *consumption tax.* Under the income tax, households pay taxes on all income earned. Under a consumption tax, households pay taxes only on the income they spend.

Households would pay taxes on saved income only if they spend the money at a later time. Use the market for loanable funds model to analyze the effect on saving, investment, the interest rate, and economic growth of switching from an income tax to a consumption tax.

SOLVING THE PROBLEM:

Step 1: **Review the chapter material.** This problem is about applying the market for loanable funds model, so you may want to review the section "Explaining Movements in Saving, Investment, and Interest Rates," which begins on page 709.

Step 2: **Explain the effect of switching from an income tax to a consumption tax.**
Households are interested in the return they receive from saving after they have paid their taxes. For example, consider someone who puts his savings in a certificate of deposit at an interest rate of 4 percent and whose tax rate is 25 percent. Under an income tax, this person's after-tax return to saving is 3 percent $[4 \times (1 - 0.25)]$. Under a consumption tax, income that is saved is not taxed, so the return rises to 4 percent. We can conclude that moving from an income tax to a consumption tax would increase the return to saving, causing the supply of loanable funds to increase.

Step 3: **Draw a graph of the market for loanable funds to illustrate your answer.**

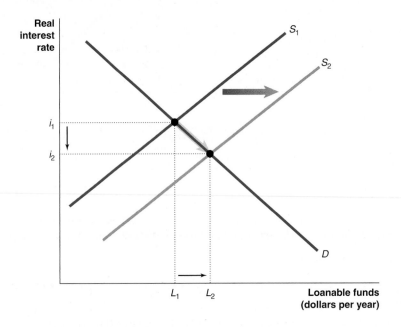

The supply curve for loanable funds will shift to the right as the after-tax return to saving increases under the consumption tax. The equilibrium interest rate will fall, and the levels of saving and investment will both increase. Because investment increases, the capital stock and the quantity of capital per hour worked will grow, and the rate of economic growth should increase. Note that the size of the fall in the interest rate and the increase in loanable funds shown in the graph are larger than the effects that most economists expect would actually result from the replacement of the income tax with a consumption tax.

>> **End Solved Problem 21-2**   **YOUR TURN:** For more practice, do related problem 2.16 on page 726 at the end of this chapter.

21.3 LEARNING OBJECTIVE   21.3 | Explain what happens during a business cycle.

The Business Cycle

Figure 21-1 on page 697 shows the tremendous increase during the last century in the standard of living of the average American. But close inspection of the figure reveals that real GDP per capita did not increase every year during this century. For example, during the first half of the 1930s, real GDP per capita *fell* for several years in a row. What accounts for these fluctuations in the long-run upward trend?

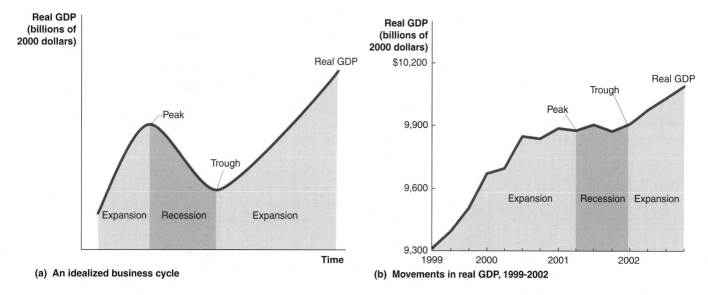

(a) An idealized business cycle

(b) Movements in real GDP, 1999-2002

Figure 21-6 | The Business Cycle

Panel (a) shows an idealized business cycle with real GDP increasing smoothly in an expansion to a business cycle peak and then decreasing smoothly in a recession to a business cycle trough, which is followed by another expansion. The periods of expansion are shown in green, and the period of recession is shown in red. In panel

(b), the actual movements in real GDP for 1999 to 2002 are shown. Real GDP fluctuates during the period around the business cycle peak of March 2001. The following recession was fairly short, and a business cycle trough was reached in November 2001, when the next expansion began.

Some Basic Business Cycle Definitions

The fluctuations in real GDP per capita shown in Figure 21-1 reflect the underlying fluctuations in real GDP. Dating back at least to the early nineteenth century, the U.S. economy has experienced a business cycle that consists of alternating periods of expanding and contracting economic activity. Because real GDP is our best measure of economic activity, the business cycle is usually illustrated using movements in real GDP.

During the *expansion phase* of the business cycle, production, employment, and income are increasing. The period of expansion ends with a *business cycle peak.* Following the business cycle peak, production, employment, and income decline as the economy enters the *recession phase* of the cycle. The recession comes to an end with a *business cycle trough*, after which another period of expansion begins. Figure 21-6 illustrates the phases of the business cycle. Panel (a) shows an idealized business cycle with real GDP increasing smoothly in an expansion to a business cycle peak and then decreasing smoothly in a recession to a business cycle trough, which is followed by another expansion. Panel (b) shows the somewhat messier reality of an actual business cycle by plotting fluctuations in real GDP during the period from 1999 to 2002. The figure shows that the expansion that began in 1991 continued through the late 1990s, until a business cycle peak was reached in March 2001. The following recession was fairly short, and a business cycle trough was reached in November 2001, when the next expansion began. But notice that real GDP declined in the third quarter of 2000, before rising in the fourth quarter of 2000, declining in the first quarter of 2001, rising in the second quarter of 2001, and then falling again in the third quarter of 2001. Inconsistent movements in real GDP around the business cycle peak can mean that the beginning and ending of a recession may not be clear-cut. In fact, some economists have argued that the recession of 2001 actually began with the fall in real GDP during the third quarter of 2000.

Making
the
Connection

The Business Cycle and the 2008 Election

Was the U.S. economy in a recession during the 2008 presidential election? Many economists, politicians, and voters believed that it was, but by election day there had not yet been any "formal" confirmation. Although the federal government publishes data about unemployment, output, and inflation, it does not determine when a recession begins or ends. Instead, the Business Cycle Dating Committee of the National Bureau of Economic Research (NBER), a private research group located in Cambridge, Massachusetts, makes that determination.

Less than one week before election day 2008, the U.S. Bureau of Economic Analysis announced its preliminary estimate that real GDP had declined during the third quarter of 2008. It was too early, though, for the NBER to decide whether the economy had entered a recession. The NBER is fairly slow in announcing business cycle dates because it takes time to gather and analyze economic statistics. Typically, the NBER will announce that the economy is in a recession only well after the recession has begun.

Whether or not the NBER has declared that a recession is underway, does the state of the economy affect which presidential candidate voters choose? There is substantial evidence that in some elections, the state of the economy can be of decisive importance. For instance, Herbert Hoover was elected president with a large majority in the 1928 presidential election. When the Great Depression began shortly after Hoover took office, his popularity rapidly faded and he was soundly defeated for reelection by Franklin Roosevelt in 1932. Similarly, George H. W. Bush was elected with 53 percent of the popular vote in 1988, but when the U.S. economy recovered only slowly following the 1991 recession, President Bush was defeated for reelection in 1992 by Bill Clinton. Even in elections that do not take place during or shortly after recessions, the state of the economy can influence voting. A careful analysis of the 2004 presidential election by Jeffrey S. DeSimone and Courtney LaFountain of the University of Texas, Austin, showed that voters who had experienced a financial decline between 2000 and 2004 were significantly less likely to vote to reelect President George W. Bush.

As of this writing, it is too early to have detailed studies of the 2008 presidential election. But it seems likely that the economic difficulties of 2008 reduced the chances that the presidential candidate of the incumbent party, John McCain, would be elected. Opinion polls showed John McCain and Barack Obama in a close election through the summer. But in the fall, as real GDP began to decline and unemployment began to rise, Barack Obama ultimately won the election by a margin in the popular vote of 53 percent to 46 percent.

The state of the U.S. economy was one factor that helped Barack Obama win the presidency in 2008.

Sources: *NBER Reporter*, Fall 2001; and Jeffrey S. DeSimone and Courtney LaFountain, "It's Still the Economy, Stupid: Economic Voting in the 2004 Presidential Election," NBER Working Paper No. 13549, October 2007.

YOUR TURN: Test your understanding by doing related problem 3.7 on page 727 at the end of this chapter.

What Happens during a Business Cycle?

Each business cycle is different. The lengths of the expansion and recession phases and which sectors of the economy are most affected are rarely the same in any two cycles. But most business cycles share certain characteristics, which we will discuss in this section. As the economy nears the end of an expansion, interest rates usually are rising, and the wages of workers usually are rising faster than prices. As a result of rising interest rates and rising wages, the profits of firms will be falling. Typically, toward the end of an expansion, both households and firms will have substantially increased their debts. These debts are the result of the borrowing firms and households undertake to help finance their spending during the expansion.

A recession will often begin with a decline in spending by firms on capital goods, such as machinery, equipment, new factories, and new office buildings, or by households on new houses and consumer durables, such as furniture and automobiles. As spending declines, firms selling capital goods and consumer durables will find their sales declining. As sales decline, firms cut back on production and begin to lay off workers. Rising unemployment and falling profits reduce income, which leads to further declines in spending.

As the recession continues, economic conditions gradually begin to improve. The declines in spending eventually come to an end; households and firms begin to reduce their debt, thereby increasing their ability to spend; and interest rates decline, making it more likely that households and firms will borrow to finance new spending. Firms begin to increase their spending on capital goods as they anticipate the need for additional production during the next expansion. Increased spending by households on consumer durables and by businesses on capital goods will finally bring the recession to an end and begin the next expansion.

The Effect of the Business Cycle on Boeing Durables are goods that are expected to last for three or more years. Consumer durables include furniture, appliances, and automobiles, and producer durables include machine tools, electric generators, and commercial airplanes. Durables are affected more by the business cycle than are nondurables—such as food and clothing—or services—such as haircuts and medical care. During a recession, workers reduce spending if they lose their jobs, fear losing their jobs, or suffer wage cuts. Because people can often continue to use their existing furniture, appliances, or automobiles, they are more likely to postpone spending on durables than spending on other goods. Similarly, when firms experience declining sales and profits during a recession, they often cut back on purchases of producer durables.

We mentioned in our discussion of Boeing at the beginning of this chapter that the firm's sales are significantly affected by the business cycle. Panel (a) of Figure 21-7 shows

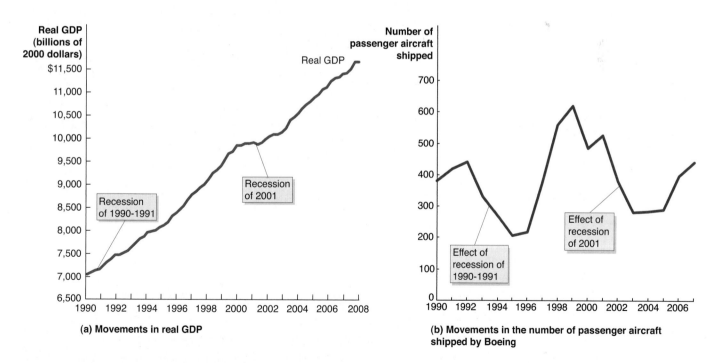

Figure 21-7 | The Effect of the Business Cycle on Boeing

Panel (a) shows movements in real GDP for each quarter from the beginning of 1990 through the end of 2007. Panel (b) shows movements in the number of passenger aircraft shipped by Boeing for the same years. In panel (b), the effects of the recessions on Boeing are more dramatic than the effects on the economy as a whole.

Sources: U.S. Bureau of Economic Analysis; Aerospace Industries Association; and Boeing.

movements in real GDP for each quarter from the beginning of 1990 through the end of 2007. We can see both the upward trend in real GDP over time and the effects of the recessions of 1990–1991 and 2001. Panel (b) shows movements in the total number of passenger aircraft shipped by Boeing during the same years. The effects of the recessions on Boeing are much more dramatic and long-lived than the effects on the economy as a whole. In each of the two recessions shown, airlines suffered a decline in ticket sales and cut back on purchases of aircraft. As a result, Boeing suffered a sharp decline in sales during each recession. In 2008, slowing growth in GDP and rising fuel prices threatened to once again reduce Boeing's sales.

The Effect of the Business Cycle on the Inflation Rate In Chapter 20, we saw that the *price level* measures the average prices of goods and services in the economy and that the *inflation rate* is the percentage increase in the price level from one year to the next. An important fact about the business cycle is that during economic expansions, the inflation rate usually increases, particularly near the end of the expansion, and during recessions, the inflation rate usually decreases. Figure 21-8 illustrates that this was true of the recession of 2001.

As Figure 21-8 shows, toward the end of the 1991–2001 expansion, the inflation rate rose from about 1.5 percent to about 3.5 percent. The recession that began in March 2001 caused the inflation rate to fall back to below 2 percent. Figure 21-9 shows that

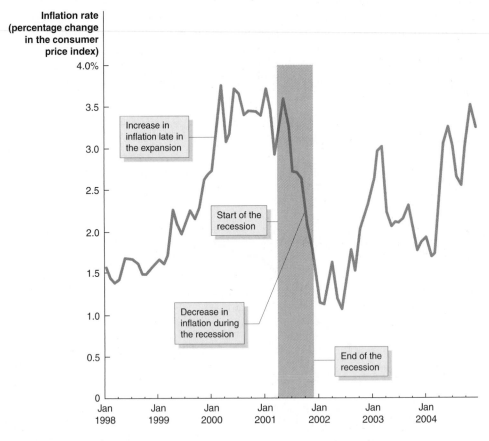

Figure 21-8 | The Effect of the 2001 Recession on the Inflation Rate

Toward the end of the 1991–2001 expansion, the inflation rate began to rise. The recession that began in March 2001, marked by the shaded vertical bar, caused the inflation rate to fall. By the end of the recession in November 2001, the inflation rate was significantly below what it had been at the beginning of the recession.

Note: The points on the figure represent the annual inflation rate measured by the change in the CPI for the year ending in the indicated month.

Source: U.S. Bureau of Labor Statistics.

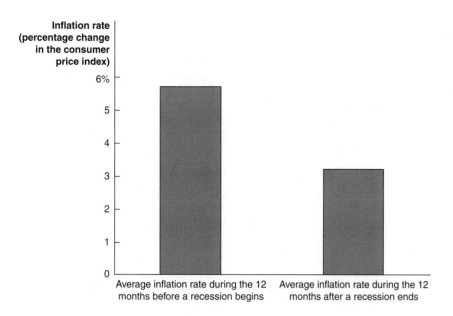

Figure 21-9 | The Impact of Recessions on the Inflation Rate

In every recession since 1950, the inflation rate has been lower during the 12 months after the business cycle trough than it was during the 12 months before the business cycle peak. The average decline in the inflation rate has been 2.5 percentage points.
Source: U.S. Bureau of Labor Statistics.

recessions have consistently had the effect of lowering the inflation rate. In every recession since 1950, the inflation rate has been lower during the 12 months after the recession ends than it was during the 12 months before the recession began. The average decline in the inflation rate has been about 2.5 percentage points. This result is not surprising. During a business cycle expansion, spending by businesses and households is strong, and producers of goods and services find it easier to raise prices. As spending declines during a recession, firms have a more difficult time selling their goods and services and are likely to increase prices less than they otherwise might have.

The Effect of the Business Cycle on the Unemployment Rate Recessions cause the inflation rate to fall, but they cause the unemployment rate to increase. As firms see their sales decline, they begin to reduce production and lay off workers. Figure 21-10 shows the impact of the recession of 2001 on the unemployment rate. As the recession began in March

Don't Let This Happen to **YOU!**

Don't Confuse the Price Level and the Inflation Rate

Do you agree with the following statement: "The consumer price index is a widely used measure of the inflation rate"? This statement may sound plausible, but it is incorrect. As we saw in Chapter 20, the consumer price index is a measure of the *price level*, not of the inflation rate. We can measure the inflation rate as the *percentage change* in the consumer price index from one year to the next. In macroeconomics, it is important not to confuse the level of a variable with the change in the variable. To give another example, real GDP does not measure economic growth. Economic growth is measured by the percentage change in real GDP from one year to the next.

YOUR TURN: Test your understanding by doing related problem 3.6 on page 727 at the end of this chapter.

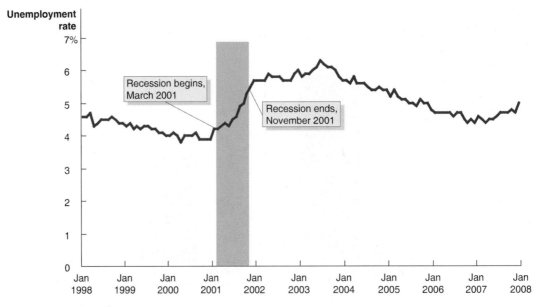

Figure 21-10 | How the Recession of 2001 Affected the Unemployment Rate

The reluctance of firms to hire new employees during the early stages of a recovery means that the unemployment rate usually continues to rise even after the recession has ended.
Source: U.S. Bureau of Labor Statistics.

2001, the unemployment rate started to rise. The rate continued to rise even after the end of the recession in November 2001. This pattern is typical and is due to two factors. First, during the business cycle, discouraged workers drop out of and then return to the labor force, as we discussed in Chapter 20. When discouraged workers drop out of the labor force during a recession, they keep the measured unemployment rate from increasing as much as it would if these workers were counted as unemployed. When discouraged workers return to the labor force as the recession ends, they increase the measured unemployment rate because they are now counted as being unemployed. Second, firms continue to operate well below their capacity even after a recession has ended and production has begun to increase. As a result, at first, firms may not hire back all the workers they have laid off and may even continue for a while to lay off more workers.

As the U.S. economy began to recover from the 2001 recession, the *Wall Street Journal* published an article giving advice to small firms on their hiring policies during the period after a recession has ended. One piece of advice was "Just because some new orders arrived, don't run out and hire a bunch of new workers." The owner of one small accounting firm suggested that during the early stages of an expansion, companies should use overtime by existing employees to meet sales rather than hire new workers.

Figure 21-11 shows that for the recessions since 1950, the unemployment rate has risen on average by about 1.2 percentage points during the 12 months after a recession has begun. So, on average, more than a million more workers have been unemployed during the 12 months after a recession has begun than during the previous 12 months.

Recessions Have Been Milder and the Economy Has Been More Stable Since 1950 Although today the U.S. economy still experiences business cycles, just as it has for at least the past 175 years, the cycles have become milder. Figure 21-12, which shows the year-to-year percentage changes in real GDP since 1900, illustrates a striking change in fluctuations in real GDP beginning around 1950. Before 1950, real GDP went through much

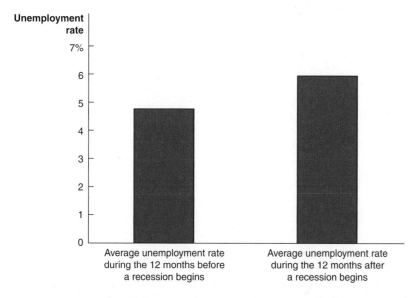

Figure 21-11 | The Impact of Recessions on the Unemployment Rate

Unemployment rises in every recession. For the recessions since 1950, the unemployment rate has risen, on average, by about 1.2 percentage points during the 12 months after a recession has begun.
Source: U.S. Bureau of Labor Statistics.

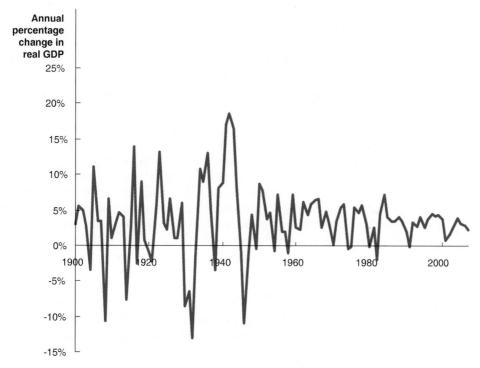

Figure 21-12 | Fluctuations in Real GDP, 1900–2007

In the first half of the twentieth century, real GDP had much more severe swings than in the second half of the twentieth century.
Sources: Louis D. Johnston and Samuel H. Williamson, "The Annual Real and Nominal GDP for the United States, 1790–Present," Economic History Services, April 1, 2008, www.eh.net/hmit/gdp; and U.S. Bureau of Economic Analysis.

TABLE 21-1

The Business Cycle Has
Become Milder

PERIOD	AVERAGE LENGTH OF EXPANSIONS	AVERAGE LENGTH OF RECESSIONS
1870–1900	26 months	26 months
1900–1950	25 months	19 months
1950–2001	61 months	9 months

Note: The World War I and World War II periods have been omitted from the computations in the table, as has the expansion that began in November 2001.

Source: National Bureau of Economic Research.

greater year-to-year fluctuations than it has since that time. During the past 50 years, the U.S. economy has not experienced anything similar to the sharp fluctuations in real GDP that occurred during the early 1930s.

Another way to compare changes in the severity of business cycles over time is to look at changes in the lengths of expansions and recessions. Table 21-1 shows that in the late nineteenth century, the average length of recessions was the same as the average length of expansions. During the first half of the twentieth century, the average length of expansions decreased slightly, and the average length of recessions decreased significantly. As a result, expansions were about six months longer than recessions during these years. The most striking change came after 1950, when the length of expansions greatly increased and the length of recessions fell. In the second half of the twentieth century, expansions were more than six times as long as recessions. In other words, in the late nineteenth century, the U.S. economy spent as much time in recession as it did in expansion. During the second half of the twentieth century, the U.S. economy experienced long expansions interrupted by relatively short recessions.

Why Is the Economy More Stable?

Shorter recessions, longer expansions, and less severe fluctuations in real GDP have resulted in a significant improvement in the economic well-being of Americans. Economists have offered three explanations of why the economy has been more stable since 1950:

- *The increasing importance of services and the declining importance of goods.* As services, such as medical care or investment advice, have become a much larger fraction of GDP, there has been a corresponding decline in the production of goods. For example, at one time, manufacturing production accounted for about 40 percent of GDP, while today it accounts for only about 12 percent. Manufacturing production, particularly production of durable goods such as automobiles, fluctuates more than the production of services. Because durable goods are more expensive, during a recession, households will cut back more on purchases of them than they will on purchases of services.

- *The establishment of unemployment insurance and other government transfer programs that provide funds to the unemployed.* Before the 1930s, programs such as unemployment insurance, which provides government payments to workers who lose their jobs, and Social Security, which provides government payments to retired and disabled workers, did not exist. These and other government programs make it possible for workers who lose their jobs during recessions to have higher incomes and, therefore, to spend more than they would otherwise. This additional spending may have helped to shorten recessions.

- *Active federal government policies to stabilize the economy.* Before the Great Depression of the 1930s, the federal government did not attempt to end recessions or prolong expansions. Because the Great Depression was so severe, with the unemployment rate rising to more than 25 percent of the labor force and real GDP declining by almost 30 percent, public opinion began favoring attempts by the government to stabilize the economy. In the Employment Act of 1946, the federal government committed itself to "foster and promote . . . conditions under which there will be afforded useful employment to those able, willing, and seeking to work; and to promote maximum employment, production, and purchasing power." Beginning in the 1930s, economists also began to increase their understanding of why GDP fluctuates. As we will see in later chapters, the models economists developed to understand fluctuations in GDP also made it possible to evaluate the effects government policy would have on the economy. In the years since World War II, the federal government has actively tried to use policy measures to end recessions and prolong expansions. Many economists believe that these government policies have played a key role in stabilizing the economy. Other economists, however, argue that active policy has had little effect. This macroeconomic debate is an important one, so we will consider it further in Chapters 26 and 27 when we discuss the federal government's *monetary* and *fiscal policies.*

Economics in YOUR Life!

>> Continued from page 695

At the beginning of the chapter, we posed a question: How do you respond to your roommate's assertion that your decision to save instead of consume will reduce economic growth? In answering this question, this chapter has shown that consumption spending promotes the production of more consumption goods and services—such as jeans and haircuts—and fewer investment goods and services—such as physical capital and worker education. This is because saving—and, so, not consuming—is necessary to fund investment expenditure. Because an economy uses investment goods and services to produce other goods and services, your decision to save instead of consume will promote, rather than reduce, economic growth.

Conclusion

The U.S. economy remains a remarkable engine for improving the well-being of Americans. The standard of living of Americans today is much higher than it was 100 years ago. But households and firms are still subject to the ups and downs of the business cycle. In the following chapters, we will continue our analysis of this basic fact of macroeconomics: Ever-increasing long-run prosperity is achieved in the context of short-run instability.

Read *An Inside Look at Policy* on the next page to learn why China's domestic aviation market is struggling and what role the government plays in addressing the problem.

China's Airlines Are Failing to Translate Rapid Growth into Profits

ECONOMIST, FEBRUARY 23, 2006

Chinese Aviation: On a Wing and a Prayer

Despite a rousing flying display from the gigantic new Airbus A380, visitors at this week's Asian Aerospace show, which opened on February 21st, were looking to the north as much as up. After a quarter of a century at Singapore's Changi Exhibition Centre, Asian Aerospace—the world's third biggest air show—will move to Hong Kong from next year. The reason, as so often these days, is the growing pull of China.

Granted, there is excitement about India, Dubai and south-east Asia. But for the aerospace industry, China's combination of rapid growth and huge absolute numbers is the real prize. Chinese airlines carried 138M passengers last year, a number that has doubled in the past five years and already turned the mainland into the second largest aviation market behind America. The Chinese government expects the figure to double again over the next five years. Freight volumes are growing even faster, increasing by 20% last year.

As a result, China is buying aircraft as never before. In 2005, it accounted for 219 planes, or fully one-fifth of Airbus's global orders in a record year. Boeing's latest analysis forecasts that over the next two decades, China will need 2,600 new planes, worth more than $213 billion.

But while airframe-makers and their suppliers are rubbing their hands,

China's airlines are so far experiencing almost profitless growth. True, China has done wonders to mobilise the country, building the infrastructure needed to support the growth of its aviation industry and improving its safety. China now has 130 airports handling more than 1M passengers a year, with another 55 international airports planned by 2020. But despite a big jump in passenger numbers and revenues, the entire sector has reported measly profits of just 10 billion yuan ($1.2 billion) in the past five years.

This year, Air China is the only one of the big three carriers expected to be in the black. China Southern and China Eastern have already warned of sharp losses. . . .

Part of the airlines' failure to make profits is simply the consequence of rapid expansion. Investing in all those new planes means most Chinese airlines are heavily in debt. A more serious issue, despite limited liberalization over the past few years, is the continued presence of the state's dead hand. Ticket prices, for example, remain more or less regulated, preventing carriers from practising the sophisticated yield management of western peers. . . . Meanwhile, a domestic jet-fuel monopoly means fuel accounts for an average of 40% of costs at Chinese airlines, compared with 24% for airlines worldwide.

Another issue is rising labour costs due to a lack of qualified staff. In particular, China will need more than 1,000 pilots a year over the next decade, but with only one state flying school,

Guanghan near Chengdu in Sichuan province, it can train 600 at most. Air China admitted this month that its planned introduction of 20–30 new aircraft in 2006 depended on it being able to man them. The suppliers are aware of this problem. Airbus has a training centre in Beijing and is setting up simulators elsewhere—as is Boeing. China is also allowing some private training schools to spring up, while China Southern already has its own training centre in Australia. But the shortage is acute and Chinese airlines are now talking of recruiting, reluctantly, pilots from overseas. Not only do they regard this as a blow to national pride; foreign crews also cost more.

Their weak profitability, coupled with ambitious plans to expand capacity, leaves the mainland carriers exposed to even a temporary slowdown in traffic growth. Further consolidation, allowing an attack on their structurally high costs, is one remedy. Another would be to liberalise the market for both fares and fuel. A braver step would be to let in foreign operators to boost competition. . . . Whichever route the government chooses, it needs to act rapidly. After all, the industry has been hit by at least one major shock every three years, from terrorist attacks to the SARS virus. After a couple of good years, the next bad one is due some time soon.

Key Points in the Article

This article discusses the rapidly expanding Chinese airline industry. It explains that China's domestic aviation market has grown dramatically in the past few years. In 2005, China's airlines carried a record 138 million passengers and ordered 219 new Airbus and Boeing airplanes. Today, the Chinese mainland comprises the second-largest airline market in the world; only the U.S. domestic airline market is larger. Nonetheless, Chinese airlines have struggled to earn a profit. According to the article, this struggle has to do with three common factors associated with long-run growth: the Chinese airline industry's recent large investments in new planes; the Chinese government's failure to liberalize markets for air travel; and a shortage of human capital, including pilots. The last problem has become so acute that Airbus and Boeing, both of which stand to gain from China's growth, have established pilot-training centers, complete with flight simulators, throughout China.

Analyzing the News

(a) To help the Chinese domestic airline industry grow, the Chinese government has sought to improve the country's infrastructure. The government has constructed and modernized 130 airports and invested in the technology necessary to improve air safety. These improvements, along with a large and growing domestic market for air travel, have fostered dramatic growth among China's airlines. This pattern is shown in Figure 1, where China Southern Airlines and China Eastern Airlines—two of China's three largest carriers—ranked among the top 10 airlines in the world in 2005, according to passengers carried on domestic flights. Nonetheless, China's airlines do not lead the industry in profitability. Figure 2 shows that none of China's carriers ranked among the top 10 airlines in the world in 2006 according to profitability; and only Air China—the other of China's three largest carriers—reported a profit, which earned it a rank of fifteenth in the world for profitability.

(b) One reason China's airlines are struggling to generate profits is their recent large investments in new airplanes. A more important reason China's airlines are struggling has to do with the Chinese government's failure to liberalize markets, including the market for air travel. As you read in this chapter, a requirement for economic growth—and profitability—is that governments facilitate the development of efficient markets. To do so, governments should avoid interfering with markets by setting prices or prohibiting entry into those markets. However, China's government continues to regulate ticket prices, while a government-sanctioned domestic jet-fuel monopoly has effectively raised the cost of operating airlines in China.

(c) China's airline industry faces a shortage of human capital, especially airline pilots. According to the article, if China's airline industry continues to grow at its current rate, it will need 1,000 additional pilots every year for the next decade; meanwhile, the country's single state-run flying school can produce only 600 pilots a year. This shortage of human capital is a problem for airplane manufacturers Airbus and Boeing, which stand to gain from China's growth. So, with permission from the Chinese government, both companies have established pilot-training centers throughout China.

Thinking Critically About Policy

1. Suppose the Chinese government ceased to regulate airline ticket prices and allowed foreign firms to sell jet fuel to China's domestic air carriers. How might such a change in policy affect the airlines' profitability?

2. Suppose the Chinese government decided to provide low-interest loans to domestic air carriers, regardless of their creditworthiness, in an attempt to foster long-term profitability in the industry. Would such a policy be likely to succeed?

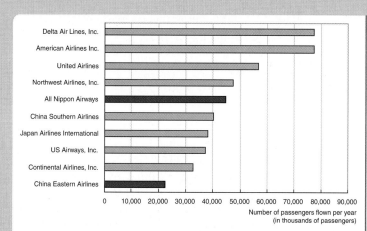

Figure 1. Airlines ranked by passengers carried on domestic flights, 2005.

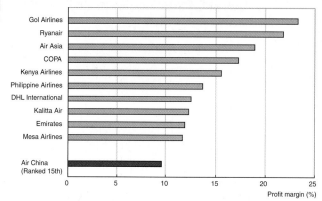

Figure 2. Airlines ranked by operating profit margin, 2005.

Key Terms

Business cycle, p. 696

Capital, p. 700

Crowding out, p. 710

Financial intermediaries, p. 705

Financial markets, p. 704

Financial system, p. 704

Labor productivity, p. 700

Long-run economic growth, p. 697

Market for loanable funds, p. 707

Potential GDP, p. 703

21.1 LEARNING OBJECTIVE 21.1 | Discuss the importance of long-run economic growth, **pages 696–703.**

Long-Run Economic Growth

Summary

The U.S. economy has experienced both *long-run economic growth* and the *business cycle*. The **business cycle** refers to alternating periods of economic expansion and economic recession. **Long-run economic growth** is the process by which rising productivity increases the standard of living of the typical person. Because of economic growth, the typical American today can buy almost eight times as much as the typical American of 1900. Long-run growth is measured by increases in real GDP per capita. Increases in real GDP per capita depend on increases in labor productivity. **Labor productivity** is the quantity of goods and services that can be produced by one worker or by one hour of work. Economists believe two key factors determine labor productivity—the quantity of capital per hour worked and the level of technology. **Capital** refers to manufactured goods that are used to produce other goods and services. *Human capital* is the accumulated knowledge and skills workers acquire from education training or their life experiences. Economic growth occurs if the quantity of capital per hour worked increases and if technological change occurs. Economists often discuss economic growth in terms of growth in **potential GDP**, which is the level of GDP attained when all firms are producing at capacity.

myeconlab Visit www.myeconlab.com to complete these exercises
Get Ahead of the Curve online and get instant feedback.

Review Questions

1.1 By how much did real GDP per capita increase in the United States between 1900 and 2007? Discuss whether the increase in real GDP per capita is likely to be greater or smaller than the true increase in living standards.

1.2 What is the most important factor in explaining increases in real GDP per capita in the long run?

1.3 What two key factors cause labor productivity to increase over time?

1.4 What is potential real GDP? Does potential real GDP remain constant over time?

Problems and Applications

1.5 Briefly discuss whether you would rather live in the United States of 1900 with an income of $1,000,000 per year or the United States of 2008 with an income of $50,000 per year. Assume that the incomes for both years are measured in 2000 dollars.

1.6 A question from Chapter 19 asked about the relationship between real GDP and the standard of living in a country. Based on what you read about economic growth in this chapter, elaborate on the importance of growth in GDP, particularly real GDP per capita, to the quality of life of a country's citizens.

1.7 (Related to the *Making the Connection* on page 698) Think about the relationship between economic prosperity and life expectancy. What implications does this relationship have for the size of the health care sector of the economy? In particular, is this sector likely to expand or contract in coming years?

1.8 Use the table to answer the following questions.

YEAR	REAL GDP (BILLIONS OF 2000 DOLLARS)
1990	$7,113
1991	7,101
1992	7,337
1993	7,533
1994	7,836

   a. Calculate the growth rate of real GDP for each year from 1991 to 1994.

   b. Calculate the average annual growth rate of real GDP for the period from 1991 to 1994.

1.9 Real GDP per capita in the United States, as mentioned in the chapter, grew from about $4,900 in 1900 to about $38,000 in 2007, which represents an annual growth rate of 1.9 percent. If the United States continues to grow at this rate, how many years will it take for real GDP per capita to double?

1.10 The economy of China has boomed since the late 1970s, having periods during which real GDP per capita has grown at rates of 9 percent per year or more. At a 9 percent growth rate in real GDP per capita, how many years will it take to double?

1.11 Labor productivity in the agricultural sector of the United States is more than 31 times higher than in the agricultural sector of China. What factors would cause U.S. labor productivity to be so much higher than Chinese labor productivity?

Source: "China: Awakening Giant," Federal Reserve Bank of Dallas, *Southwest Economy*, September/October 2003, p. 2.

1.12 (Related to *Solved Problem 21-1* on page 701) Two reasons for the rapid economic growth of China over the past two to three decades have been the massive movement of workers from agriculture to manufacturing jobs and the transformation of parts of its economy into a market system. In China, labor productivity in manufacturing substantially exceeds labor productivity in agriculture, and as many as 150 million Chinese workers will move from agriculture to manufacturing over the next decade or so. In 1978, China began to transform its economy

into a market system, and today, nearly 40 percent of Chinese workers are employed in private firms (up from 0 percent in 1978). In the long run, which of these two factors—movement of workers from agriculture to manufacturing or transforming the economy into a market system—will be more important for China's economic growth? Briefly explain.

Source: "China: Awakening Giant," Federal Reserve Bank of Dallas, *Southwest Economy*, September/October 2003.

1.13 A newspaper story on labor productivity in the United States includes the following observation: "Productivity is the vital element needed to boost living standards." Briefly explain whether you agree. Make clear in your answer what you mean by living standards.

Source: Martin Crutsinger, "Productivity Rebounds in Fourth Quarter," Associated Press, February 8, 2007.

1.14 (Related to the *Making the Connection* on page 702) If the keys to Botswana's rapid economic growth seem obvious, why have other countries in the region had so much difficulty following them?

>> **End Learning Objective 21.1**

21.2 LEARNING OBJECTIVE   21.2 | Discuss the role of the financial system in facilitating long-run economic growth, **pages 703–712.**

Saving, Investment, and the Financial System

Summary

Financial markets and financial intermediaries together comprise the **financial system**. A well-functioning financial system is an important determinant of economic growth. Firms acquire funds from households, either directly through financial markets—such as the stock and bond markets—or indirectly through financial intermediaries—such as banks. The funds available to firms come from *saving*. There are two categories of saving in the economy: *private saving* by households and *public saving* by the government. The value of total saving in the economy is always equal to the value of total investment spending. In the model of the **market for loanable funds**, the interaction of borrowers and lenders determines the market interest rate and the quantity of loanable funds exchanged.

Review Questions

2.1 Why is the financial system of a country important for long-run economic growth? Why is it essential for economic growth that firms have access to adequate sources of funds?

2.2 How does the financial system—either financial markets or financial intermediaries—provide risk sharing, liquidity, and information for savers and borrowers?

2.3 Briefly explain why the total value of saving in the economy must equal the total value of investment.

2.4 What are loanable funds? Why do businesses demand loanable funds? Why do households supply loanable funds?

Problems and Applications

2.5 Suppose you can receive an interest rate of 3 percent on a certificate of deposit at a bank that is charging borrowers 7 percent on new car loans. Why might you be unwilling to loan money directly to someone who wants to borrow from you to buy a new car, even if that person offers to pay you an interest rate higher than 3 percent?

2.6 An article argues that a main barrier to continued rapid economic growth in China is "its fragile banking system." Why might a weak banking system make economic growth difficult?

Source: "The Real Great Leap Forward," *Economist*, September 30, 2004.

2.7 According to an article in the *Wall Street Journal*, the government of Indonesia forecast that its budget deficit would increase from 1.1 percent of GDP in 2007 to 1.8 percent in 2008. Assuming that other factors that affect the demand and supply of loanable funds remain the same, what would be the effect of this larger budget deficit on the equilibrium real interest rate and the quantity of loanable funds? What would be the effect on the equilibrium quantity of saving and investment? Illustrate your answer using a graph showing the market for loanable funds in Indonesia.

Source: "Jakarta Forecasts Growth of as Much as 7% in 2008," *Wall Street Journal*, May 23, 2007.

2.8 Consider the following data for a closed economy:

$Y = \$11$ trillion
$C = \$8$ trillion
$I = \$2$ trillion
$TR = \$1$ trillion
$T = \$3$ trillion

Use the data to calculate the following.
a. Private saving
b. Public saving
c. Government purchases
d. The government budget deficit or budget surplus

2.9 Consider the following data for a closed economy:

$Y = \$12$ trillion
$C = \$8$ trillion
$G = \$2$ trillion
$S_{public} = -\$0.5$ trillion
$T = \$2$ trillion

Use the data to calculate the following.
a. Private saving
b. Investment spending
c. Transfer payments
d. The government budget deficit or budget surplus

2.10 In problem 2.9, suppose that government purchases increase from $2 trillion to $2.5 trillion. If the values for Y and C are unchanged, what must happen to the values of S and I? Briefly explain.

2.11 Use the graph to answer the following questions.

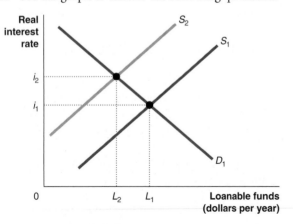

a. Does the shift from S_1 to S_2 represent an increase or a decrease in the supply of loanable funds?
b. With the shift in supply, what happens to the equilibrium quantity of loanable funds?
c. With the change in the equilibrium quantity of loanable funds, what happens to the quantity of saving? What happens to the quantity of investment?

2.12 Use the graph to answer the following questions.

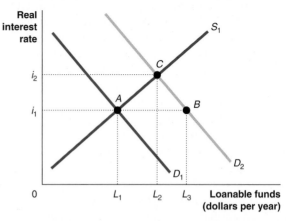

a. With the shift in the demand for loanable funds, what happens to the equilibrium real interest rate and the equilibrium quantity of loanable funds?
b. How can the equilibrium quantity of loanable funds increase when the real interest rate increases? Doesn't the quantity of loanable funds demanded decrease when the interest rate increases?
c. How much would the quantity of loanable funds demanded have increased if the interest rate had remained at i_1?
d. How much does the quantity of loanable funds supplied increase with the increase in the interest rate from i_1 to i_2?

2.13 Suppose that the economy is currently in a recession and that economic forecasts indicate that the economy will soon enter an expansion. What is the likely effect of the expansion on the expected profitability of new investment in plant and equipment? In the market for loanable funds, graph and explain the effect of the forecast of an economic expansion, assuming that borrowers and lenders believe the forecast is accurate. What happens to the equilibrium real interest rate and the quantity of loanable funds? What happens to the quantity of saving and investment?

2.14 Firms care about their after-tax rate of return on investment projects. In the market for loanable funds, graph and explain the effect of an increase in taxes on business profits. (For simplicity, assume no change in the federal budget deficit or budget surplus.) What happens to the equilibrium real interest rate and the quantity of loanable funds? What will be the effect on the quantity of investment by firms and the economy's capital stock in the future?

2.15 Use a market for loanable funds graph to illustrate the effect of the federal budget surpluses of the late 1990s. What happens to the equilibrium real interest rate and the quantity of loanable funds? What happens to the quantity of saving and investment?

2.16 (Related to *Solved Problem 21-2* on page 711) As discussed in Chapter 20, savers are taxed on the nominal interest payments they receive rather than the real interest payments. Suppose the government shifted from taxing nominal interest payments to taxing only real interest payments. Use a market for loanable funds graph to analyze the effects of this change in tax policy. What happens to the equilibrium real interest rate and the equilibrium quantity of loanable funds? What happens to the quantity of saving and investment?

2.17 (Related to the *Making the Connection* on page 708) The *Making the Connection* claims that Ebenezer Scrooge promoted economic growth more when he was a miser and saved most of his income

than when he reformed and began spending freely. Suppose, though, that most of his spending after he reformed involved buying food for the Cratchits and other poor families. Many economists believe there is a close connection between how much very poor people eat and how much they are able to work and how productive they are while working. Does this fact affect the conclusion about whether the pre-reform or post-reform Scrooge had a more positive impact on economic growth? Briefly explain.

>> **End Learning Objective 21.2**

21.3 LEARNING OBJECTIVE   21.3 | Explain what happens during a business cycle, **pages 712–721.**

The Business Cycle

Summary

During the expansion phase of a business cycle, production, employment, and income are increasing. The period of expansion ends with a business cycle peak. Following the business cycle peak, production, employment, and income decline during the recession phase of the cycle. The recession comes to an end with a business cycle trough, after which another period of expansion begins. The inflation rate usually rises near the end of a business cycle expansion and then falls during a recession. The unemployment rate declines during the later part of an expansion and increases during a recession. The unemployment rate often continues to increase even after an expansion has begun. Economists have not found a method to predict when recessions will begin and end. Recessions are difficult to predict because they have more than one cause. Recessions have been milder and the economy has been more stable since 1950.

myeconlab Visit www.myeconlab.com to complete these exercises *Get Ahead of the Curve* online and get instant feedback.

Review Questions

3.1 What are the names of the following events in a business cycle?
   a. The high point of economic activity
   b. The low point of economic activity
   c. The period between the high point of economic activity and the following low point
   d. The period between the low point of economic activity and the following high point

3.2 Briefly describe the effect of the business cycle on the inflation rate and the unemployment rate.

3.3 Briefly compare the severity of recessions in the first half of the twentieth century with recessions in the second half. Do economists agree on how to explain this difference?

Problems and Applications

3.4 (Related to the *Chapter Opener* on page 694) Briefly explain whether production of each of the following goods is likely to fluctuate more or less than real GDP does during the business cycle.
   a. Ford F-150 trucks
   b. McDonald's Big Macs
   c. Kenmore refrigerators
   d. Huggies diapers
   e. Caterpillar industrial tractors

3.5 The National Bureau of Economic Research, a private group, is responsible for declaring when recessions begin and end. Can you think of reasons why the Bureau of Economic Analysis, part of the federal government, might not want to take on this responsibility?

3.6 (Related to the *Don't Let This Happen to You!* on page 717) "Real GDP in 2007 was $11.6 trillion. This value is a large number. Therefore, economic growth must have been high during 2007." Briefly explain whether you agree or disagree with this statement.

3.7 (Related to the *Making the Connection* on page 714) Many researchers who have studied presidential elections believe that the state of the economy often plays a large role in the voting. In particular, presidents who run for reelection during a year when real GDP is declining and unemployment is increasing are usually defeated. Is the current state of the economy a good reason for voting for or against an incumbent president running for reelection? Briefly explain your argument.

3.8 Imagine you own a business and that during the next recession you lay off 20 percent of your workforce. When economic activity picks up and your sales begin to increase, why might you not immediately start rehiring workers?

>> **End Learning Objective 21.3**

Chapter 22

Long-Run Economic Growth: Sources and Policies

MySpace Meets the Chinese Economic Miracle

MySpace.com was founded in 2003 by Tom Anderson and Chris DeWolfe, who intended the site to be a virtual meeting place for (fellow) striving musicians in the Los Angeles area. In July 2005, one month after web traffic on MySpace.com exceeded that on Google, Rupert Murdoch's News Corporation bought MySpace for $580 million. Since then, the company has been aggressively expanding into international markets, including China—home to roughly 135 million Internet users in their twenties and thirties. But to enter the Chinese market, News Corporation must overcome a crucial challenge: a government that regulates the Internet for speech that it deems subversive. To deal with this problem, News Corporation needed to find a Chinese partner who can keep the Chinese version of MySpace from breaking the law. Or, in the words of

Fan Bao, chief executive of an investment banking firm in Beijing, "what it takes to be successful in China is a local entrepreneur."

Entrepreneurship is a relatively new resource in China. From the time the Communist Party seized control of China in 1949, until the late 1970s, the government controlled production, and there was little place for private businesses run by entrepreneurs. China moved away from a *centrally planned economy* in 1976, with the death of Communist Party Leader Mao Zedong. Mao's successor, Deng Xiaoping, introduced market-oriented reforms in 1978. Real GDP per capita had grown very slowly between 1949 and 1978. Following Deng's reforms, real GDP per capita grew at a rate of 6.5 percent per year between 1979 and 1995 and at the white-hot rate of more than 9 percent per year between 1996 and 2007. If this growth rate continues, per capita GDP in China will double every eight years. These rapid growth rates have transformed the

Chinese economy. Not only is real GDP per capita 10 times higher than it was 50 years ago, but it is now possible for the typical family in China to aspire for the first time to own an automobile, a television set, a refrigerator, an air-conditioner, and other goods that have long been taken for granted by consumers in high-income countries.

Despite its very rapid recent growth, as the experience of MySpace has shown, China is not a democracy, and the Chinese government still intervenes in the economy in sometimes arbitrary ways. China has failed to fully establish the rule of law, particularly with respect to the consistent enforcement of property rights. This is a problem for the long-term prospects of the Chinese economy because entrepreneurs cannot fulfill their role in the market system of bringing together the factors of production—labor, capital, and natural resources—to produce goods and services unless the government establishes the rule of law.

For another example of how economic institutions can promote or inhibit entrepreneurship, read **AN INSIDE LOOK** on **page 758**, which discusses why Europe's economy has proven unable to grow at rates similar to those of the United States.

Sources: Patricia Sellers, "MySpace Cowboys," *Fortune*, August 29, 2006; and Geoffrey A. Fowler and Jason Dean, "In China, MySpace May Need to Be 'OurSpace,'" *Wall Street Journal*, February 2, 2007, p. B1.

LEARNING Objectives

After studying this chapter, you should be able to:

22.1 Define **economic growth**, calculate economic growth rates, and describe global trends in economic growth, page 730.

22.2 Use the **economic growth model** to explain why growth rates differ across countries, page 735.

22.3 Discuss **fluctuations** in **productivity growth** in the United States, page 742.

22.4 Explain **economic catch-up** and discuss why many poor countries have not experienced rapid economic growth, page 747.

22.5 Discuss **government policies** that foster economic growth, page 754.

Economics in YOUR Life!

Would You Be Better Off without China?

Suppose that you could choose to live and work in a world with the Chinese economy growing very rapidly or a world with the Chinese economy like it was before 1978—very poor and growing slowly. Which world would you choose to live in? How does the current high-growth, high-export Chinese economy affect you as a consumer? How does it affect you as someone about to start a career? As you read the chapter, see if you can answer these questions. You can check your answers against those we provide at the end of the chapter. >> Continued on page 757

E conomic growth is not inevitable. For most of human history, no sustained increases in output per capita occurred, and, in the words of the philosopher Thomas Hobbes, the lives of most people were "poor, nasty, brutish, and short." Sustained economic growth first began with the Industrial Revolution in England in the late eighteenth century. From there, economic growth spread to the United States, Canada, and the countries of Western Europe. Following World War II, rapid economic growth also began in Japan, but the economies of most other countries stagnated, leaving their people mired in poverty.

Real GDP per capita is the best measure of a country's standard of living because it represents the ability of the average person to buy goods and services. Economic growth occurs when real GDP per capita increases. Why have countries such as the United States and the United Kingdom, which had high standards of living at the beginning of the twentieth century, continued to grow rapidly? Why have countries such as Argentina, which at one time had relatively high standards of living, failed to keep pace? Why was the Soviet Union unable to sustain the rapid growth rates of its early years? Why are some countries that were very poor at the beginning of the twentieth century still very poor today? And why have some countries, such as South Korea and Japan, that once were very poor now become much richer? What explains China's very rapid recent growth rates? In this chapter, we will develop a *model of economic growth* that helps us answer these important questions.

22.1 | Define economic growth, calculate economic growth rates, and describe global trends in economic growth.

Economic Growth Over Time and Around the World

You live in a world that is very different from the world when your grandparents were young. You can listen to music on a thin iPod. Your grandparents played vinyl records on large stereo systems. You can pick up a cell phone or send an e-mail to someone in another city, state, or country. Your grandparents mailed letters that took days or weeks to arrive. More importantly, you have access to health care and medicines that have prolonged life and improved its quality. In many poorer countries, however, people endure grinding poverty and have only the bare necessities of life, just as their great-grandparents did.

The difference between you and people in poor countries is that you live in a country that has experienced substantial economic growth. With economic growth, an economy produces both increasing quantities of goods and services and better goods and services. It is only through economic growth that living standards can increase, but through most of human history, no economic growth took place. Even today, billions of people are living in countries where economic growth is extremely slow.

Economic Growth from 1,000,000 B.C. to the Present

In 1,000,000 B.C., our ancestors survived by hunting animals and gathering edible plant life. Farming was many years in the future, and production was limited to food, clothing, shelter, and simple tools. Bradford DeLong, an economist at the University of California, Berkeley, estimates that in these primitive circumstances, GDP per capita was about $123 per year in 2006 dollars, which was the bare amount necessary to sustain life. DeLong estimates that real GDP per capita worldwide was still $123 in the year 1300 A.D. In other words, no sustained economic growth occurred between 1,000,000 B.C. and 1300 A.D.

A peasant toiling on a farm in France in the year 1300 was no better off than his ancestors thousands of years before. In fact, for most of human existence, the typical person had the bare minimum of food, clothing, and shelter necessary to sustain life. Few people survived beyond the age of forty, and most people suffered from debilitating illnesses.

Significant economic growth did not begin until the **Industrial Revolution**, which started in England around the year 1750. The production of cotton cloth in factories using machinery powered by steam engines marked the beginning of the Industrial Revolution. Before that time, production of goods had relied almost exclusively on human or animal power. Mechanical power spread to the production of many other goods, greatly increasing the quantity of goods each worker could produce. First England, and then other countries, such as the United States, France, and Germany, experienced *long-run economic growth*, with sustained increases in real GDP per capita that eventually raised living standards in these countries to the high levels of today.

Industrial Revolution The application of mechanical power to the production of goods, beginning in England around 1750.

Making the Connection | Why Did the Industrial Revolution Begin in England?

The Industrial Revolution was a key turning point in human history. Before the Industrial Revolution, economic growth was slow and halting. After the Industrial Revolution, in a number of countries economic growth became rapid and sustained. Although historians and economists agree on the importance of the Industrial Revolution, they have not reached a consensus on why it happened where and when it did. Why the eighteenth century and not the sixteenth century or the twenty-first century? Why England and not China or India or Africa or Japan?

There is always a temptation to read history backward. We know when and where the Industrial Revolution occurred; therefore, it had to happen where it did and when it did. But what was so special about England in the eighteenth century? Nobel laureate Douglass North, of Washington University in St. Louis, has argued that institutions in England differed significantly from those in other countries in ways that greatly aided economic growth. North believes that the Glorious Revolution of 1688 was a key turning point. After that date, the British Parliament, rather than the king, controlled the government. The British court system also became independent of the king. As a result, the British government was able credibly to commit to upholding private property rights, protecting wealth, and eliminating arbitrary increases in taxes. These institutional changes gave entrepreneurs the incentive to make the investments necessary to use the important technological developments of the second half of the eighteenth century—particularly the spinning jenny and the water frame, which were used in the production of cotton textiles, and the steam engine, which was used in mining and in the manufacture of textiles and other products. Without the institutional changes, entrepreneurs would have been reluctant to risk having their property seized or their wealth confiscated by the government.

Although not all economists agree with North's specific argument about the origins of the Industrial Revolution, we will see that most economists accept the idea that economic growth is not likely to occur unless a country's government provides the type of institutional framework North describes.

The British government's guarantee of property rights set the stage for the Industrial Revolution.

Sources: Douglass C. North, *Understanding the Process of Economic Change*, Princeton, NJ: Princeton University Press, 2005; and Douglass C. North and Barry R. Weingast, "Constitutions and Commitment: The Evolution of Institutions Governing Public Choice in Seventeenth-Century England," *Journal of Economic History*, Vol. 49, No. 4, December 1989.

YOUR TURN: Test your understanding by doing related problem 1.3 on page 760 at the end of this chapter.

Figure 22-1

Average Annual Growth Rates for the World Economy

World economic growth was essentially zero in the years before 1300, and it was very slow—an average of only 0.2 percent per year—before 1800. The Industrial Revolution made possible the sustained increases in real GDP per capita that have allowed some countries to attain a high standard of living.
Source: J. Bradford DeLong, "Estimating World GDP, One Million B.C.–Present," working paper, University of California, Berkeley.

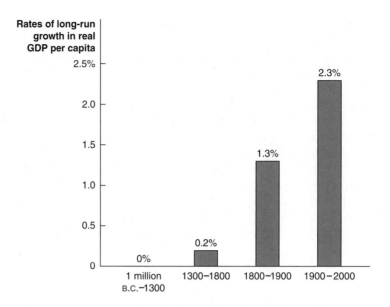

Figure 22-1 shows how growth rates of real GDP per capita for the entire world have changed over long periods. Prior to 1300 A.D., there were no sustained increases in real GDP per capita. Over the next 500 years, to 1800, there was very slow growth. Significant growth began in the nineteenth century as a result of the Industrial Revolution. A further acceleration in growth occurred during the twentieth century as the average annual growth rate increased from 1.3 percent per year to 2.3 percent per year.

Small Differences in Growth Rates Are Important

The difference between 1.3 percent and 2.3 percent may seem trivial but, over long periods, small differences in growth rates can have a large impact. For example, suppose you have $100 in a savings account earning an interest rate of 1.3 percent, which means you will receive an interest payment of $1.30 this year. If the interest rate on the account is 2.3 percent, you will earn $2.30. The difference of an extra $1.00 interest payment seems insignificant. But if you leave the interest as well as the original $100 in your account for another year, the difference becomes greater because now the higher interest rate is applied to a larger amount—$102.30—and the lower interest rate is applied to a smaller amount—$101.30. This process, known as *compounding*, magnifies even small differences in interest rates over long periods of time. Over a period of 50 years, your $100 would grow to $312 at an interest rate of 2.3 percent but to only $191 at an interest rate of 1.3 percent.

What applies to interest rates also applies to growth rates. For example, in 1950, real GDP per capita in Argentina was $6,942 (measured in 2000 dollars), which was larger than France's real GDP per capita of $5,921. Over the next 57 years, the economic growth rate in France averaged 2.7 percent per year, while in Argentina, it was only 1.0 percent per year. Although this difference in growth rates of less than two percentage points may seem small, in 2007, real GDP per capita in France had risen to $27,742, while real GDP per capita in Argentina was only $12,268. In other words, because of a relatively small difference in the growth rates of the two economies, the standard of living of the typical person in France went from being below that of the typical person in Argentina to being much higher. The important point to keep in mind is this: *In the long run, small differences in economic growth rates result in big differences in living standards.*

Why Do Growth Rates Matter?

Why should anyone care about growth rates? Growth rates matter because an economy that grows too slowly fails to raise living standards. In some countries in Africa and Asia, very little economic growth has occurred in the past 50 years, so many people remain in

Don't Let This Happen to **YOU!**

Don't Confuse the Average Annual Percentage Change with the Total Percentage Change

When economists talk about growth rates over a period of more than one year, the numbers are always *average annual percentage changes* and *not* total percentage changes. For example, in the United States, real GDP per capita was $11,752 in 1950 and $38,316 in 2007. The percentage change in real GDP per capita between these two years is:

$$\left(\frac{\$38,316 - \$11,752}{\$11,752}\right) \times 100 = 226\%.$$

However, this is *not* the growth rate between the two years. The growth rate between these two years is the rate at which $11,752 in 1950 would have to grow on average *each year* to end up as $38,316 in 2007, which is 2.1 percent.

YOUR TURN: Test your understanding by doing related problem 1.6 on page 761 at the end of this chapter.

---

severe poverty. In high-income countries, only 4 out of every 1,000 babies die before the age of one. In the poorest countries, more than 100 out of every 1,000 babies die before the age of one, and millions of children die each year from diseases that could be avoided by access to clean water or cured by medicines that cost only a few dollars.

Although their problems are less dramatic, countries that experience slow growth have also missed an opportunity to improve the lives of their citizens. For example, the failure of Argentina to grow as rapidly as the other countries that had similar levels of GDP per capita in 1950 has left many of its people in poverty. Life expectancy in Argentina is several years lower than in the United States and other high-income countries, and more than twice times as many babies in Argentina die before the age of one.

Making the Connection | The Benefits of an Earlier Start: Standards of Living in China and Japan

We noted at the beginning of this chapter that China has experienced very high growth rates in recent years. Between 1996 and 2007, real GDP per capita in China grew at an average annual rate of 9.1 percent. Japan, in contrast, grew at the much slower rate of 2.1 percent. Between 1950 and 1978, however, China had grown relatively slowly while Japan was growing rapidly. As a result, in 2007, the standard of living in China was still well below that in Japan. For example, GDP per capita measured in U.S. dollars was $5,478 in China in 2007 but $33,603—or more than six times higher—in Japan. The following table shows other measures of the standard of living for China and Japan.

Sustained high rates of economic growth have helped Japan attain high living standards.

	CHINA	JAPAN
Life expectancy at birth	72.5 years	82.3 years
Infant mortality (per 1,000 live births)	23	3
Percentage of the population surviving on less than $2 per day	35%	0%
Percentage of the population with access to improved water source	77%	100%
Percentage of the population with access to improved sanitation	44%	100%
Internet users per 1,000 people	85	668

In each of the measures shown in the preceding table, China continues to lag behind Japan as well as the United States and other high-income countries. If the

Chinese economy can sustain the high growth rates of recent years, it will continue to close the gap with Japan in real GDP per capita and other measures of the standard of living. The moral of the story is that only by sustaining high rates of economic growth over many years will the currently low-income countries be able to attain the high living standards people in Japan, the United States, and other high-income countries enjoy today.

Source: United Nations Development Programme, *Human Development Report, 2007/2008*, New York: Palgrave Macmillan, 2007.

YOUR TURN: Test your understanding by doing related problem 1.7 on page 761 at the end of this chapter.

"The Rich Get Richer and . . . "

We can divide the world's economies into two groups: the *high-income countries*, sometimes also referred to as the industrial countries, and the poorer countries, or *developing countries*. The high-income countries include the countries of Western Europe, Australia, Canada, Japan, New Zealand, and the United States. The developing countries include most of the countries of Africa, Asia, and Latin America. In the 1980s and 1990s, a small group of countries, mostly East Asian countries such as Singapore, South Korea, and Taiwan, experienced high rates of growth and are sometimes referred to as the *newly industrializing countries*. Figure 22-2 shows the levels of GDP per capita around the world in 2007. GDP is measured in U.S. dollars, corrected for differences across countries in the cost of living. In 2007, GDP per capita ranged from a high of $80,500 in Luxembourg to a low of $600 in Somalia. To understand why the gap between rich and poor countries exists, we need to look at what causes economies to grow.

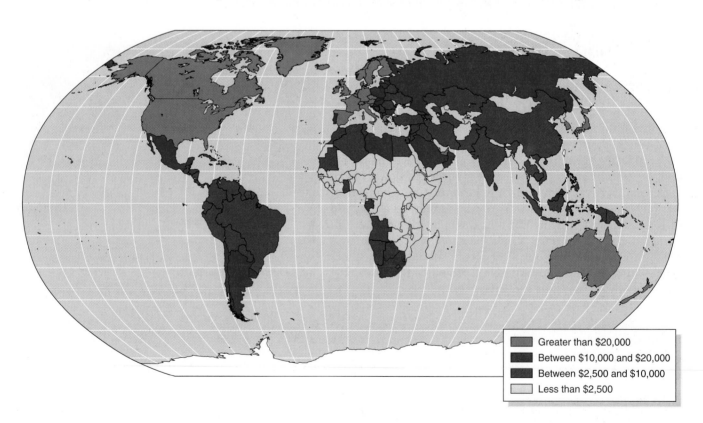

▨	Greater than $20,000
▨	Between $10,000 and $20,000
▨	Between $2,500 and $10,000
▢	Less than $2,500

Figure 22-2   │   **GDP per Capita, 2007**

GDP per capita is measured in U.S. dollars corrected for differences across countries in the cost of living.

22.2 | Use the economic growth model to explain why growth rates differ across countries.

What Determines How Fast Economies Grow?

To explain changes in economic growth rates over time within countries and differences in growth rates among countries, we need to develop an *economic growth model*. An **economic growth model** explains growth rates in real GDP per capita over the long run. As we noted in Chapter 21, the average person can buy more goods and services only if the average worker produces more goods and services. Recall that **labor productivity** is the quantity of goods and services that can be produced by one worker or by one hour of work. Because of the importance of labor productivity in explaining economic growth, the economic growth model focuses on the causes of long-run increases in labor productivity.

How can a country's workers become more productive? Economists believe two key factors determine labor productivity: the quantity of capital per hour worked and the level of technology. Therefore, the economic growth model focuses on technological change and changes over time in the quantity of capital available to workers in explaining changes in real GDP per capita. Recall that **technological change** is a change in the quantity of output firms can produce using a given quantity of inputs.

There are three main sources of technological change:

- *Better machinery and equipment.* Beginning with the steam engine during the Industrial Revolution, the invention of new machinery has been an important source of rising labor productivity. Today, continuing improvements in computers, factory machine tools, electric generators, and many other machines contribute to increases in labor productivity.

- *Increases in human capital.* Capital refers to *physical capital*, including computers, factory buildings, machine tools, warehouses, and trucks. The more physical capital workers have available, the more output they can produce. **Human capital** is the accumulated knowledge and skills that workers acquire from education and training or from their life experiences. As workers increase their human capital through education or on-the-job training, their productivity also increases. The more educated workers are, the greater is their human capital.

- *Better means of organizing and managing production.* Labor productivity increases if managers can do a better job of organizing production. For example, the *just-in-time system*, first developed by Toyota Motor Corporation, involves assembling goods from parts that arrive at the factory at the exact time they are needed. With this system, fewer workers are needed to store and keep track of parts in the factory, so the quantity of goods produced per hour worked increases.

It is important to note that technological change is *not* the same thing as more physical capital. New capital can embody technological change, as when a new processor is embodied in a new computer. But simply adding more capital of the same kind as existing capital is not technological change. To summarize, we can say that the more capital workers have available on their jobs, the better the capital, the more human capital workers have, and the better job business managers do in organizing production, the higher a country's standard of living will be.

Economic growth model A model that explains growth rates in real GDP per capita over the long run.

Labor productivity The quantity of goods and services that can be produced by one worker or by one hour of work.

Technological change A change in the quantity of output a firm can produce using a given quantity of inputs.

Human capital The accumulated knowledge and skills that workers acquire from education and training or from their life experiences.

The Per-Worker Production Function

The economic growth model explains increases in real GDP per capita over time as resulting from increases in just two factors: the quantity of physical capital available to workers and technological change. Often when analyzing economic growth, we look at increases in real GDP *per hour worked* and increases in capital *per hour worked*. We use

Figure 22-3

The Per-Worker Production Function

The per-worker production function shows the relationship between capital per hour worked and real GDP per hour worked, holding technology constant. Increases in capital per hour worked increase output per hour worked but at a diminishing rate. For example, an increase in capital per hour worked from $20,000 to $30,000 increases real GDP per hour worked from $200 to $350. An increase in capital per hour worked from $30,000 to $40,000 increases real GDP per hour worked only from $350 to $475. Each additional $10,000 increase in capital per hour worked results in progressively smaller increases in output per work.

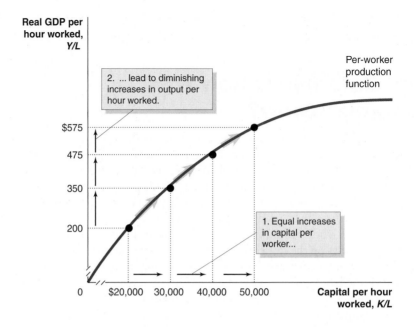

Per-worker production function
The relationship between real GDP per hour worked and capital per hour worked, holding the level of technology constant.

measures of GDP and capital per hour rather than per person so we can analyze changes in the underlying ability of an economy to produce more goods with a given amount of labor without having to worry about changes in the fraction of the population working or in the length of the workday. We can illustrate the economic growth model using the **per-worker production function**, which is the relationship between real GDP per hour worked and capital per hour worked, *holding the level of technology constant*. Figure 22-3 shows the per-worker production function as a graph. In the figure, we measure capital per hour worked along the horizontal axis and real GDP per hour worked along the vertical axis. Letting K stand for capital, L stand for labor, and Y stand for real GDP, real GDP per hour worked is Y/L, and capital per hour worked is K/L. The curve represents the production function. Notice that we do not explicitly show technological change in the figure. We assume that as we move along the production function shown in the figure, the level of technology remains constant. As we will see, we can illustrate technological change using this graph by *shifting up* the curve representing the production function.

The figure shows that increases in the quantity of capital per hour worked result in movements up the per-worker production function, increasing the quantity of output each worker produces. When *holding technology constant*, however, equal increases in the amount of capital per hour worked lead to *diminishing* increases in output per hour worked. For example, increasing capital per hour worked from $20,000 to $30,000 increases real GDP per hour worked from $200 to $350, an increase of $150. Another $10,000 increase in capital per hour worked, from $30,000 to $40,000, increases real GDP per hour worked from $350 to $475, an increase of only $125. Each additional $10,000 increase in capital per hour worked results in progressively smaller increases in real GDP per hour worked. In fact, at very high levels of capital per hour worked, further increases in capital per hour worked will not result in any increase in real GDP per hour worked. This effect results from the *law of diminishing returns*, which states that as we add more of one input—in this case, capital—to a fixed quantity of another input—in this case, labor—output increases by smaller additional amounts.

Why are there diminishing returns to capital? Consider a simple example in which you own a copy store. At first you have 10 employees but only 1 copy machine, so each of your workers is able to produce relatively few copies per day. When you buy a second copy machine, your employees will be able to produce more copies. Adding additional copy machines will continue to increase your output—but by increasingly smaller amounts. For example, adding a twentieth copy machine to the 19 you already have will not increase the copies each worker is able to make by nearly as much as adding a second copy machine did. Eventually, adding additional copying machines will not increase your output at all.

Which Is More Important for Economic Growth: More Capital or Technological Change?

Technological change helps economies avoid diminishing returns to capital. Let's consider a couple of simple examples of the effects of technological change. First, suppose you have 10 copy machines in your copy store. Each of the copy machines can produce 10 copies per minute. You don't believe that adding an eleventh machine identical to the 10 you already have will significantly increase the number of copies your employees can produce in a day. Then you find out that a new copy machine has become available that produces 20 copies per minute. If you replace your existing machines with the new machines, the productivity of your workers will increase. The replacement of existing capital with more productive capital is an example of technological change.

Or suppose you realize that the layout of your store could be improved. Maybe the paper for the machines is on shelves at the back of the store, which requires your workers to waste time walking back and forth whenever the machines run out of paper. By placing the paper closer to the copy machines, you can improve the productivity of your workers. Reorganizing how production takes place so as to increase output is also an example of technological change.

Technological Change: The Key to Sustaining Economic Growth

Figure 22-4 shows the impact of technological change on the per-worker production function. Technological change shifts up the per-worker production function and allows an economy to produce more real GDP per hour worked with the same quantity of capital per hour worked. For example, if the current level of technology puts the economy on Production function$_1$, then when capital per hour worked is $50,000, real GDP per hour worked is $575. Technological change that shifts the economy to Production function$_2$ makes it possible to produce $675 in goods and services per hour worked with the same level of capital per hour worked. Further increases in technology that shift the economy to higher production functions result in further increases in real GDP per

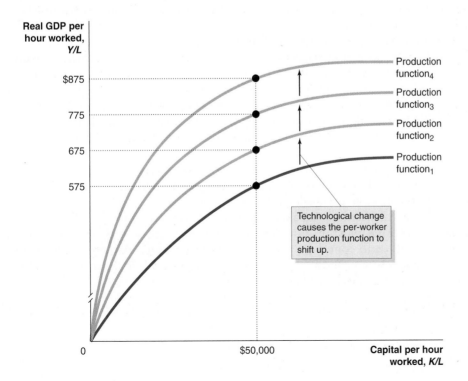

Figure 22-4

Technological Change Increases Output per Hour Worked

Technological change shifts up the production function and allows more output per hour worked with the same amount of capital per hour worked. For example, along Production function$_1$ with $50,000 in capital per hour worked, the economy can produce $575 in real GDP per hour worked. However, an increase in technology that shifts the economy to Production function$_2$ makes it possible to produce $675 in real GDP per hour worked with the same level of capital per hour worked.

hour worked. Because of diminishing returns to capital, continuing increases in real GDP per hour worked can be sustained only if there is technological change. Remember that a country will experience increases in its standard of living only if it experiences increases in real GDP per hour worked. Therefore, we can draw the following important conclusion: *In the long run, a country will experience an increasing standard of living only if it experiences continuing technological change.*

The fall of the Berlin Wall in 1989 symbolized the failure of Communism.

Making the Connection | What Explains the Economic Failure of the Soviet Union?

The economic growth model can help explain one of the most striking events of the twentieth century: the economic collapse of the Soviet Union. The Soviet Union was formed from the old Russian Empire following the Communist revolution of 1917. Under Communism, the Soviet Union was a centrally planned economy where the government owned nearly every business and made all production and pricing decisions. In 1960, Nikita Khrushchev, the leader of the Soviet Union, addressed the United Nations in New York City. He declared to the United States and the other democracies, "We will bury you. Your grandchildren will live under Communism."

Many people at the time took Khrushchev's boast seriously. Capital per hour worked grew rapidly in the Soviet Union from 1950 through the 1980s. At first, these increases in capital per hour worked also produced rapid increases in real GDP per hour worked. Rapid increases in real GDP per hour worked during the 1950s caused some economists in the United States to predict incorrectly that the Soviet Union would someday surpass the United States economically. In fact, diminishing returns to capital meant that the additional factories the Soviet Union was building resulted in smaller and smaller increases in real GDP per hour worked.

The Soviet Union did experience some technological change—but at a rate much slower than in the United States and other industrial countries. Why did the Soviet Union fail the crucial requirement for growth: implementing new technologies? The key reason is that in a centrally planned economy, the persons in charge of running most businesses are government employees and not entrepreneurs or independent business-people, as is the case in market economies. Soviet managers had little incentive to adopt new ways of doing things. Their pay depended on producing the quantity of output specified in the government's economic plan, not on discovering new, better, and lower-cost ways to produce goods. In addition, these managers did not have to worry about competition from either domestic or foreign firms.

Entrepreneurs and managers of firms in the United States, by contrast, are under intense competitive pressure from other firms. They must constantly search for better ways of producing the goods and services they sell. Developing and using new technologies is an important way to gain a competitive edge and higher profits. The drive for profit provides an incentive for technological change that centrally planned economies are unable to duplicate. In market economies, decisions about which investments to make and which technologies to adopt are made by entrepreneurs and managers who have their own money on the line. In the Soviet system, these decisions were usually made by salaried bureaucrats trying to fulfill a plan formulated in Moscow. Nothing concentrates the mind like having your own funds at risk.

In hindsight, it is clear that a centrally planned economy, such as the Soviet Union's, could not, over the long run, grow faster than a market economy. The Soviet Union collapsed in 1991, and contemporary Russia now has a more market-oriented system, although the government continues to play a much larger role in the economy than does the government in the United States.

YOUR TURN: Test your understanding by doing related problems 2.10 and 2.11 on pages 762–763 at the end of this chapter.

Solved Problem | 22-2

Using the Economic Growth Model to Analyze the Failure of the Soviet Union's Economy

Use the economic growth model and the information in the *Making the Connection* on page 738 to analyze the economic problems the Soviet Union encountered.

SOLVING THE PROBLEM:

Step 1: **Review the chapter material.** This problem is about using the economic growth model to explain the failure of the Soviet economy, so you may want to review the *Making the Connection* on page 738.

Step 2: **Draw a graph like Figure 22-3 to illustrate the economic problems of the Soviet Union.** For simplicity, we can assume that the Soviet Union experienced no technological change.

The Soviet Union experienced rapid increases in capital per hour worked from 1950 through the 1980s, but its failure to implement new technology meant that output per hour worked grew at a slower and slower rate.

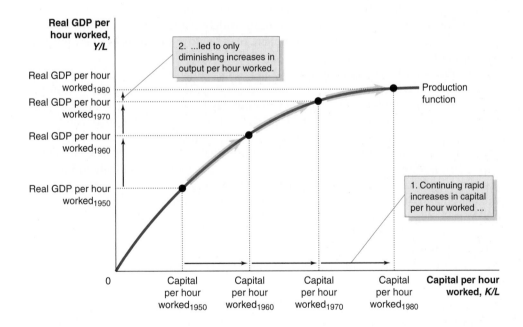

EXTRA CREDIT: The Soviet Union hoped to raise the standard of living of its citizens above that enjoyed in the United States and other high-income countries. Its strategy was to make continuous increases in the quantity of capital available to its workers. The economic growth model helps us understand the flaws in this policy for achieving economic growth.

YOUR TURN: For more practice, do related problems 2.7 and 2.8 on page 762 at the end of this chapter.

≫ End Solved Problem 22-2

New Growth Theory

The economic growth model we have been using was first developed in the 1950s by Nobel laureate Robert Solow, of MIT. According to this model, productivity growth is the key factor in explaining long-run growth in real GDP per capita. In recent years, some economists have become dissatisfied with this model because it does not explain the factors that determine productivity growth. What has become known as the **new growth theory** was developed by Paul Romer, an economist at Stanford University, to provide a better explanation of the sources of productivity change. Romer argues that the rate of technological change is influenced by how individuals and firms respond to economic incentives. Earlier accounts of economic growth left technological change unexplained or attributed it to factors such as chance scientific discoveries.

Romer argues that the accumulation of *knowledge capital* is a key determinant of economic growth. Firms add to an economy's stock of knowledge capital when they engage in research and development or otherwise contribute to technological change. We have seen that accumulation of physical capital is subject to diminishing returns: Increases in capital per hour worked lead to increases in real GDP per hour worked but at a decreasing rate. Romer argues that the same is true of knowledge capital *at the firm level*. As firms add to their stock of knowledge capital, they increase their output but at a decreasing rate. At the level of the economy, however, Romer argues that knowledge capital is subject to *increasing returns*. Increasing returns can exist because knowledge, once discovered, becomes available to everyone. The use of physical capital, such as a computer or machine tool, is *rival* because if one firm uses it other firms cannot, and it is *excludable* because the firm that owns the capital can keep other firms from using it. The use of knowledge capital, such as the chemical formula for a drug that cures cancer, is nonrival, however, because one firm's using that knowledge does not prevent another firm's using it. Knowledge capital is also nonexcludable because once something like a chemical formula becomes known, it becomes widely available for other firms to use (unless, as we discuss shortly, the government gives the firm that invents a new product the legal right to exclusive use of it).

Because knowledge capital is nonrival and nonexcludable, firms can *free ride* on the research and development of other firms. Firms free ride when they benefit from the results of research and development they did not pay for. For example, transistor technology was first developed at Western Electric's Bell Laboratories in the 1950s and served as the basic technology of the information revolution. Bell Laboratories, however, received only a tiny fraction of the immense profits that were eventually made by all the firms that used this technology. Romer points out that firms are unlikely to invest in research and development up to the point where the marginal cost of the research equals the marginal return from the knowledge gained because much of the marginal return will be gained by *other* firms. Therefore, there is likely to be an inefficiently small amount of research and development, slowing the accumulation of knowledge capital and economic growth.

Government policy can help increase the accumulation of knowledge capital in three ways:

- *Protecting intellectual property with patents and copyrights.* Governments can increase the incentive to engage in research and development by giving firms the exclusive rights to their discoveries for a period of years. The U.S. government grants patents to companies that develop new products or new ways of making existing products. A **patent** gives a firm the exclusive legal right to a new product for a period of 20 years from the date the product is invented. For example, a pharmaceutical firm that develops a drug that cures cancer can secure a patent on the drug, keeping other firms from manufacturing the drug without permission. The profits earned during the period the patent is in force provide an incentive for undertaking the research and development. The patent system has drawbacks, however. In filing for a patent, a firm must disclose information about the product or process. This information enters the public record and may help competing firms develop

New growth theory A model of long-run economic growth which emphasizes that technological change is influenced by economic incentives and so is determined by the working of the market system.

Patent The exclusive right to a product for a period of 20 years from the date the product is invented.

products or processes that are similar but that do not infringe on the patent. To avoid this problem, a firm may try to keep the results of its research a *trade secret*, without patenting it. A famous example of a trade secret is the formula for Coca-Cola. Tension also arises between the government's objectives of providing patent protection that gives firms the incentive to engage in research and development and making sure that the knowledge gained through the research is widely disseminated for the greatest impact on the economy. Economists debate the features of an ideal patent system.

Just as a new product or a new method of making a product receives patent protection, books, films, and software receive *copyright* protection. Under U.S. law, the creator of a book, film, or piece of software has the exclusive right to use the creation during the creator's lifetime. The creator's heirs retain this exclusive right for 70 years after the creator's death.

- *Subsidizing research and development.* The government can use subsidies to increase the quantity of research and development that takes place. In the United States, the federal government carries out some research directly. For example, the National Institutes of Health conducts medical research. The government also subsidizes research by providing grants to researchers in universities through the National Science Foundation and other agencies. Finally, the government provides tax benefits to firms that invest in research and development.

- *Subsidizing education.* People with technical training carry out research and development. If firms are unable to capture all the profits from research and development, the wages and salaries paid to technical workers will be reduced. These lower wages and salaries reduce the incentive to workers to receive this training. If the government subsidizes education, it can increase the number of workers who have technical training. In the United States, the government subsidizes education by directly providing free education from grades kindergarten through 12 and by providing support for public colleges and universities. The government also provides student loans at reduced interest rates.

These government policies can bring the accumulation of knowledge capital closer to the optimal level.

Joseph Schumpeter and Creative Destruction

The new growth theory has revived interest in the ideas of Joseph Schumpeter. Schumpeter was born in Austria in 1883. He served briefly as that country's finance minister, before becoming an economics professor at Harvard in 1932. Schumpeter developed a model of growth that emphasized his view that new products unleash a "gale of creative destruction" in which older products—and, often, the firms that produced them—are driven out of the market. According to Schumpeter, the key to rising living standards is not small changes to existing products but, rather, new products that meet consumer wants in qualitatively better ways. For example, in the early twentieth century, the automobile displaced the horse-drawn carriage by meeting consumer demand for personal transportation in a way that was qualitatively better. In the early twenty-first century, the DVD and the DVD player displaced the VHS tape and the VCR by better meeting consumer demand for watching films at home.

To Schumpeter, the entrepreneur is central to economic growth: "The function of entrepreneurs is to reform or revolutionize the pattern of production by exploiting an invention or, more generally, an untried technological possibility for producing new commodities or producing an old one in a new way."

The profits an entrepreneur hopes to earn provide the incentive for bringing together the factors of production—labor, capital, and natural resources—to start new firms and introduce new goods and services. Successful entrepreneurs can use their profits to finance the development of new products and are better able to attract funds from investors.

22.3 | Discuss fluctuations in productivity growth in the United States.

Economic Growth in the United States

The economic growth model can help us understand the record of growth in the United States. Figure 22-5 shows average annual growth rates in real GDP per hour worked since 1800. As the United States experienced the Industrial Revolution during the nineteenth century, U.S. firms increased the quantities of capital per hour worked. New technologies such as the steam engine, the railroad, and the telegraph also became available. Together, these factors resulted in an average annual growth rate of real GDP per worker of 1.3 percent from 1800 to 1900. Real GDP per capita grew at a slower rate of 1.1 percent during this period. At this growth rate, real GDP per capita would double about every 63 years, which means that living standards were growing steadily, but relatively slowly.

By the twentieth century, technological change had been institutionalized. Many large corporations began to set up research and development facilities to improve the quality of their products and the efficiency with which they produced them. Universities also began to conduct research that had business applications. After World War II, many corporations began to provide significant funds to universities to help pay for research. In 1950, the federal government created the National Science Foundation, whose main goal is to support university researchers. The accelerating rate of technological change led to more rapid growth rates.

Economic Growth in the United States since 1950: Fast, Then Slow, Then Fast Again

Continuing technological change allowed the U.S. economy to avoid the diminishing returns to capital that stifled growth in the Soviet economy. In fact, until the 1970s, the growth rate of the U.S. economy accelerated over time. As Figure 22-5 shows, growth in the first half of the twentieth century was faster than growth during the nineteenth century, and growth from 1950 to 1972 was faster yet. Then the unexpected happened: For more than 20 years, from 1973 to 1994, the growth rate of real GDP per hour worked slowed. The growth rate during these years was more than one percentage point per year lower than during the 1950–1972 period. Measured in 2000 dollars, real GDP per hour worked in the United States was $25,903 in 1972. If it had continued to grow from 1973

Figure 22-5

Average Annual Growth Rates in Real GDP per Hour Worked in the United States

The growth rate in the United States increased from 1800 through the mid-1970s. Then, for more than 20 years, growth slowed before increasing again in the mid-1990s.
Note: The values for 1800–1900 are real GDP per worker. The values for 1900–2007 are real GDP per hour worked and are the authors' calculations, based on data in Neville Francis and Valerie A. Ramey, "The Source of Historical Economic Fluctuations: An Analysis Using Long-Run Restrictions," in Jeffrey Frankel, Richard Clarida, and Francesco Giavazzi, eds., *International Seminar in Macroeconomics*, Chicago: University of Chicago Press, 2005; the authors thank Neville Francis for kindly providing these data.

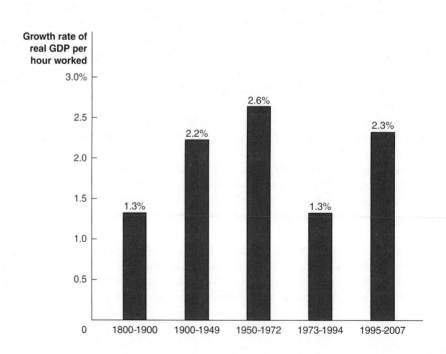

to 1994 at the same rate it had been growing from 1950 to 1972, it would have been about $45,500 in 1994, which is 30 percent higher than it actually was. The United States would today be a significantly richer country if the growth in the productivity of U.S. workers had not slowed down from the mid-1970s to the mid-1990s.

What Caused the Productivity Slowdown of 1973-1994?

Several explanations have been offered for the productivity slowdown of the mid-1970s to mid-1990s, but none is completely satisfying. We can briefly discuss three possible explanations for the slowdown:

- Measurement problems
- High oil prices
- A decline in labor quality

Was It a Measurement Problem? Some economists argue that productivity really didn't slow down from the mid-1970s to mid-1990s. They argue it only *appears* to have slowed down because of problems in measuring productivity accurately. After 1970, services—such as haircuts and financial advice—became a larger fraction of GDP, and goods—such as automobiles and hamburgers—became a smaller fraction. It is more difficult to measure increases in the output of services than to measure increases in the output of goods. Beginning in the 1970s, advances in information technology improved the convenience of some services without actually increasing the quantity of the services offered. For example, before banks began using automated teller machines (ATMs) in the 1980s, to withdraw money, you would have to go to a bank before closing time—which was usually 3:00 P.M. Once ATMs became available, you could withdraw money at any time of the day or night at a variety of locations. This increased convenience from ATMs does not show up in GDP. If it did, measured output per hour worked would have grown more rapidly.

There may also be a measurement problem in accounting for improvements in the environment and in health and safety. The Clean Air Act, passed in 1970, was the first of several federal laws that required firms to significantly reduce pollution. Other laws passed during the 1970s were aimed at promoting health and safety. The Occupational Safety and Health Administration (OSHA) and the Consumer Product Safety Commission were also given the authority to issue guidelines that firms are legally required to obey. As a result, firms had to spend billions of dollars reducing pollution, improving workplace safety, and redesigning products to improve their safety. This spending did not result in additional output that would be included in GDP—although it may have increased overall well-being. If these increases in well-being had been included in GDP, measured output per hour worked would have grown more rapidly.

It is possible that these changes in the economy during the 1970s—increased production of services and increased spending by firms to comply with environmental, safety, and health regulations—account for some of the slowdown in the growth rate of output per hour worked. However, most economists do not believe that the effect of these factors is large enough to be the whole explanation.

Was It the Effect of High Oil Prices? In 1973, the Organization of Petroleum Exporting Countries (OPEC) increased the price of a barrel of oil from less than $3 to more than $10. A second sharp increase in oil prices occurred in the late 1970s, when the price of a barrel of oil rose from about $20 to more than $35. These higher oil prices increased production costs for many firms in the United States. Some firms use oil directly in the production process. Other firms use products, such as plastics, that are made from oil. Some utilities burn oil to generate electricity, so electricity prices rose. Rising oil prices led to rising gasoline prices, which raised transportation costs for many firms. To conserve oil and use less energy, firms reorganized production in ways that reduced output per hour worked.

In the early 1980s, many economists thought the oil price increases explained the productivity slowdown, but the productivity slowdown continued after U.S. firms had fully adjusted to high oil prices. In fact, it continued into the late 1980s and early 1990s, when oil prices declined.

Was It the Declining Quality of Labor? Some economists argue that deterioration in the U.S. educational system may have contributed to the slowdown in growth from the mid-1970s to mid-1990s. Scores on some standardized tests began to decline in the 1970s. This decline may indicate that, on average, workers entering the labor force were less well educated and less productive than in earlier decades. A more subtle argument is that the skills required to perform many jobs increased during the 1970s and 1980s, while the preparation that workers had received in school did not keep pace. It is difficult to quantify the skill requirements of jobs and the skills of workers. So, it is difficult to estimate how much of the growth slowdown may have been due to the failure of worker skills to keep pace with the skill requirements of jobs.

The Productivity Slowdown Affected All Industrial Countries In assessing possible causes of the productivity slowdown, it is important to note that the United States was not alone in experiencing the slowdown in productivity. All the leading industrial countries experienced a growth slowdown between the mid-1970s and the mid-1990s. Therefore, explanations for the slowdown that rely on factors affecting only the United States—such as the deterioration in the quality of education—are not likely to be correct. Because all the industrial economies began producing more services and fewer goods and enacted stricter environmental regulations at about the same time, explanations of the productivity slowdown that emphasize measurement problems become more plausible. In the end, though, economists have not yet reached a consensus on why the productivity slowdown took place.

The Productivity Boom: Are We in a "New Economy"?

The productivity slowdown began abruptly in the mid-1970s and ended just as abruptly in the mid-1990s. As Figure 22-5 shows, productivity growth in the United States between 1995 and 2007 was almost as fast as before the growth slowdown. Some economists argue that the development of a "new economy" based on information technology caused the higher productivity growth that began in the mid-1990s. The spread of ever faster and increasingly less expensive computers has made communication and data processing easier and faster than ever before. Today, a single desktop computer has more computing power than all the mainframe computers NASA used to control the Apollo spacecrafts that landed on the moon in the late 1960s and early 1970s.

Faster data processing has had a major impact on nearly every firm. Business record keeping, once done laboriously by hand, is now done more quickly and accurately by computer. The increase in Internet use during the 1990s brought changes to the ways firms sell to consumers and to each other. Cell phones, laptop computers, and wireless Internet access allow people to work away from the office, whether at home or while traveling. These developments have significantly increased labor productivity.

Many economists are optimistic that the increases in productivity that began in the mid-1990s will continue. The use of computers, as well as information and communications technology in general, increases as prices continue to fall. By 2008, well-equipped desktop computers could be purchased for less than $300. Further innovations in information and communications technology may continue to contribute to strong productivity growth. Some economists are skeptical, however, about the ability of the economy to continue to sustain high rates of productivity growth. These economists argue that in the 1990s, innovations in information and communications technology—such as the development of the World Wide Web, Windows 95, and computerized inventory control systems—raised labor productivity by having a substantial effect on how businesses operated. By the early 2000s, these economists argue, innovations in information and communications technology were having a greater impact on consumer products, such as cell phones, than on the processes internal to firms that would lead to higher productivity.

If the rapid increases in output per hour worked that began in the mid-1990s do continue, this trend will be good news for increases in living standards in the United States.

Why Has Productivity Growth Been Faster in the United States than in Other Countries?

One notable aspect of the increase in productivity after 1995 is that, unlike the earlier productivity slowdown, it has not been experienced equally by all of the leading industrial countries. Figure 22-6 shows labor productivity growth during the years from 1996 to 2007 for the leading industrial countries, known collectively as the *Group of Seven*, or the *G-7* countries. Productivity growth was significantly higher in the United States than in the other countries, with the exception of the United Kingdom. Japan, France, Germany, and Italy actually experienced *slower* productivity growth during these years than during the years from 1973 to 1995.

Why has productivity growth in the United States been more rapid than in most other industrial countries? Many economists believe there are two main explanations: the greater flexibility of U.S. labor markets and the greater efficiency of the U.S. financial system. U.S. labor markets are more flexible than labor markets in other countries for several reasons. In many European countries, government regulations make it difficult for firms to fire workers. These regulations make firms reluctant to hire workers. As a result, many younger workers have difficulty finding jobs, and once a job is found, a worker tends to remain in it even if his or her skills and preferences are not a good match for the characteristics of the job. In the United States, by contrast, government regulations are less restrictive, workers have an easier time finding jobs, and workers also change jobs fairly frequently. For example, a typical young worker in the United States will hold seven different jobs during the worker's first 10 years in the labor force. This high rate of job mobility ensures a better match between workers' skills and preferences and the characteristics of jobs, which increases labor productivity. The higher productivity translates into higher wages: One-third of the increase in wages experienced by young workers results from job changes. Workers can also build skills through being exposed to a variety of different jobs. Workers in the United States may acquire as much as half of their skills through job mobility, on-the-job learning, and workplace education.

Many European countries also have restrictive work rules that limit the flexibility of firms to implement new technologies. Some of these work rules are imposed by government regulation, others are negotiated by labor unions. Because these rules restrict the tasks workers can be asked to perform and the hours during the day they can be asked to

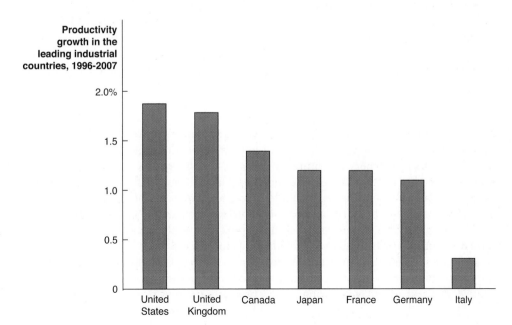

Figure 22-6

Productivity Growth in the Leading Industrial Economies, 1996–2007

Productivity growth as measured by the average annual growth rate of labor productivity was more rapid in the United States than in the other leading industrial countries during the years between 1996 and 2007.

Source: Organization for Economic Cooperation and Development, *Economic Outlook*, June 2008, Annex Table 12.

work, they reduce the ability of firms to use new technologies that may require workers to learn new skills, perform new tasks, or work during the night or early mornings. Firms must often negotiate with workers before introducing new products or relocating facilities. The hours that retail stores may be open are regulated in most European countries. These regulations reduce the revenue firms can generate from implementing new technologies and therefore reduce the incentives that firms have to adopt the technologies.

Workers in the United States tend to enter the labor force earlier, retire later, and experience fewer long spells of unemployment than do workers in Europe. These differences between the labor force experiences of U.S. and European workers, including the greater tendency for U.S. teenagers and college students to work at least part time, can be explained in several ways. One key difference, however, is the design of the systems of government-provided unemployment insurance. As we noted in Chapter 20, unemployed workers in the United States are usually eligible to receive unemployment insurance payments equal to about half their previous wage for only six months. After that time, the opportunity cost of continuing to search for a job rises. In many other high-income countries, such as Canada and most of the countries of Western Europe, workers are eligible to receive unemployment payments for a year or more, and the payments may equal 70 percent to 80 percent of their previous wage. Because the opportunity cost of being unemployed is lower in those countries, the unemployment rate tends to be higher, and the fraction of the labor force that is unemployed for more than one year also tends to be higher. Studies have shown that workers who are employed for longer periods tend to have greater skills, greater productivity, and higher wages. Many economists believe that the design of the U.S. unemployment insurance program has contributed to the greater flexibility of U.S. labor markets and to higher rates of growth in labor productivity.

As we have seen, technological change is essential for rapid productivity growth. To obtain the funds needed to implement new technologies, firms turn to the financial system. It is important that funds for investment be not only available but also allocated efficiently. In the Soviet Union, there was no shortage of funds available for investment, but the funds were directed by the government mainly into building additional factories that employed old technologies rather than being directed by entrepreneurs into funding the innovations that would have raised productivity and living standards. We saw in Chapter 7 that large corporations can raise funds by selling stocks and bonds in financial markets. U.S. corporations benefit from the efficiency of U.S. financial markets. The level of legal protection of investors is relatively high in U.S. financial markets, which encourages both U.S. and foreign investors to buy stocks and bonds issued by U.S. firms. The volume of trading in U.S. financial markets also assures investors that they will be able to quickly sell the stocks and the bonds they buy. This *liquidity* also serves to attract investors to U.S. markets.

Smaller firms that are unable to issue stocks and bonds often obtain funding from banks. However, entrepreneurs founding new firms, particularly firms that are based on new technologies, often cannot rely on banks or on sales of stocks and bonds in financial markets. Investors are usually unwilling to buy the stocks and bonds of a new firm that lacks a track record of profitability. Banks are similarly reluctant to lend money to a firm whose business plan is based on introducing a new product or a new way of producing an existing product. Many firms that are established to bring new technologies to market obtain funds from *venture capital firms*. Venture capital firms raise funds from institutional investors, such as pension funds, and from wealthy individuals, to invest in start-up firms. The owners of venture capital firms closely examine the business plans of start-up firms, looking for those that appear most likely to succeed. In exchange for providing funding, a venture capital firm often becomes part owner of the start-up, placing its representative on the start-up's board of directors and sometimes even playing a role in managing the firm. A successful venture capital firm is able to attract investors who would not otherwise be willing to provide funds to start-up firms because the investors would lack sufficient credible information on any start-up's prospectus. The ability of venture capital firms to finance technology-driven start-up firms may be giving the United States an advantage in bringing new products and new processes to market.

22.4 | Explain economic catch-up and discuss why many poor countries have not experienced rapid economic growth.

Why Isn't the Whole World Rich?

The economic growth model tells us that economies grow when the quantity of capital per hour worked increases and when technological change takes place. This model seems to provide a good blueprint for developing countries to become rich: Increase the quantity of capital per hour worked and use the best available technology. There are economic incentives for both of these things to happen in poor countries. The profitability of using additional capital or better technology is generally greater in a developing country than in a high-income country. For example, replacing an existing computer with a new, faster computer will generally have a relatively small payoff for a firm in the United States. In contrast, installing a new computer in a Zambian firm where records are kept by hand is likely to have an enormous payoff.

This observation leads to the following important conclusion: *The economic growth model predicts that poor countries will grow faster than rich countries.* If this prediction is correct, we should observe poor countries catching up to the rich countries in levels of GDP per capita (or income per capita). Has this **catch-up**—or *convergence*—actually occurred? Here we come to a paradox: The lower-income *industrial* countries have been catching up to the higher-income industrial countries, but the developing countries as a group have not been catching up to the industrial countries as a group.

Catch-up The prediction that the level of GDP per capita (or income per capita) in poor countries will grow faster than in rich countries.

Catch-up: Sometimes, but Not Always

We can construct a graph that makes it easier to see whether catch-up is happening. In Figure 22-7 the horizontal axis shows the initial level of GDP per capita, and the vertical axis shows the rate at which GDP per capita is growing. We can then plot points on the graph for rich and poor countries. Each point represents the combination of a country's initial level of GDP per capita and its growth rate over the following years. Low-income countries should be in the upper-left part of the graph because they would have low initial levels of GDP per capita but fast growth rates. High-income countries should be in the lower-right part of the graph because they would have high initial levels of GDP per capita but slow growth rates.

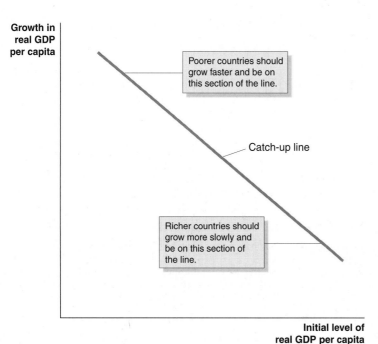

Figure 22-7

The Catch-up Predicted by the Economic Growth Model

According to the economic growth model, countries that start with lower levels of GDP per capita should grow faster (points near the top of the line) than countries that start with higher levels of GDP per capita (points near the bottom of the line).

Figure 22-8

There Has Been Catch-up among Industrial Countries

The industrial countries such as Ireland and Japan that had the lowest incomes in 1960 grew the fastest between 1960 and 2004. Countries like Switzerland and the United States that had the highest incomes in 1960 grew the slowest.

Note: Data are real GDP per capita in 2000 dollars. Each point in the figure represents one industrial country.

Source: Authors' calculations from data in Alan Heston, Robert Summers, and Bettina Aten, *Penn World Table Version 6.2*, Center for International Comparisons of Production, Income and Prices at the University of Pennsylvania, September 2006.

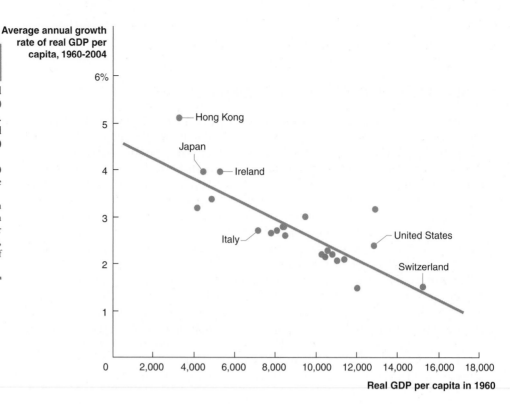

Catch-up Among the Industrial Countries If we look at only the industrial countries, we can see the catch-up predicted by the economic growth model. Figure 22-8 shows that the industrial countries that had the lowest incomes in 1960, such as Ireland and Japan, grew the fastest between 1960 and 2004. Countries that had the highest incomes in 1960, such as Switzerland and the United States, grew the slowest.

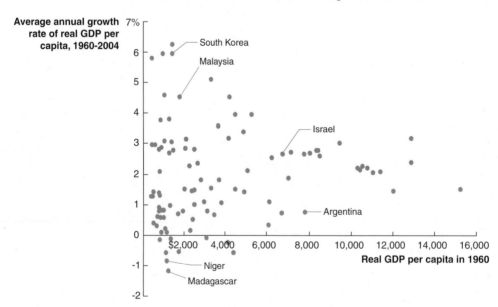

Figure 22-9 | Most of the World Hasn't Been Catching Up

Looking at all countries for which statistics are available does not show the catch-up predicted by the economic growth model. Some countries, such as Niger and Madagascar, that had low levels of real GDP per capita in 1960 actually experienced *negative* economic growth. Other countries, such as Malaysia and South Korea, that started with low levels of real GDP per capita grew rapidly. Some middle-income countries in 1960, such as Argentina, hardly grew between 1960 and 2004, while others, such as Israel, experienced significant growth.

Note: Data are real GDP per capita in 2000 dollars. Each point in the figure represents one country.
Source: Authors' calculations from data in Alan Heston, Robert Summers, and Bettina Aten, *Penn World Table Version 6.2*, Center for International Comparisons of Production, Income and Prices at the University of Pennsylvania, September 2006.

Are the Developing Countries Catching Up to the Industrial Countries? If we expand the analysis to include every country for which statistics are available, it becomes more difficult to find the catch-up predicted by the economic growth model. Figure 22-9 does not show a consistent relationship between the level of real GDP in 1960 and growth from 1960 to 2004. Some countries, such as Niger and Madagascar, that had low levels of real GDP per capita in 1960 actually experienced *negative* economic growth: They had *lower* levels of real GDP per capita in 2004 than in 1960. Other countries, such as Malaysia and South Korea, that started with low levels of real GDP per capita grew rapidly. Some middle-income countries in 1960, such as Argentina, hardly grew between 1960 and 2004, while others, such as Israel, experienced significant growth.

Solved Problem | 22-4

The Economic Growth Model's Prediction of Catch-up

The economic growth model makes predictions about the relationship between an economy's initial level of real GDP per capita relative to other economies and how fast the economy will grow in the future.

a. Consider the statistics in the following table.

COUNTRY	REAL GDP PER CAPITA IN 1960 (2000 DOLLARS)	ANNUAL GROWTH IN REAL GDP PER CAPITA, 1960–2004
Taiwan	$1,443	6.26%
Tunisia	2,102	3.13
Brazil	2,643	2.36
Algeria	3,843	1.04
Argentina	7,838	0.76

Are these statistics consistent with the economic growth model? Briefly explain.

b. Now consider the statistics in the following table.

COUNTRY	REAL GDP PER CAPITA IN 1960 (2000 DOLLARS)	ANNUAL GROWTH IN REAL GDP PER CAPITA, 1960–2004
Japan	$4,509	3.94%
Italy	7,167	2.70
France	8,531	2.58
United Kingdom	10,323	2.19

Are these statistics consistent with the economic growth model? Briefly explain.

c. Construct a new table that lists all nine countries, from lowest real GDP per capita in 1960 to highest. Are the statistics in your new table consistent with the economic growth model?

SOLVING THE PROBLEM:

Step 1: **Review the chapter material.** This problem is about catch-up in the economic growth model, so you may want to review the section "Why Isn't the Whole World Rich?" which begins on page 747.

Step 2: **Explain whether the statistics in the first table are consistent with the economic growth model.** These statistics are consistent with the economic growth model. The countries with the lowest levels of real GDP per capita in 1960 had the fastest growth rates between 1960 and 2004, and the countries with the highest levels of real GDP per capita had the slowest growth rates.

Step 3: **Explain whether the statistics in the second table are consistent with the economic growth model.** These statistics are also consistent with the economic growth model. Once again, the countries with the lowest levels of real GDP per capita in 1960 had the fastest growth rates between 1960 and 2004, and the countries with the highest levels of real GDP per capita had the slowest growth rates.

Step 4: Construct a table that includes all nine countries from the tables in questions (a) and (b) and discuss the results.

COUNTRY	REAL GDP PER CAPITA IN 1960 (2000 DOLLARS)	ANNUAL GROWTH IN REAL GDP PER CAPITA, 1960–2004
Taiwan	$1,443	6.26%
Tunisia	2,102	3.13
Brazil	2,643	2.36
Algeria	3,843	1.04
Japan	4,509	3.94
Italy	7,167	2.70
Argentina	7,838	0.76
France	8,531	2.58
United Kingdom	10,323	2.19

The statistics in the new table are not consistent with the predictions of the economic growth model. For example, France and the United Kingdom had higher levels of real GDP per capita in 1960 than did Algeria and Argentina. The economic growth model predicts that France and the United Kingdom should, therefore, have grown more slowly than Algeria and Argentina. The data in the table show, however, that they grew faster. Similarly, Italy grew faster than Brazil even though its real GDP per capita was already much higher than Brazil's in 1960.

EXTRA CREDIT: The statistics in these tables confirm what we saw in Figures 22-8 and 22-9: There has been catch-up among the industrial countries, but there has not been catch-up if we include all the countries of the world in the analysis.

>> **End Solved Problem 22-4**

YOUR TURN: For more practice, do problems 4.4 and 4.5 on page 764 at the end of this chapter.

Why Don't More Low-Income Countries Experience Rapid Growth?

The economic growth model predicts that the countries that were very poor in 1960 should have grown rapidly over the next 40 years. As we have just seen, a few did, but most did not. Why are many low-income countries growing so slowly? There is no single answer, but most economists point to four key factors:

- Failure to enforce the rule of law

- Wars and revolutions

- Poor public education and health

- Low rates of saving and investment

Failure to Enforce the Rule of Law In the years since 1960, increasing numbers of developing countries, including China, have abandoned centrally planned economies in favor of more market-oriented economies. For entrepreneurs in a market economy to succeed, however, the government must guarantee private **property rights** and enforce contracts. Unless entrepreneurs feel secure in their property, they will not risk starting a business. It is also very difficult for businesses to operate successfully in a market economy unless they can use an independent court system to enforce contracts. The failure of many developing countries to guarantee private property rights and to enforce contracts has hindered their economic growth.

Consider, for example, the production of shoes in a developing country. Suppose the owner of a shoe factory signs a contract with a leather supplier to deliver a specific quantity of leather on a particular date for a particular price. On the basis of this

Property rights The rights individuals or firms have to the exclusive use of their property, including the right to buy or sell it.

contract, the owner of the shoe factory signs a contract to deliver a specific quantity of shoes to a shoe wholesaler. This contract specifies the quantity of shoes to be delivered, the quality of the shoes, the delivery date, and the price. The owner of the tannery that produces the leather uses the contract with the shoe factory to enter into a contract with cattle ranchers for the delivery of hides. The shoe wholesaler enters into contracts to deliver shoes to retail stores, where they are sold to consumers. For the flow of goods from cattle ranchers to shoe customers to operate efficiently, each business must carry out the terms of the contract it has signed. In developed countries, such as the United States, businesses know that if they fail to carry out a contract, they may be sued in court and forced to compensate the other party for any economic damages.

Many developing countries do not have functioning, independent court systems. Even if a court system does exist, a case may not be heard for many years. In some countries, bribery of judges and political favoritism in court rulings are common. If firms cannot enforce contracts through the court system, they will insist on carrying out only face-to-face cash transactions. For example, the shoe manufacturer will wait until the leather producer brings the hides to the factory and will then buy them for cash. The wholesaler will wait until the shoes have been produced before making plans for sales to retail stores. Production still takes place, but it is carried out more slowly and inefficiently. In these circumstances, firms have difficulty finding investors willing to provide them with the funds they need to expand.

The **rule of law** refers to the ability of a government to enforce the laws of the country, particularly with respect to protecting private property and enforcing contracts. The World Bank is an agency of the United Nations whose role is to provide financial aid and policy advice to low-income countries. Economists at the World Bank have ranked 118 developing countries on the basis of how well their governments enforce the rule of law. Figure 22-10 shows the difference in average annual growth rates between the 20 developing countries that do the best job of enforcing the rule of law, such as the Czech Republic and Israel, and the 20 countries that do the worst job, such as the Congo and

Rule of law The ability of a government to enforce the laws of the country, particularly with respect to protecting private property and enforcing contracts.

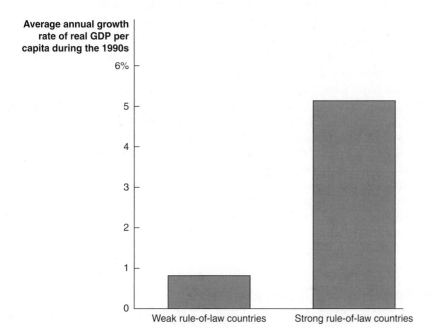

Figure 22-10 | The Rule of Law and Growth

The 20 developing countries that have the strongest rule of law, such as the Czech Republic and Israel, grew more than six times faster during the 1990s than the 20 developing countries that have the weakest rule of law, such as the Congo and Albania.

Source: Authors' calculation from data in David Dollar and Aart Kraay, "Property Rights, Political Rights, and the Development of Poor Countries in the Post-Colonial Period," World Bank Development Research Group working paper, October 2000.

Albania. Real GDP per capita in the 20 countries with the strongest rule of law grew more than six times faster during the 1990s than real GDP per capita in the 20 countries with the weakest rule of law.

Wars and Revolutions Many of the countries that were very poor in 1960 have experienced extended periods of war or violent changes of government during the years since. These wars have made it impossible for countries such as Afghanistan, Angola, Ethiopia, the Central African Republic, and the Congo to accumulate capital or adopt new technologies. In fact, conducting any kind of business has been very difficult. The positive effect on growth of ending war was shown in Mozambique, which suffered through almost two decades of civil war and declining real GDP per capita. With the end of civil war, Mozambique experienced a strong annual growth rate of 4.5 percent in real GDP per capita from 1990 to 2006.

Poor Public Education and Health We have seen that human capital is one of the determinants of labor productivity. Many low-income countries have weak public school systems, so many workers are unable to read and write. Few workers acquire the skills necessary to use the latest technology.

Many low-income countries suffer from diseases that are either nonexistent or treated readily in high-income countries. For example, few people in developed countries suffer from malaria, but more than one million Africans die from it each year. Treatments for AIDS have greatly reduced deaths from this disease in the United States and Europe. But millions of people in low-income countries continue to die from AIDS. Low-income countries often lack the resources, and their governments are often too ineffective, to provide even routine medical care, such as childhood vaccinations.

People who are sick work less and are less productive when they do work. Poor nutrition or exposure to certain diseases in childhood can leave people permanently weakened and can affect their intelligence as adults. Poor health has a significant negative impact on the human capital of workers in developing countries.

Low Rates of Saving and Investment To invest in factories, machinery, and computers, firms need funds. Some of the funds can come from the owners of the firm and from their friends and family, but as we noted in Chapter 21, firms in high-income countries raise most of their funds from bank loans and selling stocks and bonds in financial markets. In most developing countries, stock and bond markets do not exist, and often the banking system is very weak. In high-income countries, the funds that banks lend to businesses come from the savings of households. In high-income countries, many households are able to save a significant fraction of their income. In developing countries, many households barely survive on their incomes and, therefore, have little or no savings.

The low savings rates in developing countries contribute to a *vicious cycle* of poverty. Because households have low incomes, they save very little. Because households save very little, few funds are available for firms to borrow. Lacking funds, firms do not invest in the new factories, machinery, and equipment needed for economic growth. Because the economy does not grow, household incomes remain low, as do their savings, and so on.

The Benefits of Globalization

One way for a developing country to break out of the vicious cycle of low saving and investment and low growth is through foreign investment. **Foreign direct investment (FDI)** occurs when corporations build or purchase facilities in foreign countries. **Foreign portfolio investment** occurs when an individual or a firm buys stock or bonds issued in another country. Foreign direct investment and foreign portfolio investment can give a low-income country access to funds and technology that otherwise would not be available. Until recently, many developing countries were reluctant to take advantage of this opportunity.

Foreign direct investment (FDI) The purchase or building by a corporation of a facility in a foreign country.

Foreign portfolio investment The purchase by an individual or a firm of stock or bonds issued in another country.

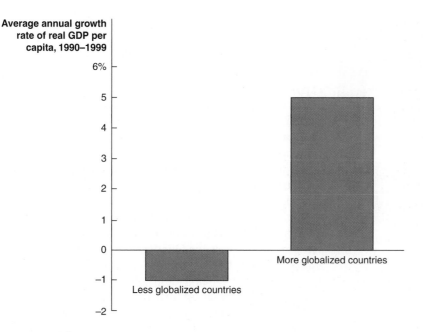

Figure 22-11 | Globalization and Growth

Developing countries that were more open to foreign trade and investment grew much faster during the 1990s than developing countries that were less open.
Source: David Dollar, "Globalization, Inequality, and Poverty since 1980," *World Bank Research Observer*, Vol. 20, No. 2, Fall 2005, pp. 145–175.

From the 1940s through the 1970s, many developing countries sealed themselves off from the global economy. They did this for several reasons. During the 1930s and early 1940s, the global trading and financial system collapsed as a result of the Great Depression and World War II. Developing countries that relied on exporting to the industrial countries were hurt economically. The example of the Soviet Union indicated that it might be possible to achieve rapid growth without participating in the global economy. Also, many countries in Africa and Asia achieved independence from the colonial powers of Europe during the 1950s and 1960s and were afraid of being dominated by them economically. As a result, many developing countries imposed high tariffs on foreign imports and strongly discouraged or even prohibited foreign investment. This made it difficult to break out of the vicious cycle of poverty.

The policies of high tariff barriers and avoiding foreign investment failed to produce much growth, so by the 1980s, many developing countries began to change policies. The result was *globalization*. **Globalization** refers to the process of countries becoming more open to foreign trade and investment.

If we measure globalization by the fraction of a country's GDP accounted for by exports, we see that globalization and growth are strongly positively associated. Figure 22-11 shows that developing countries that were more globalized grew faster during the 1990s than developing countries that were less globalized. Globalization has benefited developing countries by making it easier for them to get investment funds and technology.

Globalization The process of countries becoming more open to foreign trade and investment.

Making	**Globalization and the Spread**
the	**of Technology in Bangladesh**
Connection	

Today, Bangladesh exports more than $2 billion worth of shirts and other clothing. But the manufacture of clothing in factories only began in Bangladesh in 1980, when a local entrepreneur, Noorul

The spread of technology spurred Bangladesh's booming clothing industry.

Quader, started Desh Garments Ltd. This firm had just one shirt factory that employed 40 workers and produced only $55,550 worth of shirts its first year. Initially, Quader relied on an agreement with Daewoo Corporation of South Korea. Daewoo could export only limited numbers of shirts from Korea to the United States and Europe because the U.S. and European governments placed restrictions on clothing imports from Korea in an effort to protect domestic clothing producers. These restrictions did not apply to imports from Bangladesh.

Under the agreement with Daewoo, Quader was responsible for setting up and running the clothing factory. Daewoo would provide the most critical ingredient: training for 130 Desh workers at one of Daewoo's plants in Korea. In return, Quader would pay Daewoo an 8 percent royalty on each shirt sold. The business was a tremendous success for Quader, with production soaring from 43,000 shirts in 1980 to 2.3 million in 1987 and to 9.6 million in 2006. It was an even greater success for Bangladesh. Almost all the 130 Desh workers trained in Korea eventually left Desh to set up their own firms. In addition to making shirts, these new firms began producing coats, pants, and other clothing. The Desh workers, trained by Daewoo in garment-making technology, became the basis of Bangladesh's booming clothing industry.

This story illustrates not only how globalization can aid the spread of technology to the developing world but also the important difference between capital and technology: Although there are diminishing returns to capital, there actually may be increasing returns to technology. The investment Daewoo made in developing the best way to manufacture clothing and export it to high-income countries provided a return not only to Daewoo but also to Desh and then to the other companies in Bangladesh founded by workers who left Desh. Unlike with a piece of machinery, there is no limit to the number of people who can use knowledge about the best way to produce a good. As we discussed previously, the idea that there may be increasing returns to technology has been an important part of recent developments in the theory of economic growth. From this perspective, technological advance is not just a matter of new scientific discoveries but also depends on the incentives given to entrepreneurs to find new and better ways of producing goods and services.

Source: William Easterly, *The Elusive Quest for Growth: Economists' Adventures and Misadventures in the Tropics*, Cambridge, MA: MIT Press, 2001, pp. 146–150.

YOUR TURN: Test your understanding by doing related problems 4.7 and 4.8 on page 764 at the end of this chapter.

22.5 LEARNING OBJECTIVE   22.5 | Discuss government policies that foster economic growth.

Growth Policies

What can governments do to promote long-run economic growth? We have seen that even small differences in growth rates compounded over the years can lead to major differences in standards of living. Therefore, there is potentially a very high payoff to government policies that increase growth rates. We have already discussed some of these policies in this chapter. In this section, we explore additional policies.

Enhancing Property Rights and the Rule of Law

We have seen that a market system cannot work well unless property rights are enforced. Entrepreneurs are unlikely to risk their own funds, and investors are unlikely to lend their funds to entrepreneurs, unless property is safe from being arbitrarily seized. In many developing countries, the rule of law and property rights are undermined by *corruption*. With corruption, government officials may require bribes to carry out their obligations or may steal government property and resources. For example, in some developing countries, it is impossible for an entrepreneur to obtain a permit to start a business without paying bribes, often to several different officials. In some countries, tax revenues and foreign aid also frequently end up in the pockets of government officials. Research has shown that countries where corruption is most widespread grow much more slowly than countries where corruption is less of a problem.

Although today the United States ranks among the least corrupt countries, recent research by economists Edward Glaeser and Claudia Goldin of Harvard University has shown that in the late nineteenth and early twentieth centuries, corruption was a significant problem in the United States. The fact that political reform movements and crusading newspapers helped to reduce corruption in the United States to relatively low levels by the 1920s provides some hope for reform movements that aim to reduce corruption in developing countries today.

Property rights are unlikely to be secure in countries that are afflicted by wars and civil strife. For a number of countries, increased political stability is a necessary prerequisite to economic growth.

Improving Health and Education

Recently, many economists have become convinced that poor health is a major impediment to growth in some countries. As we saw in Chapter 21, the research of Nobel laureate Robert Fogel has emphasized the important interaction between health and economic growth. As people's health improves and they became taller, stronger, and less susceptible to disease, they also became more productive. Recent initiatives in developing countries to increase vaccinations against infectious diseases, to improve access to treated water, and to improve sanitation have begun to reduce rates of illness and death.

We discussed earlier in this chapter Paul Romer's argument that there are increasing returns to knowledge capital. Nobel laureate Robert Lucas, of the University of Chicago, has made a similar argument that there are increasing returns to *human* capital. Lucas argues that productivity increases as the total stock of human capital increases but that these productivity increases are not completely captured by individuals as they decide how much education to purchase. Therefore, the market may produce an inefficiently low level of education and training unless education is supported by the government. Some researchers have been unable to find evidence of increasing returns to human capital, but many economists believe that government subsidies to education have played an important role in promoting economic growth.

The rising incomes that result from economic growth can help developing countries deal with the *brain drain*. The brain drain refers to highly educated and successful individuals leaving developing countries for high-income countries. This migration occurs when successful individuals believe that economic opportunities are very limited in the domestic economy. Rapid economic growth in India and China in recent years has resulted in more entrepreneurs, engineers, and scientists deciding to remain in those countries rather than leave for the United States or other high-income countries.

Policies with Respect to Technology

One of the lessons from the economic growth model is that technological change is more important than increases in capital in explaining long-run growth. Government policies that facilitate access to technology are crucial for low-income countries. The easiest way for developing countries to gain access to technology is through foreign direct investment in which foreign firms are allowed to build new facilities or to buy domestic firms.

Recent economic growth in India has been greatly aided by the Indian government's relaxation of regulations on foreign investment. Relaxing these regulations made it possible for India to have access to the technology of Dell, Microsoft, and other multinational corporations.

In high-income countries, government policies can aid the growth of technology by subsidizing research and development. As we noted previously, in the United States, the federal government conducts some research and development on its own and also provides grants to researchers in universities. Tax breaks to firms undertaking research and development also facilitate technological change.

Policies with Respect to Saving and Investment

We noted in Chapter 21 that firms turn to the loanable funds market to finance expansion and research and development. Policies that increase the incentives to save and invest will increase the equilibrium level of loanable funds and may increase the level of real GDP per capita. As we also discussed in Chapter 21, tax incentives can lead to increased savings. In the United States, many workers are able to save for retirement by placing funds in 401(k) or 403(b) plans or in Individual Retirement Accounts (IRAs). Income placed in these accounts is not taxed until it is withdrawn during retirement. Because the funds are allowed to accumulate tax free, the return is increased, which raises the incentive to save.

Governments also increase incentives for firms to engage in investment in physical capital by using *investment tax credits*. Investment tax credits allow firms to deduct from their taxes some fraction of the funds they have spent on investment. Reductions in the taxes firms pay on their profits also increase the after-tax return on investments.

Is Economic Growth Good or Bad?

Although we didn't state so explicitly, in this chapter, we have assumed that economic growth is desirable and that governments should undertake policies that will increase growth rates. It seems undeniable that increasing the growth rates of very low-income countries would help relieve the daily suffering that many people in those countries must endure. But some people are unconvinced that, at least in the high-income countries, further economic growth is desirable.

The arguments against further economic growth tend to be motivated either by concern about the effects of growth on the environment or by concern about the effects of the globalization process that has accompanied economic growth in recent years. In 1973, the Club of Rome published a controversial book titled *The Limits to Growth*, which predicted that economic growth would likely grind to a halt in the United States and other high-income countries because of increasing pollution and the depletion of natural resources, such as oil. Although these dire predictions have not yet come to pass, many remain concerned that economic growth may be contributing to global warming, deforestation, and other environmental problems.

In Chapter 8, we discussed the opposition to globalization. We noted that some people believe that globalization has undermined the distinctive cultures of many countries, as imports of food, clothing, movies, and other goods displace domestically produced goods. We have seen that allowing foreign direct investment is an important way in which low-income countries can gain access to the latest technology. Some people, however, see multinational firms that locate in low-income countries as paying very low wages and as failing to follow the same safety and environmental regulations they are required to follow in the high-income countries.

As with many other normative questions, economic analysis can contribute to the ongoing political debate over the consequences of economic growth, but it cannot settle the issue.

Economics in YOUR Life!

>> Continued from page 729

At the beginning of the chapter, we posed the question: Suppose that you could choose to live and work in a world with the Chinese economy growing very rapidly or a world with the Chinese economy being very poor and growing slowly. Which world would you choose to live in? It's impossible to walk into stores in the United States without seeing products imported from China. Many of these products were at one time made in the United States. Imports from China replace domestically produced goods when the imports are either less expensive or of higher quality than the domestic goods they replace. Therefore, the rapid economic growth that has enabled Chinese firms to be competitive with firms in the United States has been a benefit to you as a consumer; you have lower-priced goods and better goods available to buy than you would if China had remained very poor. As you begin your career, there are some U.S. industries that, because of competition from Chinese firms, will have fewer jobs to offer. But, as we saw when discussing international trade in Chapter 8, expanding trade changes the types of products each country makes, and, therefore, the types of jobs available, but it does not affect the total number of jobs. So, the economic rise of China will affect the mix of jobs available to you in the United States but will not make finding a job any more difficult.

Conclusion

For much of human history, most people have had to struggle to survive. Even today, two-thirds of the world's population lives in extreme poverty. The differences in living standards among countries today are the result of many decades of sharply different rates of economic growth. According to the economic growth model, increases in the quantity of capital per hour worked and increases in technology determine how rapidly real GDP per hour worked and a country's standard of living will increase. The keys to higher living standards seem straightforward enough: Establish the rule of law, provide basic education and health care for the population, increase the amount of capital per hour worked, adopt the best technology, and participate in the global economy. However, for many countries, these policies have proved very difficult to implement.

Having discussed what determines the growth rate of economies, we will turn in the following chapters to the question of why economies experience short-run fluctuations in output, employment, and inflation. First, read *An Inside Look* on the next page for a discussion of recent economic growth in Europe.

ECONOMIST, FEBRUARY 19, 2007

Feeling Brighter

Competition for the title of "sick man of Europe" has been stiff for the past few years. Contenders included Germany, still feeling the lingering effects of unification. Italy, seemingly unable to keep its manufacturers competitive without devaluing its currency, had a good claim. Their problems were replicated across the continent: how to stay competitive with rigidly regulated labour and services markets. Crafting monetary policy for a currency zone that includes Ireland's boom and Italy's bust was a troublesome affair.

After the gloom, sunshine now seems to be breaking through all over. Despite high energy prices, tighter money, and economic slowdown in America, the economies of the Europe Union have prospered. Industrial production in Europe rose by 1% in December compared with the month before, and by 4% for the year as a whole, much better than anticipated. Foreign trade rose briskly too. And three of the big economies—Germany, France and Italy—look very strong. Preliminary estimates of fourth quarter GDP released on Tuesday, February 13th show them exceeding expectations, and in the case of Italy and Germany by a wide margin.

The future looks brighter still. On February 16th the European Commission released its interim forecast for 2007. This suggests that the European economy as a whole will grow by 2.7% this year, substantially exceeding its earlier estimate of 2.4%. In 2006 3M new jobs were created, driving the unemployment rate down to 7.5% (in the euro area), and labour markets are expected to remain strong. Inflation should come down too, as energy prices fall further.

Germany is doing particularly well, thanks to a restructuring of its labour markets that has improved competitiveness. Unemployment, though still high, has dropped sharply over the past few years. Germans have also resisted immodest wage increases, unlike faster growers, such as Spain, which have seen their competitive position eroded by soaring labour costs. Even with its new-found strength, however, Europe is barely outstripping America. Ben Bernanke, the chairman of the Federal Reserve, anticipates a slowdown to more sustainable growth rates of 2.5–3% in America's immediate future—roughly the same pace that is exciting Europeans. The question of whether Europe will ever catch up is still much in the news in America.

Edmund Phelps, winner of the 2006 Nobel prize for economics for his work on savings and labour markets, argues that the structural explanation for Europe's slower growth rates masks deeper problems with dynamism. Countries like France, Germany and Italy display markedly lower rates of commercially successful innovation. There is less churn in the top ranks of companies, and employees are given less latitude to innovate and make decisions. In part he believes that the problem is economic institutions: regulatory barriers to entrepreneurship, a financial system that favours insiders, and a high level of input from labour, which tends to be biased towards the status quo. But he also points to cultural differences that might impede Europe's growth even if those regulatory barriers are swept away: workers in Europe's big economies are less likely to regard the opportunity for innovation, autonomy and interesting work as vital components of a job.

This is one possible explanation for the difference between Europe's rapid growth in the decades following the second world war, and its current, more lackadaisical pace. Barry Eichengreen, a professor of economics at Berkeley, has just published a book arguing that Europe is very good at "extensive growth"—roughly, producing more of what we already know how to make—and less good at "intensive growth", which involves finding new products and new ways of doing things. Mr Eichengreen argues that Europe's "co-ordinated capitalism" served the first task well (and better than the messily undirected market), but has balked at pushing back new economic frontiers.

Of course, 15 years ago Americans were bombarded with books promising that Germany or Japan was poised to depose them as the world's economic powerhouse. It is always dangerous to extrapolate too much from current trends, especially since idiosyncratic factors (such as Germany's need to absorb an economy left crippled by communism) often come into play. But perhaps optimism should be tempered with at least a smidgen of European caution.

Key Points in the Article

This article discussed the relatively strong performance of Europe's largest economies in the last couple of years. But the article also discusses what many economists believe to be the reason for Europe's relatively lackluster growth over the longer term: a relative lack of innovation. The article also raises the question of why Europe was unable to sustain the rapid growth that it achieved in the decades immediately following World War II. Finally, the article discusses Barry Eichengreen's argument that this earlier rapid growth occurred with relatively few technological innovations and, hence, was particularly vulnerable to diminishing returns.

Analyzing the News

(a) Europe's economies have prospered in recent years, and growth in three of its largest economies—Germany, France, and Italy—has exceeded economists' expectations. This prosperity is particularly impressive given that it comes at a time of rising energy prices, relatively high interest rates, and a slowing U.S. economy. High energy prices and high interest rates reduce the growth in consumption spending and business investment spending, and a slowing U.S. economy reduces the growth in European exports to the United States.

(b) Despite its strong growth in the last couple of years, the European economy have been growing more slowly than the United States. The 2.7 percent growth that Europe will likely achieve in 2007 is high by European standards, but only moderate by U.S. standards. Europe's relatively low unemployment rate of 7.5 percent is also very high by U.S. standards. According to Edmund Phelps, the European economy lacks the economic institutions necessary to promote entrepreneurship. This is a problem because, as you read in this chapter, many economists believe that the innovation required to sustain strong economic growth is, to a large extent, dependent on economic incentives and the entrepreneurs who respond to those incentives.

(c) Europe's relatively sluggish growth in recent years is particularly curious given that the European economy achieved extremely rapid growth in the decades immediately following World War II. According to Barry Eichengreen, Europe's earlier rapid growth was not sustainable because it was based on goods and services that Europe produced with existing technology. This was a problem because this so-called extensive growth increased output per hour worked but at a decreasing rate due to the law of diminishing returns. This point is illustrated in Figure 1, where, holding technological change constant, an increase in capital per hour worked from $(K/L)_1$ to $(K/L)_2$ leads to an increase in output per hour worked from $(Y/L)_1$ to $(Y/L)_2$. For Europe to sustain strong economic growth, it must produce new goods and services in innovative ways. Intensive growth of this type helps economies avoid the law of diminishing returns. This pattern is shown in Figure 2, where technological change shifts up the production function and allows output per hour worked to increase from $(Y/L)_1$ to $(Y/L)_2$ while the amount of capital per hour worked remains at $(K/L)_1$.

Thinking Critically

1. Suppose European governments remove restrictions on employers' rights to fire workers. What effect would this policy likely have on the extent of European entrepreneurship and, hence, innovation?

2. Because economic growth requires innovation and change, it can lead to structural unemployment. What are some policies that governments can implement in order to relieve the social and economic strains that intensive economic growth can place on an economy's labor force?

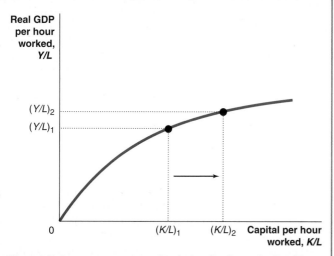

Figure 1. To increase output per worker during the aftermath of World War II, Europe increased capital per worker.

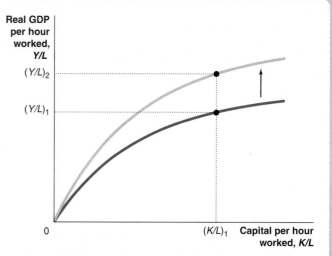

Figure 2. To increase output per worker today, Europe must find new and innovative ways to produce.

Key Terms

22.1 LEARNING OBJECTIVE   22.1 | Define economic growth, calculate economic growth rates, and describe global trends in economic growth, **pages 730–734.**

Economic Growth Over Time and Around the World

Summary

Until around the year 1300 A.D., most people survived with barely enough food. Living standards began to rise significantly only after the **Industrial Revolution** began in England in the 1700s with the application of mechanical power to the production of goods. The best measure of a country's standard of living is its level of real GDP per capita. Economic growth occurs when real GDP per capita increases, thereby increasing the country's standard of living.

 Visit www.myeconlab.com to complete these exercises online and get instant feedback.

Review Questions

1.1 Why does a country's rate of economic growth matter?

1.2 Explain the difference between the total percentage increase in real GDP between 1997 and 2007 and the average annual growth rate in real GDP between the same years.

Problems and Applications

1.3 (Related to the *Making the Connection* on page 731) Recently, economists Carol Shiue and Wolfgang Keller of the University of Texas at Austin published a study of "market efficiency" in the eighteenth century in England, other European countries, and China. If the markets in a country are efficient, a product should have the same price wherever in the country it is sold, allowing for the effect of transportation costs. If prices are not the same in two areas within a country, it is possible to make profits by buying the product where its price is low and reselling it where its price is high. This trading will drive prices to equality. Trade is most likely to occur, however, if

entrepreneurs feel confident that their gains will not be seized by the government and that contracts to buy and sell can be enforced in the courts. Therefore, in the eighteenth century, the more efficient a country's markets, the more its institutions favored long-run growth. Shiue and Keller found that in 1770, the efficiency of markets in England was significantly greater than the efficiency of markets elsewhere in Europe and in China. How does this finding relate to Douglas North's argument concerning why the Industrial Revolution occurred in England?

Source: Carol H. Shiue and Wolfgang Keller, "Markets in China and Europe on the Eve of the Industrial Revolution," forthcoming, *American Economic Review*, 2007.

1.4 Use the data on real GDP in the following table to answer the questions.

COUNTRY	2003	2004	2005	2006
Australia	$445.1	$457.0	$469.8	$481.1
Hungary	54.2	56.9	59.3	61.6
Poland	182.4	192.0	198.3	210.4

Note: All values are in billions of 2000 U.S. dollars.
Source: Organisation for Economic Cooperation and Development (OECD).

a. Which country experienced the highest rate of economic growth during 2004?
b. Which country experienced the highest rate of economic growth during 2005?
c. Which country experienced the highest average annual growth rate between 2004 and 2006?

1.5 Andover Bank and Lowell Bank each sell one-year certificates of deposit (CDs). The interest rates on these CDs are given in the following table for a three-year period.

BANK	2007	2008	2009
Andover Bank	2%	9%	10%
Lowell Bank	7%	7%	7%

Suppose you deposit $1,000 in a CD in each bank at the beginning of 2007. At the end of 2007, you take your $1,000 and any interest earned and invest it in a CD for the following year. You do this again at the end of 2008. At the end of 2009, will you have earned more on your Andover Bank CDs or on your Lowell Bank CDs? Briefly explain.

1.6 **(Related to the *Don't Let This Happen to You!* on page 733)** Use the data for the United States in the table to answer the following questions.

YEAR	REAL GDP PER CAPITA (2000 PRICES)
2003	$35,466
2004	36,412
2005	37,187
2006	37,889
2007	38,316

a. What was the percentage increase in real GDP per capita between 2003 and 2007?

b. What was the average annual growth rate in real GDP per capita between 2003 and 2007? (*Hint:* Remember from the previous chapter that the average annual growth rate for relatively short periods can be approximated by averaging the growth rate for each year.)

1.7 **(Related to the *Making the Connection* on page 733)** Between 1950 and 1978, Japan experienced high rates of economic growth while China was hardly growing. Today, the standard of living in Japan is higher than the standard of living in China. Would you expect this relationship between when a country began to experience economic growth and its relative standard of living today will always be true? That is, will it always be true that if country A first experienced rapid economic growth at an earlier date than country B, then country A will have a higher standard of living today than country B?

>> **End Learning Objective 22.1**

22.2 LEARNING OBJECTIVE   22.2 | Use the economic growth model to explain why growth rates differ across countries, **pages 735–741.**

What Determines How Fast Economies Grow?

Summary

An **economic growth model** explains changes in real GDP per capita in the long run. **Labor productivity** is the quantity of goods and services that can be produced by one worker or by one hour of work. Economic growth depends on increases in labor productivity. Labor productivity will increase if there is an increase in the amount of *capital* available to each worker or if there is an improvement in *technology*. **Technological change** is a change in the ability of a firm to produce a given level of output with a given quantity of inputs. There are three main sources of technological change: better machinery and equipment, increases in human capital, and better means of organizing and managing production. **Human capital** is the accumulated knowledge and skills that workers acquire from education and training or from their life experiences. To summarize, we can say that an economy will have a higher standard of living the more capital it has per hour worked, the more human capital its workers have, the better its capital, and the better the job its business managers do in organizing production. **The per-worker production function** shows the relationship between capital per hour worked and output per hour worked, holding technology constant. *Diminishing returns to capital* mean that increases

in the quantity of capital per hour worked will result in diminishing increases in output per hour worked. Technological change shifts up the per-worker production function, resulting in more output per hour worked at every level of capital per hour worked. The economic growth model stresses the importance of changes in capital per hour worked and technological change in explaining growth in output per hour worked. *New growth theory* is a model of long-run economic growth that emphasizes that technological change is influenced by how individuals and firms respond to economic incentives. One way governments can promote technological change is by granting **patents**, which are exclusive rights to a product for a period of 20 years from the date the product is invented. To Joseph Schumpeter, the entrepreneur is central to the "creative destruction" by which the standard of living increases as qualitatively better products replace existing products.

myeconlab Visit www.myeconlab.com to complete these exercises *Get Ahead of the Curve* online and get instant feedback.

Review Questions

2.1 Using the per-worker production function graph, show the effect on real GDP per hour worked of an increase in capital per hour worked, holding technology constant. Now, again using the per-worker production function graph, show the effect on real GDP per hour worked of an increase in technology, holding constant the quantity of capital per hour worked.

2.2 What are the consequences for growth of diminishing returns to capital? How are some economies able to maintain high growth rates despite diminishing returns to capital?

2.3 Why did some economists in the 1950s predict that the Soviet Union would continue to grow faster than the United States for decades to come? Why did this prediction turn out to be wrong?

2.4 Why are firms likely to underinvest in research and development, which slows the accumulation of knowledge capital, slowing economic growth? Briefly discuss three ways in which government policy can increase the accumulation of knowledge capital.

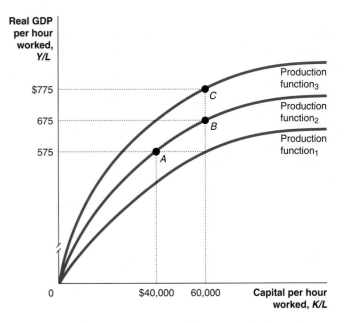

Problems and Applications

2.5 According to a study by an economist at the Federal Reserve Bank of Minneapolis, during the middle 1980s, managers at iron mines in Canada and the United States increased output per hour worked by 100 percent through changes in work rules that increased workers' effort per hour worked and increased the efficiency of workers' effort. Briefly explain whether this increase in output per hour worked is an example of an improvement in technology.

Source: James A. Schmitz, Jr., "What Determines Labor Productivity? Lessons from the Dramatic Recovery of the U.S. and Canadian Iron-Ore Industries Following Their Early 1980s Crisis," Federal Reserve Bank of Minneapolis Research Department Staff Report 286, February 2005.

2.6 Which of the following will result in a movement along Japan's per-worker production function, and which will result in a shift of Japan's per-worker production function? Briefly explain.
 a. Capital per hour worked increases from ¥5 million per hour worked to ¥6 million per hour worked.
 b. The Japanese government doubles its spending on support of university research.
 c. A reform of the Japanese school system results in more highly trained Japanese workers.

2.7 (Related to *Solved Problem 22-2* on page 739) Use the graph in the next column to answer the questions.
 a. True or false: The movement from point *A* to point *B* shows the effects of technological change.

 b. True or false: The economy can move from point *B* to point *C* only if there are no diminishing returns to capital.
 c. True or false: To move from point *A* to point *C*, the economy must increase the amount of capital per hour worked and experience technological change.

2.8 (Related to *Solved Problem 22-2* on page 739) Shortly before the fall of the Soviet Union, the economist Gur Ofer of Hebrew University of Jerusalem, wrote this: "The most outstanding characteristic of Soviet growth strategy is its consistent policy of very high rates of investment, leading to a rapid growth rate of [the] capital stock." Explain why this turned out to be a very poor growth strategy.

Source: Gur Ofer, "Soviet Economic Growth, 1928–1985," *Journal of Economic Literature*, December 1987, p. 1,784.

2.9 Why is the role of the entrepreneur much more important in the new growth theory than in the traditional economic growth model?

2.10 (Related to the *Making the Connection* on page 738) The *Making the Connection* on the economy of the Soviet Union argues that a key difference between market economies and centrally planned economies, like that of the former Soviet Union, is:

> In market economies, decisions about which investments to make and which technologies to adopt are made by entrepreneurs and managers with their own money on the line. In the Soviet system, these decisions were usually made by salaried bureaucrats trying to fulfill a plan formulated in Moscow.
>
> But in large corporations, investment decisions are often made by salaried managers who do not, in

fact, have their own money on the line. These managers are spending the money of the firm's shareholders, rather than their own money. Why then do the investment decisions of salaried managers in the United States tend to be better for the long-term growth of the economy than were the decisions of salaried bureaucrats in the Soviet Union?

2.11 (Related to the *Making the Connection* on page 738) The *Making the Connection* on the economy of the Soviet Union argues that a key problem for the Soviet economy was that "[Soviet managers'] pay depended on producing the quantity of output specified in the government's economic plan, not on discovering new, better, and lower-cost ways to produce goods." How might a centrally planned economy get around the problem of managers lacking incentives to discover and make use of new technologies? What are the main obstacles to solving this problem?

>> **End Learning Objective 22.2**

22.3 LEARNING OBJECTIVE   22.3 | Discuss fluctuations in productivity growth in the United States, **pages 742–746.**

Economic Growth in the United States

Summary

Productivity in the United States grew rapidly from the end of World War II until the mid-1970s. Growth then slowed down for 20 years before increasing again after 1995. Economists continue to debate the reasons for the growth slowdown of the mid-1970s to mid-1990s. Leading explanations for the productivity slowdown are measurement problems, high oil prices, and a decline in labor quality. Because Western Europe and Japan experienced a productivity slowdown at the same time as the United States, explanations that focus on factors affecting only the United States are unlikely to be correct. Some economists argue that the development of a "new economy" based on information technology caused the higher productivity growth that began in the mid-1990s.

myeconlab Visit www.myeconlab.com to complete these exercises
Get Ahead of the Curve online and get instant feedback.

Review Questions

3.1 Describe the record of productivity growth in the United States from 1800 to the present. What explains the slowdown in productivity growth from the mid-1970s to the mid-1990s? Why did productivity growth increase beginning in 1996?

3.2 Compare productivity growth in the United States with productivity growth in Europe in the period between 1996 and the present.

Problems and Applications

3.3 Figure 22-5 on page 742 shows growth rates in real GDP per hour worked in the United States for various periods from 1900 onward. How might the growth rates in the figure be different if they were calculated for real GDP *per capita* instead of per hour worked? (*Hint:* How do you think the number of hours worked per person has changed in the United States since 1900?)

3.4 In early 2007, revised data from the federal government on the performance of the U.S. economy during the fourth quarter of 2006 indicated that real GDP had grown more slowly than previously estimated and that the number of hours worked had grown more rapidly than previously estimated. Keeping these revised data in mind, do you think the Bureau of Labor Statistics increased or decreased its previous estimate of the growth rate in labor productivity during the fourth quarter of 2006? Briefly explain.

3.5 According to an article in the *Wall Street Journal:*

> Henry Harteveldt, travel analyst at tech-consulting firm Forrester Research, says checking in a passenger at such a kiosk costs an airline just 14 cents on average, compared with $3.02 using an agent. From 2000 to 2005, the share of passengers using such a kiosk at least once leapt from close to zero to 63%. But in 2006, that figure merely crept up to 66%.

Assuming that Harteveldt's data are correct, what would be the implications of his analysis for future increases in labor productivity at the airlines?

Source: Greg Ip, "Productivity Lull Might Signal Growth Is Easing," *Wall Street Journal,* March 31, 2007, p. A1.

3.6 Figure 22-6 on page 745 shows the annual growth rate of labor productivity in the leading industrial economies for 1996 to 2007. Using the rule of 70 from Chapter 21, indicate why the countries of Western Europe, such as Germany, should be concerned about their current growth rates.

>> **End Learning Objective 22.3**

Why Isn't the Whole World Rich?

Summary

The economic growth model predicts that poor countries will grow faster than rich countries, resulting in **catch-up**. In recent decades, some poor countries have grown faster than rich countries, but many have not. Some poor countries do not experience rapid growth for four main reasons: wars and revolutions, poor public education and health, failure to enforce the rule of law, and low rates of saving and investment. The **rule of law** refers to the ability of a government to enforce the laws of the country, particularly with respect to protecting private property and enforcing contracts. **Globalization** has aided countries that have opened their economies to foreign trade and investment. **Foreign direct investment (FDI)** is the purchase or building by a corporation of a facility in a foreign country. **Foreign portfolio investment** is the purchase by an individual or firm of stock or bonds issued in another country.

Review Questions

4.1 Why does the economic growth model predict that poor countries should catch up to rich countries in income per capita? Have poor countries been catching up to rich countries?

4.2 What are the main reasons many poor countries have experienced slow growth?

4.3 What does globalization mean? How have developing countries benefited from globalization?

Problems and Applications

4.4 (Related to *Solved Problem 22-4* on page 749) Briefly explain whether the statistics in the following table are consistent with the economic growth model's predictions of catch-up.

COUNTRY	REAL GDP PER CAPITA IN 1960	GROWTH IN REAL GDP PER CAPITA, 1960–2004
Uganda	$873	0.57%
China	448	5.79
Madagascar	1,268	−1.18
Ireland	5,294	3.94
United States	12,892	2.37

4.5 (Related to *Solved Problem 22-4* on page 749) In the following figure, each dot represents a country, with its initial real GDP per capita and its growth rate of real GDP per capita.

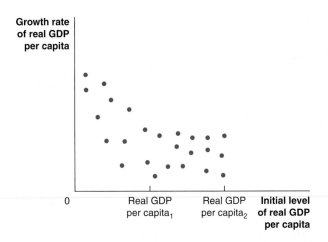

a. For the range of initial GDP per capita from 0 to Real GDP per capita$_2$, does the figure support the economic growth model's prediction of catch-up? Why or why not?

b. For the range of initial GDP per capita from 0 to Real GDP per capita$_1$, does the figure support the catch-up prediction? Why or why not?

c. For the range from initial Real GDP per capita$_1$ to Real GDP per capita$_2$, does the figure support the catch-up prediction? Why or why not?

4.6 An opinion column in the *Economist* argued, "Globalisation, far from being the greatest cause of poverty, is its only feasible cure." What does globalization have to do with reducing poverty?

Source: Clive Crook, "Globalisation and Its Critics," *Economist*, September 27, 2001.

4.7 (Related to the *Making the Connection* on page 753) How might multinational corporations that establish facilities in developing countries help break the vicious cycle of poverty in those countries?

4.8 (Related to the *Making the Connection* on page 753) What does the experience of Bangladesh suggest about the ability of poor countries to catch-up to the income levels of the rich countries? What policies would make it easier for countries like Bangladesh to catch-up?

4.9 An opinion column by Hernando De Soto in the *New York Times* argues:

Those who favor the market [have] forgotten that the only way capitalism can help the poor prosper is by bringing them into the capitalist system. But that has not happened. . . . The poor in the vast majority of nations cannot yet take advantage of legal structures that are central to the production of wealth.

What does De Soto mean by "legal structures"? Why would they have anything to do with the production of wealth?

Source: Hernando De Soto, "The Constituency of Terror," *New York Times*, October 15, 2001.

4.10 A columnist in the *New York Times* argues that "if you really want to reduce world poverty, you should be cheering on those guys in pinstripe suits at the free-trade negotiations and those investors jetting around the world." What do free-trade negotiations and

investors jetting around the world have to do with reducing poverty?

Source: David Brooks, "Good News About Poverty," *New York Times*, November 27, 2004.

4.11 The Roman Empire lasted from 27 B.C. to 476 A.D. The empire was wealthy enough to build such monuments as the Roman Coliseum. Roman engineering skill was at a level high enough that aqueducts built during the empire to carry water long distances remained in use for hundreds of years. Yet the growth rate of real GDP per capita during the empire was very low, perhaps zero. Why didn't the Roman Empire experience sustained economic growth? What would the world be like today if it had? (There are no definite answers to this question; it is intended to get you to think about the preconditions for economic growth.)

>> **End Learning Objective 22.4**

22.5 LEARNING OBJECTIVE   22.5 | Discuss government policies that foster economic growth, **pages 754–756.**

Growth Policies

Summary

Governments can attempt to increase economic growth through policies that enhance property rights and the rule of law, improve health and education, subsidize research and development, and provide incentives for savings and investment. Whether continued economic growth is desirable is a normative question that cannot be settled by economic analysis.

 Visit www.myeconlab.com to complete these exercises
Get Ahead of the Curve online and get instant feedback.

Review Questions

5.1 Briefly describe three government policies that can increase economic growth.

5.2 Can economics arrive at the conclusion that economic growth will always improve economic well-being? Briefly explain.

Problems and Applications

5.3 **(Related to the** *Chapter Opener* **on page 728)**
Writing in summer 2008, the *Economist* magazine noted:

> And there are . . . clear limits to the march of freedom in China; although personal and economic freedoms have multiplied, political freedoms have been disappointingly constrained since Hu Jintao became president in 2003."

Briefly discuss whether the limits on political freedom in China are likely to eventually become an obstacle to its continued rapid economic growth.

Source: "China's Dash for Freedom," *Economist*, July 31, 2008.

5.4 Is it likely to be easier for the typical developing country to improve the state of public health or to improve the average level of education? Briefly explain.

5.5 Briefly explain which of the following policies are likely to increase the rate of economic growth in the United States.
    a. Congress passes an investment tax credit, which reduces a firm's taxes if it installs new machinery and equipment.
    b. Congress passes a law that allows taxpayers to reduce their income taxes by the amount of state sales taxes they pay.
    c. Congress provides more funds for low-interest loans to college students.

5.6 Economist George Ayittey, in an interview on PBS about economic development in Africa, states that of the 54 African countries, only 8 have a free press. For Africa's economic development, Ayittey argues strongly for the establishment of a free press. Why would a free press be vital for the enhancement of property rights and the rule of law? How could a free press help reduce corruption?

Source: George Ayittey, *Border Jumpers*, Anchor Interview Transcript, WideAngle, PBS.org, July 24, 2005.

5.7 More people in high-income countries than in low-income countries tend to believe that rapid rates of economic growth are not desirable. Recall the concept of a "normal good" from Chapter 3. Does this concept provide insight into why some people in high-income countries might be more concerned with certain consequences of rapid economic growth than are people in low-income countries?

>> **End Learning Objective 22.5**

Chapter 23

Output and Expenditure in the Short Run

Fluctuating Demand at Cisco Systems

In spring 2001, Cisco Systems, Inc., the leading seller of hardware for computer networks in the world, announced it would cut production, sell off hardware it had already manufactured at deeply discounted prices, and lay off 6,000 of its 44,000 employees. Less than one year earlier, Cisco had rapidly expanded its workforce, purchased large amounts of hardware components, and even loaned $600 million to its suppliers to encourage them to speed up production. What had happened? Cisco had sold much less than it had forecast. As a result, Cisco had hired more people than it needed and produced more computer hardware than it could sell.

Fast forward to spring 2007: Cisco announces record sales and profits, with employment rising to more than 49,000. Why the big swings in Cisco's performance? Because Cisco's main business is selling expensive switches and routers for computer networks, its sales depend on both underlying long-run trends in Internet usage and on the short-run willingness of its business customers to spend on investment goods. During the Internet boom of the late 1990s, many firms spent heavily to establish a presence on the Internet. In addition, telecommunications firms laid more than 39 million miles of fiber-optic cable, anticipating that the volume of high-speed Internet traffic would increase rapidly. Unfortunately for Cisco and other firms, the Internet bubble popped in late 2000. The slower-than-expected growth of the Internet was bad news for Cisco, and its sales in the first three months of 2001 were 30 percent below what they had been during the last three months of 2000.

However, something beyond the Internet bust was happening to the U.S. economy during spring 2001. Firms far removed from the Internet and telecommunications were also experiencing problems. Sales at General Motors and Ford dropped 15 percent from spring 2000 to spring 2001. Delivery of two- and three-day packages at FedEx was down about 10 percent. These firms were all experiencing the effects of a slowdown in the total amount of spending, or *aggregate expenditure*, in the economy. This slowdown caused the U.S. economy to move into recession. In 2007, the explosion in using the Internet to download movies, music, and television programs led firms to expand the capacity of their computer networks. This was good news for Cisco. But Cisco and many other firms also benefited for most of 2007 from the increase in aggregate expenditures in the economy. The news was not so good in late 2007 and on into 2008, though, as aggregate expenditures grew much more slowly. In this chapter, we will explore the reasons for changes in aggregate expenditures and how these changes affect the level of total production in the economy.

AN INSIDE LOOK on **page 800** discusses the factors causing U.S. GDP to change during the first quarter of 2007.

Sources: Bobby White, "Cisco Rides Web-Traffic Growth," *Wall Street Journal*, March 7, 2006; and Bobby White and Roger Cheng, "Cisco to Acquire WebEx," *Wall Street Journal*, March 16, 2007.

Economics in YOUR Life!

Consumer Confidence Falls—Is Your Job at Risk?

Suppose that you work part time assembling desktop computers for a large computer company. One morning, you read in the local newspaper that consumer confidence in the economy has fallen and, consequently, many households expect their future income to be dramatically less than their current income. Should you be concerned about losing your job? What factors should you consider in deciding how likely your company is to lay you off? As you read the chapter, see if you can answer these questions. You can check your answers against those we provide at the end of the chapter.

>> Continued on page 799

Aggregate expenditure (*AE*) The total amount of spending in the economy: the sum of consumption, planned investment, government purchases, and net exports.

I n Chapter 22, we analyzed the determinants of long-run growth in the economy. In the short run, as we saw in Chapter 21, the economy also experiences a business cycle around the long-run upward trend in real GDP. In this chapter, we begin exploring the causes of the business cycle by examining the effect of changes in total spending on real GDP.

During some years, total spending in the economy, or **aggregate expenditure (*AE*)**, increases as much as does the production of goods and services. If this happens, most firms will sell about what they expected to sell, and they probably will not increase or decrease production or the number of workers hired. During other years, total spending in the economy increases more than the production of goods and services. In these years, firms will increase production and hire more workers. But at other times, such as spring 2001, total spending does not increase as much as total production. As a result, firms cut back on production and lay off workers, and the economy moves into a recession. In this chapter, we will explore why changes in total spending play such an important role in the economy.

23.1 LEARNING OBJECTIVE

23.1 | Understand how macroeconomic equilibrium is determined in the aggregate expenditure model.

The Aggregate Expenditure Model

The business cycle involves the interaction of many economic variables. To understand the relationships among some of the most important of these variables, we begin our study of the business cycle in this chapter with a simple model called the *aggregate expenditure model*. Recall from Chapter 19 that GDP is the value of all the final goods and services produced in an economy during a particular year. Real GDP corrects nominal GDP for the effects of inflation. The **aggregate expenditure model** focuses on the short-run relationship between total spending and real GDP. An important assumption of the model is that the price level is constant. In Chapter 24, we will develop a more complete model of the business cycle that relaxes the assumption of constant prices.

Aggregate expenditure model A macroeconomic model that focuses on the relationship between total spending and real GDP, assuming that the price level is constant.

The key idea of the aggregate expenditure model is that *in any particular year, the level of GDP is determined mainly by the level of aggregate expenditure.* To understand the relationship between aggregate expenditure and real GDP, we need to look more closely at the components of aggregate expenditure.

Aggregate Expenditure

Economists first began to study the relationship between changes in aggregate expenditure and changes in GDP during the Great Depression of the 1930s. The United States, the United Kingdom, and other industrial countries suffered declines in real GDP of 25 percent or more during the early 1930s. In 1936, the English economist John Maynard Keynes published a book, *The General Theory of Employment, Interest, and Money*, that systematically analyzed the relationship between changes in aggregate expenditure and changes in GDP. Keynes identified four categories of aggregate expenditure that together equal GDP (these are the same four categories we discussed in Chapter 19):

- *Consumption (C).* This is spending by households on goods and services, such as automobiles and haircuts.

- *Planned Investment (I).* This is planned spending by firms on capital goods, such as factories, office buildings, and machine tools, and by households on new homes.

- *Government Purchases (G).* This is spending by local, state, and federal governments on goods and services, such as aircraft carriers, bridges, and the salaries of FBI agents.

- *Net Exports (NX).* This is spending by foreign firms and households on goods and services produced in the United States minus spending by U.S. firms and households on goods and services produced in other countries.

So, we can write:

Aggregate expenditure = Consumption + Planned investment +
Government purchases + Net exports,

or:

$$AE = C + I + G + NX.$$

Governments around the world gather statistics on aggregate expenditure on the basis of these four categories. Economists and business analysts usually explain changes in GDP in terms of changes in these four categories of spending.

The Difference between Planned Investment and Actual Investment

Before considering further the relationship between aggregate expenditure and GDP, we need to consider an important distinction: Notice that it is *planned* investment spending, rather than actual investment spending, that is a component of aggregate expenditure. You might wonder how the amount that businesses plan to spend on investment can be different from the amount they actually spend. We can begin resolving this puzzle by remembering that goods that have been produced but have not yet been sold are referred to as **inventories**. Changes in inventories are included as part of investment spending along with spending on machinery, equipment, office buildings, and factories. We assume that the amount businesses plan to spend on machinery and office buildings is equal to the amount they actually spend, but the amount businesses plan to spend on inventories may be different from the amount they actually spend.

For example, Doubleday may print 1.5 million copies of the latest John Grisham novel, expecting to sell them all. If Doubleday does sell all 1.5 million, its inventories will be unchanged, but if it sells only 1.2 million, it will have an unplanned increase in inventories. In other words, changes in inventories depend on sales of goods, which firms cannot always forecast with perfect accuracy.

For the economy as a whole, we can say that actual investment spending will be greater than planned investment spending when there is an unplanned increase in inventories. Actual investment spending will be less than planned investment spending when there is an unplanned decrease in inventories. *Therefore, actual investment will equal planned investment only when there is no unplanned change in inventories.* In this chapter, we will use *I* to represent planned investment. We will also assume that the government data on investment spending compiled by the U.S. Bureau of Economic Analysis represents planned investment spending. This is a simplification, however, because the government collects data on actual investment spending, which equals planned investment spending only when unplanned changes in inventories are zero.

Macroeconomic Equilibrium

Macroeconomic equilibrium is similar to microeconomic equilibrium. In microeconomics, equilibrium in the apple market occurs at the point at which the demand for apples equals the supply of apples. When we have equilibrium in the apple market, the quantity of apples produced and sold will not change unless the demand for apples or the supply of apples changes. For the economy as a whole, macroeconomic equilibrium occurs where total spending, or aggregate expenditure, equals total production, or GDP:

Aggregate expenditure = GDP.

As we saw in Chapter 22, over the long run, real GDP in the United States grows and the standard of living rises. In this chapter, we are interested in understanding why GDP fluctuates in the short run. To simplify the analysis of macroeconomic equilibrium, we assume that the economy is not growing. In the next chapter, we discuss the more realistic case of macroeconomic equilibrium in a growing economy. If we assume that the economy is not growing, then equilibrium GDP will not change unless aggregate expenditure changes.

Inventories Goods that have been produced but not yet sold.

Adjustments to Macroeconomic Equilibrium

The apple market isn't always in equilibrium because sometimes the quantity of apples demanded is greater than the quantity supplied, and sometimes the quantity supplied is greater than the quantity demanded. The same outcome holds for the economy as a whole. Sometimes the economy is in macroeconomic equilibrium, and sometimes it isn't. When aggregate expenditure is greater than GDP, the total amount of spending in the economy is greater than the total amount of production. With spending being greater than production, many businesses will sell more goods and services than they had expected. For example, the manager of a Home Depot store might like to keep 50 refrigerators in stock to give customers the opportunity to see a variety of different sizes and models. If sales are unexpectedly high, the store may end up with only 20 refrigerators. In that case, the store will have an unplanned decrease in inventories: Its inventory of refrigerators declines by 30.

How will the store manager react when more refrigerators are sold than expected? The manager is likely to order more refrigerators. If other stores selling refrigerators are experiencing similar sales increases and are also increasing their orders, then General Electric, Whirlpool, and other refrigerator manufacturers will significantly increase their production. These manufacturers may also increase the number of workers they hire. If the increase in sales is affecting not just refrigerators but also other appliances, automobiles, furniture, computers, and other goods and services, then GDP and total employment will begin to increase. In summary, *when aggregate expenditure is greater than GDP, inventories will decline, and GDP and total employment will increase.*

Now suppose that aggregate expenditure is less than GDP. With spending being less than production, many businesses will sell fewer goods and services than they had expected, so their inventories will increase. For example, the manager of the Home Depot store who wants 50 refrigerators in stock may find that because of slow sales, the store has 75 refrigerators, so the store manager will cut back on orders for new refrigerators. If other stores also cut back on their orders, General Electric and Whirlpool will reduce production and lay off workers.

If the decrease in sales is affecting not just refrigerators but also many different goods and services, GDP and total employment will begin to decrease. These events happened at many firms during spring 2001. In summary, *when aggregate expenditure is less than GDP, inventories will increase, and GDP and total employment will decrease.*

Only when aggregate expenditure equals GDP will firms sell what they expected to sell. In that case, their inventories will be unchanged, and they will not have an incentive to increase or decrease production. The economy will be in macroeconomic equilibrium. Table 23-1 summarizes the relationship between aggregate expenditure and GDP.

Increases and decreases in aggregate expenditure cause the year-to-year changes in GDP. Economists devote considerable time and energy to forecasting what will happen to each component of aggregate expenditure. If economists forecast that aggregate expenditure will decline in the future, that is equivalent to forecasting that GDP will decline and that the economy will enter a recession. Individuals and firms closely watch these forecasts because changes in GDP can have dramatic consequences. When GDP is increasing, so are wages, profits, and job opportunities. Declining GDP can be bad news for workers, firms, and job seekers.

TABLE 23-1	IF ...	THEN ...	AND ...
The Relationship between Aggregate Expenditure and GDP	Aggregate expenditure is *equal* to GDP	inventories are *unchanged*	the economy is in *macroeconomic equilibrium.*
	Aggregate expenditure is *less* than GDP	inventories *rise*	GDP and employment *decrease.*
	Aggregate expenditure is *greater* than GDP	inventories *fall*	GDP and employment *increase.*

When economists forecast that aggregate expenditure is likely to decline and that the economy is headed for a recession, the federal government may implement *macroeconomic policies* in an attempt to head off the fall in expenditure and keep the economy from falling into recession. We discuss these macroeconomic polices in Chapters 26 and 27.

23.2 | Discuss the determinants of the four components of aggregate expenditure and define the marginal propensity to consume and the marginal propensity to save.

Determining the Level of Aggregate Expenditure in the Economy

To better understand how macroeconomic equilibrium is determined in the aggregate expenditure model, we look more closely at the components of aggregate expenditure. Table 23-2 lists the four components of aggregate expenditure for the year 2007. Each component is measured in *real* terms, meaning that it is corrected for inflation by being measured in billions of 2000 dollars. Consumption is clearly the largest component of aggregate expenditure. Investment and government purchases are of roughly similar size. Net exports are negative because in 2007, as in most years since the early 1970s, the United States imported more goods and services than it exported. Next, we consider the variables that determine each of the four components of aggregate expenditure.

Consumption

Figure 23-1 shows movements in real consumption for the years 1979 to 2007. Notice that consumption follows a smooth, upward trend. Only during periods of recession does the growth in consumption slow or decline.

The following are the five most important variables that determine the level of consumption:

- Current disposable income

- Household wealth

- Expected future income

- The price level

- The interest rate

We can discuss how changes in each of these variables affect consumption.

Current Disposable Income The most important determinant of consumption is the current disposable income of households. Recall from Chapter 19 that disposable income is the income remaining to households after they have paid the personal income tax and received government *transfer payments*, such as Social Security payments. For most households, the higher their disposable income, the more they spend, and the

EXPENDITURE CATEGORY	REAL EXPENDITURE (BILLIONS OF 2000 DOLLARS)
Consumption	$8,278
Investment	1,826
Government	2,022
Net exports	−556

Source: U.S. Bureau of Economic Analysis.

TABLE 23-2

Components of Real Aggregate Expenditure, 2007

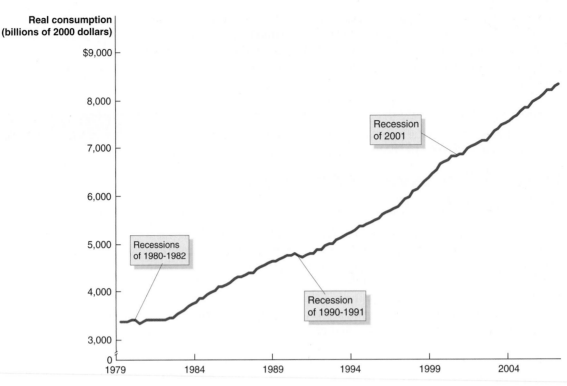

Figure 23-1 | Real Consumption, 1979–2007

Consumption follows a smooth, upward trend, interrupted only infrequently by brief recessions.

Note: The values are quarterly data seasonally adjusted at an annual rate.
Source: U.S. Bureau of Economic Analysis.

lower their income, the less they spend. Macroeconomic consumption is the total of all the consumption of U.S. households. So, we would expect consumption to increase when the current disposable income of households increases and to decrease when the current disposable income of households decreases. As we discussed in Chapter 19, total income in the United States expands during most years. Only during recessions, which happen infrequently, does total income decline. The main reason for the general upward trend in consumption shown in Figure 23-1 is that disposable income has followed a similar upward trend.

Household Wealth Consumption also depends on the wealth of households. A household's *wealth* is the value of its *assets* minus the value of its *liabilities*. Recall from Chapter 7 that an asset is anything of value owned by a person or a firm, and a liability is anything owed by a person or a firm. A household's assets include its home, stock and bond holdings, and bank accounts. A household's liabilities include any loans that it owes. A household with $10 million in wealth is likely to spend more than a household with $10,000 in wealth, even if both households have the same disposable income. Therefore, when the wealth of households increases, consumption should increase, and when the wealth of households decreases, consumption should decrease. Shares of stock are an important category of household wealth. When stock prices increase, household wealth will increase, and so should consumption. For example, a family whose stock holdings increase in value from $50,000 to $100,000 may be willing to spend a larger fraction of its income because it is less concerned with adding to its savings. A decline in stock prices should lead to a decline in consumption. Economists who have studied the determinants of consumption have concluded that permanent increases in wealth have a larger impact than temporary increases. A recent estimate of the effect of changes in wealth on consumption spending indicates that, for every permanent one-dollar increase in household wealth, consumption spending will increase by between four and five cents per year.

Expected Future Income Consumption also depends on expected future income. Most people prefer to keep their consumption fairly stable from year to year, even if their income fluctuates significantly. Real estate brokers, for example, earn most of their income from commissions (fixed percentages of the sale price) on houses they sell. Real estate brokers might have very high incomes some years and much lower incomes in other years. Most brokers keep their consumption steady and do not increase it during good years and then drastically cut back during slower years. If we looked just at a broker's current income, we might have difficulty estimating the broker's current consumption. Instead, we need to take into account the broker's expected future income. We can conclude that current income explains current consumption well *but only when current income is not unusually high or unusually low compared with expected future income.*

The Price Level Recall from Chapter 20 that the *price level* measures the average prices of goods and services in the economy. Consumption is affected by changes in the price level. It is tempting to think that an increase in prices will reduce consumption by making goods and services less affordable. In fact, the effect of an increase in the price of *one* product on the quantity demanded of that product is different from the effect of an increase in the price level on *total* spending by households on goods and services. Changes in the price level affect consumption mainly through their effect on household wealth. An increase in the price level will result in a decrease in the *real* value of household wealth. For example, if you have $2,000 in a checking account, the higher the price level, the fewer goods and services you can buy with your money. If the price level falls, the real value of your $2,000 would increase. Therefore, as the price level rises, the real value of your wealth declines, and so will your consumption, at least a little. Conversely, if the price level falls—which happens very rarely in the United States—your consumption will increase.

The Interest Rate Finally, consumption also depends on the interest rate. When the interest rate is high, the reward to saving is increased, and households are likely to save more and spend less. In Chapter 20, we discussed the distinction between the *nominal interest rate* and the *real interest rate*. The nominal interest rate is the stated interest rate on a loan or a financial investment such as a bond. The real interest rate corrects the nominal interest rate for the impact of inflation and is equal to the nominal interest rate minus the inflation rate. Because households are concerned with the payments they will make or receive after the effects of inflation are taken into account, consumption spending depends on the real interest rate.

We saw in Chapter 19 that consumption spending is divided into three categories: spending on *services*, such as medical care, education, and haircuts; spending on *nondurable goods*, such as food and clothing; and spending on *durable goods*, such as automobiles and furniture. Spending on durable goods is most likely to be affected by changes in the interest rate because a high real interest rate increases the cost of spending financed by borrowing. The monthly payment on a four-year car loan will be higher if the real interest rate on the loan is 4 percent than if the real interest rate is 2 percent.

The Consumption Function Panel (a) in Figure 23-2 illustrates the relationship between consumption and disposable income during the years 1960–2007. In panel (b), we draw a straight line through the points representing consumption and disposable income. The fact that most of the points lie almost on the line shows the close relationship between consumption and disposable income. Because changes in consumption depend on changes in disposable income, we can say that *consumption is a function of disposable income.* The relationship between consumption spending and disposable income illustrated in panel (b) of Figure 23-2 is called the **consumption function**.

The slope of the consumption function is equal to the change in consumption divided by the change in disposable income and is referred to as the **marginal propensity to consume** (*MPC*). Using the Greek letter delta, Δ, to represent "change in," C to

Consumption function The relationship between consumption spending and disposable income.

Marginal propensity to consume (*MPC*) The slope of the consumption function: The amount by which consumption spending changes when disposable income changes.

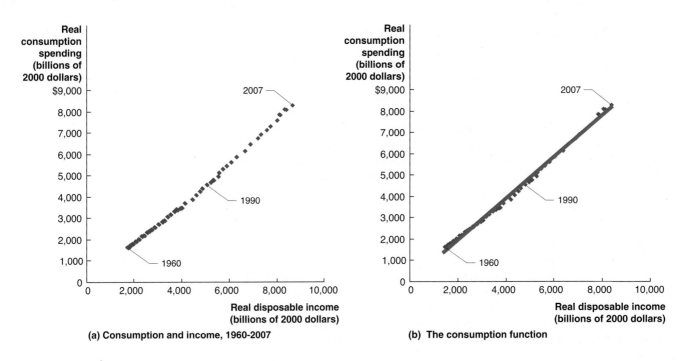

Figure 23-2 | The Relationship between Consumption and Income, 1960–2007

Panel (a) shows the relationship between consumption and income. The points represent combinations of real consumption spending and real disposable income for the years between 1960 and 2007. In panel (b), we draw a straight line through the points from panel (a). The line represents the relationship between consumption and disposable income and is called the *consumption function*. The slope of the consumption function is the marginal propensity to consume.

represent consumption spending, and *YD* to represent disposable income, we can write the expression for the *MPC* as follows:

$$MPC = \frac{\text{Change in consumption}}{\text{Change in disposable income}} = \frac{\Delta C}{\Delta YD}.$$

For example, between 1999 and 2000, consumption spending increased by $301 billion, while disposable income increased by $333 billion. The marginal propensity to consume was, therefore:

$$\frac{\Delta C}{\Delta YD} = \frac{\$301 \text{ billion}}{\$333 \text{ billion}} = 0.90.$$

The value for the *MPC* tells us that households in 2000 spent 90 percent of the increase in their household income.

We can also use the *MPC* to determine how much consumption will change as income changes. To see this relationship, we rewrite the expression for the *MPC*:

$$MPC = \frac{\text{Change in consumption}}{\text{Change in disposable income}},$$

or:

$$\text{Change in consumption} = \text{Change in disposable income} \times MPC.$$

For example, with an *MPC* of 0.90, a $10 billion increase in disposable income will increase consumption by $10 billion × 0.90, or $9 billion.

The Relationship between Consumption and National Income

We have seen that consumption spending by households depends on disposable income. We now shift our focus slightly to the similar relationship that exists between consumption spending and GDP. We make this shift because we are interested in using the aggregate expenditure model to explain changes in real GDP rather than changes in disposable income. The first step in examining the relationship between consumption and GDP is to recall from Chapter 19 that the differences between GDP and national income are small and can be ignored without affecting our analysis. In fact, in this and the following chapters, we will use the terms *GDP* and *national income* interchangeably. Also recall that disposable income is equal to national income plus government transfer payments minus taxes. Taxes minus government transfer payments are referred to as *net taxes*. So, we can write the following:

$$\text{Disposable income} = \text{National income} - \text{Net taxes.}$$

We can rearrange the equation like this:

$$\text{National income} = \text{GDP} = \text{Disposable income} + \text{Net taxes.}$$

The table in Figure 23-3 shows hypothetical values for national income (or GDP), net taxes, disposable income, and consumption spending. Notice that national income and disposable income differ by a constant amount, which is equal to net taxes of $1,000

National income or GDP (billions of dollars)	Net taxes (billions of dollars)	Disposable income (billions of dollars)	Consumption (billions of dollars)	Change in national income (billions of dollars)	Change in disposable income (billions of dollars)
$1,000	$1,000	$0	$750	—	—
3,000	1,000	2,000	2,250	2,000	2,000
5,000	1,000	4,000	3,750	2,000	2,000
7,000	1,000	6,000	5,250	2,000	2,000
9,000	1,000	8,000	6,750	2,000	2,000
11,000	1,000	10,000	8,250	2,000	2,000
13,000	1,000	12,000	9,750	2,000	2,000

Figure 23-3

The Relationship between Consumption and National Income

Because national income differs from disposable income only by net taxes—which, for simplicity, we assume are constant—we can graph the consumption function using national income rather than disposable income. We can also calculate the *MPC*, which is the slope of the consumption function, using either the change in national income or the change in disposable income and always get the same value. The slope of the consumption function between point *A* and point *B* is equal to the change in consumption—$1,500 billion—divided by the change in national income—$2,000 billion—or 0.75.

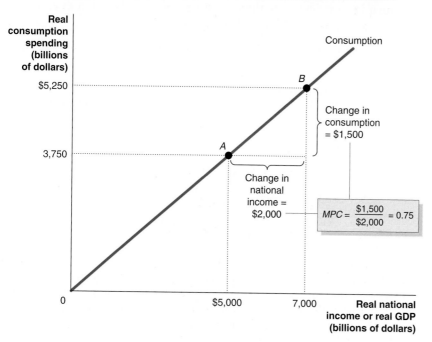

billion. In reality, net taxes are not a constant amount because they are affected by changes in income. As income rises, net taxes rise because some taxes, such as the personal income tax, increase and some government transfer payments, such as government payments to unemployed workers, fall. Nothing important is affected in our analysis, however, by our simplifying assumption that net taxes are constant. The graph in Figure 23-3 shows a line representing the relationship between consumption and national income. The line is very similar to the consumption function shown in panel (b) of Figure 23-2. We defined the marginal propensity to consume (*MPC*) as the change in consumption divided by the change in disposable income, which is the slope of the consumption function. In fact, notice that if we calculate the slope of the line in Figure 23-3 between points *A* and *B*, we get a result that will not change whether we use the values for national income or the values for disposable income. Using the values for national income:

$$\frac{\Delta C}{\Delta Y} = \frac{\$5,250 \text{ billion} - \$3,750 \text{ billion}}{\$7,000 \text{ billion} - \$5,000 \text{ billion}} = 0.75.$$

Using the corresponding values for disposable income from the table:

$$\frac{\Delta C}{\Delta YD} = \frac{\$5,250 \text{ billion} - \$3,750 \text{ billion}}{\$6,000 \text{ billion} - \$4,000 \text{ billion}} = 0.75.$$

It should not be surprising that we get the same result in either case. National income and disposable income differ by a constant amount, so changes in the two numbers always give us the same value, as is shown by the last two columns of the table in Figure 23-3. Therefore, we can graph the consumption function using national income rather than using disposable income. We can also calculate the *MPC* using either the change in national income or the change in disposable income and always get the same value.

Income, Consumption, and Saving

To complete our discussion of consumption, we can look briefly at the relationships among income, consumption, and saving. Households either spend their income, save it, or use it to pay taxes. For the economy as a whole, we can write the following:

National income = Consumption + Saving + Taxes.

When national income increases, there must be some combination of an increase in consumption, an increase in saving, and an increase in taxes:

Change in national income = Change in consumption + Change in saving + Change in taxes.

Using symbols, where *Y* represents national income (and GDP), *C* represents consumption, *S* represents saving, and *T* represents taxes, we can write the following:

$$Y = C + S + T$$

and,

$$\Delta Y = \Delta C + \Delta S + \Delta T.$$

To simplify, we can assume that taxes are always a constant amount, in which case $\Delta T = 0$, so the following is also true:

$$\Delta Y = \Delta C + \Delta S.$$

Marginal propensity to save (*MPS*)
The change in saving divided by the change in disposable income.

We have already seen that the marginal propensity to consume equals the change in consumption divided by the change in income. We can define the **marginal propensity to save (*MPS*)** as the amount by which saving increases when disposable income increases and measure the *MPS* as the change in saving divided by the change in disposable income. In calculating the *MPS*, as in calculating the *MPC*, we can safely ignore the difference between national income and disposable income.

If we divide the last equation on the previous page by the change in income, ΔY, we get an equation that shows the relationship between the marginal propensity to consume and the marginal propensity to save:

$$\frac{\Delta Y}{\Delta Y} = \frac{\Delta C}{\Delta Y} + \frac{\Delta S}{\Delta Y}$$

or,

$$1 = MPC + MPS.$$

This last equation tells us that when taxes are constant, the marginal propensity to consume plus the marginal propensity to save must always equal 1. They must add up to 1 because part of any increase in income is consumed, and whatever remains must be saved.

Solved Problem | 23-2

Calculating the Marginal Propensity to Consume and the Marginal Propensity to Save

Fill in the blanks in the following table. For simplicity, assume that taxes are zero. Show that the MPC plus the MPS equals 1.

NATIONAL INCOME AND REAL GDP (Y)	CONSUMPTION (C)	SAVING (S)	MARGINAL PROPENSITY TO CONSUME (MPC)	MARGINAL PROPENSITY TO SAVE (MPS)
$9,000	$8,000		—	—
10,000	8,600			
11,000	9,200			
12,000	9,800			
13,000	10,400			

SOLVING THE PROBLEM:

Step 1: **Review the chapter material.** This problem is about the relationship among income, consumption, and saving, so you may want to review the section "Income, Consumption, and Saving," which begins on page 776.

Step 2: **Fill in the table.** We know that $Y = C + S + T$. With taxes equal to zero, this equation becomes $Y = C + S$. We can use this equation to fill in the "Saving" column. We can use the expressions for the MPC and the MPS to fill in the other two columns:

$$MPC = \frac{\Delta C}{\Delta Y}$$
$$MPS = \frac{\Delta S}{\Delta Y}$$

For example, to calculate the value of the MPC in the second row, we have:

$$MPC = \frac{\Delta C}{\Delta Y} = \frac{\$8,600 - \$8,000}{\$10,000 - \$9,000} = \frac{\$600}{\$1,000} = 0.6.$$

To calculate the value of the MPS in the second row, we have:

$$MPS = \frac{\Delta S}{\Delta Y} = \frac{\$1,400 - \$1,000}{\$10,000 - \$9,000} = \frac{\$400}{\$1,000} = 0.4.$$

NATIONAL INCOME AND REAL GDP (Y)	CONSUMPTION (C)	SAVING (S)	MARGINAL PROPENSITY TO CONSUME (MPC)	MARGINAL PROPENSITY TO SAVE (MPS)
$9,000	$8,000	$1,000	—	—
10,000	8,600	1,400	0.6	0.4
11,000	9,200	1,800	0.6	0.4
12,000	9,800	2,200	0.6	0.4
13,000	10,400	2,600	0.6	0.4

Step 3: **Show that the *MPC* plus the *MPS* equals 1.** At every level of national income, the *MPC* is 0.6 and the *MPS* is 0.4. Therefore, the *MPC* plus the *MPS* is always equal to 1.

>> **End Solved Problem 23-2**

YOUR TURN: For more practice, do related problem 2.11 on page 804 at the end of this chapter.

Planned Investment

Figure 23-4 shows movements in real investment spending for the years 1979–2007. Notice that, unlike consumption, investment does not follow a smooth, upward trend. Investment declined significantly during the recessions of 1980, 1981–1982, 1990–1991, and 2001. Following the recovery from the 1981–1982 recession, real investment increased only slowly, so that in 1992, it was at about the same level as in 1984. But during the mid- to late 1990s, investment increased very rapidly, led by increases in spending on computers and other information technology, partly as a result of the growth of the Internet. In 2000, real investment spending had risen to nearly twice its 1992 level before declining by 10 percent between 2000 and 2002. Real investment spending increased by more than 30 percent between 2002 and mid-2006, as the economy recovered from the 2001 recession, before declining as the economy slowed during 2007.

The four most important variables that determine the level of investment are:

- Expectations of future profitability

- The interest rate

- Taxes

- Cash flow

Figure 23-4

Real Investment, 1979–2007

Investment is subject to more changes than is consumption. Investment declined significantly during the recessions of 1980, 1981–1982, 1990–1991, and 2001. Following the recovery from the 1981–1982 recession, investment increased only slowly, so that in 1992, it was at about the same level as in 1984. But during the mid- to late 1990s, investment increased very strongly, partly because the growth of the Internet led firms to increase spending on computers and other information technology. In 2000, real investment had risen to nearly twice its 1992 level before declining by more than 10 percent in 2001.

Note: The values are quarterly data seasonally adjusted at an annual rate.

Source: U.S. Bureau of Economic Analysis.

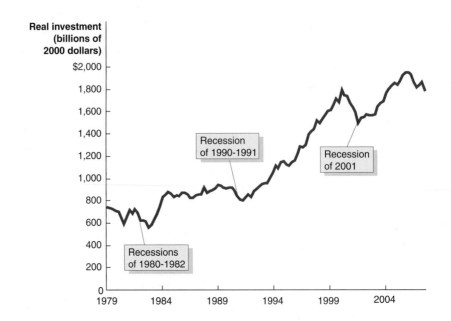

Expectations of Future Profitability Investment goods, such as factories, office buildings, and machinery and equipment, are long lived. A firm is unlikely to build a new factory unless it is optimistic that the demand for its product will remain strong for a period of at least several years. When the economy moves into a recession, many firms postpone buying investment goods even if the demand for their own product is strong because they are afraid that the recession may become worse. The reverse may be true during an expansion. In the late 1990s, many firms increased their investment spending, expecting that capital goods that embodied new information and telecommunication technologies would prove very profitable. The key point is this: *The optimism or pessimism of firms is an important determinant of investment spending.*

The Interest Rate A significant fraction of business investment is financed by borrowing. This borrowing takes the form of issuing corporate bonds or borrowing from banks. Households also borrow to finance most of their spending on new homes. The higher the interest rate, the more expensive it becomes for firms and households to borrow. Because households and firms are interested in the cost of borrowing after taking into account the effects of inflation, investment spending depends on the real interest rate. Therefore, holding the other factors that affect investment spending constant, there is an inverse relationship between the real interest rate and investment spending: *A higher real interest rate results in less investment spending, and a lower real interest rate results in more investment spending.*

Taxes Taxes also affect the level of investment spending. Firms focus on the profits that remain after they have paid taxes. The federal government imposes a *corporate income tax* on the profits corporations earn, including profits from the new buildings, equipment, and other investment goods they purchase. A reduction in the corporate income tax increases the after-tax profitability of investment spending. An increase in the corporate income tax decreases the after-tax profitability of investment spending. *Investment tax incentives* also increase investment spending. An investment tax incentive provides firms with a tax reduction when they spend on new investment goods. For example, in 2002, Congress enacted an investment tax incentive for new investment in equipment and software. This incentive expired at the end of 2004. Partially as a result of this incentive, spending on equipment and software increased from $801 billion at an annual rate in the first quarter of 2002 to $996 billion in the fourth quarter of 2004.

Cash Flow Most firms do not borrow to finance spending on new factories, machinery, and equipment. Instead, they use their own funds. **Cash flow** is the difference between the cash revenues received by a firm and the cash spending by the firm. Noncash receipts or noncash spending would not be included in cash flow. For example, tax laws allow firms to count as a cost an amount for depreciation to replace worn out or obsolete machinery and equipment even if new machinery and equipment have not actually been purchased. Because this is noncash spending, it would not be included when calculating cash flow. The largest contributor to cash flow is profit. The more profitable a firm is, the greater its cash flow and the greater its ability to finance investment. During periods of recession, many firms experience reduced profits, which in turn reduces their ability to finance spending on new factories or machinery and equipment.

Cash flow The difference between the cash revenues received by a firm and the cash spending by the firm.

Making the Connection | Cisco Rides the Roller Coaster of Information Technology Spending

We saw at the beginning of this chapter that Cisco Systems was taken by surprise by the decline in demand for its routers, switches, and other equipment during the first quarter of 2001. In fact, the Internet and telecommunications busts of 2001 were unusual in their severity. The following graph shows that spending on information processing equipment and software followed a fairly smooth, upward trend from the beginning of 1990 to the end of 2000. Measured in 2000 dollars, real spending on information processing equipment and software increased from $101 billion at an annual rate in the first quarter of 1990 to $488 billion in the fourth quarter of 2000. Spending then declined sharply and did not regain the level of the fourth quarter of 2000 until almost three years later, in the third quarter of 2003.

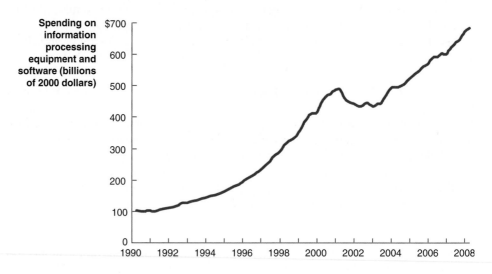

Note: The values are seasonally adjusted at an annual rate.
Source: U.S. Bureau of Economic Analysis.

Cisco benefited greatly from the increased spending on information technology in the 1990s. By the end of 2000, Cisco was second to only Microsoft in the total value of its shares of stock. In early 2000, John Chambers, Cisco's chief executive officer, predicted that by 2004, the firm's annual revenues would rise from $12.2 billion to $50 billion and that the total value of its stock would rise from $454 billion to $1 trillion. Unfortunately, the Internet and telecommunications busts made these goals impossible to attain. Cisco made an accounting profit of $2.1 billion in 2000, but by 2002, that profit had turned into a $1 billion loss as revenues declined. By 2006, Cisco's revenues had risen back to $28 billion, and the firm made a $5.6 billion accounting profit.

What explains Cisco's roller-coaster ride? As we have seen, a key determinant of investment spending is firms' expectations of the future profitability of their purchases of investment goods. In the 1990s, many firms investing in equipment to establish Web sites or to use the fiber-optic cable networks being built overestimated how profitable their investments in this equipment would be. When forecasts of future profitability were adjusted sharply downward in 2001, spending on information technology plummeted. By 2007, however, the spread of high-speed Internet access and the popularity of using the Internet for telephone service and to download movies and television programs led industry analysts to forecast that Internet traffic would be increasing by 70 percent or more per year. Cisco was still selling 70 percent to 85 percent of all network switches and routers, which left the firm well positioned to profit from this future growth. In fact, at least through mid-2008, spending on information processing equipment and software remained strong despite the slowing in the growth of aggregate demand.

Sources: Dana Cimilluca, "Thinking the Unthinkable: A Blockbuster Buyout by Cisco," *Wall Street Journal*, May 9, 2007; and "Growing Pains of the Cisco Kid," *Economist*, November 11, 2004.

YOUR TURN: Test your understanding by doing related problem 2.7 on page 803 at the end of this chapter.

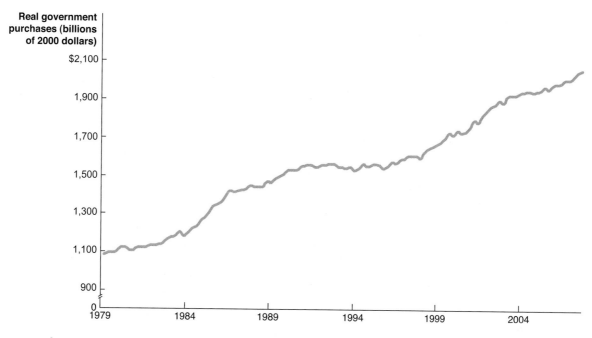

Figure 23-5 | Real Government Purchases, 1979–2007

Government purchases grew steadily for most of the 1979–2007 period, with the exception of the mid-1990s, when concern about the federal budget deficit caused real government purchases to fall for three years, beginning in 1992.

Note: The values are quarterly data seasonally adjusted at an annual rate. Source: Bureau of Economic Analysis.

Government Purchases

Total government purchases include all spending by federal, local, and state governments for goods and services. Recall from Chapter 19 that government purchases do not include transfer payments, such as Social Security payments by the federal government or pension payments by local governments to retired police officers and firefighters because the government does not receive a good or service in return.

Figure 23-5 shows levels of real government purchases during the years 1979–2007. Government purchases grew steadily for most of this period, with the exception of the mid-1990s, when concern that spending by the federal government was growing much faster than tax receipts led Congress and Presidents George H. W. Bush and Bill Clinton to enact a series of spending reductions. As a result, real government purchases declined for three years, beginning in 1992. Contributing to the slow growth of government purchases during the 1990s was the end of the Cold War between the United States and the Soviet Union in 1989. Real federal government spending on national defense declined from $479 billion in 1990 to $365 billion in 1998 before rising again to $505 billion in 2007 in response to the war on terrorism and the wars in Iraq and Afghanistan.

Net Exports

Net exports equal exports minus imports. We can calculate net exports by taking the value of spending by foreign firms and households on goods and services produced in the United States and *subtracting* the value of spending by U.S. firms and households on goods and services produced in other countries. Figure 23-6 illustrates movements in real net exports during the years 1979–2007. During nearly all these years, the United States imported more goods and services than it exported, so net exports were negative. Net exports usually increase when the U.S. economy is in recession—although this did not happen during the 2001 recession—and fall when the U.S. economy is expanding. We will explore further the behavior of net exports in Chapter 29.

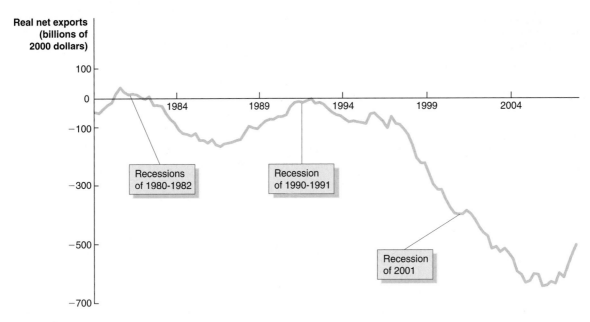

Figure 23-6 | Real Net Exports, 1979–2007

Net exports were negative in most years between 1979 and 2007. Net exports have usually increased when the U.S. economy is in recession and decreased when the U.S. economy is expanding, although they fell during the 2001 recession.

Note: The values are quarterly data seasonally adjusted at an annual rate.
Source: Bureau of Economic Analysis.

The following are the three most important variables that determine the level of net exports:

- The price level in the United States relative to the price levels in other countries

- The growth rate of GDP in the United States relative to the growth rates of GDP in other countries

- The exchange rate between the dollar and other currencies

The Price Level in the United States Relative to the Price Levels in Other Countries

If inflation in the United States is lower than inflation in other countries, prices of U.S. products increase more slowly than the prices of products of other countries. This difference in price levels increases the demand for U.S. products relative to the demand for foreign products. So, U.S. exports increase and U.S. imports decrease, which increases net exports. The reverse happens during periods when the inflation rate in the United States is higher than the inflation rates in other countries: U.S. exports decrease and U.S. imports increase, which decreases net exports.

The Growth Rate of GDP in the United States Relative to the Growth Rates of GDP in Other Countries

As GDP increases in the United States, the incomes of households rise, leading them to increase their purchases of goods and services. Some of the additional goods and services purchased with rising incomes are produced in the United States, but some are imported. When incomes rise faster in the United States than in other countries, U.S. consumers' purchases of foreign goods and services will increase faster than foreign consumers' purchases of U.S. goods and services. As a result, net exports will fall. When incomes in the United States rise more slowly than incomes in other countries, net exports will rise.

The Exchange Rate Between the Dollar and Other Currencies

As the value of the U.S. dollar rises, the foreign currency price of U.S. products sold in other countries rises, and the dollar price of foreign products sold in the United States falls. For example, suppose that the exchange rate between the Japanese yen and the U.S. dollar is 100

Japanese yen for one U.S. dollar, or ¥100 = $1. At this exchange rate, someone in the United States could buy ¥100 for $1, or someone in Japan could buy $1 for ¥100. Leaving aside transportation costs, at this exchange rate, a U.S. product that sells for $1 in the United States will sell for ¥100 in Japan, and a Japanese product that sells for ¥100 in Japan will sell for $1 in the United States. If the exchange rate changes to ¥150 = $1, then the value of the dollar will have risen because it takes more yen to buy $1. At the new exchange rate, the U.S. product that still sells for $1 in the United States will now sell for ¥150 in Japan, reducing the quantity demanded by Japanese consumers. The Japanese product that still sells for ¥100 in Japan will now sell for only $0.67 in the United States, increasing the quantity demanded by U.S. consumers. An increase in the value of the dollar will reduce exports and increase imports, so net exports will fall. A decrease in the value of the dollar will increase exports and reduce imports, so net exports will rise.

23.3 | Use a 45°-line diagram to illustrate macroeconomic equilibrium.

Graphing Macroeconomic Equilibrium

Having examined the components of aggregate expenditure, we can now look more closely at macroeconomic equilibrium. We saw earlier in the chapter that macroeconomic equilibrium occurs when GDP is equal to aggregate expenditure. We can use a graph called the *45°-line diagram* to illustrate macroeconomic equilibrium. (The 45°-line diagram is also sometimes referred to as the *Keynesian cross* because it is based on the analysis of John Maynard Keynes.) To become familiar with this diagram, consider Figure 23-7, which is a 45°-line diagram that shows the relationship between the quantity of Pepsi sold (on the vertical axis) and the quantity of Pepsi produced (on the horizontal axis).

The line on the diagram forms an angle of 45° with the horizontal axis. The line represents all the points that are equal distances from both axes. So, points such as *A* and *B*, where the number of bottles of Pepsi produced equals the number of bottles sold, are on the 45° line. Points such as *C*, where the quantity sold is greater than the quantity produced, lie above the line. Points such as *D*, where the quantity sold is less than the quantity produced, lie below the line.

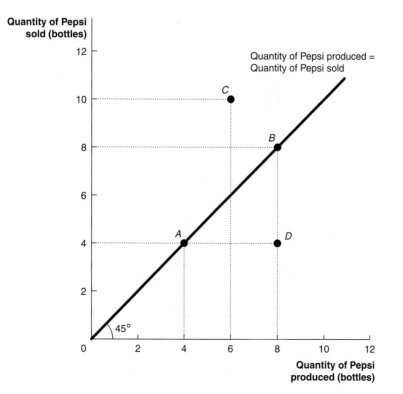

Figure 23-7

An Example of a 45°-Line Diagram

The 45° line shows all the points that are equal distances from both axes. Points such as *A* and *B*, at which the quantity produced equals the quantity sold, are on the 45° line. Points such as *C*, at which the quantity sold is greater than the quantity produced, lie above the line. Points such as *D*, at which the quantity sold is less than the quantity produced, lie below the line.

Figure 23-8

The Relationship between Planned Aggregate Expenditure and GDP on a 45°-Line Diagram

Every point of macroeconomic equilibrium is on the 45° line, where planned aggregate expenditure equals GDP. At points above the line, planned aggregate expenditure is greater than GDP. At points below the line, planned aggregate expenditure is less than GDP.

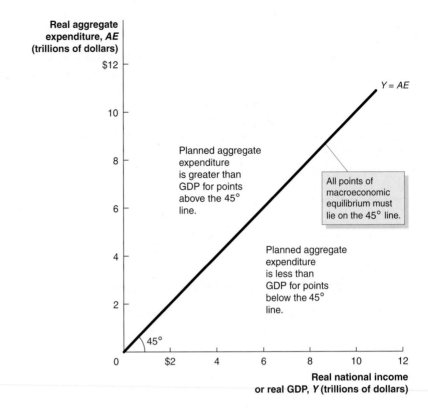

Figure 23-8 is very similar to Figure 23-7, except now we are measuring real national income or real GDP (Y) on the horizontal axis and planned real aggregate expenditure (AE) on the vertical axis. Because macroeconomic equilibrium occurs where planned aggregate expenditure equals GDP, *we know that all points of macroeconomic equilibrium must lie along the 45° line.* For all points above the 45° line, planned aggregate expenditure will be greater than GDP. For all points below the 45° line, planned aggregate expenditure will be less than GDP.

The 45° line shows many potential points of macroeconomic equilibrium. During any particular year, only one of these points will represent the actual level of equilibrium real GDP, given the actual level of planned real expenditure. To determine this point, we need to draw a line on the graph showing the *aggregate expenditure function.* The aggregate expenditure function shows us the amount of planned aggregate expenditure that will occur at every level of national income or GDP.

Changes in GDP have a much greater impact on consumption than on planned investment, government purchases, or net exports. We assume for simplicity that the variables that determine planned investment, government purchases, and net exports all remain constant, as do the variables other than GDP that affect consumption. For example, we assume that a firm's level of planned investment at the beginning of the year will not change during the year, even if the level of GDP changes.

Figure 23-9 shows the aggregate expenditure function on the 45°-line diagram. The lowest upward-sloping line, C, represents the consumption function, as shown in Figure 23-2 on page 774. The quantities of planned investment, government purchases, and net exports are constant because we assumed that the variables they depend on are constant. So, the level of planned aggregate expenditure at any level of GDP is the amount of consumption spending at that level of GDP plus the sum of the constant amounts of planned investment, government purchases, and net exports. In Figure 23-9, we add each component of spending successively to the consumption function line to arrive at the line representing planned aggregate expenditure (AE). The $C + I$ line is higher than the C line by the constant amount of planned investment; the $C + I + G$ line is higher than the $C + I$ line by the constant amount of government purchases; and

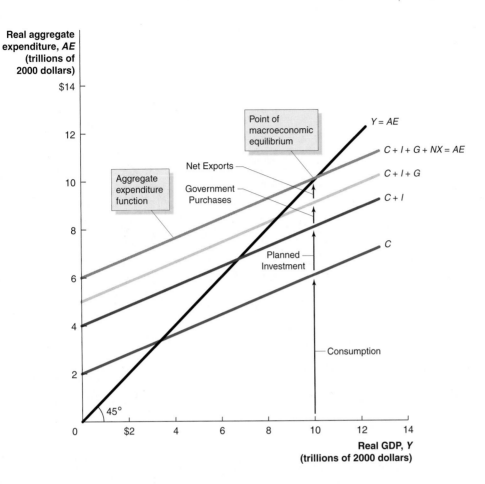

Figure 23-9

Macroeconomic Equilibrium on the 45°-Line Diagram

Macroeconomic equilibrium occurs where the aggregate expenditure line (AE) crosses the 45° line. The lowest upward-sloping line, C, represents the consumption function. The quantities of planned investment, government purchases, and net exports are constant because we assumed that the variables they depend on are constant. So, the total of planned aggregate expenditure at any level of GDP is just the amount of consumption at that level of GDP plus the sum of the constant amounts of planned investment, government purchases, and net exports. We successively add each component of spending to the consumption function line to arrive at the line representing aggregate expenditure.

the $C + I + G + NX$ line is higher than the $C + I + G$ line by the constant amount of NX. (Notice that in many years, NX is negative, which causes the $C + I + G + NX$ line to be *below* the $C + I + G$ line.) The $C + I + G + NX$ line shows all four components of expenditure and is the aggregate expenditure (AE) function. At the point where the AE line crosses the 45° line, planned aggregate expenditure is equal to GDP, and the economy is in macroeconomic equilibrium.

Figure 23-10 makes the relationship between planned aggregate expenditure and GDP clearer by showing only the 45° line and the AE line. The figure shows that the AE line intersects the 45° line at a level of real GDP of $10 trillion. Therefore, $10 trillion represents the equilibrium level of real GDP. To see why this is true, consider the situation if real GDP were only $8 trillion. By moving vertically from $8 trillion on the horizontal axis up to the AE line, we see that planned aggregate expenditure will be greater than $8 trillion at this level of real GDP. Whenever total spending is greater than total production, firms' inventories will fall. The fall in inventories is equal to the vertical distance between the AE line, which shows the level of total spending, and the 45° line, which shows the $8 trillion of total production. Unplanned declines in inventories lead firms to increase their production. As real GDP increases from $8 trillion, so will total income and, therefore, consumption. The economy will move up the AE line as consumption increases. The gap between total spending and total production will fall, but as long as the AE line is above the 45° line, inventories will continue to decline, and firms will continue to expand production. When real GDP rises to $10 trillion, inventories stop falling, and the economy will be in macroeconomic equilibrium.

As Figure 23-10 shows, if GDP initially is $12 trillion, planned aggregate expenditure will be less than GDP, and firms will experience an unplanned increase in inventories. Rising inventories lead firms to decrease production. As GDP falls from $12 trillion, so will consumption, which causes the economy to move down the AE line. The gap between planned aggregate expenditure and GDP will fall, but as long as the AE line is

Figure 23-10

Macroeconomic Equilibrium

Macroeconomic equilibrium occurs where the *AE* line crosses the 45° line. In this case, that occurs at GDP of $10 trillion. If GDP is less than $10 trillion, the corresponding point on the *AE* line is above the 45° line, planned aggregate expenditure is greater than total production, firms will experience an unplanned decrease in inventories, and GDP will increase. If GDP is greater than $10 trillion, the corresponding point on the *AE* line is below the 45° line, planned aggregate expenditure is less than total production, firms will experience an unplanned increase in inventories, and GDP will decrease.

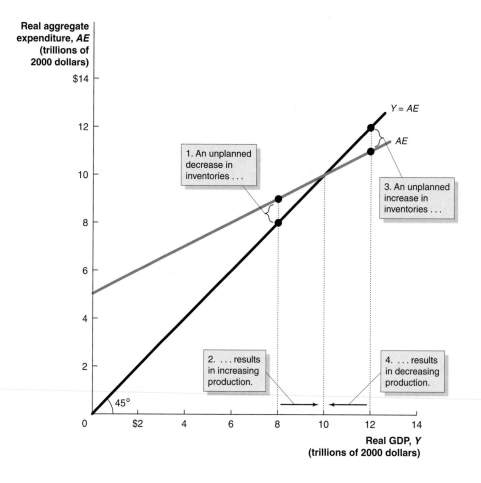

below the 45° line, inventories will continue to rise, and firms will continue to cut production. When GDP falls to $10 trillion, inventories will stop rising, and the economy will be in macroeconomic equilibrium.

Showing a Recession on the 45°-Line Diagram

Notice that *macroeconomic equilibrium can occur at any point on the 45° line.* Ideally, we would like equilibrium to occur at *potential real GDP.* At potential real GDP, firms will be operating at their normal level of capacity, and the economy will be at the *natural rate of unemployment.* As we saw in Chapter 20, at the natural rate of unemployment, the economy will be at *full employment:* Everyone in the labor force who wants a job will have one, except the structurally and frictionally unemployed. However, for equilibrium to occur at the level of potential real GDP, planned aggregate expenditure must be high enough. As Figure 23-11 shows, if there is insufficient total spending, equilibrium will occur at a lower level of real GDP. Many firms will be operating below their normal capacity, and the unemployment rate will be above the natural rate of unemployment.

Suppose that the level of potential real GDP is $10 trillion. As Figure 23-11 shows, when GDP is $10 trillion, planned aggregate expenditure is below $10 trillion, perhaps because business firms have become pessimistic about their future profitability and have reduced their investment spending. The shortfall in planned aggregate expenditure that leads to the recession can be measured as the vertical distance between the *AE* line and the 45° line at the level of potential real GDP. The shortfall in planned aggregate expenditure is exactly equal to the unplanned increase in inventories that would occur if the economy were initially at a level of GDP of $10 trillion. The unplanned increase in inventories measures the amount by which current planned aggregate expenditure is too low for the current level of production to be the equilibrium level. Or, put another way, if any of the four components of aggregate expenditure increased by this amount, the

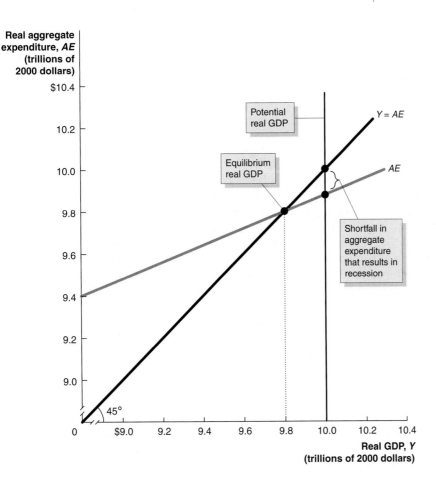

Real aggregate
expenditure, *AE*
(trillions of
2000 dollars)

Potential
real GDP

$Y = AE$

Equilibrium
real GDP

AE

Shortfall in
aggregate
expenditure
that results in
recession

45°

Real GDP, *Y*
(trillions of 2000 dollars)

Figure 23-11

**Showing a Recession
on the 45°-Line Diagram**

When the aggregate expenditure line intersects the 45° line at a level of GDP below potential real GDP, the economy is in recession. The figure shows that potential real GDP is $10 trillion, but because planned aggregate expenditure is too low, the equilibrium level of GDP is only $9.8 trillion, where the *AE* line intersects the 45° line. As a result, some firms will be operating below their normal capacity, and unemployment will be above the natural rate of unemployment. We can measure the shortfall in planned aggregate expenditure as the vertical distance between the *AE* line and the 45° line at the level of potential real GDP.

AE line would shift upward and intersect the 45° line at GDP of $10 trillion, and the economy would be in macroeconomic equilibrium at full employment.

Figure 23-11 shows that macroeconomic equilibrium will occur when real GDP is $9.8 trillion. Because this is 2 percent below the potential level of real GDP of $10 trillion, many firms will be operating below their normal capacity, and the unemployment rate will be well above the natural rate of unemployment. The economy will remain at this level of real GDP until there is an increase in one or more of the components of aggregate expenditure.

The Important Role of Inventories

Whenever planned aggregate expenditure is less than real GDP, some firms will experience an unplanned increase in inventories. If firms do not cut back their production promptly when spending declines, they will accumulate inventories. If firms accumulate excess inventories, then even if spending quickly returns to its normal levels, firms will have to sell these excess inventories before they can return to producing at normal levels. The possibility that firms will accumulate excess inventories explains why a brief decline in spending can result in a fairly long recession. In the early twentieth century, the inability of many firms to control their inventories contributed to the length and severity of recessions. By the 1980s and 1990s, many firms used improved systems of inventory control, which helped make recessions shorter and less severe.

**Making
the
Connection**

Business Attempts to Control
Inventories, Then . . . and Now

A failure to control inventories can cause a firm to suffer losses or even drive it into bankruptcy. For example, early in the twentieth century, excessive accumulation of inventories was a serious problem for the automobile

Dell Computer uses supply chain management to keep its inventory low.

industry. In his memoirs, Alfred Sloan, president of General Motors during the 1920s, described checking on inventory by traveling around the country by train and literally counting the number of unsold cars on dealers' lots. Not too surprisingly, this weak method of inventory control caused General Motors to suffer severe financial losses in 1920 and again in 1924. Eventually, automobile firms improved their inventory control methods, although not before a number of firms, including United States Motors, the predecessor of Chrysler Corporation, were driven into bankruptcy.

Modern computer firms, such as Dell and Hewlett-Packard, can also suffer significant losses if they accumulate large inventories of computer components because the prices of the components they buy from their suppliers can decline significantly, even from one week to the next. A firm that has large inventories of components may find that its costs of assembling computers are significantly greater than the costs of competitors who hold smaller inventories.

Dell Computer has pioneered in reducing costs by controlling inventories. Dell does not begin to assemble a new computer until it receives an order from a customer by telephone or over the Internet. As a result, Dell holds no inventories of finished computers. Dell still must hold some inventories of computer components, most of which are purchased from outside suppliers. Dell developed a system of *supply chain management* by which it quickly communicates orders to its suppliers and closely monitors their ability to fill its orders promptly. By the mid-1990s, Dell's suppliers could provide Dell with computer components in only two or three days. Dissatisfied with even this strong performance, in 1999, Dell set up an Internet site for suppliers to monitor Dell's need for components minute by minute and to track the components as they move through Dell's computer assembly process. As a result, the amount of time suppliers take to provide Dell with components has dropped to only six hours. When Dell assembles a computer, suppliers will have manufactured many of the components only a few hours earlier. The inventory control techniques that allow Dell to be a low-cost seller of computers also help the firm to respond quickly to sales declines without a significant buildup of inventories.

At the beginning of this chapter, we discussed Cisco's difficulties during 2001. Unlike Dell, Cisco failed to track demand well or to monitor its supply chain closely. The result was that Cisco was stuck during 2001 with large amounts of unsold inventories and had to trim production and lay off workers.

YOUR TURN: Test your understanding by doing related problem 3.6 on page 804 at the end of this chapter.

A Numerical Example of Macroeconomic Equilibrium

In forecasting real GDP, economists rely on quantitative models of the economy. We can increase our understanding of the causes of changes in real GDP by considering a simple numerical example of macroeconomic equilibrium. Although simplified, this example captures some of the key features contained in the quantitative models used by economic forecasters. Table 23-3 shows several hypothetical combinations of real GDP and planned aggregate expenditure. The first column lists real GDP. The next four columns list levels of the four components of planned aggregate expenditure that occur at the corresponding level of real GDP. We assume that planned investment, government purchases, and net exports do not change as GDP changes. Because consumption depends on GDP, it increases as GDP increases.

In the first row, GDP of $8,000 billion (or $8 trillion) results in consumption of $6,200 billion. Adding consumption, planned investment, government purchases, and net exports across the row gives planned aggregate expenditure of $8,700 billion, which is shown in the sixth column. Because planned aggregate expenditure is greater than GDP, inventories will fall by $700 billion. This unplanned decline in inventories will lead firms to increase production, and GDP will increase. GDP will continue to increase until

TABLE 23-3 | **Macroeconomic Equilibrium**

REAL GDP (Y)	CONSUMPTION (C)	PLANNED INVESTMENT (I)	GOVERNMENT PURCHASES (G)	NET EXPORTS (NX)	PLANNED AGGREGATE EXPENDITURE (AE)	UNPLANNED CHANGE IN INVENTORIES	REAL GDP WILL...
$8,000	$6,200	$1,500	$1,500	−$500	$8,700	−$700	increase
9,000	6,850	1,500	1,500	−500	9,350	−350	increase
10,000	7,500	1,500	1,500	−500	10,000	0	be in equilibrium
11,000	8,150	1,500	1,500	−500	10,650	+350	decrease
12,000	8,800	1,500	1,500	−500	11,300	+700	decrease

Note: The values are in billions of 2000 dollars.

it reaches $10,000 billion. At that level of GDP, planned aggregate expenditure is also $10,000 billion, unplanned changes in inventories are zero, and the economy is in macroeconomic equilibrium.

In the last row of Table 23-3, GDP of $12,000 billion results in consumption of $8,800 billion and planned aggregate expenditure of $11,300 billion. Because planned aggregate expenditure is less than GDP, inventories will increase by $700 billion. This unplanned increase in inventories will lead firms to decrease production, and GDP will decrease. GDP will continue to decrease until it reaches $10,000 billion, unplanned changes in inventories are zero, and the economy is in macroeconomic equilibrium.

Only when real GDP equals $10,000 billion will the economy be in macroeconomic equilibrium. At other levels of real GDP, planned aggregate expenditure will be higher or lower than GDP, and the economy will be expanding or contracting.

Don't Let This Happen to **YOU!**

Don't Confuse Aggregate Expenditure with Consumption Spending

Macroeconomic equilibrium occurs where planned aggregate expenditure equals GDP. But, remember that planned aggregate expenditure equals the sum of consumption spending, planned investment spending, government purchases, and net exports, *not* consumption spending by itself. If GDP were equal to consumption, the economy would not be in equilibrium. Planned investment plus government purchases plus net exports will always be a positive number. Therefore, if consumption were equal to GDP, aggregate expenditure would have to be greater than GDP. In that case, inventories would be decreasing, and GDP would be *increasing*; GDP would not be in equilibrium.

Test your understanding of macroeconomic equilibrium with this problem:

Question: Do you agree with the following argument?

The chapter says macroeconomic equilibrium occurs where planned aggregate expenditure equals GDP. GDP is equal to national income. So, at equilibrium, planned aggregate expenditure must equal national income. But, we know that consumers do not spend all of their income: They save at least some and use some to pay taxes. Therefore, aggregate expenditure will never equal national income, and the basic macro story is incorrect.

Answer: As was discussed in Chapter 19, national income does equal GDP (disregarding, as we have throughout this chapter, depreciation and indirect business taxes). So, it is correct to say that in macroeconomic equilibrium, planned aggregate expenditure must equal national income. But the last sentence of the argument is incorrect because it assumes that aggregate expenditure is the same as consumption spending. Because of saving and taxes, consumption spending is always much less than national income, but in equilibrium, the sum of consumption spending, planned investment spending, government purchases, and net exports do, in fact, equal GDP and national income. So, the argument is incorrect because it has confused consumption spending with aggregate expenditure.

YOUR TURN: Test your understanding by doing related problem 3.10 on page 805 at the end of this chapter.

Solved Problem ｜ 23-3

Determining Macroeconomic Equilibrium

Fill in the blanks in the following table and determine the equilibrium level of real GDP.

REAL GDP (Y)	CONSUMPTION (C)	PLANNED INVESTMENT (I)	GOVERNMENT PURCHASES (G)	NET EXPORTS (NX)	PLANNED AGGREGATE EXPENDITURE (AE)	UNPLANNED CHANGE IN INVENTORIES
$8,000	$6,200	$1,675	$1,675	−$500		
9,000	6,850	1,675	1,675	−500		
10,000	7,500	1,675	1,675	−500		
11,000	8,150	1,675	1,675	−500		
12,000	8,800	1,675	1,675	−500		

Note: The values are in billions of 2000 dollars.

SOLVING THE PROBLEM:

Step 1: **Review the chapter material.** This problem is about determining macroeconomic equilibrium, so you may want to review the section "A Numerical Example of Macroeconomic Equilibrium," which begins on page 788.

Step 2: **Fill in the missing values in the table.** We can calculate the missing values in the last two columns by using two equations:

$$\text{Planned aggregate expenditure } (AE) = \text{Consumption } (C) + \text{Planned investment } (I) + \text{Government } (G) + \text{Net exports } (NX)$$

and:

$$\text{Unplanned change in inventories} = \text{Real GDP } (Y) - \text{Planned aggregate expenditure } (AE).$$

For example, to fill in the first row, we have AE = $6,200 billion + $1,675 billion + $1,675 billion + (−$500 billion) = $9,050 billion; and Unplanned change in inventories = $8,000 billion − $9,050 billion = −$1,050 billion.

REAL GDP (Y)	CONSUMPTION (C)	PLANNED INVESTMENT (I)	GOVERNMENT PURCHASES (G)	NET EXPORTS (NX)	PLANNED AGGREGATE EXPENDITURE (AE)	UNPLANNED CHANGE IN INVENTORIES
$8,000	$6,200	$1,675	$1,675	−$500	$9,050	−$1,050
9,000	6,850	1,675	1,675	−500	9,700	−700
10,000	7,500	1,675	1,675	−500	10,350	−350
11,000	8,150	1,675	1,675	−500	11,000	0
12,000	8,800	1,675	1,675	−500	11,650	350

Step 3: **Determine the equilibrium level of real GDP.** Once you fill in the table, you should see that equilibrium real GDP must be $11,000 billion because only at that level is real GDP equal to planned aggregate expenditure.

>> End Solved Problem 23-3　　　**YOUR TURN:** For more practice, do related problem 3.12 on page 805 at the end of this chapter.

23.4 | Define the multiplier effect and use it to calculate changes in equilibrium GDP.

The Multiplier Effect

To this point, we have seen that aggregate expenditure determines real GDP in the short run and how the economy adjusts if it is not in equilibrium. We have also seen that whenever aggregate expenditure changes, there will be a new level of equilibrium real GDP. In this section, we will look more closely at the effects of a change in aggregate expenditure on equilibrium real GDP. We begin the discussion with Figure 23-12, which illustrates the effects of an increase in planned investment spending. We assume that the economy starts in equilibrium at point A, at which real GDP is $9.6 trillion. Firms then become more optimistic about their future profitability and increase spending on factories, machinery, and equipment by $100 billion. This increase in investment spending shifts the AE line up by $100 billion, from the dark tan line (AE_1) to the light tan line (AE_2). The new equilibrium occurs at point B, at which real GDP is $10.0 trillion, which equals potential real GDP.

Notice that the initial $100 billion increase in planned investment spending results in a $400 billion increase in equilibrium real GDP. The increase in planned investment spending has had a *multiplied effect* on equilibrium real GDP. It is not only investment spending that will have this multiplied effect; any increase in *autonomous expenditure* will shift up the aggregate expenditure function and lead to a multiplied increase in equilibrium GDP. **Autonomous expenditure** does not depend on the level of GDP. In the aggregate expenditure model we have been using, planned investment spending, government spending, and net exports are all autonomous expenditures. Consumption actually has both an autonomous component, which does not depend on the level of GDP, and a nonautonomous—or *induced*—component that does depend on the level of GDP. For example, if households decide to spend more of their incomes—and save less—at every level of income, there will be an autonomous increase in consumption spending, and the aggregate expenditure function will shift up. If, however, real GDP increases and households increase their consumption spending, as indicated by the consumption function, the economy will move up the aggregate expenditure function, and the increase in consumption spending will be nonautonomous.

The ratio of the increase in equilibrium real GDP to the increase in autonomous expenditure is called the **multiplier**. The series of induced increases in consumption

Autonomous expenditure
An expenditure that does not depend on the level of GDP.

Multiplier The increase in equilibrium real GDP divided by the increase in autonomous expenditure.

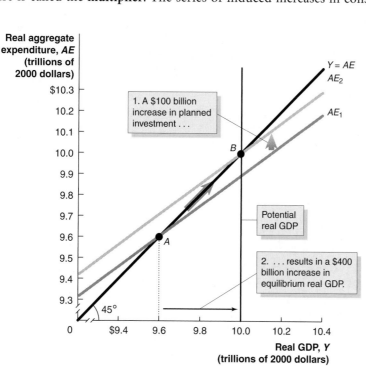

Real aggregate expenditure, AE (trillions of 2000 dollars)

1. A $100 billion increase in planned investment . . .

Potential real GDP

2. . . . results in a $400 billion increase in equilibrium real GDP.

45°

Real GDP, Y (trillions of 2000 dollars)

Figure 23-12

The Multiplier Effect

The economy begins at point A, at which equilibrium real GDP is $9.6 trillion. A $100 billion increase in planned investment shifts up aggregate expenditure from AE_1 to AE_2. The new equilibrium is at point B, where real GDP is $10.0 trillion, which is potential real GDP. Because of the multiplier effect, a $100 billion increase in investment results in a $400 billion increase in equilibrium real GDP.

Multiplier effect The process by which an increase in autonomous expenditure leads to a larger increase in real GDP.

spending that results from an initial increase in autonomous expenditure is called the **multiplier effect**. The multiplier effect happens because an initial increase in autonomous expenditure will set off a series of increases in real GDP.

In Figure 23-12, we look more closely at the multiplier effect. Suppose the whole $100 billion increase in investment spending shown in the figure consists of firms buying additional factories and office buildings. Initially, this additional spending will cause the construction of factories and office buildings to increase by $100 billion, so GDP will also increase by $100 billion. Remember that increases in production result in equal increases in national income. So, this increase in real GDP of $100 billion is also an increase in national income of $100 billion. In this example, the income is received as wages and salaries by the employees of the construction firms, as profits by the owners of the firms, and so on. After receiving this additional income, these workers, managers, and owners will increase their consumption of cars, televisions, DVD players, and many other products. If the marginal propensity to consume (*MPC*) is 0.75, we know this increase in consumption spending will be $75 billion. This additional $75 billion in spending will cause the firms making the cars, televisions, and other products to increase production by $75 billion, so GDP will rise by $75 billion. This increase in GDP means national income has also increased by another $75 billion. This increased income will be received by the owners and employees of the firms producing the cars, televisions, and other products. These workers, managers, and owners in turn will increase their consumption spending, and the process of increasing production, income, and consumption will continue.

Eventually, the total increase in consumption will be $300 billion (we will soon show how we know this is true). This $300 billion increase in consumption combined with the initial $100 billion increase in investment spending will result in a total change in equilibrium GDP of $400 billion. Table 23-4 summarizes how changes in GDP and spending

TABLE 23-4

The Multiplier Effect in Action

	ADDITIONAL AUTONOMOUS EXPENDITURE (INVESTMENT)	ADDITIONAL INDUCED EXPENDITURE (CONSUMPTION)	TOTAL ADDITIONAL EXPENDITURE = TOTAL ADDITIONAL GDP
ROUND 1	$100 billion	$0	$100 billion
ROUND 2	0	75 billion	175 billion
ROUND 3	0	56 billion	231 billion
ROUND 4	0	42 billion	273 billion
ROUND 5	0	32 billion	305 billion
⋮	⋮	⋮	⋮
ROUND 10	0	8 billion	377 billion
⋮	⋮	⋮	⋮
ROUND 15	0	2 billion	395 billion
⋮	⋮	⋮	⋮
ROUND 19	0	1 billion	398 billion
⋮	⋮	⋮	⋮
n	0	0	400 billion

caused by the initial $100 billion increase in investment will result in equilibrium GDP rising by $400 billion. We can think of the multiplier effect occurring in rounds of spending. In round 1, there is an increase of $100 billion in autonomous expenditure—the $100 billion in planned investment spending in our example—which causes GDP to rise by $100 billion. In round 2, induced expenditure rises by $75 billion (which equals the $100 billion increase in real GDP in round 1 multiplied by the *MPC*). The $75 billion in induced expenditure in round 2 causes a $75 billion increase in real GDP, which leads to a $56 billion increase in induced expenditure in round 3, and so on. The final column sums up the total increases in expenditure, which equal the total increase in GDP. In each round, the additional induced expenditure becomes smaller because the *MPC* is less than 1. By round 10, additional induced expenditure is only $8 billion, and the total increase in GDP from the beginning of the process is $377 billion. By round 19, the process is almost complete: Additional induced expenditure is only about $1 billion, and the total increase in GDP is $398 billion. Eventually, the process will be finished, although we cannot say precisely how many spending rounds it will take, so we simply label the last round "*n*" rather than give it a specific number.

We can calculate the value of the multiplier in our example by dividing the increase in equilibrium real GDP by the increase in autonomous expenditure:

$$\frac{\Delta Y}{\Delta I} = \frac{\text{Change in real GDP}}{\text{Change in investment spending}} = \frac{\$400\,\text{billion}}{\$100\,\text{billion}} = 4.$$

With a multiplier of 4, each increase in autonomous expenditure of $1 will result in an increase in equilibrium GDP of $4.

Making the Connection | The Multiplier in Reverse: The Great Depression of the 1930s

An increase in autonomous expenditure causes an increase in equilibrium real GDP, but the reverse is also true: A decrease in autonomous expenditure causes a decrease in real GDP. Many Americans became aware of this fact in the 1930s when reductions in autonomous expenditure were magnified by the multiplier into the largest decline in real GDP in U.S. history.

In August 1929, the economy reached a business cycle peak, and a downturn in production began. In October, the stock market crashed, destroying billions of dollars of wealth and increasing pessimism among households and firms. Both consumption spending and planned investment spending declined. The passage by the U.S. Congress of the Smoot–Hawley Tariff in June 1930 helped set off a trade war that reduced net exports. A series of banking crises that began in fall 1930 limited the ability of households and firms to finance consumption and investment. As aggregate expenditure declined, many firms experienced declining sales and began to lay off workers. Falling levels of production and income induced further declines in consumption spending, which led to further cutbacks in production and employment, leading to further declines in income, and so on, in a downward spiral. The following table shows the severity of the economic downturn by contrasting the business cycle peak of 1929 with the business cycle trough of 1933.

The multiplier effect contributed to the very high levels of unemployment during the Great Depression.

YEAR	CONSUMPTION	INVESTMENT	NET EXPORTS	REAL GDP	UNEMPLOYMENT RATE
1929	$661 billion	$91.3 billion	–$9.4 billion	$865 billion	3.2%
1933	$541 billion	$17.0 billion	–$10.2 billion	$636 billion	24.9%

Note: The values are in 2000 dollars.
Sources: U.S. Bureau of Economic Analysis; and U.S. Bureau of Labor Statistics.

We can use a 45°-line diagram to illustrate the multiplier effect working in reverse during these years. The economy was at potential real GDP in 1929 before the declines in aggregate expenditure began. Declining consumption, planned investment, and net exports shifted the aggregate expenditure function down from AE_{1929} to AE_{1933}, reducing equilibrium real GDP from $865 billion in 1929 to $636 billion in 1933. The depth and length of this economic downturn led to its being labeled the Great Depression.

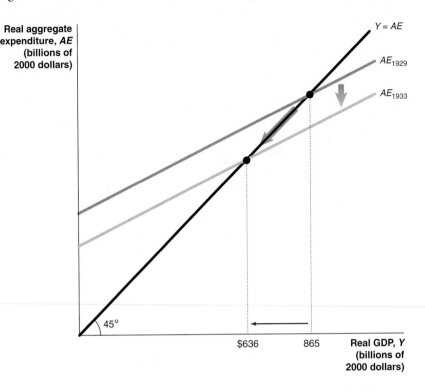

The severity of the Depression meant bankruptcy for thousands of firms. Even firms that survived experienced sharp declines in sales. By 1933, production at U.S. Steel had declined by 90 percent, and production at General Motors had declined by more than 75 percent. High rates of unemployment forced many families into poverty and a daily struggle for survival. Recovery from the business cycle trough in 1933 was slow. Real GDP did not regain its 1929 level until 1936, and a growing labor force meant that the unemployment rate did not fall below 10 percent until the United States entered World War II in 1941.

YOUR TURN: Test your understanding by doing related problem 4.9 on page 806 at the end of this chapter.

A Formula for the Multiplier

Table 23-4 shows that during the multiplier process, each round of increases in consumption is smaller than in the previous round, so eventually, the increases will come to an end, and we will have a new macroeconomic equilibrium. But how do we know that when we add all the increases in GDP, the total will be $400 billion? We can show this is true by first writing out the total change in equilibrium GDP:

The total change in equilibrium real GDP equals the initial increase in planned investment spending = $100 billion

Plus the first induced increase in consumption = $MPC \times$ $100 billion

Plus the second induced increase in consumption = $MPC \times (MPC \times$ 100 billion$) = MPC^2 \times$ $100 billion

Plus the third induced increase in consumption = $MPC \times (MPC^2 \times$ 100 billion$) = MPC^3 \times$ $100 billion

Plus the fourth induced increase in consumption = $MPC \times (MPC^3 \times \$100 \text{ billion})$
= $MPC^4 \times \$100$ billion

And so on . . .

Or:

Total change in GDP = $\$100$ billion + $MPC \times \$100$ billion + $MPC^2 \times$
$\$100$ billion + $MPC^3 \times \$100$ billion + $MPC^4 \times \$100$ billion + . . .

where the ellipsis (. . .) indicates that the expression contains an infinite number of similar terms.

If we factor out the $100 billion from each expression, we have:

Total change in GDP = $\$100$ billion $\times (1 + MPC + MPC^2 + MPC^3 + MPC^4 + \ldots)$

Mathematicians have shown that an expression like the one in the parenthesis sums to:

$$\frac{1}{1 - MPC}.$$

In this case, the *MPC* is equal to 0.75. So, we can now calculate that the change in equilibrium GDP = $\$1$ billion $\times [1/(1 - 0.75)] = \$100$ billion $\times 4 = \$400$ billion. We have also derived a general formula for the multiplier:

$$\text{Multiplier} = \frac{\text{Change in equilibrium real GDP}}{\text{Change in autonomous expenditure}} = \frac{1}{1 - MPC}.$$

In this case, the multiplier is $1/(1 - 0.75)$ or 4, which means that for each additional $1 of autonomous spending, equilibrium GDP will increase by $4. A $100 billion increase in planned investment spending results in a $400 billion increase in equilibrium GDP. Notice that the value of the multiplier depends on the value of the *MPC*. In particular, the larger the value of the *MPC*, the larger the value of the multiplier. For example, if the *MPC* were 0.9 instead of 0.75, the value of the multiplier would increase from 4 to $1/(1 - 0.9) = 10$.

Summarizing the Multiplier Effect

You should note four key points about the multiplier effect:

1 The multiplier effect occurs both when autonomous expenditure increases and when it decreases. For example, with an *MPC* of 0.75, a *decrease* in planned investment of $100 billion will lead to a *decrease* in equilibrium income of $400 billion.

2 The multiplier effect makes the economy more sensitive to changes in autonomous expenditure than it would otherwise be. When firms decided to cut back their spending on information technology following the Internet and telecommunications busts of 2001, the decision did not only affect firms such as Cisco that made computer and telecommunications equipment. Because the initial decline in investment spending set off a series of declines in production, income, and spending, firms such as automobile dealerships and furniture stores, which are far removed from the computer and telecommunications industries, also experienced sales declines.

3 The larger the *MPC*, the larger the value of the multiplier. With an *MPC* of 0.75, the multiplier is 4, but with an *MPC* of 0.50, the multiplier is only 2. This inverse relationship between the value of the *MPC* and the value of the multiplier holds true because the larger the *MPC*, the more additional consumption takes place after each rise in income during the multiplier process.

4 The formula for the multiplier, $1/(1 - MPC)$, is oversimplified because it ignores some real-world complications, such as the effect that an increasing GDP can have on imports, inflation, and interest rates. These effects combine to cause the simple formula to overstate the true value of the multiplier. Beginning in Chapter 24, we will start to take into account these real-world complications.

Solved Problem | 23-4

Using the Multiplier Formula

Use the information in the table to answer the following questions.

REAL GDP (Y)	CONSUMPTION (C)	PLANNED INVESTMENT (I)	GOVERNMENT PURCHASES (G)	NET EXPORTS (NX)
$8,000	$6,900	$1,000	$1,000	−$500
9,000	7,700	1,000	1,000	−500
10,000	8,500	1,000	1,000	−500
11,000	9,300	1,000	1,000	−500
12,000	10,100	1,000	1,000	−500

Note: The values are in billions of 2000 dollars.

a. What is the equilibrium level of real GDP?

b. What is the *MPC*?

c. Suppose government purchases increase by $200 billion. What will be the new equilibrium level of real GDP? Use the multiplier formula to determine your answer.

SOLVING THE PROBLEM:

Step 1: **Review the chapter material.** This problem is about the multiplier process, so you may want to review the section "The Multiplier Effect," which begins on page 791.

Step 2: **Determine equilibrium real GDP.** Just as in Solved Problem 23-2 on page 777, we can find macroeconomic equilibrium by calculating the level of planned aggregate expenditure for each level of real GDP.

REAL GDP (Y)	CONSUMPTION (C)	PLANNED INVESTMENT (I)	GOVERNMENT PURCHASES (G)	NET EXPORTS (NX)	PLANNED AGGREGATE EXPENDITURE (AE)
$8,000	$6,900	$1,000	$1,000	−$500	$8,400
9,000	7,700	1,000	1,000	−500	9,200
10,000	8,500	1,000	1,000	−500	10,000
11,000	9,300	1,000	1,000	−500	10,800
12,000	10,100	1,000	1,000	−500	11,600

We can see that macroeconomic equilibrium will occur when real GDP equals $10,000 billion.

Step 3: **Calculate *MPC*.**

$$MPC = \frac{\Delta C}{\Delta Y}.$$

In this case,

$$MPC = \frac{\$800 \text{ billion}}{\$1,000 \text{ billion}} = 0.8.$$

Step 4: **Use the multiplier formula to calculate the new equilibrium level of real GDP.** We could find the new level of equilibrium real GDP by constructing a new table with government purchases increased from $1,000 to $1,200. But the multiplier allows us to calculate the answer directly. In this case:

$$\text{Multiplier} = \frac{1}{1 - MPC} = \frac{1}{1 - 0.8} = 5.$$

So:

Change in equilibrium real GDP = Change in autonomous expenditure × 5.

Or:

Change in equilibrium real GDP = $200 billion × 5 = $1,000 billion.

Therefore:

The new level of equilibrium GDP = $10,000 billion + $1,000 billion = $11,000 billion.

YOUR TURN: For more practice, do related problem 4.3 on page 806 at the end of this chapter.

>> **End Solved Problem 23-4**

23.5 | Understand the relationship between the aggregate demand curve and aggregate expenditure.

23.5 LEARNING OBJECTIVE

The Aggregate Demand Curve

When demand for a product increases, firms usually respond by increasing production, but they are also likely to increase prices. Similarly, when demand falls, production falls, but often, prices also fall. We would expect, then, that an increase or a decrease in aggregate expenditure would affect not just real GDP but also the *price level*. So far, we haven't taken into account the effect of changes in the price level on the components of aggregate expenditure. In fact, as we will see, increases in the price level cause aggregate expenditure to fall, and decreases in the price level cause aggregate expenditure to rise. There are three main reasons for this inverse relationship between changes in the price level and changes in aggregate expenditure. We discussed the first two reasons earlier in this chapter when considering the factors that determine consumption and net exports:

* A rising price level decreases consumption by decreasing the real value of household wealth; a falling price level has the reverse effect.

* If the price level in the United States rises relative to the price levels in other countries, U.S. exports will become relatively more expensive, and foreign imports will become relatively less expensive, causing net exports to fall. A falling price level in the United States has the reverse effect.

* When prices rise, firms and households need more money to finance buying and selling. If the central bank (the Federal Reserve in the United States) does not increase the money supply, the result will be an increase in the interest rate. We will analyze in more detail why this happens in Chapter 25. As we discussed earlier in this chapter, at a higher interest rate, investment spending falls as firms borrow less money to build new factories or to install new machinery and equipment, and households borrow less money to buy new houses. A falling price level has the reverse effect. Other things equal, interest rates will fall and investment spending will rise.

We can now incorporate the effect of a change in the price level into the basic aggregate expenditure model in which equilibrium real GDP is determined by the intersection of the aggregate expenditure (*AE*) line and the 45° line. Remember that we measure the price level as an index number with a value of 100 in the base year. If the price level rises from, say, 100 to 103, consumption, planned investment, and net exports will all fall, causing the *AE* line to shift down on the 45°-line diagram. The *AE* line shifts down because with higher prices, less spending will occur in the economy at every level of GDP. Panel (a) of Figure 23-13 shows that the downward shift of the *AE* line results in a lower level of equilibrium real GDP.

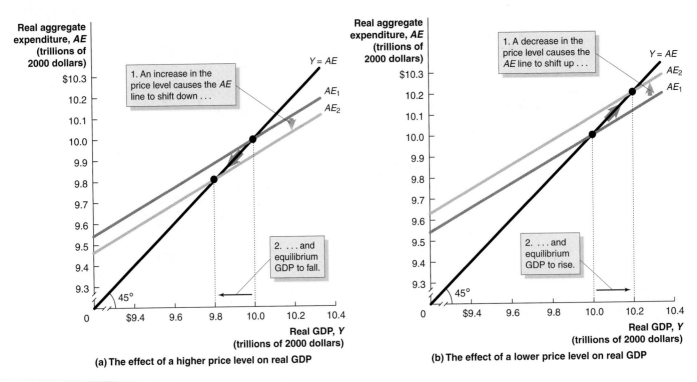

(a) The effect of a higher price level on real GDP

(b) The effect of a lower price level on real GDP

Figure 23-13 | The Effect of a Change in the Price Level on Real GDP

In panel (a), an increase in the price level results in declining consumption, planned investment, and net exports and causes the aggregate expenditure line to shift down from AE_1 to AE_2. As a result, equilibrium real GDP declines from $10.0 trillion to $9.8 trillion. In panel (b), a decrease in the price level results in rising consumption,

planned investment, and net exports and causes the aggregate expenditure line to shift up from AE_1 to AE_2. As a result, equilibrium real GDP increases from $10.0 trillion to $10.2 trillion.

Aggregate demand curve A curve that shows the relationship between the price level and the level of planned aggregate expenditure in the economy, holding constant all other factors that affect aggregate expenditure.

If the price level falls from, say, 100 to 97, then investment, consumption, and net exports would all rise. As panel (b) of Figure 23-13 shows, the AE line would shift up, which would cause equilibrium real GDP to increase.

Figure 23-14 summarizes the effect of changes in the price level on real GDP. The table shows the combinations of price level and real GDP from Figure 23-13. The figure plots the numbers from the table. In the figure, the price level is measured on the vertical axis, and real GDP is measured on the horizontal axis. The relationship shown in Figure 23-14 between the price level and the level of planned aggregate expenditure is known as the **aggregate demand curve**, or *AD* curve.

Figure 23-14

The Aggregate Demand Curve

The aggregate demand curve, labeled *AD*, shows the relationship between the price level and the level of planned aggregate expenditure in the economy. When the price level is 97, real GDP is $10.2 trillion. An increase in the price level to 100 causes consumption, investment, and net exports to fall, which reduces real GDP to $10.0 trillion.

Price level	Equilibrium real GDP
97	$10.2 trillion
100	10.0 trillion
103	9.8 trillion

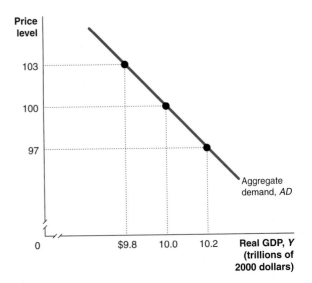

Economics in YOUR Life!

>> Continued from page 767

At the beginning of this chapter, we asked you to suppose that you work part time assembling desktop computers for a large computer company. You have learned that consumer confidence in the economy has fallen and that many households expect their future income to be dramatically less than their current income. Should you be concerned about losing your job? We have seen in this chapter that if consumers expect their future incomes to decline, they will cut their consumption spending, and consumption spending is about 70 percent of aggregate expenditure. So, there is some chance that consumption spending will fall, which would reduce aggregate expenditures and GDP. If the economy does move into a recession, spending on computers by households and firms may slow down, which could reduce your firm's sales and possibly cost you a job. Before you panic, though, keep in mind that surveys of consumer confidence do not have a good track record in predicting recessions, so you may not have to move back in with your parents after all.

Conclusion

In this chapter, we learned a key macroeconomic idea: In the short run, the level of GDP is determined mainly by the level of aggregate expenditure. When economists forecast changes in GDP, they do so by forecasting changes in the four components of aggregate expenditure. We constructed an aggregate demand curve by taking into account the effect on aggregate expenditure of changes in the price level.

But our story is incomplete. In the next chapter, we will analyze the *aggregate supply curve*. Then, we will use the aggregate demand curve and the aggregate supply curve to show how equilibrium real GDP *and* the equilibrium price level are simultaneously determined.

We also need to discuss the role the financial system and government policy play in determining real GDP and the price level in the short run. We will cover these important topics in the next three chapters. Before moving on, read *An Inside Look* on the next page, which discusses the factors causing U.S. GDP to change during the first quarter of 2007.

WALL STREET JOURNAL, APRIL 28, 2007

Economy Slows but May Hold Seeds of Growth

The U.S. economy started 2007 with its weakest growth in four years, as a housing slump continued to hobble expansion. But consumers spent freely and business investment picked up....

The Commerce Department reported that real gross domestic product, the broadest measure of economic activity adjusted for inflation, grew at a seasonally adjusted annual rate of 1.3% in the first three months of the year. That was down sharply from growth of 2.5% in the fourth quarter of 2006 ... Residential investment, a proxy for the housing market, was the biggest drag on first-quarter growth, falling at an annualized rate of 17% and slashing one percentage point off GDP....

(a) Among the more encouraging signs, the GDP report found consumer spending, which accounts for about 70% of economic activity, grew at a 3.8% annual rate in the first quarter. That is down from a 4.2% rate in the prior quarter, but higher than the 3.2% rate for all of 2006. The rise in business investment—up 2.0% compared with a decline of 3.1% last quarter—was a surprise given recent reports that suggested businesses are taking a more cautious outlook and cutting back investments accordingly. Another positive sign: Businesses continued to slow the rate of inventory accumulation, which could foretell an increase in production down the line.

That view was bolstered by news that the dollar declined again Friday on foreign-exchange markets, a trend that should give U.S. exports an edge and thus help lift factory production....

The first-quarter GDP report was "probably the low point in the cycle," said Nariman Behravesh, chief economist at consulting firm Global Insight. "It suggests that in fact we may be setting the stage for a very slight rebound this quarter." Mr. Behravesh believes the economy will be growing at a rate of close to 3% by the end of the year.

Still, the economy faces plenty of lingering challenges. Housing continues to be a significant drag, with residential investment falling for six consecutive quarters. And falling house prices could eventually affect consumers' willingness and ability to spend....

Also, many economists expect some slowdown in the buoyant job market, which has helped consumers by pushing up wages. Sharp declines in residential investment, for example, should ultimately translate into more job losses in housing construction.

There are some signs consumers are losing steam. In a separate report yesterday, the Reuters/University of Michigan consumer sentiment index fell 1.3 points to 87.1 in April, the third-consecutive monthly decline and the lowest level in seven months. High gasoline prices and the housing troubles weighed on consumers, the survey reported, even as some felt optimistic about rising wages and the stock market's recent rally....

(b) One puzzling aspect of yesterday's report was exports, which declined 1.2% in the first three months of the year, compared with a rise of 10.6% in the fourth quarter of last year. Exports have been a driver of the U.S. economy in recent months, thanks to a weakened dollar and growth throughout Europe and Asia. Many economists viewed yesterday's exports decline as a fluke, which will either be revised upward or bounce back next quarter. Compared with the first quarter of last year, exports were up 5.5%. "The important thing is to have continued growth around the world," said U.S. Commerce Secretary Carlos M. Gutierrez. "We've got a good thing going with exports, and we want to keep it going."

The strong global economy is one reason economists are especially upbeat about the prospect for corporate profits. U.S. companies in recent weeks have reported stronger-than-expected first-quarter earnings, often because of growing overseas operations that made up for sluggishness at home....

Stronger growth in places such as Europe, Japan and China does more than just add to U.S. companies' foreign sales. The change in relative growth rates has also pushed up the value of currencies such as the euro, as investors attracted by improved prospects outside the U.S. put more money into foreign securities. That provides U.S. companies with an added boost when they convert their foreign sales into dollars. Relative to the currencies of U.S. trading partners, the dollar is down about 3% from a year earlier....

Separately, the Labor Department reported Friday that its employment-cost index increased 0.8% in the first three months of the year, compared with gains of 0.9% in the previous three quarters. This was due mostly to a tiny increase in benefits costs as rising stock prices enabled firms to make smaller contributions to defined-benefit pension plans. Wages and salaries still rose briskly.

(c) Economists also have been watching how much businesses boost inventories. Businesses continued to slow the rate of inventory accumulation for the second straight quarter, trimming 0.3 percentage points from growth, after knocking 1.16 points off growth in the fourth quarter. That could actually bode well for future GDP: By keeping a tight rein on inventories, firms are less likely to respond to a sales shortfall with big cuts in production and employment. And if sales accelerate, they are more likely to boost output.

Key Points in the Article

This article discusses a Department of Commerce report on real GDP growth in the United States during the first quarter of 2007. The report indicated that real GDP grew just 1.3 percent in that quarter—far less than economists had expected and far less than the 2.5 percent growth that the U.S. economy had achieved in the fourth quarter of 2006. Economists attributed the disappointing report to a 17 percent drop in residential construction due to a slowdown in the U.S. housing market. Nonetheless, economists were encouraged by strong consumer and business investment spending, which together comprise over 85 percent of aggregate expenditures in the U.S. economy. The article also discusses a surprise in the report: a decline in exports despite a fall in the foreign exchange value of the U.S. dollar. Finally, the article explains that economists were encouraged by the slow growth in business inventories.

Analyzing the News

(a) The Commerce Department report indicated that consumer expenditure grew by a respectable 3.8 percent annual rate in the first quarter of 2007. This is important for overall growth in the U.S. economy because consumption expenditure comprises over 70 percent of aggregate expenditure. So, even small changes in consumption can have a significant effect on real GDP. The report also indicated that business investment expenditure rose at an unexpectedly high 2.0 percent annual rate. This is important for overall growth in the U.S. economy because, although business investment expenditure comprises only about 16 percent of aggregate expenditure, it is typically volatile from quarter to quarter. Moreover, changes in business investment expenditure often lead to additional changes in consumer expenditure, income, and employment.

(b) U.S. exports fell by 1.2 percent in the first quarter of 2007. This fact puzzled economists because the foreign exchange value of the U.S. dollar had fallen in recent months, and a relatively cheaper U.S. dollar lowers the prices U.S. goods sell for overseas. So, U.S. exports should have risen, as

in the previous quarter when they rose by 10.6 percent. Nonetheless, most economists remain confident that exports will increase in future quarters, as the economies of the major trading partners of the United States continue to grow. This is because when the growth rate of GDP in foreign countries exceeds that of the United States, U.S. exports and, therefore, aggregate expenditure tend to rise.

(c) Economists were encouraged by the slow growth of business inventories. This is because, as you read in this chapter, when firms' sales drop unexpectedly, they accumulate (unplanned) inventories. In response, they typically reduce production, which causes income and employment to fall. All else equal, unplanned increases in inventories are followed by slower growth in real GDP in the short run. This relationship is shown in the figure, where the economy begins in equilibrium at point E, and then aggregate expenditure falls from AE_1 to AE_2. Because planned aggregate expenditure is now less than Y_1, unplanned inventories increase. In response, firms decrease production, income, and employment until the economy reaches equilibrium at Y_2. (point A). Therefore, the fact that in the first quarter of 2007, firms slowed the rate at which they accumulated inventories was good news.

Thinking Critically About Policy

1. Suppose the U.S. government mailed every taxpayer in the United States a check for $500, which taxpayers did not have to repay. What effect would this tax policy have on U.S. aggregate expenditure?

2. Suppose that Congress enacts a law prohibiting imports from China. What will be the effect of this law on aggregate expenditure and equilibrium real GDP? Does your answer depend on how the governments of other countries react to the law? Briefly explain.

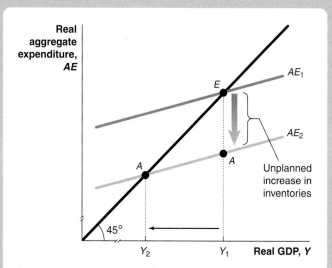

A decrease in aggregate expenditure causes an unplanned increase in inventories and a decrease in real GDP.

Key Terms

Aggregate demand curve, p. 798

Aggregate expenditure (*AE*), p. 768

Aggregate expenditure model, p. 768

Autonomous expenditure, p. 791

Cash flow, p. 779

Consumption function, p. 773

Inventories, p. 769

Marginal propensity to consume (*MPC*), p. 773

Marginal propensity to save (*MPS*), p. 776

Multiplier, p. 791

Multiplier effect, p. 792

23.1 LEARNING OBJECTIVE 23.1 │ Understand how macroeconomic equilibrium is determined in the aggregate expenditure model, **pages 768–771.**

The Aggregate Expenditure Model

Summary

Aggregate expenditure (*AE*) is the total amount of spending in the economy. The **aggregate expenditure model** focuses on the relationship between total spending and real GDP in the short run, assuming that the price level is constant. In any particular year, the level of GDP is determined by the level of total spending, or aggregate expenditure, in the economy. The four components of aggregate expenditure are consumption (*C*), planned investment (*I*), government purchases (*G*), and net exports (*NX*). When aggregate expenditure is greater than GDP, there is an unplanned decrease in **inventories**, which are goods that have been produced but not yet sold, and GDP and total employment will increase. When aggregate expenditure is less than GDP, there is an unplanned increase in inventories, and GDP and total employment will decline. When aggregate expenditure is equal to GDP, firms will sell what they expected to sell, production and employment will be unchanged, and the economy will be in macroeconomic equilibrium.

 Visit www.myeconlab.com to complete these exercises *Get Ahead of the Curve* online and get instant feedback.

Review Questions

1.1 What is the main reason for changes in GDP in the short run?

1.2 What are inventories? What usually happens to inventories at the beginning of a recession? At the beginning of an expansion?

Problems and Applications

1.3 Into which category of aggregate expenditures would each of the following transactions fall?
   a. The Jones family buys a new car.
   b. The San Diego Unified School District buys 12 new school busses.
   c. The Jones family buys a new house.
   d. A consumer in Japan orders a computer online from Dell.
   e. Prudential Insurance Company purchases 250 new computers from Dell.

1.4 Suppose Apple plans to produce 16.2 million iPods this year. It expects to sell 16.1 million and add 100,000 to the inventories in its stores.
   a. Suppose that at the end of the year, Apple has sold 15.9 million iPods. What was Apple's planned investment spending? What was Apple's actual investment spending?
   b. Now suppose that at the end of the year, Apple has sold 16.3 million iPods. What was Apple's planned investment spending? What was Apple's actual investment spending?

1.5 In the second quarter of 2005, business inventories declined by $10 billion. What does this information tell us about the relationship between aggregate expenditure and GDP during the second quarter of 2005?

1.6 Suppose you read that business inventories increased dramatically last month. What does this tell you about the state of the economy? Would your answer be affected by whether the increase in inventories was taking place at the end of a recession or the end of an expansion? Briefly explain.

≫ End Learning Objective 23.1

23.2 | Discuss the determinants of the four components of aggregate expenditure and define the marginal propensity to consume and the marginal propensity to save, **pages 771–783.**

Determining the Level of Aggregate Expenditure in the Economy

Summary

The five determinants of consumption are current disposable income, household wealth, expected future income, the price level, and the interest rate. The **consumption function** is the relationship between consumption and disposable income. The **marginal propensity to consume** (*MPC*) is the change in consumption divided by the change in disposable income. The **marginal propensity to save (***MPS***)** is the change in saving divided by the change in disposable income. The determinants of planned investment are expectations of future profitability, the real interest rate, taxes, and **cash flow**, which is the difference between the cash revenues received by a firm and the cash spending by the firm. Government purchases include spending by the federal government and by local and state governments for goods and services. Government purchases do not include *transfer payments*, such as Social Security payments by the federal government or pension payments by local governments to retired police officers and firefighters. The three determinants of net exports are the price level in the United States relative to the price levels in other countries, the growth rate of GDP in the United States relative to the growth rates of GDP in other countries, and the exchange rate between the dollar and other currencies.

 Visit www.myeconlab.com to complete these exercises *Get Ahead of the Curve* online and get instant feedback.

Review Questions

2.1 What are the four categories of aggregate expenditure? Give an example of each.

2.2 What are the five main determinants of consumption spending? Which of these is the most important?

2.3 Compare what happened to real investment between 1979 and 2006 with what happened to real consumption.

Problems and Applications

2.4 **(Related to the *Chapter Opener* on page 766)** Suppose a major U.S. furniture manufacturer is forecasting demand for its products during the next year. How will the forecast be affected by each of the following?
a. A decrease in consumer spending in the economy
b. An increase in real interest rates

c. An increase in the exchange rate value of the U.S. dollar
d. A decrease in planned investment spending in the economy

2.5 Many people have difficulty borrowing as much money as they would like, even if they are confident that their incomes in the future will be high enough to pay it back easily. For example, many students in medical school will earn high incomes after they graduate and become physicians. If they could, they would probably borrow now in order to live more comfortably while in medical school and pay the loans back out of their higher future income. Unfortunately, banks are usually reluctant to make loans to people who currently have low incomes, even if there is a good chance their incomes will be much higher in the future. If people could always borrow as much as they would like, would you expect consumption to become more or less sensitive to current income? Why?

2.6 An economics student raises the following objection: "The textbook said that a higher interest rate lowers investment, but this doesn't make sense. I know that if I can get a higher interest rate, I am certainly going to invest more in my savings account." Do you agree with this reasoning?

2.7 **(Related to the *Making the Connection* on page 779)** We can use Figure 23-4 on page 778 and the graph in the *Making the Connection* on page 779 to compare movements in real investment between 1990 and 2007 with movements in spending on information processing equipment and software. In 1990, spending on information processing equipment and software was roughly what fraction of real investment? How had this fraction changed by 2007? Compare movements in real investment with movements in spending on information and processing equipment and software during the recessions of 1990–1991 and 2001.

2.8 Unemployed workers receive unemployment insurance payments from the government. Does the existence of unemployment insurance make it likely that consumption will fluctuate more or fluctuate less over the business cycle than it would in the absence of unemployment insurance? Briefly explain.

2.9 Explain whether you agree or disagree with the following argument: "Transfer payments should be counted as part of government purchases when we calculate aggregate expenditure. After all, spending is spending. Why does it matter whether the spending is for an aircraft carrier or for a Social Security payment to a retired person?"

2.10 Suppose we drop the assumption that net exports do not depend on real GDP. Draw a graph with the value of net exports on the vertical axis and the value of real GDP on the horizontal axis. Now, add a line representing the relationship between net exports and real GDP. Briefly explain why you drew the graph the way you did.

2.11 (Related to *Solved Problem 23-2* on page 777) Fill in the blanks in the table in the next column. Assume for simplicity that taxes are zero.

NATIONAL INCOME AND REAL GDP (*Y*)	CONSUMPTION (*C*)	SAVING (*S*)	MARGINAL PROPENSITY TO CONSUME (*MPC*)	MARGINAL PROPENSITY TO SAVE (*MPS*)
$9,000	$8,000		—	—
10,000	8,750			
11,000	9,500			
12,000	10,250			
13,000	11,000			

>> **End Learning Objective 23.2**

23.3 LEARNING OBJECTIVE 23.3 | Use a 45°-line diagram to illustrate macroeconomic equilibrium,
pages 783–790.

Graphing Macroeconomic Equilibrium

Summary

The 45°-line diagram shows all the points where aggregate expenditure equals real GDP. On the 45°-line diagram, macroeconomic equilibrium occurs where the line representing the aggregate expenditure function crosses the 45° line. The economy is in recession when the aggregate expenditure line intersects the 45° line at a level of GDP that is below potential GDP. Numerically, macroeconomic equilibrium occurs when:

Consumption + Planned investment +
Government purchases + Net exports = GDP.

Review Questions

3.1 Use a 45°-line diagram to illustrate macroeconomic equilibrium. Make sure your diagram shows the aggregate expenditure function and the level of equilibrium real GDP and that your axes are properly labeled.

3.2 What is the macroeconomic consequence if firms accumulate large amounts of unplanned inventory at the beginning of a recession?

3.3 What is the difference between aggregate expenditure and consumption spending?

Problems and Applications

3.4 At point *A* in the following graph, is planned aggregate expenditure greater than, equal to, or less than GDP? What about at point *B*? At point *C*? For points

A and *C*, indicate the vertical distance that measures the unintended change in inventories.

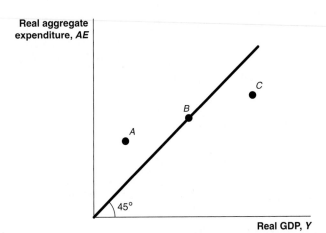

3.5 Is it possible for the economy to be in macroeconomic equilibrium at a level of real GDP that is greater than the potential level of real GDP? Illustrate using a 45°-line diagram.

3.6 (Related to the *Making the Connection* on page 787) In a Federal Reserve Board publication, the following observation was made: "The impact of inventory increases on the business cycle depends upon whether they are planned or unplanned." Do you agree? Briefly explain.

3.7 An article in *BusinessWeek* observes the following: "A further ebbing in the inventory drawdown is probably adding to GDP growth this quarter." What does the article mean by "inventory drawdown"? What component of aggregate expenditure would be affected by an inventory drawdown? Why would this add to GDP growth?

Source: James C. Cooper and Kathleen Madigan, "Forward Spin from a Backward Glance at GDP," *BusinessWeek*, April 29, 2002.

3.8 In each of the following situations, indicate what happens to the firm's inventories and whether the firm will be likely to increase or decrease its production in the future.
  a. General Electric expected to sell 120,000 microwaves during the current month but actually sold 100,000.
  b. Ford expected to sell 80,000 Explorers during the current month but actually sold 90,000.

3.9 In November 2006, U.S. exports increased to $124.76 billion from $123.67 billion in October. U.S. imports increased to $183 billion from $182.47 billion in October. An article in the *Wall Street Journal* argued that these statistics "could mean a boost for the economy." Briefly explain the author's reasoning.

Source: Jeff Bater, "U.S. Trade Gap Narrowed to $58.2 Billion in November," *Wall Street Journal*, January 10, 2007.

3.10 (Related to the *Don't Let This Happen to You!* on page 789) Briefly explain whether you agree with the following argument: "The equilibrium level of GDP is determined by the level of aggregate expenditure. Therefore, GDP will decline only if households decide to spend less on goods and services."

3.11 An article in the *New York Times* makes the following observation:

> Business spending is a powerful force. It can lift an economy when companies invest in machinery, software, office buildings, factories, trucks, aircraft and all the other tools used in the production of goods and services—or sink an economy when companies cut back.

> What does the article mean by "business spending"? How can business spending "lift an economy" or "sink" it? Use a 45°-line diagram to illustrate your answer.

Source: Louis Uchitelle and Jennifer Bayot, "Business Spending Helps to Offset Lag in Refinancing," *New York Times*, August 9, 2003.

3.12 (Related to *Solved Problem 23-3* on page 790) Fill in the missing values in the following table. Assume that the value of the *MPC* does not change as real GDP changes.

REAL GDP (Y)	CONSUMPTION (C)	PLANNED INVESTMENT (I)	GOVERNMENT PURCHASES (G)	NET EXPORTS (NX)	PLANNED AGGREGATE EXPENDITURE (AE)	UNPLANNED CHANGE IN INVENTORIES
$9,000	$7,600	$1,200	$1,200	–$400		
10,000	8,400	1,200	1,200	–400		
11,000		1,200	1,200	–400		
12,000		1,200	1,200	–400		
13,000		1,200	1,200	–400		

  a. What is the value of the *MPC*?
  b. What is the value of equilibrium real GDP?

>> End Learning Objective 23.3

23.4 LEARNING OBJECTIVE 23.4 | Define the multiplier effect and use it to calculate changes in equilibrium GDP, pages 791–797.

The Multiplier Effect

Summary

Autonomous expenditure is expenditure that does not depend on the level of GDP. An autonomous change is a change in expenditure not caused by a change in income. An *induced change* is a change in aggregate expenditure caused by a change in income. An autonomous change in expenditure will cause rounds of induced changes in expenditure. Therefore, an autonomous change in expenditure will have a *multiplier effect* on equilibrium GDP. The **multiplier effect** is the process by which an increase in autonomous expenditure leads to a larger increase in real GDP. The **multiplier** is the ratio of the change in equilibrium GDP to the change in autonomous expenditure. The formula for the multiplier is:

$$\frac{1}{1 - MPC}.$$

myeconlab Visit www.myeconlab.com to complete these exercises *Get Ahead of the Curve* online and get instant feedback.

Review Questions

4.1 What is the multiplier effect? Use a 45°-line diagram to illustrate the multiplier effect of a decrease in government purchases.

4.2 What is the formula for the multiplier? Explain why this formula is considered to be too simple.

Problems and Applications

4.3 (Related to *Solved Problem 23-4* on page 796) Use the information in the following table to answer the following questions.

REAL GDP (Y)	CONSUMPTION (C)	PLANNED INVESTMENT (I)	GOVERNMENT PURCHASES (G)	NET EXPORTS (NX)
$8,000	$7,300	$1,000	$1,000	–$500
9,000	7,900	1,000	1,000	–500
10,000	8,500	1,000	1,000	–500
11,000	9,100	1,000	1,000	–500
12,000	9,700	1,000	1,000	–500

   a. What is the equilibrium level of real GDP?
   b. What is the *MPC*?
   c. Suppose net exports increase by $400 billion. What will be the new equilibrium level of real GDP? Use the multiplier formula to determine your answer.

4.4 The following is from a letter to the *Economist* magazine:

> The arithmetic contribution of net exports to Asia's growth may have been only one percentage point, or two points in the case of China, but including multiplier effects the total growth impact has been two to three times higher.

> What does this writer mean by "multiplier effects"? What does he mean by "total growth impact"? Why would the multiplier effect increase the impact of exports on economic growth in China and other Asian countries?

Source: "On China's Economy, the Meaning of Africa, Iraq, New York, Cheesesteaks," *Economist*, November 9, 2006.

4.5 Explain whether you agree or disagree with the following statement:

> Many economists claim that the recession of 2001 was caused by a decline in investment. This can't be true. If there had just been a decline in investment, the only firms hurt would have been construction firms, computer firms, and other firms selling investment goods. In fact, many firms experienced falling sales during that recession, including automobile firms and furniture firms.

4.6 Suppose a booming economy in Europe causes net exports to rise by $75 billion in the United States. If the

MPC is 0.8, what will be the change in equilibrium GDP?

4.7 Would a larger multiplier lead to longer and more severe recessions or shorter and less severe recessions? Briefly explain.

4.8 Use the following graph to answer the questions.

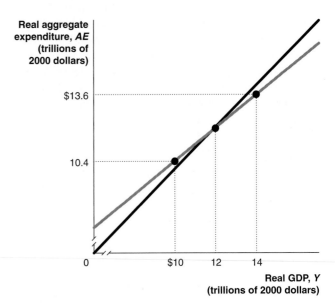

   a. What is the value of equilibrium real GDP?
   b. What is the value of the *MPC*?
   c. What is the value of the multiplier?
   d. What is the value of unplanned changes in inventories when real GDP has each of the following values?
     • $10 trillion
     • $12 trillion
     • $14 trillion

4.9 (Related to the *Making the Connection* on page 793) If the multiplier had a value of 4 in 1929, how large must the change in autonomous expenditure have been to cause the decline in real GDP between 1929 and 1933 shown in the table on page 793? If the multiplier had a value of 2, how large must the change in autonomous expenditure have been?

4.10 In an article on Microsoft expanding the number of buildings and employees at its Redmond, Washington headquarters, Bill McSherry, director of economic development at the Puget Sound Regional Council in Seattle, was quoted as saying: "The real reason you want these jobs is for the multiplier effect." How is the multiplier effect McSherry is referring to related to the multiplier effect discussed in this chapter?

Source: Kristina Shevory, "Microsoft Is Looking for More Elbow Room, *New York Times*, July 5, 2006.

>> End Learning Objective 23.4

23.5 LEARNING OBJECTIVE   23.5 | Understand the relationship between the aggregate demand curve and aggregate expenditure, **pages 797–798.**

The Aggregate Demand Curve

Summary

Increases in the price level cause a reduction in consumption, investment, and net exports. This causes the aggregate expenditure function to shift down on the 45°-line diagram, leading to a lower equilibrium real GDP. A decrease in the price level leads to a higher equilibrium real GDP. The **aggregate demand curve** shows the relationship between the price level and the level of aggregate expenditure, holding constant all factors that affect aggregate expenditure other than the price level.

 Visit www.myeconlab.com to complete these exercises *Get Ahead of the Curve* online and get instant feedback.

Review Questions

5.1 Briefly explain the difference between aggregate expenditure and aggregate demand.

5.2 Briefly explain which components of aggregate expenditure are affected by a change in the price level.

Problems and Applications

5.3 Briefly explain why the aggregate expenditure line is upward sloping, while the aggregate demand curve is downward sloping.

5.4 Briefly explain whether you agree with the following statement: "The reason that the aggregate demand curve slopes downward is that when the price level is higher, people cannot afford to buy as many goods and services."

5.5 Suppose that exports become more sensitive to changes in the price level in the United States. That is, when the price level in the United States rises, exports decline by more than they previously did. Will this change make the aggregate demand curve steeper or less steep? Briefly explain.

>> **End Learning Objective 23.5**

Appendix

The Algebra of Macroeconomic Equilibrium

Apply the algebra of macroeconomic equilibrium.

In this chapter, we relied primarily on graphs and tables to illustrate the aggregate expenditure model of short-run real GDP. Graphs help us understand economic change *qualitatively*. When we write down an economic model using equations, we make it easier to make *quantitative estimates*. When economists forecast future movements in GDP, they often rely on *econometric models*. An econometric model is an economic model written in the form of equations, where each equation has been statistically estimated, using methods similar to the methods used in estimating demand curves that we briefly described in Chapter 3. We can use equations to represent the aggregate expenditure model described in this chapter.

The following equations are based on the example shown in Table 23-3 on page 789. *Y* stands for real GDP, and the numbers (with the exception of the *MPC*) represent billions of dollars.

1	$C = 1{,}000 + 0.65\,Y$	Consumption function
2	$I = 1{,}500$	Planned investment function
3	$G = 1{,}500$	Government spending function
4	$NX = -500$	Net export function
5	$Y = C + I + G + NX$	Equilibrium condition

The first equation is the consumption function. The *MPC* is 0.65, and 1,000 is autonomous consumption, which is the level of consumption that does not depend on income. If we think of the consumption function as a line on the 45°-line diagram, 1,000 would be the intercept, and 0.65 would be the slope. The "functions" for the other three components of planned aggregate expenditure are very simple because we have assumed that these components are not affected by GDP and, therefore, are constant. Economists who use this type of model to forecast GDP would, of course, use more realistic investment, government, and net export functions. The *parameters* of the functions—such as the value of autonomous consumption and the value of the *MPC* in the consumption function—would be estimated statistically using data on the values of each variable over a period of years.

In this model, equilibrium GDP occurs where GDP is equal to planned aggregate expenditure. Equation 5—the equilibrium condition—shows us how to calculate equilibrium in the model: To calculate equilibrium, we substitute equations 1 through 4 into equation 5. This gives us the following:

$$Y = 1{,}000 + 0.65Y + 1{,}500 + 1{,}500 - 500.$$

We need to solve this expression for *Y* to find equilibrium GDP. The first step is to subtract 0.65*Y* from both sides of the equation:

$$Y - 0.65Y = 1{,}000 + 1{,}500 + 1{,}500 - 500.$$

Then, we solve for Y:

$$0.35Y = 3,500.$$

Or:

$$Y = \frac{3,500}{0.35} = 10,000.$$

To make this result more general, we can replace particular values with general values represented by letters:

1   $C = \overline{C} + MPC(Y)$ Consumption function
2   $I = \overline{I}$ Planned investment function
3   $G = \overline{G}$ Government spending function
4   $NX = \overline{NX}$ Net export function
5   $Y = C + I + G + NX$ Equilibrium condition

The letters with bars over them represent fixed, or autonomous, values. So, $\overline{C}$ represents autonomous consumption, which had a value of 1,000 in our original example. Now, solving for equilibrium, we get:

$$Y = \overline{C} + MPC(Y) + \overline{I} + \overline{G} + \overline{NX},$$

or:

$$Y - MPC(Y) = \overline{C} + \overline{I} + \overline{G} + \overline{NX},$$

or:

$$Y(1 - MPC) = \overline{C} + \overline{I} + \overline{G} + \overline{NX},$$

or:

$$Y = \frac{\overline{C} + \overline{I} + \overline{GX} + \overline{NX}}{1 - MPC}.$$

Remember that $1/(1-MPC)$ is the multiplier, and all four variables in the numerator of the equation represent autonomous expenditure. Therefore an alternative expression for equilibrium GDP is:

Equilibrium GDP = Autonomous expenditure $\times$ Multiplier.

LEARNING OBJECTIVE   Apply the algebra of macroeconomic equilibrium, **pages 808–809.**

 Visit www.myeconlab.com to complete these exercises
Get Ahead of the Curve online and get instant feedback.

Problems and Applications

23A.1 Write a general expression for the aggregate expenditure function. If you think of the aggregate expenditure function as a line on the 45°-line diagram, what would be the intercept and what would be the slope, using the general values represented by letters?

23A.2 Find equilibrium GDP using the following macroeconomic model (the numbers, with the exception of the *MPC*, represent billions of dollars).
   a. $C = 1,500 + 0.75\ Y$ Consumption function
   b. $I = 1,250$ Planned investment function

   c. $G = 1,250$ Government spending function
   d. $NX = -500$ Net export function
   e. $Y = C + I + G + NX$ Equilibrium condition

23A.3 For the macroeconomic model in problem 23.2A, write the aggregate expenditure function. For GDP of $16,000, what is the value of aggregate expenditure, and what is the value of the unintended change in inventories? For GDP of $12,000, what is the value of aggregate expenditure, and what is the value of the unintended change in inventories?

23A.4 Suppose that autonomous consumption is 500, government purchases are 1,000, planned investment spending is 1,250, net exports is −250, and the *MPC* is 0.8. What is equilibrium GDP?

>> **End Appendix Learning Objective**

Aggregate Demand and Aggregate Supply Analysis

The Fortunes of FedEx Follow the Business Cycle

When Alan Greenspan was chairman of the Federal Reserve, he spoke regularly with Fred Smith, the chairman of Federal Express. Greenspan believed that changes in the number of packages FedEx shipped gave a good indication of the overall state of the economy. FedEx plays such a large role in moving packages around the country that most economists agree with Greenspan that there is a close relationship between fluctuations in FedEx's business and fluctuations in GDP. Some Wall Street analysts refer to this relationship as the "FedEx Indicator" of how the economy is doing.

Like many successful businesses, FedEx began with a single bright idea by a young entrepreneur. In 1965, as an undergraduate, Fred Smith was assigned to write a term paper for an economics course. In the paper, Smith argued that the system for shipping freight by air in the United States was inefficient. At that time, nearly all air freight was shipped on regular passenger planes. This made freight

dependent on airline schedules and meant that if airlines cut back on flights to an area, firms in that area were left with reduced freight service. Smith proposed an entirely new system: One firm would control shipping freight from pickup to delivery. The firm would operate its own planes on a "hub-and-spoke" system: Packages would be collected and flown to a central hub, where they would be sorted and then flown to their destination for final delivery by truck. Moreover, by breaking free of airline schedules, the new firm could promise overnight delivery, which most freight companies in the 1960s couldn't do. Smith can't quite remember the grade he received (he has been quoted as saying it may have been a C), but the system he outlined in that term paper became the basis for the FedEx company of today.

Headquartered in Memphis, Tennessee, FedEx earns over $35 billion in annual revenues and has more than 240,000 employees in 220 countries and territories. Despite FedEx's tremendous success over the past 30 years, as Greenspan knew, the business cycle has always affected the company. For example, during the U.S. recession of 2001, the company's profits fell 38 percent in six months as businesses and

individuals cut back on shipping packages. When the annual growth rate of real GDP slowed to 1 percent in the first quarter of 2008, FedEx reported that the number of shipments it handled in the United States had declined, and that it had suffered its first loss after 11 straight years of profits.

To understand why FedEx and other firms are affected by the business cycle, we need to explore the effects that recessions and expansions have on production, employment, and prices. As you will read in this chapter, although no two business cycles are identical, economists use the aggregate demand and aggregate supply model to explain their general features. In later chapters, we use aggregate demand and aggregate supply to understand how the federal government can employ fiscal policy and monetary policy to reduce the severity of business cycles.

AN INSIDE LOOK on **page 838** discusses how a decline in the growth of real GDP affected UPS, one of FedEx's competitors.

Sources: David Gaffen, "The FedEx Indicator," *Wall Street Journal*, February 20, 2007; Roger Frock, *Changing How the World Does Business*, San Francisco: Berrett-Koehler Publishers, 2006; and Corey Dade and Shara Tibken, "FedEx Has First Quarterly Loss in 11 years," *Wall Street Journal*, June 19, 2008.

Economics in YOUR Life!

Is an Employer Likely to Cut Your Pay During a Recession?

Suppose that you have worked as a barista for a local coffeehouse for two years. From on-the-job training and experience, you have honed your coffee-making skills and mastered the perfect latte. Suddenly, the economy moves into a recession, and sales at the coffeehouse decline. Is the owner of the coffeehouse likely to cut the prices of lattes and other drinks? Suppose the owner asks to meet with you to discuss your wages for next year. Is the owner likely to cut your pay? As you read the chapter, see if you can answer these questions. You can check your answers against those we provide at the end of the chapter. >> Continued on page 837

We saw in Chapter 21 that the U.S. economy has experienced a long-run upward trend in real gross domestic product (GDP). This upward trend has resulted in the standard of living in the United States being much higher today than it was 50 years ago. In the short run, however, real GDP fluctuates around this long-run upward trend because of the business cycle. Fluctuations in GDP lead to fluctuations in employment. These fluctuations in real GDP and employment are the most visible and dramatic part of the business cycle. During recessions, for example, we are more likely to see factories close, small businesses declare bankruptcy, and workers lose their jobs. During expansions, we are more likely to see new businesses open and new jobs created. In addition to these changes in output and employment, the business cycle causes changes in wages and prices. Some firms react to a decline in sales by cutting back on production, but they may also cut the prices they charge and the wages they pay. Even more firms respond to a recession by raising prices and workers' wages by less than they would have otherwise.

In this chapter, we expand our story of the business cycle by developing the aggregate demand and aggregate supply model. This model will help us analyze the effects of recessions and expansions on production, employment, and prices.

24.1 LEARNING OBJECTIVE

24.1 | Identify the determinants of aggregate demand and distinguish between a movement along the aggregate demand curve and a shift of the curve.

Aggregate Demand

Aggregate demand and aggregate supply model A model that explains short-run fluctuations in real GDP and the price level.

Aggregate demand curve A curve that shows the relationship between the price level and the quantity of real GDP demanded by households, firms, and the government.

To understand what happens during the business cycle, we need an explanation of why real GDP, the unemployment rate, and the inflation rate fluctuate. We have already seen that fluctuations in the unemployment rate are caused mainly by fluctuations in real GDP. In this chapter, we use the **aggregate demand and aggregate supply model** to explain fluctuations in real GDP and the price level. As Figure 24-1 shows, real GDP and the price level in this model are determined in the short run by the intersection of the *aggregate demand curve* and the *aggregate supply curve*. Fluctuations in real GDP and the price level are caused by shifts in the aggregate demand curve or in the aggregate supply curve.

The **aggregate demand curve**, labeled *AD*, shows the relationship between the price level and the quantity of real GDP demanded by households, firms, and the government.

Figure 24-1

Aggregate Demand and Aggregate Supply

In the short run, real GDP and the price level are determined by the intersection of the aggregate demand curve and the short-run aggregate supply curve. In the figure, real GDP is measured on the horizontal axis, and the price level is measured on the vertical axis by the GDP deflator. In this example, the equilibrium real GDP is $10.0 trillion, and the equilibrium price level is 100.

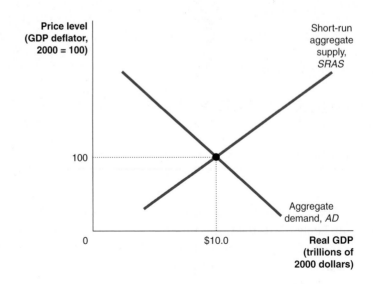

The **short-run aggregate supply curve**, labeled *SRAS*, shows the relationship in the short run between the price level and the quantity of real GDP supplied by firms. The aggregate demand and short-run aggregate supply curves in Figure 24-1 look similar to the individual market demand and supply curves we studied in Chapter 3. However, because these curves apply to the whole economy, rather than to just a single market, the aggregate demand and aggregate supply model is very different from the model of demand and supply in individual markets. Because we are dealing with the economy as a whole, we need *macroeconomic* explanations of why the aggregate demand curve is downward sloping, why the short-run aggregate supply curve is upward sloping, and why the curves shift. We begin by explaining why the aggregate demand curve is downward sloping.

Short-run aggregate supply curve
A curve that shows the relationship in the short run between the price level and the quantity of real GDP supplied by firms.

Why Is the Aggregate Demand Curve Downward Sloping?

We saw in Chapter 19 that GDP has four components: consumption (C), investment (I), government purchases (G), and net exports (NX). If we let Y stand for GDP, we can write the following:

$$Y = C + I + G + NX.$$

The aggregate demand curve is downward sloping because a fall in the price level increases the quantity of real GDP demanded. To understand why this is true, we need to look at how changes in the price level affect each of the components of aggregate demand. We begin with the assumption that government purchases are determined by the policy decisions of lawmakers and are not affected by changes in the price level. We can then consider the effect of changes in the price level on each of the other three components: consumption, investment, and net exports.

The Wealth Effect: How a Change in the Price Level Affects Consumption

Current income is the most important variable determining the consumption of households. As income rises, consumption will rise, and as income falls, consumption will fall. But consumption also depends on household wealth. A household's wealth is the difference between the value of its assets and the value of its debts. Consider two households, both with incomes of $80,000 per year. The first household has wealth of $5 million, whereas the second household has wealth of $50,000. The first household is likely to spend more of its income than the second household. So, as total household wealth rises, consumption will rise. Some household wealth is held in cash or other *nominal assets* that lose value as the price level rises and gain value as the price level falls. For instance, if you have $10,000 in cash, a 10 percent increase in the price level will reduce the purchasing power of that cash by 10 percent. When the price level rises, the *real value* of household wealth declines, and so will consumption. When the price level falls, the real value of household wealth rises, and so will consumption. This impact of the price level on consumption is called the *wealth effect*.

The Interest-Rate Effect: How a Change in the Price Level Affects Investment

When prices rise, households and firms need more money to finance buying and selling. Therefore, when the price level rises, households and firms will try to increase the amount of money they hold by withdrawing funds from banks, borrowing from banks, or selling financial assets, such as bonds. These actions tend to drive up the interest rate charged on bank loans and the interest rate on bonds. (In Chapter 26, we analyze in more detail the relationship between money and interest rates.) A higher interest rate raises the cost of borrowing for firms and households. As a result, firms will borrow less to build new factories or to install new machinery and equipment, and households will borrow less to buy new houses. To a smaller extent, households will also borrow less to finance spending on automobiles, furniture, and other durable goods. Consumption will therefore be reduced.

A lower price level will have the reverse effect, leading to an increase in investment and—to a lesser extent—consumption. This impact of the price level on investment is known as the *interest-rate effect*.

The International-Trade Effect: How a Change in the Price Level Affects Net Exports Net exports equal spending by foreign households and firms on goods and services produced in the United States minus spending by U.S. households and firms on goods and services produced in other countries. If the price level in the United States rises relative to the price levels in other countries, U.S. exports will become relatively more expensive, and foreign imports will become relatively less expensive. Some consumers in foreign countries will shift from buying U.S. products to buying domestic products, and some U.S. consumers will also shift from buying U.S. products to buying imported products. U.S. exports will fall, and U.S. imports will rise, causing net exports to fall. A lower price level in the United States has the reverse effect, causing net exports to rise. This impact of the price level on net exports is known as the *international-trade effect*.

Shifts of the Aggregate Demand Curve versus Movements Along It

An important point to remember is that the aggregate demand curve tells us the relationship between the price level and the quantity of real GDP demanded, *holding everything else constant*. If the price level changes but other variables that affect the willingness of households, firms, and the government to spend are unchanged, the economy will move up or down a stationary aggregate demand curve. If any variable changes other than the price level, the aggregate demand curve will shift. For example, if government purchases increase and the price level remains unchanged, the aggregate demand curve will shift to the right at every price level. Or, if firms become pessimistic about the future profitability of investment and cut back spending on factories and machinery, the aggregate demand curve will shift to the left.

The Variables That Shift the Aggregate Demand Curve

The variables that cause the aggregate demand curve to shift fall into three categories:

- Changes in government policies
- Changes in the expectations of households and firms
- Changes in foreign variables

Don't Let This Happen to **YOU!**

Be Clear Why the Aggregate Demand Curve Is Downward Sloping

The aggregate demand curve and the demand curve for a single product are both downward sloping—but for different reasons. When we draw a demand curve for a single product, such as apples, we know that it will slope downward because as the price of apples rises, apples become more expensive relative to other products—like oranges—and consumers buy fewer apples and more of the other products. In other words, consumers substitute other products for apples. When the overall price level rises, the prices of all domestically produced goods and services are rising, so consumers have no other domestic products to which they can switch. The aggregate demand curve slopes downward for the reasons given on pages 813–814: A lower price level raises the real value of household wealth (which increases consumption), lowers interest rates (which increases investment and consumption), and makes U.S. exports less expensive and foreign imports more expensive (which increases net exports).

YOUR TURN: Test your understanding by doing related problem 1.5 on page 840 at the end of this chapter.

Changes in Government Policies As we will discuss further in Chapters 26 and 27, the federal government uses monetary policy and fiscal policy to shift the aggregate demand curve. **Monetary policy** involves the actions the Federal Reserve—the nation's central bank—takes to manage the money supply and interest rates to pursue macroeconomic policy objectives. When the Federal Reserve takes actions to reduce interest rates, it lowers the cost to firms and households of borrowing. Lower borrowing costs increase consumption and investment spending, which shifts the aggregate demand curve to the right. Higher interest rates shift the aggregate demand curve to the left. **Fiscal policy** involves changes in federal taxes and purchases that are intended to achieve macroeconomic policy objectives, such as high employment, price stability, and high rates of economic growth. Because government purchases are one component of aggregate demand, an increase in government purchases shifts the aggregate demand curve to the right, and a decrease in government purchases shifts the aggregate demand curve to the left. An increase in personal income taxes reduces the amount of spendable income available to households. Higher personal income taxes reduce consumption spending and shift the aggregate demand curve to the left. Lower personal income taxes shift the aggregate demand curve to the right. Increases in business taxes reduce the profitability of investment spending and shift the aggregate demand curve to the left. Decreases in business taxes shift the aggregate demand curve to the right.

Monetary policy The actions the Federal Reserve takes to manage the money supply and interest rates to pursue macroeconomic policy objectives.

Fiscal policy Changes in federal taxes and purchases that are intended to achieve macroeconomic policy objectives, such as high employment, price stability, and high rates of economic growth.

Changes in the Expectations of Households and Firms If households become more optimistic about their future incomes, they are likely to increase their current consumption. This increased consumption will shift the aggregate demand curve to the right. If households become more pessimistic about their future incomes, the aggregate demand curve will shift to the left. Similarly, if firms become more optimistic about the future profitability of investment spending, the aggregate demand curve will shift to the right. If firms become more pessimistic, the aggregate demand curve will shift to the left.

Changes in Foreign Variables If firms and households in other countries buy fewer U.S. goods or if firms and households in the United States buy more foreign goods, net exports will fall, and the aggregate demand curve will shift to the left. As we saw in Chapter 19, when real GDP increases, so does the income available for consumers to spend. If real GDP in the United States increases faster than real GDP in other countries, U.S. imports will increase faster than U.S. exports, and net exports will fall, which is what happened during the late 1990s through the mid-2000s. Net exports will also fall if the *exchange rate* between the dollar and foreign currencies rises because the price in foreign currency of U.S. products sold in other countries will rise, and the dollar price of foreign products sold in the United States will fall. For example, if the current exchange rate is $1 = €1, then a $300 iPod exported from the United States to France will cost €300 in France, and a €50 bottle of French wine will cost $50 in the United States. But if the exchange rises to $1 = €1.50, then the iPod's price will rise to €450 in France, causing its sales to decline, and the price of the French wine will fall to $33.33 per bottle in the United States, causing its sales to increase. U.S. exports will fall, U.S. imports will rise, and the aggregate demand curve will shift to the left.

An increase in net exports at every price level will shift the aggregate demand curve to the right. Net exports will increase if real GDP grows more slowly in the United States than in other countries or if the value of the dollar falls against other currencies. A change in net exports that results from a change in the price level in the United States will *not* cause the aggregate demand curve to shift.

Making the Connection | In a Global Economy, How Can You Tell the Imports from the Domestic Goods?

Some U.S. firms appeal to the patriotism of U.S. consumers by urging them to buy products made in the United States. For example, an executive vice president of Ford Motor Company was quoted as saying, "Americans really do want to

Is the Toyota Sienna as American as apple pie?

buy American brands. We will compete vigorously to be America's car company." What could be more All-American than the famous Ford Mustang sports car? And what is more obviously an import than the Toyota Sienna minivan? After all, Toyota's headquarters is in Japan, and competition from cars made by Toyota, Honda, and Nissan has helped cause plummeting employment and production at Ford and the other U.S. "Big Three" automakers. But things are not so simple in the modern global economy. While the Mustang is assembled in Flat Rock, Michigan, the Sienna is not assembled in Japan but in Princeton, Indiana. What is more, most firms that sell products, such as automobiles, that have many parts, purchase those parts from suppliers who may be located anywhere in the world. In fact, according to the U.S. National Highway Traffic Safety Administration, only 65 percent of the content of the Ford Mustang was produced by Ford itself or by firms located in the United States or Canada. The other 35 percent of the content was imported from firms located in other countries. By contrast, 90 percent of the content of the Toyota Sienna is produced in the United States or Canada, and only 10 percent is imported from firms located in other countries. So, a consumer in the United States who buys a Toyota Sienna actually contributes more to increasing U.S. aggregate demand than does a consumer purchasing a Ford Mustang.

The U.S. Bureau of Economic Analysis (BEA), which is in charge of gathering data on imports, as well as the other components of aggregate demand, is well aware of this complication. The BEA is careful to include in the category of imports the parts purchased by U.S.-based firms from foreign suppliers even when the final product being sold is mainly composed of U.S.-made parts.

Source: Jathon Sapsford and Norihiko Shirouzu, "Mom, Apple Pie and . . . Toyota?" *Wall Street Journal*, May 11, 2006, p. B1.

YOUR TURN: Test your understanding by doingrelated problem 1.8 on page 841 at the end of this chapter.

Solved Problem | 24-1

Movements along the Aggregate Demand Curve versus Shifts of the Aggregate Demand Curve

Suppose the current price level is 120, and the current level of real GDP is $12.2 trillion. Illustrate each of the following situations on a graph.

a. The price level rises to 125, while all other variables remain constant.

b. Firms become pessimistic and reduce their investment. Assume that the price level remains constant.

SOLVING THE PROBLEM:

Step 1: **Review the chapter material.** This problem is about understanding the difference between movements along an aggregate demand curve and shifts of an aggregate demand curve, so you may want to review the section "Shifts of the Aggregate Demand Curve versus Movements Along It," which begins on page 814.

Step 2: **To answer question (a), draw a graph that shows a movement along the aggregate demand curve.** Because there will be a movement along the aggregate demand curve but no shift of the aggregate demand curve, your graph should look like this:

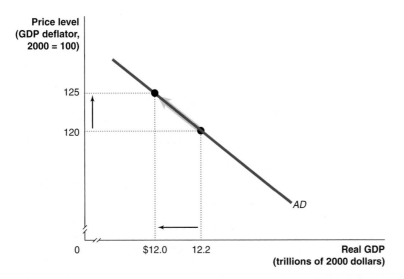

We don't have enough information to be certain what the new level of real GDP will be. We only know that it will be less than the initial level of $12.2 trillion; the graph shows the value as $12.0 trillion.

Step 3: **To answer question (b), draw a graph that shows a shift of the aggregate demand curve.** We know that the aggregate demand curve will shift to the left, but we don't have enough information to know how far to the left it will shift. Let's assume that the shift is $300 billion (or $0.3 trillion). In that case, your graph should look like this:

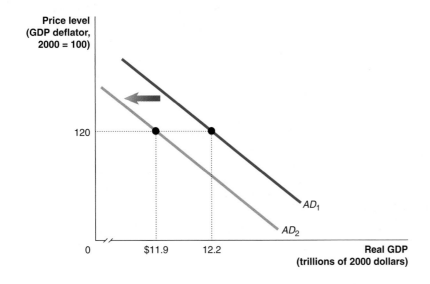

The graph shows a parallel shift in the aggregate demand curve so that at every price level, the quantity of real GDP demanded declines by $300 billion. For example, at a price level of 120, the quantity of real GDP demanded declines from $12.2 trillion to $11.9 trillion.

YOUR TURN: For more practice, do related problem 1.6 on page 841 at the end of this chapter.

>> **End Solved Problem 24-1**

Table 24-1 summarizes the most important variables that cause the aggregate demand curve to shift. It is important to notice that the table shows the shift in the aggregate demand curve that results from an increase in each of the variables. A *decrease* in these variables would cause the aggregate demand curve to shift in the opposite direction.

TABLE 24-1

Variables That Shift the Aggregate Demand Curve

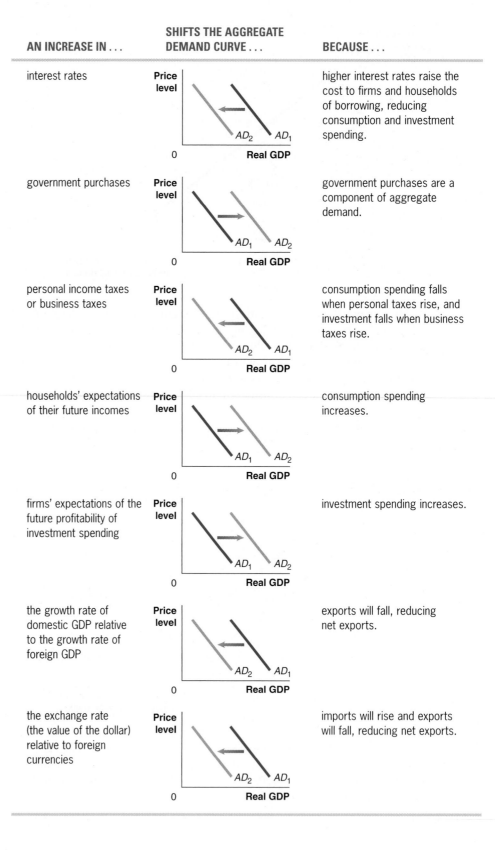

AN INCREASE IN ...	SHIFTS THE AGGREGATE DEMAND CURVE ...	BECAUSE ...
interest rates		higher interest rates raise the cost to firms and households of borrowing, reducing consumption and investment spending.
government purchases		government purchases are a component of aggregate demand.
personal income taxes or business taxes		consumption spending falls when personal taxes rise, and investment falls when business taxes rise.
households' expectations of their future incomes		consumption spending increases.
firms' expectations of the future profitability of investment spending		investment spending increases.
the growth rate of domestic GDP relative to the growth rate of foreign GDP		exports will fall, reducing net exports.
the exchange rate (the value of the dollar) relative to foreign currencies		imports will rise and exports will fall, reducing net exports.

24.2 | Identify the determinants of aggregate supply and distinguish between a movement along the short-run aggregate supply curve and a shift of the curve.

Aggregate Supply

We just discussed the aggregate demand curve, which is one component of the aggregate demand and aggregate supply model. Now we turn to aggregate supply, which shows the effect of changes in the price level on the quantity of goods and services that firms are willing and able to supply. Because the effect of changes in the price level on aggregate supply is very different in the short run than in the long run, we use two aggregate supply curves: one for the short run and one for the long run. We start by considering the *long-run aggregate supply curve.*

The Long-Run Aggregate Supply Curve

In Chapter 22, we saw that in the long run, the level of real GDP is determined by the number of workers, the *capital stock*—including factories, office buildings, and machinery and equipment—and the available technology. Because changes in the price level do not affect the number of workers, the capital stock, or technology, *in the long run, changes in the price level do not affect the level of real GDP*. Remember that the level of real GDP in the long run is called *potential GDP* or *full-employment GDP*. At potential GDP, firms will operate at their normal level of capacity, and everyone who wants a job will have one, except the structurally and frictionally unemployed. There is no reason for this normal level of capacity to change just because the price level has changed. The **long-run aggregate supply curve** is a curve, labeled *LRAS*, that shows the relationship in the long run between the price level and the quantity of real GDP supplied. As Figure 24-2 shows, the price level was 120 in 2007, and potential real GDP was $11.7 trillion. If the price level had been 110, or if it had been 130, long-run aggregate supply would still have been a constant $11.7 trillion. Therefore, the *LRAS* curve is a vertical line.

Figure 24-2 also shows that the long-run aggregate supply curve shifts to the right every year. This shift occurs because potential real GDP increases each year, as the number of workers in the economy increases, the economy accumulates more machinery and equipment, and technological change occurs. As Figure 24-2 shows, potential real GDP increased from $11.7 trillion in 2007 to $12.0 trillion in 2008 and to $12.3 trillion in 2009.

Long-run aggregate supply curve A curve that shows the relationship in the long run between the price level and the quantity of real GDP supplied.

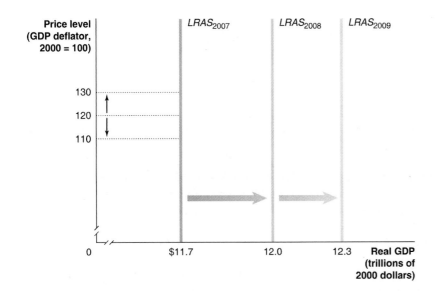

Figure 24-2

The Long-Run Aggregate Supply Curve

Changes in the price level do not affect the level of aggregate supply in the long run. Therefore, the long-run aggregate supply curve, labeled *LRAS*, is a vertical line at the potential level of real GDP. For instance, the price level was 120 in 2007, and potential real GDP was $11.7 trillion. If the price level had been 110, or if it had been 130, long-run aggregate supply would still have been a constant $11.7 trillion. Each year, the long-run aggregate supply curve shifts to the right as the number of workers in the economy increases, more machinery and equipment are accumulated, and technological change occurs.

The Short-Run Aggregate Supply Curve

Although the *LRAS* curve is vertical, the short-run aggregate supply curve, or *SRAS curve*, is upward sloping. The *SRAS* curve is upward sloping because, over the short run, as the price level increases, the quantity of goods and services firms are willing to supply will increase. The main reason firms behave this way is that, *as prices of final goods and services rise, prices of inputs—such as the wages of workers or the price of natural resources—rise more slowly.* Profits rise when the prices of the goods and services firms sell rise more rapidly than the prices they pay for inputs. Therefore, a higher price level leads to higher profits and increases the willingness of firms to supply more goods and services. A secondary reason the *SRAS* curve slopes upward is that, as the price level rises or falls, some firms are slow to adjust their prices. A firm that is slow to raise its prices when the price level is increasing may find its sales increasing and, therefore, will increase production. A firm that is slow to reduce its prices when the price level is decreasing may find its sales falling and, therefore, will decrease production.

Why do some firms adjust prices more slowly than others, and why might the wages of workers and the prices of other inputs change more slowly than the prices of final goods and services? Most economists believe the explanation is that *some firms and workers fail to predict accurately changes in the price level.* If firms and workers could predict the future price level exactly, the short-run aggregate supply curve would be the same as the long-run aggregate supply curve.

But how does the failure of workers and firms to predict the price level accurately result in an upward-sloping *SRAS* curve? Economists are not in complete agreement on this point, but we can briefly discuss the three most common explanations:

1　Contracts make some wages and prices "sticky."

2　Firms are often slow to adjust wages.

3　Menu costs make some prices sticky.

Contracts Make Some Wages and Prices "Sticky" Prices or wages are said to be "sticky" when they do not respond quickly to changes in demand or supply. Contracts can make wages or prices sticky. For example, suppose General Motors negotiates a three-year contract with the United Automobile Workers union at a time when demand for cars is increasing slowly. Suppose that after the contract is signed, the demand for cars starts to increase rapidly, and prices of cars rise. General Motors will find that producing more cars will be profitable because it can increase car prices, while the wages it pays its workers are fixed by contract. Or a steel mill might have signed a multiyear contract to buy coal, which is used in making steel, at a time when the demand for steel was stagnant. If steel demand and steel prices begin to rise rapidly, producing additional steel will be profitable because coal prices will remain fixed by contract. In both of these cases, rising prices lead to higher output. If these examples are representative of enough firms in the economy, a rising price level should lead to a greater quantity of goods and services supplied. In other words, the short-run aggregate supply curve will be upward sloping.

Notice, though, that if the workers at General Motors or the managers of the coal companies had accurately predicted what would happen to prices, this prediction would have been reflected in the contracts, and General Motors and the steel mill would not have earned greater profits when prices rose. In that case, rising prices would not have led to higher output.

Firms Are Often Slow to Adjust Wages We just noted that the wages of many union workers remain fixed by contract for several years. Many nonunion workers also have their wages or salaries adjusted only once a year. For instance, suppose you accept a job at a management consulting firm in June at a salary of $45,000 per year. The firm probably will not adjust your salary until the following June, even if the prices it can charge for its services later in the year are higher or lower than the firm had expected them to be when you were first hired. If firms are slow to adjust wages, a rise in the price level will increase the profitability of hiring more workers and producing more output. A fall in the price level will decrease the profitability of hiring more workers and producing more output. Once again, we have an explanation for why the short-run aggregate supply curve slopes upward.

It is worth noting that firms are often slower to *cut* wages than to increase them. Cutting wages can have a negative effect on the morale and productivity of workers and can also cause some of a firm's best workers to quit and look for jobs elsewhere.

Menu Costs Make Some Prices Sticky Firms base their prices today partly on what they expect future prices to be. For instance, a restaurant has to decide ahead of time the prices it will charge for meals before printing menus. Many firms print catalogs that list the prices of their products. If demand for their products is higher or lower than the firms had expected, they may want to charge prices that are different from the ones printed in their menus or catalogs. Changing prices would be costly, however, because it would involve printing new menus or catalogs. The costs to firms of changing prices are called **menu costs**. To see why menu costs can lead to an upward-sloping short-run aggregate supply curve, consider the effect of an unexpected increase in the price level. In this case, firms will want to increase the prices they charge. Some firms, however, may not be willing to increase prices because of menu costs. Because of their relatively low prices, these firms will find their sales increasing, which will cause them to increase output. Once again, we have an explanation for a higher price level leading to a larger quantity of goods and services supplied.

Menu costs The costs to firms of changing prices.

Shifts of the Short-Run Aggregate Supply Curve versus Movements Along It

It is important to remember the difference between a shift in a curve and a movement along a curve. The short-run aggregate supply curve tells us the short-run relationship between the price level and the quantity of goods and services firms are willing to supply, *holding constant all other variables that affect the willingness of firms to supply goods and services*. If the price level changes but other variables are unchanged, the economy will move up or down a stationary aggregate supply curve. If any variable other than the price level changes, the aggregate supply curve will shift.

Variables That Shift the Short-Run Aggregate Supply Curve

We now briefly discuss the five most important variables that cause the short-run aggregate supply curve to shift.

Increases in the Labor Force and in the Capital Stock A firm will supply more output at every price if it has more workers and more physical capital. The same is true of the economy as a whole. So, as the labor force and the capital stock grow, firms will supply more output at every price level, and the short-run aggregate supply curve will shift to the right. In Japan, the population is aging, and the labor force is decreasing. Holding other variables constant, this decrease in the labor force causes the short-run aggregate supply curve in Japan to shift to the left.

Technological Change As technological change takes place, the productivity of workers and machinery increases, which means firms can produce more goods and services with the same amount of labor and machinery. This improvement reduces the firms' costs of production and, therefore, allows them to produce more output at every price level. As a result, the short-run aggregate supply curve shifts to the right.

Expected Changes in the Future Price Level If workers and firms believe that the price level is going to increase by 3 percent during the next year, they will try to adjust their wages and prices accordingly. For instance, if a labor union believes there will be

Figure 24-3

How Expectations of the Future Price Level Affect the Short-Run Aggregate Supply

The *SRAS* curve shifts to reflect worker and firm expectations of future prices.

1. If workers and firms expect that the price level will rise by 3 percent, from 100 to 103, they will adjust their wages and prices by that amount.
2. Holding constant all other variables that affect aggregate supply, the short-run aggregate supply curve will shift to the left. If workers and firms expect that the price level will be lower in the future, the short-run aggregate supply curve will shift to the right.

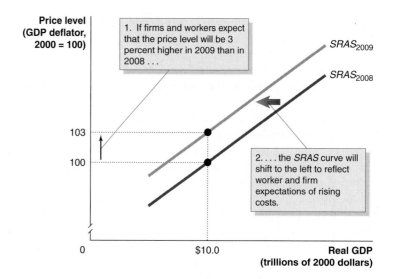

3 percent inflation next year, it knows that wages must rise 3 percent to preserve the purchasing power of those wages. Similar adjustments by other workers and firms will result in costs increasing throughout the economy by 3 percent. The result, shown in Figure 24-3, is that the short-run aggregate supply curve will shift to the left, so that any level of real GDP is now associated with a price level that is 3 percent higher. In general, *if workers and firms expect the price level to increase by a certain percentage, the* SRAS *curve will shift by an equivalent amount*, holding constant all other variables that affect the *SRAS* curve.

Adjustments of Workers and Firms to Errors in Past Expectations about the Price Level Workers and firms sometimes make wrong predictions about the price level. As time passes, they will attempt to compensate for these errors. Suppose, for example, that the United Automobile Workers signs a contract with General Motors that contains only small wage increases because the company and the union expect only small increases in the price level. If increases in the price level turn out to be unexpectedly large, the union will take this into account when negotiating the next contract. The higher wages General Motors' workers receive under the new contract will increase General Motors' costs and result in General Motors needing to receive higher prices to produce the same level of output. If workers and firms across the economy are adjusting to the price level being higher than expected, the *SRAS* curve will shift to the left. If they are adjusting to the price level being lower than expected, the *SRAS* curve will shift to the right.

Unexpected Changes in the Price of an Important Natural Resource An unexpected increase or decrease in the price of an important natural resource can cause firms' costs to be different from what they had expected. Oil prices can be particularly volatile. Some firms use oil in the production process. Other firms use products, such as plastics, that are made from oil. If oil prices rise unexpectedly, the costs of production will rise for these firms. Some utilities also burn oil to generate electricity, so electricity prices will rise. Rising oil prices lead to rising gasoline prices, which raise transportation costs for many firms. Because firms face rising costs, they will only supply the same level of output at higher prices, and the short-run aggregate supply curve will shift to the left. An unexpected event that causes the short-run aggregate supply curve to shift is known as a **supply shock**. Supply shocks are often caused by an unexpected increase or decrease in the price of an important natural resource. In September 2005, the U.S. economy was hit with a different type of supply shock when hurricane Katrina slammed into the Gulf Coast region. Many people were killed, the city of New Orleans had to be evacuated, and as many as one million people in the region were forced to relocate. The Congressional Budget Office estimated that up to 400,000 jobs were temporarily lost because of the hurricane. About one-quarter

Supply shock An unexpected event that causes the short-run aggregate supply curve to shift.

of U.S. oil and natural gas output comes from the Gulf Coast, and Katrina disrupted about half of this output. The fall in oil production caused prices to soar, with the price of gasoline rising above $3 per gallon.

Because the U.S. economy has experienced inflation every year since the 1930s, workers and firms always expect next year's price level to be higher than this year's price level. Holding everything else constant, expectations of a higher price level will cause the *SRAS* curve to shift to the left. But everything else is not constant because every year the U.S. labor force and the U.S. capital stock expand and changes in technology occur, which cause the *SRAS* curve to shift to the right. Whether in any particular year the *SRAS* curve shifts to the left or to the right depends on which of these variables has the largest impact during that year.

Table 24-2 summarizes the most important variables that cause the *SRAS* curve to shift. It is important to notice that the table shows the shift in the *SRAS* curve that results from an *increase* in each of the variables. A *decrease* in these variables would cause the *SRAS* curve to shift in the opposite direction.

TABLE 24-2

Variables That Shift the Short-Run Aggregate Supply Curve

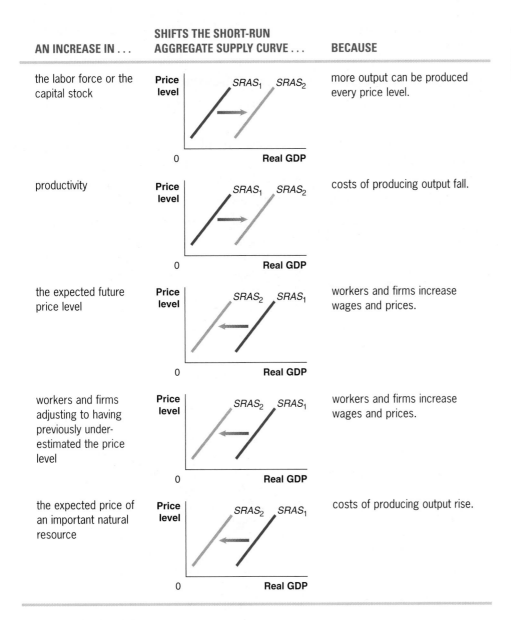

AN INCREASE IN . . .	SHIFTS THE SHORT-RUN AGGREGATE SUPPLY CURVE . . .	BECAUSE
the labor force or the capital stock		more output can be produced every price level.
productivity		costs of producing output fall.
the expected future price level		workers and firms increase wages and prices.
workers and firms adjusting to having previously under-estimated the price level		workers and firms increase wages and prices.
the expected price of an important natural resource		costs of producing output rise.

24.3 | Use the aggregate demand and aggregate supply model to illustrate the difference between short-run and long-run macroeconomic equilibrium.

Macroeconomic Equilibrium in the Long Run and the Short Run

Now that we have discussed the components of the aggregate demand and aggregate supply model, we can use it to analyze changes in real GDP and the price level. In Figure 24-4, we bring the aggregate demand curve, the short-run aggregate supply curve, and the long-run aggregate supply curve together in one graph, to show the *long-run macroeconomic equilibrium* for the economy. In the figure, equilibrium occurs at real GDP of $10.0 trillion and a price level of 100. Notice that in long-run equilibrium, the short-run aggregate supply curve and the aggregate demand curve intersect at a point on the long-run aggregate supply curve. Because equilibrium occurs at a point along the long-run aggregate supply curve, we know the economy is at potential real GDP: Firms will be operating at their normal level of capacity, and everyone who wants a job will have one, except the structurally and frictionally unemployed. We know, however, that the economy is often not in long-run macroeconomic equilibrium. In the following section, we discuss the economic forces that can push the economy away from long-run equilibrium.

Recessions, Expansions, and Supply Shocks

Because the full analysis of the aggregate demand and aggregate supply model can be complicated, we begin with a simplified case, using two assumptions:

1 The economy has not been experiencing any inflation. The price level is currently 100, and workers and firms expect it to remain at 100 in the future.

2 The economy is not experiencing any long-run growth. Potential real GDP is $10.0 trillion and will remain at that level in the future.

These assumptions are simplifications because in reality, the U.S. economy has experienced at least some inflation every year since the 1930s, and the potential real GDP also increases every year. However, the assumptions allow us to understand more easily the key ideas of the aggregate demand and aggregate supply model. In this section, we examine the short-run and long-run effects of recessions, expansions, and supply shocks.

Figure 24-4

Long-Run Macroeconomic Equilibrium

In long-run macroeconomic equilibrium, the *AD* and *SRAS* curves intersect at a point on the *LRAS* curve. In this case, equilibrium occurs at real GDP of $10.0 trillion and a price level of 100.

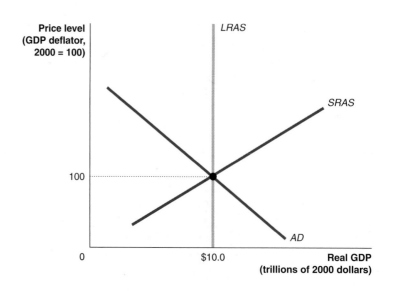

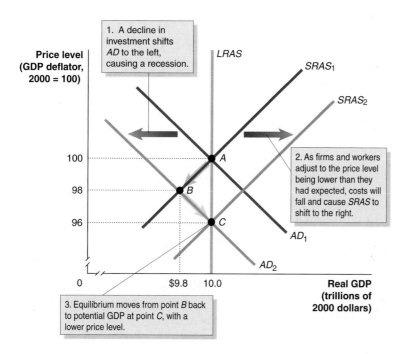

Figure 24-5

The Short-Run and Long-Run Effects of a Decrease in Aggregate Demand

In the short run, a decrease in aggregate demand causes a recession. In the long run, it causes only a decrease in the price level.

Recession

The short-run effect of a decline in aggregate demand. Suppose that an outbreak of fighting in the Middle East causes firms to become pessimistic about the future profitability of new spending on factories and equipment. The decline in investment that results will shift the aggregate demand curve to the left, from AD_1 to AD_2, as shown in Figure 24-5. The economy moves from point A to a new *short-run macroeconomic equilibrium*, where the AD_2 curve intersects the *SRAS* curve at point B. In the new short-run equilibrium, real GDP has declined from $10.0 trillion to $9.8 trillion and is below its potential level. This lower level of GDP will result in declining profitability for many firms and layoffs for some workers: The economy will be in recession.

Adjustment back to potential GDP in the long run. We know that the recession will eventually end because there are forces at work that push the economy back to potential GDP in the long run. Figure 24-5 also shows how the economy moves from recession back to potential GDP. The shift from AD_1 to AD_2 initially leads to a short-run equilibrium with the price level having fallen from 100 to 98 (point B). Workers and firms will begin to adjust to the price level being lower than they had expected it to be. Workers will be willing to accept lower wages—because each dollar of wages is able to buy more goods and services—and firms will be willing to accept lower prices. In addition, the unemployment resulting from the recession will make workers more willing to accept lower wages, and the decline in demand will make firms more willing to accept lower prices. As a result, the SRAS curve will shift to the right, from $SRAS_1$ to $SRAS_2$. At this point, the economy will be back in long-run equilibrium (point C). The shift from $SRAS_1$ to $SRAS_2$ will not happen instantly. It may take the economy several years to return to potential GDP. The important conclusion is that a decline in aggregate demand causes a recession in the short run, but in the long run, it causes only a decline in the price level.

Economists refer to the process of adjustment back to potential GDP just described as an *automatic mechanism* because it occurs without any actions by the government. An alternative to waiting for the automatic mechanism to end the recession is for the government to use monetary and fiscal policy to shift the AD curve to the right and restore potential GDP more quickly. We will discuss monetary and fiscal policy in Chapters 26 and 27. Economists debate whether it is better to wait for the automatic mechanism to end recessions or whether it is better to use monetary and fiscal policy.

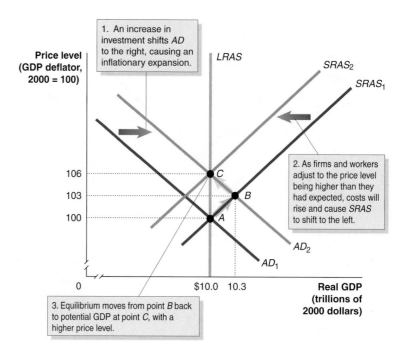

Figure 24-6 | The Short-Run and Long-Run Effects of an Increase

in Aggregate Demand

In the short run, an increase in aggregate demand causes an increase in real GDP. In the long run, it causes only an increase in the price level.

Expansion

The short-run effect of an increase in aggregate demand. Suppose that instead of becoming pessimistic, many firms become optimistic about the future profitability of new investment, as happened during the information technology and telecommunications booms of the late 1990s. The resulting increase in investment will shift the AD curve to the right, as shown in Figure 24-6. Equilibrium moves from point A to point B. Real GDP rises from $10.0 trillion to $10.3 trillion, and the price level rises from 100 to 103. The economy will be above potential real GDP: Firms are operating beyond their normal level of capacity, and some workers are employed who ordinarily would be structurally or frictionally unemployed or who would not be in the labor force.

Adjustment back to potential GDP in the long run. Just as an automatic mechanism brings the economy back to potential GDP from a recession, an automatic mechanism brings the economy back from a short-run equilibrium beyond potential GDP. Figure 24-6 illustrates this mechanism. The shift from AD_1 to AD_2 initially leads to a short-run equilibrium, with the price level rising from 100 to 103 (point B). Workers and firms will begin to adjust to the price level being higher than they had expected. Workers will push for higher wages—because each dollar of wages is able to buy fewer goods and services—and firms will charge higher prices. In addition, the low levels of unemployment resulting from the expansion will make it easier for workers to negotiate for higher wages, and the increase in demand will make it easier for firms to receive higher prices. As a result, the SRAS curve will shift to the left, from $SRAS_1$ to $SRAS_2$. At this point, the economy will be back in long-run equilibrium. Once again, the shift from

$SRAS_1$ to $SRAS_2$ will not happen instantly. The process of returning to potential GDP may stretch out for more than a year.

Supply Shock

The short-run effect of a supply shock. Suppose oil prices increase substantially. This supply shock will increase many firms' costs and cause the $SRAS$ curve to shift to the left, as shown in panel (a) of Figure 24-7. Notice that the price level is higher in the new short-run equilibrium (102 rather than 100), but real GDP is lower ($9.7 trillion rather than $10 trillion). This unpleasant combination of inflation and recession is called **stagflation**.

Stagflation A combination of inflation and recession, usually resulting from a supply shock.

Adjustment back to potential GDP in the long run. The recession caused by a supply shock increases unemployment and reduces output. This eventually results in workers being willing to accept lower wages and firms being willing to accept lower prices. In panel (b) of Figure 24-7, the short-run aggregate supply curve shifts from $SRAS_2$ to $SRAS_1$, moving the economy from point B back to point A. Potential GDP is regained at the original price level. It may take several years for this process to be completed. An alternative would be to use monetary and fiscal policy to shift the aggregate demand to the right. Using policy in this way would bring the economy back to potential GDP more quickly but would result in a permanently higher price level.

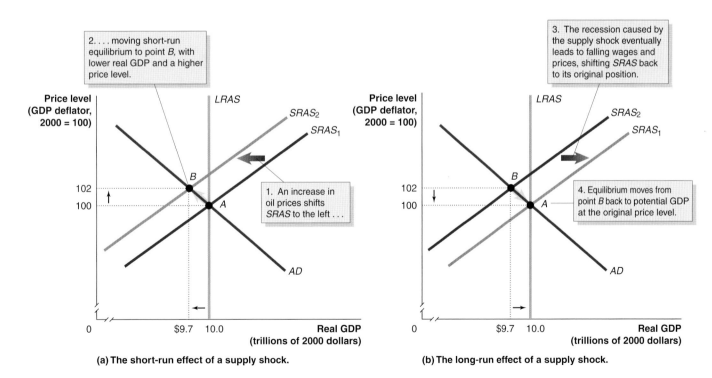

(a) The short-run effect of a supply shock.

(b) The long-run effect of a supply shock.

Figure 24-7 | The Short-Run and Long-Run Effects of a Supply Shock

Panel (a) shows that a supply shock, such as a large increase in oil prices, will cause a recession and a higher price level in the short run. The recession caused by the supply shock increases unemployment and reduces output. In panel (b), rising unemployment and falling output result in workers being willing to accept lower wages and firms being willing to accept lower prices. The short-run aggregate supply curve shifts from $SRAS_2$ to $SRAS_1$. Equilibrium moves from point B back to potential GDP and the original price level at point A.

24.4 | Use the dynamic aggregate demand and aggregate supply model to analyze macroeconomic conditions.

A Dynamic Aggregate Demand and Aggregate Supply Model

The basic aggregate demand and aggregate supply model used so far in this chapter gives us important insights into how short-run macroeconomic equilibrium is determined. Unfortunately, the model also gives us some misleading results. For instance, it incorrectly predicts that a recession caused by the aggregate demand curve shifting to the left will cause the price level to fall, which has not happened for an entire year since the 1930s. The difficulty with the basic model arises from the following two assumptions we made: (1) that the economy does not experience continuing inflation and (2) that the economy does not experience long-run growth. We can develop a more useful aggregate demand and aggregate supply model by dropping these assumptions. The result will be a model that takes into account that the economy is not *static*, with an unchanging level of potential real GDP and no continuing inflation, but *dynamic*, with potential real GDP that grows over time and inflation that continues every year. We can create a *dynamic aggregate demand and aggregate supply model* by making three changes to the basic model.

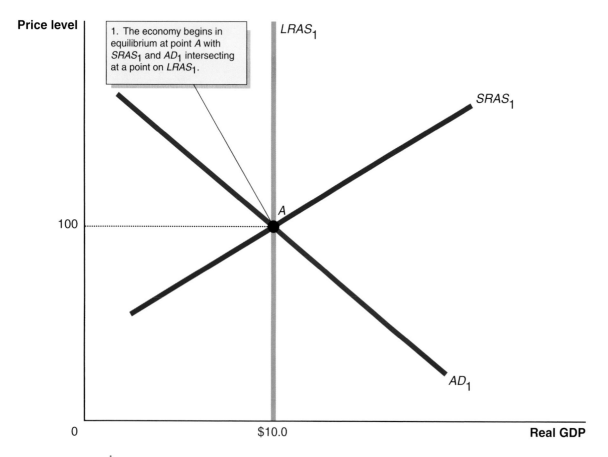

Figure 24-8 | A Dynamic Aggregate Demand and Aggregate Supply Model

We start with the basic aggregate demand and aggregate supply model.

These changes recognize the following important macroeconomic facts:

- Potential real GDP increases continually, shifting the long-run aggregate supply curve to the right.

- During most years, the aggregate demand curve will be shifting to the right.

- Except during periods when workers and firms expect high rates of inflation, the short-run aggregate supply curve will be shifting to the right.

Figure 24-8 incorporates these three changes to the basic aggregate demand and aggregate supply model. We start with $SRAS_1$ and AD_1 intersecting at point A at a price level of 100 and real GDP of $10.0 trillion. Because this intersection occurs at a point on $LRAS_1$, we know the economy is in long-run equilibrium. The long-run aggregate supply curve shifts to the right from $LRAS_1$ to $LRAS_2$. This shift occurs because during the year potential real GDP increases as the U.S. labor force and the U.S. capital stock increase and technological progress occurs. The short-run aggregate supply curve shifts from $SRAS_1$ to $SRAS_2$. This shift occurs because the same variables that cause the long-run aggregate supply to shift to the right will also increase the quantity of goods and services that firms are willing to supply in the short run. Finally, the aggregate demand curve shifts to the right from AD_1 to AD_2. The aggregate demand curve shifts for several reasons: As population grows and incomes rise, consumption will increase over time. As the economy grows, firms will expand capacity, and new firms will be formed, increasing investment. An expanding population and an expanding economy require increased government services, such as more police officers and teachers, so government purchases will increase.

The new equilibrium in Figure 24-8 occurs at point B, where AD_2 intersects $SRAS_2$ on $LRAS_2$. In the new equilibrium, the price level remains at 100, while real GDP increases to $10.5 trillion. Notice that there has been no inflation because the price level is unchanged at 100. There was no inflation because aggregate demand and aggregate supply shifted to the right by exactly as much as long-run aggregate supply. We would not expect this to be the typical situation for two reasons: First, the $SRAS$ curve is also affected by workers' and firms' expectations of future changes in the price level and by supply shocks. These variables can partially, or completely, offset the normal tendency of the $SRAS$ curve to shift to the right over the course of a year. Second, we know that sometimes consumers, firms, and the government may cut back expenditures. This reduced spending will result in the aggregate demand curve shifting to the right less than it normally would or, possibly, shifting to the left. In fact, as we will see shortly, *changes in the price level and in real GDP in the short run are determined by the shifts in the* SRAS *and* AD *curves.*

What Is the Usual Cause of Inflation?

The dynamic aggregate demand and aggregate supply model provides a more accurate explanation than the basic model of the source of most inflation. If total spending in the economy grows faster than total production, prices rise. Figure 24-9 illustrates this point by showing that if the AD curve shifts to the right by more than the $LRAS$ curve, inflation results because equilibrium occurs at a higher price level, point B. In the new equilibrium, point B, the $SRAS$ curve has shifted to the right by less than the $LRAS$ curve because the anticipated increase in prices offsets some of the technological change and increases in the labor force and capital stock that occur during the year. Although inflation is generally the result of total spending growing faster than total production, a shift to the left of the short-run aggregate supply curve can also cause an increase in the price level, as we saw earlier in the discussion of supply shocks.

As we saw in Figure 24-8, if aggregate demand increases by the same amount as short-run and long-run aggregate supply, the price level will not change. In this case, the economy experiences economic growth without inflation.

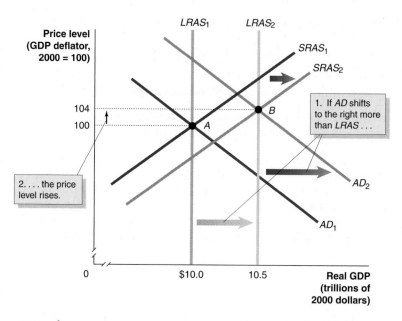

Figure 24-9 | Using Dynamic Aggregate Demand and Aggregate Supply to Understand Inflation

The most common cause of inflation is total spending increasing faster than total production.
1. The economy begins at point *A*, with real GDP of $10.0 trillion and a price level of 100. An increase in full-employment real GDP from $10.0 trillion to $10.5 trillion causes long-run aggregate supply to shift from *LRAS*$_1$ to *LRAS*$_2$. Aggregate demand shifts from *AD*$_1$ to *AD*$_2$.
2. Because *AD* shifts to the right by more than the *LRAS* curve, the price level in the new equilibrium rises from 100 to 104.

The Slow Recovery from the Recession of 2001

We can use the dynamic aggregate demand and aggregate supply model to analyze the slow recovery from the recession of 2001. The recession began in March 2001, as the long economic expansion of the 1990s ended. The recession was caused by a decline in aggregate demand. Several factors contributed to this decline:

-   *The end of the stock market "bubble."* In the late 1990s, stock prices increased rapidly. Higher stock prices partly resulted from higher corporate profits, but as we saw in Chapter 1, they were also due to the excessive optimism of investors about the future of dot-com companies. The increase in stock prices between 1995 and 2000 increased the wealth of U.S. households by $9 trillion. Stock prices began to fall in spring 2000 and eventually fell almost as far as they had risen. By 2002, the total value of stocks had declined by $7 trillion from their peak of two years before. The fall in stock prices reduced spending by households and firms. Firms that had financed investment spending by issuing new stock now had a more difficult time raising funds.

-   *Excessive investment in information technology.* During the late 1990s, many firms overestimated the future profitability of investment in information technology. For example, telecommunications firms laid many more miles of fiber-optic cable than there was demand in the short run. Some firms also invested in computers and software in anticipation of the year 2000 (Y2K) problem. This problem arose from the technical difficulty many older computers had in correctly interpreting dates in years after 1999. Once older software and computers had been replaced, spending declined. Similarly, many firms had invested heavily to establish a presence on the Internet. When their Internet sales proved disappointing, the companies had more computers than they needed. For these reasons, by spring 2001, many companies had sharply cut back on their investment spending.

- ***The terrorist attacks of September 11, 2001.*** The terrorist attacks on New York and Washington, DC, increased the level of uncertainty in the economy. Many feared further attacks would occur, and they were uncertain how the economy would respond. When firms and households face uncertainty, they often postpone spending until the uncertainty is resolved.

- ***The corporate accounting scandals.*** As we saw in Chapter 7, the top managers of some corporations, such as WorldCom, Tyco, and Enron, manipulated their financial statements during the stock market boom to make their corporations appear more profitable than they actually were. When these accounting manipulations were finally brought to light, some investors lost faith in the accuracy of corporate financial statements, which helped depress stock prices and added to the uncertainty in the economy.

Few economists were surprised that the long expansion of the 1990s eventually ended in recession. Although forecasting the exact date the recession would begin was very difficult, it was inevitable that the expansion would end, just as all previous expansions had. Some economists were surprised, however, at the weakness of the expansion that began when the recession ended in November 2001. Figure 24-10 illustrates the changes in the economy from 2001 to 2002 and shows that the economy remained well below potential GDP during 2002.

In Figure 24-10, the *AD* curve shifts to the right much less than does the *LRAS* curve. As a result, the price level increases only from 102.4 in 2001 to 104.2 in 2002, for a very low inflation rate of 1.8 percent. Real GDP increases only from $9.9 trillion to $10.1 trillion,

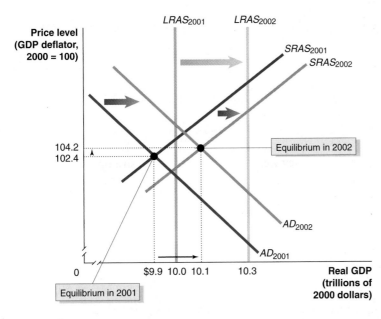

Figure 24-10 | Using Dynamic Aggregate Demand and Aggregate Supply to Understand the Recovery from the 2001 Recession

Between 2001 and 2002, *AD* shifted to the right but not by nearly enough to offset the shift to the right of *LRAS*, which represented the increase in potential real GDP from $10.0 trillion to $10.3 trillion. Although real GDP increased from $9.9 trillion in 2001 to $10.1 trillion in 2002, this was still far below the potential real GDP, shown by $LRAS_{2002}$. As a result, the unemployment rate rose from 4.7 percent in 2001 to 5.8 percent in 2002. Because the increase in aggregate demand was small, the price level increased only from 102.4 in 2001 to 104.2 in 2002, so the inflation rate for 2002 was only 1.8 percent.

which is below the potential level of $10.3 trillion, shown by $LRAS_{2002}$. Not surprisingly, the unemployment rate actually rose from 4.7 percent in 2001 to 5.8 percent in 2002.

The increase in aggregate demand during 2002 was weak because the factors that had caused the recession continued to weigh on the economy. Stock prices did not begin to rise significantly until 2003. Many firms still did not feel the need to increase investment spending, particularly on information technology, on which they had spent heavily during the late 1990s. Uncertainty remained high as the federal government continued the war on terrorism and prepared for the invasion of Iraq. Finally, each week during 2002 seemed to bring the revelation of a new corporate accounting scandal.

Making
the
Connection

Does Rising Productivity Growth Reduce Employment?

We saw in Chapter 22 that growth in output per worker—labor productivity—is the key to rising living standards over the long run. But if firms can produce more output with the same number of workers, are they less likely to hire additional workers? Some observers argued that this was happening during 2002 and 2003, as productivity and real GDP rose yet employment grew very little. The following two graphs show that productivity—measured as total output of all nonfarm businesses produced per hour worked—did in fact grow very rapidly during 2002 and 2003 and that employment, as measured by the Bureau of Labor Statistics establishment survey, declined.

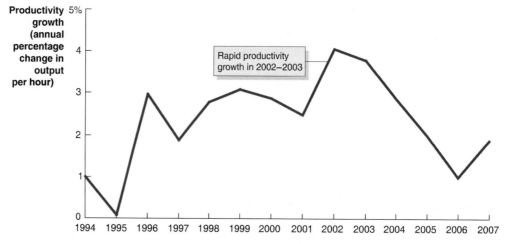

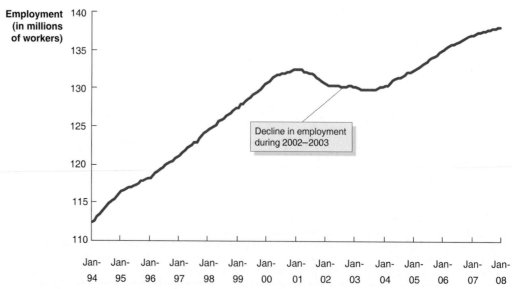

In the dynamic aggregate demand and aggregate supply model, the higher the growth of productivity during a year, the further to the right the *LRAS* and *SRAS* curves will shift. But rising productivity also leads to rising incomes, in part because rising output per worker makes it possible for firms to pay higher wages. These rising incomes raise consumption spending and allow the *AD* curve to shift to the right by enough to maintain GDP at its potential level. In 2002–2003, however, the economy was still operating below potential GDP, and many firms appeared reluctant to expand employment as rapidly as typically happens during an economic recovery. In these circumstances, rising productivity made it possible for at least some firms to expand output without expanding employment. Most economists agree that rapid productivity growth probably played some role in the slow employment growth of 2002 and 2003, but the effect was only temporary. We know that over the long run, the level of employment is determined by population growth and by factors—such as the level of retirement benefits and government unemployment insurance payments—that affect the fraction of the population in the labor force. The level of employment is not determined in the long run by the rate of productivity growth. In fact, between 1994 and 2007, the level of productivity in the U.S. economy increased by 38 percent, while during the same period, the number of people employed increased by almost 26 million. If we look at the two graphs for the whole period, we can see that productivity growth only affects employment in the short run. Productivity fluctuated considerably over those 13 years, while except for a few years after the 2001 recession, employment followed a steady upward trend.

YOUR TURN: Test your understanding by doingrelated problem 4.6 on page 844 at the end of this chapter.

The More Rapid Recovery of 2003-2004

The recovery from the recession of 2001 accelerated in the second half of 2003 and through 2004. For several reasons, aggregate demand increased more rapidly than it had during 2002 and early 2003. Low interest rates spurred spending on new houses and helped increase investment spending by firms. Tax cuts increased both consumption and investment spending. Rising stock prices contributed to increased consumption and investment spending. Finally, the value of the dollar declined against most foreign currencies, which helped exports.

Figure 24-11 shows the results of the more rapid increase in aggregate demand during 2004. In 2003, real GDP was 3.7 percent below its potential level, while the unemployment rate was 6.0 percent. The figure shows that the large shift in aggregate demand during 2004 led to an increase in real GDP from $10.3 trillion to $10.8 trillion. This level was still below potential real GDP of $11.0 trillion, but the gap had narrowed to 1.8 percent. As a result, the unemployment rate fell from 6.0 percent to 5.2 percent. The rapid increase in aggregate demand caused a rise in the inflation rate. The price level increased from 106.3 in 2003 to 109.1 in 2004, for an inflation rate of 2.6 percent. This was higher than the inflation rate of 2.0 percent during 2003.

The Economy in 2008: A Growth Slowdown, Recession, or Stagflation?

The business cycle expansion that began with the end of the 2001 recession continued through 2007. By that time, the expansion had lasted longer than the average expansion during the period since 1950. Economic growth was slowing, however, with real GDP falling 0.2 percent in the last quarter of 2007, and rising only 0.9 percent in the first quarter of 2008. Inflation was running at the relatively high rate of 2.7 percent during 2007 and the first quarter of 2008. Rising inflation reflected the rising prices of oil and other commodities. The price of a barrel of oil had been below $30 in 2004 but was

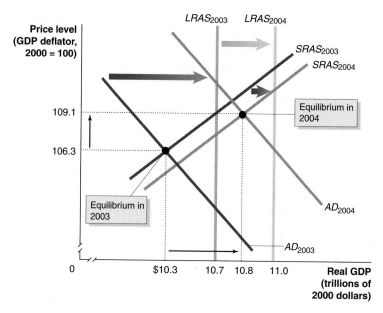

Figure 24-11 | Using Dynamic Aggregate Demand and Aggregate Supply

to Understand the More Rapid Recovery of 2003–2004

The figure shows that the large shift in aggregate demand during 2004 led to an increase in real GDP from $10.3 trillion to $10.8 trillion. This was still below the potential real GDP of $11.0 trillion, but the gap had narrowed to 1.8 percent. As a result, the unemployment rate fell from 6.0 percent to 5.2 percent. The rapid increase in aggregate demand caused a rise in the inflation rate. The price level increased from 106.3 in 2003 to 109.1 in 2004, for an inflation rate of 2.6 percent.

above $140 in mid-2008. Gasoline prices rose from $1.50 per gallon in early 2004 to more than $4.00 per gallon in mid-2008. Rising oil prices resulted in the SRAS being to the left of where it would have been, which increased inflation and deceased real GDP growth. Many economists believe that rising gasoline prices also reduced the growth in aggregate demand by reducing spending on other goods and services. Managers at Wal-Mart believed that the slow increase in sales at many of their stores was due to consumers having less income left to spend after filling up their cars.

The economy in 2008 was also feeling the effects of hard times in the housing market. When the economy began to fall into recession during 2001, the Federal Reserve had taken actions to lower interest rates. As the interest rates on mortgage loans declined, more consumers began to buy new homes. New home sales rose 46 percent, from 877,000 in 2000 to 1,283,000 in 2005. This increase in new home sales helped reduce the severity of the 2001 recession and sustain the following expansion. But by 2005, it had become clear that some new construction and some part of the rapidly rising prices for new and existing homes was due to a speculative "bubble." A bubble occurs when people become less concerned with the underlying value of an asset—either a physical asset, such as a house, or a financial asset, such as a stock—and focus instead on expectations of the price of the asset increasing. In some areas of the country, many houses were being purchased by investors who intended to resell them for higher prices than they paid for them and did not intend to live in them. Speculative bubbles eventually come to an end, and the housing bubble began to deflate in 2006. By mid-2008, new home sales were running at an annual rate of less than 525,000, down more than 60 percent from the peak in mid-2005. Housing prices were declining as well. The decline in the housing market slowed the growth of aggregate demand as spending on residential construction—a component of investment spending—declined. In addition, many banks that had been lending money to borrowers with weak credit histories began to tighten their lending standards, resulting in a "credit crunch" as households and firms had greater difficulty obtaining loans.

In mid-2008, economists were divided over whether higher oil prices, a declining housing sector, and a credit crunch would be sufficient to push the economy into a recession. While rising oil and food prices caused hardships for some consumers, the overall inflation rate remained well below what had been experienced during periods of stagflation in the 1970s. At the very least, though, slowing growth in real GDP was leading to rising unemployment and falling profits.

Solved Problem | 24-4

Showing the Oil Shock of 1974–1975 on a Dynamic Aggregate Demand and Aggregate Supply Graph

The 1974–1975 recession clearly illustrates how a supply shock affects the economy. Following the Arab–Israeli War of 1973, the Organization of Petroleum Exporting Countries (OPEC) increased the price of a barrel of oil from less than $3 to more than $10. Use this information and the statistics in the following table to draw a dynamic aggregate demand and aggregate supply graph showing macroeconomic equilibrium for 1974 and 1975. Assume that the

aggregate demand curve did not shift between 1974 and 1975. Provide a brief explanation of your graph.

	ACTUAL REAL GDP	POTENTIAL REAL GDP	PRICE LEVEL
1974	$4.32 trillion	$4.35 trillion	34.7
1975	$4.31 trillion	$4.50 trillion	38.0

Source: U.S. Bureau of Economic Analysis.

SOLVING THE PROBLEM:

Step 1: Review the chapter material. This problem is about using the dynamic aggregate demand and aggregate supply model, so you may want to review the section "A Dynamic Aggregate Demand and Aggregate Supply Model," which begins on page 828.

Step 2: Use the information in the table to draw the graph. You need to draw five curves: SRAS and LRAS for both 1974 and 1975 and AD, which is the same for both years. You know that the two LRAS curves will be vertical lines at the values given for potential GDP in the table. Because of the large supply shock, you know that the SRAS curve shifted to the left. You are instructed to assume that the AD curve did not shift. Your graph should look like this:

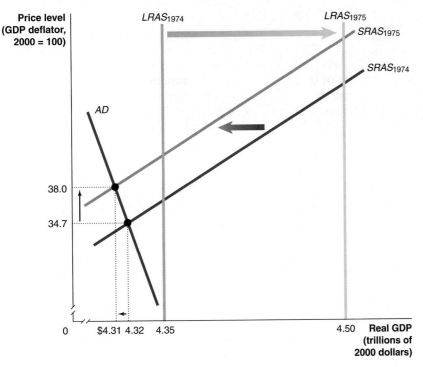

Step 3: **Explain your graph.** $LRAS_{1974}$ and $LRAS_{1975}$ are at the levels of potential real GDP for each year. Macroeconomic equilibrium for 1974 occurs where the AD curve intersects the $SRAS_{1974}$ curve, with real GDP of \$4.32 trillion and a price level of 34.7. Macroeconomic equilibrium for 1975 occurs where the AD curve intersects the $SRAS_{1975}$ curve, with real GDP of \$4.31 trillion and a price level of 38.0.

EXTRA CREDIT: As a result of the supply shock, the economy moved from an equilibrium output just below potential GDP in 1974 (the recession actually began right at the end of 1973) to an equilibrium well below potential GDP in 1975. With real GDP in 1975 about 4.2 percent below its potential level, the unemployment rate soared from 5.6 percent in 1974 to 8.5 percent in 1975.

YOUR TURN: For more practice, do related problems 4.4 and 4.5 on page 844 at the end of this chapter.

>> **End Solved Problem 24-4**

Making
the
Connection

Can FedEx and the U.S. Economy Withstand High Oil Prices?

FedEx burns a lot of gasoline and jet fuel to power its 70,000 trucks and 672 aircraft worldwide. An increase in oil prices causes FedEx to raise the prices it charges its customers, which reduces the quantity of packages those customers ship. If rising oil prices affect enough firms, the short-run aggregate supply curve will shift to the left, potentially pushing the economy into recession. This outcome occurred when oil prices rose from \$3 per barrel to \$10 per barrel in the early 1970s, pushing the U.S. economy into recession during 1974 and 1975. During those years, real GDP declined, and the unemployment rate rose to 9 percent.

FedEx's trucks and jets have become more fuel efficient.

The effects on the economy of earlier "oil shocks" led some economists during the mid-2000s to predict that the United States would experience a recession as oil prices rose from about \$34 per barrel in 2004 to over \$140 per barrel in mid-2008. The increase in the price of oil appeared to be caused by increased demand in rapidly growing economies, particularly India and China, and by the difficulty in developing new supplies of oil in the short run. Surprisingly, at least through mid-2008, real GDP continued to grow despite soaring oil prices. Had the economy become less vulnerable to high oil prices? Some economists argued that, in fact, this was the case. Because of earlier increases in the price of oil, by the mid-2000s, many firms had switched to less-oil-dependent production processes. For example, FedEx and other firms used more fuel efficient jets and trucks. As a result, the U.S. economy was consuming almost 60 percent less oil per dollar of GDP than it had in the mid-1970s. Today, oil price increases do not shift the short-run aggregate supply curve as far to the left as similar increases did 30 years ago.

In addition, the oil price increases of the mid-2000s occurred gradually, which gave individuals and firms time to adjust. Earlier increases in the price of oil had occurred more abruptly—usually as a result of conflict in the Middle East, where at the time more than half of world oil production took place. Finally, the oil price increases of the mid-2000s took place at a time when the U.S. economy was growing, so it was easier to absorb the adverse effects of higher oil prices. Economist Keith Sill of the Federal Reserve Bank of Philadelphia has estimated that a 10 percent increase in oil prices will result in a temporary reduction in the annual growth of real GDP of about 0.5 percent. So, higher oil prices reduced the increases in real GDP during the mid-2000s but at least through mid-2008 had not yet tipped the economy into recession. It remained to be seen, though, whether the impact on aggregate demand of $4.00 per gallon gasoline and rising food prices would eventually lead to a recession.

Sources: Justin Lahart and Connor Dougherty, "U.S. Retools Economy, Curbing Thirst for Oil," *Wall Street Journal*, August 12, 2008, p. A1; and Keith Sill, "The Macroeconomics of Oil Shocks," *Business Review*, First Quarter 2007, pp. 21–31.

YOUR TURN: Test your understanding by doingrelated problem 4.13 on page 845 at the end of this chapter.

Economics in YOUR Life!

>> Continued from page 811

At the beginning of this chapter, we asked you to consider whether during a recession your employer is likely to reduce your pay and cut the prices of the products he or she sells. In this chapter, the dynamic aggregate demand and aggregate supply model showed that even during a recession, the price level rarely falls. In fact, the price level in the United States has not fallen from one year to the next since the 1930s. A typical firm is therefore unlikely to cut its prices during a recession. So, the owner of the coffeehouse you work in will probably not cut the price of lattes unless sales have declined drastically. We also saw that most firms are more reluctant to cut wages than to increase them because wage cuts can have a negative effect on worker morale and productivity. Given that you are a highly skilled barista, your employer is particularly unlikely to cut your wages for fear that you might quit and work for a competitor.

Conclusion

Chapter 3 demonstrated the power of the microeconomic model of demand and supply in explaining how the prices and quantities of individual products are determined. This chapter showed that we need a different model to explain the behavior of the whole economy. We saw that the macroeconomic model of aggregate demand and aggregate supply explains fluctuations in real GDP and the price level.

One of the great disagreements among economists and political leaders is whether the federal government should intervene to try to reduce fluctuations in real GDP and keep the unemployment and inflation rates low. We explore this important issue in Chapters 26 and 27, but first, in Chapter 25, we consider the role money plays in the economy.

Read *An Inside Look* on the next page to learn how a decline in the growth rate of real GDP affected UPS.

Profits at UPS Signal Slow Growth in the U.S. Economy

WALL STREET JOURNAL, APRIL 26, 2007

Freight Carrier Weakness Shows Retailer Uncertainty

(a) Profit declines and lackluster outlooks from three freight-transportation giants, led by United Parcel Service Inc., indicate rising uncertainty about the economy among retailers and other big customers ahead of the important holiday-shipping season.

Preparations for the holiday-freight rush—when goods from Asia and other overseas suppliers fill ships, trains, planes and trucks—gear up months before the surge later in the year. Slowness now casts growing doubt on a turnaround in shipping volumes that had been predicted for this summer and fall.

"The boom in cargo imports has buoyed the whole shipping system for the last three years, but we can't count on that again this year," said Paul Bingham, a principal at Global Insight Inc., a consulting firm in Waltham, Mass., that expects U.S. containerized imports to rise 6% this year, down from its previous forecast of 7% growth.

(b) Major freight carriers, such as UPS, which posted its first quarterly decline in net income in more than three years, are deep in discussions with their largest customers about how to handle their holiday-season cargo. Early indications aren't encouraging,

with some customers waiting longer than usual to order inventory and line up shipping capacity because of uncertainty about the economy, according to some freight-industry analysts and company executives.

"In talking to our customer base, today they are not real optimistic" about the peak season, Scott Davis, UPS vice chairman and chief financial officer, said in an interview. "They are concerned with where their customers are."

In the first quarter, package-delivery volume at Atlanta-based UPS rose 0.4% from the year earlier to an average of 15.1 million packages a day. That was the slowest growth rate in two years. U.S. deliveries, generating nearly 90% of the company's volume, posted their first decline in four years. Mr. Davis said the economy has slowed "more than we anticipated," adding that UPS is considering "hundreds of initiatives" to trim expenses amid the slump.

In addition to UPS's profit decline of 14%, railroad operator Norfolk Southern Corp. said its first-quarter profit fell 6.6%, hurt by continued weakness in the automotive and housing sectors. Trucking carrier Arkansas Best Corp., Fort Smith, Ark., saw its profit shrink by 22%, but said a cost-cutting program begun last fall helped it offset weakened freight demand.

(c) The stubbornly persistent freight slowdown that began last year has been

particularly tough on trucking companies, which are facing overcapacity and pressure to cut prices because they increased truck purchases before stricter engine-emission standards took effect. Railroad shipments fell nearly 5% in the first quarter, but tight capacity has helped railroad operators maintain their pricing power so far. Norfolk Southern, of Norfolk, Va., said pricing remained strong in the first quarter.

Norfolk Southern didn't indicate when it anticipates a rebound in freight volume. But railroad Burlington Northern Santa Fe Corp. warned earlier this week that it is concerned traffic levels could remain soft for the rest of the year.

For the past two years, retailers and importers were placing orders by now with non-U.S. suppliers for merchandise to sell in the second half, including Christmas, said Mr. Bingham, the freight-industry consultant. Ordering early helped reduce the risk of delay or lost sales if ports and rail lines became congested. This year, though, many importers are less confident of growth prospects and less worried about logistical snags, so ocean-shipping lines are seeing lower booking levels for the holiday-shipping season. . . .

Source: Daniel Machalaba and Corey Dade, "Freight Carrier Weakness Shows Retailer Uncertainty," *Wall Street Journal,* April 26, 2007, p. A4. Reprinted by permission of the *Wall Street Journal* via Copyright Clearance Center.

Key Points in the Article

This article discusses why UPS and other freight-transportation companies reported weak earnings for the first quarter of 2007 and indicates that this weakness might persist for much of the year. The article explains that UPS attributed its weak earnings to the slowing growth rate of the U.S. economy. Freight-transportation companies' earnings are dependent on the volume of shipments to retailers; in a slowing economy, retailers typically reduce their orders from manufacturers as they carry smaller planned inventories than usual. Finally, the article mentions that this slowdown in freight transportation has been particularly hard on trucking companies, which find themselves with excess capacity—too many trucks—thanks to the combination of a fall in ground-freight transportation volume and a 2007 environmental regulation that introduced a new—and relatively untested—heavy-truck engine technology. To reduce their dependence on higher-priced trucks with the new engine technology, many trucking firms increased their purchases of trucks during 2006.

Analyzing the News

(a) UPS, together with railroad-operator Norfolk Southern and truck-carrier Arkansas Best, warned investors of weak profit growth for 2007. Meanwhile, the Department of Commerce announced that the growth in U.S. real GDP slowed to 0.6 percent in the first quarter of the year, and some economists forecast that the U.S. economy would continue to grow slowly through much of 2007. UPS attributed its falling profits to the slow growth of the U.S. economy. During the second and third quarters of each year, transportation companies such as UPS typically generate a large portion of their annual profits by shipping goods to retailers, which accumulate planned inventories as they prepare for the holiday shopping season in the fourth quarter of the year. However, in a slowing economy, retailers typically carry relatively smaller planned inventories and, hence, have relatively less need for the freight-transportation services of companies such as UPS.

(b) Although the volume of goods that UPS shipped in the first quarter of 2007 grew from a year earlier, the growth was just 0.4 percent, reflecting the weak growth of the U.S. economy over the same period. Put differently, earnings at UPS did not suffer because U.S. aggregate demand fell, rather, earnings suffered because the short-run increase in real GDP was less than the increase in potential real GDP. We can use the dynamic aggregate demand and aggregate supply model that you learned about in this chapter to analyze what happened to the U.S. economy from the first quarter of 2006 to the first quarter of 2007. The figure shows that in the first quarter of 2006, the U.S. economy was in a short-run macroeconomic equilibrium with real GDP of $11.2 trillion and a price level—as measured by the GDP implicit price deflator—of 115.4. During the remainder of 2006 and the early part of 2007, aggregate demand, short-run aggregate supply, and long-run aggregate supply all shifted to the right. Consequently, short-run real GDP rose to $11.4 trillion, and the price level rose to 118.8. So, from the first quarter of 2006 to the first quarter of 2007, the U.S. economy experienced growth in real GDP of only 1.8 percent, while the inflation rate was 2.9 percent.

(c) As of the first quarter of 2007, the slowdown in ground-freight transportation had been particularly hard on trucking companies, which had too much capacity thanks to a combination of a fall in ground-freight transportation volume and large truck purchases during 2006. Many ground-freight transportation firms rushed to purchase heavy trucks in 2006, before new environmental regulations—with resulting higher prices—took effect. These firms therefore found themselves with too few goods to ship volume and too many trucks in early 2007.

Thinking Critically

1. Between the first quarter of 2006 and the first quarter of 2007, when U.S. real GDP growth slowed to 0.6 percent, the foreign exchange value of the U.S. dollar fell against most of its major trading partners' currencies. What effect, if any, did this fall in the value of the U.S. dollar have on the magnitude of the rightward shift of *AD* shown in the figure on this page?

2. Freight-transportation companies such as UPS provide domestic shipping services in many countries. How, if at all, might this geographic diversification alter how UPS's earnings would otherwise respond to a slowing U.S. economy?

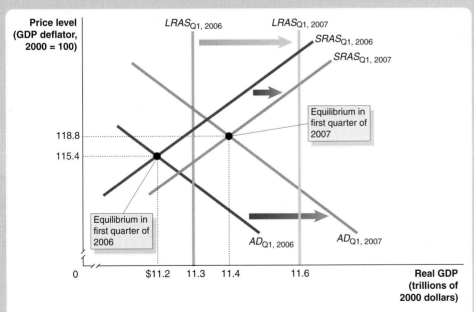

The U.S. economic expansion from the first quarter of 2006 to the first quarter of 2007.

Source: U.S. Bureau of Economic Analysis.

Key Terms

Aggregate demand and aggregate supply model, p. 812

Aggregate demand curve, p. 812

Fiscal policy, p. 815

Long-run aggregate supply curve, p. 819

Menu costs, p. 821

Monetary policy, p. 815

Short-run aggregate supply curve, p. 813

Stagflation, p. 827

Supply shock, p. 822

24.1 | Identify the determinants of aggregate demand and distinguish between a movement along the aggregate demand curve and a shift of the curve, **pages 812–818.**

Aggregate Demand

Summary

The **aggregate demand and aggregate supply model** enables us to explain short-run fluctuations in real GDP and price level. The **aggregate demand curve** shows the relationship between the price level and the level of planned aggregate expenditures by households, firms, and the government. The **short-run aggregate supply curve** shows the relationship in the short run between the price level and the quantity of real GDP supplied by firms. The **long-run aggregate supply curve** shows the relationship in the long run between the price level and the quantity of real GDP supplied. The four components of aggregate demand are consumption (C), investment (I), government purchases (G), and net exports (NX). The aggregate demand curve is downward sloping because a decline in the price level causes consumption, investment, and net exports to increase. If the price level changes but all else remains constant, the economy will move up or down a stationary aggregate demand curve. If any variable other than the price level changes, the aggregate demand curve will shift. The variables that cause the aggregate demand curve to shift are divided into three categories: changes in government policies, changes in the expectations of households and firms, and changes in foreign variables. For example, **monetary policy** involves the actions the Federal Reserve takes to manage the money supply and interest rates to pursue macroeconomic policy objectives. When the Federal Reserve takes actions to change interest rates, consumption and investment spending will change, shifting the aggregate demand curve. **Fiscal policy** involves changes in federal taxes and purchases that are intended to achieve macroeconomic policy objectives. Changes in federal taxes and purchases shift the aggregate demand curve.

[myeconlab] Visit www.myeconlab.com to complete these exercises
Get Ahead of the Curve online and get instant feedback.

Review Questions

1.1 Explain the three reasons the aggregate demand curve slopes downward.

1.2 What are the differences between the AD curve and the demand curve for an individual product, such as apples?

1.3 What are the variables that cause the AD curve to shift? For each variable, identify whether an increase in that variable will cause the AD curve to shift to the right or to the left.

Problems and Applications

1.4 Explain how each of the following events would affect the aggregate demand curve.
   a. An increase in the price level
   b. An increase in government purchases
   c. Higher state income taxes
   d. Higher interest rates
   e. Faster income growth in other countries

1.5 (Related to the *Don't Let This Happen to You!* on page 814) A student was asked to draw an aggregate demand and aggregate supply graph to illustrate the effect of an increase in aggregate supply. The student drew the following graph:
The student explained the graph as follows:

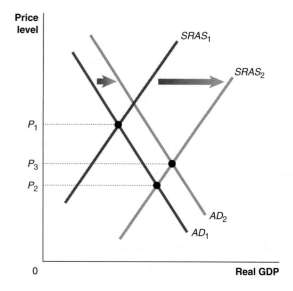

An increase in aggregate supply causes a shift from $SRAS_1$ to $SRAS_2$. Because this shift in the aggregate supply curve results in a lower price level, consumption, investment, and net exports will increase. This change causes the aggregate demand curve to shift to the right, from AD_1 to AD_2. We know that real GDP will increase, but we can't be sure whether the price level will rise or fall because that depends on whether the aggregate supply curve or the aggregate demand curve has shifted farther to the right. I assume that aggregate supply shifts out farther than aggregate demand, so I show the final price level, P_3, as being lower than the initial price level, P_1.

Explain whether you agree or disagree with the student's analysis. Be careful to explain exactly what—if anything—you find wrong with this analysis.

1.6 (Related to *Solved Problem 24-1* on page 816) Explain whether each of the following will cause a shift of the *AD* curve or a movement along the *AD* curve.
a. Firms become more optimistic and increase their spending on machinery and equipment.
b. The federal government increases taxes in an attempt to reduce a budget deficit.
c. The U.S. economy experiences 4 percent inflation.

1.7 According to an article published in *BusinessWeek* in October 2002, "The stock market plunge is weighing heavily on both businesses and consumers." Why would a decline in stock prices "weigh heavily" on businesses and consumers? What were the consequences of this for the economy?

Source: James C. Cooper and Kathleen Madigan, "Consumers: Still Some Pluses among the Minuses," *BusinessWeek*, October 21, 2002.

1.8 (Related to the *Making the Connection* on page 815) Suppose that a consumer in Germany buys a Ford Mustang for a price of $30,000. Do U.S. exports increase by $30,000? Briefly explain.

>> End Learning Objective 24.1

24.2 LEARNING OBJECTIVE | 24.2 | Identify the determinants of aggregate supply and distinguish between a movement along the short-run aggregate supply curve and a shift of the curve, **pages 819–823.**

Aggregate Supply

Summary

 Visit www.myeconlab.com to complete these exercises online and get instant feedback.

The **long-run aggregate supply curve** is a vertical line because in the long run, real GDP is always at its potential level and is unaffected by the price level. The short-run aggregate supply curve slopes upward because workers and firms fail to predict accurately the future price level. The three main explanations of why this failure results in an upward-sloping aggregate supply curve are that (1) contracts make wages and prices "sticky," (2) businesses often adjust wages slowly, and (3) menu costs make some prices sticky. **Menu costs** are the costs to firms of changing prices on menus or catalogs. If the price level changes but all else remains constant, the economy will move up or down a stationary aggregate supply curve. If any variable other than the price level changes, the aggregate supply curve will shift. The aggregate supply curve shifts as a result of increases in the labor force and capital stock, technological change, expected increases or decreases in the future price level, adjustments of workers and firms to errors in past expectations about the price level, and unexpected increases or decreases in the price of an important raw material. A **supply shock** is an unexpected event that causes the short-run aggregate supply curve to shift.

Review Questions

2.1 Explain why the long-run aggregate supply curve is vertical.

2.2 What variables cause the long-run aggregate supply curve to shift? For each variable, identify whether an increase in that variable will cause the long-run aggregate supply curve to shift to the right or to the left.

2.3 Why does the short-run aggregate supply curve slope upward?

2.4 What variables cause the short-run aggregate supply curve to shift? For each variable, identify whether an increase in that variable will cause the short-run aggregate supply curve to shift to the right or to the left.

Problems and Applications

2.5 Explain how each of the following events would affect the long-run aggregate supply curve.
a. A higher price level
b. An increase in the labor force

c. An increase in the quantity of capital goods

d. Technological change

2.6 Explain how each of the following events would affect the short-run aggregate supply curve.

a. An increase in the price level

b. An increase in what the price level is expected to be in the future

c. A price level that is currently higher than expected

d. An unexpected increase in the price of an important raw material

e. An increase in the labor force

2.7 Suppose that workers and firms could always predict next year's price level with perfect accuracy. Briefly explain whether in these circumstances the *SRAS* curve still slopes upward.

2.8 Workers and firms often enter into contracts that fix prices or wages, sometimes for years at a time. If the price level turns out to be higher or lower than was expected when the contract was signed, one party to

the contract will lose out. Briefly explain why, despite knowing this, workers and firms still sign long-term contracts.

2.9 A newspaper article noted, "About 50 percent of U.S. Steel's domestic production is tied up right now in long-term contracts pegged below market value price."

a. Why would U.S. Steel have entered into contracts to sell steel below the market price?

b. What impact is U.S. Steel selling steel below the current market price likely to have on its production and on the production of companies that buy its steel?

Source: Charles Sheehan, "Happy Days Are Here Again for U.S. Steel Corp.," (Allentown, Pennsylvania) *Morning Call*, November 28, 2004.

2.10 What are menu costs? How has the widespread use of computers and the Internet affected menu costs? If menu costs were eliminated, would the short-run aggregate supply curve be a vertical line? Briefly explain.

>> **End Learning Objective 24.2**

24.3 LEARNING OBJECTIVE | 24.3 | Use the aggregate demand and aggregate supply model to illustrate the difference between short-run and long-run macroeconomic equilibrium, **pages 824–827.**

Macroeconomic Equilibrium in the Long Run and the Short Run

Summary

In long-run macroeconomic equilibrium, the aggregate demand and short-run aggregate supply curves intersect at a point *on* the long-run aggregate supply curve. In short-run macroeconomic equilibrium, the aggregate demand and short-run aggregate supply curves often intersect at a point *off* the long-run aggregate supply curve. An automatic mechanism drives the economy to long-run equilibrium. If short-run equilibrium occurs at a point below potential real GDP, wages and prices will fall, and the short-run aggregate supply curve will shift to the right until potential GDP is restored. If short-run equilibrium occurs at a point beyond potential real GDP, wages and prices will rise, and the short-run aggregate supply curve will shift to the left until potential GDP is restored. Real GDP can be temporarily above or below its potential level, either because of shifts in the aggregate demand curve or because supply shocks lead to shifts in the aggregate supply curve. **Stagflation** is a combination of inflation and recession, usually resulting from a supply shock.

Review Questions

3.1 What is the relationship among the *AD*, *SRAS*, and *LRAS* curves when the economy is in macroeconomic equilibrium?

3.2 What is a supply shock? Why might a supply shock lead to stagflation?

3.3 Why are the long-run effects of an increase in aggregate demand on price and output different from the short-run effects?

Problems and Applications

3.4 Draw a basic aggregate demand and aggregate supply graph (with *LRAS* constant) that shows the economy in long-run equilibrium.

a. Now assume that there is an increase in aggregate demand. Show the resulting short-run equilibrium on your graph. Explain how the economy adjusts back to long-run equilibrium.

b. Now assume that there is an unexpected increase in the price of an important raw material. Show the resulting short-run equilibrium on your graph. Explain how the economy adjusts back to long-run equilibrium.

3.5 Many economists believe that some wages and prices are "sticky downward," meaning that these wages and prices increase quickly when demand is increasing but decrease slowly, if at all, when demand is decreasing. Discuss the consequences of this for the automatic mechanism that brings the economy back to potential GDP after an increase in aggregate demand. Would your answer change if aggregate demand decreased rather than increased? Explain.

3.6 Consider the data in the following table for the years 1969 and 1970 (the values for real GDP are in 2000 dollars).

YEAR	ACTUAL REAL GDP	POTENTIAL REAL GDP	UNEMPLOYMENT RATE
1969	$3.77 trillion	$3.67 trillion	3.5%
1970	$3.77 trillion	$3.80 trillion	4.9%

Sources: U.S. Department of Commerce; and Bureau of Economic Analysis.

a. In 1969, actual real GDP was greater than potential real GDP. Explain how this is possible.
b. Even though real GDP in 1970 was the same as real GDP in 1969, the unemployment rate increased substantially from 1969 to 1970. Why did this increase in unemployment occur?
c. Was the inflation rate in 1970 likely to have been higher or lower than the inflation rate in 1969? Does your answer depend on whether the recession was caused by a change in a component of aggregate demand or by a supply shock?

3.7 Use the following graph to answer the questions.

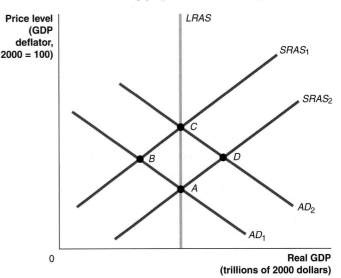

a. Which of the points A, B, C, or D can represent a long-run equilibrium?
b. Suppose that initially the economy is at point A. If aggregate demand increases from AD_1 to AD_2, which point represents the economy's short-run equilibrium? Which point represents the eventual long-run equilibrium? Briefly explain how the economy adjusts from the short-run equilibrium to the long-run equilibrium.

>> **End Learning Objective 24.3**

24.4 LEARNING OBJECTIVE   24.4 | Use the dynamic aggregate demand and aggregate supply model to analyze macroeconomic conditions, **pages 828–837.**

A Dynamic Aggregate Demand and Aggregate Supply Model

Summary

To make the aggregate demand and aggregate supply model more realistic, we need to make it *dynamic* by incorporating three facts that were left out of the basic model: (1) Potential real GDP increases continually, shifting the long-run aggregate supply curve to the right; (2) during most years, aggregate demand will be shifting to the right; and (3) except during periods when workers and firms expect high rates of inflation, the aggregate supply curve will be shifting to the right. The dynamic aggregate demand and aggregate supply model allows us to analyze macroeconomic conditions, including the recovery from the 2001 recession.

myeconlab Visit www.myeconlab.com to complete these exercises
Get Ahead of the Curve online and get instant feedback.

Review Questions

4.1 What are the key differences between the basic aggregate demand and aggregate supply model and the dynamic aggregate demand and aggregate supply model?

4.2 In the dynamic aggregate demand and aggregate supply model, what is the result of aggregate demand increasing faster than potential real GDP? What is the result of aggregate demand increasing slower than potential real GDP?

Problems and Applications

4.3 Draw a dynamic aggregate demand and aggregate supply graph showing the economy moving from potential GDP in 2006 to potential GDP in 2007, with no inflation. Your graph should contain the *AD*, *SRAS*, and *LRAS* curves for both 2006 and 2007 and should indicate the short-run macroeconomic equilibrium for each year and the directions in which the curves have shifted. Identify what must happen to have growth during 2007 without inflation.

4.4 (Related to *Solved Problem 24-4* on page 835) Consider the information in the following table for the first two years of the Great Depression (the values for real GDP are in 2000 dollars).

YEAR	ACTUAL REAL GDP	POTENTIAL REAL GDP	PRICE LEVEL
1929	$865.2 billion	$865.2 billion	12.0
1930	$790.7 billion	$895.7 billion	11.5

Sources: U.S. Department of Commerce; and Bureau of Economic Analysis.

a. The table shows that something happened during 1929–1930 that has not happened during the recessions of the past 50 years. What is it?

b. Draw a dynamic aggregate demand and aggregate supply graph to illustrate what happened during these years. Your graph should contain the *AD*, *SRAS*, and *LRAS* curves for both 1929 and 1930 and should indicate the short-run macroeconomic equilibrium for each year and the directions in which the curves have shifted.

4.5 (Related to *Solved Problem 24-4* on page 835) Look again at Solved Problem 24-4 on the supply shock of 1974–1975. In the table, the price level for 1974 is given as 34.7, and the price level for 1975 is given as 38.0. The values for the price level are well below 100. Does this indicate that inflation must have been low during these years? Briefly explain.

4.6 (Related to the *Making the Connection* on page 832) Briefly explain whether you agree or disagree with the following argument: "Whenever productivity increases, it is possible to produce the same amount of goods and services with fewer workers. Therefore, over the long run, as productivity increases, total employment should fall."

4.7 In the graph in the next column, suppose that the economy moves from point *A* in year 1 to point *B* in year 2. Using the graph, briefly explain your answers to each of the questions.

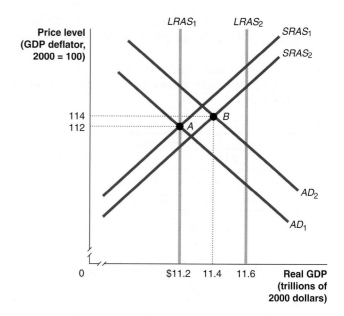

a. What is the growth rate in potential real GDP from year 1 to year 2?

b. Is the unemployment rate in year 2 higher or lower than in year 1?

c. What is the inflation rate in year 2?

d. What is the growth rate of real GDP in year 2?

4.8 Explain whether you agree or disagree with the following statement:

> The dynamic aggregate demand and aggregate supply model predicts that a recession caused by a decline in *AD* will cause the inflation rate to fall. I know that the 2001 recession was caused by a fall in *AD*, but the inflation rate was not lower after the recession. The prices of most products were definitely higher in 2002 than they were in 2001, so the inflation rate could not have fallen.

4.9 An economist at the Federal Reserve Bank of St. Louis wrote the following about the recovery from the 2001 recession:

> [Since the end of the recession,] real business fixed investment (BFI)—expenditures on structures, equipment and software—has declined at a 2.2 percent annual rate. By contrast, in the first four quarters of the typical recovery, real BFI *increases* a little more than 8 percent.
>
> Why didn't investment spending increase after the 2001 recession as much as it normally does in the year following the end of a recession?

Source: Kevin L. Kliesen, "Waiting for the Investment Boom? It Might Be a While," *National Economic Trends*, May 2003.

4.10 An article in the *New York Times* in August 2003 stated the following: "A cutback in business spending when the Internet and stock market bubbles burst brought on the recession of 2001 and the prolonged weakness that has existed since then."

a. What does the article mean by "business spending"?

b. What does it mean by the "Internet and stock market bubbles"?

c. Why would the bursting of these bubbles affect business spending?

Source: Louis Uchitelle and Jennifer Bayot, "Business Spending Helps to Offset Lag in Refinancing," *New York Times*, August 9, 2003.

4.11 The following excerpt is from an article in the *New York Times*: "The number of Americans living below the poverty line increased by more than 1.3 million [during 2002], even though the economy technically edged out of recession during the same period." Briefly discuss why poverty increased during 2002 even though the economy was in the expansion phase of the business cycle.

Source: Lynette Clemetson, "Census Shows Ranks of Poor Rose by 1.3 Million," *New York Times*, September 3, 2003.

4.12 (Related to the *Chapter Opener* on page 810) In the chapter opener, we mentioned that former Federal Reserve Chairman Alan Greenspan used to meet regularly with FedEx Chairman Fred Smith because Greenspan believed that changes in the volume of packages being shipped by FedEx was a good indicator of how the general economy was doing. Briefly compare how sensitive FedEx's sales are to changes in the business cycle to how sensitive the following firms' sales are to changes in the business cycle: Ford Motor Company, Starbucks, Toll Brothers (home builders), and Paramount Pictures (movies). In other words, do FedEx's sales fluctuate more or less than the sales of each of these other firms as the economy moves from recession to expansion and back to recession?

4.13 (Related to the *Making the Connection* on page 836) Suppose the price of a barrel of oil increases from $100 to $130. Use a basic aggregate demand and aggregate supply graph to show the short-run and long-run effects on the economy.

>> End Learning Objective 24.4

Appendix

Macroeconomic Schools of Thought

Understand macroeconomic schools of thought.

Macroeconomics as a separate field of economics began with the publication in 1936 of John Maynard Keynes's book *The General Theory of Employment, Interest, and Money*. Keynes, an economist at the University of Cambridge in England, was attempting to explain the devastating Great Depression of the 1930s. As we discussed in Chapter 23, real GDP in the United States declined by more than 25 percent between 1929 and 1933 and did not return to its potential level until the United States entered World War II in 1941. The unemployment rate soared to 25 percent by 1933 and did not return to its 1929 level until 1942. Keynes developed a version of the aggregate demand and aggregate supply model to explain these facts. The widespread acceptance during the 1930s and 1940s of Keynes's model became known as the **Keynesian revolution**.

Keynesian revolution The name given to the widespread acceptance during the 1930s and 1940s of John Maynard Keynes's macroeconomic model.

In fact, the aggregate demand and aggregate supply model remains the most widely accepted approach to analyzing macroeconomic issues. Because the model has been modified significantly from Keynes's day, many economists who use the model today refer to themselves as *new Keynesians*. The new Keynesians emphasize the importance of the stickiness of wages and prices in explaining fluctuations in real GDP. A significant number of economists, however, dispute whether the aggregate demand and aggregate supply model, as we have discussed it in this chapter, is the best way to analyze macroeconomic issues. These alternative *schools of thought* use models that differ significantly from the standard aggregate demand and aggregate supply model. We can briefly consider each of the three major alternative models:

1 The monetarist model

2 The new classical model

3 The real business cycle model

The Monetarist Model

The monetarist model—also known as the neo-Quantity Theory of Money model—was developed beginning in the 1940s by Milton Friedman, an economist at the University of Chicago who was awarded the Nobel Prize in Economics in 1976. Friedman argued that the Keynesian approach overstates the amount of macroeconomic instability in the economy. In particular, he argued that the economy will ordinarily be at potential real GDP. In the book *A Monetary History of the United States: 1867–1960*, written with Anna Jacobson Schwartz, Friedman argued that most fluctuations in real output were caused by fluctuations in the money supply rather than by fluctuations in consumption spending or investment spending. Friedman and Schwartz argued that the severity of the Great Depression was caused by the Federal Reserve's allowing the quantity of money in the economy to fall by more than 25 percent between 1929 and 1933.

In the United States, the Federal Reserve is responsible for managing the quantity of money. As we will discuss further in Chapter 26, the Federal Reserve has typically focused more on controlling interest rates than on controlling the money supply. Friedman has argued that the Federal Reserve should change its practices and adopt a **monetary growth rule**, which is a plan for increasing the quantity of money at a fixed rate. Friedman believed that adopting a monetary growth rule would reduce fluctuations in real GDP, employment, and inflation.

Friedman's ideas, which are referred to as **monetarism**, attracted significant support during the 1970s and early 1980s, when the economy experienced high rates of unemployment and inflation. The support for monetarism declined during the late 1980s and 1990s, when the unemployment and inflation rates were relatively low. In Chapter 25, we will discuss the *quantity theory of money*, which underlies the monetarist model.

The New Classical Model

The new classical model was developed in the mid-1970s by a group of economists including Nobel laureate Robert Lucas of the University of Chicago, Thomas Sargent of New York University, and Robert Barro of Harvard University. Some of the views held by the new classical macroeconomists are similar to those held by economists before the Great Depression. Keynes referred to the economists before the Great Depression as "classical economists." Like the classical economists, the new classical macroeconomists believe that the economy normally will be at potential real GDP. They also believe that wages and prices adjust quickly to changes in demand and supply. Put another way, they believe the stickiness in wages and prices emphasized by the new Keynesians is unimportant.

Lucas argued that workers and firms have *rational expectations*, meaning that they form their expectations of the future values of economic variables, such as the inflation rate, by making use of all available information, including information on variables—such as changes in the quantity of money—that might affect aggregate demand. If the actual inflation rate is lower than the expected inflation rate, the actual real wage will be higher than the expected real wage. These higher real wages will lead to a recession because they will cause firms to hire fewer workers and cut back on production. As workers and firms adjust their expectations to the lower inflation rate, the real wage will decline, and employment and production will expand, bringing the economy out of recession. The ideas of Lucas and his followers are referred to as the **new classical macroeconomics**. Supporters of the new classical model agree with supporters of the monetarist model that the Federal Reserve should adopt a monetary growth rule. They argue that a monetary growth rule will make it easier for workers and firms to accurately forecast the price level, thereby reducing fluctuations in real GDP.

The Real Business Cycle Model

Beginning in the 1980s, some economists, including Nobel laureates Finn Kydland of Carnegie Mellon University and Edward Prescott of Arizona State University, argued that Lucas was correct in assuming that workers and firms formed their expectations rationally and that wages and prices adjust quickly to supply and demand but wrong about the source of fluctuations in real GDP. They argued that fluctuations in real GDP are caused by temporary shocks to productivity. These shocks can be negative, such as a decline in the availability of oil or other raw materials, or positive, such as technological change that makes it possible to produce more output with the same quantity of inputs.

According to this school of thought, shifts in the aggregate demand curve have no impact on real GDP because the short-run aggregate supply curve is vertical. Other schools of thought all believe that the short-run aggregate supply curve is upward sloping and that only the *long-run* aggregate supply curve is vertical. Fluctuations in real GDP occur when a negative productivity shock causes the short-run aggregate supply curve to shift to the left—reducing real GDP—or a positive productivity shock causes the short-run aggregate supply curve to shift to the right—increasing real GDP. Because this model focuses on "real" factors—productivity shocks—rather than changes in the quantity of money to explain fluctuations in real GDP, it is known as the **real business cycle model**.

Monetary growth rule A plan for increasing the quantity of money at a fixed rate that does not respond to changes in economic conditions.

Monetarism The macroeconomic theories of Milton Friedman and his followers; particularly the idea that the quantity of money should be increased at a constant rate.

New classical macroeconomics The macroeconomic theories of Robert Lucas and others, particularly the idea that workers and firms have rational expectations.

Real business cycle model A macroeconomic model that focuses on real, rather than monetary, causes of the business cycle.

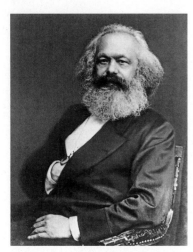

Karl Marx predicted that a final economic crisis would lead to the collapse of the market system.

Making the Connection

Karl Marx: Capitalism's Severest Critic

The schools of macroeconomic thought we have discussed in this appendix are considered part of mainstream economic theory because of their acceptance of the market system as the best means of raising living standards in the long run. One quite influential critic of mainstream economic theory was Karl Marx. Marx was born in Trier, Germany, in 1818. After graduating from the University of Berlin in 1841, he began a career as a political journalist and agitator. His political activities caused him to be expelled first from Germany and then from France and Belgium. In 1849, he moved to London, where he spent the remainder of his life.

In 1867, he published the first volume of his greatest work, *Das Kapital*. Marx read closely the most prominent mainstream economists, including Adam Smith, David Ricardo, and John Stuart Mill. But Marx believed that he understood how market systems would evolve in the long run much better than those earlier authors. Marx argued that the market system would eventually be replaced by a Communist economy in which the workers would control production. He believed in the *labor theory of value*, which attributed all of the value of a good or service to the labor that was embodied in it. According to Marx, the owners of businesses—capitalists—did not earn profits by contributing anything of value to the production of goods or services. Instead, capitalists earned profits because their "monopoly of the means of production"—their ownership of factories and machinery—allowed them to exploit workers by paying them wages that were much less than the value of workers' contribution to production.

Marx argued that wages of workers would be driven to levels that allowed only bare survival. He also argued that small firms would eventually be driven out of business by larger firms, forcing owners of small firms into the working class. Control of production would ultimately be concentrated in the hands of a few firms. These few remaining firms would have difficulty selling the goods they produced to the impoverished masses. A final economic crisis would lead the working classes to rise up, seize control of the economy, and establish Communism. Marx died in 1883 without providing a detailed explanation of how the Communist economy would operate.

Marx had relatively little influence on mainstream thinking in the United States, but several political parties in Europe were guided by his ideas. In 1917, the Bolshevik party seized control of Russia and established the Soviet Union, the first Communist state. Although the Soviet Union was a vicious dictatorship under Vladimir Lenin and his successor, Joseph Stalin, its prestige rose when it avoided the macroeconomic difficulties that plagued the market economies during the 1930s. By the late 1940s, Communist parties had also come to power in China and the countries of Eastern Europe. Poor economic performance contributed to the eventual collapse of the Soviet Union and its replacement by a market system, although one in which government intervention is still widespread. The Communist Party remains in power in China, but the economy is evolving toward a market system. Today, only North Korea and Cuba have economies that claim to be based on the ideas of Karl Marx.

Key Terms

Chapter 25

Money, Banks, and the Federal Reserve System

McDonald's Money Problems in Argentina

The McDonald's Big Mac is one of the most widely available products in the world. McDonald's 30,000 restaurants in 119 countries serve 50 million customers per day. Although some McDonald's restaurants are owned by the firm, many are franchises. A *franchise* is a business with the legal right to sell a good or service in a particular area. When a firm uses franchises, local entrepreneurs are able to buy and run the stores in their area. As McDonald's began expanding to other countries in the late 1960s, it relied on the franchise system. Franchisees in other countries were able to adapt the restaurants to the tastes of local customers. For example, although all 200 McDonald's restaurants in Argentina offer Big Macs and French fries, they also offer gourmet coffees and other foods not available in McDonald's restaurants in the United States.

In 2001, McDonald's restaurants in Argentina began to suffer from the macroeconomic problems plaguing that country. Argentina's woes centered on "money." Households and firms had begun to lose faith in the Argentine peso, the country's official money. They believed that the peso would rapidly lose its value, reducing their ability to buy goods and services. Many people converged on banks and tried to withdraw their money so they could either immediately buy goods and services or exchange Argentine pesos for U.S. dollars. To stop the outflow of money from the banking system, the government limited the amount of Argentine currency that could be withdrawn to $1,000 per account per month. This action further weakened the economy by reducing the funds households and firms had available to spend. In addition, banks became cautious about making loans, which in turn led to additional reductions in spending. An Argentine doctor was quoted as saying, "Now there's a lack of cash. . . . None of my patients can pay." Another person observed, "The chain of payments has been broken. There are millions of people forced to resort to bartering—an old sweater, anything, for goods just to survive." A cell phone dealer said, "These days, if customers want to pay us in tomatoes, I'll consider making a deal."

During the currency crisis, one Argentine province decided to issue its own currency, which it called the *patacone*. Because the patacone was not part of Argentina's official currency, there were doubts that local firms would accept it. McDonald's restaurants in the province decided to accept the new currency as payment for a meal they labeled the "Patacombo": two cheeseburgers, an order of French fries, and a soft drink.

Although the crisis in Argentina eventually passed, confidence in money remains vitally important. When you buy a DVD from a store, you get something of value. You give the store clerk dollar bills, or you might write a check with your name and the name of a bank on it or use a debit card linked to your checking account. Dollar bills and checks are pieces of paper that have no value in and of themselves. You and the store owner consider them valuable because others consider them valuable. This confidence and trust are hallmarks of money.

Confidence and trust cannot be taken for granted. As this example from Argentina shows, households and firms losing faith in an official money can harm trade and economic activity in an economy. **AN INSIDE LOOK AT POLICY** on **page 878** discusses how China's central bank is trying to control the money supply by slowing bank lending.

Sources: Tony Smith, "Freeze Has Argentines Crying All the Way to the Bank," Associated Press, December 11, 2001; and Matt Moffett, "Unfunny Money," *Wall Street Journal*, August 21, 2001.

LEARNING Objectives

After studying this chapter, you should be able to:

25.1 Define **money** and discuss its four functions, page 852.

25.2 Discuss the **definitions** of the **money supply** used in the United States today, page 856.

25.3 Explain how **banks create money**, page 860.

25.4 Discuss the three **policy tools** the **Federal Reserve** uses to manage the money supply, page 868.

25.5 Explain the **quantity theory of money** and use it to explain how high rates of inflation occur, page 872.

Economics in YOUR Life!

What if Money Became Increasingly Valuable?

Most people are used to the fact that as prices rise each year, the purchasing power of money falls. You will be able to buy fewer goods and services with $1,000 one year from now than you can today and even fewer goods and services the year after that. In fact, with an inflation rate of just 3 per-cent, in 25 years, $1,000 will buy only what $475 can buy today. Suppose, though, that you could live in an economy where the purchasing power of money rose each year? What would be the advan-tages and disadvantages of living in such an economy? As you read the chapter, see if you can answer these questions. You can check your answers against those we provide at the end of the chapter. **>> Continued on page 877**

I n this chapter, we will explore the role of money in the economy. We will see how the banking system creates money and what policy tools the Federal Reserve uses to manage the quantity of money. At the end of the chapter, we will explore the link between changes in the quantity of money and changes in the price level. What you learn in this chapter will serve as an important foundation for understanding monetary policy and fiscal policy, which we study in the next three chapters.

25.1 | Define money and discuss its four functions.

What Is Money and Why Do We Need It?

Could an economy function without money? We know the answer to this is "yes" because there are many historical examples of economies where people traded goods for other goods rather than using money. For example, a farmer on the American frontier during colonial times might have traded a cow for a plow. Most economies, though, use money. What is money? The economic definition of **money** is any asset that people are generally willing to accept in exchange for goods and services or for payment of debts. Recall from Chapter 7 that an **asset** is anything of value owned by a person or a firm. There are many possible kinds of money: In West Africa, at one time, cowrie shells served as money. During World War II, prisoners of war used cigarettes as money.

> **Money** Assets that people are generally willing to accept in exchange for goods and services or for payment of debts.
>
> **Asset** Anything of value owned by a person or a firm.

Barter and the Invention of Money

To understand the importance of money, let's consider further the situation in economies that do not use money. These economies, where goods and services are traded directly for other goods and services, are called *barter economies*. Barter economies have a major shortcoming. To illustrate this shortcoming, consider a farmer on the American frontier in colonial days. Suppose the farmer needed another cow and proposed trading a spare plow to a neighbor for one of the neighbor's cows. If the neighbor did not want the plow, the trade would not happen. For a barter trade to take place between two people, each person must want what the other one has. Economists refer to this requirement as a *double coincidence of wants*. The farmer who wants the cow might eventually be able to obtain one if he first trades with some other neighbor for something the neighbor with the cow wants. However, it may take several trades before the farmer is ultimately able to trade for what the neighbor with the cow wants. Locating several trading partners and making several intermediate trades can take considerable time and energy.

The problems with barter provide an incentive to identify a product that most people will accept in exchange for what they have to trade. For example, in colonial times, animal skins were very useful in making clothing. The first governor of Tennessee actually received a salary of 1,000 deerskins per year, and the secretary of the treasury received 450 otter skins per year. A good used as money that also has value independent of its use as money is called a **commodity money**. Historically, once a good became widely accepted as money, people who did not have an immediate use for it would be willing to accept it. A colonial farmer—or the governor of Tennessee—might not want a deerskin, but as long as he knew he could use the deerskin to buy other goods and services, he would be willing to accept it in exchange for what he had to sell.

> **Commodity money** A good used as money that also has value independent of its use as money.

Trading goods and services is much easier when money becomes available. People only need to sell what they have for money and then use the money to buy what they want. If the colonial family could find someone to buy their plow, they could use the money to buy the cow they wanted. The family with the cow would accept the money because they knew they could use it to buy what they wanted. When money is available, families are less likely to produce everything or nearly everything they need themselves and more likely to specialize.

Most people in modern economies are highly specialized. They do only one thing—work as a nurse, an accountant, or an engineer—and use the money they earn to buy everything else they need. As we discussed in Chapter 2, people become much more productive by specializing because they can pursue their *comparative advantage*. The high income levels in modern economies are based on the specialization that money makes possible. We can now answer the question, "Why do we need money?" *By making exchange easier, money allows for specialization and higher productivity.*

The Functions of Money

Anything used as money—whether a deerskin, a cowrie seashell, cigarettes, or a dollar bill—should fulfill the following four functions:

- Medium of exchange
- Unit of account
- Store of value
- Standard of deferred payment

Medium of Exchange Money serves as a medium of exchange when sellers are willing to accept it in exchange for goods or services. When the local supermarket accepts your $5 bill in exchange for bread and milk, the $5 bill is serving as a medium of exchange. To go back to our earlier example, with a medium of exchange, the farmer with the extra plow does not have to want a cow, and the farmer with the extra cow does not have to want a plow. Both can exchange their products for money and use the money to buy what they want. An economy is more efficient when a single good is recognized as a medium of exchange.

Unit of Account In a barter system, each good has many prices. A cow may be worth two plows, 20 bushels of wheat, or six axes. Using a good as a medium of exchange confers another benefit: It reduces the need to quote many different prices in trade. Instead of having to quote the price of a single good in terms of many other goods, each good has a single price quoted in terms of the medium of exchange. This function of money gives buyers and sellers a *unit of account*, a way of measuring value in the economy in terms of money. Because the U.S. economy uses dollars as money, each good has a price in terms of dollars.

Store of Value Money allows value to be stored easily: If you do not use all your accumulated dollars to buy goods and services today, you can hold the rest to use in the future. In fact, a fisherman and a farmer would be better off holding money rather than inventories of their perishable goods. The acceptability of money in future transactions depends on its not losing value over time. Money is not the only store of value. Any asset—shares of Google stock, Treasury bonds, real estate, or Renoir paintings, for example—represents a store of value. Indeed, financial assets offer an important benefit relative to holding money because they generally pay a higher rate of interest or offer the prospect of gains in value. Other assets also have advantages relative to money because they provide services. A house, for example, offers you a place to sleep.

Why, then, would you bother to hold any money? The answer has to do with *liquidity*, or the ease with which a given asset can be converted into the medium of exchange. When money is the medium of exchange, it is the most liquid asset. You incur costs when you exchange other assets for money. When you sell bonds or shares of stock to buy a car, for example, you pay a commission to your broker. If you have to sell your house on short notice to finance an unexpected major medical expense, you pay a commission to a real estate agent and probably have to accept a lower price to exchange the house for money quickly. To avoid such costs, people are willing to hold some of their wealth in the form of money, even though other assets offer a greater return as a store of value.

Standard of Deferred Payment Money is useful because it can serve as a standard of deferred payment in borrowing and lending. Money can facilitate exchange at a *given point in time* by providing a medium of exchange and unit of account. It can facilitate exchange *over time* by providing a store of value and a standard of deferred payment. For example, a furniture maker may be willing to sell you a chair today in exchange for money in the future.

How important is it that money be a reliable store of value and standard of deferred payment? People care about how much food, clothing, and other goods and services their dollars will buy. The value of money depends on its purchasing power, which refers to its ability to buy goods and services. Inflation causes a decline in purchasing power because rising prices cause a given amount of money to purchase fewer goods and services. With deflation, the value of money increases because prices are falling.

You have probably heard relatives or friends exclaim, "A dollar doesn't buy what it used to!" They really mean that the purchasing power of a dollar has fallen, that a given amount of money will buy a smaller quantity of the same goods and services than it once did.

What Can Serve as Money?

Having a medium of exchange helps to make transactions easier, allowing the economy to work more smoothly. The next logical question is this: What can serve as money? That is, which assets should be used as the medium of exchange? We saw earlier that an asset must, at a minimum, be generally accepted as payment to serve as money. In practical terms, however, it must be even more.

Five criteria make a good suitable to use as a medium of exchange:

1   The good must be *acceptable* to (that is, usable by) most people.

2   It should be of *standardized quality* so that any two units are identical.

3   It should be *durable* so that value is not lost by spoilage.

4   It should be *valuable* relative to its weight so that amounts large enough to be useful in trade can be easily transported.

5   The medium of exchange should be *divisible* because different goods are valued differently.

Dollar bills meet all these criteria. What determines the acceptability of dollar bills as a medium of exchange? Basically, it is through self-fulfilling expectations: You value something as money only if you believe that others will accept it from you as payment. A society's willingness to use green paper dollars as money makes them an acceptable medium of exchange. This property of acceptability is not unique to money. Your personal computer has the same keyboard organization of letters as other computer keyboards because manufacturers agreed on a standard layout. You learned to speak English because it is probably the language that most people around you speak.

Commodity Money Commodity money meets the criteria for a medium of exchange. Gold, for example, was a common form of money in the nineteenth century because it was a medium of exchange, a unit of account, a store of value, and a standard of deferred payment. But commodity money has a significant problem: Its value depends on its purity. Therefore, someone who wanted to cheat could mix impure metals with a precious metal. Unless traders trusted each other completely, they needed to check the weight and purity of the metal at each trade. In the Middle Ages, respected merchants, who were the predecessors of modern bankers, solved this problem by assaying metals and stamping them with a mark certifying weight and purity and earned a commission in the process. Unstamped (uncertified) commodity money was acceptable only at a discount. Another problem with using gold as money was that the money supply was difficult to control because it depended partly on unpredictable discoveries of new gold fields.

Fiat Money It can be inefficient for an economy to rely on only gold or other precious metals for its money supply. What if you had to transport bars of gold to settle your transactions? Not only would doing so be difficult and costly, but you would also run the risk of being robbed. To get around this problem, private institutions or governments began to store gold and issue paper certificates that could be redeemed for gold. In modern economies, paper currency is generally issued by a *central bank*, which is an agency of the government that regulates the money supply. The **Federal Reserve System** is the central bank of the United States. Today, no government in the world issues paper currency that can be redeemed for gold. Paper currency has no value unless it is used as money and is therefore not a commodity money. Instead, paper currency is a **fiat money**, which has no value except as money. If paper currency has no value except as money, why do consumers and firms use it?

If you look at the top of a U.S. dollar bill, you will see that it is actually a *Federal Reserve Note*, issued by the Federal Reserve. Because U.S. dollars are fiat money, the Federal Reserve is not required to give you gold or silver for your dollar bills. Federal Reserve currency is *legal tender* in the United States, which means the federal government requires that it be accepted in payment of debts and requires that cash or checks denominated in dollars be used in payment of taxes. Despite being legal tender, without everyone's acceptance, dollar bills would not be a good medium of exchange and could not serve as money. In practice, you, along with everyone else, agree to accept Federal Reserve currency as money. The key to this acceptance is that *households and firms have confidence that if they accept paper dollars in exchange for goods and services, the dollars will not lose much value during the time they hold them.* Without this confidence, dollar bills would not serve as a medium of exchange.

Federal Reserve System The central bank of the United States.

Fiat money Money, such as paper currency, that is authorized by a central bank or governmental body and that does not have to be exchanged by the central bank for gold or some other commodity money.

Making the Connection | Money without a Government? The Strange Case of the Iraqi Dinar

The value of the Iraqi dinar was rising against the U.S. dollar. This result may not seem surprising. We saw in Chapter 24 that the exchange rate, or the value of one currency in exchange for another currency, fluctuates—but this was May 2003. The Iraqi government of Saddam Hussein had collapsed the month before, following an invasion by U.S. and British forces. No new Iraqi government had been formed yet, but people continued to use Iraqi paper currency with pictures of Saddam for buying and selling.

U.S. officials in Iraq had expected that as soon as the war was over and Saddam had been forced from power, the currency with his picture on it would lose all its value. This result had seemed inevitable once the United States had begun paying Iraqi officials in U.S. dollars. However, many Iraqis continued to use the dinar because they were familiar with that currency. As one Iraqi put it, "People trust the dinar more than the dollar. It's Iraqi." In fact, for some weeks after the invasion, increasing demand for the dinar caused its value to rise against the dollar. In early April, when U.S. troops first entered Baghdad, it took about 4,000 dinar to buy 1 U.S. dollar. Six weeks later, in mid-May, it took only 1,500 dinar.

Many Iraqis continued to use currency with Saddam's picture on it, even after he was forced from power.

Eventually, a new Iraqi government was formed, and the government ordered that dinars with Saddam's picture be replaced by a new dinar. The new dinar was printed in factories around the world, and 27 Boeing 747s filled with paper dinars were flown to Baghdad. By January 2004, 2 billion paper dinars in varying denominations had been distributed to banks throughout Iraq, and the old Saddam dinars disappeared from circulation. That dinars issued by Saddam's government actually increased in value for a period after his government had collapsed illustrates an important fact about money: *Anything can be used as money as long as people are willing to accept it in exchange for goods and services,* even paper currency issued by a government that no longer exists.

Sources: Edmund L. Andrews, "His Face Still Gives Fits as Saddam Dinar Soars," *New York Times*, May 18, 2003; Yaroslav Trofimov, "Saddam Hussein Is Scarce, but Not the Saddam Dinar," *Wall Street Journal*, April 24, 2003; and "A Tricky Operation," *Economist*, June 24, 2004.

YOUR TURN: Test your understanding by doing related problem 1.8 on page 881 at the end of this chapter.

25.2 | Discuss the definitions of the money supply used in the United States today.

How Is Money Measured in the United States Today?

The definition of money as a medium of exchange depends on beliefs about whether others will use the medium in trade now and in the future. This definition offers guidance for measuring money in an economy. Interpreted literally, this definition says that money should include only those assets that obviously function as a medium of exchange: currency, checking account deposits, and traveler's checks. These assets can easily be used to buy goods and services and thus act as a medium of exchange.

This strict interpretation is too narrow, however, as a measure of the money supply in the real world. Many other assets can be used as a medium of exchange, but they are not as liquid as a checking account deposit or cash. For example, you can convert your savings account at a bank to cash. Likewise, if you have an account at a brokerage firm, you can write checks against the value of the stocks and bonds the firm holds for you. Although these assets have restrictions on their use and there may be costs to converting them into cash, they can be considered part of the medium of exchange.

In the United States, the Federal Reserve has conducted several studies of the appropriate definition of money. The job of defining the money supply has become more difficult during the past two decades as innovation in financial markets and institutions has created new substitutes for the traditional measures of the medium of exchange. During the 1980s, the Fed changed its definitions of money in response to financial innovation. Outside the United States, other central banks use similar measures. Next we will look more closely at the Fed's definitions of the money supply.

M1: The Narrowest Definition of the Money Supply

M1 The narrowest definition of the money supply: The sum of currency in circulation, checking account deposits in banks, and holdings of traveler's checks.

Figure 25-1 illustrates the definitions of the money supply. The narrowest definition of the money supply is called **M1**. It includes:

1 *Currency*, which is all the paper money and coins that are in circulation, where "in circulation" means not held by banks or the government

2 The value of all checking account deposits at banks

3 The value of traveler's checks (although this last category is so small—less than $7 billion in May 2008—we will ignore it in our discussion of the money supply)

Although currency has a larger value than checking account deposits, checking account deposits are used much more often than currency to make payments. More than 80 percent of all expenditures on goods and services are made with checks rather than with currency. In fact, the total amount of currency in circulation—$763 billion in May 2008—is a misleading number. This amount is more than $2,500 for every man, woman, and child in the United States. If this sounds like an unrealistically large amount of currency to be held per person, it is. Economists estimate that about 60 percent of U.S. currency is actually outside the borders of the United States.

Who holds these dollars outside the United States? Foreign banks and foreign governments hold some dollars, but most are held by households and firms in countries where there is not much confidence in the local currency. When inflation rates are very high, many households and firms do not want to hold their domestic currency because it is losing its value too rapidly. The value of the U.S. dollar will be much more stable. If enough people are willing to accept dollars as well as—or instead of—domestic currency, then dollars become a second currency for the country. In some countries, such as Russia and many Latin American countries, large numbers of U.S. dollars are in circulation.

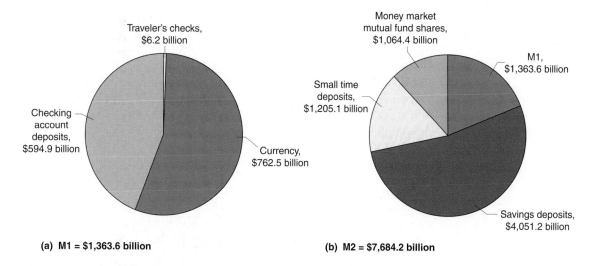

(a) **M1 = $1,363.6 billion**

(b) **M2 = $7,684.2 billion**

Figure 25-1 | Measuring the Money Supply, May 2008

The Federal Reserve uses two different measures of the money supply: M1 and M2. M2 includes all the assets in M1, as well as additional assets.
Source: Board of Governors of the Federal Reserve System, *Federal Reserve Statistical Release, H6*, June 19, 2008.

Making the Connection

Do We Still Need the Penny?

We have seen that fiat money has no value except as money. Governments actually make a profit from issuing fiat money because fiat money is usually produced using paper or low-value metals that cost far less than the face value of the money. For example, it only costs about four cents for the federal Bureau of Engraving and Printing to manufacture a $20 bill. The government's profit from issuing fiat money—which is equal to the difference between the face value of the money and its production cost—is called *seigniorage*.

With small-denomination coins—like pennies or nickels—there is always the possibility that the coins will cost more to produce than their face value. This was true in the early 1980s when the rising price of copper meant the federal government was spending more than one cent to produce a penny. That led the government to switch from making pennies from copper to making them from zinc. Unfortunately, by 2007, the rising price of zinc meant that once again, the penny cost more than one cent to produce. Many economists began to ask whether the penny should simply be abolished. Not only does it cost more to produce than it is worth, but inflation has eroded its purchasing power to such an extent that some people just find the penny to be a nuisance. Seeing a penny on the sidewalk, many people will walk on by, not bothering to pick it up. In fact, several other countries, including Great Britain, Canada, Australia, and the European countries that use the euro, have eliminated their lowest-denomination coins.

Some economists, though, have argued that eliminating the penny would subject consumers to a "rounding tax." For example, a good that had been priced at $2.99 will cost $3.00 if the penny is eliminated. Some estimates have put the cost to consumers of the rounding tax as high as $600 million. But Robert Whaples, an economist at Wake Forest University, after analyzing almost 200,000 transactions from a convenience store chain, concluded that "the 'rounding tax' is a myth. In reality, the number of times consumers' bills would be rounded upward is almost exactly equal to the number of times they would be rounded downward."

Unfortunately, these cost the government more than a penny to produce.

François Velde, an economist at the Federal Reserve Bank of Chicago, has come up with perhaps the most ingenious solution to the problem of the penny: The federal government would simply declare that Lincoln pennies are now worth five cents. There would then be two five-cent coins in circulation—the current Jefferson nickels and the current Lincoln pennies—and no one-cent coins. In the future, only the Lincoln coins—now worth five cents—would be minted. This would solve the problem of consumers and retail stores having to deal with pennies, it would make the face value of the Lincoln five-cent coin greater than its cost of production, and it would also deal with the problem that the current Jefferson nickel costs more than five cents to produce. But would Lincoln pennies actually be accepted as being worth five cents simply because the government says so? The answer is "yes" because as long as the government was willing to exchange 20 Lincoln coins for a paper dollar, everyone else would be willing to do so as well. Of course, if this plan was adopted, anyone with a hoard of pennies would find their money would be worth five times as much overnight!

Whether or not turning pennies into nickels ends up happening, it seems very likely that one way or another, the penny will eventually disappear from the U.S. money supply.

Sources: Robert Whaples, "Why Keeping the Penny No Longer Makes Sense," *USA Today*, July 12, 2006; Austan Goolsbee, "Now That a Penny Isn't Worth Much, It's Time to Make It Worth 5 Cents," *New York Times*, February 1, 2007; and François Velde, "What's a Penny (or a Nickel) Really Worth?" Federal Reserve Bank of Chicago, *Chicago Fed Letter*, Number 235a, February 2007.

YOUR TURN: Test your understanding by doing related problem 2.8 on page 882 at the end of this chapter.

M2: A Broader Definition of Money

Before 1980, U.S. law prohibited banks from paying interest on checking account deposits. Households and firms held checking account deposits primarily to buy goods and services. M1 was, therefore, very close to the function of money as a medium of exchange. Almost all currency, checking account deposits, and traveler's checks were held with the intention of buying and selling, not to store value. People could store value and receive interest by placing funds in savings accounts in banks or by buying other financial assets, such as stocks and bonds. In 1980, the law was changed to allow banks to pay interest on certain types of checking accounts. This change reduced the difference between checking accounts and savings accounts, although people are still not allowed to write checks against their savings account balances.

M2 A broader definition of the money supply: M1 plus savings account balances, small-denomination time deposits, balances in money market deposit accounts in banks, and noninstitutional money market fund shares.

After 1980, economists began to pay closer attention to a broader definition of the money supply, **M2**. M2 includes everything that is in M1, plus savings account deposits, small-denomination time deposits, such as certificates of deposit (CDs), balances in money market deposit accounts in banks, and noninstitutional money market fund shares. Small-denomination time deposits are similar to savings accounts, but the deposits are for a fixed period of time—usually from six months to several years—and withdrawals before that time are subject to a penalty. Mutual fund companies sell shares to investors and use the funds raised to buy financial assets such as stocks and bonds. Some of these mutual funds, such as Vanguard's Treasury Money Market Fund or Fidelity's Cash Reserves Fund, are called *money market mutual funds* because they invest in very short-term bonds, such as U.S. Treasury bills. The balances in these funds are included in M2. Each week, the Federal Reserve publishes statistics on M1 and M2. In the discussion that follows, we will use the M1 definition of the money supply because it corresponds most closely to money as a medium of exchange.

Don't Let This Happen to **YOU!**

Don't Confuse Money with Income or Wealth

According to *Forbes* magazine, Bill Gates's wealth of more than $55 billion makes him the richest person in the world. He also has a very large income, but how much money does he have? A person's *wealth* is equal to the value of his assets minus the value of any debts he has. A person's *income* is equal to his earnings during the year. Bill Gates's earnings as chairman of Microsoft and from his investments are very large. But his *money* is just equal to what he has in currency and in checking accounts. Only a small proportion of Gates's more than $50 billion in wealth is likely to be in currency or checking accounts. Most of his wealth is invested in stocks and bonds and other financial assets that are not included in the definition of money.

In everyday conversation, we often describe someone who is wealthy or who has a high income as "having a lot of money." But when economists use the word *money*, they are usually referring to currency plus checking account deposits. It is important to keep straight the differences between wealth, income, and money.

Just as money and income are not the same for a person, they are not the same for the whole economy. National income in the United States was equal to $12.2 trillion in 2007. The money supply in 2007 was $1.4 trillion (using the M1 measure). There is no reason national income in a country should be equal to the country's money supply, nor will an increase in a country's money supply necessarily increase the country's national income.

YOUR TURN: Test your understanding by doing related problem 2.6 on page 882 at the end of this chapter.

There are two key points about the money supply to keep in mind:

1 The money supply consists of *both* currency and checking account deposits.

2 Because balances in checking account deposits are included in the money supply, banks play an important role in the process by which the money supply increases and decreases. We will discuss this second point further in the next section.

Solved Problem | **25-2**

The Definitions of M1 and M2

Suppose you decide to withdraw $2,000 from your checking account and use the money to buy a bank certificate of deposit (CD). Briefly explain how this will affect M1 and M2.

SOLVING THE PROBLEM:

Step 1: **Review the chapter material.** This problem is about the definitions of the money supply, so you may want to review the section "How Is Money Measured in the United States Today?" which begins on page 856.

Step 2: **Use the definitions of M1 and M2 to answer the problem.** Funds in checking accounts are included in both M1 and M2. Funds in certificates of deposit are included in only M2. It is tempting to answer this problem by saying that shifting $2,000 from a checking account to a certificate of deposit reduces M1 by $2,000 and increases M2 by $2,000, but the $2,000 in your checking account was already counted in M2. So, the correct answer is that your action reduces M1 by $2,000 but leaves M2 unchanged.

YOUR TURN: For more practice, do related problems 2.4 and 2.5 on pages 881–882 at the end of this chapter.

>> End Solved Problem 25-2

What about Credit Cards and Debit Cards?

Many people buy goods and services with credit cards, yet credit cards are not included in definitions of the money supply. The reason is that when you buy something with a credit card, you are in effect taking out a loan from the bank that issued the credit card. Only when you pay your credit card bill at the end of the month—often with a check or an electronic transfer from your checking account—is the transaction complete. In contrast, with a debit card, the funds to make the purchase are taken directly from your checking account. In either case, the cards themselves do not represent money.

25.3 LEARNING OBJECTIVE

25.3 | Explain how banks create money.

How Do Banks Create Money?

We have seen that the most important component of the money supply is checking accounts in banks. To understand the role money plays in the economy, we need to look more closely at how banks operate. Banks are profit-making private businesses, just like bookstores and supermarkets. Some banks are quite small, with just a few branches, and they do business in a limited area. Others are among the largest corporations in the United States, with hundreds of branches spread across many states. The key role that banks play in the economy is to accept deposits and make loans. By doing this, they create checking account deposits.

Bank Balance Sheets

To understand how banks create money, we need to briefly examine a typical bank balance sheet. Recall from Chapter 7 that on a balance sheet, a firm's assets are listed on the left and its liabilities and stockholders' equity are listed on the right. Assets are the value of anything owned by the firm, liabilities are the value of anything the firm owes, and stockholders' equity is the difference between the total value of assets and the total value of liabilities. Stockholders' equity represents the value of the firm if it had to be closed, all its assets were sold, and all its liabilities were paid off. A corporation's stockholders' equity is also referred to as its *net worth*.

ASSETS (IN MILLIONS)		LIABILITIES AND STOCKHOLDERS' EQUITY (IN MILLIONS)	
Reserves	$30,573	Deposits	$449,129
Loans	457,447	Short-term borrowing	51,817
Deposits with other banks	3,057	Long-term debt	161,007
Securities	115,037	Other liabilities	44,071
Buildings and equipment	6,605	Total liabilities	$706,024
Other assets	170,177		
		Stockholders' equity	76,872
Total assets	$782,896	Total liabilities and stockholders' equity	$782,896

Figure 25-2 | Balance Sheet for Wachovia Bank, December 31, 2007

The items on a bank's balance sheet of greatest economic importance are its reserves, loans, and deposits. Notice that the difference between the value of Wachovia's total assets and its total liabilities is equal to its stockholders' equity. As a consequence, the left side of the balance sheet always equals the right side.

Note: Some entries have been combined to simplify the balance sheet.

Source: Wachovia Corporation and Subsidiaries Consolidated Balance Sheets from Wachovia Corporation, *Annual Report*, 2007.

Don't Let This Happen to **YOU!**

Know When a Checking Account Is an Asset and When It Is a Liability

Consider the following reasoning: "How can checking account deposits be a liability to a bank? After all, they are something of value that is in the bank. Therefore, checking account deposits should be counted as a bank *asset* rather than as a bank liability."

This statement is incorrect. The balance in a checking account represents something the bank *owes* to the owner of the account. Therefore, it is a liability to the bank, although it is an asset to the owner of the account. Similarly, your car loan is a liability to you—because it is a debt you owe to the bank—but it is an asset to the bank.

YOUR TURN: Test your understanding by doing related problem 3.11 on page 883 at the end of this chapter.

Figure 25-2 shows the balance sheet of Wachovia Bank, which is based in Charlotte, North Carolina, and in 2008 had branches in 21 states. The key assets on a bank's balance sheet are its *reserves*, loans, and holdings of securities, such as U.S. Treasury bills. **Reserves** are deposits that a bank has retained, rather than loaned out or invested by, for instance, buying U.S. Treasury bills. Banks keep reserves either physically within the bank, as *vault cash*, or on deposit with the Federal Reserve. Banks are required by law to keep as reserves 10 percent of their checking account deposits above a threshold level, which in 2008 was $43.9 million. (In 2008, the required reserve ratio was zero on a bank's first $9.3 million in checking account deposits, 3 percent on deposits between $9.3 million and $43.9 million, and 10 percent on deposits above $43.9 million. For simplicity, we will assume that banks are required to keep 10 percent of all reserves.) These reserves are called **required reserves**. The minimum fraction of deposits that banks are required to keep as reserves is called the **required reserve ratio**. We can abbreviate the required reserve ratio as *RR*. Any reserves banks hold over and above the legal requirement are called **excess reserves**. The balance sheet in Figure 25-2 shows that loans are Wachovia's largest asset, which is true of most banks.

Reserves Deposits that a bank keeps as cash in its vault or on deposit with the Federal Reserve.

Required reserves Reserves that a bank is legally required to hold, based on its checking account deposits.

Required reserve ratio The minimum fraction of deposits banks are required by law to keep as reserves.

Excess reserves Reserves that banks hold over and above the legal requirement.

Banks make *consumer loans* to households and *commercial loans* to businesses. A loan is an asset to a bank because it represents a promise by the person taking out the loan to make certain specified payments to the bank. A bank's reserves and its holdings of securities are also assets because they are things of value owned by the bank.

As with most banks, Wachovia's largest liability is its deposits. Deposits include checking accounts, savings accounts, and certificates of deposit. Deposits are liabilities to banks because they are owed to the households or firms that have deposited the funds. If you deposit $100 in your checking account, the bank owes you the $100, and you can ask for it back at any time.

Using T-Accounts to Show How a Bank Can Create Money

It is easier to show how banks create money by using a T-account rather than a balance sheet. A T-account is a stripped-down version of a balance sheet that shows only how a transaction *changes* a bank's balance sheet. For example, suppose you deposit $1,000 in currency into an account at Wachovia Bank. This transaction raises the total deposits at Wachovia by $1,000 and also raises Wachovia's reserves by $1,000. We can show this on the following T-account:

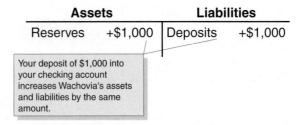

Assets		Liabilities	
Reserves	+$1,000	Deposits	+$1,000

Your deposit of $1,000 into your checking account increases Wachovia's assets and liabilities by the same amount.

Remember that because the total value of all the entries on the right side of a balance sheet must always be equal to the total value of all the entries on the left side of a balance sheet, any transaction that increases (or decreases) one side of the balance sheet must also increase (or decrease) the other side of the balance sheet. In this case, the T-account shows that we increased both sides of the balance sheet by $1,000.

Initially, this transaction does not increase the money supply. The currency component of the money supply declines by $1,000 because the $1,000 you deposited is no longer in circulation and, therefore, is not counted in the money supply. But the decrease in currency is offset by a $1,000 increase in the checking account deposit component of the money supply.

This initial change is not the end of the story, however. Banks are required to keep 10 percent of deposits as reserves. Because banks do not earn interest on reserves, they have an incentive to loan out or buy securities with the other 90 percent. In this case, Wachovia can keep $100 as required reserves and loan out the other $900, which represents excess reserves. Suppose Wachovia loans out the $900 to someone to buy a very inexpensive used car. Wachovia could give the $900 to the borrower in currency, but usually banks make loans by increasing the borrower's checking account. We can show this with another T-account:

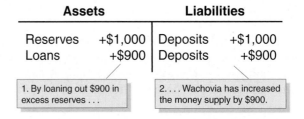

Assets		Liabilities	
Reserves	+$1,000	Deposits	+$1,000
Loans	+$900	Deposits	+$900

1. By loaning out $900 in excess reserves . . .

2. . . . Wachovia has increased the money supply by $900.

A key point to recognize is that *by making this $900 loan, Wachovia has increased the money supply by $900.* The initial $1,000 in currency you deposited into your checking account has been turned into $1,900 in checking account deposits—a net increase in the money supply of $900.

But the story does not end here. The person who took out the $900 loan did so to buy a used car. To keep things simple, let's suppose he buys the car for exactly $900 and pays by writing a check on his account at Wachovia. The owner of the used car will now deposit the check in her bank. That bank may also be a branch of Wachovia, but in most cities, there are many banks, so let's assume that the seller of the car has her account at a branch of PNC Bank. Once she deposits the check, PNC Bank will send it to Wachovia Bank to *clear* the check and collect the $900. We can show the result using T-accounts:

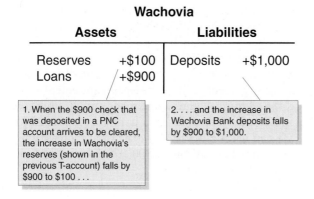

Wachovia

Assets		Liabilities	
Reserves	+$100	Deposits	+$1,000
Loans	+$900		

1. When the $900 check that was deposited in a PNC account arrives to be cleared, the increase in Wachovia's reserves (shown in the previous T-account) falls by $900 to $100 . . .

2. . . . and the increase in Wachovia Bank deposits falls by $900 to $1,000.

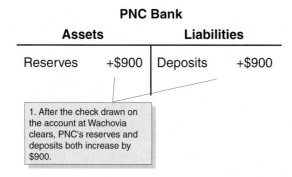

PNC Bank

Assets		Liabilities	
Reserves	+$900	Deposits	+$900

1. After the check drawn on the account at Wachovia clears, PNC's reserves and deposits both increase by $900.

Once the car buyer's check has cleared, Wachovia has lost $900 in deposits—the amount loaned to the car buyer—and $900 in reserves—the amount it had to pay PNC when PNC sent Wachovia the car buyer's check. PNC has an increase in checking account deposits of $900—the deposit of the car seller—and an increase in reserves of $900—the amount it received from Wachovia.

PNC has 100 percent reserves against this new $900 deposit, when it only needs 10 percent reserves. The bank has an incentive to keep $90 as reserves and to loan out the other $810, which are excess reserves. If PNC does this, we can show the change in its balance sheet using another T-account:

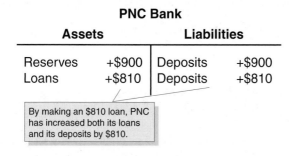

PNC Bank

Assets		Liabilities	
Reserves	+$900	Deposits	+$900
Loans	+$810	Deposits	+$810

By making an $810 loan, PNC has increased both its loans and its deposits by $810.

In loaning out the $810 in excess reserves, PNC creates a new checking account deposit of $810. The initial deposit of $1,000 in currency into Wachovia Bank has now resulted in the creation of $1,000 + $900 + $810 = $2,710 in checking account deposits. The money supply has increased by $2,710 − $1,000 = $1,710.

The process is still not finished. The person who borrows the $810 will spend it by writing a check against his account. Whoever receives the $810 will deposit it in her bank, which could be a Wachovia branch or a PNC branch or a branch of some other bank. That new bank—if it's not PNC—will send the check to PNC and will receive $810 in new reserves. That new bank will have an incentive to loan out 90 percent of these reserves—keeping 10 percent to meet the legal requirement—and the process will go on. At each stage, the additional loans being made and the additional deposits being created are shrinking by 10 percent, as each bank has to withhold that amount as required reserves. We can use a table to show the total increase in checking account deposits set off by your initial deposit of $1,000. The dots in the table represent additional rounds in the money creation process:

BANK	INCREASE IN CHECKING ACCOUNT DEPOSITS	
Wachovia	$1,000	
PNC	+ 900	(= 0.9 × $1,000)
Third Bank	+ 810	(= 0.9 × $900)
Fourth Bank	+ 729	(= 0.9 × $810)
•	+ •	
•	+ •	
•	+ •	
Total change in checking account deposits	= $10,000	

The Simple Deposit Multiplier

Your initial deposit of $1,000 increased the reserves of the banking system by $1,000 and led to a total increase in checking account deposits of $10,000. The ratio of the amount of deposits created by banks to the amount of new reserves is called the **simple deposit multiplier**. In this case, the simple deposit multiplier is equal to $10,000/$1,000 = 10. Why 10? How do we know that your initial $1,000 deposit ultimately leads to a total increase in deposits of $10,000?

There are two ways to answer this question. First, each bank in the process is keeping reserves equal to 10 percent of its deposits. For the banking system as a whole, the total increase in reserves is $1,000—the amount of your original currency deposit. Therefore, the system as a whole will end up with $10,000 in deposits, because $1,000 is 10 percent of $10,000.

A second way to answer the question is by deriving an expression for the simple deposit multiplier. The total increase in deposits equals:

$$\$1,000 + [0.9 \times \$1,000] + [(0.9 \times 0.9) \times \$1,000] + [(0.9 \times 0.9 \times 0.9) \times \$1,000] + \ldots$$

Or:

$$\$1,000 + [0.9 \times \$1,000] + [0.9^2 \times \$1,000] + [0.9^3 \times \$1,000] + \ldots$$

Or:

$$\$1,000 \times (1 + 0.9 + 0.9^2 + 0.9^3 + \ldots).$$

The rules of algebra tell us that an expression like the one in the parentheses sums to:

$$\frac{1}{1-0.9}.$$

Simple deposit multiplier The ratio of the amount of deposits created by banks to the amount of new reserves.

Simplifying further, we have:

$$\frac{1}{0.10} = 10.$$

So:

$$\text{Total increase in deposits} = \$1,000 \times 10 = \$10,000.$$

Note that 10 is equal to 1 divided by the required reserve ratio, *RR*, which in this case is 10 percent, or 0.10. This gives us another way of expressing the simple deposit multiplier:

$$\text{Simple deposit multiplier} = \frac{1}{RR}.$$

This formula makes it clear that the higher the required reserve ratio, the smaller the simple deposit multiplier. With a required reserve ratio of 10 percent, the simple deposit multiplier is 10. If the required reserve ratio were 20 percent, the simple deposit multiplier would fall to 1/0.20, or 5. We can use this formula to calculate the total increase in checking account deposits from an increase in bank reserves due to, for instance, currency being deposited in a bank:

$$\text{Change in checking account deposits} = \text{Change in bank reserves} \times \frac{1}{RR}.$$

For example, if $100,000 in currency is deposited in a bank and the required reserve ratio is 10 percent, then:

$$\text{Change in checking account deposits} = \$100,000 \times \frac{1}{0.10} = \$100,000 \times 10 = \$1,000,000.$$

Solved Problem | 25-3

Showing How Banks Create Money

Suppose you deposit $5,000 in currency into your checking account at a branch of PNC Bank, which we will assume has no excess reserves at the time you make your deposit. Also assume that the required reserve ratio is 0.10.

a. Use a T-account to show the initial effect of this transaction on PNC's balance sheet.

b. Suppose that PNC makes the maximum loan it can from the funds you deposited. Use a T-account to show the initial effect on PNC's balance sheet from granting the loan. Also include in this T-account the transaction from question (a).

c. Now suppose that whoever took out the loan in question (b) writes a check for this amount and that the person receiving the check deposits it in Wachovia Bank. Show the effect of these transactions on the balance sheets of PNC Bank and Wachovia Bank *after the check has been cleared*. On the T-account for PNC Bank, include the transactions from questions (a) and (b).

d. What is the maximum increase in checking account deposits that can result from your $5,000 deposit? What is the maximum increase in the money supply? Explain.

SOLVING THE PROBLEM:

Step 1: **Review the chapter material.** This problem is about how banks create checking account deposits, so you may want to review the section "Using T-Accounts to Show How a Bank Can Create Money," which begins on page 861.

Step 2: **Answer question (a) by using a T-account to show the impact of the deposit.** Keeping in mind that T-accounts show only the changes in a balance sheet that result from the relevant transaction and that assets are on the left side of the account and liabilities are on the right side, we have:

PNC Bank

Assets		Liabilities	
Reserves	+$5,000	Deposits	+$5,000

Because the bank now has your $5,000 in currency in its vault, its reserves (and, therefore, its assets) have risen by $5,000. But this transaction also increases your checking account balance by $5,000. Because the bank owes you this money, the bank's liabilities have also risen by $5,000.

Step 3: **Answer question (b) by using a T-account to show the impact of the loan.** The problem tells you to assume that PNC Bank currently has no excess reserves and that the required reserve ratio is 10 percent. This requirement means that if the bank's checking account deposits go up by $5,000, the bank must keep $500 as reserves and can loan out the remaining $4,500. Remembering that new loans usually take the form of setting up, or increasing, a checking account for the borrower, we have:

PNC Bank

Assets		Liabilities	
Reserves	+$5,000	Deposits	+$5,000
Loans	+$4,500	Deposits	+$4,500

The first line of the T-account shows the transaction from question (a). The second line shows that PNC has loaned out $4,500 by increasing the checking account of the borrower by $4,500. The loan is an asset to PNC because it represents a promise by the borrower to make certain payments spelled out in the loan agreement.

Step 4: **Answer question (c) by using T-accounts for PNC and Wachovia to show the impact of the check clearing.** We now show the effect of the borrower having spent the $4,500 he received as a loan from PNC. The person who received the $4,500 check deposits it in her account at Wachovia. We need two T-accounts to show this:

PNC Bank

Assets		Liabilities	
Reserves	+$500	Deposits	+$5,000
Loans	+$4,500		

Wachovia Bank

Assets		Liabilities	
Reserves	+$4,500	Deposits	+$4,500

Look first at the T-account for PNC. Once Wachovia sends the check written by the borrower to PNC, PNC loses $4,500 in reserves and Wachovia gains $4,500 in reserves. The $4,500 is also deducted from the account of the borrower. PNC is now satisfied with the result. It received a $5,000 deposit in currency from you. When that money was sitting in the bank vault, it wasn't earning any interest for PNC. Now $4,500 of the $5,000 has been loaned out and is earning interest. These interest payments allow PNC to cover its costs and earn a profit, which it has to do to remain in business.

Wachovia now has an increase in deposits of $4,500, resulting from the check deposited by the contractor, and an increase in reserves of $4,500. Wachovia is in the same situation as PNC was in question (a): It has excess reserves as a result of this transaction and a strong incentive to lend them out in order to earn some interest.

Step 5: **Answer question (d) by using the simple deposit multiplier formula to calculate the maximum increase in checking account deposits and the maximum increase in the money supply.** The simple deposit multiplier expression is (remember that RR is the required reserve ratio):

$$\text{Change in checking account deposits} = \text{Change in bank reserves} \times \frac{1}{RR}.$$

In this case, bank reserves rose by $5,000 as a result of your initial deposit, and the required reserve ratio is 0.10, so:

$$\text{Change in checking account deposits} = \$5,000 \times \frac{1}{0.10} = \$5,000 \times 10 = \$50,000.$$

Because checking account deposits are part of the money supply, it is tempting to say that the money supply has also increased by $50,000. Remember, though, that your $5,000 in currency was counted as part of the money supply while you had it, but it is not included when it is sitting in a bank vault. Therefore:

$$\text{Change in the money supply} = \text{Increase in checking account deposits} -$$
$$\text{Decline in currency in circulation} = \$50,000 - \$5,000 = \$45,000.$$

YOUR TURN: For more practice, do related problem 3.9 on page 883 at the end of the chapter.

>> End Solved Problem 25-3

The Simple Deposit Multiplier versus the Real-World Deposit Multiplier

The story we have told about the way an increase in reserves in the banking system leads to the creation of new deposits and, therefore, an increase in the money supply has been simplified in two ways. First, we assumed that banks do not keep any excess reserves. That is, we assumed that when you deposited $1,000 in currency into your checking account at Wachovia Bank, Wachovia loaned out $900, keeping only the $100 in required reserves. In fact, banks often keep at least some excess reserves to guard against the possibility that many depositors may simultaneously make withdrawals from their accounts. The more excess reserves banks keep, the smaller the deposit multiplier. Imagine an extreme case where Wachovia keeps your entire $1,000 as reserves. If Wachovia does not loan out any of your deposit, the process described earlier of loans leading to the creation of new deposits, leading to the making of additional loans, and so on will not take place. The $1,000 increase in reserves will lead to a total increase of $1,000 in deposits, and the deposit multiplier will be only 1, not 10.

Second, we assumed that the whole amount of every check is deposited in a bank; no one takes any of it out as currency. In reality, households and firms keep roughly constant the amount of currency they hold relative to the value of their checking account balances. So, we would expect to see people increasing the amount of currency they hold as the balances in their checking accounts rise. Once again, think of the extreme case. Suppose that when Wachovia makes the initial $900 loan to the borrower who wants to buy a used car, the seller of the car cashes the check instead of depositing it. In that case, PNC does not receive any new reserves and does not make any new loans. Once again, the $1,000 increase in your checking account at Wachovia is the only increase in deposits, and the deposit multiplier is 1.

The effect of these two factors is to reduce the real-world deposit multiplier to about 2.5. That means that a $1 increase in the reserves of the banking system results in about a $2.50 increase in deposits.

Although the story of the deposit multiplier can be complicated, the key point to bear in mind is that the most important part of the money supply is the checking account balance component. When banks make loans, they increase checking account balances, and the money supply expands. Banks make new loans whenever they gain reserves. The whole process can also work in reverse. If banks lose reserves, they reduce their outstanding loans and deposits, and the money supply contracts.

We can summarize these important conclusions:

1 Whenever banks gain reserves, they make new loans, and the money supply expands.

2 Whenever banks lose reserves, they reduce their loans, and the money supply contracts.

25.4 LEARNING OBJECTIVE

25.4 | Discuss the three policy tools the Federal Reserve uses to manage the money supply.

The Federal Reserve System

Many people are surprised to learn that banks do not keep in their vaults all the funds that are deposited into checking accounts. In fact, in May 2008, the total amount of checking account balances in all banks in the United States was $595 billion, while total reserves were only $44 billion. The United States, like nearly all other countries, has a *fractional reserve banking system*. In a **fractional reserve banking system**, banks keep less than 100 percent of deposits as reserves. When people deposit money in a bank, the bank loans most of the money to someone else. What happens, though, if depositors want their money back? This would seem to be a problem because banks have loaned out most of the money and can't get it back easily.

Fractional reserve banking system A banking system in which banks keep less than 100 percent of deposits as reserves.

In practice, though, withdrawals are usually not a problem for banks. On a typical day, about as much money is deposited as is withdrawn. If a small amount more is withdrawn than deposited, banks can cover the difference from their excess reserves or by borrowing from other banks. Sometimes depositors lose confidence in a bank when they question the value of the bank's underlying assets, particularly its loans. Often, the reason for a loss of confidence is bad news, whether true or false. When many depositors simultaneously decide to withdraw their money from a bank, there is a **bank run**. If many banks experience runs at the same time, the result is a **bank panic**. It is possible for one bank to handle a run by borrowing from other banks, but if many banks simultaneously experience runs, the banking system may be in trouble.

Bank run A situation in which many depositors simultaneously decide to withdraw money from a bank.

Bank panic A situation in which many banks experience runs at the same time.

A *central bank*, like the Federal Reserve in the United States, can help stop a bank panic by acting as a *lender of last resort*. In acting like a lender of last resort, a central bank makes loans to banks that cannot borrow funds elsewhere. The bank can use these loans to pay off depositors. When the panic ends and the depositors put their money back in their accounts, the bank can repay the loan to the central bank.

Making the Connection | The 2001 Bank Panic in Argentina

The Argentine central bank was unable to stop the bank panic of 2001.

We saw at the beginning of this chapter that Argentina suffered a bank panic in 2001. Some unusual aspects of the Argentine banking system made it very difficult for the Argentine central bank to act as a lender of last resort. As an alternative policy to stop the bank panic, the Argentine government limited the amount of Argentine currency that depositors could withdraw to $1,000 per account per month. Consumers cut back on their spending because much of the money in their bank accounts could not be withdrawn. Firms like McDonald's experienced declining sales as the country's recession worsened.

The inability of the Argentine central bank to act as a lender of last resort resulted from a decision made by the Argentine government in 1991 to fix the value of the Argentine peso relative to the U.S. dollar at one to one. This policy was meant to restore public faith in the ability of the Argentine currency to retain its value. Argentina had suffered through several periods of high inflation. In 1990, the inflation rate had been a staggering 2,300 percent. These inflationary episodes had caused the purchasing power of the currency to decline rapidly. Although the policy of fixing the value of the peso against the dollar was successful in greatly reducing inflation, it ultimately placed the banking system in an awkward situation. After 1991, Argentine banks were encouraged to take in U.S. dollar deposits and to make U.S. dollar loans, and U.S. dollars were legally recognized as a means of payment within Argentina. By 1994, 60 percent of time deposits and 50 percent of loans were in U.S. dollars. The Argentine central bank was allowed to issue pesos only in exchange for dollars, which limited its ability to provide pesos to banks experiencing a bank run.

By 2000, many observers had begun to doubt the ability of the Argentine government to maintain the one-to-one exchange rate. As a result, Argentine households and firms, as well as foreign investors, began moving funds out of pesos and into dollars. By late 2001, fully 80 percent of time deposits in Argentine banks were in dollars rather than in pesos. In addition, many depositors began withdrawing money from their accounts. Forty-seven of the top 50 Argentine banks experienced major withdrawals by December 2001. In January 2002, the crisis was ended when the government abandoned its commitment to the one-to-one exchange rate between the peso and the dollar and decreed that dollar deposits in banks would be converted to peso deposits at a rate of 1.4 pesos to the dollar. Although some financial stability was restored, the damage to the banking system from the crisis contributed to a decline in real GDP of 11.5 percent during 2002.

Source: Kathryn M. E. Dominguez and Linda Tesar, "International Borrowing and Macroeconomic Performance in Argentina," in Sebastian Edwards, ed., *Capital Controls and Capital Flows in Emerging Economies: Policies, Practices, and Consequences*, Chicago: University of Chicago Press, 2007.

YOUR TURN: Test your understanding by doing related problem 4.7 on page 884 at the end of this chapter.

The Organization of the Federal Reserve System

Bank panics lead to severe disruptions in business activity because neither households nor firms can gain access to their accounts. Not surprisingly, in the United States, each bank panic in the late nineteenth and early twentieth centuries was accompanied by a recession. With the intention of putting an end to bank panics, in 1913, Congress passed the Federal Reserve Act setting up the Federal Reserve System—often referred to as "the Fed." The system began operation in 1914. The Fed acts as a lender of last resort to banks and as a bankers' bank, providing services such as check clearing to banks. The Fed also takes actions to control the money supply.

The Fed's first test as a lender of last resort came in the early years of the Great Depression of the 1930s, when many banks were hit by bank runs as depositors pulled funds out of checking and savings accounts. Although the Fed had been established to act as a lender of last resort, Fed officials were worried that many of the banks experiencing runs had made bad loans and other investments. The Fed believed that making loans to banks that were in financial trouble because of bad investments might reduce the incentive bank managers had to be careful in their investment decisions. Partly due to the Fed's unwillingness to act as a lender of last resort, more than 5,000 banks failed during the early 1930s. Today, many economists are critical of the Fed's decisions in the early 1930s because they believe these decisions made the Great Depression more severe. In 1934, Congress took action to set up the Federal Deposit Insurance Corporation (FDIC), to insure deposits in most banks up to a limit, which is currently $100,000 per deposit. Deposit insurance has largely stopped bank panics because it has reassured depositors that their deposits are safe even if their bank goes out of business. Today, acting as a lender of last resort is no longer the most important activity of the Fed.

To aid the Fed in carrying out its responsibilities, Congress divided the country into 12 Federal Reserve districts, as shown in Figure 25-3. Each district has its own Federal Reserve bank, which provides services to banks in that district. The real power of the Fed, however, lies in Washington, DC, with the Board of Governors. There are seven members of the Board of Governors, who are appointed by the president of the United States to 14-year, nonrenewable terms. Board members come from banking, business, and academic backgrounds. One of the seven board members is appointed chairman for a four-year, renewable term. Chairmen of the Board of Governors since World War II have come from various backgrounds, including Wall Street (William McChesney Martin), academia (Arthur Burns and Ben Bernanke), business (G. William Miller), public service (Paul Volcker), and economic forecasting (Alan Greenspan).

How the Federal Reserve Manages the Money Supply

Although Congress established the Fed to stop bank panics by acting as a lender of last resort, today a more important activity for the Fed is managing the money supply. As we

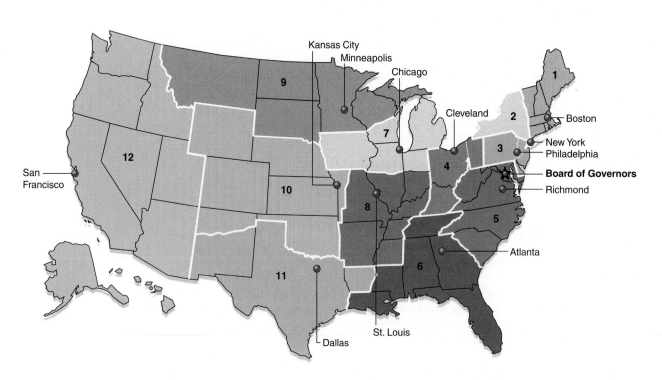

Figure 25-3 | Federal Reserve Districts

The United States is divided into 12 Federal Reserve districts, each of which has a Federal Reserve bank. The real power within the Federal Reserve System, however, lies in Washington, DC, with the Board of Governors.

Source: Board of Governors of the Federal Reserve System.

will discuss in more detail in Chapter 26, managing the money supply is part of **monetary policy**, which the Fed undertakes to pursue economic objectives.

To manage the money supply, the Fed uses three *monetary policy tools*:

1 Open market operations

2 Discount policy

3 Reserve requirements

Remember that the most important component of the money supply is checking account deposits. Not surprisingly, all three of the Fed's policy tools are aimed at affecting the reserves of banks as a means of changing the volume of checking account deposits.

Open Market Operations Eight times per year, the **Federal Open Market Committee (FOMC)** meets in Washington, DC, to discuss monetary policy. The committee has 12 members: the seven members of the Federal Reserve's Board of Governors, the president of the Federal Reserve Bank of New York, and four presidents from the other 11 Federal Reserve banks. These four presidents serve one-year rotating terms on the FOMC.

The U.S. Treasury borrows money by selling bills, notes, and bonds. Remember that the *maturity* of a financial asset is the period of time until the purchaser receives payment of the face value or principal. Usually, bonds have face values of $1,000. Treasury bills have maturities of 1 year or less, Treasury notes have maturities of 2 years to 10 years, and Treasury bonds have maturities of 30 years. To increase the money supply, the FOMC directs the *trading desk*, located at the Federal Reserve Bank of New York, to *buy* U.S. Treasury securities—most frequently bills but sometimes notes or bonds—from the public. When the sellers of the Treasury securities deposit the funds in their banks, the reserves of banks rise. This increase in reserves starts the process of increasing loans and checking account deposits that increases the money supply. To decrease the money supply, the FOMC directs the trading desk to *sell* Treasury securities. When the buyers of the Treasury securities pay for them with checks, the reserves of their banks fall. This decrease in reserves starts a contraction of loans and checking account deposits that reduces the money supply. The buying and selling of Treasury securities is called **open market operations.**

There are three reasons the Fed conducts monetary policy principally through open market operations. First, because the Fed initiates open market operations, it completely controls their volume. Second, the Fed can make both large and small open market operations. Third, the Fed can implement its open market operations quickly, with no administrative delay or required changes in regulations. Many other central banks, including the European Central Bank and the Bank of Japan, also use open market operations to conduct monetary policy.

The Federal Reserve is responsible for putting the paper currency of the United States into circulation. Recall that if you look at the top of a dollar bill, you see the words "Federal Reserve Note." When the Fed takes actions to increase the money supply, commentators sometimes say that it is "printing more money." The main way the Fed increases the money supply, however, is not by printing more money but by buying Treasury securities. Similarly, to reduce the money supply, the Fed does not set fire to stacks of paper currency. Instead, it sells Treasury securities. We will spend more time discussing how and why the Fed manages the money supply in Chapter 26, when we discuss monetary policy.

Discount Policy The loans the Fed makes to banks are called **discount loans**, and the interest rate it charges on the loans is called the **discount rate**. When a bank receives a loan from the Fed, its reserves increase by the amount of the loan. By lowering the discount rate, the Fed can encourage banks to take additional loans and thereby increase their reserves. With more reserves, banks will make more loans to households and firms, which will increase checking account deposits and the money supply. Raising the discount rate will have the reverse effect.

Monetary policy The actions the Federal Reserve takes to manage the money supply and interest rates to pursue macroeconomic policy objectives.

Federal Open Market Committee (FOMC) The Federal Reserve committee responsible for open market operations and managing the money supply in the United States.

Open market operations The buying and selling of Treasury securities by the Federal Reserve in order to control the money supply.

Discount loans Loans the Federal Reserve makes to banks.

Discount rate The interest rate the Federal Reserve charges on discount loans.

In 2008, the Fed changed its discount policy because of problems in the market for "subprime" mortgages, which are loans granted to people with flawed credit histories. Many mortgages are bundled into financial securities similar to bonds and then sold to investors. These *mortgage-backed securities* are owned by both commercial banks and *investment banks*. Investment banks earn a profit by helping other firms to sell stocks and bonds. By 2008, some subprime borrowers were defaulting on their mortgages. This reduced the value of many mortgage-backed securities and caused both commercial banks and investment banks to incur heavy losses. The Fed decided to make discount loans to investment banks to help them deal with what were hoped to be short-term problems. Because, in practice, the Fed had previously limited discount loans to helping commercial banks experiencing temporary problems with deposit withdrawals, the new policy of making loans to investment banks was somewhat controversial.

Reserve Requirements When the Fed reduces the required reserve ratio, it converts required reserves into excess reserves. For example, suppose a bank has $100 million in checking account deposits and the required reserve ratio is 10 percent. The bank will be required to hold $10 million as reserves. If the Fed reduces the required reserve ratio to 8 percent, the bank will need to hold only $8 million as reserves. The Fed has converted $2 million worth of reserves from required to excess. This $2 million is now available for the bank to lend out. If the Fed *raises* the required reserve ratio from 10 percent to 12 percent, it would have the reverse effect.

The Fed changes reserve requirements much more rarely than it conducts open market operations or changes the discount rate. Because changes in reserve requirements require significant alterations in banks' holdings of loans and securities, frequent changes would be disruptive. Also, because reserves earn no interest, the use of reserve requirements to manage the money supply effectively places a tax on banks' deposit-taking and lending activities, which can be costly for the economy.

Putting It All Together: Decisions of the Nonbank Public, Banks, and the Fed

Using its three tools—open market operations, the discount rate, and reserve requirements—the Fed has substantial influence over the money supply, but that influence is not absolute. Two other actors—the nonbank public and banks—also influence the money supply.

The nonbank public—households and firms—must decide how much money to hold as deposits in banks. The larger the money holdings in deposits, the greater the reserves of banks and the more money the banking system can create. The smaller the money holdings in deposits, the lower the reserves of banks and the less money the banking system can create. In addition, the Fed can influence, but does not control, the amount bankers decide to lend. Banks create money only if they lend their reserves. If bankers retain excess reserves, they make a smaller volume of loans and create less money.

The roles of the nonbank public and banks in the money supply process do not mean that the Fed lacks meaningful control of the money supply. The Fed's staff monitors information on banks' reserves and deposits every week, and the Fed can respond quickly to shifts in behavior by depositors or banks. The Fed can therefore steer the money supply close to the level it desires.

25.5 LEARNING OBJECTIVE

25.5 | Explain the quantity theory of money and use it to explain how high rates of inflation occur.

The Quantity Theory of Money

People have been aware of the connection between increases in the money supply and inflation for centuries. In the sixteenth century, the Spanish conquered Mexico and Peru and shipped large quantities of gold and silver back to Spain. The gold and silver were minted into coins and spent across Europe to further the political ambitions of the Spanish kings. Prices in Europe rose steadily during these years, and many observers discussed the relationship between this inflation and the flow of gold and silver into Europe from the Americas.

Connecting Money and Prices: The Quantity Equation

In the early twentieth century, Irving Fisher, an economist at Yale, formalized the connection between money and prices using the *quantity equation*:

$$M \times V = P \times Y.$$

The equation states that the money supply (M) multiplied by the *velocity of money* (V) equals the price level (P) multiplied by real output (Y). Fisher defined the **velocity of money**, often referred to simply as "velocity," as the average number of times each dollar of the money supply is used to purchase goods and services included in GDP. Rewriting the original equation by dividing both sides by M, we have the equation for velocity:

Velocity of money The average number of times each dollar in the money supply is used to purchase goods and services included in GDP.

$$V = \frac{P \times Y}{M}.$$

We can use M1 to measure the money supply, the GDP price deflator to measure the price level, and real GDP to measure real output. Then the value for velocity for 2007 was:

$$V = \frac{1.197 \times \$11{,}567 \text{ billion}}{\$1{,}368 \text{ billion}} = 10.1$$

This result tells us that, on average during 2006, each dollar of M1 was spent about 10 times on goods or services included in GDP.

Because velocity is *defined* to be equal to $(P \times Y)/M$, we know that the quantity equation must always hold true: The left side *must* be equal to the right side. A theory is a statement about the world that might possibly be false. Therefore, the quantity equation is not a theory. Irving Fisher turned the quantity equation into the **quantity theory of money** by asserting that velocity was constant. He argued that the average number of times a dollar is spent depends on how often people get paid, how often they do their grocery shopping, how often businesses mail bills, and other factors that do not change very often. Because this assertion may be true or false, the quantity theory of money is, in fact, a theory.

Quantity theory of money A theory of the connection between money and prices that assumes that the velocity of money is constant.

The Quantity Theory Explanation of Inflation

The quantity equation gives us a way of showing the relationship between changes in the money supply and changes in the price level, or inflation. To see this relationship more clearly, we can use a handy mathematical rule that states that an equation where variables are multiplied together is equal to an equation where the *growth rates* of these variables are *added* together. So, we can transform the quantity equation from:

$$M \times V = P \times Y$$

to:

Growth rate of the money supply + Growth rate of velocity =
Growth rate of the price level (or inflation rate) + Growth rate of real output.

This way of writing the quantity equation is more useful for investigating the effect of changes in the money supply on the inflation rate. Remember that the growth rate for any variable is just the percentage change in the variable from one year to the next.

The growth rate of the price level is just the inflation rate, so we can rewrite the quantity equation to help us understand the factors that determine inflation:

$$\text{Inflation rate} = \text{Growth rate of the money supply} +$$
$$\text{Growth rate of velocity} - \text{Growth rate of real output}.$$

If Irving Fisher was correct that velocity is constant, then the growth rate of velocity will be zero. That is, if velocity is, say, always 10.1, then its percentage change from one year to the next will always be zero. This assumption allows us to rewrite the equation one last time:

$$\text{Inflation rate} = \text{Growth rate of the money supply} - \text{Growth rate of real output}.$$

This equation leads to the following predictions:

1 If the money supply grows at a faster rate than real GDP, there will be inflation.

2 If the money supply grows at a slower rate than real GDP, there will be deflation. (Recall that *deflation* is a decline in the price level.)

3 If the money supply grows at the same rate as real GDP, the price level will be stable, and there will be neither inflation nor deflation.

It turns out that Irving Fisher was wrong in asserting that the velocity of money is constant. From year to year, there can be significant fluctuations in velocity. As a result, the predictions of the quantity theory of money do not hold every year, but most economists agree that the quantity theory provides a useful insight into the long-run relationship between the money supply and inflation: *In the long run, inflation results from the money supply growing at a faster rate than real GDP.*

High Rates of Inflation

Why do governments allow high rates of inflation? The quantity theory can help us to understand the reasons for high rates of inflation, such as that experienced in Argentina during the 1980s. Very high rates of inflation—in excess of hundreds or thousands of percentage points per year—are known as *hyperinflation*. Hyperinflation is caused by central banks increasing the money supply at a rate far in excess of the growth rate of real GDP. A high rate of inflation causes money to lose its value so rapidly that households and firms avoid holding it. If the inflation becomes severe enough, people stop using paper currency, so it no longer serves the important functions of money discussed earlier in this chapter. Economies suffering from high inflation usually also suffer from very slow growth, if not severe recession.

Given the dire consequences that follow from high inflation, why do governments allow it by expanding the money supply so rapidly? The main reason is that governments often want to spend more than they are able to raise through taxes. Developed countries, such as the United States, can usually bridge gaps between spending and taxes by borrowing through selling bonds to the public. Developing countries often have difficulty selling bonds because the public is skeptical of their ability to pay back the money. If they are unable to sell bonds to the public, governments in developing countries will force their central banks to purchase them. As we discussed previously, when a central bank buys bonds, the money supply will increase.

High Inflation in Argentina

The link between rapid money growth and high inflation was evident in the experience of Argentina during the 1980s. Panel (a) of Figure 25-4 shows rates of growth of the money supply and the inflation rate in Argentina in the years from 1981 to 1991. Both the average annual growth rate of the money supply and the average annual inflation

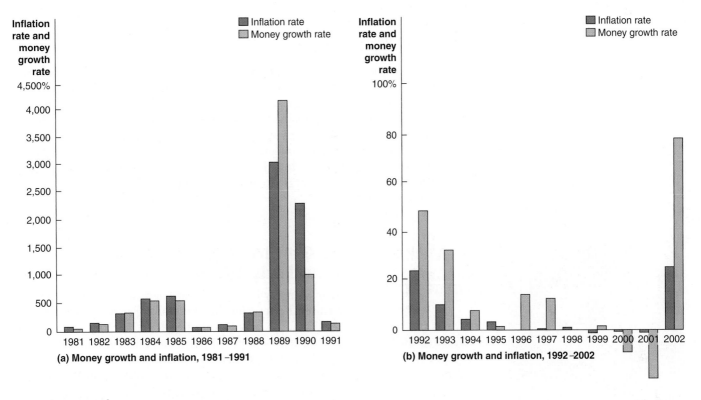

Figure 25-4 | Money Growth and Inflation in Argentina

Panel (a) shows rates of growth of the money supply and the inflation rate in Argentina in the years from 1981 to 1991. Both the average annual growth rate of the money supply and the average annual inflation rate from 1981 to 1990 were greater than 750 percent. In 1991, the Argentine government enacted a new policy that fixed the exchange rate of the peso versus the U.S. dollar at one to one. As panel (b) shows,

the new policy greatly reduced increases in the money supply and the inflation rate. (Notice that the scale of panel (b) is different from the scale of panel (a), which partly disguises the fall in money growth and inflation.)
Source: International Monetary Fund.

rate from 1981 to 1990 were greater than 750 percent. With prices rising so quickly, Argentine currency could not fulfill the normal functions of money. Not surprisingly, the Argentine economy struggled during these years, with real GDP in 1990 ending up 6 percent lower than it had been in 1981.

This weak economic performance was particularly frustrating to many people in Argentina because early in the twentieth century, the country had had one of the highest standards of living in the world. In 1910, only the United States and Great Britain had higher levels of real GDP per capita than Argentina. In U.S.-made films of the 1920s and 1930s, the rich foreigner was often from Argentina.

It was clear to policymakers in Argentina that the only way to bring inflation under control was to limit increases in the money supply. As we saw in the *Making the Connection* on page 869, in 1991, the Argentine government enacted a new policy that fixed the exchange rate of the peso versus the U.S. dollar at one to one. In addition, the Argentine central bank was allowed to issue pesos only in exchange for dollars. As panel (b) in Figure 25-4 shows, the new policy greatly reduced increases in the money supply and the inflation rate. (Notice that the scale of panel (b) is different from the scale of panel (a), which partly disguises the fall in money growth and inflation.) Economic growth also revived, with real GDP increasing at an average annual rate of almost 6 percent from 1991 to 1998. Unfortunately, though, Argentina had not come to grips with several underlying economic problems, perhaps the most important of which was the continuing gap between government expenditures and tax receipts.

By 2000, many observers expected that the Argentine government would not be able to maintain the one-to-one exchange rate between the peso and the U.S. dollar. As Argentine firms and households, along with foreign investors, began exchanging pesos for dollars, the Argentine money supply declined. The money supply declined by 9 percent in 2000 and by an additional 20 percent in 2001. Argentina experienced falling prices, or deflation, during both years, along with falling real GDP. Finally, in January 2002, the Argentine government abandoned its commitment to the one-to-one exchange rate between the peso and the dollar, and the money supply increased rapidly. During 2002, the money supply increased by nearly 80 percent, and deflation was transformed to an inflation rate of 25 percent. Although the inflation rate declined over the next few years, Argentina continues to struggle to keep its money supply from growing at rates likely to result in high inflation.

During the hyperinflation of the 1920s, people in Germany used paper currency to light their stoves.

Making the Connection | The German Hyperinflation of the Early 1920s

When Germany lost World War I, a revolution broke out that overthrew Kaiser Wilhelm II and installed a new government known as the Weimar Republic. In the peace treaty of 1919, the Allies—the United States, Great Britain, France, and Italy—imposed payments called *reparations* on the new German government. The reparations were meant as compensation to the Allies for the damage Germany had caused during the war. It was very difficult for the German government to use tax revenue to cover both its normal spending and the reparations.

The German government decided to pay for the difference between its spending and its tax revenues by selling bonds to the central bank, the Reichsbank. After a few years, the German government fell far behind in its reparations payment. In January 1923, the French government sent troops into the German industrial area known as the Ruhr to try to collect the payments directly. German workers in the Ruhr went on strike, and the German government decided to support them by paying their salaries. Raising the funds to do so was financed by an inflationary monetary policy—the German government sold bonds to the Reichsbank, thereby increasing the money supply.

The inflationary increase in the money supply was very large: The total number of marks—the German currency—in circulation rose from 115 million in January 1922 to 1.3 billion in January 1923 and then to 497 billion *billion*, or 497,000,000,000,000,000,000, in December 1923. Just as the quantity theory predicts, the result was a staggeringly high rate of inflation. The German price index that stood at 100 in 1914 and 1,440 in January 1922 had risen to 126,160,000,000,000 in December 1923. The German mark became worthless. The German government ended the hyperinflation by (1) negotiating a new agreement with the Allies that reduced its reparations payments, (2) reducing other government expenditures and raising taxes to balance its budget, and (3) replacing the existing mark with a new mark. Each new mark was worth 1 trillion old marks. The German central bank was also limited to issuing a total of 3.2 billion new marks.

These steps were enough to bring the hyperinflation to an end—but not before the savings of anyone holding the old marks had been wiped out. Most middle-income Germans were extremely resentful of this outcome. Many historians believe that the hyperinflation greatly reduced the allegiance of many Germans to the Weimar Republic and may have helped pave the way for Hitler and the Nazis to seize power 10 years later.

Source: Thomas Sargent, "The End of Four Big Hyperinflations," in *Rational Expectations and Inflation*, New York: Harper and Row, 1986.

YOUR TURN: Test your understanding by doing related problem 5.7 on page 885 at the end of this chapter.

Economics in YOUR Life!

≫ Continued from page 851

At the beginning of the chapter, we asked you to consider whether you would like to live in an economy in which the purchasing power of money rose every year. The first thing to consider when thinking about the advantages and disadvantages of this situation is that the only way for the purchasing power of money to increase is for the price level to fall; in other words, *deflation* must occur. Because the price level in the United States hasn't fallen over the course of a year since the 1930s, most people alive today have experienced only rising price levels—and declining purchasing power of money. Would replacing rising prices with falling prices necessarily be a good thing? It might be tempting to say yes, because if you have a job, then your salary will buy more goods and services each year. But, in fact, just as a rising price level results in most wages and salaries rising each year, a falling price level is likely to mean falling wages and salaries each year. So, it is likely that, on average, people would not see the purchasing power of their incomes increase, even if the purchasing power of any currency they hold would increase. There can also be a significant downside to deflation, particularly if the transition from inflation to deflation happens suddenly. In Chapter 20, we defined the real interest rate as being equal to the nominal interest rate minus the inflation rate. If an economy experiences deflation, then the real interest rate will be greater than the nominal interest rate. A rising real interest rate can be bad news for anyone who has borrowed, including homeowners who may have substantial mortgage loans. So, you are probably better off living in an economy experiencing mild inflation rather than one experiencing deflation.

Conclusion

Money plays a key role in the functioning of an economy by facilitating trade in goods and services and by making specialization possible. Without specialization, no advanced economy can prosper. Households and firms, banks, and the central bank (the Federal Reserve in the United States) are participants in the process of creating the money supply. In Chapter 26, we will explore how the Federal Reserve uses monetary policy to promote its economic objectives.

An Inside Look at Policy on the next page discusses how China's central bank is trying to control the money supply by slowing bank lending.

WALL STREET JOURNAL, APRIL 30, 2007

China Lifts Bank Reserves in Bid to Cool Growth

(a) For the seventh time in less than a year, China's central bank raised the share of deposits banks must keep on reserve as the government struggles to soak up capital and keep the country's economy from overheating.

The move, which was announced yesterday and takes effect May 15, follows accelerated economic growth and an uptick in inflation indicators. The government announced this month that gross domestic product, or the total value of goods and services produced, expanded at a faster-than-expected 11.1% in the first quarter from a year earlier.

Economists had expected the government to take further measures to tighten money supply around tomorrow's May Day holiday and said that in coming weeks the People's Bank of China could implement even more measures—including a rate increase—to contain upward pressure on prices and slow growth from the blistering pace of the first quarter.

The central bank said on its Web site yesterday that the increase in reserve ratio is aimed at "strengthening the management of liquidity in the banking system" and guiding "the reasonable growth of credit."

(b) Still, economists said increases to the reserve ratio have so far achieved little, if any, of their desired effect. The newly announced increase will bring the reserve-requirement ratio—the share of deposits that lenders must keep with the central bank—up half a percentage point to 11% for most banks. The increase, in theory, reduces the amount available to banks to lend, though in practice many Chinese banks already keep more than the minimum on reserve.

"The past two years of experience in China has shown that [reserve-ratio] changes are an ineffective policy tool to control monetary expansion," Hong Liang, a Hong Kong–based Goldman Sachs economist, said in a research note after the increase was announced. Such ratio increases are "simply not binding on banks' capabilities to lend," Ms. Liang said.

Behind the flush liquidity in the domestic economy is China's booming trade surplus, or margin by which exports exceed imports, and the central bank's intervention to keep the value of the domestic currency from appreciating too quickly as a result. The central bank pays out yuan to banks to buy their dollars, pumping cash into the economy.

Because many investors believe the reserve-requirement increase signals the government's resolve to continue employing tightening measures, the move could cause traders to push domestic shares lower in trading today—the last day China's markets are open before a weeklong holiday. But any selling is likely to be limited, analysts said.

"The People's Bank tightened at this juncture to give the markets a little time to digest this increase," said Jing Ulrich, chairwoman of China equities at J.P. Morgan & Co. "This one hike alone won't trigger a major selloff."

(c) The acceleration in China's economic growth, driven in significant part by bank lending to new investment projects, has forced Beijing to pull a variety of monetary-policy levers since last year. It has also enacted administrative measures to cool sectors such as property and steel, which threaten to push prices higher. The latest reserve-ratio increase is the second in a month.

China's consumer-price index rose 3.3% in March and 2.7% in the first quarter, compared with a year earlier. That pickup has sparked concerns that after muted inflation in recent years, rising production capacity might no longer be able to counterbalance demand, and a surge in prices could be ahead for the world's fastest-growing major economy.

"If the inflation rate continues to climb, if the momentum of fixed-asset investment growth doesn't slow down, and if the asset prices rise too quickly, the central bank definitely will tighten further," said Yu Yongding, a professor and former member of central bank's monetary-policy committee.

Key Points in the Article

This article discusses how China's central bank has attempted to slow the growth of bank lending—and, hence, the money supply—by raising banks' reserve requirement. As of May 15, 2007, China's central bank had raised the ratio seven times in less than a year. Although changing the required reserve ratio can be a relatively disruptive monetary policy tool, the central bank is using it to slow the growth of China's economy. In the first quarter of 2007, real GDP grew at an annual rate of 11.1 percent, which is probably to be sustained without causing the inflation rate to increase. The central bank's efforts to reduce bank lending have been largely ineffective because the reserve requirements are not binding; most banks already hold more than the required reserve amount. And, ironically, this is because the supply of bank reserves is growing, thanks to the exchange-rate policies of China's central bank. Finally, the article notes that China's central bank is right to be concerned because China's consumer price index rose 2.7 percentage points more in the first quarter of 2007 than it did in the first quarter of 2006.

Analyzing the News

(a) China's central bank has used reserve requirements—a monetary policy tool that the U.S. Federal Reserve rarely uses today—for the seventh time in less than 12 months in order to slow the growth of bank lending in China. As you read in this chapter, changes in reserve requirements can be disruptive to banks because they necessitate significant changes in banks' holdings of loans and securities. A bank that has no excess reserves will be forced to reduce its holdings of loans and securities if the required reserve ratio is increased. Nonetheless, the Chinese government continues to raise reserve requirements as it attempts to slow the economy, which grew at a very rapid annual rate of 11.1 percent in the first quarter of 2007. By comparison, the U.S. economy grew at an annual rate of 1.3 percent in the same quarter. China's policymakers are concerned that a high rate of growth in the money supply will cause the inflation rate to increase.

(b) As of May 15, 2007, the required reserve ratio for most Chinese banks will be 11 percent. Nonetheless, the government's attempt to reduce bank lending by raising reserve requirements has been relatively ineffective for two reasons. First, the reserve requirement is not binding because many of China's banks already hold more than the minimum amount of required reserves. So, raising the required reserve ratio has little effect on these banks' lending practices. Second, bank reserves have been rising in part due to China's large trade surplus. And, ironically, this trade surplus is, to some extent, the product of the Chinese government's strategy of fixing the value of its currency—the yuan—to the U.S. dollar. Since the mid-1990s, the Chinese government has purchased U.S. dollars—and, consequently, sold yuan—in the foreign exchange market in order to keep the yuan from increasing in value against the U.S. dollar. This pattern is shown in the figure, which plots the Chinese yuan/U.S. dollar foreign exchange rate. By keeping the value of the yuan nearly fixed against the dollar, China effectively keeps the dollar-price of its exports relatively low. Because Chinese exporters are accumulating large amounts of dollars, when these dollars are exchange for yuan they ultimately end up in Chinese banks in the form of bank reserves.

(c) Recent data on inflation has China's monetary policymakers concerned. In particular, China's consumer price index rose 2.7 percentage points more in the first quarter of 2007 than it did in the first quarter of 2006. Most economists agree that this inflation has occurred because the growth in China's aggregate demand is outpacing the growth in its aggregate supply. This is precisely what the quantity theory, which you read about in this chapter, predicts: In the long run, inflation results from the money supply growing at a faster rate than real GDP.

Thinking Critically
About Policy

1. Suppose China's reserve requirement were binding. Explain how a rise in the required reserve ratio would slow bank lending in China.
2. In light of the success that the United States has had with open market operations, why doesn't China use a similar tool to buy yuan in the open market and, hence, slow the growth of bank reserves that way?

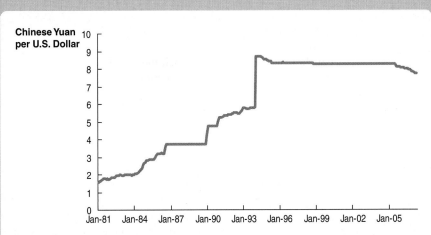

Fixing the value of the yuan against the U.S. dollar has effectively fueled the growth in China's bank reserves.

Key Terms

25.1 LEARNING OBJECTIVE   25.1 | Define money and discuss its four functions, **pages 852-855.**

What Is Money and Why Do We Need It?

Summary

A *barter economy* is an economy that does not use money and in which people trade goods and services directly for other goods and services. Barter trade occurs only if there is a *double coincidence of wants*, where both parties to the trade want what the other one has. Because barter is inefficient, there is strong incentive to use **money**, which is any **asset** that people are generally willing to accept in exchange for goods or services or in payment of debts. An *asset* is anything of value owned by a person or a firm. A *commodity money* is a good used as money that also has value independent of its use as money. Money has four functions: It is a medium of exchange, a unit of account, a store of value, and a standard of deferred payment. The *gold standard* was a monetary system under which the government produced gold coins and paper currency that were convertible into gold. The gold standard collapsed in the early 1930s. Today, no government in the world issues paper currency that can be redeemed for gold. Instead, paper currency is **fiat money**, which has no value except as money.

myeconlab Visit www.myeconlab.com to complete these exercises
Get Ahead of the Curve online and get instant feedback.

Review Questions

1.1 A baseball fan with an Albert Pujols baseball card wants to trade it for a Derek Jeter baseball card, but everyone the fan knows who has a Jeter card doesn't want a Pujols card. What do economists call the problem this fan is having?

1.2 What is the difference between commodity money and fiat money?

1.3 What are the four functions of money? Can something be considered money if it does not fulfill all four functions?

Problems and Applications

1.4 The English economist Stanley Jevons described a world tour during the 1880s by a French singer, Mademoiselle Zélie. One stop on the tour was a theater in the Society Islands, part of French Polynesia in the South Pacific. She performed for her usual fee, which was one-third of the receipts. This turned out to be three pigs, 23 turkeys, 44 chickens, 5,000 coconuts, and "considerable quantities of bananas, lemons, and oranges." She estimated that all of this would have had a value in France of 4,000 francs. According to Jevons, "as Mademoiselle could not consume any considerable portion of the receipts herself, it became necessary in the meantime to feed the pigs and poultry with the fruit." Do the goods Mademoiselle Zélie received as payment fulfill the four functions of money described in the chapter? Briefly explain.

Source: W. Stanley Jevons, *Money and the Mechanism of Exchange*, New York: D. Appleton and Company, 1889, pp. 1–2.

1.5 In the late 1940s, the Communists under Mao Zedong were defeating the government of China in a civil war. The paper currency issued by the Chinese government was losing much of its value, and most businesses refused to accept it. At the same time, there was a paper shortage in Japan. During these years, Japan was still under military occupation by the United States, following its defeat in World War II. Some of the U.S. troops in Japan realized that they could use dollars to buy up vast amounts of paper currency in China, ship it to Japan to be recycled into paper, and make a substantial profit. Under these circumstances, was the Chinese paper currency a commodity money or a fiat money? Briefly explain.

1.6 In the 1970s, Pol Pot, the dictator of Cambodia, proclaimed that he intended to do away with money in his country because money represents the decadence of the West (Western Europe and the United States). Historically, did money only exist in the West? What effect would the elimination of money have on the economy?

1.7 According to a news story, during 2007, businesses in the city of Magdeburg, Germany, were printing their own currency called the Urstromtaler. The lawyer who started the currency was quoted as saying, "All the businesses have signed contracts, and it's official. We have our own banknotes and we have an issuing office in the city centre." The new currency is issued at a rate of one for one against the euro: Anyone bringing euros to the issuing office in the city will receive the same number of Urstomtalers in exchange. Although issuing this local currency is apparently technically illegal, the German government has taken no action. Unlike euros, the local currency no longer has value after a certain date, which means consumers have an incentive to spend it quickly. Does this local German currency fulfill the four functions of money described in the chapter? Briefly explain.

Source: Tristana Moore, "Germans Take Pride in Local Money," BBC News, February 6, 2007.

1.8 **(Related to the *Making the Connection* on page 855)** According to Peter Heather, a historian at the University of Oxford, during the Roman Empire, the German tribes east of the Rhine River produced no coins of their own but used Roman coins instead:

> Although no coinage was produced in Germania, Roman coins were in plentiful circulation and could easily have provided a medium of exchange (already in the first century, Tacitus tells us, Germani of the Rhine region were using good-quality Roman silver coins for this purpose).

a. What is a medium of exchange?

b. What does the author mean when he writes that Roman coins could have provided the German tribes with a medium of exchange?

c. Why would any member of a German tribe have been willing to accept a Roman coin from another member of the tribe in exchange for goods or services when the tribes were not part of the Roman Empire and were not governed by Roman law?

Source: Peter Heather, *The Fall of the Roman Empire: A New History of Rome and the Barbarians*, New York: Oxford University Press, 2006, p. 89.

>> **End Learning Objective 25.1**

25.2 LEARNING OBJECTIVE   25.2 | Discuss the definitions of the money supply used in the United States today, **pages 856–860.**

How Is Money Measured in the United States Today?

Summary

The narrowest definition of the money supply in the United States today is **M1**, which includes currency, checking account balances, and traveler's checks. A broader definition of the money supply is **M2**, which includes everything that is in M1, plus savings accounts, small-denomination time deposits (such as certificates of deposit [CDs]), money market deposit accounts in banks, and noninstitutional money market fund shares.

myeconlab Visit www.myeconlab.com to complete these exercises *Get Ahead of the Curve* online and get instant feedback.

Review Questions

2.1 What is the main difference between the M1 and M2 definitions of the money supply?

2.2 Why does the Federal Reserve use two definitions of the money supply rather than one?

Problems and Applications

2.3 Briefly explain whether each of the following is counted in M1.
   a. The coins in your pocket
   b. The funds in your checking account
   c. The funds in your savings account
   d. The traveler's check that you have left over from a trip
   e. Your Citibank Platinum MasterCard

2.4 **(Related to *Solved Problem 25-2* on page 859)** Suppose you have $2,000 in currency in a shoebox in your closet. One day, you decide to deposit the money in a checking account. Briefly explain how this will affect M1 and M2.

2.5 (Related to *Solved Problem 25-2* on page 859) Suppose you decide to withdraw $100 in currency from your checking account. What is the effect on M1? Ignore any actions the bank may take as a result of your having withdrawn the $100.

2.6 (Related to the *Don't Let This Happen to You!* on page 859) Briefly explain whether you agree or disagree with the following statement: "I recently read that more than half of the money issued by the government is actually held by people in foreign countries. If that's true, then the United States is less than half as wealthy as government statistics indicate."

2.7 The paper currency of the United States is technically called "Federal Reserve notes." The following excerpt is from the Federal Reserve Act: "Federal reserve notes . . . shall be redeemed in lawful money on demand at the Treasury Department of the United States, in the city of Washington, District of Columbia, or at any Federal Reserve bank." If you took a $20 bill to the Treasury Department or a Federal Reserve bank, with what type of "lawful money" is the government likely to redeem it?

2.8 (Related to the *Making the Connection* on page 857) There are currently about 1.4 billion pennies in circulation. Suppose the proposal of economist François Velde to make the current penny worth five cents were adopted. What would be the effect on the value of M1? Is this change likely to have much impact on the economy? (*Hint:* According to the information given in this chapter, what is the current value of M1?)

Source: Austan Goolsbee, "Now That a Penny Isn't Worth Much, It's Time to Make It Worth 5 Cents," *New York Times*, February 1, 2007.

>> **End Learning Objective 25.2**

25.3 LEARNING OBJECTIVE   25.3 | Explain how banks create money, **pages 860–868.**

How Do Banks Create Money?

Summary

On a bank's balance sheet, *reserves* and loans are assets, and deposits are liabilities. **Reserves** are deposits that the bank has retained rather than loaned out or invested. **Required reserves** are reserves that banks are legally required to hold. The fraction of deposits that banks are required to keep as reserves is called the **required reserve ratio.** Any reserves banks hold over and above the legal requirement are called **excess reserves.** When a bank accepts a deposit, it keeps only a fraction of the funds as reserves and loans out the remainder. In making a loan, a bank increases the checking account balance of the borrower. When the borrower uses a check to buy something with the funds the bank has loaned, the seller deposits the check in his bank. The seller's bank keeps part of the deposit as reserves and loans out the remainder. This process continues until no banks have excess reserves. In this way, the process of banks making new loans increases the volume of checking account balances and the money supply. This money creation process can be illustrated with T-accounts, which are stripped-down versions of balance sheets that show only how a transaction changes a bank's balance sheet. The **simple deposit multiplier** is the ratio of the amount of deposits created by banks to the amount of new reserves. An expression for the simple deposit multiplier is $1/RR$.

Review Questions

3.1 What are the largest asset and the largest liability of a typical bank?

3.2 Suppose you decide to withdraw $100 in cash from your checking account. Draw a T-account showing the effect of this transaction on your bank's balance sheet.

3.3 Give the formula for the simple deposit multiplier. If the required reserve ratio is 20 percent, what is the maximum increase in checking account deposits that will result from an increase in bank reserves of $20,000?

Problems and Applications

3.4 The following is from a newspaper story on local, or community, banks: "Community banks . . . are awash in liabilities these days, and they couldn't be happier about it." To which "liabilities" does the story refer? Why would these banks be happy about being "awash" in these liabilities?

Source: Christian Millman, "Bank Deposits on the Rise as People Flee the Stock Market," (*Allentown, Pennsylvania*) *Morning Call*, August 11, 2002, pp. D1, D4.

3.5 The president of a local bank described deposits this way: "That's the fuel we use to be able to go out and make loans and mortgages." Briefly explain what he means.

Source: Christian Millman, "Bank Deposits on the Rise as People Flee the Stock Market," (*Allentown, Pennsylvania*) *Morning Call*, August 11, 2002, pp. D1, D4.

3.6 The following is from an article on community banks: "Their commercial-lending businesses, funded by their stable deposit bases, make them steady earners."

What is commercial lending? In what sense are loans "funded" by deposits?

Source: Karen Richardson, "Clean Books Bolster Traditional Lenders," *Wall Street Journal*, April 30, 2007, p. C1.

3.7 "Most of the money supply of the United States is created by banks making loans." Briefly explain whether you agree or disagree with this statement.

3.8 Would a series of bank runs in a country decrease the total quantity of M1? Wouldn't a bank run simply move funds in a checking account to currency in circulation? How could that movement of funds decrease the quantity of money?

3.9 (Related to *Solved Problem 25-3* on page 865) Suppose you deposit $2,000 in currency into your checking account at a branch of Bank of America, which we will assume has no excess reserves at the time you make your deposit. Also assume that the required reserve ratio is 0.20.

   a. Use a T-account to show the initial impact of this transaction on Bank of America's balance sheet.

   b. Suppose that Bank of America makes the maximum loan it can from the funds you deposited. Using a T-account, show the initial impact of granting the loan on Bank of America's balance sheet. Also include on this T-account the transaction from (a).

   c. Now suppose that whoever took out the loan in (b) writes a check for this amount and that the person receiving the check deposits it in a branch of Citibank. Show the effect of these transactions on the balance sheets of Bank of America and Citibank *after the check has been cleared*. (On the T-account for Bank of America, include the transactions from [a] and [b].)

   d. What is the maximum increase in checking account deposits that can result from your $2,000 deposit? What is the maximum increase in the money supply? Explain.

3.10 Consider the following simplified balance sheet for a bank.

Assets		Liabilities	
Reserves	$10,000	Deposits	$70,000
Loans	$66,000	Stockholders' equity	$6,000

   a. If the required reserve ratio is 10 percent, how much in excess reserves does the bank hold?

   b. What is the maximum amount by which the bank can expand its loans?

   c. If the bank makes the loans in (b), show the *immediate* impact on the bank's balance sheet.

3.11 (Related to the *Don't Let This Happen to You!* on page 861) Briefly explain whether you agree or disagree with the following statement: "Assets are things of value that people own. Liabilities are debts. Therefore, a bank will always consider a checking account deposit to be an asset and a car loan to be a liability."

3.12 "Banks don't really create money, do they?" was the challenge that a retired professor of economics was known to have used in his upper-division American economic history course to ascertain what his students remembered from introductory macroeconomics about the creation of money. He reported that few students were confident enough or remembered enough to reply correctly to his question. How would you reply?

>> **End Learning Objective 25.3**

25.4 LEARNING OBJECTIVE 25.4 | Discuss the three policy tools the Federal Reserve uses to manage the money supply, **pages 868–872.**

The Federal Reserve System

Summary

The United States has a **fractional reserve banking system** in which banks keep less than 100 percent of deposits as reserves. In a **bank run**, many depositors decide simultaneously to withdraw money from a bank. In a **bank panic**, many banks experience runs at the same time. The **Federal Reserve System** ("the Fed") is the central bank of the United States. It was originally established in 1913 to stop bank panics, but today its main role is to carry out *monetary policy*. **Monetary policy** refers to the actions the Federal Reserve takes to manage the money supply and interest rates to pursue macroeconomic policy objectives. The Fed's three monetary policy tools are open market operations, discount policy, and reserve requirements. **Open market operations** are the buying and selling of Treasury securities by the Federal Reserve. The loans the Fed makes to banks are called **discount loans**, and the interest rate the Fed charges on discount loans is the **discount rate**. The **Federal Open Market Committee (FOMC)** meets in Washington, DC, eight times per year to discuss monetary policy.

Review Questions

4.1 Why did Congress decide to set up the Federal Reserve System in 1913? Today, what is the most important role of the Federal Reserve in the U.S. economy?

4.2 What are the policy tools the Fed uses to control the money supply? Which tool is the most important?

Problems and Applications

4.3 The text explains that the United States has a "fractional reserve banking system." Why do most depositors seem to be unworried that banks loan out most of the deposits they receive?

4.4 Suppose that you are a bank manager, and the Federal Reserve raises the required reserve ratio from 10 percent to 12 percent. What actions would you need to take? How would your actions and those of other bank managers end up affecting the money supply?

4.5 Reserve requirements have been referred to as a "tax on bank profits." Briefly explain whether you agree. How would your answer change if the Fed began paying interest on banks' reserve accounts?

4.6 Suppose that the Federal Reserve makes a $10 million discount loan to the First National Bank by increasing FNB's account at the Fed.
  a. Use a T-account to show the impact of this transaction on FNB's balance sheet. Remember that the funds a bank has on deposit at the Fed count as part of its reserves.
  b. Assume that before receiving the discount loan, FNB has no excess reserves. What is the maximum amount of this $10 million that FNB can lend out?
  c. What is the maximum total increase in the money supply that can result from the Fed's discount loan? Assume that the required reserve ratio is 10 percent.

4.7 **(Related to the *Making the Connection* on page 869)** Argentina suffered a severe bank panic in 2001. The United States has not suffered a bank panic since the 1930s. What differences between the Argentine and U.S. financial systems can account for their differing vulnerability to bank panics?

>> End Learning Objective 25.4

25.5 LEARNING OBJECTIVE   25.5 | Explain the quantity theory of money and use it to explain how high rates of inflation occur, **pages 872–876.**

The Quantity Theory of Money

Summary

The *quantity equation* relates the money supply to the price level: $M \times V = P \times Y$, where M is the money supply, V is the *velocity of money*, P is the price level, and Y is real output. The **velocity of money** is the average number of times each dollar in the money supply is spent during the year. Economist Irving Fisher developed the **quantity theory of money**, which assumes that the velocity of money is constant. If the quantity theory of money is correct, the inflation rate should equal the rate of growth of the money supply minus the rate of growth of real output. Although the quantity theory of money is not literally correct because the velocity of money is not constant, it is true that in the long run, inflation results from the money supply growing faster than real GDP. When governments attempt to raise revenue by selling large quantities of bonds to the central bank, the money supply will increase rapidly, resulting in a high rate of inflation.

Review Questions

5.1 What is the quantity theory of money? How does the quantity theory explain why inflation occurs?

5.2 What is hyperinflation? Why do governments sometimes allow it to occur?

Problems and Applications

5.3 If the money supply is growing at a rate of 6 percent per year, real GDP is growing at a rate of 3 percent per year, and velocity is constant, what will the inflation rate be? If velocity is increasing 1 percent per year instead of remaining constant, what will the inflation rate be?

5.4 Suppose that during one period, the velocity of money is constant and during another period, it undergoes large fluctuations. During which period will the quantity theory of money be more useful in explaining changes in the inflation rate? Briefly explain.

5.5 The following is from an article in the *Wall Street Journal*: "[Japan's] money supply is surging. If that doesn't curtail Japan's debilitating price deflation, a lot of economics textbooks may need to be rewritten."
   a. What is "price deflation"?
   b. If rapid increases in the money supply don't stop deflation, why will economics textbooks need to be rewritten?
   c. (This is a more difficult question.) Why might price deflation in Japan be "debilitating"? (*Hint:* What reaction might consumers have to price deflation?)

Source: Peter Landers, "Japan Shows Vague Signs of Recovery," *Wall Street Journal*, March 5, 2002.

5.6 **(Related to the *Chapter Opener* on page 850)** During the Civil War, the Confederate States of America printed lots of its own currency—Confederate dollars—to fund the war. By the end of the war, nearly 1.5 billion paper dollars had been printed by the Confederate government. How would such a large quantity of Confederate dollars have affected the value of the Confederate currency? With the war drawing to an end, would Southerners have been as willing to use and accept Confederate dollars? How else could they have made exchanges?

Source: Textual Transcript of Confederate Currency, Federal Reserve Bank of Richmond.

5.7 **(Related to the *Making the Connection* on page 876)** During the German hyperinflation of the 1920s, many households and firms in Germany were hurt economically. Did you think any groups in Germany benefited from the hyperinflation? Briefly explain.

5.8 In the summer of 2006, the African country of Zimbabwe decided to change its currency. At the end of the day on August 21, 2006, the old dollar would no longer be legal tender. It would be replaced with new currency, with each new dollar worth 1,000 times what the old dollar was worth. According to a newspaper article "Under the changeover rules, individuals were permitted to exchange a limit of 100 million old Zimbabwe dollars ($40) for new currency in a single transaction each week since Aug. 1." Predict what happened to prices in Zimbabwe in terms of the old dollar as the August 21 deadline approached. What would the government of Zimbabwe hope to gain from swapping a new currency for an old currency?

Source: "Zimbabwe Swaps Currency Amid Runaway Inflation," *Wall Street Journal*, August 21, 2006.

5.9 An article in the *Economist* on Zimbabwe, described conditions in summer 2007: "inflation is hovering around 4,500%, and eight Zimbabweans in ten do not have formal jobs." Is there a connection between the very high inflation rate and the high rate of unemployment? Briefly explain.

Source: "Rumblings Within," *Economist*, June 21, 2007.

>> **End Learning Objective 25.5**

Chapter 26

Monetary Policy

Monetary Policy, Toll Brothers, and the Housing Market

Few firms experienced such dramatic swings in sales as homebuilder Toll Brothers, Inc., did between 2001 and 2008. In March 2001, the U.S. economy moved into recession. During a typical recession, sales of new homes decline sharply as unemployment increases and incomes fall. Homebuilders are usually among the businesses hit hardest during recessions. For example, during the recession of 1974–1975, spending on residential construction declined by more than 30 percent. Homebuilders fared even worse during the recessions of 1980–1982, when spending on residential construction plummeted by more than 40 percent.

So, when the recession began in 2001, Toll Brothers should have experienced a decline in sales. But look at the following excerpt from the company's report to shareholders for the third quarter of 2001:

> Amid continuing sluggishness in the U.S. economy, Toll Brothers once again posted record results. Thanks to hard work and efficient planning and the [housing] market's ability to weather the downturn, we have just completed the best third quarter and first nine months in our history.

Other homebuilders also did unexpectedly well during 2001, as spending on residential construction actually *rose* by 5 percent. The success of Toll Brothers during 2001 was not the result of good luck but rather of a policy decision made by the Federal Reserve's Federal

new home less expensive, and millions of families responded, flooding Toll Brothers with orders.

A few years later, the situation for Toll Brothers and other homebuilders looked very different. The strong housing market of 2001 had turned

Open Market Committee (FOMC). In early 2001, the members of the FOMC concluded that a recession was about to begin and implemented an expansionary monetary policy to keep the recession as short and mild as possible. By driving down interest rates, the Fed succeeded in heading off what some economists had predicted would be a prolonged and severe recession. Low interest rates made borrowing to buy a

into a housing "bubble" by 2005. In a housing bubble, prices soar to levels that are not sustainable, and homebuilders buy more land and erect more houses than they end up being able to sell for a profit. In February 2007, Toll Brothers reported a 67 percent drop in its profits for the previous quarter and warned investors that neither the housing market nor the firm's profitability would likely improve any time soon.

The warning turned out to be accurate, as Toll Brothers suffered losses of more than $425 million between August 2007 and April 2008.

This time, the Federal Reserve delayed in cutting interest rates to rescue the housing market. As we will see in this chapter, in addition to being concerned about recessions, the Fed tries to keep the inflation rate at a low level. During 2006 and 2007, the inflation rate was at or above the level the Fed considers acceptable. Lowering interest rates might worsen inflation if it led to a large increase in spending by households and firms, but fears of recession finally moved the Fed to reduce interest beginning in September 2007. In 2008, the Fed was forced to turn to new policies as it tried to keep the economy out of recession while still keeping inflation in check.

AN INSIDE LOOK AT POLICY on **page 918** compares the effects of a slowing housing market on the United States and Europe.

Sources: Judy Lam and Michael Corkery, "Toll Brothers Net Falls 67%; Outlook Is Cut," *Wall Street Journal*, February 23, 2007, p. A3; and Shawn Tully, "Toll Brothers: The New King of the Real Estate Boom," *Fortune*, April 5, 2005.

LEARNING Objectives

After studying this chapter, you should be able to:

26.1 Define **monetary policy** and describe the Federal Reserve's **monetary policy goals**, page 888.

26.2 Describe the Federal Reserve's monetary policy targets and explain how **expansionary** and **contractionary monetary policies** affect the **interest rate**, page 890.

26.3 Use aggregate demand and aggregate supply graphs to show the **effects** of **monetary policy** on **real GDP** and the **price level**, page 897.

26.4 Discuss the Fed's setting of **monetary policy targets**, page 910.

26.5 Discuss the steps the Federal Reserve took during 2007 and 2008 to respond to the **crisis** in the **housing market**, page 914.

Economics in YOUR Life!

Should You Buy a House During a Recession?

If you are like most college students, buying a house is one of the farthest things from your mind. But suppose you think forward a few years to when you might be married and maybe even (gasp!) have children. Leaving years of renting apartments behind, you are considering buying a house. But, suppose that according to an article in the *Wall Street Journal*, a majority of economists are predicting that a recession is likely to begin soon. What should you do? Would this be a good time or a bad time to buy a house? As you read the chapter, see if you can answer these questions. You can check your answers against those we provide at the end of the chapter. >> Continued on page 917

In Chapter 25, we saw that banks play an important role in creating the money supply. We also saw that the Fed manages the money supply to achieve its policy goals. As we will see in this chapter, the Fed has four policy goals: (1) price stability, (2) high employment, (3) economic growth, and (4) stability of financial markets and institutions. In this chapter, we will explore how the Federal Reserve decides which *monetary policy* actions to take to achieve its goals.

26.1 | Define monetary policy and describe the Federal Reserve's monetary policy goals.

What Is Monetary Policy?

In 1913, Congress passed the Federal Reserve Act, creating the Federal Reserve System ("the Fed"). The main responsibility of the Fed was to make discount loans to banks suffering from large withdrawals by depositors. In other words, the Fed was charged with preventing the bank panics you learned about in Chapter 25. As a result of the Great Depression of the 1930s, Congress amended the Federal Reserve Act to give the Federal Reserve's Board of Governors broader responsibility to act "so as to promote effectively the goals of maximum employment, stable prices, and moderate long-term interest rates."

Since World War II, the Federal Reserve has carried out an active *monetary policy*. **Monetary policy** refers to the actions the Fed takes to manage the money supply and interest rates to pursue its macroeconomic policy objectives.

Monetary policy The actions the Federal Reserve takes to manage the money supply and interest rates to pursue its macroeconomic policy objectives.

The Goals of Monetary Policy

The Fed has set four *monetary policy goals* that are intended to promote a well-functioning economy:

1 Price stability

2 High employment

3 Economic growth

4 Stability of financial markets and institutions

We briefly consider each of these goals.

Price Stability As we have seen in previous chapters, rising prices erode the value of money as a medium of exchange and a store of value. Especially after inflation rose dramatically and unexpectedly during the 1970s, policymakers in most industrial countries have price stability as a policy goal. Figure 26-1 shows that from the early 1950s until 1968, the inflation rate remained below 4 percent per year. Inflation was above 4 percent for most of the 1970s. In early 1979, the inflation rate increased to more than 10 percent, where it remained until late 1981, when it began to rapidly fall back to the 4 percent range. From 1992 until late 2005, the inflation rate was below 4 percent. But since then it has occasionally risen above 4 percent, which has caused concern at the Fed.

The inflation rates during the years 1979–1981 were the highest the United States has ever experienced during peacetime. When Paul Volcker became chairman of the Federal Reserve's Board of Governors in August 1979, he made fighting inflation his top policy goal. Alan Greenspan, who succeeded Volcker in August 1987, and Ben Bernanke, who succeeded Greenspan in January 2006, continued to focus on inflation. Volcker, Greenspan, and Bernanke argued that if inflation is low over the long run, the Fed will have the flexibility it needs to lessen the impact of recessions. And many economists agree.

High Employment High employment, or a low rate of unemployment, is another monetary policy goal. Unemployed workers and underused factories and office buildings reduce GDP below its potential level. Unemployment causes financial distress and decreases self-esteem for workers who lack jobs. The goal of high employment extends beyond the Fed to

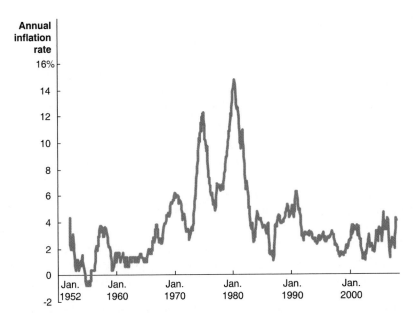

Figure 26-1

The Inflation Rate, 1952–2007

For most of the 1950s and 1960s, the inflation rate in the United States was 4 percent or less. During the 1970s, the inflation rate increased, peaking during 1979–1981, when it averaged more than 10 percent. From 1992 until late 2005, the inflation rate was less than 4 percent. Since late 2005, the inflation rate has occasionally been above 4 percent.

Note: The inflation rate is measured as the percentage increase in the consumer price index (CPI) from the same month in the previous year.

Source: U.S. Bureau of Labor Statistics.

other branches of the federal government. At the end of World War II, Congress passed the Employment Act of 1946, which stated that it was the "responsibility of the Federal Government . . . to foster and promote . . . conditions under which there will be afforded useful employment, for those able, willing, and seeking to work, and to promote maximum employment, production, and purchasing power."

Economic Growth We discussed in Chapters 21 and 22 the importance of economic growth to raising living standards. Policymakers aim to encourage *stable* economic growth because stable growth allows households and firms to plan accurately and encourages the long-run investment that is needed to sustain growth. Policy can spur economic growth by providing incentives for saving to ensure a large pool of investment funds, as well as by providing direct incentives for business investment. Policies to increase saving and investment may be better carried out by Congress and the president than by the Fed, however. For example, Congress and the president can change the tax laws to increase the return to saving and investing. In fact, some economists question whether the Fed can play a role in promoting economic growth beyond attempting to meet its goals of price stability and high employment. These economists note that high employment typically occurs only when real GDP is near potential GDP and growing at a sustained rate. So, in attaining its goal of high employment, the Fed will also have promoted economic growth. Similarly, most economists believe that economic growth is generally slow during periods of high inflation. So, in achieving price stability, the Fed will also be promoting economic growth.

Stability of Financial Markets and Institutions When financial markets and institutions are not efficient in matching savers and borrowers, resources are lost. Firms with the potential to produce goods and services valued by consumers cannot obtain the financing they need to design, develop, and market those products. Savers waste resources looking for satisfactory investments. The Fed promotes the stability of financial markets and institutions so that an efficient flow of funds from savers to borrowers will occur. For example, during the turmoil in the market for subprime mortgages in 2007 and 2008, the Fed decided to expand its role as a lender of last resort.

The crisis in the mortgage market during 2007 and 2008 was similar to the banking crises that led Congress to create the Federal Reserve System in 1913. A key difference is that while earlier banking crises affected commercial banks, investment banks were heavily involved in the events of 2007–2008. Investment banks can be subject to *liquidity problems* because they often borrow short term—sometimes as short as overnight—and invest the funds in longer term investments. Commercial banks borrow from households and firms in the form of checking and saving deposits, while investment banks borrow primarily from other financial firms, such as other investment banks, mutual funds, or hedge funds, which are similar to mutual funds but typically engage in more complex—and risky—investment strategies. Just as commercial banks can experience a crisis if depositors begin to withdraw funds, investment banks can experience a crisis if other financial firms stop offering them short-term loans. In 2008, the Fed decided to ease the liquidity problems facing investment banks by allowing them to take out discount loans, which had previously been available only to commercial banks. Later in this chapter, we will discuss in more detail the new policies the Fed enacted to help deal with the crisis in the mortgage market.

In the next section, we will look at how the Fed attempts to attain its monetary policy goals. Although the Fed has multiple monetary policy goals, during most periods, the most important goals of monetary policy have been price stability and high employment. But the turmoil in the mortgage markets during 2007 and 2008 led the Fed to put a new emphasis on the goal of financial market stability.

26.2 LEARNING OBJECTIVE

26.2 | Describe the Federal Reserve's monetary policy targets and explain how expansionary and contractionary monetary policies affect the interest rate.

The Money Market and the Fed's Choice of Monetary Policy Targets

The Fed's objective in undertaking monetary policy is to use its policy tools to achieve its monetary policy goals. Recall from Chapter 25 that the Fed's policy tools are open market operations, discount policy, and reserve requirements. At times, the Fed encounters conflicts between its policy goals. For example, as we will discuss later in this chapter, the Fed can raise interest rates to reduce the inflation rate. But, as we saw in Chapter 24, higher interest rates typically reduce household and firm spending, which may result in slower growth and higher unemployment. So, a policy that is intended to achieve one monetary policy goal, such as lower inflation, may have an adverse effect on another policy goal, such as high employment. Some members of Congress have introduced legislation that would force the Fed to focus almost entirely on achieving price stability, and many economists support such a focus. Although so far this legislation has not passed Congress, the debate has gained momentum within the Federal Reserve.

Monetary Policy Targets

The Fed tries to keep both the unemployment and inflation rates low, but it can't affect either of these economic variables directly. The Fed cannot tell firms how many people to employ or what prices to charge for their products. Instead, the Fed uses variables, called *monetary policy targets*, that it can affect directly and that, in turn, affect variables, such as real GDP, employment, and the price level, that are closely related to the Fed's policy goals. The two main monetary policy targets are the money supply and the interest rate. As we will see, the Fed typically uses the interest rate as its policy target.

The Demand for Money

The Fed's two monetary policy targets are related in an important way. To see this relationship, we first need to examine the demand and supply for money. Figure 26-2 shows the demand curve for money. The interest rate is on the vertical axis, and the quantity of money is on the horizontal axis. Here we are using the M1 definition of money, which equals currency in circulation plus checking account deposits. Notice that the demand curve for money is downward sloping.

To understand why the demand curve for money is downward sloping, consider that households and firms have a choice between holding money and holding other financial assets, such as U.S. Treasury bills. Money has one particularly desirable characteristic: You can use it to buy goods, services, or financial assets. Money also has one undesirable

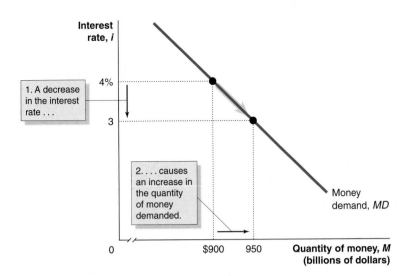

Figure 26-2

The Demand for Money

The money demand curve slopes downward because lower interest rates cause households and firms to switch from financial assets like U.S. Treasury bills to money. All other things being equal, a fall in the interest rate from 4 percent to 3 percent will increase the quantity of money demanded from $900 billion to $950 billion. An increase in the interest rate will decrease the quantity of money demanded.

characteristic: It earns either no interest or a very low rate of interest. The currency in your wallet earns no interest, and the money in your checking account earns either no interest or very little interest. Alternatives to money, such as U.S. Treasury bills, pay interest but have to be sold if you want to use the funds to buy something. When interest rates rise on financial assets such as U.S. Treasury bills, the amount of interest that households and firms lose by holding money increases. When interest rates fall, the amount of interest households and firms lose by holding money decreases. Remember that *opportunity cost* is what you have to forgo to engage in an activity. The interest rate is the opportunity cost of holding money.

We now have an explanation for why the demand curve for money slopes downward: When interest rates on Treasury bills and other financial assets are low, the opportunity cost of holding money is low, so the quantity of money demanded by households and firms will be high; when interest rates are high, the opportunity cost of holding money will be high, so the quantity of money demanded will be low. In Figure 26-2, a decrease in interest rates from 4 percent to 3 percent causes the quantity of money demanded by households and firms to rise from $900 billion to $950 billion.

Shifts in the Money Demand Curve

We saw in Chapter 3 that the demand curve for a good is drawn holding constant all variables, other than the price, that affect the willingness of consumers to buy the good. Changes in variables other than the price cause the demand curve to shift. Similarly, the demand curve for money is drawn holding constant all variables, other than the interest rate, that affect the willingness of households and firms to hold money. Changes in variables other than the interest rate cause the demand curve to shift. The two most important variables that cause the money demand curve to shift are real GDP and the price level.

An increase in real GDP means that the amount of buying and selling of goods and services will increase. This additional buying and selling increases the demand for money as a medium of exchange, so the quantity of money households and firms want to hold increases at each interest rate, shifting the money demand curve to the right. A decrease in real GDP decreases the quantity of money demanded at each interest rate, shifting the money demand curve to the left. A higher price level increases the quantity of money required for a given amount of buying and selling. Eighty years ago, for example, when the price level was much lower and someone could purchase a new car for $500 and a salary of $30 per week put you in the middle class, the quantity of money demanded by households and firms was much lower than today, even adjusting for the effect of the lower real GDP and smaller population of those years. An increase in the price level increases the quantity of money demanded at each interest rate, shifting the money demand curve to the right. A decrease in the price level decreases the quantity of money demanded at each interest rate, shifting the money demand curve to the left. Figure 26-3 illustrates shifts in the money demand curve.

Figure 26-3

Changes in real GDP or the price level cause the money demand curve to shift. An increase in real GDP or an increase in the price level will cause the money demand curve to shift from MD_1 to MD_2. A decrease in real GDP or a decrease in the price level will cause the money demand curve to shift from MD_1 to MD_3.

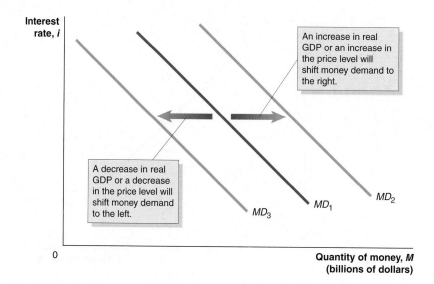

How the Fed Manages the Money Supply: A Quick Review

Having discussed money demand, we now turn to money supply. In Chapter 25, we saw how the Federal Reserve manages the money supply. Eight times per year, the FOMC meets in Washington, DC. If the FOMC decides to increase the money supply, it orders the trading desk at the Federal Reserve Bank of New York to purchase U.S. Treasury securities. The sellers of these Treasury securities deposit the funds they receive from the Fed in banks, which increases the banks' reserves. The banks loan out most of these reserves, which creates new checking account deposits and expands the money supply. If the FOMC decides to decrease the money supply, it orders the trading desk to sell Treasury securities, which decreases banks' reserves and contracts the money supply.

Equilibrium in the Money Market

In Figure 26-4, we include both the money demand and money supply curves. We can use this figure to see how the Fed affects both the money supply and the interest rate. For simplicity, we assume that the Federal Reserve is able to completely fix the money supply (although, in fact, the behavior of the public and banks can also affect the money supply). Therefore, the money supply curve is a vertical line, and changes in the interest rate

Figure 26-4

When the Fed increases the money supply, households and firms will initially hold more money than they want, relative to other financial assets. Households and firms buy Treasury bills and other financial assets with the money they don't want to hold. This increase in demand drives up the prices of these assets and drives down their interest rates. Eventually, interest rates will fall enough that households and firms will be willing to hold the additional money the Fed has created. In the figure, an increase in the money supply from $900 billion to $950 billion causes the money supply curve to shift to the right, from MS_1 to MS_2, and causes the equilibrium interest rate to fall from 4 percent to 3 percent.

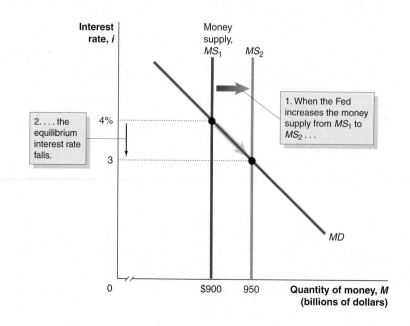

have no effect on the quantity of money supplied. Just as with other markets, equilibrium in the *money market* occurs where the money demand curve crosses the money supply curve. If the Fed increases the money supply, the money supply curve will shift to the right, and the equilibrium interest rate will fall. In Figure 26-4, when the Fed increases the money supply from $900 billion to $950 billion, the money supply curve shifts from MS_1 to MS_2, and the equilibrium interest rate falls from 4 percent to 3 percent.

In the money market, the adjustment from one equilibrium to another equilibrium is a little different from the adjustment in the market for a good. In Figure 26-4, the money market is initially in equilibrium with an interest rate of 4 percent and a money supply of $900 billion. When the Fed increases the money supply by $50 billion, households and firms have more money than they want to hold at an interest rate of 4 percent. What do households and firms do with the extra $50 billion? They are most likely to use the money to buy short-term financial assets, such as Treasury bills. Short-term financial assets have maturities—the date when the last payment by the seller is made—of one year or less. By buying short-term assets, households and firms drive up their prices and drive down their interest rates.

To see why an increasing demand for Treasury bills will lower their interest rate, recall from Chapter 7 that *the prices of financial assets and their interest rates move in opposite directions.* Suppose you buy a U.S. Treasury bill today for $962 that matures in one year, at which time the Treasury will pay you $1,000. The government sells Treasury bills at a price below their face value of $1,000. The difference between the price of the bill and its $1,000 face value represents the return to investors for lending their money to the Treasury. In this case, you will earn $38 in interest on your investment of $962. The interest rate on the Treasury bill is:

$$\left(\frac{\$38}{\$962}\right) \times 100 = 4\%.$$

Now suppose that many households and firms increase their demand for Treasury bills. This increase in demand will have the same effect on Treasury bills that an increase in the demand for apples has on apples: The price will rise. Suppose the price of Treasury bills rises from $962 to $971. Now if you buy a Treasury bill, you will receive only $29 in interest on your investment of $971. The interest rate on the Treasury bill is now:

$$\left(\frac{\$29}{\$971}\right) \times 100 = 3\%.$$

Therefore, as the price of a Treasury bill increases, the interest rate on the Treasury bill falls.

As the interest rate on Treasury bills and other financial assets falls, the opportunity cost of holding money also falls. Households and firms move down the money demand curve. Eventually the interest rate will have fallen enough that households and firms are willing to hold the additional $50 billion worth of money the Fed has created, and the money market will be back in equilibrium. To summarize: *When the Fed increases the money supply, the short-term interest rate must fall until it reaches a level at which households and firms are willing to hold the additional money.*

Figure 26-5 shows what happens when the Fed decreases the money supply. The money market is initially in equilibrium, at an interest rate of 4 percent and a money supply of $900 billion. If the Fed decreases the money supply to $850 billion, households and firms will be holding less money than they would like—relative to other financial assets—at an interest rate of 4 percent. To increase their money holdings, they will sell Treasury bills and other financial assets. The increased supply of Treasury bills for sale will decrease their prices and increase their interest rates. Rising short-term interest rates increase the opportunity cost of holding money, causing households and firms to move up the money demand curve. Equilibrium is finally restored at an interest rate of 5 percent.

Figure 26-5

The Impact on Interest Rates When the Fed Decreases the Money Supply

When the Fed decreases the money supply, households and firms will initially hold less money than they want, relative to other financial assets. Households and firms will sell Treasury bills and other financial assets, reducing their prices and increasing their interest rates. Eventually, interest rates will rise to the point at which households and firms will be willing to hold the smaller amount of money that results from the Fed's actions. In the figure, a reduction in money supply from $900 billion to $850 billion causes the money supply curve to shift to the left, from MS_1 to MS_2, and causes the equilibrium interest rate to rise from 4 percent to 5 percent.

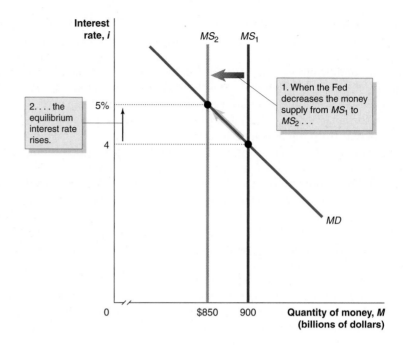

2. . . . the equilibrium interest rate rises.

1. When the Fed decreases the money supply from MS_1 to MS_2 . . .

Solved Problem | 26-2

The Relationship between Treasury Bill Prices and Their Interest Rates

What is the price of a Treasury bill that pays $1,000 in one year, if its interest rate is 4 percent? What is the price of the Treasury bill if its interest rate is 5 percent?

SOLVING THE PROBLEM:

Step 1: **Review the chapter material.** This problem is about the relationship between Treasury bill prices and interest rates, so you may want to review the section "Equilibrium in the Money Market," which begins on page 892.

Step 2: **Use the formula for calculating interest rates to determine the Treasury bill price when the interest rate is 4 percent.** In this situation, the interest rate will be equal to the percentage increase from the initial purchase price of the bill to the $1,000 buyers will receive in one year. We can set up the problem like this, where P is the purchase price of the Treasury bill:

$$\left(\frac{\$1,000 - P}{P} \right) \times 100 = 4.$$

Dividing both sides by 100 and multiplying both sides by P, we get:

$$\$1,000 - P = 0.04P,$$

or:

$$\$1,000 = 1.04P,$$

or:

$$\frac{\$1,000}{1.04} = P,$$

or, rounding to the nearest dollar:

$$P = \$962.$$

Step 3: **Use the formula for calculating interest rates to determine the Treasury bill price when the interest rate is 5 percent.** We can apply the same formula to find the price when the interest rate is 5 percent:

$$\left(\frac{\$1,000 - P}{P} \right) \times 100 = 5.$$

Once again, dividing both sides by 100 and multiplying both sides by P, we get:

$$\$1,000 - P = 0.05P,$$

or:

$$\$1,000 = 1.05P,$$

or:

$$\frac{\$1,000}{1.05} = P,$$

or:

$$P = \$952.$$

EXTRA CREDIT: The interest rate on a Treasury bill or other financial asset is also called its *yield*. It's important to remember that prices of financial assets and their yields move in opposite directions. Consider this excerpt from the credit market column in the *Wall Street Journal*: "The benchmark 10-year [U.S. Treasury] note was down . . . $5 per $1,000 face value, to . . . [$964.69]. Its yield rose to 4.955% from 4.892% Thursday, as yields move inversely to prices." A similar reminder that a bond's yield moves inversely to its price appears in this newspaper column every day. Any fact that the *Wall Street Journal* feels is important enough to remind its readers of every day is probably worth remembering!

Source: Laurence Norman, "Bond Prices Decline on Mixed U.S. Data," *Wall Street Journal*, June 2, 2007.

YOUR TURN: For more practice, do problem 2.6 on page 921 at the end of this chapter.

>> End Solved Problem 26-2

A Tale of Two Interest Rates

In Chapter 21, we discussed the loanable funds model of the interest rate. In that model, the equilibrium interest rate was determined by the demand and supply for loanable funds. Why do we need two models of the interest rate? The answer is that the loanable funds model is concerned with the *long-term real rate of interest*, and the money-market model is concerned with the *short-term nominal rate of interest*. The long-term real rate of interest is the interest rate that is most relevant when savers consider purchasing a long-term financial investment such as a corporate bond. It is also the rate of interest that is most relevant to firms that are borrowing to finance long-term investment projects such as new factories or office buildings, or to households that are taking out mortgage loans to buy new homes.

When conducting monetary policy, however, the short-term nominal interest rate is the most relevant interest rate because it is the interest rate most affected by increases and decreases in the money supply. Often—but not always—there is a close connection between movements in the short-term nominal interest rate and movements in the long-term real interest rate. So, when the Fed takes actions to increase the short-term nominal interest, usually the long-term real interest rate also increases. In other words, as we will discuss in the next section, when the interest rate on Treasury bills rises, the real interest rate on mortgage loans usually also rises, although sometimes only after a delay.

Choosing a Monetary Policy Target

As we have seen, the Fed uses monetary policy targets to affect economic variables such as real GDP or the price level, which are closely related to the Fed's policy goals. The Fed chooses the money supply or the interest rate as its monetary policy target. As Figure 26-5 shows, the Fed is capable of affecting both. The Fed has generally focused more on the interest rate than on the money supply. After 1980, deregulation and financial innovations, including paying interest on checking accounts and the introduction of money market mutual funds, have made M1 less relevant as a measure of the medium of exchange. These developments led the Fed to rely for a time on M2, a broader measure of the money supply that had a more stable historical relationship to economic growth. Even this relationship broke down in the early 1990s. In July 1993, then Fed Chairman Alan Greenspan informed the U.S. Congress that the Fed would cease using M1 or M2 targets to guide the conduct of monetary policy. The Fed has correspondingly increased its reliance on interest rate targets.

There are many different interest rates in the economy. For purposes of monetary policy, the Fed has targeted the interest rate known as the *federal funds rate*. In the next section, we discuss the federal funds rate before examining how targeting the interest rate can help the Fed achieve its monetary policy goals.

The Importance of the Federal Funds Rate

Federal funds rate The interest rate banks charge each other for overnight loans.

Recall from Chapter 25 that every bank must keep 10 percent of its checking account deposits above a certain threshold as reserves, either as currency held in the bank or as deposits with the Fed. Banks receive no interest on their reserves, so they have an incentive to invest reserves above the 10-percent minimum. Banks that need additional reserves can borrow in the *federal funds market* from banks that have reserves available. The **federal funds rate** is the interest rate banks charge on loans in the federal funds market. The loans in the federal funds market are usually very short term, often just overnight.

Despite the name, the federal funds rate is not set administratively by the Fed. Instead, the rate is determined by the supply of reserves relative to the demand for them. Because the Fed can increase and decrease the supply of bank reserves through open market operations, it can set a target for the federal funds rate and come very close to hitting it. The FOMC announces a target for the federal funds rate after each meeting. In Figure 26-6, the orange line shows the Fed's targets for the federal funds rate since 1997. The jagged green line represents the actual federal funds rate on a weekly basis.

The federal funds rate is not directly relevant for households and firms. No households or firms, except banks, can borrow or lend in the federal funds market. However, changes in the federal funds rate usually result in changes in interest rates on other

Figure 26-6

Federal Funds Rate Targeting, January 1997–May 2008

The Fed does not set the federal funds rate, but its ability to increase or decrease bank reserves quickly through open market operations keeps the actual federal funds rate close to the Fed's target rate. The orange line is the Fed's target for the federal funds rate, and the jagged green line represents the actual value for the federal funds rate on a weekly basis.
Source: Board of Governors of the Federal Reserve System.

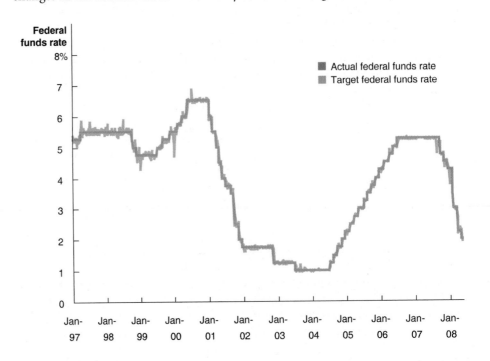

short-term financial assets, such as Treasury bills, and changes in interest rates on long-term financial assets, such as corporate bonds and mortgages. The effect of a change in the federal funds rate on long-term interest rates is usually smaller than it is on short-term interest rates, and the effect may occur only after a lag in time. Although a majority of economists support the Fed's choice of the interest rate as its monetary policy target, some economists believe the Fed should concentrate on the money supply instead. We will discuss the views of these economists later in this chapter.

26.3 | Use aggregate demand and aggregate supply graphs to show the effects of monetary policy on real GDP and the price level.

Monetary Policy and Economic Activity

Remember that the Fed uses the federal funds rate as a monetary policy target because it has good control of the federal funds rate through open market operations and because it believes that changes in the federal funds rate will ultimately affect economic variables that are related to its monetary policy goals. Here it is important to consider again the distinction between the nominal interest rate and the real interest rate. Recall that we calculate the real interest rate by subtracting the inflation rate from the nominal interest rate. Ultimately, the ability of the Fed to use monetary policy to affect economic variables such as real GDP depends on its ability to affect real interest rates, such as the real interest rates on mortgages and corporate bonds. Because the federal funds rate is a short-term nominal interest rate, the Fed sometimes has difficulty affecting long-term real interest rates. Nevertheless, for purposes of the following discussion, we will assume that the Fed is able to use open market operations to affect long-term real interest rates.

How Interest Rates Affect Aggregate Demand

Changes in interest rates affect *aggregate demand*, which is the total level of spending in the economy. Recall from Chapter 24 that aggregate demand has four components: consumption, investment, government purchases, and net exports. Changes in interest rates will not affect government purchases, but they will affect the other three components of aggregate demand in the following ways:

- *Consumption.* Many households finance purchases of consumer durables, such as automobiles and furniture, by borrowing. Lower interest rates lead to increased spending on durables because they lower the total cost of these goods to consumers by lowering the interest payments on loans. Higher interest rates raise the cost of consumer durables, and households will buy fewer of them. Lower interest rates also reduce the return to saving, leading households to save less and spend more. Higher interest rates increase the return to saving, leading households to save more and spend less.

- *Investment.* Firms finance most of their spending on machinery, equipment, and factories out of their profits or by borrowing. Firms borrow either from the financial markets by issuing corporate bonds or from banks. Higher interest rates on corporate bonds or on bank loans make it more expensive for firms to borrow, so they will undertake fewer investment projects. Lower interest rates make it less expensive for firms to borrow, so they will undertake more investment projects. Lower interest rates can also increase investment through their impact on stock prices. As interest rates decline, stocks become a more attractive investment relative to bonds. The increase in demand for stocks raises their price. An increase in stock prices sends a signal to firms that the future profitability of investment projects has increased. By issuing additional shares of stocks, firms can acquire the funds they need to buy new factories and equipment, thereby increasing investment.

  Finally, spending by households on new homes is also part of investment. When interest rates on mortgage loans rise, the cost of buying new homes rises, and fewer new homes will be purchased. When interest rates on mortgage loans fall, more new homes will be purchased.

- *Net exports.* Recall that net exports are equal to spending by foreign households and firms on goods and services produced in the United States minus spending by U.S. households and firms on goods and services produced in other countries. The value of net exports depends partly on the exchange rate between the dollar and foreign currencies. When the value of the dollar rises, households and firms in other countries will pay more for goods and services produced in the United States, but U.S. households and firms will pay less for goods and services produced in other countries. As a result, the United States will export less and import more, so net exports fall. When the value of the dollar falls, net exports will rise. If interest rates in the United States rise relative to interest rates in other countries, investing in U.S. financial assets will become more desirable, causing foreign investors to increase their demand for dollars, which will increase the value of the dollar. As the value of the dollar increases, net exports will fall. If interest rates in the United States decline relative to interest rates in other countries, the value of the dollar will fall, and net exports will rise.

New home sales dropped 60 percent between July 2005 and May 2008.

Making the Connection

The Inflation and Deflation of the Housing Market "Bubble"

We have seen that low interest rates helped boost demand for housing during the 2001 recession and for several years thereafter. By 2005, however, many economists argued that a "bubble" had formed in the housing market. As we discussed in Chapter 7, the price of any asset reflects the returns the owner of the asset expects to receive. For example, the price of a share of stock reflects the profitability of the firm issuing the stock because the owner of a share of stock has a claim on the firm's profits and its assets. Many economists believe, however, that sometimes a stock market bubble can form when the prices of stocks rise above levels that can be justified by the profitability of the firms issuing the stock. Bubbles end when enough investors decide stocks are overvalued and begin to sell. Why would an investor be willing to pay more for a share of stock than would be justified by its underlying value? There are two main explanations: The investor may be caught up in the enthusiasm of the moment and, by failing to gather sufficient information, may overestimate the true value of the stock; or the investor may expect to profit from buying stock at inflated prices if the investor can sell the stock at an even higher price before the bubble bursts.

The price of a house should reflect the value of the housing services the house provides. We can use the rents charged for comparable houses in the area to measure the value of housing services. By 2005, some economists argued that in some cities, the prices of houses had risen so much that monthly mortgage payments were far above the monthly rent on comparable houses. In addition, in some cities, there was an increase in the number of buyers who did not intend to live in the houses they purchased but were using them as investments. Like stock investors during a stock market bubble, these housing investors were expecting to make a profit by selling houses at a higher price than they had paid for them, and they were not concerned about whether the prices of the houses were above the value of the housing services provided. Changes in the mortgage market also fueled the housing bubble. In particular, "subprime" mortgages and "exotic" mortgages became more widespread. A subprime mortgage is a mortgage granted to a borrower whose credit history is not very good, perhaps because of late bill payments. In 2007, about 15 percent of existing mortgages were subprime. An exotic mortgage might allow a borrower to make loan payments at a very low interest rate—or perhaps a zero interest rate—for several years, before having to make payments at a much higher rate for the remaining life of the mortgage. Many borrowers who took out these mortgages probably would not have otherwise been able to afford a home or would have purchased a much lower-priced home. But these new mortgages increased the risk that in the future, the borrowers would not be able to make payments on their loans, thereby defaulting on them.

During 2006 and 2007, it was clear that the air was rapidly escaping from the housing bubble. The following figure shows new home sales for each month from January 2000 through May 2008. New home sales rose by 60 percent between January 2000 and July 2005 and then fell by 60 percent between July 2005 and May 2008. Sales of existing homes followed a similar pattern. Although some housing markets, such as Manhattan and Houston, remained strong, prices of new and existing homes in most markets began to decline, and the inventory of unsold homes offered for sale soared. Some home buyers with subprime mortgages began having trouble making their loan payments. Between mid-2005 and mid-2008, the percentage of delinquent subprime loans doubled. When lenders foreclosed on some of these loans, the homes were offered for sale by the lenders, causing housing prices to decline further. In addition, some mortgage lenders that had concentrated on making subprime loans suffered heavy losses and went out of business, and most banks and other lenders tightened the requirements for borrowers. This *credit crunch* made it more difficult for potential homebuyers to obtain mortgages, further depressing the market.

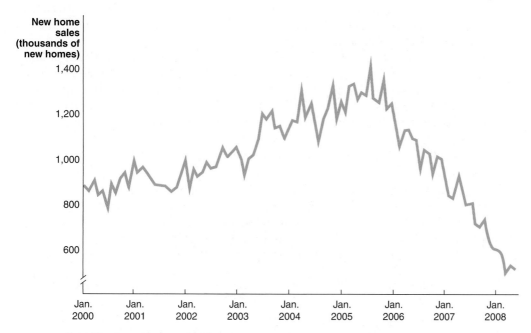

Note: The data are seasonally adjusted at an annual rate.

Source: U.S. Bureau of the Census.

The decline in the housing market affected other markets as well. With home prices falling, consumption spending on furniture, appliances, and home improvements declined as many households found it more difficult to borrow against the value of their homes. According to one estimate, more than 300,000 jobs related to housing were lost between March 2006 and May 2007.

The deflation of the housing bubble left the Fed in a dilemma. Reducing the target for the federal funds rate might bring down mortgage interest rates and help increase spending on new homes, thereby stimulating aggregate demand and reducing the likelihood of a recession. But, with the inflation rate running higher than the Fed would like, lower interest rates might also undermine progress toward price stability. Finally, in September 2007 the Fed decided that an expansionary policy was needed to head off recession. By April 2008, it had cut the target for the federal funds rate from 5.25 percent to 2 percent.

Source: James R. Hagerty, Jonathan Karp, and Mark Whitehouse, "Economists See Housing Slump Enduring Longer," *Wall Street Journal*, June 9, 2007, p. A1.

YOUR TURN: Test your understanding by doing related problems 3.17, 3.18, and 3.19 on page 924 at the end of this chapter.

The Effects of Monetary Policy on Real GDP and the Price Level: An Initial Look

Expansionary monetary policy
The Federal Reserve's increasing the money supply and decreasing interest rates to increase real GDP.

In Chapter 24, we developed the *aggregate demand and aggregate supply model* to explain fluctuations in real GDP and the price level. In the basic version of the model, we assume that there is no economic growth, so the long-run aggregate supply curve does not shift. In panel (a) of Figure 26-7, we assume that the economy is in short-run equilibrium at point *A*, where the aggregate demand curve (AD_1) intersects the short-run aggregate supply curve (*SRAS*). Real GDP is below potential real GDP, as shown by the *LRAS* curve, so the economy is in recession, with some firms operating below normal capacity and some workers having been laid off. To reach its goal of high employment, the Fed needs to carry out an **expansionary monetary policy** by increasing the money supply and decreasing interest rates. Lower interest rates cause an increase in consumption, investment, and net exports, which shifts the aggregate demand curve to the right, from AD_1 to AD_2. Real GDP increases from $12.2 trillion to potential GDP of $12.4 trillion, and the price level rises from 98 to 100 (point *B*). The policy successfully returns real GDP to its potential level. Rising production leads to increasing employment, allowing the Fed to achieve its goal of high employment.

Contractionary monetary policy
The Federal Reserve's adjusting the money supply to increase interest rates to reduce inflation.

In panel (b) of Figure 26-7, the economy is in short-run equilibrium at point *A*, with real GDP of $12.6 trillion, which is above potential real GDP of $12.4 trillion. With some firms producing beyond their normal capacity and the unemployment rate very low, wages and prices are increasing. To reach its goal of price stability, the Fed needs to carry out a **contractionary monetary policy** by decreasing the money supply and increasing rates. Higher interest rates cause a decrease in consumption, investment, and net exports, which shifts the aggregate demand curve from AD_1 to AD_2.

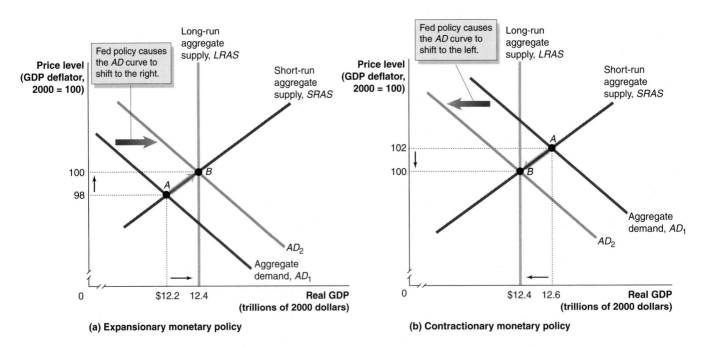

(a) Expansionary monetary policy

(b) Contractionary monetary policy

Figure 26-7 | Monetary Policy

In panel (a), the economy begins in recession at point *A*, with real GDP of $12.2 trillion and a price level of 98. An expansionary monetary policy causes aggregate demand to shift to the right, from AD_1 to AD_2, increasing real GDP from $12.2 trillion to $12.4 trillion and the price level from 98 to 100 (point *B*). With real GDP back at its potential level, the Fed can meet its goal of high employment. In panel (b), the economy begins at point *A*, with real GDP at $12.6 trillion and the price level at 102.

Because real GDP is greater than potential GDP, the economy experiences rising wages and prices. A contractionary monetary policy causes aggregate demand to shift to the left, from AD_1 to AD_2, decreasing real GDP from $12.6 trillion to $12.4 trillion and the price level from 102 to 100 (point *B*). With real GDP back at its potential level, the Fed can meet its goal of price stability.

Real GDP decreases from $12.6 trillion to $12.4 trillion, and the price level falls from 102 to 100 (point *B*). Why would the Fed want to intentionally cause real GDP to decline? Because in the long run, real GDP cannot continue to remain above potential GDP. Attempting to keep real GDP above potential GDP would result in rising inflation. As aggregate demand declines and real GDP returns to its potential level, upward pressure on wages and prices will be reduced, allowing the Fed to achieve its goal of price stability.

We can conclude that the Fed can use monetary policy to affect the price level and, in the short run, the level of real GDP, allowing it to attain its two most important policy goals: high employment and price stability.

The Effects of Monetary Policy on Real GDP and the Price Level: A More Complete Account

The overview of monetary policy we just finished contains a key idea: The Fed can use monetary policy to affect aggregate demand, thereby changing the price level and the level of real GDP. The account is simplified, however, because it ignores two important facts about the economy: (1) The economy experiences continuing inflation, with the price level rising every year, and (2) the economy experiences long-run growth, with the *LRAS* curve shifting to the right every year. In Chapter 24, we developed a *dynamic aggregate demand and aggregate supply model* that took these two facts into account. In this section, we use the dynamic model to gain a more complete understanding of monetary policy. Let's briefly review the dynamic model: Recall from Chapter 24 that over time, the U.S. labor force and U.S. capital stock will increase. Technological change will also occur. The result will be an increase in potential real GDP, which we show by the long-run aggregate supply curve shifting to the right. These factors will also result in firms supplying more goods and services at any given price level in the short run, which we show by the short-run aggregate supply curve shifting to the right. During most years, the aggregate demand curve will also shift to the right, indicating that aggregate expenditure will be higher at every price level. There are several reasons aggregate expenditure usually increases: As population grows and incomes rise, consumption will increase over time. Also, as the economy grows, firms expand capacity, and new firms are established, increasing investment spending. Finally, an expanding population and an expanding economy require increased government services, such as more police officers and teachers, so government purchases will expand.

During certain periods, however, *AD* does not increase enough during the year to keep the economy at potential GDP. This slow growth in aggregate demand may be due to households and firms becoming pessimistic about the future state of the economy, leading them to cut back their spending on consumer durables, houses, and factories. Other possibilities exist, as well: The federal government might decide to balance the budget by cutting back its purchases, or recessions in other countries might cause a decline in U.S. exports. In Figure 26-8, in the first year, the economy is in equilibrium, at potential real GDP of $12.0 trillion and a price level of 100 (point *A*). In the second year, *LRAS* increases to $12.4 trillion, but *AD* increases only to $AD_{2(\text{without policy})}$, which is not enough to keep the economy in macroeconomic equilibrium at potential GDP. If the Fed does not intervene, the short-run equilibrium will occur at $12.3 trillion (point *B*). The $100 billion gap between this level of real GDP and potential real GDP at $LRAS_2$ means that some firms are operating at less than their normal capacity. Incomes and profits will fall, firms will begin to lay off workers, and the unemployment rate will rise.

The economists at the Federal Reserve closely monitor the economy and continually update forecasts of future levels of real GDP and prices. When these economists anticipate that aggregate demand is not growing fast enough to allow the economy to remain at full employment, they present their findings to the FOMC, which decides whether circumstances require a change in monetary policy. For example, suppose that the FOMC meets and considers a forecast from the staff indicating that during the following year a

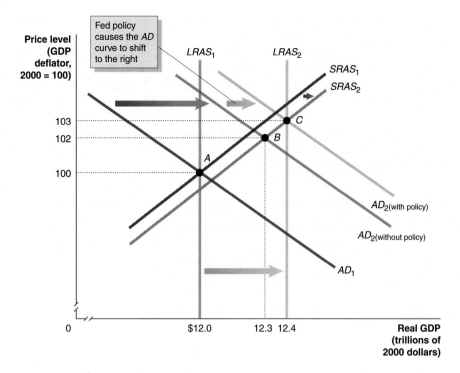

Figure 26-8 | An Expansionary Monetary Policy

The economy begins in equilibrium at point A, with real GDP of $12.0 trillion and a price level of 100. Without monetary policy, aggregate demand will shift from AD_1 to $AD_{2(without\ policy)}$, which is not enough to keep the economy at full employment because long-run aggregate supply has shifted from $LRAS_1$ to $LRAS_2$. The economy will be in short-run equilibrium at point B, with real GDP of $12.3 trillion and a price level of 102. By lowering interest rates, the Fed increases investment, consumption, and net exports sufficiently to shift aggregate demand to $AD_{2(with\ policy)}$. The economy will be in equilibrium at point C, with real GDP of $12.4 trillion, which is its full employment level, and a price level of 103. The price level is higher than it would have been if the Fed had not acted to increase spending in the economy.

gap of $100 billion will open between equilibrium real GDP and potential real GDP. In other words, the situation shown in Figure 26-8 will occur. The FOMC may then decide to carry out an expansionary monetary policy to lower interest rates to stimulate aggregate demand. The figure shows the results of a successful attempt to do this: AD has shifted to the right, and equilibrium occurs at potential GDP (point C). The Fed will have successfully headed off the falling incomes and rising unemployment that otherwise would have occurred.

Notice that in Figure 26-8, the expansionary monetary policy caused the inflation rate to be higher than it would have been. Without the expansionary policy, the price level would have risen from 100 to 102, so the inflation rate for the year would have been 2 percent. By shifting the aggregate demand curve, the expansionary policy caused the price level to increase from 102 to 103, raising the inflation rate from 2 percent to 3 percent.

Making
the
Connection
The Fed Responds to the Terrorist Attacks of September 11, 2001

When the Fed was founded, its main purpose was to make discount loans to banks suffering from deposit withdrawals. Today, discount loans have become relatively less important in the operations of the Fed. For example, the average weekly amount of discount loans outstanding in 2001 through September 11 was only $34 million. This volume of discount loans is very small compared with total bank reserves of more than $66 *billion*.

Still, discount loans remain an effective way for the Fed to make funds quickly available to banks in an emergency. The banks can use these funds to provide cash or loans to households and firms. The day after the terrorist attacks of September 11, 2001, the Fed made massive discount loans to banks. Discount loans rose from $99 million on September 5 to $45.5 *billion* on September 12, or to 500 times their normal level. In the end, households and firms did not withdraw excessive amounts from their bank accounts following the attacks, and the volume of discount loans returned to normal levels very quickly. By September 19, discount loans had fallen to $2.6 billion, and by September 26, they had fallen to only $20 million. As we will discuss later in this chapter, the Fed also relied on discount loans to cushion the banking and financial systems from potential instability during the subprime mortgage crisis of 2007 and 2008.

Although the modern Fed concentrates on its objectives for inflation and economic growth, which it implements through open market operations, it still retains its original purpose of dealing with potential financial panics. For this purpose, discount loans are an effective tool.

The day after the terrorist attacks of September 11, 2001, the Fed made massive discount loans to banks and succeeded in preventing a financial panic. Alan Greenspan, pictured here, was the chairman of the Fed at the time of the attacks.

Source: Federal Reserve Board of Governors, *Statistical Release H.4.1*, various weekly issues.

YOUR TURN: Test your understanding by doing related problem 3.21 on page 924 at the end of this chapter.

Can the Fed Eliminate Recessions?

Figure 26-8 shows an expansionary monetary policy that performs so well that no recession actually takes place. The Fed manages to shift the *AD* curve to keep the economy continually at potential GDP. In fact, however, this ideal is very difficult for the Fed to achieve. Keeping recessions shorter and milder than they would otherwise be is usually the best the Fed can do. The recession of 2001 shows the Fed performing about as well as it can in the real world. Let's review the events leading up to the 2001 recession and the actions the Fed took in response.

In spring 2000, stock prices began to decline. Hardest hit were the dot-coms because online retailing failed to grow as rapidly as many Wall Street analysts had predicted. As we saw in Chapter 24, when stock prices fall, the wealth of households declines, and, as a result, consumption falls. At the same time, many firms began to cut their expenditure on information technology.

On December 19, 2000, at the last FOMC meeting of the year, the committee left the target for the federal funds rate unchanged, although committee members believed the risk of recession had increased. Within a few days, increasing evidence indicated that the growth of aggregate demand was slowing, and the committee held a telephone conference meeting on January 3, 2001, four weeks before its regularly scheduled meeting. During the telephone conference, the committee decided to reduce the target for the federal funds rate from 6.5 percent to 6 percent. The committee continued to reduce the federal funds target at subsequent meetings. By December 2001, it had reduced the rate to 1.75 percent. Further decreases brought the federal funds rate to 1 percent in June 2003, the lowest it had been in more than 40 years.

Falling interest rates were not enough to head off a recession, which began in March 2001. The recession was milder than many economists had expected, despite the impact of the September 11, 2001, terrorist attacks. Real GDP declined only during two quarters in 2001, and GDP was actually higher for 2001 as a whole than it had been during 2000. We saw in Chapter 24 that the recovery from the recession was weaker than had been expected. The unemployment rate rose from 4.3 percent at the beginning of the recession to 5.6 percent at the end of the recession and to a peak of 6.3 percent in June 2003. Even at its peak, though, this was a relatively low unemployment rate compared to the more severe recessions of the post–World War II period, such as the 1981–1982 recession, when the unemployment rate was above 10 percent. Household purchases of consumer durables and new homes remained strong during 2001, keeping real GDP from falling too far below its potential level. Many homebuilders, like Toll Brothers, enjoyed a surprisingly good year in 2001. Although home building is usually hit hard during recessions, new home construction increased by more than 2 percent, from less than 1.57 million units in 2000 to more than 1.60 million units in 2001.

Although the Fed was able to use expansionary monetary policy successfully to reduce the severity of the 2001 recession, it was unable to entirely eliminate it. In fact, the Fed has no realistic hope of "fine-tuning" the economy to eliminate the business cycle and achieve absolute price stability.

Using Monetary Policy to Fight Inflation

In addition to using monetary policy to reduce the severity of recessions, the Fed can also use a contractionary monetary policy to keep aggregate demand from expanding so rapidly that the inflation rate begins to increase. Figure 26-9 shows the situation during 1999 and 2000, when the Fed faced this possibility. During 1999, the economy was at equilibrium beyond potential GDP, although the inflation rate for the entire year was only about 1.5 percent. By December, Alan Greenspan and other members of the FOMC were worried that aggregate demand was increasing so rapidly that the inflation rate would begin to accelerate. In fact, during the last three months of 1999, inflation

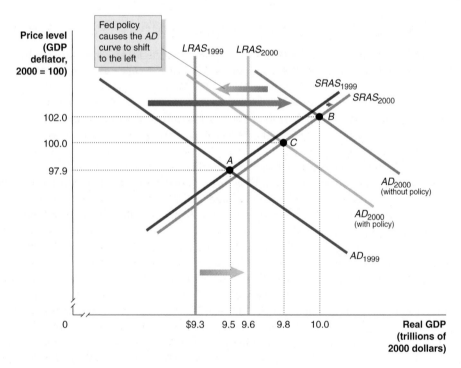

Figure 26-9 | A Contractionary Monetary Policy in 2000

The economy began 1999 in equilibrium at point A, with real GDP of $9.5 trillion and a price level of 97.9. From 1999 to 2000, potential real GDP increased from $9.3 trillion to $9.6 trillion, as long-run aggregate supply increased from $LRAS_{1999}$ to $LRAS_{2000}$. The Fed raised interest rates because it believed aggregate demand was increasing too rapidly. Without the increase in interest rates, aggregate demand would have shifted from AD_{1999} to $AD_{2000(\text{without policy})}$, and the new short-run equilibrium would have occurred at point B. Real GDP would have been $10.0 trillion—$200 billion higher than it actually was—and the price level would have been 102.0. The increase in interest rates resulted in aggregate demand increasing only to $AD_{2000(\text{with policy})}$. Equilibrium occurred at point C, with real GDP of $9.8 trillion and the price level rising only to 100.0.

had increased to an annual rate of about 2.5 percent. The FOMC issues a statement after each meeting that summarizes the committee's views on the current state of the economy and gives some indication of how monetary policy might change in the near future. After its meeting on December 21, 1999, the FOMC included the following remarks in its statement:

> The Committee remains concerned with the possibility that over time increases in demand will continue to exceed the growth in potential supply. . . . Such trends could foster inflationary imbalances that would undermine the economy's exemplary performance. . . . At its next meeting the Committee will assess available information on the likely balance of supply and demand, conditions in financial markets, and the possible need for adjustment in the stance of policy to contain inflationary pressures.

At its next meeting, on February 2, 2000, the committee raised the target for the federal funds rate from 5.5 percent to 5.75 percent. According to the minutes of the meeting:

> The Committee's decision . . . was intended to help bring the growth of aggregate demand into better alignment with the expansion of sustainable aggregate supply in an effort to avert rising inflationary pressures in the economy.

The committee raised the target for the federal funds rate twice more in following meetings, until it reached 6.5 percent in May, where it remained for the rest of 2000. Although it is impossible to know exactly what would have happened during 2000 without the Fed's policy change, Figure 26-9 presents a plausible scenario. The figure shows that without the Fed's actions to increase interest rates, aggregate demand would have shifted farther to the right, and equilibrium would have occurred at a level of real GDP that was even further beyond the potential level. The price level would have risen from 97.9 in 1999 to 102.0 in 2000, meaning that the inflation rate would have been above 4 percent. Because the Fed kept aggregate demand from increasing as much as it otherwise would have, equilibrium occurred closer to potential real GDP, and the price level in 2000 rose to only 100.0, keeping the inflation rate to a little over 2 percent. Notice that in this case, as with its policy actions during the 2001 recession, the Fed was unable to fine-tune the economy: In both 1999 and 2000, real GDP was above its potential level.

Solved Problem | 26-3

The Effects of Monetary Policy

The hypothetical information in the following table shows what the values for real GDP and the price level will be in 2011 if the Fed does *not* use monetary policy.

YEAR	POTENTIAL REAL GDP	REAL GDP	PRICE LEVEL
2010	$13.3 trillion	$13.3 trillion	140
2011	13.7 trillion	13.6 trillion	142

a. If the Fed wants to keep real GDP at its potential level in 2011, should it use an expansionary policy or a contractionary policy? Should the trading desk buy Treasury bills or sell them?

b. Suppose the Fed's policy is successful in keeping real GDP at its potential level in 2011. State whether each of

the following will be higher or lower than if the Fed had taken no action:

  i. Real GDP

  ii. Potential real GDP

  iii. The inflation rate

  iv. The unemployment rate

c. Draw an aggregate demand and aggregate supply graph to illustrate your answer. Be sure that your graph contains *LRAS* curves for 2010 and 2011; *SRAS* curves for 2010 and 2011; *AD* curve for 2010 and 2011, with and without monetary policy action; and equilibrium real GDP and the price level in 2011, with and without policy.

SOLVING THE PROBLEM:

Step 1: **Review the chapter material.** This problem is about the effects of monetary policy on real GDP and the price level, so you may want to review the section "The Effects of Monetary Policy on Real GDP and the Price Level: A More Complete Account," which begins on page 901.

Step 2: **Answer question (a) by explaining how the Fed can keep real GDP at its potential level.** The information in the table tells us that without monetary policy, the economy will be below potential real GDP in 2011. To keep real GDP at its potential level, the Fed must undertake an expansionary policy. To implement an expansionary policy, the trading desk needs to buy Treasury bills. Buying Treasury bills will increase reserves in the banking system. Banks will increase their loans, which will increase the money supply and lower the interest rate.

Step 3: **Answer question (b) by explaining the effect of the Fed's policy.** policy is successful, real GDP in 2011 will increase from the level given in the table of $13.3 trillion to its potential level of $13.7 trillion. Potential real GDP is not affected by monetary policy, so its value will not change. Because the level of real GDP will be higher, the unemployment rate will be lower than it would have been without policy. The expansionary monetary policy shifts the *AD* curve to the right, so short-run equilibrium will move up the short-run aggregate supply curve (*SRAS*), and the price level will be higher.

Step 4: **Answer question (c) by drawing the graph.** Your graph should look similar to Figure 26-8.

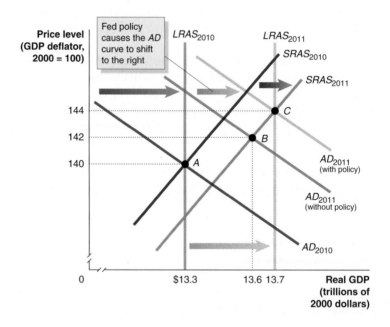

The economy starts in equilibrium in 2010 at point *A*, with the *AD* and *SRAS* curves intersecting along the *LRAS* curve. Real GDP is at its potential level of $13.3 trillion, and the price level is 140. Without monetary policy, the *AD* curve shifts to $AD_{2011(\text{without policy})}$, and the economy is in short-run equilibrium at point *B*. Because potential real GDP has increased from $13.3 trillion to $13.7 trillion, short-run equilibrium real GDP of $13.6 trillion is below the potential level. The price level has increased from 140 to 142. With policy, the *AD* curve shifts to $AD_{2011(\text{with policy})}$, and the economy is in equilibrium at point *C*. Real GDP is at its potential level of $13.7 trillion. We don't have enough information to be sure of the new equilibrium price level.

We do know that it will be higher than 142. The graph shows the price level rising to 144. Therefore, without policy, the inflation rate in 2011 would have been about 1.4 percent. With policy, it will be about 2.9 percent.

EXTRA CREDIT: It's important to bear in mind that in reality, the Fed is unable to use monetary policy to keep real GDP exactly at its potential level, as this problem suggests. In a later section, we will discuss some of the difficulties the Fed encounters in conducting monetary policy.

YOUR TURN: For more practice, do problem 3.12 and 3.13 on page 923 at the end of this chapter.

>> **End Solved Problem 26-3**

A Summary of How Monetary Policy Works

Table 26-1 compares the steps involved in expansionary and contractionary monetary policies. We need to add a very important qualification to this summary. At every point, we should add the phrase "relative to what would have happened without the policy." Table 26-1 is isolating the impact of monetary policy, *holding constant all other factors affecting the variables involved*. In other words, we are invoking the *ceteris paribus condition*, discussed in Chapter 3. This point is important because, for example, a contractionary monetary policy does not cause the price level to fall. As Figure 26-9 on page 904 shows, a contractionary monetary policy causes the price level *to rise by less than it would have without the policy*. One final note on terminology: An expansionary monetary policy is sometimes referred to as a *loose* or an *easy* policy. A contractionary monetary policy is sometimes referred to as a *tight* policy.

Table 26-1 | Expansionary and Contractionary Monetary Policies

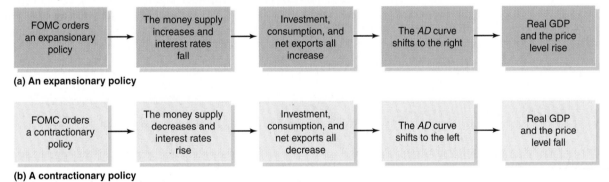

(a) An expansionary policy

FOMC orders an expansionary policy → The money supply increases and interest rates fall → Investment, consumption, and net exports all increase → The *AD* curve shifts to the right → Real GDP and the price level rise

(b) A contractionary policy

FOMC orders a contractionary policy → The money supply decreases and interest rates rise → Investment, consumption, and net exports all decrease → The *AD* curve shifts to the left → Real GDP and the price level fall

Making the Connection	**Why Does Wall Street Care about Monetary Policy?**

You have probably seen newspaper headlines similar to these:

"Fed Rate Cut Fuels Stock Gains"
"Stocks Fall in Anticipation of Fed Rate Increase"
"Worries of Fed Rate Increase Send Stocks Lower"

Before most meetings of the FOMC, newspapers report stock traders' predictions of possible Fed actions and whether those actions will cause stock prices to increase or decrease. Some Wall Street analysts are known as *Fed watchers* because they study the Fed and attempt to forecast future changes in the target for the federal funds rate. Why

The stock market reacts when the Fed either raises or lowers interest rates.

do changes in the federal funds rate affect the stock market? There are two main explanations. In thinking about both explanations, remember that changes in the federal funds rate usually cause changes in other interest rates.

The first reason that stock prices react to the Fed raising or lowering interest rates is because changes in interest rates affect the economy. As we have seen, lower interest rates usually result in increases in real GDP. Fundamentally, the value of a share of stock depends on the profitability of the firm that issued the stock. When real GDP is increasing, the profitability of many firms is also increasing. Stock prices tend to rise when investors expect that the Fed will be lowering interest rates to stimulate the economy. When investors expect that the Fed will be raising interest rates to slow down an economy at risk of rising inflation, stock prices tend to fall.

The second reason that stock prices react to changes in interest rates is that changes in interest rates make it more or less attractive for people to invest in stock rather than in other financial assets. Investors look for the highest return possible on their investments, holding constant the risk level of the investments. If the interest rates on Treasury bills, bank certificates of deposit, and corporate bonds are all low, an investment in stocks will be more attractive. When interest rates are high, an investment in stocks will be less attractive.

YOUR TURN: Test your understanding by doing related problem 3.22 on page 924 at the end of this chapter.

Can the Fed Get the Timing Right?

The Fed's ability to quickly recognize the need for a change in monetary policy is a key to its success. If the Fed is late in recognizing that a recession has begun or that the inflation rate is increasing, it may not be able to implement a new policy soon enough to do much good. In fact, if the Fed implements a policy too late, it may actually destabilize the economy. To see how this can happen, consider Figure 26-10. The straight line represents the long-run growth trend in real GDP in the United States. On average, real GDP grows about 3.5 percent per year. The actual path of real GDP differs from the underlying

Don't Let This Happen to **YOU!**

Remember That with Monetary Policy, It's the Interest Rates—Not the Money— That Counts

It is tempting to think of monetary policy working like this: If the Fed wants more spending in the economy, it increases the money supply, and people spend more because they now have more money. If the Fed wants less spending in the economy, it decreases the money supply, and people spend less because they now have less money. In fact, that is *not* how monetary policy works. Remember the important difference between money and income: The Fed increases the money supply by buying Treasury bills. The sellers of the Treasury bills have just exchanged one asset—Treasury bills—for another asset—a check from the Fed; the sellers have *not* increased their income. Even though the money supply is now larger, no one's income has increased, so no one's spending should be affected.

It is only when this increase in the money supply results in lower interest rates that spending is affected. When interest rates are lower, households are more likely to buy new homes and automobiles, and businesses are more likely to buy new factories and computers. Lower interest rates also lead to a lower value of the dollar, which lowers the prices of exports and raises the prices of imports, thereby increasing net exports. It isn't the increase in the money supply that has brought about this additional spending; *it's the lower interest rates.* To understand how monetary policy works, and to interpret news reports about the Fed's actions, remember that it is the change in interest rates, not the change in the money supply, that is most important.

YOUR TURN: Test your understanding by doing related problem 3.14 on page 923 at the end of this chapter.

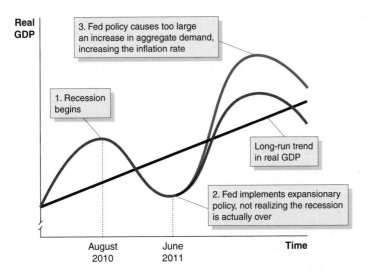

Figure 26-10 | The Effect of a Poorly Timed Monetary Policy on the Economy

The upward-sloping straight line represents the long-run growth trend in real GDP. The red curving line represents the path real GDP takes because of the business cycle. If the Fed implements a change in monetary policy too late, real GDP will follow the blue curving line. The Fed's expansionary monetary policy results in too great an increase in aggregate demand during the next expansion, which causes an increase in the inflation rate.

trend because of the business cycle, which is shown by the red curving line. As we saw in Chapter 21, the actual business cycle is more irregular than the stylized cycle shown here.

Suppose that a recession begins in August 2010. Because it takes months for economic statistics to be gathered by the Commerce Department, the Census Bureau, the Bureau of Labor Statistics, and the Fed itself, there is often a *lag*, or delay, before the Fed recognizes that a recession has begun. Then it takes time for the Fed's economists to analyze the data. Finally, in June 2011, the FOMC concludes that the economy is in recession and begins an expansionary monetary policy. As it turns out, June 2011 is actually the trough of the recession, meaning that the recession has already ended, and an expansion has begun. In these circumstances, the Fed's expansionary policy is not needed to end the recession. The increase in aggregate demand caused by the Fed's lowering interest rates is likely to push the economy beyond potential real GDP and cause a significant acceleration in inflation. Real GDP ends up following the path indicated by the curving blue line. The Fed has inadvertently engaged in a *procyclical policy*, which increases the severity of the business cycle, as opposed to a *countercyclical policy*, which is meant to reduce the severity of the business cycle, and which is what the Fed intends to use.

It is not unusual for employment or manufacturing production to decline for a month or two in the middle of an expansion. Distinguishing these minor ups and downs from the beginning of a recession is difficult. The National Bureau of Economic Research (NBER) announces dates for the beginning and ending of recessions that are generally accepted by most economists. An indication of how difficult it is to determine when recessions begin and end is that the NBER generally makes its announcements only after a considerable delay. The NBER did not announce that a recession had begun in March 2001 until November 2001, which is the same month it later determined the recession had ended. It did not announce that a recession had begun in July 1990 until April 1991, which was one month *after* it later determined the recession had ended. Failing to react until well after a recession has begun (or ended) can be a serious problem for the Fed.

A Closer Look at the Fed's Setting of Monetary Policy Targets

We have seen that in carrying out monetary policy, the Fed changes its target for the federal funds rate depending on the state of the economy. Is using the federal funds rate as a target the best way to conduct monetary policy? If the Fed targets the federal funds rate, how should it decide what the target level should be? In this section, we consider some important issues concerning the Fed's targeting policy.

Should the Fed Target the Money Supply?

Some economists have argued that rather than use an interest rate as its monetary policy target, the Fed should use the money supply. Many of the economists who make this argument belong to a school of thought known as *monetarism*. The leader of the monetarist school was Nobel laureate Milton Friedman, who was critical of the Fed's ability to correctly time changes in monetary policy.

Friedman and his followers favored replacing *monetary policy* with a *monetary growth rule*. Ordinarily, we expect monetary policy to respond to changing economic conditions: When the economy is in recession, the Fed reduces interest rates, and when inflation is increasing, the Fed raises interest rates. A monetary growth rule, in contrast, is a plan for increasing the money supply at a constant rate that does not change in response to economic conditions. Friedman and his followers proposed a monetary growth rule of increasing the money supply every year at a rate equal to the long-run growth rate of real GDP, which is 3.5 percent. If the Fed adopted this monetary growth rule, it would stick to it through changing economic conditions.

But what happens under a monetary growth rule if the economy moves into recession? Shouldn't the Fed abandon the rule to drive down interest rates? Friedman argued that the Fed should stick to the rule even during recessions because, he believed, active monetary policy destabilizes the economy, increasing the number of recessions and their severity. By keeping the money supply growing at a constant rate, Friedman argued, the Fed would greatly increase economic stability.

Although during the 1970s some economists and politicians pressured the Federal Reserve to adopt a monetary growth rule, most of that pressure has disappeared in recent years. A key reason is that the fairly close relationship between movements in the money supply and movements in real GDP and the price level that existed before 1980 has become much weaker. Since 1980, the growth rate of M1 has been unstable. In some years, it has grown more than 10 percent, while in other years, it has actually fallen. Yet despite these wide fluctuations in the growth of M1, growth in real GDP has been fairly stable, and inflation has remained low.

Why Doesn't the Fed Target Both the Money Supply and the Interest Rate?

Most economists believe that an interest rate is the best monetary policy target, but, as we have just seen, other economists believe the Fed should target the money supply. Why doesn't the Fed satisfy both groups by targeting both the money supply and an interest rate? The simple answer to this question is that the Fed can't target both at the same time. To see why, look at Figure 26-11, which shows the money market.

Remember that the Fed controls the money supply, but it does not control money demand. Money demand is determined by decisions of households and firms as they weigh the trade-off between the convenience of money and its low interest rate compared with other financial assets. Suppose the Fed is targeting the interest rate and

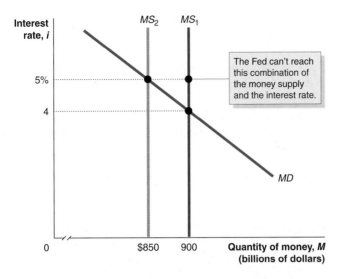

Figure 26-11 | The Fed Can't Target Both the Money Supply and the Interest Rate

The Fed is forced to choose between using either an interest rate or the money supply as its monetary policy target. In this figure, the Fed can set a target of a money supply of $900 billion or a target of an interest rate of 5 percent, but it can't have both because only combinations of the interest rate and the money supply that represent equilibrium in the money market are possible.

decides, given conditions in the economy, that the interest rate should be 5 percent. Or, suppose the Fed is targeting the money supply and decides that the money supply should be $900 billion. Figure 26-11 shows that the Fed can bring about an interest rate of 5 percent, or a money supply of $900 billion, but it can't bring about both. The point representing an interest rate of 5 percent and a money supply of $900 billion is not on the money demand curve, so it can't represent an equilibrium in the money market. Only combinations of the interest rate and the money supply that represent equilibrium in the money market are possible.

The Fed has to choose between targeting an interest rate and targeting the money supply. For most of the period since World War II, the Fed has chosen an interest rate target.

The Taylor Rule

How does the Fed choose a target for the federal funds rate? The discussions at the meetings of the FOMC can be complex, and they take into account many economic variables. John Taylor of Stanford University has analyzed the factors involved in Fed decision making and developed the **Taylor rule** to explain federal funds rate targeting. The Taylor rule begins with an estimate of the value of the equilibrium real federal funds rate, which is the federal funds rate—adjusted for inflation—that would be consistent with real GDP being equal to potential real GDP in the long run. According to the Taylor rule, the Fed should set the target for the federal funds rate so that it is equal to the sum of the inflation rate, the equilibrium real federal funds rate, and two additional terms. The first of these additional terms is the *inflation gap*—the difference between current inflation and a target rate; the second is the *output gap*—the percentage difference between real GDP and potential real GDP. The inflation gap and output gap are each given "weights" that reflect their influence on the federal funds target rate. With weights of 1/2 for both gaps, we have the following Taylor rule:

Taylor rule A rule developed by John Taylor that links the Fed's target for the federal funds rate to economic variables.

Federal funds target rate = Current inflation rate +
Real equilibrium federal funds rate + (1/2) × Inflation gap + (1/2) × Output gap.

The Taylor rule includes expressions for the inflation gap and the output gap because the Fed is concerned about both inflation and fluctuations in real GDP. Taylor demonstrated that if the equilibrium real federal funds rate is 2 percent and the target rate of inflation is 2 percent, the preceding expression does a good job of explaining changes in the Fed's target for the federal funds rate. Consider an example in which the current inflation rate is 1 percent, and real GDP is 1 percent below potential real GDP. In that case, the inflation gap is 1 percent − 2 percent = −1 percent, and the output gap is also −1 percent. Inserting these values in the Taylor rule, we can calculate the predicted value for the federal funds target rate:

$$\text{Federal funds target rate} = 1\% + 2\% + ((1/2) \times -1\%) + ((1/2) \times -1\%)$$
$$= 2\%.$$

The Taylor rule accurately predicted changes in the federal funds target during the period of Alan Greenspan's leadership of the Federal Reserve. For the period of the late 1970s and early 1980s, when Paul Volcker was chairman of the Federal Reserve, the Taylor rule predicts a federal funds rate target *lower* than the actual target used by the Fed. This indicates that Chairman Volcker kept the federal funds rate at an unusually high level to bring down the very high inflation rates plaguing the economy in the late 1970s and early 1980s. In contrast, using data from the chairmanship of Arthur Burns from 1970 to 1978, the Taylor rule predicts a federal funds rate target *higher* than the actual target. This indicates that Chairman Burns kept the federal funds rate at an unusually low level during these years, which can help explain why the inflation rate grew worse.

Although the Taylor rule does not account for changes in the target inflation rate or the equilibrium interest rate, many economists view the rule as a convenient way to analyze the federal funds target.

Should the Fed Target Inflation?

Inflation targeting Conducting monetary policy so as to commit the central bank to achieving a publicly announced level of inflation.

Over the past decade, many economists and central bankers, including the current Fed chairman, Ben Bernanke, have proposed using *inflation targeting* as a framework for carrying out monetary policy. With **inflation targeting**, the central bank commits to conducting policy to achieve a publicly announced inflation target of, for example, 2 percent. Inflation targeting need not impose an inflexible rule on the central bank. The central bank would still be free, for example, to take action in case of a severe recession. Nevertheless, monetary policy goals and operations would focus on inflation and inflation forecasts. Inflation targeting has been adopted by the central banks of New Zealand (1989), Canada (1991), the United Kingdom (1992), Finland (1993), Sweden (1993), and Spain (1994), and by the European Central Bank. Inflation targeting has also been used in some newly industrializing countries, such as Chile, South Korea, Mexico, and South Africa, as well as in some transition economies in Eastern Europe, such as the Czech Republic, Hungary, and Poland. Experience with inflation targeting has varied, but typically, the move to inflation targeting has been accompanied by lower inflation (sometimes at the cost of temporarily higher unemployment).

Should the Fed adopt an inflation target? Arguments in favor of inflation targeting focus on four points. First, as we have already discussed, in the long run, real GDP returns to its potential level, and potential real GDP is not affected by monetary policy. Therefore, in the long run, the Fed can have an impact on inflation but not on real GDP. Having an explicit inflation target would draw the public's attention to this fact. Second, by announcing an inflation target, the Fed would make it easier for households and firms to form accurate expectations of future inflation, improving their planning and the efficiency of the economy. Third, an announced inflation target would help institutionalize good U.S. monetary policy. It would be less likely that abrupt changes in policy would occur as members join and leave the FOMC. Finally, an inflation target would promote accountability for the Fed by providing a yardstick against which its performance could be measured.

Inflation targeting also has opponents, who typically raise three points. First, having a numerical target for inflation reduces the flexibility of monetary policy to address other policy goals. Second, inflation targeting assumes that the Fed can accurately forecast future inflation rates, which is not always the case. Finally, holding the Fed accountable only for an inflation goal may make it less likely that the Fed will achieve other important policy goals.

The Fed's performance in the 1980s, 1990s, and 2000s, even without a formal inflation target, has generally received high marks from economists. The 1990s, for example, saw low inflation and a substantial economic expansion. In recent years, the Fed has acted to head off the threat of future inflation before it can become established. Even without a formal inflation target, the Fed has been successful at building public support for the idea that low inflation is important to the efficient performance of the economy. The Fed's strategy is not without risk, however. The Fed's prestige during the past two decades has been dependent on public trust in the effectiveness of Fed leadership in containing inflation while maintaining economic growth. But the Fed's leadership changes over time, which highlights what may be a need for more formal procedures to reassure both the public and elected officials about the continuity of policy. As Ben Bernanke assumed the chairmanship of the Fed in early 2006, his support for inflation targeting has increased the chances that the Fed would adopt such a policy.

Making the Connection | How Does the Fed Measure Inflation?

In recent years, the Federal Reserve has put increased emphasis on the goal of price stability. The Fed has therefore had to consider carefully the best way to measure the inflation rate. As we saw in Chapter 20, the consumer price index (CPI) is the most widely used measure of inflation. But we also saw that the CPI suffers from biases that cause it to overstate the true underlying rate of inflation. An alternative measure of changes in consumer prices can be constructed from the data gathered to calculate GDP. We saw in Chapter 19 that the GDP deflator is a broad measure of the price level that includes the price of every good or service that is in GDP. Changes in the GDP deflator are not a good measure of inflation experienced by the typical consumer, worker, or firm, however, because the deflator include prices of goods, such as industrial equipment, that are not widely purchased. The *personal consumption expenditures price index* (PCE) is a measure of the price level that is similar to the GDP deflator, except it includes only the prices of goods from the consumption category of GDP.

In 2000, the Fed announced that it would rely more on the PCE than on the CPI in tracking inflation. The Fed noted three advantages that the PCE has over the CPI:

1 The PCE is a so-called chain-type price index, as opposed to the market-basket approach used in constructing the CPI. As we saw in Chapter 20, because consumers shift the mix of products they buy each year, the market-basket approach makes the CPI overstate actual inflation. A chain-type price index allows the mix of products to change each year.

2 The PCE includes the prices of more goods and services than the CPI, so it is a broader measure of inflation.

3 Past values of the PCE can be recalculated as better ways of computing price indexes are developed and as new data become available. This allows the Fed to better track historical trends in the inflation rate.

In 2004, the Fed announced that it would begin to rely on a subcategory of the PCE: the so-called core PCE, which excludes food and energy prices. Prices of food and energy tend to fluctuate up and down for reasons that may not be related to the causes of general inflation and that cannot easily be controlled by monetary policy. Oil prices, in particular, have moved dramatically up and down in recent years. Therefore, a price index that includes food and energy prices may not give a clear view of underlying trends in inflation. The following graph shows movements in the CPI, the PCE, and the core PCE over a 12-year period. Although the three measures of inflation move roughly together, the core PCE has been more stable than the others. If you want to know what the Fed thinks the current inflation rate is, the best idea is to look at data on the core PCE. These data are published monthly by the Bureau of Economic Analysis.

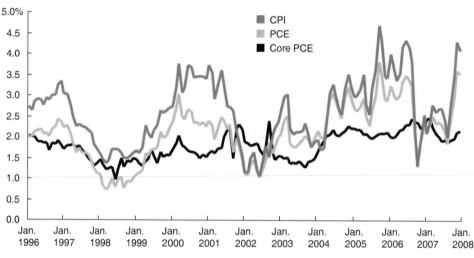

Sources: Bureau of Economic Analysis; and Bureau of Labor Statistics.

YOUR TURN: Test your understanding by doing related problem 4.7 on page 925 at the end of this chapter.

26.5 LEARNING OBJECTIVE

26.5 | Discuss the steps the Federal Reserve took during 2007 and 2008 to respond to the financial crisis.

The Fed Responds to the Financial Crisis

The *Making the Connection* on pages 898–899 discusses the housing market bubble that began to deflate in 2006. The Federal Reserve responded by cutting its target for the federal funds rate eight times between September 2007 and October 2008. Because the decline in the housing market caused wider problems in the financial system, the Fed and the U.S. Treasury Department implemented new policies to provide liquidity and restore confidence. The problems in the financial system were partly due to changes in the market for mortgage loans. We need to review these changes before considering the new policies the Fed and the Treasury put into place.

The Changing Mortgage Market

Mortgages are loans people take out to buy houses. The house serves as *collateral* so that if the borrower stops making payments on the loan, the lender can legally sell the house to pay off the loan. Until the 1970s, the commercial banks and savings and loans that granted mortgages kept the loans until the borrowers paid them off.

A financial asset—such as a loan or a stock or bond—is considered a *security* if it can be bought and sold in a *financial market* as, for instance, shares of stock issued by the Coca-Cola Company can be bought and sold on the New York Stock Exchange. (Some financial assets, such as checking accounts in banks, are not financial securities because they cannot be resold.) When a financial asset is first sold, the sale takes place in the *primary market*. Subsequent sales take place in the *secondary market*. Prior to 1970, most mortgages were not securities because they were rarely resold in a secondary market. Congress, however, wanted to increase home ownership by creating a secondary market in mortgages. If banks and savings and loans could resell mortgages, then, in effect, individual investors would be able to provide funds for mortgages. The process would work like this: If a bank or savings and loan granted a mortgage and then resold the mortgage to an investor, the bank could use the funds received from the investor to grant another mortgage. In this way, banks and savings and loans could grant more mortgage loans because they would no longer depend only on deposits for the funds needed to make the loans. One barrier to creating a secondary market in mortgages was that most investors were unwilling to buy mortgages because they were afraid of losing money if the borrower stopped making payments, or *defaulted*, on the loan.

Congress moved to reassure investors using two institutions: the Federal National Mortgage Association ("Fannie Mae") and the Federal Home Loan Mortgage Corporation ("Freddie Mac"). These two institutions stand between investors and banks that grant mortgages. Fannie and Freddie sell bonds to investors and use the funds to purchase mortgages from banks. By the 1990s, a large secondary market existed in mortgages with funds flowing from investors through Fannie Mae and Freddie Mac to banks and, ultimately, to individuals and families borrowing money to buy houses.

The Role of Investment Banks

By the 2000s, further changes had taken place in the mortgage market. First, investment banks became significant participants in the secondary market for mortgages. Investment banks, such as Goldman Sachs and Morgan Stanley, differed from commercial banks in that they did not take in deposits and rarely lent directly to households. Instead, they concentrated on providing advice to firms issuing stocks and bonds or considering mergers with other firms. Investment banks began buying mortgages, bundling large numbers of them together as bonds known as *mortgage-backed securities*, and reselling them to investors. Mortgage-backed securities proved very popular with investors because they often paid higher interest rates than other securities with comparable default risk.

Second, at the height of the housing bubble in 2005 and early 2006, lenders began to loosen the standards for obtaining a mortgage loan. Traditionally, only borrowers with good credit histories and who were willing to make a down payment equal to at least 20 percent of the value of the house they were buying would be able to receive a mortgage. By 2005, however, many mortgages were being issued to "subprime" borrowers with flawed credit histories. In addition, borrowers who stated—but did not document—their incomes and borrowers who made very small down payments found it easier to take out loans. In addition, lenders created new types of mortgages that allowed borrowers to pay a very low interest rate for the first few years of the mortgage before paying a higher rate in later years. The chance that these nontraditional mortgages would default was higher than for traditional mortgages. Why would borrowers take out mortgages if they doubted they could make the payments, and why would lenders grant these mortgages? The answer seems to be that both borrowers and lenders were anticipating that housing prices would continue to rise, which would reduce the chance that borrowers would default on the mortgages and would also make it easier for borrowers to convert to more traditional mortgages in the future.

Unfortunately, the decline in housing prices led to rising defaults among subprime borrowers and borrowers with nontraditional mortgages. When borrowers began defaulting on mortgages, the value of many mortgage-backed securities declined sharply. Investors feared that if they purchased these securities they would not receive the promised payments because the payments on the securities depended on borrowers making their mortgage payments, which an increasing number were failing to do. Many commercial and investment banks owned these mortgage-backed securities, so the decline in the value of the securities caused these banks to suffer heavy losses. The decline in the value of mortgage-backed securities and the large losses suffered by commercial and investment banks caused turmoil in the financial system. Many investors refused to buy mortgage-backed securities and some investors would only buy bonds issued by the U.S. Treasury.

The Fed and the Treasury Department Respond

Fed Chairman Ben Bernanke and U.S. Treasury Secretary Henry Paulson responded to the financial crisis by intervening in financial markets in unprecedented ways. First, although the Fed traditionally made loans only to commercial banks, it decided to make *primary dealers*—firms that participate in regular open market transactions with the Fed—eligible for discount loans. In addition, the Fed began lending directly to non-financial corporations by purchasing *commercial paper*, which corporations use for short-term borrowing. Second, at the urging of the Fed and the Treasury, Congress passed the Emergency Economic Stabilization Act of 2008, which authorized the Treasury to purchase mortgage-backed securities and other troubled assets from banks. In addition, this act authorized the Treasury to increase the financial strength of banks by buying stock in them. Third, the Fed and the Treasury took direct action to keep some large financial institutions from bankruptcy. In March 2008, they helped JPMorgan Chase acquire the investment bank Bear Stearns, which was on the edge of failing. The Fed agreed that if JPMorgan Chase would acquire Bear Stearns, the Fed would guarantee any losses JPMorgan Chase suffered on Bear Stearns's holdings of mortgage-backed securities, up to a limit of $29 billion. In September, the Fed agreed to provide an $85 billion loan to the American International Group (AIG) insurance company—the largest insurance company in the United States—in exchange for an 80 percent ownership stake, effectively giving the federal government control of the company. Finally, in September the Treasury moved to have the federal government take control of Fannie Mae and Freddie Mac. Although Fannie Mae and Freddie Mac had been sponsored by the federal government, they were actually private businesses whose stock was bought and sold on the New York Stock Exchange. Under the Treasury's plan, Fannie Mae and Freddie Mac were each provided with up to $100 billion in exchange for 80 percent ownership of the firms. The firms were placed under the supervision of the Federal Housing Finance Agency.

While the Fed and Treasury were taking these actions, the investment banking industry underwent dramatic changes. As noted earlier, in March 2008 Bear Stearns disappeared in a merger with JP Morgan Chase. In September, Lehman Brothers declared bankruptcy, Merrill Lynch sold itself to Bank of America, and Goldman Sachs and Morgan Stanley received approval from the Fed to convert themselves to bank holding companies, which allowed them to set up commercial banking operations. With these developments, the era of large, stand-alone Wall Street investment banks appeared to have come to an end.

Although the Treasury and the Fed did not take action to save Lehman Brothers from bankruptcy, they did save other large financial firms, such as Bear Stearns and AIG, from failing because they feared that the failure of large firms could damage the financial system. If a large financial firm goes bankrupt and sells its holdings of securities, the prices of these securities can decline sharply, increasing the possibility that other firms holding these securities will suffer losses and also fail. The failure of one or more large firms may make savers reluctant to make any but the safest investments and

In 2008, Fed Chairman Ben Bernanke (left) and U.S. Treasury Secretary Henry Paulson (right) took unprecedented steps to strengthen the financial system.

can make financial firms reluctant to lend money to each other. Defenders of the Treasury and the Fed argue that their actions were necessary to preserve the stability of the financial system and to prevent the flow of funds from lenders to borrowers from drying up. Critics, though, argue that by intervening so extensively in financial markets, the Treasury and Fed interfered with the usual market mechanism by which the owners and investors in successful firms gain the profits from success, while the owners and investors in unsuccessful firms suffer losses. By not allowing some large firms to fail, these critics argue, the Fed and the Treasury increased the likelihood that other firms will engage in risky behavior in the future with the expectation that the government will save them from failure. The Fed and the Treasury have defended their actions by pointing out that the owners and managers of firms receiving government support have typically still suffered heavy losses.

As we have seen, the financial crisis of 2008 led the Fed and the Treasury to try new approaches to policy. What remains to be seen is whether these new approaches will become part of the policy toolbox or whether policy will return to more traditional approaches.

Economics in YOUR Life!

>> **Continued from page 887**

At the beginning of this chapter, we asked whether buying a house during a recession is a good idea. Clearly, there are many considerations to keep in mind when buying a house, which is the largest purchase you are likely to make in your lifetime. Included among these considerations are the price of the house relative to other comparable houses in the neighborhood, whether house prices in the neighborhood have been rising or falling, and the location of the house relative to stores, work, and good schools. Also important, though, is the interest rate you will have to pay on the mortgage loan you would need in order to buy the house. As we have seen in this chapter, during a recession, the Fed often takes actions to lower interest rates. So, mortgage rates are typically lower during a recession than at other times. You may well want to take advantage of these low interest rates to buy a house during a recession. But, recessions are also times of rising unemployment, and you would not want to make a commitment to borrow a lot of money for 15 or more years if you were in significant danger of losing your job. We can conclude, then, that if your job seems secure, buying a house during a recession may actually be a good idea.

Conclusion

Monetary policy is one way governments pursue goals for inflation, employment, and financial stability. Many journalists and politicians refer to the chairman of the Federal Reserve as second only to the president of the United States in his ability to affect the U.S. economy. Congress and the president, however, also use their power over spending and taxes to try to stabilize the economy. In the next chapter, we discuss how *fiscal policy*—changes in government spending and taxes—affect the economy.

Read *An Inside Look at Policy* on the next page for a comparison of how a slowing housing market affects the United States and Europe.

WALL STREET JOURNAL, APRIL 20, 2007

Slowing Housing Market Isn't Big Worry in Europe

Europe's decade-long boom in house prices is coming to an end, much as in the U.S. But on Europe's side of the pond, the slowing property market isn't triggering the same concerns that it could stall the wider economy.

More-conservative lending practices, a smaller rise in interest rates and a lack of home-equity withdrawals mean that most of Europe isn't seeing the big pickup in mortgage defaults and bankruptcies that is worrying economists in the U.S. The difference is showing up in growth forecasts for the world's two biggest economies, as well as in interest-rate policies that have driven the euro to near-record highs against the dollar.

(a) While worrying property-market data have prompted economists to cut U.S. growth forecasts lately, the International Monetary Fund last week increased its projection for euro-zone growth this year to 2.3%. That is a shade faster than the IMF's 2.2% forecast for the U.S., which Europe has been trailing for years.

Far from considering interest-rate cuts to ease borrowers' burdens, the European Central Bank, which sets monetary policy for the 13 countries that use the euro, signaled last week that it is likely to increase its key rate to 4% in June, while further increases could follow, making the euro more attractive.

"There'll be some problems in the housing market, but they'll be very localized, and we won't see anything like the contagion we've seen in the U.S." said Julian Callow, chief European economist for Barclays Capital in London.

Spain, one of the euro zone's most vibrant property markets, saw home prices last year slip from years of double-digit percentage growth to post a 9.1% annual increase; Spanish bank BBVA predicts prices will rise between 3% and 5% this year. Fellow euro-zone hot spot France has seen house prices more than double since 1997, but the annual rate is expected to drop below 5% this year. Irish and Italian house prices are also slowing in **(c)** the wake of similar booms.

But while Spain, Ireland and the U.K. are potential trouble spots, most economists don't worry that a slowing housing market will spur a broader slowdown in euro-zone consumer spending.

(b) In part, that is because banks in most of Europe—in contrast to those in the U.S. and the U.K.—don't offer home-equity withdrawal. As a result, most Europeans can't treat their houses like giant automated-teller machines, relying on rising property values to free up cash to go shopping. Consumer spending in such places as France or Italy depends more on changes in employment levels and wages, which are expected to rise steadily this year in the euro zone.

Mortgage markets also help explain the U.S.–European contrast. The vast majority of existing euro-zone mortgages are still of the long-term, fixed-rate variety. Until recently, the U.S.'s profile was similar. But in 2006, as much as 45% of new mortgages sold in the U.S., when measured by dollar value,

were adjustable rate. As a result, when the U.S. Federal Reserve changes its key lending rate, mortgage owners feel it in their pockets quickly.

In continental Europe, there has also been far less proliferation of the innovative interest-only or hybrid loans that helped spur the U.S. boom. Subprime mortgages—loans made to home buyers with poor credit records—are also rare in Europe, removing a major source of concern.

"There's just been much less innovation in financial instruments," says Mr. Callow of Barclays Capital.

Interest rates are another key difference. Since the U.S. Federal Reserve's key lending rate bottomed out at a historical low of 1% in June 2003, the Fed has raised it 17 times, to 5.25%—making money more than five times as expensive to borrow. The ECB has raised its key lending rate, too, but by a factor of less than two—to 3.75% from a low of 2% a few years ago. So most European homeowners aren't getting pinched as hard as Americans.

To be sure, some European property markets are starting to cause concern. In Spain, more than 700,000 new houses were built last year, more than in Germany and France combined, even though those two countries together have more than three times as many residents. Spaniards tend to take out variable-interest mortgages, exposing them to rate changes, and Spanish banks have been more lax about mortgage terms, allowing buyers to borrow more.

BUILD YOUR
TOLL BROTHERS
HOME HERE
LOT

Key Points in the Article

This article discusses the macroeconomic effects of housing market slowdowns in the United States and Europe. Although the prices of houses are increasing more slowly in both economies, only the U.S. economy has slowed as a result of this weakness. Because of the housing market slowdown, economists have lowered their 2007 forecasts for U.S. economic growth to 2.2 percent, while they have raised their forecasts for euro-zone growth to 2.3 percent. (The "euro zone" is the 13 countries of Europe that use the euro as a common currency.) This article attributes these very different macroeconomic responses to the prevalence of home-equity loans and adjustable-rate mortgages in the United States, as well as the Federal Reserve's relatively aggressive contractionary monetary policy.

Analyzing the News

(a) The United States and the European Monetary Union experienced a housing boom over the past decade, as home prices in some regions of both economies appreciated by more than 10 percent annually. However, by the first half of 2007, house-price appreciation began to weaken on both sides of the Atlantic, and many economists declared that these twin booms had come to an end. While the end of the housing boom has slowed the U.S. economy, it has had a smaller effect on the European economy. Economists have recently raised their forecasts for euro-zone growth to 2.3 percent, marking the first time in many years that euro-zone growth has outpaced U.S. growth.

(b) While home-equity loans are readily available to U.S. homeowners, they are not readily available to euro-zone homeowners. This is important because a home-equity loan allows a homeowner to borrow against—and, in effect, spend—the difference between the values of a home and the amount of the mortgage loan on the home. Therefore, in an economy in which home equity loans are prevalent, consumption spending may rise and fall with house prices; however, in an economy where home equity loans are not prevalent, consumption spending may not be much affected by changes in house prices. According to the article, the weak housing market slowed consumption spending in the United States, but had relatively little effect on consumption spending in the euro-zone economy.

Adjustable-rate mortgages—which offer borrowers mortgage rates that rise and fall with other interest rates in the economy—are also readily available to U.S. homeowners. This is important because, over the past few years, both the U.S. Federal Reserve and the European Central Bank implemented monetary policies that raised interest rates. While these higher rates have increased interest payments for U.S. homeowners with adjustable-rate mortgages, the higher rates did not affect European homeowners.

(c) Finally, although the Federal Reserve and the European Central Bank both implemented policies that raised interest rates, the Federal Reserve implemented a relatively larger and more abrupt increase in interest rates. This pattern is shown in the figure, which plots the U.S. federal funds rate and the euro interbank offered rate, both of which represent the rates that banks charge one another for overnight reserves. In the United States, the federal funds rate rose from a relatively low 1 percent to a relatively high 5.25 percent from June 2003 to May 2007; meanwhile, in the euro zone, the interbank rate rose from 2 percent to a relatively moderate 4 percent. According to the article, this difference in interest rate increases is due to the Fed's relatively more contractionary monetary policy and helps explain why the U.S. economy grew relatively more slowly during 2006 and 2007 compared to Europe.

Thinking Critically About Policy

1. Compare the effects on aggregate demand of a contractionary monetary policy when adjustable-rate mortgages are prevalent in the economy versus when they are not.

2. Most economists agree that the effectiveness of monetary policy—for example, the extent to which a central bank must raise interest rates in order to slow an economy—varies with the economy's degree of openness. Is monetary policy relatively more or less effective in an open economy, as opposed to a closed economy? Briefly explain why.

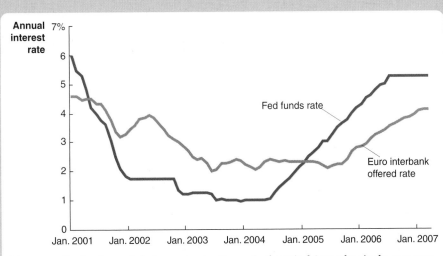

Monetary policy has been relatively more contractionary in the United States than in the euro zone during the past few years.

Key Terms

26.1 LEARNING OBJECTIVE   26.1 | Define monetary policy and describe the Federal Reserve's monetary
policy goals, **pages 888–889.**

What Is Monetary Policy?

Summary

Monetary policy is the actions the Federal Reserve takes to
manage the money supply and interest rates to pursue its
macroeconomic policy objectives. The Fed has set four
monetary policy goals that are intended to promote a well-
functioning economy: price stability, high employment,
economic growth, and stability of financial markets and
institutions.

 Visit www.myeconlab.com to complete these exercises
Get Ahead of the Curve online and get instant feedback.

Review Questions

1.1 When Congress established the Federal Reserve in
1913, what was its main responsibility? When did
Congress broaden the Fed's responsibilities?

1.2 What are the Fed's four monetary policy goals?

Problems and Applications

1.3 What is a banking panic? What role did banking
panics play in the decision by Congress to establish
the Federal Reserve?

1.4 Why is price stability one of the Fed's monetary policy goals? What problems can high inflation rates
cause for the economy?

1.5 A Federal Reserve official argues that at the Fed, "the
objectives of price stability and low long-term interest rates are essentially the same objective." Briefly
explain his reasoning.

Source: William Poole, "Understanding the Fed," *Federal Reserve Bank of
St. Louis Review*, Vol. 89, No. 1, January/February 2007, p. 4.

1.6 Stock prices rose rapidly in the late 1990s and then
fell rapidly beginning in early 2000. Housing prices
in many parts of the country rose rapidly in the
early 2000s and then declined to some extent
beginning in 2006. Some economists have argued
that rapid increases and decreases in the prices of
assets such as shares of stock or houses can damage
the economy. Currently, stabilizing asset prices is
not one of the Federal Reserve's policy goals. In
what ways would a goal of stabilizing asset prices be
different from the four goals listed on page 888? Do
you believe that stabilizing asset prices should be
added to the list of the Fed's policy goals? Briefly
explain.

>> End Learning Objective 26.1

26.2 LEARNING OBJECTIVE   26.2 | Describe the Federal Reserve's monetary policy targets and explain how
expansionary and contractionary monetary policies affect the interest rate, **pages 890–897.**

The Money Market and the Fed's Choice of Monetary Policy Targets

Summary

The Fed's *monetary policy targets* are economic variables that
it can affect directly and that in turn affect variables such as
real GDP and the price level that are closely related to the
Fed's policy goals. The two main monetary policy targets are
the money supply and the interest rate. The Fed has most
often chosen to use the interest rate as its monetary policy
target. The Federal Open Market Committee announces a

target for the **federal funds rate** after each meeting. The federal funds rate is the interest rate banks charge each other for
overnight loans. To fight a recession, the Fed conducts an
expansionary policy by increasing the money supply. The
increase in the money supply lowers the interest rate. To
reduce the inflation rate, the Fed conducts a *contractionary
monetary policy* by adjusting the money supply to increase
the interest rate. In a graphical analysis of the money market,
an *expansionary monetary policy* shifts the money supply

curve to the right, causing a movement down the money demand curve and a new equilibrium at a lower interest rate. A contractionary policy shifts the money supply curve to the left, causing a movement up the money demand curve and a new equilibrium at a higher interest rate.

 Visit www.myeconlab.com to complete these exercises online and get instant feedback.

Review Questions

2.1 What is a monetary policy target? Why does the Fed use policy targets?

2.2 Draw a demand and supply graph showing equilibrium in the money market. Suppose the Fed wants to lower the equilibrium interest rate. Show on the graph how the Fed would accomplish this objective.

2.3 Explain the effect an open market purchase has on the equilibrium interest rate.

2.4 What is the federal funds rate? What role does it play in monetary policy?

Problems and Applications

2.5 A "basis point" is one one-hundredth of a percentage point. If an interest rate increases by 50 basis points, it has gone up by one-half of a percentage point. "Monetary aggregates" are measures of the money supply, such as M1 and M2. A Federal Reserve publication from February 2002 made the following observation: "As the economy slipped into recession last year, the FOMC reduced its target level for the overnight federal funds rate by 475 basis points to 1.75 percent. Also during the year, growth of the monetary aggregates jumped sharply."
   a. If the target for the federal funds rate was reduced by 475 basis points, to 1.75 percent, what was its original level?

b. Is there a connection between the federal funds rate falling and the money supply increasing? Briefly explain.

Source: Richard G. Anderson, "Interpreting Monetary Growth," *Monetary Trends*, Federal Reserve Bank of St. Louis, February 2002.

2.6 (Related to *Solved Problem 26-2* on page 894) Suppose the interest rate is 2 percent on a Treasury bill that will pay its owner $1,000 when it matures in one year.
   a. What is the price of the Treasury bill?
   b. Suppose that the Fed engages in open market sales resulting in the interest rate on one-year Treasury bills rising to 3 percent. What will the price of these bills be now?

2.7 In this chapter, we depict the money supply curve as a vertical line. Is there any reason to believe the money supply curve might actually be upward sloping? (*Hint:* Think about the role of banks in the process of creating the money supply.) Draw a money demand and money supply graph with an upward-sloping money supply curve. Suppose that households and firms decide they want to hold more money at every interest rate. Show the result on your graph. What is the impact on the size of M1? How does this differ from the impact if the money supply curve were a vertical line?

2.8 If the Federal Reserve purchases $100 million worth of U.S. Treasury bills from the public, predict what will happen to the money supply. Explain your reasoning.

2.9 A 2004 editorial in the *New York Times* made the following observation about the federal funds rate: "The Federal Reserve Board announced yesterday that it would keep its overnight interest rate where it has been for nine months—at 1 percent, its lowest level since 1958. Factor in inflation, and Alan Greenspan is essentially lending money at a loss." What is another name for the "overnight interest rate" mentioned in this editorial? Do you agree with the author of this editorial that the Federal Reserve lends money at this interest rate? Briefly explain.

Source: "The Cost of Cheap Money," *New York Times*, March 17, 2004.

>> End Learning Objective 26.2

26.3 LEARNING OBJECTIVE   26.3 | Use aggregate demand and aggregate supply graphs to show the effects of monetary policy on real GDP and the price level, **pages 897–909.**

Monetary Policy and Economic Activity

Summary

An **expansionary monetary policy** lowers interest rates to increase consumption, investment, and net exports. This increased spending causes the aggregate demand curve (*AD*) to shift out more than it otherwise would, raising the level of real GDP and the price level. An expansionary monetary policy can help the Fed achieve its goal of high employment. A **contractionary monetary policy** raises interest rates to decrease consumption, investment, and net exports. This decreased spending causes the aggregate demand curve to shift out less than it otherwise would, reducing both the level of real GDP and the inflation rate below what they would be in the absence of policy. A contractionary monetary policy can help the Fed achieve its goal of price stability.

Review Questions

3.1 How does an increase in interest rates affect aggregate demand? Briefly discuss how each component of aggregate demand is affected.

3.2 If the Fed believes the economy is about to fall into recession, what actions should it take? If the Fed believes the inflation rate is about to increase, what actions should it take?

Problems and Applications

3.3 A newspaper headline in early 2002 read, "Companies Invest as Interest Rates Are at a 40-Year Low." Explain the connection between this headline and the monetary policy pursued by the Federal Reserve during that time.

Source: Brendan Murray, "Companies Invest as Interest Rates Are at a 40-Year Low," Bloomberg News, March 28, 2002.

3.4 (Related to the *Chapter Opener* on page 886) In an article in the *Wall Street Journal* in March 2002, Lawrence Yun, senior economist for the National Association of Realtors, was quoted as saying, "In the current [2001] brief recession, the housing-market indicators were in record territories." Economists normally expect that during a recession, the housing market does badly because of rising unemployment and falling incomes. Why did the housing market do so well during the 2001 recession?

Source: Erin Schulte, "Housing's Strength Raises Another Bubble Concern," *Wall Street Journal*, March 29, 2002.

3.5 (Related to the *Chapter Opener* on page 886) An article in the *New York Times* in March 2002 reported that the housing market had been surprisingly strong during the previous year. According to the article, "In trying to explain the resilience of the housing market in the face of rising unemployment, shrinking stock portfolios and a soft economy, economists start with the Federal Reserve." Why start with the Federal Reserve in trying to explain the strength of the housing market during a recession?

Source: Daniel Altman, "Economy's Rock: Homes, Homes, Homes," *New York Times*, March 30, 2002.

3.6 In December 2001, some Fed officials were worried that the U.S. economy might make only a slow recovery from the 2001 recession. An article in the *New York Times* quoted the views of these officials as follows:

> The main force inhibiting a strong comeback, Fed officials say, is the perception among businesses that the rates of return available to them from investing in new equipment remain too low given the uncertainty about demand for their products, the overall health of the economy and the risks associated with the campaign against terrorism.

How might firms' expectations that the rates of return on new investments are too low make monetary policy less effective in ending a recession?

Source: Richard W. Stevenson and Louis Uchitelle, "Fed Now Says '02 Recovery to Be Gradual," *New York Times*, December 4, 2001.

3.7 According to an article in the *New York Times*, an official at the Bank of Japan had the following explanation of why monetary policy was not pulling the country out of recession: "Despite recent major increases in the money supply, he said, the money stays in banks." Explain what the official meant by the phrase "the money stays in banks." Where does the money go if an expansionary monetary policy is successful?

Source: James Brooke, "Critics Say Koizumi's Economic Medicine Is a Weak Tea," *New York Times*, February 27, 2002.

3.8 According to an April 2007 article in the *Wall Street Journal*:

> In February . . . [Japan's] gauge of core consumer prices slipped 0.1% from a year earlier. . . . The Bank of Japan said last year it would regard prices as stable if they rose from zero to 2% a year. . . . The Bank of Japan's target for short-term interest rates is just 0.5%, compared with the Federal Reserve's 5.25% target for the U.S. and the European Central Bank's 3.75% for the euro zone. . . . "It will be very difficult for the BOJ [Bank of Japan] to raise interest rates when prices are below the range it defines as stable," says Teizo Taya, special counselor for the Daiwa Institute of Research and a former BOJ policy board member.

a. What is the term for a falling price level?
b. Why would the Bank of Japan, the Japanese central bank, be reluctant to raise its target for short-term interest rates if the price level is falling?
c. Why would a country's central bank consider a falling price level to be undesirable?

Source: Yuka Hayashi, "Japan's Consumer Prices May Threaten Economy," *Wall Street Journal*, April 25, 2007, p. A6.

3.9 According to an article in the *Wall Street Journal*, in mid-2007, many investors were expecting that the Federal Reserve would lower its target of the federal funds rate. But the article said that after the most recent meeting of the Federal Open Market Committee, "the Federal Reserve signaled continued wariness on inflation, leaving interest rates unchanged and giving no sign it is inching toward an interest-rate cut."

  a. What does "continued wariness on inflation" mean?

  b. If the Fed is wary of inflation, why might it be reluctant to lower the target for the federal funds rate?

Source: Greg Ip, "Inflation Risk Keeps Fed on Alert," *Wall Street Journal*, May 10, 2007, p. A3.

3.10 Most of the countries of Western Europe use a common currency, the euro, and have a common monetary policy determined by the European Central Bank. An article in the *Economist* magazine noted the following:

> The European Central Bank (ECB) raised its key interest rate by 0.25 percentage points, to 4%. The bank has now raised rates eight times since December 2005. . . . Inflation is, for the moment, on the ECB's target: consumer prices rose by 1.9% in the year to May.

If the inflation rate is "on the ECB's target," why would the ECB be increasing interest rates?

Source: "Overview," *Economist*, June 7, 2007.

3.11 William McChesney Martin, who was Federal Reserve chairman from 1951 to 1970, was once quoted as saying, "The role of the Federal Reserve is to remove the punchbowl just as the party gets going." What did he mean?

3.12 **(Related to *Solved Problem 26-3* on page 905)** Use the following graph page to answer the questions.

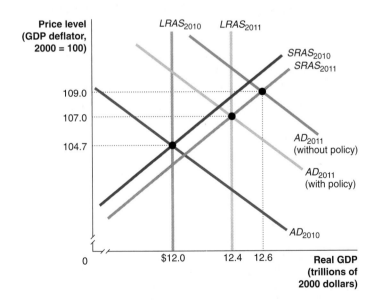

  a. If the Fed does not take any policy action, what will be the level of real GDP and the price level in 2011?

  b. If the Fed wants to keep real GDP at its potential level in 2011, should it use an expansionary policy or a contractionary policy? Should the trading desk be buying Treasury bills or selling them?

  c. If the Fed takes no policy action, what will be the inflation rate in 2011? If the Fed uses monetary policy to keep real GDP at its full-employment level, what will be the inflation rate in 2011?

3.13 **(Related to *Solved Problem 26-3* on page 905)** The hypothetical information in the following table shows what the situation will be in 2011 if the Fed does *not* use monetary policy:

YEAR	POTENTIAL REAL GDP	REAL GDP	PRICE LEVEL
2010	$12.8 trillion	$12.8 trillion	140
2011	13.3 trillion	13.4 trillion	147

  a. If the Fed wants to keep real GDP at its potential level in 2011, should it use an expansionary policy or a contractionary policy? Should the trading desk be buying T-bills or selling them?

  b. If the Fed's policy is successful in keeping real GDP at its potential level in 2011, state whether each of the following will be higher, lower, or the same as it would have been if the Fed had taken no action:

   i. Real GDP

   ii. Potential real GDP

   iii. The inflation rate

   iv. The unemployment rate

  c. Draw an aggregate demand and aggregate supply graph to illustrate your answer. Be sure that your graph contains *LRAS* curves for 2010 and 2011; *SRAS* curves for 2010 and 2011; *AD* curves for 2010 and 2011, with and without monetary policy action; and equilibrium real GDP and the price level in 2011, with and without policy.

3.14 **(Related to the *Don't Let This Happen to You!* on page 908)** Briefly explain whether you agree or disagree with the following statement: "The Fed has an easy job. Say it wants to increase real GDP by $200 billion. All it has to do is increase the money supply by that amount."

3.15 Some businesspeople believe that the active monetary policy of the Fed makes the economy less stable rather than more stable. Writing in the *New York Times*, T. J. Rodgers, chief executive of Cypress Semiconductor, argued:

> There is a fundamental flaw in the Fed's operational assumption that it can know enough about the future to fine-tune the economy without continually making mistakes. Events likely to alter the economy—wars, severe winters, technology breakthroughs and so on—are not predictable. . . . Fed action is just as likely to exacerbate an economic problem as it is to mitigate it.

Do you agree with Mr. Rodgers's argument? Explain.

Source: T. J. Rodgers, "A Computer Would Do Better than the Fed," *New York Times*, April 7, 2001.

3.16 The following appears in a Federal Reserve publication:

> In practice, monetary policymakers do not have up-to-the-minute, reliable information about the state of the economy and prices. Information is limited because of lags in the publication of data. Also, policymakers have less-than-perfect understanding of the way the economy works, including the knowledge of when and to what extent policy actions will affect aggregate demand. The operation of the economy changes over time, and with it the response of the economy to policy measures. These limitations add to uncertainties in the policy process and make determining the appropriate setting of monetary policy . . . more difficult.

If the Fed itself admits that there are many obstacles in the way of effective monetary policy, why does it still engage in active monetary policy rather than use a monetary growth rule, as suggested by Milton Friedman and his followers?

Source: Board of Governors of the Federal Reserve System, *The Federal Reserve System: Purposes and Functions*, Washington, DC, 1994.

3.17 **(Related to the *Making the Connection* on page 898)** In a speech in mid-2007, Federal Reserve Chairman Ben Bernanke made the following observation:

> Real gross domestic product has expanded a little more than 2 percent over the past year, compared with an average annual growth rate of 3-3/4 percent over the preceding three years. The cooling of the housing market is an important source of this slowdown.

a. What did Bernanke mean by "the cooling of the housing market"?
b. How would the cooling of the housing market contribute to slower economic growth?

Source: Ben Bernanke, "The Subprime Mortgage Market," speech delivered at the Federal Reserve Bank of Chicago's 43rd Annual Conference on Bank Structure and Competition, Chicago, May 17, 2007.

3.18 **(Related to the *Making the Connection* on page 898)** Federal Reserve Chairman Ben Bernanke has defined *subprime mortgages* this way: "Subprime mortgages are loans made to borrowers who are perceived to have high credit risk, often because they lack a strong credit history or have other characteristics that are associated with high probabilities of default." Why would some lenders be willing to grant mortgages to borrowers "who are perceived to have credit risk"? Why might many borrowers have been particularly willing to take on mortgage debt during the early 2000s, even if their credit was not very good? What risks to the economy might this type of lending involve?

Source: Ben Bernanke, "The Subprime Mortgage Market," speech delivered at the Federal Reserve Bank of Chicago's 43rd Annual Conference on Bank Structure and Competition, Chicago, May 17, 2007.

3.19 **(Related to the *Making the Connection* on page 898)** At the beginning of 2005, Robert Toll, CEO of Toll Brothers, argued that the United States was not experiencing a housing bubble. Instead, he argued that higher house prices reflected restrictions imposed by local governments on building new houses. He argued that the restrictions resulted from "NIMBY"—"Not in My Back Yard"—politics. Many existing homeowners are reluctant to see nearby farms and undeveloped land turned into new housing developments. As a result, according to Toll, "Towns don't want anything built." Why would the factors mentioned by Robert Toll cause housing prices to rise? How would it be possible to decide whether these factors or a bubble was the cause of rising housing prices?

Source: Shawn Tully, "Toll Brothers: The New King of the Real Estate Boom," *Fortune*, April 5, 2005.

3.20 In 1975, Ronald Reagan stated that inflation "has one cause and one cause alone: government spending more than government takes in." Briefly explain whether you agree.

Source: Edward Nelson, "Budget Deficits and Interest Rates," *Monetary Trends*, Federal Reserve Bank of St. Louis, March 2004.

3.21 **(Related to the *Making the Connection* on page 902)** Some economists and members of Congress have argued that because of deposit insurance, bank runs and bank panics no longer occur, and the Fed no longer needs to act as a lender of last resort. Therefore, the Federal Reserve Act should be amended to eliminate the ability of the Fed to make discount loans. Briefly evaluate this argument.

3.22 **(Related to the *Making the Connection* on page 907)** The following is from an article in the *Wall Street Journal*:

> The immediate catalyst for yesterday's gains [in stock prices] was a Federal Reserve report. . . . Some investors interpreted the comments to mean that if the economy proves resilient, the Fed won't stifle it with a rate increase and if it proves weaker than expected, the Fed might even cut rates.

Why would stock prices increase if investors believe that the Federal Reserve will not be raising interest rates and may even be cutting them?

Source: Peter A. McKay and E. S. Browning, "S&P Joins Record Club," *Wall Street Journal*, May 31, 2007, p. C1.

>> End Learning Objective 26.3

26.4 LEARNING OBJECTIVE   26.4 | Discuss the Fed's setting of monetary policy targets, **pages 910–914.**

A Closer Look at the Fed's Setting of Monetary Policy Targets

Summary

Some economists have argued that the Fed should use the money supply, rather than an interest rate, as its monetary target. Milton Friedman and other monetarists argued that the Fed should adopt a monetary growth rule of increasing the money supply every year at a fixed rate. Support for this proposal declined after 1980 because the relationship between movements in the money supply and movements in real GDP and the price level weakened. John Taylor has analyzed the factors involved in Fed decision making and developed the *Taylor rule* for federal funds targeting. The *Taylor rule* links the Fed's target for the federal funds rate to economic variables. Over the past decade, many economists and central bankers have expressed significant interest in using **inflation targeting**, under which monetary policy is conducted to commit the central bank to achieving a publicly announced inflation target. A number of foreign central banks have adopted inflation targeting, but the Fed has not. The Fed's performance in the 1980s, 1990s, and early 2000s generally received high marks from economists, even without formal inflation targeting.

> **myeconlab** Visit www.myeconlab.com to complete these exercises
> *Get Ahead of the Curve* online and get instant feedback.

Review Questions

4.1 What is a monetary rule, as opposed to a monetary policy? What monetary rule would Milton Friedman have liked the Fed to follow? Why has support for a monetary rule of the kind advocated by Friedman declined since 1980?

4.2 For more than 20 years, the Fed has used the federal funds rate as its monetary policy target. Why doesn't it target the money supply at the same time?

Problems and Applications

4.3 Suppose that the equilibrium real federal funds rate is 2 percent, and the target rate of inflation is 2 percent. Use the following information and the Taylor rule to calculate the federal funds rate target:

Current inflation rate = 4 percent

Potential real GDP = $14.0 trillion

Real GDP = $14.14 trillion

4.4 According to an article in the *Economist*:

> Calculations by David Mackie, of J.P. Morgan, show that virtually throughout the past six years, interest rates in the euro area have been lower than a Taylor rule would have prescribed, refuting the popular wisdom that the [European Central Bank] cares less about growth than does the Fed.

Why would keeping interest rates unusually low be an indication that the European Central Bank was very concerned about economic growth rather than inflation?

Source: "The European Central Bank: Haughty Indifference, or Masterly Inactivity?" *Economist*, July 14, 2005.

4.5 This chapter states, "Experience with inflation targeting has varied, but typically, the move to inflation targeting has been accompanied by lower inflation (sometimes at the cost of temporarily higher unemployment)." Why might a move to inflation targeting temporarily increase the unemployment rate?

4.6 William Poole, the president of the Federal Reserve Bank of St. Louis in 2007 stated, "Although my own preference is for zero inflation properly managed, I believe that a central bank consensus on some other numerical goal of reasonably low inflation is more important than the exact number." Briefly explain why the economy might gain the benefits of an explicit inflation target even if the target chosen is not a zero rate of inflation.

Source: William Poole, "Understanding the Fed," *Federal Reserve Bank of St. Louis Review*, Vol. 89, No. 1, January/February 2007, p. 4.

4.7 **(Related to the *Making the Connection* on page 913)** If the core PCE is a better measure of the inflation rate than is the CPI, why is the CPI more widely used? In particular, can you think of reasons why the federal government uses the CPI when deciding how much to increase Social Security payments to retired workers to keep the purchasing power of the payments from declining?

>> End Learning Objective 26.4

26.5 LEARNING OBJECTIVE   26.5 | Discuss the steps the Federal Reserve took during 2007 and 2008 to respond to the financial crisis, **pages 914–917.**

The Fed Responds to the Financial Crisis

Summary

The Federal Reserve responded to the housing market crisis by cutting its target for the federal funds rate eight times between September 2007 and October 2008. Because the decline in the housing market caused wider problems in the financial system, the Fed and the U.S. Treasury Department implemented new policies to provide liquidity and restore confidence. First, the Fed made *primary dealers*—firms that participate in regular open market transactions with the Fed—eligible for discount loans. Second, at the urging of the Fed and the Treasury, Congress passed the Emergency Economic Stabilization Act of 2008, which authorized the Treasury to purchase mortgage-backed securities and other troubled assets from banks, and also to increase the financial strength of banks by buying stock in them. Third, the Fed and the Treasury took direct action to keep Bear Stearns and the American International Group from bankruptcy.

myeconlab Visit www.myeconlab.com to complete these exercises
Get Ahead of the Curve online and get instant feedback.

Review Questions

5.1 What is a mortgage? What were the important developments in the mortgage market during the years after 1970?

5.2 In 2008, Fed Chairman Ben Bernanke and U.S. Treasury Secretary Henry Paulson responded to the financial crisis by intervening in financial markets in unprecedented ways. Describe the actions of the Fed and Treasury.

Problems and Applications

5.3 Some economists argue that one cause of the financial problems resulting from the housing crisis was the fact that lenders who grant mortgages no longer typically hold the mortgages until they are paid off. Instead lenders usually resell their mortgages in secondary markets. How might a lender act differently if the lender intended to resell a mortgage than if the lender intended to hold the mortgage?

5.4 An article in a Federal Reserve publication observes:

> 20 or 30 years ago, local financial institutions were the only option for some

borrowers. Today, borrowers have access to national (and even international) sources of mortgage finance.

What caused this change in the sources of mortgage finance? What would the likely consequence of this change be for the interest rates borrowers have to pay on mortgages? Briefly explain.

Source: Daniel J. McDonald and Daniel L. Thornton, "A Primer on the Mortgage Market and Mortgage Finance," *Federal Reserve Bank of St. Louis Review*, January/February 2008.

5.5 In commenting on the Emergency Economic Stabilization Act of 2008, an article in the *Economist* argues that:

> Even if it staves off disaster, the [act] will cause huge problems. It creates . . . a visible safety net [that] encourages risky behaviour. It may also politicise lending.

In what way might the act encourage risky behavior? What does it mean to say that bank loans might become politicized? How does the act make this more likely?

Source: "Capitalism at Bay," *Economist*, October 16, 2008.

5.6 "Securitization" is the process of turning a loan, such as a mortgage, into a bond that can be bought and sold in secondary markets. An article in the *Economist* notes:

> That securitization caused more subprime mortgages to be written is not in doubt. By offering access to a much deeper pool of capital, securitization helped to bring down the cost of mortgages and made home-ownership more affordable for borrowers with poor credit histories.

What is a "subprime mortgage"? What is a "deeper pool of capital"? Why would securitization give mortgage borrowers access to a deeper pool of capital? Would a subprime borrower be likely to pay a higher or a lower interest rate than a borrower with a better credit history? Under what circumstances might a lender prefer to loan money to a borrower with a poor credit history rather than to a borrower with a good credit history? Briefly explain.

Source: "Ruptured Credit," *Economist*, May 15, 2008.

>> End Learning Objective 26.5

Chapter 27

Fiscal Policy

A Boon for H&R Block

As the April deadline for filing their 2008 federal income tax forms neared, some taxpayers were confused. Earlier in 2008, many policymakers and economists had been concerned that the slow growth in aggregate demand might cause the U.S. economy to fall into recession. In response, Congress and the president had used the *discretionary fiscal policy* of cutting income taxes to increase household spending. Under this new legislation enacted in February, most households would receive a *tax rebate*, meaning that money they had already paid in taxes would be returned to them. Single taxpayers would receive rebates of $600, while married taxpayers would receive $1,200. In addition, families would receive additional rebates of $300 per child. Taxpayers with incomes of more than $75,000 would receive less than the full amount.

Unfortunately, some taxpayers were confused about how they would receive their rebate. These taxpayers believed that they could simply deduct the amount of the rebate from the taxes they would otherwise be paying. In fact, though, the rebate would actually take the form of checks

mailed out starting in May to anyone filing a tax return by the April 15 deadline. The tax rebate of 2008 is one of many provisions in the tax laws that have caused an increasing number of people to decide that they would be better off relying on the help of professional tax preparers rather than trying to fill out their own returns.

Probably the best-known professional tax preparation firm is H&R Block. In 1946, 24-year old Henry Bloch started the United Business Company, which provided accounting services to small businesses in Kansas City, Missouri. When the local office of the United States Internal Revenue Service (IRS) announced in 1955 that it would no longer provide free preparation of individual income tax forms, Henry and his brother Richard recognized an entrepreneurial opportunity. They founded a new firm, H&R Block, dedicated to preparing individual income tax returns. When the IRS announced that it would stop offering any tax preparation services at its New York City offices in 1956, the Blochs decided to expand to that city by opening seven offices close to existing IRS offices. By 2008, the firm employed more than 80,000 tax preparers to prepare more than 19.5 million tax returns a year and earned revenue of $4.9 billion.

The tax laws have become increasingly complicated. In 1955, when H&R Block was founded, the 1040 individual income tax form had 16 pages of instructions. In 2008, there were 201 pages of instructions. Even Albert Einstein supposedly remarked, "The hardest thing in the world to understand is the income tax." It is not surprising that millions of Americans have given up filling out their own income tax forms, or have to rely on software such as Intuit's TurboTax or H&R Block's TaxCut.

The tax laws are complicated because Congress and the president change them repeatedly to achieve economic and social policy goals. As we will see, some changes in tax law are the result of discretionary fiscal policy and are intended to achieve macroeconomic goals of high employment, economic growth, and price stability. Other changes in tax law are intended to achieve goals such as energy conservation.

AN INSIDE LOOK AT POLICY on **page 960** describes the debate in Congress over the alternative minimum tax (AMT).

Source: David M. Herszenhorn, "Congress Votes for Stimulus of $168 Billion," *New York Times,* February 8, 2008; and Tom Herman, "Don't Cheat (Yourself) on Taxes," *Wall Street Journal,* March 21, 2007. p. D1.

Economics in YOUR Life!

What Would You Do with $500?
Suppose that the federal government announces that it will immediately mail you, and everyone else in the economy, a $500 tax rebate. In addition, you expect that in future years, your taxes will also be $500 less than they would otherwise have been. How will you respond to this increase in your disposable income? What effect will this tax rebate likely have on equilibrium real GDP in the short run? As you read the chapter, see if you can answer these questions. You can check your answers against those we provide at the end of the chapter. **>> Continued on page 958**

I n Chapter 26, we discussed how the Federal Reserve uses monetary policy to pursue macroeconomic policy goals, including price stability and high employment. In this chapter, we will explore how the government uses *fiscal policy*, which involves changes in taxes and government purchases, to achieve similar policy goals. As we have seen, in the short run, the price level and the levels of real GDP and total employment in the economy depend on aggregate demand and short-run aggregate supply. The government can affect the levels of both aggregate demand and aggregate supply through fiscal policy. We will explore how Congress and the president decide which fiscal policy actions to take to achieve their goals. We will also discuss the disagreements among economists and policymakers over the effectiveness of fiscal policy.

27.1   │   Define fiscal policy.

Fiscal Policy

Since the end of World War II, the federal government has been committed under the Employment Act of 1946 to intervening in the economy "to promote maximum employment, production, and purchasing power." As we saw in Chapter 26, the Federal Reserve closely monitors the economy, and the Federal Open Market Committee meets eight times per year to decide whether to change monetary policy. Less frequently, Congress and the president also make changes in taxes and government purchases to achieve macroeconomic policy objectives, such as high employment, price stability, and high rates of economic growth. Changes in federal taxes and spending that are intended to achieve macroeconomic policy objectives are called **fiscal policy**.

Fiscal policy Changes in federal taxes and purchases that are intended to achieve macroeconomic policy objectives, such as high employment, price stability, and high rates of economic growth.

What Fiscal Policy Is and What It Isn't

In the United States, the federal, state, and local governments all have responsibility for taxing and spending. Economists restrict the term *fiscal policy* to refer only to the actions of the federal government. State and local governments sometimes change their taxing and spending policies to aid their local economies, but these are not fiscal policy actions because they are not intended to affect the national economy. The federal government makes many decisions about taxes and spending, but not all of these decisions are fiscal policy actions because they are not intended to achieve macroeconomic policy goals. For example, a decision to cut the taxes of people who buy hybrid cars is an environmental policy action, not a fiscal policy action. Similarly, the defense and homeland security spending increases in the years after 2001 to fund the war on terrorism and the wars in Iraq and Afghanistan were part of defense and homeland security policy, not fiscal policy.

Automatic Stabilizers versus Discretionary Fiscal Policy

There is an important distinction between *automatic stabilizers* and *discretionary fiscal policy*. Some types of government spending and taxes, which automatically increase and decrease along with the business cycle, are referred to as **automatic stabilizers**. The word *automatic* in this case refers to the fact that changes in these types of spending and taxes happen without actions by the government. For example, when the economy is expanding and employment is increasing, government spending on unemployment insurance payments to workers who have lost their jobs will automatically decrease. During a recession, as employment declines, this type of spending will automatically increase. Similarly, when the economy is expanding and incomes are rising, the amount the government collects in taxes will increase as people pay additional taxes on their higher incomes. When the economy is in recession, the amount the government collects in taxes will fall.

Automatic stabilizers Government spending and taxes that automatically increase or decrease along with the business cycle.

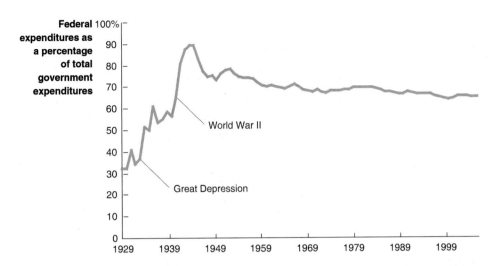

Figure 27-1

The Federal Government's Share of Total Government Expenditures, 1929–2007

Until the Great Depression of the 1930s, the majority of government spending in the United States occurred at the state and local levels. Since World War II, the federal government's share of total government expenditures has been between two-thirds and three-quarters. Source: U.S. Bureau of Economic Analysis.

With discretionary fiscal policy, the government is taking actions to change spending or taxes. The tax cuts Congress passed in 2008 are an example of a discretionary fiscal policy action.

An Overview of Government Spending and Taxes

To provide a context for understanding fiscal policy, it is important to understand the big picture of government taxing and spending. Before the Great Depression of the 1930s, the majority of government spending took place at the state and local levels. As Figure 27-1 shows, the size of the federal government expanded significantly during the crisis of the Great Depression. Since World War II, the federal government's share of total government expenditures has been between two-thirds and three-quarters.

Economists often measure government spending relative to GDP. Remember that there is a difference between federal government *purchases* and federal government *expenditures*. When the federal government purchases an aircraft carrier or the services of a Federal Bureau of Investigation (FBI) agent, it receives a good or service in return. Federal government expenditures include purchases plus all other federal government spending. As Figure 27-2 shows, federal government *purchases* as a percentage of GDP have actually been falling since the end of the Korean War in the early 1950s. Total federal *expenditures* as a percentage of GDP rose from 1950 to the early 1990s and fell from 1992 to 2001, before rising again. The decline in expenditures between 1992 and 2001 was partly the result of the end of the Cold War between the Soviet Union and the United States, which allowed for a substantial reduction in defense spending. Real federal government spending on national defense declined from $479 billion in 1990 to $365 billion in 1998, before rising again to $505 billion in 2007 in response to the war on terrorism and the wars in Iraq and Afghanistan.

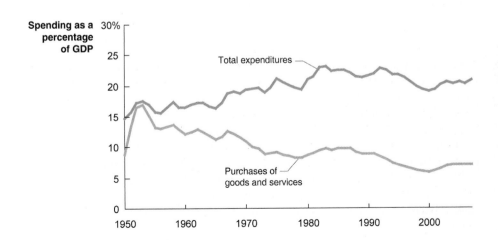

Figure 27-2

Federal Purchases and Federal Expenditures as a Percentage of GDP, 1950–2007

As a fraction of GDP, the federal government's *purchases* of goods and services have been declining since the Korean War in the early 1950s. Total *expenditures* by the federal government—including transfer payments—as a fraction of GDP slowly rose from 1950 through the early 1990s and fell from 1992 to 2001, before rising again. Source: U.S. Bureau of Economic Analysis.

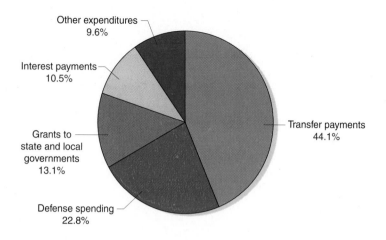

Figure 27-3 | Federal Government Expenditures, 2007

Federal government *purchases* can be divided into defense spending—which makes up about 23 percent of the federal budget—and spending on everything else the federal government does—from paying the salaries of FBI agents, to operating the national parks, to supporting scientific research—which makes up less than 10 percent of the budget. In addition to purchases, there are three other categories of federal government *expenditures*: interest on the national debt, grants to state and local governments, and transfer payments. Transfer payments have risen from about 25 percent of federal government expenditures in the 1960s to about 44 percent in 2007.
Source: U.S. Bureau of Economic Analysis.

In addition to purchases, there are three other categories of federal government expenditures: *interest on the national debt, grants to state and local governments*, and *transfer payments*. Interest on the national debt represents payments to holders of the bonds the federal government has issued to borrow money. Grants to state and local governments are payments made by the federal government to support government activity at the state and local levels. For example, to help reduce crime, Congress and the Clinton administration implemented a program of grants to local governments to hire more police officers. The largest and fastest-growing category of federal expenditures is transfer payments. Some of these programs, such as Social Security and unemployment insurance, began in the 1930s. Others, such as Medicare, which provides health care to the elderly, or the food stamps and Temporary Assistance for Needy Families programs, which are intended to aid the poor, began in the 1960s or later.

Figure 27-3 shows that in 2007, transfer payments were about 44 percent of federal government expenditures. In the 1960s, transfer payments were only about 25 percent of federal government expenditures. As the U.S. population ages, federal government spending on the Social Security and Medicare programs will continue to increase, causing transfer payments to rise above 50 percent of federal government expenditures by 2010. Figure 27-3 shows that spending on most of the federal government's day-to-day activities—including running federal agencies such as the Environmental Protection Agency, the FBI, the National Park Service, and the Immigration and Naturalization Service—makes up less than 10 percent of federal government expenditures.

Figure 27-4 shows that in 2007, the federal government raised about 44 percent of its revenue from the individual income tax. Payroll taxes to fund the Social Security and Medicare programs raised almost 36 percent of federal revenues. The tax on corporate profits raised about 14 percent of federal revenues. The remaining 6.6 percent of federal revenues were raised from sales taxes on certain products, such as cigarettes and gasoline, from tariffs on products imported from other countries, and from other sources, such as payments by companies that cut timber on federal lands.

Excise and other
taxes,
6.6%

Corporate income
taxes,
14.3%

Individual income
taxes,
43.5%

Social insurance
taxes,
35.7%

Figure 27-4 | Federal Government Revenue, 2007

In 2007, the individual income tax raised about 44 percent of the federal government's revenues. The corporate income tax raised over 14 percent of revenue. Payroll taxes to fund the Social Security and Medicare programs have risen from less than 10 percent of federal government revenues in 1950 to almost 36 percent in 2007. The remaining 6.6 percent of revenues were raised from sales taxes, tariffs on imports, and other fees.

Note: The excise and other taxes category includes a small amount of other revenue received by the federal government.

Source: U.S. Bureau of Labor Statistics.

Making the Connection

Is Spending on Social Security and Medicare a Fiscal Time Bomb?

Social Security, established in 1935 to provide payments to retired workers, began as a "pay-as-you-go" system, meaning that payments to current retirees were paid from taxes collected from current workers. In the early years of the program, many workers were paying into the system, and there were relatively few retirees. For example, in 1940, more than 35 million workers were paying into the system, and only 222,000 people were receiving benefits—a ratio of more than 150 workers to each beneficiary. In those early years, most retirees received far more in benefits than they had paid in taxes. For example, the first beneficiary was a legal secretary named Ida May Fuller. She worked for three years while the program was in place and paid total taxes of only $24.75. During her retirement, she collected $22,888.92 in benefits.

The Social Security and Medicare programs have been a great success in reducing poverty among elderly Americans, but in recent years, the ability of the federal government to finance current promises has been called into doubt. After World War II, the United States experienced a "baby boom" as birth rates rose and remained high through the early 1960s. Falling birth rates after 1965 have meant long-run problems for the Social Security system, as the number of workers per retiree has continually declined. Currently, there are only about three workers per retiree, and that ratio will probably decline to two workers per retiree in the coming decades. Congress has attempted to deal with this problem by raising the age to receive full benefits from 65 to 67 and by increasing payroll taxes. In 1940, the combined payroll tax paid by workers and firms was 2 percent; in 2008, it was 15.3 percent.

Under the Medicare program, which was established in 1965, the federal government provides health care coverage to people age 65 and over. The long-term financial situation for Medicare is also a cause for concern. As Americans live longer and as new—and expensive—medical procedures are developed, the projected expenditures under the Medicare program will eventually far outstrip projected tax revenues. The federal government also faces increasing expenditures under the Medicaid program, which is administered by state governments and provides health care coverage to low-income people. In 2007, federal spending on Social Security, Medicare, and Medicaid was 8.7 percent of GDP. As the following graph shows, forecasts by the Congressional Budget Office show spending on these three programs rising to 15.2 percent of GDP in 2030

Will the federal government be able to keep the promises made by the Social Security and Medicare programs?

and 19.0 percent of GDP by 2050. In other words, by 2050, the federal government will be spending, as a fraction of GDP, as much on these three programs as it currently does on all programs. Over the coming decades, the gap between the benefits projected to be paid under the Social Security and Medicare programs and projected tax revenues is a staggering $72 *trillion*, or more than five times the value of GDP in 2008. If current projections are accurate, policymakers are faced with the choice of significantly restraining spending on these programs, greatly increasing taxes on households and firms, or implementing some combination of reductions in spending increases and higher taxes. The alternatives will all clearly involve considerable pain. A report from the Congressional Budget Office concluded, "Even if taxation reached levels that were unprecedented in the United States, current spending policies could become financially unsustainable."

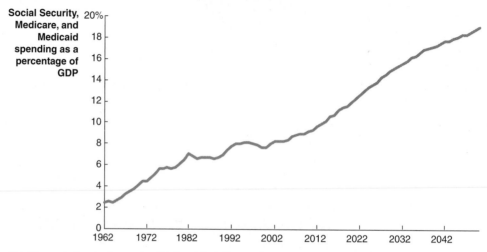

Note: The graph gives the Congressional Budget Office's "intermediate projection" of future spending.

A lively political debate has taken place over the future of the Social Security and Medicare programs. Some policymakers have proposed increasing taxes to fund future benefit payments. The tax increases needed, however, could be as much as 50 percent higher than current rates, and tax increases of that magnitude could discourage work effort, entrepreneurship, and investment, thereby slowing economic growth. There have also been proposals to slow the rate of growth of future benefits, while guaranteeing benefits to current recipients. While this strategy would avoid the need to raise taxes significantly, it would also require younger workers to save more for their retirement. Some economists and policymakers have argued for slower benefit growth for higher-income workers while leaving future benefits unchanged for lower-income workers.

Whatever changes are ultimately made, for young people, the debate over Social Security and Medicare is among the most important policy issues.

Sources: Congressional Budget Office, *Baseline Projections of Mandatory Outlays*, March 2008; "The 2005 Annual Report of the Board of Trustees of the Federal Old-Age and Survivors Insurance and Disability Insurance Trust Funds," 109th Congress, 1st Session, House Document 109-18, April 5, 2005; Congressional Budget Office, *The Long-Term Budget Outlook*, December 2005; and the Social Security Administration Web site (www.ssa.gov).

YOUR TURN: Test your understanding by doing related problems 1.6 and 1.7 on page 962 at the end of this chapter.

27.2 LEARNING OBJECTIVE

27.2 | Explain how fiscal policy affects aggregate demand and how the government can use fiscal policy to stabilize the economy.

The Effects of Fiscal Policy on Real GDP and the Price Level

The federal government uses stabilization policy to offset the effects of the business cycle on the economy. We saw in Chapter 26 that the Federal Reserve carries out monetary policy through changes in the money supply and interest rates. Congress and the president carry out fiscal policy through changes in government purchases and taxes. Because changes in government purchases and taxes lead to changes in aggregate demand, they can affect the level of real GDP, employment, and the price level. When the economy is in a recession, *increases* in government purchases or *decreases* in taxes will increase aggregate demand. As we saw in Chapter 24, the inflation rate may increase when real GDP is beyond potential GDP. Decreasing government purchases or raising taxes can slow the growth of aggregate demand and reduce the inflation rate.

Expansionary and Contractionary Fiscal Policy: An Initial Look

Expansionary fiscal policy involves increasing government purchases or decreasing taxes. An increase in government purchases will increase aggregate demand directly because government expenditures are a component of aggregate demand. A cut in taxes has an indirect effect on aggregate demand. Remember from Chapter 19 that the income households have available to spend after they have paid their taxes is called *disposable income*. Cutting the individual income tax will increase household disposable income and consumption spending. Cutting taxes on business income can increase aggregate demand by increasing business investment.

Figure 27-5 shows the results of an expansionary fiscal policy using the basic version of the aggregate demand and aggregate supply model. In this model, there is no economic growth, so the long-run aggregate supply curve does not shift. Notice that this figure is very similar to Figure 26-7 on page 900, which showed the effects of an expansionary monetary policy. The goal of both expansionary monetary policy and expansionary fiscal policy is to increase aggregate demand relative to what it would have been without the policy.

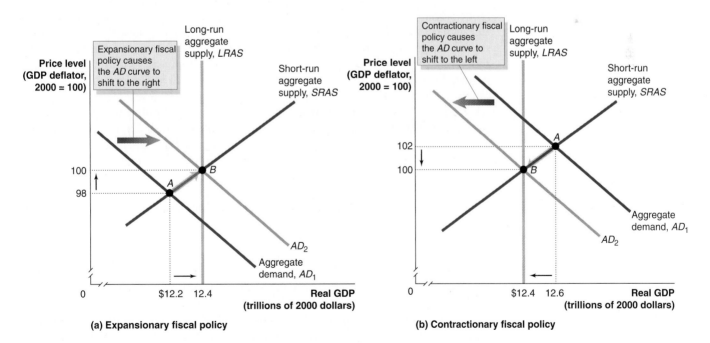

Figure 27-5 | Fiscal Policy

In panel (a), the economy begins in recession at point *A*, with real GDP of $12.2 trillion and a price level of 98. An expansionary fiscal policy will cause aggregate demand to shift to the right, from AD_1 to AD_2, increasing real GDP from $12.2 trillion to $12.4 trillion and the price level from 98 to 100 (point *B*). In panel (b), the economy begins at point *A*, with real GDP at $12.6 and the price level at 102. Because real GDP is greater than potential GDP, the economy will experience rising wages and prices. A contractionary fiscal policy will cause aggregate demand to shift to the left, from AD_1 to AD_2, decreasing real GDP from $12.6 trillion to $12.4 trillion and the price level from 102 to 100 (point *B*).

In panel (a) of Figure 27-5, we assume that the economy is in short-run equilibrium at point A, where the aggregate demand curve (AD_1) intersects the short-run aggregate supply curve ($SRAS$). Real GDP is below potential real GDP, so the economy is in recession, with some firms operating below normal capacity and some workers having been laid off. To bring real GDP back to potential GDP, Congress and the president increase government purchases or cut taxes, which will shift the aggregate demand curve to the right, from AD_1 to AD_2. Real GDP increases from $12.2 trillion to potential GDP of $12.4 trillion, and the price level rises from 98 to 100 (point B). The policy has successfully returned real GDP to its potential level. Rising production will lead to increasing employment, reducing the unemployment rate.

Contractionary fiscal policy involves decreasing government purchases or increasing taxes. Policymakers use contractionary fiscal policy to reduce increases in aggregate demand that seem likely to lead to inflation. In panel (b) of Figure 27-5, the economy is in short-run equilibrium at point A, with real GDP of $12.6 trillion, which is above potential real GDP of $12.4 trillion. With some firms producing beyond their normal capacity and the unemployment rate very low, wages and prices will be increasing. To bring real GDP back to potential GDP, Congress and the president decrease government purchases or increase taxes, which will shift the aggregate demand curve from AD_1 to AD_2. Real GDP falls from $12.6 trillion to $12.4 trillion, and the price level falls from 102 to 100 (point B).

We can conclude that Congress and the president can attempt to stabilize the economy by using fiscal policy to affect the price level and the level of real GDP.

Using Fiscal Policy to Influence Aggregate Demand: A More Complete Account

In this section, we use the *dynamic model of aggregate demand and aggregate supply* to gain a more complete understanding of fiscal policy. To briefly review the dynamic model, recall that over time, potential real GDP increases, which we show by the long-run aggregate supply curve shifting to the right. The factors that cause the *LRAS* curve to shift also cause firms to supply more goods and services at any given price level in the short run, which we show by the short-run aggregate supply curve shifting to the right. Finally, during most years, the aggregate demand curve will also shift to the right, indicating that aggregate expenditure will be higher at every price level.

Figure 27-6 shows the results of an expansionary fiscal policy using the dynamic aggregate demand and aggregate supply model. Notice that this figure is very similar to Figure 26-8 on page 902, which showed the effects of an expansionary monetary policy. The goal of both expansionary monetary policy and expansionary fiscal policy is to increase aggregate demand relative to what it would have been without the policy.

In the hypothetical situation shown in Figure 27-6, the economy begins in equilibrium at potential real GDP of $12.0 trillion and a price level of 100 (point A). In the second year, *LRAS* increases to $12.4 trillion, but *AD* increases only to $AD_{2(\text{without policy})}$, which is not enough to keep the economy in macroeconomic equilibrium at potential GDP. Let's assume that the Fed does not react to the situation with an expansionary monetary policy. In that case, without an expansionary fiscal policy of spending increases or tax reductions, the short-run equilibrium will occur at $12.3 trillion (point B). The $100 billion gap between this level of real GDP and the potential level means that some firms are operating at less than their full capacity. Incomes and profits will be falling, firms will begin to lay off workers, and the unemployment rate will rise.

Increasing government purchases or cutting taxes can shift aggregate demand to $AD_{2(\text{with policy})}$. The economy will be in equilibrium at point C, with real GDP of $12.4 trillion, which is its potential level, and a price level of 103. The price level is higher than it would have been if expansionary fiscal policy had not been used.

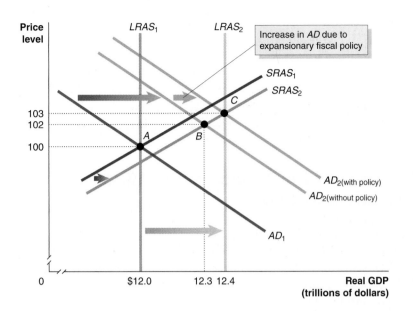

Figure 27-6

An Expansionary Fiscal Policy

The economy begins in equilibrium at point A, at potential real GDP of $12.0 trillion and a price level of 100. Without an expansionary policy, aggregate demand will shift from AD_1 to $AD_{2(\text{without policy})}$, which is not enough to keep the economy at potential GDP because long-run aggregate supply has shifted from $LRAS_1$ to $LRAS_2$. The economy will be in short-run equilibrium at point B, with real GDP of $12.3 trillion and a price level of 102. Increasing government purchases or cutting taxes will shift aggregate demand to $AD_{2(\text{with policy})}$. The economy will be in equilibrium at point C, with real GDP of $12.4 trillion, which is its potential level, and a price level of 103. The price level is higher than it would have been if expansionary fiscal policy had not been used.

Contractionary fiscal policy involves decreasing government purchases or increasing taxes. Policymakers use contractionary fiscal policy to reduce increases in aggregate demand that seem likely to lead to inflation. In Figure 27-7, the economy again begins at potential real GDP of $12.0 trillion and a price level of 100 (point A). Once again, *LRAS* increases to $12.4 trillion in the second year. In this scenario, the shift in aggregate demand to $AD_{2(\text{without policy})}$ results in a short-run macroeconomic equilibrium beyond potential GDP (point B). If we assume, once again, that the Fed does not respond to the situation with a contractionary monetary policy, the economy will experience a rising inflation rate. Decreasing government purchases or increasing taxes can keep real GDP from moving beyond its potential level. The result, shown in Figure 27-7, is that in the new equilibrium at point C, the inflation rate is 3 percent rather than 5 percent.

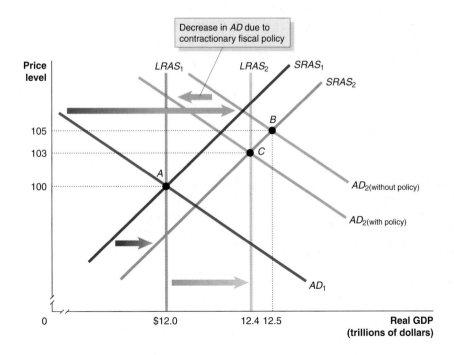

Figure 27-7

A Contractionary Fiscal Policy

The economy begins in equilibrium at point A, with real GDP of $12.0 trillion and a price level of 100. Without a contractionary policy, aggregate demand will shift from AD_1 to $AD_{2(\text{without policy})}$, which results in a short-run equilibrium beyond potential GDP at point B, with real GDP of $12.5 trillion and a price level of 105. Decreasing government purchases or increasing taxes can shift aggregate demand to $AD_{2(\text{with policy})}$. The economy will be in equilibrium at point C, with real GDP of $12.4 trillion, which is its potential level, and a price level of 103. The inflation rate will be 3 percent as opposed to the 5 percent it would have been without the contractionary fiscal policy.

TABLE 27-1

Countercyclical Fiscal Policy

PROBLEM	TYPE OF POLICY	ACTIONS BY CONGRESS AND THE PRESIDENT	RESULT
Recession	Expansionary	Increase government spending or cut taxes	Real GDP and the price level rise.
Rising inflation	Contractionary	Decrease government spending or raise taxes	Real GDP and the price level fall.

A Summary of How Fiscal Policy Affects Aggregate Demand

Table 27-1 summarizes how fiscal policy affects aggregate demand. Just as we did with monetary policy, we must add a very important qualification to this summary of fiscal policy: The table isolates the impact of fiscal policy *by holding constant monetary policy and all other factors affecting the variables involved.* In other words, we are again invoking the *ceteris paribus* condition we discussed in Chapter 3. This point is important because, for example, a contractionary fiscal policy does not cause the price level to fall. A contractionary fiscal policy causes the price level *to rise by less than it would have without the policy,* which is the situation shown in Figure 27-7.

27.3 LEARNING OBJECTIVE

27.3 | Explain how the government purchases and tax multipliers work.

The Government Purchases and Tax Multipliers

Suppose that during a recession, the government decides to use discretionary fiscal policy to increase aggregate demand by spending $100 billion more on constructing subway systems in several cities. How much will equilibrium real GDP increase as a result of this

---

Don't Let This Happen to **YOU!**

Don't Confuse Fiscal Policy and Monetary Policy

If you keep in mind the definitions of *money, income,* and *spending,* the difference between monetary policy and fiscal policy will be clearer. A common mistake is to think of monetary policy as the Fed fighting recessions by increasing the money supply so people will have more money to spend and to think of fiscal policy as Congress and the president fighting recessions by spending more money. In this view, the only difference between fiscal policy and monetary policy would be the source of the money.

To understand what's wrong with the descriptions of fiscal policy and monetary policy just given, first remember that the problem during a recession is not that there is too little *money* —currency plus checking account deposits— but too little *spending.* There may be too little spending for a number of reasons. For example, households may cut back on their spending on cars and houses because they are pessimistic about the future. Firms may cut back their spending because they have lowered their estimates of the future profitability of new machinery and factories. Or the

major trading partners of the United States—such as Japan and Canada—may be suffering from recessions, which cause households and firms in those countries to cut back their spending on U.S. products.

The purpose of expansionary monetary policy is to lower interest rates, which in turn increases aggregate demand. When interest rates fall, households and firms are willing to borrow more to buy cars, houses, and factories. The purpose of expansionary fiscal policy is to increase aggregate demand either by having the government directly increase its own purchases or by cutting taxes to increase household disposable income and, therefore, consumption spending.

Just as increasing or decreasing the money supply does not have any direct effect on government spending or taxes, increasing or decreasing government spending or taxes will not have any direct effect on the money supply. Fiscal policy and monetary policy have the same goals, but they have different effects on the economy.

YOUR TURN: Test your understanding by doing related problem 2.5 on page 963 at the end of this chapter.

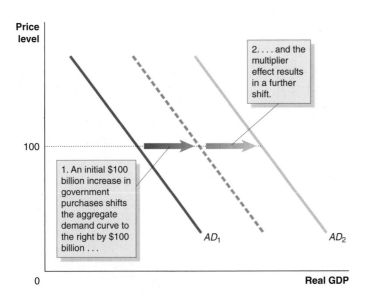

Figure 27-8

The Multiplier Effect and Aggregate Demand

An initial increase in government purchases of $100 billion causes the aggregate demand curve to shift to the right from AD_1 to the dotted AD curve and represents the impact of the initial increase of $100 billion in government purchases. Because this initial increase raises incomes and leads to further increases in consumption spending, the aggregate demand curve will ultimately shift further to the right, to AD_2.

increase in government purchases? We know that the answer is greater than $100 billion because we know the initial increase in aggregate demand will lead to additional increases in income and spending. To build the subways, the government hires private construction firms. These firms will hire more workers to carry out the new construction projects. Newly hired workers will increase their spending on cars, furniture, appliances, and other products. Sellers of these products will increase their production and hire more workers, and so on. At each step, real GDP and income will rise, thereby increasing consumption spending and aggregate demand.

Economists refer to the initial increase in government purchases as *autonomous* because it does not depend on the level of real GDP. The increases in consumption spending that result from the initial autonomous increase in government purchases are *induced* because they are caused by the initial increase in autonomous spending. Economists refer to the series of induced increases in consumption spending that result from an initial increase in autonomous expenditures as the **multiplier effect**.

Figure 27-8 illustrates how an increase in government purchases affects the aggregate demand curve. The initial increase in government purchases causes the aggregate demand to shift to the right because total spending in the economy is now higher at every price level. The shift to the right from AD_1 to the dotted AD curve represents the impact of the initial increase of $100 billion in government purchases. Because this initial increase in government purchases raises incomes and leads to further increases in consumption spending, the aggregate demand curve will ultimately shift from AD_1 all the way to AD_2.

To understand the multiplier effect, let's start with a simplified analysis in which we assume that the price level is constant. In other words, initially we will ignore the effect of an upward-sloping *SRAS*. Figure 27-9 shows how spending and real GDP increase over a number of periods, beginning with the initial increase in government purchases in the first period, holding the price level constant. The initial spending in the first period raises real GDP and total income in the economy by $100 billion. How much additional consumption spending will result from $100 billion in additional income? We know that in addition to increasing their consumption spending on domestically produced goods, households will save some of the increase in income, use some to pay income taxes, and use some to purchase imported goods, which will have no direct effect on spending and production in the U.S. economy. In Figure 27-9, we assume that in the second period, households increase their consumption spending by one-half of the increase in income from the first period—or by $50 billion. This spending in the second period will, in turn, increase real GDP and income by an additional $50 billion. In the third period, consumption spending will increase by $25 billion, or one-half of the $50 billion increase in income from the second period.

The multiplier effect will continue through a number of periods, with the additional consumption spending in each period being half of the income increase from the previous

Multiplier effect The series of induced increases in consumption spending that results from an initial increase in autonomous expenditures.

Period	Additional spending this period	Cumulative increase in spending and real GDP
1	$100 billion in government purchases	$100 billion
2	$50 billion in consumption spending	$150 billion
3	$25 billion in consumption spending	$175 billion
4	$12.5 billion in consumption spending	$187.5 billion
5	$6.25 billion in consumption spending	$193.75 billion
6	$3.125 billion in consumption spending	$196.875 billion
⋮	⋮	⋮
n	0	$200 billion

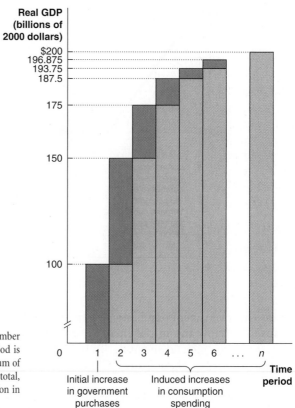

Figure 27-9 │ The Multiplier Effect of an Increase in Government Purchases

Following an initial increase in government purchases, spending and real GDP increase over a number of periods due to the multiplier effect. The new spending and increased real GDP in each period is shown in green, and the level of spending from the previous period is shown in orange, so the sum of the orange and green areas represents the cumulative increase in spending and real GDP. In total, equilibrium real GDP will increase by $200 billion as a result of an initial increase of $100 billion in government purchases.

period. Eventually, the process will be complete, although we cannot say precisely how many periods it will take, so we simply label the final period *n* rather than give it a specific number. In the graph in Figure 27-9, the new spending and increased real GDP in each period is shown in green, and the level of spending from the previous period is shown in orange, so the sum of the orange and green areas represents the cumulative increase in spending and real GDP.

How large will the total increase in equilibrium real GDP be as a result of the initial increase of $100 billion in government purchases? The ratio of the change in equilibrium real GDP to the initial change in government purchases is known as the *government purchases multiplier*:

$$\text{Government purchases multiplier} = \frac{\text{Change in equilibrium real GDP}}{\text{Change in government purchases}}.$$

Economists have estimated that the government purchases multiplier has a value of about 2. Therefore, an increase in government purchases of $100 billion should increase equilibrium real GDP by 2 × $100 billion = $200 billion. We show this in Figure 27-9 by having the cumulative increase in real GDP equal $200 billion.

Tax cuts also have a multiplier effect. Cutting taxes increases the disposable income of households. When household disposable income rises, so will consumption spending. These increases in consumption spending will set off further increases in real GDP and income, just as increases in government purchases do. Suppose we consider a change in taxes of a specific amount—say, a tax cut of $100 billion—with the tax *rate* remaining unchanged. The expression for this tax multiplier is:

$$\text{Tax multiplier} = \frac{\text{Change in equilibrium real GDP}}{\text{Change in taxes}}.$$

The tax multiplier is a negative number because changes in taxes and changes in real GDP move in opposite directions: An increase in taxes reduces disposable income, consumption, and real GDP, and a decrease in taxes raises disposable income, consumption, and real GDP. For example, if the tax multiplier is −1.6, a $100 billion *cut* in taxes will increase real GDP by −1.6 × −$100 billion = $160 billion. We would expect the tax multiplier to be smaller in absolute value than the government purchases multiplier. To see why, think about the difference between a $100 billion increase in government purchases and a $100 billion decrease in taxes. The whole of the $100 billion in government purchases results in an increase in aggregate demand. But households will save rather than spend some portion of a $100 billion decrease in taxes, and spend some portion on imported goods. The fraction of the tax cut that households save or spend on imports will not increase aggregate demand. Therefore, the first period of the multiplier process will see a smaller increase in aggregate demand than occurs when there is an increase in government purchases, and the total increase in equilibrium real GDP will be smaller.

Fiscal Policy in Action: The Tax Rebate of 2008

As we have seen, Congress and the president can use tax cuts to increase aggregate demand to avoid a recession or to shorten the length or severity of a recession that is already underway. In early 2008, economists advising President George W. Bush believed that the housing crisis, the resulting credit crunch, and rising oil prices had increased the risk that the economy would fall into recession. We saw in Chapter 26 that the Federal Reserve attempted to increase aggregate demand by cutting the target for the federal funds rate during late 2007 and early 2008. Cutting taxes would also increase aggregate demand by increasing household disposable income, which would in turn increase consumption spending. As we saw in the chapter opener, the tax cut took the form of rebates of taxes already paid. The rebates were sent as checks that most taxpayers received during the summer of 2008.

How effective were the rebates in increasing consumption spending? At this point, it is too early to tell, but economic analysis can give us some insight as can the study of a similar rebate that Congress and the president used during the recession of 2001. Many economists believe that consumers base their spending on their *permanent income*, rather than just on their *current income*. A consumer's permanent income reflects the consumer's expected future income. By basing spending on permanent income, a consumer can smooth out consumption over a period of years, rather than having to adjust spending to every blip in current income. For example, a real estate agent may have income that is quite high during some years when the real estate market is booming and much lower in other years when the real estate market is declining. The agent will find it less disruptive to keep her consumption roughly constant by basing it on her average income over a number of years, rather than to increase and decrease her consumption as her current income fluctuates. Similarly, a medical student may have very low current income, but a high expected future income. The student may borrow against this high expected future income, rather than having to consume at a very low level in the present. Some people, however, have difficulty borrowing against their future income because banks or other lenders may not be convinced that a borrower's future income really will be significantly higher than his or her current income. Consumers who have difficulty smoothing out their consumption spending on the basis of their permanent income are said to be *liquidity constrained*. The spending of consumers who are liquidity constrained is more likely to depend on their current income than is the spending of consumers who are better able to borrow against their future income. One-time tax rebates, such as those used in 2001 and 2008, increase consumers' current income, but not their permanent income. Only a permanent decrease in taxes increases consumers' permanent income. Therefore, a tax rebate is likely to increase consumption spending less than would a permanent tax cut and is likely to have its greatest effect on the spending of consumers who are liquidity constrained.

The tax rebate of 2001 was similar to the tax rebate of 2008, with single taxpayers receiving checks for $300 and married taxpayers receiving checks for $600. David Johnson of the Bureau of Labor Statistics, Jonathan Parker of Princeton University, and Nicholas Souleles of the University of Pennsylvania have studied the effect of the 2001 tax rebate on consumption spending using data from the federal government's Consumer Expenditure Survey. They found that consumers spent roughly two-thirds of the amount of the tax rebate within six months of receiving it. This is a higher level of spending than might have been expected if most consumers base their spending on their permanent incomes. As economic analysis predicts, however, consumers who were liquidity constrained spent more of the rebate and saved less of it than did consumers who were not liquidity constrained. The 2008 tax rebates totaled $100 billion. If consumers reacted as they did in 2001, then consumption spending in 2008 would have increased by more than $65 billion as a result of the rebate, which would be a significant increase, although less than 1 percent of total consumption spending. Circumstances in 2008 were somewhat different than in 2001, however, with many households having higher levels of debt. This high level of debt may have caused consumers to use more of the rebate to pay off credit cards and loans, rather than to spend it directly.

As of this writing, it is unclear whether the tax rebate, combined with the actions taken by the Federal Reserve that were described in Chapter 26, would be sufficient to keep the U.S. economy from falling into recession.

The Effect of Changes in Tax Rates

A change in tax *rates* has a more complicated effect on equilibrium real GDP than does a tax cut of a fixed amount. To begin with, the value of the tax rate affects the size of the multiplier effect. The higher the tax rate, the smaller the multiplier effect. To see why, think about the size of the additional spending increases that take place in each period following an increase in government purchases. The higher the tax rate, the smaller the amount of any increase in income that households have available to spend, which reduces the size of the multiplier effect. So, a cut in tax rates affects equilibrium real GDP through two channels: (1) A cut in tax rates increases the disposable income of households, which leads them to increase their consumption spending, and (2) a cut in tax rates increases the size of the multiplier effect.

Taking into Account the Effects of Aggregate Supply

To this point, as we discussed the multiplier effect, we assumed that the price level was constant. We know, though, that because the *SRAS* curve is upward sloping, when the *AD* curve shifts to the right, the price level will rise. As a result of the rise in the price level, equilibrium real GDP will not increase by the full amount the multiplier effect indicates. Figure 27-10 illustrates how an upward-sloping *SRAS* curve affects the size of the multiplier. To keep the graph relatively simple, assume that the *SRAS* and *LRAS* curves do not shift. The economy starts at point *A*, with real GDP below its potential level. An increase in government purchases shifts the aggregate demand curve from AD_1

Figure 27-10

The economy is initially at point *A*. An increase in government purchases causes the aggregate demand to shift to the right, from AD_1 to the dotted *AD* curve. The multiplier effect results in the aggregate demand curve shifting further to the right, to AD_2 (point *B*). Because of the upward-sloping supply curve, the shift in aggregate demand results in a higher price level. In the new equilibrium at point *C*, both real GDP and the price level have increased. The increase in real GDP is less than indicated by the multiplier effect with a constant price level.

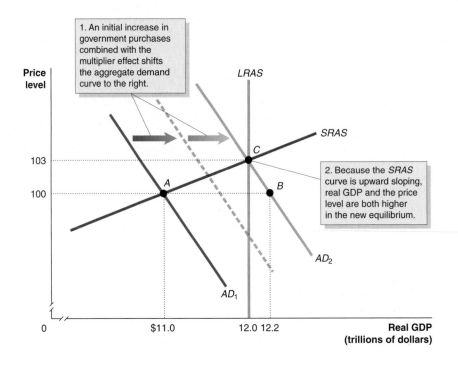

to the dotted *AD* curve. Just as in Figure 27-8, the multiplier effect causes a further shift in aggregate demand to AD_2. If the price level remained constant, real GDP would increase from $11.0 trillion at point *A* to $12.2 trillion at point *B*. However, because the *SRAS* curve is upward sloping, the price level rises from 100 to 103, reducing the total quantity of goods and services demanded in the economy. The new equilibrium occurs at point *C*, with real GDP having risen to $12.0 trillion, or by $200 billion less than if the price level had remained unchanged. We can conclude that the actual change in real GDP resulting from an increase in government purchases or a cut in taxes will be less than indicated by the simple multiplier effect with a constant price level.

The Multipliers Work in Both Directions

Increases in government purchases and cuts in taxes have a positive multiplier effect on equilibrium real GDP. Decreases in government purchases and increases in taxes also have a multiplier effect on equilibrium real GDP, only in this case, the effect is negative. For example, an increase in taxes will reduce household disposable income and consumption spending. As households buy fewer cars, furniture, refrigerators, and other products, the firms that sell these products will cut back on production and begin laying off workers. Falling incomes will lead to further reductions in consumption spending. A reduction in government spending on defense would set off a similar process of decreases in real GDP and income. The cutback would be felt first by defense contractors selling directly to the government, but then it would spread to other firms.

We look more closely at the government purchases multiplier and the tax multiplier in the appendix to this chapter.

Solved Problem | 27-3

Fiscal Policy Multipliers

Briefly explain whether you agree or disagree with the following statement: "Real GDP is currently $12.2 trillion, and potential real GDP is $12.4 trillion. If Congress and the president would increase government purchases by $200 billion or cut taxes by $200 billion, the economy could be brought to equilibrium at potential GDP."

SOLVING THE PROBLEM:

Step 1: **Review the chapter material.** This problem is about the multiplier process, so you may want to review the section "The Government Purchases and Tax Multipliers," which begins on page 938.

Step 2: **Explain how the necessary increase in purchases or cut in taxes is less than $200 billion because of the multiplier effect.** The statement is incorrect because it neglects the multiplier effect. Because of the multiplier effect, an increase in government purchases or a decrease in taxes of less than $200 billion is necessary to increase equilibrium real GDP by $200 billion. For instance, assume that the government purchases multiplier is 2 and the tax multiplier is −1.6. We can then calculate the necessary increase in government purchases as follows:

$$\text{Government purchases multiplier} = \frac{\text{Change in equilibrium real GDP}}{\text{Change in government purchases}}$$

$$2 = \frac{\$200 \text{ billion}}{\text{Change in government purchases}}$$

$$\text{Change in government purchases} = \frac{\$200 \text{ billion}}{2} = \$100 \text{ billion.}$$

And the necessary change in taxes:

$$\text{Tax multiplier} = \frac{\text{Change in equilibrium real GDP}}{\text{Change in taxes}}$$

$$-1.6 = \frac{\$200 \text{ billion}}{\text{Change in taxes}}$$

$$\text{Change in taxes} = \frac{\$200 \text{ billion}}{-1.6} = -\$125 \text{ billion}.$$

>> End Solved Problem 27-3

YOUR TURN: For more practice, do related problem 3.5 on page 964 at the end of this chapter.

Making the Connection

Fiscal Policy and the New Administration

Fiscal policy once again emerged as a key policy battleground following the 2008 election. Candidates Barack Obama and John McCain disagreed sharply over the level and composition of taxes and spending. But beyond the political skirmishing, two bigger questions surfaced: Should fiscal policy try to stimulate the flagging U.S. economy, which was still mired in a credit crunch as the new Obama administration took shape? And what trade-offs would emerge from the large long-term tax changes proposed by the new administration, the most ambitious tax agenda since President Ronald Reagan?

The weak U.S. economy brought calls for an economic stimulus package. An earlier such effort, passed in February 2008 and centered on tax rebates to households, had not succeeded in reviving U.S. GDP growth for an extended period. Early indications pointed toward a stimulus effort of $175 billion, centered on aid to states, infrastructure spending, and bankruptcy reform to allow judges to modify a troubled borrower's mortgage terms to make the loan more affordable. Proponents argued that the plan offered a tonic to put economic growth back on track. Other commentators expressed concerns that the plan would do little to address the problem of falling house prices. Indeed, the proposed bankruptcy law change, by raising risk to lenders, could raise lenders' required rate of return and, therefore, future mortgage rates. Higher mortgage rates would reduce house prices by raising the future cost of home ownership.

The more significant fiscal policy debate concerned the future level and structure of federal taxes. The expiration of the large tax cuts enacted in 2001 and 2003 and a budget deficit that could exceed $750 billion in 2009 are factors that will drive the debate.

The new administration's proposed tax changes include refundable tax credits to low- and middle-income taxpayers and making permanent the 2001 tax cuts for those same taxpayers. These tax reductions would be paid for by raising marginal tax rates on high-income workers and increasing dividend and capital gains taxes for investors. Proponents of these changes focused their arguments on fairness and inclusion; high-income workers garnered most of the large economic gains of the past quarter century, and aggressive tax changes were needed to distribute these gains more broadly. Opponents stressed costs in economic efficiency: The tax changes would discourage work, saving, and entrepreneurship for high-income taxpayers and reduce asset prices (by taxing asset returns more heavily). This debate over the level and structure of taxes will likely continue for some time.

Lurking in the background of the debate remains the U.S. budget deficit, with the U.S. downturn and the cost of the financial rescue package (Emergency Economic Stabilization Act of 2008) taking the deficit's absolute size into new territory. The looming shortfalls in Social Security and Medicare, combined with the new administration's ambitious plans for spending on health care, guarantee a starring role for the budget deficit in the not-so-distant future.

President-elect Obama discusses policy with his advisers.

YOUR TURN: Test your understanding by doing related problem 3.7 on page 964 at the end of this chapter.

27.4 | Discuss the difficulties that can arise in implementing fiscal policy.

The Limits of Using Fiscal Policy to Stabilize the Economy

Poorly timed fiscal policy, like poorly timed monetary policy, can do more harm than good. As we discussed in Chapter 26, it takes time for policymakers to collect statistics and identify changes in the economy. If the government decides to increase spending or cut taxes to fight a recession that is about to end, the effect may be to increase the inflation rate. Similarly, cutting spending or raising taxes to slow down an economy that has actually already moved into recession can make the recession longer and deeper.

Getting the timing right can be more difficult with fiscal policy than with monetary policy for two main reasons. Control over monetary policy is concentrated in the hands of the Federal Open Market Committee, which can change monetary policy at any of its meetings. By contrast, the president and a majority of the 535 members of Congress have to agree on changes in fiscal policy. The delays caused by the legislative process can be very long. For example, in 1962, President John F. Kennedy concluded that the U.S. economy was operating below potential GDP and proposed a tax cut to stimulate aggregate demand. Congress eventually agreed to the tax cut—but not until 1964.

Once a change in fiscal policy has been approved, it takes time to implement the policy. Suppose Congress and the president agree to increase aggregate demand by spending $30 billion more on constructing subway systems in several cities. It will probably take at least several months to prepare detailed plans for the construction. Local governments will then ask for bids from private construction companies. Once the winning bidders have been selected, they will usually need several months to begin the project. Only then will significant amounts of spending actually take place. This delay may push the spending beyond the end of the recession that the spending was intended to fight.

The events of 2001 showed that it is possible to change fiscal policy in a timely manner. When President George W. Bush came into office in January 2001, he immediately proposed a tax cut. Congress passed the tax cut, and the president signed it into law in early June 2001. As mentioned at the beginning of this chapter, the federal government put the tax cut into effect by mailing checks to taxpayers during summer 2001. This increase in household disposable income helped increase consumption spending and contributed in part to the 2001 recession being short and relatively mild. In 2008, Congress and the president again moved quickly to enact a tax cut as economic growth slowed. But Congress and the president use fiscal policy relatively infrequently because they are well aware of the timing problem. The Fed plays a larger role in stabilizing the economy because it can quickly change monetary policy in response to changing economic conditions.

Does Government Spending Reduce Private Spending?

In addition to the timing problem, using increases in government purchases to increase aggregate demand presents another potential problem. We have been assuming that when the federal government increases its purchases by $30 billion, the multiplier effect will cause the increase in aggregate demand to be greater than $30 billion. However, the size of the multiplier effect may be limited if the increase in government purchases causes one of the nongovernment, or private, components of aggregate expenditures—consumption, investment, or net exports—to fall. A decline in private expenditures as a result of an increase in government purchases is called **crowding out**.

Crowding out A decline in private expenditures as a result of an increase in government purchases.

Crowding Out in the Short Run

First, consider the case of a temporary increase in government purchases. Suppose the federal government decides to fight a recession by spending $30 billion more this year on subway construction. When the $30 billion has been spent, the program will end, and

Figure 27-11

An Expansionary Fiscal Policy Increases Interest Rates

If the federal government increases spending, the demand for money will increase from Money demand$_1$ to Money demand$_2$ as real GDP and income rise. With the supply of money constant, at $950 billion, the result is an increase in the equilibrium interest rate from 3 percent to 5 percent, which crowds out some consumption, investment, and net exports.

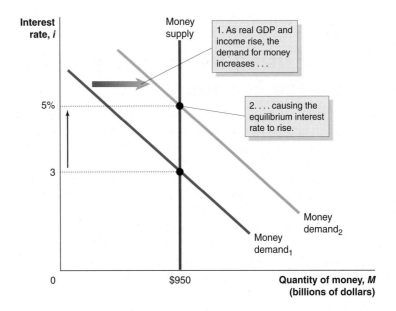

government spending will drop back to its previous level. As the spending takes place, income and real GDP will increase. These increases in income and real GDP will cause households and firms to increase their demand for currency and checking account balances to accommodate the increased buying and selling. Figure 27-11 shows the result, using the money market graph introduced in Chapter 26.

At higher levels of real GDP and income, households and firms demand more money at every level of the interest rate. When the demand for money increases, the equilibrium interest rate will rise. Higher interest rates will result in a decline in each component of private expenditures. Consumption spending and investment spending will decline because households will borrow less to buy cars, furniture, and appliances, and firms will borrow less to buy factories, computers, and machine tools. Net exports will also decline because higher interest rates in the United States will attract foreign investors. German, Japanese, and Canadian investors will want to exchange the currencies of their countries for U.S. dollars to invest in U.S. Treasury bills and other U.S. financial assets. This increased demand for U.S. dollars will cause an increase in the exchange rate between the dollar and other currencies. When the dollar increases in value, the prices of U.S. products in foreign countries rise—causing a reduction in U.S. exports—and the prices of foreign products in the United States fall—causing an increase in U.S. imports. Falling exports and rising imports mean that net exports are falling.

The greater the sensitivity of consumption, investment, and net exports to changes in interest rates, the more crowding out will occur. In a deep recession, many firms may be so pessimistic about the future and have so much excess capacity that investment spending falls to very low levels and is unlikely to fall much further, even if interest rates rise. In this case, crowding out is unlikely to be a problem. If the econ omy   is close to potential GDP, however, and firms are optimistic about the future, then an increase in interest rates may result in a significant decline in investment spending.

Figure 27-12 shows that crowding out may reduce the effectiveness of an expansionary fiscal policy. The economy begins in short-run equilibrium at point A, with real GDP at $12.2 trillion. Real GDP is below potential GDP, so the economy is in recession. Suppose that Congress and the president decide to increase government purchases to bring the economy back to potential GDP. In the absence of crowding out, the increase in government purchases would shift aggregate demand to $AD_{2(\text{no crowding out})}$ and bring the economy to equilibrium at real GDP of $12.4 trillion, which is the potential level of GDP (point B). But the higher interest rate resulting from the increased government purchases reduces consumption, investment, and net exports, causing aggregate demand to shift back to $AD_{2(\text{crowding out})}$. The result is a new short-run equilibrium at point C, with real GDP of $12.3 trillion, which is $100 billion short of potential GDP.

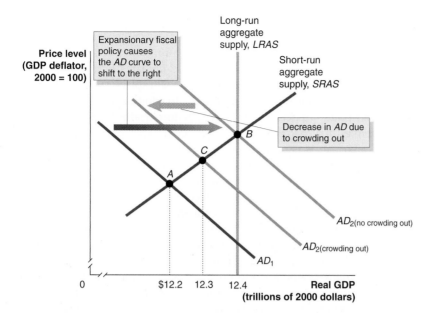

Figure 27-12

The Effect of Crowding Out in the Short Run

The economy begins in a recession with real GDP of $12.2 trillion (point *A*). In the absence of crowding out, an increase in government purchases would shift aggregate demand to $AD_{2(\text{no crowding out})}$ and bring the economy to equilibrium at potential real GDP of $12.4 trillion (point *B*). But the higher interest rate resulting from the increased government purchases reduces consumption, investment, and net exports, causing aggregate demand to shift to $AD_{2(\text{crowding out})}$. The result is a new short-run equilibrium at point *C*, with real GDP of $12.3 trillion, which is $100 billion short of potential real GDP.

Crowding Out in the Long Run

Most economists agree that in the short run, an increase in government spending results in partial, but not complete, crowding out. What is the long-run effect of a *permanent* increase in government spending? In this case, most economists agree that the result is complete crowding out. In the long run, the decline in investment, consumption, and net exports exactly offsets the increase in government purchases, and aggregate demand remains unchanged. To understand crowding out in the long run, recall from Chapter 24 that *in the long run, the economy returns to potential GDP*. Suppose that the economy is currently at potential GDP and that government purchases are 35 percent of GDP. In that case, private expenditures—the sum of consumption, investment, and net exports—will make up the other 65 percent of GDP. If government purchases are increased permanently to 37 percent of GDP, in the long run, private expenditures must fall to 63 percent of GDP. There has been complete crowding out: Private expenditures have fallen by the same amount that government purchases have increased. If government spending is taking a larger share of GDP, then private spending must take a smaller share.

An expansionary fiscal policy does not have to cause complete crowding out in the short run. If the economy is below potential real GDP, it is possible for both government purchases and private expenditures to increase. But in the long run, any permanent increase in government purchases must come at the expense of private expenditures. Keep in mind, however, that it may take several—possibly many—years to arrive at this long-run outcome.

Making the Connection | Is Losing Your Job Good for Your Health?

Recessions cause lost output and cyclical unemployment, which reduce welfare. It makes sense, then, that monetary and fiscal policies that shorten recessions would increase welfare. Someone experiencing cyclical unemployment will clearly experience declining income. Will the unemployed also suffer from declining health? For many years, most economists believed that they would. If this belief were correct, effective macroeconomic policies would improve welfare by both raising the incomes and improving the health of people who might otherwise be cyclically unemployed.

Recently, however, Christopher Ruhm, an economist at the University of North Carolina, Greensboro, has found substantial evidence that during recessions, the unemployed may on average experience improving health. Ruhm analyzed data gathered by the federal Centers for Disease Control. He found that during recessions, people tend to smoke less, drink less alcohol, eat a healthier diet, lose weight, and exercise more. As a

Recent research shows that, surprisingly, the health of people who are temporarily unemployed may improve.

result, death rates and sickness rates decline during business cycle recessions and increase during business cycle expansions. Why do recessions apparently have a positive impact on health? The reasons are not completely clear, but Ruhm offers several possibilities. The unemployed may have more time available to exercise, prepare healthy meals, and visit the doctor. Temporary joblessness also may reduce the workplace stress that some people attempt to relieve by smoking and drinking alcohol. In addition, during a recession, traffic congestion and air pollution decline, which may reduce deaths from coronary heart disease. In fact, Ruhm estimates that during business cycle expansions, a one percent decline in the unemployment rate is associated with an additional 3,900 deaths from heart disease.

Ruhm has found that health problems, such as cancer, that tend to develop over many years, are not affected by the business cycle. In addition, unlike physical health, mental health apparently does decline during recessions and improve during expansions. It is important to understand that Ruhm's research is analyzing the effects on health of temporary fluctuations in output and employment during the business cycle. Over the long-run, economic research has shown that rising incomes result in better health.

The results of the new research on health and the business cycle do not mean that the federal government should abandon using monetary and fiscal policy to stabilize the economy. Although the physical health of the unemployed may, on average, increase during recessions, their incomes and their mental health may decline. No one doubts that losing your job can be a heavy blow, as the rising suicide rate during recessions shows. So, most economists would still agree that a successful policy that reduced the severity of the business cycle would improve average well-being in the economy.

Sources: Christopher J. Ruhm, "A Healthy Economy Can Break Your Heart," forthcoming, *Demography*, 2007; Christopher J. Ruhm, "Healthy Living in Hard Times," *Journal of Health Economics*, Vol. 24, No. 2, March 2005, pp. 341–363; and Christopher J. Ruhm, "Are Recessions Good for Your Health?" *Quarterly Journal of Economics*, Vol. 115, No. 2, May 2000, pp. 617–650.

YOUR TURN: Test your understanding by doing related problem 4.7 on page 965 at the end of this chapter.

27.5 LEARNING OBJECTIVE

27.5 | Define federal budget deficit and federal government debt and explain how the federal budget can serve as an automatic stabilizer.

Deficits, Surpluses, and Federal Government Debt

Budget deficit The situation in which the government's expenditures are greater than its tax revenue.

Budget surplus The situation in which the government's expenditures are less than its tax revenue.

The federal government's budget shows the relationship between its expenditures and its tax revenue. If the federal government's expenditures are greater than its revenue, a **budget deficit** results. If the federal government's expenditures are less than its tax revenue, a **budget surplus** results. As with many other macroeconomic variables, it is useful to consider the size of the surplus or deficit relative to the size of the overall economy. Figure 27-13 shows that, as a percentage of GDP, the largest deficits of the twentieth century came during World Wars I and II. During major wars, higher taxes only partially offset massive increases in government expenditures, leaving large budget deficits. Figure 27-13 also shows large deficits during recessions. During recessions, government spending increases and tax revenues fall, increasing the budget deficit. In 1970, the federal government entered into a long period of continuous budget deficits. From 1970 through 1997, the federal government's budget was in deficit every year. From 1998 through 2001, there were four years of budget surpluses. The recession of 2001, tax cuts, and increased government spending on homeland security and the wars in Iraq and Afghanistan helped keep the budget in deficit in the years after 2001.

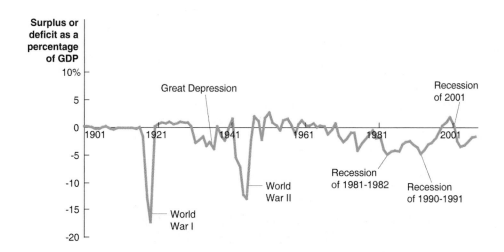

Figure 27-13

The Federal Budget Deficit, 1901–2007

During wars, government spending increases far more than tax revenues, increasing the budget deficit. The budget deficit also increases during recessions, as government spending increases and tax revenues fall.
Sources: *Budget of the United States Government, Fiscal Year 2003, Historical Tables*, Washington, DC: U.S. Government Printing Office, 2002; and U.S. Bureau of Economic Analysis.

How the Federal Budget Can Serve as an Automatic Stabilizer

The federal budget deficit sometimes increases during recessions because of discretionary fiscal policy actions. Discretionary increases in spending or cuts in taxes to increase aggregate demand during a recession will increase the budget deficit. For example, the decision to cut taxes during 2001 reduced federal revenues, holding constant other factors that affect the budget. As we saw earlier, in many recessions no significant fiscal policy actions are taken. In fact, most of the increase in the federal budget deficit during recessions takes place without Congress and the president taking any action because of the effects of the *automatic stabilizers* we briefly mentioned earlier in this chapter.

Deficits occur automatically during recessions for two reasons: First, during a recession, wages and profits fall, causing government tax revenues to fall. Second, the government automatically increases its spending on transfer payments when the economy moves into recession. The government's contribution to the unemployment insurance program will increase as unemployment rises. Spending will also increase on programs to aid poor people, such as the food stamps, Temporary Assistance for Needy Families, and Medicaid programs. These spending increases take place without Congress and the president taking any action. Existing laws already specify who is eligible for unemployment insurance and these other programs. As the number of eligible persons increases during a recession, so does government spending on these programs.

Because budget deficits automatically increase during recessions and decrease during expansions, economists often look at the *cyclically adjusted budget deficit or surplus*, which can provide a more accurate measure of the effects on the economy of the government's spending and tax policies than the actual budget deficit or surplus. The **cyclically adjusted budget deficit or surplus** measures what the deficit or surplus would be if the economy were at potential GDP. An expansionary fiscal policy should result in a cyclically adjusted budget deficit, and a contractionary fiscal policy should result in a cyclically adjusted budget surplus.

Cyclically adjusted budget deficit or surplus The deficit or surplus in the federal government's budget if the economy were at potential GDP.

Automatic budget surpluses and deficits can help to stabilize the economy. When the economy moves into a recession, wages and profits fall, which reduces the taxes that households and firms owe the government. In effect, households and firms have received an automatic tax cut, which keeps their spending higher than it otherwise would have been. In a recession, workers who have been laid off receive unemployment insurance payments, and households whose incomes have dropped below a certain level become eligible for food stamps and other government transfer programs. As a result of receiving this extra income, these households will spend more than they otherwise would have spent. This extra spending helps reduce the length and severity of the recession. Many economists argue that lack of an unemployment insurance system and other government transfer programs contributed to the severity of the Great Depression. During the Great Depression, workers who lost their jobs saw their wage incomes drop to zero and had to rely on their savings, what they could borrow, or what they received from private charities. As a result, many cut back drastically on their spending, which made the downturn worse.

When GDP increases above its potential level, households and firms have to pay more taxes to the federal government, and the federal government makes fewer transfer payments. Higher taxes and lower transfer payments cause total spending to rise by less than it otherwise would have, which helps reduce the chance that the economy will experience higher inflation.

Although government spending increased during the Great Depression, the cyclically adjusted budget was in surplus most years.

Making the Connection | Did Fiscal Policy Fail during the Great Depression?

Modern macroeconomics began during the 1930s with publication of *The General Theory of Employment, Interest, and Money* by John Maynard Keynes. One conclusion many economists drew from Keynes's book was that an expansionary fiscal policy would be necessary to pull the United States out of the Great Depression. When Franklin D. Roosevelt became president in 1933, federal government expenditures increased, and there was a federal budget deficit each remaining year of the decade, except for 1937. The U.S. economy recovered very slowly, however, and did not reach potential real GDP again until the outbreak of World War II in 1941.

Some economists and policymakers at the time argued that because the economy recovered slowly despite increases in government spending, fiscal policy had been ineffective. In separate studies, economists E. Cary Brown of MIT and Larry Peppers of Washington and Lee University argued that, in fact, fiscal policy had not been expansionary during the 1930s. The following table provides the data supporting the arguments of Brown and Peppers (all variables in the table are nominal rather than real). The second column shows federal government expenditures increasing from 1933 to 1936, falling in 1937, and then increasing in 1938 and 1939. The third column shows a similar pattern, with the federal budget being in deficit each year after 1933, with the exception of 1937. The fourth column, though, shows that in each year after 1933, the federal government ran a cyclically adjusted budget *surplus*. Because the level of income was so low and the unemployment rate was so high during these years, tax collections were far below what they would have been if the economy had been at potential GDP. As the fifth column shows, in 1933 and again in the years 1937 to 1939, the cyclically adjusted surpluses were quite large relative to GDP.

YEAR	FEDERAL GOVERNMENT EXPENDITURES (BILLIONS OF DOLLARS)	ACTUAL FEDERAL BUDGET DEFICIT OR SURPLUS (BILLIONS OF DOLLARS)	CYCLICALLY ADJUSTED BUDGET DEFICIT OR SURPLUS (BILLIONS OF DOLLARS)	CYCLICALLY ADJUSTED BUDGET DEFICIT OR SURPLUS AS A PERCENTAGE OF GDP
1929	$2.6	$1.0	$1.24	1.20%
1930	2.7	0.2	0.81	0.89
1931	4.0	−2.1	−0.41	−0.54
1932	3.0	−1.3	0.50	0.85
1933	3.4	−0.9	1.06	1.88
1934	5.5	−2.2	0.09	0.14
1935	5.6	−1.9	0.54	0.74
1936	7.8	−3.2	0.47	0.56
1937	6.4	0.2	2.55	2.77
1938	7.3	−1.3	2.47	2.87
1939	8.4	−2.1	2.00	2.17

Although President Roosevelt did propose many new government spending programs, he had also promised during the 1932 presidential election campaign to balance the federal budget. He achieved a balanced budget only in 1937, but his reluctance to allow the actual budget deficit to grow too large helps explain why the cyclically adjusted budget remained in surplus. Many economists today would agree with E. Cary Brown's conclusion: "Fiscal policy, then, seems to have been an unsuccessful recovery device in the 'thirties—not because it did not work, but because it was not tried."

Sources: E. Cary Brown, "Fiscal Policy in the 'Thirties: A Reappraisal," *American Economic Review*, Vol. 46, No. 5, December 1956, pp. 857–879; Larry Peppers, "Full Employment Surplus Analysis and Structural Changes," *Explorations in Economic History*, Vol. 10, Winter 1973, pp. 197–210; and Bureau of Economic Analysis.

YOUR TURN: Test your understanding by doing related problem 5.9 on page 966 at the end of this chapter.

Solved Problem | 27-5

The Effect of Economic Fluctuations on the Budget Deficit

The federal government's budget deficit was $207.8 billion in 1983 and $185.4 billion in 1984. A student comments, "The government must have acted during 1984 to raise taxes or cut spending or both." Do you agree? Briefly explain.

SOLVING THE PROBLEM:

Step 1: **Review the chapter material.** This problem is about the federal budget as an automatic stabilizer, so you may want to review the section "How the Federal Budget Can Serve as an Automatic Stabilizer," which begins on page 949.

Step 2: **Explain how changes in the budget deficit can occur without Congress and the president acting.** If Congress and the president take action to raise taxes or cut spending, the federal budget deficit will decline. But the deficit will also decline automatically when GDP increases, even if the government takes no action. When GDP increases, rising household incomes and firm profits result in higher tax revenues. Increasing GDP also usually means falling unemployment, which reduces government spending on unemployment insurance and other transfer payments. So, you should disagree with the comment. A falling deficit does not mean that the government *must* have acted to raise taxes or cut spending.

EXTRA CREDIT: Although you don't have to know it to answer the question, GDP did increase from $3.5 trillion in 1983 to $3.9 trillion in 1984.

YOUR TURN: For more practice, do related problem 5.6 on page 966 at the end of this chapter.

>> End Solved Problem 27-5

Should the Federal Budget Always Be Balanced?

Although many economists believe that it is a good idea for the federal government to have a balanced budget when the economy is at potential GDP, few economists believe that the federal government should attempt to balance its budget every year. To see why economists take this view, consider what the government would have to do to keep the budget balanced during a recession, when the federal budget automatically moves into deficit. To bring the budget back into balance, the government would have to raise taxes or cut spending, but these actions would reduce aggregate demand, thereby making the recession worse. Similarly, when GDP increases above its potential level, the budget automatically moves into surplus. To eliminate this surplus, the government would have to cut taxes or increase government spending. But these actions would increase aggregate demand, thereby increasing GDP further beyond potential GDP and raising the risk of higher inflation. To balance the budget every year, the government might have to take actions that would destabilize the economy.

Some economists argue that the federal government should normally run a deficit, even at potential GDP. When the federal budget is in deficit, the U.S. Treasury sells bonds to investors to raise the funds necessary to pay the government's bills. Borrowing to pay the bills is a bad policy for a household, firm, or government when the bills are for current expenses, but it is not a bad policy if the bills are for long-lived capital goods. For instance, most families pay for a new home by taking out a 15- to 30-year mortgage. Because houses last many years, it makes sense to pay for a house out of the income the family makes over a long period of time rather than out of the income received in the year the house is bought. Businesses often borrow the funds to buy machinery, equipment, and factories by selling 30-year corporate bonds. Because these capital goods generate profits for the businesses over many years, it makes sense to pay for them over a period of years as well. By similar reasoning, when the federal government contributes to the building of a new highway, bridge, or subway, it may want to borrow funds by selling Treasury bonds. The alternative is to pay for these long-lived capital goods out of the tax revenues received in the year the goods were purchased. But that means that the taxpayers in that year have to bear the whole burden of paying for the projects, even though taxpayers for many years in the future will be enjoying the benefits.

The Federal Government Debt

Every time the federal government runs a budget deficit, the Treasury must borrow funds from investors by selling Treasury securities. For simplicity, we will refer to all Treasury securities as "bonds." When the federal government runs a budget surplus, the Treasury pays off some existing bonds. Figure 27-13 on page 949 shows that there are many more years of federal budget deficits than years of federal budget surpluses. As a result, the total number of Treasury bonds has grown over the years. The total value of U.S. Treasury bonds outstanding is referred to as the *federal government debt* or, sometimes, as the *national debt*. Each year the federal budget is in deficit, the federal government debt grows. Each year the federal budget is in surplus, the debt shrinks.

Figure 27-14 shows federal government debt as a percentage of GDP over the past 100 years. The ratio of debt to GDP increased during World Wars I and II and the

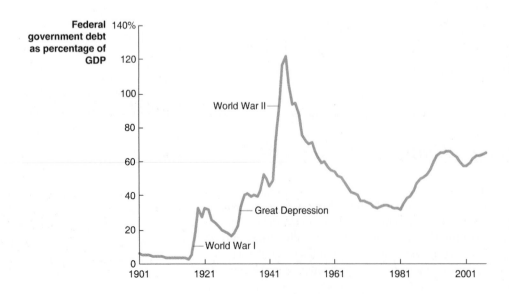

Figure 27-14

The Federal Government Debt, 1901–2007

The federal government debt increases whenever the federal government runs a budget deficit. The large deficits incurred during World Wars I and II, the Great Depression, and the 1980s and early 1990s increased the ratio of debt to GDP.

Sources: U.S. Bureau of the Census, *Historical Statistics of the United States, Colonial Times to 1970*, Washington, DC: U.S. Government Printing Office, 1975; *Budget of the United States Government, Fiscal Year 2003, Historical Tables*, Washington, DC: U.S. Government Printing Office, 2002; and Federal Reserve Bank of St. Louis, *National Economic Trends*, June 2008.

Great Depression, reflecting the large government budget deficits of those years. After the end of World War II, GDP grew faster than the debt until the early 1980s, which caused the ratio of debt to GDP to fall. The large budget deficits of the 1980s and early 1990s sent the debt-to-GDP ratio climbing. The budget surpluses of 1998 to 2001 caused the debt-to-GDP ratio to fall, but it rose again with the return of deficits beginning in 2002.

At the end of May 2008, the federal government debt was $9.4 trillion, but more than half of this debt was actually held by agencies of the federal government, including the Federal Reserve. In effect, the Treasury had borrowed more than half the debt from other agencies of the federal government. It may seem strange that other agencies of the federal government have purchased more than half of the bonds, or debt, issued by the Treasury. This has happened for two reasons. First, as discussed in Chapter 25, the Federal Reserve increases the money supply by buying Treasury bonds. As the economy grows, the Fed provides additional money to households and firms by adding more and more Treasury bonds to its holdings. By the end of May 2008, the Fed had accumulated $483 billion worth of Treasury bonds. Second, the impact of the baby boom on the Social Security and Medicare systems has led the *Social Security and Medicare trust fund* to acquire $4.1 trillion worth of Treasury debt. When the baby boomers retire, the trust fund will sell these bonds to make payments to retirees.

Is Government Debt a Problem?

Debt can be a problem for a government for the same reasons that debt can be a problem for a household or a business. If a family has difficulty making the monthly mortgage payment, it will have to cut back spending on other things. If the family is unable to make the payments, it will have to *default* on the loan and will probably lose their house. The federal government is in no danger of defaulting on its debt. Ultimately, the government can raise the funds it needs through taxes to make the interest payments on the debt. If the debt becomes very large relative to the economy, however, the government may have to raise taxes to high levels or cut back on other types of spending to make the interest payments on the debt. Interest payments are currently about 10 percent of total federal expenditures. At this level, tax increases or significant cutbacks in other types of federal spending are not required.

In the long run, a debt that increases in size relative to GDP can pose a problem. As we discussed previously, crowding out of investment spending may occur if an increasing debt drives up interest rates. Lower investment spending means a lower capital stock in the long run and a reduced capacity of the economy to produce goods and services. This effect is somewhat offset if some of the government debt was incurred to finance improvements in *infrastructure*, such as bridges, highways, and ports; to finance education; or to finance research and development. Improvements in infrastructure, a better-educated labor force, and additional research and development can add to the productive capacity of the economy.

27.6 | Discuss the effects of fiscal policy in the long run.

27.6 LEARNING OBJECTIVE

The Effects of Fiscal Policy in the Long Run

Some fiscal policy actions are intended to meet short-run goals of stabilizing the economy. Other fiscal policy actions are intended to have long-run effects by expanding the productive capacity of the economy and increasing the rate of economic growth. Because these policy actions primarily affect aggregate supply rather than aggregate demand, they are sometimes referred to as *supply-side economics*. Most fiscal policy actions that attempt to increase aggregate supply do so by changing taxes to increase the incentives to work, save, invest, and start a business.

The Long-Run Effects of Tax Policy

Tax wedge The difference between the pretax and posttax return to an economic activity.

The difference between the pretax and posttax return to an economic activity is known as the **tax wedge**. The tax wedge applies to the *marginal tax rate*, which is the fraction of each additional dollar of income that must be paid in taxes. For example, the U.S. federal income tax has several tax brackets, which are the income ranges within which a tax rate applies. In 2008, for a single taxpayer, the tax rate was 10 percent on the first $8,025 earned during a year. The tax rate rose for higher income brackets, until it reached 35 percent on income earned above $357,700. Suppose you are paid a wage of $20 per hour. If your marginal income tax rate is 25 percent, then your after-tax wage is $15, and the tax wedge is $5. When discussing the model of demand and supply in Chapter 3, we saw that increasing the price of a good or service increases the quantity supplied. So, we would expect that reducing the tax wedge by cutting the marginal tax rate on income would result in a larger quantity of labor supplied because the after-tax wage would be higher. Similarly, we saw in Chapter 21 that a reduction in the income tax would increase the after-tax return to saving, causing an increase in the supply of loanable funds, a lower equilibrium interest rate, and an increase in investment spending. In general, economists believe that the smaller the tax wedge for any economic activity—such as working, saving, investing, or starting a business—the more of that economic activity that will occur.

We can look briefly at the effects on aggregate supply of cutting each of the following taxes:

- *Individual income tax.* As we have seen, reducing the marginal tax rates on individual income will reduce the tax wedge faced by workers, thereby increasing the quantity of labor supplied. Many small businesses are *sole proprietorships*, whose profits are taxed at the individual income tax rates. Therefore, cutting the individual income tax rates also raises the return to entrepreneurship, encouraging the opening of new businesses. Most households are also taxed on their returns from saving at the individual income tax rates. Reducing marginal income tax rates, therefore, also increases the return to saving.

- *Corporate income tax.* The federal government taxes the profits earned by corporations under the corporate income tax. In 2008, most corporations faced a marginal corporate tax rate of 35 percent. Cutting the marginal corporate income tax rate would encourage investment spending by increasing the return corporations receive from new investments in equipment, factories, and office buildings. Because innovations are often embodied in new investment goods, cutting the corporate income tax can potentially increase the pace of technological change.

- *Taxes on dividends and capital gains.* Corporations distribute some of their profits to shareholders in the form of payments known as *dividends*. Shareholders also may benefit from higher corporate profits by receiving *capital gains*. A capital gain is the change in the price of an asset, such as a share of stock. Rising profits usually result in rising stock prices and capital gains to shareholders. Individuals pay taxes on both dividends and capital gains (although the tax on capital gains can be postponed if the stock is not sold). As a result, the same earnings are, in effect, taxed twice: once when corporations pay the corporate income tax on their profits and a second time when the profits are received by individual investors in the form of dividends or capital gains. Economists debate the costs and benefits of a separate tax on corporate profits. With the corporate income tax remaining in place, one way to reduce the "double taxation" problem is to reduce the taxes on dividends and capital gains. These taxes were, in fact, reduced in 2003, and currently the marginal tax rates on dividends and capital gains are well below the top marginal tax rate on individual income. Lowering the tax rates on dividends and capital gains increases the supply of loanable funds from household to firms, increasing saving and investment and lowering the equilibrium real interest rate.

Tax Simplification

In addition to the potential gains from cutting individual taxes, there are also gains from tax simplification. As we saw at the beginning of the chapter, the complexity of the tax code has created a whole industry of tax preparation services, such as H&R Block. The tax code is extremely complex and is almost 3,000 pages long. The Internal Revenue Service estimates that taxpayers spend more than 6.4 billion hours each year filling out their tax forms, or about 45 hours per tax return. Households and firms have to deal with more than 480 tax forms to file their federal taxes. It is not surprising that there are more H&R Block offices around the country than Starbucks coffeehouses.

If the tax code were greatly simplified, the economic resources currently used by the tax preparation industry would be available to produce other goods and services. In addition to wasting resources, the complexity of the tax code may also distort the decisions made by households and firms. For example, the tax rate on dividends has clearly affected whether corporations pay dividends. When Congress passed a reduction in the tax on dividends in 2003, many firms—including Microsoft—began paying a dividend for the first time. A simplified tax code would increase economic efficiency by reducing the number of decisions households and firms make solely to reduce their tax payments.

Making *the* Connection	**Should the United States Adopt the "Flat Tax"?**

In thinking about fundamental tax reform, some economists and policymakers have advocated simplifying the individual income tax by adopting a "flat tax." A flat tax would replace the current individual income tax system, with its many tax brackets, exemptions, and deductions, with a new system containing few, or perhaps no, deductions and exemptions and a single tax rate.

The proposal received publicity in the United States during the 2000 presidential election campaign, when candidate Steve Forbes proposed that the tax system be changed so that a family of four would pay no taxes on the first $36,000 of income and be taxed at a flat rate of 17 percent on income above that level. Under Forbes's proposal, corporate profits would also be taxed at a flat rate of 17 percent. The marginal tax rate of 17 percent is well below the top marginal tax rates on individual and corporate income. During the campaign, Forbes declared, "The flat tax would be so simple, you could fill out your tax return on a postcard."

In 1994, Estonia became the first country to adopt a flat tax when it began imposing a single tax rate of 26 percent on individual income. As the table shows, a number of other countries in Eastern Europe have followed Estonia's lead. Although all these countries have a flat tax rate on income, they vary in the amount of annual income they allow to be exempt from the tax and on which income is taxable. For example, Estonia does not tax corporate profits directly, although it does tax dividends paid by corporations to shareholders.

The flat tax would simplify tax preparation.

COUNTRY	FLAT TAX RATE	YEAR FLAT TAX WAS INTRODUCED
Estonia	26%	1994
Lithuania	33	1994
Latvia	25	1995
Russia	13	2001
Serbia	14	2003
Ukraine	13	2004
Slovakia	19	2004
Georgia	12	2005
Romania	16	2005

Governments in Eastern Europe are attracted by the simplicity of the flat tax. It is easy for taxpayers to understand and easy for the government to administer. The result has been greater compliance with the tax code. A study of the effects of Russia's moving to a flat tax found that, before tax reform, Russians whose incomes had placed them in the two highest tax brackets had on average been reporting only 52 percent of their income to the government. In 2001, with the new single 13 percent tax bracket in place, these high-income groups on average reported 68 percent of their income to the government.

In the United States and Western Europe, proponents of the flat tax have focused on the reduction in paperwork and compliance cost and the potential increases in labor supply, saving, and investment that would result from a lower marginal tax rate. Opponents of the flat tax believe it has two key weaknesses. First, they point out that many of the provisions that make the current tax code so complex were enacted for good reasons. For example, currently taxpayers are allowed to deduct from their taxable income the interest they pay on mortgage loans. For many people, this provision of the tax code reduces the after-tax cost of owning a home, thereby aiding the government's goal of increasing home ownership. Similarly, the limited deduction for educational expenses increases the ability of many people to further their or their children's educations. The tax credit of up to $3,000 in 2008 for the purchase of hybrid cars that combine an electric motor with a gasoline-powered engine was intended to further the goal of reducing air pollution and oil consumption. These and other deductions would be eliminated under most flat tax proposals, thereby reducing the ability of the government to pursue some policy goals. Second, opponents of the flat tax believe that it would make the distribution of income more unequal by reducing the marginal tax rate on high-income taxpayers. Because high-income taxpayers now can sometimes use the intricacies of the tax code to shelter some of their income from taxes, it is unclear whether the amount of taxes paid by high-income people actually would decrease under a flat tax.

Sources: "The Case for Flat Taxes," *Economist*, April 14, 2005; and Juan Carlos Conesa and Dirk Krueger, "On the Optimal Progressivity of the Income Tax Code," *Journal of Monetary Economics*, Vol. 53, No. 7, October 2006, pp. 1425–1450.

YOUR TURN: Test your understanding by doing related problem 6.7 on page 967 at the end of this chapter.

The Economic Effect of Tax Reform

We can analyze the economic effects of tax reduction and simplification by using the aggregate demand and aggregate supply model. Figure 27-15 shows that without tax changes, the long-run aggregate supply curve will shift from $LRAS_1$ to $LRAS_2$. This shift

Figure 27-15

The Supply-Side Effects of a Tax Change

The economy's initial equilibrium is at point A. With no tax change, long-run aggregate supply shifts to the right, from $LRAS_1$ to $LRAS_2$. Equilibrium moves to point B, with the price level falling from P_1 to P_2 and real GDP increasing from Y_1 to Y_2. With tax reductions and simplifications, long-run aggregate supply shifts further to the right, to $LRAS_3$, and equilibrium moves to point C, with the price level falling to P_3 and real GDP increasing to Y_3.

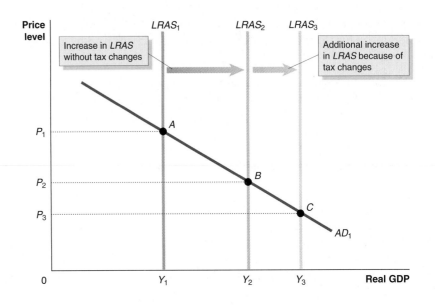

represents the increases in the labor force and the capital stock and the technological change that would occur even without tax reduction and simplification. As we know from our discussion of the *AD–AS* model in Chapter 24, during any year, the aggregate demand and short-run aggregate supply curves will also shift. To focus on the impact of tax changes on aggregate supply, we will ignore the short-run aggregate supply curve, and we will assume that the aggregate demand remains unchanged, at AD_1. In this case, equilibrium moves from point *A* to point *B*, with real GDP increasing from Y_1 to Y_2 and the price level decreasing from P_1 to P_2.

If tax reduction and simplification are effective, the economy will experience increases in labor supply, saving, investment, and the formation of new firms. Economic efficiency will also be improved. Together these factors will result in an increase in the quantity of real GDP supplied at every price level. We show the effects of the tax changes in Figure 27-15 by a shift in the long-run aggregate supply curve to $LRAS_3$. With aggregate demand remaining unchanged, the equilibrium in the economy moves from point *A* to point *C* (rather than to point *B*, which is the equilibrium without tax changes), with real GDP increasing from Y_1 to Y_3 and the price level decreasing from P_1 to P_3. An important point to notice is that compared with the equilibrium without tax changes (point *B*), the equilibrium with tax changes (point *C*) occurs at a lower price level and a higher level of real GDP. We can conclude that the tax changes have benefited the economy by increasing output and employment while at the same time reducing the price level.

Clearly, our analysis is unrealistic because we have ignored the changes in aggregate demand and short-run aggregate supply that will actually occur. How would a more realistic analysis differ from the simplified one in Figure 27-15? The change in real GDP would be the same because in the long run, real GDP is equal to its potential level, which is represented by the long-run aggregate supply curve. The results for the price level would be different, however, because we would expect both aggregate demand and short-run aggregate supply to shift to the right. The likeliest case is that the price level would end up higher in the new equilibrium than in the original equilibrium. However, because the position of the long-run aggregate supply curve is further to the right as a result of the tax changes, the increase in the price level will be smaller; that is, the price level at point *C* is likely to be lower than at point *B*, even if it is higher than at point *A*, although—as we will discuss in the next section—not all economists would agree. We can conclude that a successful policy of tax reductions and simplifications will benefit the economy by increasing output and employment and, at the same time, may result in smaller increases in the price level.

How Large Are Supply-Side Effects?

Most economists would agree that there are supply-side effects to reducing taxes: Decreasing marginal income tax rates will increase the quantity of labor supplied, cutting the corporate income tax will increase investment spending, and so on. The magnitude of the effects is subject to considerable debate, however. For example, some economists argue that the increase in the quantity of labor supplied following a tax cut will be limited because many people work a number of hours set by their employers and lack the opportunity to work additional hours. Similarly, some economists believe that tax changes have only a small effect on saving and investment. In this view, saving and investment are affected much more by changes in income or changes in expectations of the future profitability of new investment due to technological change or improving macroeconomic conditions than they are by tax changes.

Economists who are skeptical of the magnitude of supply-side effects believe that tax cuts have their greatest impact on aggregate demand rather than on aggregate supply. In their view, focusing on the impact of tax cuts on aggregate demand, while ignoring any impact on aggregate supply, yields accurate forecasts of future movements in real GDP and the price level, which indicates that the supply-side effects must be small. If tax changes have only small effects on aggregate supply, it is unlikely that they will reduce the size of price increases, as they did in the analysis in Figure 27-15.

Ultimately, the size of the supply-side effects of tax policy can be resolved only through careful study of the effects of differences in tax rates on labor supply and saving and investment decisions. Some recent studies have arrived at conflicting conclusions, however. For example, a study by Nobel laureate Edward Prescott of Arizona State University concludes that the differences between the United States and Europe with respect to the average number of hours worked per week and the average number of weeks worked per year are due to differences in taxes. The lower marginal tax rates in the United States compared with Europe increase the return to working for U.S. workers and result in a larger quantity of labor supplied. But another study by Alberto Alesina and Edward Glaeser of Harvard University and Bruce Sacerdote of Dartmouth College argues that the more restrictive labor market regulations in Europe explain the shorter work weeks and longer vacations of European workers and that differences in taxes have only a small effect.

As in other areas of economics, over time, differences among economists in their estimates of the supply-side effects of tax changes may narrow as additional studies are undertaken.

Economics in YOUR Life!

>> Continued from page 929

At the beginning of the chapter we posed the question: How will you respond to a $500 tax rebate? and What effect will this tax rebate likely have on equilibrium real GDP in the short run? This chapter has shown that tax cuts increase disposable income, and, when there is a permanent increase in disposable income, consumption spending increases. So, you will likely respond to a permanent $500 increase in your disposable income by increasing your spending. In addition, this chapter has also shown that tax cuts such as this one have a multiplier effect on the economy. That is, an increase in consumption spending sets off further increases in real GDP and income. So, if the economy is not already at potential GDP, this tax rebate will likely increase equilibrium real GDP in the short run.

Conclusion

In this chapter, we have seen how the federal government uses changes in government purchases and taxes to achieve its economic policy goals. We have seen that economists debate the effectiveness of discretionary fiscal policy actions intended to stabilize the economy. Congress and the president share responsibility for economic policy with the Federal Reserve. In Chapter 28, we will discuss further some of the challenges that the Federal Reserve encounters as it carries out monetary policy. In Chapters 29 and 30, we will look more closely at the international economy, including how monetary and fiscal policy are affected by the linkages between economies.

Read *An Inside Look at Policy* on the next page for a discussion of the debate in Congress about the alternative minimum tax (AMT).

Can Congress Afford to Fix the Alternative Minimum Tax?

WALL STREET JOURNAL, APRIL 14, 2007

Congress's Taxing Hurdle: The AMT

The alternative minimum tax originally was created to prevent the wealthy from using heavy deductions to legally avoid paying income tax. But because it is not adjusted for inflation, the tax increasingly ensnares upper-middle-class taxpayers who never were intended to be its targets.

Repealing the tax is supported by members of Congress but is costly. The government could lose $1 trillion in revenue over the next decade if it were eliminated. That has Congress looking at a partial repeal and also at ways to ramp up tax collections by, among other things, trying to close the estimated $290 billion "tax gap"—the difference between what taxpayers should have paid and what they actually pay.

While the alternative minimum tax means a significant boost in the tax bills of many Americans, proposals to close the tax gap—by increasing resources for the tax collector—could be costly for many, too. Here's what's at stake:

(a) What is the alternative minimum tax? The AMT is a separate system from the regular income tax, and it operates under many different rules. There are two rates—26% and 28%. Some popular deductions that many people claim under the regular system, such as state and local taxes, aren't allowed under the AMT. Because of the AMT, taxpayers at certain income levels have to figure out their taxes both ways and pay the higher amount.

How many people are affected? Four million taxpayers will pay the AMT in their 2006 taxes, but that could rise to 23 million for taxes filed next year. Those who pay the tax face an average increase in their tax bill of $6,800.

The problem has become more pronounced because President Bush's tax cuts lowered income-tax obligations for those who pay through the regular tax system without addressing the growing numbers that are subject to the alternative minimum tax.

(b) Who is most likely to get hit by the AMT? The tax tends to hit those with annual incomes between $100,000 and $500,000 the most, but it could reach some who earn as little as $50,000 to $75,000 on next year's taxes. White-collar professionals in high-tax states like California and in the Northeast tend to bear the brunt of the tax, because it doesn't give credits for state and local taxes. Taxpayers with large families or high medical expenses also are hit harder because it doesn't provide credits for dependents and has a higher threshold for deductions for medical expenses.

What will Congress do? In past years, Congress and the president have prevented the growing reach of the AMT with a series of one-year fixes. Congress passed such a fix for taxes filed this year, but hasn't passed one yet for next year's taxes. Democrats have suggested that they want to permanently overhaul the tax, but because they have passed pay-as-you-go spending rules, the government would have to pay for the lost revenue by increasing taxes or cutting spending. Ultimately, Congress may defer action until after the 2008 election, when it also will consider the fate of the Bush tax cuts.

If Congress boosts the resources of the Internal Revenue Service, who will be affected? The difference between what taxpayers should have paid and what they actually paid on time was $345 billion in 2001. After enforcement efforts, it collected $55 billion, leaving a net gap of $290 billion. The IRS estimates the overall compliance rate at about 84%.

(c) President Bush's budget for the 2008 fiscal year proposes a $410 million spending increase for compliance programs in order to bring in $29 billion in increased taxes over the next decade. Congress might increase that even more.

As a result, the number of families who are audited could rise. Right now, about 1% of all filings are audited. The odds of an audit are higher for those with higher incomes. Around 6% of individuals with an annual income exceeding $1 million were audited last year.

Small businesses and the self-employed are estimated to be the largest source of the tax gap, and therefore would likely bear the brunt of more aggressive enforcement efforts. One proposal would require banks to report to the IRS merchants' annual credit-card payments so that the IRS could compare the tax returns of small businesses with the payments to determine any underreporting of income. Small-business groups are fighting back by arguing that more intrusive regulation would add to their already high tax-preparation costs.

Source: Nick Timiraos, "Congress's Taxing Hurdle: The AMT," *Wall Street Journal*, April 14, 2007, p. A7. Reprinted by permission of the *Wall Street Journal* via Copyright Clearance Center.

Key Points in the Article

This article discusses the alternative minimum tax (AMT), which Congress established in order to ensure that wealthy individuals pay a minimum amount of income tax. In recent years, the AMT has come under scrutiny from taxpayers and Congress because middle-income households are increasingly subject to the AMT, which, unlike the regular income tax, does not adjust income brackets for inflation. Although Congress wants to permanently overhaul, if not eliminate, the AMT, it may not be able to do so. This is because the current Congress operates under pay-as-you-go rules, which require that any reduction in revenue be offset by either an increase in revenue elsewhere or a reduction in spending. Eliminating the AMT would reduce revenue that would be politically difficult to replace.

Analyzing the News

(a) The AMT is an income tax that Congress established in 1970 to ensure that high-income individuals do not take advantage of deductions and exemptions to reduce or eliminate their income tax liability. The AMT operates alongside the traditional income tax so that individuals must pay the AMT if it exceeds their standard income tax liability. For example, in 2006, individuals who were subject to the AMT paid, on average, $6,800 more in taxes than they would have under the traditional income tax. In recent years, the AMT has come under scrutiny from taxpayers and Congress. This is, in part, because Congress has not adjusted the AMT's tax brackets for inflation, as is done with the regular income tax. In other words, the AMT taxes individuals' nominal incomes as if they were real incomes. Therefore, as the average price level in the economy rises, so does the number of middle-income individuals who are subject to the AMT. In 2006, about 4 million taxpayers were subject to the AMT. However, under current tax law, this number is likely to rise substantially in 2007 and beyond. The figure charts the estimated numbers of individuals who will be subject to the AMT in the future if Congress does not change the current tax law.

(b) Until recently, individuals earning between $100,000 and $500,000 have been the group most likely to pay the AMT. However, because the AMT does not adjust for inflation, economists expect the tax to apply in 2007 to individuals who earn between $50,000 and $75,000. Moreover, because the AMT does not credit individuals for any state and local income taxes they pay, those living in California and the Northeast—where state and local taxes are highest—are disproportionately affected by the AMT. Because the AMT does not allow individuals to claim dependents—such as their children or other persons these individuals support financially—or deduct as many health expenses, those with large families and medical expenses are also disproportionately affected. To date, Congress has addressed these problems on a year-by-year basis. This is why the number of taxpayers affected by the AMT has so far not increased substantially. Although many in Congress support a permanent overhaul of the AMT, action on reform has been slow. An overhaul of the AMT would reduce tax revenue, and the current Congress operates under pay-as-you-go rules, which require that any reduction in revenue must be offset by either an increase in revenue elsewhere or a reduction in spending.

(c) One way for Congress to offset the revenue lost from permanently overhauling the AMT is to improve tax compliance—in other words, to collect taxes from the roughly 16 percent of those who owe but do not pay their taxes. President Bush's budget for 2008 allocates $400 million to improve compliance; the administration expects these improvements to enable the IRS to collect an estimated $29 billion of heretofore uncollected taxes. Efforts to improve compliance include increasing the number of audits and regulating small businesses more closely.

Thinking Critically

About Policy

1. Suppose that Congress passes—and the president signs into law—increased spending for an expansionary fiscal policy. All else being equal, is the policy's effect on aggregate demand relatively larger or smaller if a pay-as-you-go rule is in effect? Briefly explain your reasoning.

2. Suppose that Congress announces that it will not renew President Bush's 2001 tax cuts when they expire in 2010. How is this announcement likely to affect aggregate demand today?

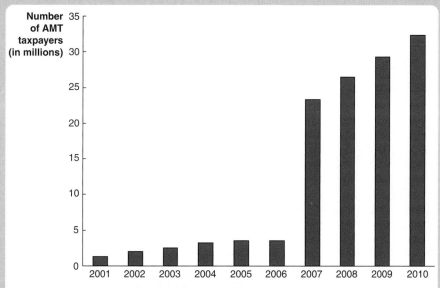

The number of taxpayers affected by the AMT will increase substantially under current U.S. tax laws.

Key Terms

Automatic stabilizers, p. 930

Budget deficit, p. 948

Budget surplus, p. 948

Crowding out, p. 945

Cyclically adjusted budget deficit or surplus, p. 949

Fiscal policy, p. 930

Multiplier effect, p. 939

Tax wedge, p. 954

27.1 LEARNING OBJECTIVE 27.1 | Define fiscal policy, **pages 930–934.**

Fiscal Policy

Summary

Fiscal policy involves changes in federal taxes and purchases that are intended to achieve macroeconomic policy objectives. **Automatic stabilizers** are government spending and taxes that automatically increase or decrease along with the business cycle. Since World War II, the federal government's share of total government expenditures has been between two-thirds and three-quarters. Federal government *expenditures* as a percentage of GDP rose from 1950 to the early 1990s and fell between 1992 and 2001, before rising again. Federal government *purchases* have declined as a percentage of GDP since the end of the Korean War in the early 1950s. The largest component of federal expenditures is transfer payments. The largest source of federal government revenue is social insurance taxes, which are used to fund the Social Security and Medicare systems.

 Visit www.myeconlab.com to complete these exercises *Get Ahead of the Curve* online and get instant feedback.

Review Questions

1.1 What is fiscal policy? Who is responsible for fiscal policy?

1.2 What is the difference between fiscal policy and monetary policy?

1.3 What is the difference between federal purchases and federal expenditures? Are federal purchases higher today as a percentage of GDP than they were in 1960? Are federal expenditures higher?

Problems and Applications

1.4 Why have federal government expenditures been increasing more rapidly than federal government purchases? What effect will the increasing average age of the U.S. population have on federal government purchases in the coming years?

1.5 From the discussion in this chapter, which source of government revenue shown in Figure 27-4 on page 933 is likely to increase the most in the future? Briefly explain.

1.6 (Related to the *Making the Connection* on page 933) According to a Congressional Budget Office report:

> The baby boomers will start becoming eligible for Social Security retirement benefits in 2008, when the first members of that generation turn 62. As a result, the annual growth rate of Social Security spending is expected to increase from about 4.5 percent in 2008 to 6.5 percent by 2017.

Who are the "baby boomers"? Why should their retirement cause such a large increase in the growth rate of spending by the federal government on Social Security?

Source: Congressional Budget Office, *The Budget and Economic Outlook: Fiscal Years 2008 to 2017*, January 2007, p. xiii.

1.7 (Related to the *Making the Connection* on page 933) According to a Congressional Budget Office report, "The number of people age 65 or older will more than double by 2050, and the number of adults under age 65 will increase by about 16 percent." Briefly explain what the implications of these facts are for federal government spending as a percentage of GDP in 2050.

Source: Congressional Budget Office, *The Budget and Economic Outlook: Fiscal Years 2008 to 2017*, January 2007, p. 10.

>> End Learning Objective 27.1

27.2 LEARNING OBJECTIVE   27.2 | Explain how fiscal policy affects aggregate demand and how the government can use fiscal policy to stabilize the economy, **pages 934–938.**

The Effects of Fiscal Policy on Real GDP and the Price Level

Summary

To fight recessions, Congress and the president can increase government purchases or cut taxes. This expansionary policy causes the aggregate demand curve to shift out more than it otherwise would, raising the level of real GDP and the price level. To fight rising inflation, Congress and the president can decrease government purchases or raise taxes. This contractionary policy causes the aggregate demand curve to shift out less than it otherwise would, reducing the increase in real GDP and the price level.

myeconlab   Visit www.myeconlab.com to complete these exercises
Get Ahead of the Curve online and get instant feedback.

Review Questions

2.1 What is an expansionary fiscal policy? What is a contractionary fiscal policy?

2.2 If Congress and the president decide an expansionary fiscal policy is necessary, what changes should they make in government spending or taxes? What changes should they make if they decide a contractionary fiscal policy is necessary?

Problems and Applications

2.3 Briefly explain whether you agree or disagree with the following statements: "An expansionary fiscal policy involves an increase in government purchases or an increase in taxes. A contractionary fiscal policy involves a decrease in government purchases or a decrease in taxes."

2.4 Identify each of the following as (i) part of an expansionary fiscal policy, (ii) part of a contractionary fiscal policy, or (iii) not part of fiscal policy.
    a. The corporate income tax rate is increased.
    b. Defense spending is increased.
    c. Families are allowed to deduct all their expenses for daycare from their federal income taxes.
    d. The individual income tax rate is decreased.
    e. The State of New Jersey builds a new highway in an attempt to expand employment in the state.

2.5 (Related to the *Don't Let This Happen to You!* on page 938) Briefly explain whether you agree with the following remark: "Real GDP is $250 billion

below its full-employment level. With a multiplier of 2, if Congress and the president increase government purchases by $125 billion or the Fed increases the money supply by $125 billion, real GDP can be brought back to its full-employment level."

2.6 Use the graph to answer the following questions.

a. If the government does not take any policy actions, what will be the values of real GDP and the price level in 2012?
b. If the government purchases multiplier is 2, how much will government purchases have to be increased to bring real GDP to its potential level in 2012? (Assume that the multiplier value takes into account the impact of a rising price level on the multiplier effect.)
c. If the tax multiplier is −1.6, how much will taxes have to be cut to bring real GDP to its potential level in 2012? (Again, assume that the multiplier value takes into account the impact of a rising price level.)
d. If the government takes no policy actions, what will be the inflation rate in 2012? If the government uses fiscal policy to keep real GDP at its potential level, what will be the inflation rate in 2012?

>> End Learning Objective 27.2

27.3 | Explain how the government purchases and tax multipliers work, **pages 938–944.**

The Government Purchases and Tax Multipliers

Summary

Because of the **multiplier effect**, an increase in government purchases or a cut in taxes will have a multiplied effect on equilibrium real GDP. The *government purchases multiplier* is equal to the change in equilibrium real GDP divided by the change in government purchases. The *tax multiplier* is equal to the change in equilibrium real GDP divided by the change in taxes. Increases in government purchases and cuts in taxes have a positive multiplier effect on equilibrium real GDP. Decreases in government purchases and increases in taxes have a negative multiplier effect on equilibrium real GDP.

 Visit www.myeconlab.com to complete these exercises *Get Ahead of the Curve* online and get instant feedback.

Review Questions

3.1 Why does a $1 increase in government purchases lead to more than a $1 increase in income and spending?

3.2 Define the government purchases multiplier and the tax multiplier.

Problems and Applications

3.3 In *The General Theory of Employment, Interest, and Money*, John Maynard Keynes wrote this:

> If the Treasury were to fill old bottles with banknotes, bury them at suitable depths in disused coal mines which are then filled up to the surface with town rubbish, and leave it to private enterprise . . . to dig the notes up again . . . there need be no more unemployment and, with the help of the repercussions, the real income of the community . . . would probably become a good deal greater than it is.

Which important macroeconomic effect is Keynes discussing here? What does he mean by "repercus-

sions"? Why does he appear unconcerned if government spending is wasteful?

3.4 Suppose that real GDP is currently $13.1 trillion, potential real GDP is $13.5 trillion, the government purchases multiplier is 2, and the tax multiplier is –1.6.
  a. Holding other factors constant, by how much will government purchases need to be increased to bring the economy to equilibrium at potential GDP?
  b. Holding other factors constant, by how much will taxes have to be cut to bring the economy to equilibrium at potential GDP?
  c. Construct an example of a *combination* of increased government spending and tax cuts that will bring the economy to equilibrium at potential GDP.

3.5 (Related to *Solved Problem 27-3* on page 944) Briefly explain whether you agree or disagree with the following statement: "Real GDP is currently $12.7 trillion, and potential real GDP is $12.4 trillion. If Congress and the president would decrease government purchases by $200 billion or increase taxes by $200 billion, the economy could be brought to equilibrium at potential GDP."

3.6 If the short-run aggregate supply curve (*SRAS*) were a horizontal line, what would be the impact on the size of the government purchases and tax multipliers?

3.7 (Related to the *Making the Connection* on page 944) An article published after the presidential election argued:

> In passing a tax bill, the Congress and Mr. Obama will have to balance the long-term deficit problem with the need for shorter-term stimulus.

Why might the U.S. economy have needed a stimulus in early 2009? What type of tax policy would be used to give the economy a short-term stimulus? What is meant by the United States having a long-term deficit problem? What type of tax policy might be used to address a long-term deficit problem?

Source: Floyd Norris, "For Obama, Long-Term Ills and Short-Term Pain," *New York Times*, November 5, 2008.

>> **End Learning Objective 27.3**

The Limits of Using Fiscal Policy to Stabilize the Economy

Summary

Poorly timed fiscal policy can do more harm than good. Getting the timing right with fiscal policy can be difficult because obtaining approval from Congress for a new fiscal policy can be a very long process and because it can take months for an increase in authorized spending to actually take place. Because an increase in government purchases may lead to a higher interest rate, it may result in a decline in consumption, investment, and net exports. A decline in private expenditures as a result of an increase in government purchases is called **crowding out**. Crowding out may cause an expansionary fiscal policy to fail to meet its goal of keeping the economy at potential GDP.

myeconlab Visit www.myeconlab.com to complete these exercises *Get Ahead of the Curve* online and get instant feedback.

Review Questions

4.1 Which can be changed more quickly: monetary policy or fiscal policy? Briefly explain.

4.2 What is meant by crowding out? Explain the difference between crowding out in the short run and in the long run.

Problems and Applications

4.3 In a column published in the *Wall Street Journal* on July 19, 2001, David Wessel wrote, "Most economic forecasters don't foresee recession this year or next." In fact, a recession had already begun in March 2001. Does this tell us anything about the difficulty of Congress and the president implementing a fiscal

policy that stabilizes rather than destabilizes the economy?

Source: David Wessel, "Economic Forecasting in Three Steps," *Wall Street Journal*, July 19, 2001, p. A1.

4.4 Figure 27-11 on page 946 shows the equilibrium interest rate rising as the demand for money increases. Describe what must be happening in the market for Treasury bills.

4.5 Some economists argue that because increases in government spending crowd out private spending, increased government spending will reduce the long-run growth rate of real GDP.
   a. Is this most likely to happen if the private spending being crowded out is consumption spending, investment spending, or net exports? Briefly explain.
   b. In terms of its effect on the long-run growth rate of real GDP, would it matter if the additional government spending involves (i) increased spending on highways and bridges or (ii) increased spending on the national parks? Briefly explain.

4.6 In his column in the *Wall Street Journal*, David Wessel wrote, "Global financial markets, politicians, corporate executives and ordinary Americans have confidence in [the Federal Reserve chairman's] ability to steer the U.S. economy, particularly during times of crisis." But isn't it Congress and the president, and not the chairman of the Fed, who steer the U.S. economy? Briefly discuss.

Source: David Wessel, "Four Hard-to-Predict Factors That Will Shape the Economy," *Wall Street Journal*, April 4, 2002.

4.7 (Related to the *Making the Connection* on page 947) Why might the effects on health of a temporary increase or decrease in income be different than the effects of a permanent increase or decrease?

>> **End Learning Objective 27.4**

Deficits, Surpluses, and Federal Government Debt

Summary

A **budget deficit** occurs when the federal government's expenditures are greater than its tax revenues. A **budget surplus** occurs when the federal government's expenditures are less than its tax revenues. The budget deficit automatically increases during recessions and decreases during expansions. The automatic movements in the federal budget help to stabilize the economy by cushioning the fall in spending during recessions and restraining the increase in spending during expansions. The **cyclically adjusted budget deficit or surplus** is the deficit or surplus in the federal government's budget if the economy were at potential GDP. The federal government debt is the value of outstanding bonds issued by the U.S. Treasury. More than half of the national debt is actually owned by other federal agencies. The national debt is a problem if interest payments on it require taxes to be raised substantially or require other federal expenditures to be cut.

 Visit www.myeconlab.com to complete these exercises online and get instant feedback.

Review Questions

5.1 In what ways does the federal budget serve as an automatic stabilizer for the economy?

5.2 What is the cyclically adjusted budget deficit or surplus? Suppose that the economy is currently at potential GDP and the federal budget is balanced. If the economy moves into recession, what will happen to the federal budget?

5.3 Why do few economists argue that it would be a good idea to balance the federal budget every year?

5.4 What is the difference between the federal budget deficit and federal government debt?

5.5 In the United States, why is more than half of federal government debt actually owned by the federal government?

Problems and Applications

5.6 (Related to *Solved Problem 27-5* on page 951) The federal government's budget deficit was $221.4 billion in 1990 and $269.2 billion in 1991. What does this information tell us about fiscal policy actions that Congress and the president took during these years?

5.7 The following is from an article in the *Wall Street Journal*: "The Treasury Department said it expected to borrow a net $1 billion during the April-to-June quarter—not repay a net $89 billion, as it said it would earlier this year." Why does the Treasury Department borrow? When the Treasury "repays," who is it repaying? Why would the Treasury say it was going to repay debt and then end up borrowing?

Source: Rebecca Christie and Deborah Lagomarsino, "U.S. Debt Is Set to Rise in Quarter as Tax Receipts Come Up Short," *Wall Street Journal*, April 30, 2002.

5.8 The federal government calculates its budget on a fiscal year that begins each year on October 1 and ends on the following September 30. At the beginning of the 1997 fiscal year, the Congressional Budget Office (CBO) forecast that the federal budget deficit would be $127.7 billion. The actual budget deficit for fiscal 1997 was only $21.9 billion. Federal expenditures were $30.3 billion less than the CBO had forecast, and federal revenue was $75.5 billion more than the CBO had forecast.

a. Is it likely that the economy grew faster or slower during fiscal 1997 than the CBO had expected? Explain your reasoning.

b. Suppose that Congress and the president were committed to balancing the budget each year. Does what happened during 1997 provide any insight

into difficulties they might run into in trying to balance the budget every year?

5.9 (Related to the *Making the Connection* on page 950) The following is from a message by President Hoover to Congress, dated May 5, 1932:

I need not recount that the revenues of the Government as estimated for the next fiscal year show a decrease of about $1,700,000,000 below the fiscal year 1929, and inexorably require a broader basis of taxation and a drastic reduction of expenditures in order to balance the Budget. Nothing is more necessary at this time than balancing the Budget.

Do you think President Hoover was correct in saying that, in 1932, nothing was more necessary than balancing the federal government's budget? Explain.

5.10 Nobel laureate Paul Samuelson, an economist at MIT, argued that "it was harmful to let a large budget surplus develop in the weak 1959–60 revival and thereby help to choke off that recovery." Why would a large budget surplus "choke off" a recovery from economic recession? What could the federal government have done to have kept a large budget surplus from developing?

Source: Paul A. Samuelson, "Economic Policy for 1962," *American Economic Review*, Vol. 44, No. 1 (February 1962), p. 6.

5.11 In testifying before Congress in 2003, then Federal Reserve Chairman Alan Greenspan observed, "There is no question that if you run substantial and excessive deficits over time you are draining savings from the private sector." What did Greenspan mean by "draining savings from the private sector"? How might this be bad for the economy?

Source: Martin Crutsinger, "Greenspan Warns of Rising Deficits," Associated Press, July 17, 2003.

5.12 An editorial in the *Wall Street Journal* declares that: "We don't put much stock in future budget forecasts because they depend on so many variables." What variables would a forecast of future federal budget deficits depend on? What is it about these variables that makes future budget deficits difficult to predict?

Source: "Fiscal Revelation," *Wall Street Journal*, February 6, 2007, p. A 16.

5.13 According to an article in the *Wall Street Journal* "U.S. tax revenue for fiscal 2006, . . . is expected to be 5%—or $115 billion—higher, than the administration projected in February. Largely as a result, the budget deficit is expected to be $296 billion this year, instead of $423 billion." Why would higher than expected tax revenues cause the budget deficit to be smaller than expected? What might make tax revenues be higher than expected? (Hint: For one possibility, note the title of the article given in the source line below.)

Source: Greg Ip and Deborah Solomon, "As Bigger Piece of Economic Pie Shifts to Wealthiest, U.S. Deficit Heads Downward," *Wall Street Journal*, July 17, 2006, p. A2.

5.14 During 2003, China ran large government budget deficits to stimulate its economy. The *Wall Street Journal* quoted an official in China's ministry of finance as saying, "The proactive fiscal policy has brought some negative effects because it has squeezed out the private investor." What did the official mean by a "proactive fiscal policy"? Why would such a policy "squeeze out" the private investor? Does that mean the policy should not have been used?

Source: Karby Leggett and Kathy Chen, "China's Rising Debt Raises Questions about the Future," *Wall Street Journal*, January 20, 2003.

5.15 A political columnist wrote the following:

> Today . . . the main purpose [of government's issuing bonds] is to let craven politicians

launch projects they know the public, at the moment, would rather not fully finance. The tab for these projects will not come due, probably, until after the politicians have long since departed for greener (excuse the expression) pastures.

Do you agree with this commentator's explanation for why some government spending is financed through tax receipts and other government spending is financed through borrowing, by issuing bonds? Briefly explain.

Source: Paul Carpenter, "The Bond Issue Won't Be Repaid by Park Tolls," *(Allentown, PA) Morning Call*, May 26, 2002, p. B1.

>> **End Learning Objective 27.5**

27.6 LEARNING OBJECTIVE   27.6 | Discuss the effects of fiscal policy in the long run, **pages 953–958.**

The Effects of Fiscal Policy in the Long Run

Summary

Some fiscal policy actions are intended to have long-run effects by expanding the productive capacity of the economy and increasing the rate of economic growth. Because these policy actions primarily affect aggregate supply rather than aggregate demand, they are sometimes referred to as *supply-side economics*. The difference between the pretax and posttax return to an economic activity is known as the **tax wedge**. Economists believe that the smaller the tax wedge for any economic activity—such as working, saving, investing, or starting a business—the more of that economic activity will occur. Economists debate the size of the supply-side effects of tax changes.

myeconlab Visit www.myeconlab.com to complete these exercises *Get Ahead of the Curve* online and get instant feedback.

Review Questions

6.1 What is meant by supply-side economics?

6.2 What is the "tax wedge"?

Problems and Applications

6.3 (Related to the *Chapter Opener* on page 928) It would seem that both households and businesses would benefit if the federal income tax were simpler and tax forms were easier to fill out. Why then have the tax laws become increasingly complicated?

6.4 Suppose a political candidate hired you to develop two arguments in favor of a flat tax. What two arguments would you advance? Alternatively, if you were

hired to develop two arguments against the flat tax, what two arguments would you advance?

6.5 Suppose that an increase in marginal tax rates on individual income affects both aggregate demand and aggregate supply. Briefly describe the effect of the tax increase on equilibrium real GDP and the equilibrium price level. Will the changes in equilibrium real GDP and the price level be larger or smaller than they would be if the tax increase affected only aggregate demand? Briefly explain.

6.6 An editorial in the *Wall Street Journal* in early 2007 observed: "The other news you won't often hear concerns the soaring tax revenues in the wake of the 2003 supply-side tax cuts. Tax collections have risen by $757 billion, among the largest revenue gushers in history." What is a "supply-side" tax cut? How would a supply-side tax cut lead to higher tax revenues? Would a supply-side tax cut always result in higher tax revenues?

Source: "Fiscal Revelation," *Wall Street Journal*, February 6, 2007.

6.7 (Related to the *Making the Connection* on page 955) As the Czech Republic considered converting to a flat tax, an editorial in the *Wall Street Journal* noted, "If the [Czech] Prime Minister manages to push his plans through a divided parliament in June, it would bring to 14 the number of single-rate tax systems in the world, all but four of them in Eastern Europe. (Hong Kong, Iceland, Mongolia and Kyrgyzstan are the exceptions.)" Why would the countries of eastern Europe and the other small countries mentioned be more likely to adopt a flat tax than the United States, Canada, Japan, or the countries of Western Europe?

Source: "Flat Czechs," *Wall Street Journal*, April 13, 2007.

>> **End Learning Objective 27.6**

Appendix

A Closer Look at the Multiplier

Apply the multiplier formula.

In this chapter, we saw that changes in government purchases and changes in taxes have a multiplied effect on equilibrium real GDP. In this appendix, we will build a simple economic model of the multiplier effect. When economists forecast the effect of a change in spending or taxes, they often rely on *econometric models*. As we saw in the appendix to Chapter 23, an econometric model is an economic model written in the form of equations, where each equation has been statistically estimated, using methods similar to those used in estimating demand curves, as briefly described in Chapter 3. In this appendix, we will start with a model similar to the one we used in the appendix to Chapter 23.

An Expression for Equilibrium Real GDP

We can write a set of equations that includes the key macroeconomic relationships we have studied in this and previous chapters. It is important to note that in this model, we will be assuming that the price level is constant. We know that this is unrealistic because an upward-sloping *SRAS* curve means that when the aggregate demand curve shifts, the price level will change. Nevertheless, our model will be approximately correct when changes in the price level are small. It also serves as an introduction to more complicated models that take into account changes in the price level. For simplicity, we also start out by assuming that taxes, T, do not depend on the level of real GDP, Y. We also assume that there are no government transfer payments to households. Finally, we assume that we have a closed economy, with no imports or exports. The numbers (with the exception of the *MPC*) represent billions of dollars:

(1) $C = 1,000 + 0.75(Y - T)$ Consumption function

(2) $I = 1,500$ Planned investment function

(3) $G = 1,500$ Government purchases function

(4) $T = 1,000$ Tax function

(5) $Y = C + I + G$ Equilibrium condition

The first equation is the consumption function. The marginal propensity to consume, or *MPC*, is 0.75, and 1,000 is the level of autonomous consumption, which is the level of consumption that does not depend on income. We assume that consumption depends on disposable income, which is $Y - T$. The functions for planned investment spending, government spending, and taxes are very simple because we have assumed that these variables are not affected by GDP and, therefore, are constant. Economists who use this type of model to forecast GDP would, of course, use more realistic planned investment, government purchases, and tax functions.

Equation (5)—the equilibrium condition—states that equilibrium GDP equals the sum of consumption spending, planned investment spending, and government purchases. To calculate a value for equilibrium real GDP, we need to substitute equations (1) through (4) into equation (5). This substitution gives us the following:

$$Y = 1{,}000 + 0.75(Y - 1{,}000) + 1{,}500 + 1{,}500$$

$$= 1{,}000 + 0.75Y - 750 + 1{,}500 + 1{,}500.$$

We need to solve this equation for Y to find equilibrium GDP. The first step is to subtract $0.75Y$ from both sides of the equation:

$$Y - 0.75Y = 1{,}000 - 750 + 1{,}500 + 1{,}500.$$

Then, we solve for Y:

$$0.25Y = 3{,}250$$

or:

$$Y = \frac{3{,}250}{0.25} = 13{,}000.$$

To make this result more general, we can replace particular values with general values represented by letters:

$$(1)\ \ C = \bar{C} + MPC(Y - T) \qquad \text{Consumption function}$$

$$(2)\ \ I = \bar{I} \qquad \qquad \qquad \qquad \text{Planned investment function}$$

$$(3)\ \ G = \bar{G} \qquad \qquad \qquad \qquad \text{Government purchases function}$$

$$(4)\ \ T = \bar{T} \qquad \qquad \qquad \qquad \text{Tax function}$$

$$(5)\ \ Y = C + I + G \qquad \qquad \text{Equilibrium condition}$$

The letters with "bars" represent fixed, or *autonomous*, values that do not depend on the values of other variables. So, $\bar{C}$ represents autonomous consumption, which had a value of 1,000 in our original example. Now, solving for equilibrium, we get:

$$Y = \bar{C} + MPC(Y - \bar{T}) + \bar{I} + \bar{G}$$

or:

$$Y - MPC(Y) = \bar{C} - (MPC \times \bar{T}) + \bar{I} + \bar{G}$$

or:

$$Y(1 - MPC) = \bar{C} - (MPC \times \bar{T}) + \bar{I} + \bar{G}$$

or:

$$Y = \frac{\bar{C} - (MPC \times \bar{T}) + \bar{I} + \bar{G}}{1 - MPC}.$$

A Formula for the Government Purchases Multiplier

To find a formula for the government purchases multiplier, we need to rewrite the last equation for changes in each variable rather than levels. Letting Δ stand for the change in a variable, we have:

$$\Delta Y = \frac{\Delta \overline{C} - (MPC \times \Delta \overline{T}) + \Delta \overline{I} + \Delta \overline{G}}{1 - MPC}.$$

If we hold constant changes in autonomous consumption spending, planned investment spending, and taxes, we can find a formula for the government purchases multiplier, which is the ratio of the change in equilibrium real GDP to the change in government purchases:

$$\Delta Y = \frac{\Delta G}{1 - MPC}$$

or:

$$\text{Government purchases multiplier} = \frac{\Delta Y}{\Delta G} = \frac{1}{1 - MPC}.$$

For an MPC of 0.75, the government purchases multiplier will be:

$$\frac{1}{1 - 0.75} = 4.$$

A government purchases multiplier of 4 means that an increase in government spending of $10 billion will increase equilibrium real GDP by $4 \times \$10$ billion = $40 billion.

A Formula for the Tax Multiplier

We can also find a formula for the tax multiplier. We start again with this equation:

$$\Delta Y = \frac{\Delta \overline{C} - (MPC \times \Delta \overline{T}) + \Delta \overline{I} + \Delta \overline{G}}{1 - MPC}.$$

Now we hold constant the values of autonomous consumption spending, planned investment spending, and government purchases, but we allow the value of taxes to change:

$$\Delta Y = \frac{-MPC \times \Delta T}{1 - MPC}.$$

Or:

$$\text{The tax multiplier} = \frac{\Delta Y}{\Delta T} = \frac{-MPC}{1 - MPC}.$$

For an MPC of 0.75, the tax multiplier will be:

$$\frac{-0.75}{1 - 0.75} = -3.$$

The tax multiplier is a negative number because an increase in taxes causes a decrease in equilibrium real GDP, and a decrease in taxes causes an increase in equilibrium real GDP. A tax multiplier of −3 means that a decrease in taxes of $10 billion will increase equilibrium real GDP by $-3 \times -\$10$ billion = $30 billion. In this chapter, we discussed the economic reasons for the tax multiplier being smaller than the government spending multiplier.

The "Balanced Budget" Multiplier

What will be the effect of equal increases (or decreases) in government purchases and taxes on equilibrium real GDP? At first, it might appear that the tax increase would exactly offset the government purchases increase, leaving real GDP unchanged. But we have just seen that the government purchases multiplier is larger (in absolute value) than the tax multiplier. We can use our formulas for the government purchases multiplier and the tax multiplier to calculate the net effect of increasing government purchases by $10 billion at the same time that taxes are increased by $10 billion:

Increase in real GDP from the increase in government purchases =

$$\$10 \text{ billion} \times \frac{1}{1 - MPC}$$

Decrease in real GDP from the increase in taxes = $\$10 \text{ billion} \times \dfrac{-MPC}{1 - MPC}$

So, the combined effect equals:

$$\$10 \text{ billion} \times \left[\left(\frac{1}{1 - MPC} \right) + \left(\frac{-MPC}{1 - MPC} \right) \right]$$

or:

$$\$10 \text{ billion} \times \left(\frac{1 - MPC}{1 - MPC} \right) = \$10 \text{ billion}.$$

The balanced budget multiplier is, therefore, equal to $(1 - MPC)/(1 - MPC)$, or 1. Equal dollar increases and decreases in government purchases and in taxes lead to the same dollar increase in real GDP in the short run.

The Effects of Changes in Tax Rates on the Multiplier

We now consider the effect of a change in the tax *rate*, as opposed to a change in a fixed amount of taxes. Changing the tax rate actually changes the value of the multiplier. To see this, suppose the tax rate is 20 percent, or 0.2. In that case, an increase in household income of $10 billion will increase *disposable income* by only $8 billion [or $10 billion × $(1 - 0.2)$]. In general, an increase in income can be multiplied by $(1 - t)$ to find the increase in disposable income, where t is the tax rate. So, we can rewrite the consumption function as:

$$C = \bar{C} + MPC(1 - t)Y.$$

We can use this expression for the consumption function to find an expression for the government purchases multiplier using the same method we used previously:

$$\text{Government purchases multiplier} = \frac{\Delta Y}{\Delta G} = \frac{1}{1 - MPC(1 - t)}.$$

We can see the effect of changing the tax rate on the size of the multiplier by trying some values. First, assume that $MPC = 0.75$ and $t = 0.2$. Then:

$$\text{Government purchases multiplier} = \frac{\Delta Y}{\Delta G} = \frac{1}{1 - 0.75(1 - 0.2)} = \frac{1}{1 - 0.6} = 2.5.$$

This value is smaller than the multiplier of 4 that we calculated by assuming that there was only a fixed amount of taxes (which is the same as assuming that the marginal tax *rate* was zero). This multiplier is smaller because spending in each period is now reduced by the amount of taxes households must pay on any additional income they earn. We can calculate the multiplier for an *MPC* of 0.75 and a lower tax rate of 0.1:

$$\text{Government purchases multiplier} = \frac{\Delta Y}{\Delta G} = \frac{1}{1 - 0.75(1 - 0.1)} = \frac{1}{1 - 0.675} = 3.1.$$

Cutting the tax rate from 20 percent to 10 percent increased the value of the multiplier from 2.5 to 3.1.

The Multiplier in an Open Economy

Up to now, we have assumed that the economy is closed, with no imports or exports. We can consider the case of an open economy by including net exports in our analysis. Recall that net exports equal exports minus imports. Exports are determined primarily by factors—such as the exchange value of the dollar and the levels of real GDP in other countries—that we do not include in our model. So, we will assume that exports are fixed, or autonomous:

$$\text{Exports} = \overline{\text{Exports}}.$$

Imports will increase as real GDP increases because households will spend some portion of an increase in income on imports. We can define the *marginal propensity to import* (*MPI*) as the fraction of an increase in income that is spent on imports. So, our expression for imports is:

$$\text{Imports} = MPI \times Y.$$

We can substitute our expressions for exports and imports into the expression we derived earlier for equilibrium real GDP:

$$Y = \overline{C} + MPC(1 - t)Y + \overline{I} + \overline{G} + [\overline{\text{Exports}} - (MPI \times Y)],$$

where the expression $\overline{\text{Exports}} - (MPI \times Y)$, represents net exports. We can now find an expression for the government purchases multiplier by using the same method as we did previously:

$$\text{Government purchases multiplier} = \frac{\Delta Y}{\Delta G} = \frac{1}{1 - [MPC(1 - t) - MPI]}.$$

We can see the effect of changing the value of the marginal propensity to import on the size of the multiplier by trying some values of key variables. First, assume $MPC = 0.75$, $t = 0.2$, and $MPI = 0.1$. Then:

$$\text{Government purchases multiplier} = \frac{\Delta Y}{\Delta G} = \frac{1}{1 - (0.75(1 - 0.2) - 0.1)} = \frac{1}{1 - 0.5} = 2.$$

This value is smaller than the multiplier of 2.5 that we calculated by assuming that there were no exports or imports (which is the same as assuming that the marginal propensity to import was zero). This multiplier is smaller because spending in each period is now reduced by the amount of imports households buy with any additional income they earn. We can calculate the multiplier with $MPC = 0.75$, $t = 0.20$, and a higher MPI of 0.2:

$$\text{Government purchases multiplier} = \frac{\Delta Y}{\Delta G} = \frac{1}{1 - (0.75(1 - 0.2) - 0.2)} = \frac{1}{1 - 0.4} = 1.7.$$

Increasing the marginal propensity to import from 0.1 to 0.2 decreases the value of the multiplier from 2 to 1.7. We can conclude that countries with a higher marginal propensity to import will have smaller multipliers than countries with a lower marginal propensity to import.

It is always important to bear in mind that the multiplier is a short-run effect which assumes that the economy is below the level of potential real GDP. In the long run, the economy is at potential real GDP, so an increase in government purchases causes a decline in the nongovernment components of real GDP, but it leaves the level of real GDP unchanged.

The analysis in this appendix is simplified compared to what would be carried out by an economist forecasting the effects of changes in government purchases or changes in taxes on equilibrium real GDP in the short run. In particular, our assumption that the price level is constant is unrealistic. However, looking more closely at the determinants of the multiplier has helped us see more clearly some important macroeconomic relationships.

LEARNING OBJECTIVE   Apply the multiplier formula, **pages 968–973.**

 Visit www.myeconlab.com to complete these exercises
Get Ahead of the Curve online and get instant feedback.

Problem and Applications

27A.1 Assuming a fixed amount of taxes and a closed economy, calculate the value of the government purchases multiplier, the tax multiplier, and the balanced budget multiplier if the marginal propensity to consume equals 0.6.

27A.2 Calculate the value of the government purchases multiplier if the marginal propensity to consume equals 0.8, the tax rate equals 0.25, and the marginal propensity to import equals 0.2.

27A.3 Show on a graph the change in the aggregate demand curve resulting from an increase in government purchases if the government purchases multiplier equals 2. Now, on the same graph, show the change in the aggregate demand curve resulting from an increase in government purchases if the government purchases multiplier equals 4.

27A.4 Using your understanding of the multiplier process, explain why an increase in the tax rate would decrease the size of the government purchases multiplier. Similarly, explain why a decrease in the marginal propensity to import would increase the size of the government purchases multiplier.

>> End Appendix Learning Objective

Inflation, Unemployment, and Federal Reserve Policy

Why Does Whirlpool Care about Monetary Policy?

How does inflation affect monetary policy, and how does monetary policy affect inflation? Testifying before Congress in July 2008, Federal Reserve Chairman Ben Bernanke said this:

Following a significant reduction in its [target for the federal funds] rate over the second half of 2007, the Federal Open Market Committee (FOMC) eased policy considerably further through the spring to counter . . . weakness in economic growth. . . . At present, . . . appropriately balancing the risks to the outlook for growth and inflation is a significant challenge for monetary policy makers. The possibility of higher energy prices, tighter credit conditions, and a still-deeper contraction in housing markets all represent significant downside risks to the outlook for growth. At the same time, upside risks to the inflation outlook have intensified lately, as the rising prices of energy and some other commodities have led to a sharp pickup in inflation. . . .

In other words, the Fed was hoping that its lowering the target for the federal funds rate to fight the negative effects on aggregate demand of the housing crisis, the credit crunch, and rising oil prices would not lead to an increase in the inflation rate.

We saw in Chapter 3 when introducing the model of demand and supply that the ability of firms to increase prices is determined partly by microeconomic factors. This statement by Chairman Bernanke indicates that macroeconomic factors, including monetary policy, also play a role.

For example, during 2005, with the housing boom in full swing and demand for appliances growing rapidly, Whirlpool was able to increase the prices of its products from 5 percent to 10 percent. But by 2008, the macroeconomic environment was not as strong for Whirlpool. The housing bubble had burst, with home sales declining in most parts of the country. Most new homes contain new built-in appliances, and many buyers of existing homes also buy at least some new appliances. Fewer home sales beginning in 2006 meant less demand for the appliances Whirlpool sells. Whirlpool expected that during 2008 their sales in the United States would decline by 7 percent, while at the same time, the rising cost of raw materials, including oil-based products and metals, led the firm to raise prices. Falling demand and rising costs is not a good combination for any firm.

Whirlpool was founded in 1911 by brothers Louis, Frederick, and Emory Upton. In 2007, Whirlpool, headquartered in Benton Harbor, Michigan, had 73,000 employees and $19 billion in annual sales. In 2001 and the following years, Whirlpool clearly benefited from the effects of monetary policy. As we saw in Chapter 26, expansionary monetary policy in 2001 and several years thereafter resulted in low real interest rates on home mortgage loans, which led to the boom in residential housing construction. As Chairman Bernanke's testimony indicates, however, by 2008, the Fed was attempting to balance the slowdown in economic growth caused by the bursting of the housing bubble and rising oil prices against the fear that inflation might remain high. As Whirlpool's situation showed, a slowdown in the growth of aggregate demand coupled with an aggregate supply shock can lead to slower growth in GDP and increases in the price level.

AN INSIDE LOOK AT POLICY on **page 998** discusses new research about the role the public's expectations of future inflation play in determining the inflation rate.

Sources: "Testimony of Chairman Ben S. Bernanke Before the Joint Economic Committee, U.S. Congress," March 28, 2007; and Ilan Brat and Henry Sanderson, "Whirlpool Likely to Keep Lift from Global Sales," *Wall Street Journal*, April 25, 2007, p. C8.

>> Continued on page 997

LEARNING Objectives

After studying this chapter, you should be able to:

28.1 Describe the **Phillips curve** and the nature of the **short-run trade-off** between **unemployment** and **inflation**, page 976.

28.2 Explain the relationship between the **short-run** and **long-run Phillips curves**, page 981.

28.3 Discuss how **expectations** of the **inflation rate** affect monetary policy, page 986.

28.4 Use a Phillips curve graph to show how the **Federal Reserve** can permanently **lower** the **inflation rate**, page 989.

Economics in YOUR Life!

How Big of a Raise Should You Ask For?

Suppose that you meet with your boss to discuss your raise for next year. One factor in deciding how big an increase to request is your expectation of what the inflation rate will be. If the Federal Reserve pledges to keep the unemployment rate at 3 percent in the long run, what effect will this pledge have on the size of the raise you request? As you read this chapter, see if you can answer this question. You can check your answer against the one we provide at the end of the chapter.

s we saw in Chapter 26, two of the Federal Reserve's monetary policy goals are price stability and high employment. These goals can sometimes be in conflict, however. Chairman Bernanke's testimony indicates that in 2008 the Fed was concerned that economic growth was slowing but also concerned that inflation would remain above acceptable levels. An important consideration for the Fed is that in the short run, there can be a trade-off between unemployment and inflation: Lower unemployment rates can result in higher inflation rates. In the long run, however, this trade-off disappears, and the unemployment rate is independent of the inflation rate. In this chapter, we will explore the relationship between inflation and unemployment in both the short run and the long run, and we will discuss what this relationship means for monetary policy.

28.1 | Describe the Phillips curve and the nature of the short-run trade-off between unemployment and inflation.

The Discovery of the Short-Run Trade-off between Unemployment and Inflation

Unemployment and inflation are the two great macroeconomic problems the Fed must deal with in the short run. As we saw in Chapter 24, when aggregate demand increases, unemployment usually falls and inflation rises. When aggregate demand decreases, unemployment usually rises and inflation falls. As a result, there is a *short-run trade-off* between unemployment and inflation: Higher unemployment is usually accompanied by lower inflation, and lower unemployment is usually accompanied by higher inflation. As we will see later in this chapter, this trade-off exists in the short run—a period that may be as long as several years—but disappears in the long run.

Although today the short-run trade-off between unemployment and inflation plays a role in the Fed's monetary policy decisions, this trade-off was not widely recognized until the late 1950s. In 1957, New Zealand economist A. W. Phillips plotted data on the unemployment rate and the inflation rate in Great Britain and drew a curve showing their average relationship. Since that time, a graph showing the short-run relationship between the unemployment rate and the inflation rate has been called a **Phillips curve**. (Phillips actually measured inflation by the percentage change in wages rather than by the percentage change in prices. Because wages and prices usually move together, this difference is not important to our discussion.) Figure 28-1 shows a graph similar to the one Phillips prepared. Each point on the Phillips curve represents a possible combination of

Phillips curve A curve showing the short-run relationship between the unemployment rate and the inflation rate.

Figure 28-1

The Phillips Curve

A. W. Phillips was the first economist to show that there is usually an inverse relationship between unemployment and inflation. Here we can see this relationship at work: In the year represented by point *A*, the inflation rate is 4 percent and the unemployment rate is 5 percent. In the year represented by point *B*, the inflation rate is 2 percent and the unemployment rate is 6 percent.

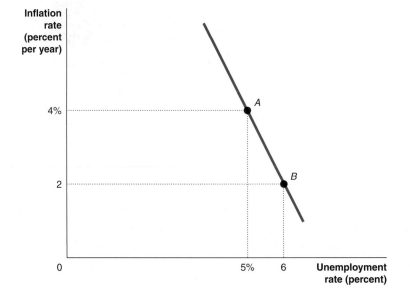

the unemployment rate and the inflation rate that might be observed in a given year. Point *A* represents a year in which the inflation rate is 4 percent and the unemployment rate is 5 percent, and point *B* represents a different year in which the inflation rate is 2 percent and the unemployment rate is 6 percent. Phillips documented that there is usually an *inverse relationship* between unemployment and inflation. During years when the unemployment rate is low, the inflation rate tends to be high, and during years when the unemployment rate is high, the inflation rate tends to be low.

Explaining the Phillips Curve with Aggregate Demand and Aggregate Supply Curves

The inverse relationship between unemployment and inflation that Phillips discovered is consistent with the aggregate demand and aggregate supply analysis we developed in Chapter 24. Figure 28-2 shows the factors that cause this inverse relationship.

Panel (a) shows the aggregate demand and aggregate supply *(AD–AS)* model from Chapter 24, and panel (b) shows the Phillips curve. For simplicity, in panel (a), we are using the basic *AD–AS* model, which assumes that the long-run aggregate supply curve and the short-run aggregate supply curve do not shift. Assume that the economy in 2011 is at point *A*, with real GDP of $14.0 trillion and a price level of 100. If there is weak growth in aggregate demand, in 2012, the economy moves to point *B*, with real GDP of $14.3 trillion and a price level of 102. The inflation rate is 2 percent and the unemployment rate is 6 percent, which corresponds to point *B* on the Phillips curve in panel (b). If there is strong growth in aggregated demand, in 2012, the economy moves to point *C*, with real GDP of $14.5 trillion and a price level of 104. Strong aggregate demand growth results in a higher inflation of 4 percent but a lower unemployment rate of 5 percent.

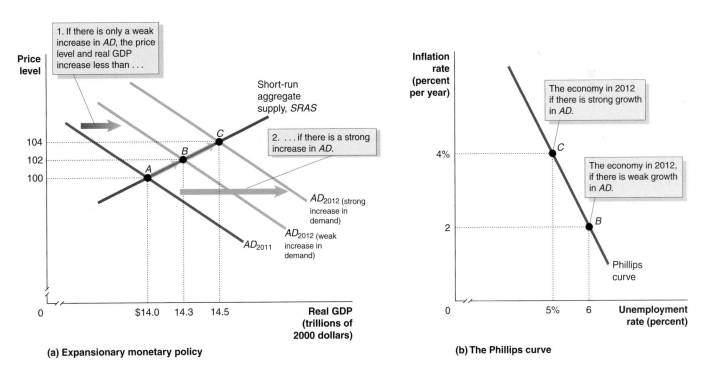

(a) Expansionary monetary policy

(b) The Phillips curve

Figure 28-2 | Using Aggregate Demand and Aggregate Supply to Explain the Phillips Curve

In panel (a), the economy in 2011 is at point *A*, with real GDP of $14.0 trillion and a price level of 100. If there is weak growth in aggregate demand, in 2012, the economy moves to point *B*, with real GDP of $14.3 trillion and a price level of 102. The inflation rate is 2 percent and the unemployment rate is 6 percent, which corresponds to point *B* on the Phillips curve in panel (b). If there is strong growth in aggregated demand,

in 2012, the economy moves to point *C*, with real GDP of $14.5 trillion and a price level of 104. Strong aggregate demand growth results in a higher inflation rate of 4 percent but a lower unemployment rate of 5 percent. This combination of higher inflation and lower unemployment is shown as point *C* on the Phillips curve in panel (b).

This combination of higher inflation and lower unemployment is shown as point *C* on the Phillips curve in panel (b).

To summarize, the *AD–AS* model indicates that slow growth in aggregate demand leads to both higher unemployment and lower inflation. This relationship explains why there is a short-run trade-off between unemployment and inflation, as shown by the downward-sloping Phillips curve. The *AD–AS* model and the Phillips curve are different ways of illustrating the same macroeconomic events. The Phillips curve has an advantage over the *AD–AS* model, however, when we want to analyze explicitly *changes* in the inflation and unemployment rates.

Is the Phillips Curve a Policy Menu?

Structural relationship A relationship that depends on the basic behavior of consumers and firms and remains unchanged over long periods.

During the 1960s, some economists argued that the Phillips curve represented a *structural relationship* in the economy. A **structural relationship** depends on the basic behavior of consumers and firms and remains unchanged over long periods. Structural relationships are useful in formulating economic policy because policymakers can anticipate that these relationships are constant—that is, the relationships will not change as a result of changes in policy.

If the Phillips curve were a structural relationship, it would present policymakers with a reliable menu of combinations of unemployment and inflation. Potentially, policymakers could use expansionary monetary and fiscal policies to choose a point on the curve that had lower unemployment and higher inflation. They could also use contractionary monetary and fiscal policies to choose a point that had lower inflation and higher unemployment. Because many economists and policymakers in the 1960s viewed the Phillips curve as a structural relationship, they believed it represented a *permanent trade-off between unemployment and inflation*. As long as policymakers were willing to accept a permanently higher inflation rate, they would be able to keep the unemployment rate permanently lower. Similarly, a permanently lower inflation rate could be attained at the cost of a permanently higher unemployment rate. As we discuss in the next section, however, economists came to realize that the Phillips curve did *not*, in fact, represent a permanent trade-off between unemployment and inflation.

Is the Short-Run Phillips Curve Stable?

During the 1960s, the basic Phillips curve relationship seemed to hold because a stable trade-off appeared to exist between unemployment and inflation. In the early 1960s, the inflation rate was low, and the unemployment rate was high. In the late 1960s, the unemployment rate had declined, and the inflation rate had increased. Then in 1968, in his presidential address to the American Economic Association, Milton Friedman of the University of Chicago argued that the Phillips curve did *not* represent a *permanent* trade-off between unemployment and inflation. At almost the same time, Edmund Phelps of Columbia University published an academic paper making a similar argument. Friedman and Phelps noted that economists had come to agree that the long-run aggregate supply curve was vertical (a point we discussed in Chapter 24). If this observation were true, the Phillips curve could not be downward sloping in the long run. A critical inconsistency existed between a vertical long-run aggregate supply curve and a long-run Phillips curve that is downward sloping. Friedman and Phelps argued, in essence, that there is no trade-off between unemployment and inflation in the long run.

The Long-Run Phillips Curve

Natural rate of unemployment The unemployment rate that exists when the economy is at potential GDP.

To understand the argument that there is no permanent trade-off between unemployment and inflation, first recall that the level of real GDP in the long run is also referred to as *potential real GDP*. At potential real GDP, firms will operate at their normal level of capacity, and everyone who wants a job will have one, except the structurally and frictionally unemployed. Friedman defined the **natural rate of unemployment** as the unemployment rate that exists when the economy is at potential GDP. The actual unemployment

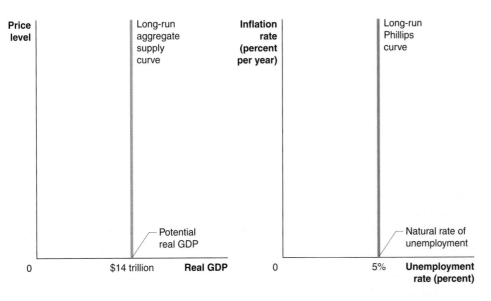

Figure 28-3

A Vertical Long-Run Aggregate Supply Curve Means a Vertical Long-Run Phillips Curve

Milton Friedman and Edmund Phelps argued that there is no trade-off between unemployment and inflation in the long run. If real GDP automatically returns to its potential level in the long run, the unemployment rate must return to the natural rate of unemployment in the long run. In this figure, we assume that potential real GDP is $14 trillion and the natural rate of unemployment is 5 percent.

rate will fluctuate in the short run but will always come back to the natural rate in the long run. In the same way, the actual level of real GDP will fluctuate in the short run but will always come back to its potential level in the long run.

In the long run, a higher or lower price level has no effect on real GDP because real GDP is always at its potential level in the long run. In the same way, in the long run, a higher or lower inflation rate will have no effect on the unemployment rate because the unemployment rate is always equal to the natural rate in the long run. Figure 28-3 illustrates Friedman's conclusion that the long-run aggregate supply curve is a vertical line at the potential real GDP, and *the long-run Phillips curve is a vertical line at the natural rate of unemployment.*

The Role of Expectations of Future Inflation

If the long-run Phillips curve is a vertical line, *no trade-off exists between unemployment and inflation in the long run.* This conclusion seemed to contradict the experience of the 1950s and 1960s, which showed a stable trade-off between unemployment and inflation. Friedman argued that the statistics from those years actually showed only a short-run trade-off between inflation and unemployment.

The short-run trade-off existed—but only because workers and firms sometimes expected the inflation rate to be either higher or lower than it turned out to be. Differences between the expected inflation rate and the actual inflation rate could lead the unemployment rate to rise above or dip below the natural rate. To see why, consider a simple case of General Motors negotiating a wage contract with the United Automobile Workers (UAW) union. Remember that both General Motors and the UAW are interested in the real wage, which is the nominal wage, corrected for inflation. Suppose, for example, that General Motors and the UAW agree on a wage of $31.50 per hour to be paid during 2012. Both General Motors and the UAW expect that the price level will increase from 100 in 2011 to 105 in 2012, so the inflation rate will be 5 percent. We can calculate the real wage General Motors expects to pay and the UAW expects to receive as follows:

$$\text{Real wage} = \frac{\text{Nominal wage}}{\text{Price level}} \times 100 = \frac{\$31.50}{105} \times 100 = \$30.$$

But suppose that the actual inflation rate turns out to be higher or lower than the expected inflation rate of 5 percent. Table 28-1 shows the effect on the actual real wage. If the price level rises only to 102 during 2012, the inflation rate will be 2 percent, and the actual real wage will be $30.88, which is higher than General Motors and

TABLE 28-1

The Impact of Unexpected Price Level Changes on the Real Wage

NOMINAL WAGE	EXPECTED REAL WAGE	ACTUAL REAL WAGE	
	Expected P_{2012} = 105	Actual P_{2012} = 102	Actual P_{2012} = 108
	Expected inflation = 5%	Actual inflation = 2%	Actual inflation = 8%
$31.50	$\dfrac{\$31.50}{105} \times 100 = \$30$	$\dfrac{\$31.50}{102} \times 100 = \$30.88$	$\dfrac{\$31.50}{108} \times 100 = \$29.17$

the UAW had expected. With a higher real wage, General Motors will hire fewer workers than it had planned to at the expected real wage of $30. If the inflation rate is 8 percent, the actual real wage will be $29.17, and General Motors will hire more workers than it had planned. If General Motors and the UAW expected a higher or lower inflation rate than actually occurred, other firms and workers probably made the same mistake.

If actual inflation is higher than expected inflation, actual real wages in the economy will be lower than expected real wages, and many firms will hire more workers than they had planned to hire. Therefore, the unemployment rate will fall. If actual inflation is lower than expected inflation, actual real wages will be higher than expected; many firms will hire fewer workers than they had planned to hire, and the unemployment rate will rise. Table 28-2 summarizes this argument.

Friedman and Phelps concluded that *an increase in the inflation rate increases employment (and decreases unemployment) only if the increase in the inflation rate is unexpected.* Friedman argued that in 1968, the unemployment rate was 3.6 percent rather than 5 percent only because the inflation rate of 4 percent was above the 1 percent to 2 percent inflation that workers and firms had expected: "There is always a temporary trade-off between inflation and unemployment; there is no permanent trade-off. The temporary trade-off comes not from inflation per se, but from unanticipated inflation."

TABLE 28-2

The Basis for the Short-Run Phillips Curve

IF . . .	THEN . . .	AND . . .
actual inflation is greater than expected inflation,	the actual real wage is less than the expected real wage,	the unemployment rate falls.
actual inflation is less than expected inflation,	the actual real wage is greater than the expected real wage,	the unemployment rate rises.

Will her wage increases keep up with inflation?

Making the Connection

Do Workers Understand Inflation?

A higher inflation rate can lead to lower unemployment if *both* workers and firms mistakenly expect the inflation rate to be lower than it turns out to be. But this same result might be due to firms forecasting inflation more accurately than workers do or to firms understanding better the effects of inflation. Some large firms employ economists to help them gather and analyze information that is useful in forecasting inflation. Many firms also have human resources or employee compensation departments that gather data on wages paid at competing firms and analyze trends in compensation. Workers generally rely on much less systematic information about wages and prices. Workers also often fail to realize a fact we discussed in Chapter 20: *Expected inflation increases the value of total production and the value of total income by the same amount.* Therefore, although not all wages will rise as prices rise, inflation will increase the average wage in the economy at the same time that it increases the average price.

Robert Shiller, an economist at Yale University, conducted a survey on inflation and discovered that, although most economists believe an increase in inflation will lead quickly to an increase in wages, a majority of the general public thinks otherwise. In one question, Shiller asked how "the effect of general inflation on wages or salary relates to your own experience and your own job." The most popular response was: "The price increase will create extra profits for my employer, who can now sell output for more; there will be no effect on my pay. My employer will see no reason to raise my pay."

Shiller also asked the following question:

> Imagine that next year the inflation rate unexpectedly doubles. How long would it probably take, in these times, before your income is increased enough so that you can afford the same things as you do today? In other words, how long will it be before a full inflation correction in your income has taken place?

Eighty-one percent of the public answered either that it would take several years for the purchasing power of their income to be restored or that it would never be restored.

If workers fail to understand that rising inflation leads over time to comparable increases in wages, then when inflation increases, in the short run, firms can increase wages by less than inflation without needing to worry about workers quitting or their morale falling. Once again, we have a higher inflation rate, leading in the short run to lower real wages and lower unemployment. In other words, we have an explanation for a downward-sloping short-run Phillips curve.

Source: Robert J. Shiller, "Why Do People Dislike Inflation?" in *Reducing Inflation: Motivation and Strategy*, Christina D. Romer and David H. Romer, eds., Chicago: University of Chicago Press, 1997.

YOUR TURN: Test your understanding by doing related problems 1.12 and 1.13 on page 1001 at the end of this chapter.

28.2 LEARNING OBJECTIVE

28.2 | Explain the relationship between the short-run and long-run Phillips curves.

The Short-Run and Long-Run Phillips Curves

If there is both a short-run Phillips curve and a long-run Phillips curve, how are the two curves related? We can begin answering this question with the help of Figure 28-4, which represents macroeconomic conditions in the United States during the 1960s. In the late

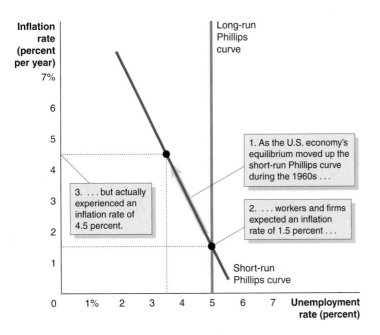

Figure 28-4

The Short-Run Phillips Curve of the 1960s and the Long-Run Phillips Curve

In the late 1960s, U.S. workers and firms were expecting the 1.5 percent inflation rates of the recent past to continue. However, expansionary monetary and fiscal policies moved the short-run equilibrium up the short-run Phillips curve to an inflation rate of 4.5 percent and an unemployment rate of 3.5 percent.

1960s, workers and firms were still expecting the inflation rate to be about 1.5 percent, as it had been from 1960 to 1965. Expansionary monetary and fiscal policies, however, had moved the short-run equilibrium up the short-run Phillips curve to an inflation rate of 4.5 percent and an unemployment rate of 3.5 percent. This very low unemployment rate was possible only because the real wage rate was unexpectedly low.

Once workers and firms began to expect that the inflation rate would continue to be about 4.5 percent, they changed their behavior. Firms knew that only nominal wage increases of more than 4.5 percent would increase real wages. Workers realized that unless they received a nominal wage increase of at least 4.5 percent, their real wage would be falling. Higher expected inflation rates had an impact throughout the economy. For example, as we saw in Chapter 25, when banks make loans, they are interested in the *real interest rate* on the loan. The real interest rate is the nominal interest rate minus the expected inflation rate. If banks need to receive a real interest rate of 3 percent on home mortgage loans and expect the inflation rate to be 1.5 percent, they will charge a nominal interest rate of 4.5 percent. If banks revise their expectations of the inflation rate to 4.5 percent, they will increase the nominal interest rate they charge on mortgage loans to 7.5 percent.

Shifts in the Short-Run Phillips Curve

The new, higher expected inflation rate can become *embedded* in the economy, meaning that workers, firms, consumers, and the government all take the inflation rate into account when making decisions. The short-run trade-off between unemployment and inflation now takes place from this higher, less favorable level, as shown in Figure 28-5.

As long as workers and firms expected the inflation rate to be 1.5 percent, the short-run trade-off between unemployment and inflation was the more favorable one shown by the lower Phillips curve. Along this Phillips curve, an inflation rate of 4.5 percent was enough to drive down the unemployment rate to 3.5 percent. Once workers and firms adjusted their expectations to an inflation rate of 4.5 percent, the short-run trade-off deteriorated to the one shown by the higher Phillips curve. At this higher expected inflation rate, the real wage rose, causing some workers to lose their jobs, and the economy's equilibrium returned to the natural rate of unemployment of 5 percent, but now with an

Figure 28-5

Expectations and the Short-Run Phillips Curve

By the end of the 1960s, workers and firms had revised their expectations of inflation from 1.5 percent to 4.5 percent. As a result, the short-run Phillips curve shifted up, which made the short-run trade-off between unemployment and inflation worse.

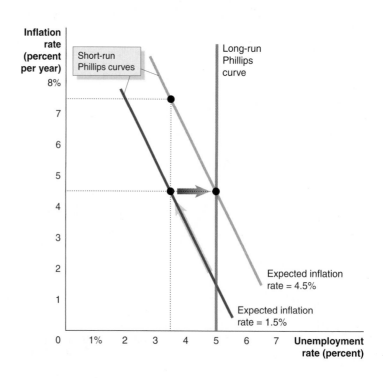

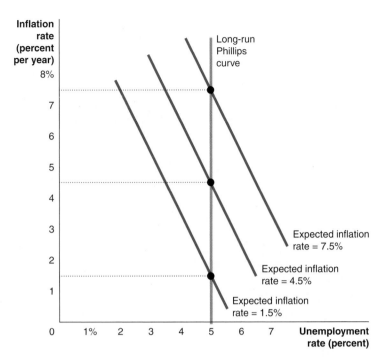

There is a different short-run Phillips curve for every expected inflation rate. Each short-run Phillips curve intersects the long-run Phillips curve at the expected inflation rate.

inflation rate of 4.5 percent rather than 1.5 percent. On the higher short-run Phillips curve, an inflation rate of 7.5 percent would be necessary to reduce the unemployment rate to 3.5 percent. An inflation rate of 7.5 percent would keep the unemployment rate at 3.5 percent only until workers and firms revised their expectations of inflation up to 7.5 percent. In the long run, the economy's equilibrium would return to the 5 percent natural rate of unemployment.

As Figure 28-6 shows, there is a short-run Phillips curve for every level of expected inflation. Each short-run Phillips curve intersects the long-run Phillips curve at the expected inflation rate.

How Does a Vertical Long-Run Phillips Curve Affect Monetary Policy?

By the 1970s, most economists accepted the argument that the long-run Phillips curve is vertical. In other words, economists realized that the common view of the 1960s had been wrong: It was *not* possible to buy a permanently lower unemployment rate at the cost of a permanently higher inflation rate. The moral of the vertical long-run Phillips curve is that *in the long run, there is no trade-off between unemployment and inflation.* In the long run, the unemployment rate always returns to the natural rate, no matter what the inflation rate is.

Figure 28-7 shows that the inflation rate is stable only when the unemployment rate is equal to the natural rate. If the Federal Reserve were to attempt to use expansionary monetary policy to push the economy to a point such as *A*, where the unemployment rate is below the natural rate, the result would be increasing inflation as the economy moved up the short-run Phillips curve. If the economy remained below the natural rate long enough, the short-run Phillips curve would shift up as workers and firms adjusted to the new, higher inflation rate. During the 1960s and 1970s, the short-run Phillips curve did shift up, presenting the economy with a more unfavorable short-run trade-off between unemployment and inflation.

If the Federal Reserve used contractionary policy to push the economy to a point such as *B*, where the unemployment rate is above the natural rate, the inflation rate would decrease. If the economy remained above the natural rate long enough, the short-run Phillips curve would shift down as workers and firms adjusted to the new, lower inflation

Figure 28-7

The Inflation Rate and the Natural Rate of Unemployment in the Long Run

The inflation rate is stable only if the unemployment rate equals the natural rate of unemployment (point *C*). If the unemployment rate is below the natural rate (point *A*), the inflation rate increases, and, eventually, the short-run Phillips curve shifts up. If the unemployment rate is above the natural rate (point *B*), the inflation rate decreases, and, eventually, the short-run Phillips curve shifts down.

Nonaccelerating inflation rate of unemployment (NAIRU) The unemployment rate at which the inflation rate has no tendency to increase or decrease.

rate. Only at a point such as *C*, where the unemployment rate is equal to the natural rate, will the inflation rate be stable. As a result, the natural rate of unemployment is sometimes called the **nonaccelerating inflation rate of unemployment (NAIRU)**. We can conclude this: *In the long run, the Federal Reserve can affect the inflation rate but not the unemployment rate.*

What makes the natural rate of unemployment increase or decrease?

Making the Connection

Does the Natural Rate of Unemployment Ever Change?

Life would be easier for the Federal Reserve if it knew exactly what the natural rate of unemployment was and if that rate never changed. Unfortunately for the Fed, the natural rate does change over time. Remember that at the natural rate of unemployment, only frictional and structural unemployment remain. Frictional or structural unemployment can change—thereby changing the natural rate—for several reasons:

- *Demographic changes.* Younger and less skilled workers have higher unemployment rates, on average, than do older and more skilled workers. Because of the baby boom, the United States had an unusually large number of younger and less skilled workers during the 1970s and 1980s. As a result, the natural rate of unemployment rose from about 5 percent in the 1960s to about 6 percent in the 1970s and 1980s. As the number of younger and less skilled workers declined as a fraction of the labor force during the 1990s, the natural rate returned to about 5 percent.

- *Labor market institutions.* As we discussed in Chapter 20, labor market institutions such as the unemployment insurance system, unions, and legal barriers to firing workers can increase the economy's unemployment rate. Because many European countries have generous unemployment insurance systems, strong unions, and restrictive policies on firing workers, the natural rate of unemployment in most Europeans countries has been well above the rate in the United States.

- *Past high rates of unemployment.* Evidence indicates that if high unemployment persists for a period of years, the natural rate of unemployment may increase. When workers have been unemployed for longer than a year or two, their skills deteriorate, they may lose confidence that they can find and hold a job, and they may become dependent on government payments to survive. Robert Gordon, an economist at Northwestern University, has argued that in the late 1930s, so many U.S. workers had been out of work for so long that the natural rate of unemployment may have risen to more than 15 percent. He has pointed out that even though the unemployment rate in the United States was 17 percent in 1939, the inflation rate did not change. Similarly, many economists have argued that the high unemployment rates experienced by European countries during the 1970s increased their natural rates of unemployment.

YOUR TURN: Test your understanding by doing related problem 2.7 on page 1003 at the end of this chapter.

Solved Problem | 28-2

Changing Views of the Phillips Curve

Writing in a Federal Reserve publication, Bennett McCallum, an economist at Carnegie Mellon University, argues that during the 1970s, the Fed was "acting under the influence of 1960s academic ideas that posited the existence of a long-run and exploitable Phillips-type tradeoff between inflation and unemployment rates." What does he mean by a "long-run and exploitable Phillips-type trade-off"? How would the Fed have attempted to exploit this long-run trade-off? What would be the consequences for the inflation rate?

SOLVING THE PROBLEM:

Step 1: **Review the chapter material.** This problem is about the relationship between the short-run and long-run Phillips curves, so you may want to review the section "The Short-Run and Long-Run Phillips Curves," which begins on page 981.

Step 2: **Explain what a "long-run exploitable Phillips-type tradeoff" means.** A "long-run exploitable Phillips-type tradeoff" means a Phillips curve that in the long run is downward sloping rather than vertical. An "exploitable" trade-off is one that the Fed could take advantage of to *permanently* reduce unemployment at the expense of higher inflation or to permanently reduce inflation at the expense of higher unemployment.

Step 3: **Explain how the inflation rate will accelerate if the Fed tries to exploit a long-run trade-off between unemployment and inflation.** As we have seen, during the 1960s, the Fed conducted expansionary monetary policies to move up what it thought was a stationary short-run Phillips curve. By the late 1960s, these policies resulted in very low unemployment rates. In the long run, there is no stable trade-off between unemployment and inflation. Attempting to permanently keep the unemployment rate at very low levels leads to a rising inflation rate, which is what happened in the late 1960s and early 1970s.

Source: Bennett T. McCallum, "Recent Developments in Monetary Policy Analysis: The Roles of Theory and Evidence," Federal Reserve Bank of Richmond, *Economic Quarterly*, Winter 2002, p. 73.

YOUR TURN: For more practice, do related problem 2.4 on page 1002 at the end of this chapter.

>> End Solved Problem 28-2

28.3 | Discuss how expectations of the inflation rate affect monetary policy.

Expectations of the Inflation Rate and Monetary Policy

How long can the economy remain at a point that is on the short-run Phillips curve, but not on the long-run Phillips curve? It depends on how quickly workers and firms adjust their expectations of future inflation to changes in current inflation. The experience in the United States over the past 50 years indicates that how workers and firms adjust their expectations of inflation depends on how high the inflation rate is. There are three possibilities:

- *Low inflation.* When the inflation rate is low, as it was during most of the 1950s, the early 1960s, the 1990s, and the early 2000s, workers and firms tend to ignore it. For example, if the inflation rate is low, a restaurant may not want to pay for printing new menus that would show slightly higher prices.

- *Moderate but stable inflation.* For the four-year period from 1968 to 1971, the inflation rate in the United States stayed in the narrow range between 4 percent and 5 percent. This rate was high enough that workers and firms could not ignore it without seeing their real wages and profits decline. It was also likely that the next year's inflation rate would be very close to the current year's inflation rate. In fact, workers and firms during the 1960s acted as if they expected changes in the inflation rate during one year to continue into the following year. People are said to have *adaptive expectations* of inflation if they assume that future rates of inflation will follow the pattern of rates of inflation in the recent past.

- *High and unstable inflation.* Inflation rates above 5 percent during peacetime have been rare in U.S. history, but the inflation rate was above 5 percent every year from 1973 through 1982. Not only was the inflation rate high during these years, it was also unstable—rising from 6 percent in 1973 to 11 percent in 1974, before falling below 6 percent in 1976 and rising again to 13.5 percent in 1980. In the mid-1970s, Nobel laureate Robert Lucas of the University of Chicago and Thomas Sargent of New York University argued that the gains to forecasting inflation accurately had dramatically increased. Workers and firms that failed to correctly anticipate the fluctuations in inflation during these years could experience substantial declines in real wages and profits. Therefore, Lucas and Sargent argued, people should use all available information when forming their expectations of future inflation. Expectations formed by using all available information about an economic variable are called **rational expectations**.

Rational expectations Expectations formed by using all available information about an economic variable.

The Effect of Rational Expectations on Monetary Policy

Lucas and Sargent pointed out an important consequence of rational expectations: An expansionary monetary policy would not work. In other words, there might not be a trade-off between unemployment and inflation, even in the short run. By the mid-1970s, most economists had accepted the idea that an expansionary monetary policy could cause the actual inflation rate to be higher than the expected inflation rate. This gap between actual and expected inflation would cause the actual real wage to fall below the expected real wage, and the unemployment rate would be pushed below the natural rate. The economy's short-run equilibrium would move up the short-run Phillips curve.

Lucas and Sargent argued that this explanation of the Phillips curve assumed that workers and firms either ignored inflation or used adaptive expectations in making their forecasts of inflation. If workers and firms have rational expectations, they will use all

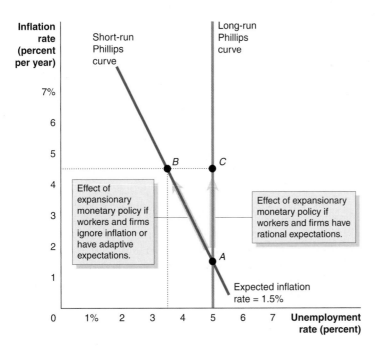

Figure 28-8

Rational Expectations and the Phillips Curve

If workers and firms ignore inflation, or if they have adaptive expectations, an expansionary monetary policy will cause the short-run equilibrium to move from point *A* on the short-run Phillips curve to point *B*; inflation will rise, and unemployment will fall. If workers and firms have rational expectations, an expansionary monetary policy will cause the short-run equilibrium to move up the long-run Phillips curve from point *A* to point *C*. Inflation will still rise, but there will be no change in unemployment.

available information, *including knowledge of the effects of Federal Reserve policy*. If workers and firms know that an expansionary monetary policy will raise the inflation rate, they should use this information in their forecasts of inflation. If they do, an expansionary monetary policy will not cause the actual inflation rate to be above the expected inflation rate. Instead, the actual inflation rate will equal the expected inflation rate, the actual real wage will equal the expected real wage, and the unemployment rate will not fall below the natural rate.

Figure 28-8 illustrates this argument. Suppose the economy begins at point *A*, where the short-run Phillips curve intersects the long-run Phillips curve. The actual and expected inflation rates are both equal to 1.5 percent, and the unemployment rate equals the natural rate of 5 percent. Then suppose the Fed engages in an expansionary monetary policy. If workers ignore inflation or if they form their expectations adaptively, the expansionary monetary policy will cause the actual inflation rate to be higher than the expected inflation rate, and the short-run equilibrium will move from point *A* on the short-run Phillips curve to point *B*. The inflation rate will rise to 4.5 percent, and the unemployment rate will fall to 3.5 percent. The decline in unemployment will be only temporary, however. Eventually, workers and firms will adjust to the fact that the actual inflation rate is 4.5 percent, not the 1.5 percent they had expected. The short-run Phillips curve will shift up, and the unemployment rate will return to 5 percent at point *C*.

Lucas and Sargent argued that if workers and firms have rational expectations, they will realize that the Fed's expansionary policy will result in an inflation rate of 4.5 percent. Therefore, as soon as the new policy is announced, workers and firms should adjust their expectations of inflation from 1.5 percent to 4.5 percent. There will be no temporary decrease in the real wage, leading to a temporary increase in employment and real GDP. Instead, the short-run equilibrium will move immediately from point *A* to point *C* on the long-run Phillips curve. The unemployment rate will never drop below 5 percent, and the *short-run* Phillips curve will be vertical.

Is the Short-Run Phillips Curve Really Vertical?

The claim by Lucas and Sargent that the short-run Phillips curve was vertical and that an expansionary monetary policy could not reduce the unemployment rate below the natural rate surprised many economists. An obvious objection to the argument of Lucas and Sargent was that the record of the 1950s and 1960s seemed to show that there was a short-run trade-off between unemployment and inflation and that, therefore, the short-run Phillips curve was downward sloping and not vertical. Lucas and Sargent argued that the apparent short-run trade-off was actually the result of *unexpected* changes in monetary policy. During those years, the Fed did not announce changes in policy, so workers, firms, and financial markets had to *guess* when the Fed had begun using a new policy. In that case, an expansionary monetary policy might cause the unemployment rate to fall because workers and firms would be taken by surprise, and their expectations of inflation would be too low. Lucas and Sargent argued that a policy that was announced ahead of time would not cause a change in unemployment.

Many economists have remained skeptical of the argument that the short-run Phillips curve is vertical. The two main objections raised are that (1) workers and firms actually may not have rational expectations, and (2) the rapid adjustment of wages and prices needed for the short-run Phillips curve to be vertical will not actually take place. Many economists doubt that people are able to use information on the Fed's monetary policy to make a reliable forecast of the inflation rate. If workers and firms do not know what impact an expansionary monetary policy will have on the inflation rate, the actual real wage may still end up being lower than the expected real wage. Also, firms may have contracts with their workers and suppliers that keep wages and prices from adjusting quickly. If wages and prices adjust slowly, then even if workers and firms have rational expectations, an expansionary monetary policy may still be able to reduce the unemployment rate in the short run.

Real Business Cycle Models

During the 1980s, some economists, including Nobel laureates Finn Kydland of Carnegie Mellon University and Edward Prescott of Arizona State University, argued that Robert Lucas was correct in assuming that workers and firms formed their expectations rationally and that wages and prices adjust quickly, but that he was wrong in assuming that fluctuations in real GDP are caused by unexpected changes in the money supply. Instead, they argued that fluctuations in "real" factors, particularly *technology shocks*, explained deviations of real GDP from its potential level. Technology shocks are changes to the economy that make it possible to produce either more output—a positive shock—or less output—a negative shock—with the same number of workers, machines, and other inputs. Real GDP will be above its previous potential level following a positive technology shock and below its previous potential level following a negative technology shock. Because these models focus on real factors—rather than on changes in the money supply—to explain fluctuations in real GDP, they are known as **real business cycle models**.

Real business cycle models
Models that focus on real rather than monetary explanations of fluctuations in real GDP.

The approach of Lucas and Sargent and the real business cycle models are sometimes grouped together under the label *the new classical macroeconomics* because these approaches share the assumptions that people have rational expectations and that wages and prices adjust rapidly. Some of the assumptions of the new classical macroeconomics are similar to those held by economists before the Great Depression of the 1930s. John Maynard Keynes, in his 1936 book *The General Theory of Employment, Interest, and Money*, referred to these earlier economists as "classical economists." Like the classical economists, the new classical macroeconomists believe that the economy will normally be at its potential level.

Economists who find the assumptions of rational expectations and rapid adjustment of wages and prices appealing are likely to accept the real business cycle model approach. Other economists are skeptical of these models because the models explain recessions as being caused by negative technology shocks. Negative technology shocks are uncommon and, apart from the oil price increases of the 1970s, real business cycle theorists have had difficulty identifying shocks that would have been large enough to cause recessions. Some economists have begun to develop real business cycle models that allow for the possibility that changes in the money supply may affect the level of real GDP. If real business cycle models continue to develop along these lines, they may eventually converge with the approaches used by the Fed.

28.4 | Use a Phillips curve graph to show how the Federal Reserve can permanently lower the inflation rate.

How the Fed Fights Inflation

We have already seen that the high inflation rates of the late 1960s and early 1970s were due in part to the Federal Reserve's attempts to keep the unemployment rate below the natural rate. By the mid-1970s, the Fed also had to deal with the inflationary impact of the OPEC oil price increases. By the late 1970s, as the Fed attempted to deal with the problem of high and worsening inflation rates, it received conflicting policy advice. Many economists argued that the inflation rate could be reduced only at the cost of a temporary increase in the unemployment rate. Followers of the Lucas–Sargent rational expectations approach, however, argued that a painless reduction in the inflation rate was possible. Before analyzing the actual policies used by the Fed, we can look at why the oil price increases of the mid-1970s made the inflation rate worse.

The Effect of a Supply Shock on the Phillips Curve

As we saw in Chapter 24, the increases in oil prices in 1974 resulting from actions by the Organization of Petroleum Exporting Countries (OPEC) caused the short-run aggregate supply curve to shift to the left. This shift is shown in panel (a) of Figure 28-9. (For simplicity, in this panel, we use the basic rather than dynamic *AD–AS* model.) The result was a higher price level and a lower level of real GDP. On a Phillips curve graph—panel (b) of Figure 28-9—we can shift the short-run Phillips curve up to show that the inflation rate and unemployment rate both increased.

As the Phillips curve shifted up, the economy moved from an unemployment rate of about 5 percent and an inflation rate of about 5.5 percent in 1973 to an unemployment

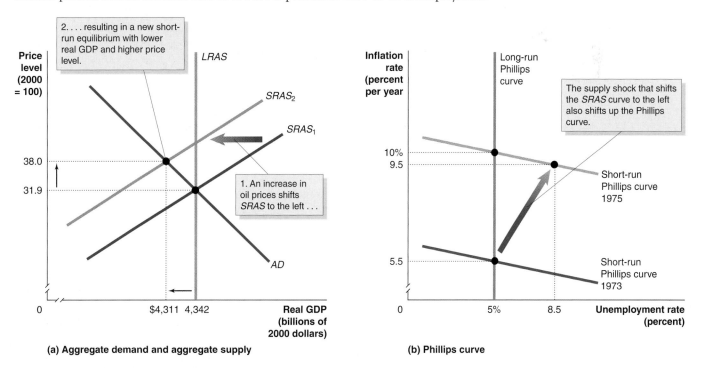

Figure 28-9 | A Supply Shock Shifts the *SRAS* and the Short-Run Phillips Curve

When OPEC increased the price of a barrel of oil from less than $3 to more than $10, in panel (a), the *SRAS* curve shifted to the left. Between 1973 and 1975, real GDP declined from $4,342 billion to $4,311 billion, and the price level rose from 31.9 to 38.0. Panel (b) shows that the supply shock shifted up the Phillips curve. In 1973, the

U.S. economy had an inflation rate of about 5.5 percent and an unemployment rate of about 5 percent. By 1975, the inflation rate had risen to about 9.5 percent and the unemployment rate to about 8.5 percent.

rate of 8.5 percent and an inflation rate of about 9.5 percent in 1975. This combination of rising unemployment and rising inflation placed the Federal Reserve in a difficult position. If the Fed used an expansionary monetary policy to fight the high unemployment rate, the *AD* curve would shift to the right, and the economy's equilibrium would move up the short-run Phillips curve. Real GDP would increase, and the unemployment rate would fall—but at the cost of higher inflation. If the Fed used a contractionary monetary policy to fight the high inflation rate, the *AD* curve would shift to the left, and the economy's equilibrium would move down the short-run Phillips curve. As a result, real GDP would fall, and the inflation rate would be reduced—but at the cost of higher unemployment. In the end, the Fed chose to fight high unemployment with an expansionary monetary policy, even though that decision worsened the inflation rate.

Paul Volcker and Disinflation

By the late 1970s, the Federal Reserve had gone through a two-decade period of continually increasing the rate of growth of the money supply. In August 1979, President Jimmy Carter appointed Paul Volcker as chairman of the Board of Governors of the Federal Reserve System. Along with most other economists, Volcker was convinced that high inflation rates were inflicting significant damage on the economy and should be reduced. To reduce inflation, Volcker decided to reduce the annual growth rate of the money supply. This contractionary monetary policy raised interest rates, causing a decline in aggregate demand. Figure 28-10 uses the Phillips curve model to analyze the movements in unemployment and inflation from 1979 to 1989.

The Fed's contractionary monetary policy shifted the economy's short-run equilibrium down the short-run Phillips curve, lowering the inflation rate from 11 percent in

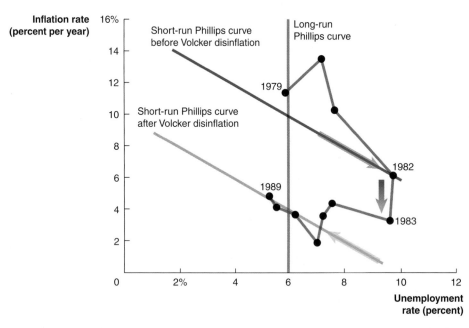

Figure 28-10 | The Fed Tames Inflation, 1979–1989

The Fed, under Chairman Paul Volcker, began fighting inflation in 1979 by reducing the growth of the money supply, thereby raising interest rates. By 1982, the unemployment rate had risen to 10 percent, and the inflation rate had fallen to 6 percent. As workers and firms lowered their expectations of future inflation, the short-run Phillips curve shifted down, improving the short-run trade-off between unemployment and inflation. This adjustment in expectations allowed the Fed to switch to an expansionary monetary policy, which by 1987 brought the economy back to the natural rate of unemployment, with an inflation rate of about 4 percent. The orange line shows the actual combinations of unemployment and inflation for each year from 1979 to 1989. Note that during these years, the natural rate of unemployment was estimated to be about 6 percent.

1979 to 6 percent in 1982—but at a cost of raising the unemployment rate from 6 percent to 10 percent. As workers and firms lowered their expectations of future inflation, the short-run Phillips curve shifted down, improving the short-run trade-off between unemployment and inflation. This adjustment in expectations allowed the Fed to switch to an expansionary monetary policy. By 1987, the economy was back to the natural rate of unemployment, which during these years was about 6 percent. The orange line in Figure 28-10 shows the actual combinations of unemployment and inflation for each year from 1979 to 1989.

Under Volcker's leadership, the Fed had reduced the inflation rate from more than 10 percent to less than 5 percent. The inflation rate has generally remained below 5 percent ever since. A significant reduction in the inflation rate is called **disinflation**. In fact, this episode is often referred to as the "Volcker disinflation." The disinflation had come at a very high price, however. From September 1982 through June 1983, the unemployment rate was above 10 percent. This period is the only one since the end of the Great Depression of the 1930s when unemployment has been above 10 percent in the United States.

Disinflation A significant reduction in the inflation rate.

Some economists argue that the Volcker disinflation provided evidence against the view that workers and firms have rational expectations. Volcker's announcement in October 1979 that he planned to use a contractionary monetary policy to bring down the inflation rate was widely publicized. If workers and firms had had rational expectations, we might have expected them to have quickly reduced their expectations of future inflation. The economy should have moved smoothly down the long-run Phillips curve. As we have seen, however, the economy moved down the existing short-run Phillips curve, and only after several years of high unemployment did the Phillips curve shift down. Apparently, workers and firms had adaptive expectations—only changing their expectations of future inflation after the current inflation rate had fallen.

Robert Lucas and Thomas Sargent argue, however, that a less painful disinflation would have occurred if workers and firms had *believed* Volcker's announcement that he was fighting inflation. The problem was that previous Fed chairmen had made similar promises throughout the 1970s, but inflation had continued to get worse. By 1979, the credibility of the Fed was at a low point. Some support for Lucas's and Sargent's argument comes from surveys of business economists at the time, which showed that they also reduced their forecasts of future inflation only slowly, even though they were well aware of Volcker's announcement of a new policy.

Don't Let This Happen to **YOU!**

Don't Confuse Disinflation with Deflation

Disinflation refers to a decline in the *inflation rate*. *Deflation* refers to a decline in the *price level*. Paul Volcker and the Federal Reserve brought about a substantial disinflation in the United States during the years between 1979 and 1983. The inflation rate fell from over 11 percent in 1979 to below 5 percent in 1984. Yet even in 1984, there was no deflation: The price level was still rising—but at a slower rate.

The last period of significant deflation in the United States was in the early 1930s during the Great Depression. The following table shows the consumer price index for those years:

YEAR	CONSUMER PRICE INDEX	DEFLATION RATE
1929	17.1	—
1930	16.7	−2.3%
1931	15.2	−9.0
1932	13.7	−9.9
1933	13.0	−5.1

Because the price level fell each year from 1929 to 1933, there was deflation.

YOUR TURN: Test your understanding by doing related problem 4.5 on page 1004 at the end of this chapter.

Solved Problem | 28-4

Using Monetary Policy to Lower the Inflation Rate

Consider the following hypothetical situation: The economy is currently at the natural rate of unemployment of 5 percent. The actual inflation rate is 6 percent and, because it has remained at 6 percent for several years, this is also the rate that workers and firms expect to see in the future.

The Federal Reserve decides to reduce the inflation rate permanently to 2 percent. How can the Fed use monetary policy to achieve this objective? Be sure to use a Phillips curve graph in your answer.

SOLVING THE PROBLEM:

Step 1: **Review the chapter material.** This problem is about using a Phillips curve graph to show how the Fed can fight inflation, so you may want to review the section "Paul Volcker and Disinflation," which begins on page 990.

Step 2: **Explain how the Fed can use monetary policy to reduce the inflation rate.** To reduce the inflation rate significantly, the Fed will have to raise the target for the federal funds rate. Higher interest rates will reduce aggregate demand, raise unemployment, and move the economy's equilibrium down the short-run Phillips curve.

Step 3: **Illustrate your argument with a Phillips curve graph.** How much the unemployment rate would have to rise to drive down the inflation rate from 6 percent to 2 percent depends on the steepness of the short-run Phillips curve. Here we have assumed that the unemployment rate would have to rise from 5 percent to 7 percent.

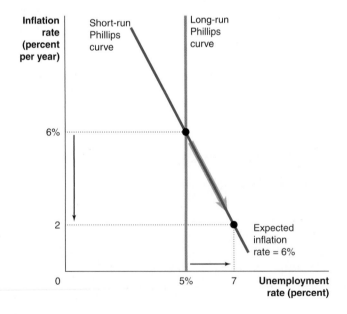

Step 4: **Show on your graph the reduction in the inflation rate from 6 percent to 2 percent.** For the decline in the inflation rate to be permanent, the expected inflation rate has to decline from 6 percent to 2 percent. We can show this on our graph:

Once the short-run Phillips curve has shifted down, the Fed can push the economy back to the natural rate of unemployment with an expansionary monetary policy. This policy is similar to the one carried out by the Fed after Paul Volcker became chairman in 1979. The downside to these policies of disinflation is that they lead to significant increases in unemployment.

EXTRA CREDIT: A follower of the new classical macroeconomics approach would have a more optimistic view of the consequences of using monetary policy to lower the inflation rate from 6 percent to 2 percent. According to this approach, the Fed's policy announcement should cause people to immediately revise downward their expectations of future inflation from 6 percent to 2 percent. The economy's short-run equilibrium would move directly down the long-run Phillips curve from an inflation rate of 6 percent to an inflation rate of 2 percent, while keeping the unemployment rate constant at 5 percent. For the reasons discussed in this chapter, many economists are skeptical that disinflation can be brought about that painlessly.

YOUR TURN: For more practice, do related problems 4.7 and 4.8 on page 1005 at the end of this chapter.

>> End Solved Problem 28-4

Alan Greenspan and the Importance of a Credible Monetary Policy

President Ronald Reagan appointed Alan Greenspan to succeed Paul Volcker as Fed chairman in 1987. Like Volcker, Greenspan was determined to keep the inflation rate low. Table 28-3 shows that the average annual inflation rate was lower during Greenspan's term than it was during the terms of his three most immediate predecessors. Inflation crept up slightly under Ben Bernanke, Greenspan's successor. Under Greenspan's leadership of the Fed, inflation was reduced nearly to the low levels experienced during the term of Chairman William McChesney Martin in the 1950s and 1960s. As we discussed in Chapter 22, beginning in the mid-1990s, the U.S. economy experienced an increase in the growth of labor productivity. By increasing the capacity of the economy, productivity growth caused a more rapid increase in potential GDP. The greater capacity of the economy to produce goods and services at every price level contributed to the low rates of inflation experienced in the United States during the late 1990s and early 2000s.

TABLE 28-3

The Record of Fed Chairmen and Inflation

FEDERAL RESERVE CHAIRMAN	TERM	AVERAGE ANNUAL INFLATION RATE DURING TERM
William McChesney Martin	April 1952–January 1970	2.0%
Arthur Burns	February 1970–January 1978	6.5
G. William Miller	March 1978–August 1979	9.2
Paul Volcker	August 1979–August 1987	6.2
Alan Greenspan	August 1987–January 2006	3.1
Ben Bernanke	January 2006–	3.4

Note: Data for Bernanke are through July 2008.

De-emphasizing the Money Supply

We saw in Chapter 25 that during the 1980s and 1990s, the close relationship between growth in the money supply and inflation broke down. Before 1987, the Fed would announce annual targets for how much M1 and M2 would increase during the year. In February 1987, near the end of Paul Volcker's term, the Fed announced that it would no longer set targets for M1. In July 1993, Alan Greenspan announced that the Fed also would no longer set targets for M2. Instead, the Federal Open Market Committee (FOMC) has relied on setting targets for the federal funds rate to meet its goals of price stability and high employment.

The Importance of Fed Credibility

The Fed learned an important lesson during the 1970s: Workers, firms, and investors in stock and bond markets have to view Fed announcements as credible if monetary policy is to be effective. As inflation worsened throughout the late 1960s and 1970s, the Fed announced repeatedly that it would take actions to reduce inflation. In fact, inflation rose. These repeated failures to follow through on announced policies had greatly reduced the Fed's credibility by the time Paul Volcker took office in August 1979. The contractionary monetary policy that the Fed announced in October 1979 had less impact on the expectations of workers, firms, and investors than it would have had if the Fed's credibility had been greater. It took a severe recession to convince people that this time, the inflation rate really was coming down. Only then were workers willing to accept lower nominal wage increases, banks willing to accept lower interest rates on mortgage loans, and investors willing to accept lower interest rates on bonds.

Over the past two decades, the Fed has taken steps to enhance its credibility. Most importantly, whenever a change in Fed policy has been announced, the change has actually taken place. In addition, Greenspan revised the previous Fed policy of keeping secret the target for the federal funds rate. Since February 1994, any change in the target rate has been announced at the conclusion of the FOMC meeting at which the change is made. In addition, the minutes of the FOMC meetings are now made public after a brief delay. Finally, in February 2000, the Fed helped make its intentions for future policy clearer by announcing at the end of each FOMC meeting whether it considered the economy in the future to be at greater risk of higher inflation or of recession. During Greenspan's terms as Fed chairman, the U.S. economy experienced only two brief recessions and no periods of high inflation.

Monetary Policy Credibility after Greenspan

Even now, debate continues over policies to increase the Fed's credibility. Some economists and policymakers believe that central banks are more credible if they adopt and follow rules. A *rules strategy* for monetary policy involves the central bank's following specific and publicly announced guidelines for policy. This strategy requires that when the central bank chooses a rule, it follows the rule, whatever the state of the economy. For example, the Fed might commit to increasing the money supply 5 percent each year, regardless of whether the economy enters a recession or suffers a financial crisis. (Note that support among economists for a monetary growth rule of this type has declined over the past 25 years.) The rule the Fed adopts should apply to variables that the Fed can control. For example, a rule stating that the Fed was committed to maintaining the growth rate of real GDP at 4 percent per year would not be useful because the Fed has no direct control over GDP.

Economists and policymakers who oppose the rules strategy support a *discretion strategy* for monetary policy. With a discretion strategy, the central bank should adjust monetary policy as it sees fit to achieve its policy goals, such as price stability and high employment. This approach differs from the rules strategy in that it allows the Fed to adjust its policy based on changes in the economy. In practice, the Fed has generally followed a discretion strategy.

Many economists believe a middle course between a rules strategy and a discretion strategy is desirable. In this view, the central bank should be free to make adjustments in policy as long as the adjustments are stated as part of the rules. The *Taylor rule*, which we discussed in Chapter 26, is an example of a modified rule of this type, although it has never been adopted explicitly by the Fed. According to the Taylor rule, the Fed should set the target for the federal funds rate according to an equation that includes the inflation rate, the equilibrium real federal funds rate, the "inflation gap," and the "output gap." Even a modified rule isn't foolproof. Rules are credible because they reduce central bank flexibility, thereby giving firms, workers, and investors more confidence that the central bank will actually do what it says it will do. But the same lack of flexibility that can make a rule credible can also limit the central bank's ability to respond during a financial crisis, such as a stock market crash.

Most economists believe the best way to achieve commitment to rules is to remove political pressures on the central bank. When the central bank is free of political pressures, the public is more likely to believe the central bank's announcements. In the early 2000s, many economists also suggested that the Federal Reserve should be more transparent about its objectives for inflation, a call embraced by Greenspan's successor, Ben Bernanke. In 2008, however, many economists inside and outside of the Federal Reserve System wondered whether the credibility of the Fed's commitment to price stability was being undermined. The Fed continued to keep its target for the federal funds at the low level of 2 percent even though the inflation rate was above 4 percent.

A Failure of Credibility at the Bank of Japan

Is it possible for the inflation rate to be too *low*? The answer is yes, particularly if inflation becomes deflation. Since the early 1990s, the Japanese economy has been plagued by slow growth and significant periods of *deflation*—or a falling price level. Deflation can contribute to slow growth by raising real interest rates, increasing the real value of debts, and causing consumers to postpone purchases in the hope of experiencing even lower prices in the future. The Bank of Japan attempted to end deflation and spur economic growth by using expansionary monetary policy to drive down interest rates and stop deflation.

By 1999, the Bank of Japan had reduced the target interest rate on overnight bank loans—the equivalent of the U.S. federal funds rate—to zero. Because Japan was experiencing deflation, however, the *real* interest rate on these loans was greater than zero. The real interest rate on mortgages and long-term bonds also remained too high to stimulate the increase in investment spending needed to bring the Japanese economy back to potential GDP. Why was the Bank of Japan unable to end deflation and reduce real interest rates? Some economists argue that the key problem was that the Bank of Japan's policies lacked credibility. Because firms, workers, and participants in financial markets doubted the Bank of Japan's willingness to continue an expansionary monetary policy long enough to end the deflation, the price level continued to fall, and real interest rates remained high. In fact, this view was reinforced when the Bank of Japan raised the target interest rate on overnight bank loans in August 2000, even though deflation continued. The lack of credibility also may have stemmed in part from the unwillingness of the Bank of Japan to state an explicit target for inflation. An explicit inflation rate target of, say, 2 percent may have caused firms, workers, and investors to raise their expectations of inflation, which could have brought the deflation to an end. Some officials at the Bank of Japan also appeared reluctant to pursue too aggressive an expansionary policy for fear of reigniting the inflation in stock prices and real estate prices that Japan had experienced in the 1980s.

Although deflation was not the only reason economic growth in Japan was so weak, failing to end deflation made other problems, such as reform of the banking system, harder to manage. The Bank of Japan's failure of credibility helps to explain its weak performance compared with the performance of the Federal Reserve during the same period.

Federal Reserve Policy and Whirlpool's "Pricing Power"

We saw in the chapter opener that during 2008, Whirlpool was suffering from declining sales of appliances in the United States at the same time that its cost were rising as raw materials prices increased. The success of any firm, particularly a firm like Whirlpool that produces consumer durables, will be determined partly by its ability to compete against rival firms and partly by macroeconomic conditions. The strength of Whirlpool's competitive position in the home appliance market was shown by its ability to acquire rival appliance maker Maytag in 2006 and by its ability to expand sales and market share in Europe and Latin America.

During and immediately after the recession of 2001, Whirlpool had clearly benefited from the effects of expansionary monetary policy. As we discussed in Chapter 21, during a typical business cycle recession, consumers reduce expenditures on new homes and on durable goods, such as household appliances. Whirlpool has a double exposure to recession because it may lose direct sales to consumers buying new or replacement appliances and also sales to builders buying appliances to be included in new home construction. In 2001 and the following years, expansionary monetary policy lessened the effects of recession by lowering interest rates. As we saw in Chapter 26, spending on new housing actually increased during 2001, as did Whirlpool's sales. Whirlpool acknowledged the importance of monetary policy to its performance in its 2004 annual report: "Consumer demand remained strong throughout 2004 as low interest rates in the United States helped maintain the momentum of new housing starts."

But in 2008, both Whirlpool and the Fed were caught in a dilemma: The declining housing market caused Whirlpool's sales to decline, while rising raw materials prices meant that its costs were increasing. Raising appliance prices to offset rising costs could further damage sales. The Fed was wrestling with a similar problem at the macroeconomic policy level: It had reduced the target for the federal funds rate to deal with the declining growth rate of GDP and rising unemployment, but was concerned that the inflation rate was still above the level consistent with meeting its goal of price stability. By mid-2008, it was unclear whether the Fed would be able to succeed in its policy of cooling off the economy enough to restrain inflation while still avoiding a recession.

Economics in YOUR Life!

>> Continued from page 975

At the beginning of the chapter, we posed this question: If the Federal Reserve pledges to keep the economy's long-run unemployment rate below 3 percent, what effect will this pledge have on the size of the raise you request? To answer this question, recall that the long-run, or natural, rate of unemployment is determined by the economy's long-run aggregate supply curve, not monetary policy, and is probably about 5 percent. The Federal Reserve's attempt to keep the economy's long-run unemployment rate below its natural level will cause the inflation rate to increase and eventually raise the public's expectations of future inflation and, by doing so, will keep inflation relatively high. Therefore, you should ask your boss for a relatively large wage increase in order to preserve the future purchasing power of your wage.

Conclusion

The workings of the contemporary economy are complex. The attempts by the Federal Reserve to keep the U.S. economy near the natural rate of unemployment with a low rate of inflation have not always been successful. Economists continue to debate the best way for the Fed to proceed.

An Inside Look at Policy on the next page discusses new research from the Federal Reserve, which indicates that inflation is driven largely by the public's expectation of inflation.

The Fed Rethinks the Phillips Curve

WALL STREET JOURNAL, FEBRUARY 26, 2007

Policy Makers at Fed Rethink Inflation's Roots

For decades, a simple rule has governed how the Federal Reserve views the nation's economy: When unemployment falls too low, inflation goes up, and vice versa.

(a) But Fed officials have rethought that notion. They believe it takes a far bigger change in unemployment to affect inflation today than it did 25 years ago. Now, when inflation fluctuates, they are far more likely to blame temporary factors, such as changes in oil prices or rents, than a change in the jobless rate.

One explanation for why inflation is influenced less by changes in unemployment is that the American public has come to expect inflation to remain stable. When inflation moves up or down, it is less likely to get stuck at the new level because companies and workers don't factor the change into their expectations—or their behavior. Another explanation is that the Fed is better at adjusting interest rates in anticipation of swings in unemployment before those swings can affect inflation.

This new view of the economy, formed in recent years, helps explain why the Fed stopped raising interest rates last summer while core inflation, which excludes food and energy prices, was rising. And it helps explain why the Fed is reluctant to cut rates now even though it sees inflation edging lower over the next two years. . . .

(b) In the late 1950s, economists discovered a tendency for inflation to rise when unemployment was low and to fall when unemployment was high. At lower unemployment rates, they concluded, companies paid more to attract scarce workers and recouped the higher wage costs by raising prices. This relationship was shown on a chart called the Phillips Curve, after Alban William Phillips, one of the first economists to identify it.

In the 1960s, American presidents and Fed officials sought to exploit the Phillips Curve by letting inflation edge higher in exchange for lower unemployment. But in the late 1960s economists Milton Friedman, who died last year, and Edmund Phelps, both of whom would later become Nobel laureates, independently deduced that the reduction in unemployment would be temporary.

Once workers began to expect higher inflation, they would want higher wages. In the long run, the economists argued, unemployment would gravitate to some "natural" level no matter what inflation did.

Although economists concluded there wasn't a *long-run* tradeoff between inflation and unemployment, they still believed there could be a *short-run* tradeoff. From 1979 to 2003, Fed Chairman Paul Volcker and his successor, Alan Greenspan, exploited this idea, periodically using interest rates to push unemployment higher to achieve lasting reductions in inflation.

But even as they were doing so, the short-run impact of unemployment on inflation began to diminish. Though the trend has been under way for 25 years, only recently has intensive research by Fed economists and others incorporated it into mainstream thinking. . . .

Core inflation, now running at a 2.2% rate by the Fed's preferred measure, remains higher than the 2% ceiling most Fed officials are comfortable with. But Janet Yellen, president of the Federal Reserve Bank of San Francisco, noted earlier this year that over the past decade, when inflation has drifted away from the 1.75% to 2% range, it has later reverted to it. For this reason it "may move down from its elevated level faster than many forecasters expect. . . ."

(c) Mr. Phelps says the new thinking on the Phillips Curve doesn't change the implications of his Nobel-winning work. If the Fed never responded to higher inflation, consumers and businesses eventually would begin to expect higher inflation, and "then the game is up."

Fed officials agree. While a given drop in unemployment is less likely to spark inflation, the potential is still there. The Fed's staff estimates it takes up to twice as much additional unemployment to achieve a percentage drop in inflation as it did before 1984. "Imbalances between demand and potential supply [may] be slow to show through convincingly to inflation, but when they do, they may be costly to correct," Fed Vice Chairman Donald Kohn said in late 2005.

That's one reason the Fed, though it expects core inflation to ease this year, isn't relaxing. With unemployment currently 4.6%, at or below the Fed's view of its natural rate, inflation may edge up after the temporary impacts of energy and rent subside. That could require the Fed to raise interest rates enough to push unemployment up sharply and bring inflation down.

Key Points in the Article

This article discusses new economic research from the Federal Reserve that indicates that inflation is influenced to a large extent by the public's expectation of future inflation, as well as by temporary factors, including changes in oil prices and housing rents. These findings have led Federal Reserve researchers to rethink the shape of the short-run Phillips curve because the findings suggest that the inflation rate has become less sensitive to changes in the unemployment rate.

Analyzing the News

(a) New economic research indicates that when temporary factors increase inflation, inflation is less likely to remain elevated for long. Why? The U.S. public—including both workers and firms—has come to expect stable inflation over time. So, when a temporary factor increases inflation, workers and employers do not alter their expectations of future inflation; instead, they expect inflation to return to its original level. These findings have also led Federal Reserve researchers to rethink the shape of the short-run Phillips curve. In

particular, the Fed is relatively less concerned today that a fall in the unemployment rate will fuel inflation.

(b) Shortly after A. W. Phillips identified the tendency for inflation and unemployment rates to move in opposite directions, economic policymakers sought to exploit this tendency. In the 1960s, Milton Friedman and Edmund Phelps made the case that such a trade-off does not exist in the long run. Both economists reasoned that the unemployment rate ultimately returns to its natural level, which is determined by the economy's long-run aggregate supply curve; hence, the Phillips curve does not represent a structural relationship. Friedman and Phelps argued that, in the long run, a relatively high inflation rate only raises the public's expectations of future inflation and, by doing so, keeps inflation relatively high. This pattern is shown in the figure, where the inflation rate is 2 percent when the economy's unemployment rate equals the natural rate of unemployment of 5 percent (point A); however, if the economy's unemployment rate is 4 percent, which is below its natural rate of unemployment, the inflation rate increases to 3 percent (point B) and, eventually, the short-run Phillips curve shifts up so that the economy returns to its natural rate of unemployment (point C).

(c) According to the Fed's estimates, to achieve a 1-percentage-point reduction in inflation today, the unemployment must rise by twice as much as it would have before 1984. So, the short-run Phillips curve is effectively flatter than it once was. Nonetheless, Fed researchers agree that their findings underscore Friedman's and Phelps's early work on the role of expectations in determining inflation. That is, a monetary policy that seeks to lower unemployment below its natural rate will ultimately only increase inflation.

Thinking Critically About Policy

1. According to this new Federal Reserve research, would a temporary increase in the inflation rate brought about by Fed policy have a larger or smaller immediate effect on unemployment today than it would have had decades ago?

2. Suppose the U.S. public does not believe that the Federal Reserve's commitment to maintain price stability is credible. Would this situation strengthen or weaken the Fed's ability to lower the unemployment rate below its natural rate?

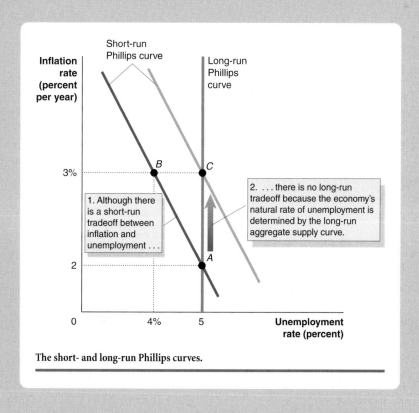

The short- and long-run Phillips curves.

Key Terms

Disinflation, p. 991

Natural rate of unemployment, p. 978

Nonaccelerating inflation rate of unemployment (NAIRU), p. 984

Phillips curve, p. 976

Rational expectations, p. 986

Real business cycle models, p. 988

Structural relationship, p. 978

28.1 LEARNING OBJECTIVE 28.1 | Describe the Phillips curve and the nature of the short-run trade-off between unemployment and inflation, **pages 976–981.**

The Discovery of the Short-Run Trade-off between Unemployment and Inflation

Summary

The **Phillips curve** illustrates the short-run trade-off between the unemployment rate and the inflation rate. The inverse relationship between unemployment and inflation shown by the Phillips curve is consistent with the aggregate demand and aggregate supply analysis developed in Chapter 23. The *AD–AS* model indicates that slow growth in aggregate demand leads to both higher unemployment and lower inflation, and rapid growth in aggregate demand leads to both lower unemployment and higher inflation. This relationship explains why there is a short-run trade-off between unemployment and inflation. Many economists initially believed that the Phillips curve was a **structural relationship** that depended on the basic behavior of consumers and firms and that remained unchanged over time. If the Phillips curve were a stable relationship, it would present policymakers with a menu of combinations of unemployment and inflation from which they could choose. Nobel laureate Milton Friedman argued that there is a **natural rate of unemployment**, which is the unemployment rate that exists when the economy is at potential GDP and to which the economy always returns. As a result, there is no trade-off between unemployment and inflation in the long run, and the long-run Phillips curve is a vertical line at the natural rate of unemployment.

myeconlab Visit www.myeconlab.com to complete these exercises *Get Ahead of the Curve* online and get instant feedback.

Review Questions

1.1 What is the Phillips curve? Draw a graph of a short-run Phillips curve.

1.2 What actions should the Fed take if it wants to move from a point on the short-run Phillips curve representing high unemployment and low inflation to a point representing lower unemployment and higher inflation?

1.3 Why did economists during the early 1960s think of the Phillips curve as a "policy menu"? Were they correct to think of it in this way? Briefly explain.

1.4 Why did Milton Friedman argue that the Phillips curve did not represent a permanent trade-off between unemployment and inflation? In your answer, be sure to explain what Friedman meant by the "natural rate of unemployment."

Problems and Applications

1.5 In fall 2003, the economy had not yet returned to the natural rate of unemployment following the end of the recession of 2001. An article in the *Wall Street Journal* noted the following:

> Perhaps the best cure for [unemployed workers'] woes would be a return to the unusually strong economy of the late 1990s, when unemployment fell so low that employers couldn't be picky. President Bush and Federal Reserve Chairman Alan Greenspan are working on that, [using] tax cuts and interest-rate cuts.

a. Which of these two actions (tax cuts and interest-rate cuts) is fiscal policy and which is monetary policy?

b. Briefly explain how tax cuts and interest-rate cuts reduce unemployment.

Source: David Wessel, "Clues to the Cure for Unemployment Begin to Emerge," *Wall Street Journal*, October 13, 2003.

1.6 Use the graphs in the next column to answer the following questions.

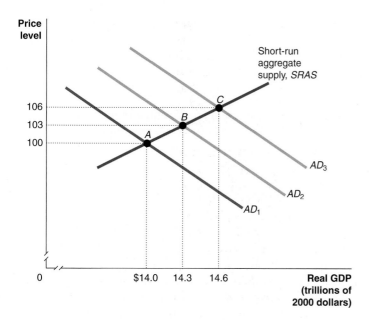

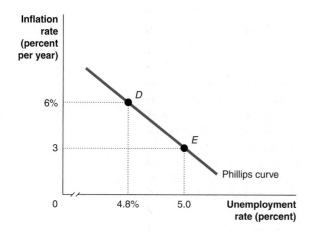

a. Briefly explain which point on the Phillips curve graph represents the same economic situation as point *B* on the aggregate demand and aggregate supply graph.

b. Briefly explain which point on the Phillips curve graph represents the same economic situation as point *C* on the aggregate demand and aggregate supply graph.

1.7 Given that the Phillips curve is derived from the aggregate demand and aggregate supply model, why use the Phillips curve analysis? What benefits does the Phillips curve analysis offer compared to the *AD–AS* model?

1.8 Briefly explain whether you agree or disagree with the following statement: "Any economic relationship that changes as economic policy changes is not a structural relationship."

1.9 In macroeconomics courses in the 1960s and early 1970s, some professors taught that one of the U.S. political parties was willing to have higher unemployment in order to achieve lower inflation and that the other major political party was willing to have higher inflation in order to achieve lower unemployment. Why might such views of the trade-off between inflation and unemployment have existed in the 1960s? Why are such views rare today?

1.10 General Juan Perón, the former dictator of Argentina, once said of the labor market in his country, "Prices have gone up the elevator, and wages have had to use the stairs." In this situation, what was happening to real wages in Argentina? Was unemployment likely to have been relatively high or relatively low?

Source: Robert J. Shiller, "Why Do People Dislike Inflation?" in Christina D. Romer and David H. Romer, eds., *Reducing Inflation: Motivation and Strategy*, Chicago: University of Chicago Press, 1997.

1.11 This chapter argues that if the price level increases, over time, the average wage should increase by the same amount. Why is this true?

1.12 (Related to the *Making the Connection* on page 981) Robert Shiller asked a sample of the general public and a sample of economists the following question: "Do you agree that preventing high inflation is an important national priority, as important as preventing drug abuse or preventing deterioration in the quality of our schools?" Fifty-two percent of the general public, but only 18 percent of economists, fully agreed. Why does the general public believe inflation is a bigger problem than economists do?

1.13 (Related to the *Making the Connection* on page 981) When Shiller asked a sample of the general public what they thought caused inflation, the most frequent answer he received was "greed." Do you agree that greed causes inflation? Briefly explain.

1.14 (Related to the *Chapter Opener* on page 972) Why would Whirlpool Corporation pay more attention than most other firms to the Federal Reserve raising or lowering interest rates? In other words, why do interest rates particularly affect Whirlpool?

1.15 Use the following information to draw a graph showing the short-run and long-run Phillips curves:
Natural rate of unemployment = 5 percent
Current rate of unemployment = 4 percent
Expected inflation rate = 4 percent
Current inflation rate = 6 percent

Be sure your graph shows the point where the short-run and long-run Phillips curves intersect.

>> End Learning Objective 28.1

The Short-Run and Long-Run Phillips Curves

Summary

There is a short-run trade-off between unemployment and inflation only if the actual inflation rate differs from the inflation rate that workers and firms had expected. There is a different short-run Phillips curve for every expected inflation rate. Each short-run Phillips curve intersects the long-run Phillips curve at the expected inflation rate. With a vertical long-run Phillips curve, it is not possible to buy a permanently lower unemployment rate at the cost of a permanently higher inflation rate. If the Federal Reserve attempts to keep the economy below the natural rate of unemployment, the inflation rate will increase. Eventually, the expected inflation rate will also increase, which causes the short-run Phillips curve to shift up and pushes the economy back to the natural rate of unemployment. The reverse happens if the Fed attempts to keep the economy above the natural rate of unemployment. In the long run, the Federal Reserve can affect the inflation rate but not the unemployment rate.

 Visit www.myeconlab.com to complete these exercises online and get instant feedback.

Review Questions

2.1 What is the relationship between the short-run Phillips curve and the long-run Phillips curve?

2.2 Why is it inconsistent to believe that the long-run aggregate supply curve is vertical and the long-run Phillips curve is downward sloping?

Problems and Applications

2.3 In 1968, Herbert Stein, who would later serve on President Nixon's Council of Economic Advisers, wrote, "Some who would opt for avoiding inflation would say that in the long run such a policy would cost little, if any, additional unemployment." Was Stein correct? Did most economists in 1968 agree with him? Briefly explain.

Source: Herbert Stein, *The Fiscal Revolution in America*, Chicago: University of Chicago Press, 1969, p. 382.

2.4 (Related to *Solved Problem 28-2* on page 985) In a speech in September 1975, then Fed chairman Arthur Burns said the following:

There is no longer a meaningful trade-off between unemployment and inflation. In the current environment, a rapidly rising level of consumer prices will not lead to the creation of new jobs. . . . Highly expansionary monetary and fiscal policies might, for a short time, provide some additional thrust to economic activity. But inflation would inevitably accelerate—a development that would create even more difficult economic problems than we have encountered over the past year.

How do Burns's views in this speech compare with the views at the Fed in the late 1960s? Why do you think he specifically says "in the current environment" there is no trade-off between unemployment and inflation?

Source: Arthur F. Burns, "The Real Issues of Inflation and Unemployment," in Federal Reserve Bank of New York, *Federal Reserve Readings on Inflation*, February 1979.

2.5 In testifying before Congress, former Federal Reserve Chairman Alan Greenspan remarked, "The challenge of monetary policy is to interpret data on the economy and financial markets with an eye to anticipating future inflationary forces and to countering them by taking action in advance." Why should the Fed take action in anticipation of inflation becoming worse? Why not just wait until the increase in the inflation rate has occurred?

Source: Nicoletta Batini and Andrew G. Haldane, "Forward-Looking Rules for Monetary Policy," in John B. Taylor, ed., *Monetary Policy Rules*, Chicago: University of Chicago Press, 1999, p. 157.

2.6 (Related to the *Chapter Opener* on page 974) In congressional testimony during 2007, Federal Reserve Chairman Ben Bernanke said:

Another significant factor influencing medium-term trends in inflation is the public's expectations of inflation. These expectations have an important bearing on whether transitory influences on prices, such as changes in energy costs, become embedded in wage and price decisions and so leave a lasting imprint on the rate of inflation.

What did Bernanke mean when he said that the public's expectations of inflation could "become embedded in wage and price decisions"? What would be the effect on the short-run Phillips curve of the public coming to expect a higher inflation rate?

Source: "Testimony of Chairman Ben S. Bernanke Before the Joint Economic Committee, U.S. Congress," March 28, 2007.

2.7 (Related to the *Making the Connection* on page 984) An article in the *Economist* magazine discussing the natural rate of unemployment, makes the observation: "'Natural' does not mean optimal."

Do you agree that the natural rate of unemployment is not the optimal rate of unemployment? In your answer, be sure to explain what you mean by *optimal*.

Source: "A Natural Choice," *Economist*, October 12, 2006.

>> End Learning Objective 28.2

28.3 LEARNING OBJECTIVE   28.3 | Discuss how expectations of the inflation rate affect monetary policy, pages 986–988.

Expectations of the Inflation Rate and Monetary Policy

Summary

When the inflation rate is moderate and stable, workers and firms tend to have *adaptive expectations*. That is, they form their expectations under the assumption that future inflation rates will follow the pattern of inflation rates in the recent past. During the high and unstable inflation rates of the mid- to late 1970s, Robert Lucas and Thomas Sargent argued that workers and firms would have *rational expectations*. **Rational expectations** are formed by using all the available information about an economic variable, including the effect of the policy being used by the Federal Reserve. Lucas and Sargent argued that if people have rational expectations, expansionary monetary policy will not work. If workers and firms know that an expansionary monetary policy is going to raise the inflation rate, the actual inflation rate will be the same as the expected inflation rate. Therefore, the unemployment rate won't fall. Many economists remain skeptical of Lucas and Sargent's argument in its strictest form. **Real business cycle models** focus on "real" factors—technology shocks—rather than changes in the money supply to explain fluctuations in real GDP.

(X) myeconlab Visit www.myeconlab.com to complete these exercises
Get Ahead of the Curve online and get instant feedback.

Review Questions

3.1 Why do workers, firms, banks, and investors in financial markets care about the future rate of inflation? How do they form their expectations of future inflation? Do current conditions in the economy have any bearing on how they form their expectations?

3.2 What does it mean to say that workers and firms have rational expectations?

3.3 Why did Robert Lucas and Thomas Sargent argue that the Phillips curve might be vertical in the short run? What difference would it make for monetary policy if they were right?

Problems and Applications

3.4 During a time when the inflation rate is increasing each year for a number of years, are adaptive expectations or rational expectations likely to give the more accurate forecasts? Briefly explain.

3.5 An article in the *Economist* notes: "A government's inability to demonstrate sincerity in achieving low inflation can . . . lead consumers to make high inflation a self-fulfilling prophecy." What does "a government's inability to demonstrate sincerity in achieving low inflation" mean in terms of Fed policy? If consumers have rational expectations, why will this policy failure make high inflation a self-fulfilling prophecy?

Source: "Cycles and Commitment," *Economist*, October 10, 2004.

3.6 Would a monetary policy intended to bring about disinflation cause a greater increase in unemployment if workers and firms have adaptive expectations or if they have rational expectations? Briefly explain.

3.7 If both the short-run and long-run Phillips curves are vertical, what will be the effect on the inflation rate and the unemployment rate of an expansionary monetary policy? Use a Phillips curve graph to illustrate your answer.

3.8 An article in the *Wall Street Journal* contained the following about the views of William Poole, the president of the Federal Reserve Bank of St. Louis:

> Mr. Poole said both inflation expectations and the output gap—the spare room the economy has between what it's producing and what it could potentially produce—go into the inflation process. But "inflation expectations . . . trump the gap. If inflation expectations were to rise, that development by itself would tend to drag the inflation rate up . . . and it might take a very long time before the (output gap) would be able to offset what's going on with inflation expectations."

a. Explain using the short-run and long-run Phillips curves what Poole meant in saying that both inflation expectations and the output gap affect the current inflation rate.

b. In terms of Phillips curve analysis, what are the implications of Poole's claim that "it might take a very long time before the (output gap) would

be able to offset what's going on with inflation expectations"?

c. Why might inflation expectations be slow to respond to the output gap?

Source: Greg Ip, "Fed Policy Maker Warns of Rising Inflation," *Wall Street Journal,* June 6, 2006.

>> **End Learning Objective 28.3**

28.4 LEARNING OBJECTIVE   28.4 | Use a Phillips curve graph to show how the Federal Reserve can permanently lower the inflation rate, **pages 989–996.**

How the Fed Fights Inflation

Summary

Inflation worsened through the 1970s. Paul Volcker became Fed chairman in 1979, and, under his leadership, the Fed used contractionary monetary policy to reduce inflation. A significant reduction in the inflation rate is called **disinflation**. This contractionary monetary policy pushed the economy down the short-run Phillips curve. As workers and firms lowered their expectations of future inflation, the short-run Phillips curve shifted down, improving the short-run trade-off between unemployment and inflation. This change in expectations allowed the Fed to switch to an expansionary monetary policy to bring the economy back to the natural rate of unemployment. During Alan Greenspan's terms as Fed chairman, inflation remained low, and the credibility of the Fed increased. Some economists and policymakers believe a central bank's credibility is increased if it follows a *rules strategy* for monetary policy, which involves the central bank's following specific and publicly announced guidelines for policy. Other economists and policymakers support a *discretion strategy* for monetary policy, under which the central bank adjusts monetary policy as it sees fit to achieve its policy goals, such as price stability and high employment.

myeconlab Visit www.myeconlab.com to complete these exercises *Get Ahead of the Curve* online and get instant feedback.

Review Questions

4.1 What was the "Volcker disinflation"? What happened to the unemployment rate during the period of the Volcker disinflation?

4.2 Why does Ben Bernanke believe that the credibility of the Fed's policy announcements is particularly important?

Problems and Applications

4.3 According to an article in *BusinessWeek,* many workers who retired in the year 2000 expected to live off the interest they would receive from bank certificates of deposit or money market mutual funds. "Then came disinflation—and a steep fall in interest rates." What is disinflation and why should it lead to a fall in interest rates?

Source: Peter Coy, "The Surprise Threat to Nest Eggs," *BusinessWeek,* July 28, 2003.

4.4 Marvin Goodfriend, an economist at Carnegie Mellon University, argues that one of the advances in macroeconomic thinking since 1979 is "the proven power of monetary policy to reduce and stabilize inflation and inflation expectations at a low rate." How has monetary policy proven its power to reduce inflation and inflation expectations?

Source: Marvin Goodfriend, "The Monetary Policy Debate Since October 1979: Lessons for Theory and Practice," Federal Reserve Bank of St. Louis *Review,* March/April 2005, Vol. 87, No. 2, Part 2, pp. 243–262.

4.5 **(Related to the *Don't Let This Happen to You!* on page 991)** Look again at the table on prices during the early 1930s in the *Don't Let This Happen to You!* Was there disinflation during 1933? Briefly explain.

4.6 Suppose the current inflation rate and the expected inflation rate are both 4 percent. The current unemployment rate and the natural rate of unemployment are both 5 percent. Use a Phillips curve graph to show the effect on the economy of a severe supply shock. If the Federal Reserve keeps monetary policy unchanged, what will happen eventually to the unemployment rate? Show this on your Phillips curve graph.

4.7 (Related to *Solved Problem 28-4* on page 992) Suppose the inflation rate has been 15 percent for the past four years. The unemployment rate is currently at the natural rate of unemployment of 5 percent. The Federal Reserve decides that it wants to permanently reduce the inflation rate to 5 percent. How can the Fed use monetary policy to achieve this objective? Be sure to use a Phillips curve graph in your answer.

4.8 (Related to *Solved Problem 28-4* on page 992) In 1995, some economists argued that the natural rate of unemployment was 6 percent. Then Fed Chairman Alan Greenspan was convinced that the natural rate was actually about 5 percent. If Greenspan had accepted the view that the natural rate was 6 percent, how might monetary policy have been different during the late 1990s?

4.9 The following statement appeared in an article in the *Wall Street Journal* in early 2007, when it was unclear whether the Fed would soon raise the target for the federal funds rate: "Federal Reserve officials appear to believe unemployment can go lower than they previously thought without generating inflation, a potentially important shift that some economists think could make interest-rate increases this year less likely."

  a. Does this statement have anything to do with the Fed's estimate of the natural rate of unemployment? Briefly explain.

  b. Why would the author of this article believe that the Fed's changed views would have an impact on

how likely the Fed was to raise the target for the federal funds rate?

Source: Greg Ip, "Fed Suggests It Is Loosening Employment–Inflation Link," *Wall Street Journal*, February 16, 2007, p. A2.

4.10 According to an article in the *Wall Street Journal*, "J.P. Morgan Chase economist Michael Feroli finds that in the past two decades it has taken a far larger drop in the jobless rate to boost inflation by one percentage point than it did in the previous 25 years." If this economist is correct, has the short-run Phillips curve become steeper during the past 25 years or less steep? If true, would this fact have any implications for monetary policy? Briefly explain.

Source: Greg Ip, "Fed Sees Inflation Rise as Fleeting," *Wall Street Journal*, August 4, 2006, p. A2.

4.11 Would a rules strategy for monetary policy be more important to increasing the credibility of the Federal Reserve during the 1970s or today? Briefly explain.

4.12 Robert Lucas was recently quoted as saying: "In practice, it is much more painful to put a modern economy through a deflation than the monetary theory we have would lead us to expect. I take this to mean that we have 'price stickiness.'" What does Lucas mean by "the monetary theory we have"? What events may have led him to conclude that it is more painful to reduce the inflation rate than theory would predict? Why does he conclude the U.S. economy apparently has "price stickiness"?

Source: Paul A. Samuelson and William A. Barnett, eds., *Inside the Economist's Mind: Conversations with Eminent Economists*, Malden, MA: Blackwell Publishing, 2007, p. 63.

>> End Learning Objective 28.4

Chapter 29

Macroeconomics
in an **Open Economy**

NewPage Paper versus China

Mark Suwyn is the CEO of NewPage, a paper manufacturer headquartered in Dayton, Ohio. NewPage specializes in the glossy paper used in catalogs and magazines. At one time, the most important competition for NewPage came from U.S.-based firms. In recent years, though, the firm's strongest competitors have been Chinese firms. Chinese exports of glossy paper to the United States in 2006 were 10 times higher than they were in 2002. Chinese firms have the advantage of paying their workers the equivalent of about $2.10 per hour, while U.S. firms pay their workers at least 10 times as much. In addition, NewPage claims that Chinese firms have received subsidies from the Chinese government in the form of special tax breaks and low-cost loans. Under existing international trade agreements, governments are not allowed to subsidize firms that export to other countries, and NewPage filed a complaint with the U.S. Department of Commerce. According to Suwyn, "We've had to shut down machines and lay off people because [Chinese firms] are dumping product way below their costs." In March 2007, the Department of Commerce announced that in response to NewPage's complaint, it was imposing tariffs of 10 percent to 20 percent on imports of glossy paper from China. Although U.S. paper manufacturers such as NewPage applauded the tariffs, U.S. publishing firms that use glossy paper complained that their costs would rise and U.S. consumers would face rising prices for magazines and other publications.

Of course, Chinese firms were exporting much more than just paper to the United States. In 2007, total Chinese exports to the United States were $323 billion, while Chinese imports from the United States were only $65 billion. The Chinese government has found that high levels of exports have led to political problems not only with the United States but also with Japan and the countries of the European Union. As we will see in this chapter, any country that has a high level of net exports must also have a high level of *net foreign investment*. When the foreign investment takes the form of buying foreign stocks and bonds, relatively little political friction usually results. But when the foreign investment takes the form of purchasing foreign firms, it can result in political difficulties. For example, in 2005, Chinese firms attempted to buy the U.S. oil company Unocal Corporation and the U.S. appliance maker Maytag. Ultimately, neither purchase was successful, and Cnooc, the Chinese oil company that failed to buy Unocal, blamed the political environment in the United States and "the unprecedented political opposition."

AN INSIDE LOOK on **page 1030** discusses why most global investors aren't worried about America's current account deficit.

Sources: James Hanah, "U.S. Paper Mills See Glimmer of Hope," *Charlotte Observer*, June 8, 2007; Gregg Hitt, "U.S. Sets New China Duties," *Wall Street Journal*, March 31, 2007, p. A3; and Matt Pottinger, Russell Gold, Michael M. Phillips, and Kate Linebaugh, "Cnooc Drops Offer for Unocal, Exposing U.S.–Chinese Tensions," *Wall Street Journal*, August 3, 2005, p. A1.

Economics in YOUR Life!

The South Korean Central Bank and Your Car Loan

Suppose that you are shopping for a new car, which you plan to finance with a loan from a local bank. One morning, as you head out the door to visit another automobile dealership, you hear the following newsflash on the radio: "The Bank of Korea, South Korea's central bank, announces it will sell its large holdings of U.S. Treasury bonds." What effect will the Bank of Korea's decision to sell its U.S. Treasury bonds likely have on the interest rate that you pay on your car loan? As you read this chapter, see if you can answer this question. You can check your answer against the one we provide at the end of the chapter. **>> Continued on page 1028**

In Chapter 8, we looked at the basics of international trade. In this chapter, we look more closely at the linkages among countries at the macroeconomic level. Countries are linked by trade in goods and services and by flows of financial investment. We will see how policymakers in all countries take these linkages into account when conducting monetary and fiscal policy.

29.1 | Explain how the balance of payments is calculated.

The Balance of Payments: Linking the United States to the International Economy

Open economy An economy that has interactions in trade or finance with other countries.

Closed economy An economy that has no interactions in trade or finance with other countries.

Balance of payments The record of a country's trade with other countries in goods, services, and assets.

Today, consumers, firms, and investors routinely interact with consumers, firms, and investors in other economies. A consumer in France may use a computer produced in the United States, listen to music on a CD player made in Japan, and wear a sweater made in Italy. A firm in the United States may sell its products in dozens of countries around the world. An investor in London may sell a U.S. Treasury bill to an investor in Mexico City. Nearly all economies are **open economies** and have extensive interactions in trade or finance with other countries. Open economies interact by trading goods and services and by making investments in each other's economies. A **closed economy** has no interactions in trade or finance with other countries. No economy today is completely closed. A few countries, such as North Korea, have very limited economic interactions with other countries.

The best way to understand the interactions between one economy and other economies is through the *balance of payments*. The **balance of payments** is a record of a country's trade with other countries in goods, services, and assets. Just as the U.S. Department of Commerce is responsible for collecting data on the GDP, it is also responsible for collecting data on the balance of payments. Table 29-1 shows the balance of payments for the United States in 2007. Notice that the table contains three "accounts": the *current account*, the *financial account*, and the *capital account*.

The Current Account

Current account The part of the balance of payments that records a country's net exports, net investment income, and net transfers.

The **current account** records *current*, or short-term, flows of funds into and out of a country. The current account for the United States includes imports and exports of goods and services (*net exports*), income received by U.S. residents from investments in other countries, income paid on investments in the United States owned by residents of other countries (*net investment income*), and the difference between transfers made to residents of other countries and transfers received by U.S. residents from other countries (*net transfers*). If you make a donation to a charity caring for orphans in Afghanistan, it would be included in net transfers. Any payments received by U.S. residents are positive numbers in the current account, and any payments made by U.S. residents are negative numbers in the current account.

Balance of trade The difference between the value of the goods a country exports and the value of the goods a country imports.

The Balance of Trade Part of the current account is the **balance of trade**, which is the difference between the value of the goods a country exports and the value of the goods a country imports. The balance of trade is the largest item in the current account and is often a topic politicians and the media discuss. If a country exports more than it imports, it has a *trade surplus*. If it exports less than it imports, it has a *trade deficit*. In 2007, the United States had a trade deficit of $816 billion. In the same year, Japan had a trade surplus of $105 billion, and China had a trade surplus of

CURRENT ACCOUNT

TABLE 29-1

**The Balance of Payments
of the United States, 2007
(billions of dollars)**

Exports of goods	$1,149	
Imports of goods	−1,965	
Balance of trade		−816
Exports of services	479	
Imports of services	−372	
Balance of services		107
Income received on investments	782	
Income payments on investments	−708	
Net income on investments		74
Net transfers		−104
Balance on current account		−739

FINANCIAL ACCOUNT

Increase in foreign holdings of assets in the United States	1,864	
Increase in U.S. holdings of assets in foreign countries	−1,206	
Balance on financial account		658

BALANCE ON CAPITAL ACCOUNT   −2

Statistical discrepancy	83
Balance of payments	0

Source: U.S. Department of Commerce, *Survey of Current Business*, June 2008.

$316 billion. Figure 29-1 shows imports and exports of goods between the United States and its trading partners and between Japan and its trading partners. The data show that the United States ran a trade deficit in 2007 with all its major trading partners and with every region of the world. Japan ran trade deficits with China, the Middle East, and Africa and trade surpluses with other regions. (Note that exports from the United States to Japan in panel (a) of Figure 29-1 should equal imports by Japan from the United States in panel (b). That the two numbers are different is an indication that international trade statistics are not measured exactly.)

Net Exports Equals the Sum of the Balance of Trade and the Balance of Services In previous chapters, we saw that *net exports* is a component of aggregate expenditures. Net exports is not explicitly shown in Table 29-1, but we can calculate it by adding together the balance of trade and the balance of services. The *balance of services* is the difference between the value of the services a country exports and the value of the services a country imports. Notice that, technically, net exports is *not* equal to the current account balance because the current account balance also includes net investment income and net transfers. But these other two items are relatively small, so it is often a convenient simplification to think of net exports as equal to the current account balance, as we will see later in this chapter.

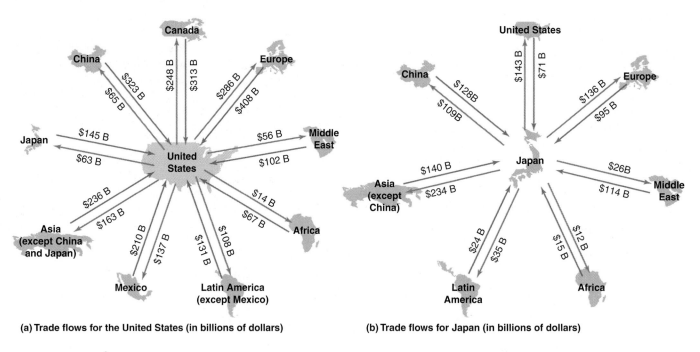

(a) Trade flows for the United States (in billions of dollars)

(b) Trade flows for Japan (in billions of dollars)

Figure 29-1 | Trade Flows for the United States and Japan, 2007

Panel (a) shows that in 2007, the United States ran a trade deficit with all its major trading partners and with every region of the world. Panel (b) shows that Japan ran trade deficits with China, the Middle East, and Africa, and trade surpluses with other regions. In each panel, the green arrows represent exports from the United States or Japan, and the red arrows represent imports.

Note: Japanese data are converted from yen to dollars at the average 2007 exchange rate of 117.76 yen per dollar.
Sources: U.S. International Trade Commission; and Japanese Ministry of Finance.

The Financial Account

Financial account The part of the balance of payments that records purchases of assets a country has made abroad and foreign purchases of assets in the country.

The **financial account** records purchases of assets a country has made abroad and foreign purchases of assets in the country. The financial account records long-term flows of funds into and out of a country. There is a *capital outflow* from the United States when an investor in the United States buys a bond issued by a foreign company or government or when a U.S. firm builds a factory in another country. There is a *capital inflow* into the United States when a foreign investor buys a bond issued by a U.S. firm or by the government or when a foreign firm builds a factory in the United States. Notice that we are using the word *capital* here to apply not just to physical assets, such as factories, but also to financial assets, such as shares of stock. When firms build or buy facilities in foreign countries, they are engaging in *foreign direct investment*. When investors buy stock or bonds issued in another country, they are engaging in *foreign portfolio investment*.

Another way of thinking of the balance on the financial account is as a measure of *net capital flows*, or the difference between capital inflows and capital outflows. (Here we are omitting a few transactions included in the capital account, as discussed in the next section.) A closely related concept to net capital flows is **net foreign investment**, which is equal to capital outflows minus capital inflows. Net capital flows and net foreign investment are always equal but have opposite signs: When net capital flows are positive, net foreign investment is negative, and when net capital flows are negative, net foreign investment is positive. Net foreign investment is also equal to net foreign direct investment plus net foreign portfolio investment. Later in this chapter, we will use the relationship between the balance on the financial account and net foreign investment to understand an important aspect of the international economic system.

Net foreign investment The difference between capital outflows from a country and capital inflows, also equal to net foreign direct investment plus net foreign portfolio investment.

The Capital Account

A third, less important, part of the balance of payments is called the *capital account*. The **capital account** records relatively minor transactions, such as migrants' transfers—which consist of goods and financial assets people take with them when they leave or enter a country—and sales and purchases of nonproduced, nonfinancial assets. A nonproduced, nonfinancial asset is a copyright, patent, trademark, or right to natural resources. The definitions of the financial account and the capital account are often misunderstood because the capital account prior to 1999 recorded all the transactions included now in both the financial account and the capital account. In other words, capital account transactions went from being a very important part of the balance of payments to being a relatively unimportant part. Because the balance on what is now called the capital account is so small, for simplicity we will ignore it in the remainder of this chapter.

> **Capital account** The part of the balance of payments that records relatively minor transactions, such as migrants' transfers, and sales and purchases of nonproduced, nonfinancial assets.

Why Is the Balance of Payments Always Zero?

The sum of the current account balance, the financial account balance, and the capital account balance equals the balance of payments. Table 29-1 shows that the balance of payments for the United States in 2007 was zero. It's not just by chance that this balance was zero; *the balance of payments is always zero*. Notice that the current account balance in 2007 was –$739 billion. This value is not quite equal (with opposite sign) to the balance on the financial account, which was $658 billion. To make the balance on the current account equal the balance on the financial account, the balance of payments includes an entry called the *statistical discrepancy*. (Remember that we are ignoring the balance on the capital account. If we included the balance on the capital account, we would say that the statistical discrepancy takes on a value equal to the difference between the current account balance and the sum of the balance on the financial account and the balance on the capital account.)

Why does the U.S. Department of Commerce include the statistical discrepancy entry to force the balance of payments to equal zero? The department knows that the sum of the current account balance and the financial account balance must equal zero. If the sum does not equal zero, some imports or exports of goods and services or some capital inflows or capital outflows were not measured accurately.

To understand why the balance of payments must equal zero every year, consider the following: In 2007, the United States spent $739 billion more on goods, services, and other items in the current account than it received. What happened to that $739 billion? We know that every dollar of that $739 billion was used by foreign individuals or firms to invest in the United States or was added to foreign holdings of dollars. We know this because logically there is nowhere else for the dollars to go: If the dollars weren't spent on U.S. goods and services—and we know they weren't because in that case they would have shown up in the current account—they must have been spent on investments in the United States or not spent at all. Dollars that aren't spent are added to foreign holdings of dollars. Changes in foreign holdings of dollars are known as *official reserve transactions*. Foreign investment in the United States or additions to foreign holdings of dollars both show up as positive entries in the U.S. financial account. Therefore, a current account deficit must be exactly offset by a financial account surplus, leaving the balance of payments equal to zero. Similarly, a country that runs a current account surplus, such as China or Japan, must run a financial account deficit of exactly the same size. If a country's current account surplus is not exactly equal to its financial account deficit, or if a country's current account deficit is not exactly equal to its financial account surplus, some transactions must not have been accounted for. The statistical discrepancy is included in the balance of payments to compensate for these uncounted transactions.

Solved Problem | 29-1

Understanding the Arithmetic of Open Economies

Test your understanding of the relationship between the current account and the financial account by evaluating the following assertion by a political commentator: "The industrial countries are committing economic suicide. Every year, they invest more and more in developing countries. Every year, more U.S., Japanese, and European manufacturing firms move their factories to developing countries. With extensive new factories and low wages, developing countries now export far more to the industrial countries than they import."

SOLVING THE PROBLEM:

Step 1: **Review the chapter material.** This problem is about the relationship between the current account and the capital account, so you may want to review the section "Why Is the Balance of Payments Always Zero?" which begins on page 1011.

Step 2: **Explain the errors in the commentator's argument.** The argument sounds plausible. It would be easy to find similar statements to this one in recent books and articles by well-known political commentators. But the argument contains an important error: The commentator has failed to understand the relationship between the current account and the financial account. The commentator asserts that developing countries are receiving large capital inflows from industrial countries. In other words, developing countries are running financial account surpluses. The commentator also asserts that developing countries are exporting more than they are importing. In other words, they are running current account surpluses. As we have seen in this section, it is impossible to run a current account surplus *and* a financial account surplus simultaneously. A country that runs a current account surplus *must* run a financial account deficit and vice versa.

EXTRA CREDIT: Most emerging economies that have received large inflows of foreign investment during the past decade, such as South Korea, Thailand, and Malaysia, have run current account deficits: They import more goods and services than they export. Emerging economies, such as Singapore, that run current account surpluses also run financial account deficits: They invest more abroad than other countries invest in them.

The point here is not obvious, otherwise it wouldn't confuse so many intelligent politicians, journalists, and political commentators. Unless you understand the relationship between the current account and the financial account, you won't be able to understand a key aspect of the international economy.

YOUR TURN: For more practice, do related problems 1.7, 1.8, and 1.9 on page 1032 at the end of this chapter.

>> **End Solved Problem 29-1**

29.2 LEARNING OBJECTIVE

29.2 | Explain how exchange rates are determined and how changes in exchange rates affect the prices of imports and exports.

The Foreign Exchange Market and Exchange Rates

A firm that operates entirely within the United States will price its products in dollars and will use dollars to pay suppliers, workers, interest to bondholders, and dividends to

Don't Let This Happen to **YOU!**

Don't Confuse the Balance of Trade, the Current Account Balance, and the Balance of Payments

The terminology of international economics can be tricky. Remember that the *balance of trade* includes only trade in goods; it does not include services. This observation is important because the United States, for example, usually imports more *goods* than it exports, but it usually exports more *services* than it imports. As a result, the U.S. trade deficit is almost always larger than the current account deficit. The *current account balance* includes the balance of trade, the balance of services, net investment income, and net transfers. Net investment income and net transfers are much smaller than the balance of trade and the balance of services.

Even though the *balance of payments* is equal to the sum of the current account balance and the financial account balance—and must equal zero—you may

sometimes see references to a balance of payments "surplus" or "deficit." These references have two explanations. The first is that the person making the reference has confused the balance of payments with either the balance of trade or the current account balance. This is a very common mistake. The second explanation is that the person is not including official reserve transactions in the financial account. If we separate changes in U.S. holdings of foreign currencies and changes in foreign holdings of U.S. dollars from other financial account entries, the current account balance and the financial account balance do not have to sum to zero, and there can be a balance of payments surplus or deficit. This may sound complicated—and it is! But don't worry. How official reserve transactions are accounted for is not crucial to understanding the basic ideas behind the balance of payments.

YOUR TURN: Test your understanding by doing related problem 1.6 on page 1032 at the end of this chapter.

shareholders. A multinational corporation, in contrast, may sell its product in many different countries and receive payment in many different currencies. Its suppliers and workers may also be spread around the world and may have to be paid in local currencies. Corporations may also use the international financial system to borrow in a foreign currency. During the 1990s, for example, many large firms located in East Asian countries, such as Thailand and South Korea, received dollar loans from foreign banks. When firms make extensive use of foreign currencies, they must deal with fluctuations in the exchange rate.

The **nominal exchange rate** is the value of one country's currency in terms of another country's currency. Economists also calculate the *real exchange rate*, which corrects the nominal exchange rate for changes in prices of goods and services. We discuss the real exchange rate later in this chapter. The nominal exchange rate determines how many units of a foreign currency you can purchase with $1. For example, the exchange rate between the U.S. dollar and the Japanese yen can be expressed as ¥100 = $1. (This exchange rate can also be expressed as how many U.S. dollars are required to buy 1 Japanese yen: $0.01 = ¥1.) The market for foreign exchange is very active. Every day, the equivalent of more than $1 trillion worth of currency is traded in the foreign exchange market. The exchange rates that result from this trading are reported each day in the business or financial sections of most newspapers.

Banks and other financial institutions around the world employ currency traders, who are linked together by computer. Rather than exchange large amounts of paper currency, they buy and sell deposits in banks. A bank buying or selling dollars will actually be buying or selling dollar bank deposits. Dollar bank deposits exist not just in banks in the United States but also in banks around the world. Suppose that the Credit Lyonnais bank in France wishes to sell U.S. dollars and buy Japanese yen. It may exchange U.S. dollar deposits that it owns for Japanese yen deposits owned by the Deutsche Bank in Germany. Businesses and individuals usually obtain foreign currency from banks in their own country.

Nominal exchange rate The value of one country's currency in terms of another country's currency.

The financial pages of most newspapers provide information on exchange rates.

Making the Connection | Exchange Rates in the Financial Pages

The business pages of most newspapers list the exchange rates between the dollar and other important currencies. The exchange rates in the following table are for July 2, 2008. The euro is the common currency used by 15 European countries, including France, Germany, and Italy.

EXCHANGE RATE BETWEEN THE DOLLAR AND THE INDICATED CURRENCY		
CURRENCY	UNITS OF FOREIGN CURRENCY PER U.S. DOLLAR	U.S. DOLLARS PER UNIT OF FOREIGN CURRENCY
Canadian dollar	1.014	0.987
Japanese yen	106.000	0.009
Mexican peso	10.390	0.096
British pound	0.502	1.992
Euro	0.630	1.587

Notice that the expression for the exchange rate stated as units of foreign currency per U.S. dollar is the *reciprocal* of the exchange rate stated as U.S. dollars per unit of foreign currency. So, the exchange rate between the U.S. dollar and the British pound can be stated as either 0.502 British pounds per U.S. dollar or 1/0.502 = 1.992 U.S. dollars per British pound.

Banks are the most active participants in the market for foreign exchange. Typically, banks buy currency for slightly less than the amount for which they sell it. This spread between the buying and selling prices allows banks to cover their expenses from currency trading and to make a profit. Therefore, when most businesses and individuals buy foreign currency from a bank, they receive fewer units of foreign currency per dollar than would be indicated by the exchange rate printed in the newspaper.

Source: *Wall Street Journal,* July 2, 2008.

YOUR TURN: Test your understanding by doing related problem 2.5 on page 1033 at the end of this chapter.

The market exchange rate is determined by the interaction of demand and supply, just as other prices are. Let's consider the demand for U.S. dollars in exchange for Japanese yen. There are three sources of foreign currency demand for the U.S. dollar:

1 Foreign firms and households who want to buy goods and services produced in the United States.

2 Foreign firms and households who want to invest in the United States either through foreign direct investment—buying or building factories or other facilities in the United States—or through foreign portfolio investment—buying stocks and bonds issued in the United States.

3 Currency traders who believe that the value of the dollar in the future will be greater than its value today.

Equilibrium in the Market for Foreign Exchange

Figure 29-2 shows the demand and supply of U.S. dollars for Japanese yen. Notice that as we move up the vertical axis in Figure 29-2, the value of the dollar increases relative to the value of the yen. When the exchange rate is ¥150 = $1, the dollar is worth 1.5 times as much relative to the yen as when the exchange rate is ¥100 = $1. Consider, first, the demand curve for dollars in exchange for yen. The demand curve has the normal downward slope. When the value of the dollar is high, the quantity of dollars demanded will be low. A Japanese investor will be more likely to buy a $1,000 bond

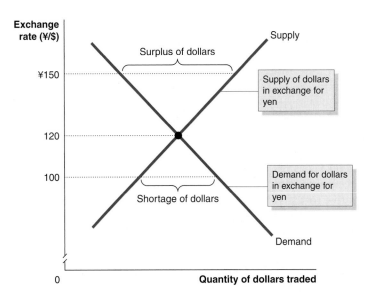

Figure 29-2

Equilibrium in the Foreign Exchange Market

When the exchange rate is ¥150 to the dollar, it is above its equilibrium level, and there will be a surplus of dollars. When the exchange rate is ¥100 to the dollar, it is below its equilibrium level, and there will be a shortage of dollars. At an exchange rate of ¥120 to the dollar, the foreign exchange market is in equilibrium.

issued by the U.S. Treasury when the exchange rate is ¥100 = $1 and the investor pays only ¥100,000 to buy $1,000 than when the exchange rate is ¥150 = $1 and the investor must pay ¥150,000. Similarly, a Japanese firm is more likely to buy $150 million worth of microchips from Intel Corporation when the exchange rate is ¥100 = $1 and the microchips can be purchased for ¥15 billion than when the exchange rate is ¥150 = $1 and the microchips cost ¥22.5 billion.

Consider, now, the supply curve of dollars in exchange for yen. The supply curve has the normal upward slope. When the value of the dollar is high, the quantity of dollars supplied in exchange for yen will be high. A U.S. investor will be more likely to buy a ¥200,000 bond issued by the Japanese government when the exchange rate is ¥200 = $1 and he needs to pay only $1,000 to buy ¥200,000 than when the exchange rate is ¥100 = $1 and he must pay $2,000. The owner of a U.S. electronics store is more likely to buy ¥20 million worth of television sets from the Sony Corporation when the exchange rate is ¥200 = $1 and she only needs to pay $100,000 to purchase the televisions than when the exchange rate is ¥100 = $1 and she must pay $200,000.

Don't Let This Happen to **YOU!**

Don't Confuse What Happens When a Currency Appreciates with What Happens When It Depreciates

One of the more confusing aspects of exchange rates is that they can be expressed in two ways. We can express the exchange rate between the dollar and the yen either as how many yen can be purchased with $1 or as how many dollars can be purchased with ¥1. That is, we can express the exchange rate as ¥100 = $1 or as $0.01 = ¥1. When a currency appreciates, it increases in value relative to another currency. When it depreciates, it decreases in value relative to another currency.

If the exchange rate changes from ¥100 = $1 to ¥120 = $1, the dollar has appreciated and the yen has depreciated because it now takes more yen to buy $1. If the exchange rate changes from $0.01 = ¥1 to $0.015 = ¥1,

however, the dollar has depreciated and the yen has appreciated because it now takes more dollars to buy ¥1. This situation can appear somewhat confusing because the exchange rate seems to have "increased" in both cases. To determine which currency has appreciated and which has depreciated, it is important to remember that an appreciation of the domestic currency means that it now takes *more* units of the foreign currency to buy one unit of the domestic currency. A depreciation of the domestic currency means it takes *fewer* units of the foreign currency to buy one unit of the domestic currency. This observation holds no matter which way we express the exchange rate.

YOUR TURN: Test your understanding by doing related problem 2.4 on page 1033 at the end of the chapter.

As in any other market, equilibrium occurs in the foreign exchange market where the quantity supplied equals the quantity demanded. In Figure 29-2, ¥120 = $1 is the equilibrium exchange rate. At exchange rates above ¥120 = $1, there will be a surplus of dollars and downward pressure on the exchange rate. The surplus and the downward pressure will not be eliminated until the exchange rate falls to ¥120 = $1. If the exchange rate is below ¥120 = $1, there will be a shortage of dollars and upward pressure on the exchange rate. The shortage and the upward pressure will not be eliminated until the exchange rate rises to ¥120 = $1. Surpluses and shortages in the foreign exchange market are eliminated very quickly because the volume of trading in major currencies such as the dollar and the yen is very large, and currency traders are linked together by computer.

Currency appreciation An increase in the market value of one currency relative to another currency.

Currency depreciation A decrease in the market value of one currency relative to another currency.

Currency appreciation occurs when the market value of a country's currency increases relative to the value of another country's currency. **Currency depreciation** occurs when the market value of a country's currency decreases relative to the value of another country's currency.

How Do Shifts in Demand and Supply Affect the Exchange Rate?

Shifts in the demand and supply curves cause the equilibrium exchange rate to change. Three main factors cause the demand and supply curves in the foreign exchange market to shift:

1 Changes in the demand for U.S.-produced goods and services and changes in the demand for foreign-produced goods and services

2 Changes in the desire to invest in the United States and changes in the desire to invest in foreign countries

3 Changes in the expectations of currency traders about the likely future value of the dollar and the likely future value of foreign currencies

Shifts in the Demand for Foreign Exchange Consider how the three factors listed above will affect the demand for U.S. dollars in exchange for Japanese yen. During an economic expansion in Japan, the incomes of Japanese households will rise, and the demand by Japanese consumers and firms for U.S. goods will increase. At any given exchange rate, the demand for U.S. dollars will increase, and the demand curve will shift to the right. Similarly, if interest rates in the United States rise, the desirability of investing in U.S. financial assets will increase, and the demand curve for dollars will also shift to the right. Some buyers and sellers in the foreign exchange market are *speculators*. **Speculators** buy and sell foreign exchange in an attempt to profit from changes in exchange rates. If a speculator becomes convinced that the value of the dollar is going to rise relative to the value of the yen, the speculator will sell yen and buy dollars. If the current exchange rate is ¥120 = $1, and the speculator is convinced that it will soon rise to ¥140 = $1, the speculator could sell ¥600,000,000 and receive $5,000,000 (= ¥600,000,000/¥120) in return. If the speculator is correct and the value of the dollar rises against the yen to ¥140 = $1, the speculator will be able to exchange $5,000,000 for ¥700,000,000 (= $5,000,000 × ¥140), leaving a profit of ¥100,000,000.

Speculators Currency traders who buy and sell foreign exchange in an attempt to profit from changes in exchange rates.

To summarize, the demand curve for dollars shifts to the right when incomes in Japan rise, when interest rates in the United States rise, or when speculators decide that the value of the dollar will rise relative to the value of the yen.

During a recession in Japan, Japanese incomes will fall, reducing the demand for U.S.-produced goods and services and shifting the demand curve for dollars to the left. Similarly, if interest rates in the United States fall, the desirability of investing in U.S. financial assets will decrease, and the demand curve for dollars will shift to the left. Finally, if speculators become convinced that the future value of the dollar will be lower than its current value, the demand for dollars will fall, and the demand curve will shift to the left.

Shifts in the Supply of Foreign Exchange The factors that affect the supply curve for dollars are similar to those that affect the demand curve for dollars. An economic expansion in the United States increases the incomes of Americans and increases their demand for goods and services, including goods and services made in Japan. As U.S. consumers and firms increase their spending on Japanese products, they must supply dollars in exchange for yen, which causes the supply curve for dollars to shift to the right. Similarly, an increase in interest rates in Japan will make financial investments in Japan more attractive to U.S. investors. These higher Japanese interest rates will cause the supply of dollars to shift to the right, as U.S. investors exchange dollars for yen. Finally, if speculators become convinced that the future value of the yen will be higher relative to the dollar than it is today, the supply curve of dollars will shift to the right as traders attempt to exchange dollars for yen.

A recession in the United States will decrease the demand for Japanese products and cause the supply curve for dollars to shift to the left. Similarly, a decrease in interest rates in Japan will make financial investments in Japan less attractive and cause the supply curve of dollars to shift to the left. If traders become convinced that the future value of the yen will be lower relative to the dollar, the supply curve will also shift to the left.

Adjustment to a New Equilibrium The factors that affect the demand and supply for currencies are constantly changing. Whether the exchange rate increases or decreases depends on the direction and size of the shifts in the demand curve and supply curve. For example, as Figure 29-3 shows, if the demand curve for dollars in exchange for Japanese yen shifts to the right by more than the supply curve does, the equilibrium exchange rate will increase.

Making the Connection	**The Incredible Falling Dollar**

An American vacationing in Paris during the spring of 2002 could have bought a meal for €50 and paid the equivalent of $44 for it. In the spring of 2008, that same €50 meal would have cost the equivalent of $79. Between 2002 and 2008, the dollar had lost nearly 45 percent of its value against the euro. And it wasn't just against the euro that the dollar was losing value. The graph below shows fluctuations for the period from 1990 to mid-2008 in an index of the value of the dollar against an average of other major currencies, such as the euro, the British pound, the Canadian dollar, and the Japanese yen. From a peak in early 2002, this index had fallen by more than 50 percent by summer 2008.

What explains the recent decline in the value of the dollar? We have just seen that an increase in the demand by foreign investors for U.S. financial assets can increase the value of the dollar, and a decrease in the demand for U.S. financial assets can decrease the value of the dollar. The increase in the value of the dollar in the late 1990s, as shown in the graph, was driven by strong demand from foreign investors for U.S. stocks and bonds, particularly U.S. Treasury securities. This increase in demand was not primarily due to higher U.S. interest rates, but to problems in the international financial system that we will discuss in Chapter 30. U.S. financial assets were seen by many investors as a safe haven in times of financial problems because the chance that the U.S. Treasury would default on its bonds was believed to be very small.

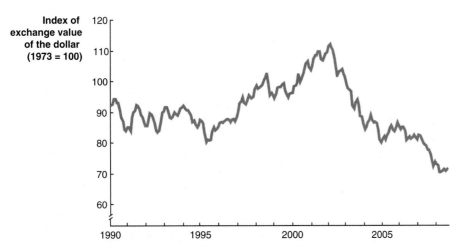

Source: Federal Reserve Bank of St. Louis.

Conditions began to change in 2002, however, for a couple of reasons. First, as we saw in Chapter 26, the Fed began aggressively cutting the target for the federal funds rate to deal with the recession of 2001 and the initially slow recovery that followed. By May 2003, the target for the federal funds rate was at a historically low level of 1 percent. Low U.S. interest rates mean that investors are likely to buy foreign assets rather than U.S. assets, which depresses the demand for dollars and lowers the exchange value of the dollar. Although the Fed did begin raising the target for the federal funds rate in 2004, it resumed cutting the target in fall 2007. In August 2008, the Fed's target for the federal funds rate was 2 percent. The corresponding interest rates at European central banks were considerably higher. The interest rate at the Bank of England was 5 percent, and the interest rate at the European Central Bank was 4.25 percent. Low U.S. interest rates have played a role in the declining value of the dollar. Second, many investors and some central banks became convinced that the value of the dollar was too high in 2002 and that it was likely to decline in the future. As we will see later in this chapter, the United States ran large current account deficits during the early 2000s. Many investors believed that the substantial increase in the supply of dollars in exchange for foreign currencies that resulted from these current account deficits would ultimately result in a significant decline in the value of the dollar. Once investors become convinced that the value of a country's currency will decline, they become reluctant to hold that country's financial assets. For example, Japanese purchases of U.S. financial assets declined from $59 billion in 2006 to only $277 million in 2007. European purchases, for all countries other than the United Kingdom, dropped from $128 billion in 2006 to $4 billion in 2007. A decreased willingness by foreign investors to buy U.S. financial assets decreases the demand for dollars and lowers the exchange value of the dollar.

The fall in the value of the dollar has been bad news for U.S. tourists traveling abroad and for anyone in the United States buying foreign goods and services. It has been good news, however, for U.S. firms exporting goods and services to other countries.

YOUR TURN: Test your understanding by doing related problem 2.13 on page 1034 at the end of this chapter.

Some Exchange Rates Are Not Determined by the Market

To this point, we have assumed that exchange rates are determined in the market. This assumption is a good one for many currencies, including the U.S. dollar, the euro, the Japanese yen, and the British pound. Some currencies, however, have *fixed exchange rates* that do not change over long periods. For example, for more than 10 years, the value of the Chinese yuan was fixed against the U.S. dollar at a rate of 8.28 yuan to the dollar.

Figure 29-3

Shifts in the Demand and Supply Curve Resulting in a Higher Exchange Rate

Holding other factors constant, an increase in the supply of dollars will decrease the equilibrium exchange rate. An increase in the demand for dollars will increase the equilibrium exchange rate. In the case shown in this figure, the demand curve and the supply curve have both shifted to the right. Because the demand curve has shifted to the right by more than the supply curve, the equilibrium exchange rate has increased from ¥120 to $1 at point *A* to ¥130 to $1 at point *B*.

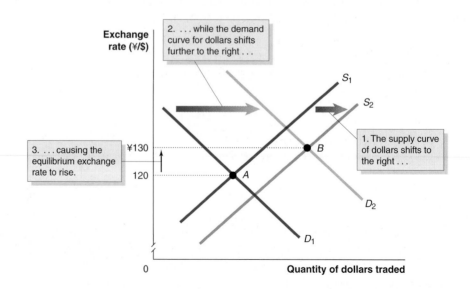

As we will discuss in more detail in Chapter 30, a country's central bank has to intervene in the foreign exchange market to buy and sell its currency to keep the exchange rate fixed.

How Movements in the Exchange Rate Affect Exports and Imports

When the market value of the dollar increases, the foreign currency price of U.S. exports rises, and the dollar price of foreign imports falls. For example, suppose that initially the market exchange rate between the U.S. dollar and the euro is $1 = €1. In that case, an Apple iPod Nano that has a price of $200 in the United States will have a price of €200 in France. A bottle of French wine that has a price of €50 in France will have a price of $50 in the United States. Now suppose the market exchange rate between the U.S. dollar and the euro changes to $1.20 = €1. Because it now takes more dollars to buy a euro, the dollar has *depreciated* against the euro, and the euro has *appreciated* against the dollar.

The depreciation of the dollar has decreased the euro price of the iPod from €200 to $200/(1.20 dollars/euro) = €167. The dollar price of the French wine has risen from $50 to €50 × 1.20 dollars/euro = $60. As a result, we would expect more iPods to be sold in France and less French wine to be sold in the United States. To generalize, we can conclude that a depreciation in the domestic currency will increase exports and decrease imports, thereby increasing net exports. As we saw in previous chapters, net exports is a component of aggregate demand. If the economy is currently below potential GDP, then, holding all other factors constant, a depreciation in the domestic currency should increase net exports, aggregate demand, and real GDP. An appreciation in the domestic currency should have the opposite effect: Exports should fall, and imports should rise, which will reduce net exports, aggregate demand, and real GDP.

Solved Problem | 29-2

The Effect of Changing Exchange Rates on the Prices of Imports and Exports

In March 2001, the average price of goods imported into the United States from Canada fell 3.3 percent. This decline was the largest since the federal government began gathering such statistics in 1992. Is it likely that the value of the U.S. dollar appreciated or depreciated versus the Canadian dollar during this period? Is it likely that the average price in Canadian dollars of goods exported from the United States to Canada during March 2001 rose or fell?

SOLVING THE PROBLEM:

Step 1: **Review the chapter material.** This problem is about changes in the value of a currency, so you may want to review the section "How Movements in the Exchange Rate Affect Exports and Imports," which appears on this page.

Step 2: **Explain whether the value of the U.S. dollar appreciated or depreciated against the Canadian dollar.** We know that if the U.S. dollar appreciates against the Canadian dollar, it will take more Canadian dollars to purchase one U.S. dollar, and, equivalently, fewer U.S. dollars will be required to purchase one Canadian dollar. A Canadian consumer or business will need to pay more Canadian dollars to buy products imported from the United States: A good or service that had been selling for 100 Canadian dollars will now sell for more than 100 Canadian dollars. A U.S. consumer or business will have to pay fewer U.S. dollars to buy products imported from Canada: A good or service that had been selling for 100 U.S. dollars will now sell for fewer than 100 U.S. dollars. We can conclude that if the price of goods imported into the United States from Canada fell, the value of the U.S. dollar must have appreciated versus the Canadian dollar.

Step 3: **Explain what happened to the average price in Canadian dollars of goods exported from the United States to Canada.** If the U.S. dollar appreciated relative to the Canadian dollar, the average price in Canadian dollars of goods exported from the United States to Canada will have risen.

>> **End Solved Problem 29-2**

YOUR TURN: For more practice, do related problem 2.9 on page 1034 at the end of this chapter.

The Real Exchange Rate

Real exchange rate The price of domestic goods in terms of foreign goods.

We have seen that an important factor in determining the level of a country's exports to and imports from another country is the relative prices of each country's goods. The relative prices of two countries' goods are determined by two factors: the relative price levels in the two countries and the nominal exchange rate between the two countries' currencies. Economists combine these two factors in the *real exchange rate*. The **real exchange rate** is the price of domestic goods in terms of foreign goods. Recall that the price level is a measure of the average prices of goods and services in an economy. We can calculate the real exchange rate between two currencies as:

$$\text{Real exchange rate} = \text{Nominal exchange rate} \times \left(\frac{\text{Domestic price level}}{\text{Foreign price level}} \right).$$

Notice that changes in the real exchange rate reflect both changes in the nominal exchange rate and changes in the relative price levels. For example, suppose that the exchange rate between the U.S. dollar and the British pound is $1 = £1, the price level in the United States is 100, and the price level in the United Kingdom is also 100. Then the real exchange rate between the dollar and the pound is:

$$\text{Real exchange rate} = 1 \text{ pound/dollar} \times \left(\frac{100}{100} \right) = 1.00.$$

Now suppose that the nominal exchange rate increases to 1.1 pounds per dollar, while the price level in the United States rises to 105 and the price level in the United Kingdom remains 100. In this case, the real exchange rate will be:

$$\text{Real exchange rate} = 1.1 \text{ pound/dollar} \times \left(\frac{105}{100} \right) = 1.15.$$

The increase in the real exchange rate from 1.00 to 1.15 tells us that the prices of U.S. goods and services are now 15 percent higher than they were relative to British goods and services.

Real exchange rates are reported as index numbers, with one year chosen as the base year. As with the consumer price index, the main value of the real exchange rate is in tracking changes over time—in this case, changes in the relative prices of domestic goods in terms of foreign goods.

29.3 LEARNING OBJECTIVE

29.3 | Explain the saving and investment equation.

The International Sector and National Saving and Investment

Having studied what determines the exchange rate, we are now ready to explore further the linkages between the U.S. economy and foreign economies. Until 1970, U.S. imports and exports were usually 4 percent to 5 percent of GDP. As Figure 29-4 shows, imports and exports are now more than twice as large a fraction of U.S. GDP. The figure also shows that since 1975, imports have consistently been larger than exports, meaning that net exports have been negative.

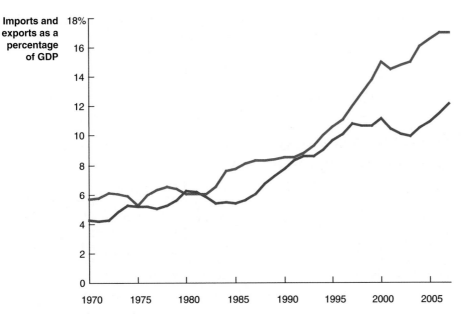

Imports and exports as a percentage of GDP

Figure 29-4

U.S. Imports and Exports, 1970–2007

Imports and exports are much larger fractions of GDP today than they were before 1970. Imports have increased faster than exports, which has made net exports negative every year since 1975.
Source: U.S. Bureau of Economic Analysis.

Net Exports Equal Net Foreign Investment

If your spending is greater than your income, what can you do? You can sell some assets—maybe those 20 shares of stock in the Walt Disney Company your grandparents gave you—or you can borrow money. A firm can be in the same situation: If a firm's costs are greater than its revenues, it has to make up the difference by selling assets or by borrowing. A country is in the same situation when it imports more than it exports. The country must finance the difference by selling assets—such as land, office buildings, or factories—or by borrowing.

In other words, for any country, a current account deficit must be exactly offset by a financial account surplus. When a country sells more assets to foreigners than it buys from foreigners, or when it borrows more from foreigners than it lends to foreigners—as it must if it is running a current account deficit—the country experiences a net capital inflow and a financial account surplus. Remember that net exports is roughly equal to the current account balance. Remember also that the financial account balance is roughly equal to net capital flows, which are in turn equal to net foreign investment but with the opposite sign. To review these two points, look again at Table 29-1 on page 1009, which shows that the current account balance is determined mainly by the balance of trade and the balance of services, and the financial account is equal to net capital flows. Also, remember the definition of net foreign investment.

When imports are greater than exports, net exports are negative, and there will be a net capital inflow as people in the United States sell assets and borrow to pay for the surplus of imports over exports. Therefore, net capital flows will be equal to net exports (but with the opposite sign), and net foreign investment will also be equal to net exports (and with the same sign). Because net exports are usually negative for the United States, in most years, the United States must be a net borrower from abroad, and U.S. net foreign investment will be negative.

We can summarize this discussion with the following equations:

$$\text{Current account balance} + \text{Financial account balance} = 0$$

or:

$$\text{Current account balance} = -\text{Financial account balance}$$

or:

$$\text{Net exports} = \text{Net foreign investment.}$$

This equation tells us, once again, that countries such as the United States that import more than they export must borrow more from abroad than they lend abroad: If net exports are negative, net foreign investment will also be negative by the same amount. Countries such as Japan and China that export more than they import must lend abroad more than they borrow from abroad: If net exports are positive, net foreign investment will also be positive by the same amount.

Domestic Saving, Domestic Investment, and Net Foreign Investment

As we saw in Chapter 21, the total saving in any economy is equal to saving by the private sector plus saving by the government sector, which we called *public saving*. When the government runs a budget surplus by spending less than it receives in taxes, it is saving. When the government runs a budget deficit, public saving is negative. Negative saving is also known as *dissaving*. We can write the following expression for the level of saving in the economy:

$$\text{National saving} = \text{Private saving} + \text{Public saving}$$

or:

$$S = S_{\text{private}} + S_{\text{public}}.$$

Private saving is equal to what households have left of their income after spending on consumption goods and paying taxes (for simplicity, we assume that transfer payments are zero):

$$\text{Private saving} = \text{National income} - \text{Consumption} - \text{Taxes}$$

or:

$$S_{\text{private}} = Y - C - T.$$

Public saving is equal to the difference between government spending and taxes:

$$\text{Government saving} = \text{Taxes} - \text{Government spending}$$

or:

$$S_{\text{public}} = T - G.$$

Finally, remember the basic macroeconomic equation for GDP or national income:

$$Y = C + I + G + NX.$$

We can use this last equation, our definitions of private and public saving, and the fact that net exports equal net foreign investment to arrive at an important relationship, known as the **saving and investment equation**:

$$\text{National saving} = \text{Domestic investment} + \text{Net foreign investment}$$

or:

$$S = I + NFI.$$

Saving and investment equation An equation that shows that national saving is equal to domestic investment plus net foreign investment.

This equation is an *identity* because it must always be true, given the definitions we have used.

The saving and investment equation tells us that a country's saving will be invested either domestically or overseas. If you save $1,000 and use the funds to buy a bond issued by General Motors, GM may use the $1,000 to renovate a factory in the United States (*I*) or to build a factory in China (*NFI*) as a joint venture with a Chinese firm.

Solved Problem | 29-3

Arriving at the Saving and Investment Equation

Use the definitions of private and public saving, the equation for GDP or national income, and the fact that net exports must equal net foreign investment to arrive at the saving and investment equation.

SOLVING THE PROBLEM:

Step 1: **Review the chapter material.** This problem is about the saving and investment equation, so you may want to review the section "Domestic Saving, Domestic Investment, and Net Foreign Investment," which begins on page 1022.

Step 2: **Derive an expression for national saving (S) in terms of national income (Y), consumption (C), and government purchases (G).**
We can bring together the four equations we need to use:

1. $S_{private} = Y - C - T$
2. $S_{public} = T - G$
3. $Y = C + I + G + NX$
4. $NX = NFI$

Because national saving (S) appears in the saving and investment equation, we need to find an equation for it in terms of the other variables. Adding equation 1. plus equation 2. yields national saving:

$$S = S_{private} + S_{public} = (Y - C - T) + (T - G) = Y - C - G.$$

Step 3: **Use the result from step 2 to derive an expression for national saving in terms of investment (I) and net exports (NX).** Because GDP (Y) does not appear in the saving and investment equation, we need to substitute the expression for it given in equation 3.:

$$S = (C + I + G + NX) - C - G$$

and simplify:

$$S = I + NX.$$

Step 4: **Use the results of steps 2 and 3 to derive the saving and investment equation.** Finally, substitute net foreign investment for net exports:

$$S = I + NFI.$$

YOUR TURN: For more practice, do related problem 3.8 on page 1035 at the end of this chapter.

>> End Solved Problem 29-3

A country such as the United States that has negative net foreign investment must be saving less than it is investing domestically. To see this, rewrite the saving and investment equation by moving domestic investment to the left side:

$$S - I = NFI.$$

If net foreign investment is negative—as it is for the United States nearly every year—domestic investment (I) must be greater than national saving (S).

The level of saving in Japan has been well above domestic investment. The result has been high levels of Japanese net foreign investment. For example, Japanese automobile companies Toyota, Honda, and Nissan have all constructed factories in the United States. Sony purchased the Columbia Pictures film studio. Japanese investors are also estimated to hold more than $200 billion worth of U.S. Treasury bonds. Japan has made many similar investments in countries around the world, which has sometimes caused resentment in these countries. There were some protests in the United States in the 1980s, for example, when Japanese investors purchased the Pebble Beach golf course in California and the Rockefeller Center complex in New York City.

Japan needs a high level of net exports to help offset a low level of domestic investment. When exports of a product begin to decline and imports begin to increase, governments are often tempted to impose tariffs or quotas to reduce imports. (See Chapter 8 to review tariffs and quotas and their negative effects on the economy.) In fact, many Japanese firms have been urging the Japanese government to impose trade restrictions on exports from China.

29.4 LEARNING OBJECTIVE

29.4 | Explain the effect of a government budget deficit on investment in an open economy.

The Effect of a Government Budget Deficit on Investment

The link we have just developed among saving, investment, and net foreign investment can help us understand some of the effects of changes in a government's budget deficit. When the government runs a budget deficit, national saving will decline unless private saving increases by the amount of the budget deficit, which is unlikely. As the saving and investment equation ($S = I + NFI$) shows, the result of a decline in national saving must be a decline in either domestic investment or net foreign investment. Why, though, does an increase in the government budget deficit cause a fall in domestic investment or net foreign investment?

To understand the answer to this question, remember that if the federal government runs a budget deficit, the U.S. Treasury must raise an amount equal to the deficit by selling bonds. To attract investors, the Treasury may have to raise the interest rates on its bonds. As interest rates on Treasury bonds rise, other interest rates, including those on corporate bonds and bank loans, will also rise. Higher interest rates will discourage some firms from borrowing funds to build new factories or to buy new equipment or computers. Higher interest rates on financial assets in the United States will attract foreign investors. Investors in Canada, Japan, or China will have to buy U.S. dollars to be able to purchase bonds in the United States. This greater demand for dollars will increase their value relative to foreign currencies. As the value of the dollar rises, exports from the United States will fall, and imports to the United States will rise. Net exports and, therefore, net foreign investment will fall.

When a government budget deficit leads to a decline in net exports, the result is sometimes referred to as the *twin deficits*, which refers to the possibility that a government budget deficit will also lead to a current account deficit. The twin deficits idea first became widely discussed in the United States during the early 1980s when the federal government ran a large budget deficit that resulted in high interest rates, a high exchange value of the dollar, and a large current account deficit.

Figure 29-5 shows that in the early 1980s, the United States had large federal budget deficits and large current account deficits. The figure also shows, however, that the twin deficits idea does not match the experience of the United States after 1990. The large federal budget deficits of the early 1990s occurred at a time of relatively small current

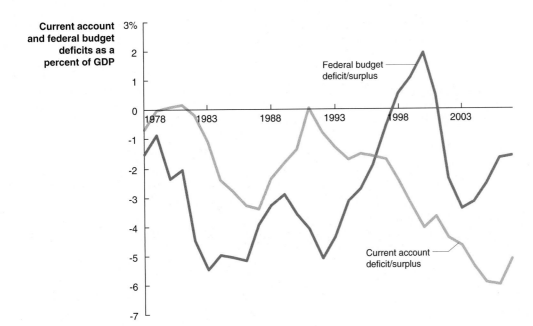

Figure 29-5 | The Twin Deficits, 1978–2007

During the early 1980s, large federal budget deficits occurred at the same time as large current account deficits, but twin deficits did not occur in the 1990s.
Source: U.S. Bureau of Economic Analysis.

account deficits, and the budget surpluses of the late 1990s occurred at a time of then-record current account deficits. Both the current account deficit and the federal budget deficit increased in the early 2000s, but the federal budget deficit declined in the mid-2000s much more than did the current account deficit.

The experience of other countries also shows only mixed support for the twin deficits idea. Germany ran large budget deficits and large current account deficits during the early 1990s, but both Canada and Italy ran large budget deficits during the 1980s without running current account deficits. The saving and investment equation shows that an increase in the government budget deficit will not lead to an increase in the current account deficit, provided that either private saving increases or domestic investment declines. According to the twin deficits idea, when the federal government ran budget surpluses in the late 1990s, the current account should also have been in surplus, or at least the current account deficit should have been small. In fact, the increase in national saving due to the budget surpluses was more than offset by a sharp decline in private saving, and the United States ran very large current account deficits.

Making **the** **Connection** | ## Why Is the United States Called the "World's Largest Debtor"?

The following graph shows the current account balance as a percentage of GDP for the United States for the period 1950–2007. The United States has had a current account deficit every year since 1982, with the exception of 1991. Between 1950 and 1975, the United States ran a current account deficit in only five years. Many economists believe that the current account deficits of the 1980s were closely related to the federal budget deficits of those years. High interest rates attracted foreign investors to U.S. bonds, which raised the exchange rate between the dollar and foreign currencies. The high exchange rate reduced U.S. exports and increased imports, leading to current account deficits.

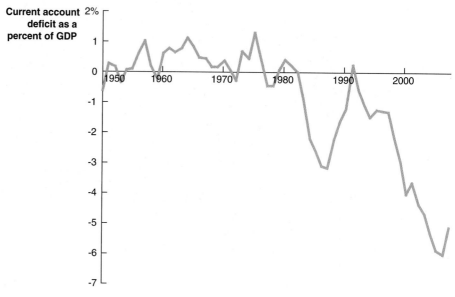

Source: Bureau of Economic Analysis.

As the federal budget deficit narrowed in the mid-1990s and disappeared in the late 1990s, the foreign exchange value of the dollar remained high—and large current account deficits continued—because foreign investors persisted in investing in the United States despite low interest rates. In the late 1990s, a number of countries around the world, such as South Korea, Indonesia, Brazil, and Russia, suffered severe economic problems. In a process known as a *flight to quality*, many investors sold their investments in those countries and bought investments in the United States. In addition, the strong performance of the U.S. stock market through the spring of 2000 attracted many investors. Finally, the sharp decline in private saving in the United States that began during the late 1990s also contributed to the U.S. current account deficit. The sharp decline in the value of the dollar during 2007 and 2008 helped reduce the size of the current account deficit, although the deficit still remained substanital.

Large current account deficits have resulted in foreign investors purchasing large amounts of U.S. assets.

Do persistent current account deficits represent a problem for the United States? Current account deficits result in U.S. net foreign investment being negative. Each year, foreign investors accumulate many more U.S. assets than U.S. investors accumulate foreign assets. At the end of 2007, foreign investors owned about $2.9 trillion more of U.S. assets—such as stocks, bonds, and factories—than U.S. investors owned of foreign assets, which is why the United States is sometimes called "the world's largest debtor." But the continued willingness of foreign investors to buy U.S. stocks and bonds and foreign companies to build factories in the United States can be seen as a vote of confidence in the strength of the U.S. economy and the buying power of U.S. consumers. With private saving rates having declined in the United States to historically low levels, only the continued flow of funds from foreign investors has made it possible for the United States to maintain the high levels of domestic investment required for economic growth.

YOUR TURN: Test your understanding by doing related problem 4.6 on page 1036 at the end of this chapter.

29.5 | Discuss the difference between the effectiveness of monetary
and fiscal policy in an open economy and in a closed economy.

Monetary Policy and Fiscal Policy in an Open Economy

When we discussed monetary and fiscal policy in Chapters 26 and 27, we did not emphasize that the United States is an open economy. Now that we have explored some of the links between economies, we can look at the difference between how monetary and fiscal policy work in an open economy as opposed to a closed economy. Economists refer to the ways in which monetary and fiscal policy affect the domestic economy as *policy channels*. An open economy has more policy channels than does a closed economy.

Monetary Policy in an Open Economy

When the Federal Reserve engages in an expansionary monetary policy, it buys Treasury securities to lower interest rates and stimulate aggregate demand. In a closed economy, the main effect of lower interest rates is on domestic investment spending and purchases of consumer durables. In an open economy, lower interest rates will also affect the exchange rate between the dollar and foreign currencies. Lower interest rates will cause some investors in the United States and abroad to switch from investing in U.S. financial assets to investing in foreign financial assets. This switch will lower the demand for the dollar relative to foreign currencies and cause its value to decline. A lower exchange rate will decrease the price of U.S. products in foreign markets and increase the price of foreign products in the United States. As a result, net exports will increase. This additional policy channel will increase the ability of an expansionary monetary policy to affect aggregate demand.

When the Fed wants to reduce the rate of economic growth to reduce inflation, it engages in contractionary monetary policy. The Fed sells Treasury securities to increase interest rates and reduce aggregate demand. In a closed economy, the main effect is once again on domestic investment spending and purchases of consumer durables. In an open economy, higher interest rates will lead to a higher foreign exchange value of the dollar. The prices of U.S. products in foreign markets will increase, and the prices of foreign products in the U.S. will fall. As a result, net exports will fall. The contractionary policy will have a larger impact on aggregate demand, and therefore it will be more effective in slowing down the growth in economic activity. To summarize: *Monetary policy has a greater impact on aggregate demand in an open economy than in a closed economy.*

Fiscal Policy in an Open Economy

To engage in an expansionary fiscal policy, the federal government increases its purchases or cuts taxes. Increases in government purchases directly increase aggregate demand. Tax cuts increase aggregate demand by increasing household disposable income and business income, which results in increased consumption spending and investment spending. An expansionary fiscal policy may result in higher interest rates. In a closed economy, the main effect of higher interest rates is to reduce domestic investment spending and purchases of consumer durables. In an open economy, higher interest rates will also lead to an increase in the foreign exchange value of the dollar and a decrease in net exports. Therefore, in an open economy, an expansionary fiscal policy may be less effective because the *crowding out effect* may be larger. In a closed economy, only consumption and investment are crowded out by an expansionary fiscal policy. In an open economy, net exports may also be crowded out.

The government can fight inflation by using a contractionary fiscal policy to slow the rate of economic growth. A contractionary fiscal policy cuts government purchases or raises taxes to reduce household disposable income and consumption spending. It also reduces the federal budget deficit (or increases the budget surplus), which may lower interest rates. Lower interest rates will increase domestic investment and purchases of consumer durables, thereby offsetting some of the reduction in government spending and increases in taxes. In an open economy, lower interest rates will also reduce the foreign exchange value of the dollar and increase net exports. Therefore, in an open economy, a contractionary fiscal policy will have a smaller impact on aggregate demand and therefore will be less effective in slowing down an economy. In summary: *Fiscal policy has a smaller impact on aggregate demand in an open economy than in a closed economy.*

Economics in YOUR Life!

>> Continued from page 1007

At the beginning of the chapter, we posed this question: What effect will the Bank of Korea's decision to sell its U.S. Treasury bonds likely have on the interest rate that you pay on your car loan? To sell its holdings of Treasury bonds, South Korea's central bank may have to offer them at a lower price. When the prices of bonds fall, the interest rates on them rise. As the interest rates on U.S. Treasury bonds increase, the interest rates on corporate bonds and bank loans, including car loans, may also increase. So, the decision of the Bank of Korea has the potential to increase the interest rate you pay on your car loan. In practice, the interest rate on your car loan is likely to be affected only if the Bank of Korea sells a very large number of bonds and if investors consider it likely that other foreign central banks may soon do the same thing. The basic point is important, however: Economies are interdependent, and interest rates in the United States are not determined entirely by the actions of people in the United States.

Conclusion

At one time, U.S. policymakers—and economics textbooks—ignored the linkages between the United States and other economies. In the modern world, these linkages have become increasingly important, and economists and policymakers must take them into account when analyzing the economy. In the next chapter, we will discuss further how the international financial system operates.

Read *An Inside Look* on the next page for a discussion of how the U.S. current account deficit affects global investors.

Can the U.S. Current Account Deficit Be Sustained?

ECONOMIST, MARCH 15, 2007

Sustaining the Unsustainable

Sour subprime mortgages, sluggish retail sales, the spectre of a broader retreat in credit and consumer spending. These are the American shadows that spooked investors across the globe this week, once again sending share prices tumbling from Manhattan to Mumbai.

(a) For years, the longest shadow of all was cast by America's imposing current-account deficit. But in these fretful times, no one seems to be fretting much about the country's heavy reliance on foreign funding. New figures released on March 14th showed that Americans spent some $857 billion more than they produced in 2006, the equivalent of 6.5% of GDP, and a new record. . . .

China's government, one of America's best creditors, has announced it is seeking a better return on a chunk of its foreign-exchange reserves. It will create a new investment agency, which looks sure to diversify some of the central bank's assets out of the American Treasury bonds that now dominate its portfolio. . . .

(b) None of this had much effect on the dollar. Measured on a trade-weighted basis, it has fallen by a mere 0.04% since the recent financial turbulence began on February 27th. And as investors yawn at America's deficit, so too do policymakers. A year ago, finance ministers and central bankers from the G7 group of big, rich countries promised to take "vigorous action" to resolve the imbalances between the world's savers (particularly China, Japan and the oil exporters) and borrowers (especially America). The IMF was hoping to reinvent itself as the overseer of this grand macroeconomic bargain. A year later the venture has fizzled. . . .

What explains this nonchalance? By some measures, the world is already rebalancing. The dollar after all has fallen by 16% from its 2002 peak in real terms. Compared with the previous quarter, America's current-account deficit shrank in the last three months of 2006 and was below $200 billion for the first time in more than a year. . . . That decline owes a lot to lower oil prices. But even excluding oil, America's trade balance seems to be stabilising as exports boom and imports slow. . . . A few years ago most economists argued that the spectacle of poor countries bankrolling America's deficits was the perverse and unsustainable consequence of American profligacy. Economic theory suggested that capital should flow from rich countries to poor ones, and that America could not increase its foreign borrowing forever. Empirical studies showed that deficits of more than 5% of GDP caused trouble.

Since then, economists have vied with each other to overturn this orthodoxy. Indeed, rejecting the conventional wisdom is now itself entirely conventional, as Jeffrey Frankel, an economist at Harvard University, has pointed out. . . .

In 2005 Ben Bernanke, now chairman of the Federal Reserve, pointed out that global interest rates were oddly low, suggesting a glut of saving abroad, not a shortfall of saving at home, was responsible for the flow of capital to America.

More recent papers have picked up similar threads, arguing that imbalances might prove to be both more persistent and less perverse than once thought. A study last summer by three economists at the IMF, for instance, showed that poor countries which export capital have grown faster than those which rely on importing it from abroad.

(c) One reason may be the feebleness of their financial markets. That is a thesis explored by Ricardo Caballero and Emmanuel Farhi of the Massachusetts Institute of Technology, as well as Pierre-Olivier Gourinchas of the University of California, Berkeley. They point out that emerging economies have been frantically accumulating real assets, such as assembly lines and office towers, but their generation of financial assets has not kept pace. Thanks to weak property rights, fear of expropriation and poor bankruptcy procedures, many newly rich countries are unable to create enough trustworthy claims on their future incomes. Lacking vehicles for saving at home, the thrifty buy assets abroad instead. In China, Mr. Caballero argues, this is done indirectly through the state, which buys foreign securities, such as Treasuries, then issues bonds of its own, which are held by Chinese banks, companies and households.

Because emerging economies' supply of financial instruments is so unreliable, people may hoard more of them as a precautionary measure. Firms and households fear they will not be able to borrow to tide themselves over bad times, therefore they choose to save for a rainy day instead. Because they cannot transfer purchasing power from the future to the present, they must store it from the past. . . .

Key Points in the Article

This article discusses the U.S. balance of payments and, in particular, the country's large current account deficit. The U.S. current account deficit in 2006 was $857 billion, or 6.5 percent of U.S. GDP. The article explains why economists have long argued that large current account deficits are unsustainable and why some economists believe that the U.S. current account deficit may prove to be the exception to this rule.

Analyzing the News

(a) Most macroeconomists contend that large deficits in a country's current account—the part of the balance of payments that records a country's net exports, net investment income, and net transfers—are unsustainable. This is because a country's current account deficit is matched by foreigners' (net) purchases of the country's real and financial assets. Hence, current account deficits can last only as long as foreigners are willing to hold the deficit country's currency, which typically decreases in value as its supply in the world market increases. For example, the U.S. current account deficit in 2006 was $857 billion, or 6.5 percent of U.S. GDP.

(b) As the U.S. current account deficit increases, so does the supply of U.S. dollars in the foreign exchange market. And, as you read in this chapter, an increase in the supply of dollars decreases the foreign exchange value of the dollar. Nonetheless, despite the growing U.S. current account deficit and, the resulting increase in the supply of U.S. dollars, the foreign exchange value of the U.S. dollar has not fallen as much as most economists and policymakers had expected. This pattern is shown in the figure below, where the trade-weighted exchange value of the U.S. dollar remained relatively stable through 2005 and 2006, during which time the U.S. current account deficit continued to increase. (The trade-weighted exchange rate shows the value of the U.S. dollar against an average of other countries' currencies, with the average determined by how much trade the United States does with each country.) This apparent resilience of the U.S. dollar has—for better or worse—eased the concerns of policymakers.

(c) Economists have developed several theories that explain why the U.S. dollar remains so resilient and, consequently, the United States continues to run a current account deficit. One explanation focuses on the fact that many investors in developing countries are unable to buy stocks and bonds issued by domestic firms because relatively weak property rights and court systems have made it difficult for financial markets to function in these countries So, investors in developing countries who wish to buy stocks and bonds have chosen to invest abroad, particularly in the United States. This explains, in part, foreigners' willingness to hold U.S. dollars, despite the enormous current account deficit of the United States.

Thinking Critically

1. Suppose the foreign exchange value of the U.S. dollar fell to an extent that reflected the country's large current account deficit. What segment of the U.S. economy would, all else being equal, benefit from such an adjustment? Why?

2. As you read in this article, the United States has a larger trade deficit with China than with any other country. How would China's economy be affected by a significant decline in the value of the U.S. dollar? Briefly explain your reasoning.

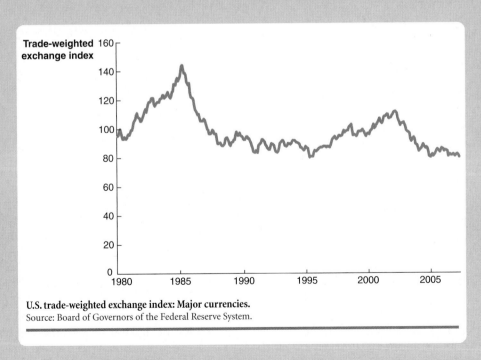

U.S. trade-weighted exchange index: Major currencies.
Source: Board of Governors of the Federal Reserve System.

Key Terms

Balance of payments, p. 1008

Balance of trade, p. 1008

Capital account, p. 1011

Closed economy, p. 1008

Currency appreciation, p. 1016

Currency depreciation, p. 1016

Current account, p. 1008

Financial account, p. 1010

Net foreign investment, p. 1010

Nominal exchange rate, p. 1013

Open economy, p. 1008

Real exchange rate, p. 1020

Saving and investment equation, p. 1022

Speculators, p. 1016

29.1 LEARNING OBJECTIVE   29.1 | Explain how the balance of payments is calculated, **pages 1008–1012.**

The Balance of Payments: Linking the United States to the International Economy

Summary

Nearly all economies are **open economies** that trade with and invest in other economies. A **closed economy** has no transactions in trade or finance with other economies. The **balance of payments** is the record of a country's trade with other countries in goods, services, and assets. The **current account** records a country's net exports, net investment income, and net transfers. The **financial account** shows investments a country has made abroad and foreign investments received by the country. The **balance of trade** is the difference between the value of the goods a country exports and the value of the goods a country imports. **Net foreign investment** is the difference between capital outflows from a country and capital inflows. The **capital account** is a part of the balance of payments that records relatively minor transactions. Apart from measurement errors, the sum of the current account and the financial account must equal zero. Therefore, the balance of payments must also equal zero.

myeconlab Visit www.myeconlab.com to complete these exercises
Get Ahead of the Curve online and get instant feedback.

Review Questions

1.1 What is the relationship among the current account, the financial account, and the balance of payments?

1.2 What is the difference between net exports and the current account balance?

1.3 Explain why you agree or disagree with the following statement: "The United States has run a balance of payments deficit every year since 1982."

Problems and Applications

1.4 In 2007, France had a current account deficit of $31 billion. Did France experience a net capital outflow or a net capital inflow during 2007? Briefly explain.

1.5 Use the information in the following table to prepare a balance of payments account, like the one shown in

Table 29-1 on page 1009. Assume that the balance on the capital account is zero.

Increase in foreign holdings of assets in the United States	$1,181
Exports of goods	856
Imports of services	−256
Statistical discrepancy	?
Net transfers	−60
Exports of services	325
Income received on investments	392
Imports of goods	−1,108
Increase in U.S. holdings of assets in foreign countries	−1,040
Income payments on investments	−315

1.6 (Related to the *Don't Let This Happen to You!* on page 1013) In 2007, Germany had a trade surplus of $282 billion and a current account balance of $252 billion. Explain how Germany's current account surplus could be smaller than its trade surplus. In 2007, would we expect that Germany's balance on financial account would have been −$252 billion? Briefly explain.

1.7 (Related to *Solved Problem 29-1* on page 1012) Is it possible for a country to run a trade deficit and a financial account deficit simultaneously? Briefly explain.

1.8 (Related to *Solved Problem 29-1* on page 1012) Suppose we know that a country has been receiving large inflows of foreign investment. What can we say about its current account balance?

1.9 (Related to *Solved Problem 29-1* on page 1012) The United States ran a current account surplus every year during the 1960s. What must have been true about the U.S. financial account balance during those years?

1.10 The only year since 1982 that the United States has run a current account surplus was 1991. In that year, Japan made a large payment to the United States to help pay for the Gulf War. Explain the connection between these two facts. (*Hint:* Where would Japan's payment to the United States appear in the balance of payments?)

1.11 According to this chapter, the U.S. trade deficit is almost always larger than the U.S. current account deficit. Why is this true?

1.12 According to an article in *BusinessWeek*, "The U.S. is depending on an ever-rising influx of foreign funds to pay for all the imported automobiles, TVs, and clothing that U.S. consumers crave." Convert this sentence into a statement about changes in the U.S. current account and the U.S. financial account.

Source: Rich Miller and David Fairlamb, "The Greenback's Setback: Cause for Concern?" *BusinessWeek*, May 20, 2002, p. 44.

>> End Learning Objective 29.1

29.2 LEARNING OBJECTIVE | 29.2 | Explain how exchange rates are determined and how changes in exchange rates affect the prices of imports and exports, **pages 1012–1020.**

The Foreign Exchange Market and Exchange Rates

Summary

The **nominal exchange rate** is the value of one country's currency in terms of another country's currency. The exchange rate is determined in the foreign exchange market by the demand and supply of a country's currency. Changes in the exchange rate are caused by shifts in demand or supply. The three main sets of factors that cause the supply and demand curves in the foreign exchange market to shift are changes in the demand for U.S.-produced goods and services and change in the demand for foreign-produced goods and services; changes in the desire to invest in the United States and changes in the desire to invest in foreign countries; and changes in the expectations of currency traders—particularly **speculators**—concerning the likely future values of the dollar and the likely future values of foreign currencies. **Currency appreciation** occurs when a currency's market value increases relative to another currency. **Currency depreciation** occurs when a currency's market value decreases relative to another currency. The **real exchange rate** is the price of domestic goods in terms of foreign goods. The real exchange rate is calculated by multiplying the nominal exchange rate by the ratio of the domestic price level to the foreign price level.

myeconlab Visit www.myeconlab.com to complete these exercises
Get Ahead of the Curve online and get instant feedback.

Review Questions

2.1 If the exchange rate between the Japanese yen and the U.S. dollar expressed in terms of yen per dollar is ¥110 = $1, what is the exchange rate when expressed in terms of dollars per yen?

2.2 Suppose that the current exchange rate between the dollar and the euro is 1.1 euros per dollar. If the exchange rate changes to 1.2 euros per dollar, has the euro appreciated or depreciated against the dollar?

2.3 What are the three main sets of factors that cause the supply and demand curves in the foreign exchange market to shift?

Problems and Applications

2.4 (Related to the *Don't Let This Happen to You!* on page 1015) If we know the exchange rate between Country A's currency and Country B's currency and we know the exchange rate between Country B's currency and Country C's currency, then we can compute the exchange rate between Country A's currency and Country C's currency.

   a. Suppose the exchange rate between the Japanese yen and the U.S. dollar is currently ¥120 = $1 and the exchange rate between the British pound and the U.S. dollar is £0.60 = $1. What is the exchange rate between the yen and the pound?

   b. Suppose the exchange rate between the yen and dollar changes to ¥130 = $1 and the exchange rate between the pound and dollar changes to £0.50 = $1. Has the dollar appreciated or depreciated against the yen? Has the dollar appreciated or depreciated against the pound? Has the yen appreciated or depreciated against the pound?

2.5 (Related to the *Making the Connection* on page 1014) Beginning January 1, 2002, 12 of the 15 member countries of the European Union eliminated their own individual currencies and began using a new common currency, the euro. For a three-year period from January 1, 1999, through December 31, 2001, these 12 countries priced goods and services in terms of both their own currencies and the euro. During this period, the value of their currencies was fixed against each other and against the euro. So during this time, the dollar had an exchange rate against each of these currencies and against the euro. The information in the following table shows the fixed exchange rates of four European currencies against the euro and their exchange rates against the U.S. dollar on March 2, 2001. Use the information on the next page to calculate the exchange rate between the dollar and the euro (in euros per dollar) on March 2, 2001.

CURRENCY	UNITS PER EURO (FIXED)	UNITS PER U.S. DOLLAR (AS OF MARCH 2, 2001)
German mark	1.9558	2.0938
French franc	6.5596	7.0223
Italian lira	1,936.2700	2,072.8700
Portuguese escudo	200.4820	214.6300

2.6 Graph the demand and supply of U.S. dollars for euros and label each axis. Show graphically and explain the effect of an increase in interest rates in Europe by the European Central Bank (ECB) on the demand and supply of dollars and the resulting change in the exchange rate of euros for U.S. dollars.

2.7 Graph the demand and supply of U.S. dollars for euros and label each axis. Show graphically and explain the effect of an increase in U.S. government budget deficits that increase U.S. interest rates on the demand and supply of dollars and the resulting change in the exchange rate of euros for U.S. dollars. Why might the change in the exchange rate lead to a current account deficit?

2.8 Use the graph to answer the following questions.

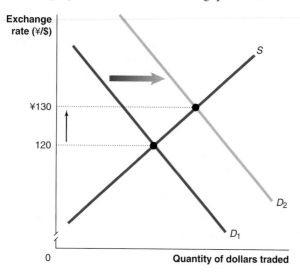

a. Briefly explain whether the dollar appreciated or depreciated against the yen.
b. Which of the following events could have caused the shift in demand shown in the graph?
   i. Interest rates in the United States have declined.
   ii. Income rises in Japan.
   iii. Speculators begin to believe the value of the dollar will be higher in the future.

2.9 **(Related to *Solved Problem* 29-2 on page 1020)** When a country's currency appreciates, is this generally good news or bad news for the country's consumers? Is it generally good news or bad news for the country's businesses? Explain your reasoning.

2.10 The following appeared in an article in the *Wall Street Journal*: ". . . Japanese exporters got a lift from the sagging yen."
a. What does the reporter mean by a "sagging yen"?

b. Why would the yen's sagging help Japanese exporters?

Source: Tim Annett, "Housing Still Hurting," *Wall Street Journal*, February 22, 2007.

2.11 **(Related to the *Chapter Opener* on page 1006)** Some U.S. firms, such as the paper manufacturer NewPage, argued that the Chinese government was keeping the value of the yuan artificially low against the dollar, which gave Chinese exporters an advantage when selling their products in the United States. Why would a low value of the yuan in exchange for the dollar help Chinese firms exporting to the United States?

2.12 Phil Treadway is president and owner of Erie Molded Plastics, Inc., which is located in Erie, Pennsylvania, and makes electrical connectors and plastic bottle caps. Treadway was quoted as follows in the *New York Times*: "Our customers have a market without borders, and we know that. We can compete against China's low labor costs. . . . But we cannot compete with them if they have a 20 percent to 40 percent currency advantage." What does Treadway mean by a "currency advantage"? How would a currency advantage make it hard for his firm to compete with Chinese firms?

Source: Elizabeth Becker and Edmund L. Andrews, "Currency of China Is Emerging as Tough Business Issue in U.S.," *New York Times*, August 26, 2003.

2.13 **(Related to the *Making the Connection* on page 1017)** An article in the Wall Street Journal contained the following observations on the foreign exchange market:

> Many eyes in currency markets Friday were on Mexico, where the dollar fell below 10 pesos for the first time since October 2002. . . . The peso's rise to its strongest level in nearly six years has been largely attributed to the widening of yield spreads—U.S. interest rates have been kept low to counter economic weakness, and the Bank of Mexico has raised rates to keep inflation expectations in check.
>
> Over in Australia, however, the U.S. dollar came out on the winning end Friday. Australia's dollar fell to a 2 1/2-month low of $0.9298 Friday as investors began betting that Australia's central bank may reduce its relatively high lending rates before the end of the year.

Why would interest rates in Mexico being higher than interest rates in the United States cause the value of the peso to be high relative to the U.S. dollar? Why would the expectation that Australia's central bank will reduce its lending rates cause the value of the Australian dollar to fall relative to the value of the U.S. dollar?

Source: Dan Molinski, "Jobs Data Lift Dollar Against Euro," *Wall Street Journal*, August 1, 2008.

The International Sector and National Saving and Investment

Summary

A current account deficit must be exactly offset by a financial account surplus. The financial account is equal to net capital flows, which is equal to net foreign investment but with the opposite sign. Because the current account balance is roughly equal to net exports, we can conclude that net exports will equal net foreign investment. National saving is equal to private saving plus government saving. Private saving is equal to national income minus consumption and minus taxes. Government saving is the difference between taxes and government spending. As we saw in previous chapters, GDP (or national income) is equal to the sum of investment, consumption, government spending, and net exports. We can use this fact, our definitions of private and government saving, and the fact that net exports equal net foreign investment, to arrive at an important relationship known as the **saving and investment equation**: $S = I + NFI$.

myeconlab Visit www.myeconlab.com to complete these exercises
Get Ahead of the Curve online and get instant feedback.

Review Questions

3.1 Explain the relationship between net exports and net foreign investment.

3.2 What is the saving and investment equation? If national saving declines, what will happen to domestic investment and net foreign investment?

3.3 If a country saves more than it invests domestically, what must be true of its net foreign investment?

Problems and Applications

3.4 Writing in the *Wall Street Journal*, David Wessel makes the following observation:

> Trend one: The U.S. has been buying more than $1 billion a day more from the rest of the world than it has been selling. . . .
> Trend two: Foreigners have been investing more than $1 billion a day of their savings in U.S. stocks, bonds, office towers, factories, and companies.

Is it coincidence that both of his "trends" involve $1 billion per day? Briefly explain.

Source: David Wessel, "Pain from the Dollar's Decline Will Mostly Be Felt Overseas," *Wall Street Journal*, June 13, 2002.

3.5 In 2006, domestic investment in Japan was 24.1 percent of GDP, and Japanese net foreign investment was

3.9 percent of GDP. What percentage of GDP was Japanese national saving?

3.6 In 2006, France's net foreign investment was negative. Which was larger in France in 2006: national saving or domestic investment? Briefly explain.

3.7 Briefly explain whether you agree with the following statement: "Because in 2006 national saving was a smaller percentage of GDP in the United States than in the United Kingdom, domestic investment must also have been a smaller percentage of GDP in the United States than in the United Kingdom."

3.8 (Related to *Solved Problem 29-3* on page 1023) Look again at Solved Problem 29-3, in which we derived the saving and investment equation $S = I + NX$. In deriving this equation, we assumed that national income was equal to Y. But Y only includes income *earned* by households. In the modern U.S. economy, households receive substantial transfer payments—such as Social Security payments and unemployment insurance payments—from the government. Suppose that we define national income to be equal to $Y + TR$, where TR equals government transfer payments, and we also define government spending to be equal to $G + TR$. Show that after making these adjustments, we end up with the same saving and investment equation.

3.9 Use the saving and investment equation to explain why the United States experienced large current account deficits in the late 1990s.

3.10 Former Congressman and presidential candidate Richard Gephardt once proposed that tariffs be imposed on imports from countries with which the United States has a trade deficit. If this proposal were enacted and if it were to succeed in reducing the U.S. current account deficit to zero, what would be the likely effect on domestic investment spending within the United States? Assume that no other federal government economic policy is changed. (*Hint:* Use the saving and investment equation to answer this question.)

3.11 (Related to the *Chapter Opener* on page 1006) Suppose that the U.S. government decides to raise tariffs on Chinese exports of paper to the United States even higher. Discuss the impact on the following:
a. U.S. paper manufacturers
b. Chinese paper manufacturers
c. U.S. consumers
d. U.S. net exports
e. U.S. net foreign investment

3.12 According to an article in *BusinessWeek*, "In the past year, foreign purchases of stocks and bonds are down 24%, and foreign direct investment is off 63%. . . .

And a key victim is the dollar, down 12% vs. the euro and 10% vs. the yen." From the U.S. point of view, do the changes mentioned in the first sentence represent an increase or a decrease in net foreign investment?

Why would this change in net foreign investment cause the exchange value of the dollar to decline?

Source: James C. Cooper and Kathleen Madigan, "The Twin Deficits Are Back—And as Dangerous as Ever," *BusinessWeek*, July 8, 2002, pp. 29–30.

>> End Learning Objective 29.3

29.4 LEARNING OBJECTIVE   29.4 | Explain the effect of a government budget deficit on investment in an open economy, **pages 1024–1026.**

The Effect of a Government Budget Deficit on Investment

Summary

When the government runs a budget deficit, national saving will decline unless private saving increases by the full amount of the budget deficit, which is unlikely. As the saving and investment equation ($S = I + NFI$) shows, the result of a decline in national saving must be a decline in either domestic investment or net foreign investment.

myeconlab Visit www.myeconlab.com to complete these exercises *Get Ahead of the Curve* online and get instant feedback.

Review Questions

4.1 What happens to national saving when the government runs a budget surplus? What is the twin deficits idea? Did it hold for the United States in the 1990s? Briefly explain.

4.2 Why were the early and mid-1980s particularly difficult times for U.S. exporters?

Problems and Applications

4.3 Writing in the April 1997 issue of *International Economic Trends*, published by the Federal Reserve Bank of St. Louis, economist Michael Pakko observed the following:

> The current account . . . reached a deficit of $165 billion in 1996, second only to the deficit of $167 billion in 1987. . . . The evidence suggests that strong investment demand underlies the current economic expansion. Since the recession of 1990–91, real fixed investment spending has been growing at a rate of 6.9 percent . . . compared to 2.6 percent growth of GDP. . . .

Only time will tell what the payoff to these investments will be, but they do give some reason to interpret the U.S. current account deficit with less apprehension.

Why should the fact that investment spending in the United States has been strong reduce apprehension about the size of the current account deficit? What does the current account deficit have to do with investment spending?

4.4 Lee Morgan, chairman of Caterpillar, was quoted in 1985 as saying this of his company's difficulties in exporting: "We believe that there should be a 25% to 30% improvement in the exchange rate with the Japanese yen, because U.S. manufacturers are finding themselves disadvantaged by that amount." When Morgan talked about an "improvement" in the exchange rate between the dollar and the yen, did he want the dollar to exchange for more yen or for fewer yen? Why was the exchange value of the dollar particularly high during the mid-1980s?

4.5 The text states, "The budget surpluses of the late 1990s occurred at a time of then-record current account deficits." Holding everything else constant, what would the likely impact have been on domestic investment in the United States if the current account had been balanced instead of being in deficit?

4.6 (Related to the *Making the Connection* on page 1025) Why might "the continued willingness of foreign investors to buy U.S. stocks and bonds and foreign companies to build factories in the United States" result in the United States running a current account deficit?

>> End Learning Objective 29.4

29.5 LEARNING OBJECTIVE 29.5 | Discuss the difference between the effectiveness of monetary and fiscal policy in an open economy and in a closed economy, **pages 1027-1028.**

Monetary Policy and Fiscal Policy in an Open Economy

Summary

When the Federal Reserve engages in an expansionary monetary policy, it buys government bonds to lower interest rates and increase aggregate demand. In a closed economy, the main effect of lower interest rates is on domestic investment spending and purchases of consumer durables. In an open economy, lower interest rates will also cause an increase in net exports. When the Fed wants to slow the rate of economic growth to reduce inflation, it engages in a contractionary monetary policy. With a contractionary policy, the Fed sells government bonds to increase interest rates and reduce aggregate demand. In a closed economy, the main effect is once again on domestic investment and purchases of consumer durables. In an open economy, higher interest rates will also reduce net exports. We can conclude that monetary policy has a greater impact on aggregate demand in an open economy than in a closed economy. To engage in an expansionary fiscal policy, the government increases government spending or cuts taxes. An expansionary fiscal policy can lead to higher interest rates. In a closed economy, the main effect of higher interest rates is on domestic investment spending and spending on consumer durables. In an open economy, higher interest rates will also reduce net exports. A contractionary fiscal policy will reduce the budget deficit and may lower interest rates. In a closed economy, lower interest rates increase domestic investment and spending on consumer durables. In an open economy, lower interest rates also increase net exports. We can conclude that fiscal policy has a smaller impact on aggregate demand in an open economy than in a closed economy.

Ⓧ myeconlab Visit www.myeconlab.com to complete these exercises
Get Ahead of the Curve online and get instant feedback.

Review Questions

5.1 Why does monetary policy have a greater effect on aggregate demand in an open economy than in a closed economy?

5.2 Why does fiscal policy have a smaller impact in an open economy than in a closed economy?

Problems and Applications

5.3 What is meant by a "policy channel"? Why would an open economy have more policy channels than a closed economy?

5.4 Suppose that Federal Reserve policy leads to higher interest rates in the United States.
   a. How will this policy affect real GDP in the short run if the United States is a closed economy?
   b. How will this policy affect real GDP in the short run if the United States is an open economy?
   c. How will your answer to part b change if interest rates also rise in the countries that are the major trading partners of the United States?

5.5 An economist remarks, "In the 1960s, fiscal policy would have been a better way to stabilize the economy, but now I believe that monetary policy is better." What has changed about the U.S. economy that might have led the economist to this conclusion?

5.6 Suppose the federal government increases spending without also increasing taxes. In the short run, how will this action affect real GDP and the price level in a closed economy? How will the effects of this action differ in an open economy?

>> End Learning Objective 29.5

Chapter 30

The **International Financial System**

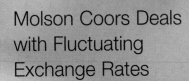

Molson Coors Deals with Fluctuating Exchange Rates

In 2004, two of North America's oldest brewers, Molson, Inc., based in Montreal, Canada, and Adolph Coors Company, based in Golden, Colorado, officially announced their plans to merge and create Molson Coors Brewing Company. Today, the combined company is the fifth-largest brewer in the world. It employs nearly 10,000 people, generates annual sales of nearly $6 billion, and operates breweries in Canada, the United Kingdom, and Golden, Colorado. The company sells 40 brands of beer in 30 markets across North America, Latin America, Europe, and Asia. Some of its most familiar brands are Molson Canadian and Carling, the best-selling beers in Canada and the United Kingdom, respectively, as well as Coors Original, Coors Light, Keystone, and Zima XXX. Because the company sells in many different markets, it is vulnerable to fluctuations in the foreign exchange value of the U.S. dollar. In its 2006 annual report to shareholders, the company noted that it faced risk from "exchange rate exposure which could materially and adversely affect [the company's] operating results." The

"exchange rate exposure" results from Molson Coors earning revenue and incurring costs in several currencies, particularly the U.S. dollar, the Canadian dollar, and the British pound. When the company converts its profits in the United Kingdom, Canada, and other countries into dollars, the amount of profits it earns depends on how many dollars it receives in exchange for those other currencies. For example, if the value of the dollar falls relative to the British pound, then Molson Coors' profits will rise because it receives more dollars when it converts the pounds it earns in the United Kingdom into U.S. dollars.

Before its merger with Coors, Molson had faced a different kind of exposure to fluctuating exchange rates. Molson had purchased the Montreal Canadiens hockey team in 1957. During the time Molson owned the team, it had to deal with a problem posed by a provision in the labor agreement between the National Hockey League and its players. This agreement required Molson to pay the Canadiens players in U.S. dollars rather than in Canadian dollars. Because the Canadiens play most of their games in the United States, many of the team's other expenses also had to be paid in U.S. dollars. Most

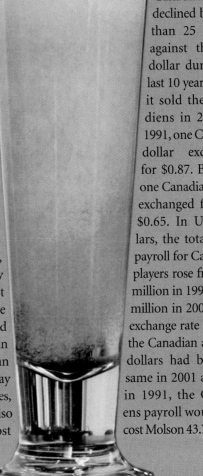

of the team's revenues from ticket sales and local television and radio broadcasts, however, were received in Canadian dollars.

Unfortunately for Molson, the value of the Canadian dollar declined by more than 25 percent against the U.S. dollar during the last 10 years before it sold the Canadiens in 2001. In 1991, one Canadian dollar exchanged for $0.87. By 2001, one Canadian dollar exchanged for only $0.65. In U.S. dollars, the total salary payroll for Canadiens players rose from $10 million in 1991 to $38 million in 2001. If the exchange rate between the Canadian and U.S. dollars had been the same in 2001 as it was in 1991, the Canadiens payroll would have cost Molson 43.7 million

Canadian dollars. Because of the decline in the value of the Canadian dollar, Molson actually had to pay 58.5 million to meet the Canadiens' payroll. In this chapter, we will explore why exchange rates fluctuate and how central banks sometimes intervene to try to control movements in exchange rates.

AN INSIDE LOOK AT POLICY on **page 1058** discusses whether governments should try to limit speculation in currencies.

Sources: Molson Coors Brewing Company, *Annual Report: 2006*; and "Lessons from a Lockout," *Economist*, July 21, 2005.

Economics in YOUR Life!

Exchange Rate Risk in Your Life

Suppose that you decide to take a job in Spain. Your plan is to work there for the next 10 years, build up some savings, and then return to the United States. As you prepare for your move, you read that economists expect the average productivity of Spanish firms to grow faster than the average productivity of U.S. firms over the next 10 years. If economists are correct, then, all else being equal, will the savings that you accumulate (in euros) be worth more or less in U.S. dollars than it would have been worth without the relative gains in Spanish productivity? As you read this chapter, see if you can answer this question. You can check your answer against the one we provide at the end of the chapter. **≫ Continued on page 1057**

A key fact about the international economy is that the exchange rates among the major currencies fluctuate. These fluctuations have important consequences for firms, consumers, and governments. In Chapter 29, we discussed the basics of how exchange rates are determined. We also looked at the relationship between a country's imports and exports, as well as at capital flows into and out of a country. In this chapter, we will look further at the international financial system and at the role central banks play in the system.

30.1 LEARNING OBJECTIVE

30.1 | Understand how different exchange rate systems operate.

Exchange Rate Systems

Floating currency The outcome of a country allowing its currency's exchange rate to be determined by demand and supply.

Exchange rate system An agreement among countries on how exchange rates should be determined.

Managed float exchange rate system The current exchange rate system, under which the value of most currencies is determined by demand and supply, with occasional government intervention.

Fixed exchange rate system A system under which countries agree to keep the exchange rates among their currencies fixed.

A country's exchange rate can be determined in several ways. Some countries simply allow the exchange rate to be determined by demand and supply, just as other prices are. A country that allows demand and supply to determine the value of its currency is said to have a **floating currency**. Some countries attempt to keep the exchange rate between their currency and another currency constant. For example, China kept the exchange rate constant between its currency, the yuan, and the U.S. dollar, from 1994 until 2005, when it announced it would allow greater exchange-rate flexibility. When countries can agree on how exchange rates should be determined, economists say that there is an **exchange rate system**. Currently, many countries, including the United States, allow their currencies to float most of the time, although they will occasionally intervene to buy and sell their currency or other currencies to affect exchange rates. In other words, many countries attempt to *manage* the float of their currencies. As a result, the current exchange rate system is a **managed float exchange rate system**.

Historically, the two most important alternatives to the managed float exchange rate system were the *gold standard* and the *Bretton Woods system*. These were both **fixed exchange rate systems**, where exchange rates remained constant for long periods. Under the gold standard, a country's currency consisted of gold coins and paper currency that the government was committed to redeem for gold. When countries agree to keep the value of their currencies constant, there is a fixed exchange rate system. The gold standard was a fixed exchange rate system that lasted from the nineteenth century until the 1930s.

Under the gold standard, exchange rates were determined by the relative amounts of gold in each country's currency, and the size of a country's money supply was determined by the amount of gold available. To rapidly expand its money supply during a war or an economic depression, a country would need to abandon the gold standard. Because of the Great Depression, by the mid-1930s, most countries, including the United States, had abandoned the gold standard. Although during the following decades there were occasional discussions about restoring the gold standard, no serious attempt to do so occurred.

A conference held in Bretton Woods, New Hampshire, in 1944 set up an exchange rate system in which the United States pledged to buy or sell gold at a fixed price of $35 per ounce. The central banks of all other members of the new Bretton Woods system pledged to buy and sell their currencies at a fixed rate against the dollar. By fixing their exchange rates against the dollar, these countries were fixing the exchange rates among their currencies as well. Unlike under the gold standard, neither the United States nor any other country was willing to redeem its paper currency for gold domestically. The United States would redeem dollars for gold only if they were presented by a foreign central bank. Fixed exchange rate regimes can run into difficulties because exchange rates are not free to adjust quickly to changes in demand and supply for currencies. As

Don't Let This Happen to **YOU!**

Remember That Modern Currencies Are Fiat Money

Although the United States has not been on the gold standard since 1933, many people still believe that somehow gold continues to "back" U.S. currency. The U.S. Department of the Treasury still owns billions of dollars worth of gold bars, most of which are stored at the Fort Knox Bullion Depository in Kentucky. (Even more gold is stored in a basement of the Federal Reserve Bank of New York, which holds about one-quarter of the world's gold supply—almost 10 percent of all the gold ever mined.

This gold, however, is entirely owned by foreign governments and international agencies.) The gold in Fort Knox no longer has any connection to the amount of paper money issued by the Federal Reserve. As we saw in Chapter 25, U.S. currency—like the currencies of other countries—is fiat money, which means it has no value except as money. The link between gold and money that existed for centuries has been broken in the modern economy.

YOUR TURN: Test your understanding by doing related problem 1.3 on page 1060 at the end of this chapter.

we will see in the next section, central banks often encounter difficulty if they are required to keep an exchange rate fixed over a period of years. By the early 1970s, the difficulty of keeping exchange rates fixed led to the end of the Bretton Woods system. The appendix to this chapter contains additional discussion of the gold standard and the Bretton Woods system.

30.2 | Discuss the three key features of the current exchange rate system.

30.2 LEARNING OBJECTIVE

The Current Exchange Rate System

The current exchange rate system has three important aspects:

1 The United States allows the dollar to float against other major currencies.

2 Most countries in Western Europe have adopted a single currency, the **euro**.

3 Some developing countries have attempted to keep their currencies' exchange rates fixed against the dollar or another major currency.

Euro The common currency of many European countries.

We begin our discussion of the current exchange rate system by looking at the changing value of the dollar over time. In discussing the value of the dollar, we can look further at what determines exchange rates in the short run and in the long run.

The Floating Dollar

Since 1973, the value of the U.S. dollar has fluctuated widely against other major currencies. Panel (a) of Figure 30-1 shows the exchange rate between the U.S. dollar and the Canadian dollar between 1973 and 2007, and panel (b) shows the exchange rate between the U.S. dollar and the Japanese yen for the same years. Remember that the dollar increases in value when it takes more units of foreign currency to buy $1, and it falls in value when it takes fewer units of foreign currency to buy $1. From the beginning of 1973 to the end of 2007, the U.S. dollar lost more than 60 percent in value against the yen, while it has ended up roughly constant in value against the Canadian dollar.

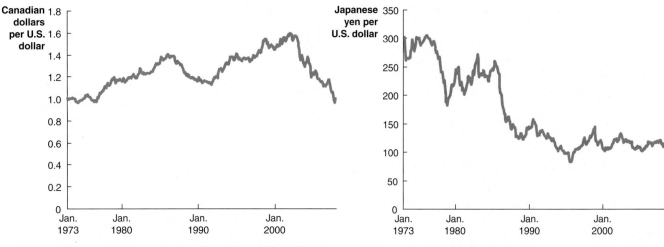

(a) The exchange rate between the Canadian dollar and the U.S. dollar   (b) The exchange rate between the Japanese yen and the U.S. dollar

Figure 30-1 | U.S. Dollar-Canadian Dollar and U.S. Dollar-Yen Exchange Rates, 1973–2007

Panel (a) shows that today the U.S. dollar has roughly the same value versus the Canadian dollar as it did at the end of the Bretton Woods system in 1973. Panel (b) shows during the same period, the U.S. dollar has lost value against the Japanese year.
Source: Federal Reserve Board of Governors.

The Toronto Blue Jays have benefited from the rising value of the Canadian dollar.

Making the Connection

The Toronto Blue Jays Gain from the Rising Value of the Canadian Dollar

In December 2000, the Canadian firm Rogers Communications, Inc., purchased the Toronto Blue Jays baseball team from Interbrew, a Canadian beer company. Rogers is based in Toronto and is the largest provider of cable television in Canada. We saw at the beginning of this chapter that Molson was hurt as the value of the Canadian dollar declined against the U.S. dollar for most of the period from 1991 to 2001, during which Molson owned the Montreal Canadiens ice hockey team. A close look at panel (a) of Figure 30-1 shows that Rogers was in a much better situation than Molson because after 2000, the number of Canadian dollars necessary to buy one U.S. dollar was declining; that is, the value of the Canadian dollar was rising. When Rogers bought the Blue Jays in December 2000, one Canadian dollar exchanged for $0.66. By July 2008, one Canadian dollar exchanged for $0.98, an increase of almost 50 percent.

Like the Canadiens, the Blue Jays have to pay their players in U.S. dollars and, because all the other major league baseball teams play in the United States, most of the Blue Jays' expenses for travel and lodging for their players also must be paid in U.S. dollars. In 2008, the total salary payroll for Blue Jays players was 97 million U.S. dollars. If the exchange rate between the Canadian and U.S. dollars had remained what it had been in December 2000, the Blue Jays payroll would have cost Rogers 147 million Canadian dollars. Because the Canadian dollar had risen in value against the U.S. dollar, Rogers actually only had to pay 99 million Canadian dollars. Rogers's other U.S. dollar expenses for the Blue Jays were correspondingly lower, and the firm benefited from the rise in the value of the Canadian dollar in other ways as well. The Blue Jays play spring training games in Dunedin, Florida. The high value of the Canadian dollar led many more Canadians to travel to Florida and buy tickets to the games there. Between 2004 and 2005 alone, ticket sales rose by nearly 33 percent. Overall, the Blue Jays improved from losing 71 million Canadian dollars in 2001 to making a profit of 33 million Canadian dollars in 2006. A team official attributed 70 percent of the improvement in the team's financial situation to the stronger Canadian dollar. Blue Jays president Paul Godfrey was quoted as saying: "We check the box scores first, then we check the attendance, and then we check the dollar." Of course, the Blue Jays remained vulnerable to the possibility that the Canadian dollar could again decline in value.

Sources: Joe Christensen, "Baseball Insider," *Knight Ridder Tribune Business News*, May 27, 2007; Rob Neyer, "Good Young Pitchers in Toronto's System," ESPN.com, August 8, 2005; and Alan Snel, "Springing Back," *Tampa Tribune*, March 14, 2005.

YOUR TURN: Test your understanding by doing related problem 2.7 on page 1061 at the end of this chapter.

What Determines Exchange Rates in the Long Run?

Over the past 30 years, why did the value of the U.S. dollar fall against the Japanese yen but end up roughly constant against the Canadian dollar? In the short run, the two most important causes of exchange rate movements are changes in interest rates—which cause investors to change their views of which countries' financial investments will yield the highest returns—and changes in investors' expectations about the future values of currencies. Over the long run, other factors are important in explaining movements in exchange rates.

The Theory of Purchasing Power Parity It seems reasonable that, in the long run, exchange rates should be at a level that makes it possible to buy the same amount of goods and services with the equivalent amount of any country's currency. In other words, the purchasing power of every country's currency should be the same. The idea that in the long run, exchange rates move to equalize the purchasing powers of different currencies is referred to as the theory of **purchasing power parity**.

Purchasing power parity The theory that in the long run, exchange rates move to equalize the purchasing powers of different currencies.

To make the theory of purchasing power parity clearer, consider a simple example. Suppose that a Hershey candy bar has a price of $1 in the United States and £1 in the United Kingdom and that the exchange rate is $1 per pound. In that case, at least with respect to candy bars, the dollar and the pound have equivalent purchasing power. If the price of a Hershey bar increases to £2 in the United Kingdom but stays at $1 in the United States, the exchange rate will have to change to £2 per $1 in order for the pound to maintain its relative purchasing power. As long as exchange rates adjust to reflect purchasing power, it will be possible to buy a Hershey bar for $1 in the United States or to exchange $1 for £2 and buy the candy bar in the United Kingdom.

If exchange rates are not at the values indicated by purchasing power parity, it appears that there are opportunities to make profits. For example, suppose a Hershey candy bar sells for £2 in the United Kingdom and $1 in the United States, and the exchange rate between the dollar and the pound is £1 = $1. In this case, it would be possible to exchange £1 million for $1 million and use the dollars to buy 1 million Hershey bars in the United States. The Hershey bars could then be shipped to the United Kingdom, where they could be sold for £2 million. The result of these transactions would be a profit of £1 million (ignoring any shipping costs). In fact, if the dollar–pound exchange rate does not reflect the purchasing power for many products—not just Hershey bars—this process could be repeated until extremely large profits were made. In practice, though, as people attempted to make these profits by exchanging pounds for dollars, they would bid up the value of the dollar until it reached the purchasing power exchange rate of £2 = $1. Once the exchange rate reflected the purchasing power of the two currencies, there would be no further opportunities for profit. This mechanism appears to guarantee that exchange rates will be at the levels determined by purchasing power parity.

Three real-world complications, though, keep purchasing power parity from being a complete explanation of exchange rates, even in the long run:

- *Not all products can be traded internationally.* Where goods are traded internationally, profits can be made whenever exchange rates do not reflect their purchasing power parity values. However, more than half of all goods and services produced in the United States and most other countries are not traded internationally. When goods are not traded internationally, their prices will not be the same in every country. For instance, suppose that the exchange rate is £1 for $1, but the price for having a cavity filled by a dentist is twice as high in the United States as it is in the United Kingdom. In this case, there is no way to buy up the low-priced British service and resell it in the United States. Because many goods and services are not traded internationally, exchange rates will not reflect exactly the relative purchasing powers of currencies.

- *Products and consumer preferences are different across countries.* We expect the same product to sell for the same price around the world, but if a product is similar but not identical to another product, their prices might be different. For example, a 3-ounce Hershey candy bar may sell for a different price in the United States than does a 3-ounce Cadbury candy bar in the United Kingdom. Prices of the same product may also differ across countries if consumer preferences differ. If consumers in the United Kingdom like candy bars more than do consumers in the United States, a Hershey candy bar may sell for more in the United Kingdom than in the United States.

Tariff A tax imposed by a government on imports.

Quota A government-imposed limit on the quantity of a good that can be imported.

- *Countries impose barriers to trade.* Most countries, including the United States, impose *tariffs* and *quotas* on imported goods. A **tariff** is a tax imposed by a government on imports. A **quota** is a limit on the quantity of a good that can be imported. For example, the United States has a quota on imports of sugar. As a result, the price of sugar in the United States is much higher than the price of sugar in other countries. Because of the quota, there is no way to buy up the cheap foreign sugar and resell it in the United States.

Making the Connection | The Big Mac Theory of Exchange Rates

In a lighthearted attempt to test the accuracy of the theory of purchasing power parity, the *Economist* magazine regularly compares the prices of Big Macs in different countries. If purchasing power parity holds, you should be able to take the dollars required to buy a Big Mac in the United States and exchange them for the amount of foreign currency needed to buy a Big Mac in any other country. The following table is for July 2008, when Big Macs were selling for an average price of $3.57 in the United States. The implied exchange rate shows what the exchange rate would be if purchasing power parity held for Big Macs. For example, a Big Mac sold for ¥280 in Japan and $3.57 in the United States, so for purchasing power parity to hold, the exchange rate should have been ¥280/$3.57, or ¥78 = $1. The actual exchange rate in July 2008 was ¥107 = $1. So, on Big Mac purchasing power parity grounds, the yen was *undervalued* against the dollar by 27 percent $(((¥107 - ¥78)/¥107) \times 100 = 27$ percent). That is, if Big Mac purchasing power parity held, it would have taken 27 percent fewer yen to buy a dollar than it actually did.

Could you take advantage of this difference between the purchasing power parity exchange rate and the actual exchange rate to become fabulously wealthy by buying up low-priced Big Macs in Tokyo and reselling them at a higher price in San Francisco? Unfortunately, the low-priced Japanese Big Macs would be a soggy mess by the time you got them to San Francisco. The fact that Big Mac prices are not the same around the world illustrates one reason why purchasing power parity does not hold exactly: Many goods are not traded internationally.

Is the price of a Big Mac in Beijing the same as the price of a Big Mac in Chicago?

COUNTRY	BIG MAC PRICE	IMPLIED EXCHANGE RATE	ACTUAL EXCHANGE RATE
Argentina	11.0 pesos	3.08 pesos per dollar	3.02 pesos per dollar
Japan	280 yen	78 yen per dollar	107 yen per dollar
Britain	2.29 pounds	0.64 pound per dollar	0.50 pound per dollar
Switzerland	6.50 Swiss francs	1.82 Swiss francs per dollar	1.02 Swiss francs per dollar
Indonesia	18,700 rupiahs	5,238 rupiahs per dollar	9,152 rupiahs per dollar
Canada	4.09 Canadian dollars	1.15 Canadian dollars per U.S. dollar	1.00 Canadian dollars per U.S. dollar
China	12.5 yuan	3.50 yuan per dollar	6.83 yuan per dollar

Source: "The Big Mac Index," *Economist*, July 24, 2008.

YOUR TURN: Test your understanding by doing related problem 2.13 on page 1061 at the end of this chapter.

Solved Problem | 30-2A

Calculating Purchasing Power Parity Exchange Rates Using Big Macs

Fill in the missing values in the following table. Remember that the implied exchange rate shows what the exchange rate would be if purchasing power parity held for Big Macs. Assume that the Big Mac is selling for $3.57 in the United States. Explain whether the U.S. dollar is overvalued or undervalued relative to each currency and predict what will happen in the future to each exchange rate. Finally, calculate the implied exchange rate between the Polish zloty and the Brazilian real and explain which currency is overvalued in terms of Big Mac purchasing power parity.

COUNTRY	BIG MAC PRICE	IMPLIED EXCHANGE RATE	ACTUAL EXCHANGE RATE
Brazil	7.50 reals		1.58 reals per dollar
Poland	7.00 zlotys		2.03 zlotys per dollar
South Korea	3,200 won		1,018 won per dollar
Czech Republic	66.1 korunas		14.5 korunas per dollar

SOLVING THE PROBLEM:

Step 1: **Review the chapter material.** This problem is about the theory of purchasing power parity as illustrated by prices of Big Macs, so you may want to review the sections "The Theory of Purchasing Power Parity," which begins on page 1043, and the *Making the Connection* "The Big Mac Theory of Exchange Rates," which begins on page 1044.

Step 2: **Fill in the table.** To calculate the purchasing power exchange rate, divide the foreign currency price of a Big Mac by the U.S. price. For example, the implied exchange rate between the Brazilian real and the U.S. dollar is 7.50 reals/$3.57, or 2.10 reals per dollar.

COUNTRY	BIG MAC PRICE	IMPLIED EXCHANGE RATE	ACTUAL EXCHANGE RATE
Brazil	7.50 reals	2.10 reals per dollar	1.58 reals per dollar
Poland	7.00 zlotys	1.96 zlotys per dollar	2.03 zlotys per dollar
South Korea	3,200 won	896 won per dollar	1,018 won per dollar
Czech Republic	66.1 korunas	18.5 korunas per dollar	14.5 korunas per dollar

Step 3: **Explain whether the U.S. dollar is overvalued or undervalued against the other currencies.** The dollar is overvalued if the actual exchange rate is greater than the implied exchange rate, and undervalued if the actual exchange rate is less than the implied exchange rate. In this case, the dollar is overvalued against the zloty and won, but undervalued against the real and the koruna. So, we would predict that in the future the value of the dollar should rise against the real and koruna, but fall against the zloty and the won.

Step 4: **Calculate the implied exchange rate between the zloty and the real.** The implied exchange rate between the zloty and the real is 7.00 zlotys/7.50 reals, or 0.93 zlotys per real. We can calculate the actual exchange rate by taking the ratio of zlotys per dollar to reals per dollar: 2.03 zlotys/1.58 reals, or 1.28 zlotys per real. The zloty is undervalued relative to the real.

Source: "The Big Mac Index," *Economist*, July 24, 2008.

>> **End Solved Problem 30-2A**

YOUR TURN: For more practice, do related problem 2.14 on page 1062 at the end of this chapter.

The Four Determinants of Exchange Rates in the Long Run We can take into account the shortcomings of the theory of purchasing power parity to develop a more complete explanation of how exchange rates are determined in the long run. There are four main determinants of exchange rates in the long run:

- *Relative price levels.* The purchasing power parity theory is correct in arguing that in the long run, the most important determinant of exchange rates between two countries' currencies is their relative price levels. If prices of goods and services rise faster in Canada than in the United States, the value of the Canadian dollar has to decline to maintain demand for Canadian products. Over the past 30 years, prices in Canada have risen at about the same rate on average as prices in the United States, while prices in Japan have risen more slowly. The relationship among inflation rates helps explain why the U.S. dollar has ended up roughly constant in value against the Canadian dollar while losing value against the Japanese yen.

- *Relative rates of productivity growth.* When the productivity of a firm increases, it is able to produce more goods and services using fewer workers, machines, or other inputs. The firm's costs of production fall, and usually so do the prices of its products. If the average productivity of Japanese firms increases faster than the average productivity of U.S. firms, Japanese products will have relatively lower prices than U.S. products, which increases the quantity demanded of Japanese products relative to U.S. products. As a result, the value of the yen should rise against the dollar. For most of the period from the early 1970s to the early 1990s, Japanese productivity increased faster than U.S. productivity, which contributed to the fall in the value of the dollar versus the yen. However, between 1992 and 2008, U.S. productivity increased faster than Japanese productivity.

- *Preferences for domestic and foreign goods.* If consumers in Canada increase their preferences for U.S. products, the demand for U.S. dollars will increase relative to the demand for Canadian dollars, and the U.S. dollar will increase in value relative to the Canadian dollar. During the 1970s and 1980s, many U.S. consumers increased their preferences for Japanese products, particularly automobiles and consumer electronics. This greater preference for Japanese products helped to increase the value of the yen relative to the dollar.

- *Tariffs and quotas.* The U.S. sugar quota forces firms like Hershey Foods Corporation to buy expensive U.S. sugar rather than less expensive foreign sugar. The quota increases the demand for dollars relative to the currencies of foreign sugar producers and, therefore, leads to a higher exchange rate. Changes in tariffs and quotas have not been a significant factor in explaining trends in the U.S. dollar–Canadian dollar or U.S. dollar–yen exchange rates.

Because these four factors change over time, the value of one country's currency can increase or decrease by substantial amounts in the long run. These changes in exchange rates can create problems for firms. A decline in the value of a country's currency lowers the foreign currency prices of the country's exports and increases the prices of imports. An increase in the value of a country's currency has the reverse effect. Firms can be both helped and hurt by exchange rate fluctuations. For example, the 15 percent decline in the value of the U.S. dollar against the Canadian dollar between 2005 and 2008 helped Molson Coors sell more Coors beer in Canada, but it hurt the firm's sales of Molson beer in the United States.

The Euro

A second key aspect of the current exchange rate system is that most western European countries have adopted a single currency. After World War II, many of the countries of western Europe wanted to more closely integrate their economies. In 1957, Belgium, France, West Germany, Italy, Luxembourg, and the Netherlands signed the Treaty of Rome, which established the European Economic Community, often referred to as the European Common Market. Tariffs and quotas on products being shipped within the Common Market were greatly reduced. Over the years, Britain, Sweden, Denmark, Finland, Austria, Greece, Ireland, Spain, and Portugal joined the European Economic Community, which was renamed the European Union (EU) in 1991. By 2008, 27 countries were members of the EU.

EU members decided to move to a common currency beginning in 1999. Three of the 15 countries that were then members of the EU—the United Kingdom, Denmark, and Sweden—decided to retain their domestic currencies. The move to a common currency took place in several stages. On January 1, 1999, the exchange rates of the 12 (now 15) participating countries were permanently fixed against each other and against the common currency, the *euro*. At first the euro was a pure *unit of account*. No euro currency was actually in circulation, although firms began quoting prices in both domestic currency and euros. On January 1, 2002, euro coins and paper currency were introduced, and on June 1, 2002, the old domestic currencies were withdrawn from circulation. Figure 30-2 shows the countries in the EU that have adopted the euro.

Figure 30-2

Countries Adopting the Euro

The 15 member countries of the European Union that have adopted the euro as their common currency as of 2008 are shaded with red hatch marks. The members of the EU that have not adopted the euro are colored tan. Countries in white are not members of the EU.

A new European Central Bank (ECB) was also established. Although the central banks of the member countries continue to exist, the ECB has assumed responsibility for monetary policy and for issuing currency. The ECB is run by a governing council that consists of a six-member executive board—appointed by the participating governments—and the governors of the central banks of the 15 member countries that have adopted the euro. The ECB represents a unique experiment in allowing a multinational organization to control the domestic monetary policies of independent countries.

Economists are divided over whether the creation of the euro will help growth in the EU countries. Having a common currency makes it easier for consumers and firms to buy and sell across borders. It is no longer necessary for someone in France to exchange francs for marks in order to do business in Germany. This change should reduce costs and increase competition. However, the participating countries are no longer able to run independent monetary policies. In addition, with fixed exchange rates, the value of one country's currency cannot fall during a recession, thereby expanding net exports to help revive aggregate demand. The experiences of the countries using the euro will provide economists with additional information on the costs and benefits to countries from using the same currency.

Making	**Was the Euro Undervalued**
the	**or Overvalued in 2007?**
Connection	

Making the Connection

Was the Euro Undervalued or Overvalued in 2007?

Whether a currency is undervalued or overvalued can have both economic and political significance. As we saw in Chapter 29, a declining exchange rate can boost a country's exports and reduce its imports; a rising exchange rate can have the opposite effect. In 2007, whether some country's currencies were chronically undervalued against the dollar became a political issue in the United States. A bill was introduced in the Senate that would punish countries whose exchange rates were "fundamentally misaligned" against the dollar. The bill seemed to be aimed at China because some politicians and economists argued that the Chinese government was taking actions to keep the Chinese yuan undervalued against the dollar. An undervalued yuan would make it easier for Chinese firms to export to the United States and harder for U.S. firms to export to China.

But is it easy to tell whether a country's currency is undervalued or overvalued against another country's currency? In fact, it is very difficult. One possible approach would be to use the model of purchasing power parity we discussed earlier in this chapter. But, as we have seen, we only expect purchasing power parity to explain exchange rates in the long run, so it does not provide a good guide to whether a currency is correctly valued at any particular time. Because investment firms buy and sell different currencies, they have an interest in knowing whether currencies are correctly valued. Economist Stephen Jen of the investment firm Morgan Stanley has analyzed whether the euro is undervalued or overvalued against the dollar. The graph on the next page shows movements in the exchange rate between the dollar and the euro from January 2002 through May 2007.

Determining whether a currency is undervalued or overvalued can be difficult.

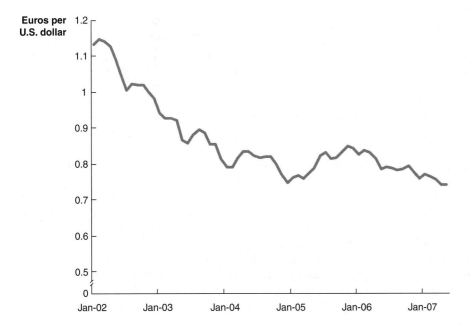

During this period, the value of the dollar declined from 1.13 euros to 0.74 euros, or by about 35 percent. Is this decline justified by changing economic conditions, or had the euro become overvalued (and, therefore, the dollar undervalued)? To see, Jen studied which economic variables had been correlated with exchange rate movements in the past. He then used current values of these variables, including productivity growth rates and the relative prices of imports and exports, to determine whether the euro was undervalued or overvalued. To account for the uncertainty in determining whether an exchange rate is at its "fair value," Jen constructed 13 estimates of what the euro's value should be. These estimates ranged from a low of 0.98 euros to the dollar to a high of 0.78 euros to the dollar. Because Jen's highest estimate was lower than the actual value of 0.74 euros to the dollar, he concluded that the euro was overvalued.

Jen's estimates have a very wide range, but even so, not every economist would agree with his conclusion that the euro is overvalued. This uncertainty in assessing the value of the euro indicates the practical difficulty of determining whether a currency is undervalued or overvalued.

Source: "Misleading Misalignments," *Economist*, June 21, 2007.

YOUR TURN: Test your understanding by doing related problem 2.17 on page 1062 at the end of this chapter.

Pegging against the Dollar

A final key aspect of the current exchange rate system is that some developing countries have attempted to keep their exchange rates fixed against the dollar or another major currency. Having a fixed exchange rate can provide important advantages for a country that has extensive trade with another country. When the exchange rate is fixed, business planning becomes much easier. For instance, if the South Korean won increases in value relative to the dollar, Hyundai, the Korean car manufacturer, may have to raise the dollar price of cars it exports to the United States, thereby reducing sales. If the exchange rate between the Korean won and the dollar is fixed, Hyundai's planning is much easier.

In the 1980s and 1990s, an additional reason for having fixed exchange rates developed. During those decades, the flow of foreign investment funds to developing countries, particularly those in East Asia, increased substantially. It became possible for firms in countries such as Korea, Thailand, Malaysia, and Indonesia to borrow dollars directly from foreign investors or indirectly from foreign banks. For example, a Thai firm might borrow U.S. dollars from a Japanese bank. If the Thai firm wants to build a new factory in Thailand with the borrowed dollars, it has to exchange the dollars for the equivalent amount of Thai currency, the baht. When the factory opens and production begins, the Thai firm will be earning the additional baht it needs to exchange for dollars to make the interest payments on the loan. A problem arises if the value of the baht falls against the dollar. Suppose that the exchange rate is 25 baht per dollar when the firm takes out the loan. A Thai firm making an interest payment of $100,000 dollars per month on a dollar loan could buy the necessary dollars for 2.5 million baht. But if the value of the baht declines to 50 baht to the dollar, it would take 5 million baht to buy the dollars necessary to make the interest payment. These increased payments might be a crushing burden for the Thai firm. The government of Thailand would have a strong incentive to avoid this problem by keeping the exchange rate between the baht and the dollar fixed.

Finally, some countries feared the inflationary consequences of a floating exchange rate. When the value of a currency falls, the prices of imports rise. If imports are a significant fraction of the goods consumers buy, a fall in the value of the currency may significantly increase the inflation rate. During the 1990s, an important part of Brazil's and Argentina's anti-inflation policies was a fixed exchange rate against the dollar. (As we will see, though, there are difficulties with following a fixed exchange rate policy, and, ultimately, both Brazil and Argentina abandoned fixed exchange rates.)

The East Asian Exchange Rate Crisis of the Late 1990s When a country keeps its currency's exchange rate fixed against another country's currency, it is **pegging** its currency. It is not necessary for both countries involved in a peg to agree to it. When a developing country has pegged the value of its currency against the dollar, the responsibility for maintaining the peg has been entirely with the developing country.

Countries attempting to maintain a peg can run into problems, however. We saw in Chapter 4 that when the government fixes the price of a good or service, the result can be persistent surpluses or shortages. Figure 30-3 shows the exchange rate between the

Pegging The decision by a country to keep the exchange rate fixed between its currency and another currency.

Figure 30-3

By 1997, the Thai Baht Was Overvalued against the Dollar

The government of Thailand pegged the value of the baht against the dollar to make it easier for Thai firms to export to the United States and to protect Thai firms that had taken out dollar loans. The pegged exchange rate of $0.04 per baht was well above the equilibrium exchange rate of $0.03 per baht. In the example in this figure, the overvalued exchange rate created a surplus of 70 million baht, which the Thai central bank had to purchase with dollars.

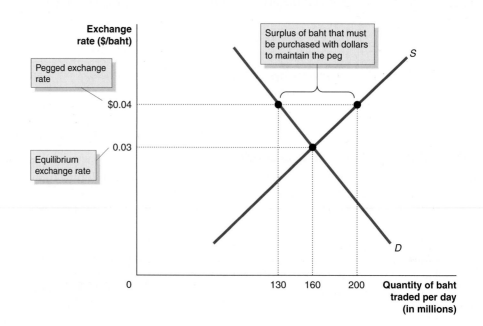

dollar and the Thai baht. The figure is drawn from the Thai point of view, so we measure the exchange rate on the vertical axis as dollars per baht. The figure represents the situation in the 1990s when the government of Thailand pegged the exchange rate between the dollar and the baht above the equilibrium exchange rate as determined by demand and supply. A currency pegged at a value above the market equilibrium exchange rate is said to be *overvalued*. A currency pegged at a value below the market equilibrium exchange rate is said to be *undervalued*.

Pegging made it easier for Thai firms to export products to the United States and protected Thai firms that had taken out dollar loans. The pegged exchange rate was 25.19 baht to the dollar, or about $0.04 to the baht. By 1997, this exchange rate was well above the market equilibrium exchange rate of 35 baht to the dollar, or about $0.03 to the baht. The result was a surplus of baht on the foreign exchange market. To keep the exchange rate at the pegged level, the Thai central bank, the Bank of Thailand, had to buy these baht with dollars. In buying baht with dollars, the Bank of Thailand gradually used up its holdings of dollars, or its *dollar reserves*. To continue supporting the pegged exchange rate, the Bank of Thailand borrowed additional dollar reserves from the International Monetary Fund (IMF). It also raised interest rates to attract more foreign investors to investments in Thailand, thereby increasing the demand for the baht. The Bank of Thailand took these actions even though allowing the value of the baht to decline against the dollar would have helped Thai firms exporting to the United States by reducing the dollar prices of their goods. The Thai government was afraid of the negative consequences of abandoning the peg even though it had led to the baht being overvalued.

Although higher domestic interest rates helped attract foreign investors, they made it more difficult for Thai firms and households to borrow the funds they needed to finance their spending. As a consequence, domestic investment and consumption declined, pushing the Thai economy into recession. International investors realized that there were limits to how high the Bank of Thailand would be willing to push interest rates and how many dollar loans the IMF would be willing to extend to Thailand. They began to speculate against the baht by exchanging baht for dollars at the official, pegged exchange rate. If, as they expected, Thailand was forced to abandon the peg, they would be able to buy back the baht at a much lower exchange rate, making a substantial profit. Because these actions by investors make it more difficult to maintain a fixed exchange rate, they are referred to as *destabilizing speculation*. Figure 30-4 shows the results of this destabilizing speculation. The decreased demand for baht shifted the demand curve for

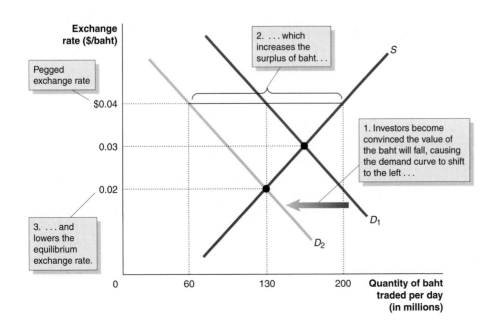

Figure 30-4

Destabilizing Speculation against the Thai Baht

In 1997, the pegged exchange rate of $0.04 = 1 baht was above the equilibrium exchange rate of $0.03 = 1 baht. As investors became convinced that Thailand would have to abandon its pegged exchange against the dollar and allow the value of the baht to fall, they decreased their demand for baht from D_1 to D_2. The new equilibrium exchange rate became $0.02 = 1 baht. This increased the quantity of baht the Bank of Thailand had to purchase in exchange for dollars from 70 million per day to 140 million to defend the pegged exchange rate. The *destabilizing speculation* by investors caused Thailand to abandon its pegged exchange rate in July 1997.

baht from D_1 to D_2, increasing the quantity of baht the Bank of Thailand needed to buy in exchange for dollars.

Foreign investors also began to sell off their investments in Thailand and exchange the baht they received for dollars. This *capital flight* forced the Bank of Thailand to run through its dollar reserves. Dollar loans from the IMF temporarily allowed Thailand to defend the pegged exchange rate. Finally, on July 2, 1997, Thailand abandoned its pegged exchange rate against the dollar and allowed the baht to float. Thai firms that had borrowed dollars were now faced with interest payments that were much higher than they had planned. Many firms were forced into bankruptcy, and the Thai economy plunged into a deep recession.

Many currency traders became convinced that other East Asian countries, such as South Korea, Indonesia, and Malaysia, would have to follow Thailand and abandon their pegged exchange rates. The result was a wave of speculative selling of these countries' currencies. These waves of selling—sometimes referred to as *speculative attacks*—were difficult for countries to fight off. Even if a country's currency was not initially overvalued at the pegged exchange rate, the speculative attacks would cause a large reduction in the demand for its currency. The demand curve for its currency would shift to the left, which would force the country's central bank to quickly run through its dollar reserves. Within the space of a few months, South Korea, Indonesia, the Philippines, and Malaysia abandoned their pegged currencies. All these countries also plunged into recession.

The Decline in Pegging Following the disastrous events experienced by the East Asian countries, the number of countries with pegged exchange rates declined sharply. Most countries that continue to use pegged exchange rates are small and trade primarily with one, much larger, country. So, for instance, several Caribbean countries continue to peg against the dollar, and several former French colonies in Africa that formerly pegged against the French franc now peg against the euro. Overall, the trend has been toward replacing pegged exchange rates with managed floating exchange rates.

The Chinese Experience with Pegging As we discussed in Chapter 22, in 1978, China began to move away from central planning and toward a market system. The result was a sharp acceleration in economic growth. Real GDP per capita grew at a rate of 6.5 percent per year between 1979 and 1995, and at the very rapid rate of 9.1 percent per year between 1996 and 2006. An important part of Chinese economic policy was the decision in 1994 to peg the value of the Chinese currency, the yuan, to the dollar at a fixed rate of 8.28 yuan to the dollar. Pegging against the dollar ensured that Chinese exporters would face stable dollar prices for the goods they sold in the United States. By the early 2000s, many economists argued that the yuan was undervalued against the dollar, possibly significantly so. Many U.S. firms claimed that the undervaluation of the yuan gave Chinese firms an unfair advantage in competing with U.S. firms.

To support the undervalued exchange rate, the Chinese central bank had to buy large amounts of dollars with yuan. By 2005, the Chinese government had accumulated more than $700 billion, a good portion of which it had used to buy U.S. Treasury bonds. In addition, China was coming under pressure from its trading partners to allow the yuan to increase in value. Chinese exports of textile products were driving some textile producers out of business in Japan, the United States, and Europe. China has also begun to export more sophisticated products, including televisions, personal computers, and cell phones. Politicians in other countries were anxious to protect their domestic industries from Chinese competition, even if the result was higher prices for domestic consumers. The Chinese government was reluctant to revalue the yuan, however, because it believed high levels of exports were needed to maintain rapid economic growth. The Chinese economy needs to create as many as 20 million new nonagricultural jobs per year to keep up with population growth and the shift of workers from rural areas to cities. Because of China's large holdings of dollars, it will also incur significant losses if the yuan increases in value.

By July 2005, the pressure on China to revalue the yuan had become too great. The government announced that it would switch from pegging the yuan against the dollar to linking the value of the yuan to the average value of a basket of currencies including the dollar, the Japanese yen, the euro, the Korean won, and several other currencies. The immediate effect was a fairly small increase in the value of the yuan from 8.28 to the dollar to 8.11 to the dollar. The Chinese central bank declared that it had switched from a peg to a managed floating exchange rate. Some economists and policymakers were skeptical, however, that much had actually changed because the initial increase in the value of yuan had been small and because the Chinese central bank did not explain the details of how the yuan would be linked to the basket of other currencies. Two years later, in mid-2008, the value of the yuan had increased to 6.83 to the dollar. But this limited increase made it clear that the value of the yuan was still not very responsive to changes in demand and supply in the foreign exchange markets.

Making the Connection | Crisis and Recovery in South Korea

Korea spent the first part of the twentieth century as a colony of Japan. In 1945, at the end of World War II, Korea was divided into Communist North Korea and democratic South Korea. North Korea's invasion of South Korea in June 1950 set off the Korean War, which devastated South Korea, before ending in 1953. Despite these difficult beginnings, by the 1960s, the South Korean economy was growing rapidly. As one of the *newly industrializing countries*, South Korea was a model for other developing countries.

To make it easier for firms like Hyundai to export to the United States and to protect firms that had taken out dollar loans, the South Korean government pegged the value of its currency, the won, to the U.S. dollar. Following Thailand's decision in July 1997 to abandon its peg, large-scale destabilizing speculation took place against the won. Foreign investors scrambled to sell their investments in Korea and to convert their won into dollars. South Korea was unable to defend the peg and allowed the won to float in October 1997.

Like other countries that underwent an exchange rate crisis, South Korea had attempted to maintain the value of the won by raising domestic interest rates. The result was a sharp decline in aggregate demand and a severe recession. However, unlike other East Asian countries—particularly Thailand and Indonesia—that made only slow progress in recovering from exchange rate crises, South Korea bounced back rapidly. The figure shows that after experiencing falling real GDP through 1999, South Korea quickly returned to high rates of growth.

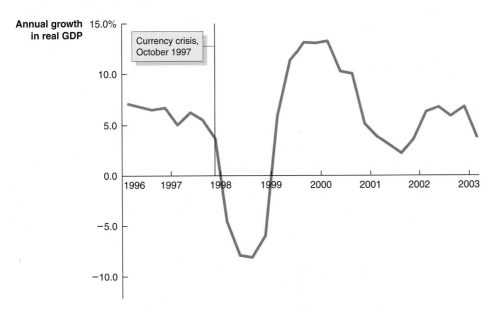

Why was the performance of South Korea so much better than that of other East Asian countries? Jahyeong Koo and Sherry L. Kiser, economists at the Federal Reserve Bank of Dallas, cite several factors:

- South Korea benefited from a $21 billion loan from the IMF in December 1997. This loan helped stabilize the value of the won.

- Even though South Korean banks were badly hurt in the crisis and cut back their loans, South Korean firms were able to obtain financing for investment projects from the stock and bond markets.

- The South Korean labor market was flexible enough to allow wage reductions, which offset some of the negative impact of the crisis on corporate profits.

South Korean firms remain saddled with large debts, and the Korean banking system has yet to fully recover. But South Korea was able to emerge from its exchange rate crisis without suffering the political and social upheavals that occurred in countries such as Indonesia.

Sources: Korea National Statistical Office; and Jahyeong Koo and Sherry L. Kiser, "Recovery from a Financial Crisis: The Case of South Korea," Federal Reserve Bank of Dallas, *Economic and Financial Review*, Fourth Quarter 2001.

YOUR TURN: Test your understanding by doing related problem 2.28 on page 1063 at the end of this chapter.

Solved Problem | 30-2B

Coping with Fluctuations in the Value of the U.S. Dollar

Analyze the following excerpt from an article in the *New York Times*: "Some economists say that if the flow of capital into the United States dries up, the dollar could fall sharply in value, reigniting the threat of inflation and putting pressure on the Fed to raise interest rates."

Use a foreign exchange market graph in your analysis and be sure to explain what the value of the dollar has to do with the U.S. inflation rate, as well as why a falling value of the dollar puts pressure on the Fed to raise interest rates.

SOLVING THE PROBLEM:

Step 1: **Review the chapter material.** This problem is about the determinants of exchange rates, so you may want to review the section "The Current Exchange Rate System," which begins on page 1041.

Step 2: **Draw the graph.** Draw a graph to show the effect of a decline in the flow of capital into the United States. "Flow of capital into the United States" refers to foreign investors engaging in portfolio investment (such as buying U.S. stocks and bonds) or direct investment (such as building factories in the United States). To invest in the United States, foreign investors must exchange their currencies for dollars. If they decide to cut back on investing in the United States, their demand for dollars will fall. This reduction is shown in the following figure by the shift from D_1 to D_2. The equilibrium exchange falls from ¥130 = $1 to ¥120 = $1.

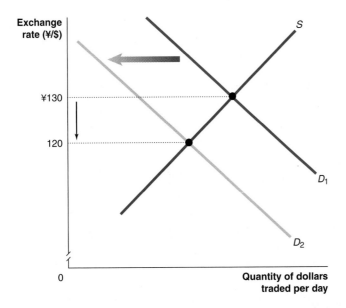

Step 3: **Explain why a falling value of the dollar puts pressure on the Fed to raise interest rates.** If the value of the dollar falls, the prices of imports will rise. Rising import prices add to the inflation rate. If the Fed wanted to increase the value of the dollar (or keep it from falling further), it would raise interest rates to make U.S. financial investments more attractive to foreign investors. In the graph, this would result in shifting the demand for dollars back to the right.

Source: Richard W. Stevenson, "Dollar Falls as Top Official Casts Doubts on Intervention," *New York Times*, May 2, 2002.

YOUR TURN: For more practice, do related problem 2.29 on page 1063 at the end of this chapter.

>> **End Solved Problem 30-2B**

30.3 LEARNING OBJECTIVE

30.3 | Discuss the growth of international capital markets.

International Capital Markets

One important reason exchange rates fluctuate is that investors seek out the best investments they can find anywhere in the world. For instance, if Chinese investors increase their demand for U.S. Treasury bills, the demand for dollars will increase, and the value of the dollar will rise. But if interest rates in the United States decline, foreign investors may sell U.S. investments, and the value of the dollar will fall.

Shares of stock and long-term debt, including corporate and government bonds and bank loans, are bought and sold on *capital markets*. Before 1980, most U.S. corporations raised funds only in U.S. stock and bond markets or from U.S. banks. U.S. investors rarely invested in foreign capital markets. In the 1980s and 1990s, European governments removed many restrictions on foreign investments in financial markets. It became possible for U.S. and other foreign investors to freely invest in Europe and for European investors to freely invest in foreign markets. Improvements in communications and computer technology made it possible for U.S. investors to receive better and more timely information about foreign firms and for foreign investors to receive better information about U.S. firms. The growth in economies around the world also made more savings available to be invested.

Although at one time the U.S. capital market was larger than all other capital markets combined, this is no longer true. Today there are large capital markets in Europe and Japan, and there are smaller markets in Latin America and East Asia. The three most important international financial centers today are New York, London, and Tokyo. Each day, the *Wall Street Journal* provides data not just on the Dow Jones

Figure 30-5

Growth of Foreign Portfolio Investment in the United States

Since 1995, a large rise has occurred in foreign purchases of bonds issued by U.S. corporations and by the federal government. Falling stock prices in the United States caused a fall in foreign purchases of corporate stocks in the years immediately after 2001. By 2007, however, foreign investment in these securities was at record levels.

Sources: International Monetary Fund, *International Capital Markets*, August 2001; and U.S. Department of the Treasury, *Treasury Bulletin*, June 2008.

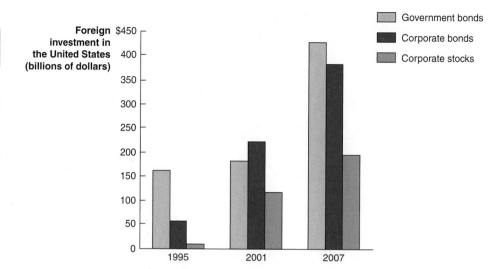

Industrial Average and the Standard & Poor's 500 stock indexes of U.S. stocks but also on the Nikkei 225 average of Japanese stocks, the FTSE 100 index of stocks on the London Stock Exchange, and the Euro STOXX 50 index of European stocks. By 2008, corporations, banks, and governments raised more than $1 trillion in funds on global financial markets.

Beginning in the 1990s, the flow of foreign funds into U.S. stocks and bonds—or *portfolio investments*—increased substantially. As Figure 30-5 shows, a dramatic increase in foreign purchases of bonds issued by corporations and by the federal government has occurred since 1995. Even though falling stock prices in the United States caused a fall in foreign purchases of corporate stocks in the years immediately after 2001, by 2007, foreign investment in these securities was at record levels.

Figure 30-6 shows the distribution of foreign portfolio investment in the United States by country. Investors in the United Kingdom accounted for about 54 percent of all foreign purchases of U.S. stocks and bonds. Investors in China accounted for 11 percent, and investors in other Asian countries accounted for 12 percent.

The globalization of financial markets has helped increase growth and efficiency in the world economy. Now it is possible for the savings of households around the world to be channeled to the best investments available. It is also possible for firms in nearly every country to tap the savings of foreign households to gain the funds needed for expansion. No longer are firms forced to rely only on the savings of domestic households to finance investment.

Figure 30-6

The Distribution of Foreign Purchases of U.S. Stocks and Bonds by Country, 2007

Investors in the United Kingdom accounted for about 54 percent of all foreign purchases of U.S. stocks and bonds, while investors in China accounted for 11 percent, and investors in all other Asian countries accounted for 12 percent.
Source: U.S. Department of the Treasury, *Treasury Bulletin*, June 2008.

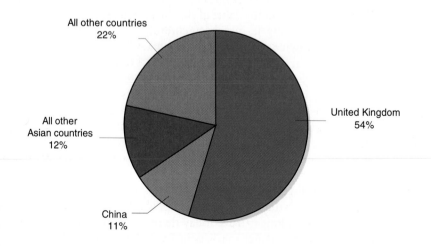

Economics in YOUR Life!

>> Continued from page 1039

At the beginning of the chapter, we posed this question: If economists are correct about the relative rates of average productivity growth between Spain and the United States in the next decade, then, all else being equal, will the savings that you accumulate (in euros) be worth more or less in U.S. dollars than it would have been worth without the relative gains in Spanish productivity? To answer this question, we saw in this chapter that when the average productivity of firms in one country increases faster than the average productivity of firms in another country, the value of the faster-growing country's currency should—all else being equal—rise against the slower-growing country's currency. Of course, Spain is only one of the 13 countries using the euro, so the impact of productivity increases in Spain on the value of the euro may not be large. But the savings that you accumulate in euros while you are in Spain are likely to be worth more in U.S. dollars than they would have been worth without the gains in Spanish productivity.

Conclusion

Fluctuations in exchange rates continue to cause difficulties for firms and governments. From the gold standard to the Bretton Woods system to currency pegging, governments have attempted to find a workable system of fixed exchange rates. Fixing exchange rates runs into the same problems as fixing any price: As demand and supply shift, surpluses and shortages will occur unless the price adjusts. Most of the countries of Western Europe are attempting to avoid this problem by using a single currency. Economists are looking closely at the results of that experiment.

Read *An Inside Look at Policy* on the next page for a discussion of whether governments should try to limit speculation in currencies.

Should the International Financial System Limit Currency Speculation?

WALL STREET JOURNAL, APRIL 5, 2007

Can Asia Control the "Hot Money"?

Asian finance officials plan to meet in Thailand Thursday, and high on the agenda: doing something about the money pouring into their countries from foreign investors, so it doesn't whipsaw their economies on the way back out.

Capital-control regulations can be controversial. Last year when Thailand slapped controls on moving foreign investments out of the country, Thai shares fell a record 15% in one day as overseas investors fled.

Yet many foreign investors are starting to warm to the idea of controls on "hot money"—speculative investors who move in and out quickly. Analysts say limited restrictions help prevent highflying markets from collapsing if foreigners decide to suddenly pull up stakes, potentially causing economic damage. . . .

Increased restriction would be a step back from the trend of the past decade or so toward more-open markets. That move toward openness to money from abroad has helped make stock markets in India, Brazil and Russia some of the best performers in the world. . . .

Some U.S. mutual-fund managers say the sort of controls they consider potentially helpful are those that would target hot money but wouldn't necessarily disrupt longer-term investors. These restrictions cover a range of measures intended to manage speculative investment flows. In Brazil, for instance, there is a tax on some transactions of securities sold within 30 days of being bought. In India, foreigners are restricted from participating in some of the domestic derivative markets, while foreign investors in Argentina are subject to a 180-day minimum holding period for all debt purchases. . . .

In Vietnam, where Hanoi is grappling with what many analysts say is a stock-market bubble that threatens to burst, some investors say they would actually welcome state action. "You'd want the government to prevent a stock-market meltdown," says Cliff Quisenberry, who manages the Eaton Vance Structured Emerging Markets Fund and invests in Vietnamese stocks. "Controls may be useful."

When Thailand's shares tanked late last year, after the government tried to make it tougher for foreigners to move money out of the country, Mark Headley, of Matthews International Capital Management in San Francisco, says he viewed it as a buying opportunity. This despite the fact that he has been burned in the past: In 1998, he was among the investors whose money got trapped inside Malaysia when the government there barred foreigners from repatriating funds amid the Asian economic crisis then unfolding.

Today Mr. Headley takes a more benign view of Thailand's actions. He says the new Thai government was worried about a strengthening currency hurting Thai exporters, "and they panicked. That's profoundly different from Malaysia, where they were trying to stick it to foreign investors." Thailand later rolled back its restrictions slightly. . . .

"Where Malaysia tried to keep foreigners from getting out, the controls today are aimed at keeping overeager money from coming in," he says. "That's a big difference." Not to everyone, however. Some say any government interference is bound to create inefficiencies and is doomed to fail. "It takes a sure policy-making hand to avoid trouble," says Stuart Schweitzer, global-markets strategist for JP Morgan Private Bank. "Markets do a better job." . . .

Not all investment restrictions are done for the same reason. Colombia in 2004 imposed a one-year "residency requirement" that prevented investors from withdrawing their money from the country for 12 months. The stated rationale was to prevent hot-money flows from causing the Colombian peso to appreciate. But analysts say it was really a bow to political pressure from exporters, who wanted the currency to stay weak.

The currency appreciated anyway because direct foreign investment in Colombian companies continued. When the stock market started to tumble last year, the government abruptly removed the lockup rule in hopes of luring foreign fund managers back.

Three months after Thailand's move, officials scrapped restrictions on stock investors. But controls on currency trading remain. Some think those controls may actually have helped the country weather more recent market turbulence. . . .

Source: Craig Karmin, "Can Asia Control the 'Hot Money'?" *Wall Street Journal*, April 5, 2007, p. C1. Reprinted by permission of the *Wall Street Journal* vis Copyright Clearance Center.

Key Points in the Article

This article discusses government-imposed capital controls, which restrict foreign investors' ability to speculate in a country's financial markets. Although foreign investors have typically resisted capital controls, a growing number of them now support some form of controls on very short-term investment flows, which can disrupt the returns of relatively long-term foreign investors. Most investors, however, continue to believe that capital controls are bad for the international financial system, which, they contend, allocates capital most efficiently when it is run by markets rather than governments.

Analyzing the News

ⓐ Private investors in the international financial system have typically resisted government-imposed capital controls designed to limit hot money—large flows of speculative foreign portfolio investments that quickly enter and exit a country's financial markets. Any government restrictions on foreign investors' ability to sell a country's stocks, bonds, or currency make it less likely that foreign investors will buy these assets. Recently, the Thai government imposed a so-called 30 percent withholding rule that required foreigners to deposit 30 percent of their foreign portfolio investments in non-interest-earning accounts at the central bank for one year. Foreigners demonstrated their opposition to the withholding rule by pulling their funds from the country. Although the Thai government later exempted stocks and some other types of investments from the rule, it has left the capital control largely in place.

Hot money enters a country's economy through its foreign exchange market; that is, speculators must buy the country's currency in order to buy the country's financial assets. Speculators buy a country's currency when they believe the currency—or the financial investments denominated in that currency—will increase in value. This pattern is shown in the figure, where the demand curve for Thai baht shifts to the right from D_1 to D_2, and the value of the baht increases from $0.03 to $0.06. Similarly, speculators sell a country's currency when they believe it will decrease in value.

ⓑ Hot money flows can disrupt the returns of other foreign investors who intend to invest in a country's assets over a long period of time. A growing number of foreign investors support some form of capital controls on short-term flows while agreeing that long-term foreign portfolio investments and foreign direct investments should remain exempt from such controls. For example, Brazil taxes foreign investors who hold select securities for less than 30 days; meanwhile, Argentina requires that foreign investors hold debt securities, such as bonds, for a minimum of 180 days. Of course, another reason some foreign investors tolerate or even support capital controls may be that foreign portfolio investments in many of these countries with capital controls are earning very high returns. If these high returns were to deteriorate, foreign investors' support for capital controls might fade.

ⓒ Capital controls today differ from those that governments imposed even a decade ago. While today's controls seek to keep speculators from entering the financial systems of these countries, earlier controls sought to keep speculators from exiting them. In other words, today, countries such as Thailand are trying to stave off a run-up in the values of their currencies, rather than avoid a collapse in their currencies' value.

Thinking Critically
About Policy

1. Suppose a small, open-economy, such as Thailand, imposes capital controls so that foreign investors who buy its currency must hold it for at least two years. Would a contractionary monetary policy, with the central bank effectively raising interest rates to slow the growth rate of GDP, be relatively more or less effective as a result of the capital controls? Briefly explain your reasoning.

2. Why do governments impose short-term capital controls on foreign portfolio investment rather than on foreign direct investment?

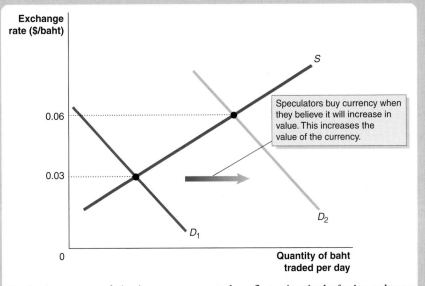

Foreign investors speculating in a currency create large fluctuations in the foreign exchange value of that currency.

Key Terms

30.1 LEARNING OBJECTIVE   30.1 │ Understand how different exchange rate systems operate, **pages 1040–1041.**

Exchange Rate Systems

Summary

When countries agree on how exchange rates should be determined, economists say that there is an **exchange rate system**. A **floating currency** is the outcome of a country allowing its currency's exchange rate to be determined by demand and supply. The current exchange rate system is a **managed float exchange rate system** under which the value of most currencies is determined by demand and supply, with occasional government intervention. A **fixed exchange rate system** is a system under which countries agree to keep the exchange rates among their currencies fixed. Under the gold standard, the exchange rate between two currencies was automatically determined by the quantity of gold in each currency. By the end of the Great Depression of the 1930s, every country had abandoned the gold standard. Under the Bretton Woods system, which was in place between 1944 and the early 1970s, the United States agreed to exchange dollars for gold at a price of $35 per ounce. The central banks of all other members of the system pledged to buy and sell their currencies at a fixed rate against the dollar.

> myeconlab   Visit www.myeconlab.com to complete these exercises
> *Get Ahead of the Curve* online and get instant feedback.

Review Questions

1.1 What is an exchange rate system? What is the difference between a fixed exchange rate system and a managed float exchange rate system?

1.2 How were exchange rates determined under the gold standard? How did the gold standard differ from the Bretton Woods system?

Problems and Applications

1.3 (Related to the *Don't Let This Happen to You!* on page 1041) Briefly explain whether you agree with the following statement: "The Federal Reserve is limited in its ability to issue paper currency by the amount of gold the federal government has in Fort Knox. To issue more paper currency, the government first has to buy more gold."

1.4 The United States and most other countries abandoned the gold standard during the 1930s. Why would the 1930s have been a particularly difficult time for countries to have remained on the gold standard? (*Hint:* Think about the macroeconomic events of the 1930s and about the possible problems with carrying out an expansionary monetary policy while remaining on the gold standard.)

1.5 If a country is on the gold standard, what is likely to happen to the country's money supply if new gold deposits are discovered in the country, as happened in the United States with the gold discoveries in California in 1849? Is this change in the money supply desirable? Briefly explain.

>> End Learning Objective 30.1

30.2 LEARNING OBJECTIVE   30.2 │ Discuss the three key features of the current exchange rate system,
pages 1041–1055.

The Current Exchange Rate System

Summary

The three key aspects of the current exchange rate system are: (1) the U.S. dollar floats against other major currencies; (2) most countries in western Europe have adopted a common currency; and (3) some developing countries have fixed their currencies' exchange rates against the dollar or against another major currency. Since 1973, the value of the U.S. dollar has fluctuated widely against other major currencies. The theory of **purchasing power parity** states that in the long run, exchange rates move to equalize the purchasing power of different currencies. This theory helps to explain some of the long-run movements in the value of the U.S. dollar relative to other currencies. Purchasing power parity does not provide a complete explanation of movements in exchange rates for several reasons, including the existence of *tariffs* and *quotas*. A **tariff** is a tax imposed by a government on imports. A **quota** is a government-imposed limit on the quantity of a good that can be imported. Currently, 15 countries of the European Union use a common currency, known as the **euro**. The experience of the countries using the euro will provide economists with information on the costs and benefits to countries from using the same currency. When a country keeps its currency's exchange rate fixed against another country's currency, it is **pegging** its currency. Pegging can result in problems similar to the problems countries encountered with fixed exchange rates under the Bretton Woods system. If investors become convinced that a country pegging its exchange rate will eventually allow the exchange rate to decline to a lower level, the demand curve for the currency will shift to the left. This illustrates the difficulty of maintaining a fixed exchange rate in the face of destabilizing speculation.

myeconlab Visit www.myeconlab.com to complete these exercises online and get instant feedback.

Review Questions

2.1 What is the theory of purchasing power parity? Does it give a complete explanation for movements in exchange rates in the long run? Briefly explain.

2.2 Briefly describe the four determinants of exchange rates in the long run.

2.3 Which European countries currently use the euro as their currencies? Why did these countries agree to replace their previous currency with the euro?

2.4 What does it mean when one currency is "pegged" against another currency? Why do countries peg their currencies? What problems can result from pegging?

2.5 If you owned a firm in Indonesia and wanted to export your product to the United States, would you like the Indonesian government to peg the value of the rupiah against the dollar? Briefly explain.

2.6 Briefly describe the Chinese experience with pegging the yuan.

Problems and Applications

2.7 (Related to the *Making the Connection* on page 1042) Suppose you are a baseball player for the Toronto Blue Jays, and your salary is paid in U.S. dollars. If you and your family live in Toronto, would you be helped or hurt by an increase in the value of the Canadian dollar relative to the U.S. dollar? Briefly explain.

2.8 Consider this newspaper report: "DuPont said that soft currency overseas, particularly in Europe and Asia, had dragged down its sales 2 percent worldwide, ultimately costing it $35 million in net income." What

is a "soft currency"? Why would soft currency overseas hurt DuPont's sales?

Source: Danny Hakim and Greg Winter, "G.M. Official Says Dollar Is Too Strong," *New York Times*, August 9, 2001.

2.9 Consider this statement: "It usually takes more than 100 yen to buy 1 U.S. dollar and more than 1.5 dollars to buy 1 British pound. These values show that the United States must be a much wealthier country than Japan, and that the United Kingdom must be wealthier than the United States." Do you agree with this reasoning? Briefly explain.

2.10 The following is from an article in the *Wall Street Journal*:

In Japan, demand for videogame machines is declining. In the past three years, the number of videogame players sold there has declined by more than 8%, while more household members say they are not interested in playing, according to an annual survey by the Japanese industry group Computer Entertainment Supplier's Association. Sales of both hardware and software have fallen about 20% to 496.5 billion yen ($4.3 billion) in 2005 from 623.2 billion yen ($5.7 billion) in 2000, according to the group.

a. According to the information in this article, what was the exchange rate between the yen and the dollar in 2000? What was the exchange rate between the yen and the dollar in 2005?

b. Was the change in the yen–dollar exchange rate between 2000 and 2005 good news or bad news for Japanese firms, such as Sony, that export video game consoles to the United States? Was the change in the yen–dollar exchange rate good news or bad news for U.S. consumers who buy Sony video game consoles? Briefly explain.

Source: Yukari Iwatani Kane and Nick Wingfield, "Amid Videogame Arms Race, Nintendo Slows Things Down," *Wall Street Journal*, November 2, 2006, p. A1.

2.11 An article in the *Wall Street Journal* is headlined "Pain from the Dollar's Decline Will Mostly Be Felt Overseas." Briefly explain the reasoning behind this headline.

Source: David Wessel, "Pain from the Dollar's Decline Will Mostly Be Felt Overseas," *Wall Street Journal*, June 13, 2002.

2.12 According to the theory of purchasing power parity, if the inflation rate in Australia is higher than the inflation rate in New Zealand, what should happen to the exchange rate between the Australian dollar and the New Zealand dollar? Briefly explain.

2.13 (Related to the *Making the Connection* on page 1044) Look again at the table on page 1045 that shows the prices of Big Macs and the implied and actual exchange rates. Indicate which countries listed in the table have undervalued currency versus the U.S. dollar and which have overvalued currency.

2.14 (Related to *Solved Problem 30-2A* on page 1046) Fill in the missing values in the following table. Assume that the Big Mac is selling for $3.57 in the United States. Explain whether the U.S. dollar is overvalued or undervalued relative to each currency and predict what will happen in the future to each exchange rate. Finally, calculate the implied exchange rate between the Russian ruble and the New Zealand dollar and explain which currency is overvalued in terms of Big Mac purchasing power parity.

COUNTRY	BIG MAC PRICE	IMPLIED EXCHANGE RATE	ACTUAL EXCHANGE RATE
Chile	1,550 pesos		494 pesos per dollar
Estonia	32.0 kroons		9.93 kroons per dollar
Russia	59.0 rubles		23.2 rubles per dollar
New Zealand	4.90 New Zealand dollars		1.32 New Zealand dollars per U.S. dollar

2.15 Britain decided not to join with other European Union countries and use the euro as its currency. One British opponent of adopting the euro argued, "It comes down to economics. We just don't believe that it's possible to manage the entire economy of Europe with just one interest rate policy. How do you alleviate recession in Germany and curb inflation in Ireland?" What interest-rate policy would be used to alleviate recession in Germany? What interest-rate policy would be used to curb inflation in Ireland? What does adopting the euro have to do with interest-rate policy?

Source: Alan Cowell, "Nuanced Conflict Over Euro in Britain," *New York Times*, June 22, 2001.

2.16 When the euro was introduced in January 1999, the exchange rate was $1.19 per euro. In July 2008, the exchange rate was $1.56 per euro. Was this change in the dollar–euro exchange rate good news or bad news for U.S. firms exporting goods and services to Europe? Was it good news or bad news for European consumers buying goods and services imported from the United States? Briefly explain.

2.17 (Related to the *Making the Connection* on page 1048) Suppose that Stephen Jen is correct that the euro was overvalued relative to the dollar in mid-2007. Would we then expect that in the future, the euro would exchange for more dollars or for fewer dollars? Would this movement in the euro be good news or bad news for European firms that export to the United States? Briefly explain.

2.18 Construct a numeric example that shows how an investor could have made a profit by selling Thai baht for dollars in 1997.

2.19 The following statement is from an article in the *New York Times*: "Government action to support [its] currency cannot be effective in the long run if it runs counter to the collective judgment of the financial markets." What does it mean to say a government is taking action to "support" its currency? Do you agree with the conclusion that this action is not effective in the long run if it runs counter to the judgment of financial markets? Briefly explain.

Source: Richard W. Stevenson, "Dollar Falls as Top Official Casts Doubts on Intervention," *New York Times*, May 2, 2002.

2.20 Use the graph to answer the following questions.

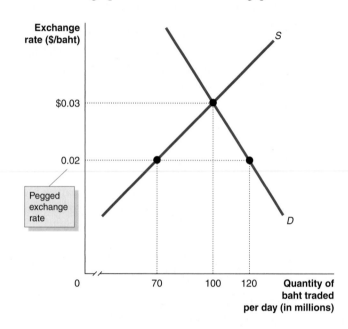

a. According to the graph, is there a surplus or a shortage of baht in exchange for U.S. dollars? Briefly explain.

b. To maintain the pegged exchange rate, will the Thai central bank need to buy baht in exchange for dollars or sell baht in exchange for dollars? How many baht will the Thai central bank need to buy or sell?

2.21 For many years, Argentina suffered from high rates of inflation. As part of its program to fight inflation, in the 1990s, the Argentine government pegged the value of the Argentine peso to the U.S. dollar at a rate of one peso per dollar. In January 2002, the government decided to abandon the peg and allow the peso to float. Just before the peg was abandoned, firms in Buenos Aires posted signs urging customers to come in and shop and take advantage of the "Last 72 Hours of One to One." What was likely to happen to the exchange rate between the dollar and the peso when Argentina abandoned the peg? Why would customers find it better to shop before the peg ended than after?

Source: Larry Rohter, "Argentina Unlinks Peso from Dollar, Bracing for Devaluation," *New York Times*, January 7, 2002.

2.22 The *Economist* observed the following: "In Argentina, many loans were taken out in dollars: this had catastrophic consequences for borrowers once the peg collapsed." What does it mean that Argentina's "peg collapsed"? Why was this catastrophic for borrowers in Argentina who had taken out dollar loans?

Source: "Spoilt for Choice," *Economist*, June 3, 2002.

2.23 According to the *Economist*, during the period in which Argentina pegged the value of its currency to the dollar, "Argentina's monetary policy was, in effect, made in Washington and was often inappropriate for Argentina's needs." Explain the sense in which Argentina's monetary policy was made in Washington during those years.

Source: "Spoilt for Choice," *Economist*, June 3, 2002.

2.24 A newspaper story discussing the effects of a decline in the exchange value of the dollar contained the following two observations:
a. "The weaker dollar will also mean higher inflation in this country."
b. "The biggest danger in coming months is that a declining dollar will make foreigners less willing to invest in the United States."
Explain whether you agree or disagree with these two observations.

Source: Martin Crutsinger, "Mighty Dollar Fading," Associated Press, May 30, 2002.

2.25 Suppose that a developing country pegs the value of its currency against the U.S. dollar. Further, suppose that the exchange rate between the dollar and the yen and between the dollar and the euro increases. What will be the impact on the ability of the developing country to export goods and services to Japan and Europe? Briefly explain.

2.26 Graph the demand and supply of Chinese yuan for U.S. dollars and label each axis. To maintain its pegged exchange rate, the Chinese central bank used yuan to buy large quantities of U.S. dollars. Indicate whether the pegged exchange rate was above or below the market equilibrium exchange rate and show on the graph the quantity of yuan the Chinese central bank would have to supply each trading period.

2.27 According to a newspaper story, "American manufacturers contend the yuan is undervalued by as much as 40 percent. . . . The [Bush] administration is under growing pressure to take a get-tough approach with the Chinese in light of soaring trade deficits. They include an imbalance of $233 billion last year with China alone, the largest ever recorded with a single country." What does it mean to say the yuan is undervalued? Why would American manufacturers be concerned that the yuan is undervalued? How does the yuan exchange rate affect the balance of trade in the United States and China?

Source: Martin Crutsinger, "Beijing Prodded on Currency Issue," *Houston Chronicle*, June 20, 2007.

2.28 (Related to the *Making the Connection* on page 1053) The following is from an article in the *Wall Street Journal* on changes in the Korean economy:

The biggest is a change in where Korean companies are finding growth. It is no longer just the U.S. and Europe, markets where Samsung, Hyundai and other big exporters have long focused on. Instead, it is in places like China, central Asia and the Middle East. . . . The broader trend is that global economic growth is less tied to the U.S., a phenomenon that has been called "decoupling."

If the trend identified in this article is correct, what are the implications for the policy of the Korean government with respect to the dollar–won exchange rate?

Source: Evan Ramstad, "Korean Stock Rally Shows a Different Picture," *Wall Street Journal*, June 19, 2007, p. C3.

2.29 (Related to *Solved Problem 30-2B* on page 1055) An article in the *Wall Street Journal* stated the following:

Romania's central bank vowed to intervene to defend the country's currency, the leu. . . . But traders said authorities will have to work quickly to maintain confidence in the currency. . . . With reserves at just $1.59 billion . . . the central bank's arsenal for staving off further speculation is limited.

Is it likely that the Romanian central bank was trying to defend an exchange rate that is above or below the exchange rate that would prevail in the absence of intervention? Draw a graph to illustrate your answer. Briefly explain what traders would have to gain by speculating against the leu and what the Romanian central bank's dollar reserves have to do with its ability to defend the value of the Romanian currency.

Source: John Reed, "Romania Vows to Defend Currency if Necessary," *Wall Street Journal*, March 19, 1999.

2.30 (Related to the *Chapter Opener* on page 1038) For 35 years, the Montreal Expos played major league baseball in the French-speaking Canadian province of Quebec, before relocating in 2005 to Washington, DC. All but one of the other 29 major league baseball teams were based in cities in the United States. Before they moved to Washington (and became the Nationals), an analysis of the Expos contained the following observation: "Numerous factors, from the language barrier to the floating Canadian dollar, conspire to make baseball in Quebec a difficult proposition." What is meant by a "floating" Canadian dollar? Why would a floating Canadian dollar make it difficult to operate a major league baseball team in Montreal?

Source: Jeff Bower et al., *Baseball Prospectus, 2002*, Washington, DC: Brassey, 2002, p. 358.

2.31 **(Related to the *Chapter Opener* on page 1038)** In 2001, Molson, a Canadian firm, sold the Montreal Canadiens ice hockey team to George Gillett, Jr., a U.S. ski resort operator. What was a key problem that Molson encountered in operating the Canadiens? Would Gillett, as a U.S. citizen, be better able to deal with this problem? Briefly explain.

>> **End Learning Objective 30.2**

30.3 LEARNING OBJECTIVE   30.3 | Discuss the growth of international capital markets, **pages 1055–1056.**

International Capital Markets

Summary

A key reason that exchange rates fluctuate is that investors seek out the best investments they can find anywhere in the world. Since 1980, the markets for stocks and bonds have become global. Foreign purchases of U.S. corporate bonds and stocks and U.S. government bonds have increased greatly just in the period since 1995. As a result, firms around the world are no longer forced to rely only on the savings of domestic households for funds.

myeconlab Visit www.myeconlab.com to complete these exercises
Get Ahead of the Curve online and get instant feedback.

Review Questions

3.1 What were the main factors behind the globalization of capital markets in the 1980s and 1990s?

3.2 Are foreign investors more likely to buy U.S. government bonds, U.S. corporate bonds, or U.S. corporate stocks?

Problems and Applications

3.3 Why are foreign investors more likely to invest in U.S. government bonds than in U.S. corporate stocks and bonds?

3.4 The text states that "the globalization of financial markets has helped increase growth and efficiency in the world economy." Briefly explain which aspects of globalization help to increase growth in the world economy.

>> **End Learning Objective 30.3**

Appendix

The Gold Standard and the Bretton Woods System

LEARNING OBJECTIVE

Explain the gold standard and the Bretton Woods system.

It is easier to understand the current exchange rate system by considering further two earlier systems: the gold standard and the Bretton Woods system, which together lasted from the early nineteenth century through the early 1970s.

The Gold Standard

As we saw in this chapter, under the gold standard, the currency of a country consisted of gold coins and paper currency that could be redeemed in gold. Great Britain adopted the gold standard in 1816, but as late as 1870, only a few nations had followed. In the late nineteenth century, however, Great Britain's share of world trade had increased, as had its overseas investments. The dominant position of Great Britain in the world economy motivated other countries to adopt the gold standard. By 1913, every country in Europe, except Spain and Bulgaria, and most countries in the Western Hemisphere had adopted the gold standard.

Under the gold standard, the exchange rate between two currencies was automatically determined by the quantity of gold in each currency. If there was one-fifth of an ounce of gold in a U.S. dollar and one ounce of gold in a British pound, the price of gold in the United States would be $5 per ounce, and the price of gold in Britain would be £1 per ounce. The exchange rate would be $5 = £1.

The End of the Gold Standard

From a modern point of view, the greatest drawback to the gold standard was that the central bank lacked control of the money supply. The size of a country's money supply depended on its gold supply, which could be greatly affected by chance discoveries of gold or by technological change in gold mining. For example, the gold discoveries in California in 1849 and Alaska in the 1890s caused rapid increases in the U.S. money supply. Because the central bank cannot determine how much gold will be discovered, it lacks the control of the money supply necessary to pursue an active monetary policy. During wartime, countries usually went off the gold standard to allow their central banks to expand the money supply as rapidly as was necessary to pay for the war. Britain abandoned the gold standard at the beginning of World War I in 1914 and did not resume redeeming its paper currency for gold until 1925.

When the Great Depression began in 1929, governments came under pressure to abandon the gold standard to allow their central banks to pursue active monetary policies. In 1931, Great Britain became the first major country to abandon the gold standard.

A number of other countries also went off the gold standard that year. The United States remained on the gold standard until 1933, and a few countries, including France, Italy, and Belgium, stayed on even longer. By the late 1930s, the gold standard had collapsed.

The earlier a country abandoned the gold standard, the easier time it had fighting the Depression with expansionary monetary policies. The countries that abandoned the gold standard by 1932 suffered an average decline in production of only 3 percent between 1929 and 1934. The countries that stayed on the gold standard until 1933 or later suffered an average decline of more than 30 percent. The devastating economic performance of the countries that stayed on the gold standard the longest during the 1930s is the key reason no attempt was made to bring back the gold standard in later years.

The Bretton Woods System

In addition to the collapse of the gold standard, the global economy had suffered during the 1930s from tariff wars. The United States had started the tariff wars in June 1930 by enacting the Smoot-Hawley Tariff, which raised the average U.S. tariff rate to more than 50 percent. Many other countries raised tariffs during the next few years, leading to a collapse in world trade.

As World War II was coming to an end, economists and government officials in the United States and Europe concluded that they had to restore the international economic system to avoid another depression. In 1947, the United States and most other major countries, apart from the Soviet Union, began participating in the General Agreement on Tariffs and Trade (GATT), under which they worked to reduce trade barriers. The GATT was very successful in sponsoring rounds of negotiations among countries, which led to sharp declines in tariffs. U.S. tariffs dropped from an average rate of more than 50 percent in the early 1930s to an average rate of less than 2 percent today. In 1995, the GATT was replaced by the World Trade Organization (WTO), which has similar objectives.

The effort to develop a new exchange rate system to replace the gold standard was more complicated than establishing the GATT. A conference held in Bretton Woods, New Hampshire, in 1944 set up a system in which the United States pledged to buy or sell gold at a fixed price of $35 per ounce. The central banks of all other members of the new **Bretton Woods system** pledged to buy and sell their currencies at a fixed rate against the dollar. By fixing their exchange rates against the dollar, these countries were fixing the exchange rates among their currencies as well. Unlike under the gold standard, neither the United States nor any other country was willing to redeem its paper currency for gold domestically. The United States would redeem dollars for gold only if they were presented by a foreign central bank. The United States continued the prohibition, first enacted in the early 1930s, against private citizens owning gold, unless they were jewelers or rare coin collectors. The prohibition was not lifted until the 1970s, when it again became possible for Americans to own gold as an investment.

Bretton Woods system An exchange rate system that lasted from 1944 to 1971, under which countries pledged to buy and sell their currencies at a fixed rate against the dollar.

Under the Bretton Woods system, central banks were committed to selling dollars in exchange for their own currencies. This commitment required them to hold *dollar reserves*. If a central bank ran out of dollar reserves, it could borrow them from the newly created **International Monetary Fund (IMF)**. In addition to providing loans to central banks that were short of dollar reserves, the IMF would oversee the operation of the system and approve adjustments to the agreed-on fixed exchange rates.

International Monetary Fund (IMF) An international organization that provides foreign currency loans to central banks and oversees the operation of the international monetary system.

Under the Bretton Woods system, a fixed exchange rate was known as a *par exchange rate*. If the par exchange rate was not the same as the exchange rate that would have been determined in the market, the result would be a surplus or a shortage. For example, Figure 30A-1 shows the exchange rate between the dollar and the British pound. The figure is drawn from the British point of view, so we measure the exchange rate on the vertical axis as dollars per pound. In this case, the par exchange rate between the dollar and the pound is above the equilibrium exchange rate as determined by supply and demand.

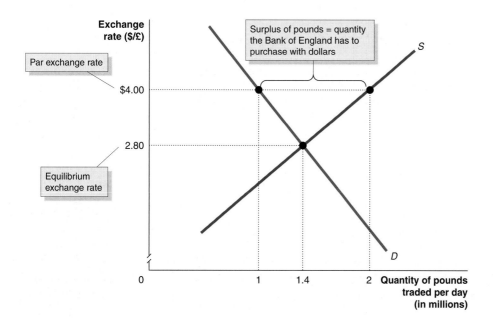

Figure 30A-1

A Fixed Exchange Rate above Equilibrium Results in a Surplus of Pounds

Under the Bretton Woods system, if the par exchange rate was above equilibrium, the result would be a surplus of domestic currency in the foreign exchange market. If the par exchange rate was below equilibrium, the result would be a shortage of domestic currency. In the figure, the par exchange rate between the pound and the dollar is $4 = £1, whereas the equilibrium exchange rate is $2.80 = £1. This gap forces the Bank of England to buy £1 million per day in exchange for dollars.

In this example, at the par exchange rate of $4 per pound, the quantity of pounds demanded by people wanting to buy British goods and services or wanting to invest in British assets is smaller than the quantity of pounds supplied by people who would like to exchange them for dollars. As a result, the Bank of England must use dollars to buy the surplus of £1 million per day. Only at an exchange rate of $2.80 per pound would the surplus be eliminated. If the par exchange rate were below the equilibrium exchange rate, there would be a shortage of domestic currency in the foreign exchange market.

A persistent shortage or surplus of a currency under the Bretton Woods system was seen as evidence of a *fundamental disequilibrium* in a country's exchange rate. After consulting with the IMF, countries in this position were allowed to adjust their exchange rates. In the early years of the Bretton Woods system, many countries found that their currencies were *overvalued* versus the dollar, meaning that their par exchange rates were too high. A reduction in a fixed exchange rate is a **devaluation**. An increase in a fixed exchange rate is a **revaluation**. In 1949, there was a devaluation of several currencies, including the British pound, reflecting the fact that those currencies had been overvalued against the dollar.

Devaluation A reduction in a fixed exchange rate.

Revaluation An increase in a fixed exchange rate.

The Collapse of the Bretton Woods System

By the late 1960s, the Bretton Woods system faced two severe problems. The first was that after 1963, the total number of dollars held by foreign central banks was larger than the gold reserves of the United States. In practice, most central banks—the Bank of France was the main exception—rarely redeemed dollars for gold. But the basis of the system was a credible promise by the United States to redeem dollars for gold if called upon to do so. By the late 1960s, as the gap between the dollars held by foreign central banks and the gold reserves of the United States grew larger and larger, the credibility of the U.S. promise to redeem dollars for gold was called into question.

The second problem the Bretton Woods system faced was that some countries with undervalued currencies, particularly West Germany, were unwilling to revalue their currencies. Governments resisted revaluation because it would have increased the prices of their countries' exports. Many German firms, such as Volkswagen, put pressure on the government not to endanger their sales in the U.S. market by raising

Figure 30A-2

West Germany's Undervalued Exchange Rate

The Bundesbank, the German central bank, was committed under the Bretton Woods system to defending a par exchange rate of $0.27 per deutsche mark (DM). Because this exchange rate was lower than what the equilibrium market exchange rate would have been, there was a shortage of deutsche marks in the foreign exchange market. The Bundesbank had to supply deutsche marks equal to the shortage in exchange for dollars. The shortage in the figure is equal to 1 billion deutsche marks per day.

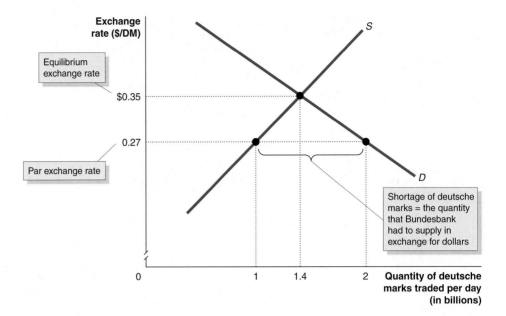

Capital controls Limits on the flow of foreign exchange and financial investment across countries.

the exchange rate of the deutsche mark against the dollar. Figure 30A-2 shows the situation faced by the German government in 1971. The figure takes the German point of view, so the exchange rate is expressed in terms of dollars per deutsche mark.

Under the Bretton Woods system, the Bundesbank, the German central bank, was required to buy and sell deutsche marks for dollars at a rate of $0.27 per deutsche mark. The equilibrium that would have prevailed in the foreign exchange market if the Bundesbank had not intervened was about $0.35 per deutsche mark. Because the par exchange rate was below the equilibrium exchange rate, the quantity of deutsche marks demanded by people wanting to buy German goods and services or wanting to invest in German assets was greater than the quantity of deutsche marks supplied by people who wanted to exchange them for dollars. To maintain the exchange rate at $0.27 per deutsche mark, the Bundesbank had to buy dollars and sell deutsche marks. The number of deutsche marks supplied by the Bundesbank was equal to the shortage of deutsche marks at the par exchange rate.

By selling deutsche marks and buying dollars to defend the par exchange rate, the Bundesbank was increasing the West German money supply, risking an increase in the inflation rate. Because Germany had suffered a devastating hyperinflation during the 1920s, the fear of inflation was greater in Germany than in any other industrial country. No German government could survive politically if it allowed a significant increase in inflation. Knowing this fact, many investors in Germany and elsewhere became convinced that eventually, the German government would have to allow a revaluation of the mark.

During the 1960s, most European countries, including Germany, relaxed their *capital controls*. **Capital controls** are limits on the flow of foreign exchange and financial investment across countries. The loosening of capital controls made it easier for investors to *speculate* on changes in exchange rates. For instance, an investor in the United States could sell $1 million and receive about 3.7 million deutsche marks at the par exchange rate of $0.27 per deutsche mark. If the exchange rate rose to $0.35 per deutsche mark, the investor could then exchange deutsche marks for dollars, receiving $1.3 million at the new exchange rate: a return of 30 percent on an initial $1 million investment. The more convinced investors became that Germany would have to allow a revaluation, the more dollars they exchanged for deutsche marks. Figure 30A-3 shows the results.

The increased demand for deutsche marks by investors hoping to make a profit from the expected revaluation of the mark shifted the demand curve for marks to the right, from D_1 to D_2. Because of this expectation, the Bundesbank had to increase the

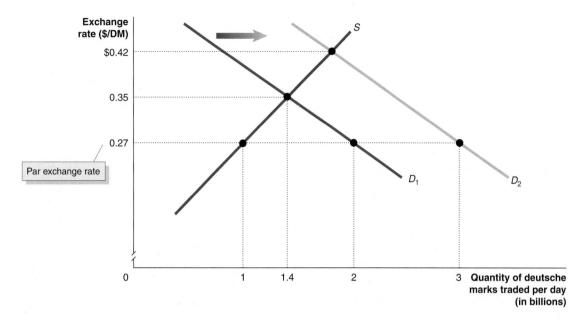

Figure 30A-3 | Destabilizing Speculation against the Deutsche Mark, 1971

In 1971, the par exchange rate of $0.27 = DM1 was below the equilibrium exchange rate of $0.35 = DM1. As investors became convinced that West Germany would have to revalue the deutsche mark, they increased their demand for marks from D_1 to D_2.

The new equilibrium exchange rate became $0.42 = DM1. This increase in demand raised the quantity of marks the Bundesbank had to supply in exchange for dollars to defend the par exchange rate from DM1 billion to DM2 billion per day.

marks it supplied in exchange for dollars, raising further the risk of inflation in Germany. As we saw in the chapter, because these actions by investors make it more difficult to maintain a fixed exchange rate, they are referred to as *destabilizing speculation*. By May 1971, the Bundesbank had to buy more than $1 billion per day to support the fixed exchange rate against the dollar. Finally, on May 5, the West German government decided to allow the mark to float. In August, President Richard Nixon decided to abandon the U.S. commitment to redeem dollars for gold. Attempts were made over the next two years to reach a compromise that would restore a fixed exchange rate system, but by 1973, the Bretton Woods system was effectively dead.

Key Terms

Bretton Woods system, p. 1066

Capital controls, p. 1068

Devaluation, p. 1067

International Monetary Fund (IMF), p. 1066

Revaluation, p. 1067

LEARNING OBJECTIVE   Explain the gold standard and the Bretton Woods system, **pages 1065–1069.**

 Visit www.myeconlab.com to complete these exercises
Get Ahead of the Curve online and get instant feedback.

Review Questions

30A.1 What determined the exchange rates among currencies under the gold standard? Why did the gold standard collapse?

30A.2 Briefly describe how the Bretton Woods system operated.

30A.3 What is the difference between a devaluation and a revaluation?

30A.4 What are capital controls?

30A.5 What role did the International Monetary Fund play in the Bretton Woods system?

30A.6 What is destabilizing speculation? What role did it play in the collapse of the Bretton Woods system?

Problems and Applications

30A.7 Suppose that under the gold standard, there was one-fifth of an ounce of gold in a U.S. dollar and one ounce of gold in a British pound. Demonstrate that if the exchange rate between the dollar and the pound was $4 = £1, rather than $5 = £1, you could make unlimited profits by buying gold in one country and selling it in the other. If the exchange rate was $6 = £1, how would your strategy change? For simplicity, assume that there was no cost to shipping gold from one country to the other.

30A.8 An article in the *Economist* observes that "Enthusiasm for the gold standard evaporated in the 1930s, when it made dreadful conditions worse." How did the gold standard make dreadful conditions worse during the 1930s?

Source: "Heading for a Fall, by Fiat?" *Economist*, February 26, 2004.

30A.9 According to an article in the *Economist*, when most countries left the gold standard in the 1930s, in South Africa, "the mining industry flourished." Briefly explain why the end of the gold standard might be good news for the owners of gold mines.

Source: "Johannesburg," *Economist*, August 18, 2004.

30A.10 By the mid-1960s, the price of gold on the London market had increased to more than $35 per ounce. (Remember that it was not legal during these years for investors in the United States to own gold.) Would this have happened if foreign investors had believed that the U.S. commitment to buy and sell gold at $35 per ounce under the Bretton Woods system would continue indefinitely? Briefly explain.

30A.11 An article in the *New York Times* states that during the 1970s, the "United States abandon[ed] the gold standard, a decision that sent the yen rocketing." Is the author of this article correct that the United States abandoned the gold standard in the 1970s? What action of the United States during the 1970s would have caused the value of the yen to rise against the dollar?

Source: Ken Belson, "Did He Fiddle While Japan Burned?" *New York Times*, February 26, 2003.

30A.12 An article summarizing the United Kingdom's experience with the gold standard makes the following statement about an event in August 1927: "The New York Federal Reserve Bank cuts its rediscount rate to 3.5% from 4%, partly in order to help the U.K. to stay on the gold standard." Why would a fall in interest rates in the United States help the United Kingdom to stay on the gold standard?

Source: Worth Civils, "A History of the Pound: 1925–2007," *Wall Street Journal*, April 18, 2007.

30A.13 One economist has argued that the East Asian exchange rate crisis of the late 1990s was due to "the simple failure of governments to remember the lessons from the breakdown of the Bretton Woods System." What are the lessons from the breakdown of the Bretton Woods system? In what sense did the East Asian governments fail to learn these lessons?

Source: Thomas D. Willett, "Crying for Argentina," *Milken Institute Review*, Second Quarter 2002, p. 54.

30A.14 An article in the *Wall Street Journal* argues that "The Bretton Woods system ran into trouble in the 1960s, in part because U.S. trade deficits mounted." Why would increases in the U.S. trade deficit cause problems for the Bretton Woods system?

Source: Jon E. Hilsenrath and Mary Kissel, "Currency Decision Marks Small Shift toward Flexibility," *Wall Street Journal*, July 22, 2005.

30A.15 Thomas Mayer, an economist at the German bank, Deutsche Bank, wrote that "following the breakup of the Bretton Woods system that had kept the mark tied to the U.S. dollar, the Bundesbank adopted a monetary policy strategy that allowed it to keep its eyes on ensuring price stability in the long run." Why might keeping the mark tied to the value of the dollar have made it difficult for the Bundesbank to pursue a policy of price stability?

Source: Thomas Mayer, "Euro Down," *Wall Street Journal*, July 21, 2005.

30A.16 In 2007, Jean-Claude Trichet, the president of the European Central Bank, argued that "the [Bretton Woods] system's collapse in the '70s seriously threatened the process of economic integration in Europe. However, Europe's leaders rose to the challenge." Why would the collapse of the Bretton Woods system have threatened economic integration in Europe? How did the European countries eventually replace the system?

Source: Jean-Claude Trichet, "Europe Turns 50," *Wall Street Journal*, March 23, 2007, p. A11.

>> End Appendix Learning Objective

Glossary

A

Absolute advantage The ability of an individual, a firm, or a country to produce more of a good or service than competitors, using the same amount of resources.

Accounting profit A firm's net income measured by revenue minus operating expenses and taxes paid.

Adverse selection The situation in which one party to a transaction takes advantage of knowing more than the other party to the transaction.

Aggregate demand and aggregate supply model A model that explains short-run fluctuations in real GDP and the price level.

Aggregate demand curve A curve that shows the relationship between the price level and the quantity of real GDP demanded by households, firms, and the government.

Aggregate expenditure (*AE*) The total amount of spending in the economy: the sum of consumption, planned investment, government purchases, and net exports.

Aggregate expenditure model A macroeconomic model that focuses on the relationship between total spending and real GDP, assuming that the price level is constant.

Allocative efficiency A state of the economy in which production represents consumer preferences; in particular, every good or service is produced up to the point where the last unit provides a marginal benefit to consumers equal to the marginal cost of producing it.

Antitrust laws Laws aimed at eliminating collusion and promoting competition among firms.

Arrow impossibility theorem A mathematical theorem that holds that no system of voting can be devised that will consistently represent the underlying preferences of voters.

Asset Anything of value owned by a person or a firm.

Asymmetric information A situation in which one party to an economic transaction has less information than the other party.

Autarky A situation in which a country does not trade with other countries.

Automatic stabilizers Government spending and taxes that automatically increase or decrease along with the business cycle.

Autonomous expenditure An expenditure that does not depend on the level of GDP.

Average fixed cost Fixed cost divided by the quantity of output produced.

Average product of labor The total output produced by a firm divided by the quantity of workers.

Average revenue (*AR*) Total revenue divided by the quantity of the product sold.

Average tax rate Total tax paid divided by total income.

Average total cost Total cost divided by the quantity of output produced.

Average variable cost Variable cost divided by the quantity of output produced.

B

Balance of payments The record of a country's trade with other countries in goods, services, and assets.

Balance of trade The difference between the value of the goods a country exports and the value of the goods a country imports.

Balance sheet A financial statement that sums up a firm's financial position on a particular day, usually the end of a quarter or year.

Bank panic A situation in which many banks experience runs at the same time.

Bank run A situation in which many depositors simultaneously decide to withdraw money from a bank.

Barrier to entry Anything that keeps new firms from entering an industry in which firms are earning economic profits.

Behavioral economics The study of situations in which people make choices that do not appear to be economically rational.

Black market A market in which buying and selling take place at prices that violate government price regulations.

Bond A financial security that represents a promise to repay a fixed amount of funds.

Brand management The actions of a firm intended to maintain the differentiation of a product over time.

Bretton Woods System An exchange rate system that lasted from 1944 to 1971, under which countries pledged to buy and sell their currencies at a fixed rate against the dollar.

Budget constraint The limited amount of income available to consumers to spend on goods and services.

Budget deficit The situation in which the government's expenditures are greater than its tax revenue.

Budget surplus The situation in which the government's expenditures are less than its tax revenue.

Business cycle Alternating periods of economic expansion and economic recession.

Business strategy Actions taken by a firm to achieve a goal, such as maximizing profits.

C

Capital Manufactured goods that are used to produce other goods and services.

Capital account The part of the balance of payments that records relatively minor transactions, such as migrants' transfers, and sales and purchases of nonproduced, nonfinancial assets.

Capital controls Limits on the flow of foreign exchange and financial investment across countries.

Cartel A group of firms that collude by agreeing to restrict output to increase prices and profits.

Cash flow The difference between the cash revenues received by a firm and the cash spending by the firm.

Catch-up The prediction that the level of GDP per capita (or income per capita) in poor countries will grow faster than in rich countries.

Centrally planned economy An economy in which the government decides how economic resources will be allocated.

***Ceteris paribus* ("all else equal")** The requirement that when analyzing the relationship between two variables—such as price and quantity demanded—other variables must be held constant.

Circular-flow diagram A model that illustrates how participants in markets are linked.

Closed economy An economy that has no interactions in trade or finance with other countries.

Coase theorem The argument of economist Ronald Coase that if transactions costs are low, private bargaining will result in an efficient solution to the problem of externalities.

Collusion An agreement among firms to charge the same price or otherwise not to compete.

Command and control approach An approach that involves the government imposing quantitative limits on the amount of pollution firms are allowed to emit or requiring firms to install specific pollution control devices.

Commodity money A good used as money that also has value independent of its use as money.

Common resource A good that is rival but not excludable.

Comparative advantage The ability of an individual, a firm, or a country to produce a good or service at a lower opportunity cost than competitors.

Compensating differentials Higher wages that compensate workers for unpleasant aspects of a job.

Competitive market equilibrium A market equilibrium with many buyers and many sellers.

Complements Goods and services that are used together.

Constant returns to scale The situation when a firm's long-run average costs remain unchanged as it increases output.

Consumer price index (CPI) An average of the prices of the goods and services purchased by the typical urban family of four.

Consumer surplus The difference between the highest price a consumer is willing to pay and the price the consumer actually pays.

Consumption Spending by households on goods and services, not including spending on new houses.

Consumption function The relationship between consumption spending and disposable income.

Contractionary monetary policy The Federal Reserve's adjusting the money supply to increase interest rates to reduce inflation.

Cooperative equilibrium An equilibrium in a game in which players cooperate to increase their mutual payoff.

Copyright A government-granted exclusive right to produce and sell a creation.

Corporate governance The way in which a corporation is structured and the effect a corporation's structure has on the firm's behavior.

Corporation A legal form of business that provides owners with protection from losing more than their investment should the business fail.

Coupon payment An interest payment on a bond.

Cross-price elasticity of demand The percentage change in quantity demanded of one good divided by the percentage change in the price of another good.

Crowding out A decline in private expenditures as a result of an increase in government purchases.

Currency appreciation An increase in the market value of one currency relative to another currency.

Currency depreciation A decrease in the market value of one currency relative to another currency.

Current account The part of the balance of payments that records a country's net exports, net investment income, and net transfers.

Cyclical unemployment Unemployment caused by a business cycle recession.

Cyclically adjusted budget deficit or surplus The deficit or surplus in the federal government's budget if the economy were at potential GDP.

D

Deadweight loss The reduction in economic surplus resulting from a market not being in competitive equilibrium.

Deflation A decline in the price level.

Demand curve A curve that shows the relationship between the price of a product and the quantity of the product demanded.

Demand schedule A table showing the relationship between the price of a product and the quantity of the product demanded.

Demographics The characteristics of a population with respect to age, race, and gender.

Derived demand The demand for a factor of production that is derived from the demand for the good the factor produces.

Devaluation A reduction in a fixed exchange rate.

Direct finance A flow of funds from savers to firms through financial markets, such as the New York Stock Exchange.

Discount loans Loans the Federal Reserve makes to banks.

Discount rate The interest rate the Federal Reserve charges on discount loans.

Discouraged workers People who are available for work but have not looked for a job during the previous four weeks because they believe no jobs are available for them.

Diseconomies of scale The situation when a firm's long-run average costs rise as the firm increases output.

Disinflation A significant reduction in the inflation rate.

Dividends Payments by a corporation to its shareholders.

Dominant strategy A strategy that is the best for a firm, no matter what strategies other firms use.

Dumping Selling a product for a price below its cost of production.

E

Economic discrimination Paying a person a lower wage or excluding a person from an occupation on the basis of an irrelevant characteristic such as race or gender.

Economic efficiency A market outcome in which the marginal benefit to consumers of the last unit produced is equal to its marginal cost of production and in which the sum of consumer surplus and producer surplus is at a maximum.

Economic growth The ability of an economy to produce increasing quantities of goods and services.

Economic growth model A model that explains growth rate changes in real GDP per capita in the long run.

Economic loss The situation in which a firm's total revenue is less

than its total cost, including all implicit costs.

Economic model A simplified version of reality used to analyze real-world economic situations.

Economic profit A firm's revenues minus all its costs, implicit and explicit.

Economic rent (or pure rent) The price of a factor of production that is in fixed supply.

Economic surplus The sum of consumer surplus and producer surplus.

Economic variable Something measurable that can have different values, such as the wages of software programmers.

Economics The study of the choices people make to attain their goals, given their scarce resources.

Economies of scale The situation when a firm's long-run average costs fall as it increases output.

Efficiency wage A higher-than-market wage that a firm pays to increase worker productivity.

Elastic demand Demand is elastic when the percentage change in quantity demanded is *greater* than the percentage change in price, so the price elasticity is *greater* than 1 in absolute value.

Elasticity A measure of how much one economic variable responds to changes in another economic variable.

Endowment effect The tendency of people to be unwilling to sell a good they already own even if they are offered a price that is greater than the price they would be willing to pay to buy the good if they didn't already own it.

Entrepreneur Someone who operates a business, bringing together the factors of production—labor, capital, and natural resources—to produce goods and services.

Equity The fair distribution of economic benefits.

Euro The common currency of many European countries.

Excess burden The efficiency loss to the economy that results from a tax causing a reduction in the quantity of a good produced; also known as the deadweight loss.

Excess reserves Reserves that banks hold over and above the legal requirement.

Exchange rate system An agreement among countries on how exchange rates should be determined.

Excludability The situation in which anyone who does not pay for a good cannot consume it.

Expansion The period of a business cycle during which total production and total employment are increasing.

Expansion path A curve that shows a firm's cost-minimizing combination of inputs for every level of output.

Expansionary monetary policy The Federal Reserve's increasing the money supply and decreasing interest rates to increase real GDP.

Explicit cost A cost that involves spending money.

Exports Goods and services produced domestically but sold to other countries.

External economies Reductions in a firm's costs that result from an increase in the size of an industry.

Externality A benefit or cost that affects someone who is not directly involved in the production or consumption of a good or service.

F

Factor markets Markets for the factors of production, such as labor, capital, natural resources, and entrepreneurial ability.

Factors of production Labor, capital, natural resources, and other inputs used to produce goods and services.

Federal funds rate The interest rate banks charge each other for overnight loans.

Federal Open Market Committee (FOMC) The Federal Reserve committee responsible for open market

operations and managing the money supply in the United States.

Federal Reserve System The central bank of the United States.

Fiat money Money, such as paper currency, that is authorized by a central bank or governmental body and that does not have to be exchanged by the central bank for gold or some other commodity money.

Final good or service A good or service purchased by a final user.

Financial account The part of the balance of payments that records purchases of assets a country has made abroad and foreign purchases of assets in the country.

Financial intermediaries Firms, such as banks, mutual funds, pension funds, and insurance companies, that borrow funds from savers and lend them to borrowers.

Financial markets Markets where financial securities, such as stocks and bonds, are bought and sold.

Financial system The system of financial markets and financial intermediaries through which firms acquire funds from households.

Fiscal policy Changes in federal taxes and purchases that are intended to achieve macroeconomic policy objectives, such as high employment, price stability, and high rates of economic growth.

Fixed costs Costs that remain constant as output changes.

Fixed exchange rate system A system under which countries agree to keep the exchange rates among their currencies fixed.

Floating currency The outcome of a country allowing its currency's exchange rate to be determined by demand and supply.

Foreign direct investment (FDI) The purchase or building by a corporation of a facility in a foreign country.

Foreign portfolio investment The purchase by an individual or

a firm of stocks or bonds issued in another country.

Fractional reserve banking system A banking system in which banks keep less than 100 percent of deposits as reserves.

Free market A market with few government restrictions on how a good or service can be produced or sold or on how a factor of production can be employed.

Free riding Benefiting from a good without paying for it.

Free trade Trade between countries that is without government restrictions.

Frictional unemployment Short-term unemployment that arises from the process of matching workers with jobs.

G

Game theory The study of how people make decisions in situations in which attaining their goals depends on their interactions with others; in economics, the study of the decisions of firms in industries where the profits of each firm depend on its interactions with other firms.

GDP deflator A measure of the price level, calculated by dividing nominal GDP by real GDP and multiplying by 100.

Globalization The process of countries becoming more open to foreign trade and investment.

Government purchases Spending by federal, state, and local governments on goods and services.

Gross domestic product (GDP) The market value of all final goods and services produced in a country during a period of time, typically one year.

H

Horizontal merger A merger between firms in the same industry.

Human capital The accumulated knowledge and skills that workers acquire from education and training or from their life experiences.

I

Implicit cost A nonmonetary opportunity cost.

Imports Goods and services bought domestically but produced in other countries.

Income effect The change in the quantity demanded of a good that results from the effect of a change in price on consumer purchasing power, holding all other factors constant.

Income elasticity of demand A measure of the responsiveness of quantity demanded to changes in income, measured by the percentage change in quantity demanded divided by the percentage change in income.

Income statement A financial statement that sums up a firm's revenues, costs, and profit over a period of time.

Indifference curve A curve that shows the combinations of consumption bundles that give the consumer the same utility.

Indirect finance A flow of funds from savers to borrowers through financial intermediaries such as banks. Intermediaries raise funds from savers to lend to firms (and other borrowers).

Industrial Revolution The application of mechanical power to the production of goods, beginning in England around 1750.

Inelastic demand Demand is inelastic when the percentage change in quantity demanded is *less* than the percentage change in price, so the price elasticity is *less* than 1 in absolute value.

Inferior good A good for which the demand increases as income falls and decreases as income rises.

Inflation rate The percentage increase in the price level from one year to the next.

Inflation targeting Conducting monetary policy so as to commit the central bank to achieving a publicly announced level of inflation.

Interest rate The cost of borrowing funds, usually expressed as a percentage of the amount borrowed.

Intermediate good or service A good or service that is an input into another good or service, such as a tire on a truck.

International Monetary Fund (IMF) An international organization that provides foreign currency loans to central banks and oversees the operation of the international monetary system.

Inventories Goods that have been produced but not yet sold.

Investment Spending by firms on new factories, office buildings, machinery, and additions to inventories, and spending by households on new houses.

Isocost line All the combinations of two inputs, such as capital and labor, that have the same total cost.

Isoquant A curve that shows all the combinations of two inputs, such as capital and labor, that will produce the same level of output.

K

Keynesian revolution The name given to the widespread acceptance during the 1930s and 1940s of John Maynard Keynes's macroeconomic model.

L

Labor force The sum of employed and unemployed workers in the economy.

Labor force participation rate The percentage of the working-age population in the labor force.

Labor productivity The quantity of goods and services that can be produced by one worker or by one hour of work.

Labor union An organization of employees that has the legal right to bargain with employers about wages and working conditions.

Law of demand The rule that, holding everything else constant, when the price of a product falls, the quantity demanded of the product will increase, and when the price of a product rises, the quantity demanded of the product will decrease.

Law of diminishing marginal utility The principle that consumers experience diminishing additional satisfaction as they consume more of a good or service during a given period of time.

Law of diminishing returns The principle that, at some point, adding more of a variable input, such as labor, to the same amount of a fixed input, such as capital, will cause the marginal product of the variable input to decline.

Law of supply The rule that, holding everything else constant, increases in price cause increases in the quantity supplied, and decreases in price cause decreases in the quantity supplied.

Liability Anything owed by a person or a firm.

Limited liability The legal provision that shields owners of a corporation from losing more than they have invested in the firm.

Long run The period of time in which a firm can vary all its inputs, adopt new technology, and increase or decrease the size of its physical plant.

Long-run aggregate supply curve A curve that shows the relationship in the long run between the price level and the quantity of real GDP supplied.

Long-run average cost curve A curve showing the lowest cost at which a firm is able to produce a given quantity of output in the long run, when no inputs are fixed.

Long-run competitive equilibrium The situation in which the entry and exit of firms has resulted in the typical firm breaking even.

Long-run economic growth The process by which rising productivity increases the average standard of living.

Long-run supply curve A curve that shows the relationship in the long run between market price and the quantity supplied.

Lorenz curve A curve that shows the distribution of income by arraying incomes from lowest to highest on the horizontal axis and indicating the cumulative fraction of income earned by each fraction of households on the vertical axis.

M

M1 The narrowest definition of the money supply: The sum of currency in circulation, checking account deposits in banks, and holdings of traveler's checks.

M2 A broader definition of the money supply: M1 plus savings account balances, small-denomination time deposits, balances in money market deposit accounts in banks, and noninstitutional money market fund shares.

Macroeconomics The study of the economy as a whole, including topics such as inflation, unemployment, and economic growth.

Managed float exchange rate system The current exchange rate system, under which the value of most currencies is determined by demand and supply, with occasional government intervention.

Marginal analysis Analysis that involves comparing marginal benefits and marginal costs.

Marginal benefit The additional benefit to a consumer from consuming one more unit of a good or service.

Marginal cost The change in a firm's total cost from producing one more unit of a good or service.

Marginal product of labor The additional output a firm produces as a result of hiring one more worker.

Marginal productivity theory of income distribution The theory that the distribution of income is determined by the marginal productivity of the factors of production that individuals own.

Marginal propensity to consume (MPC) The slope of the consumption function: The amount by which consumption spending changes when disposable income changes.

Marginal propensity to save (MPS) The change in saving divided by the change in disposable income.

Marginal rate of substitution (MRS) The slope of an indifference curve, which represents the rate at which a consumer would be willing to trade off one good for another.

Marginal rate of technical substitution (MRTS) The slope of an isoquant, or the rate at which a firm is able to substitute one input for another while keeping the level of output constant.

Marginal revenue (MR) Change in total revenue from selling one more unit of a product.

Marginal revenue product of labor (MRP) The change in a firm's revenue as a result of hiring one more worker.

Marginal tax rate The fraction of each additional dollar of income that must be paid in taxes.

Marginal utility (MU) The change in total utility a person receives from consuming one additional unit of a good or service.

Market A group of buyers and sellers of a good or service and the institution or arrangement by which they come together to trade.

Market demand The demand by all the consumers of a given good or service.

Market economy An economy in which the decisions of households and firms interacting in markets allocate economic resources.

Market equilibrium A situation in which quantity demanded equals quantity supplied.

Market failure A situation in which the market fails to produce the efficient level of output.

Market for loanable funds The interaction of borrowers and lenders that determines the market interest rate and the quantity of loanable funds exchanged.

Market power The ability of a firm to charge a price greater than marginal cost.

Marketing All the activities necessary for a firm to sell a product to a consumer.

Median voter theorem The proposition that the outcome of a majority vote is likely to represent the preferences of the voter who is in the political middle.

Menu costs The costs to firms of changing prices.

Microeconomics The study of how households and firms make choices, how they interact in markets, and how the government attempts to influence their choices.

Minimum efficient scale The level of output at which all economies of scale are exhausted.

Mixed economy An economy in which most economic decisions result from the interaction of buyers and sellers in markets but in which the government plays a significant role in the allocation of resources.

Monetarism The macroeconomic theories of Milton Friedman and his followers; particularly the idea that the quantity of money should be increased at a constant rate.

Monetary growth rule A plan for increasing the quantity of money at a fixed rate that does not respond to changes in economic conditions.

Monetary policy The actions the Federal Reserve takes to manage the money supply and interest rates to pursue macroeconomic policy objectives.

Money Assets that people are generally willing to accept in exchange for goods and services or for payment of debts.

Monopolistic competition A market structure in which barriers to entry are low and many firms compete by selling similar, but not identical, products.

Monopoly A firm that is the only seller of a good or service that does not have a close substitute.

Monopsony The sole buyer of a factor of production.

Moral hazard The actions people take after they have entered into a transaction that make the other party to the transaction worse off.

Multinational enterprise A firm that conducts operations in more than one country.

Multiplier The increase in equilibrium real GDP divided by the increase in autonomous expenditure.

Multiplier effect The series of induced increases in consumption spending that results from an initial increase in autonomous expenditure.

N

Nash equilibrium A situation in which each firm chooses the best strategy, given the strategies chosen by other firms.

Natural monopoly A situation in which economies of scale are so large that one firm can supply the entire market at a lower average total cost than can two or more firms.

Natural rate of unemployment The normal rate of unemployment, consisting of frictional unemployment plus structural unemployment.

Net exports Exports minus imports.

Net foreign investment The difference between capital outflows from a country and capital inflows, also equal to net foreign direct investment plus net foreign portfolio investment.

Network externalities The situation where the usefulness of a product increases with the number of consumers who use it.

New classical macroeconomics The macroeconomic theories of Robert Lucas and others, particularly the idea that workers and firms have rational expectations.

New growth theory A model of long-run economic growth that emphasizes that technological change is influenced by economic incentives and so is determined by the working of the market system.

Nominal exchange rate The value of one country's currency in terms of another country's currency.

Nominal GDP The value of final goods and services evaluated at current-year prices.

Nominal interest rate The stated interest rate on a loan.

Nonaccelerating inflation rate of unemployment (NAIRU) The unemployment rate at which the inflation rate has no tendency to increase or decrease.

Noncooperative equilibrium An equilibrium in a game in which players do not cooperate but pursue their own self-interest.

Normal good A good for which the demand increases as income rises and decreases as income falls.

Normative analysis Analysis concerned with what ought to be.

O

Oligopoly A market structure in which a small number of interdependent firms compete.

Open economy An economy that has interactions in trade or finance with other countries.

Open market operations The buying and selling of Treasury securities by the Federal Reserve in order to control the money supply.

Opportunity cost The highest-valued alternative that must be given up to engage in an activity.

P

Partnership A firm owned jointly by two or more persons and not organized as a corporation.

Patent The exclusive right to a product for a period of 20 years from the date the product is invented.

Payoff matrix A table that shows the payoffs that each firm earns from every combination of strategies by the firms.

Pegging The decision by a country to keep the exchange rate fixed between its currency and another currency.

Perfectly competitive market A market that meets the conditions of (1) many buyers and sellers, (2) all firms selling identical products, and (3) no barriers to new firms entering the market.

Perfectly elastic demand The case where the quantity demanded is infinitely responsive to price, and the price elasticity of demand equals infinity.

Perfectly inelastic demand The case where the quantity demanded is completely unresponsive to price, and the price elasticity of demand equals zero.

Personnel economics The application of economic analysis to human resources issues.

Per-worker production function The relationship between real GDP per hour worked and capital per hour worked, holding the level of technology constant.

Phillips curve A curve showing the short-run relationship between the unemployment rate and the inflation rate.

Pigovian taxes and subsidies Government taxes and subsidies intended to bring about an efficient level of output in the presence of externalities.

Positive analysis Analysis concerned with what is.

Potential GDP The level of GDP attained when all firms are producing at capacity.

Poverty line A level of annual income equal to three times the amount of money necessary to purchase the minimal quantity of food required for adequate nutrition.

Poverty rate The percentage of the population that is poor according to the federal government's definition.

Present value The value in today's dollars of funds to be paid or received in the future.

Price ceiling A legally determined maximum price that sellers may charge.

Price discrimination Charging different prices to different customers for the same product when the price differences are not due to differences in cost.

Price elasticity of demand The responsiveness of the quantity demanded to a change in price, measured by dividing the percentage change in the quantity demanded of a product by the percentage change in the product's price.

Price elasticity of supply The responsiveness of the quantity supplied to a change in price, measured by dividing the percentage change in the quantity supplied of a product by the percentage change in the product's price.

Price floor A legally determined minimum price that sellers may receive.

Price leadership A form of implicit collusion where one firm in an oligopoly announces a price change, which is matched by the other firms in the industry.

Price level A measure of the average prices of goods and services in the economy.

Price taker A buyer or seller that is unable to affect the market price.

Principal–agent problem A problem caused by an agent pursuing his own interests rather than the interests of the principal who hired him.

Prisoners' dilemma A game in which pursuing dominant strategies results in noncooperation that leaves everyone worse off.

Private benefit The benefit received by the consumer of a good or service.

Private cost The cost borne by the producer of a good or service.

Private good A good that is both rival and excludable.

Producer price index (PPI) An average of the prices received by producers of goods and services at all stages of the production process.

Producer surplus The difference between the lowest price a firm would be willing to accept and the price it actually receives.

Product markets Markets for goods—such as computers—

and services—such as medical treatment.

Production function The relationship between the inputs employed by a firm and the maximum output it can produce with those inputs.

Production possibilities frontier (PPF) A curve showing the maximum attainable combinations of two products that may be produced with available resources and current technology.

Productive efficiency The situation in which a good or service is produced at the lowest possible cost.

Profit Total revenue minus total cost.

Progressive tax A tax for which people with lower incomes pay a lower percentage of their income in tax than do people with higher incomes.

Property rights The rights individuals or firms have to the exclusive use of property, including the right to buy or sell it.

Protectionism The use of trade barriers to shield domestic firms from foreign competition.

Public choice model A model that applies economic analysis to government decision making.

Public franchise A designation by the government that a firm is the only legal provider of a good or service.

Public good A good that is both nonrivalrous and nonexcludable.

Purchasing power parity The theory that in the long run, exchange rates move to equalize the purchasing powers of different currencies.

Q

Quantity demanded The amount of a good or service that a consumer is willing and able to purchase at a given price.

Quantity supplied The amount of a good or service that a firm is willing and able to supply at a given price.

Quantity theory of money A theory of the connection between money and prices that assumes that the velocity of money is constant.

Quota A numeric limit imposed by a government on the quantity of a good that can be imported into the country.

R

Rational expectations Expectations formed by using all available information about an economic variable.

Real business cycle model A macroeconomic model that focuses on real, rather than monetary, causes of the business cycle.

Real exchange rate The price of domestic goods in terms of foreign goods.

Real GDP The value of final goods and services evaluated at base-year prices.

Real interest rate The nominal interest rate minus the inflation rate.

Recession The period of a business cycle during which total production and total employment are decreasing.

Regressive tax A tax for which people with lower incomes pay a higher percentage of their income in tax than do people with higher incomes.

Rent seeking The attempts by individuals and firms to use government action to make themselves better off at the expense of others.

Required reserve ratio The minimum fraction of deposits banks are required by law to keep as reserves.

Required reserves Reserves that a bank is legally required to hold, based on its checking account deposits.

Reserves Deposits that a bank keeps as cash in its vault or on deposit with the Federal Reserve.

Revaluation An increase in a fixed exchange rate.

Rivalry The situation that occurs when one person's consuming a

unit of a good means no one else can consume it.

Rule of law The ability of a government to enforce the laws of the country, particularly with respect to protecting private property and enforcing contracts.

S

Saving and investment equation An equation that shows that national saving is equal to domestic investment plus net foreign investment.

Scarcity The situation in which unlimited wants exceed the limited resources available to fulfill those wants.

Separation of ownership from control A situation in a corporation in which the top management, rather than the shareholders, control day-to-day operations.

Short run The period of time during which at least one of a firm's inputs is fixed.

Shortage A situation in which the quantity demanded is greater than the quantity supplied.

Short-run aggregate supply curve A curve that shows the relationship in the short run between the price level and the quantity of real GDP supplied by firms.

Shutdown point The minimum point on a firm's average variable cost curve; if the price falls below this point, the firm shuts down production in the short run.

Simple deposit multiplier The ratio of the amount of deposits created by banks to the amount of new reserves.

Social benefit The total benefit from consuming a good or service, including both the private benefit and any external benefit.

Social cost The total cost of producing a good or service, including both the private cost and any external cost.

Sole proprietorship A firm owned by a single individual and not organized as a corporation.

Speculators Currency traders who buy and sell foreign

exchange in an attempt to profit from changes in exchange rates.

Stagflation A combination of inflation and recession, usually resulting from a supply shock.

Stock A financial security that represents partial ownership of a firm.

Stockholders' equity The difference between the value of a corporation's assets and the value of its liabilities; also known as net worth.

Structural relationship A relationship that depends on the basic behavior of consumers and firms and remains unchanged over long periods.

Structural unemployment Unemployment arising from a persistent mismatch between the skills and characteristics of workers and the requirements of jobs.

Substitutes Goods and services that can be used for the same purpose.

Substitution effect The change in the quantity demanded of a good that results from a change in price making the good more or less expensive relative to other goods, holding constant the effect of the price change on consumer purchasing power.

Sunk cost A cost that has already been paid and cannot be recovered.

Supply curve A curve that shows the relationship between the price of a product and the quantity of the product supplied.

Supply schedule A table that shows the relationship between the price of a product

and the quantity of the product supplied.

Supply shock An unexpected event that causes the short-run aggregate supply curve to shift.

Surplus A situation in which the quantity supplied is greater than the quantity demanded.

T

Tariff A tax imposed by a government on imports.

Tax incidence The actual division of the burden of a tax between buyers and sellers in a market.

Tax wedge The difference between the pretax and posttax return to an economic activity.

Taylor rule A rule developed by John Taylor that links the Fed's target for the federal funds rate to economic variables.

Technological change A change in the quantity of output a firm can produce using a given quantity of inputs.

Technology The processes a firm uses to turn inputs into outputs of goods and services.

Terms of trade The ratio at which a country can trade its exports for imports from other countries.

Total cost The cost of all the inputs a firm uses in production.

Total revenue The total amount of funds received by a seller of a good or service, calculated by multiplying price per unit by the number of units sold.

Trade The act of buying or selling.

Trade-off The idea that because of scarcity, producing more of one good or service means producing less of another good or service.

Tragedy of the commons The tendency for a common resource to be overused.

Transactions costs The costs in time and other resources that parties incur in the process of agreeing to and carrying out an exchange of goods or services.

Transfer payments Payments by the government to individuals for which the government does not receive a new good or service in return.

Two-part tariff A situation in which consumers pay one price (or tariff) for the right to buy as much of a related good as they want at a second price.

U

Underground economy Buying and selling of goods and services that is concealed from the government to avoid taxes or regulations or because the goods and services are illegal.

Unemployment rate The percentage of the labor force that is unemployed.

Unit-elastic demand Demand is unit-elastic when the percentage change in quantity demanded is *equal to* the percentage change in price, so the price elasticity is equal to 1 in absolute value.

Utility The enjoyment or satisfaction people receive from consuming goods and services.

V

Value added The market value a firm adds to a product.

Variable costs Costs that change as output changes.

Velocity of money The average number of times each dollar in the money supply is used to purchase goods and services included in GDP.

Vertical merger A merger between firms at different stages of production of a good.

Voluntary exchange The situation that occurs in markets when both the buyer and seller of a product are made better off by the transaction.

Voluntary export restraint (VER) An agreement negotiated between two countries that places a numeric limit on the quantity of a good that can be imported by one country from the other country.

Voting paradox The failure of majority voting to always result in consistent choices.

W

Winner's curse The idea that the winner in certain auctions may have overestimated the value of the good, thus ending up worse off than the losers.

World Trade Organization (WTO) An international organization that oversees international trade agreements.

Company Index

Subject Index

Key terms and the page on which they are defined appear in **boldface**.

Credits

Photo

Chapter 1, *pages 2, 3, 19*, © Phototex/Sipa Press/0501050124; *page 13*, Brian Lee, CORBIS–NY.

Chapter 2, *pages 36, 37, 59*, © Car Culture/CORBIS, All Rights Reserved; *page 41*, Getty Images, Inc.; *page 51 top*, Jupiter Images Picturequest–Royalty Free; *right*, Dan Lim, Masterfile Corporation; *bottom*, Photolibrary.com; *left*, David Young Wolff, Getty Images Inc.–Stone Allstock; *page 53*, © Apple Computer/Court Mast/ Handout/Reuters/Corbis; *page 55*, Imagination Photo Design.

Chapter 3, *pages 66, 67, 91*, © Glow Images/Alamy; *page 72*, Getty Images, Inc; *page 75*, Getty Images, Inc.

Chapter 4, *pages 98, 99, 123*, © Ambient Images Inc./Alamy; *page 113*, Neil Guegan, Corbis Zefa Collection; *page 119*, Bill Aron, PhotoEdit, Inc.

Chapter 5, *pages 136, 137, 165*, Mariusz Szachowski, Shutterstock; *page 146*, AP Wide World Photos; *page 161*, Paul A. Souders, Corbis/ Bettmann.

Chapter 6, *pages 172, 173*, Getty Images, Inc.; *page 181*, Michelle D. Bridwell PhotoEdit Inc.; *page 186*, Getty Images, Inc.

Chapter 7, *pages 208, 209, 227*, AP Wide World Photos; *page 211*, Ed Pritchard, Getty Images Inc.–Stone Allstock; *page 219*, David McIntyre, Black Star.

Chapter 8, *pages 242, 243*, David R. Frazier, Photolibrary, Inc., Alamy Images; *page 246*, © Chung Sung-Jun/Getty Images; *page 254*, Ron Sherman, Photographer; *page 263*, Pallava Bagla, Corbis/Sygma; *page 265*, AP Wide World Photos; *page 280*, Michael Newman, PhotoEdit Inc.

Chapter 9, *pages 284, 285*, © Frank Micelotta/Getty Images; *page 298*, Chris Carlson, AP Wide World Photos; *page 302*, Getty Images, Inc.; *page 305*, Janet Bailey, Masterfile Stock Image Library; *page 307*, Larry Kolvoord, The Image Works.

Chapter 10, *pages 332, 333, 355*, Yoshikazu Tsuno/AFP/Getty Images; *page 334*, Getty Images, Inc.; *page 336*, Getty Images– Stockbyte; *page 340*, © Indranil Mukherjee/AFP/Getty Images; *page 350*, Keystone, Getty Images Inc.–Hulton Archive Photos; *page 372*, © Chris McGrath/Getty Images.

Chapter 11, *pages 376, 377, 403*, © Bob Daemmrich/The Image Works; *page 391*, Raymond Forbes, SuperStock, Inc.; *page 399*, Richard Heinzen, SuperStock, Inc.

Chapter 12, *pages 410, 411, 431*, Bernard Boutrit, Woodfin Camp & Associates; *page 420*, © Up The Resolution (upthere)/Alamy; *page 423*, © Adam Berry/ Bloomberg News/Landov; *page 425*, James A. Finley, AP Wide World Photos; *page 428*, Courtesy of BIC Corporation.

Chapter 13, *pages 440, 441, 463*, Ralf-Finn Hestoft, Corbis/ Bettmann; *page 447*, Dreamworks/ Universal/Eli Reed, Picture Desk, Inc./Kobal Collection; *page 449*, These materials have been reproduced with the permission of eBay Inc. Copyright © 2006 EBAY INC. All Rights Reserved; *page 451*, Ken Reid, Getty Images, Inc.–Taxi; *page 460*, David Frazier, The Image Works.

Chapter 14, *pages 472, 473, 497*, Getty Images, Inc.; *page 475*, REUTERS/Toshiyuki Aizawa/ Landov; *page 476*, Sean Cayton, The Image Works; *page 478*, Niall McDiarmid, Alamy Images.

Chapter 15, *pages 506, 507*, John M. Greim/CreativeEye/ MIRA.com. Disney characters © Disney Enterprises, Inc. Used by permission from Disney Enterprises, Inc.; *page 515*, Bruce Newman, AP Wide World Photos; *page 518*, David Young-Wolff, PhotoEdit Inc.; *page 524*, Gerd Ludwig, The Image Works.

Chapter 16, *pages 534, 535*, Getty Images, Inc.; *page 546*, Getty Images, Inc.; *page 549*, The Kobal Collection/Columbia Pictures; *page 558*, Safelite Group; *page 562*, Willard Culver/National Geographic Image Collection.

Chapter 17, *pages 574, 575, 591*, © Bubbles Photolibrary/Alamy; *page 582*, Getty Images, Inc.; *page 586*, www.indexopen.com; *page 587*, Bruce Laurance/Image Bank/Getty Images; *page 588*, © 2005 Kristen Brochmann/ Fundamental Photographs.

Chapter 18, *pages 598, 599*, Anthony P. Bolante, Corbis/ Bettmann; *page 611*, Spencer Grant, PhotoEdit Inc.; *page 614*, Paul Sakuma, AP Wide World Photos.

Chapter 19, *pages 632, 633*, © Joe Raedle/Getty Images; *page 637 left*, Eric Gevaert, Shutterstock; *top*, Jupiter Images Picturequest– Royalty Free; *right*, Bill Aron, PhotoEdit Inc.; *bottom*, Photolibrary.com; *center*, Yoshio Tomii, SuperStock, Inc.; *page 639*, Stephan Savoia, AP Wide World Photos; *page 643*, John Maier, Jr., The Image Works.

Chapter 20, *pages 658, 659*, Getty Images, Inc. *page 664*, The Kobal Collection/NBC TV; *page 670*, © Andre Durand/AFP/Getty Images, Inc.; *page 673*, Spencer Grant, PhotoEdit Inc.

Chapter 21, *pages 694, 695, 723*, John Froschauer, AP Wide World Photos; *page 709*, © John Springer Collection/CORBIS All Rights Reserved.

Chapter 22, *pages 728, 729*, Getty Images, Inc.; *page 731*, Authors Image, Alamy Images Royalty Free; *page 733*, Katsumi Kasahara, AP Wide World Photos; *page 738*, Lionel Cironneau, AP Wide World Photos; *page 754*, AP Wide World Photos.

Chapter 23, *pages 766, 767, 801*, AP Wide World Photos; *page 788*, Bloomberg News, Landov LLC; *page 793*, Minnesota Historical Society/CORBIS.

Chapter 24, *pages 810, 811*, Kristine Larsen; *page 816*, Toyota Motor Sales, USA, Inc.; *page 836*, Junji Kurokawa, AP Wide World Photos; *page 848*, © Bettmann/ CORBIS All Rights Reserved.

Chapter 25, *pages 850, 851*, Robert Fried, Alamy Images; *page 855*, Reuters/Russell Boyce, Reuters Limited; *page 857*, Tom Stack, Tom Stack & Associates, Inc.; *page 869*, Daniel Luna, AP Wide World Photos; *page 876*, Corbis/Bettmann.

Chapter 26, *pages 886, 887, 919*, Mike Mergen/Bloomberg News, Landov LLC; *page 898*, Seth Joel, Getty Images Inc.–Photographer's Choice Royalty Free; *page 903*, © Reuters/Larry Downing/ Corbis; *page 908*, UPI Photo/ Monika Graff, Landov LLC.

Chapter 27, *pages 928, 929, 961*, Getty Images, Inc.; *page 933*, Paddy Eckersley, ImageState/ International Stock Photography Ltd.; *page 947*, Getty Images, Inc.; *page 950*, AP Wide World Photos; *page 955*, © JLP/Jose L. Pelaez/ Corbis.

Chapter 28, *pages 974, 975*, Michael Fein/Bloomberg News,

Text

We use **business examples** to explain economic concepts. This table highlights the topic and **real-world** company introduced in the chapter-opening vignette and revisited throughout the chapter. This table also lists the companies that appear in our *Making the Connection* and *An Inside Look* features.